Personal Finance

FOURTEENTH EDITION

The McGraw Hill Education Series in Finance, Insurance, and Real Estate

Personal Finance

FOURTEENTH EDITION

JACK R. KAPOOR
College of DuPage

LES R. DLABAY
Lake Forest College

ROBERT J. HUGHES
Richland Campus of Dallas College

MELISSA M. HART
North Carolina State University

McGraw Hill

PERSONAL FINANCE

ISBN 978-1-265-10542-6
MHID 1-265-10542-1

Cover Image: *(background & top left): Shutterstock; (top right): Caia Image/Glow Images; (bottom left): William Perugini/Shutterstock*
Design element: *(city map): George Studio/Shutterstock*

Brief Contents

To the memory of my parents, Ram and Susheela Kapoor; and to my wife, Theresa; and my children, Karen, Kathryn, and Dave

To my wife, Linda Dlabay; my children, Carissa and Kyle; their spouses, Doug Erickson and Anne Jaspers; and my grandchildren, Lucy Dlabay and Caleb Erickson

To my wife, Robin; and to the memory of my mother, Barbara Y. Hughes

To my husband, David Hart; and my children, Alex and Madelyn

About the Authors

Jack R. Kapoor, EdD
College of DuPage

Jack Kapoor has been a professor of business and economics in the Business and Technology Division of the College of DuPage, Glen Ellyn, Illinois, where he has taught business and economics since 1969. He received his BA and MS from San Francisco State University and his EdD in Business and Economic Education from Northern Illinois University. He previously taught at Illinois Institute of Technology's Stuart School of Management, San Francisco State University's School of World Business, and other colleges. Professor Kapoor was awarded the Business and Technology Division's Outstanding Professor Award for 1999–2000. He served as an assistant national bank examiner for the U.S. Treasury Department and has been an international trade consultant to Bolting Manufacturing Co., Ltd., Mumbai, India.

Dr. Kapoor is known internationally as a coauthor of several textbooks, including *Business: A Practical Approach* (Rand McNally), *Business* (Houghton Mifflin), *Business and Personal Finance* (Glencoe), and *Focus on Personal Finance* (McGraw Hill). He served as a content consultant for two popular national television series, *The Business File: An Introduction to Business* and *Dollars & Sense: Personal Finance for the 21st Century*. He has also developed two full-length audio courses in business and personal finance. He has been quoted in many national newspapers and magazines, including *USA Today, U.S. News & World Report,* the *Chicago Sun-Times, Crain's Small Business,* the *Chicago Tribune,* and other publications.

Dr. Kapoor has traveled around the world and has studied business practices in capitalist, socialist, and communist countries.

Les R. Dlabay, EdD
Lake Forest College

"Learning for a life worth living" is the teaching vision of Les Dlabay, professor of business emeritus, who taught at Lake Forest College, Lake Forest, Illinois, for 35 years. In an effort to prepare students for diverse economic and cultural settings, he makes extensive use of field research projects and interactive learning related to food, water, health care, and education. He believes our society can assist global business development through volunteering, knowledge sharing, and financial support. Dr. Dlabay has authored or has adaptations of more than 40 textbooks in the United States, Canada, India, and Singapore. He has taught more than 30 different courses during his career and has presented over 300 workshops and seminars to academic, business, and community organizations. Professor Dlabay has a collection of cereal packages from more than 100 countries and banknotes from 200 countries, which are used to teach about the economic, cultural, and political aspects of international business environments.

His research emphasis involves informal and alternative financial services in cross-cultural and global settings. Dr. Dlabay serves on the board of Andean Aid (www.andeanaid.org), which provides tutoring assistance and spiritual guidance to school-age children in Colombia and Venezuela, and teaches community-based money management and workforce readiness classes for Love INC of Lake County (Illinois), which mobilizes local churches to transform lives and communities. Professor Dlabay has a BS (Accounting) from the University of Illinois, Chicago; an MBA from DePaul University; and an EdD in Business and Economic Education from Northern Illinois University. He received The Great Teacher award at Lake Forest College three times.

Robert J. Hughes, EdD
Dallas County Community Colleges

Financial literacy! Only two words, but Bob Hughes, professor of business at Richland Campus of Dallas College, believes that these two words can change people's lives. Whether you want to be rich or just manage the money you have, the ability to analyze financial decisions and gather financial information are skills that can always be improved. In addition to writing several college textbooks, Dr. Hughes has taught personal finance, introduction to business, business math, small business management, small business finance, and accounting since 1972. He also served as a content consultant for two popular national television series, *It's Strictly Business* and *Dollars & Sense: Personal Finance for the 21st Century,* and he is the lead author for a business math project utilizing computer-assisted instruction funded by the ALEKS Corporation. He has served as a consultant and investment adviser to individuals, businesses, and charitable organizations. Dr. Hughes is the recipient of three different Teaching in Excellence Awards at Richland College—one of seven colleges in the Dallas system. He received his BBA from Southern Nazarene University and his MBA and EdD from the University of North Texas. His hobbies include writing, investing, collecting French antiques, art, and travel.

Melissa M. Hart, CPA
North Carolina State University

Melissa Hart is a senior lecturer in the Poole College of Management at North Carolina State University. She is a member of the Academy of Outstanding Teachers. She has been nominated for the Gertrude Cox Award for Innovative Excellence in Teaching and Learning with Technology as well as the Alumni Distinguished Undergraduate Professor Award. She teaches courses in personal finance and corporate finance and has developed multiple ways to use technology to introduce real-life situations into the classroom and online environment. Spreading the word about financial literacy has always been a passion of hers. Each year she shares her commonsense approach of "No plan is a plan" with various student groups, clubs, high schools, and outside organizations. She is a member of the North Carolina Association of Certified Public Accountants (NCACPA) and the American Institute of Certified Public Accountants (AICPA). She received her BBA from the University of Maryland and an MBA from North Carolina State University. Prior to obtaining an MBA, she worked eight years in public accounting in auditing, tax compliance, and consulting. Her hobbies include keeping up with her family's many extracurricular activities and traveling.

Preface

Dear Personal Finance Students and Professors,

Everyone has a story about how the COVID-19 pandemic affected their life. Take a moment and think about how the events since the spring of 2020 changed your life. For example, did you lose your job because of nonessential business closures? Did you worry about how to pay your rent, car payment, home mortgage, or credit card bills? Did you change your educational or career plans? All good questions that describe how a pandemic can impact your health, education, and financial security. In reality, the pandemic was a wake-up call for many Americans that they needed money for unexpected events and a personal financial plan.

WHAT'S NEXT?

While there are no guarantees there won't be hardships ahead, the material in the 14th edition of *Personal Finance* can provide you with the information needed to weather another pandemic, an unexpected job loss, or the next crisis. As authors, we wrote this text with one purpose: To provide the information you need to make informed decisions that can literally change your life. Just for a moment consider the following questions:

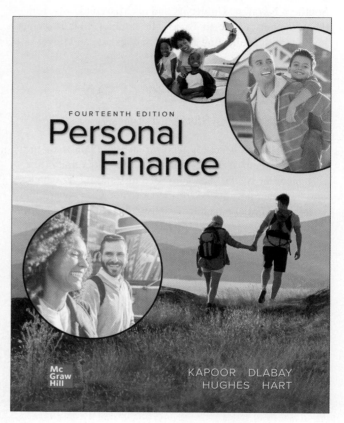

- How much money should you have in an emergency fund?
- What happens if you can't pay your bills?
- How can you balance current needs with investing for the future?
- Can you afford to buy an automobile or a home?
- How will your need for health and life insurance, employer-sponsored health care and a retirement plan, and Social Security affect your financial future?
- How can you attain your career and personal goals to create the life you really want?

Keep in mind, your answers to these questions affect not only the quality of life you have now, but also your future financial security. If you make wise financial decisions, life can become a more joyous experience. On the other hand, if you make bad decisions, life may not turn out so well. While *Personal Finance* does not guarantee that you will get the ideal job or become a millionaire, it does provide the information you need for your financial well-being.

TEXT AND DIGITAL PACKAGE

This edition of *Personal Finance* is packed with new and updated information and examples that will not only help you get a better grade in this course, but also help you plan for the future and achieve financial security. For example, we have revised important topics like taxes, banking services, college loans, health care, investments, and retirement planning to provide the most current information available. In addition, our new features *Personal FinTech* and *Digital Financial Literacy* are both designed to help you use technology to improve financial decision making.

Because more Personal Finance courses are now taught online, we worked hard to develop digital materials that help students learn and help professors teach. For students, our digital package includes an interactive e-book, practice quizzes, and short videos along with assignable auto-graded questions. We're especially proud of our new Application Based Activities. These auto-graded activities allow students to test their knowledge and skills in simulated scenarios. For professors, our digital resources include a comprehensive instructor manual, computerized test bank, and

PowerPoint presentations for each chapter. When the these components are combined, it's easy for professors to build their own online course or use a prebuilt course that enables students to learn anytime, anywhere.

OUR FOCUS ON STUDENTS AND PROFESSORS

For 14 editions, we have listened carefully to both students and professors. With each revision, we have incorporated these suggestions and ideas to create what has become a best-selling personal finance textbook. *For your suggestions, ideas, and support, we thank you.*

We invite you to examine the visual guide that follows to see how the new edition of *Personal Finance,* the McGraw Hill *Connect* learning software, and our SmartBook technology can help you achieve financial security and success.

Welcome to the new 14th edition of *Personal Finance!*

Sincerely,

Jack Kapoor	Les Dlabay	Bob Hughes	Melissa Hart
kapoorj@att.net	dlabay@lakeforest.edu	Hughespublishing@outlook.com	mmhart@ncsu.edu

ACKNOWLEDGMENTS

The extensive feedback and thoughtful comments provided by instructors in the field have greatly contributed to the quality of the 14th edition of *Personal Finance.*

Many talented professionals at McGraw Hill Higher Education have also contributed to the development of *Personal Finance,* 14th edition. We are especially grateful to Michele Janicek, Chuck Synovec, Allison McCabe-Carroll, Trina Maurer, Amy Gehl, and Emily Windelborn.

In addition, Jack Kapoor expresses special appreciation to Theresa and Dave Kapoor, Kathryn Thumme, and Karen and Joshua Tucker for their typing, proofreading, and research assistance. Les Dlabay expresses his thanks to Fred Bell, Joe Chmura, Kyle Dlabay, Linda Dlabay, Anne Jaspers, Jennifer Lazarus, Melissa Panganiban, George Seyk, Jasmine Taylor-Newton, and Ben Rohde for their help reviewing the manuscript. Finally, we thank our spouses and families for their patience, understanding, encouragement, and love throughout the years.

ASSURANCE OF LEARNING

Most educational institutions have a focus on assurance of learning, an important element of accreditation standards. *Personal Finance,* 14th edition, is designed specifically to support your assurance of learning initiatives with a simple, yet powerful, solution.

Each test bank question for *Personal Finance,* 14th edition, maps to a specific chapter learning outcome/objective listed in the text. You can use the test bank software to easily query for learning outcomes/objectives that directly relate to the learning objectives for your course. You can then use the reporting features of the software to aggregate student results in similar fashion, making the collection and presentation of assurance of learning data simple and easy.

STOCKTRAK'S PERSONAL FINANCE PRODUCT: U.S. INVESTING SIMULATION AND PERSONAL BUDGETING GAME

Students can now receive a 50% discount on access to StockTrak's market-leading simulations.

INVESTING SIMULATION

This real-time investing simulation challenges students to build a portfolio of U.S. stocks, ETFs, mutual funds, and bonds and manage it over the course of a semester. StockTrak is packed with research tools, reports, and tutorials to help students get started and real-time rankings to keep them engaged.

PERSONAL BUDGETING GAME

This budgeting simulations puts students in the role of a college graduate who just started their first job. Each participant works through a simulated year balancing their work/life balance, striving to reach savings goals, build up their credit score, maintaining a high quality of life, and deal with life's many unexpected events that will challenge students' money management skills.

For more information visit: www.StockTrak.com/Kapoor and reference access code: KAP-621 or ask your McGraw Hill representative how you can get more information.

Personal Finance Offers You Everything You Have Always Expected . . . and More!

The primary purpose of this book is to help you apply the personal finance practices you learn from the book and from your instructor to your own life. The following new features of the 14th edition expand on this principle. You can use them to assess your current personal financial literacy, identify your personal finance goals, and develop and apply a personal finance strategy to help you achieve those goals. (*For a complete list of all of the features* in Personal Finance, *14th edition, refer to the Guided Tour on pages xxvii–xxxiii.*)

FINANCIAL LITERACY IN MY LIFE

This edition continues to focus on financial literacy and financial well-being. In our many years of teaching and evaluating what knowledge and skills are most important, financial literacy—the ability to understand and interpret knowledge relating to the financial decisions we make—is of highest priority. We hope students will remember and use the details we have put so much time and care into writing, and that you put into teaching. If nothing else, though, we feel we have been successful if students come out of this course with the skills required to interpret financial information and to make wise decisions about their own money, and the confidence that comes with knowing they can solve the problems they encounter.

Throughout the text, strong emphasis is placed on financial literacy. The chapter opening questions about "Financial Literacy in My Life," and the Financial Planning features are focused to emphasize "my life"—the life and decisions that you, the student, will make. Features on financial calculations and decision making have also been altered to focus on students achieving financial literacy.

Chapter	Selected Topics	Benefits for the Teaching-Learning Environment
Chapter 1 **Personal Finance Basics and the Time Value of Money**	New content: Financial difficulties	Addresses financial difficulties caused by the pandemic and the importance of an emergency fund.
	New content: Opportunity fund	Discusses *opportunity fund,* money set aside to expand your income and net worth, or to invest in yourself with an advanced degree.
	New content: Financial literacy definition	Offers an explanation of the knowledge and skills for achieving personal, family, and community financial goals.
	New Smart Money Minute feature	Provides a warning to avoid overspending or taking on more debt when receiving a salary increase.
	New Personal FinTech feature	Presents an introduction to FinTech (financial technology), which involves apps, websites, and mobile devices for banking and personal finance activities.
	New exhibit: Goals and Actions for Personal Financial Literacy (Exhibit 1-6)	Connects attitudes and abilities with financial literacy development skills for planning short-term and long-term goals.
	Revised Financial Literacy for My Life feature	Expands the feature to create and implement SMART financial goals.
	Updated apps and websites	Presents additional online and mobile sources to consult for expanded information and assistance.
	New Digital Financial Literacy activity	Encourages students to make use of personal finance blogs to enhance their knowledge.
	Revised Your Personal Financial Plan activity	Creates a foundation for identifying and implementing short-term and long-term financial planning activities.
Chapter 2 **Financial Aspects of Career Planning**	Revised exhibit: Education and income (Exhibit 2-1)	Updates median weekly earnings for various levels of education, based on Bureau of Labor Statistics data.
	New content: Leadership	Provides a brief discussion of leadership qualities vital for career success.
	Revised Financial Literacy for My Life feature	Guides students through a personal SWOT analysis to develop a career action plan.
	New content: Negotiating salary	Suggests actions for negotiating salary in difficult economic times.
	Updated content: Industry trends	Lists job opportunities with the greatest potential in various industries.
	Expanded Financial Literacy for My Life feature	Suggests personal finance actions for people who own their own business.
	Revised Financial Literacy for My Life feature	Provides an overview of innovative benefits offered by various companies.
	New Personal FinTech feature	Discusses artificial intelligence (AI) and other technology used for identifying and hiring employees.

Chapter	*Selected Topics*	**Benefits for the Teaching-Learning Environment**
Chapter 5 (Cont.)	Updated data: Understanding interest rates	Provides data for various interest rates that affect spending, saving, borrowing, and investing decisions
	New Personal FinTech feature	Discusses *neobanks*, FinTech start-ups offering financial services through digital channels and apps.
	New content: High-yield savings accounts	Presents an introduction to high-yield savings accounts.
	New Financial Literacy for My Life feature	Suggests an array of savings accounts to effectively manage finances.
	Expanded content: Checking accounts	Provides an overview of traditional, special feature, and checkless checking accounts.
	Expanded Personal FinTech feature	Presents information on the benefits and concerns associated with Bitcoin and other cryptocurrencies.
	Updated How To: Avoid Identity Theft	Expands suggestions to prevent identity theft with an update of sources for assistance.
	New Digital Financial Literacy activity	Provides a framework for analyzing person-to-person (P2P) payment apps.
	Revised Your Personal Financial Plan activity	Suggests short-term and long-term activities for planning and implementing the use of banking services.
Chapter 6 Introduction to Consumer Credit	New introductory paragraph on consumer credit	Describes consumer credit and why it is important to understand and protect it.
	Revised section on credit	Points out how society today has popularized credit and its use.
	Updated exhibit: Volume of consumer credit (Exhibit 6-1)	Illustrates that the volume of credit has been increasing steadily, reaching $4.18 trillion in 2020.
	New example: Revised credit card section.	Explains how credit card rewards remain popular and have continued to increase in number over the last few years.
	New Smart Money Minute: Credit Card Facts	Provides the latest statistics on credit cards.
	New Smart Money Minute feature	Distinguishes between a home equity loan and a home equity line of credit.
	New Personal FinTech feature	Points out that consumers are entitled to order a free copy of their credit report every year from each of the major credit reporting agencies.
	New Smart Money Minute feature	Explains how consumers can get six credit reports every 12 months from Equifax through December 2026.
	New Personal FinTech feature	Suggests how to protect privacy and security when making mobile payments.
	Revised all Self-Test Problems	Provides updated examples.
	New Digital Financial Literacy feature	Asks students to determine what it takes to protect consumers from credit card scammers.
	New Your Personal Financial Plan feature	Asks students to complete short-term and long-term financial planning activities in establishing and maintaining a credit record.

Chapter	Selected Topics	Benefits for the Teaching-Learning Environment
Chapter 7 **Choosing a Source of Credit: The Cost of Credit Alternatives**	Revised medium-priced loans section	Updates the number of Americans who belong to credit unions, the number of credit unions, and the assets held by credit unions in the United States.
	New material in Exhibit 7-1	Adds payday loan companies and online lenders as possible sources of credit.
	New Smart Money Minute feature	Explains loan origination fees and how these fees increase the total cost of a loan.
	New Smart Money Minute feature	Reports how credit card companies provide assistance to consumers during the COVID-19 pandemic.
	New section in debt collection practices	Describes what debt collectors can or cannot do by federal law to collect debts.
	New Exhibit 7-3	Provides sample letter to inform debt collectors when and how to contact you.
	New Financial Literacy for My Life feature	Describes different ways to respond appropriately to debt collectors.
	Revised Exhibit 7-5	Updates total U.S. Chapter 7 and Chapter 13 bankruptcy filings (1980–2020).
	New Smart Money Minute feature	Explains that despite continued high unemployment due to COVID-19 pandemic, personal bankruptcies fell sharply.
	Revised Chapter 7 bankruptcy discussion	Updates information about bankruptcy fees required in 2021.
	New Personal FinTech feature	Explains that personal bankruptcy can be filed without an attorney, which is called filing pro se.
	New Digital Financial Literacy feature	Asks students to conduct a cost/benefit analysis before making any major purchase.
	New Your Personal Financial Plan feature	Asks students to research short-term or long-term financial planning activities in comparing credit services and costs, using Personal Financial Planning sheets 30 or 31.
Chapter 8 **Consumer Purchasing Strategies and Legal Protection**	New Personal FinTech feature	Presents retail technology trends enhancing the shopping experience.
	New Smart Money Minute feature	Presents information on current retailing technology trends designed to enhance the shopping experience.
	New Smart Money Minute feature	Discusses the increasing popularity of electric vehicles (EVs) along with the benefits, concerns, and types of EVs.
	Updated Financial Literacy for My Life feature	Provides updated coverage of pandemic cons, payment scams, and other fraudulent activities.
	New Smart Money Minute feature	Explains how to avoid scams of online used-car sellers.
	New Smart Money Minute feature	Points out that people who drive older vehicles save more for retirement.
	New Smart Money Minute feature	Discusses buying habits of minimalists and frugal people.

Chapter	Selected Topics	Benefits for the Teaching-Learning Environment
Chapter 8 (Cont.)	New Digital Financial Literacy activity	Provides an opportunity to better understand consumer product testing procedures.
	Revised Your Personal Financial Plan activity	Suggests short-term and long-term activities for wise buying.
Chapter 9 **The Housing Decision: Factors and Finances**	New Smart Money Minute feature	Compares ready-to-assemble home kits of the early 20th century with 3D printing of today for creating houses.
	New Personal FinTech feature	Discusses technology to plan, build, buy, sell, and manage real estate; and information on the interconnectivity of devices for smart home features.
	Revised Financial Literacy for My Life feature	Expands actions when deciding whether to pay off a mortgage early along with potential risks of an early mortgage payoff.
	New content: ATR/QM rule	Offers an explanation of the Ability-to-Repay (ATR) /Qualified Mortgage (QM) rule that requires lenders to carefully consider a borrower's financial situation.
	Updated Exhibit: Common closing costs (Exhibit 9-11)	Lists potential closing costs, the fees and charges paid when a real estate transaction is completed.
	Revised Smart Money Minute feature	Suggests upgrades that add value to a home and that have the highest payoffs when selling.
	New Personal FinTech feature	Discusses tech-oriented companies called iBuyers that will buy your home.
	New Digital Financial Literacy activity	Guides students in using online sources for comparing housing alternatives and analyzing housing costs.
	Revised Your Personal Financial Plan activity	Suggests short-term and long-term activities for housing.
Chapter 10 **Property and Motor Vehicle Insurance**	New Financial Literacy for My Life feature	Cautions readers that standard home insurance policies don't cover flood damage.
	Updated Smart Money Minute feature	Explains that for about $100 a year, homeowners can obtain $10,000 of coverage for sewage and drain backup damage.
	New examples of actual cash value and replacement value coverage	Illustrates the differences between actual value and replacement value coverage.
	Updated statistics for motor vehicle crashes	Reports that motor vehicle crashes cost over $250 billion in lost wages and medical costs.
	New Smart Money Minute feature	Cautions readers to think twice before lending their car to friends.
	New example of a deductible	Explains that a deductible may be a specific dollar amount or a percentage.
	Added two Self-Test Problems	Asks students to solve problems related to motor vehicle and homeowners insurance.

Chapter	Selected Topics	Benefits for the Teaching-Learning Environment
Chapter 10 (Cont.)	New Digital Financial Literacy feature	Asks students to gather information about careers in the insurance industry.
	New Personal Financial Plan feature	Asks students to create an insurance plan to cover financial difficulties.
Chapter 11 **Health, Disability, and Long-Term Care Insurance**	Revised content: High medical costs	Provides revised and updated information on runaway health care costs.
	Revised content: Rapid increase in medical expenditures	Updates data on medical expenditures.
	Revised Exhibit 11-1	Illustrates current and projected health care costs to year 2028.
	New Personal FinTech feature	Provides information on electronic health records.
	New Financial Literacy for My Life feature	Offers seven steps to keep medical costs and debt under control.
	New Smart Money Minute feature	Explains various government and private sources to get health insurance coverage.
	Revised Example: Deductibles and Coinsurance	Updates the deductible and coinsurance example with revised dollar amounts.
	Revised content in long-term care insurance	Updates nursing home costs in the United States.
	New Exhibit 11-7	Summarizes main features of HMO, EPO, PPO, and POS plans.
	New Smart Money Minute feature	Cautions readers not to contribute to HSAs once Medicare coverage begins.
	Revised Financial Literacy for My Life feature	Updates how HSAs work in 2021.
	New Smart Money Minute feature	Informs readers that the CARES Act of 2020 permits HSA, FSA, and HRA account holders to pay for over-the-counter medication.
	New Personal FinTech feature	Assures readers that Medicare covers the COVID-19 lab tests and vaccines.
	Revised material on Affordable Care Act	Updates Health Insurance and Patient Protection and Affordable Care Act of 2010.
	New Smart Money Minute feature	Explains that many young adults and children were uninsured in 2019.
	Revised Self-Test problems	Updates Self-Test problems.
	New Digital Financial Literacy feature	Explains why readers should care about health care costs.
	New Your Financial Plan feature	Asks students to compare health insurance plans.

Chapter	Selected Topics	Benefits for the Teaching-Learning Environment
Chapter 12 **Life Insurance**	Updated statistics for policy coverage and total coverage.	Reports current statistics for total life insurance policies and total coverage.
	Updated statistics for life insurance coverage	Reports current statistics for life insurance coverage for adult consumers.
	New Exhibit 12-1	New exhibit for top reasons that people do not have life insurance.
	Updated statistics for life expectancy	Reports current statistics for life expectancy for males and females based upon current age.
	New Exhibit 12-3	New exhibit for average face amount of policies purchased.
	Updated Smart Money Minute	Includes current information about stay-at-home moms' equivalent wage.
	Updated Smart Money Minute	Provides a possible reason why people don't purchase life insurance policies.
	New Personal FinTech feature	Asks students to calculate the amount and cost of a life insurance policy.
	New Personal Financial Plan feature	Asks students to create an insurance plan to cover financial difficulties.
	Updated Exhibit 12-8	Reports current information for credit, group, and individual policies.
	New Digital Financial Literacy feature	Asks students to research life insurance coverage and premiums post-pandemic.
	New Your Personal Finance feature	Describes short-term and long-term financial planning activities.
Chapter 13 **Investing Fundamentals**	New information on goals	Includes planning for emergencies and retirement.
	New information for budgeting apps	Provides information for four popular apps that can help budget and manage your money.
	Updated statistics for credit cards	Reports current statistics for credit cards and time required to repay credit card debt.
	Revised Smart Money feature	Provides current customer ranking for overall customer satisfaction for credit cards.
	New material in the business cycle section	Describes the effect of the COVID-19 pandemic on the business cycle.
	New example of the time value of money	Describes how $1,800 invested at 8 percent can grow to $466,302 in 40 years.
	New Exhibit 13-1	Illustrates the growth of investments that earn 2 percent or 8 percent over different time periods.
	New example of risk-return trade-off	Shows the effect of dividends and a recent price increase on the total return for an investment in Procter & Gamble stock.

Chapter	*Selected Topics*	**Benefits for the Teaching-Learning Environment**
Chapter 13 (Cont.)	New example of the effect of changing interest rates in the economy	Illustrates how bond prices for an Amazon corporate bond increase or decrease because of changes in the overall interest rates in the economy.
	New example of business failure risk	Explains what happened to investors who owned JC Penney stock or bonds when the company filed for bankruptcy.
	New statistics for investment returns	Illustrates different investment returns for stock investors over different time periods.
	New information on the largest one-day loss for the stock market	Provides information about the decline in stock values that occurred on March 16, 2020.
	Revised Smart Money Minute	Includes new statistics for income for American families.
	New example of asset allocation for older investor	Explains how many investors become more conservative as they get older.
	New example of interest calculation for a Clorox bond	Describes the options for an investor who chooses a Clorox bond that pays 3.90 percent and matures in 2028.
	New How To . . . feature	Provides information about how to open a brokerage account.
	New Personal FinTech feature	Points out how some investors are using robo advisors.
	Revised Exhibit 13-7 and Exhibit 13-8	Includes more websites and sources that investors can use to stay current with financial news.
	New Digital Financial Literacy feature	Asks students to determine what it takes to become a certified financial planner.
	New Your Personal Financial Plan feature	Asks students to complete short-term and long-term financial planning activities.
Chapter 14 **Investing in Stocks**	New information on corporate dividends	Explains why some companies don't pay dividends and some companies have a long history of paying dividends.
	Revised information on a McDonald's investment	Illustrates how an investor made money by investing in McDonald's stock over a long period of time.
	New information about stock market returns	Shows average returns for the stock market over different time periods.
	Updated Smart Money Minute	Provides new information on the percentage of people that own stock in different age groups.
	Updated Exhibit 14-1	Illustrates the record date and payable date for a recent Starbucks dividend.
	New Exhibit 14-2	Describes the total return for an investment in Clorox stock over a 12-month period.
	New information for stock splits	Describes the effect of a 4 for 1 stock split for Apple.
	New Exhibit 14-5	Illustrates the type of information available from the Yahoo! Finance website for Coca-Cola.
	New Exhibit 14-7	Illustrates a Value Line report for Walmart.

Chapter	*Selected Topics*	Benefits for the Teaching-Learning Environment
Chapter 14 (Cont.)	Updated Smart Money Minute	Shows values for the Dow Jones Industrial Average for the period 2015 to February 2021.
	New examples in the section Numerical Measures that Influence Investment Decisions	Uses current financial information for calculations that can be used to evaluate an investment.
	New example for an IPO	Describes how DoorDash raised $3.3 billion in its IPO.
	New Exhibit 14-8	Shows the amount required to open an account, the commission charge for stock trades, and specific advantages for popular online brokerage firms.
	New Personal FinTech feature	Explains how investors can practice their investment skills by using a virtual stock game.
	New examples for a limit and stop-loss order	Describes how investors can use a limit order to buy or sell Walt Disney stock and a stop-loss order for American Airlines.
	Revised Exhibit 14-9	Explains how dollar cost averaging can be used to buy Johnson & Johnson stock for the period 2015 to 2021.
	New example for day trading	Describes the volatility that investors experienced when they bought and sold GameStop in 2021.
	New Digital Financial Literacy feature	Illustrates how investors can use Yahoo! Finance to track the historical value of dividends, stock prices, and stock splits.
	New Financial Planning Case	Asks students to evaluate Walmart based on the Value Line report in Exhibit 14-7, and then make a decision to buy the stock or not.
	New Your Personal Financial Plan feature	Asks students to research different brokerage firms and also evaluate a specific company that would be a good long-term investment.
Chapter 15 **Investing in Bonds**	New example in the chapter introduction	Describes how one person chose to invest in bonds to avoid investment losses during the COVID-19 pandemic.
	Revised Smart Money Minute	Provides average interest rates for high-quality corporate bonds for the period 2000 to 2020.
	New example for convertible bonds	Explains why Southwest Airlines issued convertible bonds.
	New example for bond interest calculation	Shows the interest calculation for a Microsoft bond that pays 3.3 percent and matures in 2027.
	New example explains why bond prices fluctuate	Illustrates how the price of a bond issued by Apple can increase or decrease because of changes in the overall interest rates in the economy.
	New example to approximate the value of a bond	Uses an internet link for a bond price calculator to approximate the current value of a bond.
	New Exhibit 15-3	Explains how bond investors can make money if they purchase a Clorox bond.
	Revised Smart Money Minute	Provides average interest rates for 10-year Treasury notes for the period 2000 to 2020.

Chapter	Selected Topics	Benefits for the Teaching-Learning Environment
Chapter 15 (Cont.)	New example for tax-equivalent yield	Shows the calculation to determine the tax-equivalent yields for a taxpayer in the 24 percent tax bracket who purchases a tax-free bond that pays 3 percent.
	New Exhibit 15-5	Illustrates the tax-equivalent yields based on different tax-free returns and current individual tax rates.
	New websites for bond investors	Provides additional websites that bond investors can use to get current information.
	New Exhibit 15-6	Describes the type of bond information available on the FINRA website.
	New example for bond pricing	Calculates the current price for a bond based on a bond quotation.
	New Personal FinTech feature	Describes brokerage firm apps that can be used to help screen possible bond investments.
	Revised Exhibit 15-7	Provides current ratings information available from Moody's Investor Services and Standard & Poor's.
	Enhanced explanation of bond ratings	Provides more detailed information about what bond ratings mean.
	New example for current yield	Calculates the current yield for a Boeing bond.
	New example for yield-to-maturity	Calculates the yield-to-maturity for a Boeing bond.
	Updated Financial Literacy Calculations feature	Uses current financial information to calculate the times interest earned ratio for Home Depot.
	New Digital Financial Literacy feature	Asks students to explore the Treasury Direct website.
	New Financial Planning Case	Updates the information needed by an investor who is trying to choose between different bond investments and a conservative stock investment.
	New Your Personal Financial Plan feature	Asks students to explain the difference between stocks and bonds and also use the FINRA website to research a specific corporate bond.
Chapter 16 Investing in Mutual Funds	Updated example in the chapter introduction	Revised average return is now 16 percent for the T. Rowe Price Dividend Growth mutual fund.
	New statistics for mutual funds	Lists statistics from the Investment Company Institute about mutual fund investments.
	New Exhibit 16-1	Provides information about the number and type of securities contained in the Fidelity Blue Chip Growth Fund.
	Updated Smart Money Minute feature	Shows the percentage of fund investors for different generations.
	New statistics for different types of funds	Includes the number of closed-end, exchange-traded, and open-end funds.
	New example for net asset value	Explains how to calculate the NAV for the New American Frontiers fund.

Chapter	Selected Topics	Benefits for the Teaching-Learning Environment
Chapter 16 (Cont.)	Revised information on fees for a load fund	Explains that the average sales charge for a load fund is now 2 to 5 percent.
	Revised Exhibit 16-3	Updates the load charges, management fees, 12b-1 fees, and expense ratio for the Davis New York Venture fund.
	Increased coverage of different types of funds	Discusses why young investors often pick more growth-oriented funds and investors closer to retirement choose more conservative funds.
	New fund objective	Includes the fund objective for the Vanguard U.S. Growth fund.
	Updated Smart Money Minute feature	Shows the four top reasons why people invest in funds.
	New material on the difference between a managed fund and an index fund	Supplies additional material on the reasons why index funds often outperform managed funds.
	New Exhibit 16-4	Provides information about the three largest U.S. mutual fund families—Blackrock, Vanguard, and Fidelity.
	New Exhibit 16-5	Discusses a Morningstar research report for the Calvert Balanced A Fund.
	Updated Exhibit 16-6	Provides fund information from Kiplinger's 25 Favorite No-Load Mutual Funds.
	New example on how to make money with fund investments	Shows how an investor can make money with an investment in the T. Rowe Price Communications and Technology fund.
	Revised Financial Literacy Calculations feature	Provides information to illustrate how to compute total return and percentage of return for a fund investment.
	New Personal FinTech feature	Describes investment apps for mutual fund investors.
	New Digital Financial Literacy feature	Asks students to read a Forbes article and use the internet to research different investment apps.
	New Financial Planning Case	Asks students to determine if they would invest in a specific fund based on information from the internet and their answers to the questions on Personal Financial Planner sheet 62.
	New Your Personal Financial Plan feature	Asks students to evaluate sources of mutual fund information and also evaluate a specific mutual fund.
Chapter 17 Investing in Real Estate and Other Investment Alternatives	New material in Your Home as an Investment section	Explains that even though the global pandemic shattered the United States economy in 2020, the housing market remained strong.
	Revised Exhibit 17-2	Updates data of annual home ownership rates by age groups.
	New material in Your Vacation Home section	Explains that during the COVID-19 pandemic, the demand for vacation homes remained strong.

Chapter	Selected Topics	Benefits for the Teaching-Learning Environment
Chapter 17 (Cont.)	New material in Commercial Property section	Reveals that COVID-19 pandemic had stalled the commercial real estate market, but the market continued to recover gradually.
	Revised Financial Literacy for My Life feature	Describes that over five decades, Freddie Mac has provided more than $11 trillion to more than 69 million homeowners.
	New material in Gold Bullion Coins section	Cautions readers to ask the seller for the coin melt value when purchasing gold bullion coins.
	Revised content: Prices of precious metals	Includes the latest prices of silver, platinum, and rhodium.
	New content in Silver, Platinum, Palladium, and Rhodium section	Advises readers not to take cash from their retirement accounts and invest it in precious metals.
	New Personal FinTech feature	Cautions buyers of jewelry, precious stones, and collectibles to compare quality, price, and service from several different sellers before making the purchase.
	New Financial Literacy for My Life feature	Provides tips for buyers of Bitcoin and other cryptocurrencies.
	New Digital Financial Literacy for My Life feature	Explains that the value of bullion coins is determined mostly by their precious metals content rather than by their rarity and condition.
	New Your Personal Financial Plan feature	Cautions that speculative ventures must be considered carefully in relation to personal financial situations.
Chapter 18 **Starting Early: Retirement Planning**	Revised contents: Centenarians	Updates the number of centenarians in the United States.
	Revised content: Inflation rate	Updates annual inflation rate for 2021.
	Updated statistics for Social Security	Reports current statistics for Social Security recipients as of 2021.
	Revised Smart Money Minute feature	Provides current statistics on who receives Social Security benefits.
	Revised Smart Money Minute feature	Shows what groups are collecting Social Security benefits as of 2021.
	New Smart Money Minute feature	Explains how to protect yourself from Social Security phone scams.
	Revised content on the future of Social Security	Provides updated statistics about the future of Social Security.
	Revised Exhibit 18-8	Illustrates how the number of workers per beneficiary has plummeted over the decades.
	New content in Other Public Pension Plans	Explains how PensionHelp America assists people if they have questions about retirement plans.
	New Smart Money Minute feature	Describes how despite increasing wealth, most Americans have only modest savings relative to their retirement income needs.
	Revised content: 401(k) plans	Updates the contribution limits for 2021.

Chapter	Selected Topics	Benefits for the Teaching-Learning Environment
Chapter 18 (Cont.)	New Personal FinTech feature	Illustrates that when you change jobs, generally you have four choices about what to do with your 401(k) plan savings.
	Revised content: Pension Benefits Guaranty Corporation (PBGC)	Explains that since 1974, the PBGC has protected the pension benefits of over 34 million workers, retirees, and their families.
	Revised content: IRAs	Updates the contribution limits for 2021.
	Revised content: Rollover IRAs	Updates the contribution limits for 2021.
	Revised content: SEP-IRAs	Updates the contribution limits for 2021.
	New content: Keogh Plans	Explains that you may contribute 25 percent of your income, up to a maximum of $58,000 as of 2021.
	New Digital Financial Literacy feature	Assists readers in creating their own My Social Security account.
	New Your Personal Financial Plan feature	Helps readers to plan for retirement using Personal Financial Planning sheets 64 and 65.
Chapter 19 **Estate Planning**	Revised content: New lifestyles	Points out that the law allows $11.7 million exemption for estate taxes.
	New Personal FinTech feature	Provides rules to remember when writing a will.
	Revised content: Cost of a Will	Updates the cost of a standard will.
	Revised content: Stated dollar amount will	Updates the amount ($11.7 million) for 2021.
	Revised content: Credit-shelter trust	Provides updated new exemption amounts for 2021.
	Updated Exhibit 19-6	Includes the new exemption amounts for 2019, 2020, and 2021.
	Revised content: Estate taxes	Points out that the surviving spouse's estate in excess of $23.4 million (in 2021) faces estate tax of 40 percent.
	Revised content: Estate taxes	Explains that only 12 states and the District of Columbia impose an estate tax. Maryland imposes both estate and inheritance tax.
	Revised content: Self-test problems	Updates examples for 2021.
	Revised content: Financial Planning Problems	Updates problems for 2021 amounts.
	New Digital Financial Literacy feature	Includes student activities for making a will.
	New Your Personal Financial Plan feature	Asks students to perform short-term and long-term financial planning activities in developing an estate plan.

Learning Objectives

Learning objectives are presented at the start of each chapter. These goals are then highlighted at the start of each major section in the chapter, and appear again in the end-of-chapter summary. The learning objectives are also used to organize the end-of-chapter problems, as well as materials in the *Instructor's Manual* and *Test Bank*. Problems in *Connect* can also be organized using the objectives.

Financial Literacy in Your Life

This introductory feature covers the why and how of key chapter topics, with suggested action alternatives that a person might consider when encountering related decisions.

My Life

The *My Life* concept begins with the chapter opener. Students are presented with an engaging scenario relating what they're about to learn to their own lives. The follow-up questions are designed to get students thinking about current personal finance activities and to motivate them to try new beneficial practices. The *My Life* boxes throughout the chapters and the Learning Objectives in the chapter summary expand on this concept.

How To . . .

The *How To . . .* boxes emphasize application-driven personal finance themes. Each box highlights an issue and walks students through how to navigate the situation.

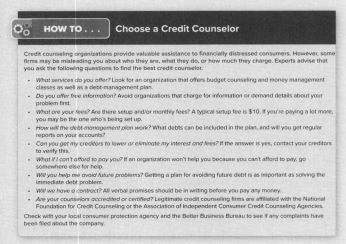

HOW TO . . . Choose a Credit Counselor

Credit counseling organizations provide valuable assistance to financially distressed consumers. However, some firms may be misleading you about who they are, what they do, or how much they charge. Experts advise that you ask the following questions to find the best credit counselor.

- *What services do you offer?* Look for an organization that offers budget counseling and money management classes as well as a debt-management plan.
- *Do you offer free information?* Avoid organizations that charge for information or demand details about your problem first.
- *What are your fees?* Are there setup and/or monthly fees? A typical setup fee is $10. If you're paying a lot more, you may be the one who's being set up.
- *How will the debt-management plan work?* What debts can be included in the plan, and will you get regular reports on your accounts?
- *Can you get my creditors to lower or eliminate my interest and fees?* If the answer is yes, contact your creditors to verify this.
- *What if I can't afford to pay you?* If an organization won't help you because you can't afford to pay, go somewhere else for help.
- *Will you help me avoid future problems?* Getting a plan for avoiding future debt is as important as solving the immediate debt problem.
- *Will we have a contract?* All verbal promises should be in writing before you pay any money.
- *Are your counselors accredited or certified?* Legitimate credit counseling firms are affiliated with the National Foundation for Credit Counseling or the Association of Independent Consumer Credit Counseling Agencies.

Check with your local consumer protection agency and the Better Business Bureau to see if any complaints have been filed about the company.

Financial Literacy for My Life

IS IT TAXABLE INCOME? IS IT DEDUCTIBLE?

Certain financial benefits individuals receive are not subject to federal income tax. Indicate whether each of the following items would or would not be included in taxable income when you compute your federal income tax.

Is it taxable income?	Yes	No
1. Lottery/Jackpot winnings		
2. Child support received		
3. Worker's compensation benefits		
4. Life insurance death benefits		
5. Cash rebate for laptop		
6. Unemployment income		

Indicate whether each of the following items would or would not be deductible when you compute your federal income tax.

Is it deductible?	Yes	No
7. Life insurance premiums		
8. Baggage fees for self-employed		
9. Fees for traffic violations		
10. Mileage for driving to volunteer work		
11. An attorney's fee for preparing a will		
12. Income tax preparation fee		

Note: These taxable income items and deductions are based on the 2018 tax year and may change due to changes in the tax code.

Answers: 1, 6, 8, 10—yes; 2, 3, 4, 5, 7, 9, 11, 12—no.

Financial Literacy for My Life

This feature offers information to assist students when faced with special situations and unique financial planning decisions. Many emphasize the use of online sources.

Financial Literacy Calculations

TAX CREDITS VERSUS TAX DEDUCTIONS

Many people confuse *tax credits* with *tax deductions*. Is one better than the other? A *tax credit*, such as eligible child care or dependent care expenses, results in a dollar-for-dollar reduction in the amount of taxes owed. A *tax deduction*, such as an itemized deduction in the form of medical expenses, mortgage interest, or charitable contributions, reduces the taxable income on which your taxes are based.

Shown at right is how a $100 tax credit compares with a $100 tax deduction:

As you might expect, tax credits are less readily available than tax deductions. To qualify for a $100 child care tax credit, you may have to spend $500 in child care expenses. In some situations, spending on deductible items may be more beneficial than qualifying for a tax credit. A knowledge of tax law and careful financial planning will help you use both tax credits and tax deductions to maximum advantage.

TAX CREDIT
$100 TAX CREDIT

Reduces your taxes by $100

TAX DEDUCTION
$100 TAX DEDUCTION

Reduces your taxable income by $100. The amount of your tax reduction depends on your tax bracket. Your taxes will be reduced by $12 if you are in the 12 percent tax bracket and $35 if you are in the 35 percent tax bracket.

35% tax bracket =

(100 dollar bill): andreynekrasov/123RF; (5, 10, 20 dollar bill): Ruslan Nassyrov/Alamy Stock Photo

Financial Literacy Calculations

This feature presents over 90 mathematical applications for various personal financial activities and decisions.

Margin notes provide connections to supplementary information. The Smart Money Minute feature provides interesting statistics and tips in personal financial planning. The Concept Check feature provides an ongoing assessment tool.

Key Terms

Key terms appear in bold type and in the margin definition boxes. The terms and their page references are also listed at the end of each chapter.

My Life Boxes

My Life boxes appear next to material that relates back to the opening *My Life* scenario and the Learning Objectives. These margin notes offer useful tips and possible solutions to help students better manage their finances.

Smart Money Minute

Each chapter contains several *Smart Money Minute* features with fun facts, information, and financial planning assistance.

Daily purchasing decisions influence cash outflows and long-term financial goals.
georgerudy/123RF

Her take-home pay is $3,100; this amount, plus earnings from savings and investments, gives her an available income of $3,196 for use during the current month.

Take-home pay may also be referred to as *disposable income,* the amount a person or household has available to spend. **Discretionary income** is money left over after paying for housing, food, and other necessities. The amount available for discretionary income will vary by age, income level, and economic conditions. During the recent pandemic many people had very limited discretionary income.

discretionary income
Money left over after paying for housing, food, and other necessities.

STEP 2: RECORD CASH OUTFLOWS Cash payments for living expenses and other items are the second component of a cash flow statement. Lin Ye divides her cash outflows into two major categories: *fixed expenses* and *variable expenses.* While every individual and household has different cash outflows, these main categories, along with the subcategories Lin uses, can be adapted to most situations.

1. *Fixed expenses* are payments that do not vary from month to month. Rent, mortgage payments, loan payments, wifi service fees, and a monthly train ticket for work are examples of constant or fixed cash outflows. For Lin, another type of fixed expense is the amount set aside each month for payments due once or twice a year. For example, Lin pays $384 every March for life insurance. Each month, she records a fixed outflow of $32 for deposit in a savings account so the money will be available when her insurance payment is due.

2. *Variable expenses* are flexible payments that change from month to month. Examples of variable cash outflows are food, clothing, utilities (electricity, cell phone, gas), recreation, medical expenses, gifts, and donations. The use of an app or other system is necessary for an accurate total of cash outflows.

my life 2

I know the details of my cash flow statement.

In what ways might the *Daily Spending Diary* (at the end of Chapter 1) be of value when preparing a personal cash flow statement?

smart money minute

Many people make the **mistake** of not having an accurate record of spending, which results in high debt levels and low saving amounts. An **action** is to use an app or a written spending record, or to track spending with sticky notes, a whiteboard, a monthly calendar, or by collecting receipts as a visual reminder. This can result in **success**—having funds for financial goals and emergencies. To reduce financial stress, potential actions include: (1) Have a low debt-to-income ratio. (2) Delay, reduce, or eliminate unnecessary expenses. (3) Build up emergency savings. (4) Seek additional income by selling unneeded items, working extra hours at your job, securing part-time work, starting a home-based or online business, turning a hobby into a business, or selling your expertise as a consultant. Search online for other ideas for increased income.

STEP 3: DETERMINE NET CASH FLOW The difference between income and outflows can be either a positive (*surplus*) or a negative (*deficit*) cash flow. A deficit exists if more cash goes out than comes in during a month. This amount must be made up by taking money from savings or by borrowing.

When you have a cash surplus, as Lin did (Exhibit 3-4), this amount is available for saving, investing, or paying off debts. Each month, Lin sets aside money for her *emergency fund* in a savings account that she could use for unexpected expenses or to pay living costs if she did not receive her salary. She deposits the additional surplus in savings and investment plans with two purposes: (1) short-term and intermediate financial goals, such as a new car, a vacation, or returning to school; (2) long-term financial security—her retirement.

A cash flow statement is the foundation for a spending, saving, and investment plan. The cash flow statement reports the *actual* spending of a household. In contrast, a budget, with a similar format, is used to *project* income and spending.

The *Financial Literacy Calculations* feature offers tools that may be used to determine how to improve your balance sheet and cash flow statement.

---

personal fintech

Innovative apps and websites are available to assist with money management activities.

- **Albert (www.meetalbert.com)** is an app to guide your financial decisions.
- **EARN (www.earn.org)** helps you to create a habit of saving.
- **Scratch (www.scratch.fi)** helps borrowers understand, manage, and repay loans.
- **SaverLife (about.saverlife.org)** helps you to create a habit of saving.
- **Axos Invest (axosinvest.com)** suggests and manages investments for financial goals.
- **Greenlight (greenlightcard.com)** teaches financial responsibility to children.
- **gohenry (gohenry.com)** helps kids build money management skills.

Personal FinTech

The *Personal FinTech* feature, new to this edition, presents ways in which apps, websites, mobile devices, and other technology are influencing how people earn, save, spend, and invest.

Examples of key concepts and calculations reinforce student learning. The Practice Quizzes provide an ongoing assessment tool.

Highlighted Examples

Worked-out examples featuring key concepts and calculations appear throughout the text for students to see practical applications of personal finance. Many examples include a *How About You?* question to guide personal applications of the topic.

EXAMPLE: Net Worth

If a household has $193,000 of assets and liabilities of $88,000, the net worth would be $105,000 ($193,000 minus $88,000).

How about you? What is an estimate of your current net worth? What actions might you take to increase your net worth?

Practice Quiz

The *Practice Quiz* at the end of each major section provides questions to help students assess their knowledge of the main ideas in that section. As shown here, many of these quizzes include references to related *Personal Financial Planning* sheets, offered both in Excel and in hard copy at the back of the book.

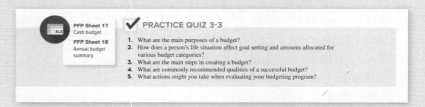

PFP Sheet 17
Cash budget

PFP Sheet 18
Annual budget summary

✓ PRACTICE QUIZ 3-3

1. What are the main purposes of a budget?
2. How does a person's life situation affect goal setting and amounts allocated for various budget categories?
3. What are the main steps in creating a budget?
4. What are commonly recommended qualities of a successful budget?
5. What actions might you take when evaluating your budgeting program?

A variety of end-of-chapter features support the concepts presented in the chapter.

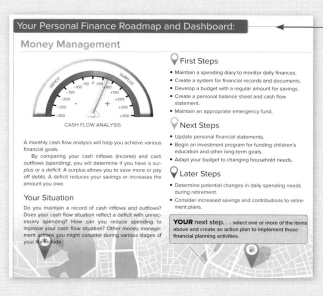

Personal Finance Roadmap and Dashboard

An increasing number of nontraditional students take personal finance. The Dashboard feature provides students of all ages with a high-level snapshot outlining how to evaluate progress for key financial planning activities. The Roadmap at the end of each chapter provides personal finance action items for students of all ages.

Financial Planning Problems

With added and revised items, these problems allow students to apply their quantitative analysis to personal financial decisions.

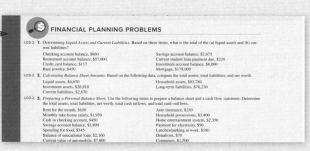

Digital Financial Literacy

The *Digital Financial Literacy* feature provides students with an opportunity to enhance their skills to identify, research, and implement money decisions as both consumers and producers of digital content.

Financial Planning Case

Students are given a hypothetical personal finance dilemma and data to work through to practice concepts learned in the chapter. Questions help students use analytic and critical thinking skills while reinforcing their mastery of chapter topics.

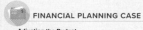

YOUR PERSONAL FINANCIAL PLAN

PERSONAL FINANCIAL STATEMENTS AND A SPENDING PLAN

Money management activities are the foundation for other financial planning actions. Creation of a financial document filing system, a personal balance sheet, a cash flow statement, and a budget provide you with tools for setting, implementing, and achieving financial goals.

Your Short-Term Financial Planning Activity

Task Create a system for financial documents and develop personal financial statements.

Research

1) Based on PFP Sheet 14, propose a filing system to organize your financial records and documents.

2) Using PFP Sheet 15 and 16 or a similar format, create a personal balance sheet and a personal cash flow statement for your current situation.

3) Considering your current situation, use PFP Sheets 17 and 18 to develop a budget and monitor your spending plan

Outcome Add these documents and files to your portfolio or to your Personal Financial Plan online folder.

Your Long-Term Financial Planning Activity

Task Plan long-term savings activities.

Research

1) As needed, use PFP Sheet 19 to plan long-term financial goals related to education.

2) Assess your current emergency fund. Develop a plan, such as automatic withdrawals, to increase your emergency fund and to achieve long-term financial goals.

Outcome Prepare an audio or written summary of your proposed actions for increased savings. What factors are creating any limitations for savings to achieve your financial goals?

Note: All *Personal Financial Planner* sheets are available at the end of the book and in an Excel spreadsheet format in *Connect Finance.*

Your Personal Financial Plan

This feature provides long- and short-term financial planning activities based on the chapter topics, and referenced to relevant *Personal Financial Planner* sheets, located at the end of the book and on Connect.

Continuing Case

The continuing case gives students the opportunity to apply course concepts in a life situation. This feature encourages students to evaluate the changes that affect real life and then respond to the resulting shift in needs, resources, and priorities through the questions at the end of each case.

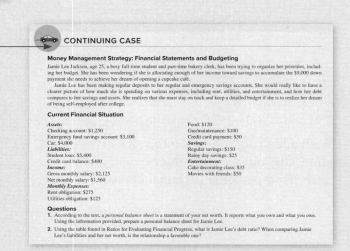

CONTINUING CASE

Money Management Strategy: Financial Statements and Budgeting

Jamie Lee Jackson, age 25, a busy full-time student and part-time bakery clerk, has been trying to organize her priorities, including her budget. She has been wondering if she is allocating enough of her income toward savings to accumulate the $9,000 down payment she needs to achieve her dream of opening a cupcake café.

Jamie Lee has been making regular deposits to her regular and emergency savings accounts. She would really like to have a clearer picture of how much she is spending on various expenses, including rent, utilities, and entertainment, and how her debt compares to her savings and assets. She realizes that she must stay on track and keep a detailed budget if she is to realize her dream of being self-employed after college.

Current Financial Situation

Assets:
Checking account: $1,250
Emergency fund savings account: $3,100
Car: $4,000
Liabilities:
Student loan: $5,400
Credit card balance: $400
Income:
Gross monthly salary: $2,125
Net monthly salary: $1,560
Monthly Expenses:
Rent obligation: $275
Utilities obligation: $125

Food: $120
Gas/maintenance: $100
Credit card payment: $50
Savings:
Regular savings: $150
Rainy day savings: $25
Entertainment:
Cake decorating class: $35
Movies with friends: $50

Questions

1. According to the text, a *personal balance sheet* is a statement of your net worth. It reports what you own and what you owe. Using the information provided, prepare a personal balance sheet for Jamie Lee.

2. Using the table found in Ratios for Evaluating Financial Progress, what is Jamie Lee's debt ratio? When comparing Jamie Lee's liabilities and her net worth, is the relationship a favorable one?

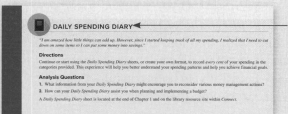

DAILY SPENDING DIARY

"I am amazed how little things can add up. However, since I started keeping track of all my spending, I realized that I need to cut down on some items so I can put some money into savings."

Directions

Continue or start using the *Daily Spending Diary* sheets, or create your own format, to record *every cent* of your spending in the categories provided. This experience will help you better understand your spending patterns and help you achieve financial goals.

Analysis Questions

1. What information from your *Daily Spending Diary* might encourage you to reconsider various money management actions?

2. How can your *Daily Spending Diary* assist you when planning and implementing a budget?

A *Daily Spending Diary* sheet is located at the end of Chapter 1 and on the library resource site within *Connect.*

Daily Spending Diary

Do you buy a latte or a soft drink every day? Do you and your friends meet for a movie once a week? How much do you spend on gas for your car each month? Do you try to donate to your favorite local charity every year?

These spending activities might go unnoticed, yet they have a significant effect on your overall financial health. The *Daily Spending Diary* sheet (following Chapter 1 and online) and end-of-chapter activities offer students a place to track their spending in various categories. Careful monitoring and assessing of spending habits can lead to better financial control and expanded personal financial understanding.

Personal Finance continues to provide instructors and students with features and materials to create a learning environment that can be adapted to any educational setting.

Personal Financial Planner Sheets

The PFP sheets that correlate with sections of the text are located at the end of the text and in an Excel format on *Connect*. Each worksheet asks students to work through the application and record their personal financial plan answers. These sheets apply concepts learned to personal situations and serve as a roadmap for your personal financial future. Students can fill them out, submit them for homework, and keep them filed for future reference!

Key websites are provided to help students research and devise their personal financial plan, and the "What's Next for Your Personal Financial Plan?" section at the end of each sheet challenges students to plan future decisions. The authors also recommend apps to guide help students with this task.

Look for one or more PFP icons next to many Practice Quizzes. The icons direct students to the *Personal Financial Planner* sheet that corresponds with the material in the preceding section.

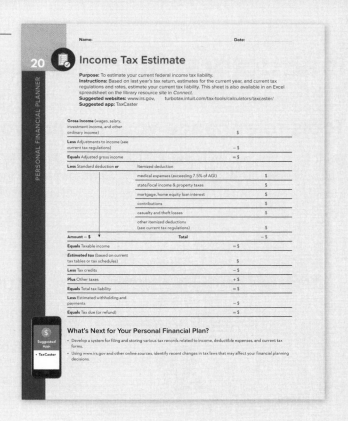

Instructors: Student Success Starts with You

Tools to enhance your unique voice

Want to build your own course? No problem. Prefer to use an OLC-aligned, prebuilt course? Easy. Want to make changes throughout the semester? Sure. And you'll save time with Connect's auto-grading too.

65%
Less Time Grading

Study made personal

Incorporate adaptive study resources like SmartBook® 2.0 into your course and help your students be better prepared in less time. Learn more about the powerful personalized learning experience available in SmartBook 2.0 at **www.mheducation.com/highered/connect/smartbook**

Affordable solutions, added value

Make technology work for you with LMS integration for single sign-on access, mobile access to the digital textbook, and reports to quickly show you how each of your students is doing. And with our Inclusive Access program you can provide all these tools at a discount to your students. Ask your McGraw Hill representative for more information.

Solutions for your challenges

A product isn't a solution. Real solutions are affordable, reliable, and come with training and ongoing support when you need it and how you want it. Visit **www.supportateverystep.com** for videos and resources both you and your students can use throughout the semester.

Students: Get Learning that Fits You

Effective tools for efficient studying

Connect is designed to help you be more productive with simple, flexible, intuitive tools that maximize your study time and meet your individual learning needs. Get learning that works for you with Connect.

Study anytime, anywhere

Download the free ReadAnywhere app and access your online eBook, SmartBook 2.0, or Adaptive Learning Assignments when it's convenient, even if you're offline. And since the app automatically syncs with your Connect account, all of your work is available every time you open it. Find out more at **www.mheducation.com/readanywhere**

> *"I really liked this app—it made it easy to study when you don't have your text-book in front of you."*
>
> - Jordan Cunningham, Eastern Washington University

Everything you need in one place

Your Connect course has everything you need—whether reading on your digital eBook or completing assignments for class, Connect makes it easy to get your work done.

Learning for everyone

McGraw Hill works directly with Accessibility Services Departments and faculty to meet the learning needs of all students. Please contact your Accessibility Services Office and ask them to email accessibility@mheducation.com, or visit **www.mheducation.com/about/accessibility** for more information.

Contents

4 | Planning Your Tax Strategy   118

2 Managing Your Personal Finaces

5 | Financial Services: Savings Plans and Payment Methods   153

6 | Introduction to Consumer Credit   185

5   Investing Your Financial Resources

6 Controlling Your Financial Future

EXHIBIT 1-1

The financial planning process

STEP 2: DEVELOP FINANCIAL GOALS

Several times a year, you should analyze your values and goals. This involves identifying how you feel about money and why you feel that way. Are your feelings about money based on factual knowledge or on the influence of others? Are your financial priorities based on social pressures, household needs, or a desire for security? How will the economy affect your goals and priorities? The purpose of this analysis is to differentiate between your needs and wants. Specific financial goals are vital to financial planning. Others can suggest financial goals for you; however, *you* must decide which goals to pursue.

EXAMPLE: Step 2 - Develop Financial Goals

Kent Mullins has several goals, including paying off his student loans, obtaining an advanced degree in global business management, and working in Latin America for a multinational company. What other goals might be appropriate for Kent?

How about you? Depending on your current (or future) life situation, describe short-term or long-term goals that might be appropriate for you.

Many believe that the quality of life should be measured by something other than money. An emphasis on family, friends, and serving others is a priority. Both financial and personal satisfaction result from an organized process that is commonly referred to as *personal money management* or *personal financial planning*.

Personal financial planning is the process of managing your money to achieve personal economic satisfaction. These actions help you control your financial situation. Since every person, family, or household has a unique financial position, every financial activity should be carefully planned to meet specific needs and goals.

Financial literacy is the use of knowledge and skills for earning, saving, spending, and investing money to achieve personal, family, and community goals. The process includes developing attitudes, behaviors, and competencies to meet current and future financial obligations. Financial literacy leads to financial well-being and a lifetime of financial security, allowing you to adapt to changing personal and economic circumstances. The advantages of being financially literate include:

- Increased effectiveness in obtaining, using, and protecting financial resources.
- Expanded control of financial activities to avoid excessive debt, bankruptcy, and dependence on others.
- Improved personal relationships with well-planned and effectively communicated financial decisions.
- Enhanced freedom from financial worries achieved by looking to the future, anticipating expenses, and achieving personal economic goals.

You make hundreds of decisions each day. Most choices are quite simple, with minimum consequences. Others are complex and have long-term effects. Personal financial activities involve three main decision areas:

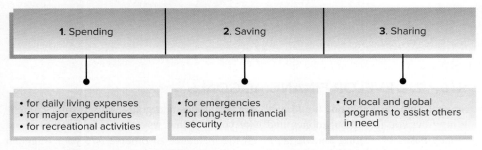

While everyone makes decisions, few people consider how to make better decisions. As Exhibit 1-1 shows, the financial planning process is a six-step procedure that can be adapted to any life situation.

STEP 1: DETERMINE YOUR CURRENT FINANCIAL SITUATION

First, determine your current financial situation regarding income, savings, living expenses, and debts. Maintaining a record of your daily spending and preparing a list of asset and debt balances are the foundation for financial decisions. The Daily Spending Diary at the end of the chapter and the personal financial statements discussed in Chapter 3 provide the information needed to match your goals with your current and future monetary resources.

> ### EXAMPLE: Step 1 - Determine Current Situation
>
> Within the next two months, Kent Mullins will complete his undergraduate studies with a major in global business development. He has worked part time in various sales jobs. He has a small savings fund ($1,700) and over $8,500 in student loans. What additional information should Kent have available when planning his personal finances?
>
> **How about you?** Depending on your current (or future) life situation, what actions might you take to determine your current financial situation?

personal financial planning The process of managing your money to achieve personal economic satisfaction.

Financial Literacy
IN YOUR LIFE

▶ **What if you . . .** needed funds for major auto repairs? Or encountered unexpected medical bills? Financial difficulties of the recent pandemic emphasized the importance of an *emergency fund* for effective personal financial planning. What actions would you take?

You might . . . reduce current spending or seek to earn additional income to start or grow your emergency fund. Tracking your spending will help you set aside money, even a small amount, for financial uncertainty. This action is a first step toward financial security. Next, you should learn to avoid common money mistakes. Your knowledge and actions will allow you to use wise financial strategies for achieving your personal goals.

Now, what would you do? What actions are you currently taking to create or expand your emergency fund? Do you have a system for tracking your spending? You will be able to monitor your progress using the Your Personal Finance Roadmap and Dashboard feature at the end of the chapter.

---

my life | HOW DO I START?

One day, you may receive news that a relative has given you a gift of $10,000. Or you might find yourself with an extensive amount of credit card debt. Or maybe you wish to contribute money to a homeless shelter or a hunger-relief organization.

Each of these financial situations involves planning and taking action. The process you use should be carefully considered so no (or only a few) surprises occur.

The main focus when making decisions is to avoid financial difficulties and legal concerns. How will you best plan to use your finances? For each of the following statements, select "yes," "no," or "uncertain" to indicate your responses to these financial planning activities.

1. When making major financial decisions, I research them using a variety of information sources.	Yes	No	Uncertain
2. My family and household situation is likely to stay fairly stable over the next year or two.	Yes	No	Uncertain
3. My specific financial goals for the next year are in writing.	Yes	No	Uncertain
4. Time value of money calculations often guide my saving and spending decisions.	Yes	No	Uncertain
5. I am able to name specific types of risks that can affect my personal financial decisions.	Yes	No	Uncertain

As you study this chapter, you will encounter "My Life" boxes with additional information and resources related to these items.

The Financial Planning Process

LO1-1

Analyze the process for making personal financial decisions.

Being "rich" means different things to different people. Some define wealth as owning expensive possessions or having a high income. People may associate being rich with not having to worry about finances by being able to pay bills. For others, being rich means donating to organizations that make a difference in our society.

People obtain financial wealth in varied ways. Starting a business or pursuing a high-paying career are common paths. Frugal living and wise investing can also result in long-term financial security. You might consider an *opportunity fund,* money set aside to expand your income and net worth, or to invest in yourself with an advanced degree.

Personal Finance Basics and the Time Value of Money

1

WAYHOME studio/Shutterstock

LEARNING OBJECTIVES

LO1-1 Analyze the process for making personal financial decisions.

LO1-2 Assess personal and economic factors that influence personal financial planning.

LO1-3 Develop personal financial goals.

LO1-4 Calculate time value of money to analyze personal financial decisions.

LO1-5 Identify strategies for achieving personal financial goals for different life situations.

The Chapter 1 Appendix provides expanded discussion of time value of money calculations and applications.

APPENDIX

STEP 3: IDENTIFY ALTERNATIVE COURSES OF ACTION

Identifying alternatives is crucial for making decisions. Although many factors can influence your alternatives, common courses of action include:

- *Continue the same course of action.* For example, you may determine that the amount you are saving each month is still appropriate.
- *Expand the current situation.* You may choose to save a larger amount each month.
- *Change the current situation.* You may decide to use a money market account instead of a regular savings account.
- *Take a new course of action.* You may decide to use your monthly savings budget to pay off credit card debts.

Financial choices require periodic evaluation.
Tetra Images/Getty Images

Not all of these alternatives will apply to every decision; however, they do represent possible courses of action. For example, if you want to stop working full time to go to school, you must generate alternatives under the category "Take a new course of action."

Creative decision-making is vital for effective choices. By considering many alternatives, you will likely make more effective decisions. For instance, most people believe they must own a car. However, other alternatives may include public transportation, carpooling, renting a car, shared car ownership, or use of a ride-sharing program.

Remember, when you decide not to take action, you elect to do nothing, which can be a dangerous alternative.

EXAMPLE: Step 3 - Identify Alternatives

Kent Mullins has several options available for the near future. He could work full time and save for graduate school; he could go to graduate school full time by taking out an additional loan; or he could go to school part time and work part time. What additional alternatives might he consider?

How about you? Depending on your current (or future) life situation, list alternatives for achieving the financial goals you identified in the previous step.

STEP 4: EVALUATE YOUR ALTERNATIVES

Next, evaluate possible courses of action, and consider your life situation, personal values, and current economic conditions. How will the ages of dependents affect your saving goals? How do you like to spend leisure time? How might changes in interest rates affect your financial situation?

opportunity cost What a person gives up by making a choice.

CONSEQUENCES OF CHOICES Every decision closes off alternatives. For example, a decision to invest in stock may mean you cannot take a vacation. A decision to go to school full time may mean you cannot work full time. **Opportunity cost** is what you give up by making a choice. This cost, commonly referred to as a *trade-off,* is not always measured in dollars. It may refer to the money you forgo by attending school rather than working, but it may also be the time you spend comparison shopping for a major purchase. Remember, the resources you give up (money or time) have a value that is lost. Since decision-making will be an ongoing part of your life, always consider the lost opportunities of a decision.

smart money minute

Some people become victims of *lifestyle inflation.* When receiving a salary increase, they overspend and take on more debt. Choose to maintain your existing spending at a frugal level. Instead of buying a bigger house or a new car, pay off debts and save for future needs. Keep living expenses and housing costs low; upgrade, maintain, and improve your current home. Increase your automatic savings amounts. Avoid the temptation to increase your spending just because you have more money.

EVALUATING RISK   Uncertainty is a part of every decision. Selecting a college major and choosing a career field involve risk. What if you don't like working in this field or cannot obtain employment? Some decisions involve a very low risk, such as putting money in an insured savings account or purchasing items that cost only a few dollars. Your chances of losing something of great value are low in these situations.

In many financial decisions, identifying and evaluating risk is difficult (see Exhibit 1-2). The best way to consider risk is to gather information based on your experience and the experiences of others, and to use financial planning information sources.

FINANCIAL PLANNING INFORMATION SOURCES   When you travel, you might use a GPS or map. Traveling the path of financial planning requires a different kind of guidance. Valid information is required at each stage of the decision-making process. This book provides the foundation. Changing personal, social, and economic conditions requires that you continually update your knowledge. Exhibit 1-3 offers an overview of the resources available when making personal financial decisions.

EXAMPLE: Step 4 - Evaluate Alternatives

As Kent Mullins evaluates his alternative courses of action, he must consider his income needs for both the short term and the long term. He should also assess career opportunities based on current skills and potential situations once he obtains advanced training. What risks and trade-offs should Kent consider?

How about you? Depending on your current (or future) life situation, what types of risks might you encounter in your personal financial activities?

EXHIBIT 1-2

Types of risk

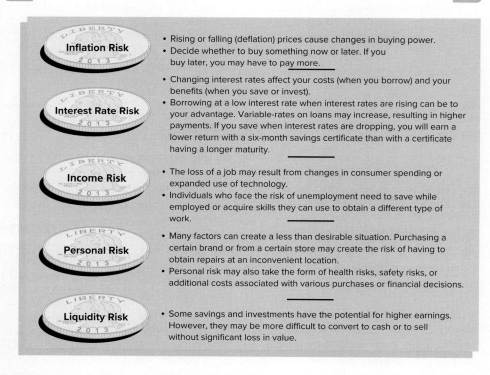

Inflation Risk
- Rising or falling (deflation) prices cause changes in buying power.
- Decide whether to buy something now or later. If you buy later, you may have to pay more.

Interest Rate Risk
- Changing interest rates affect your costs (when you borrow) and your benefits (when you save or invest).
- Borrowing at a low interest rate when interest rates are rising can be to your advantage. Variable-rates on loans may increase, resulting in higher payments. If you save when interest rates are dropping, you will earn a lower return with a six-month savings certificate than with a certificate having a longer maturity.

Income Risk
- The loss of a job may result from changes in consumer spending or expanded use of technology.
- Individuals who face the risk of unemployment need to save while employed or acquire skills they can use to obtain a different type of work.

Personal Risk
- Many factors can create a less than desirable situation. Purchasing a certain brand or from a certain store may create the risk of having to obtain repairs at an inconvenient location.
- Personal risk may also take the form of health risks, safety risks, or additional costs associated with various purchases or financial decisions.

Liquidity Risk
- Some savings and investments have the potential for higher earnings. However, they may be more difficult to convert to cash or to sell without significant loss in value.

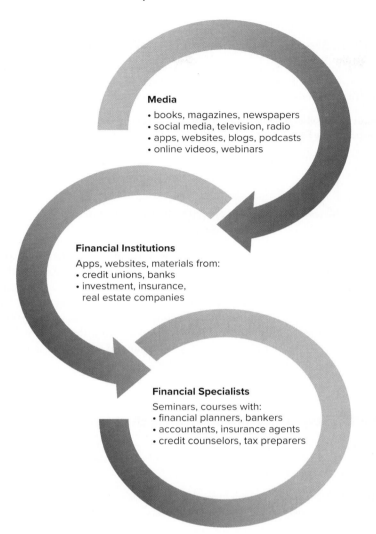

EXHIBIT 1-3
Financial planning information sources

Media
• books, magazines, newspapers
• social media, television, radio
• apps, websites, blogs, podcasts
• online videos, webinars

Financial Institutions

Apps, websites, materials from:
• credit unions, banks
• investment, insurance, real estate companies

Financial Specialists

Seminars, courses with:
• financial planners, bankers
• accountants, insurance agents
• credit counselors, tax preparers

Note: For additional guidance when using financial planning information sources, see the Chapter 3 Appendix.

STEP 5: CREATE AND IMPLEMENT YOUR FINANCIAL ACTION PLAN

The next step of the process involves developing an action plan to achieve your goals. For example, you can increase your savings by reducing spending or by working extra hours. If you are concerned about year-end tax payments, you may increase the amount withheld from your paycheck, file quarterly tax payments, use a tax-deferred retirement program, or invest in tax-exempt securities.

To implement your financial action plan, you may need assistance from others. For example, you may contact an insurance agent to purchase property insurance or use an online investment account to purchase stocks, bonds, or mutual funds.

my life | 1

When making major financial decisions, I research a situation using a variety of information sources.

Always consult several information sources when making financial decisions. In addition to apps and online sources, talk to friends, relatives, and financial planning specialists for banking, insurance, tax, and investment guidance.

EXAMPLE: Step 5 - Implement Financial Action Plan

Kent Mullins has decided to work full time for a few years while he (1) pays off his student loans, (2) saves money for graduate school, and (3) takes a couple of courses in the evenings and on weekends. What are the benefits and drawbacks of this choice?

How about you? Depending on your current (or future) life situation, describe the benefits and drawbacks of a financial situation you have encountered during the past year.

personal fintech

FinTech (financial technology) involves apps, websites, and mobile devices for banking and personal finance activities. Artificial intelligence, robotics, drones, blockchain, and other innovations will influence how you earn, save, spend, and invest. Robo-advisors, for example, offer personalized investment advice based on your income, assets, debt, financial goals, and risk tolerance. Other FinTech activities include crowdfunding, cryptocurrencies, budgeting and payment apps, and start-up insurance companies operating online.

STEP 6: REVIEW AND REVISE YOUR PLAN

Financial planning does not end when you take action. You need to regularly assess your financial decisions. Plan to do a review of your finances at least once a year. Changing personal, social, and economic factors may require more frequent reviews to adapt your financial plan. Regularly reviewing this decision-making process helps connect your financial goals and activities to your current life situation.

EXAMPLE: Step 6 - Review and Revise the Plan

Over the next 6 to 12 months, Kent Mullins should reassess his financial, career, and personal situations. What employment opportunities or family circumstances might affect his need or desire to take a different course of action?

How about you? Depending on your current (or future) life situation, what factors in your life might affect your personal financial situation and decisions in the future?

PFP Sheet 1
Personal Data

PFP Sheet 2
Financial Institutions and Advisors

✓ PRACTICE QUIZ 1-1

1. What are the main elements of every decision we make?
2. What are some risks associated with financial decisions?
3. What are common sources of financial planning information?
4. Why should you reevaluate your actions after making a personal financial decision?

Influences on Personal Financial Planning

LO1-2

Assess personal and economic factors that influence personal financial planning.

Many factors influence daily financial decisions, such as age, household size, interest rates, and inflation. An *ecosystem* is a network of activities and interconnections. Elements of the personal finance ecosystem include life situation, personal values, the financial system, and economic factors.

LIFE SITUATION AND PERSONAL VALUES

People in their 20s have different spending behaviors than those in their 50s. Personal factors such as age, income, household size, and personal beliefs influence spending and saving patterns. Life situation or lifestyle is a composite of several factors.

As society changes, different financial needs surface. In contrast to the past, people today tend to marry at a later age, and more households have two incomes. Many households are headed by single parents. Millions of women provide care for both dependent children and parents. People are also living longer; over 80 percent of Americans now living are expected to live past age 65.

The **adult life cycle**—the stages in the family situation and financial needs of an adult—influences financial activities and decisions. Your life situation is affected by marital status, household size, and employment. In addition, financial decisions will be influenced by events such as graduation (at different levels of education), the birth or adoption of a child, a career change, dependent children leaving home, changes in health, divorce, retirement, and the death of a spouse or family member.

In addition to family situation, you are defined by your **values**—the ideas and principles that you consider correct, desirable, and important. Values have a direct influence on decisions such as whether to spend now or save for the future, or whether to continue school or get a job.

my life 2

My personal situation is likely to stay fairly stable over the next year or two.

Many personal, social, and economic factors can affect your life situation. Refer to Exhibit 1-6 for further information on financial goals and personal finance activities for you to consider.

adult life cycle The stages in the family situation and financial needs of an adult.

values Ideas and principles that a person considers correct, desirable, and important.

THE FINANCIAL SYSTEM AND ECONOMIC FACTORS

The financial system and daily economic activities influence personal financial decisions. As shown in Exhibit 1-4, money in an economy flows from providers of funds to users of funds through intermediaries and financial markets. The buying and selling of investments occur in these financial settings.

While some investments involve physical items (houses, land, gold, rare art), others represent borrowing or ownership. A *security* is a financial instrument that represents debt or equity. *Debt securities,* such as bonds, represent money borrowed by companies or governments. These debt securities are often bought as an investment. In contrast, *equity securities* (stock) represent ownership in a corporation. Shares of stock are also bought by investors. In addition to stocks and bonds, other examples of securities include mutual funds, certificates of deposit (CDs), and commodity futures.

EXHIBIT 1-4 The financial system

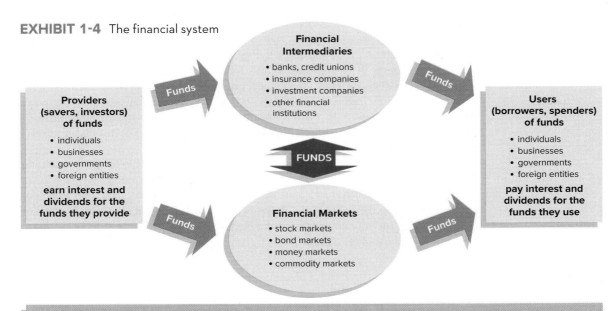

Financial Regulators: Federal Reserve System, Federal Deposit Insurance Corporation, National Credit Union Administration, Office of the Comptroller of the Currency, Consumer Financial Protection Bureau, Securities and Exchange Commission, state banking agencies, state insurance agencies.

economics The study of
how wealth is created and
distributed.

In most societies, the forces of supply and demand set prices for securities, goods, and services. **Economics** is the study of how wealth is created and distributed. The economic environment includes various institutions, such as businesses, labor, and government, that work together to satisfy needs and wants.

Several government agencies regulate financial activities (see Exhibit 1-4). The Federal Reserve System, the central bank of the United States, has significant economic responsibility. *The Fed* attempts to maintain an adequate money supply with efforts to influence borrowing, interest rates, and the buying and selling of government securities. An appropriate money supply is necessary for consumer spending and business expansion while keeping interest rates and consumer prices at an acceptable level.

GLOBAL INFLUENCES   The global economy also influences personal finance. Our economy is affected by both the financial activities of foreign investors and competition from global companies. U.S. businesses compete against foreign companies for the spending dollars of consumers.

When the value of exports of U.S.-made goods is lower than the value of imported goods, more U.S. dollars leave the country than the dollar value of foreign currency coming into the United States. This reduces the funds available for domestic spending and investment. Also, if foreign companies decide not to invest in the United States, the domestic money supply is reduced. This reduced money supply can result in higher interest rates. A *trade deficit* also affects the value of a nation's money and the cost of items being purchased by consumers. While a country may impose a *tariff,* an import tax, to reduce its trade deficit, this action may not have the intended effect.

ECONOMIC CONDITIONS   The economic conditions that most often influence personal finance are consumer prices, consumer spending, and interest rates. These and other economic factors are presented in Exhibit 1-5.

inflation A rise in the general level of prices.

1. Consumer Prices Inflation is a rise in the general level of prices. In times of inflation, the buying power of the dollar decreases. For example, if prices increased 5 percent during the last year, items that cost $100 one year ago would now cost $105. This means it now takes more money to buy the same amount of goods and services as a year ago.

The main cause of inflation is an increase in demand without a comparable increase in supply. For example, if people have more money to spend because of pay increases or borrowing but the same amounts of goods and services are available, the increased demand can bid up prices for goods and services.

Inflation is most harmful to people living on fixed incomes. Due to inflation, retired people and others with fixed incomes can afford fewer goods and services.

Inflation can also adversely affect lenders of money. Unless an adequate interest rate is charged, amounts repaid by borrowers in times of inflation have less buying power than the money borrowed. If you pay 4 percent interest on a loan and the inflation rate is 6 percent, the dollars you pay the lender have lost buying power. For this reason, interest rates rise in periods of higher inflation.

The rate of inflation varies. During the late 1950s and early 1960s, the annual inflation rate was in the 1 to 3 percent range. During the late 1970s and early 1980s, the cost of living increased 10 to 12 percent annually. At a 12 percent annual inflation rate, prices double (and the value of the dollar is cut in half) in about six years. To find out how fast prices (or your savings) will double, use the *rule of 72:* Just divide 72 by the annual inflation (or interest) rate.

EXAMPLE: Rule of 72

An annual inflation rate of 4 percent, for example, means prices will double in 18 years (72 ÷ 4 = 18). Regarding savings, if you earn 6 percent, your money will double in 12 years (72 ÷ 6 = 12).

EXHIBIT 1-5 Changing economic conditions and financial decisions

Economic Factor	What It Measures	How It Influences Financial Planning
Consumer prices	The buying power of a dollar; inflation.	If consumer prices increase faster than income, you are not able to purchase the same amount of goods and services; higher consumer prices often cause higher interest rates.
Consumer spending	The demand for goods and services by individuals and households.	Increased consumer spending usually creates more jobs and higher wages; high levels of consumer spending and borrowing may push up consumer prices and interest rates.
Interest rates	The cost of money; the cost of credit when you borrow; the return on your money when you save or invest.	Higher interest rates make buying on credit more expensive; higher interest rates make saving and investing more attractive and may discourage borrowing.
Money supply	The dollars available for spending in our economy.	Interest rates tend to decline as more people save and invest, but higher saving (and lower spending) may also reduce job opportunities.
Unemployment	The number of people without jobs who are willing and able to work.	Unemployed people should reduce spending and may need to access their emergency fund; high unemployment reduces consumer spending and future job opportunities.
Housing starts	The number of new homes being built.	Increased home building creates jobs, higher wages, more consumer spending, and overall economic expansion.
Gross domestic product (GDP)	The total value of goods and services produced within a country's borders, including items produced with foreign resources.	GDP is an indication of a nation's economic viability, resulting in jobs and opportunities for increased personal wealth.
Trade balance	The difference between a country's exports and its imports.	If a country has more exports than imports, the balance of trade deficit can result in price changes for foreign goods.
Dow Jones Average, S&P 500, other stock market indexes	The relative value of stocks represented by the index.	These indexes provide an indication of the general movement of stock prices.

Price changes for goods and services are measured with the use of a price index. The *consumer price index (CPI)*, published by the Bureau of Labor Statistics, is a measure of the average change in the prices urban consumers pay for a fixed "basket" of goods and services. For current CPI information, go to www.bls.gov.

Inflation rates can be deceptive. Most people face *hidden* inflation since the cost of necessities (food, gas, health care), on which they spend most of their money, may rise at a higher rate than the cost of nonessential items. This results in a *personal* inflation rate that is higher than the government's CPI. Cost of living also varies by geographic area. At www.nerdwallet.com/cost-of-living-calculator you can compare living costs in different cities.

Deflation, a decline in prices, can also have damaging economic effects. As prices drop, consumers tend to expect the prices to go even lower. As a result, people cut their spending, which causes damaging economic conditions. While widespread deflation is unlikely, some items may be affected with the prices of those items declining.

HOW TO . . .   Set a Path to Financial Security

Do you feel stress when you think about money? Are your financial decisions influenced by emotions or valid information? Do you often have disagreements with others about money?

To address these and other concerns, two paths exist for your money decisions. The *easy* path involves little thinking, no planning, and minimal effort, usually resulting in wasted money and financial difficulties. In contrast, the *appropriate* path takes some time and effort, but results in lower stress and better financial security.

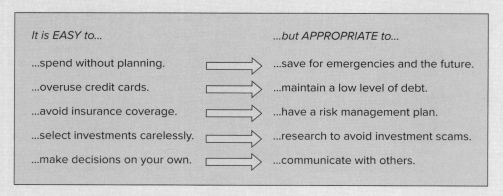

It is EASY to...   ...but APPROPRIATE to...

...spend without planning.   →   ...save for emergencies and the future.

...overuse credit cards.   →   ...maintain a low level of debt.

...avoid insurance coverage.   →   ...have a risk management plan.

...select investments carelessly.   →   ...research to avoid investment scams.

...make decisions on your own.   →   ...communicate with others.

You can start to move yourself from *easy mistakes* to *appropriate actions* with these steps:

1. **Do something.** Start small, such as saving a small amount each month. Or, reduce your credit card use.

2. **Avoid excuses.** Do not tell yourself that "I don't have time" or "It's what everyone else is doing."

3. **Rate your current situation.** Indicate on this scale where you are currently in relation to the two available paths:

Spender   Saver

Financial difficulties   Financial security

4. **Set your mission.** Create a *personal finance mission statement* with your personal values, goals, and future vision. This paragraph (or list or drawing or other format) will remind you and family members of the desired path for financial security. The wording should describe where you want to be and how you will get there. Develop a financial mission statement by talking with those who can help guide you. Your personal finance mission statement may include phrases such as "My financial mission is to change my spending habits for . . .," "I will . . . to better understand my insurance needs," or ". . . to donate (or volunteer) to local community service organizations."

Choose appropriate actions with deadlines and calendar reminders. This approach can result in reduced emotional stress, improved personal relationships, and enhanced financial security.

2. Consumer Spending Total demand for goods and services in the economy influences employment opportunities and income potential. As consumer purchasing increases, the financial resources of employees expand. This situation improves the financial condition of many households.

In contrast, reduced consumer spending can cause unemployment with staff reductions resulting from lower demand for a company's goods and services. The financial hardships of unemployment are a major concern of labor, business, and government. Retraining programs, income assistance, and job services can help people adjust.

3. Interest Rates In simple terms, interest rates are the cost of money. Like everything else, money has a price. The forces of supply and demand influence interest rates. When consumer saving and investing increase the supply of money, interest rates tend to decrease. However, as consumer, business, government, and foreign borrowing increase the demand for money, interest rates rise.

Interest rates affect financial planning. The earnings you receive as a saver or an investor reflect current interest rates as well as a *risk premium* based on the length of time your funds will be used by others, expected inflation, and the uncertainty about getting your money back. Risk is also a factor in the interest rate you pay as a borrower. People with poor credit ratings pay a higher interest rate than people with good credit ratings. Interest rates influence many financial decisions. Current interest rate data may be obtained at www.federalreserve.gov.

 **PRACTICE QUIZ 1-2**

PFP Sheet 3
Current Economic
Conditions

1. How do age, marital status, household size, employment situation, and other personal factors affect financial planning?
2. How might the uncertainty of inflation make personal financial planning difficult?
3. What factors influence the level of interest rates?

Developing Personal Financial Goals

Since the United States is one of the richest countries in the world, it is difficult to understand why so many Americans have money problems. The answer is the result of poor planning and weak money management related to spending and credit use. Achieving personal financial satisfaction starts with tracking your spending (see Daily Spending Diary at the end of the chapter) and creating clear financial goals.

LO1-3

Develop personal financial goals.

TYPES OF FINANCIAL GOALS

Two factors commonly influence your financial plans for the future. The first is the time frame in which you would like to achieve a goal. The second is the financial need that drives your goals.

TIMING OF GOALS   What would you like to do tomorrow? Believe it or not, that question involves goal setting, which may be viewed in three time frames:

A variety of personal and financial goals will motivate your actions.
Rawpixel.com/Shutterstock

1. *Short-term goals,* such as saving for a vacation or paying off small debts, might be achieved within the next year.
2. *Intermediate goals* have a time frame from one to five years.
3. *Long-term goals* involve financial plans of more than five years, such as retirement, funding children's college education, or purchase of a vacation home.

smart money minute

To become financially disciplined: (1) select a word or short phrase to describe your goal; (2) use a visual reminder—a photo, sticky note, notecard, or goal progress chart placed on your desk, computer, bathroom mirror, refrigerator, or car dashboard; (3) keep a financial diary or journal; (4) obtain support—work with a friend, roommate, spouse, or group to stay accountable.

Financial goals often lack the "why" to achieve meaningful results. If you cannot answer "why," this may indicate that a goal is not appropriate for you. What is the "why" for one of your financial goals?

Long-term goals should be coordinated with short-term and intermediate ones. Setting and achieving short-term goals is the basis for achieving long-term goals. For example, saving for a down payment to buy a house is an intermediate goal that can be the foundation for a long-term goal: owning your own home.

Goal frequency is another ingredient in the process. Some goals, such as saving for a vacation or holiday gifts, may be set annually. Other goals, such as a college education, a car, or a house, occur less frequently.

GOALS FOR DIFFERENT FINANCIAL NEEDS   A goal of obtaining increased career training is different from a goal of saving money to pay your auto insurance. *Consumable-product goals* usually occur on a periodic basis and involve items that are used up relatively quickly, such as food, clothing, and entertainment. Such purchases, if not planned, can have a negative effect on your financial situation.

Durable-product goals usually involve infrequently purchased, expensive items such as appliances, cars, or sports equipment; these are tangible items. In contrast, many people overlook *intangible-purchase goals*. These goals may relate to personal relationships, health, education, and leisure. Goal setting for these life circumstances is necessary for your overall well-being.

GOAL-SETTING GUIDELINES

An old saying goes, "If you don't know where you're going, you might end up somewhere else and not even know it." Goal setting is central to financial decision-making. Your goals are the foundation for planning, implementing, and measuring the progress of spending, saving, and investing. Exhibit 1-6 offers goals for financial literacy and long-term security, along with attitudes, abilities, and actions to achieve those goals.

Your financial goals should take a SMART approach, in that they are:

S—*specific,* so you know exactly what your goals are so you can create a plan to achieve them.

M—*measurable* with a specific amount. For example, "Accumulate $5,000 in an investment fund within three years" is easier to determine success than "Put money into an investment fund."

A—*action-oriented,* involving the personal financial activities to be taken. For example, "Reduce credit card debt" means actions must be taken to pay off amounts owed.

R—*realistic,* selecting goals based on your income and life situation. For example, it is probably not realistic to buy a new car each year if you are a full-time student.

T—*time-based,* indicating a time frame for achieving the goal, such as three years, which allows you to measure your progress.

Your financial goals are just the start of financial planning activities. Identifying and implementing actions to achieve these goals must now occur. Commit to a process with a focus on what you will do. And be ready to modify and revise goals due to uncontrollable events such as the recent COVID-19 pandemic.

my life 3

My specific financial goals for the next year are written down.

Having specific financial goals in writing that you review on a regular basis is the foundation of successful personal financial planning. To start (or continue) creating and achieving your financial goals, use the *Financial Literacy for My Life: Developing Financial Goals* feature.

PFP Sheet 4
Setting Personal
Financial Goals

✓ PRACTICE QUIZ 1-3

1. What are examples of long-term goals?
2. What are the five main characteristics of useful financial goals?

Financial Literacy for My Life

DEVELOPING FINANCIAL GOALS

Based on your current situation or expectations for the future, use the SMART format to create a financial goal that you would like to accomplish regarding saving, spending, or sharing your time, talents, or financial resources.

Example	Your Goal
Specific....... Create an emergency fund...	
Measurable....... of $1,800...	
Action-oriented....... at a credit union...	
Realistic....... by reduced spending on food away from home...	
Time-based....... within the next six months.	

What are your next actions to achieve this financial goal?
1.
2.
3.

See *Personal Financial Planner Sheet 4* to plan and implement your financial goals.

EXHIBIT 1-6 Goals and actions for personal financial literacy

PERSONAL FINANCE INFORMATION SOURCES	GOALS FOR ACTION	FINANCIAL LITERACY DEVELOPMENT
ATTITUDES, ABILITIES	**Short-term**	**EXPERIENTIAL LEARNING**
• A desire for ongoing learning in varied settings	• Obtain needed career training	... use interviews, observations, and market experiences for improved financial decisions.
• A willingness to monitor spending and saving activities	• Create a financial document system	
• Reconciliation of varied money attitudes among family and household members	• Track spending; create/implement a budget	**RETENTION, REINFORCEMENT**
• Motivation to reduce or eliminate unplanned spending and credit use	• Begin emergency fund, regular savings plan	... consistently use knowledge and skills for wise money management and personal financial decisions.
• Determination and discipline to achieve long-term goals	• Reduce/eliminate existing credit balances	
• A commitment to share time, talents, and resources with others	• Purchase appropriate insurance coverages	**CRITICAL THINKING**
	• Explore additional income sources	... creatively analyze and solve problems for financial opportunities.
	Long-term	
	• Monitor investments for changing needs	
	• Seek actions for beneficial tax planning	
	• Ongoing review of changing life situation	
	• Adapt budget, financial plan, as needed	
	• Assess changing career opportunities	
	• Plan retirement income, living situation	

Opportunity Costs and the Time Value of Money

Have you noticed that you must give up something when you make choices? In every financial decision, you sacrifice something to obtain something else that you consider more desirable. For example, you might reduce current spending to invest funds for future purchases or long-term financial security. Or you might obtain use of an item now by making credit payments from future earnings. These *opportunity costs* may be viewed in terms of both personal and financial resources (see Exhibit 1-7).

LO1-4

Calculate time value of money to analyze personal financial decisions.

PERSONAL OPPORTUNITY COSTS

A valuable personal opportunity cost involves time, which when used for one activity cannot be used for other activities. Time used for studying, working, or shopping will not

EXHIBIT 1-7

Opportunity costs and financial results should be assessed when making financial decisions

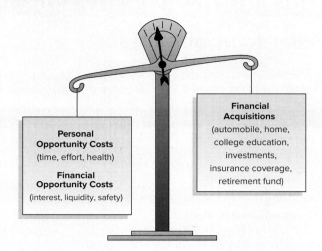

be available for other uses. The allocation of time should be viewed like other resources; select your use of time to meet your needs, achieve your goals, and satisfy personal values.

Other personal opportunity costs relate to health. Poor eating habits, lack of sleep, or avoiding exercise can result in illness, time away from school or work, increased health care costs, and reduced financial security. Like financial resources, your personal resources (time, energy, health, abilities, knowledge) require careful management.

FINANCIAL OPPORTUNITY COSTS

Would you rather have $100 today or $105 a year from now? How about $120 a year from now instead of $100 today? Your choice among these alternatives will depend on several factors, including current needs, future uncertainty, and current interest rates. If you wait to receive your money in the future, you want to be rewarded for the risk. The **time value of money** calculates increases in an amount of money as a result of interest earned. Saving or investing a dollar instead of spending it today results in a future amount greater than a dollar. Every time you spend, save, invest, or borrow money, you should consider the time value of the money as an opportunity cost. Spending money from your savings account means lost interest earnings; however, the purchase may have a higher priority than the earnings. Borrowing to make a purchase involves the opportunity cost of paying interest on the loan, but your current needs may make the trade-off worthwhile.

The opportunity cost of the time value of money is also present in these financial decisions:

- Setting aside funds in a savings plan with little or no risk has the opportunity cost of potentially higher returns from an investment with greater risk.
- Having extra money withheld from your paycheck in order to receive a tax refund has the opportunity cost of the lost interest the money could earn for you.
- Making annual deposits in a retirement account can avoid the opportunity cost of having inadequate funds later in life.
- Purchasing a new automobile or home appliance has the potential benefit of saving money on future maintenance and energy costs.

INTEREST CALCULATIONS   Three amounts are required to calculate the time value of money for savings in the form of interest earned:

1. The amount of the savings (commonly called the *principal*).

2. The annual interest rate.

3. The length of time the money is on deposit.

time value of money Increases in an amount of money as a result of interest earned.

These three items are multiplied to obtain the amount of interest. Simple interest is calculated as follows:

| Amount in savings | × | Annual interest rate | × | Time period | = | Interest |

For example, $1,000 on deposit at 3 percent for six months would earn $15 (calculated as: $1,000 × 0.03 × 6 months/12 months).

The increased value of money from interest earned involves two types of time value of money calculations: future value and present value. The amount available at a later date is called the *future value*. In contrast, the current value of an amount in the future is the *present value*. Five methods are available for calculating time value of money:

1. *Formula Calculation.* With this conventional method, math notations are used to compute future value and present value.

2. *Time Value of Money Tables.* Before calculators and computers, future value and present value tables were commonly used for easier calculations.

3. *Financial Calculator.* Specialized calculators are programmed with financial functions. Both future value and present value calculations use appropriate keystrokes.

4. *Spreadsheet Software.* Excel and other spreadsheet programs have built-in formulas for financial computations, including future value and present value.

5. *Websites and Apps.* Time-value-of-money calculators are available online and through mobile devices. These programs calculate the future value of savings as well as loan payment amounts.

future value The amount to which current savings will increase based on a certain interest rate and a certain time period; also referred to as *compounding*.

FUTURE VALUE OF A SINGLE AMOUNT Deposited money earns interest that will increase over time. **Future value** is the amount to which current savings will grow based on a certain interest rate and a certain time period. For example, $100 deposited in a 4 percent account for one year will grow to $104. This amount is computed as follows:

Future value = $100 + ($100 × 0.04 × 1 year) + $104

The same process could continue for a second, third, and fourth year, but the computations would be time-consuming. The previously mentioned calculation methods make the process easier.

An example of the future value of a single amount might involve an investment of $650 earning 8 percent for 10 years. This situation would be calculated as follows:

 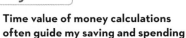 

my life **4**

Time value of money calculations often guide my saving and spending decisions.

To assist you with using future value and present value computations for achieving personal financial goals, several websites are available: for example, www.dinkytown.net, www.moneychimp.com/calculator, and cgi.money.cnn.com/tools.

Formula	Time Value of Money Table	Financial Calculator	Spreadsheet Software
$FV = PV(1+i)^n$ $FV = 650(1+.08)^{10}$ $FV = \$1,403.30$ i – interest rate n – number of time periods	Using Exhibit 1-A (Chapter Appendix), multiply the amount deposited by the factor for the interest rate and time period. $650 × 2.159 = \$1,403.35$	PV, I/Y, N, PMT, CPT FV 650 PV, 8 I/Y, 10 N, 0 PMT, CPT FV $1,403.30 (Different financial calculators will require different keystrokes.)	= FV(rate, periods, amount per period, single amount) = FV(0.08,10,0,−650) = $1,403.30

(*Note:* Expanded explanations of these time value of money calculation methods are presented in the Chapter Appendix.)

Financial Literacy Calculations

USING TIME VALUE OF MONEY FOR ACHIEVING FINANCIAL GOALS

Achieving specific financial goals may require making regular savings deposits or determining an amount to be invested. By using time value of money calculations, you can compute the amount needed to achieve a financial goal.

Situation 1. Jonie Emerson has two children who will start college in 10 years. She plans to set aside $1,500 a year for her children's college education during that period and estimates she will earn an annual interest rate of 5 percent on her savings. What amount can Jonie expect to have available for her children's college education when they start college?

Formula	Time Value of Money Table	Financial Calculator	Spreadsheet Software
$FV = \text{Annuity}\dfrac{(1+i)^n - 1}{i}$ $FV = 1500\dfrac{(1+.05)^{10} - 1}{.05}$ $FV = \$18,866.84$	Using Exhibit 1-B (Chapter Appendix), multiply the amount deposited by the factor for the interest rate and time period. $1,500 \times 12.578 = \$18,867$	[PV] [I/Y] [N] [PMT] [CPT] [FV] 0 [PV], 5 [I/Y], 10 [N], -1500 [PMT], [CPT] [FV] $18,866.84 (Different financial calculators will require different keystrokes.)	= FV(rate, periods, amount per period, amount, type) = FV(0.05,10,−1500,0,0) = $18,866.84

Conclusion. Based on these calculations, if Jonie deposits $1,500 a year at an annual interest rate of 5 percent, she would have $18,867 available for her children's college education.

Situation 2. Don Yamada wants to have $50,000 available in 10 years as a reserve fund for his parents' retirement living expenses and health care. If he earns an average of 8 percent on his investments, what amount must he invest today to achieve this goal?

Formula	Time Value of Money Table	Financial Calculator	Spreadsheet Software
$PV = \dfrac{FV}{(1+i)^n}$ $PV = \dfrac{50,000}{(1+.08)^{10}}$ $PV = \$23,159.67$	Using Exhibit 1-C (Chapter Appendix), multiply the amount desired by the factor for the interest rate and time period. $50,000 \times 0.463 = \$23,150$ (this slight difference is due to the rounding of table factors in the appendix exhibit)	[FV] [N] [I/Y] [PMT] [CPT] [PV] −50000 [FV], 10 [N], 8 [I/Y], 0 [PMT], [CPT] [PV] $23,159.67 (Different financial calculators will require different keystrokes.)	= PV(rate, periods, payment, future value amount, type) = PV(0.08,10,0,−50000) = $23,159.67

Conclusion. Don needs to invest approximately $23,160 today for 10 years at 8 percent to achieve the desired financial goal.

(*Note:* Expanded explanations of these time value of money calculation methods are presented in the Chapter Appendix.)

Future value computations are also referred to as *compounding* since interest is earned on previously earned interest. Compounding allows the future value of a deposit to grow faster than if interest were paid only on the original deposit. The sooner you make deposits, the greater the future value will be. Depositing $1,000 in a 5 percent account at age 40 will give you $3,386 at age 65. However, making the $1,000 deposit at age 25 would result in an account balance of $7,040 at age 65.

FUTURE VALUE OF A SERIES OF DEPOSITS Many savers and investors make regular deposits. An *annuity* is a series of equal deposits or payments. To determine the future value of equal yearly savings deposits, time value of money tables can be used (see Exhibit 1-B, Chapter Appendix). For this table to be used, and for an annuity to exist, the deposits must earn a constant interest rate. For example, if you deposit $50 a year at 7 percent for six years, starting at the end of the first year, you will have $357.65 at the end of that time ($50 × 7.153). The *Financial Literacy Calculations: Using Time Value of Money for Achieving Financial Goals* feature presents examples of using time value of money to achieve financial goals.

PRESENT VALUE OF A SINGLE AMOUNT   Another aspect of the time value of money involves the current value of an amount desired in the future. **Present value** is the current value for a future amount based on a particular interest rate for a certain period of time. Present value computations, also called *discounting,* determine how much to deposit now to obtain a desired amount in the future. For example, using the present value table (Exhibit 1-C, Chapter Appendix), if you want $1,000 five years from now and you earn 5 percent on your savings, you need to deposit $784 ($1,000 × 0.784).

> **present value** The current value for a future amount based on a certain interest rate and a certain time period; also referred to as *discounting.*

PRESENT VALUE OF A SERIES OF DEPOSITS   Present value computations may also be used to determine how much you need to deposit now so that you can withdraw a certain amount for a set number of years. For example, if you want to take $400 out of an investment account each year for nine years and your money is earning an annual rate of 8 percent, you can see from Exhibit 1-D (Chapter Appendix) that you need to make a current deposit of $2,498.80 ($400 × 6.247).

Additional details for the formulas, tables, and other methods for calculating time value of money are presented in the Chapter Appendix.

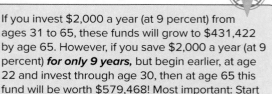

smart money minute

If you invest $2,000 a year (at 9 percent) from ages 31 to 65, these funds will grow to $431,422 by age 65. However, if you save $2,000 a year (at 9 percent) *for only 9 years,* but begin earlier, at age 22 and invest through age 30, then at age 65 this fund will be worth $579,468! Most important: Start saving and investing now!

 PRACTICE QUIZ 1-4

1. How can you use future value and present value computations to measure the opportunity cost of a financial decision?
2. Use a financial calculator or the time value of money tables in the Chapter Appendix to calculate the following:
   a. The future value of $100 at 7 percent in 10 years.
   b. The future value of $100 a year for six years earning 6 percent.
   c. The present value of $500 received in eight years with an interest rate of 8 percent.

PFP Sheet 5
Time Value
of Money
Calculations

Achieving Financial Goals

Throughout life, your needs will usually be satisfied with wise use of financial resources. By using eight major areas of personal finance to organize your financial activities, you can avoid many common money mistakes.

LO1-5

Identify strategies for achieving personal financial goals for different life situations.

COMPONENTS OF PERSONAL FINANCIAL PLANNING

This book provides a framework of eight areas for the study and planning of personal financial decisions (Exhibit 1-8). To achieve personal finance success, coordinate these components with an organized plan and wise decision-making.

OBTAINING (CHAPTER 2)   Financial resources, most often obtained from employment, investments, or business ownership, are the foundation of planning and financial decision making.

EXHIBIT 1-8

Components of personal financial planning

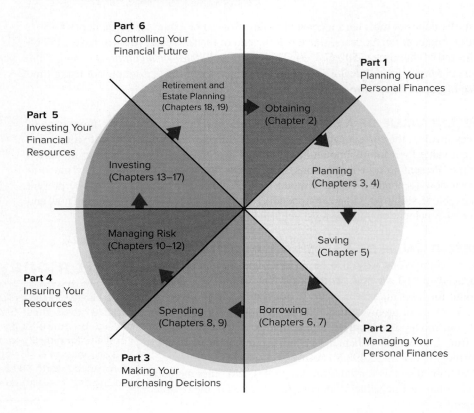

Part 6
Controlling Your
Financial Future

Part 1
Planning Your
Personal Finances

Part 5
Investing Your
Financial
Resources

Part 4
Insuring Your
Resources

Part 3
Making Your
Purchasing Decisions

Part 2
Managing Your
Personal Finances

Retirement and
Estate Planning
(Chapters 18, 19)

Obtaining
(Chapter 2)

Investing
(Chapters 13–17)

Planning
(Chapters 3, 4)

Managing Risk
(Chapters 10–12)

Saving
(Chapter 5)

Spending
(Chapters 8, 9)

Borrowing
(Chapters 6, 7)

EXAMPLE: Apps and Online Sources for Obtaining

Assistance for effective career planning and professional development may be obtained at www.careerbuilder.com and www.monster.com. Consider career apps such as Glassdoor and Interview Preparation Guide.

PLANNING (CHAPTERS 3, 4)   Planned spending with a budget is key to achieving goals and future financial security. A spending plan starts with tracking your spending (see Daily Spending Diary at the end of the chapter). Efforts to anticipate expenses and financial decisions can reduce taxes. Wise tax planning is a vital element for increasing your financial resources.

EXAMPLE: Apps and Online Sources for Planning

Budgeting is an ongoing activity, and tax planning should not occur only around April 15. For assistance, go to www.kiplinger.com/millennial-money, www.20somethingfinance.com, www.moneyunder30.com/, and www.irs.gov. Planning apps include Mint, Expense Keep, and Mvelopes.

SAVING (CHAPTER 5)   Long-term financial security starts with regular savings for emergencies, unexpected bills, replacement of major items, and future goals such as a college education, a boat, or a vacation home. Once you have established a basic savings plan, use additional funds for investments that offer greater financial growth.

Some savings must be available to meet current household needs. **Liquidity** is the ability to readily convert financial resources into cash without a loss in value. The need

liquidity The ability to readily convert financial resources into cash without a loss in value.

for liquidity will vary based on a person's age, health, job, and family situation. Savings plans such as high-yield savings accounts, money market accounts, and money market funds earn money while providing liquidity.

EXAMPLE: Apps and Online Sources for Saving

Fast updates on savings rates and other banking services are available at www.bankrate.com and www.depositaccounts.com. Savings apps include Mint and Qapital.

BORROWING (CHAPTERS 6, 7)   Appropriate credit use can contribute to your financial goals. Misuse of credit will cause a situation in which debts far exceed the resources available to pay those debts. **Bankruptcy** is the legal status of a person who is not able to pay debts owed. Federal laws exist that allow you to either restructure your debts or remove certain debts. However, people who declare bankruptcy may have avoided this trauma with wise spending and borrowing decisions. Chapter 7 discusses bankruptcy in detail.

bankruptcy The legal status of a person who is not able to pay debts owed.

EXAMPLE: Apps and Online Sources for Borrowing

Current rates for credit cards, personal loans, and other types of credit information are available at www.nerdwallet.com, www.bankrate.com, www.eloan.com, and the CreditWise app.

SPENDING (CHAPTERS 8, 9)

Financial planning is designed not to prevent enjoyment of life but to help obtain the things you want. Too often, however, people make purchases without considering the financial consequences. Some people shop compulsively, creating financial difficulties. Monitor your living expenses and other financial obligations with a spending plan. Spending less than you earn is the only way to achieve long-term financial security.

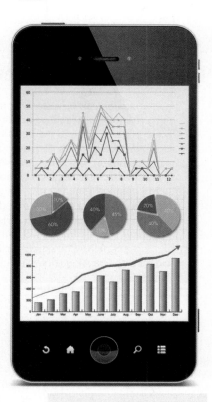

EXAMPLE: Apps and Online Sources for Spending

Consumer buying information is available at www.consumerworld.org and www.consumer.gov. To plan and research car purchases, consider www.carbuyingtips.com and www.consumerreports.org. Prospective home buyers can obtain financing online at www.hsh.com and www.realtor.com. Apps include Trulia and Zillow.

MANAGING RISK (CHAPTERS 10-12)   Adequate insurance is another component of personal financial planning. Certain types of insurance are commonly overlooked. For example, the number of people who suffer disabling injuries or diseases at age 50 is greater than the number who die at that age, so a person may need disability insurance more than life insurance. Yet surveys reveal that more people have adequate life insurance, but fewer have disability insurance. The insurance industry is often more aggressive in selling life insurance than selling disability insurance, putting the burden of obtaining disability insurance on you.

The planning component of personal finance provides a foundation for other activities.
hudiemm/Getty Images

Many households have excessive or overlapping insurance coverage. Insuring property for more than it is worth may be a waste of money, as may both marriage partners paying for complete family health insurance.

EXAMPLE: Apps and Online Sources for Managing Risk

Insurance planning assistance and rate quotes may be obtained at www.thebalance.com and www.carinsurance.com. An app to maintain a home inventory is Sortly.

INVESTING (CHAPTERS 13-17) People invest for two primary reasons. Those interested in *current income* select investments that pay regular dividends or interest. In contrast, investors who desire *long-term growth* choose stocks, mutual funds, real estate, and other investments with potential for increased value over time. Investment diversification involves a variety of assets in your *portfolio,* with stocks, bond mutual funds, real estate, precious metals, and collectibles such as rare coins or art.

When starting an investment program, select low-cost mutual funds and other investments to minimize fees and commissions. Take advantage of tax-deferred retirement programs with your employer. When young, consider more aggressive investments for greater long-term returns.

EXAMPLE: Apps and Online Sources for Investing

"Information is power"—this is especially true when investing. You can obtain company information and investment assistance at finance.yahoo.com, www.fool.com, and www.marketwatch.com. Consider apps for investing such as Stash, Robinhood, and Acorns.

smart money minute

Your education can be a significant investment, which will hopefully result in future financial and career benefits. To fund the costs of school, consider these alternatives: (1) grants from schools and government, which don't need to be repaid; (2) financial aid and work-study programs; (3) scholarships from government agencies, organizations, and other sources; (4) education loans; (5) tax credits and personal savings; (6) lower-cost living locations and tuition programs; and (7) tuition reimbursement from an employer. For additional guidance on financing your education, see the Chapter 7 Appendix.

RETIREMENT AND ESTATE PLANNING (CHAPTERS 18, 19) Due to financial difficulties resulting from the recent COVID-19 pandemic, some people withdrew funds from their retirement accounts. Efforts must be made to replace those funds and to stay on track to achieve financial security upon completion of full-time employment. Retirement planning also involves thinking about your housing situation, recreational activities, and possible part-time or volunteer work. Estate planning arranges for the transfer of finances and valuables to others when incapacity, illness, or death occurs; it also involves considering the tax implications of those actions.

Transfers of money or property to others should be timed to minimize the tax burden and maximize the benefits for those receiving the financial resources. A knowledge of property transfer methods can help select the best course of action for funding current and future living costs, educational expenses, and retirement needs of dependents.

EXAMPLE: Apps and Online Sources for Retirement and Estate Planning

Whether retirement is 40 years or 40 minutes away, you can obtain assistance at www.thebalance.com, www.aarp.org, www.estateplanninglinks.com, and from the RetirePlan app.

DEVELOPING A FLEXIBLE FINANCIAL PLAN

A **financial plan** is a formalized report that summarizes your current financial situation, analyzes your financial needs, and recommends future financial activities. You can create this document on your own, seek assistance from a financial planner, or use a money management tool. Exhibit 1-9 offers a framework for developing and implementing a financial plan with examples for several life situations.

financial plan A formalized report that summarizes your current financial situation, analyzes your financial needs, and recommends future financial activities.

IMPLEMENTING YOUR FINANCIAL PLAN

You must have a plan before you can implement it. However, once you have clearly assessed your current situation and identified financial goals, what do you do next?

A vital success strategy is to develop financial habits for both short-term satisfaction and long-term financial security, including the following:

1. Track spending to create a spending plan to live within your income while you save and invest for the future. The main cause of financial difficulties is overspending.

2. Have appropriate insurance protection to avoid financial disasters.

3. Become informed about taxes and investments to help expand your financial resources.

my life | **5**

I am able to name specific types of risks that can affect my personal financial decisions.

All decisions involve risk. Some risks are minor with limited consequences. Others can have long-term effects. Inflation and interest rates will influence your financial decisions. Information on changing economic conditions is available at www.bls.gov, www.federalreserve.gov, and www.wsj.com.

EXHIBIT 1-9   Financial planning in action for different life situations

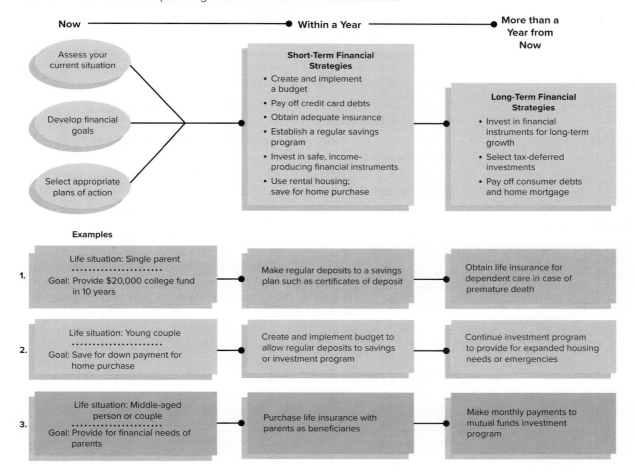

Financial Literacy for My Life

ASSESSING YOUR FINANCIAL HEALTH

To evaluate your current financial situation, respond with a YES or NO answer to the following items:

1. Do you have a budget or spending plan that guides your financial activities? Yes/No

2. Each month, do you pay your bills and credit card accounts on time? Yes/No

3. Do you maintain a complete record of your spending each month? Yes/No

4. Is your monthly spending less than your income? Yes/No

5. If you had an unexpected major expense, would you have access to funds to cover the cost? Yes/No

6. Do you know the amount in the bank account you use for daily spending? Yes/No

7. Do you have money automatically set aside each month in a saving or investment program? Yes/No

8. Does your filing system allow you to quickly locate important financial documents? Yes/No

9. Do you know the balance of your credit card accounts and other loans? Yes/No

10. Over the past year, have you avoided late fees for credit cards, loans, or bills? Yes/No

A "yes" answer to eight or more of these questions indicates a strong personal financial situation. What actions should you consider based on your responses to these items?

Financial advisors point out these common financial planning mistakes: (1) Unrealistic expectations. Use a realistic rate of return, inflation rate, and cash flow projections in your plan. (2) Emotional decision-making. Avoid allowing feelings to control goal setting and spending. (3) Inflexibility. Consider unexpected events; create an emergency fund and contingency plan. (4) Inaction. Plan your implementation steps. (5) Vague priorities. Determine the main focus for achieving financial goals.

STUDYING PERSONAL FINANCE

Useful learning tools are in each chapter of this book. The *Personal Financial Planner sheets* provide a framework for planning and implementing your financial activities. The library resource site for this book in *Connect* provides additional resources and activities. As you move forward, we recommend that you:

- Read and study this book carefully. Use the Practice Quizzes and end-of-chapter problems and activities.

- Talk to family members, friends, financial experts, and others who have knowledge of various money topics.

- Use online sources and apps for the latest information for answers to questions that result from your desire to know more.

- Remember, knowledge does not equal behavior. You must be determined to take appropriate financial actions as a result of your learning.

For successful financial planning, know where you are now, know where you want to be, and be persistent in your efforts to get there. Use the *Financial Literacy for My Life: Assessing Your Financial Health* box to assess your financial health as you get started.

smart money minute

A common *mistake* when studying personal finance is a low desire to learn. An *action* would be to develop strong study skills when using this book. This can result in *success* both in class and in gaining a satisfying personal and financial life.

✔ PRACTICE QUIZ 1-5

1. What are the main components of personal financial planning?
2. What is the purpose of a financial plan?
3. Identify some common actions taken to achieve financial goals.

Your Personal Finance Roadmap and Dashboard:

Financial Planning

MONTHS
EMERGENCY SAVINGS FUND

The creation of an emergency fund is often overlooked. Financial advisors suggest saving three to six months of living expenses for unexpected situations. A larger amount may be needed if you are self-employed or a full-time student. Most people keep their emergency fund in some type of savings account; different savings accounts are discussed in Chapter 5.

Your emergency fund can be measured with a *dashboard,* a tool used by organizations to monitor *key performance indicators* such as delivery time, product defects, or customer complaints. As an individual, you can use a *personal finance dashboard* to assess your financial situation. As with driving, a personal finance dashboard allows you to keep track of your progress to a destination.

YOUR SITUATION

Have you started your emergency fund? Do you make progress each month? Where is the needle on your

Personal Finance Dashboard for an emergency fund? Other personal financial planning actions you might consider during different stages of your life include:

 First Steps

- Track your daily spending to develop a budget.
- Create a regular savings program, that includes an emergency fund.
- Establish a plan for banking services and credit.
- Pay off any college loans.
- Continue proper spending and credit habits.

 Next Steps

- Assess progress toward long-term financial goals.
- Evaluate needed insurance as a result of changes in household or financial situation.

Later Steps

- Assess need for long-term health care coverage.
- Review your will and estate plan.
- Consider activities and locations for retirement.

YOUR next step... select one or more of the items above and create an action plan to implement those financial planning activities.

SUMMARY OF LEARNING OBJECTIVES

LO1-1

Analyze the process for making personal financial decisions. When making financial decisions, use a variety of information sources to implement the personal financial planning process: (1) determine your current financial situation, (2) develop financial goals, (3) identify alternative courses of action, (4) evaluate alternatives, (5) create and implement a financial action plan, and (6) review and revise the financial plan.

LO1-2

Assess personal and economic factors that influence personal financial planning. Financial goals and financial planning decisions are affected by a person's life situation (income, age, household size, health) and personal values, and by economic factors (prices, interest rates, and employment opportunities).

LO1-3

Develop personal financial goals. The financial goals you develop should take a SMART approach with goals that are: Specific, Measurable, Action-oriented, Realistic, and Time-based.

LO1-4

Calculate time value of money to analyze personal financial decisions. Every decision involves a trade-off with things given up. Personal opportunity costs include time, effort, and health. Financial opportunity costs are based on time value of money calculations. Future value and present value calculations enable you to measure the increased value (or lost interest) that results from a saving, investing, borrowing, or purchasing decision.

LO1-5

Identify strategies for achieving personal financial goals for different life situations. Successful financial planning requires specific goals combined with spending, saving, investing, and borrowing actions based on your personal situation along with various social and economic factors.

KEY TERMS

adult life cycle 9	future value 17	personal financial planning 3
bankruptcy 21	inflation 10	present value 19
economics 10	liquidity 20	time value of money 16
financial plan 23	opportunity cost 5	values 9

SELF-TEST PROBLEMS

1. The rule of 72 provides a guideline for determining how long it takes your money to double. This rule can also be used to determine your earning rate. If your money is expected to double in 12 years, what is your rate of return?

2. If you want to have $10,000 in savings eight years from now, what amount would you need to deposit in an account that earns 5 percent?

Self-Test Solutions

1. Using the rule of 72, if your money is expected to double in 12 years, you are earning approximately 6 percent (72 ÷ 12 years = 6 percent).

2. To calculate the present value of $10,000 for eight years at 5 percent, use a financial calculator, website or using Exhibit 1-C (Chapter Appendix): $10,000 × 0.677 = $6,770.

FINANCIAL PLANNING PROBLEMS

(*Note:* Some of these problems require the use of the time value of money tables in the Chapter Appendix.)

LO1-2 1. *Calculating the Future Value of Property.* Josh Collins plans to buy a house for $210,000. If that real estate is expected to increase in value by 3 percent each year, what will its approximate value be six years from now?

LO1-2 2. *Using the Rule of 72.* Using the rule of 72, approximate the following amounts.

    a. If the value of land in an area is increasing 6 percent a year, how long will it take for property values to double?

    b. If you earn 10 percent on your investments, how long will it take for your money to double?

    c. At an annual interest rate of 5 percent, how long will it take for your savings to double?

LO1-2 3. *Determining the Inflation Rate.* In 2018, selected automobiles had an average cost of $16,000. The average cost of those same automobiles is now $24,000. What was the rate of increase for these automobiles between the two time periods?

LO1-2 4. *Computing Future Living Expenses.* A family spends $46,000 a year for living expenses. If prices increase by 2 percent a year for the next three years, what amount will the family need for their living expenses after three years?

5. *Calculating Earnings on Savings.* What would be the yearly earnings for a person with $6,000 in savings at an annual interest rate of 2.5 percent? **LO1-4**

6. *Computing the Time Value of Money.* Using a financial calculator or time value of money tables in the Chapter Appendix, calculate the following. **LO1-4**

   a. The future value of $450 six years from now at 7 percent.

   b. The future value of $900 saved each year for 10 years at 8 percent.

   c. The amount a person would have to deposit today (present value) at a 6 percent interest rate to have $1,000 five years from now.

   d. The amount a person would have to deposit today to be able to take out $600 a year for 10 years from an account earning 8 percent.

7. *Calculating the Future Value of a Series of Amounts.* Elaine Romberg prepares her own income tax return each year. A tax preparer would charge her $70 for this service. Over a period of 10 years, how much does Elaine gain from preparing her own tax return? Assume she can earn 3 percent on her savings. **LO1-4**

8. *Calculating the Time Value of Money for Savings Goals.* If you want to have $20,000 for a down payment for a house in five years, what amount would you need to deposit today? Assume that your money will earn 4 percent. **LO1-4**

9. *Calculating the Present Value of a Series.* Pete Morton is planning to go to graduate school in a program of study that will take three years. Pete wants to have $15,000 available each year for various school and living expenses. If he earns 4 percent on his money, how much must be deposited at the start of his studies to be able to withdraw $15,000 a year for three years? **LO1-4**

10. *Using the Time Value of Money for Retirement Planning.* Carla Lopez deposits $3,400 a year into her retirement account. If these funds have an average earning of 9 percent over the 40 years until her retirement, what will be the value of her retirement account? **LO1-4**

11. *Calculating the Value of Reduced Spending.* If a person spends $15 a week on coffee (assume $750 a year), what would be the future value of that amount over 10 years if the funds were deposited in an account earning 3 percent? **LO1-4**

12. *Calculating the Present Value of Future Cash Flows.* A financial company advertises on television that they will pay you $60,000 now in exchange for annual payments of $10,000 that you are expected to receive for a legal settlement over the next 10 years. If you estimate the time value of money at 10 percent, would you accept this offer? **LO1-4**

13. *Calculating the Potential Future Value of Savings.* Mai Tran plans to set aside $2,400 a year for the next six years, earning 4 percent. What would be the future value of this savings amount? **LO1-4**

14. *Determining a Loan Payment Amount.* If you borrow $8,000 with a 5 percent interest rate, to be repaid in five equal yearly payments, what would be the amount of each payment? (*Note:* Use a financial calculator or the present value of an annuity table in the Chapter Appendix.) **LO1-4**

DIGITAL FINANCIAL LITERACY: PERSONAL FINANCE BLOGS

Extensive online resources are available for personal finance and wise money management. As both a consumer and producer of digital content, you will locate, assess, create, and share information. In addition, online safety, privacy settings, social media sharing, and fake news influence your financial well-being and career opportunities. Improving your *digital financial literacy* involves developing skills to identify, research, and implement money decisions.

Personal finance blogs offer articles, videos, podcasts, calculators, and personal observations and experiences. The blog for this textbook at https://kapoormoneyminute.com/ features summaries of current articles to expand your learning. Each blog post is connected to one or more textbook chapters with a link to the original source. Also provided are discussion questions and suggestions for enhanced learning.

Action items:

1. Using information from a personal finance blog, identify a financial goal and develop action steps to achieve the goal based on your personal life situation.

2. Create a list of questions that might be used to validate the information presented on a blog. Prepare a brief response that you might post on a personal finance blog.

FINANCIAL PLANNING CASE

You Be the Financial Planner

At some point in your life you may use a financial planner. However, your personal knowledge should be the foundation for financial decisions. For each of these situations, determine the goals, issues, and actions that might be appropriate:

Situation 1: Fran and Ed Blake, ages 43 and 47, have a daughter who is completing her first year of college and a son three years younger. Currently, they have $42,000 in savings and investment funds for their children's education. With increasing education costs, they are concerned whether this amount is adequate. In recent months, Fran's mother has required extensive medical attention and personal care assistance. Unable to live alone, she is now a resident of a long-term care facility. The monthly cost is $4,750, with annual increases of about 5 percent. While much of the cost is covered by Social Security and her pension, Fran's mother is unable to cover the entire cost. In addition, Fran and Ed are concerned about saving for their retirement. While they have consistently made annual deposits to a retirement fund, current financial demands may force them to access some of that money. The Blakes represent the millions of people with both dependent children and parents in need of assistance.

Situation 2: "While I knew it might happen someday, I didn't expect this." Due to the COVID-19 pandemic, Patrick Hamilton lost his job. In an effort to adapt to the economic climate, his company merged with another organization and moved to another state. Patrick does have some flexibility in his finances with three months of living expenses in a savings account. However, "three months can go by very quickly," as Patrick noted.

Situation 3: Nina Resendiz, age 23, recently received a $12,000 gift from a relative. Nina is considering various uses for these unexpected funds, including paying off credit card bills from her last vacation and setting aside money for a down payment on a house. Or she might invest the money in a tax-deferred retirement account. Another possibility is using the money for technology certification courses to enhance her earning power. Nina also wants to contribute some of the funds to a homeless shelter and a world hunger organization. She is overwhelmed by the choices and comments to herself, "I want to avoid the temptation of wasting the money on impulse items. I want to make sure I use the money on things with lasting value."

Questions

1. For each situation, identify the main financial planning issues that need to be addressed.

2. What additional information would you like to have before recommending actions in each situation?

3. Based on the information provided and your assessment of the situations, recommend actions related to: (a) SMART goals, (b) spending, and (c) saving, for the Blakes, Patrick, and Nina.

YOUR PERSONAL FINANCIAL PLAN

STARTING YOUR FINANCIAL PLAN

Planning is the foundation for success in every aspect of life. Assessing your current financial situation, along with setting goals is the key to successful financial planning.

Your Short-Term Financial Planning Activity

Task Develop the foundation for your personal financial plan.

Research

1) Use PFP Sheets 1, 2 to list your personal and financial information; also list the financial service organizations that you use.
2) Based on PFP Sheet 3 and "Financial Literacy for My Life: Developing Financial Goals" in Chapter 1, set financial goals for your current and future life situation.
3) Use PFP Sheet 4 to monitor current economic conditions (inflation, interest rates) for possible actions related to your personal finances.

Outcome Create a portfolio file for completed PFP sheets and other documents, or set up a computer folder of Excel PFP sheets.

Your Long-Term Financial Planning Activity

Task Plan actions to achieve financial goals.

Research

1) Use PFP Sheet 5 and Chapter 1 Appendix to calculate the savings deposits necessary to achieve a specific financial goal.
2) Based on Exhibit 1-6, identify financial planning actions for you and other household members for the next two to five years.

Outcome Add these documents and files to your portfolio or files to your Personal Financial Plan online folder. Prepare an audio or written summary of the actions you might take to achieve a specific financial goal.

Note: All *Personal Financial Planner* sheets are available at the end of the book and in an Excel spreadsheet format in *Connect Finance.*

CONTINUING CASE

Personal Finance Basics and the Time Value of Money

Jamie Lee Jackson, age 23, recently decided to switch from attending college part time to full time in order to pursue her business degree and to graduate within the next three years. She has 55 credit hours remaining to earn her bachelor's degree. She knows that it will be a challenge to complete her course of study while still working part time in the bakery department of a local grocery store, where she earns $390 a week. Jamie Lee wants to keep her part-time job, as she loves baking and creates very decorative cakes. She dreams of opening her own cupcake café within the next five years. She also realizes that by returning to school full time, she will forgo any free time that she enjoys now socializing with friends.

Jamie Lee currently shares a small apartment with a friend, and they split the living expenses, such as rent and utilities. She would really like to eventually have a place of her own. Her car is still going strong, even though it is seven years old, and she has no plans to buy a new one any time soon. She is carrying a balance on her credit card and is making regular monthly payments of $50 with hopes of paying it off within a year. Jamie recently took out a student loan to cover educational costs and expenses. She also began depositing $1,800 a year in a savings account that earns 2 percent interest, in hopes of having the $9,000 down payment needed to start the cupcake café two years after graduation.

Current Financial Situation

    Checking account: $1,250
    Emergency fund savings account: $3,100
    Car: $4,000
    Student loan: $5,400
    Credit card balance: $400
    Gross annual salary: $2,125
    Net monthly salary: $1,560

Questions

1. Using *Personal Financial Planner Sheet 3*, Personal Financial Goals, as a guide, what are Jamie Lee's short-term financial goals? How do they compare to her intermediate financial goals?

2. Review Jamie Lee's current financial situation. Using the *SMART* approach, what recommendations would you make for her to achieve her long-term goals?

3. Name two opportunity costs that might be considered in Jamie Lee's situation.

4. Jamie Lee needs to save a total of $9,000 to get started in her cupcake café venture. She is currently depositing $1,800 a year in a regular savings account earning 2 percent interest.

Using *Personal Financial Planner Sheet 5*, Time Value of Money, as a guide, how much will she have accumulated five years from now in the regular savings account, assuming she leaves her emergency fund savings account balance untouched?

DAILY SPENDING DIARY

"I first thought this process would be a waste of time, but the information has helped me become much more careful of how I spend my money."

Directions

Nearly everyone who tracks their spending has found the process to be beneficial. Using the *Daily Spending Diary* sheet, which follows, record every cent of your spending each day in the categories provided. Or you may create your own format to monitor your spending. You can indicate the use of a credit card with (CC). This experience will help you better understand your spending patterns and identify desired changes you might want to make in your spending habits.

Analysis Questions

1. What did your *Daily Spending Diary* reveal about your spending habits? What areas of spending might you consider changing?

2. How might your *Daily Spending Diary* assist you when identifying and achieving financial goals?

A *Daily Spending Diary* sheet follows, and is on the library resource site within *Connect*.

DAILY SPENDING DIARY (INSTRUCTIONS AND SHEETS)

Effective personal financial planning depends on spending less than you earn. The use of a Daily Spending Diary will provide information to help you better understand your spending patterns and to help you achieve desired financial goals.

The following sheet, which is also available on the library resource site in *Connect,* can be used to record *every cent* of your spending each day in the categories provided. Or, you can create your own format to monitor your spending. You can indicate the use of a credit card with (CC).

Other methods that might be used to track your spending include carrying a small notebook, calendar book, or index cards, saving receipts to record later, writing amounts spent on sticky notes to summarize later, or using an app to record spending. Be creative to motivate yourself to monitor your spending.

This experience will help you better understand your spending habits and may point to changes you should make. Recording comments will reflect what you have learned about your spending and can guide actions you might want to take. Ask yourself, "What spending amounts can I reduce or eliminate?"

Many people who take on this task may initially consider it a waste of time. However, nearly everyone who makes a serious effort to keep a Daily Spending Diary has found it beneficial over time. The process may seem tedious at first, but after a while recording this information becomes easier and faster. Most important, you will know where your money is going. Then you will be able to better decide if that is truly how you want to spend your available financial resources. A sincere effort will produce useful information for monitoring and controlling your spending and will create the foundation for long-term financial security.

Daily Spending Diary

Directions: Record every cent of your spending each day in the categories provided, or create your own format to monitor your spending. You can indicate the use of a credit card with (CR). Comments should reflect what you have learned about your spending patterns and desired changes you might want to make in your spending habits. (Note: As income is received, record in Date column.)

Month: _____ Amount available for spending: $ _____ Amount to be saved: $ _____

Date (Income)	Total Spending	Auto, Transportation	Housing, Utilities	Food (H) Home (A) Away	Health, Personal Care	Education	Recreation, Leisure	Donations, Gifts	Other (note item, amount)	Comments
Example	$83	$20 (gas) (CR)		$47 (H)		$2 (pen)	$4 (DVD rental)	$10 (food pantry)		This takes time but it helps me control my spending
1										
2										
3										
4										
5										
6										
7										
8										
9										
10										
11										
12										
13										
14										
Subtotal										

Date (Income)	Total Spending	Auto, Transportation	Housing, Utilities	Food (H) Home (A) Away	Health, Personal Care	Education	Recreation, Leisure	Donations, Gifts	Other (note item, amount)	Comments
15										
16										
17										
18										
19										
20										
21										
22										
23										
24										
25										
26										
27										
28										
29										
30										
31										
Total										

Total Income
$ _____

Total Spending
$ _____

Difference(+/−)
$ _____

Possible Actions: amount to savings; areas for reduced spending; other actions . . .

APPENDIX
The Time Value of Money

- "If I deposit $10,000 today, how much will I have for a down payment on a house in five years?"
- "Will $2,000 saved each year give me enough money when I retire?"
- "How much must I save today to have enough for my children's college education?"

The *time value of money,* more commonly referred to as *interest,* is the cost of money that is borrowed or lent. Interest can be compared to rent, the cost of using an apartment or other item. The time value of money is based on the fact that a dollar received today is worth more than a dollar received later, because the dollar received today can be saved or invested and will be worth more than a dollar in the future. Similarly, a dollar that will be received one year from today is currently worth less than a dollar today.

The time value of money has two major components: future value and present value. *Future value* computations, also called *compounding,* yield the amount to which a current amount will increase based on a certain interest rate and period of time. *Present value,* calculated through a process called *discounting,* is the current value of a future amount based on a certain interest rate and period of time.

In future value situations, you are given an amount to save or invest, and you calculate the amount available at some future date. With present value, you are given the amount that will be available at some future date, and you calculate the current value. Both future value and present value computations are based on interest rate calculations.

Interest Rate Basics

Simple interest is the dollar cost of borrowing or earnings from lending money. The interest is based on three elements:

- The dollar amount, called the *principal.*
- The *rate of interest.*
- The amount of *time.*

The formula and financial calculator computations are as follows:

INTEREST RATE BASICS	
Formula	**Financial Calculator***
Interest = Principal × Rate of interest (annual) × Time (years)	Interest = Amount × Rate × Number of (or portion of) years
The interest rate is stated as a percentage for a year. For example, you must convert 12 percent to either 0.12 or 12/100 before doing your calculations. The time element must also be converted to a decimal or fraction. For example, three months would be shown as 0.25, or 1/4 of a year. Interest for 2½ years would involve a time period of 2.5.	
Example A: Suppose you borrow $1,000 at 5 percent and will repay it in one payment at the end of one year. Using the simple interest calculation, the interest is $50, computed as follows:	

INTEREST RATE BASICS	
Formula	**Financial Calculator***
$\$50 = \$1{,}000 \times 0.05 \times 1$ (year)	$\$50 = 1000 \times .05 \times 1$
Example B: If you deposited $750 in a savings account paying 8 percent, how much interest would you earn in nine months? You would compute this amount as follows:	
Interest = $\$750 \times 0.08 \times 3/4$ (or 0.75 of a year) = $45	-750 [PV], 8 [I/Y], 9/12 = .75 [N], 0 [PMT], [CPT] [FV] 795. 795 − 750 = 45

Note: These financial calculator notations may require slightly different keystrokes when using various brands and models.

SAMPLE PROBLEM 1

How much interest would you earn if you deposited $300 at 6 percent for 27 months? (Answers to sample problems are on page 38.)

SAMPLE PROBLEM 2

How much interest would you pay to borrow $670 for eight months at 12 percent?

Future Value of a Single Amount

The future value of an amount consists of the original amount plus compound interest. This calculation involves the following elements:

$$FV = \text{Future value}$$
$$PV = \text{Present value}$$
$$i = \text{Interest rate}$$
$$n = \text{Number of time periods}$$

The formula and financial calculator computations are as follows:

FUTURE VALUE OF A SINGLE AMOUNT		
Formula	**Table**	**Financial Calculator**
$FV = PV(1 + i)^n$	$FV = PV$ (Table factor)	[PV], [I/Y], [N], [PMT], [CPT] [FV]
Example C: The future value of $1 at 10 percent after three years is $1.33. This amount is calculated as follows:		
$\$1.33 = \$1(1 + 0.10)^3$	Using Exhibit 1-A: $1.33 = $1.00(1.331)	-1 [PV], 10 [I/Y], 3 [N], 0 [PMT], [CPT] [FV] 1.33
Future value tables are available to help you determine compounded interest amounts (see Exhibit 1-A). Looking at Exhibit 1-A for 10 percent and three years, you can see that $1 would be worth $1.33 at that time. For other amounts, multiply the table factor by the original amount. This process may be viewed as follows:		

Future value
(rounded) $1 $1.10 $1.21   FV = $1.33
                      Interest $0.10   Interest $0.11   Interest $0.12
After year   0   1   2   3

FUTURE VALUE OF A SINGLE AMOUNT		
Formula	**Table**	**Financial Calculator**
Example D: If your savings of $400 earns 12 percent, compounded *monthly*, over a year and a half, use the table factor for 1 percent for 18 time periods; the future value would be:		
$478.46 = \$400(1 + 0.01)^{18}$	$478.40 = \$400(1.196)$	$-400\ \boxed{PV}$, 12/12 = 1 $\boxed{I/Y}$, 1.5 × 12 = 18 $\boxed{N}$, 0 $\boxed{PMT}$, $\boxed{CPT}\boxed{FV}$ 478.46
Excel formula notation for future value of a single amount	= FV(rate, nper, pmt, pv, type)	
	Example D solution = FV(0.01,18,0,−400,0) = 478.46	

SAMPLE PROBLEM 3

What is the future value of $800 at 8 percent after six years?

SAMPLE PROBLEM 4

How much would you have in savings if you kept $200 on deposit for eight years at 8 percent, compounded *semiannually*?

Future Value of a Series of Equal Amounts (an Annuity)

Future value may also be calculated for a situation in which regular additions are made to savings. The formula and financial calculator computations are as follows:

FUTURE VALUE OF A SERIES OF PAYMENTS		
Formula	**Table**	**Financial Calculator**
$FV = \text{Annuity}\ \dfrac{(1 + i)^n - 1}{i}$	Using Exhibit 1-B: Annuity × Table factor	$\boxed{PMT}$, $\boxed{N}$, $\boxed{I/Y}$, $\boxed{PV}$, $\boxed{CPT}\boxed{FV}$
This calculation assumes that (1) each deposit is for the same amount, (2) the interest rate is the same for each time period, and (3) the deposits are made at the end of each time period.		
Example E: The future value of three $1 deposits made at the end of the next three years, earning 10 percent interest, is $3.31. This is calculated as follows:		
$3.31 = \$1\ \dfrac{(1 + 0.10)^3 - 1}{0.10}$	Using Exhibit 1-B: $3.31 = \$1 × 3.31$	$-1\ \boxed{PMT}$, 3 $\boxed{N}$, 10 $\boxed{I/Y}$, 0 $\boxed{PV}$, $\boxed{CPT}\boxed{FV}$ 3.31

This may be viewed as follows:

		$1		$2.10		FV = $3.31
Future value (rounded)	Deposit $1 Interest 0		Deposit $1 Interest $0.10		Deposit $1 Interest $0.21	
After year	0		1		2	3

FUTURE VALUE OF A SERIES OF PAYMENTS		
Formula	**Table**	**Financial Calculator**
Example F: If you plan to deposit $40 a year for 10 years, earning 8 percent compounded annually, the future value of this amount is:		
$\$579.46 = \$40\,\dfrac{(1+0.08)^{10}-1}{0.08}$	Using Exhibit 1-B: $\$579.48 = \$40(14.487)$	-40 ⯀PMT, 10 ⯀N, 10 ⯀I/Y, 0 ⯀PV, ⯀CPT⯀FV 579.46
Excel formula notation for future value of a series	$= \text{FV(rate,nper,pmt,pv,type)}$	
	Example F solution $= \text{FV}(0.08,10,-40,0,0) = 579.46$	

SAMPLE PROBLEM 5

What is the future value of an annual deposit of $230 earning 6 percent for 15 years?

SAMPLE PROBLEM 6

What amount would you have in a retirement account if you made annual deposits of $375 for 25 years earning 12 percent, compounded annually?

Present Value of a Single Amount

If you want to know how much you need to deposit now to receive a certain amount in the future, the formula and financial calculator computations are as follows:

PRESENT VALUE OF A SINGLE AMOUNT		
Formula	**Table**	**Financial Calculator**
$PV = \dfrac{FV}{(1+I)^n}$	Using Exhibit 1-C: $PV = FV(\text{Table Factor})$	⯀FV, ⯀N, ⯀I/Y, ⯀PMT, ⯀CPT⯀PV
Example G: The present value of $1 to be received three years from now based on a 10 percent interest rate is calculated as follows:		
$\$0.75 = \dfrac{\$1}{(1+0.10)^3}$	Using Exhibit 1-C: $\$0.75 = \$1(0.751)$	1 ⯀FV, 3 ⯀N, 10 ⯀I/Y, 0 ⯀PMT, ⯀CPT ⯀PV .75131

This may be viewed as follows:

Present value (rounded)	$0.75	$0.83	$0.91	$1
	Discount (interest) $0.075	Discount (interest) $0.0825	Discount (interest) $0.0905	
After year	0	1	2	3

Present value tables are available to assist you in this process (see Exhibit 1-C). Notice that $1 at 10 percent for three years has a present value of $0.75. For amounts other than $1, multiply the table factor by the amount involved.

Example H: If you want to have $300 seven years from now and your savings earn 10 percent, compounded *semiannually* (which would be 5 percent for 14 time periods), finding how much you would have to deposit today is calculated as follows:		
$\$151.52 = \dfrac{\$300}{(1+0.05)^{14}}$	Using Exhibit 1-C: $\$151.50 = \$300(0.505)$	-300 ⯀FV, $7\times2=14$ ⯀N, $10/2=5$ ⯀I/Y, 0 ⯀PMT, ⯀CPT⯀PV 151.52
Excel formula notation for present value of a single amount	$= \text{PV(rate, nper, pmt, fv, type)}$	
	Example H solution: $= \text{PV}(0.05,14,0,-300,0) = 151.52$	

SAMPLE PROBLEM 7

What is the present value of $2,200 earning 15 percent for eight years?

SAMPLE PROBLEM 8

To have $6,000 for a child's education in 10 years, what amount should a parent deposit in a savings account that earns 12 percent, compounded *quarterly*?

Present Value of a Series of Equal Amounts (an Annuity)

The final time value of money situation allows you to receive an amount at the end of each time period for a certain number of periods. The formula and financial calculator computations are as follows:

PRESENT VALUE OF A SERIES OF PAYMENTS		
Formula	**Table**	**Financial Calculator**
$PV = \text{Annuity} \times \dfrac{1 - \dfrac{1}{(1 + I)^n}}{I}$	Using Exhibit 1-D: PV = Annuity(Table factor)	[PMT], [N], [I/Y], [FV], [CPT] [PV]
Example I: The present value of a $1 withdrawal at the end of the next three years would be $2.49, for money earning 10 percent. This would be calculated as follows:		
$\$2.49 = \$1 \left[\dfrac{1 - \dfrac{1}{(1 + 0.10)^3}}{0.10} \right]$	Using Exhibit 1-D: $2.49 = $1(2.487)	1 [PMT], 3 [N], 10 [I/Y], 0 [FV], [CPT] [PV] 2.48685

This may be viewed as follows:

Present value (fund balance)	$2.49	$1.74	$0.91	$0

Withdrawal – $1 Interest + $0.25 Withdrawal – $1 Interest + $0.17 Withdrawal – $1 Interest + $0.09

After year   0   1   2   3

This same amount appears in Exhibit 1-D for 10 percent and three time periods. To use the table for other situations, multiply the table factor by the amount to be withdrawn each year.

Example J: If you wish to withdraw $100 at the end of each year for 10 years from an account that earns 14 percent, compounded annually, what amount must you deposit now?

$\$521.61 = \$100 \left(\dfrac{1 - \dfrac{1}{(1 + 0.14)^{10}}}{0.14} \right)$	Using Exhibit 1-D: $521.60 = $100(5.216)	100 [PMT], 10 [N], 14 [I/Y], 0 [FV], [CPT] [PV] 521.61
Excel formula notation for present value of a series	= PV(rate, nper, pmt, fv, type)	
	Example J solution = PV(0.14,10,−100,0,0) = 521.61	

SAMPLE PROBLEM 9

What is the present value of a withdrawal of $200 at the end of each year for 14 years with an interest rate of 7 percent?

SAMPLE PROBLEM 10

How much would you have to deposit now to be able to withdraw $650 at the end of each year for 20 years from an account that earns 11 percent?

Using Present Value to Determine Loan Payments

Present value tables (Exhibit 1-D) can also be used to determine installment payments for a loan as follows:

PRESENT VALUE TO DETERMINE LOAN PAYMENTS	
Table	**Financial Calculator**
$\dfrac{\text{Amount borrowed}}{\text{Present value of series table factor (Exhibit 1-D)}} = \text{Loan payment}$	PV, I/Y, N, FV, CPT PMT
Example K: If you borrow $1,000 with a 6 percent interest rate to be repaid in three equal payments at the end of the next three years, the payments will be $374.11. This is calculated as follows:	
$\dfrac{\$1,000}{2.673} = \$374.11$	1000 PV, 6 I/Y, 3 N, 0 FV, CPT PMT 374.10981
Excel formula notation for determining loan payment amount	= PMT(rate,nper,pv,fv,type)
	Example K solution = PMT(.06,3,1000,0,0) = $374.11

SAMPLE PROBLEM 11

What would be the annual payment amount for a $20,000, 10-year loan at 7 percent?

Answers to Sample Problems (based on TVM tables)

1. $300 × 0.06 × 2.25 years (27 months) = $40.50.
2. $670 × 0.12 × 2/3 (of a year) = $53.60.
3. $800(1.587) = $1,269.60. (Based on Exhibit 1-A, 8%, 6 periods.)
4. $200(1.873) = $374.60. (Based on Exhibit 1-A, 4%, 16 periods.)
5. $230(23.276) = $5,353.48. (Based on Exhibit 1-B, 6%, 15 periods.)
6. $375(133.33) = $49,998.75. (Based on Exhibit 1-B, 12%, 25 periods.)
7. $2,200(0.327) = $719.40. (Based on Exhibit 1-C, 15%, 8 periods.)
8. $6,000(0.307) = $1,842. (Based on Exhibit 1-C, 3%, 40 periods.)
9. $200(8.745) = $1,749. (Based on Exhibit 1-D, 7%, 14 periods.)
10. $650(7.963) = $5,175.95. (Based on Exhibit 1-D, 11%, 20 periods.)
11. $20,000/7.024 = $2,847.38. (Based on Exhibit 1-D, 7%, 10 periods.)

Time Value of Money Application Exercises

1. **(Present value of an annuity)** You wish to borrow $18,000 to buy a new automobile. The rate is 8.6% over four years with monthly payments. Find the monthly payment. (Answer: $444.52)

2. **(Present value of an annuity)** How much money must you have now to finance four years of college, assuming an annual cost of $48,000 and an interest rate of 6% (applied to the principal until disbursed)? (Answer: $166,325.07)

3. **(Present value of a single amount)** How much money must you set aside at age 20 to accumulate retirement funds of $100,000 at age 65, assuming a rate of interest of 7%? (Answer: $4,761.35)

4. **(Future value of a single amount)** If you deposit $2,000 in a 5-year certificate of deposit at 5.2%, how much will it be worth in five years? (Answer: $2,576.97)

5. **(Future value of a single amount)** If you deposit $2,000 in a 5-year certificate of deposit at 5.2% with quarterly compounding, how much will it be worth in five years? (Answer: $2,589.52)

6. **(Future value of an annuity)** You choose to invest $50/month in a 401(k) that invests in an international stock mutual fund. Assuming an annual rate of return of 9%, how much will this fund be worth if you are retiring in 40 years? (Answer: $234,066.01)

7. **(Future value of an annuity)** You invest $600/year in a 401(k) that invests in an international stock mutual fund. Assuming an annual rate of return of 9%, how much will this fund be worth if you are retiring in 40 years? (Answer: $202,729.47)

Time Value of Money Calculation Methods: A Summary

The time value of money may be calculated using a variety of techniques. When achieving specific financial goals requires regular deposits to a savings or investment account, the computation may occur in one of several ways. For example, Bonnie Keller plans to deposit $10,000 in an account for the next 10 years. She estimates these funds will earn an annual rate of 5 percent. What amount can Bonnie expect to have available after 10 years?

Method	Process, Results
Formula Calculation The most basic method of calculating the time value of money involves using a formula.	For this situation, the formula would be: $$PV\,(1+i)^n = FV$$ The result should be $$\$10,000\,(1+0.05)^{10} = \$16,288.95$$
Time Value of Money Tables Instead of calculating with a formula, time value of money tables are available. The numeric factors eased the computational process.	Using the table in Exhibit 1-A: $10,000 Future value of $1, 5%, 10 years $10,000 × 1.629 = $16,290
Financial Calculator A variety of financial calculators are programmed with financial functions. Both future value and present value calculations may be performed using the appropriate keystrokes.	Using a financial calculator, the keystrokes would be: Amount −10,000 $\boxed{PV}$ Time periods 10 $\boxed{N}$ Interest rate 5 $\boxed{I}$ Result $\boxed{FV}$ $16,288.94
Spreadsheet Software Excel and other software programs have built-in formulas for various financial computations, including time value of money.	When using a spreadsheet program, this type of calculation would require this format: = FV(rate, periods, amount per period, single amount) The results of this example would be: = FV(0.05, 10, 0, −10,000) = $16,288.95
Time Value of Money Websites and Apps Many time-value-of-money calculators are also available online and for smartphones. These programs perform calculations for the future and present value of savings as well as determining loan payment amounts.	Some easy-to-use calculators for computing the time value of money and other financial computations are located at • www.kiplinger.com/tools • www.dinkytown.net • www.grunderware.com • www.calculatorsoup.com Apps: TVM;TVM Financial Calculator

Note: The slight differences in answers are the result of rounding.

EXHIBIT 1-A Future value (compounded sum) of $1 after a given number of time periods

Period	1%	2%	3%	4%	5%	6%	7%	8%	9%	10%	11%
1	1.010	1.020	1.030	1.040	1.050	1.060	1.070	1.080	1.090	1.100	1.110
2	1.020	1.040	1.061	1.082	1.103	1.124	1.145	1.166	1.188	1.210	1.232
3	1.030	1.061	1.093	1.125	1.158	1.191	1.225	1.260	1.295	1.331	1.368
4	1.041	1.082	1.126	1.170	1.216	1.262	1.311	1.360	1.412	1.464	1.518
5	1.051	1.104	1.159	1.217	1.276	1.338	1.403	1.469	1.539	1.611	1.685
6	1.062	1.126	1.194	1.265	1.340	1.419	1.501	1.587	1.677	1.772	1.870
7	1.072	1.149	1.230	1.316	1.407	1.504	1.606	1.714	1.828	1.949	2.076
8	1.083	1.172	1.267	1.369	1.477	1.594	1.718	1.851	1.993	2.144	2.305
9	1.094	1.195	1.305	1.423	1.551	1.689	1.838	1.999	2.172	2.358	2.558
10	1.105	1.219	1.344	1.480	1.629	1.791	1.967	2.159	2.367	2.594	2.839
11	1.116	1.243	1.384	1.539	1.710	1.898	2.105	2.332	2.580	2.853	3.152
12	1.127	1.268	1.426	1.601	1.796	2.012	2.252	2.518	2.813	3.138	3.498
13	1.138	1.294	1.469	1.665	1.886	2.133	2.410	2.720	3.066	3.452	3.883
14	1.149	1.319	1.513	1.732	1.980	2.261	2.579	2.937	3.342	3.797	4.310
15	1.161	1.346	1.558	1.801	2.079	2.397	2.759	3.172	3.642	4.177	4.785
16	1.173	1.373	1.605	1.873	2.183	2.540	2.952	3.426	3.970	4.595	5.311
17	1.184	1.400	1.653	1.948	2.292	2.693	3.159	3.700	4.328	5.054	5.895
18	1.196	1.428	1.702	2.026	2.407	2.854	3.380	3.996	4.717	5.560	6.544
19	1.208	1.457	1.754	2.107	2.527	3.026	3.617	4.316	5.142	6.116	7.263
20	1.220	1.486	1.806	2.191	2.653	3.207	3.870	4.661	5.604	6.727	8.062
25	1.282	1.641	2.094	2.666	3.386	4.292	5.427	6.848	8.623	10.835	13.585
30	1.348	1.811	2.427	3.243	4.322	5.743	7.612	10.063	13.268	17.449	22.892
40	1.489	2.208	3.262	4.801	7.040	10.286	14.974	21.725	31.409	45.259	65.001
50	1.645	2.692	4.384	7.107	11.467	18.420	29.457	46.902	74.358	117.391	184.565

Period	12%	13%	14%	15%	16%	17%	18%	19%	20%	25%	30%
1	1.120	1.130	1.140	1.150	1.160	1.170	1.180	1.190	1.200	1.250	1.300
2	1.254	1.277	1.300	1.323	1.346	1.369	1.392	1.416	1.440	1.563	1.690
3	1.405	1.443	1.482	1.521	1.561	1.602	1.643	1.685	1.728	1.953	2.197
4	1.574	1.630	1.689	1.749	1.811	1.874	1.939	2.005	2.074	2.441	2.856
5	1.762	1.842	1.925	2.011	2.100	2.192	2.288	2.386	2.488	3.052	3.713
6	1.974	2.082	2.195	2.313	2.436	2.565	2.700	2.840	2.986	3.815	4.827
7	2.211	2.353	2.502	2.660	2.826	3.001	3.185	3.379	3.583	4.768	6.275
8	2.476	2.658	2.853	3.059	3.278	3.511	3.759	4.021	4.300	5.960	8.157
9	2.773	3.004	3.252	3.518	3.803	4.108	4.435	4.785	5.160	7.451	10.604
10	3.106	3.395	3.707	4.046	4.411	4.807	5.234	5.695	6.192	9.313	13.786
11	3.479	3.836	4.226	4.652	5.117	5.624	6.176	6.777	7.430	11.642	17.922
12	3.896	4.335	4.818	5.350	5.936	6.580	7.288	8.064	8.916	14.552	23.298
13	4.363	4.898	5.492	6.153	6.886	7.699	8.599	9.596	10.699	18.190	30.288
14	4.887	5.535	6.261	7.076	7.988	9.007	10.147	11.420	12.839	22.737	39.374
15	5.474	6.254	7.138	8.137	9.266	10.539	11.974	13.590	15.407	28.422	51.186
16	6.130	7.067	8.137	9.358	10.748	12.330	14.129	16.172	18.488	35.527	66.542
17	6.866	7.986	9.276	10.761	12.468	14.426	16.672	19.244	22.186	44.409	86.504
18	7.690	9.024	10.575	12.375	14.463	16.879	19.673	22.901	26.623	55.511	112.455
19	8.613	10.197	12.056	14.232	16.777	19.748	23.214	27.252	31.948	69.389	146.192
20	9.646	11.523	13.743	16.367	19.461	23.106	27.393	32.429	38.338	86.736	190.050
25	17.000	21.231	26.462	32.919	40.874	50.658	62.669	77.388	95.396	264.698	705.641
30	29.960	39.116	50.950	66.212	85.850	111.065	143.371	184.675	237.376	807.794	2,619.996
40	93.051	132.782	188.884	267.864	378.721	533.869	750.378	1,051.668	1,469.772	7,523.164	36,118.865
50	289.002	450.736	700.233	1,083.657	1,670.704	2,566.215	3,927.357	5,988.914	9,100.438	70,064.923	497,929.223

EXHIBIT 1-B Future value (compounded sum) of $1 paid in at the end of each period for a given number of time periods (an annuity)

Period	1%	2%	3%	4%	5%	6%	7%	8%	9%	10%	11%
1	1.000	1.000	1.000	1.000	1.000	1.000	1.000	1.000	1.000	1.000	1.000
2	2.010	2.020	2.030	2.040	2.050	2.060	2.070	2.080	2.090	2.100	2.110
3	3.030	3.060	3.091	3.122	3.153	3.184	3.215	3.246	3.278	3.310	3.342
4	4.060	4.122	4.184	4.246	4.310	4.375	4.440	4.506	4.573	4.641	4.710
5	5.101	5.204	5.309	5.416	5.526	5.637	5.751	5.867	5.985	6.105	6.228
6	6.152	6.308	6.468	6.633	6.802	6.975	7.153	7.336	7.523	7.716	7.913
7	7.214	7.434	7.662	7.898	8.142	8.394	8.654	8.923	9.200	9.487	9.783
8	8.286	8.583	8.892	9.214	9.549	9.897	10.260	10.637	11.028	11.436	11.859
9	9.369	9.755	10.159	10.583	11.027	11.491	11.978	12.488	13.021	13.579	14.164
10	10.462	10.950	11.464	12.006	12.578	13.181	13.816	14.487	15.193	15.937	16.722
11	11.567	12.169	12.808	13.486	14.207	14.972	15.784	16.645	17.560	18.531	19.561
12	12.683	13.412	14.192	15.026	15.917	16.870	17.888	18.977	20.141	21.384	22.713
13	13.809	14.680	15.618	16.627	17.713	18.882	20.141	21.495	22.953	24.523	26.212
14	14.947	15.974	17.086	18.292	19.599	21.015	22.550	24.215	26.019	27.975	30.095
15	16.097	17.293	18.599	20.024	21.579	23.276	25.129	27.152	29.361	31.772	34.405
16	17.258	18.639	20.157	21.825	23.657	25.673	27.888	30.324	33.003	35.950	39.190
17	18.430	20.012	21.762	23.698	25.840	28.213	30.840	33.750	36.974	40.545	44.501
18	19.615	21.412	23.414	25.645	28.132	30.906	33.999	37.450	41.301	45.599	50.396
19	20.811	22.841	25.117	27.671	30.539	33.760	37.379	41.446	46.018	51.159	56.939
20	22.019	24.297	26.870	29.778	33.066	36.786	40.995	45.762	51.160	57.275	64.203
25	28.243	32.030	36.459	41.646	47.727	54.865	63.249	73.106	84.701	98.347	114.413
30	34.785	40.568	47.575	56.085	66.439	79.058	94.461	113.283	136.308	164.494	199.021
40	48.886	60.402	75.401	95.026	120.800	154.762	199.635	259.057	337.882	442.593	581.826
50	64.463	84.579	112.797	152.667	209.348	290.336	406.529	573.770	815.084	1,163.909	1,668.771

Period	12%	13%	14%	15%	16%	17%	18%	19%	20%	25%	30%
1	1.000	1.000	1.000	1.000	1.000	1.000	1.000	1.000	1.000	1.000	1.000
2	2.120	2.130	2.140	2.150	2.160	2.170	2.180	2.190	2.200	2.250	2.300
3	3.374	3.407	3.440	3.473	3.506	3.539	3.572	3.606	3.640	3.813	3.990
4	4.779	4.850	4.921	4.993	5.066	5.141	5.215	5.291	5.368	5.766	6.187
5	6.353	6.480	6.610	6.742	6.877	7.014	7.154	7.297	7.442	8.207	9.043
6	8.115	8.323	8.536	8.754	8.977	9.207	9.442	9.683	9.930	11.259	12.756
7	10.089	10.405	10.730	11.067	11.414	11.772	12.142	12.523	12.916	15.073	17.583
8	12.300	12.757	13.233	13.727	14.240	14.773	15.327	15.902	16.499	19.842	23.858
9	14.776	15.416	16.085	16.786	17.519	18.285	19.086	19.923	20.799	25.802	32.015
10	17.549	18.420	19.337	20.304	21.321	22.393	23.521	24.709	25.959	33.253	42.619
11	20.655	21.814	23.045	24.349	25.733	27.200	28.755	30.404	32.150	42.566	56.405
12	24.133	25.650	27.271	29.002	30.850	32.824	34.931	37.180	39.581	54.208	74.327
13	28.029	29.985	32.089	34.352	36.786	39.404	42.219	45.244	48.497	68.760	97.625
14	32.393	34.883	37.581	40.505	43.672	47.103	50.818	54.841	59.196	86.949	127.913
15	37.280	40.417	43.842	47.580	51.660	56.110	60.965	66.261	72.035	109.687	167.286
16	42.753	46.672	50.980	55.717	60.925	66.649	72.939	79.850	87.442	138.109	218.472
17	48.884	53.739	59.118	65.075	71.673	78.979	87.068	96.022	105.931	173.636	285.014
18	55.750	61.725	68.394	75.836	84.141	93.406	103.740	115.266	128.117	218.045	371.518
19	63.440	70.749	78.969	88.212	98.603	110.285	123.414	138.166	154.740	273.556	483.973
20	72.052	80.947	91.025	102.444	115.380	130.033	146.628	165.418	186.688	342.945	630.165
25	133.334	155.620	181.871	212.793	249.214	292.105	342.603	402.042	471.981	1,054.791	2,348.803
30	241.333	293.199	356.787	434.745	530.312	647.439	790.948	966.712	1,181.882	3,227.174	8,729.985
40	767.091	1,013.704	1,342.025	1,779.090	2,360.757	3,134.522	4,163.213	5,529.829	7,343.858	30,088.655	120,392.883
50	2,400.018	3,459.507	4,994.521	7,217.716	10,435.649	15,089.502	21,813.094	31,515.340	45,497.191	280,255.693	1,659,760.743

EXHIBIT 1-C Present value of $1 to be received at the end of a given number of time periods

Period	1%	2%	3%	4%	5%	6%	7%	8%	9%	10%	11%	12%
1	0.990	0.980	0.971	0.962	0.952	0.943	0.935	0.926	0.917	0.909	0.901	0.893
2	0.980	0.961	0.943	0.925	0.907	0.890	0.873	0.857	0.842	0.826	0.812	0.797
3	0.971	0.942	0.915	0.889	0.864	0.840	0.816	0.794	0.772	0.751	0.731	0.712
4	0.961	0.924	0.885	0.855	0.823	0.792	0.763	0.735	0.708	0.683	0.659	0.636
5	0.951	0.906	0.863	0.822	0.784	0.747	0.713	0.681	0.650	0.621	0.593	0.567
6	0.942	0.888	0.837	0.790	0.746	0.705	0.666	0.630	0.596	0.564	0.535	0.507
7	0.933	0.871	0.813	0.760	0.711	0.665	0.623	0.583	0.547	0.513	0.482	0.452
8	0.923	0.853	0.789	0.731	0.677	0.627	0.582	0.540	0.502	0.467	0.434	0.404
9	0.914	0.837	0.766	0.703	0.645	0.592	0.544	0.500	0.460	0.424	0.391	0.361
10	0.905	0.820	0.744	0.676	0.614	0.558	0.508	0.463	0.422	0.386	0.352	0.322
11	0.896	0.804	0.722	0.650	0.585	0.527	0.475	0.429	0.388	0.350	0.317	0.287
12	0.887	0.788	0.701	0.625	0.557	0.497	0.444	0.397	0.356	0.319	0.286	0.257
13	0.879	0.773	0.681	0.601	0.530	0.469	0.415	0.368	0.326	0.290	0.258	0.229
14	0.870	0.758	0.661	0.577	0.505	0.442	0.388	0.340	0.299	0.263	0.232	0.205
15	0.861	0.743	0.642	0.555	0.481	0.417	0.362	0.315	0.275	0.239	0.209	0.183
16	0.853	0.728	0.623	0.534	0.458	0.394	0.339	0.292	0.252	0.218	0.188	0.163
17	0.844	0.714	0.605	0.513	0.436	0.371	0.317	0.270	0.231	0.198	0.170	0.146
18	0.836	0.700	0.587	0.494	0.416	0.350	0.296	0.250	0.212	0.180	0.153	0.130
19	0.828	0.686	0.570	0.475	0.396	0.331	0.277	0.232	0.194	0.164	0.138	0.116
20	0.820	0.673	0.554	0.456	0.377	0.312	0.258	0.215	0.178	0.149	0.124	0.104
25	0.780	0.610	0.478	0.375	0.295	0.233	0.184	0.146	0.116	0.092	0.074	0.059
30	0.742	0.552	0.412	0.308	0.231	0.174	0.131	0.099	0.075	0.057	0.044	0.033
40	0.672	0.453	0.307	0.208	0.142	0.097	0.067	0.046	0.032	0.022	0.015	0.011
50	0.608	0.372	0.228	0.141	0.087	0.054	0.034	0.021	0.013	0.009	0.005	0.003

Period	13%	14%	15%	16%	17%	18%	19%	20%	25%	30%	35%	40%	50%
1	0.885	0.877	0.870	0.862	0.855	0.847	0.840	0.833	0.800	0.769	0.741	0.714	0.667
2	0.783	0.769	0.756	0.743	0.731	0.718	0.706	0.694	0.640	0.592	0.549	0.510	0.444
3	0.693	0.675	0.658	0.641	0.624	0.609	0.593	0.579	0.512	0.455	0.406	0.364	0.296
4	0.613	0.592	0.572	0.552	0.534	0.516	0.499	0.482	0.410	0.350	0.301	0.260	0.198
5	0.543	0.519	0.497	0.476	0.456	0.437	0.419	0.402	0.328	0.269	0.223	0.186	0.132
6	0.480	0.456	0.432	0.410	0.390	0.370	0.352	0.335	0.262	0.207	0.165	0.133	0.088
7	0.425	0.400	0.376	0.354	0.333	0.314	0.296	0.279	0.210	0.159	0.122	0.095	0.059
8	0.376	0.351	0.327	0.305	0.285	0.266	0.249	0.233	0.168	0.123	0.091	0.068	0.039
9	0.333	0.308	0.284	0.263	0.243	0.225	0.209	0.194	0.134	0.094	0.067	0.048	0.026
10	0.295	0.270	0.247	0.227	0.208	0.191	0.176	0.162	0.107	0.073	0.050	0.035	0.017
11	0.261	0.237	0.215	0.195	0.178	0.162	0.148	0.135	0.086	0.056	0.037	0.025	0.012
12	0.231	0.208	0.187	0.168	0.152	0.137	0.124	0.112	0.069	0.043	0.027	0.018	0.008
13	0.204	0.182	0.163	0.145	0.130	0.116	0.104	0.093	0.055	0.033	0.020	0.013	0.005
14	0.181	0.160	0.141	0.125	0.111	0.099	0.088	0.078	0.044	0.025	0.015	0.009	0.003
15	0.160	0.140	0.123	0.108	0.095	0.084	0.074	0.065	0.035	0.020	0.011	0.006	0.002
16	0.141	0.123	0.107	0.093	0.081	0.071	0.062	0.054	0.028	0.015	0.008	0.005	0.002
17	0.125	0.108	0.093	0.080	0.069	0.060	0.052	0.045	0.023	0.012	0.006	0.003	0.001
18	0.111	0.095	0.081	0.069	0.059	0.051	0.044	0.038	0.018	0.009	0.005	0.002	0.001
19	0.098	0.083	0.070	0.060	0.051	0.043	0.037	0.031	0.014	0.007	0.003	0.002	0
20	0.087	0.073	0.061	0.051	0.043	0.037	0.031	0.026	0.012	0.005	0.002	0.001	0
25	0.047	0.038	0.030	0.024	0.020	0.016	0.013	0.010	0.004	0.001	0.001	0	0
30	0.026	0.020	0.015	0.012	0.009	0.007	0.005	0.004	0.001	0	0	0	0
40	0.008	0.005	0.004	0.003	0.002	0.001	0.001	0.001	0	0	0	0	0
50	0.002	0.001	0.001	0.001	0	0	0	0	0	0	0	0	0

EXHIBIT 1-D Present value of $1 received at the end of each period for a given number of time periods (an annuity)

Period	1%	2%	3%	4%	5%	6%	7%	8%	9%	10%	11%	12%
1	0.990	0.980	0.971	0.962	0.952	0.943	0.935	0.926	0.917	0.909	0.901	0.893
2	1.970	1.942	1.913	1.886	1.859	1.833	1.808	1.783	1.759	1.736	1.713	1.690
3	2.941	2.884	2.829	2.775	2.723	2.673	2.624	2.577	2.531	2.487	2.444	2.402
4	3.902	3.808	3.717	3.630	3.546	3.465	3.387	3.312	3.240	3.170	3.102	3.037
5	4.853	4.713	4.580	4.452	4.329	4.212	4.100	3.993	3.890	3.791	3.696	3.605
6	5.795	5.601	5.417	5.242	5.076	4.917	4.767	4.623	4.486	4.355	4.231	4.111
7	6.728	6.472	6.230	6.002	5.786	5.582	5.389	5.206	5.033	4.868	4.712	4.564
8	7.652	7.325	7.020	6.733	6.463	6.210	5.971	5.747	5.535	5.335	5.146	4.968
9	8.566	8.162	7.786	7.435	7.108	6.802	6.515	6.247	5.995	5.759	5.537	5.328
10	9.471	8.983	8.530	8.111	7.722	7.360	7.024	6.710	6.418	6.145	5.889	5.650
11	10.368	9.787	9.253	8.760	8.306	7.887	7.499	7.139	6.805	6.495	6.207	5.938
12	11.255	10.575	9.954	9.385	8.863	8.384	7.943	7.536	7.161	6.814	6.492	6.194
13	12.134	11.348	10.635	9.986	9.394	8.853	8.358	7.904	7.487	7.103	6.750	6.424
14	13.004	12.106	11.296	10.563	9.899	9.295	8.745	8.244	7.786	7.367	6.982	6.628
15	13.865	12.849	11.938	11.118	10.380	9.712	9.108	8.559	8.061	7.606	7.191	6.811
16	14.718	13.578	12.561	11.652	10.838	10.106	9.447	8.851	8.313	7.824	7.379	6.974
17	15.562	14.292	13.166	12.166	11.274	10.477	9.763	9.122	8.544	8.022	7.549	7.120
18	16.398	14.992	13.754	12.659	11.690	10.828	10.059	9.372	8.756	8.201	7.702	7.250
19	17.226	15.678	14.324	13.134	12.085	11.158	10.336	9.604	8.950	8.365	7.839	7.366
20	18.046	16.351	14.877	13.590	12.462	11.470	10.594	9.818	9.129	8.514	7.963	7.469
25	22.023	19.523	17.413	15.622	14.094	12.783	11.654	10.675	9.823	9.077	8.422	7.843
30	25.808	22.396	19.600	17.292	15.372	13.765	12.409	11.258	10.274	9.427	8.694	8.055
40	32.835	27.355	23.115	19.793	17.159	15.046	13.332	11.925	10.757	9.779	8.951	8.244
50	39.196	31.424	25.730	21.482	18.256	15.762	13.801	12.233	10.962	9.915	9.042	8.304

Period	13%	14%	15%	16%	17%	18%	19%	20%	25%	30%	35%	40%	50%
1	0.885	0.877	0.870	0.862	0.855	0.847	0.840	0.833	0.800	0.769	0.741	0.714	0.667
2	1.668	1.647	1.626	1.605	1.585	1.566	1.547	1.528	1.440	1.361	1.289	1.224	1.111
3	2.361	2.322	2.283	2.246	2.210	2.174	2.140	2.106	1.952	1.816	1.696	1.589	1.407
4	2.974	2.914	2.855	2.798	2.743	2.690	2.639	2.589	2.362	2.166	1.997	1.849	1.605
5	3.517	3.433	3.352	3.274	3.199	3.127	3.058	2.991	2.689	2.436	2.220	2.035	1.737
6	3.998	3.889	3.784	3.685	3.589	3.498	3.410	3.326	2.951	2.643	2.385	2.168	1.824
7	4.423	4.288	4.160	4.039	3.922	3.812	3.706	3.605	3.161	2.802	2.508	2.263	1.883
8	4.799	4.639	4.487	4.344	4.207	4.078	3.954	3.837	3.329	2.925	2.598	2.331	1.922
9	5.132	4.946	4.772	4.607	4.451	4.303	4.163	4.031	3.463	3.019	2.665	2.379	1.948
10	5.426	5.216	5.019	4.833	4.659	4.494	4.339	4.192	3.571	3.092	2.715	2.414	1.965
11	5.687	5.453	5.234	5.029	4.836	4.656	4.486	4.327	3.656	3.147	2.752	2.438	1.977
12	5.918	5.660	5.421	5.197	4.988	4.793	4.611	4.439	3.725	3.190	2.779	2.456	1.985
13	6.122	5.842	5.583	5.342	5.118	4.910	4.715	4.533	3.780	3.223	2.799	2.469	1.990
14	6.302	6.002	5.724	5.468	5.229	5.008	4.802	4.611	3.824	3.249	2.814	2.478	1.993
15	6.462	6.142	5.847	5.575	5.324	5.092	4.876	4.675	3.859	3.268	2.825	2.484	1.995
16	6.604	6.265	5.954	5.668	5.405	5.162	4.938	4.730	3.887	3.283	2.834	2.489	1.997
17	6.729	6.373	6.047	5.749	5.475	5.222	4.990	4.775	3.910	3.295	2.840	2.492	1.998
18	6.840	6.467	6.128	5.818	5.534	5.273	5.033	4.812	3.928	3.304	2.844	2.494	1.999
19	6.938	6.550	6.198	5.877	5.584	5.316	5.070	4.843	3.942	3.311	2.848	2.496	1.999
20	7.025	6.623	6.259	5.929	5.628	5.353	5.101	4.870	3.954	3.316	2.850	2.497	1.999
25	7.330	6.873	6.464	6.097	5.766	5.467	5.195	4.948	3.985	3.329	2.856	2.499	2.000
30	7.496	7.003	6.566	6.177	5.829	5.517	5.235	4.979	3.995	3.332	2.857	2.500	2.000
40	7.634	7.105	6.642	6.233	5.871	5.548	5.258	4.997	3.999	3.333	2.857	2.500	2.000
50	7.675	7.133	6.661	6.246	5.880	5.554	5.262	4.999	4.000	3.333	2.857	2.500	2.000

Financial Aspects of Career Planning

2

Eva-Katalin/Getty Images

LEARNING OBJECTIVES

LO2-1 Describe activities associated with career planning and advancement.

LO2-2 Evaluate factors that influence employment opportunities.

LO2-3 Implement employment search strategies.

LO2-4 Assess financial and legal concerns related to obtaining employment.

LO2-5 Analyze techniques available for career growth and advancement.

The Chapter 2 Appendix provides expanded discussion of résumés, cover letters, and interviewing.

APPENDIX

Financial Literacy
IN **YOUR LIFE**

▶ **What if you . . .** were seeking your first job or wanted to obtain a different employment position? What actions would you take to locate available jobs?

You might . . . attend campus or community programs to meet people. Or you might use social media to make connections that could help guide your career activities. Career contacts and networking with others are vital for a successful job search. Your ability to identify, connect with, and maintain career contacts will provide the foundation for ongoing career success.

Now, what would you do? What actions are you currently taking to expand your career interactions? You will be able to monitor your progress using the Your Personal Finance Roadmap and Dashboard feature at the end of the chapter.

| my life | WORK TO LIVE, OR LIVE TO WORK? |

Few decisions in life will affect you more than your choice of employment. Your income, amount of leisure time, travel opportunities, and the people with whom you associate are greatly influenced by your work situation.

As you start (or expand) your career planning activities, consider the following statements. For each, indicate if you "agree," are "neutral," or "disagree" related to your current situation regarding career planning activities.

1.	I understand my personal interests and abilities that could create a satisfying work life.	Agree	Neutral	Disagree
2.	I stay informed of factors that influence employment opportunities in our society.	Agree	Neutral	Disagree
3.	I have the ability to ask questions of others that provide me with information about employment opportunities.	Agree	Neutral	Disagree
4.	Salary would be the most important factor for me when accepting an employment position.	Agree	Neutral	Disagree
5.	I sometimes think about what type of employment situation I would like to have three or five years from now.	Agree	Neutral	Disagree

As you study this chapter, you will encounter "My Life" boxes with additional information and resources related to these items.

Career Choice Factors

LO2-1

Describe activities associated with career planning and advancement.

"Only two days until the weekend." "Just ten more minutes of sleep!" "Oh no!" "Excellent!" These are some common responses to "It's time to get up for work."

Have you ever wondered why some people find great satisfaction in their work while others only put in their time? As with other personal financial decisions, career selection and professional growth require planning. Most people will change jobs, and careers, several times during a lifetime. Therefore, you will need to reevaluate your choice of work on a regular basis.

The lifework you select is key to financial well-being and personal satisfaction. You may obtain a **job,** an employment position obtained mainly to earn money. Many people work in one or more jobs during their lives without considering their interests or opportunities for advancement. Or you may select a **career,** a commitment to a profession that requires continued training and offers a path for professional growth.

TRADE-OFFS OF CAREER DECISIONS

While many factors affect personal and financial choices, your employment probably affects daily decisions the most. Your income, business associates, and leisure time are a direct result of the work you do.

Like other decisions, career choice and professional development alternatives have risks and opportunity costs. Many people place family relationships and personal fulfillment above monetary reward and professional recognition. Career choices require periodic evaluation of trade-offs related to personal, social, and economic factors. A person may select challenging employment with strong personal satisfaction rather than obtaining a high salary. Or, some people give up secure employment to operate their own business. Parents may opt for part-time employment or flexible hours to have more time with children.

The Mom Project (themomproject.com) connects experienced professionals with major companies that provide opportunities to keep accomplished women in the workforce during every stage of their personal and career journeys.

> **job** An employment position obtained mainly to earn money, without regard for interests or opportunities for advancement.
>
> **career** A commitment to a profession that requires continued training and offers a clear path for occupational growth.

CAREER TRAINING AND SKILL DEVELOPMENT

Level of formal training affects financial success. Exhibit 2-1 shows the influence of education on earnings. These statistics do not mean you will automatically earn a certain amount because you have a college degree. However, more education increases your *potential* earning power and reduces your chances of being unemployed. Other factors, such as field of study, experience, and the job market influence future income. For guidance on financing your education, see the Chapter 7 Appendix.

The skills gap—the difference between skills needed by employers and the skills possessed by applicants—is an ongoing concern. Also missing in many employees are *employability skills,* also called *transferable skills,* which refer to basic capabilities that are needed for obtaining, maintaining, and advancing in a career.

Your workforce readiness may be placed into two main categories:

Time with family members may be an important influence on career decisions.
LightField Studios/Shutterstock

1. **Technical skills.** Specialized career training, also referred to as *hard skills,* are needed for a specific profession. This training involves competencies in fields such as information technology, accounting, law, engineering, health care, education, marketing, real estate, insurance, and law enforcement.

2. **General skills.** In addition to technical training, employers emphasize the importance of traits adaptable to varied work situations, often called *soft skills.* While some of these abilities are acquired in school, others require experience in work settings.

The general competencies that successful people commonly possess include:

- An ability to work well with others in varied settings.
- Taking initiative to overcome obstacles and meet challenges.

EXHIBIT 2-1

Education and income

Median weekly earnings for various levels of education:

Two-year
degree

$887

Bachelor's
degree

$1,248

Master's
degree

$1,497

Professional
or doctoral
degree

$1,861

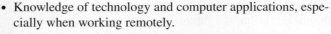

Over a lifetime, the earnings for a person with a two-year
degree exceeds $1.8 million, while a person with a professional
or doctoral degree is likely to earn nearly $4 million.

Source: Unemployment Rates and Earnings by Educational Attainment, 2019 (https://www.bls.gov/emp/chart-unemployment-earnings-education.htm).

- An interest in reading and ongoing learning to understand technical journals and financial reports.
- A willingness to cope with conflict and adapt to change.
- Knowledge of technology and computer applications, especially when working remotely.
- Creative problem solving in team settings.
- Knowledge of research techniques and resource materials.
- Effective written and oral communication skills.
- An understanding of personal motivations and the motivations of others.
- Awareness of accounting, finance, marketing, and other business fundamentals.

These competencies give people flexibility, making it easier to move from one organization to another and to change career fields. The Occupational Mobility Explorer (available at https://www.philadelphiafed.org/surveys-and-data/community-development-data/occupational-mobility-explorer), he mustloped by the Federal Reserve Bank of Philadelphia, helps workers identify training or upskilling paths for new employment and higher pay opportunities.

Leadership is also vital in many work situations. Your ability to think strategically, communicate a vision, make decisions, and delegate work will be viewed favorably. Leaders possess integrity, empathy, gratitude, creativity, a cooperative nature, and strong listening and questioning skills. You can obtain leadership experience through class projects, campus

smart money minute

To enhance success in your job search and interviews, emphasize these items:

- **Accomplishments**—instead of telling what you've done, highlight examples with a brief story to show how you made a difference in a job setting or a class project.
- **Motivation**—communicate what excites you about your work. Show your passion and desire to contribute to others.
- **Connectivity**—be prepared for casual conversation related to your background and family. Keep responses short, and don't hesitate to ask similar questions of your interviewer.
- **Company, position knowledge**—research in advance so you can confidently communicate relevant information about company trends and the job.
- **Organizational fit**—many employees fail due to cultural incompatibility. Self-awareness is vital to communicate your potential for fitting into the company culture.

Financial Literacy for My Life

DEVELOPING A CAREER ACTION PLAN

A career plan might start with a personal SWOT analysis, in which you identify your:

Strengths – your unique skills, experiences

Weaknesses – personal areas in need of improvement

Opportunities – social, economic, technological, other trends creating employment opportunities

Threats – factors limiting employment opportunities, such as technology, global competition

Next, select one of these career development activities, and describe actions using the steps below.

☐ Assess personal and career interests.

☐ Identify and expand career skills.

☐ Obtain required education and career training.

☐ Apply for an employment position.

Action Step	Your Responses
1. Describe your current situation.	
2. Set a specific goal.	
3. Identify the time frame for the goal.	
4. List actions to be taken to achieve this goal.	

activities, sports teams, and community service. What actions are you taking to develop your career and leadership skills?

PERSONAL FACTORS

A satisfying career can be identified using guidance tests. Aptitude tests, interest inventories, and other types of career assessment tests are available at your school career office and online. *Aptitudes* are natural abilities that people possess, such as the the ability to work well with numbers, problem-solving skills, creativity, and physical dexterity. *Interest inventories* determine activities that give you satisfaction in various work situations. People with strong social tendencies are usually best suited for careers interacting with people; those with investigative interests may be best suited for research-based careers.

Test results will not tell you which career to pursue. These assessments indicate your aptitudes and interests. Also important is your personality. Do you perform best in structured or high-pressure situations, or do you prefer unstructured or creative work environments? Sample career assessments may be located online by searching for "career interest inventory" and "career interest survey."

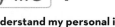

my life 1

I understand my personal interests and abilities that could create a satisfying work life.

You might ask people who know you well to point out some of your interests and abilities. Use this information to start your career planning activities using the *Financial Literacy for My Life: Developing a Career Action Plan* feature.

CAREER DECISION-MAKING

Changing personal and workplace factors requires that you continually assess your career situation. Exhibit 2-2 provides an approach to career planning, advancement, and career change. Note that different entry points depend on your personal situation. For example, people established in a certain career field may start at point C (Change employment within same career field) or D (Career advancement).

Your career goals will affect how you use this process. If you want more responsibility on the job, for example, you may obtain advanced training or change career fields. This process is a framework for planning, changing, or advancing in a career.

EXHIBIT 2-2

Stages of career planning
and advancement

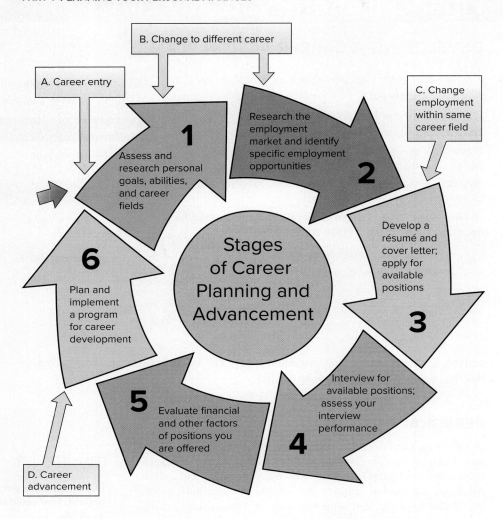

A. Career entry

B. Change to different career

C. Change employment within same career field

1 Assess and research personal goals, abilities, and career fields

Research the employment market and identify specific employment opportunities **2**

Develop a résumé and cover letter; apply for available positions **3**

6 Plan and implement a program for career development

Stages of Career Planning and Advancement

Interview for available positions; assess your interview performance **4**

5 Evaluate financial and other factors of positions you are offered

D. Career advancement

✔ **PRACTICE QUIZ 2-1**

1. How does a job differ from a career?
2. What opportunity costs are associated with career decisions?
3. What skills would be of value in most employment situations?

LO2-2

Evaluate factors that influence employment opportunities.

Career Opportunities: Now and in the Future

Your job search should start with an assessment of the career choice factors shown in Exhibit 2-3.

SOCIAL INFLUENCES

Various demographic and geographic trends influence employment opportunities. An expanded number of single and working parents increases demand for food service and child care. More leisure time can result in expanded interest in personal

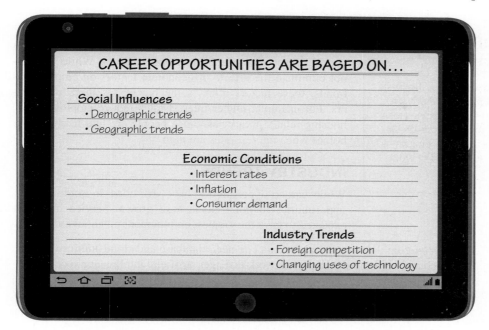

EXHIBIT 2-3

Factors influencing your career opportunities

health, physical fitness, technology, and recreational products and services. As people live longer, demand for travel services, health care, and retirement facilities grows. Working from home increases demand for various work-related and personal services.

When considering different geographic areas, also assess salary levels. Average incomes are high in metropolitan areas such as Boston, New York, Los Angeles, and Chicago; however, living costs in these areas are also high. What appears to be a high salary may actually mean a lower standard of living. For example, in recent years, the cost of living for a single employee earning $30,000 annually was 60 percent higher in the District of Columbia than the national city average. In contrast, the cost of living in Fayetteville, Arkansas, was only 90 percent of the national city average.

EXAMPLE: Geographic Cost-of-Living Differences

To compare living costs and salaries in different cities, you may use the following "Geographic Buying Power" formula:

$$\frac{\text{City 1}}{\text{City 2}} \frac{\text{Index number} \times \text{Salary}}{\text{Index number}} = \$ \text{ buying power}$$

For example,

$$\frac{\text{Chicago}}{\text{Omaha}} \frac{123 \times \$30,000}{93.3} = \$39,550$$

A person earning $30,000 in Omaha, Nebraska, would need to earn $39,550 in Chicago to have comparable buying power. Information to compare geographic cost-of-living differences is available at www.bls.gov, www.erieri.com, and www.nerdwallet.com/cost-of-living-calculator.

How about you? Describe how economic factors and the cost of living in an area might affect your decision about accepting a job.

smart money minute

ECONOMIC CONDITIONS

Interest rates, price fluctuations, or changing global demand for goods and services affect career opportunities. While you cannot eliminate the effects of economic factors on employment trends, these factors affect some businesses more than others. For example, higher interest rates reduce employment in housing-related industries, since people are less likely to buy homes when interest rates are high.

INDUSTRY TRENDS

While career opportunities have dwindled in some sectors, opportunities in other fields have grown. Service industries expected to have the greatest employment potential include:

- *Technology*—systems analyst, data engineer, database and cloud administrator, web and software developer, network manager, artificial intelligence specialist, information security analyst, service technician, and DevOps, which combines software development and IT operations.

- *Health care*—medical assistant, physical therapist, home health care aide, biotech analyst, laboratory technician, registered nurse, nurse assistant, dental hygienist, health services administrator, pandemic tester, and contact tracer.

  - *Medical technology*—microbiologist, food and drug inspector, pharmaceutical sales, public health specialist, medical laboratory manager, clinical pathologist, and toxicologist.

  - *Environmental services*—environmental auditor, environmental consultant, water quality analyst, sustainability analyst, energy analyst, and urban planner.

  - *Business services*—supply chain and logistics manager, social media consultant, foreign language translator, employee benefit manager, operations analyst, research data analyst, statistician, home office designer, and construction supervisor.

  - *Social services*—child care worker, elder care coordinator, family counselor, and social service agency administrator.

Technology influences career opportunities and required employment skills.
PeopleImages/Getty Images

- *Marketing, sales, and retailing*—digital marketing developer, social media marketing representative, customer service representative, and sales manager with technical knowledge in the areas of electronics, medical products, and financial services.

  - *Hospitality and food services*—resort and hotel administrator, food service manager, online customer service representative, and meeting planner.

  - *Management and human resources*—clerical supervisor, recruiter, interviewer, employee benefit administrator, and employment service worker.

  - *Education*—online tutor, corporate trainer, special education teacher, language teacher, adult education instructor, and teacher for elementary, secondary, or postsecondary schools.

my life 2

My actions keep me informed of various factors that influence employment opportunities in our society.

What are some personal, social, economic, and technological factors you might consider when planning the direction for your career?

ENTREPRENEURIAL CAREER OPTIONS

People start their own businesses due to: (1) limited career opportunities in their field, and (2) a desire for greater control of their work situation. Over 20 million people in the United States operate their own businesses. These range from home-based sales and consulting services to small manufacturing enterprises and online technology support. In recent years, new opportunities for start-ups included:

- *Social entrepreneurs* mix traditional business practices with innovation to address concerns such as hunger, disease, poverty, and education.

- The *gig economy* involves independent contractors and freelancers with flexibility of projects and work locations.

- The *shared economy* emphasizes renting or borrowing rather than buying, with examples such as eBay, Craigslist, Airbnb, Lyft, Uber, and co-working shared office space locations.

- The *circular economy* involves environmental activities to recover, restore, recycle, reuse, and repurpose resources. Emphasis is on renewable energy and innovations that minimize waste and ecological impact.

Personal finances must be considered by independent contractors and small business owners. Maintain a detailed record of income and expenses. Be aware of tax regulations. Obtain adequate insurance for business risks.

GETTING STARTED

If you plan to start a business, first, become familiar with the product or service. Select a market offering that solves a problem. Many new opportunities were created during the pandemic. Next, identify potential customers, select a location, and study competitors. Finally, consider the financial resources. Most entrepreneurs use a combination of personal finances and loans for start-up funding. *Microloans,* popular in many areas of the world, are available through nonprofits, community organizations, foundations, government agencies, and peer-to-peer lending networks.

QUALITIES OF SUCCESSFUL ENTREPRENEURS

Is running your own business appropriate for you? That depends on your personality and abilities. Are you a highly motivated, confident person? Do you have the ability to manage different business activities? Are you someone who enjoys challenges and is willing to take risks?

Vital skills for entrepreneurial success include sales and marketing knowledge, effective communication skills, understanding accounting and financial management, an ability to motivate and coordinate others, efficient time management, and a creative vision. To enhance your potential success, work, intern, or conduct research in the business field you are considering.

BUSINESS PLAN ELEMENTS

A business plan is used to communicate the vision and purpose of an enterprise. This document contains financial projections, product information, and a marketing plan. Business plan information is available at: www.bplans.com, www.thebalancesmb.com, canvanizer.com, and www.strategyzer.com/canvas/business-model-canvas.

When starting a business, seek guidance from a lawyer, banker, accountant, and insurance agent. Additional information on running your own business is available from the Small Business Administration (www.sba.gov), the National Association for the Self-Employed (www.nase.org), *Entrepreneur* magazine (www.entrepreneur.com), SCORE (www.score.org), and INC magazine (www.inc.com).

- *Financial services*—financial advisor, risk assessment manager, actuary, accountant, investment broker, investment banker, and other position with a knowledge of accounting, finance, economics, and taxes.

In nearly every career field, productivity while working remotely will be valued. Expanded technology and the recent pandemic expanded the number of virtual work settings, a trend that will likely continue.

 PRACTICE QUIZ 2-2

1. What are some demographic and economic factors that affect career opportunities?
2. How does technology affect available employment positions?

PFP Sheet 6
Career Research Sheet

Employment Search Strategies

LO2-3

Implement employment search strategies.

Most people have heard about job applicants who sent hundreds of résumés with little success, while others got several offers. What are the differences between these? The answer involves the level of one's experiences and the ability to effectively use job search techniques.

OBTAINING EMPLOYMENT EXPERIENCE

A common concern among people seeking employment is a lack of work experience. Many opportunities are available to obtain work-related training.

PART-TIME EMPLOYMENT   Summer and part-time work provide experience and an opportunity to see if you enjoy a career field. Temporary employees can obtain experience in varied career areas. Many workers take advantage of temporary job assignments as a path to a full-time position. Working as a "temp" can give you valuable experience as well as career contacts.

VOLUNTEER WORK   Involvement in community organizations can provide an excellent opportunity to acquire skills, develop good work habits, and make contacts. Volunteering to work at the gift shop of a museum gives you experience in retailing. Or, you might participate in a recycling project, assist at a senior center, or supervise a park district youth program. These activities help you obtain organizational experience.

INTERNSHIPS   In competitive fields, an internship can provide needed experience, while you make contacts about available jobs. The application process is similar to applying for a job. Most colleges and universities have internship academic programs. The COVID-19 pandemic resulted in an expanded number of virtual internships that involved working remotely.

CAMPUS PROJECTS   Class assignments and campus activities may be overlooked as work-related experience. You can obtain valuable career skills on campus from experience in:

- Managing, organizing, and coordinating people and activities as an officer of a campus organization or with a class team project.
- Public speaking in class, campus, and community presentations.
- Goal setting, planning, supervising, and delegating responsibility in community service and class projects.
- Financial planning and budgeting gained from organizing fund-raising projects, managing personal finances, and handling funds for campus organizations.
- Conducting research for class projects, community organizations, and campus activities.

USING CAREER INFORMATION SOURCES

Career planning, like other financial decisions, is enhanced by relevant information. Exhibit 2-4 provides an overview of the main career information sources.

Libraries and campus career offices offer many career planning resources. The *Occupational Outlook Handbook* (available at www.bls.gov/ooh/) covers career planning activities and provides detailed information on various career clusters. This handbook and other government publications are available online. Newspapers and

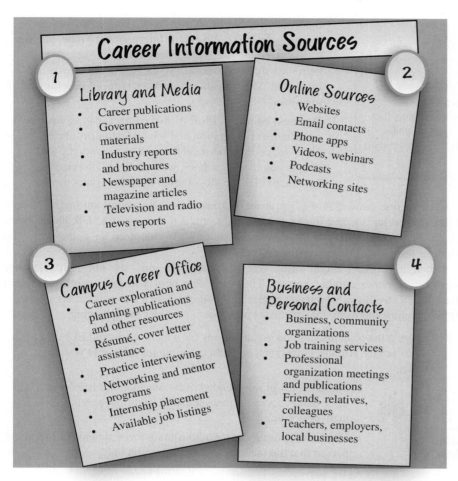

EXHIBIT 2-4
Career information sources

online sources offer articles and information about career trends, job opportunities, résumés, interviewing, and other career planning topics.

CAREER DEVELOPMENT OFFICE This campus office offers many services. Starting with career exploration, counselors assist with résumé, cover letter, and interview preparation. Networking and mentor programs provide access to alumni, employers, and opportunities for internships and available jobs. The career development staff will help you target your career focus and job search.

NETWORKING **Networking** is the process of making and using contacts to obtain and update career information. Every person you talk to is a potential career contact. These activities are especially valuable since about 70 percent of professionals find positions through personal contacts and networking; responding to job ads accounts for only about 15 percent of jobs. The main sources of networking include:

1. **Community organizations.** Every community has business and civic groups. Public meetings with industry leaders and business owners provide opportunities to make contacts.

2. **Professional associations.** All professions have organizations to promote their career areas. These organizations include the American Marketing Association,

networking The process of making and using contacts to obtain and update career information.

smart money minute

An *elevator speech,* also called an *elevator pitch,* is a short, persuasive, focused summary of your unique experiences and skills used when networking. This talk should be conversational (not forced), memorable, and sincere. Using an engaging idea or question can help keep the conversation moving forward.

informational interview A company visit or meeting at which one gathers information about a career or an organization.

my life 3

I have the ability to ask other people questions that provide me with information about career planning activities and employment opportunities.

Develop questions that you might ask in an informational interview. These questions should reflect your current knowledge of a career field and should lead the person to provide additional information. The best questions usually start with "How," "What," "Why," "Describe," "Explain," and "Tell me more about. . ."

the Council of Supply Chain Management Professionals, the Association of Women in International Trade, and the National Restaurant Association. An online search can help identify organizations for careers in which you are interested. Most organizations have reduced fees for student members.

3. **Business contacts.** Professional contacts can advise you about career preparation and job opportunities. Friends, relatives, people you meet through organizations, and people you meet at school, work, religious services, or other activities are all potential business contacts.

For effective networking: (1) prepare and practice a 30-second summary of your abilities, experiences, and interests; (2) ask questions to get others to talk about themselves, their profession, and their experiences; and (3) volunteer for committees and events of professional organizations.

Although contacts might offer you a position, if jobs are not available they might refer you to another person. They can also help you get an **informational interview,** a meeting at which you gather information about a career or an organization. When planning and using informational interviews, consider the following.

- Prepare a list of industries and organizations for which you would like to work. Talk to family, friends, coworkers, and others for names of people you might contact.
- Prepare a list of open-ended questions that will help you obtain information about current industry trends and potential employment opportunities.
- Make an appointment for a 20-minute meeting; emphasize to the person that the meeting is for information only.
- Try to interact with the person at his or her place of work for awareness of the work environment.
- Follow up with a thank-you note or email and, if possible, send some current information (such as an article) that might be of interest to your contact.

An email informational "interview" may be used in some settings. Be sure your questions are open-ended and focused on various career and industry topics. Send your email request to a specific person. As a follow-up to the email response, you may also want to meet in person or talk by telephone.

EXAMPLE: Business Cards in an Age of Social Media

While several apps are available as an alternative to business cards, a physical card for networking may be expected in some settings. Things to remember:

- Keep the format simple with necessary contact information.
- Create a brief, yet descriptive, tagline to communicate your unique skills. Search online for ideas for your business card format and content.
- Use the back of the card for competencies and accomplishments, or to have a translation of your card for international business contacts.
- Several apps are available to scan and store business cards.

How about you? Describe the content, format, and design of a business card that you might consider.

 **HOW TO . . .** **Create a Focused Career Planning Strategy**

While planning a career can be overwhelming, this summary can help you adapt to a changing employment market.

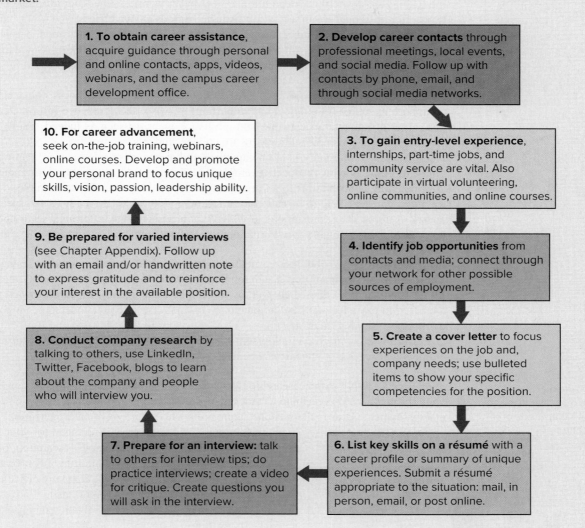

1. To obtain career assistance, acquire guidance through personal and online contacts, apps, videos, webinars, and the campus career development office.

2. Develop career contacts through professional meetings, local events, and social media. Follow up with contacts by phone, email, and through social media networks.

3. To gain entry-level experience, internships, part-time jobs, and community service are vital. Also participate in virtual volunteering, online communities, and online courses.

4. Identify job opportunities from contacts and media; connect through your network for other possible sources of employment.

5. Create a cover letter to focus experiences on the job and, company needs; use bulleted items to show your specific competencies for the position.

6. List key skills on a résumé with a career profile or summary of unique experiences. Submit a résumé appropriate to the situation: mail, in person, email, or post online.

7. Prepare for an interview: talk to others for interview tips; do practice interviews; create a video for critique. Create questions you will ask in the interview.

8. Conduct company research by talking to others, use LinkedIn, Twitter, Facebook, blogs to learn about the company and people who will interview you.

9. Be prepared for varied interviews (see Chapter Appendix). Follow up with an email and/or handwritten note to express gratitude and to reinforce your interest in the available position.

10. For career advancement, seek on-the-job training, webinars, online courses. Develop and promote your personal brand to focus unique skills, vision, passion, leadership ability.

Enhance your career planning activities with an online presence. Avoid posts that present you in less than a professional manner. To communicate an appropriate online image, consider these actions:

- DO get connected to LinkedIn and other professional networking sites.
- DON'T put items online that create an unprofessional image; search your name to assess your online presence.
- DO use keywords for capabilities and experiences expected in the industry in which you work.
- DON'T post your résumé online arbitrarily; select websites appropriate for your specific job search.
- DO regular follow-ups with online contacts; share current news and ideas on industry trends.
- DON'T join online groups in which you will not be an active participant.
- DO create a blog to enhance your online image and communicate areas of expertise.

Continually search online and use apps to update career planning activities.

IDENTIFYING JOB OPPORTUNITIES

As you plan to apply for employment, identify job openings that match your interests and abilities.

JOB ADVERTISEMENTS   Advertisements for employment opportunities were previously found in newspapers and other print media. While some still exist, nearly all job listings are now online. In addition to newspaper websites, check for available positions offered through community job listings, campus career offices, and other online sources. For opportunities in a specific field, use the websites of professional organizations for that field, such as advertising, marketing, accounting, or banking. Since many available jobs may not be advertised, other job search actions are critical.

NETWORKING AND CAREER FAIRS   Your personal and business contacts are an important source for employment opportunities. Also, seek guidance from the campus career office, alumni network, and job listing websites such as Indeed, Vault, Zip Recruiter, and Handshake with a focus for college students.

Career fairs, commonly held on campuses and at conference centers, are an opportunity to connect with prospective employers. Be prepared to quickly communicate your potential contributions to an organization. By making yourself memorable to the recruiter, you are likely to be called for a follow-up interview. Be ready to ask specific questions about the organizations in which you are interested. Additional information on career fairs is available at www.nationalcareerfairs.com.

EMPLOYMENT AGENCIES   Another source of job leads is employment agencies. These for-profit organizations match job hunters with prospective employers. Often the hiring company pays the fee charged by the employment agency. Be careful when you are asked to pay a fee and have no guarantee of a job. Be sure you understand any contracts before signing them.

Government-supported employment services are also available. Contact your state employment service or state department of labor for further information.

job creation The development of an employment position that matches your skills with the needs of an organization.

JOB CREATION   After researching a particular organization or industry, present how your abilities would contribute to that organization. **Job creation** involves developing an employment position that matches your skills with the needs of an organization.

As you develop skills you enjoy, you might be able to create a demand for your services. For example, a person who enjoys researching business and economic trends might be hired by a corporation to make presentations for managers at company offices. Or people with an ability to design promotions and advertising might be hired by a nonprofit organization that needs to enhance its visibility.

OTHER JOB SEARCH METHODS   Your ability to locate existing and potential employment positions is limited only by your imagination and initiative. Here are some often-overlooked ways to find job information:

Volunteering can make a difference in getting your foot in the door for a new job.
LightField Studios/Shutterstock

- Visit organizations where you would like to work to make in-person contacts. Create an impression as someone who can contribute. Call or visit before 8 a.m. or after 4 p.m. to talk with someone who may be available to meet with you.

- Successful organizations continually look for quality employees. An online search can provide names of organizations that employ people with your qualifications.

- Through LinkedIn or your campus career office, be in contact with alumni who work in your field of interest. Graduates who are familiar with your school and major can help you focus your career search.

To improve your job search efforts, work as many hours a week *getting* a job as you expect to work each week *on* the job. Maintaining an ongoing relationship with contacts can be a valuable source of information about future career opportunities.

smart money minute

A *mistake* for résumés and cover letters is not carefully checking the spelling and grammar. An *action* would be to seek assistance to ensure your document is error-free. After reading it several times yourself, ask a friend or family member to check for errors and clarity. This can result in *success* with high-quality documents that can improve your chances of obtaining employment.

APPLYING FOR EMPLOYMENT

Qualified people will not get the jobs they deserve without an effective presentation of their skills and experiences. This process usually involves three main elements.

1. The **résumé,** a summary of education, training, experience, and qualifications, provides prospective employers with an overview of your potential contributions to an organization.

2. A **cover letter** is the correspondence you send with a résumé to communicate your interest in a job and to obtain an interview.

3. The **interview** is the formal meeting to discuss a job candidate's qualifications in detail, which may include an online, in-person, and combination connection.

When connecting your background and potential contributions to the needs of an organization in a résumé, cover letter, or interview, consider how these examples achieve that purpose:

résumé A summary of a person's education, training, experience, and other job qualifications.

cover letter A letter that accompanies a résumé and is designed to express interest in a job and obtain an interview.

interview The formal meeting to discuss a job candidate's qualifications in detail.

A prospective employer requires that you have:	Experiences and competencies you have:	A connection you might make on a résumé or in an interview:
• Research experience	• Class research project for case study in Eastern Europe	• Researched potential markets in Eastern Europe for company expansion
• Leadership skills	• Summer camp coordinator for youth sports	• Coordinated camp volunteers for youth sports program
• Marketing background	• Prepared marketing proposal during internship	• Developed marketing proposal for community service organization

Most important, communicate how your experiences will contribute to the future needs and success of the organization. For expanded coverage of résumés, cover letters, and interview strategies, see the Chapter Appendix.

 ## PRACTICE QUIZ 2-3

PFP Sheet 7
Career Contacts

1. How can a person obtain employment-related experiences without working in a job situation?
2. What types of career information sources can be helpful in identifying job opportunities?
3. What actions might a person take to identify job opportunities that may not be advertised?

Financial and Legal Aspects of Employment

LO2-4

Assess financial and legal concerns related to obtaining employment.

"We would like you to work for us." When offered an employment position, you should consider several factors. Carefully assess the organization and the specific job responsibilities, along with the salary and other benefits.

ACCEPTING AN EMPLOYMENT POSITION

Before accepting a position, do additional research. Request information about your specific duties and expectations. If appropriate, ask to meet with someone from the department in which you will be working.

THE WORK ENVIRONMENT Investigate the organizational setting. *Corporate culture* refers to management styles, work intensity, dress codes, and social interactions within an organization. For example, some companies have rigid lines of communication, while others have an informal setting. Are the values, goals, and lifestyles of current employees similar to yours? If not, you may find yourself in an uncomfortable situation.

Consider company policies and procedures for salary increases, performance evaluations, and promotions. Talk with current workers, and observe interactions among employees, desk areas, the break room, other facilities, and remote work opportunities.

smart money minute

Some career advisors advocate a *condensed cover letter* with a single paragraph or two. Use a strong, brief opening such as a story to communicate your desire to work in the setting for which you are applying. Avoid general, vague skills that are expected of everyone, such as *communication, detail oriented,* or *desire to learn.* Don't repeat information on your résumé. Focus on actions you might take once you start working based on the job description. If possible, include solid data for work you have done. Emphasize your passion to the company mission and its future growth.

FACTORS AFFECTING SALARY Your initial salary will be based on your education and training, company size, and salaries for comparable positions. To improve your value and to enhance your salary potential:

- Ask your supervisor for professional development suggestions.
- Obtain additional training; request expanded duties.
- Take initiative to exceed performance expectations.
- Talk with coworkers for ideas to contribute to team and organizational success.

When negotiating salary, even in difficult economic times: (1) research comparable positions; (2) prepare evidence of your contributions; (3) plan the appropriate time and message for meeting with your supervisor; and (4) emphasize the value of your work for your employer. If a salary increase doesn't result, consider a request for non-monetary benefits, additional training, and the possibility to discuss the situation in the future. Express appreciation to your supervisor for the meeting and discussion.

EVALUATING EMPLOYEE BENEFITS

Health care costs, changing family situations, and retirement concerns increase the attention given to supplementary compensation benefits.

MEETING EMPLOYEE NEEDS Nonsalary employee benefits continue to expand to meet varied life situations. Increased two-income and single-parent households result in a greater need for child care benefits and leaves of absence. Elder care benefits for employees with dependent parents or grandparents have also increased. Other employee benefits designed to meet varied life situations include flexible work schedules, virtual work settings, legal assistance, counseling for health, emotional, and financial needs,

Financial Literacy for My Life

EMERGING EMPLOYEE BENEFITS

Common employee benefits include health insurance, life insurance, disability income insurance, dental insurance, retirement plans, flexible spending accounts (FSAs) and health savings accounts (HSAs), paid vacation time, paid holidays, paid medical and family leaves, flexible work schedules, child and elder care services, and education assistance. Tuition benefits help companies attract top talent, reduce turnover, and increase productivity.

Following are some examples of employee benefits in recent years that go beyond the usual:

- Life coaches to guide professional development of employees.
- Sleep pods for work-day naps.
- A soccer tournament for Bain & Company employees around the world.

- Eventbrite has a monthly wellness stipend for gym dues and juice cleanses; other companies offer on-site fitness classes, massages, and yoga.
- Deloitte offers sabbatical programs for personal or professional growth with 40 percent pay.
- Southwest Airlines offers access to Clear Skies, which is a program offering confidential counseling and legal consultation.
- Salesforce and Timberland employees are provided paid time off for volunteering.

Based on your current life situation or expectations for the future, what employee benefits might be most important to you? What is an employee benefit that you would suggest to a company?

and fitness programs. These benefits enhance the quality of life for workers and result in happier, healthier employees with fewer absences and higher productivity.

Flexible employee benefit programs, also referred to as *cafeteria-style benefits,* allow workers to base their job benefits on a credit system and on their personal needs. Flexible selection of employee benefits has become common. A married employee with children may opt for increased life and health insurance, while a single parent may use benefit credits for child care services. The *Financial Literacy for My Life: Emerging Employee Benefits* feature provides additional information on varied employee benefits.

Many organizations offer *flexible spending plans,* also called *expense reimbursement accounts.* This arrangement allows you to set aside part of your salary to pay medical or dependent care expenses. These funds are not subject to income or Social Security taxes. Under certain conditions, some money not used in one year may be carried over into the next year.

Similarly, a *medical-savings account (MSA)* or a *health savings account (HSA)* enables account holders to pay health care costs with pretax dollars. These programs have two components: (1) health insurance coverage with a high deductible and (2) a tax-deferred savings account for medical expenses. In certain situations, money in these accounts may be used for other purposes; however, the amount is taxed, along with a tax penalty based on age and health condition. While MSAs and HSAs have tax-saving implications, the high deductible may not be affordable for many households.

When matching dependent health care needs with a medical insurance plan, consider the following:

- Types of services available and location of health care providers.
- Direct costs (insurance premiums) for you.
- Anticipated out-of-pocket costs (deductibles and coinsurance amounts).

As people live longer, retirement programs are increasing in importance. In addition to Social Security benefits, some employers

> **Flexible employee benefit programs** Also referred to as cafeteria-style benefits are programs that allow workers to base their job benefits on a credit system and personal needs.

 my life **4**

Salary would be the most important factor for me when accepting an employment position.

While salary is important, research findings consistently show that people rate other factors higher when deciding to accept a position. Talk to people in various stages of their careers to obtain information about factors they have considered when selecting an employment position.

Financial Literacy Calculations

TAX-EQUIVALENT EMPLOYEE BENEFITS

Employee benefits that are nontaxable have a higher financial value than you may realize. A $100 employee benefit on which you are taxed is not worth as much as a nontaxable $100 benefit. This formula is used to calculate the *tax-equivalent value* of a nontaxable benefit:

$$\frac{\text{Value of the benefit}}{1 - \text{Tax rate}}$$

For example, receiving a life insurance policy with a nontaxable annual premium of $350 is comparable to receiving a taxable employee benefit worth $461 if you are in a 24 percent tax bracket. This tax-equivalent amount is calculated as follows:

$$\frac{\$350}{1 - 0.24} = \frac{\$350}{0.76} = \$461$$

A variation of this formula, which would give the *after-tax value* of an employee benefit, is

Taxable value of the benefit (1 − Tax rate)

For the preceding example, the calculation would be

$$\$461\,(1 - 0.24) = \$461\,(0.76) = \$350$$

In other words, a taxable benefit with a value of $461 would have an after-tax value of $350 since you would have to pay $111 ($461 × 0.24) in tax on the benefit.

These calculations can help you compare different employee benefits within a company or when considering different job offers. Remember, also evaluate the value of employee benefits in terms of your personal and family needs and goals.

contribute to a retirement plan, such as a 401(k) or, in a nonprofit organization, a 403(b). *Vesting* is the point at which retirement payments made by the organization on your behalf belong to you even if you no longer work for the organization. Vesting schedules vary, but all qualified plans (those for which an employer may deduct plan contributions for tax purposes) must (1) be 100 percent vested on completion of five years of service, or (2) have 20 percent vesting after three years and full vesting, in stages, after seven years. Vesting refers only to the employer's pension contributions; employee contributions belong to the workers regardless of the length of their service with the organization.

Workers are usually allowed to make personal contributions to company-sponsored retirement programs. These plans involve a variety of investments, making it possible for employees to create a diversified portfolio for their retirement.

COMPARING BENEFITS Two methods used to assess the monetary value of employee benefits are the market value and future value calculations.

Market value is the monetary value of an employee benefit—the cost of the benefit if you had to pay for them. For example, you may view the value of one week's vacation as 1/52 of your annual salary, or the value of a life insurance benefit as what it would cost to buy the same coverage yourself. This method can be used to compare two job offers with different salaries and employee benefits.

Future value calculations, as discussed in Chapter 1, enable you to assess the long-term worth of employee benefits such as a retirement plan. For example, you can compare the future value of payments contributed to a company retirement fund with other saving and investment options.

Also take taxes into consideration when comparing employment benefits. A *tax-exempt* benefit is one for which you won't have to pay income tax, but a *tax-deferred* benefit requires payment of income tax at some future time, such as at retirement. When assessing employment compensation and benefits, consider taxability, since an untaxed benefit of lower value may be worth more than a benefit of higher value that is subject taxes (see the *Financial Literacy Calculations: Tax-Equivalent Employee Benefits* feature).

personal fintech

The use of artificial intelligence (AI) is increasing for identifying and hiring employees. Computer-based matching of job descriptions with résumés can identify the candidates with the best fit. Algorithms are AI programs used to post openings on job boards that attract the most qualified applicants. AI video games are used to screen candidates based on personality, skills, and risk-taking tendencies. Chatbots analyze word choice, tone of voice, and eye contact during an online video interview. *Voice masking* for online interviews helps to eliminate accent bias. However, concerns exist that some desirable candidates may not be comfortable interacting with automated systems.

YOUR EMPLOYMENT RIGHTS

Employees have legal rights during the hiring process and on the job. For example, an employer cannot refuse to hire a woman or terminate her employment because of pregnancy, nor can she be forced to go on leave at an arbitrary point during her pregnancy. In addition, a woman who stops working due to pregnancy must get full credit for previous service, accrued retirement benefits, and accumulated seniority. Other employment rights include:

- A person may not be discriminated against in the selection process on the basis of age, race, color, religion, sex, marital status, national origin, mental or physical disabilities, or sexual orientation.
- Minimum-wage and overtime pay legislation apply to individuals in certain work settings.
- Worker's compensation (for work-related injury or illness), Social Security, and unemployment insurance are required benefits.

 PRACTICE QUIZ 2-4

PFP Sheet 12
Employee Benefits
Comparison

1. How does a person's life situation determine the importance of certain employee benefits?
2. What methods can be used to measure the monetary value of employee benefits?

Long-Term Career Development

A job is for today, but a career can be for a lifetime. Will you always enjoy the work you do today? Will you be successful in the career you select? These questions cannot be answered right away; however, certain skills and attitudes can lead to a fulfilling work life.

LO2-5

Analyze techniques available for career growth and advancement.

Every day you can take actions that contribute to your career success. Communicating and working well with others will enhance your chances for advancement. Flexibility and openness to new ideas will expand your abilities, knowledge, and career potential. Connect within your organization to create knowledge networks and career support relationships.

Develop efficient work habits. Use lists, goal setting, note taking, and time management techniques. Combine increased productivity with quality. All of your work activities should reflect a high level of excellence. Extra effort will be recognized and rewarded.

Finally, learn to anticipate problems and opportunities, along with potential action steps. Creativity and a willingness to assist others helps an entire organization and contributes to your work enjoyment and career growth.

TRAINING OPPORTUNITIES

Most technology careers did not exist a few years ago, and many future job skills have yet to be identified. Ongoing education and training are crucial for career stability and advancement. Continue to learn about new technology, diverse cultures, management strategies, and global business.

Formal training methods include company programs, seminars, and webinars, along with graduate and advanced college courses. Most companies encourage, and some pay for, continuing education.

Informal methods for enhanced knowledge include reading and discussion with colleagues. Webinars and online courses can expand your knowledge of business,

EXHIBIT 2-5

Stages of career development: Characteristics and concerns

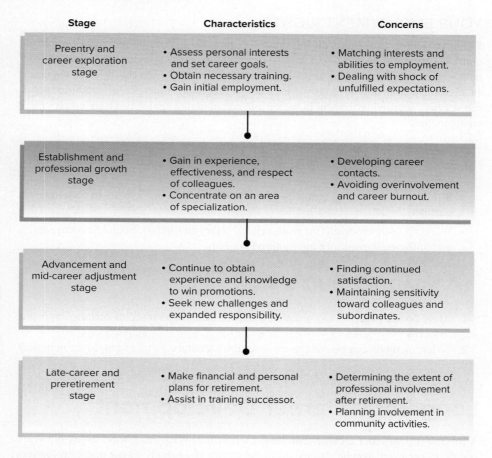

Stage	Characteristics	Concerns
Preentry and career exploration stage	• Assess personal interests and set career goals. • Obtain necessary training. • Gain initial employment.	• Matching interests and abilities to employment. • Dealing with shock of unfulfilled expectations.
Establishment and professional growth stage	• Gain in experience, effectiveness, and respect of colleagues. • Concentrate on an area of specialization.	• Developing career contacts. • Avoiding overinvolvement and career burnout.
Advancement and mid-career adjustment stage	• Continue to obtain experience and knowledge to win promotions. • Seek new challenges and expanded responsibility.	• Finding continued satisfaction. • Maintaining sensitivity toward colleagues and subordinates.
Late-career and preretirement stage	• Make financial and personal plans for retirement. • Assist in training successor.	• Determining the extent of professional involvement after retirement. • Planning involvement in community activities.

economic, and social trends. Informal meetings with others are also a valuable source of career information.

CAREER PATHS AND ADVANCEMENT

As with other financial decisions, career choices should be regularly reviewed. As Exhibit 2-5 shows, you will likely move through career stages, each with specific tasks and challenges. A successful technique for coping with the anxieties associated with career development is to get the support of an established person in your field. A **mentor** is an experienced employee who serves as a teacher and counselor for a less experienced person in a career field. A relationship with a mentor can provide such benefits as personalized training, access to influential people, and emotional support during difficult times.

Attracting a mentor starts with excellent performance. Show initiative, be creative, and be alert to meeting the needs of others. Maintain visibility and display a desire to learn and grow by asking questions and volunteering for new assignments.

Prospective mentors should be receptive to assisting others and to helping them grow in both the technical and social aspects of a career. Many organizations have formal mentor programs with an experienced employee assigned to guide the career development of a newer employee. Some mentor relationships involve retired individuals who wish to share their knowledge and experience.

CHANGING CAREERS

At some point you will probably change jobs for a better or different position within your career field, or you may move into a different career area. Changing jobs may be

mentor An experienced employee who serves as a teacher and counselor for a less experienced person in a career field.

more difficult than selecting your first job. Indications that it may be time to move on include low motivation toward your current work, physical or emotional distress caused by the job, or consistently poor performance evaluations. Other signs might be a lack of social interactions with coworkers, limited opportunity for salary or position advancement, and a poor relationship with your supervisor.

A decision to change careers may require minor adjustments (such as going from retail sales to industrial sales), or it may mean extensive retraining and starting at an entry level in a new field. When considering a career change, carefully assess the financial and personal costs along with the benefits based on your needs and goals. Giving up benefits such as health insurance may be costly to a family, but the expanded career opportunities in a new field may be worth the trade-off.

In most situations, long-term job security is a thing of the past. Company mergers, downsizing, technological advances, and economic conditions result in forced career changes. Layoffs and unemployment cause emotional and financial stress. To cope with these difficult career situations, which many people experienced during the recent pandemic, counselors recommend that you:

my life | 5

I sometimes think about what type of employment situation I would like to have three or five years from now.

Conduct an online search to locate suggestions for career development and advanced career training.

- Acknowledge stress, anxiety, frustration, and fear.
- Maintain appropriate eating, sleep, exercise, and social activities.
- Determine sources of emergency funds and cut unnecessary spending.
- Expand networking activities through personal contacts, professional organizations, community activities, and volunteering.
- Seek an assessment of your competencies and experience from others.
- Improve career skills through personal study and online courses.
- Target your job search to high-growth industries, small business start-ups, and other emerging opportunities.
- Consider opportunities with nonprofit organizations, temporary employment, consulting, or starting your own business.
- Maintain a positive outlook to communicate confidence.

✔ PRACTICE QUIZ 2-5

1. What types of activities would you recommend for people who desire career advancement and professional growth?
2. What factors should a person consider before changing jobs or career fields?

PFP Sheet 13
Career Development and Advancement

Your Personal Finance Roadmap and Dashboard:

Career Planning

MONTHLY CAREER INTERACTIONS

Successfully obtaining employment and advancing in a career is enhanced by interaction with others. Networking (in-person and online) has many benefits. Face-to-face meetings, phone conversations, informational interviews, and email exchanges allow you to obtain advice about industry trends, company activities, and career opportunities.

Using your personal finance dashboard to monitor career interactions can increase your career potential. An ability to connect and engage people in varied professional and social settings improves your interpersonal skills while also gaining employment insights.

Your Situation

Have you attended business and community events to meet potential career contacts? Do you research and prepare questions to engage your contacts? Do you follow up with career contacts to learn about their current activities? Other career planning actions you might consider during various stages of your life include . . .

 First Steps

- Obtain career competencies in class, work, and volunteer situations.
- Explore various career fields.
- Make contacts with people in various career fields.
- Create résumé and career portfolio.
- Apply for employment positions.

 Next Steps

- Expand and update career network contacts.
- Obtain additional training, advanced degree, and career advancement skills.
- Revise résumé and career portfolio.

 Later Steps

- Reassess career situation and employee benefits based on life situation.
- Enhance career competencies and organizational value to avoid complacency.
- Serve as a mentor for less-experienced workers.
- Increase contributions to retirement plans, as appropriate.

YOUR NEXT STEP . . . select one or more of the items above and create an action plan to implement those financial planning activities.

 SUMMARY OF LEARNING OBJECTIVES

LO2-1
Describe activities associated with career planning and advancement. Understanding your personal interests and abilities is the foundation of a satisfying work life. Career planning and advancement involve these steps: (1) assess and research personal goals, abilities, and career fields, (2) evaluate the employment market and identify specific employment opportunities, (3) develop a résumé and cover letter for use in applying for available positions, (4) interview for available positions, (5) evaluate financial and other elements of the positions you are offered, and (6) plan and implement a program for career development.

LO2-2
Evaluate factors that influence employment opportunities. Keep informed about factors that influence employment opportunities. Consider the selection of a career in relation to personal abilities, interests, experience, training, and goals; social influences affecting employment, such as demographic trends; changing economic conditions; and industrial and technological trends.

LO2-3
Implement employment search strategies. Asking questions to obtain information about career planning

activities and employment opportunities is the basis of successful career planning. Also consider the following: Obtain employment or related experiences by working part time or by participating in campus and community activities. Use career information sources to learn about employment fields and to identify job opportunities. Prepare a résumé and cover letter that effectively present your qualifications for a specific employment position. Practice interview skills that project enthusiasm and competence.

LO2-4

Assess financial and legal concerns related to obtaining employment. While salary is an important factor when accepting an employment position, also consider the work environment and compensation package. Assess employee benefits on the basis of their market value, future value, and taxability as well as your personal needs and goals. Prospective and current employees have legal rights regarding fair hiring practices and equal opportunities on the job.

LO2-5

Analyze techniques available for career growth and advancement. When considering what your employment situation will be three to five years from now, identify education and training opportunities available to further your professional development and facilitate career changes.

KEY TERMS

career   47

cover letter   59

flexible employee benefit
   program   61

informational interview   56

interview 59

job   46

job creation   58

mentor   64

networking   55

résumé   59

KEY FORMULAS

Topic	Formula
Geographic buying power	$\text{Geographic buying} = \dfrac{\text{City 1}}{\text{City 2}} \dfrac{\text{Index number} \times \text{Salary}}{\text{Index number}}$
	Example:
	$= \dfrac{123 \times 50{,}000}{98.8}$
	$= \$62{,}247$
Tax-equivalent employee benefits	$\text{Tax-equivalent of a nontaxable} = \dfrac{\text{Value of benefit}}{(1 - \text{Tax rate})}$
	Example:
	$= \dfrac{\$1{,}250}{(1 - 0.24)}$
	$= \$1{,}645$

SELF-TEST PROBLEMS

1. Time value of money calculations are used to determine the value of potential retirement benefits. If a person deposits $1,800 a year in a retirement account earning 6 percent for 20 years, what will be the future value of that account?

2. A nontaxable employee benefit has a greater value than the stated amount. What would be the tax-equivalent value of a nontaxable employee benefit of $392? Assume a 30 percent tax rate.

Self-Test Solutions

1. Using a financial calculator or the future value of a series (annuity) table, the result will be $66,214.80 ($1,800 × 36.786).

2. To determine the tax-equivalent value, divide the amount by 1 minus the tax rate. In this situation, $392 would be divided by 0.70 (1 − 0.3), resulting in $560.

FINANCIAL PLANNING PROBLEMS

LO2-1 1. *Determining the Future Value of Education.* Jenny Lopez estimates that as a result of completing her master's degree, she will earn an additional $10,000 a year for the next 40 years.

    a. What would be the total amount of these additional earnings?

    b. What would be the *future value* of these additional earnings based on an annual interest rate of 4 percent? (Use a financial calculator or Exhibit 1-B in the Chapter 1 Appendix.)

LO2-1 2. *Comparing Living Costs.* Luke Anderson is earning $52,000 a year in a city located in the Midwest. He is interviewing for a position in a city with a cost of living 12 percent higher than where he currently lives. What is the minimum salary Brad would need at his new job to maintain the same standard of living?

LO2-2 3. *Calculating Future Value of Salary.* During a job interview, Pam Thompson is offered a salary of $32,000. The company gives annual raises of 3 percent. What would be Pam's salary during her fifth year on the job?

LO2-3 4. *Computing Future Value.* Calculate the future value of a retirement account in which you deposit $2,000 a year for 30 years with an expected annual interest rate of 6 percent. (Use a financial calculator or the tables in the Chapter 1 Appendix.)

LO2-4 5. *Comparing Taxes for Employee Benefits.* Which of the following employee benefits has the greater value? Use the formula given in the *Financial Literacy Calculations* feature to compare these benefits. (Assume a 28 percent tax rate.)

    a. A nontaxable pension contribution of $4,300 or the use of a company car with a taxable value of $6,325.

    b. A life insurance policy with a taxable value of $450 or a nontaxable increase in health insurance coverage valued at $340.

LO2-4 6. *Comparing Employment Offers.* Bill Mason is considering two job offers. Job 1 pays a salary of $36,500 with $4,500 of nontaxable employee benefits. Job 2 pays a salary of $34,700 and $6,120 of nontaxable benefits. Which position would have the higher monetary value? Use a 28 percent tax rate.

LO2-4 7. *Calculating the After-Tax Value of Employee Benefits.* Helen Ming receives a travel allowance of $180 each week from her company for time away from home. If this allowance is taxable and she has a 24 percent income tax rate, what amount will she have to pay in taxes for this employee benefit?

LO2-5 8. *Future Value of Advanced Training.* Joshua Kelly estimates that taking some classes would result in earning $4,200 more a year for the next 30 years. Based on an annual interest rate of 4 percent, calculate the future value of these classes.

LO2-5 9. *Comparing the Value of a Career Change.* Marla Opper currently earns $50,000 a year and is offered a job in another city for $56,000. The city she would move to has 8 percent higher living expenses than her current city. What quantitative analysis should Marla consider before taking the new position?

DIGITAL FINANCIAL LITERACY: RÉSUMÉ WORD TRACKING

Many qualified job seekers are rejected before being seen in person. An applicant tracking system (ATS) screens résumés with software to collect, sort, scan, and rank prospective employees. An ATS filters for keywords and excludes résumés lacking the required items as well as ones that are poorly written or incorrectly formatted.

To avoid this career search concern, be sure to only apply for jobs for which you have the appropriate background and experience. Target your résumé to the specific position; provide vital information in an easy-to-find format. Use keywords from the job title and job description to communicate your skills, qualifications, experience, and personal qualities.

For past positions, use clear job titles that conform to generally accepted industry standards. Do not use abbreviations that might not be recognized by the ATS. Submit an appropriate file type; a graphic file may not be read by the ATS. Avoid fancy formatting such as tables, text boxes, images, columns, headers, footers, and links.

Action items:

1. Locate a recent online article related to ATS. Using the information from the article, obtain opinions from three other people about the benefits and concerns associated with ATS.

2. Based on your research, create a visual presentation, podcast, or video summary to report mistakes one should avoid when preparing a résumé that will be screened by an ATS.

FINANCIAL PLANNING CASE

Which Job? Are You Sure?

"Wow, you mean you have three job offers? How did that happen?"

"I'm not quite sure, Joan," responded Alexia. "I guess I just carefully prepared for my job search."

"Ahhh . . . could you be a bit more specific for those of us who have no job offers?" asked Joan.

"After researching various organizations, I tried to match my abilities and experiences to their needs," Alexia continued.

"Then, in addition to my résumé, I sent a portfolio with samples of my research work and creative projects."

"OK, Alexia, which of the three jobs are you going to take?" asked Joan.

"Again, I'm not quite sure. I've created a comparison of the three to help me decide," Alexia replied.

"Let me see that!" exclaimed Joan. "Wow, you take this career search stuff seriously!"

Job Offer Comparison	Position A	Position B	Position C
Position description, organization	Advertising account assistant for international promotions with global company with offices in 17 countries.	Marketing assistant for a medium-sized equipment company; sales offices in eight southeastern states.	Public relations director in office of a local nonprofit organization assisting low-income families with food and housing.
Salary situation	$53,000; performance reviews and salary increases every six months for first two years, then annually.	$49,500; annual bonus based on percentage of company sales increase.	$45,500, with annual salary increases of 2 to 3 percent.
Vacation time (paid)/year	Two weeks (first year); additional two days for each year of service.	One week after six months on the job; two additional days for each six months of service.	Two weeks (paid); additional unpaid leave time up to four weeks a year.
Health insurance coverage	Employer pays 80 percent of health premiums for doctors on list of insurance company.	Employer pays for HMO coverage with some flexibility of doctors.	Employer pays 60 percent of health premiums; employee selects own doctor.
Retirement fund	Employer contributes 5 percent of salary; additional contributions allowed.	Employer matches employee contributions (up to 10 percent).	Employer pays 2 percent of salary; employee may make tax-deferred contributions.
Educational opportunities	On-site training seminars to update employees on global cultures and advertising trends.	Tuition reimbursement (up to $6,000 a year) for graduate courses.	Two trips a year to seminars on topics related to non-profit organizations.

Questions

1. What steps might Alexia take when deciding which position to accept?
2. What additional factors would you consider when selecting an employment position?
3. Which employment position would you recommend for her? Why?

YOUR PERSONAL FINANCIAL PLAN

PLANNING YOUR CAREER

Your selection of a career and professional development activities will influence many aspects of your life, including financial resource availability, leisure time, living location, and acquaintances.

Your Short-Term Financial Planning Activity

Task Plan preliminary activities for a job search.

Research

1) Explore various career areas based on your interests, abilities, and goals using PFP Sheets 6 and 7.
2) Use PFP Sheets 8 and 9 or another format to develop a résumé and sample cover letter for use in a job search.
3) Based on PFP Sheets 10 and 11, research a prospective employer and develop a strategy for effective interviewing.

Outcome Add these documents to your portfolio or to your Personal Financial Plan online folder. Prepare a video of a practice job interview situation.

Your Long-Term Financial Planning Activity

Task Assess your needs for various employee benefits and career advancement actions.

Research

1) Use PFP Sheet 12 to analyze employee benefits based on your current and possible future financial needs.
2) Develop a plan of action for professional development using PFP Sheet 13. Also consider starting your own business.

Outcome Create an audio or written summary that communicates factors influencing employee benefits decisions and your future career development activities.

Note: All *Personal Financial Planner* sheets are available at the end of the book and in an Excel spreadsheet format in *Connect Finance.*

CONTINUING CASE

Financial Aspects of Career Planning

Jamie Lee Jackson, age 24, is graduating with her business administration degree in the next year. She has been attending college full time while working part time in the bakery department of a local grocery store. She has a strong interest in starting her own cupcake café in the next three or four years and has been saving toward that goal.

Many of Jamie's fellow students are obtaining internships at this point in their education. She has been hearing a lot from others about out-of-state positions that they are considering.

"Would this be something I would like to consider?" wonders Jamie. She knows that when weighing job offers, there is much to consider beyond the position title and the salary.

Because Jamie still has some time to consider whether to be self-employed or to work for a company, she offers help to her friend and roommate Kayla, who will be interviewing with several out-of-state companies. Kayla had been contacted by the companies to interview after attending the recent campus career fair.

Kayla is taking a personal inventory of her skills in order to learn about careers and to help her find career opportunities that would fit her skills. She knows that her educational background is strong because she is expected to graduate in the top 10 percent of her class. She asks for Jamie's help with discussing skills that may be attractive to Kayla's potential employers. She would like to create a career action plan to help her decide for which position she may be best suited.

Questions

1. Technical skills are a very important selling point for potential employees in the workforce.

   a. Prepare a comprehensive list of technical skills that you possess.

   b. Conduct online research to determine the technical skills that are most sought after by companies today, and compare them to your personal list.

   c. In which areas are you most competent?

   d. In which areas could you use training to increase your employability?

2. Thinking back on past work experiences:

   a. Prepare a list of traits that contribute to your level of social intelligence.

   b. Reflect on the traits that you might emphasize in an interview, and develop a plan to increase your skills in areas that need improvement.

3. Kayla and Jamie discuss the importance of choosing a career that is balanced between being rewarding and also in demand by companies.

   a. Based on online research, identify the most sought-after career positions in the area of your degree pathway.

   b. Are those career opportunities located locally, in specific regions of the United States, or international?

   c. What are the salary ranges for the career pathway you have chosen?

   d. Based on your research, what are the predicted future trends for the career area?

 DAILY SPENDING DIARY

"My daily work expenses could easily be reduced if I'd be more careful with lunch and coffee spending."

Directions

Continue or start using the *Daily Spending Diary* sheets, or create your own format. Record every cent of your spending in the categories provided, or set up your own categories. Knowing your spending actions can help you to achieve your financial goals.

Questions

1. What types of job-related expenses might be commonly included as part of your *Daily Spending Diary*?

2. What actions might be taken to reduce costs associated with seeking a job or with changing jobs?

A *Daily Spending Diary* sheet is located at the end of Chapter 1 and on the library resource site within *Connect*.

APPENDIX 2
Résumés, Cover Letters, and Interviews

Developing a Résumé

Every business must effectively present its product or service to potential customers. Similarly, you must market yourself to prospective employers by developing a résumé, creating a cover letter, and interviewing for available positions.

RÉSUMÉ ELEMENTS

A résumé is a summary of your education, training, experience, and other work qualifications. This personal information sheet is usually an essential component in your employment search. The main elements are typically as follows.

1. THE PERSONAL DATA SECTION   The heading includes your name, phone number, and email. Providing a mailing address is less common, although some employers may require this information.

smart money minute

Templates are available online to help you prepare your résumé content and format. You might consider various creative approaches. Be sure your presentation conveys a level of professionalism appropriate for the industry and the organization to which you are applying. Also, include required words for the position since an applicant tracking system (ATS) may screen your résumé.

2. THE CAREER PROFILE, SUMMARY SECTION   A "Career Profile" or a "Career Summary" section allows you to communicate a synopsis of your distinctive skills and experiences. A career objective is usually not included on the résumé and is best communicated in your cover letter.

3. THE EDUCATION SECTION   This section includes dates, schools attended, fields of study, and degrees earned. Courses directly related to your career field may be highlighted with information about research activities, team projects, and presentations. If your grade point average is exceptionally high, you might include it to demonstrate your ability to excel.

4. THE EXPERIENCE SECTION   Next, list organizations, dates of service, and responsibilities for previous employment, work-related school activities, and community service. Highlight computer skills, technical abilities, and other competencies. Use action verbs to communicate how your experience and talents will benefit the organization (see Exhibit 2-A). Focus this information on results and accomplishments. Consider using the S-T-A-R format to communicate your experiences and achievements:

- Achieved...
- Administered...
- Coordinated...
- Created...
- Designed...
- Developed...
- Directed...
- Edited...
- Initiated...
- Implemented...

- Managed...
- Monitored...
- Organized...
- Planned...
- Produced...
- Researched...
- Summarized...
- Supervised...
- Trained...
- Updated...

EXHIBIT 2-A
Action verbs to effectively communicate career-related experiences

S	Situation, or the setting	Served as fund-raising coordinator for campus organization
T	Task, your duties	Prepared a plan to raise funds for social service agency
A	Actions you took	Administered a team that solicited donations on campus
R	Result, the outcome	Donations of over $3,200 to a homeless shelter

On your résumé, this experience might be presented as follows:

- Coordinated fund-raising campaign to raise funds for social service agency, resulting in over $3,200 in donations to a homeless shelter.

Relate this information back to the job position for which you are applying. The S-T-A-R format may also be used when communicating your experiences during an interview.

5. THE RELATED INFORMATION SECTION Highlight unique technical expertise, computer skills, or languages spoken. List honors or awards to communicate your achievement ability, along with interests and activities that relate to your career. A brief mention of hobbies and other interests can communicate balance in your life.

REFERENCES Prepare a list of *references,* people who can verify your abilities and competencies. These individuals may include teachers, previous employers, supervisors, or business colleagues. Obtain permission from the people you plan to use as references. Also communicate what you would like them to highlight in their references.

References are usually not included on a résumé; have this information available when requested. Your reference list should include the person's name, title, organization, and contact information (address, phone, email). When selecting references, choose people who will give a balanced view of your strengths and needed improvements.

TYPES OF RÉSUMÉS

While résumé formats are evolving, the *chronological résumé,* which presents your education and experience in a reverse time sequence (the most recent item first) is still common. Exhibit 2-B provides an example of a chronological résumé along with suggestions on how to create a more effective presentation.

EXHIBIT 2-B   Résumé makeover

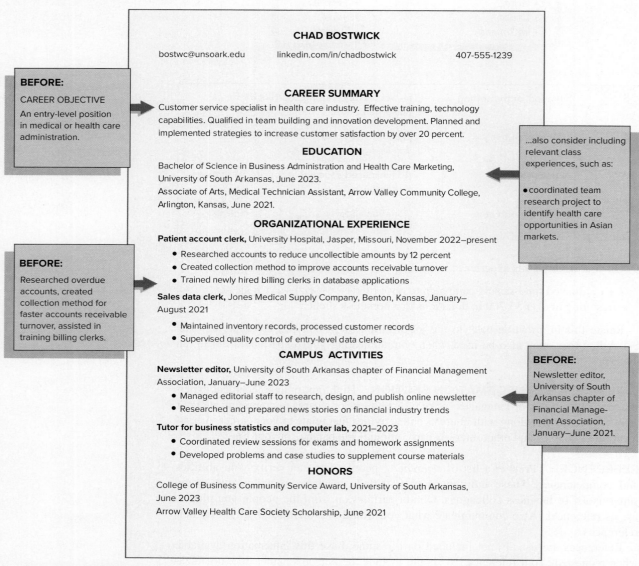

BEFORE:

CAREER OBJECTIVE

An entry-level position in medical or health care administration.

BEFORE:

Researched overdue accounts, created collection method for faster accounts receivable turnover, assisted in training billing clerks.

CHAD BOSTWICK

bostwc@unsoark.edu   linkedin.com/in/chadbostwick   407-555-1239

CAREER SUMMARY

Customer service specialist in health care industry. Effective training, technology capabilities. Qualified in team building and innovation development. Planned and implemented strategies to increase customer satisfaction by over 20 percent.

EDUCATION

Bachelor of Science in Business Administration and Health Care Marketing, University of South Arkansas, June 2023.
Associate of Arts, Medical Technician Assistant, Arrow Valley Community College, Arlington, Kansas, June 2021.

ORGANIZATIONAL EXPERIENCE

Patient account clerk, University Hospital, Jasper, Missouri, November 2022–present

- Researched accounts to reduce uncollectible amounts by 12 percent
- Created collection method to improve accounts receivable turnover
- Trained newly hired billing clerks in database applications

Sales data clerk, Jones Medical Supply Company, Benton, Kansas, January–August 2021

- Maintained inventory records, processed customer records
- Supervised quality control of entry-level data clerks

CAMPUS ACTIVITIES

Newsletter editor, University of South Arkansas chapter of Financial Management Association, January–June 2023

- Managed editorial staff to research, design, and publish online newsletter
- Researched and prepared news stories on financial industry trends

Tutor for business statistics and computer lab, 2021–2023

- Coordinated review sessions for exams and homework assignments
- Developed problems and case studies to supplement course materials

HONORS

College of Business Community Service Award, University of South Arkansas, June 2023
Arrow Valley Health Care Society Scholarship, June 2021

...also consider including relevant class experiences, such as:

- coordinated team research project to identify health care opportunities in Asian markets.

BEFORE:

Newsletter editor, University of South Arkansas chapter of Financial Management Association, January–June 2021.

Note: In recent years, many résumés are taking a more creative approach with sidebars, varied fonts, skill charts, infographics, and other visuals. Search online for résumé ideas that fit your situation. However, beware that formatting may distract when a résumé is screened by an applicant tracking system (ATS).

A *functional résumé* may be appropriate for people with diverse skills and time gaps in their experience. This format emphasizes competencies in categories such as communication, supervision, project planning, human relations, and research. A functional résumé may be used when changing careers or if recent experiences are not directly related to the new position.

To be distinctive, some applicants use creative approaches. Résumés have been submitted in the form of comic strips, "wanted" posters, advertisements, and menus, and attached to balloons, pizzas, and plants. While some were effective, most employers view them as frivolous. Some job candidates enhance their résumés with *infographics* to visually communicate skills and qualifications. This approach may be appropriate in advertising, journalism, photography, public relations, and other creative fields.

smart money minute

A valuable career skill for creative problem solving is *human-centered design* (HCD), also called *design thinking*. HCD is a three-step process: (1) **HEAR** (also called *inspiration*) involves immersion in the lives of people to listen and understand their needs. (2) **CREATE** (*ideation*) identifies business opportunities and develops prototypes based on the needs. (3) **DELIVER** (*implementation*) involves a market solution for identified needs. Successful human-centered design requires deep empathy with people, generating many ideas, building credible prototypes, seeking feedback, and putting an innovative solution into use. Additional information at: ideo.org and ideo.com.

EXAMPLE: Social Media Résumé

Résumés have become online "living entities" through social media networks. Your interactions with hiring managers may include:

- A LinkedIn profile highlighting career achievements and competencies. Links to photos, videos, and presentations can display your skills. Recommendations on LinkedIn can help you move forward in the job application process.

- Twitter to communicate unique skills and a personal brand by linking prospective employers to your website.

- Instagram, Facebook, and Pinterest to present your personal brand, résumé, photos, videos, and other visuals related to career competencies, expertise, and achievements.

- A video résumé to communicate distinctive qualities and potential contributions to the organization.

Be careful with your social media life since your private life becomes public. Employers use social media to screen candidates. Avoid negative comments, inappropriate photos, and too much personal information. Beware of an incomplete or outdated profile and not having appropriate connections in your network.

How about you? In what ways might you use social media to enhance your career planning and development?

RÉSUMÉ PREPARATION

While no exact formula exists, a résumé must look professional. The use of bulleted items, bold type, and short sentences improves readability. Your résumé needs to be readable on a phone, tablet, or other mobile device.

Limit your résumé to one page. Send a two-page résumé only if you have enough experiences to fill three pages. Then use the most relevant information to prepare an impressive two-page presentation.

Be sure to highlight how your experiences will contribute to an organization's needs. Remember, résumés are commonly scanned for keywords related to education and technical skills. Use words and phrases based on the job description and industry. Some important words include "foreign language skills," "software certification," "research experience," "problem-solving," "leadership," "team projects," "remote work experience," and "overseas experience." *Avoid* overused words such as "team player," "energetic," "results focused," "confident," "creative," and "professional." Instead of listing your ability with software (such as Excel or PowerPoint), describe how these tools were used in research or to present findings for a specific project.

When preparing an online résumé, be sure to:

- Keep the format simple. If you use varied format styles, save your résumé as a PDF.
- Avoid attached files that may be difficult to open.
- Use keywords (especially nouns) for the specific position and industry.
- Submit online applications using plain text in required fields.

PFP Sheet 8
Résumé
Worksheet

Résumés posted online may be viewed by your current employer, whom you may not want to know about your job search. Consider putting a date on your résumé so your current boss will not think your résumé from two years ago is for a current job search. Seek guidance in preparing your résumé from the campus career development office, business associates, and friends.

RÉSUMÉ SUBMISSION

Previously, résumés were mailed or delivered in person. Today, most résumés are submitted online. Most résumé posting sites are free. Never pay a large fee; scam artists have set up phony websites with an online payment system to defraud people. Be cautious of sites not based in the country in which you wish to work.

Résumés sent by email should be addressed to a specific person with a subject line referencing the specific job. Your email will usually include a cover letter to introduce yourself and to encourage the recipient to view your résumé. Properly format your résumé and include it in the body of the email or as a PDF attachment.

Follow up with a call or email to reinforce your qualifications and interest. Ask about how and when to follow up on your status in the job search process.

Most important, your résumé and cover letter should have F-O-C-U-S:

smart money minute

Identity theft can occur when you use an online résumé. Do not put your Social Security number on your résumé. Thieves will often contact you and pretend to be a prospective employer in an effort to obtain other personal information.

- **F**it—communicate your suitability for the company culture and specific position.
- **O**bjective—present a goal of your desire and interest to work in the industry.
- **C**onnect—provide examples of accomplishments that will benefit the company.
- **U**nique—emphasize your distinctive qualities and campus experiences.
- **S**kills—relate your abilities to company needs and industry trends.

EXAMPLE: Your Career Brand

Your professional image, or "brand," can be of value in your job search and should:

- Communicate unique skills, experiences, and competencies.

- Provide a vision of your potential contribution to an employer.

- Have a consistent message online, in print, and elsewhere.

- Connect to current technology and emerging business trends.

- Involve actions that communicate your image, such as "collaborator," "international expert," or "I provide ___ for ___." Search online or view LinkedIn profiles for ideas.

When communicating your personal brand, consider these questions: What problem do I solve? What am I passionate about? What do I research? What do I have results in? What business am I in? What would people be willing to buy?

How about you? What are some competencies or experiences you might communicate for your personal brand?

Creating a Cover Letter

As you target your résumé to a specific job position, a *cover letter* is designed to obtain an interview. This letter accompanies your résumé and usually consists of:

1. An *introductory paragraph* to get the reader's attention with an interesting start. Refer to the job or type of employment in which you are interested. Communicate your experience and qualifications. If applicable, mention the name of the person who referred you. Other possible approaches to start a cover letter include:

- Communicate a passion for the type of work or the organization.

- Use a personal story, class project, or campus activity that relates to the position.

- Briefly connect your experiences to the requirements of the available position.

2. One or two *development paragraphs* should highlight aspects of your background that specifically qualify you for the job. Elaborate on experiences and training. Connect your background to specific organizational needs. Refer to your résumé for more details.

3. The *concluding paragraph* should request action. Ask to meet to discuss your qualifications in more detail; in other words, get an interview! Include information to make contacting you convenient, such as telephone numbers, email address, and the times when you are available. Close your letter by summarizing how you can benefit the organization.

The key items to remember when preparing a cover letter are:

- Prepare a personalized cover letter (see Exhibit 2-C) for each position.

- Email (or address) the letter to the appropriate person. In the subject line of an email, state the job title for which you are applying.

- Emphasize your fit for the position and your desire to work in this industry.

- Communicate how your skills will serve the needs of the organization.

PFP Sheet 9
Planning a Cover Letter

A résumé and cover letter are your ticket to the interview. You may have outstanding qualifications and great potential, but you need an interview to communicate this information. The time, effort, and care you take to present yourself will help you achieve your career goal.

EXHIBIT 2-C
Sample cover letter

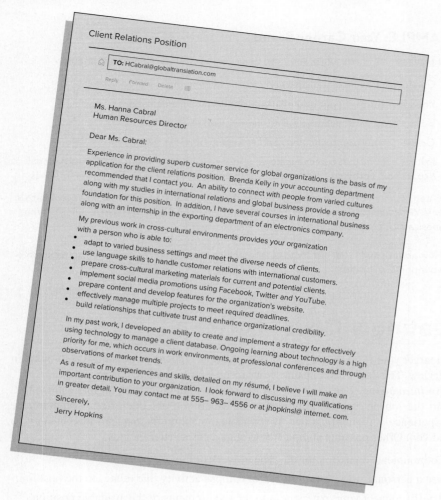

Client Relations Position

TO: HCabral@globaltranslation.com

Reply   Forward   Delete

Ms. Hanna Cabral
Human Resources Director

Dear Ms. Cabral:

Experience in providing superb customer service for global organizations is the basis of my application for the client relations position. Brenda Kelly in your accounting department recommended that I contact you. An ability to connect with people from varied cultures along with my studies in international relations and global business provide a strong foundation for this position. In addition, I have several courses in international business along with an internship in the exporting department of an electronics company.

My previous work in cross-cultural environments provides your organization with a person who is able to:

- adapt to varied business settings and meet the diverse needs of clients.
- use language skills to handle customer relations with international customers.
- prepare cross-cultural marketing materials for current and potential clients.
- implement social media promotions using Facebook, Twitter and YouTube.
- prepare content and develop features for the organization's website.
- effectively manage multiple projects to meet required deadlines.
- build relationships that cultivate trust and enhance organizational credibility.

In my past work, I developed an ability to create and implement a strategy for effectively using technology to manage a client database. Ongoing learning about technology is a high priority for me, which occurs in work environments, at professional conferences and through observations of market trends.

As a result of my experiences and skills, detailed on my résumé, I believe I will make an important contribution to your organization. I look forward to discussing my qualifications in greater detail. You may contact me at 555– 963– 4556 or at jhopkinsl@ internet. com.

Sincerely,

Jerry Hopkins

EXAMPLE: The Q Letter

A targeted cover letter is sometimes referred to as a *Q letter* (Q for *qualifications*), which provides a side-by-side comparison of your experiences with the job requirements. The two coordinated lists allow you to be quickly rated as a viable candidate for the position. For example:

Promotions Assistant Requirements	My Experiences
Implement community fund-raising activities.	• Coordinated sponsors, volunteers, and donors for fund-raising by campus organizations, raising $8,000 for world hunger prevention programs
Prepare and present proposals to potential community sponsors.	• Created more than 10 customized proposals for potential event sponsors; presented the proposals in meetings
Coordinate public and media relations and advertising campaigns.	• Promoted events through social media and other marketing materials

How about you? What are some your experiences that might apply to future employment positions?

The Job Interview

"Why should we hire you?" This may be an unexpected question; however, you may need to answer it. The interview phase is limited to candidates who possess the specific qualifications desired by the employer. Being invited for an interview puts you closer to receiving a job offer.

PREPARING FOR THE INTERVIEW

Prepare for your interview by obtaining information about your prospective employer. The best sources of company information include: (1) an online search for the annual report, company news, and industry trends; (2) observations of company activities and products; (3) informal discussions with current and past employees; and (4) conversations with people knowledgeable about the company or industry. This information will allow you to discuss your potential contributions to the organization.

PFP Sheet 10
Researching a Prospective Employer

A vital pre-interview action is to prepare questions to ask, such as:

- What qualities do your most successful employees possess?
- What are the expectations and challenges of this position?
- What do your employees like best about working here?
- What career development opportunities are available to employees?
- What market trends or actions of competitors might affect the company in the future? (You might offer your ideas for the company after receiving a response to this question.)

Also prepare questions about your specific interests, company policies, and employee benefits. Search online to identify other questions you might ask. Many interviewers judge candidates on the quality of questions they ask.

Successful interviewing requires practice. By video recording yourself or working with friends, you can develop confidence for effective interviewing. Organize ideas, speak clearly and calmly, and communicate enthusiasm. Campus organizations and career development offices offer opportunities to practice with *mock interviews*. Prepare concise answers for specific questions (see Exhibit 2-D) explaining how your experience will contribute to the company. Also, practice stories that demonstrate your skills and experiences. If appropriate, bring photos or other evidence of your past efforts.

PFP Sheet 11
Preparing for an Interview

Career counselors suggest having a "theme" for interview responses to focus your main qualifications. This theme may involve your research ability, technical skills, or personal journey to overcome adversity. Throughout the interview, come back to the central idea that communicates your potential contributions to the organization.

In some interviews, you may encounter unusual questions such as, "If you were a brick in a wall, which brick would you be and why?" or "How would you use the items in this room to survive on a deserted island?" If this occurs, stay calm. No right or wrong answer is expected. Your analysis and creativity in responding are most important. You might ask follow-up questions to clarify the situation and to communicate your thought process.

Current employees are the best source of information about how to dress. In general, dress more conservatively than current employees. A business suit is usually appropriate for both men and women. Avoid trendy and casual styles, and don't wear too much jewelry. Confirm the time and location of the interview. Be sure you have correct directions to the interview location.

Take copies of your résumé, your reference list, work samples, and paper for taking notes during the interview. Arrive about 10 minutes earlier than your appointed time.

EXHIBIT 2-D

Interview questions you
should expect

Education and Training Questions

What education and training qualify you for this job?

Why are you interested in working for this organization?

In addition to going to school, what activities have helped you expand your interests
and knowledge?   ˙

Behavioral, Competency-Based Questions

Describe the supervisors who motivated you most.

Describe some people whom you have found difficult to work with.

Describe a situation in which your determination helped you achieve a specific goal.

Describe situations in which you demonstrated creative problem solving.

Describe an example of your leadership for a project. What steps did you take to move
the situation forward to provide value for various stakeholders?

As a consultant to our organization, how would you assess the current situation? What
actions would you recommend to us?

Personal Qualities Questions

What are your major strengths?

What are your major weaknesses? What have you done to overcome your weaknesses?

What do you plan to be doing three to five years from now?

Which individuals have had the greatest influence on you?

How did you prepare for this interview?

What analytic and problem-solving skills do you possess that would be of value to our
organization?

(*NOTE*: Also, search online for sample interview questions for your specific industry
such as engineering, finance, health care, hospitality, information technology, medical
technology, sales, or social services.)

EXAMPLE: Preparing for an Online Interview

1. Prepare as you would for any interview. Be professional. Plan to wear solid colors.
2. Plan a quiet environment with door and windows closed; silence phone.
3. Eliminate clutter; select an appropriate background. Check lighting to avoid shad-
   ows, glares; use natural light, if possible.
4. Locate camera at eye level to avoid distorted angles; use a computer instead of your
   phone for a better video display.
5. Test computer connection in advance; avoid wifi that may not provide consistent
   service.
6. Conduct test run before interview day. Record practice session to view how you
   might improve.
7. Go online early to communicate punctuality. Have a professional username.
8. Maintain eye contact with the camera to project confidence and professionalism. Put
   notes on the wall behind the screen with reminders of key points and questions to ask.
9. Check your interview time, especially if in a different time zone.
10. Show energy and enthusiasm. Move around or do light exercises before you start.

How about you? Which of these actions have you considered when preparing for an online
interview?

THE INTERVIEW PROCESS

A *screening interview* is an initial, usually brief, meeting to determine the best candidates. Applicants are evaluated on an overall impression and a few general questions. Screening interviews may be conducted on campus, by phone, online, or at a job fair. A telephone screening interview requires strong verbal communication since there is no eye contact or body language.

Video platform screening interviews will ask for personal and background information. In addition, you may be asked to respond to questions such as "Would you rather have structure or flexibility in your work?" and "What approach do you use to solve difficult problems?" Online testing may be used to assess ability for job-related tasks such as those that a bank teller or retail clerk might encounter.

The next phase of the interview process can last from an hour to several days. The *selection interview,* for finalists in the job search, often involves a series of activities, including responses to questions, meetings with several staff members, and a seminar presentation.

A selection interview may start in an informal setting to help you relax and to establish rapport. Next, a brief discussion of the available position may take place. The main part of the interview involves questions to assess your abilities and potential.

Interviews often include situations or questions to determine how you react under pressure. Remain calm. *Behavioral interviewing* evaluates on-the-job potential. Applicants are asked how they might handle specific work situations. Behavioral interview questions typically begin with "describe" or "tell me about . . ." Answer clearly in a controlled manner. In the last portion of the interview, you will be expected to ask questions.

When encountering a *panel interview* with several people asking questions, make eye contact and engage all participants as you answer a question. In a *group interview*, be ready to answer a question with a slightly different response than the other job candidates.

The *case interview* involves responding to real-world problems using analytical skills and creativity. See the "How To..." feature for additional information on case interviews.

An interviewer *cannot* ask where you were born, your age, if you have any disabilities, or about marital status, religion, or responsibility for children, or other personal information protected by law. However, an interviewer *can* ask if you have the legal right to work in the United States indefinitely, if you can prove you are over 18 (if there is a minimum age requirement for the job), if you have the physical ability to perform the job for which you have applied, and if there are any days when you can't work.

Employers may use credit reports as part of the hiring process. Federal law requires that applicants be told when credit histories are used in the hiring process. Some states limit the use of a person's credit history in making employment decisions.

Near the end of an interview, show your desire for the position by asking for the job. Some questions you might use: "I believe my experiences would contribute to your organization. Is there any additional information you need from me?" "Based on my abilities in the area of _____, am I the appropriate fit for this position?" "Since my background and skills seem very appropriate for the position, what additional steps will be involved in the selection process?"

Most interviewers conclude by telling you when you can expect to hear from them. While waiting, do two things. First, within a day, send an email to every person you met to express appreciation for the opportunity to interview. Also, reinforce your skills and interest in the job. If you don't get the job, this communication can make a positive impression for future consideration. Second, do a self-evaluation of your interview performance. Note areas for improvement, and list questions you were asked that were not expected.

smart money minute

A traditional interview may not accurately predict future job performance. More organizations are using job simulations, situational interviewing, and job auditions. Candidates for a sales position may be asked to interact with potential customers. At Southwest Airlines, prospective employees participate in a *job audition,* which starts with extensive notes from the initial phone call. During the flight to the interview, gate agents, flight attendants, and others pay close attention to the candidate's behaviors. The process includes a talk to a group of other applicants. Bored or distracted audience members are disqualified. Another approach may require working on a project similar to those from the job for which you are applying. Or, job candidates may be asked for their analysis of a situation while interacting with current employees. These methods can reduce employee turnover and increase customer satisfaction.

Finally, the more interviews you have, the more effectively you will present yourself. And the more interviews you have, the better the chance of being offered a job.

EXAMPLE: A Checklist for Interview Success

To enhance your interview success, theladders.com suggests these actions:

- Don't arrive late ... or too early.
- Show respect to the receptionist, driver, and all others.
- While waiting, don't be on your phone; review notes, and be ready to shake hands.
- Have a confident handshake and a pleasant smile; don't sit before you are asked.
- If offered a drink, accept water but not coffee. A drink of cold water can help reduce sweating, and spilling it won't lead to pain or stains!
- Connect with the interviewer through common interests and background; adapt responses to questions based on the interview's age.
- Avoid looking at your watch or cell phone.
- Maintain good eye contact, an appropriate posture, proper hand positions, and professional body language.
- Make sure your voice and tone are engaging and calming.
- Communicate competency with confidence, but don't oversell yourself.
- Ask well-prepared questions that reflect your knowledge of the company and industry as well as your vision for the job position.
- Be prepared for strange questions that assess your ability to respond under pressure and determine your creative problem solving.
- Clothing color should be conservative, such as black, blue, gray, or brown.
- Within a day, send a thank-you email, and maybe a handwritten note, to all people involved in the interview.
- If you don't hear back within the time they set, contact the organization to express your continued interest.

 **HOW TO. . .**   **Prepare for a Case Interview**

"The client believes that declining profits are the result of new competitors. How might the company determine if this is the actual cause?" This question reflects what you might encounter in a *case interview,* which is commonly used by organizations as part of the interview process and may involve this sequence:

| *A screening interview* designed to determine your overall qualifications for the available position. | → | *A behavioral interview* allows you to explain how your training, experiences, and achievements prepare you for the position. | → | *A case interview* assesses problem-solving and analytical abilities for providing conclusion and recommmunications. |

A case interview allows a prospective employee to demonstrate an ability to think in a structured, creative manner when presented with a real-world problem. These case situations may address business topics such as competition, joint ventures, company financing, and supply chain or present a candidate with an open-ended question. When involved in a case interview, consider these actions:

1. Listen and read carefully to understand the background and the main problem of the situation.
2. Develop a framework to organize your analysis and the relationship among key issues.
3. Consider alternative courses of action to communicate varied approaches and versatility in thinking.
4. Use quantitative and qualitative evidence to support your analysis and suggested actions.
5. Clearly communicate your analysis process, conclusions, and recommendations.

Take these actions for improved success in a case interview:

- Prepare by using online practice cases and researching the organization.
- Talk with people who have experienced the case interview process.
- Research current business events and organizational trends.
- Ask questions of the interviewer to clarify key points.
- Stay focused on the key question for the situation and main issues.
- Avoid stock answers; popular frameworks and buzzwords may not be appropriate.
- Emphasize the process, analysis, and recommended actions rather than finding the "right" answer.
- Practice the process with others who are willing to help.

Extensive resources on case interviews are available at www.caseinterview.com or search online for "preparing for case interviews."

3

Money Management Strategy: Financial Statements and Budgeting

LEARNING OBJECTIVES

LO3-1 Recognize relationships among financial documents and money management activities.

LO3-2 Develop a personal balance sheet and cash flow statement.

LO3-3 Create and implement a budget.

LO3-4 Connect money management and savings activities to achieving financial goals.

The Chapter 3 Appendix provides additional information on money management advisors and information sources.

APPENDIX

MBI/Alamy Stock Photo

Financial Literacy
IN **YOUR LIFE**

▶ **What if you . . .** continually spend more each month than your income? If you regularly take money out of savings or overuse a credit card for living expenses, what actions would you take?

You might . . . carefully track your spending to evaluate areas for reduced spending. This would allow you to determine expenses that might be eliminated or cut back. Or you might consider actions to increase your income. Your ability to monitor and control spending provides a foundation for wise money management and long-term financial security.

Now, what would you do? What actions are you taking to improve your cash flow surplus? You will be able to examine your progress using the Your Personal Finance Roadmap and Dashboard feature at the end of the chapter.

| my life | **SAVING IS THE ONLY PATH FOR FINANCIAL SUCCESS** |

"Money not going out is like money coming in!" Reduced spending will result in lower credit card debt, more money for emergencies, and funds for long-term investing.

From a budgeting perspective, "if you only spend money on things you **really need**, you always have money for things you **really want**." Very often, people use the word *need* when they really mean *want*. As a result, overspending, increased debt, and lower savings occur.

What are your money management habits? You can start to assess your money management knowledge and skills. For each of the following statements, select the choice that best describes your current situation.

1. My money management activities are most valuable to help me
   a. avoid credit problems.
   b. achieve financial goals.
   c. enjoy spending for daily needs.
2. My system for organizing personal financial records could be described as
   a. nonexistent . . . I have documents that are missing in action!
   b. basic . . . I can find most stuff when I need to!
   c. very efficient . . . better than Google!
3. The details of my cash flow statement are
   a. simple . . . "money coming in" and "money going out."
   b. appropriate for my needs . . . enough information for me.
   c. very informative . . . I know where my money goes.
4. My budgeting activities could be described as
   a. "I don't have enough money to worry about where it goes."
   b. "I keep track of my spending with an app."
   c. "I have a written plan for spending and paying my bills on time."
5. The status of my savings goals could be described as
   a. "Good progress is being made."
   b. "If I save $100 more, I'll have $100!"
   c. "What's a savings goal?"

As you study this chapter, you will encounter "My Life" boxes with additional information and resources related to these items.

Successful Money Management

money management
Day-to-day financial activities necessary to manage current personal economic resources while working toward long-term financial security.

"Each month, I have too many days and not enough money. If the month were only 20 days long, budgeting would be easy." Most of us have heard a comment like this when it comes to budgeting and money management.

Daily spending and saving decisions are the main element of financial planning. You must coordinate these choices with your needs, goals, and personal situation. When people watch a sporting event, they usually know the score. In financial planning, knowing the score is also important.

Maintaining financial records and planning your spending are essential to successful personal financial management. The time and effort you devote to these record-keeping activities will yield benefits. **Money management** refers to the day-to-day financial activities necessary to manage current personal economic resources while working toward long-term financial security.

OPPORTUNITY COST AND MONEY MANAGEMENT

Daily decision-making is a fact of life, and trade-offs are associated with your choices. Selecting an alternative means you give up something else. For money management decisions, examples of trade-off situations, or *opportunity costs,* include the following:

- Current spending reduces money available for long-term saving and investing.
- Increased saving and investing for the future lowers what you can spend now.
- Credit payments over time reduce future income available for spending and saving.
- Using savings to buy things results in lost interest and not being able to use savings for other purposes.
- Comparison shopping results in wiser buying but uses something of value you cannot replace: your time.

As you plan money management activities, consider financial and personal costs and benefits associated with these decisions.

COMPONENTS OF MONEY MANAGEMENT

As Exhibit 3-1 shows, three major money management activities are interrelated. First, personal financial records and documents are the foundation of systematic resource use. These records provide evidence of business transactions and ownership of property, and information on legal matters. Next, personal financial statements enable you to measure and assess your financial position and progress. Finally, your spending plan, or *budget,* is the basis for effective money management.

A PERSONAL FINANCIAL RECORDS SYSTEM

Receipts, credit card statements, insurance policies, and tax forms report personal financial activities. An organized financial records system provides for (1) handling daily business activities, such as bill paying, (2) measuring financial progress, (3) completing tax forms, (4) making investment decisions, and (5) determining resources for spending. A poorly organized system can result in lost valuables and hidden assets such as U.S. savings bonds, old life insurance policies with a cash value, dormant savings accounts, old investments, and unused gift cards.

I understand the value of money management activities.

Many online sources are available to provide money management information. Locate a blog or website that you consider reliable for obtaining money management guidance. Also visit: https://kapoormoneyminute.com/ for recent articles on wise money management.

EXHIBIT 3-1 Money management activities

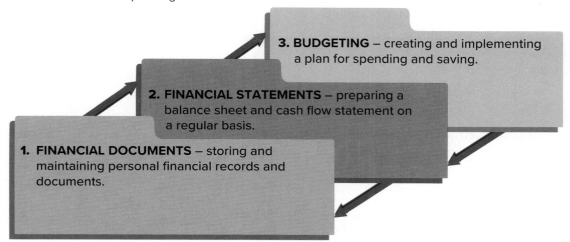

3. BUDGETING – creating and implementing a plan for spending and saving.

2. FINANCIAL STATEMENTS – preparing a balance sheet and cash flow statement on a regular basis.

1. FINANCIAL DOCUMENTS – storing and maintaining personal financial records and documents.

Most financial records are stored in one of three places: a home file, a safe deposit box, or online. A home file is best for documents for current needs and records with limited value. Your home file may be a series of folders, a file cabinet, or even a box. Your home file should be organized for quick access to needed information using 10 categories (see Exhibit 3-2). These groups correspond to the major topics in this book. You may not need all of these at present. As your financial situation changes, you may add others.

Important financial records and valuables should be kept in a location with better security than a home file. A **safe deposit box** is a private storage area at a financial institution with maximum security for valuables and difficult-to-replace documents. Access to the contents of a safe deposit box requires two keys. One key is issued to you; the other is kept by the financial institution. Items commonly kept in a safe deposit box include birth certificate, car title, passport, list of credit card numbers and insurance policies, a USB drive with vital financial documents, and valuables such as jewelry and gold coins. These documents and items may also be kept in a fireproof home safe.

When documents are in a digital format using cloud storage, consider the following actions:

- Download copies of all statements and forms to a local storage area with a system of files and folders.
- Back up files on external media or use an online backup service.
- Secure data with complex passwords and encryption.
- Scan copies of documents when you no longer need to keep paper versions.
- Take action to completely erase files when discarding items no longer needed.

Certain hard copies may be required, such as car titles, birth certificates, property deeds, and life insurance policies. Original receipts may be needed for returns or warranty service.

How long should you keep personal finance records? Records such as birth certificates, wills, and Social Security data should be kept permanently. Records for

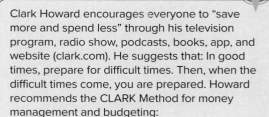

smart money minute

Clark Howard encourages everyone to "save more and spend less" through his television program, radio show, podcasts, books, app, and website (clark.com). He suggests that: In good times, prepare for difficult times. Then, when the difficult times come, you are prepared. Howard recommends the CLARK Method for money management and budgeting:
Calculate your income
List your expenses
Analyze your spending and set goals
Record everything
Knock out debt and build your savings

safe deposit box A private storage area at a financial institution with maximum security for valuables.

EXHIBIT 3-2 Where to keep your financial records

Home Files, Home Computer, or Online

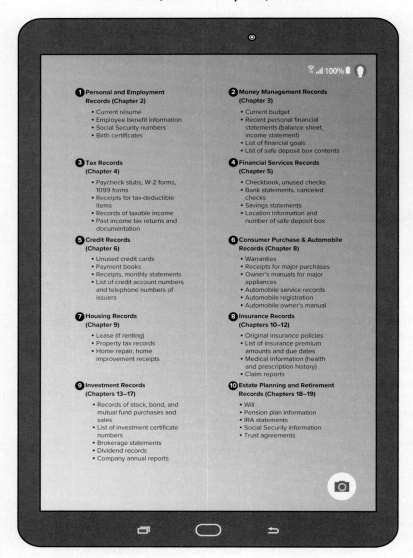

❶ Personal and Employment Records (Chapter 2)
- Current résumé
- Employee benefit information
- Social Security numbers
- Birth certificates

❸ Tax Records (Chapter 4)
- Paycheck stubs, W-2 forms, 1099 forms
- Receipts for tax-deductible items
- Records of taxable income
- Past income tax returns and documentation

❺ Credit Records (Chapter 6)
- Unused credit cards
- Payment books
- Receipts, monthly statements
- List of credit account numbers and telephone numbers of issuers

❼ Housing Records (Chapter 9)
- Lease (if renting)
- Property tax records
- Home repair, home improvement receipts

❾ Investment Records (Chapters 13–17)
- Records of stock, bond, and mutual fund purchases and sales
- List of investment certificate numbers
- Brokerage statements
- Dividend records
- Company annual reports

❷ Money Management Records (Chapter 3)
- Current budget
- Recent personal financial statements (balance sheet, income statement)
- List of financial goals
- List of safe deposit box contents

❹ Financial Services Records (Chapter 5)
- Checkbook, unused checks
- Bank statements, canceled checks
- Savings statements
- Location information and number of safe deposit box

❻ Consumer Purchase & Automobile Records (Chapter 8)
- Warranties
- Receipts for major purchases
- Owner's manuals for major appliances
- Automobile service records
- Automobile registration
- Automobile owner's manual

❽ Insurance Records (Chapters 10–12)
- Original insurance policies
- List of insurance premium amounts and due dates
- Medical information (health and prescription history)
- Claim reports

❿ Estate Planning and Retirement Records (Chapters 18–19)
- Will
- Pension plan information
- IRA statements
- Social Security information
- Trust agreements

Safe Deposit Box or Fireproof Home Safe

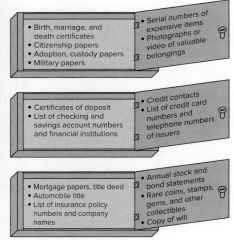

- Birth, marriage, and death certificates
- Citizenship papers
- Adoption, custody papers
- Military papers
- Serial numbers of expensive items
- Photographs or video of valuable belongings

- Certificates of deposit
- List of checking and savings account numbers and financial institutions
- Credit contacts
- List of credit card numbers and telephone numbers of issuers

- Mortgage papers, title deed
- Automobile title
- List of insurance policy numbers and company names
- Annual stock and bond statements
- Rare coins, stamps, gems, and other collectibles
- Copy of will

Computer, Tablet, Phone

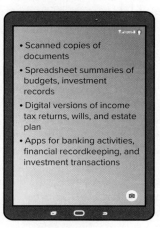

- Scanned copies of documents
- Spreadsheet summaries of budgets, investment records
- Digital versions of income tax returns, wills, and estate plan
- Apps for banking activities, financial recordkeeping, and investment transactions

What Not to Keep . . .

Wastebasket

- Receipts for small, non-tax-deductible purchases
- Expired warranties

Shredder

- Quarterly investment account statements (keep the annual summary statements)
- Documents that you no longer need with personal information such as your Social Security number or account numbers

Computer Recycle Bin

Empty recycle bin on regular basis. Make sure personal data files are completely erased.

Source: (Computer Recycle Bin): (c)Microsoft 2013.

investments should be kept as long as you own them. Federal tax documents should be kept for three years from the date you file your return. Under certain circumstances in an audit, the Internal Revenue Service may request information from further back. As a result, consider keeping your tax records for seven years. Keep documents related to the purchase and sale of real estate indefinitely.

 **PRACTICE QUIZ 3-1**

1. What opportunity costs are associated with money management activities?
2. What are the three major money management activities?
3. What are the benefits of an organized system of financial records and documents?
4. What suggestions would you give for creating a system for organizing and storing financial records and documents?

 **PFP Sheet 14** Financial Documents and Records

Personal Financial Statements

Every journey starts somewhere. You need to know where you are before you can go somewhere else. Personal financial statements are the starting point for your financial journey.

Most financial documents come from financial institutions, businesses, or government. Two documents you create, the personal balance sheet and the cash flow statement, are called *personal financial statements*. These reports provide information on your current financial position and a summary of income and spending. The main purposes of personal financial statements are to:

- Report your current financial position based on the value of items you own and amounts you owe.
- Measure your progress toward financial goals.
- Maintain information about your financial activities.
- Provide data for preparing tax forms or applying for credit.

THE PERSONAL BALANCE SHEET: WHERE ARE YOU NOW?

The current financial position of an individual or a family is a starting point for financial planning. A **balance sheet,** also called a *net worth statement* or *statement of financial position,* reports what you own and what you owe. You prepare a personal balance sheet to determine your current financial position using the following process:

$$\text{Items of value (what you own)} - \text{Amounts owed (what you owe)} = \text{Net worth (your wealth)}$$

For example, if your possessions are worth $4,500 and you owe $800 to others, your net worth is $3,700.

STEP 1: LIST ITEMS OF VALUE
Money in bank accounts combined with other items of value are the foundation of your current financial position. **Assets** are cash and other tangible property with a monetary value. The balance sheet for Rose and Edgar Gomez (Exhibit 3-3) reports their assets in four categories.

LO3-2

Develop a personal balance sheet and cash flow statement.

balance sheet A financial statement that reports what an individual or a family owns and owes; also called a *net worth statement.*

assets Cash and other property with a monetary value.

EXHIBIT 3-3 Creating a personal balance sheet

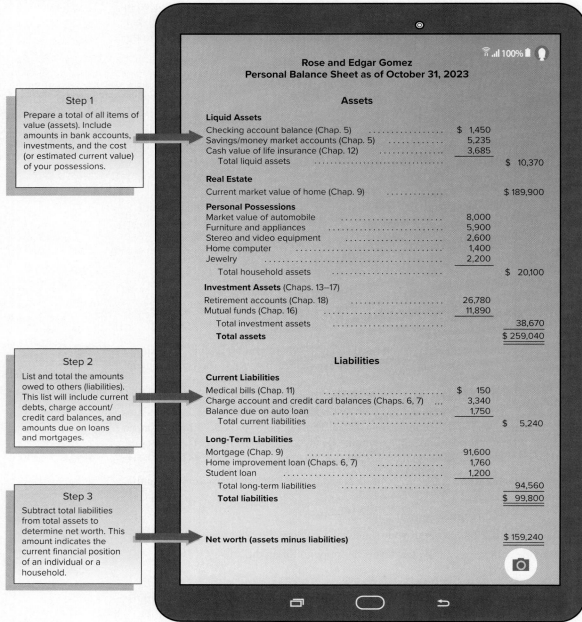

Step 1
Prepare a total of all items of value (assets). Include amounts in bank accounts, investments, and the cost (or estimated current value) of your possessions.

Rose and Edgar Gomez
Personal Balance Sheet as of October 31, 2023

🛜 .ıll 100% 🔋 💡

Assets

Liquid Assets

Checking account balance (Chap. 5)	$ 1,450	
Savings/money market accounts (Chap. 5)	5,235	
Cash value of life insurance (Chap. 12)	3,685	
Total liquid assets		$ 10,370

Real Estate

Current market value of home (Chap. 9)		$ 189,900

Personal Possessions

Market value of automobile	8,000	
Furniture and appliances	5,900	
Stereo and video equipment	2,600	
Home computer	1,400	
Jewelry	2,200	
Total household assets		$ 20,100

Investment Assets (Chaps. 13–17)

Retirement accounts (Chap. 18)	26,780	
Mutual funds (Chap. 16)	11,890	
Total investment assets		38,670
Total assets		**$ 259,040**

Step 2
List and total the amounts owed to others (liabilities). This list will include current debts, charge account/credit card balances, and amounts due on loans and mortgages.

Liabilities

Current Liabilities

Medical bills (Chap. 11)	$ 150	
Charge account and credit card balances (Chaps. 6, 7) ...	3,340	
Balance due on auto loan	1,750	
Total current liabilities		$ 5,240

Long-Term Liabilities

Mortgage (Chap. 9)	91,600	
Home improvement loan (Chaps. 6, 7)	1,760	
Student loan	1,200	
Total long-term liabilities		94,560
Total liabilities		**$ 99,800**

Step 3
Subtract total liabilities from total assets to determine net worth. This amount indicates the current financial position of an individual or a household.

Net worth (assets minus liabilities)		**$ 159,240**

Note: Various asset and liability items are discussed in the chapters listed next to them.

1. **Liquid assets** are cash and items of value that can easily be converted to cash. Money in checking and savings accounts is *liquid* and available to the Gomez family for current spending. The cash value of their life insurance may be borrowed if needed. While assets other than liquid assets can also be converted into cash, the process is not as easy.

2. *Real estate* includes a home, a condominium, vacation property, or other land that a person or family owns.

3. *Personal possessions* are a major portion of assets for most people. Included in this category are automobiles and personal belongings. While these items have value, they may be difficult to convert to cash. While you may list your possessions at their original cost, these values need to be revised over time. A three-year-old

liquid assets Cash and items of value that can easily be converted to cash.

television set is worth less now than when it was new. You may wish to list your possessions at their current value (also referred to as *market value*). This method takes into account the fact that things such as a home or rare jewelry may increase in value over time. You can estimate current value with an online search for the price of automobiles, homes, or other possessions.

4. *Investment assets* are funds set aside for long-term financial needs. The Gomez family will use their investments for financing their children's education, purchasing a vacation home, and retirement. Since investment assets fluctuate in value, the amounts listed should reflect their value at the time the balance sheet is prepared.

smart money minute

An estimated $3 billion of grants and scholarships go unused each year. A simple way to take advantage of these funds is to complete the Free Application for Federal Student Aid (FAFSA) at https://fafsa.ed.gov. In addition, www.finaid.org, www.fastweb.com, and www.cappex.com are some of the online sources for locating scholarships for which you may qualify. For additional guidance on financing your education, see the Chapter 7 Appendix.

STEP 2: DETERMINE AMOUNTS OWED Looking at the total assets of the Gomez family, you might conclude that they have a strong financial position. However, their debts must also be considered. **Liabilities** are amounts owed to others but do not include items not yet due, such as next month's rent. A liability is a debt you owe now, not something you may owe in the future. Liabilities usually have two categories:

1. **Current liabilities** are debts you must pay within a short time, usually less than a year. These liabilities include such things as medical bills, tax payments, cash loans, and charge accounts.

2. **Long-term liabilities** are debts you do not have to pay in full until more than a year from now. Common long-term liabilities include auto loans, educational loans, and mortgages. A *mortgage* is an amount borrowed to buy a house or other real estate usually repaid over a period of 15 years or more. Similarly, a home improvement loan may be repaid over the next 5 to 10 years.

The debts in the liability section of a balance sheet represent the amount owed at the moment; they do not include future interest payments or monthly expenses due at a later time. However, debt payments may include a portion of interest. Chapters 6 and 7 discuss the use of credit and the cost of borrowing.

liabilities Amounts owed to others.

current liabilities Debts that must be paid within a short time, usually less than a year.

long-term liabilities Debts that are not required to be paid in full until more than a year from now.

STEP 3: COMPUTE NET WORTH **Net worth** is the difference between your total assets and your total liabilities. This relationship can be stated as

$$\text{Assets} - \text{Liabilities} = \text{Net worth}$$

Net worth is the amount you would have if all assets were sold for the listed values and all debts were paid in full. Also, total assets equal total liabilities plus net worth. The balance sheet of a business is commonly expressed as

$$\text{Assets} = \text{Liabilities} + \text{Net worth}$$

As Exhibit 3-3 shows, Rose and Edgar Gomez have a net worth of $159,240. Since people will probably never liquidate all assets, net worth has a more practical purpose: It provides a measurement of your current financial position.

net worth The difference between total assets and total liabilities.

EXAMPLE: Net Worth

If a household has $193,000 of assets and liabilities of $88,000, the net worth would be $105,000 ($193,000 minus $88,000).

How about you? What is an estimate of your current net worth? What actions might you take to increase your net worth?

A person may have a high net worth but still have financial difficulties. Having many assets with low liquidity means not having the cash available to pay current expenses.

Insolvency is the inability to pay debts when they are due; it occurs when a person's liabilities far exceed available assets. Bankruptcy, discussed in Chapter 7, may be an alternative for a person in this position.

Actions to increase net worth are the result of (1) increasing your savings, (2) reducing spending, (3) increasing the value of investments and other possessions, and (4) reducing amounts owed. Remember, your net worth is *not* money available for use but an indication of your financial position on a given date.

insolvency The inability to pay debts when they are due because liabilities far exceed the value of assets.

EVALUATING YOUR FINANCIAL POSITION

A personal balance sheet measures progress toward financial goals. Your financial situation improves if your net worth increases each time you prepare a balance sheet. It will improve more rapidly if you can set aside money each month for saving and investing.

THE CASH FLOW STATEMENT: WHERE DID YOUR MONEY GO?

Each day, financial events affect your net worth. When you receive a paycheck or pay living expenses, your total assets and liabilities change. **Cash flow** is the actual inflow and outflow of cash during a time period. Income from employment probably represents your most important *cash inflow;* however, other income, such as interest earned on a savings account, should also be considered. In contrast, payments for items such as rent, food, and loans are *cash outflows.*

A **cash flow statement,** also called a *personal income and expenditure statement* (Exhibit 3-4), is a summary of cash receipts and payments for a time period, such as a month or a year. This report provides data on income and spending patterns, which will be helpful when preparing a budget. Your bank account can provide information for a cash flow statement. Deposits to the account are your *inflows;* checks, online payments, and debit card purchases are *outflows.* With this system, when you make a cash payment or purchase, also note these amounts for your cash flow statement.

The process for preparing a cash flow statement is

cash flow The actual inflow and outflow of cash during a given time period.

cash flow statement A financial statement that summarizes cash receipts and payments for a time period.

$$\text{Total cash received during the time period} - \text{Cash outflows during the time period} = \text{Cash surplus or deficit}$$

STEP 1: RECORD INCOME   Creating a cash flow statement starts with identifying the cash received during the time period involved. **Income** is the inflows of cash for an individual or a household. For most people, the main source of income is money received from work. Common income sources include:

income Inflows of cash to an individual or a household.

- Wages, salaries, commissions, and self-employment business income.
- Savings and investment income (interest, dividends, rent).
- Gifts, grants, scholarships, and government payments, such as Social Security, public assistance, and unemployment benefits.
- Amounts received from pension and retirement plans.
- Alimony and child support payments.

EXHIBIT 3-4 Creating a cash flow statement of income and outflows

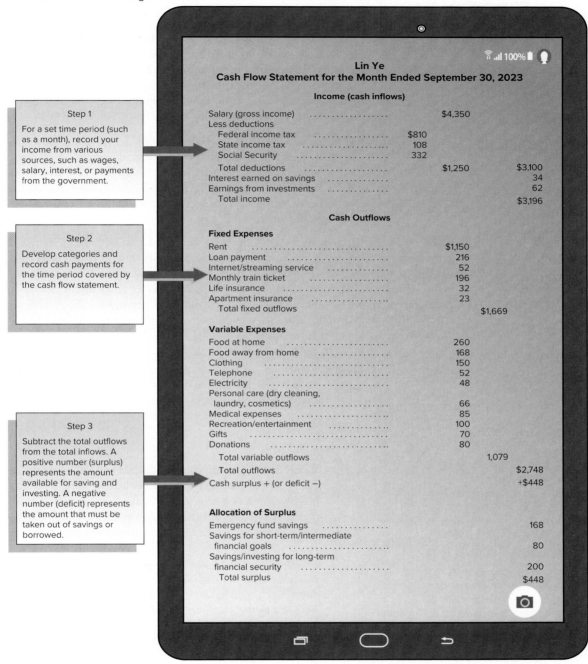

Step 1

For a set time period (such as a month), record your income from various sources, such as wages, salary, interest, or payments from the government.

Step 2

Develop categories and record cash payments for the time period covered by the cash flow statement.

Step 3

Subtract the total outflows from the total inflows. A positive number (surplus) represents the amount available for saving and investing. A negative number (deficit) represents the amount that must be taken out of savings or borrowed.

Lin Ye
Cash Flow Statement for the Month Ended September 30, 2023

Income (cash inflows)

Salary (gross income)		$4,350	
Less deductions			
Federal income tax	$810		
State income tax	108		
Social Security	332		
Total deductions		$1,250	$3,100
Interest earned on savings			34
Earnings from investments			62
Total income			$3,196

Cash Outflows

Fixed Expenses

Rent	$1,150	
Loan payment	216	
Internet/streaming service	52	
Monthly train ticket	196	
Life insurance	32	
Apartment insurance	23	
Total fixed outflows		$1,669

Variable Expenses

Food at home	260	
Food away from home	168	
Clothing	150	
Telephone	52	
Electricity	48	
Personal care (dry cleaning, laundry, cosmetics)	66	
Medical expenses	85	
Recreation/entertainment	100	
Gifts	70	
Donations	80	
Total variable outflows	1,079	
Total outflows		$2,748
Cash surplus + (or deficit −)		+$448

Allocation of Surplus

Emergency fund savings	168
Savings for short-term/intermediate financial goals	80
Savings/investing for long-term financial security	200
Total surplus	$448

In Exhibit 3-4, notice that Lin Ye's monthly salary (or *gross income*) of $4,350 is her main source of income. However, she does not have use of the entire amount. **Take-home pay,** also called *net pay,* is a person's earnings after deductions for taxes and other items. Lin's deductions for federal, state, and Social Security taxes are $1,250.

take-home pay Earnings after deductions for taxes and other items; also called *net pay.*

Daily purchasing decisions influence cash outflows and long-term financial goals.
georgerudy/123RF

discretionary income
Money left over after paying for housing, food, and other necessities.

Her take-home pay is $3,100; this amount, plus earnings from savings and investments, gives her an available income of $3,196 for use during the current month.

Take-home pay may also be referred to as *disposable income,* the amount a person or household has available to spend. **Discretionary income** is money left over after paying for housing, food, and other necessities. The amount available for discretionary income will vary by age, income level, and economic conditions. During the recent pandemic many people had very limited discretionary income.

STEP 2: RECORD CASH OUTFLOWS   Cash payments for living expenses and other items are the second component of a cash flow statement. Lin Ye divides her cash outflows into two major categories: *fixed expenses* and *variable expenses.* While every individual and household has different cash outflows, these main categories, along with the subcategories Lin uses, can be adapted to most situations.

1. *Fixed expenses* are payments that do not vary from month to month. Rent, mortgage payments, loan payments, wifi service fees, and a monthly train ticket for work are examples of constant or fixed cash outflows. For Lin, another type of fixed expense is the amount set aside each month for payments due once or twice a year. For example, Lin pays $384 every March for life insurance. Each month, she records a fixed outflow of $32 for deposit in a savings account so the money will be available when her insurance payment is due.

2. *Variable expenses* are flexible payments that change from month to month. Examples of variable cash outflows are food, clothing, utilities (electricity, cell phone, gas), recreation, medical expenses, gifts, and donations. The use of an app or other system is necessary for an accurate total of cash outflows.

my life 2

I know the details of my cash flow statement.

In what ways might the *Daily Spending Diary* (at the end of Chapter 1) be of value when preparing a personal cash flow statement?

smart money minute

Many people make the **mistake** of not having an accurate record of spending, which results in high debt levels and low saving amounts. An **action** is to use an app or a written spending record, or to track spending with sticky notes, a whiteboard, a monthly calendar, or by collecting receipts as a visual reminder. This can result in **success**—having funds for financial goals and emergencies. To reduce financial stress, potential actions include: (1) Have a low debt-to-income ratio. (2) Delay, reduce, or eliminate unnecessary expenses. (3) Build up emergency savings. (4) Seek additional income by selling unneeded items, working extra hours at your job, securing part-time work, starting a home-based or online business, turning a hobby into a business, or selling your expertise as a consultant. Search online for other ideas for increased income.

STEP 3: DETERMINE NET CASH FLOW   The difference between income and outflows can be either a positive (*surplus*) or a negative (*deficit*) cash flow. A deficit exists if more cash goes out than comes in during a month. This amount must be made up by taking money from savings or by borrowing.

When you have a cash surplus, as Lin did (Exhibit 3-4), this amount is available for saving, investing, or paying off debts. Each month, Lin sets aside money for her *emergency fund* in a savings account that she could use for unexpected expenses or to pay living costs if she did not receive her salary. She deposits the additional surplus in savings and investment plans with two purposes: (1) short-term and intermediate financial goals, such as a new car, a vacation, or returning to school; (2) long-term financial security—her retirement.

A cash flow statement is the foundation for a spending, saving, and investment plan. The cash flow statement reports the *actual* spending of a household. In contrast, a budget, with a similar format, is used to *project* income and spending.

The *Financial Literacy Calculations* feature offers tools that may be used to determine how to assess your balance sheet and cash flow statement.

Financial Literacy Calculations

RATIOS FOR EVALUATING FINANCIAL PROGRESS

Financial ratios provide guidelines for measuring the changes in your financial situation. These relationships can indicate progress toward an improved financial position.

Ratio	Calculation	Example	Interpretation
Debt ratio	Liabilities divided by assets	$25,000/$50,000 = 0.5	Shows relationship between debt and assets; a low debt ratio is best.
Current ratio	Liquid assets divided by current liabilities	$4,000/$2,000 = 2	Indicates $2 in liquid assets for every $1 of current liabilities; a high current ratio is desirable to have cash available to pay bills.
Liquidity ratio	Liquid assets divided by monthly expenses	$10,000/$4,000 = 2.5	Indicates the number of months in which living expenses can be paid if an emergency arises; a high liquidity ratio is desirable.
Debt-payments ratio	Monthly credit payments divided by take-home pay	$540/$3,600 = 0.15	Indicates how much of a person's earnings goes for debt payments (excluding a home mortgage); financial advisors recommend a debt-payments ratio of less than 20 percent.
Savings ratio	Amount saved each month divided by gross income	$648/$5,400 = 0.12	Financial advisors recommend monthly savings of 5–10 percent.

Based on the following information, calculate the ratios requested:

Liabilities $12,000

Liquid assets $2,200

Monthly credit payments $150

Monthly savings $130

Total assets $36,000

Current liabilities $550

Take-home pay $900

Gross income $1,500

    1. Debt ratio _____

    2. Current ratio _____

    3. Debt-payments ratio _____

    4. Savings ratio _____

Analysis: How do these ratios compare with the guidelines mentioned in the "Interpretation" column above?

Answers: (1) $12,000/$36,000 = 0.33, or 33%; (2) $2,200/$550 = 4.0; (3) $150/$900 = 0.167, or 16.7%; (4) $130/$1,500 = 0.087, or 8.7%

✓ PRACTICE QUIZ 3-2

    1. What are the main purposes of personal financial statements?

    2. What does a personal balance sheet tell you about your financial situation?

    3. How can you use a balance sheet for personal financial planning?

    4. What information does a cash flow statement present?

PFP Sheet 15
Personal Balance Sheet

PFP Sheet 16
Personal Cash Flow Statement

Budgeting for Skilled Money Management

LO3-3

Create and implement a budget.

budget A specific plan for spending income.

People in different situations have varied financial challenges and budgeting activities. An *achiever,* with a strong financial resource base, will encounter different money issues than those of an *explorer,* someone seeking to get to the next level of financial success. A *striver,* with minimal financial resources, must carefully plan the use of available funds.

A **budget,** or *spending plan,* is necessary for successful financial planning. Financial problems such as overuse of credit and a lack of a savings program can be reduced with budgeting. The main purposes of a budget are to: (1) live within your income; (2) spend money wisely; (3) reach financial goals; (4) prepare for financial emergencies; and (5) develop wise financial management habits.

With a budget, you will be in control of your life. Without a budget, others will be in control, such as those to whom you owe money. Use a budget to tell your money where to go, rather than having overspending and debt control your life. Budgeting may be viewed in four major phases, as shown in Exhibit 3-5.

In Phase 1 (Assess Your Current Situation), the emphasis is on recording and reviewing past spending, saving, and income. This information is the foundation for your budget. Phase 2 (Plan Your Financial Direction) involves the steps necessary for creating a budget. Phase 3 (Implement Your Budget) requires maintaining a record of spending to compare actual amounts with budgeted amounts. Finally, in Phase 4 (Evaluate Your Budget Program), review and adjust the budget for the future.

EXHIBIT 3-5

Creating and implementing a budget

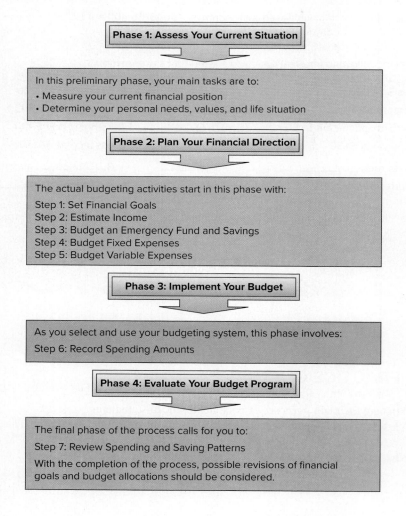

Phase 1: Assess Your Current Situation

In this preliminary phase, your main tasks are to:
• Measure your current financial position
• Determine your personal needs, values, and life situation

Phase 2: Plan Your Financial Direction

The actual budgeting activities start in this phase with:
Step 1: Set Financial Goals
Step 2: Estimate Income
Step 3: Budget an Emergency Fund and Savings
Step 4: Budget Fixed Expenses
Step 5: Budget Variable Expenses

Phase 3: Implement Your Budget

As you select and use your budgeting system, this phase involves:
Step 6: Record Spending Amounts

Phase 4: Evaluate Your Budget Program

The final phase of the process calls for you to:
Step 7: Review Spending and Saving Patterns
With the completion of the process, possible revisions of financial goals and budget allocations should be considered.

THE BUDGETING PROCESS

Financial statements and documents are the starting point for wise money management. A personal balance sheet is an effective scorecard for measuring financial progress. An improved net worth, as a result of increased assets or decreased debt, is evidence of a better financial position. Regularly evaluating your financial position is important for the budgeting process, which involves these steps.

STEP 1: SET FINANCIAL GOALS   Financial goals are plans related to your spending, saving, and investing. Exhibit 3-6 gives examples of common financial goals for varied life situations and time frames.

As discussed in Chapter 1, financial goals should take a SMART approach with goals that are **S**pecific, **M**easurable, **A**ction-oriented, **R**ealistic, and **T**ime-based. Your personal financial statements and budget guide you for achieving financial goals with

1. Your *balance sheet* reporting your current financial position—where you are now.
2. Your *cash flow statement* reporting what you received and spent.
3. Your *budget* setting a plan for spending and saving.

STEP 2: ESTIMATE INCOME   As Exhibit 3-7 shows, next estimate available money for a set time period. A common budgeting period is a month, with many payments such as rent or mortgage, utilities, and credit card payments due each month. In determining available income, include only money you are sure of receiving. Bonuses, gifts, or unexpected income should not be considered until the money is actually received.

If you get paid once a month, planning is easy since you will work with a single amount. If you get paid weekly or twice a month, plan how each paycheck will be used for expenses. If you get paid every two weeks, plan your spending based on two paychecks each month. Then, during the two months each year with three paydays, you can put additional amounts into savings, pay off debts, or make a special purchase.

smart money minute

Kakeibo, ("kah-keh-boh"), meaning "household financial ledger," has been used in Japan for over 100 years. This system requires writing of spending (no apps or computer) using four categories: (1) needs, (2) wants, (3) culture (books and museum visits), and (4) unexpected (medical costs, car repairs). Next, to become honest about your spending, reflect on these questions: How much do I have available? How much would I like to save? How much am I spending? How can I improve? *Kakeibo* may not control your spending, but it can make you more mindful of how you spend.

EXHIBIT 3-6 Common financial goals

Personal Situation	Short-Term Goals (less than 1 year)	Intermediate Goals (1–5 years)	Long-Term Goals (over 5 years)
Single person	• Complete college • Pay off auto loan • Donate to charity	• Take a vacation to Europe • Pay off education loan • Attend graduate school	• Buy a vacation home in the mountains • Provide for retirement income • Expand monthly volunteer hours
Married couple (no children)	• Take an annual vacation • Buy a new car	• Remodel lower level of home • Build a stock portfolio	• Buy a retirement home with ocean view • Provide for retirement income
Single parent (young children)	• Increase life insurance • Increase monthly savings	• Increase investments • Buy a new car	• Accumulate a college fund for children • Move to a larger home

EXHIBIT 3-7 The Fraziers develop and implement a monthly budget

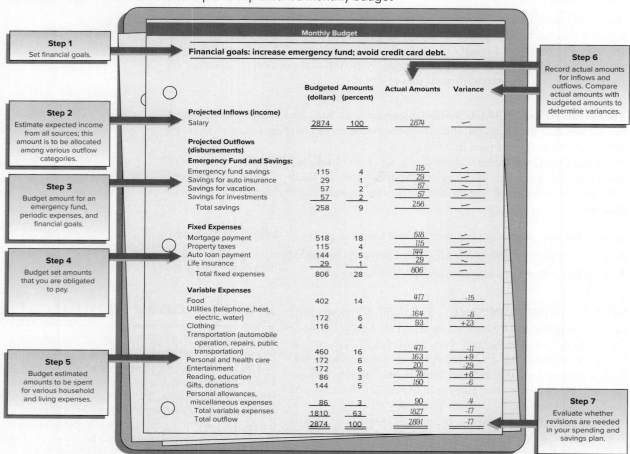

Step 1
Set financial goals.

Step 2
Estimate expected income from all sources; this amount is to be allocated among various outflow categories.

Step 3
Budget amount for an emergency fund, periodic expenses, and financial goals.

Step 4
Budget set amounts that you are obligated to pay.

Step 5
Budget estimated amounts to be spent for various household and living expenses.

Step 6
Record actual amounts for inflows and outflows. Compare actual amounts with budgeted amounts to determine variances.

Step 7
Evaluate whether revisions are needed in your spending and savings plan.

Monthly Budget

Financial goals: increase emergency fund; avoid credit card debt.

	Budgeted Amounts (dollars)	Amounts (percent)	Actual Amounts	Variance
Projected Inflows (income)				
Salary	2874	100	2874	—
Projected Outflows (disbursements)				
Emergency Fund and Savings:				
Emergency fund savings	115	4	115	—
Savings for auto insurance	29	1	29	—
Savings for vacation	57	2	57	—
Savings for investments	57	2	57	—
Total savings	258	9	258	—
Fixed Expenses				
Mortgage payment	518	18	518	—
Property taxes	115	4	115	—
Auto loan payment	144	5	144	—
Life insurance	29	1	29	—
Total fixed expenses	806	28	806	—
Variable Expenses				
Food	402	14	417	-15
Utilities (telephone, heat, electric, water)	172	6	164	-8
Clothing	116	4	93	+23
Transportation (automobile operation, repairs, public transportation)	460	16	471	-11
Personal and health care	172	6	163	+9
Entertainment	172	6	201	-29
Reading, education	86	3	78	+8
Gifts, donations	144	5	150	-6
Personal allowances, miscellaneous expenses	86	3	90	-4
Total variable expenses	1810	63	1827	-17
Total outflow	2874	100	2891	-17

Maintaining income and expense records makes the budgeting process easier.
kate_sept2004/Getty Images

Budgeting income can be difficult if your earnings vary by season or your income is irregular, as with sales commissions. Try to estimate income based on the past year and on expectations for the current year. Estimate income on the low side to avoid overspending and other financial difficulties.

STEP 3: BUDGET AN EMERGENCY FUND AND SAVINGS To set aside money for unexpected expenses and future financial security, the Fraziers (see Exhibit 3-7) budget amounts for savings and investments. Financial advisors suggest an *emergency fund* of three to six months of living expenses for unexpected financial difficulties. This amount will vary based on life situation and employment stability. A three-month emergency fund is probably adequate for a person with a stable income or secure employment, while a person with erratic or seasonal income may need an emergency fund of six months or more. Uncertainty such as the recent COVID-19 pandemic emphasized the importance of an emergency fund.

The Fraziers also set aside amounts in *sinking funds* for non-monthly expenses that occur during the year. For example, their automobile insurance is due every six months. Other sinking funds may be for vacations or year-end holiday spending. These amounts and the emergency fund may be put into separate savings accounts, which some people refer to as their *savings buckets*. The *time value of money,* discussed in Chapter 1, refers to increases in savings as a result of interest earned. Savings methods for achieving financial goals are discussed later in this chapter.

A very common mistake is to save only the amount left at the end of the month, if any. When you do that, you often have *nothing* left for savings. Since saving is vital for long-term financial security, budget a savings amount as a fixed expense.

STEP 4: BUDGET FIXED EXPENSES Definite obligations are the next element of a budget. As Exhibit 3-7 shows, the Fraziers have fixed expenses for housing, taxes, and loan payments. They also make a monthly payment of $29 for life insurance. The budgeted total for the Fraziers' fixed expenses is $806, or 28 percent of estimated available income.

Notice that a budget has a similar format to the cash flow statement. A budget, however, involves *projected* or planned income and expenses. The cash flow statement reports the *actual* income and expenses.

Assigning amounts to spending categories requires careful consideration. Sources to guide your spending include your cash flow statement, online articles and data, and estimates of your future income and expenses. Exhibit 3-8 provides suggested budget allocations for different life situations. While this information can be helpful, a detailed record of spending is the best source. Use a simple system, such as a notebook, your bank account, or the *Daily Spending Diary* (see end of Chapter 1). Remember, a budget is an *estimate* for spending and saving to help you better use your money, not to reduce your enjoyment of life.

smart money minute

Few people enjoy financial recordkeeping. To make budgeting and money management fun, consider these ideas:

- *Money Nicknames.* Name bank accounts and budget categories to personalize your money activities. Use a permanent marker to label debit and credit cards, such as "Hey, bills only!" or "Treat yourself today."

- *Bae Day* is a time set aside to plan spending. *Bae,* which stands for "before anything else," is a self-appointment that can be fun when you dress up, go to a special location, or play favorite music.

- *Money Mate Date* provides financial accountability from a person who calls you to make sure bills are paid, or sends a text to discourage impulse buying.

- *Arts and Crafts.* Create, or locate online, a poster that displays savings and debt categories to track your progress. Color in the poster little by little as you save or pay down student loans. Use photos to represent budget categories or financial goals.

Source: https://www.refinery29.com/en-us/how-to-make-budgeting-fun, accessed August 5, 2021.

EXHIBIT 3-8 Typical after-tax budget allocations for different life situations

Budget Category	Student	Working Single (no dependents)	Couple (children under 18)	Single Parent (young children)	Parents (children over 18 in college)	Couple (over 55, no dependent children)
Housing (rent or mortgage payment; utilities; furnishings; and appliances)	0–25%	30–35%	25–35%	20–30%	25–30%	25–35%
Transportation	5–10	15–20	15–20	10–18	12–18	10–18
Food (at home and away from home)	15–20	15–25	15–25	13–20	15–20	18–25
Clothing	5–12	5–15	5–10	5–10	4–8	4–8
Personal and health care (including child care)	3–5	3–5	4–10	8–12	4–6	6–12
Entertainment and recreation	5–10	5–10	4–8	4–8	6–10	5–8
Reading and education	10–30	2–4	3–5	3–5	6–12	2–4
Personal insurance and pension payments	0–5	4–8	5–9	5–9	4–7	6–8
Gifts, donations, and contributions	4–6	5–8	3–5	3–5	4–8	3–5
Savings	0–10	4–15	5–10	5–8	2–4	3–5

Sources: Bureau of Labor Statistics (stats.bls.gov); *American Demographics; Money; The Wall Street Journal.*

my life | 3

I adapt my budgeting activities for changing situations.

Spending will vary depending on household size, ages, and geographic location. Guidelines for budget allocations include the *70% rule,* which allocates 70 percent of income for necessary expenses, 20 percent for savings, and 10 percent for retirement and future financial security. A variation is the *50/30/20 rule* with three categories; 50 percent for necessities, 20 percent for financial goals, and 30 percent on other items.

budget variance The difference between the amount budgeted and the actual amount received or spent.

STEP 5: BUDGET VARIABLE EXPENSES Planning for variable expenses is not as easy as for savings or fixed expenses. Variable expenses will fluctuate by household situation, time of year, health, economic conditions, and other factors. A major portion of the Fraziers' planned spending—over 60 percent of their budgeted income—is for variable living costs.

The Fraziers base their estimates on needs and desires for the items listed and on expected cost-of-living changes. The *consumer price index (CPI)* is a measure of the general price level of consumer goods and services in the United States. This government statistic indicates changes in the buying power of a dollar. As consumer prices increase due to inflation, people must spend more to buy the same amount. Changes in the cost of living will vary depending on where you live and what you buy.

STEP 6: RECORD SPENDING AMOUNTS After establishing your spending plan, continue to keep records of actual income and expenses. In Exhibit 3-7, notice that the Fraziers' estimated amounts are presented under "Budgeted Amounts."

The family's actual spending was not always the same as planned. A **budget variance** is the difference between the amount budgeted and the actual amount received or spent. The total variance for the Fraziers was a $17 **deficit,** since their actual spending exceeded their planned spending by this amount. The Fraziers would have had a **surplus** if their actual spending had been less than they had planned.

EXAMPLE: Budget Variance

If a family budgeted $380 a month for food and spent $363, this would result in a $17 budget *surplus.* However, if the family spent $406 on food during the month, a $26 budget *deficit* would exist.

How about you? What actions would you take if you encountered a budget deficit? What would you do with money from a budget surplus?

personal fintech

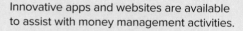

Innovative apps and websites are available to assist with money management activities.

- **Albert** (www.meetalbert.com) is an app to guide your financial decisions.
- **EARN** (www.earn.org) helps you to create a habit of saving.
- **Scratch** (www.scratch.fi) helps borrowers understand, manage, and repay loans.
- **SaverLife (**about.saverlife.org**)** helps you to create a habit of saving.
- **Axos Invest** (axosinvest.com) suggests and manages investments for financial goals.
- **Greenlight** (greenlightcard.com) teaches financial responsibility to children.
- **gohenry** (gohenry.com) helps kids build money management skills.

Variances for income are the opposite of expense variances. Less income than expected would be a deficit, while more income than expected would be a surplus.

Spending more than planned for an item may be justified by reducing spending for another item or putting less into savings. However, it may be necessary to revise your budget and financial goals.

STEP 7: REVIEW SPENDING AND SAVING PATTERNS

Like most financial activities, budgeting is an ongoing process. You need to review and revise your spending plan on a regular basis.

Review Your Financial Progress Positive budget outcomes may include extra cash in your bank account. Negative outcomes, such as falling behind in bill payments, require action. The outcomes may not always be obvious. Occasionally, you will probably have to evaluate (with other household members) where spending has been more or less than expected.

As Exhibit 3-9 shows, an annual summary compares actual spending with budgeted amounts. This summary may be prepared every three or six months. A spreadsheet program or app may be used. This summary will guide you in making needed budget changes. An annual review is valuable for successful short-term money management and long-term financial security.

Revise Your Goals and Budget Allocations   What should be cut when a budget shortage occurs? Answers will vary for different situations. The most common overspending areas are entertainment, food, and away-from-home meals. Purchasing less expensive brand items, buying quality used products, avoiding credit card purchases, and renting rather than buying are common budget adjustment techniques. Reduced spending for vacations, dining out, cleaning and lawn care, and subscription services is often recommended.

At this point, you may also revise financial goals. Are you making progress toward achieving your objectives? Have changes in your personal situation affected certain

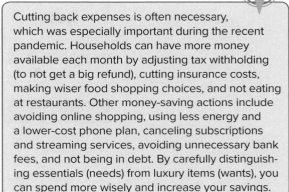

smart money minute

Cutting back expenses is often necessary, which was especially important during the recent pandemic. Households can have more money available each month by adjusting tax withholding (to not get a big refund), cutting insurance costs, making wiser food shopping choices, and not eating at restaurants. Other money-saving actions include avoiding online shopping, using less energy and a lower-cost phone plan, canceling subscriptions and streaming services, avoiding unnecessary bank fees, and not being in debt. By carefully distinguishing essentials (needs) from luxury items (wants), you can spend more wisely and increase your savings.

deficit The amount by which actual spending exceeds planned spending.

surplus The amount by which actual spending is less than planned spending.

EXHIBIT 3-9 An annual budget summary

Actual Spending (Cash Outflows)														Annual Totals	
Item	Monthly Budget	Jan.	Feb.	Mar	Apr	May	June	July	Aug.	Sept.	Oct	Nov.	Dec.	Actual	Budgeted
Income	2,730	2,730	2,730	2,730	2,940	2,736	2,730	2,730	2,730	2,856	2,850	2,850	2,850	33,450	32,760
Savings	150	150	150	200	150	90	50	30	100	250	250	150	40	1,610	1,800
Mortgage/Rent	826	826	826	826	826	826	826	826	826	826	826	826	826	9,912	9,912
Housing costs (insurance, utilities)	190	214	238	187	176	185	88	146	178	198	177	201	195	2,283	2,280
Telephone	50	43	45	67	56	54	52	65	45	43	52	49	47	618	600
Food (at home)	280	287	277	245	234	278	267	298	320	301	298	278	324	3,407	3,360
Food (away from home)	80	67	76	64	87	123	09	89	83	67	76	83	143	1,089	960
Clothing	100	98	78	123	156	86	76	111	124	87	95	123	111	1,268	1,200
Transportation (auto operation, public transportation)	340	302	312	333	345	297	287	390	373	299	301	267	301	3,807	4,000
Credit payments	249	249	249	249	249	249	249	249	249	249	249	249	249	2,988	2,908
Insurance (life, health, other)	45	–	–	135	–	–	35	–	–	135	–	–	135	540	540
Health care	140	176	145	187	122	111	56	186	166	134	189	193	147	1,912	1,680
Recreation	80	67	98	123	98	67	45	87	98	65	87	87	111	1,033	960
Heading, education	40	32	54	44	34	39	54	12	38	54	34	76	45	516	480
Gifts, donations	100	102	116	94	87	123	69	95	94	113	87	99	134	1,227	1,200
Personal miscellaneous expense	60	89	45	67	54	98	59	54	49	71	65	90	56	797	720
Total	2,730	2,702	2,705	2,984	2,674	2,626	2,642	2,638	2,743	2,892	2,786	2,771	2,864	33,007	32,760
Surplus (deficit)		26	25	(234)	266	104	86	92	(13)	(42)	64	79r	(14)	443	...

goals? Have new goals surfaced that should be given a higher priority? Addressing these issues and creating an effective saving plan will help you to achieve financial goals.

EXAMPLE: Tracking Budget Success

For a reliable picture of your financial health, take time to monitor these numbers:

Monthly Numbers	Annual Numbers	Long-term Numbers
• Income	• Taxes paid	• Home equity
• Expenses	• Yearly total expenses	• Retirement savings
• Cash flow	• Net worth	• Investment balance
• Emergency fund balance	• Credit score	• Asset allocation
• Debt payments	• Credit card interest paid	• Sector breakdown

How about you? Which numbers do you believe are most important for you to check now and in the future?

CHARACTERISTICS OF SUCCESSFUL BUDGETING

A spending plan will not eliminate financial worries. A budget will only be effective if you follow it. Changes in income, expenses, and goals will require budget revisions. A successful budget should be:

smart money minute

To develop financial literacy among children: (1) have a payday for chores, not an allowance; (2) explain opportunity cost and needs versus wants; (3) start a savings jar or bank account; (4) create a budgeting chart to show family spending; (5) create a shopping list with them; (6) talk about prices and brands when in stores; (7) sign an agreement with payment dates for money borrowed from parents; (8) have them buy shampoo, toothpaste, and snacks to prepare them to be on their own.

- *Well planned.* Take time and effort to prepare your budget. Involve everyone; children learn valuable lessons from family budgeting activities.
- *Realistic.* You may not immediately be able to start saving for an expensive car or vacation. A budget is not to prevent you from enjoying life but to help you obtain what you want most.
- *Flexible.* Unexpected expenses and unusual circumstances require a budget to be easily adapted and revised, as was the situation for many during the recent pandemic.
- *Clearly communicated.* All involved must be aware of the plan for it to work. The budget should be in writing or online, and available to all household members.

TYPES OF BUDGETING SYSTEMS

Your online payments summary provides a summary of expenses, but it does not serve as a spending plan. Some commonly used budgeting systems include:

1. A *mental budget* is in a person's mind. This simple system may be appropriate if you have very limited resources and minimal financial responsibilities. However, an "in your head" budget can be dangerous when you forget planned spending amounts.

2. A *physical budget* involves envelopes, folders, or containers to hold money or paper with amounts for planned spending. This system allows you to see where your money goes. Envelopes would contain cash or a note listing the amount in each expense category. Budget envelope apps such as Mvelopes.com and

online templates to create envelopes can help you visualize where your money is going.

3. A *written budget* provides a detailed plan in a notebook or a budget record book. A common written budget has columns for comparing budgeted and actual amounts.

4. A *digital budget* may be created with a spreadsheet, software such as Quicken, a website, or an app. Excel budget templates may be located with an online search. An online budget may be created at a website such as www.mint.com. Banks, credit unions, and other financial institutions offer online budgeting and money management tools. Budgeting apps to track, monitor, and plan your spending have costs ranging from free to a few dollars.

The budgeting system you use will depend on your personal and financial situation. Most important, select a system that best helps you to achieve your financial goals.

 HOW TO . . .   **Conduct a Money Management SWOT Analysis**

SWOT (strengths, weaknesses, opportunities, threats) is a planning tool used by businesses and other organizations. This technique can also be used for your money management activities. Listed below are examples of possible items for each SWOT category. In the areas provided, determine your strengths, weaknesses, opportunities, and threats related to budgeting and money management. Do online research and talk with others to get ideas for your personal SWOT items.

Internal (Personal) Factors	External (Economic, Social) Influences
Strengths	**Opportunities**
• Saving 5–10 percent of income	• Phone apps for monitoring finances
• Informed on personal finance topics	• Part-time work to supplement income
• No credit card debt	• Availability of no-fee bank account
• Flexible job skills	• Low-interest-rate education loan
Your strengths: _____	*Potential opportunities:* _____
_____	_____
Weaknesses	**Threats**
• High level of credit card debt	• Lower market value of retirement fund
• No emergency fund	• Possible reduced hours at part-time job
• Automobile in need of repairs	• Reduced home market value
• Low current cash inflow	• Increased living costs (inflation)
Your weaknesses: _____	*Potential threats:* _____
_____	_____

Creating a money management SWOT analysis is only a start. Next, select actions to build on your strengths, minimize your weaknesses, take advantage of opportunities, and avoid being a victim of threats. Through research and innovation, weaknesses and threats can become strengths and opportunities.

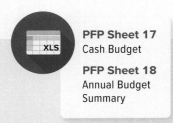

PFP Sheet 17
Cash Budget

PFP Sheet 18
Annual Budget
Summary

✓ PRACTICE QUIZ 3-3

1. What are the main purposes of a budget?
2. How does a person's life situation affect goal setting and amounts allocated for various budget categories?
3. What are the main steps in creating a budget?
4. What are commonly recommended qualities of a successful budget?
5. What actions might you take when evaluating your budgeting program?

Money Management and Achieving Financial Goals

LO3-4

Connect money management and savings activities to achieving financial goals.

Your personal financial statements and budget are designed to help you achieve financial goals with:

1. A balance sheet reporting your current financial position—where you are now.
2. A cash flow statement detailing your income and spending during a month.
3. A budget recording your plans for spending and saving for your financial goals.

People may prepare a balance sheet on a periodic basis, such as every three or six months. Between those times, a budget and cash flow statement help you plan and measure spending and saving activities. For example, you might prepare a balance sheet on January 1 and July 1 with your budget guiding your spending and saving between those points in time, while your cash flow statement documents your actual spending and saving. This relationship may be viewed as follows:

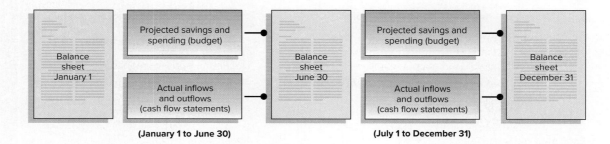

Changes in net worth result from cash inflows and outflows. When outflows exceed inflows, you must draw on savings or borrow. When this happens, lower assets (savings) or higher liabilities (due to credit use) result in a lower net worth. When inflows exceed outflows, putting money into savings or paying off debts results in a higher net worth.

IDENTIFYING SAVING GOALS

Saving current income, as well as investing (discussed in Chapters 13-17), is the basis for an improved financial position and long-term financial security. Common reasons for saving include:

- To create an emergency fund for irregular and unexpected expenses.
- To pay for the replacement of expensive items, such as appliances or an automobile, or to have money for a down payment on a house.

- To buy expensive items such as electronics or sports equipment or to pay for a vacation.
- To provide for long-term expenses such as the education of children or retirement.
- To earn income from interest on savings to pay current living expenses.

SELECTING A SAVING TECHNIQUE

For several decades, the United States ranked low among industrial nations for savings rate. Low savings affect personal financial situations. Research often indicates that most Americans do not have an adequate emergency fund.

To expand your savings: (1) use payroll deduction or an app to automatically deposit funds in a separate savings account; (2) regularly save 5 or 10 percent in your income, or a specific dollar amount; most important, "pay yourself first;" (3) take advantage of employer matching retirement fund contributions.

How you save is less important than making regular savings deposits for financial goals. Small amounts of savings can grow fast. During the recent pandemic, some people were able to continue and expand saving deposits, while others took money out of their retirement account for living expenses. Once able to do so, they were encouraged to replace the money withdrawn and to again save for future financial security.

CALCULATING SAVINGS AMOUNTS

To achieve financial objectives, convert your savings goals into specific amounts. Use of a savings or investment plan is vital to the growth of your money. As Exhibit 3-10 shows, using the time value of money calculations introduced in Chapter 1, you can help you measure progress toward financial goals.

smart money minute

If saving money is difficult for you, try some unusual actions:

- Save a certain money denomination, such as every five-dollar bill you receive in change, or save coins in a decorated jar or container.
- Instead of trying to save $150 a month, save $35 a week or $5 a day.
- Skip buying items, such as coffee, soft drinks, snacks, or other impulse items; bring your lunch.
- Use recurring payments; if you have a monthly car payment, when the vehicle is paid, keep sending that amount to your savings.
- Enroll in a round-up program, in which a purchase is rounded up to the nearest dollar with the difference transferred to savings.
- Save in short sprints; for one month, avoid eating away from home or stop another spending.
- Set aside the amount shown as "You Saved" on receipts for items on sale and store discounts.
- Pay for your drinks (or snacks) at home by setting aside the "price," such as $1 for a soft drink or $2 for a bag of chips, for savings.
- Visualize a savings goal with a photo or other graphic as a reminder of something you plan to buy (holiday gifts or a vacation).
- Place your credit card in a bag or container of water and place it in the freezer to avoid impulse purchases. Defrost it under warm water when you need to pay for an emergency. Of course, you can also freeze your credit by contacting the three major credit reporting bureaus to avoid scams and fraud. You may also delete a saved credit card on online shopping sites.

 my life **4**

I regularly review the status of my saving goals.

Reaching your financial goals will depend on the savings method used and the time value of money. How do the examples shown in Exhibit 3-10, Using Savings to Achieve Financial Goals, relate to your current or future life situation?

 PRACTICE QUIZ 3-4

1. What are some suggested methods to make saving easy?
2. What methods are available to calculate amounts needed to reach savings goals?

 PFP Sheet 19
College Education Savings Plan, Cost Analysis

EXHIBIT 3-10

Using savings to achieve financial goals

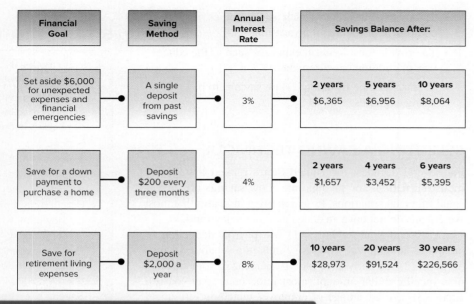

Financial Goal	Saving Method	Annual Interest Rate	Savings Balance After:		
			2 years	**5 years**	**10 years**
Set aside $6,000 for unexpected expenses and financial emergencies	A single deposit from past savings	3%	$6,365	$6,956	$8,064
			2 years	**4 years**	**6 years**
Save for a down payment to purchase a home	Deposit $200 every three months	4%	$1,657	$3,452	$5,395
			10 years	**20 years**	**30 years**
Save for retirement living expenses	Deposit $2,000 a year	8%	$28,973	$91,524	$226,566

Your Personal Finance Roadmap and Dashboard:

Money Management

CASH FLOW ANALYSIS

A monthly cash flow analysis will help you achieve various financial goals.

By comparing your cash inflows (income) and cash outflows (spending), you will determine if you have a *surplus* or a *deficit*. A surplus allows you to save more or pay off debts. A deficit reduces your savings or increases the amount you owe.

Your Situation

Do you maintain a record of cash inflows and outflows? Does your cash flow situation reflect a deficit with unnecessary spending? How can you reduce spending to improve your cash flow situation? Other money management actions you might consider during various stages of your life include:

⑨ First Steps

- Maintain a spending diary to monitor daily finances.
- Create a system for financial records and documents.
- Develop a budget with a regular amount for savings.
- Create a personal balance sheet and cash flow statement.
- Maintain an appropriate emergency fund.

⑨ Next Steps

- Update personal financial statements.
- Begin an investment program for funding children's education and other long-term goals.
- Adapt your budget to changing household needs.

⑨ Later Steps

- Determine potential changes in daily spending needs during retirement.
- Consider increased savings and contributions to retirement plans.

> **YOUR** next step. . . select one or more of the items above and create an action plan to implement those financial planning activities.

SUMMARY OF LEARNING OBJECTIVES

LO3-1
Recognize relationships among financial documents and money management activities. Successful money management requires coordination among financial records, personal financial statements, and budgeting activities. A system for organizing personal financial documents is the foundation of effective money management. This system should provide ease of access as well as security for financial records that may be impossible to replace.

LO3-2
Develop a personal balance sheet and cash flow statement. A personal balance sheet, also known as a *net worth statement* or *statement of financial position,* is prepared by listing items of value (assets) and amounts owed to others (liabilities). The difference between the total assets and total liabilities is net worth. A cash flow statement, also called a *personal income and expenditure statement,* is a summary of cash receipts and payments for a given period,

such as a month or a year. This report provides data on your income and spending patterns.

LO3-3
Create and implement a budget. Budgeting activities involve four phases: (1) assessing your current personal and financial situation, (2) planning your financial direction by setting financial goals and creating budget allowances, (3) implementing your budget, and (4) evaluating your budgeting program.

LO3-4
Connect money management and savings activities to achieving financial goals. Saving goals should be based on your personal balance sheet, cash flow statement, and budget. Saving current income provides the basis for long-term financial security. Future value and present value calculations are used to compute the increased value of savings for achieving financial goals.

KEY TERMS

assets 89	deficit 100	money management 86
balance sheet 89	discretionary income 94	net worth 91
budget 96	income 92	safe deposit box 87
budget variance 100	insolvency 92	surplus 100
cash flow 92	liabilities 91	take-home pay 93
cash flow statement 92	liquid assets 90	
current liabilities 91	long-term liabilities 91	

KEY FORMULAS

Topic	Formula
Net worth	Net worth = Total assets − Total liabilities *Example* : = $125,000 − $53,000 = $72,000
Cash surplus (or deficit)	Cash surplus (or deficit) = Total inflows − Total outflows *Example* : = $5,600 − $4,970 = $630 (surplus)
Debt ratio	Debt ratio = Liabilities/Assets *Example* : = $7,000/$21,000 = 0.33

Topic	Formula
Current ratio	Current ratio = Liquid assets/Current liabilities *Example* :　　= $8,500/$4,500 　　　　　　　= 1.88
Liquidity ratio	Liquidity ratio = Liquid assets/Monthly expenses *Example* :　　= $8,500/$3,500 　　　　　　　= 2.4
Debt-payments ratio	Debt-payments ratio = Monthly credit payments/Take-home pay *Example* :　　　　= $760/$3,800 　　　　　　　　　= 0.20
Savings ratio	Savings ratio = Amount saved per month/Gross monthly income *Example* :　　= $460/$3,800 　　　　　　　= 0.12

SELF-TEST PROBLEMS

1. The Hamilton household has $145,000 in assets and $63,000 in liabilities. What is the family's net worth?

2. Aiko Sasaki budgeted $210 for food for the month of July. She spent $227 on food during July. Does she have a budget surplus or a deficit, and what amount?

Self-Test Solutions

1. Net worth is determined by assets ($145,000) minus liabilities ($63,000) resulting in $82,000.

2. The budget *deficit* of $17 is calculated by subtracting the actual spending ($227) from the budgeted amount ($210).

FINANCIAL PLANNING PROBLEMS

LO3-2 **1.** *Determining Liquid Assets and Current Liabilities.* Based on these items, what is the total of the (a) liquid assets and (b) current liabilities?

Checking account balance, $860　　　　　　Savings account balance, $2,675
Retirement account balance, $57,000　　　Current student loan payment due, $220
Credit card balance, $117　　　　　　　　Investment account balance, $8,000
Rare jewelry, $450　　　　　　　　　　　Mortgage, $178,000

LO3-2 **2.** *Calculating Balance Sheet Amounts.* Based on the following data, compute the total assets, total liabilities, and net worth.

Liquid assets, $4,670　　　　　　　　　Household assets, $93,780
Investment assets, $26,910　　　　　　　Long-term liabilities, $76,230
Current liabilities, $2,670

LO3-2 **3.** *Preparing a Personal Balance Sheet.* Use the following items to prepare a balance sheet and a cash flow statement. Determine the total assets, total liabilities, net worth, total cash inflows, and total cash outflows.

Rent for the month, $650　　　　　　　　Auto insurance, $230
Monthly take-home salary, $1,950　　　　　Household possessions, $3,400
Cash in checking account, $450　　　　　　Home entertainment system, $2,350
Savings account balance, $1,890　　　　　　Payment for electricity, $90
Spending for food, $345　　　　　　　　　Lunches/parking at work, $180
Balance of educational loan, $2,160　　　　Donations, $70
Current value of automobile, $7,800　　　　Computers, $1,500
Telephone bill paid for month, $65　　　　　Value of stock investment, $860
Credit card balance, $235　　　　　　　　Clothing purchase, $110
Loan payment, $80　　　　　　　　　　　Restaurant spending, $130

4. *Computing Balance Sheet Amounts.* For each of the following situations, compute the missing amount. **LO3-2**

    a. Assets $48,000; liabilities $12,800; net worth $_____.

    b. Assets $78,780; liabilities $_____; net worth $13,700.

    c. Assets $44,280; liabilities $12,265; net worth $_____.

    d. Assets $_____; liabilities $38,374; net worth $53,795.

5. *Calculating Financial Ratios.* The Fram family has liabilities of $128,000 and assets of $340,000. What is their debt ratio? **LO3-2** How would you assess this?

6. *Determining Financial Progress.* Carl Lester has liquid assets of $2,680 and current liabilities of $2,436. What is his current **LO3-2** ratio? What comments do you have about this financial position?

7. *Determining Budget Variances.* Fran Bowen created the following budget: **LO3-3**

    Food, $350   Clothing, $100

    Transportation, $320   Personal expenses and recreation, $275

    Housing, $950

    She actually spent $298 for food, $337 for transportation, $982 for housing, $134 for clothing, and $231 for personal expenses and recreation. Calculate the variance for each of these categories, and indicate whether it was a *deficit* or a *surplus.*

8. *Calculating the Effect of Inflation.* Bill and Sally Kaplan have an annual spending plan that amounts to $39,500. If inflation is **LO3-3** 3 percent a year for the next three years, what amount will the Kaplans need for their living expenses three years from now?

9. *Computing the Time Value of Money for Savings.* Use future value and present value calculations (see Chapter 1 Appendix) **LO3-4** to determine the following:

    a. The future value of a $400 savings deposit after eight years at an annual interest rate of 3 percent.

    b. The future value of saving $1,800 a year for five years at an annual interest rate of 4 percent.

    c. The present value of a $6,000 savings account that will earn 2 percent interest for four years.

10. *Calculating Present Value of a Savings Fund.* You want to establish a savings fund from which a community organiza- **LO3-4** tion could draw $1,000 a year for 20 years. If the account earns 2 percent, what amount would you have to deposit now to achieve this goal?

11. *Future Value of Reduced Spending.* Brenda plans to reduce her spending by $80 a month. Calculate the future value of this **LO3-4** increase in savings over the next 10 years. (Assume an annual deposit to her savings account and an annual interest rate of 4 percent.)

12. *Future Value of Savings.* Kara Delaney received a $3,000 gift for graduation from a relative. If she deposits the entire **LO3-4** amount in an account paying 3 percent, what will be the value of this gift in 15 years?

DIGITAL FINANCIAL LITERACY: BUDGETING APPS

While a written budget provides a tangible experience, many people use apps to guide their spending. In recent years, the most popular budget apps included YNAB, Mint, Personal Capital, EveryDollar, and Zeta. Some apps emphasize investing, while others help couples coordinate money management activities.

In addition to planning and monitoring spending, other features offered in budgeting apps include:

- Coordination of financial activities, such as account balances, bill tracking, and net worth.

- Financial advice and a visual summary of progress toward suggested financial goals.

- Detailed information on spending; accounting for every dollar (zero-based budgeting).

- Spending reminders with an option to adjust amounts among categories.

- Avoiding paycheck-to-paycheck living by only spending "aged" money (at least 30 days old).

- The ability to split transactions when out to eat, and to enter cash payment transactions.

An evaluation of budgeting apps will likely include the cost (some are free). This assessment might also consider the presence of ads for financial products appropriate to your personal situation, privacy controls, and security measures.

Action items:

1. (a) Locate online reviews for budget apps. (b) Talk to several people about their experiences with budget apps. What benefits and concerns are associated with these apps?

2. Prepare a summary response for a budget app review that might be posted online to guide others when using a budgeting app.

FINANCIAL PLANNING CASE

Adjusting the Budget

In a recent month, the Constantine family had a budget deficit, which is something they want to avoid so they do not have future financial difficulties. Jason and Karen Constantine and their children (ages 10 and 12) plan to discuss the situation after dinner this evening.

While at work, Jason was talking with his friend Ken Ruiz. Ken had been a regular saver since he was very young, starting with a small savings account. Those funds were then invested in stocks and mutual funds. While in college, Ken was able to pay for his education while continuing to save between $50 and $100 a month. He closely monitored his spending. Ken realized that the few dollars here and there for snacks and other minor purchases quickly add up.

Today, Ken works as a customer service manager for the online division of a retailing company. He lives with his wife and their two young children. The family's spending plan allows for all their needs and also includes regularly saving and investing for the children's education and for retirement.

Jason asked Ken, "How come you never seem to have financial stress in your household?"

Ken replied, "Do you know where your money is going each month?"

"Not really," was Jason's response.

"You'd be surprised by how much is spent on little things you might do without," Ken responded.

"I guess so. I just don't want to have to go around with a notebook writing down every amount I spend," Jason said in a troubled voice.

"Well, you have to take some action if you want your financial situation to change," Ken countered.

That evening, the Constantine family met to discuss their budget situation:

Current Spending		Suggested Budget	
Rent	$950	Rent	$ _____
Electricity, water	120	Electricity, water	_____
Telephone	55	Telephone	_____
Wifi service	125	Wifi service	_____
Food (at home)	385	Food (at home)	_____
Food (away)	230	Food (away)	_____
Auto payment	410	Auto payment	_____
Gas, oil changes	140	Gas, oil changes	_____
Insurance	125	Insurance	_____
Clothing	200	Clothing	_____
Personal, gifts	185	Personal, gifts	_____
Donations	50	Donations	_____
Savings	35	Savings	_____
Total spending	$3,010	Total budgeted	$ _____
Total monthly amount available	$2,800	Total monthly amount available	$2,800
Surplus (deficit)	($210)	Surplus (deficit)	$ _____

Questions

1. What situations might have created the budget deficit for the Constantine family?

2. What amounts would you suggest for the various categories for the family budget?

3. Describe additional actions for the Constantine family related to their: (a) SMART goals, (b) budgeting activities, (c) spending, and (d) saving.

YOUR PERSONAL FINANCIAL PLAN

PERSONAL FINANCIAL STATEMENTS AND A SPENDING PLAN

Money management activities are the foundation for other financial planning actions. Creation of a financial document filing system, a personal balance sheet, a cash flow statement, and a budget provide you with tools for setting, implementing, and achieving financial goals.

Your Short-Term Financial Planning Activity

Task Create a system for financial documents and develop personal financial statements.

Research

1) Based on PFP Sheet 14, propose a filing system to organize your financial records and documents.

2) Using PFP Sheet 15 and 16 or a similar format, create a personal balance sheet and a personal cash flow statement for your current situation.

3) Considering your current situation, use PFP Sheets 17 and 18 to develop a budget and monitor your spending plan

Outcome Add these documents and files to your portfolio or to your Personal Financial Plan online folder.

Your Long-Term Financial Planning Activity

Task Plan long-term savings activities.

Research

1) As needed, use PFP Sheet 19 to plan long-term financial goals related to education.

2) Assess your current emergency fund. Develop a plan, such as automatic withdrawals, to increase your emergency fund and to achieve long-term financial goals.

Outcome Prepare an audio or written summary of your proposed actions for increased savings. What factors are creating any limitations for savings to achieve your financial goals?

Note: All *Personal Financial Planner* sheets are available at the end of the book and in an Excel spreadsheet format in *Connect Finance.*

CONTINUING CASE

Money Management Strategy: Financial Statements and Budgeting

Jamie Lee Jackson, age 25, a busy full-time student and part-time bakery clerk, has been trying to organize her priorities, including her budget. She has been wondering if she is allocating enough of her income toward savings to accumulate the $9,000 down payment she needs to achieve her dream of opening a cupcake café.

Jamie Lee has been making regular deposits to her regular and emergency savings accounts. She would really like to have a clearer picture of how much she is spending on various expenses, including rent, utilities, and entertainment, and how her debt compares to her savings and assets. She realizes that she must stay on track and keep a detailed budget if she is to realize her dream of being self-employed after college.

Current Financial Situation

Assets:
Checking account: $1,250
Emergency fund savings account: $3,100
Car: $4,000
Liabilities:
Student loan: $5,400
Credit card balance: $400
Income:
Gross monthly salary: $2,125
Net monthly salary: $1,560
Monthly Expenses:
Rent obligation: $275
Utilities obligation: $125

Food: $120
Gas/maintenance: $100
Credit card payment: $50
Savings:
Regular savings: $150
Rainy day savings: $25
Entertainment:
Cake decorating class: $35
Movies with friends: $50

Questions

1. According to the text, a *personal balance sheet* is a statement of your net worth. It reports what you own and what you owe. Using the information provided, prepare a personal balance sheet for Jamie Lee.

2. Using the table found in Ratios for Evaluating Financial Progress, what is Jamie Lee's debt ratio? When comparing Jamie Lee's liabilities and her net worth, is the relationship a favorable one?

3. Using the table found in Ratios for Evaluating Financial Progress, what is Jamie Lee's savings ratio? Using the rule of thumb recommended by financial experts, is she saving enough?

4. Using Exhibit 3-8, "Typical After-Tax Budget Allocations for Different Life Situations," calculate the budget allocations for Jamie Lee, using her net monthly salary (or after-tax salary) amount. Is she within the recommended parameters for a student?

 # DAILY SPENDING DIARY

"I am amazed how little things can add up. However, since I started keeping track of all my spending, I realized that I need to cut down on some items so I can put some money into savings."

Directions

Continue or start using the *Daily Spending Diary* sheets, or create your own format, to record *every cent* of your spending in the categories provided. This experience will help you better understand your spending patterns and help you achieve financial goals.

Analysis Questions

1. What information from your *Daily Spending Diary* might encourage you to reconsider various money management actions?

2. How can your *Daily Spending Diary* assist you when planning and implementing a budget?

A *Daily Spending Diary* sheet is located at the end of Chapter 1 and on the library resource site within *Connect.*

Money Management Information Sources and Advisors

While this book offers a foundation for successful financial planning, changing social trends, economic conditions, and technology will influence your future decisions. An ability to update your knowledge and skills will serve you for a lifetime. Many resources are available to assist.

Online Resources

Exhibit 3-A lists online personal finance publications and websites available to expand and update your knowledge.

Personal finance is constantly changing. Keep up with new developments with the following:

The Balance	www.thebalance.com
Bankrate	www.bankrate.com
Consumer Protection	www.consumer.gov
Consumer Reports	www.consumerreports.org
F.D.I.C.	www.fdic.gov/consumers
Federal Reserve System	www.federalreserve.gov
Financial Times	www.ft.com
Forbes	www.forbes.com
Fortune	www.fortune.com
Investopedia	www.investopedia.com
Kiplinger's Personal Finance	www.kiplinger.com
Money	www.money.com
My Money	www.mymoney.gov
Money Wise	www.moneywise.com
The Motley Fool	www.fool.com
Nerd Wallet	www.nerdwallet.com
U.S. News & World Report	money.usnews.com
The Wall Street Journal	www.wsj.com

EXHIBIT 3-A

Personal finance publications and websites

Financial Institutions

Financial advisors, such as insurance agents and investment brokers, are usually connected with financial service companies. Through marketing and promotions, banks, credit unions, insurance companies, investment brokers, and real estate offices offer suggestions on budgeting, saving, investing, and other financial planning topics. These organizations frequently offer financial planning webinars, publications, and online information.

Courses and Seminars

Colleges and universities offer courses in investments, real estate, insurance, taxes, and estate planning. The Cooperative Extension Service, funded through the U.S. Department of Agriculture, has offices in every state offering community seminars and classes on money management, housing, wise buying, health care, and food and nutrition. Libraries and community organizations sponsor free or low-cost programs on career planning, small-business management, budgeting, life insurance, tax return preparation, and investments. Free online courses, webinars, and videos are a valuable source of financial planning assistance.

Personal Finance Software and Apps

Computer software and apps can guide your personal financial planning. These programs analyze your current financial situation and project your future financial position. Specialized programs are also available for conducting investment analyses, preparing tax returns, and determining housing costs. Remember, an app cannot change your saving, spending, and borrowing habits; only *you* can do that. However, your mobile device can provide information for wiser financial decisions.

A spreadsheet program, such as Excel, can assist with financial planning tasks. Spreadsheets may be used for activities such as tracking spending, budgeting, maintaining tax records, monitoring investment values, creating a home inventory, and projecting needed amounts of life insurance and retirement income. An online search for "personal finance spreadsheets" can help you locate ready-to-use templates. Excel templates are available for each of the *Personal Financial Planner sheets* on the library resource site in *Connect.*

Financial Planning Specialists

Several professionals are available to provide specific financial assistance and advice:

- *Accountants* specialize in tax matters and personal financial statements.
- *Bankers* assist with financial services and trusts.
- *Certified financial planners* coordinate financial decisions into a single plan.
- *Credit counselors* suggest ways to reduce spending and eliminate credit problems.
- *Insurance agents* sell insurance coverage to protect your wealth and property.
- *Investment brokers* provide information and handle transactions for stocks, bonds, and other investments.
- *Lawyers* help with wills, estate planning, tax problems, and other legal matters.
- *Real estate agents* assist with buying and selling a home or other real estate.
- *Tax preparers* specialize in completing income tax returns and other tax matters.

Most specialists offer several financial planning services. The background and company of financial planners indicate their area of expertise. An accountant is likely to be most knowledgeable about tax laws, while an insurance representative will likely emphasize insurance for achieving financial goals.

WHO ARE THE FINANCIAL PLANNERS?

Many financial planners represent major insurance companies or investment businesses. Financial planners may also be individuals whose primary profession is tax accounting, real estate, or law. Over 200,000 people work as financial planners; they are commonly categorized based on four methods of compensation:

1. **Fee-only planners** charge an hourly rate from $150 to $400, or a fixed fee of about $500 to several thousand dollars. Other fee-only planners charge an annual fee from .25 percent to 1 percent of the value of assets being managed.

2. **Fee-offset planners** start with an hourly fee or annual fee. This charge is reduced by commissions earned from the sale of investments or insurance.

3. **Fee-and-commission planners** earn commissions from investment and insurance sales and charge a fixed fee (ranging from $250 to $2,000) for a financial plan.

4. **Commission-only planners** receive their income from commissions on sales of insurance, mutual funds, and other investments.

While fee-based planners are usually recommended, be cautious about the fees charged and how these fees are communicated. Studies reveal that financial planners who say they are "fee-only" may earn commissions or other financial rewards for recommendations made to clients.

DO YOU NEED A FINANCIAL PLANNER?

The two main factors that determine whether you need financial planning assistance are (1) your income and (2) your willingness to make independent decisions. If you earn less than $50,000 a year, you probably do not need a financial planner. An income of less than that amount does not allow for many major financial decisions once you have planned for spending, savings, insurance, and taxes.

Your willingness to keep up to date on investments, insurance, and tax laws reduces the need for a financial planner. These actions require an ongoing investment of time and effort; however, it will enable you to control your own financial direction.

When deciding whether to use a financial planner, also consider the services provided. First, the financial planner should assist you in assessing your current financial position. Second, the financial planner should offer a clear plan with different courses of action. Third, the planner should discuss the components of the plan and help you monitor your financial progress. Finally, the financial planner should guide you to other experts and sources of financial services as needed.

personal fintech

Robo-financial advisors are automated programs that guide financial planning. These online financial planners may be completely autonomous, or they may be combined with human assistance. The process starts by responding to questions related to income, assets, debt, goals, and risk tolerance. Then, computer algorithms suggest actions for your investment portfolio and financial plan. Digital advisors have lower fees than other financial planners and can be a good starting point for people with uncomplicated finances. Before using a robo-advisor, conduct research regarding fees, types of advice, and services available to meet your financial needs and personal goals. Search online for additional advice on selecting a robo-advisor.

HOW SHOULD YOU SELECT A FINANCIAL PLANNER?

You can locate a financial planner with an online search, or obtain references from friends, business associates, or professionals with whom you currently do business, such as insurance agents or real estate brokers.

When evaluating a financial planner, ask the following:

- Is financial planning your primary activity? What are your other business activities?
- Are you licensed as an investment broker or as a seller of life insurance?
- What is your educational background and formal training?
- What are your areas of expertise?
- Do you use experts in other areas, such as taxes, law, or insurance, to assist you with financial planning recommendations?
- What professional titles and certifications do you possess?
- Am I allowed a free initial consultation?
- How is the fee determined? (Is this an amount I can afford?)
- Do you have an independent practice, or are you affiliated with a major company?
- What are sample insurance, tax, and investment recommendations you make for clients?
- My major concern is _____. What would you suggest?
- May I see a sample of a written financial plan?
- May I see the contract you use with clients?
- Who are some of your clients whom I might contact?
- Are you a *fiduciary* (acting in my best interest)?

Make sure you are comfortable with the planner and can clearly communicate desired information. This type of investigation takes time and effort; however, remember you are considering placing your entire financial future with one person.

Most financial planning professionals have a code of ethics, but not all abide by these principles. To avoid financial difficulties and potential fraud, make sure your financial planner strictly applies industry policies regarding confidentiality, integrity, and objectivity to prevent a conflict of interest, and has a commitment to continuing education.

A *fiduciary* is a financial professional who has the legal obligation to put you first with recommendations made in your best interest. Fiduciary financial advisors must disclose conflicts of interest, execute investment trades at the best possible price, and provide the best possible advice for your financial goals. In contrast to a fiduciary, a financial advisor may operate using a *suitability* standard, meaning the advice given would be relevant for you, but not necessarily in your best interest. Fee-only advisors act as a fiduciary.

Financial advisors who work for registered firms are usually fiduciaries. They usually charge a flat fee or a small percentage of the portfolio value. This arrangement reduces potential conflicts of interest.

HOW ARE FINANCIAL PLANNERS CERTIFIED?

While state and federal regulation of financial planners exists, the requirements for becoming a financial planner vary from state to state. Some states license individual investment advisors; other states license firms but not individual advisors. A few states regulate neither individual advisors nor firms. Federal regulation requires that the Securities and Exchange Commission (SEC) monitor the largest financial advisors.

Many financial planners use abbreviations for the certifications they have earned. Some of these abbreviations are quite familiar, for example, CPA (certified public accountant), JD (doctor of law), and MBA (master of business administration). Others include:

- CFP—Certified Financial Planners have expertise in insurance, investments, taxation, employee benefits, retirement, and estate planning.
- ChFC—Chartered Financial Consultants are trained in the areas of finance, insurance, and investing.

- CFA—Chartered Financial Analysts have focused training in portfolio management and security analysis.
- RIA—Registered Investment Advisors provide investment advice and are registered with the SEC or a state securities agency.
- EA—Enrolled Agents are tax specialists certified by the Internal Revenue Service.
- RFC—Registered Financial Consultants have training in insurance, investments, taxes, and estate planning.
- AEP—Accredited Estate Planners emphasize wills, trusts, and estate taxes.
- CRP—Certified Retirement Planners address long-term financial planning activities.
- AICPA PFP—Personal Financial Planning Specialists are certified public accountants with additional financial planning training.
- AFC—Accredited Financial Counselors are certified by the Association for Financial Counseling and Planning Education.
- CEBS—Certified Employee Benefit Specialists sell and administer employee benefits with emphasis on insurance, pensions, and related topics.
- CMFC—Chartered Mutual Fund Counselors provide advice related to mutual funds and related investment vehicles.

Additional information on these and other financial planning designations may be obtained with an online search of these certifications.

While credentials provide some assurance of expertise, not all planners are licensed. The Federal Trade Commission estimates that fraudulent planners cost consumers tens of millions of dollars in bad investments and poor advice each year. Financial planning activities such as insurance and investment security sales are closely regulated. Be wary, and carefully investigate any financial planning action you are considering.

Contact these organizations and agencies for further information about certification and regulation of financial planners:

- American Institute of Certified Public Accountants at (www.aicpa.org).
- Certified Financial Planners Board of Standards at 1-800-487-1497 (www.cfp.net).
- Financial Industry Regulatory Authority at 1-301-590-6500 (www.finra.org).
- Financial Planning Association at 1-800-322-4237 (www.fpanet.org).
- National Association of Insurance Commissioners at 1-202-471-3990 (www.naic.org).
- National Association of Personal Financial Advisors at 1-888-333-6659 (www.napfa.org).
- North American Securities Administrators Association at 1-202-737-0900 (www.nasaa.org).
- Securities and Exchange Commission at 1-800-732-0330 (www.sec.gov).

The financial planning industry offers varied career opportunities. If you have an aptitude for analyzing financial data along with an ability to connect with people, you might consider this career field. Go to the websites above or search "careers in financial planning" for addition information.

4 Planning Your Tax Strategy

LEARNING OBJECTIVES

LO4-1 Describe the importance of taxes for personal financial planning.

LO4-2 Calculate taxable income and the amount owed for federal income tax.

LO4-3 Prepare a federal income tax return.

LO4-4 Identify tax assistance sources.

LO4-5 Select appropriate tax strategies for various financial and personal situations.

Shutterstock

Financial Literacy
IN YOUR LIFE

▶ **What if you . . .** receive a large tax refund each year? Or owe a large amount each year? Monitoring your tax withholding and adjusting estimated payments is important for effective personal financial planning. What actions would you take?

You might . . . make adjustments if there are changes in the size of your family, if you have multiple sources of income, or if you have a large amount of tax deductions to offset income.

Now, what would you do? Review your allowances selected through your employer and adjust accordingly. You should continue to monitor your tax situation annually as well as throughout the year if significant income or deductions occur. You will be able to monitor your progress using the Your Personal Finance Roadmap and Dashboard feature at the end of the chapter.

---

my life | PAY ONLY YOUR FAIR SHARE

Taxes are often viewed as a confusing aspect of personal financial planning. However, with a little effort, the basic elements of taxes can be understood.

THE MAIN FOCUS

The main focus when planning and paying your taxes is to pay your fair share based on current tax laws. What action do you commonly take regarding taxes? For each of the following statements, select Agree or Disagree to indicate your personal response regarding these tax-planning activities.

1. I have a good knowledge of the various taxes paid in our society.	Agree	Disagree
2. My tax records are organized to allow me to easily find needed information.	Agree	Disagree
3. I am able to file my taxes on time each year.	Agree	Disagree
4. My tax returns have never been questioned by the Internal Revenue Service.	Agree	Disagree
5. I stay informed on proposed tax changes being considered for my current tax filing status.	Agree	Disagree

As you study this chapter, you will encounter "My Life" boxes with additional information and resources related to these items.

Taxes and Financial Planning

Taxes are an everyday financial fact of life. You pay some taxes every time you get a paycheck or make a purchase. However, most people concern themselves with taxes only in April. With about one-third of each dollar you earn going to taxes, an effective tax strategy is vital for successful financial planning. Understanding tax rules and regulations can help you reduce your tax liability.

Taxes are a significant factor in financial planning. Each year, the Tax Foundation determines how long the average person works to pay taxes. In recent years, "Tax Freedom Day" came in mid-April. This means that the time people worked from January 1 until mid-April represents the portion of the year worked to pay their taxes.

LO4-1

Describe the importance of taxes for personal financial planning.

smart money minute

This financial obligation includes the many types of taxes discussed later in this section. To help you cope with these taxes, common goals related to tax planning include:

- Knowing the current tax laws and regulations that affect you.
- Maintaining complete and appropriate tax records.
- Making purchase and investment decisions that can reduce your tax liability.

Target your tax planning efforts toward paying your fair share of taxes while taking advantage of tax benefits appropriate to your personal and financial situation.

The principal purpose of taxes is to finance government activities. As citizens, we expect government to provide services such as police and fire protection, schools, road maintenance, parks and libraries, and safety inspection of food, drugs, and other products. Most people pay taxes in four major categories: taxes on purchases, taxes on property, taxes on wealth, and taxes on earnings.

excise tax A tax imposed on specific goods and services, such as gasoline, cigarettes, alcoholic beverages, tires, and air travel.

estate tax A tax imposed on the value of a person's property at the time of his or her death.

inheritance tax A tax levied on the value of property bequeathed by a deceased person.

TAXES ON PURCHASES

You probably pay *sales tax* on many of your purchases. This state and local tax is added to the purchase price of products. Many states exempt food and drugs from sales tax to reduce the economic burden of this tax on the poor. In recent years, all but five states (Alaska, Delaware, Montana, New Hampshire, and Oregon) have had a general sales tax. An **excise tax** is imposed by the federal and state governments on specific goods and services, such as gasoline, cigarettes, alcoholic beverages, tires, air travel, and telephone service.

TAXES ON PROPERTY

Real estate property tax is a major source of revenue for local governments. This tax is based on the value of land and buildings. The increasing amount of real estate property taxes is a major concern of homeowners. Retired people with limited pension incomes may encounter financial difficulties if local property taxes increase rapidly.

Some areas also impose *personal property taxes.* State and local governments may assess taxes on the value of automobiles, boats, furniture, and farm equipment.

TAXES ON WEALTH

An **estate tax** is imposed on the value of a person's property at the time of his or her death. This federal tax is based on the fair market value of the deceased individual's investments, property, and bank accounts less allowable deductions and other taxes. Estate taxes are discussed in greater detail in Chapter 19.

Real estate property taxes are the major revenue source for local government.
Artashes/Shutterstock

Money and property passed on to heirs may also be subject to a state tax. An **inheritance tax** is levied on the value of property bequeathed by a deceased person. This tax is paid for the right to acquire the inherited property.

For 2021, individuals are allowed to give money or items valued at $15,000 or less in a year to a person without being subject to taxes. Gift amounts greater than $15,000 may be subject to federal tax. Amounts given for the payment of tuition or medical expenses are not subject to federal gift taxes. Some states impose a gift tax on amounts that a person, before his or her death, transfers to another person, because the action may have been intended to avoid estate and inheritance taxes.

TAXES ON EARNINGS

The two main taxes on wages and salaries are Social Security and income taxes. The Federal Insurance Contributions Act (FICA) created the Social Security tax to fund the old-age, survivors, and disability insurance portion of the Social Security system and the hospital insurance portion (Medicare). Chapters 11 and 18 discuss various aspects of Social Security.

Income tax is a major financial planning factor for most people. Some workers are subject to federal, state, and local income taxes. Currently, nine states do not have a state income tax.

I have a good working knowledge of the various taxes paid in our society.

Prepare a list of the various taxes you pay in our society. This list might include fees and charges associated with various licenses and government services.

Throughout the year, your employer will withhold income tax payments from your paycheck, or you may be required to make estimated tax payments if you own your own business. Both types of payments are only estimates of your income taxes. When you file your tax return for the year, you may need to pay an additional amount or you may get a refund. The following sections will assist you in preparing your federal income tax return and planning your future tax strategies.

 PRACTICE QUIZ 4-1

1. How should you consider taxes in your financial planning?
2. What types of taxes do people often overlook when making financial decisions?

Income Tax Fundamentals

On December 22, 2017, the Tax Cuts and Jobs Act (TCJA) was signed into law. It included reductions in tax rates for individuals, larger standard deductions for all taxpayers, and limits to other more commonly used deductions (for example, mortgage interest and state and local taxes). These changes have been incorporated into this chapter. It is important to note that many of the changes are not considered permanent and could expire on December 31, 2025, if not extended.

The starting point for preparing your taxes is proper documentation. You are required to keep records to document tax deductions. Maintaining an organized system that allows you to quickly access this documentation is essential. Later, we will discuss how long you should keep these documents and will recommend ways to create an organized system.

Each year, millions of Americans are required to pay their share of income taxes to the federal government. The process involves computing taxable income, determining the amount of income tax owed, and comparing this amount with the income tax payments withheld or made during the year.

STEP 1: DETERMINING ADJUSTED GROSS INCOME

Taxable income is the net amount of income, after allowable deductions, on which income tax is computed. Exhibit 4-1 presents the components of taxable income and the process used to compute it.

TYPES OF INCOME Most, but not all, income is subject to taxation. Your gross, or total, income can consist of three main components:

1. **Earned income** is money received for personal effort. Earned income is usually in the form of wages, salary, commission, fees, tips, or bonuses.
2. **Investment income** (sometimes referred to as *portfolio income*) is money received in the form of dividends, interest, or rent from investments.

LO4-2

Calculate taxable income and the amount owed for federal income tax.

taxable income The net amount of income, after allowable deductions, on which income tax is computed.

earned income Money received for personal effort, such as wages, salary, commission, fees, tips, or bonuses.

investment income Money received in the form of dividends, interest, or rent from investments. Also called *portfolio income*.

EXHIBIT 4-1 Computing taxable income and your tax liability

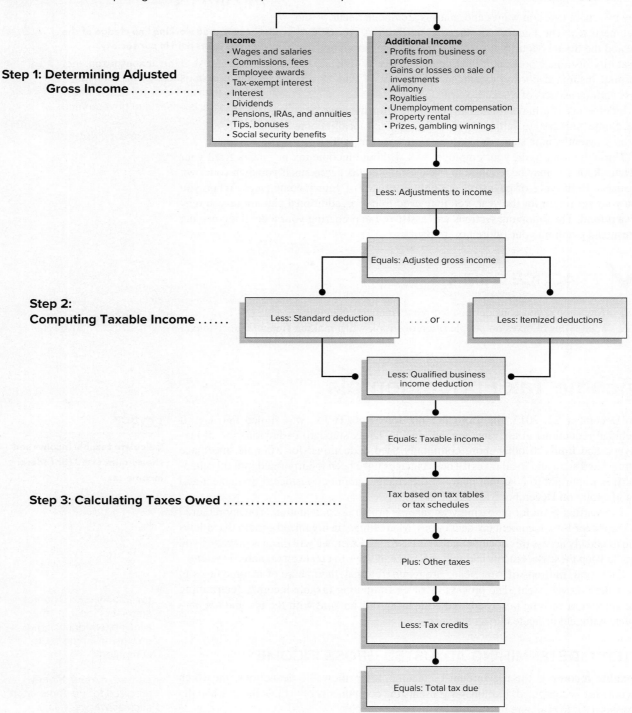

**Step 1: Determining Adjusted
Gross Income** . . . .

Income
- Wages and salaries
- Commissions, fees
- Employee awards
- Tax-exempt interest
- Interest
- Dividends
- Pensions, IRAs, and annuities
- Tips, bonuses
- Social security benefits

Additional Income
- Profits from business or profession
- Gains or losses on sale of investments
- Alimony
- Royalties
- Unemployment compensation
- Property rental
- Prizes, gambling winnings

Less: Adjustments to income

Equals: Adjusted gross income

**Step 2:
Computing Taxable Income** . . . . . .

Less: Standard deduction   . . . . or . . . .   Less: Itemized deductions

Less: Qualified business income deduction

Equals: Taxable income

Step 3: Calculating Taxes Owed . . . .

Tax based on tax tables or tax schedules

Plus: Other taxes

Less: Tax credits

Equals: Total tax due

passive income Income resulting from business activities in which you do not actively participate.

3. Passive income results from business activities in which you do not actively participate, such as a limited partnership.

Other types of income subject to federal income tax include alimony, awards, lottery winnings, and prizes. James Holzhauer won $2,462,216 in 33 appearances on "Jeopardy." Contestants are required to pay California tax (even if they are not California residents). After paying federal and state tax of 47.6 percent his net earnings were $1,290,201. For game shows that have prizes, like cars or fancy coffee makers, many contestants forfeit their prizes to avoid paying taxes on their inflated retail values.

Total income is also affected by exclusions. An **exclusion** is an amount not included in gross income. For example, the foreign earned income exclusion allows U.S. citizens working and living in another country to exclude a certain portion ($108,700, as of 2021) of their incomes from federal income taxes.

Exclusions are also referred to as **tax-exempt income,** or income that is not subject to tax. For example, interest earned on most state and city bonds is exempt from federal income tax. **Tax-deferred income** is income that will be taxed at a later date. The earnings on an individual retirement account (IRA) are an example of tax-deferred income. While these earnings are credited to the account now, you do not pay taxes on them until you withdraw them from the account.

ADJUSTMENTS TO INCOME   **Adjusted gross income (AGI)** is gross income after certain additions and reductions have been made. Additions may be rental income or business profits. Reductions, called *adjustments to income,* include contributions to an IRA or a Keogh retirement plan, penalties for early withdrawal of savings, and alimony payments (if deductible). Adjusted gross income is used as the basis for computing various income tax deductions, such as medical expenses.

Certain adjustments to income, such as tax-deferred retirement plans, are a type of tax shelter. **Tax shelters** are investments that provide immediate tax benefits and a reasonable expectation of a future financial return. In recent years, tax court rulings and changes in the tax code have disallowed various types of tax shelters that were considered excessive.

STEP 2: COMPUTING TAXABLE INCOME

DEDUCTIONS   A **tax deduction** is an amount subtracted from adjusted gross income to arrive at taxable income. Every taxpayer receives at least the **standard deduction,** a set amount on which no taxes are paid. As of 2021, single people receive a standard deduction of $12,550 (married couples filing jointly receive $25,100). Blind people and individuals 65 and older receive higher standard deductions.

Some people qualify for more than the standard deduction. **Itemized deductions** are expenses a taxpayer is allowed to deduct from adjusted gross income. Common itemized deductions include the following:

- *Medical and dental expenses,* including doctors' fees, prescription medications, hospital expenses, medical insurance premiums, hearing aids, eyeglasses, and medical travel that has not been reimbursed or paid by others. This deduction is equal to the amount by which the medical and dental expenses exceed 7.5 percent of adjusted gross income. If your AGI is $60,000, for example, you must have more than $4,500 ($60,000 x 7.5 percent) in unreimbursed medical and dental expenses before you can claim this deduction. If your medical and dental bills amount to $6,000, you qualify for a $1,500 deduction. *Note:* The 7.5 percent threshold has varied over the last decade between 7.5 and 10 percent, depending on the tax year. Most recently, the 7.5 percent threshold was voted to be permanent for the foreseeable future.

- *Taxes*—state and local income tax, real estate property tax, and state or local personal property tax. This deduction has been limited to $10,000 beginning with the 2018 tax year. You may also deduct an amount for state sales tax instead of your state income tax, whichever is larger—but not both. This deduction will benefit taxpayers in the seven states without a state income tax. Sales tax deductions are not capped at $10,000.

- *Interest*—mortgage interest (up to $750,000 loan limit), home equity loan interest (up to $100,000, if used for the home), and investment interest expense up to an amount equal to investment income.

- *Contributions* of cash or property to qualified charitable organizations. Contribution totals greater than 20 percent of adjusted gross income are subject to limitations.

---

exclusion An amount not included in gross income.

tax-exempt income Income that is not subject to tax.

tax-deferred income Income that will be taxed at a later date.

adjusted gross income (AGI) Gross income reduced by certain adjustments, such as contributions to an individual retirement account (IRA) and alimony payments.

tax shelter An investment that provides immediate tax benefits and a reasonable expectation of a future financial return.

tax deduction An amount subtracted from adjusted gross income to arrive at taxable income.

standard deduction A set amount on which no taxes are paid.

itemized deductions Expenses that can be deducted from adjusted gross income, such as medical expenses, real estate property taxes, home mortgage interest, charitable contributions, casualty losses, and certain work-related expenses

Financial Literacy for My Life

IS IT TAXABLE INCOME? IS IT DEDUCTIBLE?

Certain financial benefits individuals receive are not subject to federal income tax. Indicate whether each of the following items would or would not be included in taxable income when you compute your federal income tax.

Indicate whether each of the following items would or would not be deductible when you compute your federal income tax.

Is it taxable income?	Yes	No
1. Lottery/Jackpot winnings	___	___
2. Child support received	___	___
3. Worker's compensation benefits	___	___
4. Life insurance death benefits	___	___
5. Cash rebate for laptop	___	___
6. Unemployment income	___	___

Is it deductible?	Yes	No
7. Life insurance premiums	___	___
8. Baggage fees for self-employed	___	___
9. Fees for traffic violations	___	___
10. Mileage for driving to volunteer work	___	___
11. An attorney's fee for preparing a will	___	___
12. Income tax preparation fee	___	___

Note: These taxable income items and deductions are based on the 2018 tax year and may change due to changes in the tax code.

Answers: 1, 6, 8, 10—yes; 2, 3, 4, 5, 7, 9, 11, 12—no.

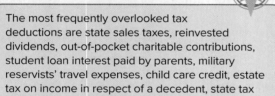

smart money minute

The most frequently overlooked tax deductions are state sales taxes, reinvested dividends, out-of-pocket charitable contributions, student loan interest paid by parents, military reservists' travel expenses, child care credit, estate tax on income in respect of a decedent, state tax you paid last spring, refinancing points, and jury pay paid to employer.

- *Casualty and theft losses*—financial losses resulting from federally declared disasters only (as of 2018). Deductions are for the amount exceeding 10 percent of AGI, less $100, for losses *not* reimbursed by an insurance company or other source. (California residents commonly report casualty losses due to earthquake damage.)

- *Moving expenses* deductions are only available to active duty military servicepersons for those who have a permanent change in duty station for tax years 2018 and beyond. Deductible moving expenses include only the cost of transporting the taxpayer and household members and the cost of moving household goods and personal property. (*Note:* Some states may still allow deductions for moving expenses for non-military taxpayers.)

- *Job-related and other miscellaneous expenses* such as unreimbursed job travel, union dues, required continuing education, work clothes or uniforms, investment expenses, tax preparation fees, and safe deposit box rental (for storing investment documents). The total of these expenses must exceed 2 percent of adjusted gross income to qualify as a deduction. The TCJA eliminated these deductions, starting with the 2018 tax year.

The standard deduction *or* total itemized deductions are subtracted from adjusted gross income to obtain your taxable income. In past years, there was a limitation on itemized deductions for high-income taxpayers. The TCJA removed the limitation, starting with the 2018 tax year.

Financial advisors recommend a filing system (see Exhibit 4-2) for organizing receipts and other tax documents. Canceled checks (or electronic copies of checks) can serve as proof of payment for such deductions as charitable contributions and medical expenses.

EXHIBIT 4-2 A tax recordkeeping system

Tax Forms and Tax Filing Information	Income Records	Expense Records
☐ Current tax forms and instruction booklets (or printouts) ☐ Reference books on current tax laws and tax-saving techniques ☐ Social Security numbers of household members ☐ Copies of federal tax returns from previous years	☐ W-2 forms reporting salary, wages, and taxes withheld ☐ W-2P forms reporting pension income ☐ 1099 forms reporting interest, dividends, and capital gains and losses from savings and investments ☐ 1099 forms for self-employment income, royalty income, unemployment, state refunds, and lump-sum payments from pension or retirement plans	☐ Receipts for medical, dependent care, charitable donations, and job-related expenses ☐ Mortgage interest (Form 1098) and other deductible interest ☐ Business, investment, and rental-property expense documents

Generally, you should keep tax records for three years from the date you file your return. However, you may be held responsible for providing back documentation up to seven years. This means keep documentation from tax year 2021, which is filed in 2022, until 2029. Records such as copies of past tax returns and home ownership documents should be kept indefinitely.

EXEMPTIONS For tax years prior to 2018, an **exemption** was allowed as a deduction from adjusted gross income for yourself, your spouse, and qualified dependents. These were eliminated with the TCJA and the standard deductions were increased significantly instead.

my life 2

My tax records are organized to allow me to easily find needed information.

To assist you in organizing your tax records, you need to be aware of what is taxable income and what is deductible. See the *Financial Literacy for My Life: Is It Taxable Income? Is It Deductible?* feature.

EXAMPLE: Taxable Income

Calculating taxable income involves the following steps:

1	Gross income (wages, profits, dividends, interest, other income)	$ 81,050
2	Less: Adjustments to income (retirement plan contributions)	− $ 4,500
3	Equals: Adjusted gross income	= $ 76,550
4	Less: Itemized deductions (or standard deduction)	− $ 25,100
5	Less: Qualified business income deduction	− $ 10,100
6	Equals: Taxable income	= $ 41,350

Qualified Business Income To provide a benefit to small business owners, a provision called Section 199A permits owners of sole proprietorships, S corporations, or partnerships to deduct up to 20 percent of the income earned by the business from their individual return to arrive at taxable income.

exemption A deduction from adjusted gross income for yourself, your spouse, and qualified dependents that is no longer allowed.

STEP 3: CALCULATING TAXES OWED

Your taxable income is the basis for computing the amount of your income tax. The use of tax rates and the benefits of tax credits are the final phase of the tax computation process.

TAX RATES   Use your taxable income in conjunction with the appropriate tax table or tax schedule. For several years previous to 1987, there were 14 tax rates, ranging from 11 to 50 percent. For 2021, the seven-rate system for federal income tax was as follows:

Rate on Taxable Income	Single Taxpayers	Married Taxpayers Filing Jointly	Head of Households
10%	Up to $9,950	Up to $19,900	Up to $14,200
12	$9,951–$40,525	$19,901–$81,050	$14,201–$54,200
22	$40,526–$86,375	$81,051–$172,750	$54,201–$86,350
24	$86,376–$164,925	$172,751–$329,850	$86,351–$164,900
32	$164,926–$209,425	329,851–418,850	$164,901–$209,400
35	$209,426–$523,600	$418,851–$628,300	$209,401–$523,600
37	$523,601 +	$628,301 +	$523,601+

A separate tax rate schedule exists for married persons who file separate income tax returns.

The 10, 12, 22, 24, 32, 35, and 37 percent rates are referred to as **marginal tax rates.** These rates are used to calculate tax on the last (and next) dollar of taxable income. After adjustments and deductions, a person in the 22 percent tax bracket pays 22 cents on their last dollar of taxable income in that bracket.

marginal tax rate The rate used to calculate tax on the last (and next) dollar of taxable income.

CALCULATING YOUR TAX   Each of the tax rates represents a range of income levels. These are often referred to as *brackets*. To calculate the tax on a specific amount of income, you must calculate the tax from each of the brackets as you progress up to your taxable income. (*Note:* This is the tax calculated prior to additional credits or other taxes, such as self-employment tax.)

The diagram below illustrates the calculation of the income tax due if your filing status is *Married Filing Jointly* and you have a taxable income of $95,000. You and your spouse are in the 22 percent tax bracket. This means you will pay tax at rates of 10, 12, and 22 percent. Although most computer programs will automatically calculate the tax owed, it is helpful to understand the process to calculate the tax due. (*Note:* For this assumption, we will assume that there is no other income at different rates, such as capital gains.)

Tax Due for Married Filing Jointly ($95,000 taxable income)

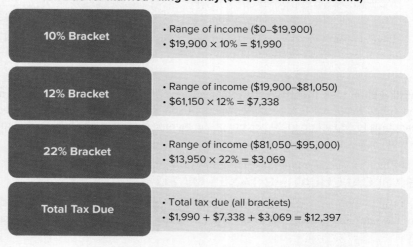

10% Bracket	• Range of income ($0–$19,900) • $19,900 × 10% = $1,990
12% Bracket	• Range of income ($19,900–$81,050) • $61,150 × 12% = $7,338
22% Bracket	• Range of income ($81,050–$95,000) • $13,950 × 22% = $3,069
Total Tax Due	• Total tax due (all brackets) • $1,990 + $7,338 + $3,069 = $12,397

In contrast, the **average tax rate** is based on the total tax due divided by taxable income. Except for taxpayers in the 10 percent bracket, this rate is less than a person's marginal tax rate. For example, a single person with taxable income of $40,000 and a total tax bill of $4,601 would have an *average tax rate* of 11.50 percent ($4,601 ÷ $40,000). Self-employed people are likely to have a higher average tax rate due to self-employment taxes, which include payments toward future Social Security benefits.

Taxpayers with high amounts of certain deductions and various types of income may be subject to an additional tax. The *alternative minimum tax (AMT)* is designed to ensure that those who receive tax breaks also pay their fair share of taxes. The AMT was originally designed to prevent those with high incomes from using special tax breaks to pay little in taxes. Some of these special tax breaks that can result in a person paying the AMT include high levels of deductions for state and local taxes, interest on second mortgages, medical expenses, and other deductions. Other items that can trigger the AMT are incentive stock options, long-term capital gains, and tax-exempt interest. AMT rules state that the taxpayer starts with gross income but excludes many of the tax breaks, which makes the taxable income much higher. The AMT allows an exemption for a certain portion of income. This exemption in previous years was not inflation adjusted. As income levels rose, more people were exposed to the AMT. The new tax rules under the TCJA significantly increased the exemption. For tax year 2021, the exemptions are $114,600 for married couples filing jointly and $73,600 for single and head of household filers. Additional information about the AMT may be obtained at www.irs.gov.

The Affordable Care Act of 2010, or Obamacare, also required that taxpayers confirm that they had health coverage for the year. For a number of years there was a penalty imposed, called the individual mandate, for failure to have health insurance during the year. The federal penalty was eliminated for tax years starting in 2019, under the Tax Cuts and Jobs Act. However, some states have now instituted their own individual mandate penalty.

TAX CREDITS The tax owed may be reduced by a **tax credit,** an amount subtracted directly from the amount of taxes owed. One example of a tax credit is the credit given for child care and dependent care expenses. This amount lowers the tax owed by an individual or a couple. A tax credit differs from a deduction in that a *tax credit* has a full dollar effect in lowering taxes, whereas a *deduction* reduces the taxable income on which the tax liability is computed. (See the *Financial Literacy Calculations: Tax Credits Versus Tax Deductions* feature.)

Low-income workers can benefit from the *earned income credit (EIC)*. This federal tax regulation, for working parents with taxable income under a certain amount ($57,414 in 2021 for three or more children), can result in a tax credit of up to $6,728. Families that do not earn enough to owe federal income taxes are also eligible for the EIC. When these families file a tax return and attach Schedule EIC, they receive a check from the IRS for the amount of their credit.

Other tax credits include:

- Foreign tax credit to avoid double taxation on income taxes paid to another country.

- Child and dependent care expense credit to cover qualifying expenses to pay for someone else to care for your child under age 13 or dependent (e.g., disabled older child, spouse, or parent) who could not care for themselves.

- Savers tax credit to encourage investment contributions to individual and employer-sponsored retirement plans by low- and middle-income taxpayers.

- Adoption tax credit to cover qualifying expenses when adopting a child.

- American Opportunity and Lifetime Learning tax credits to help offset college education expenses.

Financial Literacy Calculations

TAX CREDITS VERSUS TAX DEDUCTIONS

Many people confuse *tax credits* with *tax deductions*. Is one better than the other? A *tax credit,* such as eligible child care or dependent care expenses, results in a dollar-for-dollar reduction in the amount of taxes owed. A *tax deduction,* such as an itemized deduction in the form of medical expenses, mortgage interest, or charitable contributions, reduces the taxable income on which your taxes are based.

Shown at right is how a $100 tax credit compares with a $100 tax deduction:

As you might expect, tax credits are less readily available than tax deductions. To qualify for a $100 child care tax credit, you may have to spend $500 in child care expenses. In some situations, spending on deductible items may be more beneficial than qualifying for a tax credit. A knowledge of tax law and careful financial planning will help you use both tax credits and tax deductions to maximum advantage.

TAX CREDIT

$100 TAX CREDIT

↓

Reduces your taxes by $100

TAX DEDUCTION

$100 TAX DEDUCTION

↓

Reduces your taxable income by $100. The amount of your tax reduction depends on your tax bracket. Your taxes will be reduced by $12 if you are in the 12 percent tax bracket and $35 if you are in the 35 percent tax bracket.

35% tax bracket =

(100 dollar bill): andreynekrasov/123RF; (5, 10, 20 dollar bill): Ruslan Nassyrov/Alamy Stock Photo

- Residential energy-savings tax credit when purchasing various energy-efficient products or renewable home energy systems.
- Elderly and disabled tax credit to assist low-income people age 65 or older, and those under age 65 retired with a permanent disability and taxable disability income.
- Premium tax credit for low- to moderate-income households that purchased health insurance through the Health Insurance Marketplace.
- Alternative Motor Vehicle and Qualified Plug-in Electric Drive Tax Credit for qualified fuel cell and plug-in electric cars.

During recent economic difficulties, other tax credits were used to stimulate business activity, some of which may be extended in the future. Tax preparation software will guide you in identifying current tax credits for which you may qualify.

MAKING TAX PAYMENTS

You will make your payment of income taxes to the federal government in one of two ways: through payroll withholding or through estimated tax payments.

WITHHOLDING The pay-as-you-go system requires an employer to deduct federal income tax from your pay and send it to the government. The withheld amount is

EXHIBIT 4-3 W-2 form

a Employee's social security number		OMB No. 1545-0008	Safe, accurate, FAST! Use	IRS e~file	Visit the IRS website at www.irs.gov/efile

b Employer identification number (EIN) 37 - 19876541	1 Wages, tips, other compensation $48,212.78	2 Federal income tax withheld $5,589.93

c Employer's name, address, and ZIP code	3 Social security wages $54,212.78	4 Social security tax withheld $3,794.84
Information Data, Inc. 9834 Collins Blvd. Benton, NJ 08734	5 Medicare wages and tips $54,212.78	6 Medicare tax withheld $1,264.94
	7 Social security tips	8 Allocated tips

d Control number 123-45-6789	9	10 Dependent care benefits

e Employee's first name and initial Last name Suff.	11 Nonqualified plans	12a See instructions for box 12 D $5,000
Barbara Victor 124 Harper Lane Parmont, NJ 07819	13 Statutory employee ☐ Retirement plan ☒ Third-party sick pay ☐	12b AA $2,000
	14 Other	12c DD $4,125
f Employee's address and ZIP code		12d

15 State Employer's state ID number 37 - 19876541	16 State wages, tips, etc. $48,212.78	17 State income tax $2,592.72	18 Local wages, tips, etc.	19 Local income tax	20 Locality name

Form W-2 Wage and Tax Statement

Copy B—To Be Filed With Employee's FEDERAL Tax Return.
This information is being furnished to the Internal Revenue Service.

Department of the Treasury—Internal Revenue Service

Source: W-2 form, U.S. Department of the Treasury.

based on your filing status and any other optional adjustments to withholding claimed on the W-4 form. For example, a married person would have less withheld than a single person with the same salary, since the married person will owe less tax at year-end.

After the end of the year, you will receive a W-2 form (see Exhibit 4-3), which reports your annual earnings and the amounts that have been deducted for federal income tax, Social Security, and, if applicable, state income tax. A copy of the W-2 form is filed with your tax return to document your earnings and the amount you have paid in taxes. The difference between the amount withheld and the tax owed is either the additional amount you must pay or the refund you will receive.

Regarding wise financial decisions for your tax refund,

smart money minute

An estimated 15 million people are self-employed, an equivalent of one in nine workers. These self-employed people file Schedule C, requiring payment for Social Security and Medicare taxes. However, they will also be eligible for various business deductions against their income (including the new Qualified Business Income Deduction).

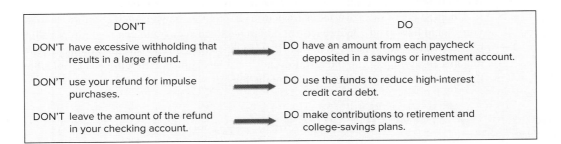

DON'T	DO
DON'T have excessive withholding that results in a large refund.	DO have an amount from each paycheck deposited in a savings or investment account.
DON'T use your refund for impulse purchases.	DO use the funds to reduce high-interest credit card debt.
DON'T leave the amount of the refund in your checking account.	DO make contributions to retirement and college-savings plans.

Students and low-income individuals may file for exemption from withholding if they paid no federal income tax last year and do not expect to pay any in the current year. Dependents may not be exempt from withholding if they have $2,200 or more of unearned income (e.g., interest) and if the earned income (e.g., wages) will be more than $12,550. Being exempt from withholding results in not having to file for a refund and allows you to make more use of your money during the year. However, even if federal income tax is not withheld, Social Security taxes will still be deducted.

ESTIMATED PAYMENTS   People with income from savings, investments, independent contracting, royalties, and lump-sum payments from pensions or retirement plans have their earnings reported on Form 1099. People in these situations and others who do not have taxes withheld may be required to make tax payments during the year (April 15, June 15, September 15, and January 15 as the last payment for the previous tax year). These payments are based on the person's estimate of taxes due at year-end. Underpayment or failure to make these estimated payments can result in penalties and interest charges. These penalties are usually avoided if withholding and estimated payments total more than your tax liability for the previous year or at least 90 percent of the current year's tax.

EXAMPLE: Refund or Amount Owed?

Taxes owed or a refund?

(1)	Compare withholding amount and payments made during the year with	$4,225
(2)	taxes due as calculated on your 1040 form, which	$4,494
(3)	would result in an amount OWED of:	$ 269

When withholding and payments are less than the amount of taxes due, an additional amount must be paid by April 15.

DEADLINES AND PENALTIES

Most people are required to file their federal income tax return each April 15. If you are not able to file on time, you can use Form 4868 to obtain an automatic six-month extension. This extension is for the 1040 form and other documents, but it does not delay your payment liability. You must submit the estimated amount owed along with Form 4868 by April 15. Failure to file on time can result in a penalty of 5 percent for just one day.

People who make quarterly deposits for estimated taxes must submit their payments by April 15, June 15, and September 15 of the current tax year, with the final payment due by January 15 of the following year.

The IRS can impose penalties and interest for violations of the tax code. Failure to file a tax return can result in a 25 percent penalty in addition to the taxes owed.

Underpayment of quarterly estimated taxes requires paying interest on the amount you should have paid. Underpayment due to negligence or fraud can result in penalties of 50 to 75 percent. The good news is that if you claim a refund several months or years late, the IRS will pay you interest. Refunds must be claimed within three years of filing the return or within two years of paying the tax.

PFP Sheet 20
Current Income
Tax Estimate

 ## PRACTICE QUIZ 4-2

1. How does tax-exempt income differ from tax-deferred income?
2. What information is needed to compute taxable income?
3. When would you use the standard deduction instead of itemized deductions?
4. What is the difference between your marginal tax rate and your average tax rate?
5. How does a tax credit affect the amount owed for federal income tax?

Filing Your Federal Income Tax Return

As you stare at those piles of papers, you know it's time to do your taxes! Submitting your federal income tax return requires several decisions and activities. First, you must determine whether you are required to file a return. Next, you need to decide which basic form best serves your needs and whether you are required to submit additional schedules or supplementary forms. Finally, you must prepare your return.

LO4-3

Prepare a federal income tax return.

WHO MUST FILE?

Every citizen or resident of the United States and every U.S. citizen who is a resident of Puerto Rico is required to file a federal income tax return if his or her income is above a certain amount. The amount is based on the person's *filing status* and other factors such as age. For example, single persons under 65 had to file a return on April 15, 2021 (for tax year 2020) if their gross income exceeded $12,400; single persons over 65 had to file if their gross income exceeded $14,050. The amount at which you are required to file will change each year based on changes in the standard deduction. If your gross income is less than this amount but taxes were withheld from your earnings, you will need to file a return to obtain a refund.

Your filing status is affected by such factors as marital status and dependents. The five filing status categories are as follows:

- *Single*—never-married, divorced, or legally separated individuals with no dependents.
- *Married, filing joint return*—combines the income of a couple.
- *Married, filing separate returns*—each spouse is responsible for his or her own tax. Under certain conditions, a married couple can benefit from this filing status.
- *Head of household*—an unmarried individual or a surviving spouse who maintains a household (paying for more than half of the costs) for a child or a dependent relative.
- *Qualifying widow or widower*—an individual whose spouse died within the past two years and who has a dependent; this status is limited to two years after the death of the spouse.

In some situations, you may have a choice of filing status. In such cases, compute your taxes under the available alternatives to determine the most advantageous filing status.

The *marriage penalty* often occurs for couples that have similar income levels. The *penalty* is the amount of additional tax that a couple will pay using a *married, filing joint* status versus a *single* filing status. It is important to note that couples who are married on the last day of the year are considered married for the entire year. A *marriage bonus* can also occur if the income levels of each person are vastly different as well. Want to calculate the amount of the penalty or bonus? The Tax Policy Center has an online calculator that you can access at http://tpc-marriage-calculator.urban.org.

EXHIBIT 4-4 Federal income tax return—Form 1040

1.
Your marriage and household situation will affect your taxable income and tax rate.

2.
Your earnings and other sources of income are reported in this section, including items from Schedule 1.

4.
In this section, you subtract your itemized deductions or the standard deduction to obtain taxable income; your tax is based on the tax tables or schedule.

3.
Adjusted gross income results from certain deductions (see Schedule 1) and will be used as a basis for computing other deductions (see Schedule A).

Form **1040**   Department of the Treasury—Internal Revenue Service   (99)
U.S. Individual Income Tax Return   OMB No. 1545-0074   IRS Use Only—Do not write or staple in this space.

Filing Status ☐ Single ☑ Married filing jointly ☐ Married filing separately (MFS) ☐ Head of household (HOH) ☐ Qualifying widow(er) (QW)
Check only one box. If you checked the MFS box, enter the name of your spouse. If you checked the HOH or QW box, enter the child's name if the qualifying person is a child but not your dependent ▶

Your first name and middle initial Darren J	Last name Brooks	Your social security number 5 6 7 8 9 1 2 3 4
If joint return, spouse's first name and middle initial Cameron S	Last name Brooks	Spouse's social security number 2 3 4 5 6 7 8 9 0

Home address (number and street). If you have a P.O. box, see instructions. 6785 Avalanche Canyon Drive   Apt. no.

Presidential Election Campaign
Check here if you, or your spouse if filing jointly, want $3 to go to this fund. Checking a box below will not change your tax or refund.   ☐ You ☐ Spouse

City, town, or post office. If you have a foreign address, also complete spaces below.   State   ZIP code
Jackson, WY 83001

Foreign country name   Foreign province/state/county   Foreign postal code

At any time during 2020, did you receive, sell, send, exchange, or otherwise acquire any financial interest in any virtual currency? ☐ Yes ☐ No

Standard Deduction Someone can claim: ☐ You as a dependent   ☐ Your spouse as a dependent
☐ Spouse itemizes on a separate return or you were a dual-status alien

Age/Blindness You: ☐ Were born before January 2, 1956 ☐ Are blind   Spouse: ☐ Was born before January 2, 1956   ☐ Is blind

Dependents (see instructions):

(1) First name Last name	(2) Social security number	(3) Relationship to you	(4) ✔ if qualifies for (see instructions): Child tax credit	Credit for other dependents
Candace Brooks	1 2 3 4 5 6 7 8 9	Daughter	☑	☐
Kendall Brooks	1 2 3 7 8 9 1 2 3	Daughter	☑	☐
Devon Brooks	1 2 4 5 6 7 1 2 3	Son	☑	☐
			☐	☐

If more than four dependents, see instructions and check here ▶ ☐

Attach Sch. B if required.

1	Wages, salaries, tips, etc. Attach Form(s) W-2		1	128371
2a	Tax-exempt interest . . . 2a	b Taxable interest	2b	215
3a	Qualified dividends . . . 3a 354	b Ordinary dividends	3b	354
4a	IRA distributions . . . 4a	b Taxable amount	4b	
5a	Pensions and annuities . . 5a	b Taxable amount	5b	
6a	Social security benefits . . 6a	b Taxable amount	6b	
7	Capital gain or (loss). Attach Schedule D if required. If not required, check here . . . ▶ ☐		7	
8	Other income from Schedule 1, line 9		8	
9	Add lines 1, 2b, 3b, 4b, 5b, 6b, 7, and 8. This is your **total income** . . . . ▶		9	128940
10	Adjustments to income:			
a	From Schedule 1, line 22 . . . . 10a			
b	Charitable contributions if you take the standard deduction. See instructions 10b			
c	Add lines 10a and 10b. These are your **total adjustments to income** . . . . . ▶		10c	
11	Subtract line 10c from line 9. This is your **adjusted gross income** . . . . . . ▶		11	128940
12	**Standard deduction or itemized deductions** (from Schedule A)		12	36850
13	Qualified business income deduction. Attach Form 8995 or Form 8995-A		13	
14	Add lines 12 and 13		14	36850
15	**Taxable income.** Subtract line 14 from line 11. If zero or less, enter -0-		15	92090

Standard Deduction for—
• Single or Married filing separately, $12,400
• Married filing jointly or Qualifying widow(er), $24,800
• Head of household, $18,650
• If you checked any box under Standard Deduction, see instructions.

For Disclosure, Privacy Act, and Paperwork Reduction Act Notice, see separate instructions.   Cat. No. 11320B

WHICH TAX FORMS AND SCHEDULES SHOULD YOU USE?

The Tax Cuts and Jobs Act (TCJA) simplified the basic form used when filing your taxes. In the past, there were three basic forms—Form 1040, Form 1040EZ, and Form 1040A—to choose from. Now there is basically one form, Form 1040, to report your cumulative income. The IRS has provided Form 1040-SR for senior citizens, which is a large print version of Form 1040. There are still about 800 additional federal tax forms and schedules that are used to report additional income, deductions, and complex tax situations. Most tax preparation software programs will guide you in selecting the appropriate tax forms for your situation.

personal fintech

Want to check on your Federal refund? Go to irs.gov/refunds, click on "check my refund status" to see when you should receive your refund.

EXHIBIT 4-4 (continued)

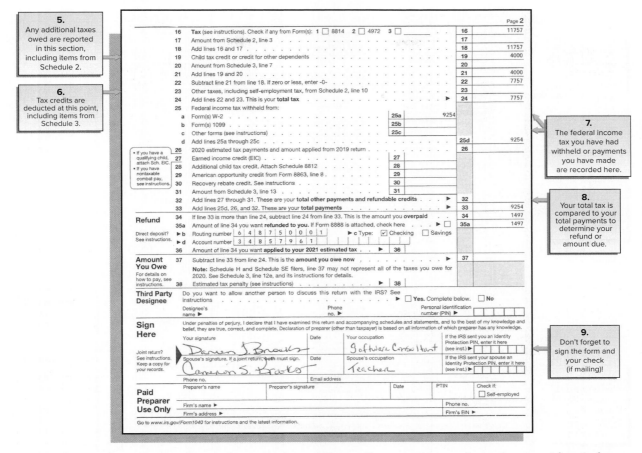

5.
Any additional taxes owed are reported in this section, including items from Schedule 2.

6.
Tax credits are deducted at this point, including items from Schedule 3.

7.
The federal income tax you have had withheld or payments you have made are recorded here.

8.
Your total tax is compared to your total payments to determine your refund or amount due.

9.
Don't forget to sign the form and your check (if mailing)!

Note: These forms were used in a recent year; the current forms may not be exactly the same. Obtain current income tax forms and current tax information from your local IRS office, post office, public library, or at www.irs.gov.

Source: Form 1040, U.S. Department of the Treasury.

COMPLETING THE FEDERAL INCOME TAX RETURN

The major sections of Form 1040 (see Exhibit 4-4) correspond to tax topics discussed in the previous sections of this chapter:

1. *Filing status.* Your tax rate is determined by your filing status as determined by yourself, your spouse, and your dependents.

2. *Income.* Earnings from your employment (as reported by your W-2 form) and other income, such as savings and investment income, are reported in this section of Form 1040.

3. *Adjustments to income.* As discussed later in the chapter, if you qualify, you may deduct contributions (up to a certain amount) to an individual retirement account (IRA) or other qualified retirement program.

4. *Taxable income.* In this section, your adjusted gross income is reduced by your itemized deductions (see Exhibit 4-5), or by the standard deduction for your tax situation. This income is the basis for determining the amount of your tax (see Exhibit 4-6).

EXHIBIT 4-5   Schedule A for itemized deductions—Form 1040

Health care expenses (not covered by insurance) are listed here, but must exceed 7.5% of adjusted gross income to be deductible.

Deductible interest payments are listed here.

A variety of other expenses may qualify under these deduction categories.

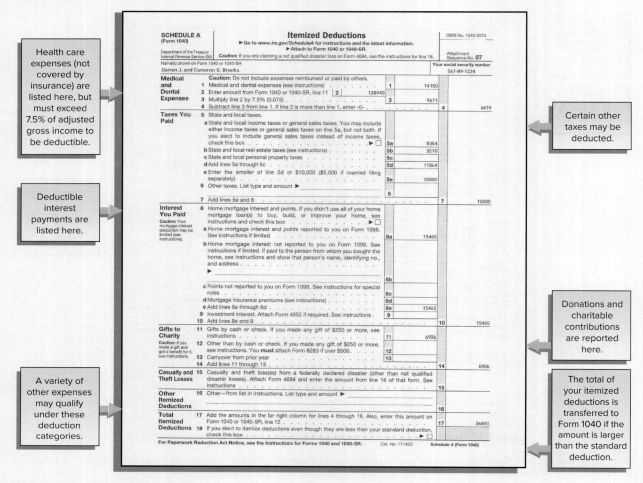

Certain other taxes may be deducted.

Donations and charitable contributions are reported here.

The total of your itemized deductions is transferred to Form 1040 if the amount is larger than the standard deduction.

Source: Form 1040, U.S. Department of the Treasury.

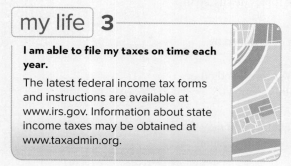

my life 3

I am able to file my taxes on time each year.

The latest federal income tax forms and instructions are available at www.irs.gov. Information about state income taxes may be obtained at www.taxadmin.org.

5. *Other taxes.* Any special taxes, such as self-employment tax, are included at this point.

6. *Tax credits.* Any tax credits for which you qualify are subtracted at this point.

7. *Payments.* Your total withholding and other payments are indicated in this section.

8. *Refund or amount you owe.* If your payments exceed the amount of income tax you owe, you are entitled to a refund. If the opposite is true, you must make an additional payment. Taxpayers who want their refunds sent directly to a bank record the necessary account information directly on Form 1040.

9. *Your signature.* Forgetting to sign a tax return is one of the most common filing errors.

EXHIBIT 4-6 Tax tables and tax rate schedules

If Taxable income is							Tax Rate Schedules

At least	But less than	Single	Married filing jointly *	Married filing separately	Head of a household
			Your tax is—		

70,000

At least	But less than	Single	Married filing jointly	Married filing separately	Head of a household
70,000	70,050	11,196	8,008	11,196	9,754
70,050	70,100	11,207	8,014	11,207	9,765
70,100	70,150	11,218	8,020	11,218	9,776
70,150	70,200	11,229	8,026	11,229	9,787
70,200	70,250	11,240	8,032	11,240	9,798
70,250	70,300	11,251	8,038	11,251	9,809
70,300	70,350	11,262	8,044	11,262	9,820
70,350	70,400	11,273	8,050	11,273	9,831
70,400	70,450	11,284	8,056	11,284	9,842
70,450	70,500	11,295	8,062	11,295	9,853
70,500	70,550	11,306	8,068	11,306	9,864
70,550	70,600	11,317	8,074	11,317	9,875
70,600	70,650	11,328	8,080	11,328	9,886
70,650	70,700	11,339	8,086	11,339	9,897
70,700	70,750	11,350	8,092	11,350	9,908
70,750	70,800	11,361	8,098	11,361	9,919
70,800	70,850	11,372	8,104	11,372	9,930
70,850	70,900	11,383	8,110	11,383	9,941
70,900	70,950	11,394	8,116	11,394	9,952
70,950	71,000	11,405	8,122	11,405	9,963

Married Filing jointly or Qualifying widow(er)

Taxable income is over—	But not over—	The tax is:	of the amount over—
$0	$19,900	$0 + 10%	$0
19,900	81,050	1,990.00 + 12%	19,900
81,050	172,750	9,328.00 + 22%	81,050
172,750	329,850	29,502.00 + 24%	172,750
329,850	418,850	67,206.00 + 32%	329,850
418,850	628,300	95,686.00 + 35%	418,850
628,300	---------	168,993.50 + 37%	628,300

Note: These were the federal income tax rates for a recent year. Current rates may vary due to changes in the tax code and adjustments for inflation. Obtain current income tax booklets from your local IRS office or at www.irs.gov.

CORRECTING THE FEDERAL RETURN

Occasionally, you will discover income that was not reported or additional deductions to which you are entitled. In this case, you should file Form 1040X to pay the additional tax or obtain a refund. This form is designed to amend a previously filed tax return. It is not recommended that you wait for the IRS to notify you of a discrepancy. Waiting could cost you penalties and interest.

FILING STATE INCOME TAX RETURNS

All but nine states have a state income tax. In most states, the tax rate ranges from 1 to 10 percent and is based on some aspect of your federal income tax return, such as adjusted gross income or taxable income. For further information about the income tax in your state, contact the state department of revenue. States usually require income tax returns to be filed when the federal income tax return is due. For help in planning your tax activities, see Exhibit 4-7.

 PRACTICE QUIZ 4-3

1. In what ways does your filing status affect preparation of your federal income tax return?
2. What is the marriage penalty?

EXHIBIT 4-7 Tax-planner calendar

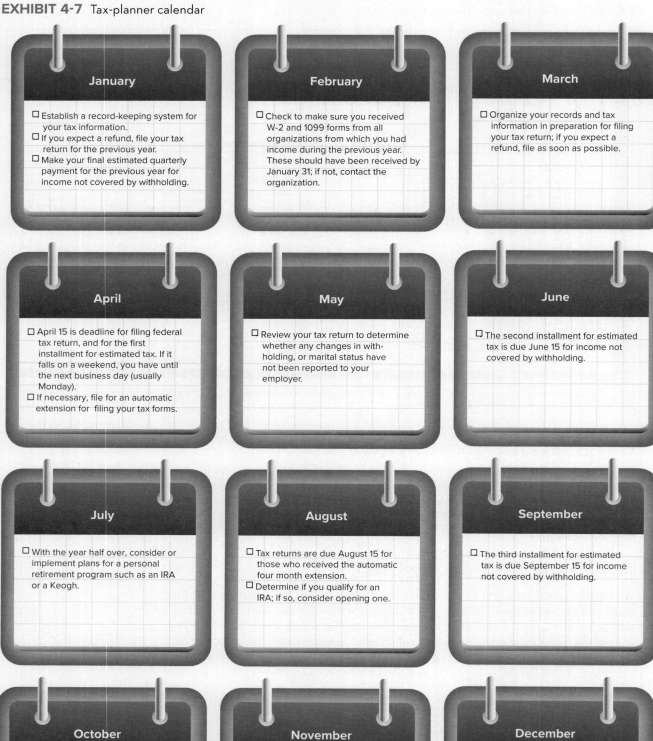

January
- ☐ Establish a record-keeping system for your tax information.
- ☐ If you expect a refund, file your tax return for the previous year.
- ☐ Make your final estimated quarterly payment for the previous year for income not covered by withholding.

February
- ☐ Check to make sure you received W-2 and 1099 forms from all organizations from which you had income during the previous year. These should have been received by January 31; if not, contact the organization.

March
- ☐ Organize your records and tax information in preparation for filing your tax return; if you expect a refund, file as soon as possible.

April
- ☐ April 15 is deadline for filing federal tax return, and for the first installment for estimated tax. If it falls on a weekend, you have until the next business day (usually Monday).
- ☐ If necessary, file for an automatic extension for filing your tax forms.

May
- ☐ Review your tax return to determine whether any changes in withholding, or marital status have not been reported to your employer.

June
- ☐ The second installment for estimated tax is due June 15 for income not covered by withholding.

July
- ☐ With the year half over, consider or implement plans for a personal retirement program such as an IRA or a Keogh.

August
- ☐ Tax returns are due August 15 for those who received the automatic four month extension.
- ☐ Determine if you qualify for an IRA; if so, consider opening one.

September
- ☐ The third installment for estimated tax is due September 15 for income not covered by withholding.

October
- ☐ Tax returns are due October 15 for those who received the automatic six-month extension.
- ☐ Determine the tax benefits of selling certain investments by year-end.

November
- ☐ Make any last-minute changes in withholding by your employer to avoid penalties for too little withholding.
- ☐ Determine if you qualify for an IRA; if so, consider opening one.

December
- ☐ Determine if it would be to your advantage to make payments for next year before December 31 of the current year.
- ☐ Decide if you can defer income or expenses in the current year until the following year, if advantageous.

Tax Assistance and the Audit Process

In the process of completing your federal income tax return, you may seek additional information or assistance. After filing your return, you may be identified for a tax audit. If this happens, several policies and procedures protect your rights.

LO4-4

Identify tax assistance sources.

TAX INFORMATION SOURCES

As with other aspects of personal financial planning, many resources are available to assist you with your taxes. The IRS offers forms, instructions, and publications at www.irs.gov.

IRS SERVICES   If you wish to do your own tax return or just to expand your knowledge of tax regulations, the IRS has several methods of assistance:

1. *Publications.* The IRS offers hundreds of free booklets and pamphlets. You can obtain these publications at a local IRS office, by mail request, or by a telephone call. Especially helpful is *Your Federal Income Tax* (IRS Publication 17). You may obtain IRS publications and tax forms by calling 1-800-TAX-FORM, online at www.irs.gov, or by fax at 703-368-9694.

2. *Phone hot line.* You can obtain information about specific problems through an IRS-staffed phone line. The appropriate telephone number is listed in your local telephone directory, or call 1-800-829-1040. You are not asked to give your name when you use this service, so your questions are anonymous.

3. *Walk-in service.* You can visit your local or district IRS office to obtain assistance with your taxes. More than 400 of these facilities are available to taxpayers. Be aware, however, that information IRS employees provide is not always reliable. Various studies in recent years have reported incorrect answers over 30 percent of the time. You are still liable for taxes owed even if you based your calculations on information provided by IRS employees.

4. *Interactive tax assistant (ITA).* The IRS has developed an interactive tool that allows taxpayers to get answers to a number of common and challenging questions. The system is designed to ask probing questions based upon a variety of tax laws. This can be a very detailed query that may generate additional questions for taxpayers to ensure that they are receiving correct information based on their specific questions.

5. *IRS2Go App.* This tool provides options for checking your refund status, requesting tax records, locating free tax preparation help, and other interactive tools.

smart money minute

Volunteer Income Tax Assistance (VITA) offers free tax help to low- and moderate-income taxpayers who cannot prepare their own tax returns. Certified volunteers provide this service at community centers, libraries, schools, shopping malls, and other locations. Most locations also offer free electronic filing. To locate the nearest VITA site, call 1-800-829-1040.

In addition, the IRS has videos, free speakers for community groups, and teaching materials for schools to assist taxpayers.

TAX PUBLICATIONS   Each year, several tax guides are published and offered for sale. These publications include *J. K. Lasser's Your Income Tax, The Ernst & Young Tax Guide,* and the *U.S. Master Tax Guide.* You can purchase them online or at local stores.

ONLINE RESOURCES   As with other personal finance topics, extensive information may be found on the Internet. The Internal Revenue Service (www.irs.gov) is a good starting point. Personal finance sources, such as *Kiplinger's Personal Finance* and CNBC (cnbc.com/personal-finance), as well as other financial planning information services, offer a variety of tax information. In addition, the websites of tax-related organizations and companies that sell tax software can be useful.

Software can reduce tax return preparation time and effort.
Calamy stock images/Alamy Stock Photo

TAX PREPARATION SOFTWARE

Today, most taxpayers use computers for tax recordkeeping and tax form preparation. A spreadsheet program can be helpful in maintaining and updating income and expense data. Software packages such as *H & R Block* and *TurboTax* allow you to complete needed tax forms and schedules to either print for mailing or file online.

Using tax software can save you many hours when preparing your Form 1040 and accompanying schedules. When selecting tax software, consider the following factors:

1. Your personal situation—are you employed or do you operate your own business?
2. Special tax situations with regard to types of income, unusual deductions, and various tax credits.
3. Features in the software, such as "audit check," future tax planning, and filing your federal and state tax forms online.
4. Technical aspects, such as the hardware and operating system requirements, and online support that is provided.

TAX PREPARATION SERVICES

Over 40 million U.S. taxpayers pay someone to do their income taxes. The fee for this service can range from $50 at a tax preparation service for a simple return to more than $2,000 to a certified public accountant for a complicated return.

TYPES OF TAX SERVICES   Doing your own taxes may not be desirable, especially if you have sources of income other than salary. The sources available for professional tax assistance include the following:

- Tax services range from local, one-person operations to national firms with thousands of offices, such as H&R Block.
- Enrolled agents—government-approved tax experts—prepare returns and provide tax advice. You may contact the National Association of Enrolled Agents at 1-800-424-4339 for information about enrolled agents in your area.
- Many accountants offer tax assistance along with other business services. A certified public accountant (CPA) with special training in taxes can help with tax planning and the preparation of your annual tax return.
- Attorneys usually do not complete tax returns; however, you can use an attorney's services when you are involved in a tax-related transaction or when you have a difference of opinion with the IRS.

EVALUATING TAX SERVICES   When planning to use a tax preparation service, consider these factors:

- What training and experience does the tax professional possess?
- How will the fee be determined? (Avoid preparers who earn a percentage of your refund.)
- Does the preparer suggest you report various deductions that might be questioned?

my life   4

My tax returns have never been questioned by the Internal Revenue Service.

You reduce your chance of a tax audit when using tax preparation software. Conduct a web search to obtain information about various tax software tools as well as the cost of these programs.

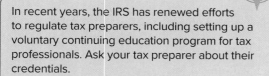

smart money minute

In recent years, the IRS has renewed efforts to regulate tax preparers, including setting up a voluntary continuing education program for tax professionals. Ask your tax preparer about their credentials.

HOW TO . . . File Your Taxes Online

In 2020 (for tax year 2019), over 184 million taxpayers filed returns electronically. The IRS has made online filing easier and in many cases free. There are three main options for filing electronically.

OPTION 1: *Free File*

For Tax Year 2020, if your income is $72,000 or less, you are eligible to use Free File, which includes free tax preparation and free e-filing through a list of predetermined companies.

- Go to the "Free File" page at www.irs.gov and select "Start Free File Now." This will take you to a list of companies, including descriptions and any limitations of their services. After you determine your eligibility for a particular company, select the link for the company's website.
- The online sites and tax software will guide you through the steps of the process. You will be prompted to enter your personal data, income amounts, deductions, and tax information.
- After you have ensured that all relevant information has been entered, you are ready to submit your federal tax form online. You will usually receive an email confirmation of your submission, and your refund will be processed within two weeks.
- Be aware: Free e-file services may not include preparation of your state tax return, or may require an additional fee.

OPTION 2: *E-File*

- The IRS offers a "Free File Fillable Forms" option. This option is available primarily for taxpayers whose income exceeds the income limitations for Free File. This may also be used by taxpayers who attempted the Free File process and encountered additional fees or issues based on additional forms needed to complete their returns. Quick, online access is available for the most commonly filed federal tax forms and schedules.
- It is strongly recommended that you print out relevant forms and perform necessary calculations before using this option. This will help to ensure accuracy and reduce the need to amend your return in the future.

OPTION 3: *Paid Preparer E-File (or Purchased Software)*

- Most tax preparation software and paid preparers now offer e-filing as part of their service. If you purchase a tax preparation software tool, you will be able to connect directly through the software to electronically file your return. In addition, paid preparers who prepare more than 10 individual returns are now required by the IRS to electronically file returns.

- Will the preparer represent you if your return is audited?
- Is tax preparation the main business activity, or does it serve as a front for selling other financial products and services?

Additional information about tax preparers may be obtained at the websites for the National Association of Enrolled Agents (www.naea.org) and the National Association of Tax Professionals (www.natptax.com).

TAX SERVICE WARNINGS   Even if you hire a professional tax preparer, you are responsible for supplying accurate and complete information. Hiring a tax preparer will not guarantee that you pay the *correct* amount. A study conducted by *Money* magazine of 41 tax preparers reported fees ranging from $375 to $3,600, with taxes due ranging from $31,846 to $74,450 for the same fictional family. If you owe more tax because your return contains errors or you have made entries that are not allowed, it is your responsibility to pay that additional tax, plus any interest and penalties.

Beware of tax preparers and other businesses that offer your refund in advance. These "refund anticipation loans" often charge very high interest rates for this type of

Financial Literacy for My Life

TAX SCAM WARNINGS FROM THE IRS

Alan Newell was attracted to the idea of reducing his taxes by running a business out of his home. However, the bogus home-based business promoted in an online advertisement did not qualify for a home office deduction.

Vanessa Elliott liked the idea of increasing the refund she would receive from her federal income tax return. For a fee, she would be informed of additional tax deductions to lower her taxable income. Vanessa avoided the offer since the refund was promised without any knowledge of her tax situation.

Ken Turner was informed that he had won a prize that required payment of the income tax on the item before it would be shipped to him. While taxes are usually due on large prizes, the amount would not be paid until later.

Fortunately, Alan, Vanessa, and Ken did not fall for these deceptive offers. These three situations are some of the many common tax scams that cost consumers billions of dollars each year. The Internal Revenue Service warns taxpayers to never give out personal and financial information without proper identification by the IRS employee.

Each year, the IRS releases its annual list of the "Dirty Dozen Tax Scams." This is a listing of the most prevalent tax scams that have occurred in the past year. For 2020, a portion of the listing includes:

IDENTITY OR FINANCIAL THEFT

- An official-looking, but phony, letter or email is sent in an attempt to trick a taxpayer into disclosing personal information and bank account numbers. This is also referred to as *phishing*. The most common tactic is informing a person that they are entitled to a tax refund from the IRS. This usually requires that the recipient reveal personal information to claim the money. The IRS has seen a significant increase in this type of activity in recent years.

RETURN PREPARER FRAUD

- Due to complex tax laws, nearly 60 percent of taxpayers hire someone to prepare their tax returns. Incidence of refund fraud and identity theft due to unscrupulous preparers is on the rise. One important reminder is that preparers should always sign the tax returns and enter their IRS Preparer Tax Identification Numbers (PTINs).

MALWARE & RANSOMWARE

- Cybercriminals may try to send you malware to support a fake charitable organization. The malware can infect your computer. It can track keystrokes and obtain sensitive data as well as lock down the computer and demand payment.

CHARITABLE ORGANIZATIONS FRAUD

- Organizations using names similar to familiar or nationally known organizations are trying to attract contributions from unsuspecting contributors. The IRS recommends donating to recognized charities only. Also, don't give or send cash. You can check the status of a charitable organization on www.irs.gov to determine if they are a recognized charity.

As with any fraud, consumers should be cautious. The opportunity to make fast money can end up being very expensive. Information about misuse of IRS insignia, seals, and symbols or help identifying theft related to taxes may be obtained at www.ustreas.gov/tigta. Suspected tax fraud can be reported using IRS Form 3949-A, which is available at www.irs.gov, or by calling 1-800-829-3676.

Source: "Dirty Dozen Tax Scams," www.irs.gov.

---

consumer credit. Studies reveal interest rates sometimes exceeding 300 percent (on an annualized basis). See *Financial Literacy for My Life: Tax Scam Warnings from the IRS* for more information on other tax preparation pitfalls to watch for.

WHAT IF YOUR RETURN IS AUDITED?

The Internal Revenue Service reviews all returns for completeness and accuracy. If you make an error, your tax is automatically refigured and you receive either a bill or a refund. If you make an entry that is not allowed, you will be notified by mail. A **tax audit** is a detailed examination of your tax return by the IRS. In most audits, the IRS requests more information to support the entries on your tax return. Be sure to keep accurate records to support your return. Keep receipts, canceled checks, and other evidence to prove amounts that you claim. Avoiding common filing mistakes (see Exhibit 4-8) helps to minimize your chances of an audit.

tax audit A detailed examination of your tax return by the Internal Revenue Service.

EXHIBIT 4-8 How to avoid common filing errors

- Organize all tax-related information for easy access.
- Follow instructions carefully. Many people deduct total medical and dental expenses rather than the amount of these expenses that exceeds a certain percentage of adjusted gross income.
- Be sure to recheck the spelling of your name that matches your Social Security card.
- Make sure to include the correct Social Security number(s) and to record amounts on the correct lines.
- Use the proper tax rate schedule or tax table column.
- Consider the alternative minimum tax that may apply to your situation. Be sure to pay self-employment tax and tax on early IRA withdrawals.
- Check your math and the accuracy of software data entries several times.
- Sign your return (both spouses must sign a joint return). For e-filers, this will require a PIN or verification using last year's tax information.
- Attach necessary documentation, such as your W-2 forms and required schedules.
- If you owe money: Make the check payable to "United States Treasury." Put your Social Security number, the tax year, and a daytime telephone number on your check—and be sure to sign the check!
- If you are due a refund: Make sure you enter the bank routing and account numbers correctly.
- Keep a copy of your return.
- Finally, check everything again—and file on time! Care taken when you file your income tax can result in "many happy returns."

WHO GETS AUDITED? Less than 1 percent of all tax filers—about 1 out of every 220 taxpayers—are audited each year. While the IRS does not reveal its basis for auditing returns, several indicators are evident. People who claim large or unusual deductions increase their chances of an audit.

Tax advisors suggest including a brief explanation or a copy of receipts for deductions that may be questioned. Individuals with high incomes who report large losses due to tax shelters or partnerships, or who have had their tax returns questioned in the past, may also be targeted for an audit.

TYPES OF AUDITS The simplest and most common type of audit is the *correspondence audit*. This mail inquiry requires you to clarify or document minor questions about your tax return. You usually have 30 days to provide the requested information.

The *office audit* requires you to visit an IRS office to clarify some aspect of your tax return. This type of audit usually takes an hour or two.

The *field audit* is more complex. An IRS agent visits you at your home, your business, or the office of your accountant to have access to your records. A field audit may be done to verify whether an individual has an office in the home as claimed.

The IRS also conducts more detailed audits for about 50,000 taxpayers. These range from random requests to document various tax return items to line-by-line reviews by IRS employees. These are commonly known as Taxpayer Compliance Measurement Program (TCMP) audits.

YOUR AUDIT RIGHTS When you receive an audit notice, you have the right to request time to prepare. Also, you can ask the IRS for clarification of items being questioned. When you are audited, use the following suggestions.

- Decide whether you will bring your tax preparer, accountant, or lawyer.
- Be on time for your appointment; bring only relevant documents.
- Present tax records and receipts in a logical, calm, and confident manner; maintain a positive attitude.

smart money minute

The Internal Revenue Service reported that they audited 1.1 million tax returns in a recent year. This represented about 0.5 percent of all returns for that tax year.

- Make sure the information you present is consistent with the tax law.
- Keep your answers aimed at the auditor's questions. Answer questions clearly and completely. Be as brief as possible; you can never tell an auditor too little.

People under stress tend to talk too much. IRS auditors are trained to create silence and listen in case the taxpayer blurts out damaging information. The five best responses to questions during an audit are "Yes," "No," "I don't recall," "I'll have to check on that," and "What specific items do you want to see?"

If you disagree with the results of an audit, you may request a conference at the Regional Appeals Office. Although most differences of opinion are settled at this stage, some taxpayers take their cases further. A person may go to the U.S. tax court, the U.S. claims court, or the U.S. district court. Some tax disputes have gone to the U.S. Supreme Court.

PFP Sheet 21
Tax Preparer
Comparison

 PRACTICE QUIZ 4-4

1. What are the main sources available to help people prepare their taxes?
2. What actions can reduce the chances of an IRS audit?
3. What appeal process do taxpayers have if they disagree with an audit decision of the IRS?

Tax Planning Strategies

LO4-5

Select appropriate tax strategies for various financial and personal situations.

tax avoidance The use of legitimate methods to reduce one's taxes.

tax evasion The use of illegal actions to reduce one's taxes.

Most people want to pay their fair share of taxes—no more, no less. They do this by practicing **tax avoidance,** the use of legitimate methods to reduce one's taxes. In contrast, **tax evasion** is the use of illegal actions to reduce one's taxes. To minimize taxes owed, follow these guidelines.

- If you expect to have the *same* or a *lower* tax rate next year, *accelerate deductions* into the current year. Pay real estate property taxes or make your January mortgage payment in December. Make charitable donations by December 31.
- If you expect to have a *lower* or the *same* tax rate next year, *delay the receipt of income* until next year. This means income will be taxed at a lower rate or at a later date.
- If you expect to have a *higher* tax rate next year, consider *delaying deductions,* since they will have a greater benefit. A $1,000 deduction at 24 percent lowers your taxes $240; at 32 percent, your taxes are lowered $320.
- If you expect to have a *higher* tax rate next year, *accelerate the receipt of income* to have it taxed at the current lower rate.

As Exhibit 4-9 shows, people in different life situations can take advantage of various tax rules. When considering financial decisions in relation to your taxes, remember that purchasing, investing, and retirement planning are the areas most heavily affected by tax laws.

CONSUMER PURCHASING

The buying decisions most directly affected by taxes are the purchase of a residence, the use of credit, and job-related expenses.

PLACE OF RESIDENCE   Owning a home is one of the best tax shelters. Both real estate property taxes and interest on the mortgage are deductible (as itemized deductions) and thus reduce your taxable income. While renting may seem less expensive than

EXHIBIT 4-9 Special tax situations

Business in your home	• You may deduct any ordinary and necessary expenses related to starting and maintaining your business, including a portion of your rent or mortgage if that portion of your home is used exclusively for business. • It must be your principal place of business. (Individuals who are employed elsewhere and claim an office at home are likely to be challenged by the IRS on this deduction.)
Divorced persons	• Child support payments have no tax consequences. They are neither deductible by the payer nor included in the recipient's income. • Divorce decrees prior to Dec. 31, 2018 are tax deductible by the payer and must be included as income by the recipient. • Divorce decrees after Dec. 31, 2018 eliminate the deduction for alimony payments. Thus, recipients of the alimony payments will not have to include them in taxable income.
Single parents	• A single parent may claim "head of household" filing status, which has greater advantages than "single" status. • Working parents may qualify for a child care tax credit. • Low-income families may qualify for the earned income credit (EIC).
Retired persons	• Individuals over age 59½ may withdraw tax-deferred funds from a retirement plan without penalty. Of course, these funds must be reported as ordinary income. • Retirees with total incomes, including Social Security, exceeding $44,000 (couples) and $34,000 (singles) pay income tax on up to 85 percent of their Social Security benefits. Those with incomes between $25,000 and $34,000 (singles) or $32,000 and $44,000 (couples) continue to be taxed on up to 50 percent of their benefits.

Note: Individual circumstances and changes in the tax laws can affect these examples.

owning, the after-tax cost of owning a home often makes owning financially advantageous. Chapter 9 presents specific calculations for comparing renting and buying.

CONSUMER DEBT Current tax laws allow homeowners to borrow for consumer purchases. You can deduct interest on loans (of up to $100,000) secured by your primary or secondary home up to the actual dollar amount you have invested in it—the difference between the market value of the home and the amount you owe on it. These *home equity loans,* which are *second mortgages,* are discussed in greater detail in Chapters 6 and 9. Current tax laws (on or after tax year 2018) will allow you to deduct the interest if you use that line of credit to buy, build, or make home improvements.

HEALTH CARE EXPENSES *Flexible spending accounts (FSAs),* a type of health savings account, allow you to reduce your taxable income when paying for medical expenses or child care costs. Workers are allowed to put pretax dollars into these employer-sponsored programs. These "deposits" result in a lower taxable income. Then, the funds in the FSA may be used to pay for various medical expenses and dependent care costs. A potential drawback of the FSA is that the amount that can be left in the account each year is limited. Any amounts exceeding this limit may be forfeited.

smart money minute

Returns must be filed to claim tax refunds and you have three years from the due date of the return. In recent years, the amount forefeited in one year was almost $1 billion.

Heath Savings Accounts (HSAs), are another type of health savings account that allows you to reduce your taxable income when paying for medical expenses. These types of accounts are paired with high deductible medical insurance plans. There are no limits to the amounts that can be carried over each year and the amounts can be taken out tax free for any reason after age 65.

INVESTMENT DECISIONS

A major area of tax planning involves the wide variety of decisions related to investing.

TAX-EXEMPT INVESTMENTS   Interest income from municipal bonds, which are issued by state and local governments, and other tax-exempt investments is not subject to federal income taxes. While municipal bonds have lower interest rates than other investments, the *after-tax* income may be higher. For example, if you are in the 24 percent tax bracket, earning $100 of tax-exempt income would be worth more to you than earning $125 in taxable investment income. The $125 would have an after-tax value of $95: $125 less $30 (24 percent of $125) for taxes. Interest on EE savings bonds is exempt from federal income tax if it is used to pay tuition at a college, university, or qualified technical school. Chapter 5 gives further details.

TAX-DEFERRED INVESTMENTS   Although, from a tax standpoint, tax-deferred investments, whose income will be taxed at a later date, are less beneficial than tax-exempt investments, they also have financial advantages. According to basic opportunity cost, paying a dollar in the future instead of today gives you the opportunity to invest (or spend) it now. Examples of tax-deferred investments include:

- *Tax-deferred annuities,* usually issued by insurance companies. These investments are discussed in Chapter 19.
- *Section 529 savings plans* are state-run, tax-deferred plans to set aside money for a child's education. The 529 is like a prepaid tuition plan in which you invest to cover future education costs. The 529 plans differ from state to state.
- *Retirement plans* such as IRA, Keogh, or 401(k) plans. The next section discusses the tax implications of these plans.

capital gains Profits from the sale of a capital asset such as stocks, bonds, or real estate.

Capital gains, profits from the sale of a capital asset such as stocks, bonds, or real estate, are also tax deferred; you do not have to pay the tax on these profits until the asset is sold. *Long-term* capital gains (on investments held more than a year) will be taxed at a rate that is lower than ordinary income that is based on taxable income amounts. For 2021, the rates are as follows:

Capital Gain Tax Rate	Single	Married Filing Jointly
0%	Up to $40,400	Up to $80,800
15%	$40,401–$445,850	$80,801–$501,600
20%	$445,851 +	$501,601 +

Certain assets, however, such as art, antiques, stamps, and other collectibles, are taxed at 28 percent.

Short-term capital gains (on investments held for less than a year) are taxed as ordinary income (see the nearby *Financial Literacy Calculations* feature).

The sale of an investment for less than its purchase price is, of course, a *capital loss.* Capital losses can be used to offset capital gains and up to $3,000 of ordinary income. Unused capital losses may be carried forward into future years to offset capital gains or ordinary income up to $3,000 per year.

Capital gains of $500,000 on the sale of a home may be excluded by a couple filing a joint return ($250,000 for singles). This exclusion is allowed each time a taxpayer sells or exchanges a principal residence—however, only once every two years.

SELF-EMPLOYMENT   Owning your own business has certain tax advantages. Self-employed persons may deduct expenses such as health and life insurance as business costs. However, business owners have to pay self-employment tax (Social Security) in addition to the regular tax rate.

Financial Literacy Calculations

SHORT-TERM AND LONG-TERM CAPITAL GAINS

You will pay a lower tax rate on the profits from stocks and other investments if you hold the asset for more than 12 months. As of 2021, a taxpayer in the 32 percent tax bracket would pay $640 in taxes on a $2,000 short-term capital gain (assets held for less than a year). However, that same taxpayer would pay only $300 on the $2,000 (a 15 percent capital gains tax) if the investment were held for more than a year.

	Short-Term Capital Gain (assets held less than a year)	Long-Term Capital Gain (assets held a year or more)
Capital gain	$2,000	$2,000
Capital gains tax rate	32%	15%
Capital gains tax	$640	$300
Tax savings		$340

CHILDREN'S INVESTMENTS In past years, parents made investments on their children's behalf and listed the children as owners. This process, known as *income shifting,* attempted to reduce the taxable income of parents by shifting the ownership of investments to children in lower tax brackets. A child under 18 with investment income of more than $2,200 (as of 2021) is taxed at the rates that are applicable to estates and trusts (which are higher than individual ordinary income rates).

RETIREMENT AND EDUCATION PLANS

A major tax strategy is the use of tax-deferred retirement and education plans such as individual retirement arrangements (IRAs), Keogh plans, 401(k) plans, and education savings accounts.

TRADITIONAL IRA When IRAs were first established, every working person was allowed to deduct up to $2,000 per year for IRA contributions. The contributions to and earnings from these accounts are not taxed until they are withdrawn. Today, the regular IRA deduction is available only to people who do not participate in employer-sponsored retirement plans or who have an adjusted gross income under a certain amount. As of 2021, the IRA contribution limit was $6,000. Older workers, age 50 and over, are allowed to contribute up to $7,000 as a "catch up" to make up for lost time saving for retirement.

In general, amounts withdrawn from deductible IRAs are included in gross income. An additional 10 percent penalty is usually imposed on withdrawals made before age 59½ unless the withdrawn funds are on account of death or disability, for medical expenses, or for qualified higher education expenses.

Variations of the IRA include the Simplified Employee Pension (SEP) Plan and the Savings Incentive Match Plans for Employees (SIMPLE Plans). These plans are designed for people who are self-employed and small business owners.

ROTH IRA The Roth IRA also allows a $6,000 (as of 2021) annual contribution, which is not tax deductible; however, the earnings on the account are tax free after five years. The funds from the Roth IRA may be withdrawn before age 59½ if the account owner is disabled, or for the purchase of a first home ($10,000 maximum).

my life 5

I stay informed on proposed tax changes being considered for my current tax filing status.

Your attempts to continually update your knowledge of income taxes will help you make better informed financial decisions. Ask several people about the actions they take to stay informed and to reduce the amount paid in taxes.

Deductible IRAs provide tax relief up front as contributions reduce current taxes. However, taxes must be paid when the withdrawals are made from the deductible IRA. In contrast, the Roth IRA does not have immediate benefits, but the investment grows in value on a tax-free basis. Withdrawals from the Roth IRA are exempt from federal and state taxes.

COVERDELL EDUCATION SAVINGS ACCOUNT The Education Savings Account is designed to assist parents in saving for the education of their children. Once again, the annual contribution (limited to $2,000) is not tax deductible and is limited to taxpayers with an adjusted gross income under a certain amount. However, as with the Roth IRA, the earnings accumulate tax free.

529 PLAN The 529 plan is another type of education savings plan that helps parents save for the college education of their children. Almost every state has a 529 plan available. There is no federal tax deduction, but the earnings grow tax free and there are no taxes when the money is taken out of the account for qualified educational expenses. In addition, you do not have to invest in the plan for your home state, but there may be tax advantages in doing so. Many states allow their residents to deduct contributions to their state plans up to a specified maximum. Make sure to check out the investment choices and performance before investing.

KEOGH PLAN If you are self-employed and own your own business, you can establish a Keogh plan. This retirement plan, also called an HR10 plan, may combine a profit-sharing plan and a pension plan of other investments purchased by the employee. In general, with a Keogh, people may contribute 25 percent of their annual income, up to a maximum of $58,000 (as of 2021), to this tax-deferred retirement plan.

401(K) PLAN The part of the tax code called 401(k) authorizes a tax-deferred retirement plan sponsored by an employer. This plan allows you to contribute a greater tax-deferred amount ($19,500 in 2021) than you can contribute to an IRA. Older workers, age 50 and over, are allowed to contribute up to $26,000. However, most companies set a limit on your contribution, such as 15 percent of your salary. Many employers provide a matching contribution in their 401(k) plans. For example, a company may contribute 50 cents for each $1 contributed by an employee up to a certain percentage of income. This results in an immediate 50 percent return on your investment.

Tax planners advise people to contribute as much as possible to a Keogh or 401(k) plan since (1) the increased value of the investment accumulates on a tax-free basis until the funds are withdrawn and (2) contributions reduce your adjusted gross income for computing your current tax liability. Chapter 18 discusses retirement plans in greater detail.

TAX-SAVINGS STRATEGIES: A SUMMARY

Someone once said that "death and taxes are the only certainties of life." Changing tax laws seem to be another certainty. Each year, the IRS modifies the tax form and filing procedures. In addition, Congress often passes legislation that changes the tax code. These changes require that you regularly determine how to take best advantage of the tax laws for personal financial planning. Some guidelines to consider when selecting effective personal tax strategies include the following:

- Time the receipt of income and payment of taxable expenses in relation to your current and future tax rate.
- Take advantage of tax credits for which you qualify.
- Maximize contributions to tax-deferred retirement programs.
- Consider tax-exempt investments, such as municipal bonds.
- Defer capital gains and accelerate capital losses.
- Take advantage of the tax benefits of owning your own business.

- Plan purchases, such as a house or health care, with tax implications in mind.
- Search out all possible itemized deductions.

Carefully monitor your personal tax strategies to best serve both your daily living needs and your long-term financial goals.

 PRACTICE QUIZ 4-5

PFP Sheet 22
Tax Planning
Activities

1. How does tax avoidance differ from tax evasion?
2. What common tax-saving methods are available to most individuals and households?

Your Personal Finance Roadmap and Dashboard:

Tax Planning

TAX REFUND OR OVERPAYMENT?

Another indicator of your financial health is your ability to organize and prepare key documents to maximize your tax situation. Whether you prepare your tax return or take it to someone to prepare, you need to have all of the key documents to pay your "fair share." You also need to monitor your tax situation throughout the year. This means understanding your tax situation and being aware of any changes.

YOUR SITUATION

Do you owe taxes each year? Do you receive an excessive tax refund? Other personal financial planning actions you might consider during various stages of your life include:

 First Steps

- Maintain a system for tax documents.
- Estimate a suitable withholding amount to avoid a large refund or large amount owed.

- Develop an understanding for preparing your own tax return.
- Sign up for your employer's tax-deferred retirement plan.
- Consider buying a home or other actions for possible tax savings.
- Revise withholding amounts based on family changes.

Next Steps

- Consider increased contributions to tax-deferred retirement plans.
- Investigate various tax-exempt investments.
- Research tax credits for which you may qualify.

Later Steps

- Contribute larger "catch-up" amounts to your retirement plan.
- Assess the financial and tax implications of withdrawals from tax-deferred retirement plans.
- Determine the age at which Social Security benefits will start.

YOUR next step...select one or more of the items above and create an action plan to implement those financial planning activities.

SUMMARY OF LEARNING OBJECTIVES

LO4-1

Describe the importance of taxes for personal financial planning. Your knowledge of the varied taxes paid in our society will provide an understanding of your tax planning, which can influence spending, saving, borrowing, and investing decisions. Knowing tax laws and maintaining accurate tax records allows you to take advantage of appropriate tax benefits. An awareness of income taxes, sales taxes, excise taxes, property taxes, estate taxes, inheritance taxes, gift taxes, and Social Security taxes is vital for successful financial planning.

LO4-2

Calculate taxable income and the amount owed for federal income tax. Organized tax records allow you to easily find needed information when calculating taxable income, which is determined by subtracting adjustments to income, deductions, and allowances for exemptions from gross income. Your total tax liability is based on the published tax tables or tax schedules, less any tax credits.

LO4-3

Prepare a federal income tax return. To file your taxes on time each year requires that you understand the major sections of Form 1040, which are (1) your filing status, (2) exemptions, (3) income from all sources, (4) adjustments to your income, (5) standard deduction or itemized deductions, (6) tax credits for which you qualify, (7) other taxes you owe, (8) amounts you have withheld or paid in advance, and (9) your refund or the additional amount you owe.

LO4-4

Identify tax assistance sources. You can find answers to your tax questions by using the following sources: IRS services and publications, other tax publications, the internet, computer software, and professional tax preparers such as commercial tax services, enrolled agents, accountants, and attorneys.

LO4-5

Select appropriate tax strategies for various financial and personal situations. Learning new tax information may reduce your tax burden when you carefully plan financial decisions related to consumer purchasing, debt, investments, and retirement planning.

KEY TERMS

adjusted gross income (AGI) 123	inheritance tax 120	tax avoidance 142
average tax rate 127	investment income 121	tax credit 127
capital gains 144	itemized deductions 123	tax deduction 123
earned income 121	marginal tax rate 126	tax-deferred income 123
estate tax 120	passive income 122	tax evasion 142
excise tax 120	standard deduction 123	tax-exempt income 123
exclusion 123	taxable income 121	tax shelter 123
exemption 125	tax audit 140	

SELF-TEST PROBLEMS

1. A person had $3,645 withheld for federal income taxes and had a tax liability of $3,400. Would there be a refund or an additional amount due? For what amount?

2. Based on the following information, what is the amount of taxable income?

Gross salary	$64,155	Interest earnings	$50
Dividend income	$155	Standard deduction	$12,550
Itemized deductions	$10,200		

Self-Test Solutions

1. To determine the amount of refund or additional tax due, compare the amount of tax liability with the amount withheld. The $3,400 tax liability minus the $3,645 would result in a refund of taxes of $245.

2. Taxable income is calculated by adding salary, income, and dividends, and then subtracting itemized deductions or the standard deduction (whichever is larger). $64,155 + $50 + $155 − $12,550 = $51,810

FINANCIAL PLANNING PROBLEMS

1. *Computing Taxable Income.* Ross Martin arrived at the following tax information: LO4-2

   Gross salary, $56,145
   Interest earnings, $205

   Dividend income, $65

   Standard deduction, $12,550

   Itemized deductions, $11,250

   Adjustments to income, $1,200

   What amount would Ross report as taxable income?

2. *Determining Tax Deductions.* If Lola Harper had the following itemized deductions, should she use Schedule A or the standard deduction? The standard deduction for her tax situation is $12,550.   LO4-2

   Donations to church and other charities, $6,050
   Medical and dental expenses exceeding 7.5% percent of adjusted gross income, $2,400.

   State income tax, $4,690

3. *Calculating Tax Deductions.* Kaye Blanchard is 50 years old. She has $30,000 of adjusted gross income and $8,000 of qualified medical expenses. She will be itemizing her tax deductions this year. How much of a tax deduction will Kaye be able to deduct (assume 7.5 percent floor for deduction)?   LO4-2

4. *Computing Taxable Income with Qualified Business Income.* Imari Brown arrived at the following tax information: LO4-2

   Gross salary, $36,145
   Additional small business income, $10,000

   Interest earnings, $205

   Dividend income, $65

   Standard deduction, $12,550

   Itemized deductions, $14,250

   Adjustments (subtractions) to income, $5,000

   What amount would Imari report as taxable income?

5. *Calculating Average Tax Rate.* What would be the average tax rate for a person who paid taxes of $4,584 on a taxable income of $41,670?   LO4-2

6. *Determining a Refund or Taxes Owed.* Based on the following data, would Ann and Carl Wilton receive a refund or owe additional taxes?   LO4-2

   Adjusted gross income: $42,686

   Standard deduction: $25,100

   Child care tax credit: $100

   Federal income tax withheld: $1,490

   Tax rate on taxable income: 10 percent

7. *Indexing Standard Deductions for Inflation.* Each year, the Internal Revenue Service adjusts the value of the standard deductions based on inflation (and rounds to the nearest $50). In a recent year, if the deduction was worth $12,550 and inflation was 3.4 percent, what would be the amount of the deduction for the upcoming tax year?   LO4-2

8. *Determining a Tax Refund.* If $4,026 was withheld during the year and taxes owed were $4,050, would the person owe an additional amount or receive a refund? What is the amount?   LO4-2

9. *Opportunity Cost of Tax Refunds.* If 400,000 people each receive an average refund of $2,450, based on an interest rate of 3 percent, what would be the lost annual income from savings on those refunds?   LO4-2

LO4-3 **10.** *Using Federal Tax Rate Schedules.* Using the tax rate schedule in Exhibit 4-6, determine the amount of taxes for the following taxable incomes:

    A. Married filing jointly: Taxable income $50,000.

    B. Married filing jointly: Taxable income $70,000.

    C. Married filing jointly: Taxable income $95,000.

LO4-3 **11.** *Using Federal Tax Tables.* Using the tax table in Exhibit 4-6, determine the amount of taxes for the following situations:

    A. A head of household with taxable income of $70,751.

    B. A single person with taxable income of $70,052.

    C. A married person filing a separate return with taxable income of $70,926.

LO4-5 **12.** *Comparing Taxes on Investments.* Would you prefer a fully taxable investment earning 8.1 percent or a tax-exempt investment earning 6.1 percent? (Assume a 24 percent tax rate.) Why?

LO4-5 **13.** *Capital Gains.* Samuel Jenkins made two investments; the first was 13 months ago and the second was 2 months ago. He just sold both investments and has a capital gain of $3,000 on each. If Samuel is single and has taxable income of $40,000, what will be the amount of capital gains tax on each investment?

LO4-5 **14.** *Future Value of a Tax Savings.* On December 30, you decide to make a $2,500 charitable donation. If you are in the 22 percent tax bracket and you expect to itemize your deductions, how much will you save in taxes for the current year? If you deposit that tax savings in a savings account for the next five years at 4 percent, what will be the future value of that account?

LO4-5 **15.** *Tax Deferred Retirement Benefits.* If a person in the 32 percent tax bracket makes a deposit of $6,000 to a tax-deferred retirement account, what amount would be saved on current taxes?

DIGITAL FINANCIAL LITERACY: TAX TOPIC RESEARCH

Understanding the tax implications of various financial planning decisions is essential as you move through various phases of your life. It's also important to recognize that the tax treatment of various items can change with tax laws. It is essential that you know where to identify important resources to help you understand how to report these items on your tax return.

Action items:

1. Visit the tax section of *Kiplinger's Personal Finance* at kiplinger.com or *The Balance* at thebalance.com to research what the most recent tax topics are today.

2. Identify the appropriate IRS tax publication (www. IRS. gov) that will give you guidance on a particular tax topic.

3. Prepare a one-page report that addresses a tax topic that might be of concern in your financial future.

FINANCIAL PLANNING CASE

A Single Father's Tax Situation

Ever since his wife's death, Eric Stanford has faced difficult personal and financial circumstances. His job provides him with a good income but keeps him away from his daughters, ages 8 and 10, nearly 20 days a month. This requires him to use in-home child care services that consume a large portion of his income. Since the Stanfords live in a small apartment, this arrangement has been very inconvenient.

Due to the costs of caring for his children, Eric has only a minimal amount withheld from his salary for federal income taxes. This makes more money available during the year, but for the last few years he has had to make large payments in April—another financial burden.

Although Eric has created an investment fund for his daughters' college education and for his retirement, he has not sought to select investments that offer tax benefits. Overall, he needs to

look at several aspects of his tax planning activities to find strategies that will best serve his current and future financial needs.

Eric has assembled the following information for the current tax year:

Earnings from wages	$94,124
Interest earned on savings	$150
IRA deduction	$6,000
Checking account interest	$80
Current standard deduction for filing status	$18,800
Amount withheld for federal income tax	$1,000
Tax credit for children	$4,000
Tax credit for child care	$5,000
Filing status	Head of household

150

Questions

1. What are Eric's major financial concerns in his current situation?

2. In what ways might Eric improve his tax planning efforts?

3. Is Eric typical of many people in our society with regard to tax planning? Why or why not?

4. What additional actions might Eric investigate with regard to taxes and personal financial planning?

5. Calculate the following:

   a. What is Eric's taxable income? (Refer to Exhibit 4-1.)

   b. What is his total tax liability? (Use Exhibit 4-6.) What is his average tax rate?

   c. Based on his withholding, will Eric receive a refund or owe additional tax? What is the amount?

YOUR PERSONAL FINANCIAL PLAN

TAX PLANNING ACTIVITIES

Taxes are an important factor of financial planning. Various actions can be taken to reduce the time and money that go toward taxes. Understanding your tax situation now and into the future is helpful for planning purposes.

Your Short-Term Financial Planning Activity

Task Evaluate your tax situation to identify action items for the current tax year.

Research

1) Use PFP Sheet 20 to estimate your current year income tax.
2) Use PFP Sheet 22 to identify any action items that may be required in the current year.

Outcome Create a personal file with summary notes that include reasons for changes as identified.

Your Long-Term Financial Planning Activity

Task Compare tax preparer costs and services you may need in the future as your tax situation becomes more complex (i.e., buying a house, making investments, starting a home-based business).

Research

1) Use PFP Sheet 21 to compare various costs and services of a local tax service, a national tax service, and a local accountant.
2) Go to IRS.gov, Free File page, to determine your options and costs for filing your taxes yourself.

Outcome Create a personal file, printed or electronic, to keep your research as a reference.

Note: All *Personal Financial Planner* sheets are available at the end of the book and in an Excel spreadsheet format in *Connect Finance*.

CONTINUING CASE

Planning Your Tax Strategy

Jamie Lee Jackson, age 26, is in her last semester of college and is waiting for graduation day, just around the corner! It is the time of year again when Jamie Lee must file her annual federal income taxes. Last year, she received an increase in salary from the bakery, which brought her gross monthly earnings to $2,550, and she also opened an IRA, to which she contributed $300. Her savings accounts earn 1 percent interest per year, and she also had received an unexpected $1,500 gift from her great aunt. Jamie was also lucky enough last year to win a raffle prize of $2,000, most of which was deposited into her regular savings account after paying off her credit card balance.

Current Financial Situation

Assets:

Checking account: $2,250
Savings account: $6,900 (Interest earned last year: $125)
Emergency fund savings account: $3,900 (Interest earned last year: $75)
IRA balance: $350 ($300 contribution made last year)
Car: $3,000

Liabilities:

Student loan: $10,800
Credit card balance: $0 (Interest paid last year: $55)

Income:

Gross monthly salary: $2,550

Monthly Expenses:

Rent obligation: $275
Utilities obligation: $135
Food: $130
Gas/maintenance: $110
Credit card payment: $0

Savings:

Regular savings monthly deposit: $175
Rainy day savings monthly deposit: $25

Entertainment:

Cake decorating class: $40
Movies with friends: $60

Questions

1. What impact on Jamie Lee's income would the gift of $1,500 from her great aunt have on her adjusted gross income? Would there be an impact on the adjusted gross income with her $2,000 raffle prize winnings? Explain your answer.

2. Using Exhibit 4-1 as a guide, calculate Jamie Lee's adjusted gross income amount by completing the following table.

Gross income	
(−) Adjustments to income	(−)
= Adjusted gross income	=

3. What would Jamie Lee's filing status be considered? Would you choose the standard deduction allowance or the itemized deduction allowance in Jamie's situation? Based on your choice, what would the deduction amount be?

4. In Jamie Lee's situation, what is her marginal tax rate? How would a marginal tax rate compare to an average tax rate?

 # DAILY SPENDING DIARY

"Sales tax on various purchases can really increase the amount of my total spending."

Directions

Continue your *Daily Spending Diary* to record and monitor your spending in various categories. Your comments should reflect what you have learned about your spending patterns and help you consider possible changes you might want to make in your spending habits.

Questions

1. What taxes do you commonly pay that are reflected (directly or indirectly) in your *Daily Spending Diary*?

2. How might you revise your spending habits to better control or reduce the amount you pay in taxes?

The *Daily Spending Diary* sheets are located at the end of Chapter 1 and on the library resource site in *Connect*.

Financial Services: Savings Plans and Payment Methods

5

Rawpixel.com/Shutterstock

LEARNING OBJECTIVES

LO5-1 Analyze factors that influence the selection and use of financial services.

LO5-2 Compare the types of financial-service providers.

LO5-3 Assess the costs and benefits of various savings plans.

LO5-4 Identify the factors used to evaluate different savings plans.

LO5-5 Evaluate the costs and benefits of different types of payment accounts.

Financial Literacy
IN YOUR LIFE

▶ **What if you . . .** would like to save funds for graduate studies or an advanced technical certificate? Or do you need an emergency fund for unexpected expenses? What actions would you take?

You might . . . reduce current spending or increase your income. Carefully selecting financial services can also result in saving money by avoiding unnecessary fees and service charges. These added savings amounts will result in achieving current financial goals while moving toward long-term financial security.

Now, what would you do? What actions are you currently taking to improve the amount in your savings? You will be able to monitor your progress using the Your Personal Finance Roadmap and Dashboard feature at the end of the chapter.

---

my life	**BANKING BASICS**

The variety and sources of financial services can be overwhelming. Many savings, checking, and credit plans are offered through local banks, online service providers, and apps. Understanding the costs associated with banking services can result in large savings and improved personal financial planning.

What are your attitudes toward financial services? For each of the following statements, indicate the choice that best describes your current situation.

1. The financial service about which I'm least informed is
   a. mobile app banking services.
   b. certificates of deposit and other savings plans.
   c. checking accounts and other payment methods.

2. My primary financial service activity involves the use of
   a. a bank or credit union.
   b. a mobile banking app.
   c. a check-cashing outlet.

3. The most appropriate savings plan for my current situation is a
   a. regular savings account.
   b. money market account.
   c. certificate of deposit.

4. When selecting a savings plan, my main concern is
   a. bank location and availability of cash machines.
   b. federal deposit insurance coverage.
   c. rate of return.

5. My checking account balance is
   a. updated in my records after every payment and deposit.
   b. based on a rough estimate in my account.
   c. only known by my financial institution.

As you study this chapter, you will encounter "My Life" boxes with additional information and resources related to these items.

Financial Services for Financial Planning

Banking activities continue to evolve from:

- standing in line for a teller . . . to using a smartphone app.
- writing a check . . . to paying with a tap and go digital wallet app.
- mailing in a deposit . . . to using remote check deposit.
- obtaining a loan from a bank . . . to borrowing through a peer-to-peer lender.

While banks traditionally processed most payment, savings, and credit transactions, many nonbanks and FinTech (financial technology) organizations now offer these and other services. Exhibit 5-1 is an overview of financial-service providers and services for managing cash flows and achieving financial goals.

LO5-1

Analyze factors that influence the selection and use of financial services.

MANAGING DAILY MONEY NEEDS

Buying groceries, paying rent, and spending require a cash management plan. Cash, check, credit card, debit card, and apps are common payment methods. Mistakes when managing cash needs include (1) overspending due to impulse buying and using credit; (2) having insufficient liquid assets to pay bills; (3) using savings or borrowing for

EXHIBIT 5-1 Financial-service providers and banking services

DEPOSIT FINANCIAL INSTITUTIONS
- Commercial bank
- Credit union
- Savings and loan association
- Mutual savings bank

NONDEPOSIT INSTITUTIONS
- Life insurance company
- Investment company
- Brokerage firm
- Credit card company
- Finance company
- Mortgage company

TYPES OF FINANCIAL SERVICES

Cash Availability	Payment Services
• Check cashing, debit cards • ATM access • Wire transfers • Foreign currency exchange	• Checking account/debit cards • Online payments • Prepaid debit cards • Cashier's checks, money orders

Savings Services	Credit Services
• Regular savings account • Money market account • Certificates of deposit • U.S. savings bonds	• Credit cards, cash advances • Auto loans, education loans • Mortgages, business loans • Home equity loans

Investment Services	Other Services
• Individual retirement accounts (IRAs) • Brokerage service • Investment advice • Mutual funds	• Insurance; trust service • Tax preparation • Safe deposit boxes • Budget counseling • Estate planning

HIGH-COST FINANCIAL SERVICE PROVIDERS
- Pawnshop
- Check-cashing outlet
- Payday loan company
- Rent-to-own center
- Car title loan company

NONBANK FINANCIAL SERVICE PROVIDERS
- Retailer stores (prepaid debit cards, other services)
- Online, mobile banks (E*Trade Bank, Varo Bank)
- Online payment services (PayPal, Venmo, Zelle)
- P2P (peer-to-peer) lending intermediaries

Information on financial services is available from many sources.
dennizn/Shutterstock

current living expenses; and (4) failing to put funds in an interest-earning savings account or investment program.

No matter how carefully you manage your money, at some time you may need more cash than you have available. To cope in that situation, you have two basic choices: use your savings or borrow. A savings account, certificate of deposit, mutual fund, or other investment may be accessed when you need funds. Or a credit card cash advance or a personal loan may be appropriate. Remember, both using savings and borrowing more reduce your current net worth and your potential for long-term financial security.

TYPES OF FINANCIAL SERVICES

Banks and other financial-service providers offer services in four main categories.

1. SAVINGS   Storage of funds for future use is a basic need. These services, often referred to as *time deposits,* include savings accounts and certificates of deposit. Selection of a savings plan is based on the interest rate, liquidity, safety, and convenience; these factors are discussed later in the chapter.

2. CASH AVAILABILITY AND PAYMENT SERVICES   Transferring money to others is necessary for daily business activities. Checking accounts, called *demand deposits* in the banking industry, and other payment methods are also covered later in the chapter.

3. BORROWING   Most people use credit at some time. Credit alternatives range from short-term accounts, such as credit cards and cash loans, to long-term borrowing, such as a home mortgage. Chapters 6 and 7 discuss the types and costs of credit.

4. INVESTING, OTHER FINANCIAL SERVICES   Insurance, investing, real estate purchases, tax assistance, and financial planning are other financial services. In some situations, someone else manages your finances. A **trust** is a legal agreement that provides for the management and control of assets by one party for the benefit of another. This arrangement is most commonly created through a commercial bank or a lawyer. Parents who want to set aside funds for their children's education may use a trust. The investments and money in the trust are managed by a bank, and the necessary amounts go to the children for their educational expenses. Trusts are discussed in more detail in Chapter 19.

To monitor several accounts, financial institutions offer an all-in-one platform. An **asset management account**, also called a *cash management account* or a *wealth management account,* provides a complete financial services program for a single fee. Investment brokers and other financial institutions offer this all-purpose account, which usually includes a checking account, a debit-credit card, online banking, an app, and a line of credit for quick loans. These accounts, also used for buying and selling investments, can have the benefits of: (1) keeping track of finances in a single location; (2) fewer monthly and quarterly statements; (3) lower fees when working with one financial institution; (4) fewer forms for tax reporting of dividends and interest; and (5) ease of communicating financial information to family members. Apps are also available that may be used to consolidate, track, and monitor your financial data.

ONLINE AND MOBILE BANKING

Online and mobile banking platforms provide both traditional services and enhanced customer experiences with FinTech applications. The recent pandemic resulted in a

trust A legal agreement that provides for the management and control of assets by one party for the benefit of another.

asset management account An all-in-one account that includes savings, checking, borrowing, investing, and other financial services for a single fee; also called a *cash management account.*

EXHIBIT 5-2 Mobile banking services

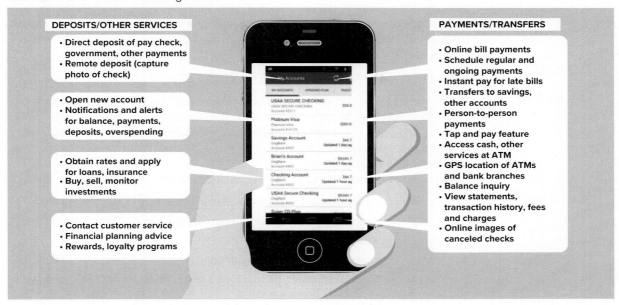

DEPOSITS/OTHER SERVICES

- Direct deposit of pay check, government, other payments
- Remote deposit (capture photo of check)

- Open new account
- Notifications and alerts for balance, payments, deposits, overspending

- Obtain rates and apply for loans, insurance
- Buy, sell, monitor investments

- Contact customer service
- Financial planning advice
- Rewards, loyalty programs

PAYMENTS/TRANSFERS

- Online bill payments
- Schedule regular and ongoing payments
- Instant pay for late bills
- Transfers to savings, other accounts
- Person-to-person payments
- Tap and pay feature
- Access cash, other services at ATM
- GPS location of ATMs and bank branches
- Balance inquiry
- View statements, transaction history, fees and charges
- Online images of canceled checks

rapid increase in using digital channels and apps for banking activities (see Exhibit 5-2), to provide social distancing and contactless transactions.

Online banking, through the website or app of a financial institution, allows access to services for various transactions. Mobile and online banking provide convenience and save time and provide instant information access. However, privacy, data security, overspending, fees, and online scams are concerns of digital banking.

Many banking transactions can be conducted with an *automatic teller machine (ATM)*, also called a *cash machine.* To minimize ATM fees: (1) compare several financial institutions, (2) use your bank's ATMs to avoid surcharges, (3) find an online bank offering no-cost ATMs, (4) withdraw larger amounts to avoid several small transactions, and (5) obtain cash back when checking out at supermarkets.

Video teller machines (VTMs) provide personalized service after bank hours with a face-to-face connection to bank representative or financial specialist. VTMs offer services beyond the typical ATM, such as answering specific account questions. The video banker can handle transactions without your debit card when you prove your identity by answering security questions and presenting a photo ID, or with a facial recognition scan. To avoid being overheard, a chat function may be available. Cash withdrawals through a VTM can involve a precise dollar amount rather than only providing twenty-dollar bills from an ATM.

A **debit card** activates banking and buying transactions. A debit card is in contrast to a *credit card,* since you are spending your money rather than borrowing money. A lost or stolen debit card can be expensive. If you notify the financial institution within two days of the lost card, your liability for unauthorized use is $50. However, you can be liable for up to $500 of unauthorized use if you wait up to 60 days to notify your bank. After 60 days, your liability can be the total amount in your account.

Some card issuers use the same rules for lost or stolen debit cards as for credit cards: a $50 maximum. Of course, you are not liable for unauthorized use, such as a con artist using your account number to make a purchase. Remember, report the fraud within 60 days of receiving your statement to protect your right not to be charged. If your debit or credit card is lost or stolen, contact the issuer to freeze the account.

With increased reliance on technology, a phone, tablet, smartwatch, or computer serves as a *virtual bank branch* to provide information, conduct transactions, and meet remotely. Enhanced video connections, artificial intelligence, voice recognition, chatbots,

debit card A plastic access card used for digital banking transactions and purchases; also called a *cash card.*

and other emerging technology provide a personalized customer experience. Alexa (Amazon), Siri (Apple), Google Assistant, and other voice-enabled devices can check bank and credit card balances, pay bills, and send money. This handsfree access is especially of value when engaged in other activities or for people with accessibility needs.

BANKING APPS AND DIGITAL WALLETS

Nearly every bank, credit union, and nonbank financial service provider has an app to access their services. Wireless transactions, such as *tap and go* and *tap and pay,* are reducing debit and credit card use with cardless banking and contactless purchases. Apps are also available with a credit card "lock and limit" feature to control spending and block unauthorized transactions.

When encountering difficulties with a banking app, actions you might take include:

- Be sure you are using the correct username and password.
- Check your email and social media accounts for any app problem notifications.
- Update app and phone software.
- Contact customer service for the bank or app.
- Login on a desktop computer, go to a bank branch, or use an ATM to do business until the app is back in operation.

Digital wallets, also called *mobile wallets* and *mobile money,* are increasing in use. These apps allow storage and use of credit, debit, and loyalty cards, contactless in-store payments, peer-to-peer (P2P) money transfers as well as storing ID cards, transit tickets, and event tickets. Not all digital wallets offer all services, and most online retailers only accept certain payment types. Common digital wallets are Apple Pay, Google Pay, PayPal, Samsung Pay, Venmo, and Zelle.

Digital wallets continue to expand services with integrated mobile payments, a credit card, investing, saving, budgeting, and cryptocurrency capabilities in a single platform. Shopping elements include features that monitor prices, promotions, coupons, and rewards along with subscriptions management and small business profiles to guide buying choices.

PREPAID DEBIT CARDS

Prepaid debit cards are a common payment method. These cards (see Exhibit 5-3) replace traditional banking services for many consumers. Prepaid payment cards are issued by financial-service providers, including banks, credit card companies, retailers (such as Walmart), and nonbank companies created to provide this financial service.

"Loading" (adding funds to) a prepaid debit card may occur by cash, check, direct deposit, online transfer, smartphone check photo, or credit card cash advance. Common

EXHIBIT 5-3

Prepaid debit card services

Prepaid debit card deposit ("loading") methods:

- Cash or check
- Direct deposit
- Online transfer
- Smartphone check photo
- Credit card cash advance

Prepaid debit card uses, other features:

- In-store, online purchases
- Person-to-person payments
- Savings account
- Usually has federal deposit insurance

VALID FROM ▶ 02/21   EXPIRES END ▶ 12/25

A N OTHER   *DEBIT*

uses include in-store and online purchases as well as peer-to-peer (P2P) payments. A savings account feature is also connected to many cards.

Extensive fees have been a concern with prepaid debit cards. Charges may include an activation fee, a monthly fee, a transaction fee, a cash withdrawal (ATM) fee, a balance-inquiry fee, a fee to add funds, an inactivity fee, and others. Federal regulations requiring disclosure of prepaid debit card fees can guide consumers to make wiser choices. Most prepaid debit cards are covered by federal deposit insurance if managed by a bank, or if the card issuer partners with a bank.

Prepaid card use can result in lower debt since the debit card controls spending and buying on credit. With credit cards, you **pay later**; with debit cards, you **pay now**; with prepaid cards, you **pay before**. Comparisons of prepaid debit card features and fees are available at www.nerdwallet .com/prepaid.

| my life | **1** |

I am well informed about financial services.

To be better informed on current financial services, search for online banks. Obtain information on the services that might be of value to you now or in the future. How could changing interest rates affect your use of various financial services?

FINANCIAL SERVICES AND ECONOMIC CONDITIONS

Changing economic conditions, such as changes in interest rates and consumer prices, influence financial services. Successful financial planning requires an awareness of current trends and future prospects for interest rates (see Exhibit 5-4), which you can learn about through these sources: *The Wall Street Journal* (www.wsj.com); business periodicals such as *Bloomberg Businessweek* (www.bloomberg.com/businessweek), *Forbes* (www.forbes.com), and *Fortune* (www.fortune.com); and other online finance sources. See the *Financial Literacy for My Life* feature in this chapter to better understand interest rates.

personal fintech

While FinTech influences every aspect of personal finance, the effect on banking and financial services may be the greatest.

What if you got paid on the day you work? Instant Financial's app allows access to 50 percent of pay each day worked. The other half is paid at the end of the pay period. This can reduce payday loan use by making funds available between pay periods, but it may discourage saving and increase debt due to a lack of funds at the end of the month. As always, wise money management by building an emergency fund and other savings is encouraged.

Cash App is a money transfer service with "cash boosts" for savings on selected purchases, a stock purchase option, and Bitcoin compatibility. Beware, money deposited with Cash App is not covered by federal deposit insurance.

Chime is a checking account without paper checks, and offers two automatic savings programs: (1) a percentage of your paycheck goes to savings, and (2) small amounts go savings when the app rounds up to the nearest dollar for purchases.

The NetSpend prepaid debit card has a savings and overdraft option (for a fee)—choose between a monthly fee and paying a fee for every transaction. Other fees may also be incurred.

Klarna features "buy now, pay later" (BNPL), allowing purchases with four interest-free payments. This service may not improve your credit score, but it could damage it as a result of missed payments. Quadpay offers a similar BNPL service.

FamZoo and Greenlight are prepaid cards that allow parents to control and monitor children's spending while teaching them wise money management.

The MoneyLion, RoarMoney, and Shake N' Bank platforms combine to offer automatic savings, a virtual debit card, contactless payments, investment suggestions, and cash-back rewards. The *Financial Heartbeat* feature rates customers with a 1 to 10 score on these categories: Save (financial preparedness), Spend (paying current expenses), Shield (insurance), and Score (credit rating.)

Lending Club, which first offered personal loans, has its own credit scoring system and emphasizes improved financial health of customers with an app for wise spending, borrowing, and increased saving.

 PRACTICE QUIZ 5-1

1. What is the relationship between financial services and your financial plan?
2. What are the major categories of financial services?
3. How might opportunity costs influence your selection of financial services?
4. How do changing economic conditions affect financial services?

PFP Sheet 23
Planning the Use of Financial Services

EXHIBIT 5-4

Changing interest rates and decisions related to financial services

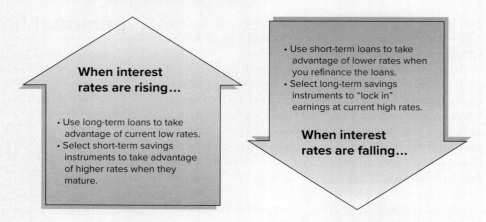

When interest rates are rising...

• Use long-term loans to take advantage of current low rates.
• Select short-term savings instruments to take advantage of higher rates when they mature.

• Use short-term loans to take advantage of lower rates when you refinance the loans.
• Select long-term savings instruments to "lock in" earnings at current high rates.

When interest rates are falling...

Financial-Service Providers

LO5-2

Compare the types of financial-service providers.

Some bank customers encounter a fancy reception desk, then enjoy a cup of private-blend coffee in an elegant lounge area. In contrast, many consumers never enter a physical location, preferring an app. As shown in Exhibit 5-1, a variety of financial-service providers are available to serve your needs.

DEPOSIT INSTITUTIONS

Financial institutions serve as intermediaries between suppliers (savers) and users (borrowers) of funds. These deposit-type institutions include commercial banks, credit unions, savings and loan associations, and mutual savings banks.

commercial bank A financial institution that offers a full range of financial services to individuals, businesses, and government agencies.

COMMERCIAL BANKS   A **commercial bank** offers a full range of financial services, including checking, savings, and lending, along with other services. Commercial banks are organized as corporations with investors (stockholders) contributing the needed capital to operate. Commercial banks include national banks, regional banks, community banks, and online-only banks.

credit union A user-owned, nonprofit, cooperative financial institution that is organized for the benefit of its members.

CREDIT UNIONS   A **credit union** is a user-owned, nonprofit, cooperative financial institution, with members traditionally having a common bond such as work location, church, or community affiliation. Credit union membership today is more flexible than in earlier times, with more than 100 million people in the United States belonging to one. Annual banking studies consistently report lower fees and lower loan rates with higher customer satisfaction levels for credit unions compared to other financial institutions. Most credit unions offer a full range of financial services.

THRIFTS   Thrift financial institutions were originally created to serve low- and middle-income customers with savings accounts and mortgages. Today, *savings and loan associations (S&Ls)* also offer financial services comparable to banks. *Mutual savings banks* are owned by depositors and specialize in savings and mortgages. The profits of a mutual savings bank go to the depositors through higher rates on savings.

OTHER FINANCIAL INSTITUTIONS

In addition to deposit institutions, services are available from other financial institutions and business organizations.

Financial Literacy for My Life

UNDERSTANDING INTEREST RATES

When people talk about higher or lower interest rates, they could be talking about one of many types. Some interest rates refer to the cost of borrowing by a business; others refer to the cost of buying a home. Your awareness of interest rates can guide your spending, saving, borrowing, and investing. The following table describes some commonly reported interest rates and gives their *annual average* for selected years.

Using the website of the Federal Reserve System (www.federalreserve.gov) or an online search, obtain current numbers for these interest rates. How might the current trend in interest rates affect your financial decisions?

	1990	1995	2000	2005	2010	2015	2020	Current
Prime rate—an indication of the rate banks charge large corporations	10.01%	8.83%	9.23%	6.19%	3.25%	3.26%	3.25%	___%
Discount rate—the rate financial institutions are charged to borrow funds from Federal Reserve banks	6.98	5.21	5.73	4.19	0.72	0.76	0.65	___
T-bill rate—the yield on short-term (13-week) U.S. government debt obligations	7.51	5.51	5.66	3.15	0.11	0.03	0.09	___
Treasury bond rate—the yield on long-term (20-year) U.S. government debt obligations	8.55	6.96	6.23	4.64	4.03	2.55	1.45	___
Mortgage rate—the cost of a 30-year loan to borrow for the purchase of a new home	10.13	7.95	8.06	5.86	4.69	3.85	2.66	___
Corporate bond rate—the cost of borrowing for large U.S. corporations	9.32	7.59	7.62	5.23	4.94	3.89	3.16	___
Certificate of deposit rate—the rate earned for a six-month time deposit at a bank or credit union	8.17	5.93	6.59	3.73	0.44	0.27	0.11	___

Source: Federal Reserve Statistical Release: *Selected Interest Rates* (H-15), www.federalreserve.gov and fred.stlouisfed.org.

LIFE INSURANCE COMPANIES While the main purpose of life insurance is to provide financial security for dependents, many life insurance policies contain savings and investment features. Chapter 12 discusses these policies. Life insurance companies also offer financial services such as investment advice and retirement planning.

INVESTMENT COMPANIES Investment companies, also referred to as *mutual funds,* offer banking services. A common service is the **money market fund**, a combination savings–investment plan in which the investment company uses your money to purchase a variety of short-term financial instruments. Unlike accounts at most banks and credit unions, investment company accounts are not covered by federal deposit insurance. Money market funds provide liquidity with check writing and online transfer of funds. Additional information on mutual funds is in Chapter 16.

BROKERAGE FIRMS A brokerage company employs investment advisors and financial planners, which serve as agents between the buyer and seller for stocks, bonds, and other investments. Their earnings come from commissions and fees (see Chapter 14). Some expanded financial services are available from brokerage firms, including checking accounts and online banking.

money market fund A savings–investment plan offered by investment companies, with earnings based on investments in various short-term financial instruments.

my life 2

My primary financial service activities are clearly identified.

Comparing financial institutions requires identifying services and costs. Credit unions consistently offer a low-cost alternative for financial services. For additional information about credit unions, go to www.asmarterchoice.org and www.mycreditunion.gov.

smart money minute

Many people make the *mistake* of paying unnecessary bank fees. An *action* would be to: (1) avoid overdraft charges by linking your checking account to savings, (2) use ATMs in your bank's network, (3) search for no- or low-minimum balance checking accounts, and (4) consider doing your banking at a credit union or with a FinTech. This can result in *success* of reduced fees and service charges. If you decide to change financial institutions, take these actions:

- Transfer money to an account in the new institution.
- Change automatic payments to the new institution.
- Be sure pending payments at your current bank have cleared.
- Notify your former bank, and destroy old checks and debit cards.

Some banks allow you to close an account online.

personal fintech

Neobanks are FinTech start-ups offering financial services through digital channels and apps. Benefits of neobanks include: (1) lower costs; (2) access to no-fee ATMs; (3) services for unbanked and underbanked consumers; (4) no overdraft fees since you only spend the amount in your account; (5) budgeting guidance; and (6) ease of loan approval. Concerns about neobanks include the absence of physical bank branches, a potential lack of government regulation, and the possibility that you may have no recourse when an app malfunctions. Many financial institutions are serving the neobank customer segment, such as GoBank, SoFi Money, Varo Money, and Wells Fargo's Greenhouse.

FINANCE COMPANIES   Making loans to consumers and small businesses is the main function of finance companies. These short- and intermediate-term loans have higher rates than most other lenders. Some finance companies offer other financial services.

CREDIT CARD COMPANIES   Specializing in funding short-term retail lending is the focus of credit card companies, discussed in Chapters 6 and 7. These networks, including Visa, MasterCard, and Discover, have also expanded into other banking and investing services.

MORTGAGE COMPANIES   Mortgage companies provide loans to purchase homes. Chapter 9 discusses the activities of mortgage companies.

OTHER FINANCIAL SERVICE PROVIDERS   Also offering financial services are retailers, Internet banks, FinTechs, and P2P (peer-to-peer) lending networks. Web-only banks operate online, providing most financial services and often with access to ATMs. Amazon offers a checking-account product, loans to small businesses, and other banking services. See the *Financial Literacy for My Life: The "Unbanked" and High-Cost Alternative Financial Services* feature for information on high-cost financial service providers.

COMPARING FINANCIAL-SERVICE PROVIDERS

When deciding where to do your banking, Exhibit 5-5 provides guidelines for selecting a financial-service provider. Some trade-offs when selecting and using financial services include: (1) higher returns for long-term savings with low liquidity; (2) convenience will usually have a cost; and (3) "no-fee" checking accounts will likely require a minimum balance. Be aware of financial service subscriptions (*bundled banking*) with several services for a monthly fee; you may be paying for services that are not used. Evaluate costs and benefits to select the financial-service business that best serve your needs.

PRACTICE QUIZ 5-2

1. What are examples of deposit financial institutions?
2. What factors might consumers consider when selecting a financial-service provider?

Financial Literacy for My Life

THE "UNBANKED" AND HIGH-COST ALTERNATIVE FINANCIAL SERVICES

Would you pay $4 to cash a $100 check? Or pay $20 to borrow $100 for two weeks? Many people without bank accounts (primarily low-income consumers) make use of financial service companies that charge high fees and excessive interest rates. Over 10 million people in the United States are "unbanked" and use alternative financial services. An additional 15 percent of the population are "underbanked" and make use of these services along with a bank account. An unbanked or underbanked person may pay as much as $2,400 a year in interest and service fees.

PAWNSHOPS

Pawnshop loans are based on the value of items such as jewelry or other valuables. Low- and moderate-income families quickly obtain cash loans at a pawnshop, which charges higher fees than other lenders. Many consumers are in need of small loans—usually $50 to $75, to be repaid in 30 to 45 days. Pawnshops are often viewed as "neighborhood bankers" and "local shopping malls," providing both lending and shopping services, selling items that borrowers do not reclaim. While states regulate pawnshops, the interest rates charged can range from 3 percent a month to over 100 percent a year.

CHECK-CASHING OUTLETS

Most banks will not cash a check unless you have an account. As an alternative, to obtain cash, some people use one of the 6,000 check-cashing outlets (CCOs) that charge between 1 and 20 percent of the value of a check; the average is 2 to 3 percent. For a low-income family, that can be a significant amount for their household budget. CCOs, sometimes called *currency exchanges,* also offer electronic tax filing, money orders, private postal boxes, utility bill payment, and prepaid debit cards. A person can often obtain these services at a lower cost at other locations.

PAYDAY LOANS

Beware of the high cost of loans, also called *cash advances, check advance loans, postdated check loans,* and *delayed deposit loans.* Borrowers pay annual rates of as much as 780 percent or more for needed cash from payday loan companies. The most frequent users are workers trapped by debts or difficult financial situations. In recent years, state and federal regulations have attempted to reduce the exploitation of payday loan clients.

With a typical payday loan, a consumer may write a check for $115 to borrow $100 for 14 days. The payday lender agrees to hold the check until the next payday. This $15 finance charge for the 14 days translates into an annual percentage rate of 391 percent. Many borrowers "roll over" their loans, paying another $15 for the $100 loan for the next 14 days. After a few rollovers, the finance charge exceeds the amount borrowed. To prevent this situation, some employers offer pay advances with loan rates in the 9 to 18 percent range.

RENT-TO-OWN CENTERS

Rental businesses offer big-screen televisions, bedroom sets, kitchen appliances, and computers. The rent-to-own (RTO) industry involves stores that lease products to consumers who can own the item if they complete a certain number of payments. A $600 computer can result in $1,900 of payments. RTO purchases may have annual interest rates of over 300 percent.

CAR TITLE LOANS

When in need of money, people with poor credit might obtain cash using their automobile title as security. These high-interest loans, usually due in 30 days, have a cost similar to those of payday loans, often exceeding 200 percent. While the process is simple, the consequences can be devastating when failure to repay the loan results in the repossession of your car.

To avoid high-cost financial service providers, carefully manage your money and do business with lower-cost financial-service providers, such as a credit union. Several FinTech companies offer apps and other products to serve unbanked and underbanked consumers.

Savings Plans

As emphasized in Chapter 3, a savings program is the basis for achieving financial goals. Alternative types of savings are presented in Exhibit 5-6.

SAVINGS ACCOUNTS

Regular savings accounts require a low minimum balance or none at all. Savers can view an online summary of transactions. A regular savings account usually allows you to withdraw money as needed. Banks and other financial institutions offer regular savings accounts. At a credit union, these savings plans are called **share accounts**.

LO5-3

Assess the costs and benefits of various savings plans.

share account A regular savings account at a credit union.

EXHIBIT 5-5 Selecting a financial-service provider

STEP 1. Identify your most important featues for a financial-service provider, related to:

Services	Fees, earnings	Convenience	Online, mobile
• types of accounts • deposit insurance • loans; investments • app/online service	• account minimum balance, ATM fees • loans rates • savings rates	• branch, ATM locations, hours • customer service • rewards program	• ease of operation • services • privacy, security • app features

STEP 2. Rank the top features based on importance and your life situation:

College student	Young family	Older consumer
• low minimum balance • ATM access; app features • waived monthly fee	• low fee, minimum balance • savings plans for future • low-cost auto, home loans	• cash withdrawal limit and fraud detection notifications • large-font documents

STEP 3. Prepare a list of local, national, and online banks and credit unions (include the name, address, phone, website, services offered).

STEP 4. Conduct online and in-person research:
• talk with people who have used various financial-service providers
• search online for services, policies, fees, and customer reviews
• if appropriate, visit the financial institution to observe and talk with staff members
• obtain a fee disclosure statement, savings rate sheet, and sample loan application

STEP 5. Based on the information collected:
• decide where to do business; you may use more than one financial institution
• take advantage of the best services at more than one institution for flexibility in the future
• before changing banks, ask about fees and charges you consider unfair
• use a "switch kit" (available online) with letters and forms to change banks

The following comparison of financial service providers can guide your decision:

Financial Institution	Benefits	Drawbacks
Large-scale bank	• Many branches, fee-free ATMs • Latest digital banking services	• Limited personal service, higher fees • Potential security concerns
Regional, community bank	• High customer satisfaction • Strong personal service	• Limited numbers of branches • May not be in ATM network
Credit union	• Strong personal service • Higher savings rates, lower fees	• Few branches, limited fee-free ATMs • May have membership eligibility
Online bank, FinTech company, neobank	• High customer satisfaction • Higher yields on savings	• Limited personal contact; no branches • May lack regulation; security concerns

Note: *Personal Financial Planner Sheets* 23, 25, 26, and 27, at the end of the book, can be used for this process. Also, see www.pewtrusts.org/banking.

High-yield savings accounts are offered by traditional financial institutions as well as online-only banks. These accounts pay many times more than regular savings accounts, but they have restrictions for the minimum balance, withdrawal limits, and fees.

CERTIFICATES OF DEPOSIT

certificate of deposit (CD) A savings plan requiring that a certain amount be left on deposit for a stated time period to earn a specified interest rate.

Higher earnings are available to savers when money is on deposit for a set time period. A **certificate of deposit (CD)** is a savings plan requiring that a certain amount be on

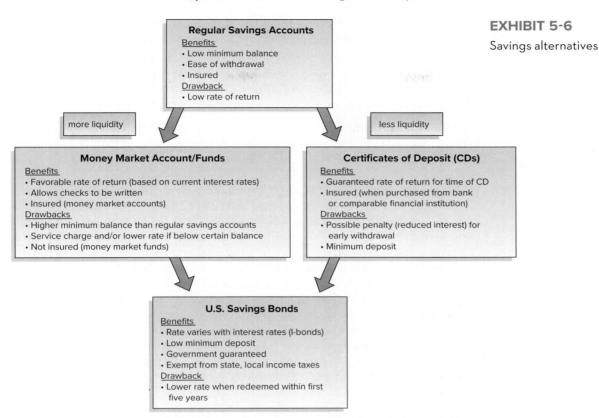

EXHIBIT 5-6

Savings alternatives

deposit for a stated time period (ranging from 30 days to five years or more) to earn a specific rate of return. These *time deposits,* called *share certificates* at a credit union, can be a beneficial and safe savings alternative.

Most financial institutions impose a penalty for early withdrawal of CD funds. For CDs of one year or less, the penalty may be three months' interest. With CDs of more than a year, you might have to forfeit six months' interest, while a five-year CD can have a penalty as high as 20 to 25 percent of the total interest to maturity. If money might be needed before maturity, search for CDs with the lowest penalties. While some CDs have penalty-free withdrawals, the interest rate will likely be lower.

TYPES OF CDs   In addition to traditional certificates of deposit, other types are available:

- *Rising-rate* or *bump-up CDs* have higher rates at set intervals, such as every six months. Beware of ads highlighting a higher future rate. This rate may be in effect for only the last few months of an 18- or 24-month CD.

- *Liquid CDs* allow withdrawal of money without a penalty. A minimum balance will likely be required. This CD may have other restrictions such as a waiting period, a lower rate, or a limit on the number of withdrawals allowed.

- A *zero-coupon CD* is purchased at a deep discount (a portion of the face value) with no interest payments. Your initial deposit ($5,000, for example) grows to the maturity value of the CD ($10,000) in 12 years, which is approximately a 6 percent annual return.

- *Indexed CDs* have earnings based on the stock market. In times of strong stock performance, your earnings can be higher than on other CDs. At other times, you may earn no interest and may even lose part of your savings. A CD based on the consumer price index can result in higher returns as inflation increases.

- *Callable CDs* start with higher rates and have long maturities, as much as 10 or 15 years. With this savings option, if interest rates drop, the bank may "call" (close) the account after a set period, such as one or two years. When the call option is exercised, the saver receives the original deposit and any earned interest.

Beware of *promotional CDs* that attempt to attract savers with gifts or special rates. These "too good to be true" rates may actually be marketing efforts to sell you high-cost financial products.

MANAGING CDs   When buying a CD or *rolling over* a CD (automatically renewing at maturity), carefully assess earnings and costs. Do not allow your financial institution to automatically roll over your money into another CD for the same term. If interest rates have dropped, you might consider a shorter maturity. Or if you believe rates are at a peak and you won't need the money for some time, consider a CD with a longer term.

Consider creating a portfolio of CDs that mature at different times. For example, $2,000 in a three-month CD, $2,000 in a six-month CD, $2,000 in a one-year CD, and $2,000 in a two-year CD. This will give you some liquidity and flexibility for your funds.

Buying CDs from an online bank can be beneficial; rates higher than a local bank may be available. Also, when interest rates are low, consider other savings alternatives such as high-yield savings accounts, savings bonds, mutual funds, and government securities. Current information about CD rates may be obtained at www.bankrate.com, www.nerdwallet.com, and www.depositaccounts.com.

MONEY MARKET ACCOUNTS AND FUNDS

money market account A savings account offered by banks and other financial institutions that requires a minimum balance and has earnings based on market interest rates.

A **money market account** is a savings account that requires a minimum balance and has earnings based on market interest rates. This savings plan will allow you to write checks or to transfer money to other accounts. Money market accounts may impose a fee if the account goes below the required minimum balance.

Both money market accounts and money market funds have earnings based on current interest rates, have minimum-balance restrictions, and allow check writing and transfers. The major difference is safety. Money market *accounts* at banks and credit unions have federal deposit insurance, which is not true of money market *funds,* a product of investment companies. Since money market funds invest in short-term (less than a year) government and corporate securities, however, they are quite safe. When interest rates are very low, be sure to consider other savings alternatives.

SAVINGS BONDS

U.S. savings bonds are low-risk, guaranteed by the federal government, and may be used to save for long-term goals or to create an emergency fund you can access quickly. The U.S. Treasury Department offers several programs for buying savings bonds.

I am aware of the most appropriate savings plan for my current situation.

Several types of savings plans are available for your financial goals and life situation. You can obtain current rates for CDs and other savings plans at www.bankrate.com. For the latest rates and information on U.S. savings bonds, go to www.savingsbonds.gov.

EE BONDS   Series EE bonds are the most common, involving amounts greater than $25. These bonds were originally in a paper format and were purchased for set values ranging from $25 to $5,000, with maturity values of $50 to $10,000. Today, EE bonds are bought and managed online, and they may be purchased for any amount.

EE bonds increase in value as interest is earned monthly and compounds semiannually. If you redeem the bonds less than five years after purchase, you forfeit the latest three months of interest;

BANK ACCOUNTS EVERYONE SHOULD HAVE

While savings and checking accounts are the foundation, consider other accounts to coordinate your finances. You don't use one file for all financial documents, so all your money shouldn't be in one account. To effectively manage your finances, these accounts are recommended:

- *Emergency savings* for funds when you face financial difficulties, such as the recent COVID-19 pandemic. An amount that can cover 6 to 12 months of living expenses is often recommended. Store this money in an "out of sight, out of mind" location, such as an online bank account, high-yield savings account, money market fund, Treasury bills, or short-term bonds.

- *Regular savings* for short-term needs, such as home repairs, vacation, auto maintenance, or new furniture. Have a goal and plan for these funds.

- *Household checking account* for paying current bills. Deposit all income in this account; use automatic transfers for bills and deposits to savings accounts. Extra funds can go to the regular savings fund.

- *Spouse-partner checking accounts* to pay items for which each person has responsibility as well as work-related costs.

- *Health savings account (HSA)* for tax-exempt payments of medical-related expenses for people with high-deductible insurance plans.

- The *extra fund* is "fun money" left over after all bills are paid, amounts are saved, and all accounts have an appropriate balance. This is the reward for spending and managing money wisely.

If all your accounts are at the same financial institution, use the online dashboard to monitor balances. If you use different banks, use a website or app to view your overall financial situation.

Source: https://funcheaporfree.com/the-7-bank-accounts-your-family-should-have-updated/accessed August 5, 2021.

---

after five years, you are not penalized. A bond must be held for one year before it can be cashed. Series EE bonds continue to earn interest for 30 years. The tax advantages of series EE bonds are (1) the interest earned is exempt from state and local taxes, and (2) federal income tax on earnings is not due until the bonds are redeemed.

Redeemed series EE bonds may be exempt from federal income tax if the funds are used to pay tuition and fees at a college, university, or qualified technical school for yourself or a dependent. The bonds must be purchased by an individual who is at least 24 years old, and they must be registered in the names of one or both parents. This provision is designed to assist low- and middle-income households; people whose incomes exceed a certain amount do not qualify for this tax exemption.

I BONDS The I bond has an interest rate based on two components: (1) a fixed rate for the life of the bond, and (2) an inflation rate calculated twice a year. Every six months a new, fixed base rate is set for new bonds. The additional interest payment is recalculated twice a year, based on the current inflation rate. I bonds are sold in any amount over $25 and are purchased at face value. As with EE bonds, the minimum holding period is one year. Interest earned on I bonds is added to the value of the bond and received when you redeem your bond. I bonds have the same tax and education benefits as EE bonds. I bonds might be considered for achieving long-term savings goals.

A person may purchase up to $10,000 worth of savings bonds of each series (EE and I bonds) a year, for a total of $20,000. This amount applies to any person, so parents may buy an additional $20,000 in each child's name. Savings bonds are commonly registered in one of three ways: (1) single owner; (2) two owners, either as co-owners or with one as primary owner; or (3) with a beneficiary, who takes ownership of the bond when the original owner dies.

A TreasuryDirect account at www.treasurydirect.gov allows you 24-hour access to buy, manage, redeem, and view the current

smart money minute

A 529 plan is a qualified tuition plan with tax advantages to encourage saving for education. These programs are sponsored by state agencies and educational institutions. *Prepaid tuition plans* allow the purchase of future college credits at current prices. *Education savings plans* are investment accounts to save for future higher education expenses, such as tuition, fees, and room and board. For additional guidance on education financing, see the Chapter 7 Appendix.

value of savings bonds. You can also invest in other Treasury securities such as bills, notes, bonds, and TIPS (Treasury inflation-protected securities), discussed in Chapter 15.

PFP Sheet 24
Using Savings to Achieve Financial Goals

✓ PRACTICE QUIZ 5-3

1. What are the main types of savings plans?
2. How does a money market *account* differ from a money market *fund*?
3. What are the benefits of U.S. savings bonds?

LO5-4

Identify the factors used to evaluate different savings plans.

rate of return The percentage of increase in the value of savings as a result of interest earned; also called *yield.*

Evaluating Savings Plans

As shown in Exhibit 5-7, your selection of a savings plan will be influenced by several factors.

RATE OF RETURN

Earnings on savings are commonly measured by the **rate of return,** or *yield,* which is the percentage of increase in the value of your savings from earned interest. The rate of return is calculated by dividing the interest earned for the year by the amount in the savings account.

EXAMPLE: Rate of Return

The *rate of return,* or *yield,* on a savings account or other investment is the ratio between the interest earned for the year and the amount in the savings account. For example, a $100 savings account that earned $3 interest for the year would have a rate of return of 3 percent.

$$\$3 \div \$100 = .03 \text{ or } 3 \text{ percent}$$

How about you? How might you use www.depositaccounts.com to obtain a higher yield on your savings?

EXHIBIT 5-7

Selecting a savings plan

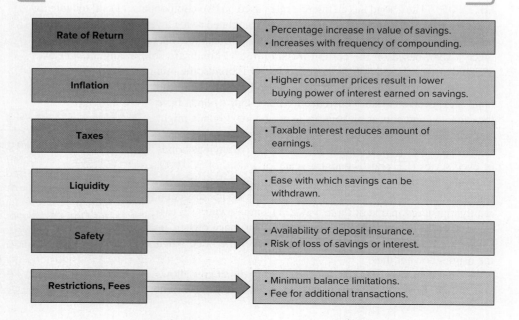

Financial Literacy Calculations

ANNUAL PERCENTAGE YIELD

The Truth in Savings law requires that financial institutions report to savings plan customers and in advertisements, if a rate is quoted, the annual percentage yield (APY). The formula for APY is

$$APY = 100 \left[(1 + \text{Interest/Principal})^{365/\text{days in term}} - 1 \right]$$

The *principal* is the amount of funds on deposit. *Interest* is the total dollar amount earned during the term on the principal. *Days in term* is the actual number of days over which interest is earned.

When the number of days in the term is 365 (i.e., where the stated maturity is 365 days) or when the account does not have a stated maturity, the APY formula is simply

$$APY = 100 \, (\text{Interest/Principal})$$

APY provides a consistent way to compare savings plans with different interest rates, different compounding frequencies, and different time periods. APY may be easily viewed in terms of a $100 deposit for a 365-day year. For example, an APY of 6.5 percent would mean $6.50 interest for a year.

End of Year	Compounding Method			
	Daily	Monthly	Quarterly	Annually
1	$10,832.78	$10,830.00	$10,824.32	$10,800.00
2	11,734.90	11,728.88	11,716.59	11,664.00
3	12,712.16	12,702.37	12,682.42	12,597.12
4	13,770.79	13,756.66	13,727.86	13,604.89
5	14,917.59	14,898.46	14,859.47	14,693.28
Annual yield	8.33%	8.30%	8.24%	8.00%

EXHIBIT 5-8
Compounding frequency affects the savings yield
Shorter compounding periods result in higher yields. This chart shows the growth of $10,000, five-year CDs paying the same rate of 8 percent, but with different compounding methods.

COMPOUNDING The yield on your savings will usually be greater than the stated interest rate. **Compounding** refers to interest that is earned on previously earned interest. Each time interest is added to your savings, the next interest amount is computed on the new balance in the account. Future value and present value calculations, introduced in Chapter 1, take compounding into account.

The more frequently the compounding occurs, the higher your rate of return will be. For example, $100 in a savings account that earns 6 percent compounded annually will increase $6 after a year. But the same $100 in a 6 percent account compounded daily will earn $6.19 for the year. Although this difference may seem slight, large amounts held in savings for long periods of time will result in far higher differences (see Exhibit 5-8).

compounding A process that calculates interest based on previously earned interest.

TRUTH IN SAVINGS The *Truth in Savings* law (Federal Reserve Regulation DD) requires financial institutions to disclose the following information on savings accounts: (1) fees on deposit accounts, (2) the stated interest rate, (3) the annual percentage yield (APY), and (4) other terms and conditions.

Truth in Savings (TIS) defines **annual percentage yield (APY)** as the percentage rate expressing the total amount of interest that would be received on a $100 deposit based on the annual rate and frequency of compounding for a 365-day period. TIS eliminates the confusion caused by the more than 8 million variations of interest calculation methods previously used by financial institutions. APY reflects the amount of interest a saver should expect to earn. (See the *Financial Literacy Calculations: Annual Percentage Yield* feature for additional information on APY.)

annual percentage yield (APY) The percentage rate expressing the total amount of interest that would be received on a $100 deposit based on the annual rate and frequency of compounding for a 365-day period.

Financial Literacy Calculations

AFTER-TAX SAVINGS RATE OF RETURN

The taxability of interest on savings reduces the real rate of return. In other words, you lose some portion of earned interest to taxes. This calculation consists of the following steps:

1. Determine your top tax bracket for federal income taxes.
2. Subtract this rate, expressed as a decimal, from 1.0.
3. Multiply the result by the yield on your savings account.
4. This number, expressed as a percentage, is your after-tax rate of return.

For example,

1. You are in the 24 percent tax bracket.
2. $1.0 - 0.24 = 0.76$.
3. If the yield on your savings account is 5 percent, $0.05 \times 0.76 = 0.038$.
4. Your after-tax rate of return is 3.8 percent.

You may use the same procedure to determine the *real rate of return* on your savings based on inflation. For example, if you are earning 6 percent on savings and inflation is 5 percent, your real rate of return (after inflation) is 5.7 percent: $0.06 \times (1 - 0.05) = 0.057$.

EXAMPLE: Annual Percentage Yield

In a situation with a $1,200 savings account balance in which $66 interest is earned over a year, the APY would be calculated as follows:

$$APY = 100 \left(\frac{\text{Interest}}{\text{Principal}} \right)$$

$$= \left(\frac{100\ 66}{1,200} \right)$$

$$= 100\ (0.055) = 5.5\%$$

In addition to setting the formula for computing the annual percentage yield, Truth in Savings (1) requires disclosure of fees and APY earned on any statements provided to customers, (2) establishes rules for advertising deposit accounts, and (3) restricts the method of calculating the balance on which interest is paid. Financial institutions are also required to calculate interest on the full principal balance in the account each day.

INFLATION

The rate of return you earn on savings should be compared with the inflation rate. At a time when the inflation rate was over 10 percent, people with money in savings accounts earning 5 or 6 percent were experiencing a loss in buying power. In general, as the inflation rate increases, the interest rates offered to savers also increase. This gives you an opportunity to select a savings option that will minimize the loss in value of your dollars on deposit.

TAX CONSIDERATIONS

Like inflation, taxes reduce interest earned on savings. For example, a 10 percent return for a saver in a 24 percent tax bracket means a real return of 7.6 percent (the *Financial Literacy Calculations: After-Tax Savings Rate of Return* feature shows how to compute the after-tax savings rate of return). As discussed in Chapter 4 and discussed further in Chapter 18, several tax-exempt and tax-deferred savings plans and investments can increase your real rate of return.

Remember, taxes are not usually withheld from taxable savings and investment income. As a result of the earnings on these savings, you may owe additional taxes at year end.

LIQUIDITY

Liquidity allows you to withdraw your money on short notice without a loss of principal or fees. Some savings plans impose penalties for early withdrawal or have other restrictions. With certain types of savings certificates and accounts, early withdrawal may be penalized by a loss of interest or a lower interest rate.

You should consider the degree of liquidity you desire in relation to your savings goals. To achieve long-term financial goals, many people trade liquidity for a higher return.

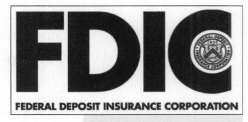

FEDERAL DEPOSIT INSURANCE CORPORATION

Federal deposit insurance reduces the risk of saving for consumers.
Source: Federal Deposit Insurance Corporation
Reproduction of image permitted under General Public License Agreement (GPL)

SAFETY

Savings accounts at nearly every bank, savings and loan, and credit union are insured by federal agencies. Federal Deposit Insurance Corporation (FDIC) coverage prevents a loss of money due to the failure of the insured institution. Credit unions obtain deposit insurance through the National Credit Union Administration (NCUA). Some state-chartered credit unions use a private insurance program. While a few financial institutions have failed in recent years, savers with deposits covered by federal insurance have not lost any money. Depositors have either been paid or have had the accounts taken over by a financially stable institution.

The FDIC insures amounts of up to $250,000 per depositor per insured financial institution. Coverage for higher amounts than this can be obtained by using different ownership categories, such as individual, joint, and trust ownership accounts. For example, a joint account, held by two people, would be covered up to $500,000, with each account owner having $250,000 of coverage. Remember, however, that different branch offices count as the same institution, and mergers in the financial service industry may bring accounts from different banks together.

The FDIC and NCUA also provide deposit insurance for some retirement accounts, up to $250,000, including traditional IRAs, Roth IRAs, Simplified Employee Pension (SEP) IRAs, and Savings Incentive Match Plans for Employees (SIMPLE) IRAs as well as self-directed Keogh accounts and various plans for state government employees. Of course, this coverage applies only to retirement accounts in financial institutions insured by the FDIC and NCUA.

To determine if all of your deposits are insured, use the Electronic Deposit Insurance Estimator (EDIE) at edie.fdic.gov. This site includes a step-by-step tutorial with deposit situations for different types of accounts and different ownership. Information about credit union deposit coverage is available at www.mycreditunion.gov/estimator and www.ncua.gov. Since a financial institution may not have federal deposit insurance, be sure to investigate this matter before opening a savings account. Additional information on regulation and consumer protection of financial institutions is in the Chapter 8 Appendix.

| my life | 4 |

I understand the major factors to consider when selecting a savings plan.

While several factors should be considered when selecting a savings plan, safety is often a major one. Be aware that some "shadow" banking services (money market funds, reloadable prepaid cards) are not covered by federal deposit insurance; additional information is available at www.fdic.gov.

EXAMPLE: Deposit Insurance

If you have a $562,000 in a joint savings account with a relative in an FDIC insured financial institution, $62,000 of the savings would not be covered by federal deposit insurance.

The $562,000 balance exceeds the $500,000 ($250,000 per person) limit by $62,000.

How about you? What actions would you take to make sure your savings are insured?

RESTRICTIONS AND FEES

Other costs and limitations can affect your savings choices. Some banks may charge a monthly fee for low-balance accounts, or an inactivity fee if no transactions occur for 6 to 24 months. Government regulations may limit the number of transfers and withdrawals you can make each month from a savings or money market account. After a certain number, you may be subject to a fee; ATM withdrawals do not count. This restriction was eased to allow easier access to savings during the recent pandemic. Also, a delay may exist between the time interest is earned and when it is added to your account.

PFP Sheet 25
Savings Plan
Comparison

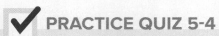 **PRACTICE QUIZ 5-4**

1. When would you prefer a savings plan with high liquidity over one with a higher rate of return?
2. What is the relationship between compounding and the future value of an amount?
3. How do inflation and taxes affect earnings on savings?

Payment Methods

LO5-5

Evaluate the costs and benefits of different types of payment accounts.

Cash and checks, once used for almost all payments, have been replaced by digital methods (Exhibit 5-9). The main trends include touchless payments, digital wallets, and QR code payments. Despite increased card and app use, cash will continue to be used. Legislation in some areas ban cashless stores because they discriminate against customers without a bank account.

Financial institutions offer convenient services through technology.
Bro Crock/Shutterstock

DIGITAL PAYMENTS

Transactions without cash, checks, or credit cards are common as a result of technology, improved security, and increased consumer acceptance.

DEBIT CARD TRANSACTIONS Retailers process debit card transactions with the purchase amount deducted from your bank account. Most debit cards can be used with either: (1) your signature, like a credit card, or (2) your personal identification number (PIN), like an ATM transaction.

When the debit card is processed like a credit card, you have more security in case of a fraudulent transaction or a purchase dispute. When using a debit card to check into a hotel, buy gas, or rent a car, a merchant may *freeze* an amount in your bank account greater than what you actually spend. This hold on your funds could result in an overdrawn account.

EXHIBIT 5-9 Payment alternatives

Electronic Payments	Checking Accounts	Other Payment Methods
• Debit (cash, check) cards	• Traditional checking accounts	• Certified checks
• Online payments, mobile transfers	• Special feature checking accounts	• Cashier's checks
• Stored-value (prepaid) cards	• Checkless checking accounts	• Money orders
• Smart cards, digital wallets		• Traveler's checks

EXAMPLE: Credit Cards vs. Debit Cards

Use a Credit Card to	Use a Debit Card to
Delay the payment for a purchase.	Limit your spending to available money.
Build a credit history with wise buying.	Avoid bills that will be paid in the future.
Buy online or for major purchases.	Avoid interest payment or an annual fee.
Earn more generous rewards points for spending.	Obtain better protection if you process a transaction as a credit card.

How about you? Describe a situation when you might use a credit card instead of a debit card.

ONLINE PAYMENTS Banks and online companies serve as third parties to facilitate online bill payments. Some online payment services give you a choice of using a credit card or a bank account, while others require one or the other. Linking a transaction to your checking account, rather than to a credit card, may not give you as much leverage when disputing a transaction.

Be sure to monitor online payment dates for your checking account, which is usually the date when the amount is to be received by the payee. However, some banks may ask for the date to start processing the payment. In that case, be sure to select a date that will allow your payment to be received by the payee by the due date.

Third-party payment services often charge a fee and may send in your payment late, resulting in another fee and possible interruption of service for utilities or a poor credit report.

People without a credit or debit card can use PayNearMe.com for online transactions. This service allows buyers to make a purchase and pay cash at a local store. The customer receives a receipt and the seller is notified of the payment. This cash transaction network may be used for online purchases, telephone orders, loan repayments, money transfers, and other transactions that might require a credit card. When using this service, be sure to consider fees, online security, and customer service availability.

MOBILE TRANSFERS Apps for mobile payments through smartphones, tablets, and other wireless devices are replacing debit and credit cards. A tap or wave of your phone at the point-of-sale terminal sensor completes the purchase.

Mobile services to transfer money to another person require registering with a debit or credit card or bank account. Peer-to-peer (P2P) payments are conducted with an app such as PayPal, Venmo, and Zelle. Fees for using a P2P service can range from less than a dollar to a percentage of the amount transferred.

Money transfer services are a fast, convenient, and safe way to send funds across the country or around the world. For a fee, companies such as MoneyGram, TransferWise, Western Union, and Xoom use highly secure systems to electronically deliver money to another person within a day or two.

STORED-VALUE (PREPAID) CARDS Prepaid cards may be used for telephone service, transit fares, highway tolls, laundry service, and school lunches as well as gift cards for retailers. While some stored-value cards are disposable, others can be reloaded with additional funds. Some prepaid cards may have an activation charge, ATM fees, and other transaction costs. Recipients of government benefits may receive Social Security and other payments on a prepaid debit card, which is practical for people without a bank account. Some states offer the option of receiving your tax refund on a debit card.

SMART CARDS, DIGITAL WALLET Smart cards, with an embedded chip, are used for banking transactions and may also store your personal data, past purchases, insurance information, and medical history. Digital wallets, such as Apple Pay and Google Pay, contain electronic versions of credit and debit cards in an app to allow contactless transactions, which people value when health and hygiene concerns are present. With these benefits, digital wallets are expected to have an expanded presence as a payment method.

TYPES OF CHECKING ACCOUNTS

While *checking account* is still the commonly accepted name, other titles are emerging such as *debit account, digital bank account, spending account,* and *transaction account.* Variations of checking accounts serve the needs of different customer segments.

TRADITIONAL CHECKING ACCOUNTS The types of checking accounts that have been used over the years include:

- *Regular checking accounts* usually have a monthly service charge that may be avoided with a minimum balance in the account. Or, the monthly fee may be waived if you keep a certain amount in savings. Avoiding the monthly service charge can be beneficial. For example, a monthly fee of $7.50 results in $90 a year. Debit cards and online banking are provided with this account.

- *Interest-earning checking accounts* require a minimum balance. If the balance goes below that amount, you may not earn interest and may incur a service charge. The annual percentage yield (APY) is a factor to consider when selecting an account. A **share draft account** is an interest-earning checking account at a credit union. Credit union checks are called *share drafts.*

> **share draft account** An interest-bearing checking account at a credit union.

- *Activity accounts* charge a fee for each check written and sometimes a fee for each deposit, in addition to a monthly service charge. However, you do not have to maintain a minimum balance. An activity account is most appropriate for people who write only a few checks each month and cannot maintain the required minimum balance.

SPECIAL FEATURE CHECKING ACCOUNTS Financial institutions offer checking accounts to serve various needs.

- *Targeted group accounts* for seniors, students, or military personnel are offered with lower fees and additional services.

- *Rewards checking accounts* earn points, cash back, or a bonus interest rate based on certain requirements such as a certain number of debit card transactions, a direct deposit, and use of a credit card from the same financial institution.

- *Premier checking accounts* offer several services (safe deposit box, low-rate loans, and travel insurance) for a single monthly fee or a high minimum balance. This option may not be a good value if you do not make use of the services in the package.

CHECKLESS CHECKING ACCOUNTS These accounts have no paper checks; all transactions are conducted with a debit card or through online banking. No overdraft fees occur since only amounts within the account balance will be processed.

EVALUATING CHECKING ACCOUNTS

Would you rather have a checking account that pays interest and requires a $1,000 minimum balance or an account that doesn't pay interest and requires a $300 minimum balance to avoid a monthly service charge? This decision requires evaluating many factors, such as restrictions, fees and charges, interest, and special services (see Exhibit 5-10).

RESTRICTIONS A common checking account limitation is the required minimum balance to earn interest or avoid a service charge. Financial institutions may also place a

CHECKING ACCOUNT SELECTION FACTORS

Restrictions	Fees and Charges
• Minimum balance	• Monthly fee
• Federal deposit insurance	• Fees for each check or deposit
• Hours and location of branch offices	• Printing of checks
• Holding period for deposited checks	• Fee to obtain canceled check copy
	• Overdraft, stop-payment order, certified check fee
	• Fees for preauthorized bill payment, fund transfer, or online banking activity

Special Services	Interest
• Direct deposit of payroll and government checks	• Interest rate
• 24-hour teller machines	• Minimum deposit to earn interest
• Overdraft protection	• Method of compounding
• Online banking and apps	• Portion of balance used to compute interest
• Discounts or free checking for certain groups (students, military, senior citizens, employees of certain companies)	• Fee charged for falling below necessary balance to earn interest
• Free or discounted services	

EXHIBIT 5-10
Checking account selection factors

overdraft protection An automatic loan made to cover the amount of checks written and payments in excess of the available balance in the checking account.

hold on the availability of funds from deposited checks; that is, they require a period of time for checks to clear before you can access the funds. The Check Clearing for the 21st Century Act (known as Check 21) shortens the processing time for clearing checks, and it allows a *substitute check,* a digital reproduction of the original paper check, to be considered a legal equivalent.

FEES AND CHARGES   Nearly all financial institutions require a minimum balance or impose service charges for checking accounts. When using an interest-bearing checking account, compare your earnings with any service charge or fee. Also, consider the cost of lost or reduced interest resulting from the requirement to maintain the minimum balance. Checking account fees have increased in recent years. The cost of items such as check printing, overdraft fees, and stop-payment orders have doubled or tripled at some institutions.

INTEREST   The interest rate, the frequency of compounding, and the interest computation method will affect checking account earnings.

OTHER SERVICES   An overdrawn account, when you exceed your balance, results in a *bounced check,* also referred to as *non-sufficient funds.* **Overdraft protection** is an automatic loan for payments in excess of the available balance. This service can be convenient but costly. An overdraft of just $1 might trigger a $50 loan along with high finance charges. However, overdraft protection can be less costly than the fee charged for a payment that exceeds your balance.

Customers can prevent overdrafts for debit card transactions and ATM withdrawals by opting out of the service to cover payments that exceed your balance. While your transaction will be denied, you will avoid an overdraft fee as high as $35. For a nominal amount, many financial institutions will cover overdrafts with an

personal fintech

Cryptocurrencies such as Bitcoin, Cardano, Ethereum, Litecoin, and Tether are increasing in popularity. Also called *cybercurrencies, digital currencies,* and *virtual currencies,* these digital assets are a payment method with flexibility, control, transparency, and security. Using digital files as money, the tokens or coins are viewed by some as a store of value, similar to gold.

Cryptocurrency transactions are processed with technology known as *blockchain* with digital records maintained through computers in a peer-to-peer network. This decentralized system results in every transaction being validated by multiple parties, rather than being controlled by one person or government. The individual records, called *blocks,* are linked together in single list, called a *chain.* This creates a public record (the blockchain) shared with all users to verify the permanence of transactions.

Recent drawbacks of virtual currencies include: (1) a lack of awareness and understanding among users and merchants; (2) the changing and often uncertain value of the currency unit; and (3) risks as new features make the digital currency more secure and accessible.

Coinbase and Celsius are two of the crypto wallet apps used to buy and hold cryptocurrencies. Digital currencies issued by the U.S. Federal Reserve and central banks in Europe are also under consideration.

HOW TO . . .   **Avoid Identity Theft**

Phishing by email, *vishing* by phone, *smishing* by text, and *pharming* involving bogus websites are scams to get your credit card number, bank account information, Social Security number, passwords, or other personal data. Email spam or pop-up messages deceive you by looking official, including logos from a financial institution or government agency. Never click on the link or disclose personal data by phone to a questionable source.

In the past, people put their Social Security and driver's license numbers on their checks, making identity theft fairly easy. With one check, a con artist could know a person's Social Security, driver's license, and bank account numbers as well as address, phone number, and perhaps even a signature sample. Identity fraud can range from passing bad checks and using stolen credit cards to theft of another person's total financial existence. Although online banking and apps is increasing, fake check scams continue; for information, go to www.consumer.ftc.gov/features/fake-check-scams.

To avoid identity theft, consider these actions:

1. Use initials and last name on checks so a person will not know how you sign checks. Use your work phone and a post office box on checks. Do not put the full account number on checks when paying a bill, only the last four digits.
2. Only download apps from an official app store. Use security features on mobile devices. Avoid sharing personal data on social media. Take advantage of biometric security systems, such as eye scan and fingerprint recognition.
3. Do not put your Social Security number on any document unless legally required. In your wallet, do not carry your Social Security card, a list of passwords, spare keys, blank checks, or extra credit cards. Keep a photocopy of your wallet contents (both sides of each item).
4. Shred or burn financial documents that contain account information or Social Security numbers.
5. Use passwords with letters, numbers, and special characters; change passwords and PINs often on accounts and phone.
6. Do not mail bills from your home mailbox. Mail checks at the post office. Promptly collect your mail each day.
7. Monitor billing cycles; contact the sender if a statement is late. Review bank and credit card statements for unauthorized transactions.
8. Each year, or more often if you suspect fraud, check your credit report for errors with the three major credit reporting services. Use fraud monitoring offered by many banks. Consider a credit monitoring or identity monitoring service or identity theft insurance.
9. Set up alerts and notifications when unusual activity occurs; freeze accounts if fraudulent transactions are suspected.
10. Have your name removed from mailing lists operated by credit agencies and companies offering credit promotions.
11. Use only secure websites of reputable companies for purchases or when providing personal data. Avoid public wifi networks. Be careful in public so others can't see your credit/debit card number or PIN. Store cards in an RFID-blocking wallet or sleeve to prevent access to personal data; wrapping cards in foil can also provide security.
12. Maintain up-to-date antivirus software with anti-spam, a secured home wireless network with a password, firewall, a locked router, virtual private network (VPN), and encrypted information.

If you suspect or are a victim of identity theft, be sure to:

- File a police report immediately in the area where the item was stolen. This proves you were diligent, and it is a first step toward any investigation.
- Call the three national credit reporting organizations to place a fraud alert on your name and Social Security number. The numbers are: Equifax, 1-800-525-6285; Experian, 1-888-397-3742; and TransUnion, 1-800-680-7289.
- Complete an ID Theft Affidavit, available at www.identitytheft.gov.
- Contact the Social Security Administration fraud line at 1-800-269-0271.
- Check with your post office to determine if a fraudulent change-of-address form was submitted.
- Maintain a record of your actions—people you contacted, dates, reports filed.

Additional information on financial privacy and identity theft is available at www.identitytheft.gov, www.ftc.gov/idtheft, www.privacyrights.org, and www.idtheftcenter.org.

automatic transfer from savings or with a link to a credit card. If available, take advantage of this service to avoid an overdraft fee, which can occur more than once each day. In a recent year, banks collected an estimated $30 billion in overdraft fees.

MANAGING YOUR CHECKING ACCOUNT

Obtaining and using a checking account involves several actions.

my life 5

I regularly maintain a record of my checking account balance.

Each year, fewer and fewer checks are written. However, debit cards and online payments are usually connected to a checking account. Compare payment accounts at several financial-service providers to determine the one that best serves your needs.

OPENING A CHECKING ACCOUNT First, decide on the owner of the account. Only one person is allowed to write checks on an *individual account*. A *joint account* has two or more owners. Both an individual account and a joint account require a *signature card*. This document is a record of the official signatures of the person or persons authorized to write checks on the account.

MAKING DEPOSITS A *deposit ticket* is used to list cash and check amounts being deposited. Each check requires an *endorsement*—your signature on the back of the check—to authorize the transfer of the funds into your account. The four common endorsements are:

- A *blank endorsement* is just your signature, and it should only be used when you deposit or cash a check in person, because a check can be cashed by anyone once it has been signed.
- A *restrictive endorsement* consists of the words "for deposit only" followed by your signature and account number, which is useful when depositing checks.
- A *special endorsement* allows the transfer of a check to someone else with the words "pay to the order of" followed by the name of the other person and then your signature.
- A *remote deposit capture* deposits a check with an app photo; it may require wording such as "for remote deposit" followed by your signature and account number. Keep the check to make sure it is deposited correctly; then it can be shredded.

WRITING CHECKS Before writing a check, record the information in your check register and deduct the amount of the check from your balance. Some consumers use duplicate checks to maintain a record of their balance. Be sure to record other payments made by debit card, phone app, or online banking.

When writing a check, follow these steps: (1) record the date, (2) write the name of the person or organization receiving payment, (3) record the check amount in figures, (4) write the check amount in words (checks for less than a dollar should be written as "only 79 cents," for example, and cross out the word *dollars* on the check), (5) sign the check, and (6) note the reason for payment. Never write a check in pencil or with red ink.

A *stop-payment order* may be necessary if a check is lost or stolen. Most banks do not honor checks with "stale" dates, usually six months old or older. The fee for a stop-payment is commonly as much as $30 or more. If several checks are missing or you lose your checkbook, closing the account and opening a new one is less costly than paying several stop-payment fees.

RECONCILING YOUR CHECKING ACCOUNT Online you will be able to access your *bank statement* summarizing deposits, checks paid, online payments, ATM withdrawals, interest earned, and fees and service charges. The balance reported on the statement will usually differ from the balance in your check register, written record, app, or spreadsheet of checks written, online payments, and cash withdrawals. Reasons for a difference may include checks that have not yet cleared, deposits not received by the bank, and interest earned.

Smart Money Minute

To determine the correct balance, prepare a *bank reconciliation* to account for differences between the bank statement and your checkbook balance. This process involves the following steps:

1. Compare checks written, payments, and withdrawals from your records with those reported as paid on the bank statement. *Subtract* from the *bank statement balance* the total of these outstanding checks and payments.

2. Determine whether any deposits made are not on the statement; *add* the amount of the outstanding deposits to the *bank statement balance.*

3. *Subtract* fees or charges reported on the bank statement, debit card payments, automatic payments, and ATM withdrawals from your *checkbook balance.*

4. *Add* any interest earned to your *checkbook balance.*

At this point, the revised balances for both the checkbook and the bank statement should be the same. If the two do not match, check your math; make sure every payment, cash withdrawal, deposit, fee, and interest earned was recorded correctly. At certain points in time, no difference may exist since most digital transactions (payments and deposits) are processed faster than paper checks.

EXAMPLE: Bank Reconciliation

To determine the true balance in your checking account:

Bank Statement		Your Checkbook	
Bank balance	$920	Checkbook balance	$1,041
Subtract: Outstanding checks, payments, withdrawals	−187	**Subtract:** Fees, ATM withdrawals	−271
Add: Outstanding deposits	+200	**Add:** Interest earned, direct deposits	+163
Adjusted bank statement balance	933	**Adjusted checkbook balance**	933

How about you? Describe actions you might take to make sure the correct amount is reported in your bank account.

A failure to reconcile your bank account each month can result in **not** knowing:

- Your exact spending habits for wise money management.
- If the correct deposit amounts have been credited to your account.
- Any unauthorized ATM withdrawals or incorrect transactions.
- If your bank is overcharging you for fees.
- Errors that your bank may have made in your account.

OTHER PAYMENT METHODS

A *certified check* is a personal check with guaranteed payment. The amount of the check is deducted from your balance when the financial institution certifies the check. A *cashier's check* is a check of a financial institution, which is purchased by paying the check amount plus a fee. A *money order* is purchased in a similar manner from financial institutions, post offices, and stores. Certified checks, cashier's checks, and money orders allow you to make payments that a recipient knows is valid, which would be useful when buying a used car from someone who doesn't know you.

Traveler's checks, popular before ATMs, allowed payments when away from home. This document required you to sign each check twice. First, you signed the traveler's checks when purchased. Then, as identification, you signed again as you used them. Electronic traveler's checks, in the form of prepaid travel cards, have become common allowing travelers from other nations to obtain local currency from an ATM.

 PRACTICE QUIZ 5-5

1. What factors are commonly considered when selecting a checking account?
2. Are checking accounts that earn interest preferable to other types of checking accounts? Why or why not?

PFP Sheet 26
Payment Account Comparison

PFP Sheet 27
Checking/
Payment Account
Cost Analysis

PFP Sheet 28
Checking Account Reconciliation

Your Personal Finance Roadmap and Dashboard:

Using Financial Services

PERCENT
SAVINGS RATE

A key indicator of your future financial success is the percentage of income saved each month. Different financial-service providers and savings instruments can be used to implement this element of your financial plan.

While most people in our society save nothing or very little, financial experts recommend a savings rate of between 5 and 10 percent of income. These funds might be used for emergencies, unexpected expenses, or short-term financial goals as well as long-term financial security.

YOUR SITUATION

Are you able to set aside an amount for savings each month? Are there expenses you can reduce, or sources of increased income that could add to the amount you save each month? An improving savings rate is the foundation for progress toward financial independence. Other financial services actions you might consider during different stages of your life include:

 First Steps

- Establish an account with a bank or credit union (seek special student accounts).
- Maintain proper spending to avoid overdraft charges.
- Use an app or online payments for convenience.
- Monitor ATM fees and other account charges.

Next Steps

- Increase the amount in your emergency fund.
- Compare fees and charges among different financial-service providers.
- Evaluate the use of other financial services such as an asset management account and a trust account.

Later Steps

- Expand your savings and investment program for funding future needs.
- Consider special "senior" accounts with lower fees and other features.
- Coordinate ownership of your bank accounts in relation to estate planning activities.

YOUR Next Step . . . select one or more of the items above and create an action plan to implement those financial planning activities.

SUMMARY OF LEARNING OBJECTIVES

LO5-1

Analyze factors that influence the selection and use of financial services. An understanding of financial services should include savings plans, payment accounts, loans, trust services, and mobile and online banking, which are used for managing daily financial activities. Technology, opportunity costs, and economic conditions influence the selection and use of financial services.

LO5-2

Compare the types of financial-service providers. When selecting a primary financial service provider, your choices include commercial banks, credit unions, thrifts, life insurance companies, investment companies, FinTech organizations, and online banks. These financial institutions should be assessed on the basis of services offered, rates and fees, safety, convenience, and special programs available to customers.

LO5-3

Assess the costs and benefits of various savings plans. The most common savings plans available to

consumers are regular savings accounts, high-yield savings accounts, certificates of deposit, money market accounts, money market funds, and U.S. savings bonds.

LO5-4

Identify the factors used to evaluate different savings plans. Evaluate a savings plan on the basis of rate of return, inflation, tax considerations, liquidity, safety, restrictions, and fees.

LO5-5

Evaluate the costs and benefits of different types of payment accounts. When considering alternatives, digital methods include debit cards, mobile and online payment systems, stored-value cards, smart cards, and digital wallets. Traditional checking accounts, special feature checking accounts, and checkless checking accounts can be compared with regard to restrictions (such as a minimum balance), fees and charges, interest, and special services. Other payment alternatives include certified checks, cashier's checks, money orders, and traveler's checks.

KEY TERMS

annual percentage yield (APY) 169	credit union 160	rate of return 168
asset management account 156	debit card 157	share account 163
certificate of deposit (CD) 164	money market account 166	share draft account 174
commercial bank 160	money market fund 161	trust 156
compounding 169	overdraft protection 175	

KEY FORMULAS

Topic	Formula
Annual percentage yield (APY)	$APY = 100[(1 + \text{Interest/Principal})^{365/\text{days in term}} - 1]$
	Principal = The amount of funds on deposit
	Interest = The total dollar amount earned on the principal
	Days in term = The actual number of days in the term of the account
When the number of days in the term is 365 or where the account does not have a stated maturity, the APY formula is simply: APY = 100 (Interest/Principal)	*Example:* $100\left[\left(1 + \dfrac{\$56.20}{\$1,000}\right)^{\frac{365}{365}} - 1\right] = 0.0562 = 5.62\%$
After-tax rate of return	Interest rate $\times$ (1 − Tax rate)
	Example: $0.05 \times (1 - 0.24) = 0.038 = 3.8\%$

SELF-TEST PROBLEMS

1. What would be the annual percentage yield (APY) for a savings account that earned $174 on a balance of $3,250 over the past 365 days?

2. If you earned a 4.2 percent return on your savings, with a 15 percent tax rate, what is the after-tax rate of return?

Self-Test Solutions

1. To calculate the APY when the number of days in the term is 365, use this formula:

   APY = 100 (Interest/Principal)

   APY = 100 (174/3250)

   APY = 100 (.0535) = 5.35%

2. To calculate the after-tax rate of return use:

   Interest rate × (1 − Tax rate)

   0.042 × (1 − 0.15) = 0.042 (0.85) = 0.0357 = 3.57%

FINANCIAL PLANNING PROBLEMS

1. *Calculating the Cost of ATM Fees.* If a person has ATM fees each month of $16 for 7 years, what would be the total cost of those banking fees? **LO5-1**

2. *Determining an Annual Interest Rate.* A payday loan company charges 4.25 percent interest for a two-week period. What is the annual interest rate? **LO5-2**

3. *Computing CD Interest.* A certificate of deposit will often result in a penalty for withdrawing funds before the maturity date. If the penalty involves two months of interest, what would be the amount for early withdrawal on a $20,000, 4 percent CD? **LO5-4**

4. *Computing Future Value.* What would be the value of a savings account started with $1,200, earning 3 percent (compounded annually) after 10 years? **LO5-4**

5. *Calculating Present Value.* Brenda Young wants to have $20,000 eight years from now for her daughter's college fund. If she will earn 4 percent (compounded annually) on her money, what amount should she deposit now? Use the present value of a single amount calculation. **LO5-4**

6. *Computing Future Value of Annual Deposits.* What amount would you have if you deposited $2,500 a year for 30 years at 8 percent (compounded annually)? (Use time value of money calculations in Chapter 1 Appendix.) **LO5-4**

7. *Comparing Taxable and Tax-Free Yields.* With a 28 percent marginal tax rate, would a tax-free yield of 7 percent or a taxable yield of 9.5 percent give you a better return on your savings? Why? **LO5-4**

8. *Computing APY.* What would be the annual percentage yield for a savings account that earned $56 in interest on $800 over the past 365 days? **LO5-4**

9. *Calculating Opportunity Cost.* What is the annual opportunity cost of a checking account that requires a $300 minimum balance to avoid service charges? Assume an interest rate of 3 percent. **LO5-5**

10. *Comparing Costs of Checking Accounts.* What would be the net *annual* cost of the following checking accounts? **LO5-5**

    a. Monthly fee, $3.75; processing fee, $0.25 per check; checks written, an average of 22 a month.

    b. Interest earnings of 6 percent with a $500 minimum balance; average monthly balance, $600; monthly service charge of $15 for falling below the minimum balance, which occurs three times a year (no interest earned in these months).

11. *Computing Checking Account Balance.* Based on the following information, determine the true balance in your checking account. (See the *Financial Literacy Calculations: Annual Percentage Yield* feature.) **LO5-5**

    Balance in your checkbook, $356   Interest earned on the account, $4
    Balance on bank statement, $472   Total of outstanding checks, $187
    Service charge and other fees, $15   Deposits in transit, $60

DIGITAL FINANCIAL LITERACY: P2P PAYMENT APPS

For many transactions, peer-to-peer, or person-to-person (P2P) payment apps have replaced cash and checks to send money to friends and family. These services allow quick transfer of funds to others, usually for free or with a small fee. Some of the most common P2P services are Zelle, Venmo, Cash App, PayPal, Google Pay, and Apple Pay. Today, most money transfers are screen based. Future developments are expected to involve artificial intelligence personal assistants, voice commands, facial recognition, and virtual reality interfaces.

Action items:

1. (a) Locate online information with reviews of P2P payment apps. (b) Talk to several people regarding their experiences with P2P apps. What benefits and concerns are associated with these services?

2. Describe a life situation for a single person or family. Visually present the features of a P2P app that would serve the financial planning needs of this person or family.

FINANCIAL PLANNING CASE

Evaluating Banking Services

"Wow! My account balance is a little lower than I expected," commented Melanie Harper as she viewed her banking app. "Wait a minute! There's nearly $20 in fees for ATM withdrawals and other service charges."

"Oh no! I also went below the minimum balance required for my *free* checking account," Melanie groaned. "That cost me $7.50!" Melanie is not alone in her frustration with fees paid for financial services. While careless money management caused most of these charges, other fees could have been reduced or eliminated by comparing costs at different financial-service providers.

Melanie has decided to investigate alternatives to her current banking services. Her preliminary research provided the following:

Mobile banking—allows faster access to account information by phone app, to quickly transfer funds and to make payments and purchases. May include access to expanded financial services, such as low-cost, online investment trading and instant loan approval.

Prepaid debit card—would prevent overspending, staying within the budgeted amount loaded to the card. Cards are usually accepted in most retail locations and online. A variety of fees might be associated with the card.

Check-cashing outlet—would result in fees only when services are used, such as money orders, cashing a check, obtaining a prepaid cash card, or paying bills online.

Many people do not realize the amount they pay each month for bank fees. Some basic research can result in saving several hundred dollars a year.

Questions

1. What benefits and drawbacks might Melanie encounter when using these financial services?

Mobile banking	Prepaid debit card	Check-cashing outlet

2. What factors should Melanie consider when selecting among different banking services?

3. Describe how an improved understanding of banking services could be of value for budgeting, money management, and achieving financial goals.

YOUR PERSONAL FINANCIAL PLAN

SELECTING SAVINGS AND PAYMENT SERVICES

Payment services and savings programs are needed for effective financial planning. Minimizing banking fees and maximizing earnings on funds are common objectives.

Your Short-Term Financial Planning Activity

Task Create a plan for selecting and using financial services.

Research

1) View Exhibit 5-5 to identify factors when selecting a financial institution. Use the websites of three financial institutions or apps and PFP Sheet 23 to identify services needed for savings, payments, and other money management activities.

2) Based on PFP Sheet 25, compare the rates of return, fees, and other factors for different savings plans.

3) Using PFP Sheet 26, compare features and costs of payment accounts at different finance-service providers.

Outcome Present the results of your findings in a table, chart, or other visual. Describe actions to minimize banking fees and maximize earnings on savings. Which of the three financial-service providers or apps would you use? Why? Add the documents and files you create to your portfolio or to your Personal Financial Plan online folder.

Your Long-Term Financial Planning Activity

Task Assess the influence of economic conditions and identify personal actions for achieving long-term savings goals.

Research

1) Use PFP Sheet 4 as a guide to determine how economic conditions (inflation, interest rates) might affect your long-term savings actions.

2) Based on PFP Sheet 24, determine savings decisions that you might consider to achieve long-term financial goals.

Outcome Prepare an audio or written summary of your economic findings and your action plan for achieving long-term savings goals. What personal factors related to the costs and benefits of financial services should you monitor as your life situation changes over time? Add the documents and files you create to your portfolio or to your Personal Financial Plan online folder.

Note: All *Personal Financial Planner* sheets are available at the end of the book and in an Excel spreadsheet format in *Connect Finance.*

 CONTINUING CASE

Financial Services: Savings Plans and Payment Accounts

Jamie Lee Jackson, age 26, is in her last semester of college and is anxiously awaiting graduation. She still works part time as a bakery clerk, has been sticking to her budget, and is on track to accumulate money to make the $9,000 down payment to open her cupcake café within the next two years.

Jamie Lee is single, shares a small apartment with a friend, and continues to split associated living expenses, such as rent and utilities. However, following a bad turn of events, she has to consider a place of her own.

One evening, after returning to the apartment after work, Jamie learned that her roommate had a couple of friends over earlier in the evening. As Jamie went to her room, she noticed that her top desk drawer had been left open and her debit card, checkbook, and Social Security card were missing. She immediately contacted the authorities, and the police instructed her to notify her financial institution. But it was late Saturday night, and Jamie thought she had to wait until Monday morning. Unfortunately, within no time, Jamie found that her checking account had been emptied!

Jamie Lee's luck worsened, as she had paid many of her monthly bills late last week. Her automobile insurance, two utility bills, and a layaway payment had all been paid for by check. Her bank almost immediately began sending overdraft alerts through her smartphone for the emptied checking account.

Current Financial Situation

Bank Accounts:

Checking account: $2,250 (before the theft)
Savings account: $6,900
Emergency fund savings account: $3,900
401(k) balance: $350

Questions

1. Jamie Lee is beside herself knowing that the thieves had unauthorized use of her debit/ATM card. What is Jamie's financial responsibility for the unauthorized use?

2. What would Jamie Lee's financial liability have been had she waited more than two days to report the debit/ATM card lost or stolen?

3. What financial service would now benefit Jamie Lee, as she had legitimate checks written to cover her monthly bills that are now in excess of the available checking account balance due to the theft? Will Jamie Lee incur fees for taking advantage of this financial service?

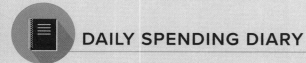

DAILY SPENDING DIARY

"My ATM fees and other bank charges take away money from other budget items."

Directions

Start (or continue) your *Daily Spending Diary* to record and monitor spending in various categories using the sheets provided at the end of Chapter 1. Or you may create your own format to monitor your spending. Your comments should reflect what you have learned about your spending patterns and help you consider possible changes you might want to make in your spending habits.

Questions

1. What banking fees do you pay each month? What actions might you take to reduce or eliminate these cash outflows?

2. What other areas of your daily spending might be reduced or revised?

A *Daily Spending Diary* sheet is located at the end of Chapter 1 and on the library resource site within *Connect*.

Introduction to Consumer Credit

6

Ariel Skelley/Getty Images

LEARNING OBJECTIVES

LO6-1 Define *consumer credit* and analyze its advantages and disadvantages.

LO6-2 Differentiate among various types of credit.

LO6-3 Assess your credit capacity and build your credit rating.

LO6-4 Describe the information creditors look for when you apply for credit.

LO6-5 Identify the steps you can take to avoid and correct credit mistakes.

LO6-6 Describe the laws that protect you if you have a complaint about consumer credit.

Financial Literacy
IN YOUR LIFE

▶ **What if you . . .** needed a loan for a car or college education? If you don't have a budget, or a spending plan, you are not ready to take on debt. Before you take on a debt, it is very important to have a good financial foundation, including your emergency savings, a budget, and your financial records.

You might . . . decide to reduce your current credit card debt, analyze your present debt, develop a strategy, and take action. For example, you might list the balance, interest rate, and monthly interest on each credit card, check your credit score, and shop for the best interest rate.

Now, what would you do? If you have good credit, you may want to take out a loan to purchase a car or to cover educational expenses. But regardless how the money is spent, a loan is a liability, or debt, and decreases your wealth. Make sure to keep your debt payments-to-income ratio to no more than 20 percent of your net (after-tax) income. You will be able to monitor your progress using Your Personal Finance Roadmap and Dashboard at the end of the chapter.

my life | CASH, CREDIT, OR DEBIT—WALKING A TIGHTROPE

Remember how thrilled you were when you graduated from high school and received an offer for a credit card? Soon afterward, you were excited when you made your first charge for some new clothes. After making a few more purchases, you reached your card limit. So you applied for two more credit cards, each with an annual interest rate of 23 percent. Then you began to charge groceries and furniture, because it was easier than paying cash. Do you know how to use credit wisely?

As you start or expand your use of credit, consider the following statements. For each of the following statements, select the letter to indicate your answers regarding these statements:

1. If I need more money for my expenses, I _____ borrow it.
   a. never
   b. sometimes
   c. often

2. I _____ pay any bills I have when they are due.
   a. always
   b. usually
   c. sometimes

3. If I want to see a copy of my credit report, I can contact
   a. a credit reporting agency.
   b. a bank.
   c. the dean of my economics department.

4. If I default (do not repay) on a loan, it will stay on my credit report for
   a. 7 years.
   b. 2 years.
   c. 6 months.

5. I can begin building a good rating by
   a. opening a savings account and making regular monthly deposits.
   b. paying most of my bills on time.
   c. opening a checking account and bouncing checks.

6. If I have serious credit problems, I should
   a. contact my creditors to explain the problem.
   b. contact only the most persistent creditors.
   c. not contact my creditors and hope they will forget about me.

SCORING: Give yourself 3 points for each "a," 2 points for each "b," and 1 point for each "c." Add up the number of points.

If you scored 6–9 points, you might want to take a closer look at how credit works before you get over your head in debt.

If you scored 10–13 points, you are off to a good start, but be sure you know the pitfalls of opening a credit account.

Source: How to Be Credit Smart (Washington, DC: Consumer Education Foundation, 1994).

As you study this chapter, you will encounter "My Life" boxes with additional information and resources related to these items.

What Is Consumer Credit?

You hear a lot about credit—credit reports, credit scores, credit freezes, and credit monitoring. What does it all mean for you? Your credit matters because if affects your ability to get a loan, a job, housing, insurance, and more. It is important to understand what credit is and how to protect it.

"Charge it!" "Cash or credit?" "Put it on my account." As these phrases indicate, the use of credit is a fact of life in personal and family financial planning. When you use credit, you satisfy needs today and pay for this satisfaction in the future. While the use of credit is often necessary and even advantageous, responsibilities and disadvantages are associated with its use.

Credit is an arrangement to receive cash, goods, or services now and pay for them in the future. **Consumer credit** refers to the use of credit for personal needs (except a home mortgage) by individuals and families, in contrast to credit used for business purposes. Many people use credit to live beyond their means, largely because of a change in perception about credit. Past generations viewed credit as a negative and used it very sparingly. Society today has popularized credit with phrases such as "It's everywhere you want to be" and "My life, My Card" slogan campaigns. That said, when used appropriately, credit can be a very useful tool.

Although Polonius cautioned, "Neither a borrower nor a lender be,"[1] using and providing credit have become a way of life for many people and businesses in today's economy. In January, you pay a bill for electricity that you used in December. A statement arrives in the mail for medical services that you received last month. You write a check for $40, a minimum payment on a $300 department store bill. With a bank loan, you purchase a new car. These are all examples of using credit: paying later for goods and services obtained now.

Most consumers have three alternatives in financing current purchases: They can draw on their savings, use their present earnings, or borrow against their expected future income. Each of these alternatives has trade-offs. If you continually deplete your savings, little will be left for emergencies or retirement income. If you spend your current income on luxuries instead of necessities, your well-being will eventually suffer. And if you pledge your future income to make current credit purchases, you will have little or no spendable income in the future.

Consumer credit is based on trust in people's ability and willingness to pay bills when due. It works because people by and large are honest and responsible. But how does consumer credit affect our economy, and how is it affected by our economy?

LO6-1

Define *consumer credit* and analyze its advantages and disadvantages.

credit An arrangement to receive cash, goods, or services now and pay for them in the future.

consumer credit The use of credit for personal needs (except a home mortgage).

THE IMPORTANCE OF CONSUMER CREDIT IN OUR ECONOMY

Consumer credit dates back to colonial times. While credit was originally a privilege of the affluent, farmers came to use it extensively. No direct finance charges were imposed; instead, the cost of credit was added to the prices of goods. With the advent of the automobile in the early 1900s, installment credit, in which the debt is repaid in equal installments over a specified period of time, exploded on the American scene.

All economists now recognize consumer credit as a major force in the American economy. Any forecast or evaluation of the economy includes consumer spending trends and consumer credit as a sustaining force. To paraphrase an old political expression, as the consumer goes, so goes the U.S. economy.

The aging of the baby boom generation (born between 1946 and 1964) has added to the growth of consumer credit. This generation currently represents about 20 percent of the population but holds nearly 60 percent of the outstanding debt. The people in this age group have always been disproportionate users of credit, since consumption is highest as families are formed and homes are purchased and furnished. Thus, while the extensive use of debt by this generation is nothing new, the fact that it has grown rapidly has added to overall debt use. Moreover, Generation X (born between 1965 and 1979) views credit as a lifeline. According to a study from Allianz Life, about half of Gen Xers and baby boomers consider credit cards to be a financial survival tool. No wonder consumer credit has been exploding in the United States. As Exhibit 6-1 shows, consumer credit reached over $4.18 trillion in 2020.

USES AND MISUSES OF CREDIT

Using credit to purchase goods and services may allow consumers to be more efficient or more productive or to lead more satisfying lives. There are many valid reasons for using credit. A medical emergency may leave a person strapped for funds. A homemaker returning to the workforce may need a car. It may be possible to buy an item now for less money than it will cost later. Borrowing for a college education is another valid reason. But it probably is not reasonable to borrow for everyday living expenses or to finance a Mustang Shelby GT350 on credit when a Ford EcoSport is all your budget allows.

"Shopaholics" and young adults are most vulnerable to misusing credit. College students are a prime target for credit card issuers, and issuers make it very easy for students to get credit cards. Wendy Leright, a 25-year-old teacher in Detroit, knows this all too well. As a college freshman, she applied for and got seven credit cards, all bearing at least an 18.9 percent interest rate and a $50 annual fee. Although unemployed, she used the cards freely, buying expensive clothes for herself, extravagant Christmas presents for friends and family, and even a one-week vacation in the Bahamas. "It got to a point where I didn't even look at the price tag," she said. By her senior year, Wendy had amassed $9,000 in credit card debt and couldn't make the monthly payments of nearly $200. She eventually turned to her parents to bail her out. "Until my mother sat me down and showed me how much interest I had to pay, I hadn't even given it a thought. I was shocked," Wendy said. "I would have had to pay it off for years."[2]

Using credit increases the amount of money a person can spend to purchase goods and services now. But the trade-off is that it decreases the amount of money that will be available to spend in the future. However, many people expect their incomes to increase and therefore expect to be able to make payments on past credit purchases and still make new purchases.

Here are some questions you should consider before you decide how and when to make a major purchase, for example, a car:

- Do I have the cash I need for the down payment?
- Do I want to use my savings for this purchase?

EXHIBIT 6-1 Volume of consumer credit (seasonally adjusted)

All economists now recognize consumer credit as a major force in the American economy.

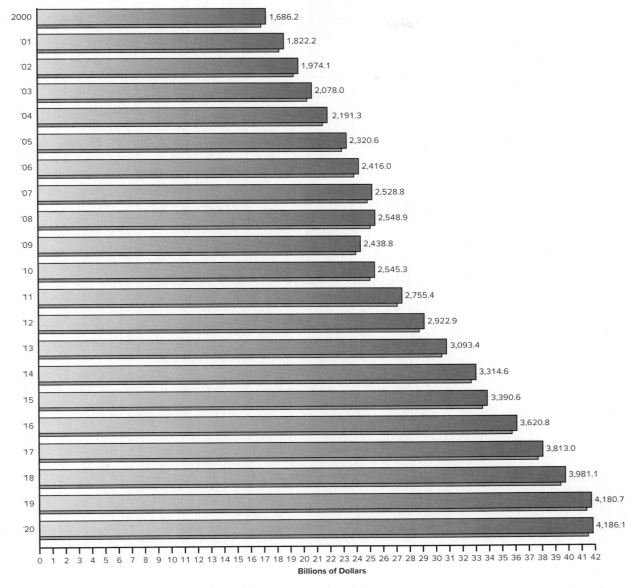

Year	Billions of Dollars
2000	1,686.2
'01	1,822.2
'02	1,974.1
'03	2,078.0
'04	2,191.3
'05	2,320.6
'06	2,416.0
'07	2,528.8
'08	2,548.9
'09	2,438.8
'10	2,545.3
'11	2,755.4
'12	2,922.9
'13	3,093.4
'14	3,314.6
'15	3,390.6
'16	3,620.8
'17	3,813.0
'18	3,981.1
'19	4,180.7
'20	4,186.1

Source: Federal Reserve Statistical Release: Consumer Credit (G-19), Consumer Credit Outstanding, www.federalreserve.gov/releases/g19/current/g19.pdf, accessed August 7, 2021.

- Does the purchase fit my budget?
- Could I use the credit I need for this purchase in some better way?
- Could I postpone the purchase?
- What are the opportunity costs of postponing the purchase (alternative transportation costs, a possible increase in the price of the car)?
- What are the dollar costs and the psychological costs of using credit (interest, other finance charges, being in debt and responsible for making a monthly payment)?

If you decide to use credit, make sure the benefits of making the purchase now (increased efficiency or productivity, a more satisfying life, etc.) outweigh the costs (financial and psychological) of using credit. Thus, credit, when effectively used, can help you have more and enjoy more. When misused, credit can result in default, bankruptcy, and loss of creditworthiness.

ADVANTAGES OF CREDIT

Consumer credit enables people to enjoy goods and services now—a car, a home, an education, help in emergencies—and pay for them through payment plans based on future income.

Credit cards permit the purchase of goods even when funds are low. Customers with previously approved credit may receive other extras, such as advance notice of sales and the right to order by phone or to buy on approval. In addition, many shoppers believe it is easier to return merchandise they have purchased on account. Credit cards also provide shopping convenience and the efficiency of paying for several purchases with one monthly payment.

It is safer to use credit, since charge accounts and credit cards let you shop and travel without carrying a large amount of cash. You need a credit card to make a hotel reservation, rent a car, and shop by phone. You may also use credit cards for identification when cashing checks, and the use of credit provides you with a record of expenses.

The use of credit cards can provide up to a 50-day "float," the time lag between when you make the purchase and when the lender deducts the balance from your checking account when the payment is due. This float, offered by many credit card issuers, includes a grace period of 21 to 25 days. During the grace period, no finance charges are assessed on current purchases if the balance is paid in full each month within 25 days after billing.

Some large corporations, such as General Electric Company and General Motors Corporation, issue their own Visa and MasterCard and offer rebates on purchases. For example, every time you make a purchase with the GM MasterCard, 5 percent of the purchase price is set aside for you in a special GM Card Rebate account. When you are ready to buy or lease a GM car or truck, you just cash in your rebate at the GM dealership. Similarly, with an AT&T MasterCard, you can earn a cash bonus of up to 5 percent based on your total purchases during the year.

Some credit cards, including gold and platinum MasterCards and Visa Signature cards, extend the manufacturer's warranty by up to one year when you buy products with their cards. American Express and Citi's Thank You Premiere cards pay up to $1,000 per claim to repair broken items or replace lost purchases within 90 days.

Platinum credit cards offered by American Express provide emergency medical evacuation for travelers. When Stephen Bradley of New York was vacationing in tiny, isolated Coruripe, Brazil, he ate something that made him gravely ill. With no doctor nearby, a friend frantically called American Express about its guarantee to arrange emergency medical evacuation and treatment for Platinum Card users. AmEx moved fast: It lined up a car to rush Bradley to the nearest large town, managed to book a room in a sold-out hotel, and sent a doctor there to make a house call. The physician even accompanied Bradley's travel partner, Richard Laermer, to a local pharmacy for medicine. "When we went home to see our doctor, he told us the physician had saved Steve's life," recalls Laermer. "For the last five years we have been indebted to Platinum."[3]

In addition, many major credit cards provide the following benefits to their customers at no extra cost.

- Accidental death and dismemberment insurance when you travel on a common carrier (train, plane, bus, or ship), up to $250,000.
- Worldwide auto rental collision damage waiver (CDW) for damage due to collision or theft for $50,000 or more.

- Roadside dispatch referral service for emergency roadside assistance, such as towing, locksmith services, and more.
- Redeem your points or miles for gift cards, cash, or to book travel—from airfare, hotels, and rental cars to vacation packages.
- Damage and theft purchase protection if your purchases are damaged or stolen within 120 days of purchase.
- Some cards, such as Capital One, don't charge foreign transaction fees.

Finally, credit indicates stability. The fact that lenders consider you a good risk usually means you are a responsible individual. However, if you do not repay your debts in a timely manner, you will find that credit has many disadvantages.

DISADVANTAGES OF CREDIT

Perhaps the greatest disadvantage of using credit is the temptation to overspend, especially during periods of inflation. It seems easy to buy today and pay tomorrow using cheaper dollars. But continual overspending can lead to serious trouble.

Whether or not credit involves security (something of value to back the loan), failure to repay a loan may result in a loss of income, valuable property, and your good reputation. It can even lead to court action and bankruptcy. Misuse of credit can create serious long-term financial problems, damage to family relationships, and a slowing of progress toward financial goals. Therefore, you should approach credit with caution and avoid using it more extensively than your budget permits.

Although credit allows more immediate satisfaction of needs and desires, it does not increase total purchasing power. Credit purchases must be paid for out of future income; therefore, credit ties up the use of future income. Furthermore, if your income does not increase to cover rising costs, your ability to repay credit commitments will diminish. Before buying goods and services on credit, consider whether they will have lasting value, whether they will increase your personal satisfaction during present and future income periods, and whether your current income will continue or increase.

Finally, credit costs money. It is a service for which you must pay. Paying for purchases over a period of time is more costly than paying for them with cash. Purchasing with credit rather than cash involves one very obvious trade-off: the fact that it will cost more due to monthly finance charges and the compounding effect of interest on interest.

SUMMARY: ADVANTAGES AND DISADVANTAGES OF CREDIT

The use of credit provides immediate access to goods and services, flexibility in money management, safety and convenience, a cushion in emergencies, a means of increasing resources, and a good credit rating if you pay your debts back in a timely manner. But remember, the use of credit is a two-sided coin. An intelligent decision as to its use demands careful evaluation of your current debt, your future income, the added cost, and the consequences of overspending.

 1

If I need more money for my expenses, I borrow it.

Remember, using credit does not increase your total purchasing power, nor does it mean that you have more money. It just allows you to buy things now for which you must pay later. Conduct an online search to locate suggestions for wise uses of credit.

 PRACTICE QUIZ 6-1

1. What is consumer credit?
2. Why is consumer credit important to our economy?
3. What are the uses and misuses of credit?
4. What are the advantages and disadvantages of credit?

Types of Credit

LO6-2

Differentiate among various types of credit.

Two basic types of consumer credit exist: closed-end credit and open-end credit. With **closed-end credit**, you pay back one-time loans in a specified period of time and in payments of equal amounts. With **open-end credit**, loans are made on a continuous basis and you are billed periodically for at least partial payment. Exhibit 6-2 shows examples of closed-end and open-end credit.

closed-end credit One-time loans that the borrower pays back in a specified period of time and in payments of equal amounts.

open-end credit A line of credit in which loans are made on a continuous basis and the borrower is billed periodically for at least partial payment.

CLOSED-END (OR INSTALLMENT) CREDIT

Closed-end credit is used for a specific purpose and involves a specified amount. Mortgage loans, automobile loans, and installment loans for purchasing furniture or appliances are examples of closed-end credit. An agreement, or contract, lists the repayment terms: the number of payments, the payment amount, and how much the credit will cost. Closed-end payment plans usually involve a written agreement for each credit purchase. A down payment or trade-in may be required, with the balance to be repaid in equal weekly or monthly payments over a period of time. Generally, the seller holds title to the merchandise until the payments have been completed.

The three most common types of closed-end credit are installment sales credit, installment cash credit, and single lump-sum credit. *Installment sales credit* is a loan that allows you to receive merchandise, usually high-priced items such as large appliances or furniture. You make a down payment and usually sign a contract to repay the balance, plus interest and service charges, in equal installments over a specified period.

Installment cash credit is a direct loan of money for personal purposes, home improvements, or vacation expenses. You make no down payment and make payments in specified amounts over a set period.

Single lump-sum credit is a loan that must be repaid in total on a specified day, usually within 30 to 90 days. Lump-sum credit is generally, but not always, used to purchase a single item.

OPEN-END (OR REVOLVING) CREDIT

Using a credit card issued by a department store, using a bank credit card (Visa, MasterCard) to make purchases at different stores, charging a meal at a restaurant, and using overdraft protection are examples of open-end credit. As you will soon see, you do not apply for open-end credit to make a single purchase, as you do with closed-end credit. Rather, you can use open-end credit to make any purchases you wish if you do not exceed your **line of credit**, the maximum dollar amount of credit the lender has made available to you. You may have to pay **interest**, a periodic charge for the use of credit, or other finance charges.

You may have had an appointment with a doctor or a dentist that you did not pay for until later. Professionals and small businesses often do not demand immediate payment but will charge interest if you do not pay the bill in full within 30 days. *Incidental credit* is a credit arrangement that has no extra costs and no specific repayment plan.

Many retailers use open-end credit. Customers can purchase goods or services up to a fixed dollar limit at any time. Usually you have the option to pay the bill in full

line of credit The dollar amount, which may or may not be borrowed, that a lender makes available to a borrower.

interest A periodic charge for the use of credit.

EXHIBIT 6-2

Examples of closed-end and open-end credit

Closed-End Credit	Open-End Credit
• Mortgage loans • Automobile loans • Installment loans (installment sales contract, installment cash credit, single lump-sum credit)	• Cards issued by department stores, bank cards (Visa, MasterCard) • Travel and entertainment cards (Diners Club, American Express) • Overdraft protection

within 30 days without interest charges or to make set monthly installments based on the account balance plus interest.

Many banks extend **revolving check credit**. Also called a *bank line of credit,* this is a prearranged loan for a specified amount that you can use by writing a special check. Repayment is made in installments over a set period. The finance charges are based on the amount of credit used during the month and on the outstanding balance.

revolving check credit A prearranged loan from a bank for a specified amount; also called a *bank line of credit.*

CREDIT CARDS   Credit cards are extremely popular. According to a recent *American Banker* survey, 7 out of 10 U.S. households carry one or more credit cards. Two out of three households have at least one retail credit card, 56 percent have one or more Visa cards, and 47 percent have at least one MasterCard.

About half of all credit card users generally pay off their balances in full each month. These cardholders are often known as *convenience users.* Others are borrowers; they carry balances beyond the grace period and pay finance charges. Consumers use more than 1.1 billion credit cards to buy clothing, meals, vacations, gasoline, groceries, doctor visits, and other goods and services on credit.

While cash advances on credit cards can look attractive, remember that interest usually accrues from the moment you accept the ATM cash, and you must also pay a transaction fee. One cash advance could cost you the money you were saving for a birthday gift for that special someone.

About 25,000 financial institutions participate in the credit card business, and the vast majority of them are affiliated with Visa International or the Interbank Card Association, which issues MasterCard. The *Financial Literacy for My Life: Choosing a Credit Card?* box provides a few helpful hints for choosing a credit card.

Co-branding is the linking of a credit card with a business trade name offering "points" or premiums toward the purchase of a product or service. Airlines were the first to offer co-branded credit cards, and hotels followed soon after. Co-branding became increasingly popular following the success of General Motors Corporation's credit card, launched in 1992. Co-branded credit cards offer rebates on products and services such as health clubs, tax preparation services from H&R Block, and gasoline purchases. Banks are realizing that co-branded credit cards help build customer loyalty.

In addition to airlines and hotels, many large retailers, such as Walmart, Amazon, Costco, and Target, have store-branded credit cards to encourage more spending in their stores and online purchases. Credit cards offering points, miles, cash back, or other rewards remain popular and have continued to increase in number over the last few years.

SMART CARDS   Smart cards are also known as smart-chip, chip-enabled smart cards, chip cards, chip-and-signature cards, and chip-and-pin cards. The ultimate plastic smart cards are embedded with a computer chip that can store 500 times the data of a credit card. Smart cards may ultimately combine credit cards, a driver's license, a health care ID with your medical history and insurance information, frequent-flier miles, and telephone cards. A single smart card, for example, could be used to buy an airline ticket, store it digitally, and track frequent-flier miles. It is estimated that between 30 and 50 billion smart cards are in circulation. Smart cards provide security, confidentiality, portability, and convenience.

At Florida State University, smart cards have become practically indispensable. Students use smart cards to pay tuition, buy meals in the cafeteria, borrow library books, and gain access to dormitories and online study groups.

DEBIT CARDS   Don't confuse credit cards with debit cards. Debit cards are often called *bank cards, ATM cards, cash cards,*

smart money minute

Credit Card Facts

- Over 1.1 billion credit cards are being used in the United States.

- About 2.8 billion credit cards are in use worldwide.

- MasterCard is among the most popular credit cards, with 97 million cardholders.

- About 14 percent of Americans have at least 10 credit cards.

- About 60 percent of Americans believe the United States will soon become a cashless society.

Source: shiftprocessing.com/credit-card/, accessed January 9, 2021.

Financial Literacy for My Life

CHOOSING A CREDIT CARD?

When choosing a credit card, it pays to shop around. Follow these suggestions to select the card that best meets your needs.

1. Department stores and gasoline companies are good places to obtain your first credit card. Pay your bills in full and on time, and you will begin to establish a good credit history.

2. Bank cards are offered through banks and savings and loan associations. Fees and finance charges vary considerably (from 8 to 21.6 percent), so shop around.

3. If you usually pay your bills in full, try to deal with a financial institution with an interest-free grace period, which is the time after a purchase has been made and before a finance charge is imposed, typically 21 to 30 days.

4. If you're used to paying monthly installments, look for a card with a low monthly finance charge. Be sure you understand how that finance charge is calculated.

5. Consider obtaining a card from an out-of-state financial institution if it offers better terms than those offered locally.

6. Be aware of some credit cards that offer "no fee" or low interest but start charging interest from the day you purchase an item.

7. Watch out for credit cards that do not charge annual fees but instead charge a "transaction fee" each time you use the card.

8. If you're paying only the minimum amounts on your monthly statement, you need to plan your budget more carefully. The longer it takes for you to pay off a bill, the more interest you pay. The finance charges you pay on an item could end up being more than the item is worth.

9. With a grace period of 25 days, you actually get a free loan when you pay bills in full each month.

10. To avoid delays that may result in finance charges, follow the card issuer's instructions as to where, how, and when to make bill payments.

11. If you have a bad credit history and problems getting a credit card, look for a savings institution that will give you a secured credit card if you open a savings account. Your line of credit will be determined by the amount you have on deposit.

12. Beware of offers of easy credit. No one can guarantee to get you credit.

13. Think twice before making a 900 number telephone call for a credit card. You will pay from $2 to $50 for the 900 call and may never receive a credit card.

14. Be aware of credit cards offered by "credit repair" companies or "credit clinics." These firms may also offer to clean up your credit history for a fee. But remember, only time and good credit habits will repair your credit report if you have a poor credit history.

15. Travel and entertainment (T&E) cards often charge higher annual fees than most credit cards. Usually you must make payment in full within 30 days of receiving your bill or typically no further purchases will be approved on the account.

16. Often additional credit cards on your account for a spouse or child (over 18) are available with a minimum additional fee or no fee at all.

17. Be aware that debit cards are not credit cards but simply a substitute for a check or cash. The amount of the sale is subtracted from your checking account.

Sources: American Institute of Certified Public Accountants; U.S. Office of Consumer Affairs; Federal Trade Commission.

debit card Electronically subtracts the amount of a purchase from the buyer's account at the moment the purchase is made.

and *check cards*. Although they may look alike, the **debit card**, as the name implies, electronically subtracts from your account at the moment you buy goods or services, while the credit card extends credit and delays your payment. Debit cards are most commonly used at automatic teller machines, but they are increasingly being used to purchase goods at point-of-sale terminals in stores and service stations.

You are never responsible for charges on a debit card you haven't accepted. If you report a lost or stolen debit card within two days, federal regulations limit your liability to $50. After two days, your liability is limited to $50 plus any amount resulting from your failure to notify the issuer. If your debit card is lost or stolen, you must work directly with the issuer. If you have a tendency to overspend with a credit card, use a debit card.

Raquel Garcia is serious about avoiding debt. The 18-year-old customer service representative for U-Haul recently canceled her credit card. Now she gets her entire paycheck deposited onto a prepaid debit card, which she uses for all her purchases. Since she can access only what's in the account, Garcia no longer worries about breaking her budget and reports: "I'm spending just what I need."

STORED-VALUE (OR GIFT) CARDS   Stored-value cards—gift cards or prepaid cards—resemble a typical debit card, using magnetic stripe technology to store information and track funds. However, unlike traditional debit cards, stored-value cards are prepaid, providing you with immediate money. By the mid-1990s, large retailers began issuing stored-value cards instead of traditional paper gift certificates. Over the past few decades, the stored-value cards have grown rapidly. Today, gift cards are being used for many purposes, including payroll, general spending, travel expenses, government benefit payments, and employee benefit and reward payments.

One market research firm estimates that holders of gift cards recently lost more than $100 million when the number of retailer bankruptcies increased sharply. Bankruptcy courts treat gift cards the same way they handle unsecured debt: If a retailer goes bankrupt, holders get pennies on the dollar at most—and in many cases nothing.

my life 2

I pay any bills I have when they are due.

If you are having trouble paying your bills and need help, contact your creditors and try to work out an adjusted repayment plan. Before taking out a loan, make sure you can afford to repay it. Exhibit 6-3 can help you determine your debt payments-to-income ratio.

TRAVEL AND ENTERTAINMENT (T&E) CARDS   T&E cards are really not credit cards, because the monthly balance is due in full. However, most people think of Diners Club or Carte Blanche cards as credit cards because they don't pay the moment they purchase goods or services. The Diners Club card, owned by Discover Financial Services, is accepted by millions of merchants in more than 200 countries and provides cash access at over 845,000 locations worldwide. An annual fee allows you to replace lost passports, buy airline tickets, find doctors, and access airport lounges around the world, and it also provides identity theft assistance and car rental discounts.

SMARTPHONES   Most smartphones are now equipped to make purchases. This concept, called *mobile commerce,* has seen a significant increase in interest from consumers, retailers, and finance companies. For example, some credit card companies, instead of providing a physical credit card, provide stickers that attach to a phone that will allow the customer to scan the code. In addition, retailers such as Starbucks have apps to quickly pay using a mobile phone. Over 80 percent of Americans have smartphones.

HOME EQUITY LOANS   A **home equity loan** is based on the difference between the current market value of your home and the amount you still owe on your mortgage. With such a loan, you can borrow up to $100,000 or more on your home. Depending on the value of the home, you can borrow up to 85 percent of its appraised value, less the amount you still owe on your mortgage. The interest you pay on a home equity loan can be tax deductible, unlike interest on other types of loans.

A home equity loan is usually set up as a revolving line of credit, typically with a variable interest rate. A *revolving line of credit* is an arrangement whereby borrowings are permitted up to a specified limit and for a stated period, usually 5 to 10 years. Once the line of credit has been established, you draw from it only the amount you need at any one time (see the *Financial Literacy Calculations: How Much Can You Borrow with a Home Equity Loan?* box). Today many lenders offer home equity lines of credit. But your home is probably your largest asset. You should use the home equity loan only for major items such as education, home improvements, or medical bills and not for daily expenses or to buy a boat or new car, or to pay for a cruise. *Remember, if you miss payments on a home equity loan, you can lose your home.* Furthermore, when you sell your home, you probably will be required to pay off your equity line in full. If you plan to sell your house in the near future, consider whether annual fees to maintain the account and other costs of setting up an equity credit line make sense.

According to the Internal Revenue Service, although restricted by the Tax Cuts and Jobs Act, you can still deduct interest on many home equity loans, home equity lines of

home equity loan A loan based on the current market value of a home less the amount still owed on the mortgage.

Financial Literacy Calculations

HOW MUCH CAN YOU BORROW WITH A HOME EQUITY LOAN?

Depending on your income and the equity in your home, you can apply for a line of credit for anywhere from $10,000 to $250,000 or more.

Some lenders let you borrow only up to 75 percent of the value of your home, less the amount of your first mortgage. At some banks you may qualify to borrow up to 85 percent! This higher lending limit may make the difference in your ability to get the money you need for home improvements, education, or other expenses.

Use the following chart to calculate your home loan value, which is the approximate amount of your home equity line of credit.

	Example	Your Home
Approximate market value of your home	$100,000	$ _____
Multiply by 0.75	× 0.75	× 0.75
Approximate loan value	75,000	_____
Subtract balance due on mortgage(s)	40,000	_____
Approximate credit limit available	$ 35,000	$ _____

In the above example, your "credit limit available" home loan value (the amount for which you could establish your account) is $35,000. Once your account is established, you can write a check for any amount you need up to $35,000.

In choosing a home equity loan,

1. Find out if your lending institution protects you against rising interest rates.
2. Compare the size of your lender's fee with those of other institutions.
3. Find out if your lender charges an inactivity fee.
4. Make sure high annual fees and other costs do not outweigh the tax advantage of a home equity loan, especially if you are borrowing only a small amount.
5. Be careful of interest-only payments on home equity loans.
6. Find out whether your lender has the right to change the terms and conditions of your loan or to terminate your loan.
7. Make sure that all of the interest you hope to finally deduct on your home equity loan is in fact deductible.
8. Carefully evaluate your reasons for using the equity in your home for loans.
9. Know the full costs and risks of home equity loans before you make a commitment to a lending institution.

Source: The Federal Reserve Board, "What You Should Know about Home Equity Lines of Credit," files.consumerfinance.gov/f/201204_CFPB_HELOC-brochure.pdf, accessed March 17, 2021.

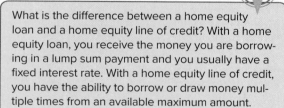

smart money minute

What is the difference between a home equity loan and a home equity line of credit? With a home equity loan, you receive the money you are borrowing in a lump sum payment and you usually have a fixed interest rate. With a home equity line of credit, you have the ability to borrow or draw money multiple times from an available maximum amount.

credit, or second mortgages (Informational Release IR 2018-32). However, the interest paid on home equity loans can be deducted only if you use the money to buy, build, or improve your home.

PROTECTING YOURSELF AGAINST DEBIT/CREDIT CARD FRAUD *Dead Man Walking* is the title of a movie, but it's also the nickname for a man arrested by postal inspectors. Using a bizarre twist on mail fraud and credit card fraud, Michael Dantorio was accused of using personal information from at least 17 deceased persons across the country to acquire credit cards in their names, resulting in fraudulent charges of over $60,000. Hence his nickname, "Dead Man Walking."

Dantorio relied on the use of several private mailboxes. He filed false changes of address for the deceased individuals and directed the credit cards to his private mailboxes. Once he received the cards, he lost no time in running up huge charges. If you have recently lost a loved one, be on the lookout for crooks who try to take advantage when you are most vulnerable.

In a country where consumers owe almost $1 trillion on their credit cards, estimates of a few billion dollars in credit fraud losses—just two to three one-thousandths of 1 percent—may not seem all that terrible. But it *is* terrible for victims of fraud. Though they may be protected financially, they are forced to endure major inconvenience. Many fraud victims are devastated emotionally. The negative effects can linger for years. Moreover, all of us pay the costs of credit card fraud through higher prices, higher interest rates, and increased inconvenience.

How can you protect yourself against credit card fraud? You can take several measures:

- Treat your cards like money. Store them in a secure place.
- Shred anything with your account number before throwing it away.
- Don't give your card number over the phone or online unless you initiate the call.
- Don't write your card number on a postcard or the outside of an envelope.
- Remember to get your card and receipt after a transaction, and double-check to be sure it's yours.
- If your billing statement is incorrect or your credit cards are lost or stolen, notify your card issuers immediately.
- If you don't receive your billing statement, notify the company immediately.

Credit card companies spend hundreds of millions of dollars to promote their credit cards. The average cardholder has more than three credit cards.
imageBROKER/Alamy Stock Photo

New technology is making it more difficult to use, alter, or counterfeit credit and debit cards. The security features being added to major credit cards include a holograph—a three-dimensional, laser-produced optical device that changes its color and image as the card is tilted. Another feature is the use of ultraviolet ink, visible only under ultraviolet light, which displays the credit card company logo.

PROTECTING YOUR CREDIT INFORMATION ON THE INTERNET   The internet has joined the smartphone and television as an important part of our lives. Every day, more consumers use the internet for financial activities such as investing, banking, and shopping.

When you make purchases online, make sure your transactions are secure, your personal information is protected, and your fraud sensors are sharpened. Although you can't control fraud or deception on the internet, you can take steps to recognize it, avoid it, and report it if it does occur. Here's how:

- *Use a secure browser,* software that encrypts or scrambles the purchase information you send over the internet, to guard the security of your online transactions. Most computers come with a secure browser already installed. You can also download some browsers for free over the internet.
- *Keep records of your online transactions.* Read your email. Merchants may send you important information about your purchases.
- *Review your monthly bank and credit card statements* for any billing errors or unauthorized purchases. Notify your credit card issuer or bank immediately if your credit card or checkbook is lost or stolen.
- *Read the policies of websites you visit,* especially the disclosures about a site's security, its refund policies, and its privacy policy on collecting and using your personal information. Some websites' disclosures are easier to find than others; look at the bottom of the home page, on order forms, or in the "About" or "FAQs" section of a site. If you can't find a privacy policy, consider shopping elsewhere.
- *Keep your personal information private.* Don't disclose personal information—your address, telephone number, Social Security number, or email address—unless you know who's collecting the information, why they're collecting it, and how they'll use it.
- *Give payment information only to businesses you know and trust* and only in appropriate places such as electronic order forms.

Financial Literacy for My Life

WHAT'S "PHISHING"?

You open an email and see messages like these: "We suspect an unauthorized transaction on your account. To ensure that your account is not compromised, please click the link below and confirm your identity." "During our regular verification of accounts, we could not verify your information. Please click here to update and verify your information." "Our records indicate that your account was overcharged. You must call us within 7 days to receive your refund." These senders are "phishing" for your information in order to commit fraud.

Regulatory agencies have published a brochure, *Internet Pirates Are Trying to Steal Your Information,* to assist you in identifying and preventing a type of internet fraud known as "phishing." With this type of scam, you receive fraudulent email messages that appear to be from your financial institution. The messages often appear authentic and may include the institution's logo and marketing slogans.

These messages usually describe a situation that requires immediate attention and state that your accounts will be terminated unless you verify your personal information by clicking on a provided Web link. The Web link then takes you to a screen that asks for confidential information, including:

- Account numbers.
- Social Security numbers.
- Passwords.
- Place of birth.
- Other information used to identify you.

Those perpetrating the fraud then use this information to access your accounts or assume your identity.
The brochure advises consumers:

- If you're not sure the email is legitimate, go to the company's site by typing in a web address that you know is authentic.
- If you think the email message might be fraudulent, *do not* click on any embedded link within the email. The link may contain a virus.
- Do not be intimidated by emails that warn of dire consequences for not following the sender's instructions.
- If you do fall victim to a phishing scam, act immediately to protect yourself by alerting your financial institution, placing fraud alerts on your credit files, and monitoring your account statements closely.
- Report suspicious emails or calls from third parties to the Federal Trade Commission, either through the internet at www.consumer.gov/idtheft or by calling 1-877-IDTHEFT.

The brochure is on the Office of the Comptroller of the Currency's website, www.occ.gov/topics/consumer-protection/fraud-resources/internet-pirates.html.

Sources: Federal Trade Commission, www.consumer.ftc.gov/articles/0003-phishing, and consumer.ftc.gov/blog/2020/09/heard-about-waiting-package-phishing-scam, accessed March 17, 2021.

- *Never give your password to anyone online,* even your internet service provider.
- *Do not download files sent to you by strangers or click on hyperlinks from people you don't know.* Opening a file could expose your computer system to a virus.[4]

The *Financial Literacy for My Life: What's Phishing?* box describes what *phishing* is and what you can do to protect yourself.

 PRACTICE QUIZ 6-2

1. What are the two main types of consumer credit?
2. What is a debit card?
3. What is a home equity loan?

Measuring Your Credit Capacity

LO6-3

Assess your credit capacity and build your credit rating.

The only way to determine how much credit you can assume is to first learn how to make an accurate and sensible personal or family budget. Budgets, as you learned in Chapter 3, are simple, carefully considered spending plans. With budgets, you first provide for basic necessities such as rent or mortgage, food, and clothing. Then you provide for items such as home furnishings and other heavy, more durable goods.

CAN YOU AFFORD A LOAN?

Before you take out a loan, ask yourself whether you can meet all of your essential expenses and still afford the monthly loan payments. You can make this calculation in two ways. One is to add up all of your basic monthly expenses and then subtract this total from your take-home pay. If the difference will not cover the monthly payment and still leave funds for other expenses, you cannot afford the loan.

A second and more reliable method is to ask yourself what you plan to give up to make the monthly loan payment. If you currently save a portion of your income that is greater than the monthly payment, you can use these savings to pay off the loan. However, if you do not, you will have to forgo spending on entertainment, new appliances, or perhaps even necessities. Are you prepared to make this trade-off? Although it is difficult to precisely measure your credit capacity, you can follow certain rules of thumb.

GENERAL RULES OF CREDIT CAPACITY

DEBT PAYMENTS-TO-INCOME RATIO The debt payments-to-income ratio is calculated by dividing your monthly debt payments (not including house payment, which is a long-term liability) by your net monthly income. Experts suggest that you spend no more than 20 percent of your net (after-tax) income on consumer credit payments. Thus, as Exhibit 6-3 shows, a person making $2,136 per month after taxes should spend no more than $427.20 on credit payments per month.

The 20 percent estimate is the maximum; however, 15 percent is much better. The 20 percent estimate is based on the average family, with average expenses; it does not take major emergencies into account. If you are just beginning to use credit, you should not consider yourself safe if you are spending 20 percent of your net income on credit payments.

DEBT-TO-EQUITY RATIO The debt-to-equity ratio is calculated by dividing your total liabilities by your net worth. In calculating this ratio, do not include the value of your home and the amount of its mortgage. If your debt-to-equity ratio is about 1—that

Monthly gross income	$3,000
Less:	
All taxes	540
Social Security	224
Monthly IRA contribution	−100
Monthly net income	$2,136
Monthly installment credit payments:	
Visa	50
MasterCard	40
Discover card	30
Education loan	—
Personal bank loan	—
Auto loan	306
Total monthly payments	$ 426
Debt payments-to-income ratio ($426/$2,136)	19.94%

EXHIBIT 6-3
How to calculate debt payments-to-income ratio
Spend no more than 20 percent of your net (after tax) income on credit payments.

Source: The Federal Reserve Board, What You Should Know about Home Equity Lines of Credit, files.consumerfinance.gov/f/201204_CFPB_HELOC-brochure.pdf, accessed March 17, 2021.

EXAMPLE: Calculating the Debt-to-Equity Ratio

Shayna's net worth is $150,000. Her liabilities of $60,000 include medical bills, charge account and credit card balances, balance due on an auto loan, and a home improvement loan. Her home has a market value of $210,000, and she owes $180,000 to the mortgage company. What is Shayna's ratio? (Use the space below to show your work.)

_____

_____

In calculating the debt-to-equity ratio, simply divide Shayna's total liabilities by her net worth. (Do not include the value of her home and the amount of its mortgage.)

$$\text{Ratio} = \frac{\text{Liabilities}}{\text{Net worth}} = \frac{\$60,000}{\$150,000} = 0.4$$

is, if your consumer installment debt roughly equals your net worth (not including your home or the mortgage)—you have probably reached the upper limit of debt obligations.

The ratio for business firms in general ranges between 0.33 and 0.50. The larger this ratio, the riskier the situation for lenders and borrowers. Of course, you can lower the ratio by paying off debts.

None of the above methods is perfect for everyone; the limits given are only guidelines. Only you, based on the money you earn, your current obligations, and your financial plans for the future, can determine the exact amount of credit you need and can afford. You must be your own credit manager.

Keep in mind that you adversely affect your credit capacity if you cosign a loan for a friend or a relative.

COSIGNING A LOAN

What would you do if a friend or a relative asked you to cosign a loan? Before you give your answer, make sure you understand what cosigning involves. Under a Federal Trade Commission rule, creditors are required to give you a notice to help explain your obligations. The cosigner's notice says,

> You are being asked to guarantee this debt. Think carefully before you do. If the borrower doesn't pay the debt, you will have to. Be sure you can afford to pay if you have to, and that you want to accept this responsibility.
>
> You may have to pay up to the full amount of the debt if the borrower does not pay. You may also have to pay late fees or collection costs, which increase this amount.
>
> The creditor can collect this debt from you without first trying to collect from the borrower. The creditor can use the same collection methods against you that can be used against the borrower, such as suing you, garnishing your wages, etc. If this debt is ever in default, that fact may become a part of *your* credit record.[5]

COSIGNERS OFTEN PAY
Some studies of certain types of lenders show that as many as three of four cosigners are asked to wholly or partially repay the loan. That statistic should not surprise you. When you are asked to cosign, you are being asked to take a risk that a professional lender will not take. The lender would not require a cosigner if the borrower met the lender's criteria for making a loan.

In most states, if you do cosign and your friend or relative misses a payment, the lender can collect the entire debt from you immediately without pursuing the borrower first. Also, the amount you owe may increase if the lender decides to sue to collect. If the lender wins the case, it may be able to take your wages and property.

IF YOU DO COSIGN Despite the risks, at times you may decide to cosign. Perhaps your child needs a first loan or a close friend needs help. Here are a few things to consider before you cosign.

1. Be sure you can afford to pay the loan. If you are asked to pay and cannot, you could be sued or your credit rating could be damaged.

2. Consider that even if you are not asked to repay the debt, your liability for this loan may keep you from getting other credit you want.

3. Before you pledge property, such as your automobile or furniture, to secure the loan, make sure you understand the consequences. If the borrower defaults, you could lose the property you pledge.

4. Check your state law. Some states have laws giving you additional rights as a cosigner.

5. Request that a copy of overdue-payment notices be sent to you so that you can take action to protect your credit history.

BUILDING AND MAINTAINING YOUR CREDIT RATING

If you apply for a charge account, credit card, car loan, personal loan, or mortgage, your credit experience, or lack of it, will be a major consideration for the creditor. Your credit experience may even affect your ability to get a job or buy life insurance. A good credit rating is a valuable asset that should be nurtured and protected. If you want a good rating, you must use credit with discretion: Limit your borrowing to your capacity to repay, and live up to the terms of your contracts. The quality of your credit rating is entirely up to you.

In reviewing your creditworthiness, a creditor seeks information from a credit bureau. Most creditors rely heavily on credit reports in considering loan applications.

CREDIT BUREAUS **Credit bureaus**, or Consumer Reporting Agencies (CRAs), collect credit and other information about consumers. There are three major credit bureaus: Experian Information Solutions (formerly TRW, Inc.), TransUnion Credit Information Company, and Equifax Services, Inc. Each bureau maintains millions of credit files on individuals based on over 2.5 billion items of information received each month from lenders. In addition, several thousand regional credit bureaus collect credit information about consumers. These firms sell the data to creditors that evaluate credit applications.

credit bureau A reporting agency that assembles credit and other information about consumers.

The Consumer Financial Protection Bureau receives more consumer complaints about credit bureaus than about any other industry, on average 36,000 a year. A common complaint involves incorrect information on credit reports and mix-ups between people with identical surnames. However, the accuracy of credit reports has improved recently, due primarily to public outcry and the threat of stricter federal laws.

A 2015 legal settlement requires Experian, Equifax, and TransUnion to reduce errors on credit reports. Beginning in 2017, the three credit bureaus began removing tax liens and civil judgment debts (court-ordered payment of damages) from consumer credit reports, if the information is incomplete. The bureaus also agreed to exclude medical debts on consumer credit reports until such debts are at least 180 days past due.

WHO PROVIDES DATA TO CREDIT BUREAUS? Credit bureaus obtain their data from banks, finance companies, merchants, credit card companies, and other creditors. These sources regularly send reports to credit bureaus containing information about the kinds of credit they extend to customers, the amounts and terms of that credit, and customers' paying habits. Credit bureaus also collect some information from other sources, such as court records.

WHAT IS IN YOUR CREDIT FILES?   The credit bureau file contains your name, address, Social Security number, and birth date. It may also include the following information.

- Your employer, position, and income.
- Your former address.
- Your former employer.
- Your spouse's name, Social Security number, employer, and income.
- Whether you own your home or rent.
- Checks returned for insufficient funds.

Your credit file may also contain detailed credit information. Each time you buy from a reporting store on credit or take out a loan at a bank, a finance company, or some other reporting creditor, a credit bureau is informed of your account number and the date, amount, terms, and type of credit. As you make payments, your file is updated to show the outstanding balance, the number and amounts of payments past due, and the frequency of 30-, 60-, or 90-day delinquencies. Any suits, judgments, or tax liens against you may appear as well. However, a federal law protects your rights if the information in your credit file is erroneous.

In summary, credit reports contain information about your bill payment history, loans, current debt, and other financial information. The report shows where you work and live, and whether you have been sued, arrested, or filed for bankruptcy.

FAIR CREDIT REPORTING   You can see that fair and accurate credit reporting is vital to both creditors and consumers. In 1971 Congress enacted the **Fair Credit Reporting Act**, which regulates the use of credit reports, requires the deletion of obsolete information, and gives consumers access to their files and the right to have erroneous data corrected. Furthermore, the act allows only authorized persons to obtain credit reports.

Credit bureaus provide lists of creditworthy consumers for companies to offer credit. These are called prescreened lists. You can remove your name from all Experian-generated mail and telephone lists by sending your full name and addresses for the past five years to Experian, Consumer Opt Out, P.O. Box 919, Allen, TX 75013. Your name will be shared with Equifax and TransUnion, the other two national credit reporting systems.

WHO MAY OBTAIN A CREDIT REPORT?   Your credit report may be issued only to properly identified persons for approved purposes. It may be furnished to prospective employers in response to a court order or in accordance with your own written request. A credit report may also be provided to someone who will use it in connection with a credit transaction, underwriting of insurance, or some other legitimate business need or in determining eligibility for a license or other benefit granted by a government agency. Your friends and neighbors may not obtain credit information about you. If they request such information, they may be subject to a fine and imprisonment.

The credit bureaus contend that current laws protect consumers' privacy, but many consumer organizations believe that anyone with internet access can easily access credit bureau files.

TIME LIMITS ON ADVERSE DATA   Most of the information in your credit file may be reported for only 7 years. If you have declared personal bankruptcy, however, that fact may be reported for 10 years. Unpaid tax liens can be reported for 15 years. After 7, 10, or 15 years, a credit reporting agency can't disclose the information in your credit file unless you are being investigated for a

Fair Credit Reporting Act Regulates the use of credit reports, requires the deletion of obsolete information, and gives consumers access to their files and the right to have erroneous data corrected.

my life 3

If I want to see a copy of my credit report, I know who to contact.

In 2005 all consumers became eligible to receive a free credit report from each of the three major credit reporting agencies (CRAs). Call 1-877-322-8228 or visit www.annualcreditreport.com. Your FICO® score is available from www.myfico.com for a fee. A good strategy is to ask for one report from a different agency every four months. That makes it easier to spot suspicious activity over the course of a year.

credit application of $75,000 or more or for an application to purchase life insurance of $150,000 or more.

INCORRECT INFORMATION IN YOUR CREDIT FILE

Credit bureaus are required to follow reasonable procedures to ensure that subscribing creditors report information accurately. However, mistakes may occur. Your file may contain erroneous data or records of someone with a name similar to yours. When you notify the credit bureau that you dispute the accuracy of its information, it must reinvestigate and modify or remove inaccurate data. You should give the credit bureau any pertinent data you have concerning an error. If you contest an item on your credit report, the reporting agency must remove the item unless the creditor verifies that the information is accurate (see Exhibit 6-4).

If you are denied credit, insurance, employment, or rental housing based on the information in the report, you can get a copy of your credit report free within 60 days of your request. You should review your credit files every year even if you are not planning to apply for a big loan. Married persons and young adults should make sure that all accounts for which they are individually and jointly liable are listed in their credit files.

personal fintech

You are entitled to order a free copy of your credit report every year from each of the major credit reporting agencies at AnnualCreditReport.com. This website is the only one that is authorized to provide you with free copies of your credit report. You may also contact the agencies directly by calling:

> Equifax: 1-866-349-5191
>
> Experian: 1-888-397-3742
>
> TransUnion: 1-800-916-8800
>
> or by mail, Annual Credit Report Service,
>
> P.O. Box 105281, Atlanta, GA 30348-5281.

If your request is denied, try to resolve the issue with the credit reporting agency, or contact the Consumer Financial Protection Bureau at 1-855-411-CFPB.

Read the *Financial Literacy for My Life: Your Identity Has Been Stolen: What Now?* feature if you are affected by the Equifax data breach.

EXHIBIT 6-4

Sample dispute letter

The law requires credit card companies to correct inaccurate or incomplete information in your credit report.

Date

Your Name
Your Address
Your City, State, Zip Code

Complaint Department
Name of Credit Reporting Agency
Address
City, State, Zip Code

Dear Sir or Madam:

I am writing to dispute the following information in my file. The items I dispute are also encircled on the attached copy of the report I received. (Identify item(s) disputed by name of source, such as creditor or tax court, and identify type of item, such as credit account, judgment, etc.)

This item is (inaccurate or incomplete) because (describe what is inaccurate or incomplete and why). I am requesting that the item be deleted (or request another specific change) to correct the information.

Enclosed are copies of (use this sentence if applicable and describe any enclosed documentation, such as payment records, court documents) supporting my position. Please reinvestigate this (these) matter(s) and (delete or correct) the disputed item(s) as soon as possible.

Sincerely,
Your name
Enclosures: (List what you are enclosing)

Source: Federal Trade Commission, www.consumer.ftc.gov/articles/0384-sample-letter-disputing-errors-your-credit-report, March 16, 2021.

Financial Literacy for My Life

YOUR IDENTITY HAS BEEN STOLEN: WHAT NOW?

If you have a credit report, there's a good chance that you're one of the 143 million American consumers whose sensitive personal information was exposed in a data breach at Equifax, one of the nation's three major credit reporting agencies.

According to Equifax, the breach lasted from mid-May through July 2017. The hackers accessed names, Social Security numbers, birth dates, addresses, and, in some instances, driver's license numbers. They also stole credit card numbers of about 209,000 Americans.

Take the following steps to protect your information from being misused. Visit Equifax's website, www.equifaxsecurity2017.com and:

- Find out if your information was exposed. Click on the "Potential Impact" tab and enter your last name and the last six digits of your Social Security number. Your Social Security number is sensitive information, so make sure you're on a secure computer and an encrypted network connection. The site will tell you if you've been affected by this breach.

- You can also access frequently asked questions at this site.

Here are some additional suggestions to help you to protect yourself after a data breach:

- Check your credit reports from Equifax, Experian, and TransUnion—for free—by visiting annualcreditreport. com. Accounts or activity that you don't recognize could indicate identity theft. Visit IdentityTheft.gov to find out what to do.

- Consider placing a credit freeze on your files. A credit freeze makes it harder for someone to open a new account in your name. Remember that a credit freeze won't prevent a thief from making charges to your existing accounts.

- Monitor your existing credit card and bank accounts closely for charges you don't recognize.

- If you decide against a credit freeze, consider placing a fraud alert on your files. An alert warns creditors that you may be an identity theft victim and they should verify that anyone seeking credit in your name is really you.

Source: https://www.consumer.ftc.gov/blog/2017/09/equifax-data-breach-what-do, accessed March 17, 2021.

WHAT ARE THE LEGAL REMEDIES? Any consumer reporting agency or user of reported information that willfully or through negligence fails to comply with the provisions of the Fair Credit Reporting Act may be sued by the affected consumer. If the agency or the user is found guilty, the consumer may be awarded actual damages, court costs and attorneys' fees, and, in the case of willful noncompliance, punitive damages as allowed by the court. The action must be brought within two years of the occurrence or within two years after the discovery of material and willful misrepresentation of information. An unauthorized person who obtains a credit report under false pretenses may be fined up to $5,000, imprisoned for one year, or both. The same penalties apply to anyone who willfully provides credit information to someone not authorized to receive it.

Exhibit 6-5 outlines the steps you can take if you are denied credit.

PFP Sheet 29
Consumer Credit Usage

 PRACTICE QUIZ 6-3

1. What are the general rules for measuring credit capacity? How is credit capacity calculated?
2. What can happen if you cosign a loan?
3. What can you do to build and maintain your credit rating?
4. What is the Fair Credit Reporting Act?
5. How do you correct erroneous information in your credit file?
6. What are your legal remedies if a credit reporting agency engages in unfair reporting practices?

EXHIBIT 6-5* What if you are denied credit?

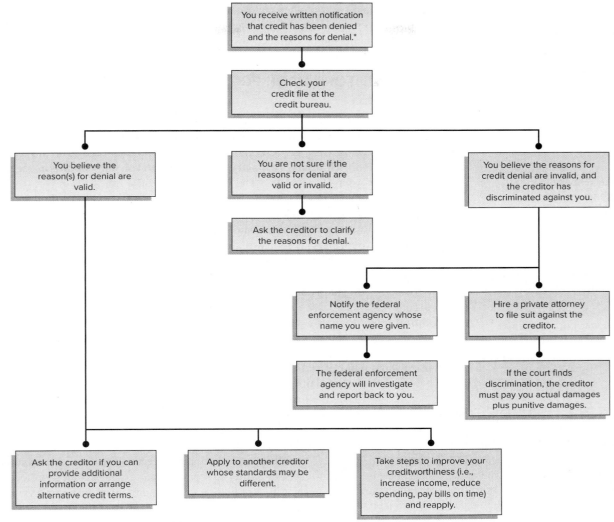

You receive written notification that credit has been denied and the reasons for denial.*

Check your credit file at the credit bureau.

You believe the reason(s) for denial are valid.

You are not sure if the reasons for denial are valid or invalid.

You believe the reasons for credit denial are invalid, and the creditor has discriminated against you.

Ask the creditor to clarify the reasons for denial.

Notify the federal enforcement agency whose name you were given.

Hire a private attorney to file suit against the creditor.

The federal enforcement agency will investigate and report back to you.

If the court finds discrimination, the creditor must pay you actual damages plus punitive damages.

Ask the creditor if you can provide additional information or arrange alternative credit terms.

Apply to another creditor whose standards may be different.

Take steps to improve your creditworthiness (i.e., increase income, reduce spending, pay bills on time) and reapply.

*If a creditor receives no more than 150 applications during a calendar year, the disclosures may be oral.

Source: Office of Public Information, Federal Reserve Bank of Minneapolis, Minneapolis, MN 55480.

Applying for Credit

A SCENARIO FROM THE PAST

Mary and John Jones have a joint income that is more than enough for them to make payments on their dream house. Yet they are turned down for a mortgage loan. The lender says Mary might become pregnant and leave her job.

In fact, however, it is illegal for a creditor to ask or assume anything about a woman's childbearing plans. It is even illegal to discourage the Joneses from applying for a loan because Mary is of childbearing age. Also, the lender must fully acknowledge Mary's income.

When you are ready to apply for credit, you should know what creditors think is important in deciding whether you are creditworthy. You should also know what they

LO6-4

Describe the information creditors look for when you apply for credit.

cannot legally consider in their decisions. The **Equal Credit Opportunity Act (ECOA)** starts all credit applicants off on the same footing. It states that race, color, age, sex, marital status, and certain other factors may not be used to discriminate against you in any part of a credit dealing. Credit rights of women are protected under the ECOA. Women should build and protect their own credit histories.

WHAT CREDITORS LOOK FOR: THE FIVE Cs OF CREDIT MANAGEMENT

When a lender extends credit to its customers, it recognizes that some customers will be unable or unwilling to pay for their purchases. Therefore, lenders must establish policies for determining who will receive credit. Most lenders build their credit policies around the *five Cs of credit:* **character**, **capacity**, **capital**, **collateral**, and **conditions** (see the *Financial Literacy for My Life* box, "The Five Cs of Credit").

character The borrower's attitude toward his or her credit obligations.

Character is the borrower's attitude toward credit obligations. Most credit managers consider character the most important factor in predicting whether you will make timely payments and ultimately repay your loan.

capacity The borrower's financial ability to meet credit obligations.

Capacity is your financial ability to meet credit obligations, that is, to make regular loan payments as scheduled in the credit agreement. Therefore, the lender checks your salary statements and other sources of income, such as dividends and interest. Your other financial obligations and monthly expenses are also considered before credit is approved.

capital The borrower's assets or net worth.

Capital refers to your assets or net worth. Generally, the greater your capital, the greater your ability to repay a loan. The lender determines your net worth by requiring you to complete certain credit application questions (see Exhibit 6-6). You must authorize your employer and financial institutions to release information to confirm the claims made in the credit application.

collateral A valuable asset that is pledged to ensure loan payments.

Collateral is an asset that you pledge to a financial institution to obtain a loan. If you fail to honor the terms of the credit agreement, the lender can repossess the collateral and then sell it to satisfy the debt.

conditions The general economic conditions that can affect a borrower's ability to repay a loan.

Conditions refer to general economic conditions that can affect your ability to repay a loan. The basic question focuses on security—of both your job and the firm that employs you.

Creditors use different combinations of the five Cs to reach their decisions. Some creditors set unusually high standards, and others simply do not make certain kinds of loans. Creditors also use different kinds of rating systems. Some rely strictly

smart money minute

ESTABLISHING YOUR CREDIT

You need a steady work record and continued residence at the same address. Open a checking account and be careful not to bounce checks. Apply for credit at a local department store or credit union. Consider a secured credit card, which requires you to deposit money as security for the charges you make on the card.

EXHIBIT 6-6

Sample credit application questions

- Amount of loan requested.
- Proposed use of the loan.
- Your name and birth date.
- Social Security and driver's license numbers.
- Present and previous street addresses.
- Present and previous employers and their addresses.
- Present salary.
- Number and ages of dependents.
- Other income and sources of other income.

- Have you ever received credit from us? If so, when and at which office?
- Checking account number, institution, and branch.
- Savings account number, institution, and branch.
- Name of nearest relative not living with you.
- Relative's address and telephone number.
- Your marital status.
- Information regarding joint applicant: same questions as above.

Financial Literacy for My Life

THE FIVE Cs OF CREDIT

Here is what lenders look for in determining your creditworthiness.

1. Character: Will you repay the loan?

CREDIT HISTORY

Do you have a good attitude toward credit obligations?

Have you used credit before?

Do you pay your bills on time?

Have you ever filed for bankruptcy?

Do you live within your means?

STABILITY

How long have you lived at your present address?

Do you own your home?

How long have you been employed by your present employer?

2. Capacity: Can you repay the loan?

INCOME

Your salary and occupation?

Place of occupation?

How reliable is your income?

Any other sources of income?

EXPENSES

Number of dependents?

Do you pay any alimony or child support?

Current debts?

3. Capital: What are your assets and net worth?

NET WORTH

What are your assets?

What are your liabilities?

What is your net worth?

4. Collateral: What if you don't repay the loan?

LOAN SECURITY

What assets do you have to secure the loan? (Car, home, furniture?)

What sources do you have besides income? (Savings, stocks, bonds, insurance?)

5. Conditions: What general economic conditions can affect your repayment of the loan?

JOB SECURITY

How secure is your job?

How secure is the firm you work for?

Source: Adapted from William M. Pride, Robert J. Hughes, and Jack R. Kapoor, *Business,* 12th ed. (Mason, OH: Cengage Learning, 2014), p. 541.

---

on their own instinct and experience. Others use a credit scoring or statistical system to predict whether an applicant is a good credit risk. They assign a certain number of points to each characteristic that has proven to be a reliable sign that a borrower will repay. Then they rate the applicant on this scale.

In addition, during the loan application process, the lender may evaluate many of the following criteria to determine whether you are a good credit risk. The other factors include:

AGE Retired couples and many older people have complained that they were denied credit because they were over a certain age or that, when they retired, their credit was suddenly cut off or reduced.

The ECOA is very specific about how a person's age may be used in credit decisions. A creditor may ask about your age, but if

my life **4**

Most of the information in your credit file may be reported for seven years. Several websites can provide current information about credit files. Visit ftc.gov, equifax.com, or experian.com for more information.

you're old enough to sign a binding contract (usually 18 or 21 years old, depending on state law), a creditor may not

- Turn you down or decrease your credit because of your age.
- Ignore your retirement income in rating your application.
- Close your credit account or require you to reapply for it because you have reached a certain age or retired.
- Deny you credit or close your account because credit life insurance or other credit-related insurance is not available to people of your age.

PUBLIC ASSISTANCE   You may not be denied credit because you receive Social Security or public assistance. But, as with age, certain information related to this source of income could have a bearing on your creditworthiness.

smart money minute

WHAT'S IN YOUR FICO SCORE?

The data from your credit report is generally grouped into five categories. The percentages in the pie diagram reflect how important each of the categories is in determining your FICO score.

- 10%
- 15%
- 10%
- 30%
- 35%

- Length of credit history
- Payment history
- Amounts owed
- Types of credit used
- New credit

Source: "How My FICO Scores Are Calculated," FICO website www.myfico.com/CreditEducation/WhatsInYourScore.aspx. This information is provided by the Fair Isaac Corporation.

my life 5

I can improve my credit score.

A credit score is a snapshot of the contents of your credit report at the time it is calculated. The first step in improving your score is to review your credit report to ensure it is accurate. Long-term, responsible credit behavior is the most effective way to improve future scores. Open a savings account and make regular monthly deposits. Pay bills on time, lower balances, and use credit wisely to improve your score over time. Read the nearby *How To . . . Improve Your Credit Score* feature.

HOUSING LOANS   The ECOA covers your application for a mortgage or a home improvement loan. It bans discrimination due to characteristics such as your race, color, or sex or due to the race or national origin of the people in the neighborhood where you live or want to buy your home. Creditors may not use any appraisal of the value of your property that considers the race of the people in your neighborhood.

FICO AND VANTAGESCORE   Typical questions in a credit application appear in Exhibit 6-6. The information in your credit report is used to calculate your FICO® credit score—a number generally between 300 and 850 that rates how risky a borrower is. The higher the score, the less risk you pose to creditors. You need about a 760 score to get the best mortgage rate, and a score of 720 to get the best deal on an auto loan. Released recently, FICO® Score 9 is the most predictive score yet. Introduced in 1989, your FICO® scores, most widely used by lenders, are available from www.myfico.com for a fee. Better yet, get your free credit score from Discover at https://www.discover.com/free-credit-score/. Free credit reports do not contain your credit score. Exhibit 6-7 shows a numerical depiction of your creditworthiness and how you can improve your credit score.

VantageScore, launched in 2006, is a scoring technique, the first to be developed collaboratively by the three credit reporting companies. This model allows for a more predictive score for consumers, even for those with limited credit histories, reducing the need for creditors to manually review credit information. Introduced in 2013, the new VantageScore 4.0:

- Features a common score range of 300 to 850 (higher scores represent lower likelihood of risks).
- Does not count debt collections that have been paid off.
- Makes up to 30 million additional consumers with short credit histories eligible for credit reports.
- Ignores negative credit history if you are affected by natural disasters, such as Hurricane Sandy.

EXHIBIT 6-7 TransUnion personal credit score

The higher your score, the less risk you pose to creditors.

Your Credit Score Is: 775

Score created on:
08/08/2021

You can purchase your credit score
for $9.95 by calling 1-866-SCORE-TU
or 1-866-726-7388.

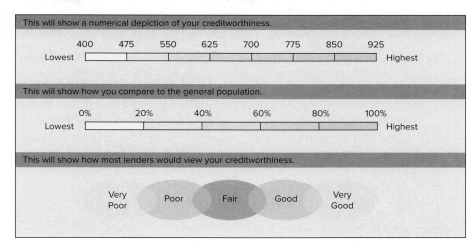

This will show a numerical depiction of your creditworthiness.

400 475 550 625 700 775 850 925
Lowest   Highest

This will show how you compare to the general population.

0%   20%   40%   60%   80%   100%
Lowest   Highest

This will show how most lenders would view your creditworthiness.

Very Poor   Poor   Fair   Good   Very Good

A key benefit of VantageScore is that as long as the three major credit bureaus have the same information regarding your credit history, you will receive the same score from each of them. A different score alerts you that there are discrepancies in your report. You can get your free VantageScore score from https://www.nerdwallet.com.

WHAT IF YOUR APPLICATION IS DENIED?

ASK QUESTIONS IF YOUR APPLICATION IS DENIED If you receive a notice that your application has been denied, the ECOA gives you the right to know the specific reasons for denial. If the denial is based on a credit report, you are entitled to know the specific information in the credit report that led to it. After you receive this information from the creditor, you should contact the local credit bureau to find out what information it reported. The bureau cannot charge you a disclosure fee if you ask for a copy of your credit report within 60 days of being notified of a denial based on a credit report. You may ask the bureau to investigate any inaccurate or incomplete information and correct its records.

HOW CAN I IMPROVE MY CREDIT SCORE? A credit score is a snapshot of the contents of your credit report at the time it is calculated. The first step in improving your score is to review your credit report to ensure it is accurate. Long-term, responsible credit behavior is the most effective way to improve future scores. Pay bills on time, lower balances, and use credit wisely to improve your score over time. (Read the nearby *How To . . . Improve Your Credit Score* feature.)

smart money minute

In addition to your free annual credit reports, all U.S. consumers are entitled to six free credit reports every 12 months from Equifax through December 2026. All you have to do is get a "myEquifax" account at equifax.com/personal/credit-report-services/free-credit-reports/ or call Equifax at 866-349-5191.

smart money minute

YOU CAN GET FREE CREDIT REPORT UPDATES

Sign up for credit monitoring with Credit Sesame (www.creditsesame.com/credit-monitoring) for email alerts. Also, Credit Karma (www.creditkarma.com/credit-monitoring) provides free daily monitoring of your TransUnion report.

HOW TO . . .   Improve Your Credit Score

1. **Get copies of your credit report—then make sure the information is correct.** Go to www.annualcreditreport.com. This is the only authorized online source for a free credit report. Under federal law, you can get a free report from each of the three national credit reporting companies every 12 months.

   You can also call 877-322-8228 or complete the *Annual Credit Report Request Form* and mail it to Annual Credit Report Request Service, P.O. Box 105281, Atlanta, GA 30348-5281.

2. **Pay your bills on time.** One of the most important steps you can take to improve your credit score is to pay your bills by the due date. You can set up automatic payments from your bank account to help you pay on time, but be sure you have enough money in your account to avoid overdraft fees.

3. **Understand how your credit score is determined.** Your credit score is usually based on the answers to these questions.

   - **Do you pay your bills on time?** The answer to this question is very important. If you have paid bills late, had an account referred to a collection agency, or have ever declared bankruptcy, this history will show up in your credit report.

   - **What is your outstanding debt?** Many scoring models compare the amount of debt you have and your credit limits. If the amount you owe is close to your credit limit, it is likely to have a negative effect on your score.

   - **How long is your credit history?** A short credit history may have a negative effect on your score, but a short history can be offset by other factors, such as timely payments and low balances.

   - **Have you applied for new credit recently?** If you have applied for too many new accounts recently, that may negatively affect your score. However, if you request a copy of your own credit report, or if creditors are monitoring your account or looking at credit reports to make prescreened credit offers, these inquiries about your credit history are not counted as applications for credit.

   - **How many and what types of credit accounts do you have?** Many credit-scoring models consider the number and type of credit accounts you have. A mix of installment loans and credit cards may improve your score. However, too many finance company accounts or credit cards might hurt your score.

   To learn more about credit scoring, see the Federal Trade Commission's website at www.ftc.gov.

4. **Learn the legal steps to take to improve your credit report.** The Federal Trade Commission's *"Building a Better Credit Report"* has information on correcting errors in your report, tips on dealing with debt and avoiding scams, and more.

5. **Beware of credit-repair scams.** Sometimes doing it yourself is the best way to repair your credit. The Federal Trade Commission's *"Credit Repair, How to Help Yourself"* explains how you can improve your creditworthiness and lists legitimate resources for low-cost or no-cost help.

Source: Board of Governors of the Federal Reserve System, https://www.federalreserve.gov/pubs/creditscore/creditscoretips_2.pdf, accessed March 17, 2021.

PRACTICE QUIZ 6-4

1. What is the Equal Credit Opportunity Act?
2. What are the five *C*s of credit?
3. What can you do if your credit application is denied?

Avoiding and Correcting Credit Mistakes

Has a department store's computer ever billed you for merchandise that you returned to the store or never received? Has a credit company ever charged you for the same item twice or failed to properly credit a payment on your account?

The best way to maintain your credit standing is to repay your debts on time. But complications may still occur. To protect your credit and save your time, money, and future credit rating, you should learn how to correct any mistakes and misunderstandings that crop up in your credit accounts. If a snag occurs, first try to deal directly with the creditor. The credit laws can help you settle your complaints.

The **Fair Credit Billing Act (FCBA)**, passed in 1975, sets procedures for promptly correcting billing mistakes, refusing to make credit card or revolving credit payments on defective goods, and promptly crediting your payments.

The act defines a billing error as any charge for something you did not buy or for something bought by a person not authorized to use your account. Also included among billing errors is any charge that is not properly identified on your bill (i.e., for an amount different from the actual purchase price) or that was entered on a date other than the purchase date. A billing error may also be a charge for something you did not accept on delivery or was not delivered according to agreement.

Billing errors also include errors in arithmetic; failure to reflect a payment or other credit to your account; failure to mail the statement to your current address, provided you notified the creditor of an address change at least 20 days before the end of the billing period; and questionable items, or items about which you need additional information.

IN CASE OF A BILLING ERROR

If you think your bill is wrong or you want more information about it, follow these steps. First, call your creditor. Many errors can be corrected over the phone. Other items that appear to be errors can be clarified. If there is a dispute or more information is needed, notify the creditor *in writing* within 60 days after the bill was mailed. Credit card issuers will mail or email a form, which then can be mailed to fulfill the 60-day mailing requirement. A telephone call will not protect your rights. Be sure to write to the address the creditor lists for billing inquiries. Give the creditor your name and account number, say that you believe the bill contains an error, and explain what you believe the error to be. State the suspected amount of the error or the item you want explained. Then pay all the parts of the bill that are not in dispute. While waiting for an answer, you do not have to pay the disputed amount or any minimum payments or finance charges that apply to it.

The creditor must acknowledge your letter within 30 days, unless it can correct your bill sooner. Within two billing periods, but in no case longer than 90 days, either your account must be corrected or you must be told why the creditor believes the bill is correct. If the creditor made a mistake, you need not pay any finance charges on the disputed amount. Your account must be corrected, and you must be sent an explanation of any amount you still owe.

If no error is found, the creditor must promptly send you an explanation of the reasons for that determination and a statement of what you owe, which may include any finance charges that have accumulated and any minimum payments you missed while you were questioning the bill. Exhibit 6-8 summarizes the steps in resolving a billing dispute, and Exhibit 6-8A shows a sample letter to dispute a billing error.

YOUR CREDIT RATING DURING THE DISPUTE

A creditor may not threaten your credit rating while you are resolving a billing dispute. Once you have written about a possible error, a creditor is prohibited from giving out information that would damage your credit reputation to other creditors or credit bureaus. And until your complaint has been answered, the creditor may not take any action to collect the disputed amount.

LO6-5

Identify the steps you can take to avoid and correct credit mistakes.

Fair Credit Billing Act (FCBA) Sets procedures for promptly correcting billing mistakes, refusing to make credit card payments on defective goods, and promptly crediting payments.

EXHIBIT 6-8* Steps in the process of resolving a billing dispute

A creditor may not threaten your credit rating while you are resolving a billing dispute.

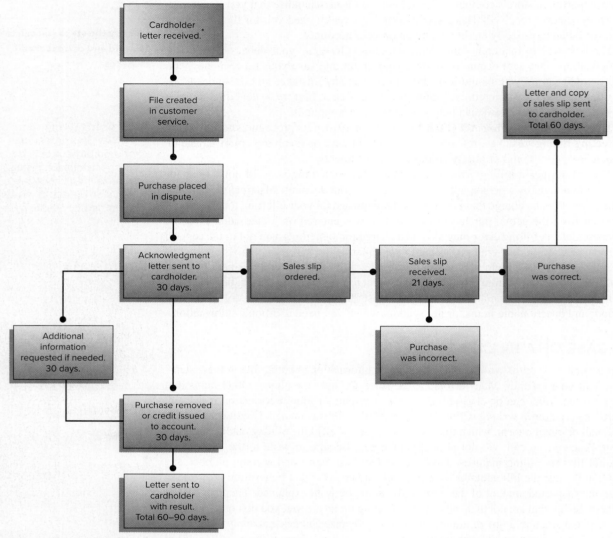

*Exhibit 6-8A shows a sample letter to dispute a billing error.

Source: Charge-It-System, Billing Errors Section, *Cardholder Tips*, March 1992, n.p.

After explaining the bill, the creditor may report you as delinquent on the amount in dispute and take action to collect if you do not pay in the time allowed. Even so, you can still disagree in writing. Then the creditor and the credit bureau must report that you have challenged your bill and give you the name and address of each recipient of information about your account. When the matter has been settled, the creditor must report the outcome to each recipient of the information. Remember, you may also place your version of the dispute in your credit record.

DEFECTIVE GOODS OR SERVICES

Your new sofa arrives with only three legs. You try to return it, but no luck. You ask the merchant to repair or replace it; still no luck. The Fair Credit Billing Act provides that you may withhold payment on any damaged or shoddy goods or poor services that you have purchased with a credit card as long as you have made a sincere attempt to resolve the problem with the merchant.

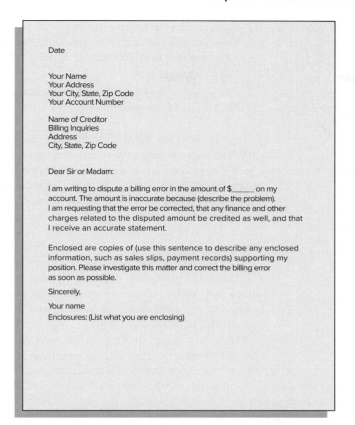

Date

Your Name
Your Address
Your City, State, Zip Code
Your Account Number

Name of Creditor
Billing Inquiries
Address
City, State, Zip Code

Dear Sir or Madam:

I am writing to dispute a billing error in the amount of $_____ on my
account. The amount is inaccurate because (describe the problem).
I am requesting that the error be corrected, that any finance and other
charges related to the disputed amount be credited as well, and that
I receive an accurate statement.

Enclosed are copies of (use this sentence to describe any enclosed
information, such as sales slips, payment records) supporting my
position. Please investigate this matter and correct the billing error
as soon as possible.

Sincerely,

Your name
Enclosures: (List what you are enclosing)

EXHIBIT 6-8A

A sample letter to dispute a
billing error

Write to the creditor at the address given
for "billing inquiries," not the address for
sending your payments.

Source: Federal Trade Commission, "Sample Letter for Disputing Billing Errors," www.consumer.ftc.gov/articles/0385-
sample-letter-disputing-billing-errors, accessed March 17, 2021.

IDENTITY CRISIS: WHAT TO DO IF YOUR IDENTITY IS STOLEN

"I don't remember charging those items. I've never even been in that store." Maybe you
never charged those goods and services, but someone else did—someone who used
your name and personal information to commit fraud. When impostors take your name,
Social Security number, credit card number, or some other piece of your personal information for their use, they are committing a crime.

The biggest problem is that you may not know your identity has been stolen until you
notice that something is amiss: You may get bills for a credit card account you never
opened, your credit report may include debts you never knew you had, a billing cycle
may pass without you receiving a statement, or you may see charges on your bills that
you didn't sign for, didn't authorize, and know nothing about.

If someone has stolen your identity, the Federal Trade Commission recommends that
you take three actions immediately:

1. *Contact the fraud departments of each of the three major credit bureaus* (see
   the table that follows). Tell them to flag your file with a fraud alert, including a
   statement that creditors should call you for permission before they open any new
   accounts in your name.

	To Report Fraud	To Order Credit Report	Website
Equifax	1-800-525-6285	1-800-685-1111	www.equifax.com
Experian	1-888-397-3742	1-888-EXPERIAN	www.experian.com
TransUnion	1-800-680-7289	1-800-916-8800	www.transunion.com

personal fintech

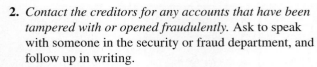

PROTECTING YOUR PRIVACY AND SECURITY WHEN YOU MAKE MOBILE PAYMENTS

Now you can use a smartphone, tablet, or other mobile devices to pay for some purchases. Mobile payments can be convenient—no need to write a check or to pull out your wallet for cash or plastic, no need to type in your payment information to buy online. But are mobile payments safe? What about your privacy? These are good questions to ask when you consider using any technology. Because you usually carry your phone or other mobile device with you, it is on most of the time, and it may contain very sensitive personal information. It is important to keep it and its contents safe and secure, especially if you want to use it to make mobile payments or conduct other financial business.

If someone steals your identity, contact credit bureaus and creditors, and file a police report immediately.
citalliance/123RF

smart money minute

The Federal Trade Commission maintains the Identity Theft Data Clearinghouse and provides information to identify theft victims. You can call toll-free 1-877-ID-THEFT or visit www.consumer.ftc.gov/features/feature-0014-identity-theft.

2. *Contact the creditors for any accounts that have been tampered with or opened fraudulently.* Ask to speak with someone in the security or fraud department, and follow up in writing.

3. *File a police report.* Keep a copy in case your creditors need proof of the crime.

To prevent an identity thief from picking up your trash to capture your personal information, tear or shred your charge receipts, copies of credit applications, insurance forms, bank checks and statements, expired charge cards, and credit offers you get in the mail.

If you believe an identity thief has accessed your bank accounts, checking account, or ATM card, close the accounts immediately. When you open new accounts, insist on password-only access. If your checks have been stolen or misused, stop payment. If your ATM card has been lost, stolen, or otherwise compromised, cancel the card and get another with a new personal identification number (PIN).

If, after taking all these steps, you are still having identity problems, stay alert to new instances of identity theft. Notify the company or creditor immediately, and follow up in writing. Also, contact the Privacy Rights Clearinghouse, which provides information on how to network with other identity theft victims. Call 619-298-3396 or visit www.privacyrights.org.

The U.S. Secret Service has jurisdiction over financial fraud cases. Although the service generally investigates cases where the dollar loss is substantial, your information may provide evidence of a larger pattern of fraud that requires its involvement. Contact your local field office.

The Social Security Administration may issue you a new Social Security number if you still have difficulties after trying to resolve problems resulting from identity theft. Unfortunately, however, there is no guarantee that a new Social Security number will resolve your problems. Call the Social Security Administration at 1-800-772-1213.

Finally, you can file a complaint with the Federal Trade Commission (FTC) through a toll-free consumer help line at 1-877-FTC-HELP at Consumer Response Center, or at its website, www.ftc.gov, using the online complaint form. Although the FTC cannot resolve individual problems for consumers, it can act against a company if it sees a pattern of possible law violations.

✔ PRACTICE QUIZ 6-5

1. What is the Fair Credit Billing Act?
2. What must you do to protect your rights if a billing error occurs?
3. What happens to your credit rating during the billing dispute?
4. What can you do if your identity is stolen?

Complaining about Consumer Credit

If you have a complaint about credit, first try to solve your problem directly with the creditor. Only if that fails should you use more formal complaint procedures. This section describes how to file a complaint with the federal agencies responsible for administering consumer credit protection laws.

COMPLAINTS ABOUT BANKS

If you have a complaint about a bank in connection with any of the federal credit laws, or if you think any part of your business with a bank has been handled in an unfair or deceptive way, you may get advice and help from the Federal Reserve System. You don't need to have an account at the bank to file a complaint. (See Exhibit 6-9.)

PROTECTION UNDER CONSUMER CREDIT LAWS

You may also take legal action against a creditor. If you decide to file a lawsuit, there are important consumer credit laws you should know about.

LO6-6

Describe the laws that protect you if you have a complaint about consumer credit.

I know what to do if I have serious credit problems.

First, try to solve your problems directly with your creditors. The National Center for Economic and Financial Education (councilforeconed.org) and the National Foundation for Consumer Credit (nfcc.org) are good internet sources of further information.

TRUTH IN LENDING AND CONSUMER LEASING ACTS If a creditor fails to disclose information required under the Truth in Lending Act or the Consumer Leasing Act, gives inaccurate information, or does not comply with the rules regarding credit cards or the right to cancel them, you may sue for actual damages, that is, any money loss you suffer. Class action suits are also permitted. A class action suit is a suit filed on behalf of a group of people with similar claims.

EQUAL CREDIT OPPORTUNITY ACT If you think you can prove that a creditor has discriminated against you for any reason prohibited by the ECOA, you may sue for actual damages plus punitive damages (i.e., damages for the fact that the law has been violated) of up to $10,000.

FAIR CREDIT BILLING ACT A creditor that fails to comply with the rules applying to the correction of billing errors automatically forfeits the amount owed on the item in question and any finance charges on it, up to a combined total of $50, even if the bill was correct. You may also sue for actual damages plus twice the amount of any finance charges.

FAIR CREDIT REPORTING ACT You may sue any credit reporting agency or creditor for violating the rules regarding access to your credit records and correction of errors in your credit file. You are entitled to actual damages plus any punitive damages the court allows if the violation is proven to have been intentional.

CONSUMER CREDIT REPORTING REFORM ACT An unfavorable credit report can force you to pay a higher interest rate on a loan or cost you a loan, an insurance policy, an apartment rental, or even a job offer. The **Consumer Credit Reporting Reform Act** of 1997 places the burden of proof for accurate credit information on the credit reporting agency rather than on you. Under this law, the creditor must certify that disputed data are accurate. If a creditor or the credit bureau verifies incorrect data, you can sue for damages. The federal government and state attorneys general can also sue creditors for civil damages.

Consumer Credit Reporting Reform Act Places the burden of proof for accurate credit information on the credit reporting agency.

EXHIBIT 6-9   Complaint form to report violations of federal credit laws

FR 1379c - OMB No. 7100-0135

Please print clearly below.
Mail or fax this completed form to:
Federal Reserve Consumer Help
PO Box 1200, Minneapolis, MN 55480
Fax: 877-888-2520

CONSUMER COMPLAINT FORM   *Required Fields   Questions? Call us at 888-851-1920

YOUR INFORMATION

Prefix: ☐ Mr. ☐ Mrs. ☐ Ms. ☐ Dr.   *First Name: _____   *Last Name: _____

*Address: _____

City   State   Zip Code   Country

E-mail: _____

*Phone: _____   Alternate Phone: _____   *Contact Preference: ☐ Mail ☐ E-Mail

REPRESENTATIVE CONTACT

Do you want us to communicate with a third party, such as an attorney or other legal representative, regarding this complaint?

☐ Yes   ☐ No   If you checked 'No', skip to Institution Information.

By selecting 'Yes', you legally authorize the Federal Reserve System to release information to and communicate directly with the party named below and for that party to act on your behalf in the processing of this complaint.

Prefix: ☐ Mr. ☐ Mrs. ☐ Ms. ☐ Dr.   *First Name: _____   *Last Name: _____

*Address: _____

City   State   Zip Code   Country

E-mail: _____

*Phone: _____   Alternate Phone: _____

INSTITUTION INFORMATION

Please provide as much information as possible about the bank or financial institution.

*Institution Name: _____

Account / Product Type: _____   Routing Number: _____

*Address: _____

City   State   Zip Code   Country

If you do not have the exact address of the bank or financial institution, provide a location, such as the nearest cross streets or major intersection.

_____

_____

E-mail: _____   Phone: _____

Financial Literacy for My Life

CREDIT CARD RULES

The Federal Reserve's rules for credit card companies mean new credit card protections for you. Here are some key changes from the law.

What your credit card company has to tell you.

1. **When they plan to increase your rate or other fees.** Your credit card company must send you a notice 45 days before they can

   - increase your interest rate;
   - change certain fees (such as annual fees, cash advance fees, and late fees) that apply to your account; or
   - make other significant changes to the terms of your card.

If your credit card company plans to make changes to the terms of your card, it must give you the option to cancel the card before certain fee increases take effect.

For example, the credit card company can require you to pay off the balance in five years, or it can double the percentage of your balance used to calculate your minimum payment (which will result in faster repayment than under the terms of your account).

The company does **not** have to send you a 45-day advance notice if

   - you have a variable interest rate tied to an index; if the index goes up, the company does not provide notice before your rate goes up;
   - your introductory rate expires and reverts to the previously disclosed "go-to" rate;
   - your rate increases because you haven't made your payments as agreed.

2. **How long it will take to pay off your balance.** Your monthly credit card bill will include information on how long it will take you to pay off your balance if you only make minimum payments. It will also tell you how much you would need to pay each month in order to pay off your balance in three years. For example, suppose you owe $3,000 and your interest rate is 14.4 percent—your bill might look like this:

New balance	$3,000.00
Minimum payment due	$ 90.00
Payment due date	4/20/22

Late Payment Warning: If we do not receive your minimum payment by the date listed above, you may have to pay a $35 late fee and your APRs may be increased up to the Penalty of 28.99%.

Minimum Payment Warning: If you make only the minimum payment each period, you will pay more interest and it will take you longer to pay off your balance. For example:

If you make no additional charges using this card and each month you pay . . .	You will pay off the balance shown on this statement in about . . .	And you will end up paying an estimated total of . . .
Only the minimum payment	11 years	$4,745
$103	3 years	$3,712
		(Savings = $1,033)

Source: Board of Governors of the Federal Reserve System.

Note: For more information about these laws, visit www.consumerfinance.gov/credit-cards/credit-card-act/.

CREDIT CARD ACCOUNTABILITY, RESPONSIBILITY, AND DISCLOSURE ACT OF 2009 Also known as the Credit CARD Act, this law provides the most sweeping changes in credit card protections for you since the Truth in Lending Act of 1968. The **Credit Card Accountability, Responsibility, and Disclosure Act** places new restrictions on credit card lending and eliminates certain fees. The *Financial Literacy for My Life: Credit Card Rules* feature summarizes credit card rules that began on February 22, 2010.

Exhibit 6-10 summarizes the major federal consumer credit laws. The Federal Reserve System has set up a separate office, the Division of Consumer and Community Affairs, to handle consumer complaints. Visit its website at federalreserve.gov. This division also writes regulations to carry out the consumer credit laws, enforces these laws for state-chartered banks that are members of the Federal Reserve System, and helps banks comply with these laws.

Credit Card Accountability Responsibility and Disclosure Act Places new restrictions on credit card lending and eliminates certain fees.

EXHIBIT 6-10 Summary of federal consumer credit laws

Act (effective date)	Major Provisions
Truth in Lending Act (July 1, 1969)	Provides specific cost disclosure requirements for the annual percentage rate and the finance charges as a dollar amount. Requires disclosure of other loan terms and conditions. Regulates the advertising of credit terms. Provides the right to cancel a contract when certain real estate is used as security.
(January 25, 1971)	Prohibits credit card issuers from sending unrequested cards; limits a cardholder's liability for unauthorized use of a card to $50.
(October 1, 1982)	Requires that disclosures for closed-end credit (installment credit) be written in plain English and appear apart from all other information. Allows a credit customer to request an itemization of the amount financed if the creditor does not automatically provide it.
Fair Credit Reporting Act (April 24, 1971)	Requires disclosure to consumers of the name and address of any consumer reporting agency that supplied reports used to deny credit, insurance, or employment. Gives consumers the right to know what is in their files, have incorrect information reinvestigated and removed, and include their version of a disputed item in the file. Requires credit reporting agencies to send the consumer's version of a disputed item to certain businesses or creditors. Sets forth identification requirements for consumers wishing to inspect their files. Requires that consumers be notified when an investigative report is being made. Limits the amount of time certain information can be kept in a credit file.
Fair Credit Billing Act (October 28, 1975)	Establishes procedures for consumers and creditors to follow when billing errors occur on periodic statements for revolving credit accounts. Requires creditors to send a statement setting forth these procedures to consumers periodically. Allows consumers to withhold payment for faulty or defective goods or services (within certain limitations) when purchased with a credit card. Requires creditors to promptly credit customers' accounts and to return overpayments if requested.
Equal Credit Opportunity Act (October 28, 1975)	Prohibits credit discrimination based on sex and marital status. Prohibits creditors from requiring women to reapply for credit upon a change in marital status. Requires creditors to inform applicants of acceptance or rejection of their credit application within 30 days of receiving a completed application. Requires creditors to provide a written statement of the reasons for adverse action.

Act (effective date)	Major Provisions
(March 23, 1977)	Prohibits credit discrimination based on race, national origin, religion, age, or the receipt of public assistance.
(June 1, 1977)	Requires creditors to report information on an account to credit bureaus in the names of both husband and wife if both use the account and both are liable for it.
Fair Debt Collection Practices Act (March 20, 1978)	Prohibits abusive, deceptive, and unfair practices by debt collectors. Establishes procedures for debt collectors contacting a credit user. Restricts debt collector contacts with a third party. Specifies that payment for several debts be applied as the consumer wishes and that no money be applied to a debt in dispute.
Consumer Credit Reporting Reform Act (September 30, 1997)	Places the burden of proof for accurate credit information on credit issuers rather than on consumers. Requires creditors to certify that disputed credit information is accurate. Requires "credit repair" companies to give consumers a written contract that can be canceled within three business days. Requires the big three credit bureaus (Experian, Equifax, and TransUnion) to establish a joint toll-free system that allows consumers to call and remove their names permanently from all prescreened lists. Places the maximum cost of a credit report at $8; however, indigent persons, welfare recipients, unemployed persons, and job hunters can get one free report annually.
Fair and Accurate Credit Transactions Act (April 28, 2003)	Requires the Federal Trade Commission to issue proposed rules to address identity theft concerns. Defines identity theft as a fraud committed or attempted using the identifying information of another person without lawful authority. Requires credit reporting agencies to develop and implement reasonable requirements for what information can be considered a consumer's proof of identity.
Credit Card Accountability, Responsibility, and Disclosure (CARD) Act (February 22, 2010)	Bans unfair rate increases on existing balances and restricts retroactive increases due to late payment. Ends late fee traps such as weekend deadlines, due dates that change every month, and deadlines that fall in the middle of the day. Requires issuers to display on monthly statement how long it would take to pay off the existing balance—and the total interest cost—if the consumer paid only the minimum due. Contains protections for college students and young adults. Requires issuers extending credit to people under 21 to obtain signature of a parent, guardian, or other individual 21 years or older who will take responsibility for the debt, or proof that the applicant has an independent means of repaying the debt.

Source: The Federal Trade Commission and the Board of Governors of the Federal Reserve System.

EXHIBIT 6-11 Federal government agencies that enforce consumer credit laws

If you think you've been discriminated against by:	You may file a complaint with the following agency:
Consumer reporting agencies, creditors and others not listed below.	Consumer Financial Protection Bureau, (consumerfinance.gov), 202-435-7000
National banks, federal branches/agencies of foreign banks (word "National" or initials "N.A." appear in or after bank's name).	Office of the Comptroller of the Currency Compliance Management, occ.treas.gov, 800-613-6743
Federal credit unions (words "Federal Credit Union" appear in institution's name).	National Credit Union Administration, ncua.gov. 800-755-1030
State-chartered banks that are not members of the Federal Reserve System.	Federal Deposit Insurance Corporation, Consumer Response Center, fdic.gov/consumers/, 877-275-3342
Air, surface, or rail common carriers regulated by former Civil Aeronautics Board or Interstate Commerce Commission.	Department of Transportation Office of Financial Management, transportation.gov, 202-366-4000

Source: Federal Trade Commission, www.ftc.gov.

YOUR RIGHTS UNDER CONSUMER CREDIT LAWS

If you believe you have been refused credit due to discrimination, you can do one or more of the following:

1. Complain to the creditor. Let the creditor know you are aware of the law.

2. File a complaint with the government. You can report any violations to the appropriate government enforcement agency (see Exhibit 6-11). Although the agencies use complaints to decide which companies to investigate, they cannot handle private cases. When you are denied credit, the creditor must give you the name and address of the appropriate agency to contact.

3. If all else fails, sue the creditor. You have the right to bring a case in a federal district court. If you win, you can recover your actual damages and punitive damages of up to $10,000. You can also recover reasonable attorneys' fees and court costs. A private attorney can advise you on how to proceed.

 PRACTICE QUIZ 6-6

1. What federal laws protect you if you have a complaint regarding consumer credit?
2. What are your rights under the consumer credit laws?

Your Personal Finance Roadmap and Dashboard:

MANAGING CREDIT

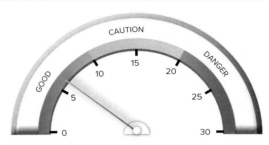

DEBT PAYMENTS-
TO-INCOME RATIO

A key indicator of creditworthiness is your capacity to handle a certain level of debt. Lenders will review your current debt payments-to-income ratio. Based on this, they will determine how much credit they will extend and at what interest rate. Lenders will be more reluctant to lend to individuals who are near the top of the acceptable range of 20 percent.

Your Situation

Do you pay your credit cards off each month when the bill is due? If you carry a balance, is it steadily increasing? Are there debts that you can eliminate to reduce the amount of your overall debt payments? An improving debt payments-to-income ratio is the foundation for progress toward financial independence. Other personal financial planning actions you might consider during various stages of your life include:

 First Steps

- If possible, get a personal credit card, or become an authorized user on your parents' credit card.
- Monitor your current spending.
- Be aware of the risks of credit card fraud.
- Set credit card limit and review monthly statements.
- Get a credit card in your own name.
- Build your own positive credit file.
- Set up a budget for credit use and pay in full when the bill arrives.

Next Steps

- Shop around for the best card.
- Avoid maxing out your credit card.
- Continue to monitor your credit card spending.

Later Steps

- Maintain a good credit rating.
- Know what is in your credit files.
- Remain a cautious guardian of your credit.
- Be debt-free.

YOUR Next Step . . . select one or more of the items above and create an action plan to implement those financial planning activities.

SUMMARY OF LEARNING OBJECTIVES

LO6-1

Define *consumer credit* and analyze its advantages and disadvantages. Consumer credit is the use of credit by individuals and families for personal needs. Among the advantages of using credit are the ability to purchase goods when needed and pay for them gradually, the ability to meet financial emergencies, convenience in shopping, and establishment of a credit rating. Disadvantages are that credit costs money, encourages overspending, and ties up future income.

LO6-2

Differentiate among various types of credit. Closed-end and open-end credit are two types of consumer credit. With closed-end credit, the borrower pays back a one-time loan in a stated period of time and with a specified number of payments. With open-end credit, the borrower is permitted to take loans on a continuous basis and is billed for partial payments periodically.

LO6-3

Assess your credit capacity and build your credit rating. Two general rules for measuring credit capacity are the debt payments-to-income ratio and the debt-to-equity ratio. In reviewing your creditworthiness, a creditor seeks information from one of the three national credit bureaus or a regional credit bureau.

LO6-4

Describe the information creditors look for when you apply for credit. Creditors determine creditworthiness on the basis of the five Cs: character, capacity, capital, collateral, and conditions.

LO6-5

Identify the steps you can take to avoid and correct credit mistakes. If a billing error occurs on your account,

notify the creditor in writing within 60 days. If the dispute is not settled in your favor, you can place your version of it in your credit file. You may also withhold payment on any defective goods or services you have purchased with a credit card as long as you have attempted to resolve the problem with the merchant.

LO6-6

Describe the laws that protect you if you have a complaint about consumer credit. If you have a complaint about credit, first try to deal directly with the creditor. If that fails, you can turn to the appropriate consumer credit law. These laws include the Truth in Lending Act, the Consumer Leasing Act, the Equal Credit Opportunity Act, the Fair Credit Billing Act, the Fair Credit Reporting Act, the Consumer Credit Reporting Reform Act, and the Fair and Accurate Credit Transactions Act.

KEY TERMS

SELF-TEST PROBLEMS

1. The current approximate value of Joshua's home is about $260,000. He still has a $150,000 balance on his mortgage. His bank has agreed to let him borrow 80 percent of the value of his home. What is the maximum home equity line of credit available to Joshua?

2. Audra has a monthly net income of $3,000. She has a house payment of $1,000 per month, a car loan with payments of $600 per month, a Visa card with payments of $100 per month, and a credit card with a local department store with payments of $200 per month. What is Audra's debt payment-to-income ratio?

3. Hannah has determined that her net worth is $120,000. She has also determined that the face value of her mortgage is $260,000. She has determined that the face value of the rest of her debt is $60,000. What is Hannah's debt-to-equity ratio?

Self-Test Solutions

1.	
Approximate market value of Joshua's house	$260,000
Multiply by 0.80	208,000
Approximate loan value	208,000
Subtract balance due on mortgage	150,000
Approximate credit limit available	$ 58,000

2. Audra's net monthly income = $3,000

   Audra's monthly expenses:

House payment	$1,000
Car loan	600
Visa card	100
Store card	200
Total expenses	1,900

   Debt payments-to-income = $\dfrac{\$1,900 - \$1,000}{\$3,000}$ = .30, or 30%

3. Hannah's net worth = $120,000

Face value of her mortgage	$260,000
Remainder of her debt	60,000
Hannah's debt-to-equity ratio	$\dfrac{60,000}{\$120,000}$ = .5

FINANCIAL PLANNING PROBLEMS

1. *Calculating the Amount for a Home Equity Loan.* A few years ago, Michael purchased a home for $200,000. Today the home is worth $300,000. His remaining mortgage balance is $100,000. Assuming Michael can borrow up to 80 percent of the market value of his home, what is the maximum amount he can borrow?   LO6-2

2. *Determining the Debt Payments-to-Income Ratio.* Louise's monthly gross income is $2,000. Her employer withholds $400 in federal, state, and local income taxes and $160 in Social Security taxes per month. Louise contributes $80 per month for her IRA. Her monthly credit payments for Visa, MasterCard, and Discover cards are $35, $30, and $20, respectively. Her monthly payment on an automobile loan is $285. What is Louise's debt payments-to-income ratio? Is Louise living within her means? Explain.   LO6-3

3. *Calculating the Debt-to-Equity Ratio.* Robert owns a $140,000 town house and still has an unpaid mortgage of $110,000. In addition to his mortgage, he has the following liabilities: LO6-3

Visa	$ 565
MasterCard	480
Discover card	395
Education loan	920
Personal bank loan	800
Auto loan	4,250
Total	$7,410

   Robert's net worth (not including his home) is about $21,000. This equity is in mutual funds, an automobile, a coin collection, furniture, and other personal property. What is Robert's debt-to-equity ratio? Has he reached the upper limit of debt obligations? Explain.

4. *Calculating the Debt Payments-to-Income Ratio.* Kim is trying to decide whether she can afford a loan she needs in order to go to chiropractic school. Right now Kim is living at home and works part-time in a shoe store, earning a gross income of $820 per month. Her employer deducts $145 for taxes from her monthly pay. Kim also pays $95 on several credit card debts each month. The loan she needs for chiropractic school will cost an additional $120 per month. Help Kim make her decision by calculating her debt payments-to-income ratio with and without the college loan. (Remember the 20 percent rule.)   LO6-3

5. *Calculating the Debt Payments-to-Income Ratio.* Suppose that your monthly net income is $2,400. Your monthly debt payments include your student loan payment and a gas credit card. They total $360. What is your debt payments-to-income ratio?   LO6-3

LO6-3   **6.** *Calculating the Debt Payments-to-Income Ratio.* What is your debt payments-to-income ratio if your debt payments total $684 and your net income is $2,000 per month?

LO6-3   **7.** *Calculating a Safe Credit Limit.* Drew's monthly net income is $4,000. What is the maximum he should use on debt payments?

LO6-3   **8.** *Credit Reduces Future Income.* The disposable income from your part-time job in 2021 was $12,000. In 2020, you borrowed $500 at 18 percent interest. You repaid your loan with interest in 2021. How much would you have available for spending in 2021?

LO6-4   **9.** *Analyzing the Feasibility of a Loan.* Fred has had a student loan, two auto loans, and three credit cards. He has always made timely payments on all obligations. He has a savings account of $2,400 and an annual income of $25,000. His current payments for rent, insurance, and utilities are about $1,100 per month. Fred has accumulated $12,800 in an individual retirement account. Fred's loan application asks for $10,000 to start up a small restaurant with some friends. Fred will not be an active manager; his partner will run the restaurant. Will he get the loan? Explain your answer.

LO6-3   **10.** *Analyzing a Spending Plan.* Carl's house payment is $1,050 per month and his car payment is $385 per month. If Carl's take-home pay is $2,800 per month, what percentage does Carl spend on his home and car?

LO6-3   **11.** *Analyzing a Spending Plan.* In the example of Problem 10, what percentage does Carl spend on his home?

LO6-4   **12.** *Analyzing a Spending Plan.* In the example of Problem 10, what percentage does Carl spend on his car payment?

DIGITAL FINANCIAL LITERACY: PROTECT CONSUMERS FROM CREDIT CARD SCAMMERS

Are you interested in a career that protects consumers from credit card scammers and to ensure that Federal Consumer Protection Laws are obeyed? Then you may want to explore the Consumer Financial Protection Bureau's website at www.consumerfinance.gov/about-us/careers/current-openings/. The Bureau looks for energetic student leaders from various backgrounds to apply for the summer internship program.

Action items:

1. Locate more information about protecting U.S. consumers. You may begin your search by visiting www.ftc.gov, www.aarp.org, www.usa.gov/consumer, or your state consumer protection agency.

2. Prepare a one-page report of your findings. Also, state in your report if you would be interested in a career assisting consumers from credit card scammers.

FINANCIAL PLANNING CASE

Don't Let Crooks Steal Your Identity: How to Protect Yourself—and Your Credit Rating

Identity theft is the fastest-growing financial crime. One of the first things the FBI discovered about the September 11 hijackers was that as many as half a dozen were using credit cards and driver's licenses with identities lifted from stolen or forged passports.

If you care at all about the privacy of your financial information—your credit history, your portfolio, your charge card numbers—you can protect yourself from criminals determined to exploit that information. The theft can be as simple as someone pilfering your credit card number and charging merchandise to your account. Or it can be as elaborate as a crook using your name, birth date, and Social Security number to take over your credit card and bank accounts, or set up new ones.

If your identity has been snatched, you're first likely to learn about it when checks start bouncing or a collection agency begins calling. The damage isn't so much in dollars, since the financial institutions are liable for the unauthorized charges. Rather, the fallout includes a checkered credit history, which could prevent you from getting a mortgage or a job, and the countless phone calls and piles of paperwork you'll need to go through to set the records straight. Guarding against identity theft is much like locking the door and activating the burglar alarm when you leave your home. By and large, the crime is a low-tech operation, despite well-publicized instances of hackers breaking into websites and stealing millions of credit card numbers. Usually, someone fishes a bank statement or credit card offer out of your trash, or a dishonest employee peeks at your personnel file.

To protect yourself, keep your Social Security number in a secure place and never carry it around with you. Provide your Social Security number only when necessary. Instead, try to use other forms of identification. Ignore email requests for your personal financial information. Shred your discarded financial records and any preapproved credit card applications. And check your credit report regularly, because credit card companies don't have to honor fraud alerts.

Finally, protect your identity by giving it a lower profile. For example, remove your name from junk mail and telemarketing lists by going to the Direct Marketing Association's website at www.thedma.org/resources/consumer-resources.

Call 1-888-567-8688 to stop receiving preapproved credit card offers.

Questions

1. What are several methods that crooks use to steal your identity?
2. How do you discover that someone has stolen your identity?
3. What steps can you take to thwart identity thieves?
4. What actions might you take to ensure that your credit cards and other financial information are secure?

 YOUR PERSONAL FINANCIAL PLAN

ESTABLISHING AND MAINTAINING A CREDIT RECORD

The wise use of credit requires knowing the process for establishing credit. In addition, you should develop an awareness of credit reports and the legal rights associated with using consumer credit.

Your Short-Term Financial Planning Activity

Task Build and maintain your credit rating.

Research

1) View Exhibit 6-3 and read general rules of measuring credit capacity. Distinguish between debt-payments-to-income and debt-to-equity ratios. Use Personal Financial Plan Sheet 29 to classify different types of debts.

2) Visit bankrate.com. credit.org, and ftc.org. Obtain information on how to check your credit report, how to deal with your student loans, and who else you can turn for help.

3) Use the Internet to locate other sources of information about how to build and maintain your credit rating.

Your Long-Term Financial Plan Activity

Task Take actions to reduce your credit card and other debts.

Research

1) Visit mymoney.gov, federalreserve.gov, or myfico.com. Gather information to help you to see a full picture of all your debt payments and to figure out when you will pay off your debts with your current repayment plan.

2) Check your credit report, which is a record of some of your bill-paying history, public record information, and prior inquiries by creditors. Get your free credit report once a year to check for any errors.

3) If you have student loans, find out if your loans are federal or private. Identify your loan payback status. Determine if you are eligible for an income-driven or alternative repayment plan. If you have federal loans, learn about the total costs on your federal loans with the "Repayment Estimator" at studentloans. gov. For private loans, contact your private loan servicer directly.

Outcome Create a table that shows your current debts, interest rate, total amount left to pay, and payoff dates. Attach this table to Personal Financial Plan Sheet 29 and review it often. Prepare an audio or written summary of your findings and your action plan for achieving your long-term debt-free goal.

Note: All *Personal Financial Planner* sheets are available at the end of the book and in an Excel spreadsheet format in *Connect Finance*.

Introduction to Consumer Credit

Jamie Lee Jackson, age 27, full-time student and part-time bakery employee, has just moved into an unfurnished bungalow-style home of her own. The house has only one bedroom, but the rent is manageable, and it is plenty of room for Jamie Lee. She decided to give notice to her roommate that she would be leaving the apartment and the shared expenses after the incident with the stolen checkbook and credit cards a few weeks back. Jamie had to dip into her emergency savings account to help cover the deposit and moving expenses, as she had not planned to move out of the apartment and be on her own this soon.

Jamie is in need of a few appliances because there is a small laundry room but no washer or dryer, nor is there a refrigerator in the kitchen. She will also need a living room set and a television, as Jamie only had a bedroom set to move in with. Jamie is excited to finally have the say in how she will furnish the bungalow, and she began shopping for her home as soon as the lease was signed.

The local home appliance store, Acme Home Goods, was the first stop as Jamie chose a stacking washer and dryer set, which would fit comfortably in the laundry space provided. A stainless-steel refrigerator with a built-in television screen was her next choice, and the salesperson quickly began to write up the order. Jamie was informed that if she opened up a credit card through the appliance store that she would receive a discount of 10 percent off her total purchase. As she waited for her credit to be approved, she decided to continue shopping for her other needed items.

Living room furniture was next on the list. Jamie continued on to the local home furnishings retailer to look at seemingly endless choices of complete sofa sets that included the coffee and end tables as well as matching lamps. Jamie chose a contemporary-style set and again was offered the tempting deal of opening a credit card through the store in exchange for a percentage off her purchase and free delivery.

Next up was the big box retailer, where Jamie chose a 52-inch 1080p LED HDTV. For the third time, a percentage off her first purchase at the big box retailer was all that was needed to get Jamie to sign on the dotted line of the credit card application. She was daydreaming of how wonderful her new home would look when a call from the appliance store came through and asked her to return to the store.

Jamie Lee had the unfortunate news that her credit application at the appliance store had been denied. She left the store only to arrive at the next two stores where she had chosen the living room set and television with the same bad news—credit application denied! She was informed that her credit score was too low for approval. "How could this be?" Jamie wondered and immediately contacted the credit bureau for further explanation.

Current Financial Situation

Assets:

Checking account: $1,800
Savings account: $7,200
Emergency fund savings account: $2,700
IRA balance: $410
Car: $2,800

Liabilities:

Student loan balance: $10,800 (Jamie is still a full-time student, so no payments are required on the loan until after graduation)
  Credit card balance: $4,250 (total of three store credit cards)

Income:

Gross monthly salary from the bakery: $2,750 (net income: $2,175)

Monthly Expenses:

Rent: $350
Utilities: $70
Food: $125
Gas/maintenance: $130
Credit card payment: $0

Questions

1. What steps should Jamie Lee take so she may discover the reason for the denial of her credit application?

2. Jamie discovers that she has become the victim of identity theft, as her credit report indicates that two credit cards have been opened in her name without her authorization! The police had already been notified the evening of the theft incident in the apartment, but what other measures should Jamie Lee take now that she has become aware of the identity theft?

3. Fortunately for Jamie, she was able to show proof of the theft to the credit bureau, and her credit applications for her apartment furnishings were approved. The purchase total for the appliances, living room furniture, and television amounted to $4,250. The minimum payments between the three accounts total $325 a month. What is Jamie Lee's debt payments-to-income ratio?

4. Oh, no! The television was finally delivered today from Acme Home Goods but was left on the porch by the delivery company. When Jamie Lee was finally able to attach all the wires and cables according to the owner's manual, it played for a half an hour and then shut off. Jamie Lee was unable to get the television to turn back on, although she read the troubleshooting guide in the manual and contacted tech support from the manufacturer. Jamie Lee lugged the television back to the store, but they would not accept a return on electronics. What should Jamie Lee do now?

5. The bills for the home furnishings are beginning to arrive, and Jamie Lee inspects each explanation and charged amount, carefully matching each to her purchase receipts. Jamie Lee notices that Acme Home Goods overcharged her by $120. It appears the bill does not reflect the 10 percent discount she received as an incentive for opening the store charge account for her large refrigerator. Using Exhibit 6-8A as a guide, compose an email or a letter to Acme Home Goods (55 Main Street, Your Town, Your State 00000) from Jamie Lee to dispute the billing error.

 DAILY SPENDING DIARY

"I admire people who are able to pay off their credit cards each month."

Directions

Your ability to monitor spending and credit use is a fundamental success for wise money management and long-term financial security. The *Daily Spending Diary* can help in this process. Use the *Daily Spending Diary* sheet provided at the end of the Chapter 1 to record all of your spending in the categories provided. Be sure to indicate the use of a credit card with (CR).

Analysis Questions

1. What do your spending habits indicate about your use of credit?

2. How might your *Daily Spending Diary* provide information for wise use of credit?

The *Daily Spending Diary* sheet is located in the appendix following Chapter 1 and on the library resource site in *Connect*.

7 Choosing a Source of Credit: The Costs of Credit Alternatives

LEARNING OBJECTIVES

LO7-1 Analyze the major sources of consumer credit.

LO7-2 Determine the cost of credit by calculating interest using various interest formulas.

LO7-3 Develop a plan to manage your debts.

LO7-4 Evaluate various private and governmental sources that assist consumers with debt problems.

LO7-5 Assess the choices in declaring personal bankruptcy.

The Chapter 7 Appendix provides coverage of education financing, loans, and scholarships.

APPENDIX

oliveromg/Shutterstock

Financial Literacy
IN YOUR LIFE

▶ **What if you . . .** suddenly become ill or lose your job and find that you cannot make your payments on time? What actions can you take to still keep your good name and maintain your credit rating?

You might . . . contact your creditors at once and try to work out a modified payment plan with them. It is most important not to wait until your account is turned over to a debt collector. If you have paid your bills promptly in the past, creditors may be willing to work with you.

Now, what would you do . . . If your creditors agree to a modified repayment plan, be sure to make payments promptly. However, if creditors don't agree to a new plan, seek a credit counselor from your local Consumer Credit Counseling Service. Remember, paying your bills on time is the foundation for progress toward good financial health. Monitor your progress using the Your Personal Finance Roadmap and Dashboard at the end of the chapter.

---

my life — CAN I AFFORD A LOAN AND REPAY IT ON TIME?

If you are thinking of taking out a loan or applying for a credit card, your first step should be to figure out how much the loan will cost you and whether you can afford it. Then you should shop for the best credit terms. But what if you are having trouble paying your bills and need help? Do you know your options? The main focus is to keep the cost of credit low and avoid the warning signs of debt problems.

For each of the following statements, select Yes, No, or Uncertain to indicate your personal response regarding these situations.

1. If I need to borrow money, my parents or family members are often the source of the least expensive loans.	Yes	No	Uncertain
2. I am aware of the two most common methods of calculating interest.	Yes	No	Uncertain
3. If my household is experiencing problems in paying bills, it is time to examine the family budget for ways to reduce expenses.	Yes	No	Uncertain
4. I am aware that everyone who is overburdened with credit obligations can phone, email, or visit the Consumer Credit Counseling Service.	Yes	No	Uncertain
5. I realize that the Bankruptcy Abuse Prevention and Consumer Protection Act of 2005 made it more difficult for consumers to file a Chapter 7 bankruptcy.	Yes	No	Uncertain

As you study this chapter, you will encounter "My Life" boxes with additional information and resources related to these items.

Sources of Consumer Credit

Credit costs got you down? Well, you are not alone. Credit costs money; therefore, always weigh the benefits of buying an item on credit now versus waiting until you have saved enough money to pay cash. We can all get into credit difficulties if we do not understand how and when to use credit.

Financial and other institutions, the sources of credit, come in all shapes and sizes. They play an important role in our economy, and they offer a broad range of financial services. By evaluating your credit options, you can reduce your finance charges. You can reconsider your decision to borrow money, discover a less expensive type of loan, or find a lender that charges a lower interest rate.

Before deciding whether to borrow money, ask yourself these three questions: Do I need a loan? Can I afford a loan? Can I qualify for a loan? We discussed the affordability

LO7-1

Analyze the major sources of consumer credit.

my life **1**

If I need to borrow money, my parents or family members are often the source of the least expensive loans.

Borrowing from relatives and friends is usually the least expensive, but make sure the loan agreement is in writing. It should state the interest rate, repayment schedule, and final payment date. Information on various sources of loans and costs is available at www.consumerworld.org and www.ftc.gov/credit.

of loans and the qualifications required to obtain loans in the last chapter. Here we wrestle with the first question.

You should avoid credit in two situations. The first situation is one in which you do not need or really want a product that will require financing. Easy access to installment loans or possession of credit cards sometimes encourages consumers to make expensive purchases they later regret. The solution to this problem is simple: After you have selected a product, resist any sales pressure to buy immediately and take a day to think it over.

The second situation is one in which you can afford to pay cash. Consider the trade-offs and opportunity costs involved. Paying cash is almost always cheaper than using credit. In fact, some stores even offer a discount for payment in cash.

WHAT KIND OF LOAN SHOULD YOU SEEK?

As discussed in the last chapter, two types of credit exist: closed-end and open-end credit. Because installment loans may carry a lower interest rate, they are the less expensive credit option for loans that are repaid over a period of many months or years. However, because credit cards usually provide a float period—a certain number of days during which no interest is charged—they represent the cheaper way to make credit purchases that are paid off in a month or two. Also, once you have a credit card, using it is always easier than taking out an installment loan. An alternative to a credit card is a travel and entertainment (T&E) card, such as an American Express or Diners Club card. A T&E card requires full payment of the balance due each month but does not impose a finance charge. Annual fees, however, can be high.

In seeking an installment loan, you may think first of borrowing from a bank or a credit union. However, less expensive credit sources are available.

INEXPENSIVE LOANS   Parents or family members are often the source of the least expensive loans. They may charge you only the interest they would have earned had they not made the loan—as little as the 1 percent they would have earned on a regular savings account. Such loans, however, can complicate family relationships. All loans to or from family members should be in writing and state the interest rate, if any, repayment schedule, and the final payment date.

Also relatively inexpensive is money borrowed on financial assets held by a lending institution, for example, a bank certificate of deposit or the cash value of a whole life insurance policy. The interest rate on such loans typically ranges from 5 to 7 percent. But the trade-off is that your assets are tied up until you have repaid the loan.

Parents often loan their children money. If you are the recipient of such a loan, make sure to come to an agreement regarding repayment.
Tetra Images/Getty Images

Another source of potentially inexpensive loans are certain types of federal financial aid, such as Stafford Loans. See the Chapter 7 Appendix (about Education Financing, Loans, and Scholarships) for additional details.

MEDIUM-PRICED LOANS   Often you can obtain medium-priced loans from commercial banks, federal savings banks (savings and loan associations), and credit unions. New-car loans, for example, may cost 2 to 5 percent; used-car loans and home improvement loans may cost slightly more.

Borrowing from credit unions has several advantages. These institutions provide free credit life insurance, are generally sympathetic to borrowers with legitimate payment problems, and provide personalized service. Credit unions can now offer the same range of consumer loans that banks and other financial institutions do. Over 124.3 million Americans belong to credit unions, and the number of credit union members has been growing steadily. About 5,100 credit unions that hold $1.84 trillion in assets exist in the United States today.[1]

EXPENSIVE LOANS   Though convenient to obtain, the most expensive loans available are from finance companies, retailers, and banks through credit cards. Finance companies often lend to people who cannot obtain credit from banks or credit unions. Typically, the

Financial Literacy Calculations

CASH ADVANCES

A cash advance is a loan billed to your credit card. You can obtain a cash advance with your credit card at a bank or an automated teller machine (ATM) or by using checks linked to your credit card account.

Most cards charge a special fee when a cash advance is taken out. The fee is based on a percentage of the amount borrowed, usually about 2 or 3 percent.

Some credit cards charge a minimum cash advance fee, as high as $5. You could get $20 in cash and be charged $5, a fee equal to 25 percent of the amount you borrowed.

Most cards do not have a grace period on cash advances. This means you pay interest every day until you repay the cash advance, even if you do not have an outstanding balance from the previous statement.

On some cards, the interest rate on cash advances is higher than the rate on purchases. Be sure you check the details on the contract sent to you by the card issuer.

Here is an example of charges that could be imposed for a $200 cash advance that you pay off when the bill arrives:

Cash advance fee = $4 (2% of $200)

Interest for one month = $3 (1.5% APR on $200)

Total cost for one month = $7 ($4 + $3)

In comparison, a $200 purchase on a card with a grace period could cost $0 if paid off promptly in full.

The bottom line: It is usually much more expensive to take out a cash advance than to charge a purchase to your credit card. Use cash advances only for real emergencies.

Source: A pamphlet provided by the office of Public Responsibility, American Express Company and Consumer Action, San Francisco, CA 94105 (n.d., n.p.).

interest ranges from 8 to 20 percent. If you are denied credit by a bank or a credit union, you should question your ability to afford the higher rate a loan company charges.

While there are no legal definitions of predatory lending, it is the unfair, deceptive, or fraudulent practices of some lenders. These lenders exploit lower-income and minority borrowers and elderly homeowners. Before you sign a loan contract, make sure to

- Explore other financing options.
- Do your homework: contact several lenders, compare interest rates, payments, terms of the loan, other fees, and costs of the loan.
- Know your rights under the law.

Check cashers, finance companies, and others make small, short-term, high-rate loans called payday loans, cash advance loans, check advance loans, postdated check loans, or deferred deposit check loans. Such loans secured by a personal check are extremely expensive. Suppose you write a personal check for $115 to borrow $100 for 14 days. The lender agrees to hold the check until your next payday, when you redeem the check by paying the $115 in cash. Your cost of this loan is a $15 finance charge that amounts to a whopping 391 percent annual percentage rate (APR).

Another expensive way to borrow money is a tax refund loan. This type of credit lets you get an advance on a tax refund. APRs as high as 774 percent have been reported. If you are short of cash, avoid these loans by asking for more time to pay a bill or seek a traditional loan. Even a cash advance on your credit card may cost less.

Borrowing from car dealers, appliance stores, department stores, and other retailers is also relatively expensive. The interest rates retailers charge are usually similar to those charged by finance companies, frequently 15 percent or more.

Banks lend funds not only through installment loans but also through cash advances on MasterCard or Visa cards. (See the nearby *Financial Literacy Calculations* box.)

One type of loan from finance companies is currently less expensive than most other credit. Loans of this kind, which often can be obtained at a rate of under 4 percent, are available from the finance companies of major automakers—General Motors Acceptance Corporation, Ford Motor Credit Company, and others. In early 2021, Toyota was offering zero percent financing for up to five years. But a car dealer that offers you such a rate may be less willing to discount the price of the car or throw in free options.

Exhibit 7-1 summarizes the major sources of consumer credit: commercial banks, consumer finance companies, credit unions, life insurance companies, savings and loan

EXHIBIT 7-1 Sources of consumer credit

Credit Source	Type of Loan	Lending Policies
Commercial banks	Single-payment loans Personal installment loans Savings account loans Check-credit loans Credit card loans Second mortgages	• Seek customers with established credit history. • Often require collateral or security. • Prefer to deal in large loans, such as vehicle, home improvement, and home modernization, with the exception of credit card and check-credit plans. • Determine repayment schedules according to the purpose of the loan. • Vary credit rates according to the type of credit, time period, customer's credit history, and the security offered. • May require several days to process a new credit application.
Consumer finance companies	Personal installment loans Second mortgages	• Often lend to consumers without established credit history. • Often make unsecured loans. • Often vary rates according to the size of the loan balance. • Offer a variety of repayment schedules. • Make a higher percentage of small loans than other lenders. • Maximum loan size limited by law. • Process applications quickly, frequently on the same day the application is made.
Credit unions	Personal installment loans Share draft–credit plans Credit card loans Second mortgages	• Lend to members only. • Make unsecured loans. • May require collateral or cosigner for loans over a specified amount. • May require payroll deductions to pay off loan. • May submit large loan applications to a committee of members for approval. • Offer a variety of repayment schedules.
Life insurance companies	Single-payment or partial-payment loans	• Lend on cash value of life insurance policy. • No date or penalty on repayment. • Deduct amount owed from the value of policy benefit if death or other maturity occurs before repayment.
Federal savings banks (savings and loan associations)	Personal installment loans (generally permitted by state-chartered savings associations) Home improvement loans Education loans Savings account loans Second mortgages	• Will lend to all credit worthy individuals. • Often require collateral. • Loan rates vary depending on size of loan, length of payment, and security involved.
Payday loan companies	Immediate cash loans Short-term loans	• High interest rates. • Lenders allow the loan to "roll over" for another pay period and charge additional fees.
Online lenders	Usually single payment, small loans Short-term, high-cost loans	• Loan applications are completed on a lender's website. • Funds are transferred by direct deposit. You authorize the lender to electronically debit the funds from your bank on the due date. • High interest rates. • More consumer protection if the lender is licensed by your state. • Providing sensitive personal and financial information on the internet may be risky.

Consumer credit is available from several types of sources. *Which sources seem to offer the widest variety of loans?*

associations, and payday and online lenders. This exhibit attempts to generalize the information and give an average picture of each source regarding the type of credit available, lending policies, and customer services. Due to the dramatic fluctuations in interest rates in recent years, it is no longer possible to provide a common range of annual percentage rates for each source of credit. Check with your local lender for current interest rates. Study and compare the differences to determine which source can best meet your needs.

Today borrowing and credit are more complex than ever. As more and more types of financial institutions crop up to offer financial services, including peer-to-peer lenders (P2Ps) such as Lending Club and Lendingtree, your choices of what and where to borrow will widen. The internet may be used to compare interest rates for different loan sources and credit cards. Shopping for credit is just as important as shopping for an automobile, furniture, or major appliances.

 **PRACTICE QUIZ 7-1**

1. What are the major sources of consumer credit?
2. What are some advantages and disadvantages of securing a loan from a credit union? From a finance company?

The Cost of Credit

The **Truth in Lending law** of 1969 was a landmark piece of legislation. For the first time, creditors were required to state the cost of borrowing as a dollar amount so that consumers would know exactly what the credit charges were and thus could compare credit costs and shop for credit.

If you are thinking of borrowing money or opening a credit account, your first step should be to figure out how much it will cost you and whether you can afford it. Then you should shop for the best terms. Two key concepts that you should remember are the finance charge and the annual percentage rate.

FINANCE CHARGE AND ANNUAL PERCENTAGE RATE

Credit costs vary. If you know the finance charge and the annual percentage rate (APR), you can compare credit prices from different sources. Under the Truth in Lending law, the creditor must inform you, in writing and before you sign any agreement, of the finance charge and the APR.

The **finance charge** is the total dollar amount you pay to use credit. It includes interest costs and sometimes other costs such as service charges, credit-related insurance premiums, or appraisal fees. For example, borrowing $100 for a year might cost you $10 in interest. If there is also a service charge of $1, the finance charge will be $11.

The **annual percentage rate (APR)** is the percentage cost (or relative cost) of credit on a yearly basis. The APR is your key to comparing costs, regardless of the amount of credit or how much time you have to repay it. Suppose you borrow $100 for one year and pay a finance charge of $10. If you can keep

LO7-2

Determine the cost of credit by calculating interest using various interest formulas.

Truth in Lending law A federal law that requires creditors to disclose the annual percentage rate (APR) and the finance charge as a dollar amount.

smart money minute

Most every time you use a credit card in a foreign country, some cards charge a 2–3 percent fee for converting the purchase or cash advance into U.S. dollars. If you travel frequently, you should investigate your credit card's policies; there are some cards issued by Bank of America, Capital One, and American Express that don't charge foreign transaction fees. And those can save you a great deal of money if you plan to spend much on your travels.

finance charge The total dollar amount paid to use credit.

annual percentage rate (APR) The percentage cost (or relative cost) of credit on a yearly basis. The APR yields a true rate of interest for comparison with other sources of credit.

the entire $100 for the whole year and then pay it all back at once, you are paying an APR of 10 percent:

Amount Borrowed	Month Number	Payment Made	Loan Balance
$100	1	$0	$100
	2	0	100
	3	0	100
	.	.	.
	.	.	.
	.	.	.
	.	.	.
	12	100	0

(plus $10 interest)

On average, you had full use of $100 throughout the year. To calculate the average use, add the loan balance during the first and last month, then divide by 2:

$$\text{Average balance} = \frac{\$100 + \$100}{2} = \$100$$

But if you repay the $100 in 12 equal monthly payments, you don't get use of the $100 for the whole year. In fact, as shown next, you get use of less and less of that $100 each month. In this case, the $10 charge for credit amounts to an APR of 18.5 percent.

Note that you are paying 10 percent interest on $100 even though you had use of only $91.67 during the second month, not $100. During the last month, you owed only $8.37 (and had use of $8.37), but the $10 interest is for the entire $100. As calculated in the previous example, the average use of the money during the year is $100 + $8.37 ÷ 2, or $54.19.

Amount Borrowed	Month Number	Payment Made	Loan Balance
$100	1	$0	$100.00
	2	8.33	91.67
	3	8.33	83.34
	4	8.33	75.01
	5	8.33	66.68
	6	8.33	58.35
	7	8.33	50.02
	8	8.33	41.69
	9	8.33	33.36
	10	8.33	25.03
	11	8.33	16.70
	12	8.33	8.37

Financial Literacy Calculations

THE ARITHMETIC OF THE ANNUAL PERCENTAGE RATE (APR)

There are two ways to calculate the APR: using an APR formula and using the APR tables. The APR tables are more precise than the formula. The formula, given below, only approximates the APR.

$$r = \frac{2 \times n \times I}{P(N + 1)}$$

where

r = Approximate APR
n = Number of payment periods in one year (12, if payments are monthly; 52, if weekly)
I = Total dollar cost of credit
P = Principal, or net amount of loan
N = Total number of payments scheduled to pay off the loan

Let us compare the APR when the $100 loan is paid off in one lump sum at the end of the year and when the same loan is paid off in 12 equal monthly payments. The stated annual interest rate is 10 percent for both loans. Using the formula, the APR for the lump-sum loan is

$$r = \frac{2 \times 1 \times \$10}{\$100(1 + 1)} = \frac{\$20}{\$100(2)} = \frac{\$20}{\$200} = 0.10$$

or 10 percent

Using the formula, the APR for the monthly payment loan is

$$r = \frac{2 \times 12 \times \$10}{\$100(12 + 1)} = \frac{\$240}{\$100(13)} = \frac{\$240}{\$1,300}$$

$$= 0.1846, \text{ or } 18.46 \text{ percent (rounded to 18.5 percent)}.$$

The *Financial Literacy Calculations: The Arithmetic of the Annual Percentage Rate (APR)* box shows how to calculate the APR. All creditors—banks, stores, car dealers, credit card companies, and finance companies—must state the cost of their credit in terms of the finance charge and the APR. The law does not set interest rates or other credit charges, but it does require their disclosure so that you can compare credit costs and tackle the trade-offs.

smart money minute

LOAN ORIGINATION FEES

A loan origination fee is what the lender charges you for the loan. It may include processing the application, underwriting and funding the loan, and other administrative services. The loan origination fees increase the cost of your loan.

TACKLING THE TRADE-OFFS

When you choose your financing, there are trade-offs between the features you prefer (term, size of payments, fixed or variable interest, or payment plan) and the cost of your loan. Here are some of the major trade-offs you should consider.

TERM VERSUS INTEREST COSTS Many people choose longer-term financing because they want smaller monthly payments. But the longer the term for a loan at a given interest rate, the greater the amount you must pay in interest charges. Consider the following analysis of the relationship between the term and interest costs.

A COMPARISON Even when you understand the terms a creditor is offering, it's easy to underestimate the difference in dollars that different terms can make. Suppose you're buying a $7,500 used car. You put $1,500 down, and you need to borrow $6,000. Compare the following three credit arrangements:

	APR	Length of Loan	Monthly Payment	Total Finance Charge	Total Cost
Creditor A	15%	3 years	$205.07	$1,382.52	$7,382.52
Creditor B	15	4 years	163.96	1,870.08	7,870.08
Creditor C	16	4 years	166.98	2,015.04	8,015.04

How do these choices compare? The answer depends partly on what you need. The lowest-cost loan is available from creditor A. If you are looking for lower monthly payments, you could repay the loan over a longer period of time. However, you would

my life 2

I am aware of the two most common methods of calculating interest.

The two most common methods of calculating interest are compound and simple interest formulas. For examples of calculating interest, be sure to read the *Financial Planning Calculations* boxes in this chapter.

have to pay more in total costs. A loan from creditor B—also at a 15 percent APR, but for four years—would add about $488 to your finance charge.

If that four-year loan were available only from creditor C, the APR of 16 percent would add another $145 to your finance charges. Other terms, such as the size of the down payment, will also make a difference. Be sure to look at all the terms before you make your choice.

LENDER RISK VERSUS INTEREST RATE   You may prefer financing that requires low fixed payments with a large final payment or only a minimum of up-front cash. But both of these requirements can increase your cost of borrowing because they create more risk for your lender.

If you want to minimize your borrowing costs, you may need to accept conditions that reduce your lender's risk. Here are a few possibilities.

Variable Interest Rate   A variable interest rate is based on fluctuating rates in the banking system, such as the prime rate. With this type of loan, you share the interest rate risks with the lender. Therefore, the lender may offer you a lower initial interest rate than it would with a fixed-rate loan.

A Secured Loan   If you pledge property or other assets as collateral, you'll probably receive a lower interest rate on your loan.

Up-Front Cash   Many lenders believe you have a higher stake in repaying a loan if you pay cash for a large portion of what you are financing. Doing so may give you a better chance of getting the other terms you want. Of course, by making a large down payment, you forgo interest that you might earn in a savings account.

A Shorter Term   As you have learned, the shorter the period of time for which you borrow, the smaller the chance that something will prevent you from repaying and the lower the risk to the lender. Therefore, you may be able to borrow at a lower interest rate if you accept a shorter-term loan, but your payments will be higher.

In the next section, you will see how the above-mentioned trade-offs can affect the cost of closed-end and open-end credit.

CALCULATING THE COST OF CREDIT

The two most common methods of calculating interest are compound and simple interest formulas. Perhaps the most basic method is the simple interest calculation. Simple interest on the declining balance, add-on interest, bank discount, and compound interest are variations of simple interest.

simple interest Interest computed on principal only and without compounding.

SIMPLE INTEREST   **Simple interest** is the interest computed on principal only and without compounding; it is the dollar cost of borrowing money. This cost is based on three elements: the amount borrowed, which is called the *principal;* the rate of interest; and the amount of time for which the principal is borrowed.

You can use the following formula to find simple interest:

$$\text{Interest} = \text{Principal} \times \text{Rate of interest} \times \text{Time}$$

or

$$I = P \times r \times T$$

EXAMPLE: Using the Simple Interest Formula

Suppose you have persuaded a relative to lend you $1,000 to purchase a laptop computer. Your relative agreed to charge only 5 percent interest, and you agreed to repay the loan at the end of one year. Using the simple interest formula, the interest will be 5 percent of $1,000 for one year, or $50, since you have the use of $1,000 for the entire year:

$$I = \$1,000 \times 0.05 \times 1$$
$$= \$5\,0$$

Using the APR formula discussed earlier,

$$APR = \frac{2 \times n \times I}{P(N+1)} = \frac{2 \times 1 \times \$50}{\$1,000(1+1)} = \frac{\$100}{\$2,000} = 0.05, \text{ or } 5 \text{ percent}$$

Note that the stated rate, 5 percent, is also the annual percentage rate.

SIMPLE INTEREST ON THE DECLINING BALANCE   When more than one payment is made on a simple interest loan, the method of computing interest is known as the **declining balance method.** Since you pay interest only on the amount of the original principal that you have not yet repaid, the more frequent the payments, the lower the interest you will pay. Most credit unions use this method for their loans.

declining balance method A method of computing interest when more than one payment is made on a simple interest loan.

EXAMPLE: Using the Simple Interest Formula on the Declining Balance

Using simple interest on the declining balance to compute interest charges, the interest on a 5 percent, $1,000 loan repaid in two payments, one at the end of the first half-year and another at the end of the second half-year, would be $37.50, as follows:

First payment:

$$I = P \times r \times T$$
$$= \$1,000 \times 0.05 \times \frac{1}{2}$$
$$= \$25 \text{ interest plus } \$500, \text{ or } \$525$$

Second payment:

$$I = P \times r \times T$$
$$= \$500 \times 0.05 \times \frac{1}{2}$$
$$= \$12.50 \text{ interest plus the remaining balance of } \$500, \text{ or } \$512.50$$

Total payment on the loan:

$$\$525 + \$512.50 = \$1,037.50$$

Using the APR formula,

$$APR = \frac{2 \times n \times I}{P(N+1)} = \frac{2 \times 2 \times \$37.50}{\$1,000(2+1)} = \frac{\$150}{\$3,000} = 0.05, \text{ or } 5 \text{ percent}$$

Note that using simple interest under the declining balance method, the stated rate, 5 percent, is also the annual percentage rate. The add-on interest, bank discount, and compound interest calculation methods differ from the simple interest method as to when, how, and on what balance interest is paid. For these methods, the real annual rate, or the annual percentage rate, differs from the stated rate.

add-on interest method A method of computing interest in which interest is calculated on the full amount of the original principal.

ADD-ON INTEREST With the **add-on interest method,** interest is calculated on the full amount of the original principal. The interest amount is immediately added to the original principal, and payments are determined by dividing principal plus interest by the number of payments to be made. When only one payment is required, this method produces the same APR as the simple interest method. However, when two or more payments are to be made, the add-on method results in an effective rate of interest that is higher than the stated rate.

Note that using the add-on interest method means that no matter how many payments you are to make, the interest will always be $50. As the number of payments increases, you have use of less and less credit over the year. For example, if you make four quarterly payments of $262.50, you have use of $1,000 during the first quarter, $737.50 during the second quarter, $475 during the third quarter, and $212.50 during the fourth and final quarter. Therefore, as the number of payments increases, the true interest rate, or APR, also increases.

EXAMPLE: Using the Add-On Method

Consider again the two-payment loan in the previous example. Using the add-on method, interest of $50 (5 percent of $1,000 for one year) is added to the $1,000 borrowed, giving $1,050 to be repaid—half (or $525) at the end of the first half-year and the other half at the end of the second half-year.

Even though your relative's stated interest rate is 5 percent, the real interest rate is

$$APR = \frac{2 \times n \times I}{P(N+1)} = \frac{2 \times 2 \times \$50}{\$1,000(2+1)} = \frac{\$200}{\$3,000} = 0.067, \text{ or } 6.7 \text{ percent}$$

---

adjusted balance method The assessment of finance charges after payments made during the billing period have been subtracted.

previous balance method A method of computing finance charges that gives no credit for payments made during the billing period.

average daily balance method A method of computing finance charges that uses a weighted average of the account balance throughout the current billing period.

COST OF OPEN-END CREDIT As discussed earlier, open-end credit includes credit cards, department store charge cards, and check overdraft accounts that allow you to write checks for more than your actual balance. You can use open-end credit again and again until you reach a prearranged borrowing limit. The Truth in Lending law requires that open-end creditors let you know how the finance charge and the APR will affect your costs.

First, creditors must tell you how they calculate the finance charge. Creditors use various systems to calculate the balance on which they assess finance charges. Some creditors add finance charges after subtracting payments made during the billing period; this is called the **adjusted balance method.** Other creditors give you no credit for payments made during the billing period; this is called the **previous balance method.** Under the third—and the fairest—method, the **average daily balance method,** creditors add your balances for each day in the billing period and then divide by the number of days in the period. The average daily balance may include or exclude new purchases during the billing period.

Here is how some different methods of calculating finance charges affect the cost of credit:

	Average Daily Balance (*including* new purchases)	Average Daily Balance (*excluding* new purchases)
Monthly rate	1.5%	1.5%
APR	18%	18%
Previous balance	$400	$400
New purchases	$50 on 18th day	$50 on 18th day
Payments	$300 on 15th day (new balance = $100)	$300 on 15th day (new balance = $100)
Average daily balance	$270*	$250**
Finance charge	$4.05 (1.5% × $270)	$3.75 (1.5% × $250)

*To figure average daily balance (*including* new purchases):
[($400 × 15 days) + ($100 × 3 days) + ($150 × 12 days)] ÷ 30 days =
($6,000 + $300 + $1,800) ÷ 30 days = $8,100 ÷ 30 days = $270

**To figure average daily balance (*excluding* new purchases):
[($400 × 15 days) + ($100 × 15 days)] ÷ 30 days =
($6,000 + $1,500) ÷ 30 days = $7,500 ÷ 30 days = $250

	Adjusted Balance	Previous Balance
Monthly rate	1.5%	1.5%
APR	18%	18%
Previous balance	$400	$400
Payments	$300	$300
Average daily balance	N/A	N/A
Finance charge	$1.50 (1.5% × $100)	$6.00 (1.5% × $400)

As the example shows, the finance charge varies for the same pattern of purchases and payments. Furthermore, some creditors used a *two-cycle average daily balance* method, which may *include* or *exclude* new purchases. Instead of using the average daily balance for one billing cycle, as described above, these creditors use the average daily balance for *two* consecutive billing cycles. The Credit CARD Act of 2009 bans a two-cycle average daily balance method.

Second, creditors must tell you when finance charges on your credit account begin, so that you know how much time you have to pay your bills before a finance charge is added. Some creditors, for example, give you a 21- to 25-day grace period to pay your balance in full before imposing a finance charge. But in most cases, the grace period applies only if you have no outstanding balance on your card. Therefore, if you want to take advantage of the interest-free period on your card, you must pay your bill in full every month.

All credit card issuers must include the following key pieces of information with their applications for credit cards. Look for a box similar to the one that follows for information about interest rates, fees, and other terms for the card you are considering.

Interest Rates and Interest Charges

Annual Percentage Rate (APR) for Purchases

8.99%, 10.99%, or 12.99% introductory APR for one year, based on your creditworthiness.

After that, your APR will be **14.99%**. This APR will vary with the market based on the Prime Rate.

APR for Balance Transfers

15.99%
This APR will vary with the market based on the prime rate.

APR for Cash Advances

21.99%
This APR will vary with the market based on the prime rate.

Penalty APR and When It Applies

28.99%
This APR may be applied to your account if you:

1. Make a late payment;
2. Go over your credit limit;
3. Make a payment that is returned; or
4. Do any of the above on another account that you have with us.

How Long Will the Penalty APR Apply? If your APRs are increased for any of these reasons, the penalty APR will apply until you make six consecutive minimum payments when due.

How to Avoid Paying Interest on Purchases

Your due date is at least 25 days after the close of each billing cycle. We will not charge you any interest on purchases if you pay your entire balance by the due date each month.

Minimum Interest Charge

If you are charged interest, the charge will be no less than $1.50.

For Credit Card Tips from the Federal Reserve Board

To learn more about factors to consider when applying for or using a credit card, visit the website of the Federal Reserve Board at www.consumerfinance.gov/data-research/credit-card-data/.

Fees

Set-up and Maintenance Fees

- Annual Fee
- Account Set-up Fee
- Participation Fee
- Additional Card Fee

NOTICE: Some of these set-up and maintenance fees will be assessed before you begin using your card and will reduce the amount of credit you initially have available. For example, if you are assigned the minimum credit limit of $250, your initial available credit will be only about $209 (or about $204 if you choose to have an additional card).

$20
$20 (one-time fee)
$12 annually ($1 per month)
$5 annually (if applicable)

Transaction Fees

- Balance Transfer
- Cash Advance
- Foreign Transaction

Either **$5** or **3%** of the amount of each transfer, whichever is greater (maximum fee: $100).
Either **$5** or **3%** of the amount of each cash advance, whichever is greater.
2% of each transaction in U.S. dollars.

Penalty Fees

- Late Payment
- Over-the-Credit Limit
- Returned Payment

$29 if balance is less than or equal to $1,000
$35 if balance is more than $1,000
$29
$35

Other Fees

Credit insurance, or debt cancellation, or debt suspension coverage

How We Will Calculate Your Balance: We use a method called "average daily balance (including new purchases)."

Loss of Introductory APR: We may end your introductory APR and apply the penalty APR if you become more than 60 days late in paying your bill.

⑫

Source: The Federal Reserve Board.

The Truth in Lending law does not set rates or tell the creditor how to make interest calculations. It requires only that the creditor tell you the method that will be used. You should ask for an explanation of any terms you don't understand.

COST OF CREDIT AND EXPECTED INFLATION   Borrowers and lenders are less concerned about dollars, present or future, than about the goods and services those dollars can buy—that is, their purchasing power.

Inflation erodes the purchasing power of money. Each percentage point increase in inflation means a decrease of 1 percent in the quantity of goods and services you can purchase with a given quantity of dollars. As a result, lenders, seeking to protect their purchasing power, add the expected rate of inflation to the interest rate they charge. You are willing to pay this higher rate because you expect inflation to enable you to repay the loan with cheaper dollars.

For example, if a lender expects a 3 percent inflation rate for the coming year and desires a 6 percent return on its loan, it will probably charge you a 9 percent nominal or stated rate (a 3 percent inflation premium plus a 6 percent "real" rate).

Return to the previous example in which you borrowed $1,000 from your relative at the bargain rate of 5 percent for one year. If the inflation rate was 4 percent during that year, your relative's real rate of return was only 1 percent (5 percent stated interest minus 4 percent inflation rate) and your "real" cost was not $50 but only $10 ($50 minus $40 inflation premium).

COST OF CREDIT AND TAX CONSIDERATIONS   Before the Tax Reform Act of 1986, the interest you paid on consumer credit reduced your taxable income. The new law did not affect the deductibility of home mortgage interest, but now you can no longer deduct interest paid on consumer loans.

smart money minute

BEWARE: OFFERS TO SKIP A PAYMENT
If your credit company invites you to skip a monthly payment without a penalty, it is not doing you a favor. You will still owe finance charges on your unpaid balance. And interest could be adding up on any purchases you make after the due date you skipped. It would be a *mistake* to take them up on this offer! The best *action* to take? Ignore the offer. *Success!* You saved money on interest.

AVOID THE MINIMUM MONTHLY PAYMENT TRAP   The "minimum monthly payment" is the smallest amount you can pay and still be a cardholder in good standing. Banks often encourage you to make the minimum payment, such as 2 percent of your outstanding balance or $20, whichever is greater. Some statements refer to the minimum as the "cardholder amount due." But that is not the total amount you owe.

Consider the following examples. In each example, the minimum payment is based on 1/36 of the outstanding balance or $20, whichever is greater.

EXAMPLE 1: Minimum Monthly Payment Trap

You are buying books for college. If you spend $500 on textbooks using a credit card charging 19.8 percent interest and make only the minimum payment, it will take you more than 2½ years to pay off the loan, adding $150 in interest charges to the cost of your purchase. The same purchase on a credit card charging 12 percent interest will cost only $78 extra.

EXAMPLE 2: Minimum Monthly Payment Trap

You purchase a $2,000 sound system using a credit card with 19 percent interest and a 2 percent minimum payment. If you pay just the minimum every month, it will take you 265 months—over 22 years—to pay off the debt and will cost you nearly $4,800 in interest payments. Doubling the amount paid each month to 4 percent of the balance owed would allow you to shorten the payment time to 88 months from 265 months—or 7 years as opposed to 22 years—and save you about $3,680.

The Credit CARD law requires creditors to include the minimum payment warning in their monthly statements. Here is an example:

Minimum Payment Warning: If you make only the minimum payment each period, you will pay more in interest and it will take you longer to pay off your balance. For example:

If you make no additional charges using this card and each month you pay ...	You will pay off the balance shown on this statement in about ...	And you will end up paying an estimated total of ...
Only the minimum payment	10 years	$3,284
$62	3 years	$2,232 (Savings = $1,052)

If you would like information about credit counseling services, call 1-800-388-CCCS.

WHEN THE REPAYMENT IS EARLY: THE RULE OF 78s

rule of 78s A mathematical formula to determine how much interest has been paid at any point in a loan term.

Creditors sometimes use tables based on a mathematical formula called the **rule of 78s,** also called *the sum of the digits,* to determine how much interest you have paid at any point in a loan. This formula favors lenders and dictates that you pay more interest at the beginning of a loan, when you have the use of more of the money, and pay less and less interest as the debt is reduced. Because all of the payments are the same in size, the part going to pay back the amount borrowed increases as the part representing interest decreases.

The laws of several states authorize the use of the rule of 78s as a means of calculating finance charge rebates when you pay off a loan early. The Truth in Lending law requires that your creditor disclose whether or not you are entitled to a rebate of the finance charge if you pay off the loan early. Loans for a year or less, however, usually do not allow for a finance charge rebate. Read the *Financial Literacy Calculations: Other Methods of Determining the Cost of Credit* feature to learn about other methods of determining the cost of credit.

smart money minute

It would take 61 years to pay off a $5,000 credit card balance if you made only the minimum monthly payment. You'd pay almost $16,000 in interest (assuming a 14 percent interest rate and minimum payment of 1.5 percent of the outstanding balance).

CREDIT INSURANCE

Credit insurance ensures the repayment of your loan in the event of death, disability, or loss of property. The lender is named the beneficiary and directly receives any payments made on submitted claims.

There are three types of credit insurance: credit life, credit accident and health, and credit property. The most commonly purchased type of credit insurance is credit life insurance, which provides for the repayment of the loan if the borrower dies. According to the Consumer Federation of America and the National Insurance Consumer Organization, most borrowers don't need credit life insurance. Those who don't have life insurance can buy term life insurance for less. Term life insurance is discussed in Chapter 12.

Credit accident and health insurance, also called *credit disability insurance,* repays your loan in the event of a loss of income due to illness or injury. Credit property insurance provides coverage for personal property purchased with a loan. It may also insure collateral property, such as a car or furniture. However, premiums for such coverages are quite high.

credit insurance Any type of insurance that ensures repayment of a loan in the event the borrower is unable to repay it.

COST OF CREDIT AND THE CREDIT CARD ACCOUNTABILITY, RESPONSIBILITY, AND DISCLOSURE ACT OF 2009 (THE CREDIT CARD ACT)

The Credit CARD Act had a sweeping effect on annual percentage rates, fees, and disclosures. The law:

- Limits card issuers' ability to increase the APR on transferred balances during the first year that the account is opened.
- Restricts card issuers from applying new (higher) interest rates to the existing card balances.
- Requires companies to inform consumers of rate increases or other significant changes at least 45 days in advance.
- States that teaser rates must stay in effect for at least 6 months.
- Requires issuers to mail monthly statements at least 21 days before payment is due.
- Makes new disclosure statements clear and more timely.
- Mandates that monthly credit card statements must prominently display the due date and potential late fees, as well as the interest you have paid during the current year and the monthly payment required to pay off the existing balance. Statements must also warn consumers about the costs of making only the minimum payments.
- Requires credit card issuers to post their standard card agreements on the internet.
- Sets a consistent due date for card payments each month. If the due date falls on a holiday or weekend, the deadline is considered the next business day.

Financial Literacy Calculations

OTHER METHODS OF DETERMINING THE COST OF CREDIT

BANK DISCOUNT METHOD

When the *bank discount rate* method is used, interest is calculated on the amount to be paid back, and you receive the difference between the amount to be paid back and the interest amount. For instance, if your relative lends you $1,000 less $50 (interest at 5 percent), you receive $950.

Example 1. Using the APR formula, you find the true interest rate, or the annual percentage rate, is 5.263 percent, not the stated 5 percent:

$$\text{APR} = \frac{2 \times n \times I}{P(N + 1)} = \frac{2 \times 1 \times \$50}{\$950(1 + 1)} = \frac{\$100}{\$1,900}$$

$$= 0.05263, \text{ or } 5.263 \text{ percent}$$

COMPOUND INTEREST

Unlike simple interest, *compound interest* is the interest paid on the original principal *plus* the accumulated interest. With interest compounding, the greater the number of periods for which interest is calculated, the more rapidly the amount of interest on interest and interest on principal builds.

Annual compounding means there is only *one* period annually for the calculation of interest. With such compounding, interest charges on a *one-year* loan are identical whether they are figured on a simple interest basis or on an annual compound basis. However, a new interest formula, based on the simple interest formula, must be used if there is annual compounding for two or more years or compounding with more than one compound period per year.

A compact formula that describes compound interest calculations is

$$F = P(1 + r)^T$$

where

F = Total future repayment value of a loan (principal *plus* total accumulated or compound interest)

P = Principal

r = Rate of interest per year, or annual interest rate

T = Time in years

Before the compound interest formula can be used for *multiple*-period compounding, two important adjustments must be made.

First, adjust the *annual* interest rate (r) to reflect the number of compounding periods per year. For example, a 5 percent annual rate of interest, compounded half-yearly, works out to 2.5 percent (5 percent divided by 2) per half-year.

Second, adjust the time factor (T), which is measured in years, to reflect the *total* number of compounding periods. For example, your loan for one year compounded half-yearly works out to two compound periods (1 year multiplied by 2 compounding periods per year) over the length of the loan.

Example 2. Suppose your relative compounds interest semiannually and you make two payments, six months apart. Using the compound interest formula, here is the annual percentage rate:

$$F = P(1 + r)^T$$
$$F = \$1,000[1 + (0.05/2)]^{1 \times 2}$$
$$= \$1,000(1 + 0.025)^2$$
$$= \$1,000(1.050625)$$
$$= \$1,050.625$$

That is, you are paying $50.63 in interest for a one-year, $1,000 loan. Now, using the APR formula, you find the APR is 6.75 percent:

$$\text{APR} = \frac{2 \times n \times I}{P(N + 1)}$$
$$= \frac{2 \times 2 \times \$50.63}{\$1,000(2 + 1)}$$
$$= \frac{\$202.50}{\$3,000}$$
$$= 0.0675, \text{ or } 6.75 \text{ percent}$$

If your relative chose to compound interest daily (365 compounding periods per year), the solution to this problem would be quite complicated. A calculator or a compound interest table can make interest calculations more manageable.

The following table summarizes the effects on the APR when the interest on a one-year, $1,000 loan is calculated using the simple interest, declining balance, add-on interest, bank discount, and compound interest methods:

Method	Amount Borrowed	Stated Interest	Total Interest	Number of Payments	APR
Simple interest*	$1,000	5%	$50.00	1	5.00%
Declining balance*	1,000	5	37.50	2	5.00
Add-on*	1,000	5	50.00	2	6.60
Bank discount	1,000(−50)	5	50.00	1	5.26
Compound interest*	1,000	5	50.63	2	6.75

*Discussed in the chapter.

- Restricts the penalties that card issuers can charge for going over the credit limit.
- Prohibits card issuers from issuing cards to consumers under 21 unless they have a cosigner or can demonstrate that they have independent means to repay the card debt.

 PRACTICE QUIZ 7-2

1. Distinguish between the finance charge and the annual percentage rate.
2. What are the three variations of the simple interest formula?
3. Distinguish among the adjusted balance, previous balance, and average daily balance methods of calculating the cost of open-end credit.
4. What is the rule of 78s?

PFP Sheet 30
Credit Card
Comparison

PFP Sheet 31
Consumer Loan
Comparison

Managing Your Debts

A sudden illness or the loss of your job may make it impossible for you to pay your bills on time. If you find you cannot make your payments, contact your creditors at once and try to work out a modified payment plan with them. If you have paid your bills promptly in the past, they may be willing to work with you. Do not wait until your account is turned over to a debt collector. At that point, the creditor has given up on you.

Automobile loans present special problems. Most automobile financing agreements permit your creditor to repossess your car any time you are in default on your payments. No advance notice is required. If your car is repossessed and sold, you will still owe the difference between the selling price and the unpaid debt, plus any legal, towing, and storage charges. Try to solve the problem with your creditor when you realize you will not be able to meet your payments. It may be better to sell the car yourself and pay off your debt than to incur the added costs of repossession.

If you are having trouble paying your bills, you may be tempted to turn to a company that claims to offer assistance in solving debt problems. Such companies may offer debt consolidation loans, debt counseling, or debt reorganization plans that are "guaranteed" to stop creditors' collection efforts. Before signing with such a company, investigate it. Be sure you understand what services the company provides and what they will cost you. Do not rely on verbal promises that do not appear in your contract. Also, check with the Better Business Bureau and your state or local consumer protection office. They may be able to tell you whether other consumers have registered complaints about the company.

A constant worry for a debtor who is behind in payments is the fear of debt collection agencies. However, as you will see in the next section, a federal agency protects certain legal rights that you possess in your dealings with such agencies.

LO7-3

Develop a plan to manage your debts.

smart money minute

Collection agencies can't:

- Contact you before 8 a.m. or after 9 p.m.
- Contact you at your place of employment.
- Harass you.
- Threaten harm.
- Make false claims, such as representing that they work for credit reporting companies, or misrepresent the amount you owe.
- Say that you will be arrested if you don't pay the debt.
- State that they are taking legal action if they don't intend to do so.

For more information about your rights or to file a complaint, contact your state's attorney general or the Federal Trade Commission.

DEBT COLLECTION PRACTICES

The Federal Trade Commission (FTC) enforces the **Fair Debt Collection Practices Act (FDCPA),** which prohibits certain practices by agencies that collect debts for creditors. The act does not apply to creditors that collect debts themselves. While the act does not erase the legitimate debts consumers owe, it does regulate the ways debt collection agencies do business. Recently, the FTC and the Consumer Financial Protection Bureau (CFPB) reported that the agencies received 84,500 debt collection complaints, making it one of the most prevalent topics of complaints about consumer finance products or services. Exhibit 7-2 summarizes the steps you may take if a debt collector calls.

Fair Debt Collection Practices Act (FDCPA)
A federal law, enacted in 1978, that regulates debt collection activities.

EXHIBIT 7-2 What to do if a debt collector calls

The Federal Trade Commission enforces the Fair Debt Collection Practices Act. The law dictates how and when a debt collector may contact you.

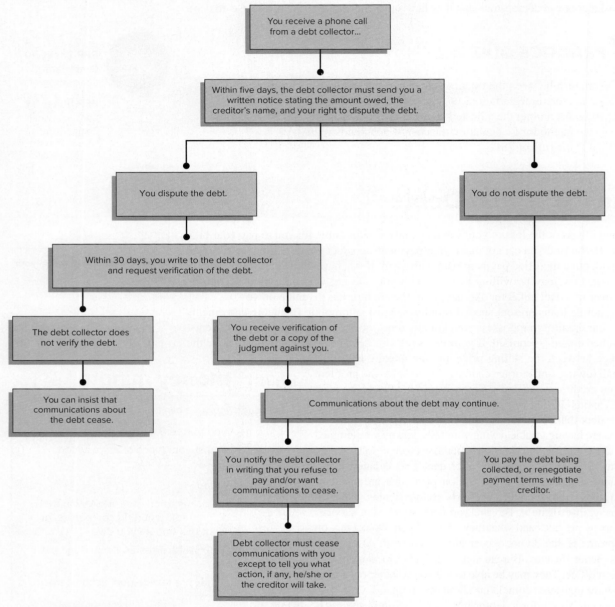

Source: Office of Public Information, Federal Reserve Bank of Minneapolis, Minneapolis, MN 55480.

smart money minute

During the coronavirus (COVID-19) pandemic, many credit card companies offered assistance by lowering or deferring monthly minimum payments, waiving or refunding late fees, reducing the interest rate, and establishing payment plans to pay off existing balances.

Debt collectors are prohibited by federal law from contacting you about a debt at a time or place they know is inconvenient for you. They also can't contact you at your place of employment if you let them know that your employer prohibits it. Use this letter if you want to restrict how a debt collector can contact you. But be careful about overdoing it: If you want to work something out, you don't want to make it too hard for the debt collector to reach you. Use the sample letter (Exhibit 7-3) if you want to tell a debt collector how they can contact you and instruct them not to contact you any other way. Read the nearby *Financial Literacy for My Life* feature to learn what to do when a debt collector contacts you.

What should I do when a debt collector contacts me?

There are different ways to respond appropriately to debt collectors. Depending on your situation, the Consumer Financial Protection Bureau has sample letters you can use if you're experiencing common problems.

When contacted, find out the following:

- Identity of the debt collector, including name, address, and phone number
- The amount of the debt, including any fees such as interest or collection costs
- What the debt is for and when the debt was incurred

- The name of the original creditor
- Information about whether you or someone else may owe the debt

When a debt collector first contacts you in writing regarding a debt, it must provide you a written notice that has certain, legally required information. If the collection agency first contacts you by phone, insist that they contact you in writing. **Do not give personal or financial information to the caller until you have confirmed it is a legitimate debt collector.**

Source: https://www.consumerfinance.gov/ask-cfpb/what-should-i-do-when-a-debt-collector-contacts-me-en-1695/, March 17, 2021.

WARNING SIGNS OF DEBT PROBLEMS

Bill Kenney, in his early 30s, has a steady job with an annual income of $65,000. Bill, his wife, and their two children enjoy a comfortable life. A new car is parked in the driveway of their home, which is furnished with such amenities as a six-burner gourmet stove, a Subzero freezer, and a large home theater system.

However, Bill Kenney is in debt. He is drowning in a sea of bills, with most of his income tied up in repaying debts. Foreclosure proceedings on his home have been instituted, and several stores have court orders to repossess practically every major appliance in it. His current car payment is overdue, and three charge accounts at local stores are several months delinquent.

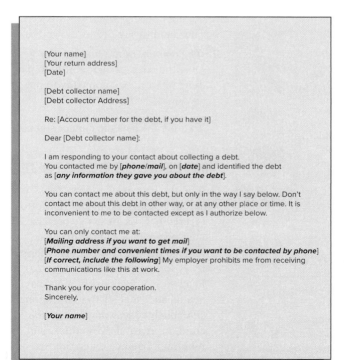

[Your name]
[Your return address]
[Date]

[Debt collector name]
[Debt collector Address]

Re: [Account number for the debt, if you have it]

Dear [Debt collector name]:

I am responding to your contact about collecting a debt.
You contacted me by [*phone/mail*], on [*date*] and identified the debt as [*any information they gave you about the debt*].

You can contact me about this debt, but only in the way I say below. Don't contact me about this debt in other way, or at any other place or time. It is inconvenient to me to be contacted except as I authorize below.

You can only contact me at:
[*Mailing address if you want to get mail*]
[*Phone number and convenient times if you want to be contacted by phone*]
[*If correct, include the following*] My employer prohibits me from receiving communications like this at work.

Thank you for your cooperation.
Sincerely,

[*Your name*]

EXHIBIT 7-3

Sample response letter

Source: Consumer Financial Protection Bureau, consumerfinance.gov/consumer-tools/debt-collection/accessed March 17, 2021.

Drowning in a sea of debt can turn your American dream into a nightmare.
Paul J. Richards/AFP/Getty Images

This case is neither exaggerated nor isolated. Unfortunately, many people are in the same floundering state. Their problem is immaturity. Mature consumers have certain information; they demonstrate self-discipline, control their impulses, and use sound judgment; they accept responsibility for money management; and they are able to postpone and govern expenditures when overextension of credit appears likely. According to the Consumer Credit Counseling Service, excessive use of credit is the most common reason consumers are unable to pay their bills on time.

Referring to overindebtedness as the nation's number one family financial problem, a nationally noted columnist on consumer affairs lists the following as frequent reasons for indebtedness:

1. *Emotional problems,* such as the need for instant gratification, as in the case of a man who can't resist buying a costly suit or a woman who impulsively purchases an expensive dress in a trendy department store.

2. *The use of money to punish,* such as a husband who buys a new car without consulting his wife, who in turn buys a diamond watch to get even.

3. *The expectation of instant comfort* among young couples who assume that by using the installment plan, they can have immediately the possessions their parents acquired after years of work.

4. *Keeping up with the Joneses,* which is more apparent than ever, not only among prosperous families but among limited-income families too.

5. *Overindulgence of children,* often because of the parents' own emotional needs, competition with each other, or inadequate communication regarding expenditures for the children.

6. *Misunderstanding or lack of communication among family members.* For example, a salesperson visited a Memphis family to sell them an expensive freezer. Although the freezer was beyond the means of this already overindebted family and too large for their needs anyway, the husband thought his wife wanted it. Not until later, in an interview with a debt counselor, did the wife relate her concern when she signed the contract; she had wanted her husband to say no.

7. *The amount of the finance charges,* which can push a family over the edge of their ability to pay, especially when they borrow from one company to pay another and these charges pyramid.

Exhibit 7-4 lists the danger signals of potential debt problems.

THE SERIOUS CONSEQUENCES OF DEBT

Just as the causes of indebtedness vary, so too do the other personal and family problems that often result from overextension of credit. Loss of a job because of garnishment proceedings may occur in a family that has a disproportionate amount of income tied up in debts. Another possibility is that such a family is forced to neglect vital areas. In the frantic effort to "rob Peter to pay Paul," skimping may seriously affect the family's health and neglect the educational needs of children. Excessive indebtedness may also result in heavy drinking, neglect of children, marital difficulties, and drug abuse. Paying only the minimum balance on credit card bills each month can lead you to a bankruptcy.

my life | **3**

If my household is experiencing problems in paying bills, it is time to examine the family budget for ways to reduce expenses.

Overindebtedness is the nation's number one family financial problem. Refer to Exhibit 7-4 for 16 danger signals of potential debt problems. For additional information, visit www.moneymanagement.org.

smart money minute

Did you make the *mistake* of getting behind on your bills? Don't wait: Take *action*. Call your creditors before a debt collector calls you. You may have *success* in avoiding the more serious consequences of debt, including declaring personal bankruptcy.

1.	Paying only the minimum balance on credit card bills each month.
2.	Increasing the total balance due on credit accounts each month.
3.	Missing payments, paying late, or paying some bills this month and others next month.
4.	Intentionally using the overdraft or automatic loan features on checking accounts or taking frequent cash advances on credit cards.
5.	Using savings to pay routine bills such as groceries or utilities.
6.	Receiving second or third payment notices from creditors.
7.	Not talking to your spouse about money or talking *only* about money.
8.	Depending on overtime, moonlighting, or bonuses to meet everyday expenses.
9.	Using up your savings.
10.	Borrowing money to pay old debts.
11.	Not knowing how much you owe until the bills arrive.
12.	Going over your credit limit on credit cards.
13.	Having little or nothing in savings to handle unexpected expenses.
14.	Being denied credit because of a negative credit bureau report.
15.	Getting a credit card revoked by the issuer.
16.	Putting off medical or dental visits because you can't afford them right now.

If your household is experiencing more than two of these warning signals, it's time to examine your budget for ways to reduce expenses.

Sources: *Advice for Consumers Who Use Credit* (Silver Springs, MD: Consumer Credit Counseling Service of Maryland, Inc.); *How to Be Credit Smart* (Washington, DC: Consumer Credit Education Foundation).

EXHIBIT 7-4

Danger signals of potential debt problems
Seek help from your local Consumer Credit Counseling Service if you experience these danger signals.

 PRACTICE QUIZ 7-3

1. What is the Fair Debt Collection Practices Act?
2. What are the most frequent reasons for indebtedness?
3. What are common danger signals of potential debt problems?

Consumer Credit Counseling Services

If you are having problems paying your bills and need help, you have several options. You can contact your creditors and try to work out an adjusted repayment plan yourself, or you can research online for a nonprofit financial counseling program to get help.

The **Consumer Credit Counseling Service (CCCS)** is a local, nonprofit organization affiliated with the National Foundation for Consumer Credit (NFCC). Branches of the CCCS provide debt counseling services for families and individuals with serious financial problems. It is not a charity, a lending institution, or a governmental or legal agency. The Consumer Credit Counseling Service is supported by contributions from banks, consumer finance companies, credit unions, merchants, and other community-minded organizations and individuals.

According to the NFCC, every year millions of consumers contact CCCS offices for help with their personal financial problems. All of the U.S. population has convenient access to CCCS services. To find an office near you, check online under Consumer Credit Counseling Service, or call 1-800-388-CCCS. All information is kept strictly confidential.

LO7-4

Evaluate various private and governmental sources that assist consumers with debt problems.

Consumer Credit Counseling Service (CCCS) A local, nonprofit organization that provides debt counseling services for families and individuals with serious financial problems.

HOW TO . . . Choose a Credit Counselor

Credit counseling organizations provide valuable assistance to financially distressed consumers. However, some firms may be misleading you about who they are, what they do, or how much they charge. Experts advise that you ask the following questions to find the best credit counselor.

- *What services do you offer?* Look for an organization that offers budget counseling and money management classes as well as a debt-management plan.
- *Do you offer free information?* Avoid organizations that charge for information or demand details about your problem first.
- *What are your fees?* Are there setup and/or monthly fees? A typical setup fee is $10. If you're paying a lot more, you may be the one who's being set up.
- *How will the debt-management plan work?* What debts can be included in the plan, and will you get regular reports on your accounts?
- *Can you get my creditors to lower or eliminate my interest and fees?* If the answer is yes, contact your creditors to verify this.
- *What if I can't afford to pay you?* If an organization won't help you because you can't afford to pay, go somewhere else for help.
- *Will you help me avoid future problems?* Getting a plan for avoiding future debt is as important as solving the immediate debt problem.
- *Will we have a contract?* All verbal promises should be in writing before you pay any money.
- *Are your counselors accredited or certified?* Legitimate credit counseling firms are affiliated with the National Foundation for Credit Counseling or the Association of Independent Consumer Credit Counseling Agencies.

Check with your local consumer protection agency and the Better Business Bureau to see if any complaints have been filed about the company.

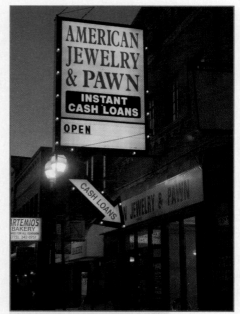

Being forced to pawn your belongings for some cash is just one of the serious consequences of debt.
Christopher Kerrigan/McGraw-Hill

WHAT THE CCCS DOES

Credit counselors are aware that most people who are in debt over their heads are basically honest people who want to clear up their indebtedness. Too often, the problems of such people arise from a lack of planning or a miscalculation of what they earn. Therefore, the CCCS is as concerned with preventing the problems as with solving them. As a result, its activities are divided into two parts:

1. Aiding families with serious debt problems by helping them manage their money better and setting up a realistic budget and plan for expenditures.

2. Helping people prevent debt problems by teaching them the necessity of family budget planning, providing education to people of all ages regarding the pitfalls of unwise credit buying, suggesting techniques for family budgeting, and encouraging credit institutions to provide full information about the costs and terms of credit and to withhold credit from those who cannot afford to repay it.

Anyone who is overburdened by credit obligations can phone, write, or visit a CCCS office. The CCCS requires that an applicant complete an application for credit counseling and then arranges an appointment for a personal interview with the applicant.

CCCS counseling is usually free. However, when the CCCS administers a debt repayment plan, it sometimes charges a nominal fee to help defray administrative costs.

Financial Literacy for My Life

CREDIT COUNSELING IN CRISIS

The National Consumer Law Center and Consumer Federation of America's comprehensive report recently indicated that a new generation of credit counseling agencies is a serious threat to debt-burdened consumers. The study found that, unlike the previous creditor-funded counseling services, these new agencies often harm debtors with improper advice, deceptive practices, excessive fees, and abuse of their nonprofit status. "Nonprofit" credit counseling agencies are increasingly performing like profit-making enterprises and pay their executives lavishly. For example, recently American Consumer Credit Counseling paid its president $462,350 in annual salary plus over $130,000 in benefits. According to Thomas Leary, a member of the Federal Trade Commission (FTC), "Some companies use their nonprofit status as a badge of trustworthiness to attract customers, who are then duped into paying large fees." For example, Mr. Leary testified that the commission filed a lawsuit against AmeriDebt, a large, Maryland-based credit counseling firm. According to the FTC complaint, the firm "aggressively advertises itself as a nonprofit and dedicated to assisting consumers with their finances. AmeriDebt advertises its services as 'free' when in fact the company retains a consumer's first payment as a 'contribution.'"[2]

Traditional credit counseling agencies offer financial and budget counseling, debt counseling, and community education as well as debt-management plans (DMP). Newer agencies, however, force consumers only into DMPs (also known as debt consolidation plans) and charge high monthly maintenance fees. Some agencies charge as much as a full month's consolidated payment, usually hundreds of dollars, simply to establish an account.

The report recommends that Congress and the states enact laws to curb abuses by credit counseling agencies. The law should:

- Prohibit false or misleading advertising and referral fees.
- Require credit counseling agencies to better inform consumers about fees, the sources of agency funding, suitability of DMPs for many consumers, and other options that consumers should consider, such as bankruptcy.
- Prohibit agencies from receiving a fee for service from a consumer until all her/his creditors have approved a DMP.
- Give consumers three days to cancel an agreement with a credit counseling agency without obligation.
- Cap fees charged by agencies at $50 for enrollment or setup. Allow only reasonable monthly charges.
- Require agencies to prominently disclose all financial arrangements with lenders or financial service providers.
- Provide consumers with the right to enforce the law in court.

Finally, the Internal Revenue Service should aggressively enforce existing standards for nonprofit credit counseling organizations, and credit counseling trade associations should set strong "best practice standards."

ALTERNATIVE COUNSELING SERVICES

In addition to the CCCS, universities, military bases, credit unions, local county extension agents, and state and federal housing authorities sometimes provide nonprofit counseling services. These organizations usually charge little or nothing for such assistance. You can also check with your local bank or consumer protection office to see whether it has a listing of reputable, low-cost financial counseling services.

Several national nonprofit organizations provide information and assist people with debt problems by phone and online.

- American Consumer Credit Counseling. Visit www.consumercredit.com or call 1-800-769-3571.
- Financial Counseling Association of America. Visit fcaa.org or call 1-866-797-2891.
- InCharge Institute of America. Visit www.incharge.org or call 1-800-565-8953.
- Money Management International. Visit www.moneymanagement.org or call 1-866-889-9347.

 my life **4**

I am aware that everyone who is over-burdened with credit obligations can phone, email, or visit the Consumer Credit Counseling Service.

In addition to the services provided by Consumer Credit Counseling Service, universities, military bases, credit unions, local county extension agents, and state and federal housing authorities provide debt counseling services. For additional information, visit Money Management International at (www.moneymanagement.org 1-866-889-9347) or InCharge Debt Solutions at www.incharge.org (1-800-565-8953).

smart money minute

Don't make the *mistake* of trusting in credit repair clinics that promise to clean up your credit report for a fee. You can take *action* and do it yourself for free. Only time and a conscientious effort to pay your debt in a timely manner will lead to the *success* of improving your credit report.

Typically, a counseling service will negotiate lower payments with your creditors, then make the payments using money you send to them each month. The creditor, not you, pays the cost of setting up this debt management plan (DMP). Read the *How To. . .* "Choose a Credit Counselor" feature on how to find the best credit counselor. Also, read the *Financial Literacy for My Life: Credit Counseling in Crisis* box to be aware of deceptive credit counseling organizations.

✔ PRACTICE QUIZ 7-4

1. What is the Consumer Credit Counseling Service?
2. What are the two major activities of the Consumer Credit Counseling Service?
3. What options other than the CCCS do consumers have for financial counseling?

Declaring Personal Bankruptcy

LO7-5

Assess the choices in declaring personal bankruptcy.

What if a debtor suffers from an extreme case of financial woes? Can there be any relief? The answer may be bankruptcy proceedings. **Bankruptcy** is a legal process in which some or all of the assets of a debtor are distributed among the creditors because the debtor is unable to pay his or her debts. Bankruptcy may also include a plan for the debtor to repay creditors on an installment basis. Declaring bankruptcy is a last resort because it severely damages your credit rating.

Jan Watson illustrates the new face of bankruptcy. A 43-year-old freelance commercial photographer from Point Reyes, California, she was never in serious financial trouble until she began incurring big medical costs last year and reached for her credit cards to pay the bills. Since Jan didn't have adequate health insurance, her debt quickly mounted and soon reached $17,000. It was too much for her to pay off with her $50,000-a-year freelance income. Her solution: Declare personal bankruptcy and enjoy the immediate freedom it would bring from creditors' demands.

my life | 5

I realize that the Bankruptcy Abuse Prevention and Consumer Protection Act of 2005 made it more difficult for consumers to file a Chapter 7 bankruptcy.

The filing process is now more difficult for debtors.

- Debtors must file more documents, including itemized statements of monthly net income, proof of income (pay stubs) for the last 60 days, and tax returns for the preceding year (four years for Chapter 13).
- Debtors must take a prefiling credit counseling and postfiling education course to have debts discharged.
- Debtors face increased filing fees, plus fees for credit counseling/education.
- The bankruptcy petition and process are more complicated, so it's very difficult to file without an attorney.

Ms. Watson's move put her in familiar company, demographically speaking. An increasing number of bankruptcy filers are well-educated, middle-class people with an overwhelming level of credit card debt. These individuals make up 30 percent of the adult population, but they account for 60 percent of personal bankruptcies. In that group, the people most likely to be in bankruptcy are between 35 and 44 years old (average age is 38), an age group that is usually assumed to be economically established.

In 1994, the U.S. Senate unanimously passed a bill that reduced the time and cost of bankruptcy proceedings. The bill strengthened creditor rights and enabled more individuals to cope with bankruptcy proceedings without selling their assets.

Unfortunately, for some debtors, bankruptcy had become an acceptable tool of credit management. According to the American Bankruptcy Institute, a record 2 million people declared bankruptcy in 2005, the highest rate since the U.S. bankruptcy code took effect in 1979 (see Exhibit 7-5). Bankruptcy courts had turned to regular Saturday sessions to handle the overflow. This drastic increase in personal bankruptcy filing led to the Bankruptcy Abuse Prevention and Consumer Protection Act of 2005.

EXHIBIT 7-5 Total U.S. consumer bankruptcy filings (Chapters 7 and 13), 1980–2020

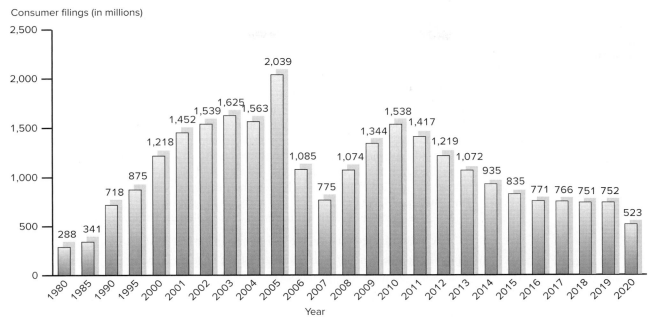

Consumer filings (in millions)

Source: Administrative Office of the U.S. Courts, www.uscourts.gov/news/2021/01/28/annual-bankruptcy-filings-fall-297-percent, accessed January 29, 2021.

THE BANKRUPTCY ABUSE PREVENTION AND CONSUMER PROTECTION ACT OF 2005

On April 20, 2005, President Bush signed the Bankruptcy Abuse Prevention and Consumer Protection Act, which remains the largest overhaul of the Bankruptcy Code since it was enacted in 1978. Signing the bill, the president declared, "Bankruptcy should always be the last resort in our legal system. In recent years too many people have abused the bankruptcy laws. Under the new law, Americans who have the ability to pay will be required to pay back at least a portion of their debts. The law will help make credit more affordable, because when bankruptcy is less common, credit can be extended to more people at better rates. Debtors seeking to erase all debts will now have to wait eight years from their last bankruptcy before they can file again. The law will also allow us to clamp down on bankruptcy mills that make their money by advising abusers on how to game the system."

Among other provisions, the law required that:

- The director of the Executive Office for U.S. Trustees develop a financial management training curriculum to educate individual debtors on how to better manage their finances and test, evaluate, and report to Congress on the curriculum's effectiveness.

- Debtors complete an approved instructional course in personal financial management.

- The clerk of each bankruptcy district maintain a list of credit counseling agencies and instructional courses on personal financial management.

Furthermore, the law required that states develop personal finance curricula designed for use in elementary and secondary schools.

The bottom line: The new law makes it more difficult for consumers to file a Chapter 7 bankruptcy and forces them into a Chapter 13 repayment plan. You have two choices in declaring personal bankruptcy: Chapter 7 (straight bankruptcy) and Chapter 13 (a wage-earner plan) bankruptcy. Both choices are undesirable, and neither should be

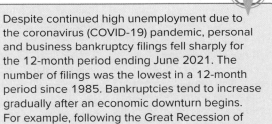

smart money minute

Despite continued high unemployment due to the coronavirus (COVID-19) pandemic, personal and business bankruptcy filings fell sharply for the 12-month period ending June 2021. The number of filings was the lowest in a 12-month period since 1985. Bankruptcies tend to increase gradually after an economic downturn begins. For example, following the Great Recession of 2007–2008, bankruptcy filings increased over a two-year period until they peaked in 2010.

bankruptcy A legal procedure for dealing with debt problems of individuals.

considered an easy way out. As shown in Exhibit 7-5, in 2020, personal bankruptcies had declined to 522,808.

CHAPTER 7 BANKRUPTCY   In a **Chapter 7 bankruptcy,** a debtor is required to draw up a petition listing his or her assets and liabilities. The debtor submits the petition to a U.S. district court and pays a filing fee. A person filing for relief under the bankruptcy code is called a *debtor;* the term *bankrupt* is not used.

Chapter 7 is a straight bankruptcy in which many, but not all, debts are forgiven. Most of the debtor's assets are sold to pay off creditors. However, certain assets of the debtor are protected to some extent. For example, Social Security payments; unemployment compensation; limited values of your equity in a home, car, or truck; household goods and appliances; trade tools; books; and so forth are protected.

In 2021, the courts must charge a $245 case filing fee, a $75 miscellaneous administrative fee, and a $15 trustee fee. If the debtor cannot pay the fees even in installments, the court may waive the fees.

In filing a petition, a debtor must provide the following information.

- A list of all creditors and the amount and nature of their claims.
- The source, amount, and frequency of the debtor's income.
- A list of all the debtor's property.
- A detailed list of the debtor's monthly expenses.

The discharge of debts in Chapter 7 bankruptcy does not affect alimony, child support, certain taxes, fines, certain debts arising from educational loans, or debts that the debtor fails to properly disclose to the bankruptcy court. At the request of a creditor, the bankruptcy judge may also exclude from the discharge debts resulting from loans the debtor received by giving the lender a false financial statement. Furthermore, debts arising from fraud, embezzlement, driving while intoxicated, larceny, or certain other willful or malicious acts may also be *excluded.* In 2020, there were 381,217 Chapter 7 bankruptcies filed.

CHAPTER 13 BANKRUPTCY   In a **Chapter 13 bankruptcy** (also called a wage-earner's plan), a debtor with a regular income proposes to a bankruptcy court a plan for extinguishing his or her debts from future earnings or other property over a period of time. In such a bankruptcy, the debtor normally keeps all or most of the property. In 2020, the total filing fee for Chapter 13 bankruptcy was $310.

During the period the plan is in effect, which can be as long as five years, the debtor makes regular payments to a Chapter 13 trustee. The trustee, in turn, distributes the money to the creditors. Under certain circumstances, the bankruptcy court may approve a plan permitting the debtor to keep all property even though the debtor repays less than the full amount of the debts. Certain debts not dischargeable in Chapter 7, such as those based on fraud, may be discharged in Chapter 13 if the debtor successfully completes the plan. In 2020, there were 154,341 Chapter 13 bankruptcies filed.

EFFECT OF BANKRUPTCY ON YOUR JOB AND YOUR FUTURE CREDIT

Different people have different experiences in obtaining credit after they file bankruptcy. Some find obtaining credit more difficult. Others find obtaining credit easier because they have relieved themselves of their prior debts or because creditors know they cannot file another bankruptcy case for a period of time. Obtaining credit may be easier for people who file a Chapter 13 bankruptcy and repay some of their debts than for people who file a Chapter 7 bankruptcy and make no effort to repay. The bankruptcy law prohibits your employer from discharging you simply because you have filed a bankruptcy case.

One caution: Don't confuse a personal bankruptcy with a business (or Chapter 11) bankruptcy. The Chapter 11 bankruptcy is a reorganization requested by a business and ordered by the court because a business is unable to pay its debts.

SHOULD A LAWYER REPRESENT YOU IN A BANKRUPTCY CASE?

When 29-year-old Lynn Jensen of San Gabriel, California, lost her $35,000-a-year job, she ended up filing for bankruptcy using a "how to file for bankruptcy" book because she could not afford a lawyer. Like Lynn, you have the right to file your own bankruptcy case and to represent yourself at all court hearings. In any bankruptcy case, however, you must complete and file with a bankruptcy court several detailed forms concerning your property, debts, and financial condition. Many people find it easier to complete these forms with the assistance of experienced bankruptcy counsel. In addition, you may discover that your case will develop complications, especially if you own a substantial amount of property or your creditors object to the discharge of your debts. Then you will require the advice and assistance of a lawyer.

Choosing a bankruptcy lawyer may be difficult. Some of the least reputable lawyers make easy money by handling hundreds of bankruptcy cases without adequately considering individual needs. Recommendations from those you know and trust and from employee assistance programs are most useful.

WHAT ARE THE COSTS?   The monetary costs to the debtor under Chapter 13 bankruptcy include the following:

1. *Court costs.* The debtor must pay a filing fee to the clerk of the court at the time of filing his or her petition. The filing fee may be paid in up to four installments if the court grants authorization.
2. *Attorneys' fees.* These fees are usually the largest single item of cost. Often the attorney does not require them to be paid in advance at the time of filing but agrees to be paid in installments after receipt of a down payment. Fees range between $2,000 and $5,000, depending on the state, the attorney, and the complexity of your bankruptcy case.
3. *Trustees' fees and costs.* The trustees' fees are established by the bankruptcy judge in most districts and by a U.S. trustee in certain other districts.

Although it is possible to reduce these costs by purchasing the legal forms in a local office supplies store and completing them yourself, an attorney is strongly recommended.

There are also intangible costs to bankruptcy. For example, obtaining credit in the future may be difficult, since bankruptcy reports are retained in credit bureaus for 10 years. Therefore, you should take the extreme step of declaring personal bankruptcy only when no other options for solving your financial problems exist.

Since you now know everything you ever wanted to know about consumer credit, read the *Financial Literacy for My Life: What's Your Credit IQ?* feature to test your credit IQ.

smart money minute

ALERT: "DEBT RELIEF" MAY BE CODE FOR BANKRUPTCY

The Federal Trade Commission cautions you to read between the lines when faced with ads in newspapers or telephone directories that promise debt relief. This relief may actually be bankruptcy. The following catch phrases are commonly used:
"Consolidate your bills into one monthly payment without borrowing."
"Keep your property."
"Stop credit harassment, foreclosures, repossessions, and garnishments."
"Wipe out your debts! Consolidate your bills!"
"Use the protection and assistance provided by federal law. For once let the law work for you."

personal fintech

Filing bankruptcy without an attorney is called *pro se*. However, seeking the advice of a qualified attorney is strongly recommended because bankruptcy has long-term financial and legal repercussions. Misunderstanding of the law or making mistakes in the process can affect your rights. Court employees and bankruptcy judges are prohibited by law from offering legal advice. If you are unable to afford an attorney, you may qualify for free legal services.

smart money minute

According to Fair Isaac Corporation (FICO), a personal bankruptcy can cause an immediate drop of up to 260 points on your credit report. This damage is serious, harmful, and long lasting.

✔ PRACTICE QUIZ 7-5

1. What is the purpose of Chapter 7 bankruptcy?
2. What is the difference between Chapter 7 and Chapter 13 bankruptcy?
3. How does bankruptcy affect your job and future credit?
4. What are the costs of declaring bankruptcy?

Financial Literacy for My Life

WHAT'S YOUR CREDIT IQ?

CREDIT-ABILITY SCORECARD

Test your credit IQ. For each question, circle the letter that best describes your credit habits.

1. **I pay my bills when they are due.**
   (A) Always
   (B) Almost always
   (C) Sometimes

2. **After paying my regular bills each month, I have money left from my income.**
   (A) Yes
   (B) Sometimes
   (C) Never

3. **I know how much I owe on my credit cards each month before I receive my bills.**
   (A) Yes
   (B) Sometimes
   (C) No

4. **When I get behind in my payments, I ignore the past-due notices.**
   (A) Never or not applicable
   (B) Sometimes
   (C) Always

5. **When I need more money for my regular living expenses, I take out a loan or use my line of credit on my credit card or checking account.**
   (A) Never
   (B) Sometimes
   (C) Often

6. **If I wanted to see a copy of my credit report, I would contact**
   (A) A credit reporting agency.
   (B) My lenders.
   (C) My lawyer.

7. **My credit record shows that I am current on all my loans and charge accounts.**
   (A) Yes
   (B) Don't know
   (C) No

8. **I pay more than the minimum balance due on my credit card accounts.**
   (A) Always
   (B) Sometimes
   (C) Never

9. **To pay off my current credit and charge card accounts, it would take me**
   (A) 4 months or less.
   (B) 5 to 8 months.
   (C) Over 8 months.

10. **My consumer loans (including auto loans, but not mortgage payment) and credit card bills each month average more than 20 percent of my take-home pay.**
    (A) No
    (B) Sometimes
    (C) Always

11. **If I had serious credit problems, I would contact my creditors to explain the problem.**
    (A) Yes
    (B) Probably
    (C) No

12. **If I default (don't repay) on a loan, that fact can stay on my credit report for**
    (A) 7 years.
    (B) 3 years.
    (C) 1 year.

Assign a score of 3 for each "A" answer, 2 for each "B" answer, and 1 for each "C" response. Total the score.

If you scored:	
31–36	You have an excellent knowledge of credit and its responsible use.
24–30	You should take steps toward better understanding your personal finances and the credit process.
18–23	You probably need to take a serious look at your personal finances; consider controlling your spending and keeping on a tight budget.
12–17	You may be heading for serious trouble; consider seeking help, such as nonprofit consumer credit counseling services.

Source: AFSA Education Foundation, How to Be Credit Smart, 1997.

Your Personal Finance Roadmap and Dashboard:

Credit Usage

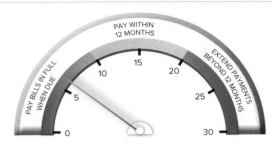

PAYING YOUR BILLS

One indicator of your sound financial health is your ability to pay your bills in a timely manner. You should figure out not only how much the loan will cost you, but whether you can pay it on time without incurring excessive interest.

Your Situation

If you need to borrow money, do you know where you can get the least expensive loan? Can you calculate interest on your loan? Do you know the consequences and costs of paying the minimum amount due on your credit card balances?

Paying your bills on time is the foundation for progress toward good financial health. Other personal financial planning actions you might consider during various stages of your life include:

 ### First Steps

- Look for a low interest rate card and no annual fees.
- Don't charge if you can't pay the full balance within one month.
- Consider contacting a credit counseling agency if you need help in managing your credit.
- Don't miss or be late on your payments, and avoid late fees.
- Check the online tools and resources at www.federal-reserve.gov to make well-informed decisions about the use and sources of credit.
- Create a realistic budget and stick to it.
- Boost your credit score.

- Pay bills on time and pay down the balances to boost your credit score.
- Build your emergency fund.
- Spend within your means.
- Don't go over your credit limit on credit cards.
- Keep your own credit account after you change your name or marital status.
- Request a free credit report every year from each of the three credit reporting agencies.

 ### Next Steps

- Check your credit report for accuracy and continue monitoring your credit score.
- Decrease the total balance due on credit accounts each month.
- Use your savings to purchase big-ticket items.
- Contact your lenders immediately if you have problems making payments.
- Remain diligent about managing your credit, and become familiar with the provisions of the CARD Act.

Later Steps

- Avoid any negative entry on your credit report and maintain an excellent credit rating.
- Don't depend on overtime, a part-time job, or bonuses to meet expenses.
- Keep balances low on credit cards and other revolving credit.
- Lower your cost of credit by consolidating your debt through a second mortgage or a home equity line of credit.
- Consider carefully before taking out a home equity loan.

> **YOUR** Next Step . . . select one or more of the items above and create an action plan to implement those financial planning activities.

SUMMARY OF LEARNING OBJECTIVES

LO7-1
Analyze the major sources of consumer credit. The major sources of consumer credit are commercial banks, savings and loan associations, credit unions, finance companies, life insurance companies, and family and friends. Each of these sources has unique advantages and disadvantages.

Parents or family members are often the source of the least expensive loans. They may charge you only the interest they would have earned had they not made the loan. Such loans, however, can complicate family relationships.

LO7-2
Determine the cost of credit by calculating interest using various interest formulas. Compare the finance charge and the annual percentage rate (APR) as you shop for credit. Under the Truth in Lending law, creditors are required to state the cost of borrowing so that you can compare credit costs and shop for credit.

For a borrower, the most favorable method of calculating the cost of open-end credit is the adjusted balance method. In this method, creditors add finance charges after subtracting payments made during the billing period. The rule of 78s favors lenders.

LO7-3
Develop a plan to manage your debts. The Fair Debt Collection Practices Act prohibits certain practices by debt collection agencies. Debt has serious consequences if a proper plan for managing it is not implemented.

Most people agree that emotional problems, the use of money to punish, the expectation of instant comfort, keeping up with the Joneses, overindulgence of children, misunderstanding or lack of communication among family members, and the amount of finance charges are common reasons for excessive indebtedness.

LO7-4
Evaluate various private and governmental sources that assist consumers with debt problems. If you cannot meet your obligations, contact your creditors immediately. Before signing up with a debt consolidation company, investigate it thoroughly. Better yet, contact your local Consumer Credit Counseling Service or other debt counseling organizations.

Such organizations help people manage their money better by setting up a realistic budget and planning for expenditures. These organizations also help people prevent debt problems by teaching them the necessity of family budget planning and providing education to people of all ages.

LO7-5
Assess the choices in declaring personal bankruptcy. A debtor's last resort is to declare bankruptcy, permitted by the U.S. Bankruptcy Act of 1978. Consider the financial and other costs of bankruptcy before taking this extreme step. A debtor can declare Chapter 7 (straight) bankruptcy or Chapter 13 (wage earner plan) bankruptcy.

Some people find obtaining credit more difficult after filing bankruptcy. Others find obtaining credit easier because they have relieved themselves of their prior debts or because creditors know they cannot file another bankruptcy case for a period of time. Obtaining credit may be easier for people who file a Chapter 13 bankruptcy and repay some of their debts than for people who file a Chapter 7 bankruptcy and make no effort to repay their debts.

The Bankruptcy Abuse Prevention and Consumer Protection Act of 2005 overhauled the Bankruptcy Code. The Act made it more difficult for consumers to file Chapter 7 bankruptcy, often forcing them into a Chapter 13 repayment plan instead.

KEY TERMS

add-on interest method   238

adjusted balance method   238

annual percentage rate (APR)   233

average daily balance method   238

bankruptcy   252

Chapter 7 bankruptcy   254

Chapter 13 bankruptcy   254

Consumer Credit Counseling
   Service (CCCS)   249

credit insurance   243

declining balance method   237

Fair Debt Collection Practices Act
   (FDCPA)   245

finance charge   233

previous balance method   238

rule of 78s   242

simple interest   236

Truth in Lending law   233

KEY FORMULAS

Topic	Formula

Calculating annual percentage rate (APR)

$$\text{APR} = \frac{2 \times \text{Number of payment periods in one year} \times \text{Dollar cost of credit}}{\text{Loan amount (Total number of payments to pay off the loan} + 1)}$$

$$= \frac{2 \times n \times I}{P(N + 1)}$$

Example:

P = Principal borrowed, $100

n = number of payments in one year, 1

I = Dollar cost of credit, $8

$$\text{APR} = \frac{2 \times 1 \times \$8}{\$100(1 + 1)} = \frac{\$16}{\$200} = 0.08, \text{ or 8 percent}$$

For 12 equal monthly payments,

$$\text{APR} = \frac{2 \times 12 \times \$8}{\$100(12 + 1)} = \frac{\$192}{\$1,300} = 0.1477, \text{ or 14.77 percent}$$

Calculating simple interest

Interest (in dollars) = Principal borrowed × Interest rate × Length of loan in years

$$I = P \times r \times T$$

Example:

From above: P = $100; r = 0.08; T = 1

$$I = \$100 \times 0.08 \times 1 = \$8$$

Calculating compound interest

Total future value of a loan = Principal (1 + Rate of interest)$^{\text{Time in years}}$

$$F = P(1 + r)^T$$

Example:

From above: P = $100; r = 0.08; T = 1

$$F = \$100(1 + 0.08)^1 = \$100(1.08) = \$108$$

SELF-TEST PROBLEMS

1. Your bank card has an APR of 18 percent and there is a 2 percent fee for cash advances. The bank starts charging you interest on cash advances immediately. You get a cash advance of $600 on the first day of the month. You get your credit card bill at the end of the month. What is the total finance charge you will pay on this cash advance for the month?

2. You borrowed $1,000 at the stated interest rate of 8 percent. You pay off the loan in one lump sum at the end of the year. What is the approximate annual percentage rate?

Self-Test Solutions

1. Cash advance fee = 2 percent of $600 = $12

   Interest for one month = ($600 × .18 × 1)/12 = $108 ÷ 12 = $9

   (Using $I = P \times r \times T$ formula)

   Total cost for one month = $12 + $9 = $21

2. Using the formula, the APR for the lump-sum loan is

$$r = \frac{2 \times n \times 1}{P(N + 1)} = \frac{2 \times 1 \times \$8}{\$1,000(1 + 1)} = \frac{\$16}{\$2,000} = .008, \text{ or 8 percent}$$

FINANCIAL PLANNING PROBLEMS

LO7-2 **1.** *Calculating the Finance Charge on a Loan.* Dave borrowed $500 for one year and paid $50 in interest. The bank charged him a $5 service charge. What is the finance charge on this loan?

LO7-2 **2.** *Calculating the Annual Percentage Rate.* In problem 1, Dave borrowed $500 on January 1, 2022, and paid it all back at once on December 31, 2022. What was the APR?

LO7-2 **3.** *Calculating the Annual Percentage Rate.* If Dave paid the $500 in 12 equal monthly payments, what was the APR?

LO7-2 **4.** *Comparing the Costs of Credit Cards.* Bobby is trying to decide between two credit cards. One has no annual fee and an 18 percent interest rate, and the other has a $40 annual fee and an 8.9 percent interest rate. Should he take the card that's free or the one that costs $40?

LO7-2 **5.** *Calculating the Cash Advance Fee and the Dollar Amount of Interest.* Sidney took a $200 cash advance by using checks linked to her credit card account. The bank charges a 2 percent cash advance fee on the amount borrowed and offers no grace period on cash advances. Sidney paid the balance in full when the bill arrived. What was the cash advance fee? What was the interest for one month at an 18 percent APR? What was the total amount she paid? What if she had made the purchase with her credit card and promptly paid off the bill in full?

LO7-2 **6.** *Comparing the Cost of Credit during Inflationary Periods.* Dorothy lacks cash to pay for a $600 dishwasher. She could buy it from the store on credit by making 12 monthly payments of $52.74. The total cost would then be $632.88. Instead, Dorothy decides to deposit $50 a month in the bank until she has saved enough money to pay cash for the dishwasher. One year later, she has saved $642—$600 in deposits plus interest. When she goes back to the store, she finds the dishwasher now costs $660. Its price has gone up 10 percent. Was postponing her purchase a good trade-off for Dorothy?

LO7-2 **7.** *Comparing Costs of Credit Using Three Calculation Methods.* You have been pricing Samsung-Galaxy SmartWatch in several stores. Three stores have the identical price of $300. Each store charges 18 percent APR, has a 30-day grace period, and sends out bills on the first of the month. On further investigation, you find that store A calculates the finance charge by using the average daily balance method, store B uses the adjusted balance method, and store C using the previous balance method. Assume you purchased the smartwatch on May 5 and made a $100 payment on June 15. What will the finance charge be if you made your purchase from store A? From store B? From store C?

LO7-2 **8.** *Determining Interest Cost Using the Simple Interest Formula.* What are the interest cost and the total amount due on a six-month loan of $1,500 at 13.2 percent simple annual interest?

LO7-2 **9.** *Calculating the Total Cost of a Purchase, the Monthly Payment, and an APR.* After visiting several automobile dealerships, Richard selects the used car he wants. He likes its $10,000 price, but financing through the dealer is no bargain. He has $2,000 cash for a down payment, so he needs an $8,000 loan. In shopping at several banks for an installment loan, he learns that interest on most automobile loans is quoted at add-on rates. That is, during the life of the loan, interest is paid on the full amount borrowed even though a portion of the principal has been paid back. Richard borrows $8,000 for a period of four years at an add-on interest rate of 11 percent. What is the total interest on Richard's loan? What is the total cost of the car? What is the monthly payment? What is the annual percentage rate (APR)?

LO7-2 **10.** *Calculating Simple Interest on a Loan.* Damon convinced his aunt to lend him $2,000 to purchase a digital TV. She has agreed to charge only 6 percent simple interest, and he has agreed to repay the loan at the end of one year. How much interest will he pay for the year?

LO7-2 **11.** *Calculating Simple Interest on a Loan.* You can buy an item for $100 on a charge with the promise to pay $100 in 90 days. Suppose you can buy an identical item for $95 cash. If you buy the item for $100, you are in effect paying $5 for the use of $95 for three months. What is the effective annual rate of interest?

LO7-2 **12.** *Calculating Interest Using the Simple Interest Formula.* Rebecca wants to buy a new saddle for her horse. The one she wants usually costs $500, but this week it is on sale for $400. She does not have $400, but she could buy it with $50 down and pay the rest in 6 months with 10 percent interest. Does Rebecca save any money buying the saddle this way?

LO7-2 **13.** *Calculating Interest Using the Simple Interest Formula.* You just bought a used car for $3,500 from your cousin. He agreed to let you make payments for 3 years with simple interest at 7 percent. How much interest will you pay?

LO7-2 **14.** *Calculating Interest Using the Bank Discount Method.* Your uncle lends you $2,000 less $100 (interest at 5 percent), and you receive $1,900. Use the APR formula to find the true annual percentage rate.

LO7-2 **15.** *Calculating the Annual Percentage Rate Using the Compound Interest Formula.* A $1,000 loan is paid off in 12 equal monthly payments. The stated annual interest rate is 10 percent. What is the annual percentage rate?

DIGITAL FINANCIAL LITERACY: COSTS OF CREDIT

As explained at the beginning of this chapter, credit costs money; therefore, you must conduct a cost/benefit analysis before making any major purchase. While most people consider credit costs, others simply ignore them and eventually find themselves in financial difficulties. To help you avoid this problem, each of the following organizations has a home page on the internet.

Debtors Anonymous offers financial counseling to debt-ridden consumers. (www.debtorsanonymous.org)

Bankrate provides rate information for mortgages, credit cards, auto loans, home equity loans, and personal loans. (www.bankrate.com)

Action items:

1. Choose one of the above organizations and visit its website and gather information about the costs of credit.

2. Prepare a report that summarizes the information the organization provides. Finally, decide how this information could help you better manage your credit and its costs.

FINANCIAL PLANNING CASE

Financing Sue's Prius

After shopping around, Sue decided on the car of her choice, a used Prius. The dealer quoted her a total price of $8,000. Sue decided to use $2,000 of her savings as a down payment and borrow $6,000. The salesperson wrote this information on a sales contract that Sue took with her when she set out to find financing.

When Sue applied for a loan, she discussed loan terms with the bank lending officer. The officer told her that the bank's policy was to lend only 80 percent of the total price of a used car. Sue showed the officer her copy of the sales

contract, indicating that she had agreed to make a $2,000, or 25 percent, down payment on the $8,000 car, so this requirement caused her no problem. Although the bank was willing to make 48-month loans at an annual percentage rate of 15 percent on used cars, Sue chose a 36-month repayment schedule. She believed she could afford the higher payments, and she knew she would not have to pay as much interest if she paid off the loan at a faster rate. The bank lending officer provided Sue with a copy of the Truth in Lending Disclosure Statement shown here.

Truth in Lending Disclosure Statement (Loans)			
Annual Percentage Rate	**Finance Charge**	**Amount Financed**	**Total of Payments, 36**
The cost of your credit as a yearly rate.	The dollar amount the credit will cost you.	The amount of credit provided to you or on your behalf.	The amount you will have paid after you have made all payments as scheduled.
15%	$1,487.71	$6,000.00	$7,487.71

You have the right to receive at this time an itemization of the Amount Financed.

☒ I want an itemization.	☐ I do not want an itemization.

Your payment schedule will be:

Number of Payments	**Amount of Payments**	**When Payments Are Due**
36	$207.99	1st of each month

Sue decided to compare the APR she had been offered with the APR offered by another bank, but the 20 percent APR of the second bank (bank B) was more expensive than the 15 percent APR of the first bank (bank A). Here is her comparison of the two loans:

	Bank A 15% APR	Bank B 20% APR
Amount financed	$6,000.00	$6,000.00
Finance charge	1,487.71	2,027.33
Total of payments	7,487.71	8,027.33
Monthly payments	207.99	222.98

The 5 percent difference in the APRs of the two banks meant Sue would have to pay $15 extra every month if she got her loan from the second bank. Of course, she got the loan from the first bank.

Questions

1. What is perhaps the most important item shown on the disclosure statement? Why?
2. What is included in the finance charge?
3. What amount will Sue receive from the bank?

YOUR PERSONAL FINANCIAL PLAN

COMPARING CREDIT SOURCES AND COSTS

Credit is available from many sources. Becoming aware of the differences among financial institutions related to borrowing costs and other factors while wisely managing your debt will help you avoid financial difficulties.

Your Short-Term Financial Planning Activity

Task Compare credit sources and costs

Research

1) Use Personal financial Planning Sheet 30 to evaluate your current use of credit cards; also compare credit card offers related to annual percentage rate, annual fee, grace period, and other fees.

2) Use Personal Financial Planning Sheet 31 to compare various credit sources for loans related to various financial needs. How are the simple interest, simple interest on the declining balance, and add-on interest formulas used in determining the cost of credit?

Outcome Add these documents and files to your portfolio or to your Personal Financial Planning folder. In your report, describe actions to minimize finance charges and annual percentage rate.

Your Long-Term Financial Planning Activity

Task Avoid debt problems and minimize the use of credit.

Research

1) Use Exhibit 7-4 to identify danger signals of potential debt problems. What actions can you take to avoid or minimize these dangers?

2) Research online a local office of the Consumer Credit Counseling Service. What assistance can debtors obtain from this office? What is the cost of assistance, if any? How can the Consumer Credit Counseling Service help you reduce (or eliminate) the use of credit cards?

3) Use the internet to locate other sources of information that might help you avoid debt problems and minimize the use of credit.

Outcome Prepare an audio or a written summary of your findings and your action plan to avoid debt problems and minimize the use of credit.

Note: All *Personal Financial Planner* sheets are available at the end of the book and in an Excel spreadsheet format in *Connect Finance.*

CONTINUING CASE

Choosing a Source of Credit: The Costs of Credit Alternatives

Jamie Lee Jackson, age 27, full-time student and part-time bakery employee, is busy setting up her new home. Her budget is a little tight now as she made the decision to move in to a place of her own, which gives her privacy and independence, but all of the expenses are now her responsibility.

Jamie Lee applied for three store credit cards when she was shopping for her furnishings. The excitement of making selections and the attractiveness of percentages off her purchases made the credit card offers too good to pass up. It was all too easy to select the new furnishings when the cash was not immediately coming from her pocket. "The payments will not be due for at least 45 days from now, by the time all the accounts are opened and the grace periods are factored in. I am sure I will have enough to cover the balances by then," Jamie Lee convinced herself.

Jamie Lee's new furnishings have been delivered, and she is quite happy with her choices. The bungalow is comfortable, and Jamie is now getting into a routine balancing the new move with work and school obligations. Unfortunately, the bills have begun to arrive in Jamie Lee's mailbox; payments are soon due for all the new furniture and appliances.

The corresponding annual interest rates on the credit card purchases were not something Jamie Lee factored in when she applied for the store credit cards. "Wow, 18.5 percent on one, and the other two have interest rates of 19 percent per year. Those interest fees can really add up quickly. The disclosure said that by making the minimum payments, I could be paid off in 14 years! I am not sure my appliances will still be working at that time, nor will the furniture still be in style 14 years from now."

Jamie Lee was starting to feel the consequences of overspending and knew she must develop a plan to pay off the purchases quickly!

Current Financial Situation

Assets:

Checking account: $1,800
Savings account: $7,200
Emergency fund savings account: $2,700
IRA balance: $410
Car: $2,800

Liabilities:

Student loan balance: $10,800 (Jamie is still a full-time student, so no payments are required on the loan until after graduation)
Credit card balance: $4,250 (total of three store credit cards)

Income:

Gross monthly salary from the bakery: $2,750 (Net income: $2,175)

Monthly Expenses:

Rent: $350
Utilities: $70
Food: $125
Gas/maintenance: $130
Credit card payment: $0

Questions

1. Jamie Lee received an offer to transfer the balance of all of her store credit cards to her bank credit card in the mail. It offered zero percent finance charges/interest for the first three months (90 days), and an 18.5 percent interest rate thereafter until the balance is paid in full. Upon reading the fine print, she saw there was a $50 transaction fee and interest accrued from the day the balance transfer was made if the balance was not paid in full within the first 90 days. How could Jamie Lee use this balance transfer offer to her advantage? How is this offer a major disadvantage to Jamie Lee?

2. Based on Jamie Lee's current financial situation, could she possibly make the balance transfer option work?

3. What solution would you recommend for Jamie Lee to get her credit cards paid off as soon as possible? What are the advantages of your choices? What are the disadvantages of your choices?

DAILY SPENDING DIARY

"Tracking my spending has helped me avoid credit problems."

Directions

Continue (or start) your *Daily Spending Diary* to record and monitor your spending in various categories. Also record comments to reflect what you have learned about your spending patterns and help you consider possible changes you might want to make in your spending habits.

Analysis Questions

1. Describe any aspects of your spending habits that might indicate an overuse of credit.

2. How might your *Daily Spending Diary* information help you avoid credit problems?

The *Daily Spending Diary* sheet is located in the appendix at the end of Chapter 1 and on the library resource site in *Connect.*

APPENDIX
Education Financing, Loans, and Scholarships

The desire to pursue higher education has grown steadily since the 1940s. According to the Census Bureau, in 1940 approximately 5 percent of the population held a bachelor's degree. Today, that percentage has grown to greater than 35 percent. The increase in demand for education has created an expansion in many areas, including the number of higher education schools, the development of different types of degree programs, and specialization in occupations, which has contributed to the overall higher cost of a college education.

What is driving the increase in demand for education? Some of the main drivers appear to be higher projected salaries with additional education and reduced potential for unemployment. Numerous studies have shown a correlation between additional education and higher salaries. In addition, lower unemployment rates are correlated with higher education levels. (See Exhibit 7-A.) However, along with additional education come the opportunity costs associated with it: lost wages while in school, and tuition and living costs to attend school. Paying for these educational pursuits is the primary focus of this appendix.

EXHIBIT 7-A Education pays

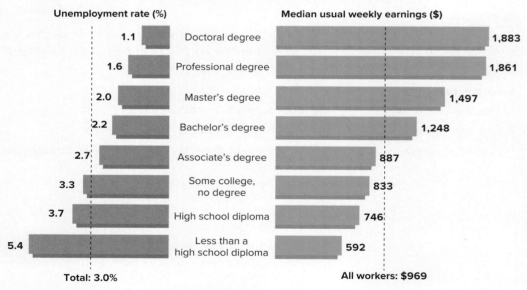

Unemployment rates and earnings by educational attainment, 2019

Unemployment rate (%)		Median usual weekly earnings ($)
1.1	Doctoral degree	1,883
1.6	Professional degree	1,861
2.0	Master's degree	1,497
2.2	Bachelor's degree	1,248
2.7	Associate's degree	887
3.3	Some college, no degree	833
3.7	High school diploma	746
5.4	Less than a high school diploma	592

Total: 3.0%   All workers: $969

Note: Data are for persons age 25 and over. Earnings are for full-time wage and salary workers.
Source: U.S. Bureau of Labor Statistics, Current Population Survey. Date accessed: February 15, 2021.

Return on Investment

For years, the business community has used the concept of return on investment (ROI). ROI is simply a profitability measure. While there are a few ways to calculate ROI, remember that what you are trying to measure is "bang for your buck." Students who are faced with increasing tuition amounts and large loan balances upon graduation are now able to review schools based upon their ROI. This will help give a general idea about how much income to expect compared to tuition costs and potential loan amounts.

INCREASING COSTS OF EDUCATION

As college enrollments have swelled, increases in tuition, especially over the last decade, have been significant. Not only are there major increases in the numbers of traditional students coming straight from high school, but the number of those who are returning to school to "retool" and change careers has risen greatly as well. A common issue for many of these students is finding ways to pay for tuition, books, school fees, and living expenses while they pursue an education.

For some students, being accepted by their "dream college" can be a euphoric experience. The more earthbound question is: How do you pay for the education? This question clearly should be asked before applying to schools, but school endowments and additional assistance provided often add to the challenge of determining the full costs until the college applications are accepted and the financial aid process begins.

The majority of students fund their education through a combination of loans, scholarships, grants, savings, and current earnings. Loans have specific repayment terms, but scholarships and grants do not need to be repaid and thus are sometimes referred to as *free money*. Yet nothing in life is free, as the saying goes, and although there are no repayment requirements, you will have to put in some time and effort to find these scholarships as well as choose a school that offers the best value.

personal fintech

Check out the ROI on your current school and other schools you considered at www.payscale.com/college-roi.

smart money minute

Average student loan debt for bachelor's degrees has risen to $29,500 at public universities and $45,300 at private for-profit schools!

Source: Educationdata.org, *accessed February 15, 2021.*

Free Application for Federal Student Aid

The very first step to funding your education, whether with loans or certain grants, is completing and submitting the Free Application for Federal Student Aid (FAFSA) form. Most state and institutional aid programs require that this form be remitted before they consider providing any type of funding. After the FAFSA has been processed, you will receive notification of your expected family contribution (EFC). For dependent students being claimed on their parents' tax return, the amount of parental income, assets, and college savings accounts will be important factors in determining the amount of the EFC. For an independent student, individual assets will also be carefully considered in determining eligibility for aid.

The schools that the student designates on the FAFSA will receive notification that the FAFSA has been processed. Once the admission application is accepted, the schools will take the FAFSA information and prepare a financial aid package. The goal is to evaluate each student's situation and provide the best possible selection of aid. In many cases, the aid package will not be able to cover the full cost of attendance. In addition, the federal student aid may be reduced based upon other aid that has been awarded (scholarships, state aid, etc.).

The financial aid package received from the school will often include a combination of grants, loans, and work-study options. The student will be sent an award letter with each portion designated (see Exhibit 7-B). The family should carefully consider their ability to fund the expected family contribution and repay the loans offered in the the aid package. These aid types will now be reviewed with the goal of understanding the repayment requirements and the terms of acceptance of each.

EXHIBIT 7-B

Sample award package

Cost of Attendance		
Tuition and fees	$22,000	
Room and meals	10,000	
Books and personal	3,500	
Travel	700	
Total Cost of Attendance (1)	**$36,200**	
Expected Family Contribution		
Student	$ 2,000	
Parent	6,000	
Total Family Contribution (2)	**$ 8,000**	
Calculated Financial Need (1-2)	$28,200	
	Fall 20XX	**Spring 20XX**
Your college grant	$ 1,000	$ 1,000
Your college scholarship	$ 1,500	$ 1,500
Federal Perkins Loan	$ 2,000	$ 2,000
Federal Subsidized Stafford Loan	$ 5,500	$ 5,500
Parent PLUS Loan Option	$ 4,100	$ 4,100
Total	**$14,100**	**$14,100**

my life 1

Financial Aid Websites:

www.finaid.org
www.fastweb.com/
studentaid.ed.gov
bigfuture.collegeboard.org

my life 2

Key Websites for Scholarships:

www.scholarships.com
bigfuture.collegeboard.org
www.collegenet.com
www.fastweb.com
www.goodcall.com/scholarships

SCHOLARSHIPS

Scholarships do not have to be repaid. Scholarships awarded from organizations outside the school have to be reported on the FAFSA or to the financial aid office, if awarded later. Big-name scholarships (e.g., Coca-Cola and Prudential) receive an extraordinary number of applicants, but there are many other places to consider. Examples include rotary clubs, churches, professional associations, and local or regional businesses. Although the reward amounts may be smaller, they might add up to big dollars, and some may have the benefit of being renewed in subsequent years. Special attention should be given to knowing the deadlines for each scholarship. Carefully research the type of candidate they are interested in helping, and tailor your information to show how you qualify, much like you would do with a résumé.

GRANTS

Grants also do not need to be repaid. They can be used to pay for education, training, books, tuition, or any school-related expenses. Students who have demonstrated financial need may receive grants. The most common type is the federal Pell Grant that offers a maximum of $6,495 for the 2021–2022 academic year. This maximum amount can change each year and has increased significantly in the past decade. For the most up-to-date numbers, visit http://studentaid.ed.gov. The Pell Grant will only be disbursed for a maximum of 12 semesters. Another grant that is available is the

Federal Supplemental Educational Opportunity Grant (FSEOG). This can be worth up to $4,000 annually. You must receive a Pell Grant to be eligible for the FSEOG grant. This grant is typically provided to those who have demonstrated exceptional financial need.

The Teacher Education Assistance for College and Higher Education (TEACH) grant may also be available, depending on the types of courses and the student's future career. This grant provides up to $4,000 annually and requires a signed TEACH grant agreement that the student will fulfill his or her teaching requirement within eight years of graduation or leaving school.

Another grant is the Iraq and Afghanistan service grant. These are available to students whose parents have died as a result of military service in Iraq or Afghanistan after 9/11. The grant award is equal to a Federal Pell Grant, or the cost of attendance, whichever is lower.

In addition to the federal grants, many states offer grants that are distributed through the schools' financial aid office, called institutional grants. Certain colleges and schools also provide grants to women, minority groups, and students in certain degree programs to encourage enrollment.

LOANS

Education loans can be a significant part of the financial aid package. These types of loans have become a significant part of the outstanding consumer debt. It has been reported by the Federal Reserve Bank of New York and the U.S. Department of Education that the total amount of student loans distributed in recent years was $100 billion annually. Additionally, they have reported that the total loan balances outstanding are expected to grow to over $1.55 trillion, an amount greater than the total owed nationally on consumer credit cards.[1]

Federal education loans that are available today originate from the Direct Loan program. Each college's financial aid office disburses the funds provided by the U.S. Department of Education. The interest rates and fees are evaluated annually, in July, and are adjusted by the federal government. The current interest rate range for 2020–2021 for federal loans dropped from 4.53% to 2.75%.[2] As a result of the recent COVID-19 pandemic, principal and interest on federal loans were suspended from March 31, 2020, to September 30, 2021.

Education loans are typically divided into four main categories:

1. *Stafford Loans*
   a. Stafford Loans were initially called the Federal Guaranteed Student Loan Program. In 1988, the loans were renamed to honor U.S. Senator Robert Stafford, based on his work with higher education.
   b. Stafford Loans are the most frequently disbursed loans. They are typically disbursed from the financial aid office directly to the student. (*Note:* The Stafford Loan can also be disbursed through a private lender, which will be discussed later.)
   c. One key element to the Stafford Loan is how the interest accrues while the student is in school. In some cases of extreme need, the federal government will make the interest payments during the time that the student is in school and for certain grace periods. This type of loan is commonly referred to as a *subsidized loan*. Subsidized loans are no longer available for graduate or professional education programs.
   d. The more common Stafford Loan makes paying the interest the responsibility of the borrower while in school and during the grace period. This type of loan is commonly referred to as an *unsubsidized loan*. Two options exist for paying the interest: pay the interest while still enrolled in school or have the interest added to the balance of the loan. The borrower must carefully calculate the cost of allowing this interest to be added onto the loan. This process is commonly called *negative amortization* and occurs when the amount of the loan exceeds the original amount borrowed. This not only adds to the amount of the loan but can extend the time for repayment.

e. The maximum amounts allowed for the Stafford Loans vary considerably based on many factors, including: the student's current year in school, type of schooling, subsidized versus unsubsidized cumulative amounts, and dependency status. The federal website with the most up-to-date information is: http://studentaid.ed.gov.

2. *Perkins Loans*

a. Perkins Loans are named after Carl D. Perkins, a former member of the U.S. House of Representatives from Kentucky. Mr. Perkins was an advocate for higher education, as well as a strong supporter of education for underprivileged students.

b. The Perkins Loan is typically provided to students who have demonstrated exceptional financial need. This program is run by the individual schools, which serve as the lender, using money provided by the federal government. This type of loan is provided only in a subsidized form; it offers a very low interest rate, a long repayment schedule of 10 years, and a slightly longer grace period to begin repayment.

c. Although each school's financial aid office will determine the amount each student receives, there are still annual and cumulative limits for this loan. For the 2021–2022 academic year, the maximum Perkins Loan allowed for undergraduate students is $5,500 with a cumulative maximum of $27,500. For graduate students, the annual maximum is $8,500 with a cumulative maximum of $60,000, including undergraduate loans.

3. *Parent Loans (PLUS loans),* formerly known as the Parent Loan for Undergraduate Students

a. There are times when parents of dependent children want to contribute financially to help with educational expenses. If they do not currently have funds to contribute, they may apply for a loan. PLUS loans are provided by the government and can only be obtained by contacting the financial aid office of the school, not a private lender. Currently, there is no maximum amount; however, the parent may only borrow amounts not covered by the student's current financial aid package, up to the total cost of attending the school.

b. For the PLUS loans, the parent is responsible for repaying the loan. The parent's creditworthiness is a factor in determining whether the loan will be granted. If the parent does not qualify, the student may have the option of taking out additional unsubsidized Stafford Loans.

c. One variant of the PLUS loan program is the Grad PLUS loan, which allows graduate students to borrow for educational expenses.

d. The PLUS loans and the Grad PLUS loans have higher interest rates than the Stafford and Perkins Loans, so they should be considered very carefully.

4. *Private Student Loans (also called Alternative Student Loans)*

a. Private student loans should also be considered very carefully. They tend to have higher interest rates than the government programs. In addition, the interest rates are commonly variable, which can make the payments more challenging to manage.

b. The three most common reasons that borrowers choose private student loans are:

1. To fund additional education expenses above the limits that the other programs provide.

2. There is no requirement for a FAFSA form to be completed. The loan is based upon the creditworthiness of the borrower.

3. To provide additional flexibility over the government loans to the borrower in terms of repayment or deferral while the student is in school.

In addition to traditional student loans, a new form of nontraditional lending has also started to be used to fund education expenses. It is known as *social lending* or *peer-to-peer lending*. This newest form of student loan comes from the private sector. The basic premise is that borrowers can post relevant information and stories regarding why they need money, and prospective lenders or individuals can view the information and choose to fund these aspirations. A large majority of social lending has been in the form of short-term lending, six months to three years. Thus, student lending has been a little slower to catch on primarily due to the time frame for repayment. However, a few websites have started to offer longer repayment periods. Examples of social lending sites are www.sofi.com, www.prosper.com, and www.lendingclub.com.

REPAYING YOUR LOANS

Acquiring the funds to attend school is only the beginning of the financial aid process. The much more lengthy part of the process is the repayment. Many of the different types of loans have differing *grace periods* before the first payment is due:

- Stafford Loans require repayment to begin six months after the student no longer attends school or has dropped below half-time enrollment.
- Perkins Loans require repayment to begin nine months after the student no longer attends school or has dropped below half-time enrollment.
- Federal PLUS loans, which are typically taken out by parents or graduate students, require repayment to begin 60 days after the loan is disbursed. The repayment can sometimes be deferred while the student is in school, but the interest will still accrue, much like an unsubsidized Stafford Loan.

Once repayment begins, federal loan borrowers have many options to consider regarding repaying the loan. The most common plans are:

1. *Standard Repayment.* This is one of the most common repayment plans. This repayment method typically has the lowest amount of interest paid. This method is a fixed monthly amount with a repayment term not to exceed 10 years (30 years for consolidated loans).

2. *Graduated Repayment.* This repayment plan allows newly graduated students to make lower payments as they start their careers and then slowly increase the amount of the monthly payment over the life of the loan. The payments usually increase every two years. This repayment term will not exceed 10 years (30 years for a consolidated loan).

3. *Extended Repayment.* This option lowers the monthly payment amounts. The length of the repayment term is up to 25 years. One point to consider is the substantial increase in the amount of total interest that will be paid over this time period.

4. *Income-Contingent Repayment.* This repayment plan is designed to provide the borrower with some leniency in terms of the amount to be repaid. The monthly payments are recalculated annually, based on the borrower's most recent reported income as well as total debt amount. The length of the repayment is up to 25 years. If the borrower follows through with the entire repayment plan, any remaining balance will be forgiven.

5. *Income-Sensitive Repayment.* This repayment plan is similar to the income-contingent repayment plan. The income-sensitive plan allows the borrower the option to set the monthly payment amount based upon a percentage of gross monthly income. The length of this repayment is limited to 15 years.

6. *Income-Based Repayment (IBR).* This repayment plan is currently calculated as 10 or 15 percent of discretionary income. To calculate discretionary income: Take your adjusted gross income (see Chapter 4) and subtract 150 percent of the poverty line for your state and family size. The plan provides a reduction to the previously discussed income-contingent and income-sensitive repayment plans. This program provides forgiveness beyond a 20- or 25-year time period, if all prior payments were made on time, depending on when the loan was first distributed.

7. *Pay as You Earn Repayment (PAYE).* The repayment amount is capped at 10 percent of discretionary income (see IBR plan above to calculate). This program provides forgiveness beyond a 20-year time period, if all prior payments were made

EXHIBIT 7-C

Education pays

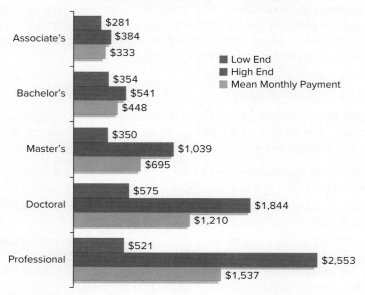

Monthly Student Loan Payments by Degree

Note: Data are for persons age 25 and over. Earnings are for full-time wage and salary workers.
Source: U.S. Bureau of Labor Statistics, Current Population Survey. Date accessed: February 15, 2021.

on time. The plan does require proof of a partial financial hardship to qualify for the more favorable terms compared to the IBR plan. This program was phased out in 2011 by the revised pay as you earn repayment plan.

8. *Revised Pay as You Earn Repayment (REPAYE).* This is the newest repayment option. This repayment plan is open to all borrowers regardless of when disbursements were made. Loan types include Stafford Loans and PLUS loans (excluding parent loans). This program provides forgiveness beyond a 20-year time period (undergraduates) and a 25-year time period (graduate), if all prior payments were made timely.

All eight plans are available for student loans, but only the first three plans are available for PLUS loans to parents. The amount paid per month can vary widely by degree obtained as well as by the amount borrowed (See Exhibit 7-C)

CONSOLIDATION LOAN Another attractive repayment option for borrowers is to combine all their student loans into one loan, and thus one convenient monthly payment. Just like the extended repayment plan, this method will lower the total monthly payment amount and increase the length of the loan up to 30 years. Remember to carefully consider the increase in the amount of total interest that will be paid over this time period. Unless you are struggling to make the individual loan payments, typically there is no advantage to consolidating loans other than ease of administration (i.e., one payment).

Private loans may have the option of refinancing to obtain a lower interest rate based on an improved credit situation for the borrower. However, in most cases, a federal consolidated loan does not offer this option.

smart money minute

One thing to keep in mind, any amounts forgiven on student loans will be considered taxable income to the borrower.

Source: https://www.irs.gov/taxtopics/tc431 (accessed February 15, 2021).

STUDENT LOAN DEFAULT STATISTICS The ease of obtaining money and the ever-increasing student loan balances that new graduates must begin to repay have created many challenges. These issues, combined with a significant number of graduates who are vying for a smaller pool of available jobs, has created some very unfortunate side effects relating to students' abilities to repay loans. The percentage of student loan borrowers who are more than 90 days late on their student loan payments has increased significantly in the last decade and has remained high compared to other types of debt (see Exhibit 7-D).

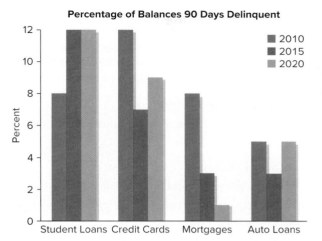

Percentage of Balances 90 Days Delinquent

EXHIBIT 7-D

Proportion of borrowers 90+ days delinquent by loan type

Source: Federal Reserve Bank of New York Consumer Credit Panel/Equifax. Date accessed: February 15, 2021.

Default rates on student loans have increased dramatically for students who have attended all types of higher education institutions: public, private, and for-profit. Student loans will typically not be included in bankruptcy. There are no limitations on the number of years that the lender can seek repayment. For federal student loans, the government can garnish wages, withhold tax refunds, or confiscate other federal benefits for which you might be eligible. Careful consideration should be given to the costs associated with repaying loans.

LOAN DEFERMENT Loan deferments allow you to temporarily stop making payments on existing student loans. The most common reasons for the deferments are reenrollment in school, demonstrated financial hardship, unemployment, and military deployment.

LOAN FORBEARANCE Loan forbearance also allows you to temporarily stop making payments on existing student loans. However, this should only be considered as a temporary solution if you are unable to make your monthly payment because a loan in forbearance will continue to accrue interest the entire time. If you are at least able to make payments to cover the interest owed, this would help with the overall balance over a long period of time.

LOAN FORGIVENESS Loan forgiveness is the option to have all or a portion of your student loan forgiven (paid off on your behalf). The most common forgiveness options are for volunteer work or public or military service.

The Public Service Loan Forgiveness Program was established by the College Cost Reduction and Access Act of 2007. Under this program, full-time, qualifying public service employees who make 120 qualifying loan payments on eligible Federal Direct Loans will have the balance of their Federal Direct Loans forgiven. Eligibility for the public service position includes working for the government or an organized nonprofit organization, service in the Peace Corps or AmeriCorps, or even working for a private organization that provides public service.

Many of the above-mentioned organizations also have specific programs to allow a portion of the loan to be canceled even sooner. For example:

- The Peace Corps provides partial cancellation of Perkins Loans (15 percent for each year of service, up to 70 percent in total).

- AmeriCorps volunteers who serve for 12 months can receive $6,345 to be used toward cancellation of their loan.

- Military service also offers a cancellation program. Students who enlist in the Army National Guard may be eligible for up to $10,000 of cancellation of student loans.

- In addition, there are a variety of other programs for teachers who serve in low-income areas, work with students with disabilities, or work in high-need schools. Law students can also find loan forgiveness programs for serving with nonprofit or public interest organizations. Medical students may also be eligible for loan forgiveness for performing certain medical research or working in low-income or remote areas. It is strongly advised that you review each program's requirements for eligibility, conditions of employment, and repayment to ensure that you are a good candidate for the program.

LOAN CANCELLATION (DISCHARGE)   In very special circumstances, student loans may be permanently canceled. The most common situations include:

- Death.
- Total and permanent disability.
- School closure (while you were enrolled).
- Fraud by the school (e.g., in the event of forged promissory notes, the school owes the lender a refund).
- Bankruptcy (very rare because the bankruptcy court would need to establish that repayment would create a significant hardship).

WORK-STUDY PROGRAMS

Aside from loans, there are other ways to earn money to pay for educational expenses. The Federal Work-Study Program is available at many schools. It is commonly included as part of the financial aid package. Students who decline this option are expected to fund the amount from another source. Some students like the options that the program offers: They can work on campus without needing additional transportation, apply to a variety of positions that interest them, and get to know faculty and staff that they may want to work with on teaching or research assignments. Some students decline the option in favor of higher-paying jobs off campus. You should consider very carefully the opportunity costs with this decision (fuel costs, commuting time, wardrobe needs, etc.).

Your Future and Financial Aid

Navigating the process of financing an education can be very daunting and time consuming, but the rewards are very high. Finding the money for school and repaying the loans in a manner that works best for your personal situation can lead to long-term success, improved credit scores, higher salaries, a lower potential for future unemployment, and higher rates of home ownership (see Exhibit 7-E). One excellent source for choosing a school, and the financial aid package for your needs, is the College Affordability and Transparency Center (http://collegecost.ed.gov/). This is a one-stop website that you can use to evaluate a college based upon net price, average student debt, state funding, graduation rates, and much more. It is very important for your financial future that you find the most affordable education that fits your budget, future career, and long-term financial goals.

EXHIBIT 7-E Home ownership and education

Home ownership by Age 30	
Bachelor's degree or higher, no student debt	40%
Bachelor's degree or higher, student debt	33%
Associate degree, no student debt	31%
Associate degree, student debt	24%
No college	22%

Sources: New York Fed Consumer Credit Panel/Equifax and National Student Clearinghouse. Accessed February 15, 2021.

Consumer Purchasing Strategies and Legal Protection

8

ichaeljung/Shutterstock

LEARNING OBJECTIVES

LO8-1 Identify strategies for effective consumer buying.

LO8-2 Implement a process for making consumer purchases.

LO8-3 Determine steps to take to resolve consumer problems.

LO8-4 Evaluate legal alternatives available to consumers.

The Chapter 8 Appendix provides expanded coverage of consumer protection agencies and organizations.

APPENDIX

Financial Literacy
IN **YOUR LIFE**

▶ **What if you . . .** continually spend more than you plan to spend? Or are you tempted by scams that promise you will "earn easy money" or "get out of debt fast"? Unplanned and careless buying reduces your potential for long-term financial security. Impulse buying activities of a few dollars a week can cost you

thousands in just a couple of years. What actions would you take?

You might . . . carefully track current spending. Then, make a list for shopping that is based on your budget and needs. Next, learn to avoid the influences of advertising and marketing to cause you to overspend. Many buying strategies are for wiser purchasing choices.

Now, what would you do? What strategies do you use to reduce unplanned spending? You will be able to monitor your progress using the Your Personal Finance Roadmap and Dashboard feature at the end of the chapter.

| my life | **BETTER SHOPPING CHOICES** |

Recreational shopping and impulse buying are major causes of financial trouble. In contrast, wise consumer decisions can result in lower spending and better long-term financial security.

For each of the following shopping behaviors, circle Agree, Neutral, or Disagree to indicate your attitude toward this action.

1. Buying brand-name items is usually the best strategy for my personal situation.　　Agree　Neutral　Disagree

2. The use of a buying process to gather information and make decisions is useful for me when planning purchases.　　Agree　Neutral　Disagree

3. I know what actions to take when complaining about a consumer purchase.　　Agree　Neutral　Disagree

4. The legal actions available to consumers may be of value to me in the future.　　Agree　Neutral　Disagree

As you study this chapter, you will encounter "My Life" boxes with additional information and resources related to these items.

Consumer Buying Activities

LO8-1

Identify strategies for effective consumer buying.

FINANCIAL IMPLICATIONS OF CONSUMER DECISIONS

Whether in a store, at a street market, or using a shopping app, every person making buying decisions is a consumer. Regardless of age, income, or household situation, we all use goods and services. Daily buying decisions involve a trade-off between current spending and saving for the future.

Economic, social, and personal factors affect daily buying habits (see Exhibit 8-1). These factors influence your spending, saving, and investing choices, and when combined with wise buying activities can contribute to your long-term financial security. The recent pandemic resulted in shopping trends including increased online buying along with expanded home delivery and curbside pickup.

EXHIBIT 8-1   Buying influences and wise spending strategies

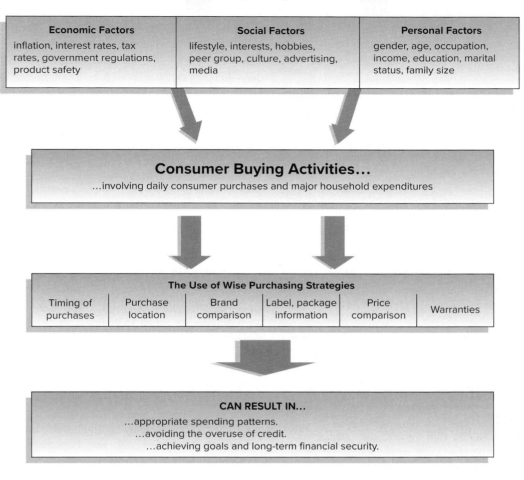

Economic Factors	Social Factors	Personal Factors
inflation, interest rates, tax rates, government regulations, product safety	lifestyle, interests, hobbies, peer group, culture, advertising, media	gender, age, occupation, income, education, marital status, family size

Consumer Buying Activities...
...involving daily consumer purchases and major household expenditures

The Use of Wise Purchasing Strategies

Timing of purchases	Purchase location	Brand comparison	Label, package information	Price comparison	Warranties

CAN RESULT IN...
...appropriate spending patterns.
...avoiding the overuse of credit.
...achieving goals and long-term financial security.

When making buying decisions, consider opportunity costs to maximize your purchasing satisfaction. Commonly overlooked trade-offs when buying include:

- Paying a more over time when buying on credit for an item needed now.
- Buying unknown, possibly poor-quality brands that are less expensive.
- Buying online to save time and money but may make it difficult to return, replace, or repair an item.
- Taking time and effort to comparison shop to save money and obtain better after-sale service.

Buying decisions reflect your personality, life situation, values, and goals. Combine this with the complexity of the marketplace, and you can see that most purchase decisions require analysis.

WISE PURCHASING STRATEGIES

Comparison shopping is the process of evaluating alternative stores, brands, and prices. In contrast, **impulse buying** is unplanned purchasing, which often creates financial problems. Psychological factors affecting compulsive shopping can be revealed by these questions: Do you have an overwhelming desire to buy things? Do you buy to change your mood? Do your shopping habits hurt your relationships? Does the amount spent damage your finances? Several buying techniques are available to avoid impulse buying and practice wise buying.

impulse buying Unplanned buying.

Financial Literacy for My Life

BUYING CALENDAR

Throughout the year, certain items tend to go on sale at the same time each year. Planning your purchases can result in great savings.

January—exercise equipment, bedding and linens, carpeting and flooring, televisions and electronics, small kitchen appliances, winter coats, winter sports equipment

February—televisions, winter apparel, winter sporting accessories, air conditioners, gardening tools, grills, mattresses, video games, Presidents Day sales

March—golf clubs, grills, digital cameras, exercise equipment, air conditioners, sewing machines, office furniture

April—vacuums, sewing machines, jewelry, carpets, computers, Tax Day specials and discounts

May—spring cleaning products, cookware, small appliances, coffee makers, blenders, mattresses, baby strollers and high chairs, paint, outdoor furniture, Memorial Day sales furniture and other items

June—cookware, small appliances, semiannual sale on undergarments, gym memberships, exercise equipment, summer sports equipment, furniture, graduation and Father's Day specials

July—summer clothing, swimsuits, paint, personal electronics, sporting goods, jewelry, furniture, patriotic items for Fourth of July celebrations

August—air conditioners, backpacks, school supplies, swimsuits, outdoor furniture, lawnmowers, snowblowers, camping equipment, end-of-summer clearance sales

September—lawnmowers, snowblowers, mattresses, smartphones, computers, paint, major appliances, Labor Day sales

October—computers, gas grills, outdoor furniture, lawnmowers, jeans, candy for Halloween

November—cookware, small appliances, tablets and laptop computers, gaming systems, gas grills, major appliances (end-of-month), televisions, Black Friday sales

December—toys, motor vehicles, gas grills, kitchen cookware, televisions, small appliances, major appliances, wedding dresses, holiday decorations late in the month.

smart money minute

Financial difficulties occur when you believe something is a NEED when it is actually a WANT. Actual needs involve food, air, water, shelter, health care, clothing, and maybe internet access. However, time online can result in unneeded purchases. To avoid this, 20SomethingFinance.com suggests:

- Don't buy an item right away. Delay a purchase to consider the value.
- Review delayed purchases in a month to determine if the urge still exists, and if money is available.
- Return items, as allowed, when the purchase does not meet expectations.
- Put a note in your wallet or on your debit card: "Do you REALLY need this?"
- Use websites and apps to compare prices and obtain coupons.
- For large purchases, don't just consider the price. Calculate how many hours you need to work to pay for the item.

cooperative A nonprofit organization whose member-owners may save money on certain products or services.

TIMING PURCHASES Certain items go on sale the same time each year. You can obtain bargains by buying winter clothing in mid- or late winter, or summer clothing in mid- or late summer. People save by buying holiday items at reduced prices in late December and early January. See the *Financial Literacy for My Life: Buying Calendar* feature for more information on timing purchases.

Weather reports and other news can help you plan. A crop failure can result in higher prices for food products. Changing economic conditions and political conflicts around the world may result in higher prices and reduced supplies of certain products. Awareness of these situations can assist you in buying when prices are lower.

PURCHASE LOCATION Your decision to buy from a certain retailer will be influenced by location, price, product selection, and services. Competition and technology have resulted in greater emphasis on superstores, specialty shops, and online buying. A changing shopping environment can provide consumers with greater choice, potentially lower prices, and a need to carefully evaluate alternatives.

A lesser-known, but useful, shopping alternative is the **cooperative,** a nonprofit organization whose member-owners save money on various products and services. As discussed in Chapter 5, a credit union is an example of a financial cooperative. Food cooperatives, often organized by a community group or church, buy grocery items in large quantities. The savings on bulk purchases are passed on to the co-op's members through lower food prices. Cooperatives have also been organized to provide child care, recreational equipment, health care, cable television, and burial services.

Buying at "dollar stores" can result in bargains on many items. However, beware of expired food products, "look-alikes" posing as famous brands, items that are more expensive than the sale price at other stores, and potentially unsafe imported products such as extension cords, toys, vitamins, and jewelry.

BRAND COMPARISON Food and other products are available in various brands. *National-brand* products are highly advertised items available in many stores. You are probably familiar with brands such as Green Giant, Nabisco, Coca-Cola, Pepsi, Kellogg's, Kraft, Apple, and Samsung. Brand-name products are usually more expensive than nonbrand products, but they offer a consistency of quality for which people are willing to pay.

Consumers have a wide variety of shopping alternatives from which to choose.
SeventyFour/Shutterstock

Store-brand and *private-label* products, sold by a store chain, are low-cost alternatives to famous-name products. These products are identified with a specific retail chain, such as Safeway, Kroger, Walgreen's, and Walmart. Since store-brand products are often produced by the same manufacturers of brand-name items, these lower-cost alternatives can result in significant savings. The *Financial Literacy Calculations: Analyzing Consumer Purchases* feature shows how these factors might be analyzed when making a purchasing decision.

LABEL INFORMATION Some label information is helpful; other information is promotional. Federal law requires that food labels contain the company name and address, ingredients, nutrients, and food allergy warnings. Product labeling for appliances includes information about operating costs, to assist you in selecting the most energy-efficient models. **Open dating** describes the freshness or shelf life of a perishable product. Phrases such as "Use before May 6, 2023" or "Not to be sold after October 8" appear on most grocery items. However, these labels can be confusing. Most expiration dates relate to quality, not safety. Items used after the "sell by" date are likely to still be safe for consumption. Canned and packaged foods, if not opened, will usually be safe beyond the expiration date.

open dating Information about freshness or shelf life found on the package of a perishable product.

PRICE COMPARISON **Unit pricing** uses a standard unit of measurement to compare the prices of packages of different sizes. To calculate the unit price, divide the price by the number of units of measurement, such as ounces, pounds, gallons, or number of sheets (for items such as paper towels and facial tissues). Then, compare the unit prices for various sizes, brands, and stores.

unit pricing The use of a standard unit of measurement to compare the prices of packages of different sizes.

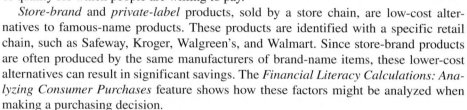

EXAMPLE: Unit Pricing

To calculate the unit price of an item, divide the cost by the number of units. For example, a 64-ounce product costing $8.32 would be calculated in this manner:

Unit price = $8.32 ÷ 64
= $0.13, or 13 cents an ounce

How about you? What are some situations in which you might use unit pricing calculations?

Coupons and rebates can provide better pricing for wise consumers. A family saving about $8 a week on their groceries by using coupons will save $416 over a year and $2,080 over five years (not counting interest). A **rebate** is a partial refund of the price of a product.

rebate A partial refund of the price of a product.

Financial Literacy Calculations

ANALYZING CONSUMER PURCHASES

NET PRESENT VALUE OF A CONSUMER PURCHASE: IS A HYBRID CAR WORTH THE COST?

The time value of money (explained in Chapter 1) may be used to evaluate the financial benefits of a consumer purchase. For example, when deciding to buy a hybrid car, the money saved on gas would be considered a cash *inflow* (since money not going out is like money coming in). The additional cost between a hybrid and a fuel-version vehicle would be the current cash *outflow*. If the car has an expected life of eight years, the *net present value* calculations might be as shown here:

Step 1: Estimate the annual savings on gas (for example, 8,000 miles at $3 a gallon), with a vehicle getting 50 miles per gallon rather than 25 miles per gallon.

Step 2: Calculate the present value (PV) of a series using either the time value of money tables (Chapter 1 Appendix) or a financial calculator. Assume a 2 percent interest rate, 8 years.

Step 3: Subtract the difference in cost of a hybrid car (compared with a gasoline-powered car).

Annual gas savings $960	PV of annual savings $7,032	–	Vehicle cost difference $ 6,000

The result: $1,032 is a positive (favorable) net present value of the savings from a hybrid car compared to a gasoline-powered car. A negative net present value would indicate that the financial aspects of the purchase are not desirable.

This analysis for buying a hybrid car or electric vehicle will vary based on other factors, such as maintenance costs, miles driven per year, and gas prices. Hybrid car cost calculators are also available online. Remember that this decision will also be influenced by personal preferences and social factors. This calculation format may be used to assess the financial benefits of consumer purchases by comparing the present value of the cost savings with the price of the item.

CONSUMER BUYING MATRIX

Buying alternatives may be evaluated based on personal values, goals, available time and money, and specific needs

(continued)

When comparing prices, remember that

- More store convenience (location, hours, sales staff) usually means higher prices.
- Ready-to-use products have higher prices.
- Large packages are usually the best buy; however, compare the unit price.
- "Sale" may not always mean saving money.
- Many websites and apps are available with prices, coupons, and rebates.

Exhibit 8-2 provides a summary of wise online buying.

WARRANTIES

warranty A written guarantee from the manufacturer or distributor of a product that specifies the conditions under which the product can be returned, replaced, or repaired.

Most products come with some assurance of quality. A **warranty** is a written guarantee from the manufacturer or distributor that specifies the conditions under which the product can be returned, replaced, or repaired. An *express warranty,* usually in written form, for product size, quality, quantity, and features. This buying matrix can be used to evaluate alternative buying choices.

In this example, the following steps are used to evaluate three brands of notebook computers.

Step 1. *Identify attributes such as features, performance, design, and warranty; assign a weight based on the importance of each attribute.*

Step 2. *Select the brands to be evaluated.*

Item __Notebook Computer__

Information Sources/Comments __Consumer magazine/brand C slow compared to__

__others tested; Friend/brand B performs well__

		Alternatives					
Attribute	**Weight**	**Brand** A **Price** $1,100		**Brand** B **Price** $950		**Brand** C **Price** $875	
		Rating (1-10)	Weighted Score	Rating (1-10)	Weighted Score	Rating (1-10)	Weighted Score
• Features	.3	6	1.8	8	2.4	10	3
• Performance	.4	9	3.6	7	2.8	5	2
• Design	.1	8	.8	8	.8	7	.7
• Warranty	.2	9	1.8	6	1.2	4	.8
■ Totals	1.0		8.0		7.2		6.5

Step 2 — (Brand row)

Step 1 — (Attribute rows)

Step 4 — (Totals row)

Step 3

Step 3. *Rate (from 1 to 10) each brand based on the attributes identified in step 1. Multiply the rating number by the weight. For example, in this example, brand A received a rating of 6 for "features," giving a weighted score of 1.8 (6 × .3).*

Step 4. *Total and assess the results. Besides the numeric evaluation, consider factors such as price, store reputation, and your needs.*

When researching a consumer purchase, identify the attributes important to you. Helpful sources are friends, salespeople, media sources such as *Consumer Reports,* and online reviews. The specific attributes will vary depending on the product or service. When evaluating services, consider price, location, employee training, experience, and reputation.

is created by the seller or manufacturer and has two forms: the full warranty and the limited warranty. A *full warranty* states that a defective product can be fixed or replaced during a reasonable amount of time. A *limited warranty* covers only certain aspects of the product, such as parts, or requires the buyer to incur part of the cost for shipping or repairs. An *implied warranty* covers a product's intended use or other basic understandings that are not in writing. For example, an implied *warranty of title* indicates that the seller has the right to sell the product. An implied *warranty of merchantability* guarantees that the product is fit for the ordinary uses for which it is intended: A toaster must toast bread, and an MP3 player must play audio files. Implied warranties vary from state to state.

my life | 1

Buying brand-name items is usually the best strategy for my personal situation.

Experienced shoppers are an excellent source of wise buying strategies. Talk with friends, relatives, and other people you know about wise buying actions that save time and money.

EXHIBIT 8-2   Wise online buying activities

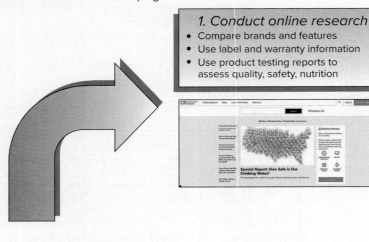

1. Conduct online research
- Compare brands and features
- Use label and warranty information
- Use product testing reports to assess quality, safety, nutrition

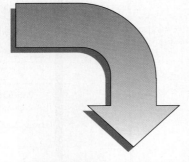

2. Compare retailers
- Consider both stores and online
- Evaluate price, service, product quality, warranties, shipping cost and time, return policy, location
- Determine reputation, customer service

4. Plan for future purchases
- Keep receipts, other documents
- Know return, complaint process
- Watch emails for special offers
- Evaluate time, effort involved

3. Make Purchase
- Use secure buying website
- Seek discounts, coupons
- Select payment method based on security, fees, other factors

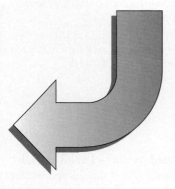

Source: ConsumerReports.org; Google LLC; PayPal; Amazon.com

service contract An agreement between a business and a consumer to cover the repair costs of a product.

USED-CAR WARRANTIES   The Federal Trade Commission (FTC) requires businesses that sell used cars to place a buyer's guide sticker in the windows of cars for sale. This disclosure must state whether the car comes with a warranty and, if so, what protection the dealer will provide. If no warranty is offered, the car is sold "as is," and the dealer assumes no responsibility for any repairs, regardless of any oral claims.

Most used cars sold by dealers come without a warranty. If you buy such a car, you will need to pay for any repairs to correct problems. Be sure to get in writing any promises made by a salesperson.

The Buyer's Guide required by the FTC encourages you to have the used car inspected by a mechanic and to get all promises in writing. You also receive a list of the 14 major systems of an automobile indicating major problems that may occur in these systems. This list is helpful when comparing vehicles and warranties offered by different dealers. FTC used-car regulations do not apply to vehicles purchased from private owners.

While a used car may not have an express warranty, most states have implied warranties that protect the rights of a used-car buyer. Because an implied warranty of merchantability guarantees a product must do what it is supposed to do, a used car is guaranteed to run—at least for a while!

Online shopping and information sources provide consumers with convenience.
Ariel Skelley/Getty Images

NEW-CAR WARRANTIES New-car warranties provide buyers with an assurance of quality. These warranties vary in the time, mileage, and parts they cover. The main conditions of a new-car warranty are (1) coverage of basic parts against defects; (2) power train coverage for the engine, transmission, and drivetrain; and (3) the corrosion warranty, which usually applies only to holes due to rust, not to surface rust. Other important conditions include whether the warranty is transferable to other owners of the car and details about the charges, if any, that will be incurred for major repairs, in the form of a *deductible.*

SERVICE CONTRACTS **Service contracts** are agreements between a business and a consumer to cover the repair costs of a product. Frequently called *extended warranties,* they are not warranties. For a fee, these agreements protect the buyer from high costs resulting from certain repairs and other losses. Beware of service contracts that offer coverage for three years but really only cover two since the item has a manufacturer's one-year warranty.

Automotive service contracts cover repairs not included in the manufacturer's warranty. Service contracts range from $800 to over $1,500, and they may not cover everything you might expect. These contracts usually cover failure of the engine cooling system; however, some contracts exclude coverage if the failure results from overheating.

Because of cost and exclusions, some service contracts may not be a wise financial decision. You can minimize your concern about expensive repairs by setting aside money to cover those costs. Then, if you need repairs, the funds will be available.

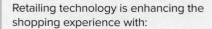

personal fintech

Retailing technology is enhancing the shopping experience with:

- Increased online buying opportunities as small retailers were forced to connect as result of the COVID-19 pandemic.
- Social media stories and video ads with an option to buy.
- AmazonGo stores that allow shoppers to pay with an app using *just walk out* technology.
- Artificial intelligence for customer service and buying recommendations.
- Shopping personalization that suggests a store movement pattern based on frequently purchased items.
- V-commerce (using virtual reality) that allows shoppers to try on products or using an item in a cyber setting.
- The Internet of Things (IoT), which connects a smart refrigerator to order needed groceries.
- Resale apps and websites to buy used designer apparel and accessories, including luxury handbags, jewelry, and watches. Several major retailers sell popular brands of preowned clothing and shoes online.

 **PRACTICE QUIZ 8-1**

 PFP Sheet 32 Unit Pricing Worksheet

1. What factors commonly influence daily buying choices?
2. How are daily buying decisions related to overall financial planning?
3. What types of brands are commonly available to consumers?
4. In what situations could comparing prices be of value in purchasing decisions?
5. How does a service contract differ from a warranty? What rights do purchasers of products have even if no written warranty exists?

Major Consumer Purchases: Buying Motor Vehicles

LO8-2

Implement a process for making consumer purchases.

Complex shopping decisions should be approached using a decision-making process. Exhibit 8-3 presents effective steps for purchasing a motor vehicle.

PHASE 1—PRESHOPPING ACTIVITIES

First, define your needs and obtain relevant product information. These activities are the foundation for buying decisions to achieve your goals.

PROBLEM IDENTIFICATION   Effective decision-making should start with an open mind. Some people always buy the same brand, when another lower-priced brand could serve their needs or another brand at the same price might provide better quality. A narrow view of the problem can be a weakness in your analysis. You may think the problem is "I need to have a car" when the real problem is "I need transportation."

INFORMATION GATHERING   Information is power. The better informed you are, the wiser buying decisions you will make. Some people spend little time gathering and evaluating buying information. At the other extreme are those who spend extensive time gathering information. While information is necessary for wise purchasing,

EXHIBIT 8-3

A research-based approach for purchasing a motor vehicle

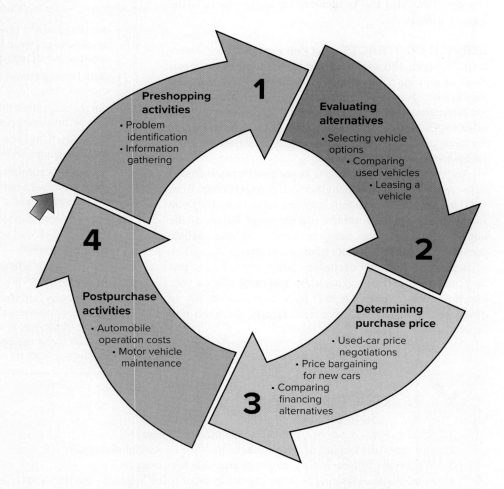

1
Preshopping activities
• Problem identification
• Information gathering

Evaluating alternatives
• Selecting vehicle options
• Comparing used vehicles
• Leasing a vehicle

2

Determining purchase price
• Used-car price negotiations
• Price bargaining for new cars
• Comparing financing alternatives

3

Postpurchase activities
• Automobile operation costs
• Motor vehicle maintenance

4

too much information can create confusion and frustration. Following are common information sources:

- *Personal contacts,* such as family, friends, and others, can provide information about product performance, brand quality, and prices.

- *Business organizations* offer advertising, product labels, and packaging with basic facts about price, ingredients, quality, and availability.

- *Media sources* (television, radio, newspapers, magazines, websites, apps) offer purchase location availability, prices, shopping suggestions, and product reviews from other consumers.

- *Independent testing organizations,* such as Consumers Union (publisher of *Consumer Reports*), report the quality of products and services. Underwriters Laboratories (UL) tests products for electrical and fire safety.

- *Government agencies,* at the local, state, and federal levels, provide information, complaint handling, and educational programs. The appendix for this chapter provides contact information for government agencies.

The use of a buying process to gather information and make decisions is useful for me when planning purchases.

As in most settings, knowledge is power. For various sources of consumer buying information, government agencies, and consumer organizations, see the appendixes following Chapter 3 and Chapter 8.

Basic information about car buying can be obtained at www.edmunds.com, www.caranddriver.com, www.autoweb.com, www.autotrader.com, and www.msn.com/en-us/autos. Consumers Union (www.ConsumerReports.org) offers a computerized car cost data service. Car-buying services, such as www.acscorp.com and www.autobytel.com, allow you to order your vehicle online.

PHASE 2—EVALUATING ALTERNATIVES

Most purchasing decisions have several acceptable alternatives. Ask yourself: Is it possible to delay the purchase or to do without the item? Should I pay with cash, an app or debit card, or use credit? Which brands should I consider? Does the price, quality, and service vary at different buying locations? Is it possible to rent the item instead of buying? Considering alternatives will result in more effective decisions.

Research shows that prices vary for all products. For a camera, prices may range from under $100 to well over $500. The price of aspirin may range from less than $1 to over $3 for 100 tablets containing 325 mg. While differences in quality and features exist among the cameras, the aspirin are equivalent in quantity and quality.

Some people believe comparison shopping is a waste of time. While this may be true in some situations, comparison shopping can be beneficial when: (1) buying expensive or complex items; (2) buying items that you purchase often; (3) the process can be done easily, such as with advertisements, catalogs, or online; (4) different sellers offer different prices and services; and (5) product quality or prices vary greatly.

SELECTING VEHICLE OPTIONS Optional equipment for cars may be viewed in three categories: (1) *mechanical devices* to improve performance, such as a larger engine; (2) *convenience options,* including power seats, air conditioning, sound systems, power locks, and tinted glass; and (3) *aesthetic features* that add to the vehicle's visual appeal, such as metallic paint, special trim, and upholstery.

High-tech safety features help us to avoid crashes. Forward-collision warning (FCW) systems alert drivers of a potential crash with signals. Automatic emergency braking (AEB) senses a potential collision and begins braking. Blind-spot warning technology provides warnings about vehicles not in the driver's line of vision. Adaptive cruise control (ACC) adjusts vehicle speed based on traffic conditions. Lane-keeping assist (LKA) and lane-departure warning (LDW) offer slight steering adjustments and

smart money minute

Electric vehicles (EVs) are increasing in popularity as a result of environmental benefits, nearly silent engine sound, potential tax credits, lower maintenance costs, and smartphone apps to program charging times and to heat or cool the cabin before driving. Concerns associated with EVs have included the higher initial cost, short driving ranges for some models, slow charging time, charging station availability, and loss of cargo space for the battery pack. The two main EV types are battery electric vehicles (BEVs) that only run on electricity, and plug-in hybrid electric vehicles (PHEVs) that use electricity for a limited distance before switching to a gas-electric hybrid mode. Some models have an onboard generator to extend driving distances.

warnings. Vehicle features to assist drivers also include larger mirrors, swivel-seat cushions, pedal extenders, and left-foot accelerators. The most recent models have sensors to provide map makers, city planners, and utility companies with data on lane markings, speeds, potholes, construction area, traffic signals, utility facilities, and pedestrians and cyclists.

COMPARING USED VEHICLES In recent years, an average used car cost about $19,000 less than a new car. However, the pandemic caused an increased demand and higher prices for vehicles as people avoided public transportation and ride sharing. Common sources to buy a used vehicle include:

- New-car dealers offer late-model vehicles and may include a warranty, resulting in higher prices than at other sources.
- Used-car dealers usually offer older vehicles. Warranties, if available, will be limited. Lower prices may be available.
- Individuals selling their own cars can be a bargain if the vehicle was well maintained. Few consumer protection regulations apply to private-party sales. Caution is highly recommended.
- Auctions and dealers sell automobiles previously owned by businesses, auto rental companies, and government agencies.
- Used-car superstores, such as CarMax, offer a large inventory of previously owned vehicles.
- Online used-car businesses, such as www.carvana.com and www.autotrader.com.

Certified, preowned (CPO) vehicles are nearly new cars with the original manufacturer's guarantee of quality. The rigorous inspection and repair process means a higher price than for other used vehicles. CPO programs were created to increase demand for low-mileage vehicles returned at the end of a lease.

The appearance of a used car can be deceptive. A well-maintained engine may be inside a body with rust; a clean, shiny exterior may conceal major operational problems. Therefore, conduct a used-car inspection as described in Exhibit 8-4. Have a trained, trusted mechanic of *your* choice check the car to estimate needed repair costs. This action will help avoid surprises. People often buy used vehicles with the odometer rolled back and pay more than they should due to fraudulent mileage totals.

LEASING A MOTOR VEHICLE *Leasing* is a contractual agreement with monthly payments for the use of an automobile over a set time period, typically three, four, or five years. At the end of the lease term, the vehicle is usually returned.

The main advantages of leasing include: (1) only a small cash outflow may be required for the security deposit, whereas buying on credit may require a large down payment; (2) monthly lease payments are often lower than monthly financing payments; (3) the lease agreement provides detailed records for business purposes; and (4) an ability to secure a more expensive vehicle for a short period, allowing you to obtain a new vehicle more often.

Major drawbacks of leasing include: (1) no ownership interest in the vehicle; (2) a need to meet requirements similar to qualifying for credit; and (3) possible additional costs incurred for extra mileage, certain repairs, returning the car early, or even moving to another state.

EXHIBIT 8-4   Checking out a used car

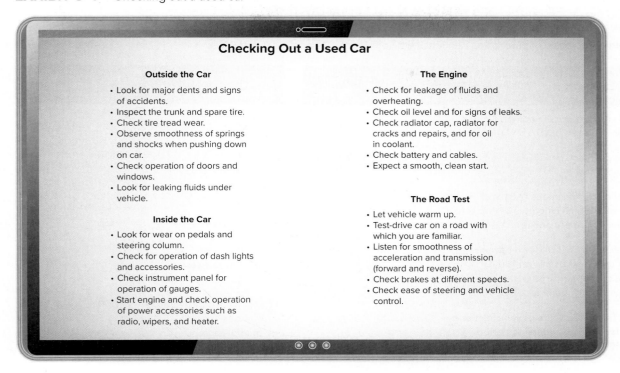

Checking Out a Used Car

Outside the Car
- Look for major dents and signs of accidents.
- Inspect the trunk and spare tire.
- Check tire tread wear.
- Observe smoothness of springs and shocks when pushing down on car.
- Check operation of doors and windows.
- Look for leaking fluids under vehicle.

Inside the Car
- Look for wear on pedals and steering column.
- Check for operation of dash lights and accessories.
- Check instrument panel for operation of gauges.
- Start engine and check operation of power accessories such as radio, wipers, and heater.

The Engine
- Check for leakage of fluids and overheating.
- Check oil level and for signs of leaks.
- Check radiator cap, radiator for cracks and repairs, and for oil in coolant.
- Check battery and cables.
- Expect a smooth, clean start.

The Road Test
- Let vehicle warm up.
- Test-drive car on a road with which you are familiar.
- Listen for smoothness of acceleration and transmission (forward and reverse).
- Check brakes at different speeds.
- Check ease of steering and vehicle control.

When leasing, the dealer sells the vehicle through a financing company. As a result, be sure you know the true cost, including:

1. The *capitalized cost,* which is the price of the vehicle. The average car buyer pays about 92 percent of the list price for a vehicle; the average leasing arrangement has a capitalized cost of 96 percent of the list price.

2. The *money factor,* which is the interest rate being paid on the capitalized cost.

3. The monthly payment and number of payments.

4. The *residual value,* which is the expected value of the vehicle at the end of the lease.

At the end of the lease, you may choose to return, keep, or sell the vehicle. If the current market value is greater than the residual value, you may be able to sell it for a profit. If the residual value is greater than the market value (which is the typical case), returning the vehicle to the leasing company is usually recommended. The *Financial Literacy Calculations: Buying versus Leasing an Automobile* feature provides additional details for this consumer decision.

PHASE 3—DETERMINING PURCHASE PRICE

Real estate and automobile purchases often involve price negotiation. Negotiation may be used in other buying situations to obtain a lower price or additional features. Two factors for effective negotiation are (1) having all necessary information about the product and buying situation, and (2) dealing with a person who has the authority to give you a lower price or additional features, such as the business owner or store manager.

USED-CAR PRICE NEGOTIATION   Determine a fair vehicle price by searching online for prices of comparable vehicles, using sources such as *Edmund's Used Car Prices* (www.edmunds.com) and the *Kelley Blue Book* (www.kbb.com). Several

Financial Literacy Calculations

BUYING VERSUS LEASING AN AUTOMOBILE

Comparing the costs of purchasing and leasing a vehicle may be analyzed as follows:

Purchase Costs	Example	Your Figures
Total vehicle cost, including sales tax ($20,000)		
Down payment (or full amount if paying cash)	$ 2,000	$_____
Monthly loan payment: $385 × 48-month length of financing (this item is zero if vehicle is not financed)	18,480	_____
Opportunity cost of down payment (or total cost of the vehicle if it is bought for cash): $2,000 × 4 years of financing/ownership × 3 percent	240	_____
Less: Estimated value of vehicle at end of loan term/ ownership period	−6,000	_____
Total cost to buy	$14,720	_____

Leasing Costs	Example	Your Figures
Security deposit ($300)		
Monthly lease payments: $295 × 48-month length of lease	$14,160	$_____
Opportunity cost of security deposit: $300 security deposit × 4 years × 3 percent	36	_____
End-of-lease charges* (if applicable)	800	_____
Total cost to lease	$14,996	_____

*Such as charges for extra mileage.

AVOIDING LEASE TRAPS

When considering a lease agreement for a motor vehicle, beware of these common pitfalls:

- Not knowing the total cost of the agreement, including the cost of the vehicle, not just the monthly payment.
- Making a larger up-front payment than is required or paying unnecessary add-on costs.
- Negotiating the monthly payment rather than the capitalized cost of the vehicle.
- Not having the value of any trade-in vehicle reflected in the lease.
- Signing a contract you don't understand.

Compare monthly payments and other terms among several leasing companies. Information on leasing terms is available at www.leasesource.com, www.leaseguide.com, and www.carinfo.com.

factors influence the price of a used car, including the number of vehicle miles and the features and options. A low-mileage car will have a higher price than a comparable car with high mileage. The vehicle condition and the demand for the model also affect price.

PRICE BARGAINING FOR NEW CARS A useful new-car price source is the *sticker price,* which is the suggested retail price printed on a vehicle label. This amount represents the base price of the car with costs of added features. The dealer's cost, or *invoice price,* is an amount less than the sticker price. The difference between the sticker price and the dealer's cost is available for negotiation. This range is larger for full-size, luxury cars with more options; smaller, less expensive vehicles usually have a smaller negotiation range. Information about dealer's cost is available from sources such as *Edmund's New Car Prices* (www.edmunds.com) and *Consumer Reports* (www.consumerreports.org).

Set-price dealers use a no-haggling selling strategy, with stated prices accepted or rejected as stated. *Car-buying services* help buyers obtain a specific vehicle at a reasonable price. Also referred to as *auto brokers,* these businesses offer desired models for prices ranging between $50 and $200 over dealer cost. The auto broker charges an initial fee for price information. Then, if you choose to buy the car, the broker arranges the purchase with a dealer near your home.

To prevent confusion in determining the true price of the new car, do not mention a trade-in vehicle until settling on the cost of the new car. Then, ask how much the dealer is willing to pay for your old car. If the offer price is not acceptable, sell the old car on your own.

A typical negotiating conversation when buying a car might go like this:

Customer: "I'm willing to pay $35,600 for the car. That's my top offer."

Auto salesperson: "Let me check with my manager." After returning, "My manager says $36,200 is the best we can do."

Customer (who should be willing to walk out at this point): "I can go to $35,650."

Auto salesperson: "We have the car you want, ready to go. How about $35,700?"

If the customer agrees, the dealer has gotten $100 more than the customer's "top offer"!

Other questionable sales techniques used in the past include:

- *Lowballing,* when quoted a very low price that increases when add-on costs are included at the last moment.
- *Highballing,* when offered a high amount for a trade-in vehicle, with the amount made up by increasing the new-car price.
- When asked "How much can you afford per month?" be sure to also ask how many months.
- "A small deposit will hold this vehicle for you." Never leave a deposit unless you are ready to buy, or are willing to lose that amount.
- "Your price is only $100 above our cost." However, many hidden costs may have been added in to get the dealer's cost.
- Beware of sales agreements with preprinted amounts. Cross out numbers you believe are not appropriate.

Research suggests that Sundays (if allowed in your state) and Tuesdays are the best days to buy a new car; the worst day is Thursday. The best deals are often obtained near the end of the month, at the end of each quarter, and on New Year's Eve, Labor Day, and Black Friday—the day after Thanksgiving. Be aware that inventory levels may be limited at these times of the year.

COMPARING FINANCING ALTERNATIVES While you may pay cash, most new cars purchased are financed. Auto loans are available from banks, credit unions, consumer finance companies, and businesses. Many lenders will *preapprove* you for a certain loan amount, which separates financing from negotiating the price of the car. Until the new-car price is set, you should not indicate that you intend to use the dealer's credit plan.

The lowest interest rate or the lowest payment does not necessarily mean the best financing option. Be sure to also consider the loan length. Otherwise, after two or three years, the value of your car may be less than the amount you still owe, a situation called *upside-down* or *negative equity.* If you default on your loan or sell the car at this time, you will have to pay the difference.

smart money minute

To avoid scams of online used-car sellers:

- Research the seller's reputation and background.
- Do a title check to confirm the seller's name and to make sure the car is not stolen; the "seller" may not actually own the vehicle being sold.
- Do an online VIN (vehicle identification number) search for price history, other information.
- Beware of photos with tempting low prices.
- Check for recalls, safety record of the vehicle.
- Don't buy a car if you're not allowed to have a mechanic inspect it.

EXAMPLE: Upside Down

A $26,000 vehicle is purchased with an initial loan of $18,000. After a period of time, the vehicle may only be worth $12,000 while you still owe $14,000. To avoid this situation, make a large down payment, have a short-term loan (less than five years), and pay off the loan faster than the decline in value of the vehicle.

How about you? What actions might be taken to avoid this situation?

smart money minute

Older car. . .wealthier you! People who drive older vehicles on average save more for retirement. Instead of making a monthly payment, that amount is saved for long-term financial security. The average monthly loan payment for a new car is over $500, and nearly $400 for a used car. Keeping a vehicle well after it is paid for allows you to invest these amounts, even if you need to set aside money for repairs and upkeep. Also consider buying a less expensive vehicle, especially one that will be reliable for 200,000 miles or more. Remember, cars are not an investment; they are an expense for providing transportation.

Automobile manufacturers may offer low-interest financing. On occasion, at the same time, they may also offer rebates, giving buyers a choice between a rebate and a low-interest loan. Carefully compare financing at various financial institutions and the rebate. Special rebates are sometimes offered to students, teachers, veterans, credit union members, real estate agents, and other groups.

The annual percentage rate (APR) indicates the true cost of credit. The federal Truth in Lending law requires that the APR be clearly stated in advertising and other communications. Low payments may seem like a good deal, but you will pay longer and your total finance charges will be higher. Consider both the APR and the finance charge when comparing credit terms of different lenders. Additional auto financing information can be obtained at www.bankrate.com and www.nerdwallet.com.

PHASE 4—POSTPURCHASE ACTIVITIES

Maintenance and ownership costs are associated with many purchases. Proper operating actions result in improved performance and fewer repairs. When repairs not covered by a warranty are needed, follow a similar pattern used when making the original purchase. Investigate, evaluate, and negotiate various servicing options.

In the past, when new car problems occurred and the warranty didn't address the situation, many consumers lacked a course of action. As a result, all 50 states and the District of Columbia enacted *lemon laws* requiring a vehicle refund after the owner made repeated attempts to obtain a resolution. These laws apply when four attempts have been made to get the same problem corrected or when the vehicle has been out of service for more than 30 days within 12 months of purchase or the first 12,000 miles. The terms of the state laws vary; for details go to www.lemonlawamerica.com.

AUTOMOBILE OPERATION COSTS   Over a lifetime, most people will spend more than $200,000 on automobile-related expenses. Your driving costs will vary based on two main factors: the size of your automobile and the number of miles you drive. These costs involve two categories:

Fixed Ownership Costs	Variable Operating Costs
Depreciation	Gasoline and oil
Interest on auto loan	Tires
Insurance	Maintenance and repairs
License, registration, taxes, and fees	Parking and tolls

The largest fixed expense associated with a new automobile is *depreciation*, the loss in vehicle value due to time and use. Since money is not paid out for depreciation, many people do not consider it an expense. However, this decreased value is a cost that owners incur. Well-maintained vehicles and certain high-quality models depreciate at a slower rate.

Costs such as gasoline, oil, and tires increase with the number of miles driven. Planning expenses is easier if the number of miles you drive is fairly constant. Unexpected trips and vehicle age will increase such costs.

Knowing the total cost of owning and operating your vehicle will help your overall financial planning. An automobile expense record should include the dates of odometer readings. Recording your mileage each time you buy gas will allow you to compute fuel efficiency. For tax-deductible travel, the Internal Revenue Service requires specific information about the mileage, locations, dates, and purposes of trips. Keep records of regular operating expenses such as gas, oil, parking, and tolls (there are apps you can use to do this, like aCar). Also, keep files on maintenance, repair, and replacement parts as well as infrequent expenses such as tires, insurance, and license and registration fees.

MOTOR VEHICLE MAINTENANCE   People who sell, repair, or drive automobiles for a living emphasize the importance of regular care. While owner's manuals and articles suggest mileage or time intervals for certain servicing, more frequent oil changes and tune-ups can minimize major repairs and maximize vehicle life. Exhibit 8-5 offers suggested maintenance areas to consider.

AUTOMOBILE SERVICING SOURCES
Businesses that offer automobile maintenance and repair service include the following:

- Car dealers have a service department with a wide range of car care services. The cost for vehicle servicing at car dealers is usually higher than other repair options.

- Independent auto repair shops service vehicles at competitive prices. Since the quality of shops can vary, obtain recommendations from customers and online reviews.

- Mass merchandise retailers emphasize the sale of tires and batteries along with services for brakes, oil changes, and tune-ups.

- Specialty shops offer brakes, tires, transmission servicing, and oil changes at a reasonable price with fast service.

Regular maintenance can reduce future repair costs and increase your vehicle's life.
michaeljung/Shutterstock

To avoid unnecessary expenses, beware of common repair frauds (see Exhibit 8-6) and do business with reputable companies. Be sure to get a written, detailed estimate in advance as well as a detailed, paid receipt for the service completed. Studies of consumer problems consistently rank auto repairs as one of the top consumer ripoffs. Some people avoid problems and minimize costs by working on their own vehicles.

- Get regular oil changes (every 3,000–7,500 miles depending on recommendations for the vehicle).
- Check fluids (brake, power steering, transmission).
- Inspect hoses and belts for wear.
- Get a tune-up (spark plugs, filters) every 10,000–50,000 miles (varies by vehicle).
- Check and clean battery cables and terminals.
- Check tire pressure regularly.
- Check spark plug wires after 50,000 miles.
- Flush radiator and service transmission every 25,000 miles.
- Keep lights, turn signals, and horn in good working condition.
- Check muffler and exhaust pipes.
- Check tires for wear; rotate tires every 7,500 miles.
- Check condition of brakes, wiper blades.

EXHIBIT 8-5

Extend vehicle life with proper maintenance

EXHIBIT 8-6

Common auto repair scams

The majority of automobile service businesses are fair and honest. Sometimes, however, consumers waste dollars when they fall prey to these tricks:

- When checking the oil, the attendant puts the dipstick only partially down and then shows you that you need oil.

- An attendant cuts a fan belt or punctures a hose. Watch carefully when someone checks under your hood.

- You are shown a dirty air filter but it's not from your car. You are told you need to buy a new air filter.

- A garage employee puts some liquid on your battery and then tries to convince you that it is leaking and you need a new battery.

- Removing air from a tire instead of adding air to it can make an unwary driver open to buying a new tire or paying for an unneeded patch on a tire that is in perfect condition.

- The attendant puts grease near a shock absorber or on the ground and then tells you your present shocks are dangerous and you need new ones.

- You are charged for two gallons of antifreeze with a radiator flush when only one gallon was put in.

Dealing with reputable businesses and having a basic knowledge of your automobile are the best methods of avoiding deceptive repair practices.

PFP Sheet 33
Consumer Purchase Comparison

PFP Sheet 34
Transportation Needs

PFP Sheet 35
Used-Car Comparison

 PRACTICE QUIZ 8-2

1. What are the major sources of consumer information?
2. What actions are appropriate when buying a used car?
3. When might leasing a motor vehicle be appropriate?
4. What maintenance activities could increase the life of your vehicle?

 PFP Sheet 36
Buying or Leasing a Motor Vehicle

 PFP Sheet 37
Comparing Cash and Credit Purchases

 PFP Sheet 38
Auto Operation Costs

Resolving Consumer Complaints

LO8-3

Determine steps to take to resolve consumer problems.

Most customer complaints result from defective or low-quality products, short product lives, unexpected costs, deceptive pricing, and fraudulent business practices. These problems are often with motor vehicles, online purchases, work-at-home businesses, landlord–tenant relations, investments, telemarketing, electronics, health clubs, diet plans, mortgages, home repairs, credit cards, debt collection, phony contests, travel services, rent-to-own companies, employment opportunities, and bogus charities. As a result of the pandemic, many people needed to take action to obtain refunds for canceled flights, hotel stays, concerts, weddings, and other events.

Federal consumer agencies estimate annual consumer losses from fraudulent business activities at over $30 billion a year for telemarketing and online purchases, $3 billion for credit card fraud and credit "repair" scams, and $10 billion for investment swindles. See the *Financial Literacy for My Life: Beware of These Common (and Not So Common) Frauds* feature for some common consumer frauds.

Financial Literacy for My Life

BEWARE OF THESE COMMON (AND NOT SO COMMON) FRAUDS

Pandemic Cons. These scams included fraudulent COVID-19 test kits, treatments, and cures, fake coronavirus charities, stimulus check swindles, work-at-home schemes, a guaranteed job, "special" unemployment benefits, and robocalls pretending to be from the Social Security Administration.

Foreign Scams. Do not reply to a letter or email from a "bank" or another foreign source promising money. Beware of a plan to receive over $100,000 for an investment of $120. This is a type of *pyramid scheme.*

Disaster-Related Fraud. Scams surface after tragedies and natural disasters, such as hurricanes and wildfires. Phony charities solicit funds for victims.

Credit Repair. Companies offer to clean up credit histories. After paying hundreds of dollars, consumers find out these companies did nothing to help.

Crowdfunding Scams. Avoid funding products already on the market elsewhere in the world. Conduct online research to determine the validity of the request.

Fraudulent Diet Products & Health Claims. Fraudulent diets have claims such as "The Amazing Skin Patch Melts Away Body Fat," and "Lose Weight While You Sleep." Be cautious of phrases such as "scientific breakthrough," "miraculous cure," "exclusive product," "secret ingredient," or "ancient remedy."

Romance Scams. Romance scammers target single, older people and others. While this scam can happen in person, it more often occurs online. Avoid giving a new friend access to credit cards, bank accounts, or other assets. Beware of Cupid's arrow striking your wallet instead of your heart!

Scholarship and Financial Aid Scams. The Federal Trade Commission warns students to avoid college financing programs with these hooks: "The scholarship is guaranteed," "You can't get this information anywhere else," "I just need your credit card or bank account number to hold this scholarship," "We'll do all the work. You just pay a processing fee," "You've been selected" by a "national foundation," or "You're a finalist" in a contest you never entered. Also beware of student loan forgiveness scams. For guidance on financing your education, see the Chapter 7 Appendix.

Phishing. Email spam or pop-up messages attempt to obtain credit card numbers, bank account information, Social Security numbers, or passwords. These messages look official, as from a financial institution, government agency, PayPal, or LinkedIn. This fraud may also occur by phone (called "vishing") and by text message ("smishing"). Never click on a link in these emails or disclose personal information.

Pharming. Malicious software or an email attachment places the virus or worm in a computer or server. Even if the correct web address is entered, the software goes to a bogus website. Be sure to have updated antivirus and anti-spyware programs.

The "Yes" Scam. This deception asks a legitimate-sounding question related to a credit card account. Questions are designed to get the victim to say "yes," with the positive answer recorded. Later, the victim is billed what appears to be a valid transaction. Beware of *one-ring scams.* If you call back, you may be charged $15 to $30. *Spoofing* makes a call look like its is from a local or familiar number. *one-ring scams*

Fake Checks. Despite increased use of online banking and apps, fake check scams continue; for information, search "fake checks" at: www.consumer.ftc.gov.

Payment Scams. Fraudsters often request payment with a gift card, wire transfer, cryptocurrency, or money-transfer app. Never send money to someone you don't know.

Further information about various frauds and deceptive business practices is available at www.fraud.org and www.ftc.gov. The AARP Fraud Watch Network offers a scam-tracking map at https://www.aarp.org/money/scams-fraud/tracking-map/ to report fraud activity based on zip code, with more than 50 types, ranging from debt collection and charities to contests and online auctions.

To minimize consumer problems: (1) obtain recommendations from friends, family, and online reviews; (2) verify company affiliations, certifications, and licenses; and (3) understand the sale terms, return policies, and warranty. Most people do not anticipate having problems with purchases. However, since problems arise, be prepared for them. The process for resolving differences between buyers and sellers includes the steps presented in Exhibit 8-7.

my life | 3

I know what actions to take when complaining about a consumer purchase.

Consumer scams are a frequent source of complaints. These deceptions can be very creative. For examples of cons, see *Financial Literacy for My Life,* "Beware of These Common (and Not So Common) Frauds."

EXHIBIT 8-7

Resolving consumer
complaints

Step 1—Initial Communication
- Return to place of purchase or contact online retailer.
- Provide a detailed explanation and the action you desire.
- Be pleasant yet persistent in your efforts to obtain a resolution.

Step 2—Communication with the Company
- Send an email with the details of the situation (Exhibit 8-8).
- Post your concerns on the company's online social media sites.
- Comment on a blog or a consumer review website.

Step 3—Consumer Agency Assistance
- Seek guidance from a local, state, or federal consumer agency.
- Determine if any laws have been violated in the situation.
- Consider the use of mediation or arbitration.

Step 4—Legal Action
- Consider bringing your case to small claims court.
- Determine if a class action suit is appropriate.
- Seek assistance from a lawyer or legal aid organization.

Before starting the complaint resolution process, know your rights and the laws for the situation; this information is located online and through apps. To ensure success when you complain, keep a file of receipts, names of people you talked to, dates of attempted repairs, copies of letters you wrote, and costs incurred. Written documents will help to resolve a problem in your favor. An automobile owner kept detailed records and receipts for all gasoline purchases, oil changes, and repairs. When a warranty dispute occurred, the owner was able to prove proper maintenance and received a refund. Perseverance is vital when companies ignore your request or delay their response.

STEP 1: INITIAL COMMUNICATION

Most consumer complaints are resolved at the original sales location. Since most businesses are concerned about their reputation, legitimate complaints are honored. When contacting a company or talking with a staff member, avoid threatening words or demanding unreasonable action. In general, a calm, rational, yet persistent approach is appropriate.

STEP 2: COMMUNICATION WITH THE COMPANY

Express your dissatisfaction to company headquarters if a problem is not resolved at the place of purchase. An email may be appropriate (see Exhibit 8-8). Obtain contact information for companies with an online search. Company websites usually provide a method to communicate with them, such as an email contact or a toll-free phone

EXHIBIT 8-8   Sample complaint email

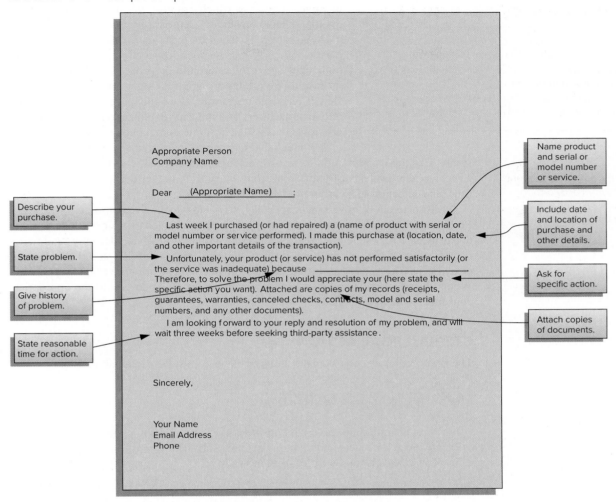

Note: Keep copies of your letter and all related documents and information.
Source: *Consumer Action Handbook* (www.usa.gov/consumer).

number. Companies often have toll-free numbers and website information on product packages. Studies reveal that reasonable consumer complaints made to a company are resolved on the first contact.

STEP 3: CONSUMER AGENCY ASSISTANCE

If you do not receive satisfaction from the company, agencies and organizations are available to assist you (see chapter appendix). These include national groups specializing in various consumer topics, and local organizations that handle complaints and provide legal guidance.

The Better Business Bureau is a network that may help resolve complaints with local merchants. These organizations are sponsored by local business organizations; member companies are not obligated to respond to complaints. The Better Business Bureau can be of value before you make a purchase by sharing information about the experiences of others with a local company.

Mediation involves the use of a third party to settle grievances. In mediation, an impartial person—the *mediator*—tries to resolve a conflict between a customer and

mediation The attempt by an impartial third party to resolve a difference between two parties through discussion and negotiation.

smart money minute

Driving a rental car to a vacation site rather than your own vehicle can have financial benefits. Fewer miles on your vehicle will result in a better resale value, and lower maintenance and repair costs. You may also get better gas mileage with a rental resulting in lower fuel costs for your trip.

arbitration The settlement of a difference by a third party whose decision is legally binding.

a business through discussion and negotiation. Mediation is a nonbinding process, which can save time and money compared to other dispute resolution methods.

Arbitration is the settlement of a difference by a third party—the *arbitrator*—whose decision is legally binding. After both sides agree to the arbitration process, each side presents its case to the arbitrator. Arbitrators are selected from professionals and volunteers trained for this purpose. Most automobile manufacturers and industry organizations have arbitration programs to resolve consumer complaints.

Without realizing it, you may sign a contract with provisions that require arbitration to resolve disputes. As a result, consumers face various risks, including rules vastly different from a jury trial, higher costs for the arbitrator's time, and selection of an arbitrator by the defendant.

A vast network of government agencies is available to resolve consumer complaints. Problems with local restaurants or food stores may be handled by a city or county health department. Every state has agencies to handle problems involving deceptive and fraudulent business practices, banking, insurance companies, and utility rates. Federal agencies help resolve consumer difficulties and provide information (see chapter appendix). When unsure of which agency to use, search online to guide you to the appropriate consumer protection agency.

STEP 4: LEGAL ACTION

The next section discusses legal actions available to resolve consumer problems.

✔ PRACTICE QUIZ 8-3

1. What are common causes of consumer problems and complaints?
2. How can most consumer complaints be resolved?
3. How does arbitration differ from mediation?

Legal Options for Consumers

LO8-4

Evaluate legal alternatives available to consumers.

small claims court A court that settles legal differences involving amounts below a set limit and employs a process in which the litigants usually do not use a lawyer.

What should you do if the previously mentioned actions fail to resolve a consumer complaint? The following legal actions might be considered.

SMALL CLAIMS COURT

Every state has a court system to settle minor disagreements. In **small claims court,** a person may file a claim involving amounts below a set dollar limit. The maximum varies from state to state, ranging from $500 to $25,000; most states have a limit of between $2,500 and $10,000. The process usually takes place without a lawyer, although in many states attorneys are allowed. To make the best use of small claims court, observe other cases to learn the process. For additional information on how to file a suit in small claims court, see the *How To . . . File a Suit in Small Claims Court* feature.

CLASS-ACTION SUITS

Several people may have the same complaint—for example, people who were injured by a defective product, customers who were overcharged by a utility company, or travelers

In every state, small claims courts are available to handle legal disputes involving minor amounts. While specific procedures vary from state to state, these actions are usually involved:

Step 1. Notify the defendant to request a payment for damages with a deadline, such as within 30 days. Note in your letter that you will initiate legal action after that time.

Step 2. Determine the appropriate location for filing the case. Decide if your type of case is allowed in small claims court in your state, and whether the amount is within the state limit. (Information on state limits is available at www.nolo.com/legal-encyclopedia/small-claims-suits-how-much-30031.html.)

Step 3. Obtain and complete the filing documents; a fee of $30 to $100 will be required. Forms can be obtained at the courthouse or online. The petition will include the plaintiff's name (you), the defendant (person or organization being sued), the amount being requested, a clear description of the claim with dates of various actions, and copies of any relevant documents (contracts, receipts).

Step 4. File the forms and pay the fee. The petition will be served to the defendant, notifying the person of the suit. After being served, the defendant may be required to file a written response, denying or not contesting the claim. If the defendant does not respond, a default judgment will likely be entered.

Step 5. Next, a hearing date will be set. Prepare evidence with a clear and concise presentation of: (a) the details of what happened and when; (b) evidence, such as contracts, leases, receipts, canceled checks, credit card statements, and photographs; and (c) testimony of people who witnessed aspects of the dispute or who are knowledgeable about the type of situation. If both parties decide to settle before the hearing, be sure that you receive payment before the case is dismissed.

Step 6. At the hearing, be clear and concise, and bring supporting documentation with you. Witnesses whom you wish to present at the hearing may involve a subpoena requiring them to appear in court.

Step 7. Once you receive a favorable judgment, you still have to collect the funds. While the court does not collect the money for you, the party may pay when the judgment is rendered. If not, a letter from you or an attorney may result in payment. More formal debt collection actions might be necessary.

Every state has different procedures and regulations for small claims court. Search online for information for your specific location. Careful and detailed preparation of your case is the key to success in small claims court.

who were cheated by a tour business. These individuals may qualify for a class-action suit. A **class-action suit** is a legal action taken by a few individuals on behalf of all the people who suffered the same alleged injustice. This group, called a *class,* is represented by a lawyer or by a group of lawyers working together.

Once a situation qualifies as a class-action suit, all affected parties are notified. At this point, a person must decide whether to opt in or opt out. Nonrespondents will not be part of the complaint. If a plaintiff chooses not to participate in the class-action suit, the person may file an individual lawsuit.

If the court ruling is favorable, the funds awarded may be divided among members of the class, used to reduce future rates, assigned to public funds for government use, or donated to charity. Past examples of class-action suits include auto owners who were sold unneeded replacement parts, investors who sued a brokerage company for unauthorized transactions resulting in high commission charges, and consumers who were charged unfair processing fees by an online concert ticket seller.

class-action suit A legal action taken by a few individuals on behalf of all the people who have suffered the same alleged injustice.

smart money minute

The **mistake** of buying fake and counterfeit products can be dangerous. A fake purse or watch may not cost much money, but other products can cost lives. Counterfeit prescription medications may not be effective, or a knockoff airbag used as a replacement part in a vehicle after an accident may not deploy properly. An **action** to take would be to carefully investigate the source of your purchases. This can result in the **success** of improved personal safety.

Complicated legal matters may require the services of an attorney.
Maskot/Getty Images

legal aid society One of a network of publicly supported community law offices that provides legal assistance to consumers who cannot afford their own attorney.

my life | 4

The legal actions available to consumers may be of value to me in the future.

At some point in your life, going to small claims court may be an appropriate action for a consumer complaint situation. To learn more, conduct an online search for small claims court procedures for your state.

USING A LAWYER

When small claims court or a class-action suit is not appropriate, you may seek the services of an attorney. Common sources of lawyers are referrals from friends, online research, and the local division of the American Bar Association.

Straightforward legal situations such as appearing in small claims court, renting an apartment, or defending yourself for a minor traffic violation will usually not need legal counsel. More complicated matters such as writing a will, settling a real estate purchase, or suing for injury damages will likely require the services of an attorney.

When selecting a lawyer, consider several questions. Is the lawyer experienced in your type of case? Will you be charged on a flat fee basis, at an hourly rate, or on a contingency basis? Is there a fee for the initial consultation? How and when will you be required to make payment for services?

Legal services can be expensive. A **legal aid society** is one of a network of publicly supported community law offices providing legal assistance to people who cannot afford their own attorney. These agencies provide assistance at a minimal or no cost.

OTHER LEGAL ALTERNATIVES

Prepaid legal services provide unlimited or reduced-fee legal assistance for a set fee. Some programs provide certain basic services, such as telephone consultation and preparation of a simple will, for an annual fee ranging from $50 to $150 or more. Complicated legal assistance will likely require an additional fee, usually at a reduced rate. That fee may not be much lower than one you could negotiate on your own. More expensive plans cover most legal services. Since most people do not make frequent use of a lawyer, carefully consider the plan's coverage and your options before signing up. Also, determine if the lawyers who provide telephone consultations are allowed to refer cases to themselves, which can result in a conflict of interest.

Websites such as LegalZoom, Nolo, and Rocket Lawyer are available to assist with basic legal documents, such as creating a will. Beyond this minimal document preparation, consumers are encouraged to consult a lawyer.

PERSONAL CONSUMER PROTECTION

While many laws, agencies, and legal tools are available to protect your rights, none will be of value unless you use them. (See *Financial Literacy for My Life: Is It Legal?*) To avoid becoming a victim of deceptive business practices, consider these actions:

1. Do business with reputable companies with consistent customer satisfaction.
2. Understand contracts or other documents you sign; if it sounds too good to be true, it probably is!

Financial Literacy for My Life

IS IT LEGAL?

The following situations are common problems for consumers. How would you respond to the question at the end of each situation?

		Yes	No
1.	You purchase a laptop computer for $650. Two days later, the same store offers the same item for $425. Is this legal?	___	___
2.	You receive an unordered sample of flower seeds in the mail. You decide to plant them to see how well they will grow in your yard. A couple of days later, you receive a bill for the seeds. Do you have to pay for the seeds?	___	___
3.	A 16-year-old injured while playing ball at a local park is taken to a hospital for medical care. The parents refuse to pay the hospital since they didn't request the service. Can the parents be held legally responsible for the charges?	___	___
4.	You purchase a shirt for a friend. The shirt doesn't fit, but when you return it to the store, you are offered an exchange since the store policy is no cash refunds. Is this legal?	___	___
5.	A manufacturer refuses to repair a motorcycle that is still under warranty. The manufacturer can prove that the motorcycle was used improperly. If this is true, must the manufacturer honor the warranty?	___	___
6.	An employee of a store incorrectly marks the price of an item at a lower amount. Is the store obligated to sell the item at the lower price?	___	___

Circumstances, interpretations of the law, store policies, and state and local laws can affect the above situations. The generally accepted answers are **yes** for 1, 3, and 4, and **no** for 2, 5, and 6.

3. Beware of websites not ending in .com, .gov, or .org.
4. Compare credit costs with paying cash; contact a bank or credit union for financing.
5. Avoid impulse buying; con artists often tell you this is your last chance.
6. STOP. . .WAIT. . .THINK. . .DON'T DO IT!

smart money minute

Minimalists and frugal people buy store brands; avoid shopping for pleasure; avoid waste; plan ahead; take advantage of free and low-cost leisure activities; buy based on utility and reliability; attempt to repair broken items; and shop for used items first. Several major retailers along with second-hand stores and apps offer top quality, preowned clothing.

✔ PRACTICE QUIZ 8-4

1. Describe some situations in which small claims court and class-action suits might be helpful.
2. Describe some situations in which you might use the services of a lawyer.

PFP Sheet 39
Legal Services
Comparison

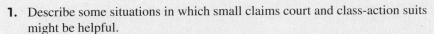

Your Personal Finance Roadmap and Dashboard:

Consumer Buying

UNPLANNED SPENDING PERCENT

 First Steps

- Maintain a spending diary to monitor daily spending activities.
- Develop research skills for making consumer purchases.
- Learn wise buying techniques and comparison-shopping strategies.
- Create a spending plan that allows for saving and avoids unnecessary spending.

Unplanned spending, often called *impulse buying,* is a common danger in preventing effective financial planning. While people may spend to feel good about themselves, that action often results in budget problems, higher debt levels, and greater financial stress. Measuring and controlling unplanned spending can contribute to your financial progress. Careful spending will result in lower debt, increased savings, and achieving your financial goals.

 Next Steps

- Save funds for the purchase of expensive items to avoid credit costs.
- Assess your needs for major consumer items.
- Update your spending activities based on changing household situations.
- Teach other household members about wise buying strategies.

YOUR SITUATION

Can you minimize the amount you spend on unplanned purchases? Are there areas of spending you might reduce? A low unplanned spending ratio can result in improved financial security. Other consumer buying actions you might consider during various stages of your life include:

Later Steps

- Save to replace major purchases, as needed.
- Determine spending needs in relation to current and future household situations.
- Plan for changes in spending activities that might occur during retirement.
- Consider the sale or donation of unneeded consumer items.

> **YOUR** next step . . . select one or more of the items above and create an action plan to implement those financial planning activities.

SUMMARY OF LEARNING OBJECTIVES

LO8-1

Identify strategies for effective consumer buying. Many economic, social, and personal factors influence daily buying decisions. Overspending and poor money management are frequent causes of credit overuse and other financial difficulties. Timing purchases, comparing buying sources and brands, using label information, computing unit prices, and evaluating warranties are common strategies for effective purchasing.

LO8-2

Implement a process for making consumer purchases. A buying process with several steps can be useful when planning purchases. A research-based approach to consumer buying involves: (1) preshopping activities, such as problem identification and information gathering; (2) evaluating alternatives; (3) determining the purchase price; and (4) postpurchase activities, such as proper operation and maintenance.

LO8-3

Determine steps to take to resolve consumer problems. Knowing what actions to take when complaining about a consumer purchase can effectively resolve a situation. This process should involve these steps: (1) return to the place of purchase, (2) contact the company's main office, (3) obtain assistance from a consumer agency, and (4) take legal action.

LO8-4

Evaluate legal alternatives available to consumers. The legal actions available to consumers include small claims court, class-action suits, the services of a lawyer, legal aid societies, and prepaid legal services. These legal means for handling consumer problems should be considered when a situation cannot be resolved through communication with the company or through the help of a consumer agency.

KEY TERMS

arbitration 294	legal aid society 296	service contract 281
class-action suit 295	mediation 293	small claims court 294
cooperative 276	open dating 277	unit pricing 277
impulse buying 275	rebate 277	warranty 278

SELF-TEST PROBLEMS

1. An item bought on credit with a $60 down payment, and monthly payments of $70 for 36 months, would have a total cost of what amount?

2. A food package with 32 ounces costing $1.76 would have a unit cost of what amount?

Self-Test Solutions

1. 36 × $70 = $2,520 plus the $60 down payment for a total of $2,580
2. $1.76 ÷ 32 = 5.5 cents an ounce

FINANCIAL PLANNING PROBLEMS

1. *Calculating Future Value.* Krista Lee can purchase a service contract for all of her major appliances for $180 a year. If the appliances are expected to last for 10 years and she earns 5 percent on her savings, what would be the future value of the amount Krista will pay for the service contract? **LO8-1**

2. *Future Value of Wise Buying.* If Eric Sanchez saves $60 a month by using coupons and doing comparison shopping, (a) what is the amount for a year? (b) What would be the future value of this annual amount over 10 years, assuming an interest rate of 2 percent? **LO8-1**

LO8-2 3. *Comparing Buying Alternatives.* Angela Simpson is considering the purchase of a home entertainment center. The product attributes she plans to consider and the weights she gives to them are as follows:

Portability   .1

Sound projection   .6

Warranty   .3

Angela rated the brands as follows:

	Portability	Sound Projection	Warranty
Brand A	6	8	7
Brand B	9	6	8
Brand C	5	9	6

Using the consumer buying matrix, conduct a quantitative product evaluation rating for each brand. What other factors is Angela likely to consider when making her purchase?

LO8-2 4. *Calculating the Cost of Credit.* Pierre Martina is comparing the cost of credit to the cash price of an item. If Pierre makes a $70 down payment and pays $34 a month for 24 months, how much more will that amount be than the cash price of $695?

LO8-2 5. *Computing Unit Prices.* Calculate the unit price of each of the following items.

Item	Price	Size	Unit Price
Motor oil	$1.95	2.5 quarts	___ cents/quart
Cereal	2.17	15 ounces	___ cents/ounce
Canned fruit	0.89	13 ounces	___ cents/ounce
Facial tissue	2.25	300 tissues	___ cents/100 tissues
Shampoo	3.96	17 ounces	___ cents/ounce

LO8-2 6. *Calculating the Present Value of a Consumer Purchase.* What would be the net present value of a microwave oven that costs $159 and will save you $68 a year in time and food away from home? Assume an average return on your savings of 4 percent for five years.

LO8-2 7. *Comparing Automobile Loans.* What would be the total vehicle cost in each of these situations?

    Vehicle 1: A down payment of $3,500 with 48 monthly payments of $312.
    Vehicle 2: A down payment of $2,700 with 60 monthly payments of $276.

LO8-2 8. *Calculating Motor Vehicle Operating Costs.* Using *Personal Financial Planner Sheet 38*, calculate the approximate yearly operating cost of the following vehicle.

Annual depreciation, $2,500   License and registration fees, $65

Annual mileage, 13,200   Average gasoline price, $3.68 per gallon

Current year's loan interest, $650   Oil changes/repairs, $370

Miles per gallon, 24   Parking/tolls, $420

Insurance, $680

LO8-2 9. *Buying versus Leasing a Motor Vehicle.* Based on the following, calculate the costs of buying and of leasing a motor vehicle.

Purchase Costs		Leasing Costs	
Down payment	$1,500	Security deposit	$500
Loan payment	$450 for 36 months	Lease payment	$450 for 36 months
Estimated value at end of loan	$4,000	End of lease charges	$600
Opportunity cost interest rate:	4%		

DIGITAL FINANCIAL LITERACY: CONSUMER PRODUCT TESTING

Consumer Reports has been published by Consumers Union since 1936 with information on product safety, food, health care, and financial services. Over 100 experts work in 40 labs to test, analyze, evaluate, and rate products purchased by staff members or anonymous "secret shoppers." Sensitive instruments such as a liquid chromatograph are used to measure the caffeine in coffee. Food tasting is done by people trained in food science, nutrition, statistics, and psychology.

The Consumer Reports Auto Test Center covers 300 acres in rural Connecticut. Each year, about 50 cars and trucks are pushed to their limits, driven hundreds of thousands of miles. Vehicles tested are those with the style and options most often bought by consumers. More than 50 vehicle aspects are assessed, including acceleration, braking, emergency handling, emissions, fuel economy, headlights, ride comfort, safety features, trunk and cargo space, and off-road capability for vehicles designed for that type of driving. Subscribers to the magazine provide vehicle reliability and satisfaction survey data.

Action items:

1. Locate an online article related to testing of appliances, food, or another product. Explain the process to another person, and have them comment on how the testing procedures might be improved.

2. With the use of an online article and visuals related to the testing of appliances, food, or another product, create a visual (photo, poster, flowchart) or brief video to report the testing procedures.

FINANCIAL PLANNING CASE

Online Car Buying

Using online research, Mackenzie enters the auto "showroom." In the past few months she had realized that the repair costs for her 11-year-old car were increasing. She thought it was time to shop for a new car, and started her online search for a vehicle. She was interested in small and mid-sized SUVs.

However, her friends suggested that Mackenzie research more than one vehicle type. They reminded her that comparable models were available from various auto manufacturers.

In her online car-buying process, Mackenzie next did a price comparison. She obtained more than one price quote by using online sources. She then prepared an overview of her online car buying experiences.

Online Car-Buying Action	Online Activities	Websites Consulted
Gather information	• Review available vehicle models and options. • Evaluate operating costs and safety features.	www.msn.com/en-us/autos www.consumerreports.org www.caranddriver.com www.motortrend.com
Compare prices	• Identify specific make, model, and features desired. • Locate availability and specific price in your geographic area.	www.edmunds.com www.kbb.com www.nada.com
Finalize purchase	• Make payment or financing arrangements. • Conduct in-person inspection. • Arrange for delivery.	www.carvana.com www.autobytel.com www.autonation.com www.autoweb.com

Mackenzie's next step was to make her final decision. After selecting what she planned to buy, she finalized the purchase online and was able to take delivery at a local dealer.

While car buying online continues to grow in popularity, be sure to make a personal examination of the vehicle before finalizing the purchase.

Questions

1. Based on Mackenzie's experience, what benefits and drawbacks are associated with online car buying?

2. What additional actions might Mackenzie consider before buying a car?

3. How might the benefits and drawbacks of shopping online affect a person's budgeting and saving activities?

YOUR PERSONAL FINANCIAL PLAN

COMPARISON SHOPPING AND BUYING MOTOR VEHICLES

Daily buying actions such as comparing prices, evaluating brands, and avoiding fraud allow you to wisely use resources for both current living expenses and long-term financial security.

Your Short-Term Financial Planning Activity

Task Develop a foundation for consumer purchasing activities.

Research

1) Use PFP Sheets 33 and 37 to compare different brands and the use of cash and credit for the purchase of a major consumer item you may need in the near future.

2) Conduct a unit pricing comparison at several stores or with online sites (see PFF Sheet 32).

3) Determine current transportation needs related to new and used motor vehicles and compare buying and leasing options using PFP Sheets 34, 35, and 36 as a guide.

Outcome Present the results of your findings in a table, chart, or other visual. Add these documents to your portfolio or to your Personal Financial Plan online folder.

Your Long-Term Financial Planning Activity

Task Plan actions for future spending.

Research

1) Determine buying guidelines for major purchases (appliances, furniture, home entertainment equipment). Identify brands, store locations, online sites, and actions to avoid buying on credit.

2) Use PFP Sheet 38 as a guide to identify motor vehicles that would provide low operating and insurance costs.

3) Identify and compare various legal services available for use (see PFP Sheet 39).

Outcome Prepare an audio or written summary of your planned future actions. Add the documents you create to your portfolio or to your Personal Financial Plan online folder.

Note: All *Personal Financial Planner* sheets are available at the end of the book and in an Excel spreadsheet format in *Connect Finance*.

CONTINUING CASE

Consumer Purchasing Strategies and Legal Protection

It sputtered and squeaked and, with a small hesitation followed by an abbreviated lunge, it was finally over. The car Jamie Lee had driven since she received her driver's license at 17 completed its last mile. Thirteen years and 140,000 miles later, it was time for a new vehicle.

After skimming the Sunday newspaper and browsing the online ads, Jamie Lee was ready to visit car dealers to see vehicles of interest to her. She was unsure if she would purchase a new or used car, and finance with a down payment or lease. "No money down and only $219 a month," Jamie Lee read, "with approved credit." This sounded like an offer she might find of interest. Jamie Lee had a good credit rating, as she made sure she paid her bills on time and kept a close eye on her credit report since being a victim of identity theft several years ago. The more she thought about the brand-new car, the more excited she became. That new car fit her personality perfectly!

As Jamie Lee inquired about the advertised vehicle with the salesperson, her excitement turned to dismay. The automobile advertised was available for $219 a month with no money down, based on approved credit, and other qualifications to get the advertised price. The salesperson explained that the information in the fine print of the advertisement stated that the price was based on all of the following criteria: being active in the military, a college graduate within the last three months, a current lessee of the automobile company, and having a top credit score, above 800. If Jamie Lee did not meet all of the qualifications, she would not receive the price advertised. But, he noted, he could get her in that vehicle—for an additional $110 per month. Two hundred and seventy-five dollars was the maximum Jamie budgeted for a monthly payment. This vehicle was outside of her financial plan.

Jamie Lee had to start over. She decided that she must fully research the vehicle purchase process before going to another dealership. She felt she was getting caught up in the moment and vowed to do her research before speaking with another salesperson.

Questions

1. Jamie Lee is considering a used vehicle but cannot decide where to begin her search. Using *Personal Financial Planner Sheet 34,* Transportation Needs, and online research, evaluate two possible choices for a used car that may be available to Jamie Lee, considering her budget.

2. Identify the advantages and disadvantages of using each source for used car purchases listed in the table below.

Source	Advantage	Disadvantage
New car dealer		
Used car dealer		
Private party sale (through individuals)		
Auctions		
Used-car superstores		

3. Jamie Lee is attracted to the low monthly payment advertised for a vehicle lease. She may be able to afford a more expensive car than she originally thought. Jamie Lee really needs to think this through. What are the advantages and disadvantages to leasing a vehicle?

4. Jamie Lee sat down with a salesperson to discuss a new vehicle and its $24,000 purchase price. Jamie Lee has heard that "no one really pays the vehicle sticker price." What guidelines may be suggested for negotiating the purchase price of a vehicle?

5. Jamie Lee decided to purchase a certified preowned vehicle. What might she expect as far as reliability and a warranty on the used car?

DAILY SPENDING DIARY

"Using the daily spending diary has helped me control impulse buying. When I have to write down every amount, I'm more careful in my spending. I can now put more in savings."

Directions

Consider continuing (or starting) the use of a *Daily Spending Diary* to record and monitor your cash outflows. Sheets are provided for you to record *every cent* of your spending in various categories. Most people who have participated in this activity have found it beneficial for monitoring and controlling their spending habits.

Analysis Questions

1. What daily spending items are amounts that might be reduced or eliminated to allow for higher savings amounts?

2. How might a *Daily Spending Diary* result in wiser consumer buying and more saving for the future?

A *Daily Spending Diary* sheet is located at the end of Chapter 1 and on the library resource site within *Connect*.

8 Consumer Protection Agencies and Organizations

Many government agencies and private organizations offer information and assistance. These groups can serve your needs when you want to:

- Research a financial decision or consumer topic.
- Obtain information when planning a purchase decision.
- Seek assistance to resolve a consumer problem.

Section 1 provides an overview of federal, state, and local agencies and other organizations you may contact for information and assistance. Section 2 covers state consumer protection offices to assist you with local matters.

Section 1

Federal agencies can be contacted online. Information on agencies and organizations available to assist you is available at www.consumer.gov and www.usa.gov/consumer, as well as the websites listed below.

EXHIBIT 8-A Federal, state, and local agencies and other organizations

Topic Area	Federal Agency	State, Local Agency; Other Organizations
Advertising False advertising; product labeling Deceptive sales practices; warranties	Federal Trade Commission 1-877-FTC-HELP? (www.ftc.gov)	State consumer protection office c/o state attorney general or governor's office National Fraud Information Center (www.fraud.org)
Air Travel Air safety; airport regulation; airline routes	Federal Aviation Administration 1-800-FAA-SURE (www.faa.gov)	AirHelp (www.airhelp.com)
Appliances/Product Safety Potentially dangerous products Complaints against retailers and manufacturers	Consumer Product Safety Commission 1-800-638-CPSC (www.cpsc.gov)	Council of Better Business Bureaus 1-800-955-5100 (www.bbb.org)

(continued)

Topic Area	Federal Agency	State, Local Agency; Other Organizations

Automobiles
New cars;
   used cars
Automobile repairs;
   auto safety
	Federal Trade Commission
	(www.ftc.gov)
	
	National Highway Traffic Safety
	   Administration
	1-800-424-9393
	(www.nhtsa.gov)
		AUTOCAP/National Automobile
		   Dealers Association
		1-800-252-6232
		(www.nada.org)
		
		Center for Auto Safety
		   (202) 328-7700
		(www.autosafety.org)

Banking and Financial Institutions
Checking and savings accounts
Deposit insurance
Financial services
	Federal Deposit Insurance
	   Corporation
	1-877-275-3342
	(www.fdic.gov)
	
	Comptroller of the Currency
	(202) 447-1600
	(www.occ.treas.gov)
	
	Federal Reserve Board
	(202) 452-3693
	(www.federalreserve.gov)
	
	National Credit Union
	   Administration
	(703) 518-6300
	(www.ncua.gov)
		State banking authority
		
		Credit Union National Association
		(608) 232-8256
		(www.cuna.org)
		
		American Bankers Association
		(202) 663-5000
		(www.aba.com)
		
		U.S. savings bond rates
		1-800-US-BONDS
		(www.savingsbonds.gov)

Career Planning
Job training; employment
   information
	Coordinator of Consumer Affairs
	   Department of Labor
	(202) 219-6060
	(www.dol.gov)
		State department of labor or state
		   employment service

Consumer Credit
Credit cards; deceptive credit
   advertising
Truth in Lending Act
Credit rights of individuals
	Consumer Financial Protection
	   Bureau
	1-855-411-2372
	(www.consumerfinance.gov)
	
	Federal Trade Commission
	1-877-FTC-HELP
	(www.ftc.gov)
		CredAbility
		1-800-251-2227
		(www.cccsatl.org)
		
		National Foundation for Credit Counseling
		(301) 589-5600
		(www.nfcc.org)

Environment
Air and water pollution
Toxic substances
	Environmental Protection
	   Agency
	1-800-438-4318 (indoor air
	   quality)
	1-800-426-4791 (drinking
	   water safety)
	(www.epa.gov)
		Clean Water Action
		(202) 895-0420
		(www.cleanwater.org)

Food Food grades Food additives Nutritional information	U.S. Department of Agriculture 1-800-424-9121 (www.usda.gov) Food and Drug Administration 1-888-463-6332 (www.fda.gov)	Center for Science in the Public Interest (202) 332-9110 (www.cspinet.org) *(continued)*

Topic Area	Federal Agency	State, Local Agency; Other Organizations
Funerals Cost disclosure Deceptive business practices	Federal Trade Commission 1-877-FTC-HELP (www.ftc.gov)	Funeral Service Help Line 1-800-228-6332 (www.nfda.org)
Housing and Real Estate Fair housing practices Mortgages Community development	Department of Housing and Urban Development 1-800-669-9777 (www.hud.gov)	National Association of Realtors (www.realtor.com) (www.move.com) National Association of Home Builders (www.nahb.com)
Insurance Policy conditions Premiums Types of coverage Consumer complaints	Federal Trade Commission (www.ftc.gov) National Flood Insurance Program 1-888-CALL-FLOOD	State insurance regulator American Council of Life Insurance (www.acli.com) Insurance Information Institute 1-800-331-9146 (www.iii.org)
Internet/Mail Order Damaged products Deceptive business practices Illegal use of U.S. mail	Internet Crime Complaint Center (www.ic3.gov) U.S. Postal Service 1-800-ASK-USPS (www.usps.gov)	Direct Marketing Association (212) 768-7277 (www.the-dma.org)
Investments Stocks, bonds, and mutual funds Commodities; investment brokers	Securities and Exchange Commission (202) 551-6551 (www.sec.gov) Commodity Futures Trading Commission (202) 418-5000 (www.cftc.gov)	Investment Company Institute (202) 293-7700 (www.ici.org) Financial Industry Regulatory Authority (301) 590-6500 (www.finra.org) National Futures Association 1-800-621-3570 (www.nfa.futures.org) Securities Investor Protection Corp. (202) 371-8300 (www.sipc.org)
Legal Matters Consumer complaints; arbitration	Department of Justice Office of Consumer Litigation (202) 514-2401	American Arbitration Association (212) 484-4000 (www.adr.org) American Bar Association 1-800-285-2221 (www.abanet.org)

(continued)

Topic Area	Federal Agency	State, Local Agency; Other Organizations
Medical Concerns Prescription medications Over-the-counter medications Medical devices; health care	Food and Drug Administration (www.fda.gov) U.S. Centers for Medicare and Medicaid Services (www.cms.gov) Health care coverage (www.healthcare.gov)	American Medical Association 1-800-336-4797 (www.ama-assn.org) Public Citizen Health Research Group (202) 588-1000 (www.citizen.org/topic/health-care/)
Retirement Old-age benefits; pension information Medicare	Social Security Administration 1-800-772-1213 (www.ssa.gov)	AARP (202) 434-2277 (www.aarp.org)
Taxes Tax information; audit procedures	Internal Revenue Service 1-800-829-1040 1-800-TAX-FORM (www.irs.gov)	Department of revenue (in your state capital city) The Tax Foundation (202) 464-6200 (www.taxfoundation.org) National Association of Enrolled Agents 1-800-424-4339 (www.naea.org)
Telemarketing 900 numbers	Federal Communications Commission 1-888-225-5322 (www.fcc.gov)	National Consumers League (202) 835-3323 (www.nclnet.org)
Utilities Cable television; utility rates	Federal Communications Commission 1-988-225-5322 (www.fcc.gov)	State utility commission (in your state capital)

Section 2

State, county, and local consumer protection offices provide online information for wise buying and handling complaints. Your state consumer protection office may be accessed through the National Association of Attorneys General at www.naag.org, or with an online search using "(*state*) consumer protection agency." In addition, each state has agencies regulating banking, insurance, securities, and utilities. These may be identified with an online search.

State departments of insurance can be accessed online at www.naic.org/state_web_map.htm.

The websites of state tax departments are available at www.taxadmin.org/state-tax-agencies or www.aicpa.org/research/externallinks/taxesstatesdepartmentsofrevenue.html.

To save time, call or email the office before sending in a complaint. Ask if the office handles the type of complaint you have, and if an online complaint form is available.

9

The Housing Decision: Factors and Finances

LEARNING OBJECTIVES

LO9-1 Evaluate available housing alternatives.

LO9-2 Analyze the costs and benefits associated with renting.

LO9-3 Explain the home-buying process.

LO9-4 Calculate the costs associated with purchasing a home.

LO9-5 Develop a strategy for selling a home.

Monkey Business Images/Shutterstock

Financial Literacy
IN YOUR LIFE

▶ **What if you . . .** wish to reduce the amount owed on your mortgage and increase the equity? This action could result in an improved financial position and the potential for more funds for use in the future. How might you achieve this goal?

You might . . . pay an additional amount each month (toward the loan principal) so the equity in your home will increase. Or you might choose a 15-year mortgage rather than one for 30 years. This would also result in faster growth of your home equity while saving many thousands of dollars of interest.

Now, what would you do? What actions might you take now or later in life to improve your mortgage equity? You will be able to monitor your progress using the Your Personal Finance Roadmap and Dashboard at the end of the chapter.

| my life | **PLANNING WHERE TO LIVE** |

Housing represents the largest expenditure for most people. Your choice of a place to live will require both time and money.

To assess your attitudes and behaviors related to housing, for each of the following statements, select the choice that best describes your current situation.

1. When selecting a place to live, what is most important for you?
   a. Being close to work or school.
   b. The costs involved.
   c. Flexibility for moving in the future.
2. A benefit of renting for me would be
   a. ease of mobility.
   b. low initial costs.
   c. There are no benefits of renting for me.
3. The type of housing I might purchase that would be best for me is
   a. a house.
   b. a condominium or town house.
   c. a mobile home.
4. The type of mortgage I am most likely to use is
   a. a fixed-rate conventional mortgage.
   b. an adjustable-rate mortgage.
   c. an FHA or VA mortgage.
5. When planning to sell my home, I would most likely
   a. sell it on my own.
   b. use the services of a real estate agent.
   c. attempt to sell it using an online service.

As you study this chapter, you will encounter "My Life" boxes with additional information and resources related to these items.

Housing Alternatives

As you travel through various areas, you see many housing types. When you consider housing alternatives, identify factors that will influence your choice of housing.

LO9-1

Evaluate available housing alternatives.

my life **1**

I consider different factors when selecting a place to live.

Use several information sources when making your housing decisions. These may range from discussions with people you know to using websites such as www.thebalance.com, www.msn.com/en-us/money/realestate, portal.hud.gov, and www.homefair.com.

YOUR CHOICE OF HOUSING

Your lifestyle, needs, values, beliefs, and attitudes are reflected in your choice of a place to live. For example, some people want a large kitchen for family gatherings. Others may want a lavish bathroom or a media room to escape the pressures of work. A separate office also became a priority for many, even before the pandemic. As you select housing, consider the alternatives in Exhibit 9-1.

While personal preferences are the foundation of a housing decision, financial factors will modify the final choice. A budget and other financial records discussed in Chapter 3 can help you evaluate your income, living costs, and other financial obligations to determine an appropriate amount for your housing expenses.

OPPORTUNITY COSTS OF HOUSING CHOICES

While selection of housing may be based on life situation and financial factors, you should also consider what you might have to give up. The opportunity costs of your housing decision include these trade-offs:

- Lost interest earnings on the down payment money when buying a home or the security deposit for an apartment.
- The time and cost of commuting to work when living in an area with less expensive housing or more living space.
- Loss of home-buying tax advantages and equity growth when you rent.

EXHIBIT 9-1

Housing for different life situations

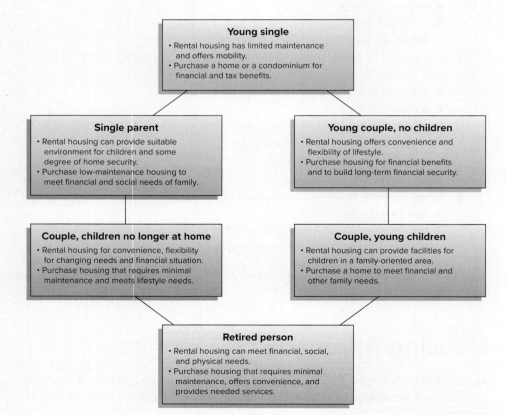

Financial Literacy Calculations

RENTING VERSUS BUYING YOUR PLACE OF RESIDENCE

Comparing the costs of renting and buying involves various factors. The following analysis and example provide a basis for assessing these two housing alternatives. The apartment in the example has a monthly rent of $1,250, and the home costs $200,000. A 28 percent tax rate is assumed.

Although the numbers in this example favor buying, remember that in any financial decision, calculations provide only part of the answer. You should also consider your needs and values, and consider the opportunity costs associated with renting and buying.

	Example	Your Figures
RENTAL COSTS		
Annual rent payments	$15,000	$_____
Renter's insurance	210	_____
Interest lost on security deposit (amount of security deposit times after-tax savings account interest rate)	36	_____
Total annual cost of renting	$15,246	_____
BUYING COSTS		
Annual mortgage payments	$15,168	$_____
Property taxes (annual costs)	4,800	_____
Homeowner's insurance (annual premium)	600	_____
Estimated maintenance and repairs (1%)	2,000	_____
After-tax interest lost on down payment and closing costs	750	_____
Less (financial benefits of home ownership):		_____
Growth in equity	−1,120	−_____
Tax savings for mortgage interest (annual mortgage interest times tax rate)	−3,048	−_____
Tax savings for property taxes (annual property taxes times tax rate)	−1,344	−_____
Estimated annual appreciation (1.5%)*	−3,000	−_____
Total annual cost of buying	$14,806	_____

*This is a nationwide average; actual appreciation of property will vary by geographic area and economic conditions.

- The time and money for repairing and improving a lower-priced home.
- The time and effort involved when having a home built to your specifications.

Like every financial choice, a housing decision requires consideration of what you give up in time, effort, and money.

RENTING VERSUS BUYING HOUSING

Living in a mobile society affects the decision as to whether to rent or buy your housing. Your choice of residence should be analyzed based on lifestyle and financial factors. Exhibit 9-2 can help you consider different housing alternatives.

EXHIBIT 9-2

Evaluating housing
alternatives

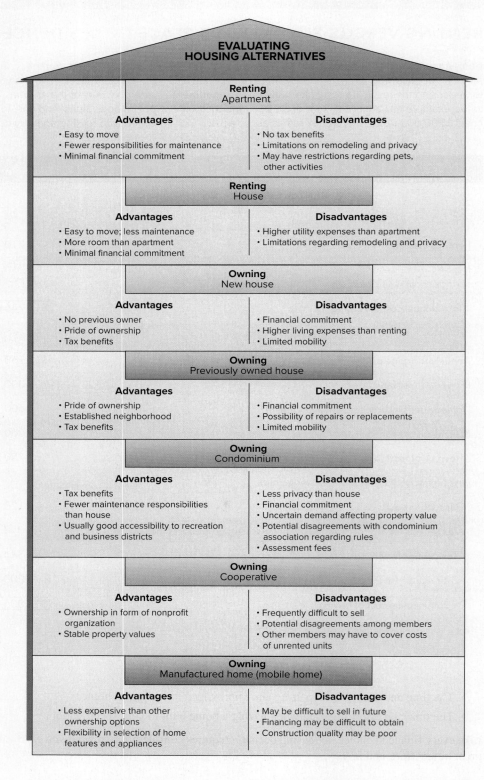

For many young people, renting may be preferred. However, if you plan to live in the same area for several years and believe real estate prices will increase, you might consider buying a home.

People who are financially able to buy a home may still choose to rent to avoid the time and money commitment needed to maintain a house. If renting, invest your savings if you decide to buy a home in the future. As you can see in the *Financial Literacy Calculations: Renting Versus Buying Your Place of Residence* feature, the choice between renting and buying is often not clear. In general, renting is less costly in the short run, but home ownership usually has long-term financial advantages.

HOUSING INFORMATION SOURCES

As with any consumer purchase, many housing information sources are available. Start your search with basic resources such as this book. Next, consult online sources and apps for information about renting, buying, financing, remodeling, and other housing topics. Other helpful sources are friends, real estate agents, and government agencies (see Chapter 8 Appendix).

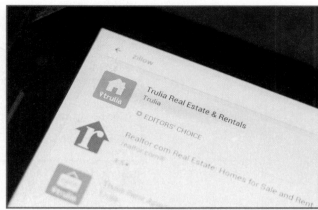

Online sources are very useful for buying, selling, or renting a home.
Sharaf Maksumov/Shutterstock

 PRACTICE QUIZ 9-1

1. How does a person's employment and household situation influence the selection of housing?
2. What are some opportunity costs associated with the selection of housing?

PFP Sheet 40
Housing Needs

PFP Sheet 41
Renting or Buying Housing

Renting Your Residence

In the past, apartment ads might include "2-bd. garden apt, a/c, crptg, mod bath, lndry, sec $1050." Which translated means a two-bedroom garden apartment (at or below ground level) with air-conditioning, carpeting, a modern bath, and laundry facilities. And a required security deposit of $1,050.

At some point in your life, you are likely to rent. You may rent when you are first on your own or later in life when you want to avoid the activities needed to maintain a home. Approximately 35 percent of U.S. households live in rental units.

As a tenant, you pay for the right to live in a residence owned by someone else. Exhibit 9-3 presents the activities involved in finding and living in a rental unit.

SELECTING A RENTAL UNIT

An apartment is the most common type of rental housing. Apartments range from modern, luxury units with extensive recreational facilities to simple one- and two-bedroom units in quiet neighborhoods. If you need more room, consider renting a house or condo. The increased space will cost more, and you may have some responsibility for maintaining the property. If you need less space, you may rent a room in a private house.

LO9-2

Analyze the costs and benefits associated with renting.

EXHIBIT 9-3

Housing rental activities

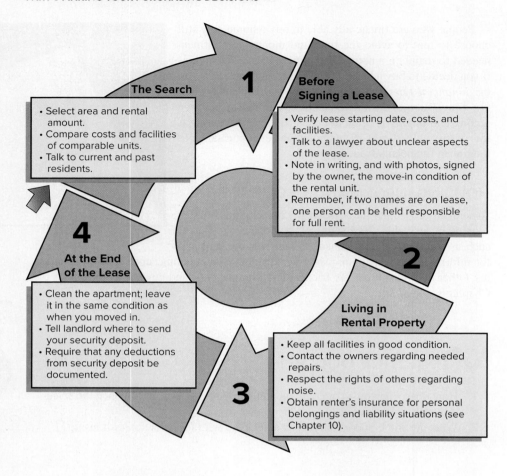

The Search
- Select area and rental amount.
- Compare costs and facilities of comparable units.
- Talk to current and past residents.

1

Before Signing a Lease
- Verify lease starting date, costs, and facilities.
- Talk to a lawyer about unclear aspects of the lease.
- Note in writing, and with photos, signed by the owner, the move-in condition of the rental unit.
- Remember, if two names are on lease, one person can be held responsible for full rent.

2

Living in Rental Property
- Keep all facilities in good condition.
- Contact the owners regarding needed repairs.
- Respect the rights of others regarding noise.
- Obtain renter's insurance for personal belongings and liability situations (see Chapter 10).

3

4

At the End of the Lease
- Clean the apartment; leave it in the same condition as when you moved in.
- Tell landlord where to send your security deposit.
- Require that any deductions from security deposit be documented.

The main information sources for available rental units are online and newspaper ads, real estate and rental offices, and people you know. When comparing rental units, consider the factors presented in Exhibit 9-4.

ADVANTAGES OF RENTING

The three main advantages of renting are mobility, fewer responsibilities, and lower initial costs.

MOBILITY   Renting offers mobility when a location change may be needed or desired. A new job, a rent increase, the need for a larger apartment, or the desire to live in a different community are reasons people relocate. Moving is easier when you are renting than when you own a home. After completing school and starting your career, renting makes job transfers easier.

FEWER RESPONSIBILITIES   Renters have fewer responsibilities than homeowners since they usually do not have to be concerned with maintenance and repairs. However, they are expected to do regular household cleaning. Renters also have fewer financial concerns. Their main housing costs are rent and utilities; homeowners incur expenses related to property taxes, property insurance, maintenance, and repairs.

LOWER INITIAL COSTS   Moving into a rental unit is less expensive than buying a home. While new tenants usually pay a security deposit, a home buyer will have a down payment and closing costs of several thousand dollars.

EXHIBIT 9-4   Selecting an apartment

Selecting an Apartment

LOCATION
- Schools, places of worship
- Shopping
- Public transportation
- Recreation

BUILDING EXTERIOR
- Condition of building, grounds
- Parking facilities and recreation

BUILDING INTERIOR
- Exits, security
- Hallway maintenance
- Condition of elevators
- Access to mailboxes

FINANCIAL ASPECTS
- Rent, length of lease
- Security deposit
- Utilities, other costs

LAYOUT AND FACILITIES
- Condition, size
- Closets, carpeting, appliances
- Type of heat, air-conditioning
- Plumbing, water pressure
- Storage area
- Room size
- Doors, locks, windows

DISADVANTAGES OF RENTING

Renting has few financial benefits, may impose a restricted lifestyle, and involves legal details.

FEW FINANCIAL BENEFITS   Renters do not have the financial advantages of homeowners. Tenants cannot take tax deductions for mortgage interest and property taxes or benefit from the potential increased value of real estate. Renters are also subject to rent increases over which they may have little control.

RESTRICTED LIFESTYLE   Renters are generally limited in the activities they can pursue in their residence. Sound from a home entertainment system or parties may be monitored closely. Tenants are often subject to restrictions regarding pets and decorating.

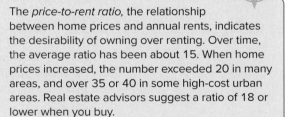

smart money minute

The *price-to-rent ratio,* the relationship between home prices and annual rents, indicates the desirability of owning over renting. Over time, the average ratio has been about 15. When home prices increased, the number exceeded 20 in many areas, and over 35 or 40 in some high-cost urban areas. Real estate advisors suggest a ratio of 18 or lower when you buy.

Also, beware of *lease-to-purchase* and *rent-with-options* for renters to become homeowners. While these offers can be beneficial, financial disasters can also occur. An up-front deposit and other purchase funds could be lost if a late rent payment is made.

LEGAL DETAILS   Most tenants sign a **lease,** a legal document that defines the conditions of a rental agreement. This document provides the following information.

- A description and address of the rental unit.
- The name and address of the owner/landlord (the *lessor*).
- The name of the tenant (the *lessee*).
- The effective date of the lease and the length of the lease.

lease A legal document that defines the conditions of a rental agreement.

- The amount of the security and pet deposit.
- The amount and due date of the monthly rent.
- The location where the rent payment is to be sent.
- The date and amount due for late rent payments.
- A list of the utilities, appliances, furniture, and other facilities included in the rent.
- Restrictions regarding certain activities (pets, remodeling); tenant's right to sublet.
- Charges for damages or for moving out of the rental unit later (or earlier) than the lease expiration date.
- The conditions under which the landlord may enter the apartment.

my life 2

I am aware of the benefits of renting.
Before signing a lease, be sure that you understand the elements of this legal document. For additional information on leases, and the potential benefits and drawbacks of renting, go to www.thespruce.com/apartment-living-4127933.

smart money minute

Renter's insurance is often overlooked by people living in an apartment. Damage or theft of personal property (clothing, furniture, television, laptop, jewelry) is usually not covered by the landlord's insurance policy. Renter's insurance is discussed in Chapter 10.

Standard lease forms may include conditions you might not want to accept. The fact that a lease is printed does not mean you must accept it as is. If you have a high credit score, you may be able to negotiate a lower rent or a reduced security deposit. Also, discuss with the landlord any lease terms you consider unacceptable. The COVID-19 pandemic caused a decrease in rental demand in some areas, which created opportunities for lower rents. To negotiate a rent cut, provide evidence of comparable area rents, your payment consistency, and, if appropriate, a job loss or financial difficulties.

Some leases give you the right to *sublet* the rental unit. Subletting may be necessary if you must move before the lease expires. Subletting allows you to have another person take over rent payments and live in the rental unit.

A lease should be in writing, but oral leases are also valid. With an oral lease, one party must give a 30-day written notice to the other party before terminating the lease or charging a rent increase. To avoid potential difficulties, make every attempt to get a lease that is in writing.

A lease provides protection to both landlord and tenant. The tenant is protected from rent increases during the lease term unless the lease contains a provision allowing an increase. In most states, the tenant cannot be locked out or evicted without a court hearing. The lease gives the landlord the right to take legal action against a tenant for nonpayment of rent or destruction of property.

COSTS OF RENTING

A *security deposit* is usually required when you sign a lease. This money is held by the landlord to cover the cost of any damages done to the rental unit during the lease period. The security deposit is usually one month's rent. However, you may be required to also pay the first and last month's rent before being allowed to move in.

Several state and local laws require the landlord to pay interest on a security deposit. After you vacate the rental unit, your security deposit should be refunded within a reasonable time. Many states require that it be returned within 30 days. If money is deducted from your security deposit, you have the right to an itemized list of repair costs.

As a renter, you will incur other living expenses besides monthly rent. For many apartments, water is included in the rent; however, other utilities may not be covered. If you rent a house, you will probably pay for heat, electricity, water, and wifi.

PRACTICE QUIZ 9-2

1. What are the main benefits and drawbacks of renting a place of residence?
2. Which components of a lease are likely to be most negotiable?

PFP Sheet 42
Apartment Rental
Comparison

The Home-Buying Process

Many people dream of having a place of residence they can call their own. Home ownership is a common financial goal. Exhibit 9-5 presents the process for achieving this goal.

STEP 1: DETERMINE HOME OWNERSHIP NEEDS

To start the home-buying process, consider the benefits and drawbacks of this financial commitment. Also, evaluate different housing units and determine the amount you can afford.

EVALUATE OWNING YOUR PLACE OF RESIDENCE

What Are the Benefits of Home Ownership?   Whether you purchase a house, a condominium, or a manufactured home, you can enjoy the pride of ownership, financial benefits, and lifestyle flexibility of home ownership.

LO9-3

Explain the home-buying process.

EXHIBIT 9-5

The home-buying process

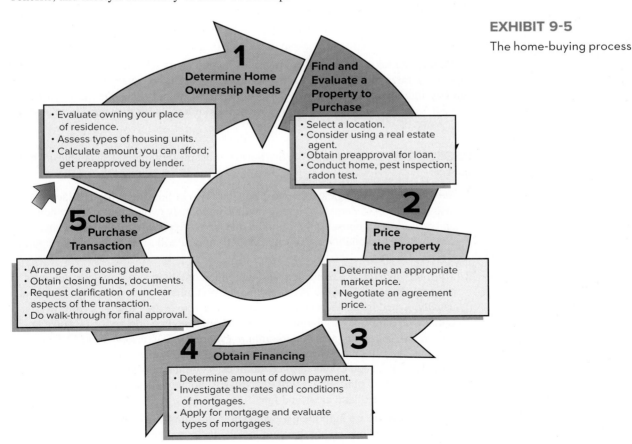

Home ownership allows you the flexibility to decorate as you desire.
M_Agency/Shutterstock

1. *Pride of ownership.* Having a place to call their own is a primary motive of many home buyers. Stability of residence and a personalized living location can be important.

2. *Financial benefits.* One financial benefit is the deductibility of mortgage interest and real estate tax payments for federal income taxes. Another benefit is potential increases in the value of the property. Finally, homeowners may be able to borrow against the equity in their homes. *Equity* is the current home value less the amount owed on the mortgage.

3. *Lifestyle flexibility.* While renting gives you mobility, home ownership gives you more opportunity to express individuality. Homeowners have greater freedom than renters for decorating and entertaining guests.

What Are the Drawbacks of Home Ownership?   The dream of owning a home does not guarantee a glamorous existence. This economic obligation can result in financial uncertainty, limited mobility, and higher living costs.

1. *Financial uncertainty.* Among the financial uncertainties associated with buying a home is obtaining money for a down payment. Qualifying for mortgage financing may be a problem due to your personal situation or current economic conditions. Finally, changing property values in an area can affect your financial investment.

2. *Limited mobility.* Home ownership is not as easy for changing living location as with renting. If changes in your situation make it necessary to sell your home, doing so may take time. High interest rates and other factors can result in a weak demand for housing.

3. *Higher living costs.* Owning your place of residence can be expensive. As a homeowner, you are responsible for maintenance, repainting, repairs, and home improvements.

Real estate taxes are a major expense of homeowners. Higher property values and higher tax rates mean higher real estate taxes. Higher taxes affect homeowners more directly than renters, who pay them in the form of higher rent. See the *How To . . . Appeal Your Property Taxes* feature to learn about appealing mistakes on your property taxes.

ASSESS TYPES OF HOUSING   Several housing options are available to home buyers.

1. *Single-family dwellings* are the most popular form of housing. These residences, also referred to as *detached* homes, include previously owned houses, new houses, and custom-built houses. Older houses may be preferred by people who want a certain style and quality of housing. Modern homes will offer a more contemporary style and features.

2. *Multiunit dwellings,* a residence with more than one living unit, include duplexes and town houses. A *duplex* is a building that contains two housing units, with each usually owned by a different homeowner. *Town houses* are buildings with two, four, or six single-family living units. These attached housing options involve land ownership, in contrast to a condominium. *Planned unit developments (PUDs)* are designed communities with varied housing (detached homes and town houses) and other land use, such as recreational facilities, a commercial center, shopping areas, and an industrial park. PUDs will likely have a homeowners association to maintain commonly owned land areas and facilities.

condominium An individually owned housing unit in a building with several such units.

3. **Condominiums** are individually owned housing units in a building with several units. Individual ownership does not include the common areas, such as hallways,

HOW TO...   Appeal Your Property Taxes

Property taxes vary from area to area, but they usually range from 2 to 4 percent of the market value of the home. Taxes are based on the *assessed value,* the amount that your local government determines your property to be worth for tax purposes. Assessed values are normally lower than the market value, often about half. A home with a market value of $180,000 may be assessed at $90,000. If the tax rate is $60 per $1,000 of assessed value, this would result in annual taxes of $5,400 ($90,000 divided by $1,000 times $60). This rate is 6 percent of the assessed value but only 3 percent of the market value.

Although higher home values are desirable, this increase means higher property assessments. Increasing property taxes are frustrating, but there are actions you can take:

Step 1: Know the appeal deadline. Call the local assessor's office. You will usually have between 14 and 90 days to initiate your appeal. Late requests are usually not accepted. Send your appeal by certified mail to have proof that you met the deadline; keep copies of all documents.

Step 2: Check for errors. The assessment office may have incorrect information. Obvious mistakes may include reporting incorrect square footage or stating that a home has four bedrooms when there are only three.

Step 3: Determine the issues to emphasize. A property tax appeal can be based on a mistake in the assessment or a higher assessment than comparable homes. Note items that negatively affect the value of your home. For example, a bridge is no longer in operation near your home, making your house much less accessible—and less valuable. Or, if a garage has been taken down to increase garden space, the home's value likely would be less. Compare your assessment with homes of the same size, age, and general location. Obtain comparisons for 5 to 10 homes.

Step 4: Prepare for the hearing. Gather evidence and prepare an organized presentation. Use photos of comparable properties. A spreadsheet can make it easy for the hearing officials to view your evidence. Suggest a specific corrected assessment, and give your reasons. Observe the hearings of others to become familiar with the process.

---

outside grounds, and recreational facilities. These areas are owned by the condominium association, which is run by the people who own the housing units. The condominium association oversees the management and operation of the housing complex. Condominium owners are charged a monthly fee to cover the maintenance, repairs, improvements, and insurance for the building and common areas. A condominium is a legal form of home ownership.

4. **Cooperative housing** is a form of housing in which the units in a building are owned by a nonprofit organization. The shareholders purchase stock to obtain the right to live in a unit in the building. While the residents do not own the units, they have the legal right to occupy a unit for as long as they own stock in the cooperative. The title for the property belongs to the co-op. This ownership arrangement is different from condominiums, in which residents own their individual living units.

cooperative housing A form of housing in which a building containing a number of housing units is owned by a nonprofit organization whose members rent the units.

HOUSING CONSTRUCTION   The construction of a living unit can vary. *Factory-built houses* are living units that are fully or partially assembled in a factory and then moved to the living site. A *prefabricated home,* with components built in a factory, is then assembled at the housing site. With this type of housing, mass production can keep building costs lower. A variation of factory-built housing is a *modular home,* in which completed pieces of the house are transported to its location and set on a concrete foundation. Since they must conform to building codes, most modular homes, once completed, are impossible to distinguish from site-built homes.

Mobile homes, legally referred to as *manufactured homes* and sometimes called *trailer homes,* are not often moved from their original sites. These housing units, which are typically less than 1,000 square feet, can offer features of a conventional house,

smart money minute

Between 1908 and 1940, the Sears company sold about 70,000 ready-to-assemble home kits in North America. The precut materials were shipped by rail and delivered to the home site by truck. With over 350 architectural styles, family members, friends, and contractors worked to assemble the mail order home. Today, 3D printing is taking a similar approach with a giant, three-dimensional device creating the footings, foundation, slab, and walls. The printing time takes about 48 hours, part of the eight-day process to build the home.

my life 3

I know how to research which housing type would be best for me.

As you start the home-buying process, consider what you can afford to spend. You can prequalify for a mortgage online at www.mortgage101.com or www.erate.com.

personal fintech

Technology to plan, build, buy, sell, and manage real estate is called *PropTech* (property technology). These digital innovations connect buyers, sellers, brokers, lenders, and landlords through artificial intelligence, virtual reality, 3D printing, drones, and crowdfunding. PropTech involves three main areas: (1) *smart home* uses digital platforms and apps; (2) *sharing real estate* facilitates leasing and renting of land, offices, storage, and apartments; (3) *real estate FinTech* includes blockchain technology to eliminate transaction paperwork.

The interconnectivity of devices with the Internet of Things (IoT) makes these smart home features possible:

- A smart thermostat to control home temperature.
- A ceiling fan that monitors temperature and humidity.
- A wifi-enabled coffee maker programmable for strength and flavor.
- A light bulb to regulate brightness and stream audio.
- An intelligent oven with sensors for cooking settings and a camera to livestream food preparation progress to your smartphone.

such as fully equipped kitchens, fireplaces, cathedral ceilings, and whirlpool baths. The site for a manufactured home may be either purchased or leased.

The safety of a manufactured home can be a concern. While fires occur no more often in these houses than in other living units, construction may allow a fire to spread faster. Today, manufacturing standards for fire safety are stricter than in the past. However, when a fire occurs, the unit is often completely destroyed. This type of housing is also vulnerable to wind damage. Another concern is the tendency to quickly depreciate in value. When this occurs, an important benefit of home ownership is eliminated. Obtaining financing for a manufactured home may also be difficult.

BUILDING A HOME Some people prefer to have a home built to their specifications. Before beginning such a project, be sure you have the necessary knowledge, money, and perseverance. When choosing a contractor to coordinate the project, consider the following:

- Does the contractor have the experience needed for the type of building project you require?
- Does the contractor have a good working relationship with the architect, material suppliers, electricians, plumbers, carpenters, and other personnel needed for the project?
- What assurance do you have about the quality of materials?
- What arrangements are required for payments during construction?
- What delays in the construction process will be considered legitimate?
- Is the contractor licensed and insured?
- Is the contractor willing to provide names, addresses, and phone numbers of satisfied customers?
- Have local consumer agencies received any complaints about this contractor?
- Does the written contract include a time schedule, cost estimates, a description of the work, and a payment schedule?

An alternative to building your own house is a DIY (do-it-yourself) "home in a box." These kits include all the materials for your custom-designed house, and they cost about half of a completed home. However, you or someone you hire will have to assemble the precut and numbered pieces.

DETERMINE HOW MUCH YOU CAN AFFORD As you determine how much of your budget you will spend on a home, consider the price of the house along with its size and quality.

Price and Down Payment The amount you can afford is affected by funds available for a down payment, your income, and your current living expenses. Other factors you should consider are current mortgage rates, the potential future value of the property, and your ability to make monthly mortgage, tax, and insurance payments. To determine how much you can afford to spend on a home, have a loan officer at a mortgage company or other financial institution *prequalify* you. This service is provided without charge.

Size and Quality You may not get all the features you want in your first home, but financial advisors suggest getting into the housing market by purchasing what you can afford. As you move up, your second or third home can include more of your desired features.

Ideally, the home you buy will be in good condition. In certain circumstances, you may be willing to buy a *handyman's special,* a home that needs work and that you can get at a lower price because of its condition. You will then need to put money into the house for repairs and improvements or invest *sweat equity* by doing some of the work yourself. Home improvement information and assistance are available from home-improvement retailers and online.

Before buying a home, be sure to inspect all aspects of the property you are considering.
Pixsooz/Shutterstock

STEP 2: FIND AND EVALUATE A PROPERTY TO PURCHASE

Next, select a location, consider using the services of a real estate agent, and conduct a home inspection.

SELECTING A LOCATION An old saying among real estate professionals is that the three most important factors to consider when buying a home are *location, location,* and *location!* Perhaps you prefer an urban, a suburban, or a rural setting. Or perhaps you want to live in a small town or in a resort area. In selecting a neighborhood, compare your values and lifestyle with those of current residents.

Be aware of **zoning laws,** restrictions on how the property in an area can be used. The location of businesses and the anticipated construction of industrial buildings or a highway may influence your buying decision.

If you have or plan to have a family, consider the school system. Educators recommend that schools be evaluated on program variety, student achievement, percentage of students who go to college, faculty dedication, facilities, school funding, and parent involvement. Homeowners without children also benefit from strong schools since the educational strengths of a community help property values.

zoning laws Restrictions on how the property in an area can be used.

USING A REAL ESTATE AGENT Real estate agents have information about housing in locations of interest to you. Their main services include (1) showing you homes in many areas based on your needs and preapproved mortgage amount; (2) presenting your offer to the seller based on a market analysis; (3) negotiating a purchase price; (4) assisting you in obtaining financing; and (5) representing you at the closing. A real estate agent may also recommend lawyers, insurance agents, home inspectors, and mortgage companies.

Since the home seller usually pays the commission, a buyer may not incur a direct cost. However, this expense is reflected in the price paid for the home. In some states, the agent could be working for the seller. In others, the agent may be working for the buyer, the seller, or as a *dual agent,* working for both the buyer and the seller. When dual agency exists, most states require that buyers sign a disclosure acknowledging that they are aware the agent is working for both buyer and seller. This agreement can limit the information provided to each party, and the agent may not be allowed to negotiate on your behalf. Many states have *buyer agents* who represent the buyer's interests and are paid by either the seller or the buyer.

smart money minute

The CLUE® (Comprehensive Loss Underwriting Exchange) report provides a five-year history of insurance losses at a property that a home buyer is considering for purchase. This disclosure report is an independent source of information.

EXHIBIT 9-6   Conducting a home inspection

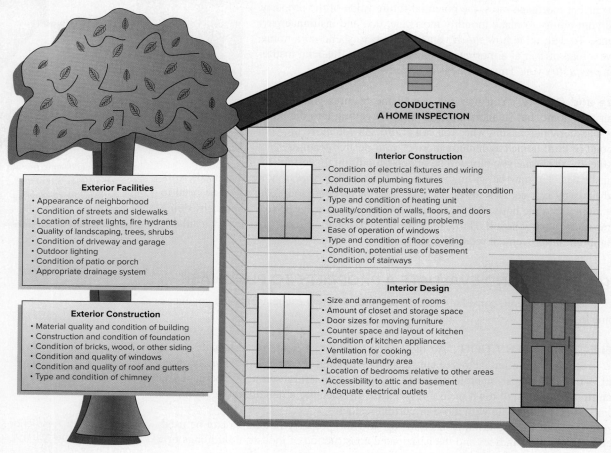

CONDUCTING A HOME INSPECTION   Before deciding on a specific home, perform a complete evaluation. Do not assume everything is in working condition just because someone lives there. A trained home inspector can minimize future problems. Being cautious will help avoid headaches and unexpected expenses. Exhibit 9-6 suggests items that an inspector and you might consider when evaluating a home. A home purchase agreement may include the right to have various professionals (roofer, plumber, electrician) inspect the property. Radon testing, pest (termite), and lead inspections are also often conducted.

Some states, cities, and lenders require inspection documents. The mortgage company will usually require an *appraisal* to determine the fair value of the property. An appraisal is not a detailed inspection, only an estimate of the market price.

STEP 3: PRICE THE PROPERTY

After you have selected a home, determine an offer price and negotiate a final buying price.

DETERMINING THE HOME PRICE   What price should you offer for the home? The main factors to consider are recent selling prices in the area, current housing demand, the length of time the home has been on the market, the owner's need to sell, financing options, and features and condition of the home. Each of these can affect your offer price. For example, you will have to offer a higher price in times of low interest rates and high demand for homes. On the other hand, a home that has been on the

Components of a Home Purchase Agreement

In a real estate transaction, the contract between buyer and seller contains the following information:

- ❏ The names and addresses of the buyer and seller
- ❏ Address and legal description of the property
- ❏ The price of the property
- ❏ The amount of the mortgage, interest rate, and approval date
- ❏ The amount of the earnest money deposit
- ❏ The date and time of the closing
- ❏ Where the closing will take place
- ❏ A provision for extension of the closing date

- ❏ A provision for disposition of the deposit money if something goes wrong
- ❏ Adjustments to be made at the closing
- ❏ Details of what is included in the sale—home appliances, drapes, carpeting, and other items
- ❏ Special conditions of the sale
- ❏ Inspections the buyer can make before the closing
- ❏ Property easements, such as the use of an area of the property for utility lines or poles

Source: *Homeownership: Guidelines for Buying and Owning a Home* (Richmond, VA: Federal Reserve Bank of Richmond).

EXHIBIT 9-7

The components of a home purchase agreement

market for over a year could mean an opportunity to offer a lower price. Housing prices fluctuate over time, such as the financial crisis of 2008 with home values hitting a low in 2012. More recently, prices recovered when demand increased after the pandemic. The services of a real estate agent or an appraiser can assist you in determining a current home value.

Your offer will be in the form of a *purchase agreement,* or contract (see Exhibit 9-7). This document constitutes your legal offer to purchase the home. Your first offer price will usually not be accepted.

NEGOTIATING THE PURCHASE PRICE If your initial offer is accepted and signed by all parties, you have a valid contract. If your offer is rejected, you have several options, depending on the seller. A *counteroffer* from the owner indicates a willingness to negotiate a price settlement. If the counteroffer is only slightly lower than the asking price, you are expected to move closer to that price with your next offer. If the counteroffer is quite a bit off the asking price, you are closer to the point where you might split the difference to arrive at the purchase price. If no counteroffer is forthcoming, you may wish to make another offer to determine whether the seller is willing to negotiate.

In times of high demand for housing, negotiating may be minimized; this situation is referred to as a *seller's market,* since the current homeowner is likely to have several offers for the property. In contrast, when home sales are slow, a *buyer's market* exists and a lower price is likely.

When you buy a previously owned home, your negotiating power is based on current market demand and the current owner's need to sell. When you buy a new home, a slow market may mean lower prices or an opportunity to obtain various amenities (fireplace, appliances, higher quality carpeting) from the builder at a lower cost.

Once a price has been agreed on, the purchase contract becomes the basis for the real estate transaction. As part of the offer, the buyer will usually submit **earnest money,** a portion of the purchase price deposited as evidence of good faith to show that the purchase offer is serious. At the closing of the home purchase, the earnest money is applied toward the down payment. This money may be returned if the sale cannot be completed due to circumstances beyond the buyer's control.

Home purchase agreements often contain a *contingency clause.* This contract condition states that the agreement is binding only if a certain event occurs. For example, a real estate contract may stipulate that the contract will not be valid unless the buyer

earnest money A portion of the price of a home that the buyer deposits as evidence of good faith to indicate a serious purchase offer.

obtains financing for the purchase within a certain period of time, or it may make the purchase of a home contingent on the sale of the buyer's current home.

 PRACTICE QUIZ 9-3

1. What are the advantages and disadvantages of owning a home?
2. What guidelines might determine the amount to spend for a home?
3. How can the quality of a school system benefit homeowners in a community who do not have school-age children?
4. What services are available to home buyers from a real estate agent?
5. How does a *seller's* market differ from a *buyer's* market?

The Finances of Home Buying

LO9-4

Calculate the costs associated with purchasing a home.

Home buyers should meet with a banker or mortgage broker early in the process to determine the amount they can afford. Financing a home purchase requires obtaining a mortgage, awareness of mortgage types, and settling the real estate transaction.

STEP 4: OBTAIN FINANCING

DETERMINE DOWN PAYMENT   The amount of cash available for a down payment affects the mortgage loan size needed. A large down payment, such as 20 percent or more, makes it easier to obtain a mortgage. Personal savings, investments or other assets, and assistance from relatives are common down payment sources. Parents can help children purchase a home. When accepting funds, be sure to assess the financial impact for family members, and evaluate the tax implications. Consider other sources and possibilities, such as setting it up as a loan rather than a gift. Also investigate government or private programs available to lower-income or first-time home buyers.

Private mortgage insurance (PMI) is usually required if the down payment is less than 20 percent. This coverage protects the lender from financial loss due to default. After building up 20 percent equity in a home, a home buyer should contact the lender to cancel PMI. The Homeowners Protection Act requires that a PMI policy be terminated automatically when the equity reaches 22 percent of the property value at the time the mortgage was executed. Homeowners can request termination earlier if they can prove the equity in the home is at least 22 percent of the current market value. FHA and VA mortgage loans, discussed later, have special provisions for mortgage insurance.

mortgage A long-term loan on a specific piece of property such as a home or other real estate.

smart money minute

A common *mistake* of home buyers is not planning for additional costs. An *action* would be to create a budget and consult with others. Determine amounts for closing costs, moving, property taxes, insurance, utilities, furniture, repairs, condo fees, and homeowner association dues. This action can result in *success* of a home that fits your budget and lifestyle. Once approved for a mortgage, do not make any significant financial transactions before closing. Obtaining a car loan or making a major credit card purchase can affect your loan qualification.

QUALIFYING AND APPLYING FOR A MORTGAGE   Do you have funds for a down payment? Do you earn enough to make mortgage payments along with other living expenses? Do you have a good credit rating? Unless you pay cash for a home, favorable responses to these questions are required.

A **mortgage** is a long-term loan on a specific piece of property such as a home or other real estate. Payments on a mortgage are usually made over 10, 15, 20, 25, or 30 years. Banks, credit unions, and mortgage companies are common sources of home financing. *Mortgage brokers* can help home buyers obtain financing, since they are in contact with several financial institutions. While online mortgage providers offer faster quotes and approval, you may be assigned a loan officer in a call center and may not receive the personal service you desire.

To qualify for a mortgage, you must meet criteria similar to other loans. The home you buy serves as security, or *collateral,* for the mortgage. The major factors that affect the affordability of your mortgage are your income, other debts, credit score, down payment amount, loan length, and current mortgage rates.

To obtain a home loan, pay down your credit cards, pay loans on time, and save for a down payment. These actions will increase your ability to qualify for a mortgage. With a credit score of at least 620, a person will usually be able to obtain home financing. A high credit score (720 or above) may allow a mortgage without a down payment and with a lower interest rate. Your credit score may vary among reporting agencies due to different calculation methods.

Applying for a mortgage involves these phases:

smart money minute

Spring is often viewed as the best time to buy a house, but with more people in the market, bidding wars can drive up prices. Instead, studies reveal that in January and February the average home sells for 5 to 6 percent less than at other times of the year. Remember, these lower prices are the result of offers made during the holidays in late December and early January when home prices are typically lowest. The worst month to buy is June; for home sellers that's the best time to be on the market.

1. *Prequalification,* which involves completing the mortgage application. The borrower provides evidence of employment, income, asset ownership, and existing debt amounts. Self-employed applicants or those with a limited credit record should provide evidence of a stable job, a good income, amounts in savings, and paying bills on time.

2. The lender obtains a credit report and verifies the borrower's financial status. A decision to approve or deny the mortgage is made with the maximum mortgage amount for which the borrower qualifies. When applying for a mortgage, the borrower will receive a *loan estimate.* This form, required by the Consumer Financial Protection Bureau at www.consumerfinance.gov, summarizes key information to help borrowers decide among various loans.

3. At this point, lenders will likely charge a fee that may be as high as $500. The loan commitment is a pledge for the funds to purchase the home, at which time the purchase contract becomes legally binding. The borrower decides whether to lock in an interest rate for 30–90 days; or, if rates are expected to decline, the borrower may *float,* locking in the rate at a later date.

The Ability-to-Repay (ATR)/Qualified Mortgage (QM) rule requires lenders to carefully consider a borrower's financial situation. ATR expects lenders to make a "reasonable and good faith determination" of repayment ability based on income, assets, employment status, liabilities, credit history, and debt-to-income (DTI) ratio. QM limits points and fees, prohibits or restricts certain mortgage features, and imposes a maximum on a borrower's DTI ratio. A concern with ATR/QM is balancing protection from exploitive lending while allowing access to a mortgage for those who desire a home loan.

Based on your situation for home financing, the results in Exhibit 9-8 include: (*a*) the monthly mortgage payment you can afford, (*b*) the mortgage amount you can afford, and (*c*) the home purchase price you can afford.

These sample calculations are typical of many financial institutions; actual qualifications will vary by lender and mortgage type. The amount will be larger when interest rates are lower. As interest rates rise, fewer people will be able to afford an average-priced home. For example, a person who can afford a monthly mortgage payment of $700 will qualify for a 30-year loan of:

$165,877 at 3 percent	$116,667 at 6 percent
$146,750 at 4 percent	$105,263 at 7 percent
$130,354 at 5 percent	$95,368 at 8 percent

EXHIBIT 9-8 Housing affordability and mortgage qualification amounts

		Example A	Example B
Step 1:	Determine your monthly gross income (annual income divided by 12).	$48,000 ÷ 12	$48,000 ÷ 12
Step 2:	With a down payment of at least 5 percent, lenders use 33 percent of monthly gross income as a guideline for PITI (principal, interest, taxes, and insurance) and 38 percent of monthly gross income as a guideline for PITI plus other debt payments.	$4,000 × .38 $1,520	$4,000 × .33 $1,320
Step 3:	Subtract other debt payments (e.g., payments on an auto loan) and an estimate of the monthly costs of property taxes and home-owner's insurance.	−380 −300	— −300
(a) Affordable monthly mortgage payment		$840	$1,020
Step 4:	Divide this amount by the monthly mortgage payment per $1,000 based on current mortgage rates—an 8 percent, 30-year loan, for example (see Exhibit 9-9)—and multiply by $1,000.	÷$7.34 × $1,000	÷$7.34 × $1,000
(b) Affordable mortgage amount		$114,441	$138,965
Step 5:	Divide your affordable mortgage amount by 1 minus the fractional portion of your down payment (e.g., 1 − .1 with a 10 percent down payment).	÷ .9	÷ .9
(c) Affordable home purchase price		$127,157	$154,405

Note: The two ratios lending institutions use (step 2) and other loan requirements may vary based on a variety of factors, including the type of mortgage, the amount of the down payment, your income level, and current interest rates. For example, with a down payment of 10 percent or more and a credit score exceeding 720, the ratios might increase to 40/45 or 45/50 percent in the above exhibit.

EXAMPLE: Calculate Mortgage Payment

To determine the amount of your monthly mortgage payment, multiply the factor from Exhibit 9-9 by the number of thousands of the loan amount. For a 30-year, 7 percent, $223,000 mortgage:

$$\text{Monthly payment amount} = 223 \times \$6.65$$
$$= \$1,482.95$$

EXHIBIT 9-9
Mortgage payment factors (principal and interest factors per $1,000 of loan amount)

Term Rate	30 Years	25 Years	20 Years	15 Years
3.0%	$4.22	$4.74	$5.55	$6.91
3.5	4.49	5.01	5.80	7.15
4.0	4.77	5.28	6.06	7.40
4.5	5.07	5.56	6.33	7.65
5.0	5.37	5.85	6.60	7.91
5.5	5.68	6.14	6.88	8.17
6.0	6.00	6.44	7.16	8.44
6.5	6.32	6.75	7.46	8.71
7.0	6.65	7.07	7.75	8.99
7.5	6.99	7.39	8.06	9.27
8.0	7.34	7.72	8.36	9.56

In addition to using the mortgage payment factors (Exhibit 9-9), the monthly payment may be calculated with a formula, a financial calculator, Excel spreadsheet, website, or app. Loan payment amounts may also be determined using the following methods.

Formula	Financial Calculator		Excel®
$M = P[i(1+i)^n]/[(1+i)^n - 1]$	(payments a year)	12 P/YR	= PMT (rate/12,30*12,loan amount)
M = mortgage payment (monthly)	(total loan payments)	360 N	= denotes a formula
P = principal of the loan (loan amount)	(interest rate)	6 I/YR	rate/12 provides monthly rate
i = interest rate divided by 12	(loan amount)	180000 PV	total number of payments, such as 12 a year for 30 years
n = number of months of the loan	(calulate monthly payment)	PMT	loan amount – beginning mortgage balance

EVALUATING POINTS When comparing mortgage companies, consider other factors than the interest rate. The down payment and the points charged will affect the interest rate. **Points** are prepaid interest charged by the lender. Each *discount point* is equal to 1 percent of the loan amount and is a premium paid for obtaining a lower mortgage rate. In deciding whether to take a lower rate with more points or a higher rate with fewer points, consider the following guidelines:

points Prepaid interest charged by a lending institution for the mortgage; each discount point is equal to 1 percent of the loan amount.

- If you plan to live in the home for a period of time (over five years, for example), the lower mortgage rate is probably the best action.
- If you plan to sell the home in the next few years, the higher mortgage rate with fewer discount points may be better.

FIXED-RATE, FIXED-PAYMENT MORTGAGES Use online research to compare current mortgage rates. Most mortgage lenders allow you to apply online; the three main types are: (1) retail banks; (2) correspondent lenders, also called independent mortgage banks, which includes recent start-ups such as LoanDepot and SoFi; and (3) mortgage wholesalers and brokers. Exhibit 9-10 shows the main types of mortgages available to home buyers.

smart money minute

Today, fewer young people are buying homes due to marrying older, having children later, and high student debts. Other obstacles include higher home prices, limited money for a down payment, a poor credit history, and not having a stable income. The home features that younger home buyers are willing to give up to live in their ideal neighborhood include a garage, updated kitchen, storage space, yard, and updated bathroom.

EXHIBIT 9-10 Types of mortgage loans

Loan Type	Benefits	Drawbacks
1. Conventional 30-year mortgage	• Fixed monthly payments for 30 years provide certainty of principal and interest payments.	• Higher initial rates than adjustables.
2. Conventional 15- or 20-year mortgage.	• Lower rate than 30-year fixed; faster equity buildup and quicker payoff of loan.	• Higher monthly payments.
3. FHA/VA fixed-rate mortgage (30-year and 15-year)	• Low down payment requirements and fully assumable with no prepayment penalties.	• May require additional processing time.
4. Adjustable-rate mortgage (ARM)—payment changes on 1-, 3-, 5-, 7-, or 10-year schedules	• Lower initial rates than fixed-rate loans, particularly on the 1-year adjustable. Offers possibility of future rate and payment decreases. Loans with rate "caps" may protect borrowers against increases in rates.	• Shifts far greater interest rate risk onto borrowers than fixed-rate loans. Risk of higher monthly payments in future years.
5. Interest-only mortgage	• Lower payments; more easily affordable.	• No decrease in amount owed; no building equity unless home value increases.

Conventional Mortgages   The **conventional mortgage** usually has equal payments over 15, 20, or 30 years based on a fixed interest rate. This mortgage offers certainty about future loan payments. The mortgage payments are set at a level that allows **amortization** of the loan; that is, the balance owed is reduced with each payment. Since the amount borrowed is large, the payments made during the early years are applied mainly to interest, with only small reductions in the principal. As the amount owed declines, the monthly payments have an increasing impact on the loan balance. Near the end of the mortgage term, most of each payment is applied to the balance.

For example, a $125,000, 30-year, 6 percent mortgage would have monthly payments of $749.44. The payments would be divided as follows for the first and final months:

	Interest	Principal	Remaining Balance
For the first month	$625.00 ($125,000 × 0.06 × 1/12)	$124.44	$124,875.56 ($125,000 − $124.44)
For the second month	$624.38 ($124,875.56 × 0.06 × 1/12)	$125.06	$124,750.50 ($124,875.56 − $125.06)
For the 360th month	$3.73 ($745.71 × 0.06 × 1/12)	$745.71	–0–

my life 4

I understand the different types of mortgages.

What are current mortgage rates in your area? The information can be obtained at www.bankrate.com, www.hsh.com, and www.interest.com, as well as from local financial institutions.

With a 15-year instead of a 30-year mortgage, a home buyer borrowing $200,000 can save over $150,000 in interest over the life of the loan. This faster equity growth and savings on interest will also occur if an extra amount is paid toward principal each month. An amortization schedule calculator is available at www.hsh.com/amortization-calculator.html.

In the past, some conventional mortgages were *assumable*. This feature allowed a home buyer to continue with the seller's original agreement. Today, most assumable mortgages are through government programs.

Government Financing Programs   Government financing programs include loans insured by the Federal Housing Authority (FHA) and loans guaranteed by the Veterans Administration (VA). These government agencies do not provide the mortgage money; rather, they help home buyers obtain low-interest, low-down-payment loans.

To qualify for an FHA-insured loan, a person must meet certain conditions related to the down payment and fees. Most low- and middle-income people can qualify for the FHA loan program. The minimum down payment starts at 3.5 percent and varies depending on loan size. A lower down payment makes it easier for a person to purchase a home. The borrower is required to pay a fee for insurance that protects the lender from default.

The VA-guaranteed loan program assists eligible armed services veterans with home purchases. As with the FHA program, the funds for VA loans come from a mortgage company, with the risk reduced by government participation. A VA loan can be obtained without a down payment, with the rate based on the borrower's credit score. However, closing costs are still required.

Both FHA-insured loans and VA-guaranteed loans can be attractive financing alternatives and are assumable by future owners when the house is sold to a qualifying buyer. Both programs limit the amount one can borrow. Approval of FHA and VA loans usually require repairs for items revealed during the home inspection and appraisal.

Another government home loan source is the United States Department of Agriculture (USDA). This program may be used to finance housing and community facilities in rural areas. USDA loans, grants, and loan guarantees are available for single- and multi-family housing as well as to buy and improve land.

ADJUSTABLE-RATE, VARIABLE-PAYMENT MORTGAGES   As shown in Exhibit 9-10, the **adjustable-rate mortgage (ARM),** also referred to as a *flexible-rate mortgage* or a *variable-rate mortgage,* has an interest rate that increases or decreases during the life of the loan. When mortgage rates were at record highs, many people used variable-rate home loans, expecting rates would eventually go down. ARMs have a lower initial interest rate than fixed-rate mortgages; however, the borrower, not the lender, bears the risk of future interest rate increases.

A **rate cap** restricts the amount that the interest rate can increase or decrease during the ARM term. This limit prevents the borrower from having to pay an interest rate significantly higher than the original agreement. Most rate caps limit increases (or decreases) in the rate to one or two percentage points in a year, and no more than five points over the life of the loan.

A **payment cap** keeps the payments on an adjustable-rate mortgage at a set level or limits the amount to which those payments can rise. When payment amounts do not rise but interest rates do, the amount owed can increase when the mortgage payment does not cover the interest owed. This increased loan balance, called *negative amortization,* means the amount of the home equity is decreasing instead of increasing. As a result of the increased amount owed, payments may be required for longer than originally planned. Some ARMs may last as long as 40 years.

Factors to consider when evaluating adjustable-rate mortgages include: (1) determine the frequency and restrictions for interest rates changes; (2) consider the frequency and restrictions for monthly payment changes; (3) investigate if the loan will be extended due to negative amortization, and determine limits on negative amortization; and (4) know what index the lending institution uses to set the mortgage rate.

Adjustable-rate mortgage rates change based on current interest rates. The London Interbank Offered Rate (LIBOR) has been the most common base index for setting rates for adjustable-rate mortgages. Studies reveal ARMs can be less costly over the life of a mortgage as long as interest rates remain fairly stable.

INTEREST-ONLY MORTGAGE   An *interest-only mortgage* allows a home buyer to have lower payments for the first few years of the loan. During that time, none of the mortgage payment goes toward the loan amount. Once the initial period ends, the mortgage adjusts to be interest-only at the new payment amount. Or a borrower may obtain a different type of mortgage to start building equity. With an interest-only mortgage, higher payments occur later in the loan. The payment will be based on the amount of the original loan since no principal has been paid. Interest-only mortgages can be dangerous if the value of the property declines.

OTHER FINANCING APPROACHES   To assist first-time home buyers, existing homeowners, and retired people, other financing plans are available.

Buy-Downs   A **buy-down** is an interest rate subsidy from a home builder or a real estate developer that reduces the mortgage payments during the first few years of the loan. This assistance is intended to encourage sales among home buyers who cannot afford conventional financing. However, the home price may be higher to cover the buy-down. After the buy-down period, the mortgage payments increase to the level that would have existed without the financial assistance. A buy-down can also be purchased with a buyer's own funds.

Second Mortgages   A **second mortgage,** more commonly called a *home equity loan,* allows a homeowner to borrow on the paid-up value (equity) of the property. Traditional second mortgages allow a homeowner to borrow a lump sum against the equity and repay

rate cap A limit on the increases and decreases in the interest rate charged on an adjustable-rate mortgage.

payment cap A limit on the payment increases for an adjustable-rate mortgage.

smart money minute

A real estate *short sale* occurs when the new selling price is less than the amount owed on a previous mortgage. This alternative to foreclosure can result in a "bargain" for a home buyer. However, beware that it may take a long time for the lender to accept the offer, if the offer is accepted at all. Also, the home is usually sold "as is," which means some expected items may be missing or damaged. When doing a short sale, be sure to use a lawyer and a negotiator, and obtain a release from any deficiencies for previous loan amounts.

A variety of mortgage companies are available to finance your home purchase.
TZIDO SUN/Shutterstock

buy-down An interest rate subsidy from a home builder or a real estate developer that reduces a home buyer's mortgage payments during the first few years of the loan.

second mortgage A cash advance based on the paid-up value of a home; also called a *home equity loan.*

it monthly, usually at a fixed rate of interest. Lenders also offer a home equity line of credit (HELOC) that allows the borrower to obtain additional funds as needed, most often with a variable interest rate. Be careful using a home equity line of credit. This revolving credit plan can keep you continually in debt as you request new cash advances.

Interest on a home equity loan may be tax deductible on your federal income tax return. However, this debt creates the risk of losing the home if payments on both the first and second mortgages are not made. To help prevent financial difficulties, home equity loans for amounts that exceed 70 percent of your equity are not allowed in many states.

Reverse Mortgages   Programs are available to assist people who have a high equity in their homes and need cash. **Reverse mortgages** provide elderly homeowners with tax-free income in the form of a loan that is paid back (with interest) when the home is sold or the homeowner dies. You must be 62 to qualify, and continue to live in the home. These financing plans, formally called *home equity conversion mortgages,* allow a person to access funds in several ways. A person may take a lump sum, a line of credit, monthly payments, or a combination of a credit line and regular payments. As with any financial decision, obtain reliable information and consider alternatives, such as a home equity loan. In response to deceptive reverse mortgage providers charging exorbitant fees and related scams, increased consumer protection now exists.

Refinancing   During the term of a mortgage, you may want to **refinance,** that is, obtain a new mortgage at a lower rate and payment. Before taking this action, consider the refinancing costs in relation to the savings with a lower monthly payment, and how long you plan to be in the home. Refinancing is often advantageous when you can get at least a 1 percent lower rate than your current rate. To assess the situation, divide the costs of refinancing by the amount saved each month to determine the number of months to cover your costs. Refinancing benefits will occur more quickly with larger mortgages. Don't refinance with a 30-year mortgage replacing a 30-year mortgage on which you have been paying for five years. Consider a mortgage with a shorter term.

Another financing decision involves making extra payments on your mortgage (see the *Financial Literacy for My Life* feature about paying a mortgage off early).

STEP 5: CLOSE THE PURCHASE TRANSACTION

Before finalizing the transaction, do a *walk-through* to inspect the condition and facilities of the home you plan to buy. Take photos or a video to collect evidence for any last-minute items you may need to negotiate.

The *closing* is a meeting among the buyer, seller, and lender of funds, or representatives of each party, to complete the transaction. Documents are signed, last-minute details are settled, and required amounts are paid. A number of expenses are incurred at the closing. The **closing costs,** also referred to as *settlement costs,* are the fees and charges paid when a real estate transaction is completed (see Exhibit 9-11).

Title insurance is one closing cost that covers two items. First, the title company defines the boundaries of the property being purchased and conducts a search to determine whether the property is free of claims, such as unpaid real estate taxes. Second, during the mortgage term, the title company protects the owner and the lender against financial loss resulting from future defects in the title and from other unforeseen property claims not excluded by the policy.

Also due at closing time is the deed recording fee. The **deed** is the document that transfers ownership of property from one party to another. With a *warranty deed,* the seller guarantees the title is good. This document certifies that the seller is the true owner of the property, there are no claims against the title, and the seller has the right to sell the property.

Mortgage insurance is another possible closing cost. If required, mortgage insurance protects the lender from loss resulting from a mortgage default.

The Real Estate Settlement Procedures Act (RESPA) helps home buyers understand the closing process and costs. This law requires loan applicants be given certain information, including an estimate of the costs, at least three days before the closing. For

reverse mortgage A loan based on the equity in a home, that provides elderly homeowners with tax-free income and is paid back with interest when the home is sold or the homeowner dies.

refinancing The process of obtaining a new mortgage on a home to get a lower interest rate and payment.

closing costs Fees and charges paid when a real estate transaction is completed; also called *settlement costs.*

title insurance Insurance that, during the mortgage term, protects the owner and lender against financial loss resulting from future defects in the title and from other unforeseen property claims not excluded by the policy.

deed A document that transfers ownership of property from one party to another.

Financial Literacy for My Life

SHOULD YOU PAY OFF YOUR MORTGAGE EARLY?

When considering paying off your mortgage early, make sure your loan does not include a *prepayment penalty;* most mortgages do not. Then, consider these actions:

1. Be warned about the risks of an early mortgage payoff. If you encounter financial difficulties and don't have an emergency (reserve) fund, you could face foreclosure. If your reserve fund earns a greater rate than your mortgage rate (taking into account tax benefits), you may decide to invest rather than pay down your mortgage. This could give more flexibility in case of an economic downturn, and allow refinancing your mortgage at a lower interest rate.

2. Assess lost tax deductions and lost earnings on money you use to pay off your loan. The larger standard deduction in recent tax law changes means fewer people qualify to itemize, no longer benefiting from the mortgage interest and property tax deductions.

3. Consider paying an extra amount each month—for example, $25—applied to the loan principal, which could save tens of thousands of dollars in interest. However, be sure to first pay off any credit cards or other high-interest debt.

4. Beware of companies that help you make extra mortgage payments. You can do this on your own, without the fee they will likely charge. These businesses often collect from you every two weeks but make a payment only once a month, which gives them the use of *your* dollars to invest.

After paying off your mortgage, set up an automatic savings payment to an investment account. The amount of your monthly home payment will now go toward long-term financial security.

EXHIBIT 9-11 Common closing costs

At the transaction settlement of a real estate purchase and sale, the buyer and seller will encounter a variety of expenses that are commonly referred to as *closing costs.*

	Cost Range Encountered	
	By the Buyer	**By the Seller**
Title search fee	$150–$375	–
Title insurance	$800—$1,800	$2,000+
Attorney's fee	$400–$700	$50–$700
Property survey	—	$400–$500
Appraisal fee (or nonrefundable application fee)	$300–$400	—
Recording fees; transfer taxes (city, county, state)	$95–$130	$15–$30
Settlement fee	$500–$1,000+	—
Wire transfer fee	$25–$100	
Lender's origination fee	1–3% of loan amount	—
Reserves for home insurance and property taxes	Varies	—
Interest paid in advance (from the closing date to the end of the month) and "points"	Varies	—
Real estate broker's commission	—	4–7% of purchase price

Note: The amounts paid by the buyer are in addition to the down payment.

escrow account Money, usually deposited with the lending financial institution, for the payment of property taxes and homeowner's insurance.

information on RESPA and the "know before you owe" rule (with the technical label TRID) go to www.consumerfinance.gov.

At the closing and when monthly payments are made, you will probably deposit money for property taxes and home insurance. The lender will require that you have property insurance. An **escrow account** is money, usually deposited with the lending

Financial Literacy for My Life

ARE YOU AWARE OF . . . ?

The Bank of Mom and Dad. With millions of satisfied customers and service that really cares about its borrowers, the "Bank of Mom and Dad" is a source of home-buying funds. Money from parents for a home purchase can increase the amount of home you can afford. With *shared-equity financing,* parents or other relatives who provide down payment money share in the appreciation of the property. A contract among the parties should detail (a) who makes the mortgage payments and gets the tax deduction, (b) how much each person will pay of the real estate taxes, and (c) how and when the equity will be shared.

Online Home Buying. After viewing homes online or in-person, technology makes it possible to complete a home purchase without meeting a mortgage broker or the title insurance representative in person. Financing activities include: (1) online mortgage prequalification, (2) comparing mortgage rates with various lenders, and (3) a web-based mortgage application. Price negotiation involves email, and the online *closing* is conducted with the mortgage provider sending the settlement documents electronically. Documents are "signed" on a specially formatted screen. The Electronic Signature in Global and National (ESIGN) Commerce Act allows this process to take place. This law recognizes an *electronic signature* as "an electronic sound, symbol, or process, attached to or logically associated with a contract or other record and executed or adopted by a person with the intent to sign the record." Traditionally, the recording of documents and issuing of the title insurance policy takes up to 45 days. Online, the process is usually completed faster.

Co-op College Housing. Students can save money by living in an off-campus co-op. This living arrangement requires that residents do chores as part of their "payment." However, the few hours a week can result in reducing housing costs by several thousands of dollars. In recent years, the North American Students of Cooperation (www.nasco.coop) has helped students organize housing cooperatives near the University of Virginia, Penn State, the University of Rochester, and Western Michigan University.

Down Payment Wire Fraud and Other Scams. Each year, billions of dollars are lost by home buyers due to email hacking, identity theft, and wire transfer fraud related to home buying. Sensitive data is hacked, and the scammer assumes the identity of a representative of the mortgage or title company. Down payment funds are diverted to a fraudulent account. Con artists disguise their phone numbers to resemble those of legitimate businesses. To avoid this scam, verify that your real estate agent, lender, and attorney use fraud-resistant procedures and are actively serving and protecting your interests. Mobile connections, unsecured websites, call centers, and bank employees are some potential points of compromise. To prevent title and deed fraud resulting from identity theft, contact your county about its *consumer-notification service,* which notifies you when a document related to your property is recorded.

Other mortgage scams can result when a person misrepresents income or the home value in an effort to obtain a loan. While banks and mortgage lenders are usually the victims, individuals may also face losses. To avoid participating in mortgage fraud, verify that a mortgage company is properly licensed, and report any incorrect information in the process.

institution, for the payment of property taxes, homeowner's insurance, and private mortgage insurance. This account protects the lender from financial loss due to unpaid real estate taxes or damage from fire or other hazards.

As a new home buyer, you might consider purchasing an agreement that gives you protection against home defects. *Implied warranties* created by state laws may cover some problem areas, but other repair costs can occur. Home builders and real estate sales companies offer warranties. Coverage commonly provides protection against structural, wiring, plumbing, heating, and other mechanical defects. Most home warranty programs have various limitations.

A homeowner may also purchase a service contract from a home warranty company, obtained through your real estate agent. This agreement warrants appliances, plumbing, air-conditioning and heating systems, and other items for one year. As with any service contract, decide whether the coverage provided and the chances of repair expenses justify the cost. For each service call, a deductible of $75 to $100 is usually charged.

HOME BUYING: A SUMMARY

Buying a home is the most expensive financial decision most people will make. As a reminder, Exhibit 9-12 summarizes the major elements to consider.

A number of other topics related to home buying that you should be aware of are covered in the *Financial Literacy for My Life: Are You Aware Of . . .?* feature.

EXHIBIT 9-12

The main elements of buying
a home

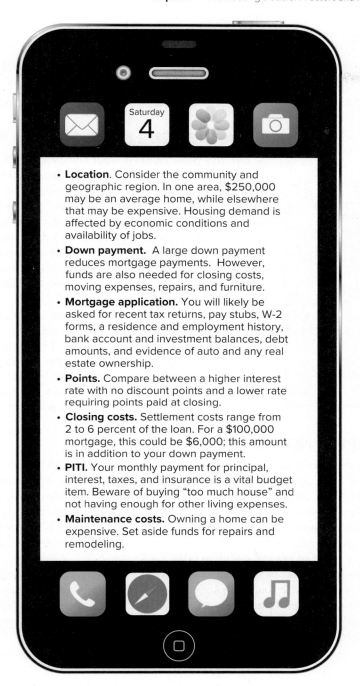

- **Location**. Consider the community and geographic region. In one area, $250,000 may be an average home, while elsewhere that may be expensive. Housing demand is affected by economic conditions and availability of jobs.

- **Down payment.** A large down payment reduces mortgage payments. However, funds are also needed for closing costs, moving expenses, repairs, and furniture.

- **Mortgage application.** You will likely be asked for recent tax returns, pay stubs, W-2 forms, a residence and employment history, bank account and investment balances, debt amounts, and evidence of auto and any real estate ownership.

- **Points.** Compare between a higher interest rate with no discount points and a lower rate requiring points paid at closing.

- **Closing costs.** Settlement costs range from 2 to 6 percent of the loan. For a $100,000 mortgage, this could be $6,000; this amount is in addition to your down payment.

- **PITI.** Your monthly payment for principal, interest, taxes, and insurance is a vital budget item. Beware of buying "too much house" and not having enough for other living expenses.

- **Maintenance costs.** Owning a home can be expensive. Set aside funds for repairs and remodeling.

 **PRACTICE QUIZ 9-4**

1. What are the main sources of down payment money?
2. What factors affect a person's ability to qualify for a mortgage?
3. How do changing interest rates affect the amount of mortgage a person can afford?
4. How do discount points affect the cost of a mortgage?
5. Under what conditions might an adjustable-rate mortgage be appropriate?
6. When might refinancing a mortgage be advisable?
7. How do closing costs affect a person's ability to afford a home purchase?

PFP Sheet 43
Housing Mortgage
Affordability

PFP Sheet 44
Mortgage
Comparison

PFP Sheet 45
Mortgage Refi-
nance Analysis

Selling Your Home

LO9-5

Develop a strategy for selling a home.

Most people who buy a home will eventually be on the other side of a real estate transaction. Selling your home requires preparation for selling, setting a price, and deciding whether to sell it yourself or use a real estate agent.

PREPARING YOUR HOME FOR SELLING

The effective presentation of your home can result in a fast and financially favorable sale. Real estate salespeople recommend that you make needed repairs, clean windows, and paint exterior and interior areas. Make sure house numbers are plainly visible. Clear the garage and exterior areas of toys, debris, and old vehicles; keep the lawn cut and the leaves raked. Keep the kitchen and bathroom clean. Avoid offensive odors by removing garbage, and keeping pets and their areas clean. Remove excess furniture and dispose of unneeded items to make the house, closets, and storage areas look larger.

When showing your home, open drapes, turn on lights, and set thermostats at a comfortable level. Consider environmentally friendly features such as energy-saving light bulbs and water-saving faucets. This effort will give your property a positive image and make it attractive to potential buyers. The use of a home staging service with rented furniture and decor can result in a more appealing presentation of your home.

smart money minute

Upgrades that add value to a home and have the highest payoffs when selling are a second-story addition, a remodeled bathroom with directional and "rainfall" showerheads, an updated kitchen, an outdoor living area, a finished basement, energy-efficient windows and lighting, a home security system, and technology-enhanced features. Media rooms are also popular with many home buyers. Recent research indicates that most rooms painted with varied shades of blue add value to a home, except the dining room for which light brown or beige is recommended. Walls painted with bright, vibrant colors can reduce a home's value.

DETERMINING THE SELLING PRICE

appraisal An estimate of the current value of a property.

Pricing your home can be difficult. You risk not selling it quickly if the price is too high, and you may not get a fair amount if the price is too low. An **appraisal,** an estimate of the current value of the property, can provide an indication of the price to set.

A home appraisal costs between $300 and $400. This expense can help people selling on their own to get a realistic property value. An asking price is influenced by recent selling prices of comparable homes in the area, housing market demand, and available financing based on current mortgage rates.

Home improvements you have made may or may not increase the selling price. A hot tub or an exercise room may have no value for some potential buyers. Among the most desirable improvements are energy-efficient features, a remodeled kitchen, an additional or remodeled bathroom, added rooms and storage space, a separate office, a finished basement, a fireplace, and an outdoor deck or patio.

The time to think about selling your home is when you buy it and every day you live there. Daily maintenance, timely repairs, and home improvements will increase the future sale price.

my life **5**

I understand actions to take when planning to sell a home.

When selling a home on your own, information sources are available. You can find assistance at www.moneyunder30.com/how-to-sell-your-house-by-owner-yourself-without-realtor and www.zillow.com/sellers-guide/how-to-sell-your-house-for-sale-by-owner/. Talking with people who have sold their home on their own is also valuable.

SALE BY OWNER

Each year, about 10 percent of home sales are made by owners. If you decide to sell your home without a real estate professional, price the home and advertise it through local newspapers, a detailed information sheet, and online. View online home listings for the information to include in the property description. Obtain the services of an experienced real estate photographer for professional photos, 3D visuals for a virtual-reality tour, and drone videos for large properties. Distribute the information and visuals online through websites, social media, and at local public areas.

When selling on your own, obtain information about available financing and financing requirements. This information will help you and potential buyers to determine whether a sale is possible. Use the services of a lawyer or title company with the contract, the closing, and other legal matters.

Require potential buyers to provide names, addresses, telephone numbers, and background information, and show your home only by appointment. As a security measure, show it only when two or more adults are at home. The pandemic required various health and safety precautions during home showings. While selling your own home can save thousands of dollars, it requires an investment of time, effort, and a strong ability to negotiate, especially if you have multiple offers.

personal fintech

Tech-oriented companies called iBuyers will buy your home, usually in a few days. These quick sales usually come with a price lower than if you used a real estate agent. Also, a 7 to 9 percent service fee is likely. An iBuyer may require certain repairs before the sale is final. While iBuyers account for a very minor portion of home sales, the industry is growing with new companies entering the market.

LISTING WITH A REAL ESTATE AGENT

If you sell using a real estate agent, consider the person's knowledge of the community and the agent's efforts to market your home. A real estate agent will provide you with services that include a suggested listing price based on a market analysis, providing advice on features to highlight, hosting open houses, and coordinating showings to potential buyers. The agent will also help negotiate a selling price and guide you through the closing.

An agent's marketing materials include promotional items such as brochures, flyers, and for-sale signs along with digital activities such as e-mail blasts, virtual tours by video, and social media content. A real estate agent will also connect you with real estate attorneys, repair companies, and other services that might be needed.

Discount real estate brokers assist sellers who are willing to take on certain duties and reduce selling costs. These companies charge a flat fee or 1 to 2 percent of the selling price instead of the customary 6 percent. Be prepared to assume some marketing, negotiating, and other home-selling activities that a full-service real estate agent would do. You will pay the buyer's agent fee of 2.5 to 3 percent. Most important when selecting an agent, decide how much attention and assistance you want during the home-selling process.

PRACTICE QUIZ 9-5

1. What actions are recommended when planning to sell your home?
2. What factors affect the selling price of a home?
3. What should you consider when deciding whether to sell your home on your own or use the services of a real estate agent?

Your Personal Finance Roadmap and Dashboard:

Money Management

MORTGAGE EQUITY PERCENTAGE

For home buyers, *home equity,* the amount of your ownership in the property, can be an indicator of financial progress. Equity is calculated by subtracting the mortgage amount owed from the current market value of the home. For example, a home worth $200,000 with $80,000 still owed on the mortgage would have equity of $120,000, which is 60 percent of the home's value.

In years when the market value of homes decline, home equity becomes lower for many homeowners. Building equity through shorter mortgages and additional principal payments might be considered.

YOUR SITUATION

Are you able to make additional mortgage payments toward the loan principal to build the equity in your home? What budget areas might be reduced to be able to pay down your mortgage? Are there home improvements you might make to increase the market value of your home? Increased equity in your home is a vital component for building long-term financial security. Other housing actions you might consider during different stages of your life include:

 ### First Steps

- Develop a positive renting reputation with the property owner.
- Obtain an understanding of leases and rental activities.
- Learn about the advantages and disadvantages of owning a home.
- Compare renting and buying your housing based on your finances and life situation.

 ### Next Steps

- Consider a savings fund that might be used for a down payment to buy a house.
- Assess different types of mortgages.
- Make additional principal payments to reduce your mortgage balance.

 ### Later Steps

- Consider refinancing your mortgage based on lower interest rates.
- Adapt your housing budget and situation based on changing family needs.
- Determine changes in housing needs resulting from changing life and household situations.
- Consider various housing situations and locations for retirement.

YOUR next step . . . select one or more of the items above and create an action plan to implement those financial planning activities.

SUMMARY OF LEARNING OBJECTIVES

LO9-1

Evaluate available housing alternatives. When selecting a place to live, consider your needs, life situation, and financial resources. Also, evaluate renting and buying alternatives in terms of financial and opportunity costs.

LO9-2

Analyze the costs and benefits associated with renting. The main benefits of renting are mobility, fewer responsibilities, and lower initial costs. Renting has the disadvantages of few financial benefits, a restricted lifestyle, and legal concerns.

LO9-3

Explain the home-buying process. When assessing the housing type that might be best for you to purchase, use the home-buying process: (1) determine home ownership needs,

(2) find and evaluate a property to purchase, (3) price the property, (4) finance the purchase, and (5) close the real estate transaction.

LO9-4

Calculate the costs associated with purchasing a home. The costs associated with purchasing a home include the down payment; mortgage origination costs; closing costs such as a deed fee, prepaid interest, attorney's fees, payment for title insurance, and a property survey; and an escrow account for homeowner's insurance and property taxes.

LO9-5

Develop a strategy for selling a home. When planning to sell a home, decide whether to make certain repairs and improvements, determine a selling price, and choose between selling the home yourself and using the services of a real estate agent.

KEY TERMS

adjustable-rate mortgage (ARM) 328	cooperative housing 319	points 327
amortization 328	deed 330	rate cap 329
appraisal 334	earnest money 323	refinancing 330
buy-down 329	escrow account 331	reverse mortgage 330
closing costs 330	lease 315	second mortgage 329
condominium 318	mortgage 324	title insurance 330
conventional mortgage 328	payment cap 329	zoning laws 321

SELF-TEST PROBLEMS

1. What would be the monthly payment for a $180,000, 20-year mortgage at 6 percent?

2. What is the total amount of a 30-year mortgage with monthly payments of $850?

Self-Test Solutions

1. Using the Exhibit 9-9 table, multiply 180 times $7.16 to determine the monthly payment of $1,288.80.

2. 360 payments (30 years × 12 months) are multiplied by $850 for a total of $306,000.

FINANCIAL PLANNING PROBLEMS

1. *Comparing Renting and Buying.* Based on the following data, would you recommend buying or renting?   LO9-1

Rental Costs	Buying Costs
Annual rent, $7,380	Annual mortgage payments, $9,800 ($9,575 is interest)
Insurance, $145	Property taxes, $1,780
Security deposit, $650	Insurance/maintenance, $1,050
	Down payment/closing costs, $4,500
	Growth in equity, $225
	Estimated annual appreciation, $1,700

Assume an after-tax savings interest rate of 6 percent and a tax rate of 28 percent.

LO9-2   **2.** *Calculating Security Deposit Interest.* Many locations require that renters be paid interest on their security deposits. If you have a security deposit of $1,800, how much would you expect a year at 3 percent?

LO9-3   **3.** *Calculating Condo Monthly Fees.* Condominiums usually require a monthly fee for various services. At $235 a month, how much would a homeowner pay over a 10-year period for living in this housing facility?

LO9-4   **4.** *Estimating a Monthly Mortgage Payment.* Estimate the affordable monthly mortgage payment, the affordable mortgage amount, and the affordable home purchase price for the following situation (see Exhibit 9-8).

     Monthly gross income, $2,950
     Down payment to be made, 15 percent of purchase price
     Other debt (monthly payment), $160
     Monthly estimate for property taxes and insurance, $210
     30-year loan at 8 percent

LO9-4   **5.** *Calculating Monthly Mortgage Payments.* Based on Exhibit 9-9, or using a financial calculator, what would be the monthly mortgage payments for each of the following situations?

     a. $120,000, 15-year loan at 5 percent.

     b. $86,000, 30-year loan at 4.5 percent.

     c. $105,000, 20-year loan at 4 percent.

     d. What relationship exists between the length of the loan and the monthly payment? How does the mortgage rate affect the monthly payment?

LO9-4   **6.** *Comparing Total Mortgage Payments.* Which mortgage would result in higher total payments?

     Mortgage A: $970 a month for 30 years
     Mortgage B: $760 a month for 5 years and $1,005 for 25 years

LO9-4   **7.** *Calculating Payment Changes.* If an adjustable-rate 30-year mortgage for $120,000 starts at 4.0 percent and increases to 5.5 percent, what is the amount of increase of the monthly payment? (Use Exhibit 9-9.)

LO9-4   **8.** *Evaluating a Refinance Decision.* Kelly and DeAndre Browne plan to refinance their mortgage to obtain a lower interest rate. They will reduce their mortgage payments by $83 a month. Their closing costs for refinancing will be $1,670. How long will it take them to recover the cost of refinancing?

LO9-4   **9.** *Saving for a Down Payment.* In an attempt to have funds for a down payment, Carmella Carlson plans to save $3,400 a year for the next five years. With an interest rate of 3 percent, what amount will Jan have available for a down payment after the five years?

LO9-4   **10.** *Calculating the Monthly Housing Payment.* Ben and Zhang Manchester plan to buy a condominium. They will obtain a $150,000, 30-year mortgage at 4 percent. Their annual property taxes are expected to be $1,800. Property insurance is $480 a year, and the condo association fee is $220 a month. Based on these items, determine the total monthly housing payment for the Manchesters.

LO9-5   **11.** *Future Value of an Amount Saved.* You estimate that you can save $3,800 by selling your home yourself rather than using a real estate agent. What would be the future value of that amount if invested for five years at 3 percent?

DIGITAL FINANCIAL LITERACY

HOUSING COSTS

If you're uncertain where to live over the next three to five years, you should probably rent; otherwise, you might buy a home. To determine if you can afford to buy, estimate monthly housing costs (mortgage payment, insurance, property taxes, and maintenance). Compare the total to your current rent, then set aside the difference for a few months. If you can regularly cover those costs, buying may be an option. The additional money you set aside can go toward a down payment.

If renting, consider utility costs, availability of public transportation, and *walkability* of the area to save on travel expenses. Apartment selection could also be influenced by

access to a dishwasher, clothes washer and dryer, pool, fitness center, parking garage, and whether pets are allowed.

Action items:

1. Locate an online rent-versus-buy calculator and a mortgage payment calculator. Describe how these tools might be used when deciding on a place to live.

2. Search online for a "home buying" article. (a) Prepare a visual (photo, poster) or brief video reporting one or more actions you might take as a result of the article. (b) Based on the article and comments from friends and relatives, prepare a summary of the information obtained that might be posted as a blog entry to help others.

FINANCIAL PLANNING CASE

Home-Buying and Mortgage Decisions

As their apartment rent increased each year, Zoe and Luis Martinez started thinking about buying a home. For a slightly higher amount each month, they could become homeowners. However, their student loan debt might be a barrier to obtaining a mortgage.

With limited funds, Zoe and Luis found some mortgages requiring only a 3 to 5 percent down payment. This financing choice would probably require mortgage insurance and could result in financial difficulties if housing prices decline. They must also consider closing costs and the real estate agent commission.

Zoe and Luis also discussed whether to use an online mortgage company or a local one. And then there's the decision of a fixed-rate or adjustable-rate mortgage.

Several weeks later, after moving forward with their home purchase, Zoe and Luis were ready to close. Their Cape Cod–style home was previously owned by a sales manager who

was transferred across the country. At the time the house went under contract, the home inspection and appraisal went smoothly. However, when Zoe and Luis arrived for the final walk-through, a few concerns surfaced: the lights on the lower level were flickering, and when the kitchen sink water was turned on, the water pressure was barely a trickle. Estimates to repair those items were $1,800.

Questions

1. What are possible sources of down payment funds for Zoe and Luis?

2. If they obtained a mortgage with a very small down payment, what concerns might Zoe and Luis encounter?

3. How might Zoe and Luis address the problems they discovered at the final walk-through?

4. Based on this situation: (a) What budgeting and saving actions would you recommend to Zoe and Luis? (b) What lessons did you learn from their experience?

YOUR PERSONAL FINANCIAL PLAN

SELECTING AND FINANCING HOUSING

Housing represents a major budget expenditure. This area of financial planning requires careful analysis of needs along with a comparison of the costs and benefits of housing alternatives.

Your Short-Term Financial Planning Activity

Task Create a plan for making housing decisions.

Research

1) Use PFP Sheet 40 to assess your current housing situation in relation to your housing needs and financial situation.

2) Conduct a financial analysis to compare renting and buying of housing using PFP Sheet 41.

3) Compare potential rental alternatives using PFP Sheet 42 as a guide.

Outcome Present the results of your findings in flowchart, video, or other visual form. Add the documents and files you create to your portfolio or to your Personal Financial Plan online folder.

Your Long-Term Financial Planning Activity

Task Consider factors that might affect future housing decisions.

Research

1) Develop a plan for assessing future housing needs and costs.

2) In planning a home purchase, use PFP Sheets 43 and 44 to determine your mortgage affordability and to compare mortgage sources.

3) Monitor changing interest rates and assess refinancing alternatives. Use PFP Sheet 45 to evaluate a potential mortgage refinance.

Outcome Add the documents and files you create to your portfolio or to your Personal Financial Plan online folder.

Note: All *Personal Financial Planner* sheets are available at the end of the book and in an Excel spreadsheet format in *Connect Finance*.

CONTINUING CASE

The Housing Decision: Factors and Finances

Five years have passed, and Jamie Lee, 34, is considering taking the plunge—she is not only engaged to be married but is also debating whether to purchase a new home.

Jamie Lee's cupcake café is a success! It has been open for over a year and has earned rave reviews in the local press and from customers, who just cannot get enough of her delicious cupcakes. One such customer, who stopped by on a whim in the café's first week of business, is Ross. After they dated for a few months, Ross, a self-employed web page designer, proposed, and Jamie Lee agreed to be his wife.

The bungalow that Jamie Lee has been renting for the past five years is too small for the soon-to-be newlyweds, so Jamie Lee and Ross are trying to decide if they should move to another rental or purchase a home of their own. They met with their local banker to get an idea of how much home they can afford based on their combined incomes.

Current Financial Situation

Assets (Jamie Lee and Ross combined):

Checking account: $4,300
Savings account: $55,200
Emergency fund savings account: $19,100
IRA balance: $24,000
Cars: $12,000 (Jamie Lee) and $20,000 (Ross)

Liabilities (Jamie Lee and Ross combined):

Student loan balance: $0
Credit card balance: $0
Car loans: $8,000

Income:

Jamie Lee: $45,000 gross income ($31,500 net income after taxes)
Ross: $70,000 gross income ($59,000 net income after taxes)

Monthly Expenses (Jamie Lee and Ross combined):

Utilities: $160
Food: $325
Gas/maintenance: $275
Credit card payment: $0
Car loan payment: $289
Entertainment: $300

Questions

1. Using *Personal Financial Planner Sheet* 40, Housing Needs, compare the advantages and the disadvantages of renting versus buying a home.

2. Jamie Lee and Ross estimate that they will be able to use $40,000 from their savings as a down payment for their home purchase. Based on a traditional financial guideline of "two and a half times your salary plus your down payment," calculate approximately how much Jamie Lee and Ross can spend on a house.

3. Using *Personal Financial Planner Sheet* 43, Housing Mortgage Affordability, calculate the affordable mortgage amount that would be suggested by a lending institution and based on Jamie Lee and Ross's income. How does this amount compare with the traditional financial guideline found in Question 2?

   Use the following amounts for Jamie Lee and Ross's calculations:

   - 10 percent down payment
   - 28 percent for TIPI
   - $500.00 per month for estimated combined property taxes and insurance
   - 5 percent interest rate for 30 years (found in Exhibit 9-9 table)

4. Jamie Lee and Ross found a brand-new, 3-bedroom, 2½-bath home in a quiet neighborhood for sale. The listing price is $275,000. They placed a bid of $260,000 on the home. The seller's counteroffer was $273,000. What should Jamie Lee and Ross do next to demonstrate to the owner that they are serious buyers?

5. Jamie Lee and Ross received a signed contract from the buyer accepting their $273,000 offer! The seller also agreed to pay two points toward Jamie Lee and Ross's mortgage. Calculate the benefit of having points paid toward the mortgage if Jamie Lee and Ross are putting a $40,000 down payment on the home.

6. Using the table found in Exhibit 9-9, or a financial calculator, calculate Jamie Lee and Ross's mortgage payment, using the 5 percent rate for 30 years on the mortgage balance of $233,000.

DAILY SPENDING DIARY

"After I pay my rent, utilities, and renter's insurance, I have very little for other expenses."

Directions

Your *Daily Spending Diary* will help you manage housing expenses to create a better spending plan. As you record daily spending, your comments should reflect what you have learned about your spending patterns and what possible changes you might want to make.

Analysis Questions

1. What portion of your daily spending involves expenses related to housing?

2. What types of housing expenses might be reduced with more careful spending habits?

A *Daily Spending Diary* sheet is located in the appendix at the end of Chapter 1 and on the library resource site within *Connect*.

Property and Motor Vehicle Insurance

10

Piyawat Nandeenopparit/Shutterstock

LEARNING OBJECTIVES

LO10-1 Develop a risk management plan using insurance.

LO10-2 Discuss the importance of property and liability insurance.

LO10-3 Explain the insurance coverage and policy types available to homeowners and renters.

LO10-4 Analyze factors that influence the amount of coverage and the cost of home insurance.

LO10-5 Identify the important types of automobile insurance coverage.

LO10-6 Evaluate factors that affect the cost of automobile insurance.

Financial Literacy
IN **YOUR LIFE**

▶ **What if . . .** damage from fire or another disastrous event prevents the use of your home and household belongings, such as computer equipment, furniture, appliances, and clothing? Hopefully, you have established a specific and measurable portion of your insurance coverage for your household belongings. If you do not have adequate personal property coverage . . .

You might . . . consider increasing your coverage for damage or loss up to at least 55 or even 70 or 75 percent of the insured value of your home.

Now, what would you do? Contact your insurance agent to review your current home insurance policy and consider a personal property floater, which covers the damage or loss of a specific item of high value. Make sure to prepare a household inventory, with purchase dates and cost information. You will be able to monitor your progress using the Your Personal Finance Roadmap and Dashboard at the end of the chapter.

---

my life | INSURING YOUR STUFF

We all have items with a financial value that require protection. While several risk management actions are available, most people purchase insurance.

The main focus when making insurance decisions is to avoid major financial losses. Do you take wise planning actions related to property and liability insurance? For each of the following statements, select Yes, No, or Uncertain to indicate your personal response regarding these insurance activities.

1.	I use various risk management actions to reduce the chance of financial loss.	Yes	No	Uncertain
2.	I have knowledge of property and liability insurance coverage.	Yes	No	Uncertain
3.	I have appropriate home or renter's insurance coverage.	Yes	No	Uncertain
4.	I understand methods to reduce my home or renter's insurance costs.	Yes	No	Uncertain
5.	I understand the main types of auto insurance coverage.	Yes	No	Uncertain
6.	I take various actions to reduce my auto insurance costs.	Yes	No	Uncertain

As you study this chapter, you will encounter "My Life" boxes with additional information and resources related to these items.

Insurance and Risk Management: An Introduction

LO10-1

Develop a risk management plan using insurance.

In today's world of the "strange but true," you can obtain insurance for just about anything. You might purchase a policy to protect yourself in the event that you are abducted by aliens. Some insurance companies will offer you protection if you think you have a risk of turning into a werewolf. If you are a fast runner, you might be able to get a discount on a life insurance policy. Some people buy wedding disaster insurance just in case something goes wrong on the big day. You may never need these types of insurance, but you'll certainly need insurance on your home, your vehicle, and your personal property. The more you know about insurance, the better able you will be to make decisions about buying it.

Insurance involves property and people. By providing protection against the risks of financial uncertainty and unexpected losses, insurance makes it possible to plan for the future.

WHAT IS INSURANCE?

Insurance is protection against possible financial loss. Although many types of insurance exist, they all have one thing in common: They give you the peace of mind that comes from knowing that money will be available to meet the needs of your survivors, pay medical expenses, protect your home and belongings, and cover personal or property damage caused by you when driving.

Life insurance replaces income that would be lost if the policyholder died. Health insurance helps meet medical expenses when the policyholder (or any family member covered by the policy) becomes ill. Automobile insurance helps cover property and personal damage caused by the policyholder's car. Home insurance covers the policy-holder's place of residence and its associated financial risks, such as damage to personal property and injuries to others.

Insurance is based on the principle of *pooling risks,* in which thousands of policyholders pay a small sum of money (*premium*) into a central pool. The pool is then large enough to meet the expenses of the small number of people who actually suffer a loss.

An **insurance company,** or **insurer,** is a risk-sharing firm that agrees to assume financial responsibility for losses that may result from an insured risk. A person joins the risk-sharing group (the insurance company) by purchasing a **policy** (a contract). Under the policy, the insurance company agrees to assume the risk for a fee (the **premium**) that the person (the **insured** or the **policyholder**) pays periodically.

Insurance can provide protection against many risks of financial uncertainty and unexpected losses. The financial consequences of failing to obtain the right amount and type of insurance can be disastrous.

TYPES OF RISKS

You face risks every day. You cross the street with some danger that you'll be hit by a car. You can't own property without taking the chance that it will be lost, stolen, damaged, or destroyed. Insurance companies offer financial protection against such dangers and losses by promising to compensate the insured for a relatively large loss in return for the payment of a much smaller but certain expense called the *premium.*

Risk, peril, and *hazard* are important terms in insurance. While in popular use these terms tend to be interchangeable, each has a distinct, technical meaning in insurance terminology.

Basically, **risk** is uncertainty or lack of predictability. In this instance, it refers to the uncertainty as to loss that a person or a property covered by insurance faces. Insurance companies frequently refer to the insured person or property as the *risk.*

Peril is the cause of a possible loss. It is the contingency that causes someone to take out insurance. People buy policies for financial protection against perils such as fire, windstorms, explosions, robbery, accidents, and premature death.

Hazard increases the likelihood of loss through some peril. For example, defective house wiring is a hazard that increases the likelihood of the peril of fire.

The most common risks are classified as personal risks, property risks, and liability risks. *Personal risks* are the uncertainties surrounding loss of income or life due to premature death, illness, disability, old age, or unemployment. *Property risks* are the uncertainties of direct or indirect losses to personal or real property due to fire, windstorms, accidents, theft, and other hazards. *Liability risks* are possible losses due to negligence resulting in bodily injury or property damage to others. Such harm or damage could be caused by an automobile, professional misconduct, injury suffered on one's property, and so on.

---

insurance Protection against possible financial loss.

insurance company A risk-sharing firm that assumes financial responsibility for losses that may result from an insured risk.

insurer An insurance company.

policy A written contract for insurance.

premium The amount of money a policyholder is charged for an insurance policy.

insured A person covered by an insurance policy.

policyholder A person who owns an insurance policy.

risk Chance or uncertainty of loss; also used to mean "the insured."

peril The cause of a possible loss.

hazard A factor that increases the likelihood of loss through some peril.

pure risk A risk in which there is only a chance of loss; also called *insurable risk.*

speculative risk A risk in which there is a chance of either loss or gain.

Personal risks, property risks, and liability risks are types of **pure risk,** or *insurable risk,* since there would be a chance of loss only if the specified events occurred. Pure risks are accidental and unintentional risks for which the nature and financial cost of the loss can be predicted.

A **speculative risk** is a risk that carries a chance of either loss or gain. Starting a small business that may or may not succeed is an example of speculative risk. So is gambling. Most speculative risks are considered to be uninsurable.

smart money minute

The Institute for Business and Home Safety (IBHS) created a six-story "disaster blaster" with 105 fans to simulate a category 3 hurricane. This chamber tests the wind resistance of structural modifications. Metal joint straps, a second roof water barrier, fortified decks, and siding attached with specialized fasteners can save more than $20 billion in home insurance claims a year. IBHS testing has also resulted in life-saving features for motor vehicles, helping to reduce auto insurance rates.

RISK MANAGEMENT METHODS

Risk management is an organized strategy for protecting assets and people. It helps reduce financial losses caused by destructive events. Risk management is a long-range planning process. People's risk management needs change at various points in their lives. If you understand risks and how to manage them, you can provide better protection for yourself and your family. In this way, you can reduce your financial losses and thereby improve your chances for economic, social, physical, and emotional well-being. Since you will probably be unable to afford to cover all risks, you need to understand how to obtain the best protection you can afford.

Most people think of risk management as buying insurance. However, insurance is not the only method of dealing with risk; in certain situations, other methods may be less costly. Four risk management techniques are commonly used.

1. RISK AVOIDANCE You can avoid the risk of being in an automobile accident by not driving or being a passenger. McDonald's can avoid the risk of product failure by not introducing new products. Risk avoidance would be practiced in both instances, but at a very high cost. You might have to give up your job, and McDonald's might lose out to competitors that introduce new products.

In some situations, however, risk avoidance is practical. At the personal level, people avoid risks by not smoking or by not walking through high-crime neighborhoods. At the business level, jewelry stores avoid losses through robbery by locking their merchandise in vaults. Obviously, no person or business can avoid all risks.

self-insurance The process of establishing a monetary fund to cover the cost of a loss.

Taking thoughtful actions can reduce the risks you face in your daily life.
Westend61/Getty Images

2. RISK REDUCTION While avoiding risks completely may not be possible, reducing risks may be a cause of action. You can reduce the risk of injury in an auto accident by wearing a seat belt. You can install smoke alarms and fire extinguishers to protect life and reduce potential fire damage. You can reduce the risk of illness by eating a balanced diet and exercising.

3. RISK ASSUMPTION Risk assumption means taking on responsibility for the loss or injury that may result from a risk. Generally, it makes sense to assume a risk when the potential loss is small, when risk management has reduced the risk, when insurance coverage is expensive, and when there is no other way to obtain protection. For instance, you might decide not to purchase collision insurance on an older car. Then, if an accident occurs, you will bear all of the costs of fixing the car.

Self-insurance is the process of establishing a monetary fund to cover the cost of a loss. Self-insurance does not eliminate risks; it only provides means for covering losses. Many people self-insure by default, not by choice, by not obtaining insurance.

4. RISK SHIFTING   The most common method of dealing with risk is to shift it. That simply means to transfer it to an insurance company or some other organization. In exchange for the fee you pay, the insurance company agrees to pay for your losses.

Most insurance policies include deductibles, which are a combination of risk assumption and risk shifting. A **deductible** is the set amount that the policyholder must pay per loss on an insurance policy. For example, if a falling tree damages your car, you may have to pay $200 toward the repairs. Your insurance company will pay the remaining amount.

deductible The set amount a policyholder must pay per loss on an insurance policy.

Exhibit 10-1 summarizes various risks and appropriate strategies for managing them.

PLANNING AN INSURANCE PROGRAM

Because all people have their own needs and goals, many of which change over the years, a personal insurance program should be tailored to those changes. In the early years of marriage, when the family is growing, most families need certain kinds of insurance protection. This protection may include property insurance on an apartment or a house, life and disability insurance for wage earners and caretakers of dependents, and adequate health insurance for all family members.

smart money minute

Deductibles are a combination of risk assumption and risk shifting. The insured person assumes part of the risk, paying the first $250, $500, or $1,000 of a claim. The majority of the risk for a large claim is shifted to another party, the insurance company.

EXHIBIT 10-1 Examples of risks and risk management strategies

| RISKS | | POSSIBLE STRATEGIES FOR REDUCING FINANCIAL IMPACT | | |
Personal Events	Financial Impact	Personal Resources	Private Sector	Public Sector
Disability	Loss of one's income Loss of services Increased expenses	Savings, investments Family observing safety precautions	Disability insurance	Disability insurance Social Security
Illness	Loss of one's income Catastrophic hospital expenses	Health-enhancing behavior	Health insurance Health maintenance organizations	Military health care Medicare, Medicaid
Death	Loss of one's income Loss of services Final expenses	Estate planning Risk reduction	Life insurance	Veteran's life insurance Social Security survivor's benefits
Retirement	Decreased income Unplanned living expenses	Savings Investments Hobbies, skills Part-time work	Retirement and/or pensions	Social Security Pension plan for government employees
Property loss	Cost to repair damage to property Repair or replacement cost of theft	Property repair and upkeep Security plans	Automobile insurance Homeowner's insurance Flood insurance (joint program with government)	Flood insurance (joint program with business)
Liability	Claims and settlement costs Lawsuits and legal expenses Loss of personal assets and income	Observing safety precautions Maintaining property	Homeowner's insurance Automobile insurance Malpractice insurance	State-operated insurance plans

Later, when the family has a higher income and a different financial situation, protection needs will change. There might be a long-range provision for the children's education, more life insurance to match higher income and living standards, and revised health insurance protection. Still later, when the children have grown and are on their own, retirement benefits will be a consideration, further changing the family's personal insurance program.

The *How To. . .Plan an Insurance Program* feature suggests several guidelines to follow in planning your insurance program. Exhibit 10-2 outlines the steps in developing a personal insurance program.

STEP 1: SET INSURANCE GOALS   In managing risks, your goals are to minimize personal, property, and liability risks. Your insurance goals should define what to do to cover the basic risks present in your life situation. Covering the basic risks means providing a financial resource to cover costs resulting from a loss.

Suppose your goal is to buy a new car. You must plan to make the purchase and to protect yourself against financial losses from accidents. Auto insurance on the car lets you enjoy the car without worrying that an auto accident might leave you worse off, financially and physically, than before.

Each individual has unique goals. Income, age, family size, lifestyle, experience, and responsibilities influence the goals you set, and the insurance you buy must reflect those goals. In general, financial advisors say that a basic risk management plan must set goals to reduce:

- Potential loss of income due to the premature death, illness, accident, or unemployment of a wage earner.

my life | **1**

Various risk management actions may be used to reduce the chance of financial loss.

A wide range of insurance coverages exist in our society. Talk with an insurance agent or financial planner to obtain recommendations about the types of insurance you may need.

EXHIBIT 10-2

Creating a personal insurance program

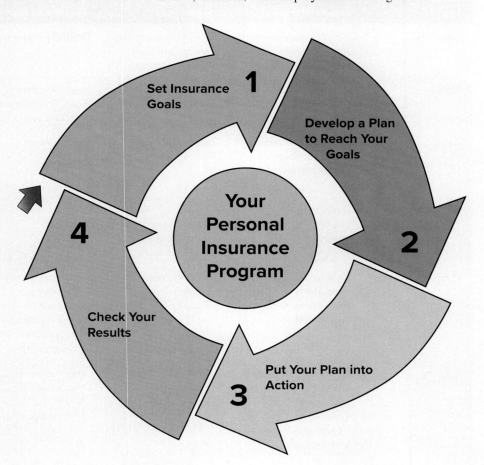

Financial Literacy for My Life

HOW TO. . .PLAN AN INSURANCE PROGRAM

Did you:	Yes	No
1. Seek advice from a competent and reliable insurance advisor?	☐	☐
2. Determine what insurance you need to provide your family with sufficient protection if you die?	☐	☐
3. Consider what portion of the family protection is met by Social Security and by group insurance?	☐	☐
4. Decide what other needs insurance must meet (funeral expenses, savings, retirement annuities, etc.)?	☐	☐
5. Decide what types of insurance best meet your needs?	☐	☐
6. Plan an insurance program and implement it except for periodic reviews of changing needs and changing conditions?	☐	☐
7. Avoid buying more insurance than you need or can afford?	☐	☐
8. Consider dropping one policy for another that provides the same coverage for less money?	☐	☐

Note: Yes answers reflect wise actions for insurance planning.

- Potential loss of income and extra expense resulting from the illness, disability, or death of a spouse.
- Additional expenses due to the injury, illness, or death of other family members.
- Potential loss of real or personal property due to fire, theft, or other hazards.
- Potential loss of income, savings, and property due to personal liability.

STEP 2: DEVELOP A PLAN TO REACH YOUR GOALS Planning is a sign of maturity, a way of taking control of life instead of letting life happen to you. What risks do you face? Which risks can you afford to take without having to back away from your goals? What resources—public programs, personal assets, family, church, or private risk-sharing plans—are available to you?

To understand and use the resources at your command, you need good information. In terms of insurance, this means a clear picture of the available insurance, the reliability of different insurers, and the comparative costs of the coverage needed.

STEP 3: PUT YOUR PLAN INTO ACTION As you carry out your plan, obtain financial and personal resources, budget them, and use them to reach risk management goals. If, for example, you find the insurance protection you have is not enough to cover your basic risks, you may purchase additional coverage, change the kind of insurance coverage, restructure your budget to cover additional insurance costs, and strengthen your savings or investment programs to reduce long-term risk.

The best risk management plans have flexibility. Savings accounts or other cash, for example, should be available as emergency funds for unexpected financial problems. The best plans are also flexible enough to allow you to respond to changing life situations. Your goal should be an insurance program that expands (or contracts) with changing protection needs.

To put your risk management plan to work, you must answer these questions: What should be insured? For how much? What kind of insurance should I buy? From whom? What amount can I afford?

STEP 4: REVIEW YOUR RESULTS Evaluate your insurance plan periodically, at least every two or three years or whenever your family circumstances change. Among the questions you should ask yourself are: Does it work? Does it adequately protect my plans and goals? An effective risk manager consistently checks the outcomes of decisions and is alert to changes that may reduce the effectiveness of the current risk management plan.

A young working couple may be entirely happy with their life and health insurance coverage. When they add an infant to the family, a review of protection is appropriate. Suddenly the risk of financial catastrophe to the family (should one or both parents die or become disabled) is much greater.

The needs of a single person differ from those of a family, a single parent, a couple, or a group of unrelated adults living in the same household. While these people face similar risks, their financial responsibility to others differs greatly. In each case, the vital question is: Have I provided the financial resources and risk management strategy needed to take care of my basic responsibilities for my own well-being and the well-being of others?

PFP Sheet 46
Insurance Policies
and Needs

✔ PRACTICE QUIZ 10-1

1. What is the purpose of insurance?
2. How are the most common risks classified?
3. What is the difference between pure risk and speculative risk?
4. What are the methods of managing risk?
5. What are the steps in planning your personal insurance coverage?

Property and Liability Insurance

LO10-2

Discuss the importance of property and liability insurance.

Property owners face a variety of risks, including fire and smoke damage.
Colin Anderson Productions pty ltd/
Getty Images

Major disasters have caused catastrophic amounts of property loss in the United States. In recent years, forest fires, hurricanes, tornadoes, and floods in various areas have caused billions of dollars of damage.

Since most people invest large amounts of money in their homes and motor vehicles, protecting these assets from loss is a great concern. Each year, homeowners and renters lose billions of dollars from more than 3 million burglaries, 500,000 fires, and 200,000 instances of damage from other hazards. The cost of injuries and property damage caused by automobiles is also very great. Most people use insurance to reduce their chances of economic loss from these risks.

The price you pay for home and automobile insurance may be viewed as an investment in financial protection against these losses. Although the costs of home and automobile insurance may seem high, the financial losses from which insurance protects you are much higher. Property and liability insurance offer protection from financial losses that may arise from a wide variety of situations.

The main types of risks related to a home and an automobile are (1) property damage or loss and (2) your responsibility for injuries or damage to the property of others.

POTENTIAL PROPERTY LOSSES

Houses, automobiles, furniture, clothing, and other personal belongings are a substantial financial commitment. Property owners face two basic types of risks. The first is *physical damage* caused by hazards such as fire, wind, water, and smoke.

These hazards can cause destruction of your property or temporary loss of its use. For example, if a windstorm causes a large tree branch to break your automobile windshield, you lose the use of the vehicle while it is being repaired. The second type of risk property owners face is *loss of use* due to robbery, burglary, vandalism, or arson.

LIABILITY PROTECTION

In a wide variety of circumstances, a person may be judged legally responsible for bodily injuries or property damages. For example, if a child walks across your property, falls, and sustains severe injuries, the child's family may be able to recover substantial damages from you as a result of the injuries. If you accidentally damage a rare painting while assisting a friend with home repairs, the friend may take legal action against you to recover the cost of the painting.

Liability is legal responsibility for the financial cost of another person's losses or injuries. Your legal responsibility is commonly caused by **negligence,** failure to take ordinary or reasonable care. Doing something in a careless manner, such as improperly supervising children at a swimming pool or failing to remove items from a frequently used staircase, may be ruled as negligence in a liability lawsuit.

Despite taking great care, a person may still be held liable in a situation. **Strict liability** is present when a person is held responsible for intentional or unintentional actions. **Vicarious liability** occurs when a person is held responsible for the actions of another person. If the behavior of a child causes financial or physical harm to others, the parent may be held responsible; if the activities of an employee cause damage, the employer may be held responsible.

my life 2

Knowledge of property and liability insurance coverages is a fundamental element of personal financial planning.

We each face various legal responsibilities in our daily lives. Conduct an online search about various types of liability insurance protection.

liability Legal responsibility for the financial cost of another person's losses or injuries.

negligence Failure to take ordinary or reasonable care in a situation.

strict liability A situation in which a person is held responsible for intentional or unintentional actions.

vicarious liability A situation in which a person is held legally responsible for the actions of another person.

 PRACTICE QUIZ 10-2

1. What property and liability risks might some people overlook?
2. How could a person's life situation influence the need for certain types of property and liability insurance?

Home and Property Insurance

Your home and personal belongings are probably a major portion of your assets. Whether you rent your dwelling or own a home, property insurance is vital. **Homeowner's insurance** is coverage for your place of residence and its associated financial risks, such as damage to personal property and injuries to others (see Exhibit 10-3).

HOMEOWNER'S INSURANCE COVERAGES

A homeowner's policy provides coverages for the house and other structures, additional living expenses, personal property, personal liability and related coverages, and specialized coverages.

HOUSE AND OTHER STRUCTURES   The main component of homeowner's insurance is protection against financial loss due to damage or destruction to a house or other structures. Your dwelling and attached structures are covered for fire and other hazards.

LO10-3

Explain the insurance coverage and policy types available to homeowners and renters.

homeowner's insurance Coverage for a place of residence and its associated financial risks.

EXHIBIT 10-3 Home insurance coverage

| House and other structures | Personal property | Loss of use/additional living expenses while home is uninhabitable | Personal liability and related coverages |

Detached structures on the property, such as a garage, toolshed, or gazebo, are also protected. The coverage will usually also include trees, shrubs, and plants.

ADDITIONAL LIVING EXPENSES   If damage from a fire or other event prevents the use of your home, *additional living expense coverage* pays for the cost of living in a temporary location while your home is being repaired. Some policies limit additional living expense coverage to 10 to 20 percent of the home's coverage and limit payments to a maximum of six to nine months; other policies pay the full cost incurred for up to a year.

PERSONAL PROPERTY   Your household belongings, such as furniture, appliances, and clothing, are covered for damage or loss up to a portion of the insured value of the home, usually 55, 70, or 75 percent. For example, a home insured for $80,000 might have $56,000 (70 percent) of coverage for household belongings.

Personal property coverage commonly has limits for the theft of certain items, such as $1,000 for jewelry, $2,000 for firearms, and $2,500 for silverware. Items with a value exceeding these limits can be protected with a **personal property floater,** which covers the damage or loss of a specific item of high value. A floater requires a detailed description of the item and periodic appraisals to verify the current value. This coverage protects the item regardless of location; thus, the item is insured while you are traveling or transporting it.

Floaters to protect home computers and other electronic equipment are recommended. This additional coverage can prevent financial loss due to damage or loss of your computer. Contact your insurance agent to determine whether the equipment is covered against damage from mischievous pets, spilled drinks, dropping, or power surges.

Personal property coverage usually provides protection against the loss or damage of articles taken with you when away from home. For example, possessions taken on vacation or used while at school are usually covered up to a policy limit. Property that you rent, such as some power tools or a rug shampoo machine, is insured while in your possession.

In the event of damage or loss of property, you must be able to prove both ownership and value. A **household inventory** is a list or other documentation of personal belongings, with purchase dates and cost information. You can get a form for such an inventory from an insurance agent or online. Exhibit 10-4 provides a reminder of the items you should include in the inventory. For items of special value, you should have receipts, serial numbers, brand names, model names, and written appraisals of value.

A household inventory can be a list, photographs, or a video of your home and contents. Photograph closets and storage areas open to see all items. Indicate the date and the value of property. Regularly update your inventory, photos, and appraisal documents. Keep information in a waterproof bag in a fireproof box with a copy in a safe-deposit box. Online inventory tools and phone apps are also available.

personal property floater Additional property insurance to cover the damage or loss of a specific item of high value.

household inventory A list or other documentation of personal belongings, with purchase dates and cost information.

EXHIBIT 10-4 Household inventory contents

PERSONAL LIABILITY AND RELATED COVERAGES Each day, you face the risk of financial loss due to injuries to others or damage to property for which you are responsible. The following are examples of this risk.

- A neighbor or guest falls on your property, resulting in permanent disability.
- A spark from burning leaves on your property starts a fire that damages a neighbor's roof.
- A member of your family accidentally breaks an expensive glass statue while at another person's house.

In each of these situations, you could be held responsible for the costs incurred. The personal liability component of a homeowner's policy protects you from financial

smart money minute

Errors and omissions (E&O) is liability insurance to protect service professionals from claims if a client holds them responsible for errors or if they fail to perform as promised. E&O coverage is used by doctors, lawyers, accountants, architects, engineers, printers, wedding planners, and others.

umbrella policy Supplementary personal liability coverage; also called a *personal catastrophe policy.*

medical payments coverage (homeowner) Home insurance that pays the cost of minor accidental injuries on one's property.

my life | 3

Appropriate home or renter's insurance coverage is a basic component of wise financial planning.

To determine the value of your property for planning insurance coverage, you should prepare a household inventory. For information about conducting a household inventory, go to www.iii.org or conduct a web search for "household inventory."

endorsement An addition of coverage to a standard insurance policy.

smart money minute

For about $100 a year, homeowners can obtain $10,000 coverage for sewage and drain backup damage. Heavy rains that clog a sewer line can cause damage to furniture and other items in a finished basement. Information on flood insurance is available at www.floodsmart.gov.

losses resulting from legal action or claims against you or family members due to damages to the property of others. This coverage includes the cost of legal defense.

Not all individuals who come to your property are covered by your liability insurance. While a babysitter or others who assist you occasionally are probably covered, regular employees, such as a housekeeper or a gardener, may require workers' compensation coverage.

Most homeowner's policies provide a basic personal liability coverage of $100,000, but additional amounts are frequently recommended. An **umbrella policy,** also called a *personal catastrophe policy,* supplements your basic personal liability coverage. This added protection covers you for personal injury claims such as libel, slander, defamation of character, and invasion of property. An umbrella policy also increases bodily injury and property damage coverages. Extended liability policies are sold in amounts of $1 million or more and are useful for individuals with substantial net worth. If you are a business owner, you may need other types of liability coverage.

Medical payments coverage (homeowner) pays the costs of minor accidental injuries on your property and minor injuries caused by you, family members, or pets. Settlements under medical payments coverage are made without determining fault. This protection allows fast processing of small claims, generally up to $5,000. Suits for more severe personal injuries are covered by the personal liability portion of the homeowner's policy. Medical payments coverage does not cover the people who live in the home being insured.

Should you or a family member accidentally damage another person's property, the *supplementary coverage* of homeowner's insurance will pay for these minor mishaps. This protection is usually limited to $500 or $1,000. Again, payments are made regardless of fault. Any property damage claims for greater amounts would require action under the personal liability coverage.

SPECIALIZED COVERAGES   Homeowner's insurance usually does not cover losses from floods and earthquakes. People living in areas with these two risks need special coverage. In various communities, the National Flood Insurance Program makes flood insurance available. This protection is separate from the homeowner's policy. An insurance agent or the Federal Emergency Management Agency can give you additional information about this coverage. Fewer than half of the people who live in flood-prone areas have this coverage. To learn more about flood insurance, read the *Financial Literacy for My Life: Do You Need Flood Insurance?* feature.

Earthquake insurance can be obtained as an **endorsement,** or addition of coverage, to the homeowner's policy. Since the most severe earthquakes occur in the Pacific Coast region, most insurance against this risk is bought in that region. Remember, however, that every state is vulnerable to earthquakes, and this insurance coverage is available in all areas. Lenders frequently require insurance against both floods and earthquakes for a mortgage to buy a home in areas with these risks.

BEWARE: WHEN HOME INSURANCE COVERAGES COLLIDE   When a disaster strikes, your home may be damaged by several factors at the same time or one right after the other. You may think that your insurance policy will protect you, but that isn't the case.

Financial Literacy for My Life

DO YOU NEED FLOOD INSURANCE?

If it can rain, it can flood. And your home insurance policy doesn't cover flood damage. To make sure your property is covered, you'll need a separate flood policy.

THE RISK

If your home is in a designated flood zone, your lender requires you to have flood insurance. A flood zone is an area that has a 1 percent chance of being flooded in any given year.

But floods can happen anywhere. More than half of homes flooded by Hurricane Harvey were outside of designated flood zones. For example, Texas is particularly prone to floods, especially in two large parts of the state: the coast and a wide band called Flash Flood Alley that extends through Central and North Texas. Almost every major city in Texas is in an area at high risk of flooding.

Flood maps are difficult to keep up to date because growth can add to flood risk. Prairies and pasture absorb excess rainfall from storms. When those lands are replaced by concrete and asphalt, it can put areas that never flooded before at risk.

FLOOD INSURANCE

Talk to your home insurance agent about getting a flood policy from the National Flood Insurance Program. If your agent doesn't sell flood insurance, call 1-800-427-4661 for help.

WHAT IT COSTS

The average flood policy costs about $700 a year. The cost will vary depending on your flood risk, the value of your home, and the amount of your deductible, among other factors. Typically, for homes that are not in a flood zone, a flood policy can be very affordable.

WHAT'S COVERED

A flood insurance policy will cover your home up to $250,000. You'll need a separate flood policy for your personal belongings, which provides coverage up to $100,000.

THERE'S A WAIT

Most flood policies have a 30-day waiting period before kicking in, so don't wait for an approaching storm before deciding to buy coverage.

RESOURCES

- Use FEMA's Historical Flood Risk and Cost data to help evaluate the flood risk in your area.
- Search for flood maps at FEMA's Flood Map Service Center.

Source: Texas Department of Insurance, https://www.tdi.texas.gov/index.html, accessed April 5, 2021.

Many home insurance policies include an anti-concurrent causation clause. These clauses give your insurer the right to reject your claim if your home is damaged by several factors, such as wind and rain. If these two or more factors together cause damage to your home, your insurer may deny your entire claim because they can't determine which factor came first and actually caused the damage. You can face a serious shock if you thought your policy protected you from such disaster.

Before disaster strikes, read your home insurance policy closely for anti-concurrent causation clauses. Ask your agent if you may opt out of that clause or pay an increased premium to have full coverage. See the *Financial Literacy for My Life: Homeowner's Policy Coverages* feature to learn what is and what is not covered in a typical homeowner's policy.

RENTER'S INSURANCE

While more than 9 out of 10 homeowners have property insurance, only about 4 out of 10 renters are covered. For people who rent, home insurance coverages include personal property protection, additional living expenses coverage, and personal liability and related coverages. Protection against financial loss due to damage or loss of personal property is the main component of renter's insurance. Often renters believe they are covered under the insurance policy of the building owner. In fact, the building owner's property insurance does not cover tenants'

smart money minute

Computers and other equipment used in a home-based business may not be covered by a home insurance policy. Contact your insurance agent to obtain needed business coverage.

Financial Literacy for My Life

HOMEOWNER'S POLICY COVERAGES

Companies may exclude coverage for certain losses. Even the most comprehensive all-risk policy will exclude certain types of damage.

The following chart shows the most common types of losses covered or excluded from a homeowner's policy.

Most Policies Cover Losses Caused by	Most Policies Do Not Cover Losses Caused by
Fire and lightning	Flooding
Sudden and accidental damage by smoke	Earthquakes
Explosion	Termites, insects, rats, or mice
Theft	Freezing pipes while your house is unoccupied (unless you turned off the water or heated the building)
Vandalism and malicious mischief	Losses if your house is vacant for the number of days specified by your policy
Riot and civil commotion	Wear and tear or maintenance
Aircraft and vehicles	Wind or hail damage to trees and shrubs
Windstorm, hurricane, and hail (this coverage may be excluded if you live on the Gulf Coast)	Mold, except what is necessary to repair or replace property damage caused by a covered water loss
Sudden and accidental water damage	Water damage resulting from continuous and repeated seepage

Source: tdi.texas.gov/pubs/consumer/cb025.html, accessed April 5, 2021.

personal property unless the building owner can be proven liable. For example, if faulty wiring causes a fire and damages a tenant's property, the renter may be able to collect for damages from the building owner.

The personal belongings of students in college housing are usually covered (up to a certain amount) on the home insurance policies of their parents. However, if students live off campus or own many expensive items, they should consider a separate policy. Renter's insurance is relatively inexpensive and provides protection from financial loss due to many of the same risks covered in homeowner's policies.

HOME INSURANCE POLICY FORMS

Until the mid-1950s, a homeowner had to buy separate coverage for fire, theft, and other risks. Then the insurance industry developed a series of package policies as shown in Exhibit 10-5. Some property is excluded from most home insurance (see Exhibit 10-6).

Manufactured housing units and mobile homes usually qualify for insurance coverage with conventional policies. However, certain mobile homes may require a special arrangement and higher rates since their construction makes them more prone to fire and wind damage. The cost of mobile home insurance coverage is most heavily affected by location and by the method used to attach the housing unit to the ground. This type of property insurance is quite expensive; a $20,000 mobile home can cost as much to insure as a $60,000 house.

EXHIBIT 10-5 Types of home insurance policies

EACH OF THE POLICIES BELOW COVERS THESE PERILS, IN ADDITION TO THE ITEMS NOTED.		

- Fire, lightning
- Windstorm, hail
- Explosion
- Riot or civil commotion
- Aircraft
- Vehicles
- Discharge of water
- Freezing
- Accidental damage from steam or electrical current
- Smoke
- Vandalism or malicious mischief
- Theft
- Glass breakage
- Volcanic eruption
- Falling objects
- Tearing apart of heating system or appliance
- Weight of ice, snow, or sleet

Special Form (All risk) (HO-3)	Covers all above perils, plus any other perils except those specifically excluded from the policy, such as • Flood • Earthquake • War • Nuclear accidents
Tenants Form (HO-4)	Covers personal belongings against the perils in the top section.
Comprehensive Form (HO-5)	Expands coverage of HO-3 to include endorsements for items such as replacement cost coverage on contents and guaranteed replacement cost coverage on buildings.
Condominium Form (HO-6)	Covers personal belongings and additions to the living unit.
Country Home Form (HO-7)	For nonfarm business rural residents with coverage on agricultural buildings and equipment.
	The other major coverages of each policy are • Personal liability • Medical payments for guests on the property • Additional living expenses

Note: HO-1 (Basic Form), HO-2 (Broad Form), and HO-8 (Modified Coverage Form for older homes with a high replacement value) are no longer being offered by most companies.

In addition to the property and liability risks previously discussed, home insurance policies include coverage for:

- Credit card fraud, check forgery, and counterfeit money.
- The cost of removing damaged property.
- Emergency removal of property to protect it from damage.
- Temporary repairs after a loss to prevent further damage.
- Fire department charges in areas with such fees.

 **PRACTICE QUIZ 10-3**

 **PFP Sheet 47** Home Inventory

1. What main coverage is included in home insurance policies?
2. What is the purpose of personal liability coverage?
3. How does renter's insurance differ from other home insurance policies?

EXHIBIT 10-6

Not everything is covered

Certain personal property is specifically excluded from the coverage provided by homeowner's insurance.
• Articles separately described and specifically insured, such as jewelry, furs, boats, or expensive electronic equipment.
• Animals, birds, or fish.
• Motorized land vehicles, except those used to service an insured's residence, that are not licensed for road use.
• Any device or instrument for the transmission and recording of sound, including any accessories or antennas, while in or on motor vehicles.
• Aircraft and parts.
• Property of roomers, boarders, and other tenants who are not related to any insured.
• Property contained in an apartment regularly rented or held for rental to others by any insured.
• Property rented or held for rental to others away from the residence premises.
• Business property in storage, or held as a sample, or for sale, or for delivery after sale.
• Business property pertaining to business actually conducted on the residence premises.
• Business property away from the residence premises.

Home Insurance Cost Factors

LO10-4

Analyze factors that influence the amount of coverage and the cost of home insurance.

Studies reveal that as many as two-thirds of homes in the United States are not insured or are underinsured. Financial losses caused by fire, theft, wind, and other risks amount to billions of dollars each year. Since most homeowners have a mortgage on their property, their lending institutions usually require insurance. When purchasing insurance, you can get the best value by selecting the appropriate coverage amount and being aware of factors that affect insurance costs.

Insurance premiums are affected by claims in your area.
michelmond/Shutterstock

HOW MUCH COVERAGE DO YOU NEED?

Several factors affect the insurance coverage needed for your home and property (see Exhibit 10-7). Your insurance protection should be based on the amount needed to rebuild or repair your house, not the amount you paid for it. As construction costs rise, you should increase the amount of coverage. In recent years, most insurance policies have had a built-in inflation clause that increases coverage as property values increase.

In the past, most homeowner's policies contained a provision requiring that the building be insured for at least 80 percent of the replacement value. Under this **coinsurance clause,** the homeowner would have to pay for part of the losses if the property was not insured for the specified percentage of the replacement value. Few companies still use coinsurance; most require full coverage.

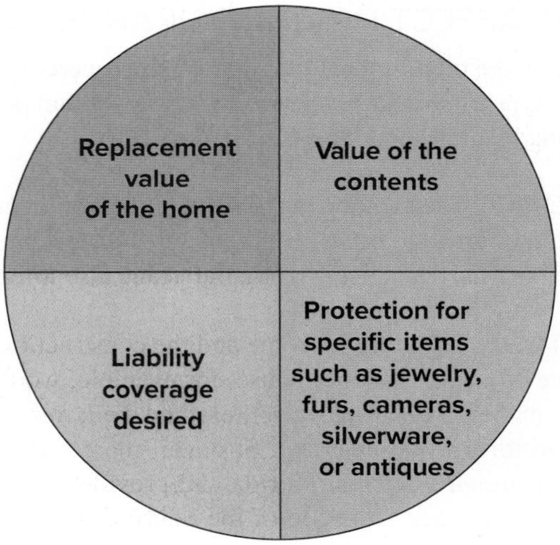

EXHIBIT 10-7
Determining the amount of home insurance you need

If you are financing a home, the lending institution will require you to have property insurance in an amount that covers its financial investment. Remember, too, that the amount of insurance on your home will determine the coverage on the contents. Personal belongings are generally covered up to an amount ranging from 55 to 75 percent of the insurance amount on the dwelling.

Insurance companies base claim settlements on one of two methods. Under the **actual cash value (ACV)** method, the payment you receive is based on the current replacement cost of a damaged or lost item less depreciation. This means you would get $180 for a five-year-old television set that cost you $400 and had an estimated life of eight years if the same set now costs $480. Your settlement amount is determined by taking the current cost of $480 and subtracting five years of depreciation from it—$300 for five years at $60 a year.

coinsurance clause
A policy provision that requires a homeowner to pay for part of the losses if the property is not insured for the specified percentage of the replacement value.

actual cash value (ACV)
A claim settlement method in which the insured receives payment based on the current replacement cost of a damaged or lost item, less depreciation.

EXAMPLE 1: Actual Cash Value Coverage

Suppose your home is insured for $200,000 with a 2 percent deductible, or $4,000. The entire roof was damaged by a storm. If it costs $10,000 to replace the roof, the insurance company will pay depending on how old the roof is.

	5-Year-Old Roof	10-Year-Old Roof	20-Year-Old Roof
Actual cash value of roof	$8,500	$7,000	$4,000
Minus deductible	−$4,000	−$4,000	−$4,000
Insurance company would pay	$4,500	$3,000	0

Under the **replacement value** method for settling claims, you receive the full cost of repairing or replacing a damaged or lost item; depreciation is not considered. However, many companies limit the replacement cost to 400 percent of the item's actual cash value. Replacement value coverage costs about 10 to 20 percent more than ACV coverage.

replacement value A claim settlement method in which the insured receives the full cost of repairing or replacing a damaged or lost item.

EXAMPLE 2: Replacement Cost Coverage

If it costs $10,000 to replace the roof, replacement cost policy will pay the same amount no matter how old is the roof. The insurance company will pay $6,000 ($10,000 − $4,000).

FACTORS THAT AFFECT HOME INSURANCE COSTS

The main influences on the premium paid for home and property insurance are the location of the home, the type of structure, the coverage amount and policy type, discounts, and differences among insurance companies.

LOCATION OF HOME   The location of the residence affects insurance rates. If more claims have been filed in an area, home insurance rates for people living there will be higher. Weather events such as a hailstorm or a hurricane also affect insurance costs.

TYPE OF STRUCTURE   The type of home and the construction materials influence the costs of insurance coverage. A brick house, for example, would cost less to insure than a similar house made of wood. However, earthquake coverage is more expensive for a brick home than for a wood dwelling. Stronger, more wind-resistant home construction can reduce insurance costs in Florida and provide greater protection against hurricane damage. Also, the age and style of the house can create potential risks and increase insurance costs.

smart money minute

In some areas, a home could be automatically rejected for insurance coverage if it has had two or three claims of any sort in the past 3 years. Homes that have encountered water damage, storm damage, and burglaries are most vulnerable to rejection.

COVERAGE AMOUNT AND POLICY TYPE   The policy you select and the financial limits of coverage affect the premium you pay. It costs more to insure a $150,000 home than a $100,000 home. The comprehensive form of homeowner's policy costs more than a tenant's policy.

The *deductible* amount in your policy also affects the cost of your insurance. If you increase the amount of your deductible, your premium will be lower since the company will pay out less in claims. The most common deductible amounts are $500 or $1,000 or higher, which can reduce the premium 15 percent or more.

EXAMPLE: Increase a Deductible to Reduce the Premium

Suppose your home insurance policy premium is $800 with a $250 deductible. If you increase the amount of your deductible to $500, you reduce the premium by 10 percent, or $80.

REDUCING HOME INSURANCE COSTS

HOME INSURANCE DISCOUNTS   Most companies offer incentives that reduce home insurance costs. Your premium may be lower if you have smoke detectors or a fire extinguisher. Deterrents to burglars, such as dead-bolt locks or an alarm system, can also save you money. Some companies offer home insurance discounts to policyholders who are nonsmokers or may give a discount for being "claim-free" for a certain number of years.

my life 4

Understanding methods to reduce home or renter's insurance costs can save you money.

To identify steps that you might take to reduce home insurance costs, talk to various people you know about actions of which they are aware.

COMPANY DIFFERENCES   Studies show that you can save more than 30 percent on homeowner's insurance by comparing companies. Contact both insurance agents who work for one company and independent agents who represent several. The information you obtain will enable you to compare rates. Home insurance rates may be compared using information from websites such as www.netquote.com.

Don't select a company on the basis of price alone. Also consider service and coverage. Not all companies settle claims in the same way. For example, a number of homeowners had two sides of their houses dented by hail. Since the type of siding used in these houses was no longer available, all of the siding had to be replaced. Some insurance companies paid for complete replacement of the siding, while others paid only for replacement of the damaged areas. State insurance commissions, other government agencies, and consumer organizations can provide information about the reputations of insurance companies. *Consumer Reports* (www.consumerreports.org) regularly publishes a satisfaction index of property insurance companies.

 **PRACTICE QUIZ 10-4**

1. What major factors influence the cost of home insurance?
2. What actions can a person take to reduce the cost of home insurance?

PFP Sheet 48
Property Insurance

PFP Sheet 49
Apartment/
Home Insurance
Comparison

Automobile Insurance Coverages

Each year, motor vehicle crashes cost over $250 billion in lost wages and medical costs. The National Traffic Safety Administration estimates that alcohol use, texting, and cell phone use are factors in more than half of all automobile accidents. Such accidents result in thousands of highway deaths and injuries and over $30 billion in costs. These automobile accidents create a risk that affects many people financially and emotionally. Automobile insurance cannot eliminate the costs of automobile accidents; however, it does reduce the financial impact.

A **financial responsibility law** is state legislation that requires drivers to prove their ability to cover the cost of damage or injury caused by an automobile accident. All states have such laws to protect the public from physical harm and property damage losses caused by drivers. When injuries or significant property damage occur in an accident, the drivers involved are required to file a report with the state and to show financial responsibility. Nearly all states have compulsory automobile insurance laws. In other states, most people meet the financial responsibility requirement by buying insurance, since very few have the financial resources to meet this legal requirement on their own.

The main coverages provided by automobile insurance fall into two categories: bodily injury coverages and property damage coverages (see Exhibit 10-8). Other coverages include wage loss insurance, towing service, accidental death, and car rental when a vehicle is undergoing repairs due to an accident or other damage.

LO10-5

Identify the important types of automobile insurance coverage.

financial responsibility law State legislation that requires drivers to prove their ability to cover the cost of damage or injury caused by an automobile accident.

MOTOR VEHICLE BODILY INJURY COVERAGES

Most money automobile insurance companies pay in claims goes for the cost of injury lawsuits, medical expenses, and related legal costs. The main bodily injury coverages are bodily injury liability, medical payments coverage, and uninsured motorist protection. No-fault systems in a number of states have influenced the process of settling bodily injury claims.

BODILY INJURY LIABILITY **Bodily injury liability** covers the risk of financial loss due to legal expenses, medical expenses, lost wages, and other expenses associated with injuries caused by an automobile accident for which you were responsible. This insurance protects you from extensive financial loss.

bodily injury liability Coverage for the risk of financial loss due to legal expenses, medical costs, lost wages, and other expenses associated with injuries caused by an automobile accident for which the insured was responsible.

EXHIBIT 10-8

Two major categories of automobile insurance

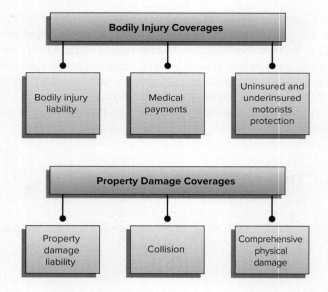

smart money minute

Think twice before lending your car to friends. If you don't have medical payment coverage, don't take passengers in your car, especially if your passengers don't have a good health care plan.

medical payments coverage Automobile insurance that covers medical expenses for people injured in one's car or as a pedestrian.

uninsured motorist protection Automobile insurance coverage for the cost of injuries to a person and members of his or her family caused by a driver with inadequate insurance or by a hit-and-run driver.

Automobile liability insurance coverage is usually expressed as a split limit, such as 50/100/25 or 100/300/50. The first two numbers represent bodily injury liability coverage. These amounts represent thousands of dollars of coverage. The first number (see Exhibit 10-9) is the limit for claims that can be paid to one person; the second number is the limit for each accident; the third number is discussed in the section on property damage coverages. With 100/300 bodily injury coverage, for example, a driver would have a limit of $100,000 for claims that could be paid to one person in an accident. In addition, there would be a $300,000 limit for all bodily injury claims from a single accident.

MEDICAL PAYMENTS COVERAGE While bodily injury liability pays for the costs of injuries to persons who were not in your automobile, **medical payments coverage** covers the costs of health care for people who were injured in your automobile, including yourself. This protection covers friends, carpool members, and others who ride in your vehicle. Medical payments insurance also provides medical benefits if you or a member of your family is struck by an automobile or injured while riding in another person's automobile.

UNINSURED MOTORIST PROTECTION If you are in an accident caused by a person without insurance, **uninsured motorist protection** covers the cost of injuries to you and your family; in most states, however, it does not cover property damage. This insurance also provides protection against financial losses due to injuries caused by a hit-and-run driver or by a driver who has insufficient coverage to cover the cost

EXHIBIT 10-9

Automobile liability insurance coverage

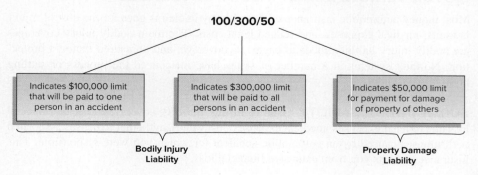

of your injuries. *Underinsured motorist coverage* provides financial protection when another driver has insurance coverage below the amount to cover the financial damages you have encountered.

NO-FAULT INSURANCE Difficulties and high costs of settling claims for medical expenses and personal injuries have resulted in the creation of the **no-fault system**, in which drivers involved in accidents collect medical expenses, lost wages, and related injury costs from their own insurance companies. The system is intended to provide fast, smooth methods of paying for damages without taking the legal action frequently necessary to determine fault.

Massachusetts was the first state to implement no-fault insurance. In recent years, nearly 30 states had some variation of the system. While no-fault automobile insurance was intended to reduce the time and cost associated with the settlement of automobile injury cases, this has not always been the result. One reason for continued difficulties is that no-fault systems vary from state to state. Some no-fault states set limits on medical expenses, lost wages, and other claim settlements, while other states allow lawsuits under certain conditions, such as permanent paralysis or death. Some states include property damage in no-fault insurance. Drivers should investigate the coverages and implications of no-fault insurance in their states.

Bodily injuries contribute to the major portion of costs for auto insurance claims.
VStock/Alamy Stock Photo

MOTOR VEHICLE PROPERTY DAMAGE COVERAGES

Three types of coverage protect you from financial loss due to damage to property of others and damage to your vehicle: (1) property damage liability, (2) collision, and (3) comprehensive physical damage. (See the *Financial Literacy for My Life: Are You Covered?* feature.)

PROPERTY DAMAGE LIABILITY When you damage the property of others, **property damage liability** protects you against financial loss. This coverage applies mainly to other vehicles; however, it also includes damage to street signs, lampposts, buildings, and other property. Property damage liability protects you and others covered by your policy when driving another person's automobile with permission. The policy limit for property damage liability is commonly stated with your bodily injury coverages. The last number in 50/100/25 and 100/300/50, for example, is for property damage liability ($25,000 and $50,000, respectively).

COLLISION When your automobile is involved in an accident, **collision** insurance pays for the damage to the automobile regardless of fault. However, if another driver caused the accident, your insurance company may attempt to recover the repair costs for your vehicle through the other driver's property damage liability. The insurance company's right to recover the amount it pays for the loss from the person responsible for the loss is called *subrogation*.

The amount you can collect with collision insurance is limited to the actual cash value of the automobile at the time of the accident. This amount is usually based on the figures provided by some appraisal service such as the *Official Used Car Guide* of the National Automobile Dealers Association (www.nada.org). If you have an automobile with many add-on features or one that is several years old and has been restored, you should obtain a documented statement of its condition and value before an accident occurs.

no-fault system An automobile insurance program in which drivers involved in accidents collect medical expenses, lost wages, and related injury costs from their own insurance companies.

property damage liability Automobile insurance coverage that protects a person against financial loss when that person damages the property of others.

collision Automobile insurance that pays for damage to the insured's car when it is involved in an accident.

personal fintech

WILL GPSs REDUCE AUTO INSURANCE COSTS?

Global positioning systems (GPSs) and other technology are being used to encourage safer driving and reduce auto insurance costs. In Britain, one insurance company adjusts premiums each month based on a driver's braking and acceleration habits. The Car Chip allows parents to monitor the speed and braking actions of young drivers.

Financial Literacy for My Life

ARE YOU COVERED?

Often people believe their insurance will cover various financial losses. For each of the following situations, name the type of home or automobile insurance that would protect you.

1. While you are on vacation, clothing and other personal belongings are stolen. _____
2. Your home is damaged by fire, and you have to live in a hotel for several weeks. _____
3. You and members of your family suffer injuries in an automobile accident caused by a hit-and-run driver. _____
4. A delivery person is injured on your property and takes legal action against you. _____
5. Your automobile is accidentally damaged by some people playing baseball. _____
6. A person takes legal action against you for injuries you caused in an automobile accident. _____
7. Water from a local lake rises and damages your furniture and carpeting. _____
8. Your automobile needs repairs because you hit a tree. _____
9. You damaged a valuable tree when your automobile hit it, and you want to pay for the damage. _____
10. While riding with you in your automobile, your nephew is injured in an accident and incurs various medical expenses. _____

Answers: (1) Personal property coverage of home insurance; (2) additional living expenses of home insurance; (3) uninsured motorist protection; (4) personal liability coverage of home insurance; (5) comprehensive physical damage; (6) bodily injury liability; (7) flood insurance—requires coverage separate from home insurance; (8) collision; (9) property damage liability of automobile insurance; (10) medical payments.

---

comprehensive physical damage Automobile insurance that covers financial loss from damage to a vehicle caused by a risk other than a collision, such as fire, theft, glass breakage, hail, or vandalism.

COMPREHENSIVE PHYSICAL DAMAGE Another protection for your automobile involves financial losses from damage caused by a risk other than a collision. **Comprehensive physical damage** covers you for risks such as fire, theft, glass breakage, falling objects, vandalism, wind, hail, flood, tornado, lightning, earthquake, avalanche, or damage caused by hitting an animal. Certain articles in your vehicle, such as some radios and stereo systems, may be excluded from this insurance. These articles may be protected by the personal property coverage of your home insurance. Like collision insurance, comprehensive coverage applies only to your car, and claims are paid without considering fault. Both collision and comprehensive coverage are commonly sold with a *deductible* to help reduce insurance costs. Deductibles keep insurance premiums lower by reducing the number of small claims companies pay. Going from full-coverage comprehensive insurance to a $100 deductible may reduce the cost of that coverage by as much as 40 percent.

EXAMPLE 1: Deductible

If a broken windshield costs $750 to replace and you have a $200 deductible on your comprehensive coverage, the insurance company will pay $550 of the damages.

EXAMPLE 2: Deductible

A deductible may be a specific dollar amount or a percentage. If a policy has a deductible that's a percentage, make sure you know how that translates to a dollar amount. Here are two examples for homes insured for $150,000:

- Policy A has a $500 deductible. A hailstorm destroys the home's roof, and the cost for repairs is $6,500. Policy A will pay $6,000 of the cost to repair the roof.
- Policy B has a 5 percent deductible—or $7,500. If the home needed $6,500 in roof repairs, Policy B would not pay anything because the amount of repairs is less than the deductible.

Financial Literacy for My Life

WERE YOU IN AN ACCIDENT CAUSED BY THE OTHER DRIVER?

As in any accident, move your car out of the way safely if you can and call 911 if there are injuries. If you think the other driver was at fault, here are some tips to keep in mind.

1. AFTER THE ACCIDENT

Exchange information, making sure to get the other driver's:

- Name, address, and phone number.
- Driver's license number and license plate number.
- Auto insurance company name and policy number. Make sure you get the exact name of the company and not just the agent's name.

Get the names and contact information of any witnesses if possible. Make sure to get a copy of the police report if there is one. It's also helpful to take photos of the damage to the vehicles.

If the other driver isn't insured or left the scene, you may be able to file a claim on your own policy, depending on your coverage.

2. AFTER YOU GET HOME

Contact your agent or insurance company to let them know about the accident. Also contact the other driver's insurance company to make sure the accident was reported to them. The other driver's insurance company should pay:

- To repair or replace your car.
- For a rental car while your car is being repaired.
- Medical and hospital bills for you and your passengers.
- For wages lost because of an injury.

The other driver's company may ask you to get an estimate for the cost of the repair, or they may send out their own adjuster. You may have a separate adjuster for any medical claims.

3. IF YOU HAVE PROBLEMS WITH YOUR CLAIM

If the costs are more than the other driver's policy limits, you may be able to file on your own policy for the difference, depending on your coverage. Also, sometimes the insurance company decides that both drivers share fault and will pay only part of the claim.

- If the other driver's company won't cover all your medical bills, file a claim for the difference with your health insurance. Another option is to file on your auto policy depending on the types of medical coverage you have.
- If the other driver's policy won't cover the full cost of fixing your car, file on your own policy if you have collision or uninsured/underinsured coverage. You'll have to pay your deductible, but your company may be able to recover that from the other driver or insurance company and pay you back.
- If the other driver's company has treated you unfairly, you can file a complaint with your state's Department of Insurance.

Source: http://tdi.texas.gov/takefive/accident-caused-by-other-driver.html, accessed April 5, 2021.

OTHER AUTOMOBILE INSURANCE COVERAGES

In addition to basic bodily injury and property damage coverages, other protection is available. *Wage loss insurance* will reimburse you for any salary or income lost due to injury in an automobile accident. Wage loss insurance is usually required in states with a no-fault insurance system; in other states, it is available on an optional basis.

Towing and emergency road service coverage pays for the cost of breakdowns and mechanical assistance. This coverage can be especially beneficial on long trips or during inclement weather. Towing and road service coverage pays for the cost of getting the vehicle to a service station or starting it when it breaks down on the highway, not for the cost of repairs. If you belong to an automobile club, your membership may include towing coverage. Purchasing duplicate coverage as part of your automobile insurance could be a waste of money. Rental reimbursement coverage pays for a rental car if your vehicle is stolen or is in the shop for repairs from an accident or for other covered damages. The *Financial Literacy for My Life: Were You in an Accident Caused by the Other Driver?* feature explains what to do if you are in an accident caused by the other driver.

 5

Knowing the main types of auto insurance coverages is vital for reducing financial risk.

Auto insurance coverage is not completely understood by many people. In an attempt to increase your knowledge and to inform others, conduct a series of informal discussions with various people about the purpose of the main types of auto insurance coverage.

PRACTICE QUIZ 10-5

1. What is the purpose of financial responsibility laws?
2. What are the main coverages included in most automobile insurance policies?
3. What is no-fault insurance?
4. How does collision coverage differ from comprehensive physical damage coverage?

Automobile Insurance Costs

LO10-6

Evaluate factors that affect the cost of automobile insurance.

Most households spend more than $1,200 for auto insurance each year. Automobile insurance premiums reflect the amounts insurance companies pay for injury and property damage claims. Your automobile insurance is directly related to coverage amounts and factors such as the vehicle, your place of residence, and your driving record.

smart money minute

Many people make the *mistake* of trying to eat messy food while driving. The foods and drinks that were reported as the most common distractions in auto accidents: coffee, hot soup, tacos, chili-covered foods, hamburgers, chicken, jelly- or cream-filled doughnuts, and soft drinks. There are, of course, other distractions available to drivers, including cell phones, razors, makeup, or other electronic devices. You can take *action* to avoid eating, drinking, and using electronic devices while driving. This will result in fewer accidents and lead to *success* in saving lives.

AMOUNT OF COVERAGE

"How much coverage do I need?" This question affects the amount you pay for insurance. Our legal environment and increasing property values influence coverage amounts.

LEGAL CONCERNS   As discussed earlier, every state has laws that require or encourage automobile liability insurance coverage. Since very few people can afford to pay an expensive court settlement with personal assets, most drivers buy automobile liability insurance.

In the past, bodily injury liability coverage of 10/20 was considered adequate. In fact, most states have only recently increased their minimum limits for financial responsibility above 10/20. However, in recent injury cases, some people have been awarded millions of dollars; thus, legal and insurance advisors now recommend 100/300. As discussed earlier in this chapter, an umbrella policy can provide additional liability coverage of $1 million or more.

PROPERTY VALUES   Just as medical expenses and legal settlements have increased, so has the cost of vehicles. Therefore, a policy limit of more than $10,000 for property damage liability is appropriate; $50,000 or $100,000 is usually suggested.

AUTOMOBILE INSURANCE PREMIUM FACTORS

Several factors influence the premium you pay for automobile insurance. The main factors are vehicle type, rating territory, and driver classification.

smart money minute

While larger cars are usually safer than smaller ones in a crash, bigger vehicles often cause more damage to other cars. Certain models of pickups, sport utility vehicles, and sedans resulted in the greatest property damage liability claims, according to the Highway Data Loss Institute.

AUTOMOBILE TYPE   The year, make, and model of your motor vehicle strongly influence automobile insurance costs. Expensive replacement parts and complicated repairs due to body style contribute to higher rates. Also, certain makes and models are stolen more often than others.

RATING TERRITORY In most states, your **rating territory** is the place of residence used to determine your automobile insurance premium. Various geographic locations have different costs due to differences in the number of claims made. For example, fewer accidents and less vandalism occur in rural areas than in large cities. New York City, Los Angeles, and Chicago have the highest incidence of automobile theft.

DRIVER CLASSIFICATION You are compared with other drivers to set your automobile insurance premium. **Driver classification** is a category based on the driver's age, sex, marital status, driving record, and driving habits; drivers' categories are used to determine automobile insurance rates. In general, young drivers (under 25) and those over 70 have more frequent and severe accidents. As a result, they pay higher premiums.

Accidents and traffic violations influence your driver classification. A poor driving record increases your insurance costs. Finally, you pay less for insurance if you do not drive to work than if you use your automobile for business. Belonging to a carpool instead of driving to work alone can reduce insurance costs.

Your credit history may also be considered when applying for auto insurance. While some states limit the use of credit scoring in auto insurance, the practice is common in other areas.

The number of claims you file with your insurance company also affects your premiums. Expensive liability settlements or extensive property damage will increase your rates. If you have many expensive claims or a poor driving record, your company may cancel your policy, making it difficult for you to obtain coverage from another company. To deal with this problem, every state has an **assigned risk pool** consisting of people who are unable to obtain automobile insurance. Some of these people are assigned to each insurance company operating in the state. They pay several times the normal rates but do get coverage. Once a good driving record is established, the driver can reapply for insurance with a lower premium.

REDUCING AUTOMOBILE INSURANCE PREMIUMS

Methods for lowering automobile insurance costs include comparing companies and taking advantage of commonly offered discounts.

COMPARING COMPANIES Rates and service vary among automobile insurance companies. Among companies in the same area, premiums can vary as much as 100 percent. If you relocate, don't assume your present company will offer the best rates in your new living area. Rates may be compared online at www.netquote.com.

Also consider the service the local insurance agent provides. Will this company representative be available to answer questions, change coverages, and handle claims as needed? You can check a company's reputation for handling automobile insurance claims and other matters with sources such as *Consumer Reports* or your state insurance department. Several states publish information with sample auto insurance rates for different companies to help consumers save money. The address and contact information of your state insurance regulator may be found online.

PREMIUM DISCOUNTS The best way to keep your rates down is to establish and maintain a safe driving record. Taking steps to avoid accidents and traffic violations will mean lower automobile insurance premiums. In addition, most insurance companies

rating territory The place of residence used to determine a person's automobile insurance premium.

driver classification A category based on the driver's age, sex, marital status, driving record, and driving habits; used to determine automobile insurance rates.

assigned risk pool Consists of people who are unable to obtain automobile insurance due to poor driving or accident records and must obtain coverage at high rates through a state program that requires insurance companies to accept some of them.

 my life 6

Various actions are available to reduce auto insurance costs.

People take various actions to reduce their auto insurance costs. Locate a blog about auto insurance coverage and costs. What advice is offered that you might consider?

personal fintech

To reduce driving accidents among teens, some parents have installed an in-car monitoring device that records seat belt use, engine speed, and tire traction. The device also beeps when preset limits for speed, braking, or sharp turns are violated.

Financial Literacy for My Life

PAY AS YOU GO CAR INSURANCE

One of the newest trends in the auto insurance industry is "pay as you go" insurance, or coverage based on, and tailored to, your driving habits.

Most of these programs offer an initial discount, but you may be required to install a device in your car that sends data about your driving back to the insurer. Data tracked may include the times of day you drive, how far you drive, and how often you hop in the car. These factors combine to determine your car insurance rates.

While the discounts are a definite perk, it is important to understand what you are signing up for. Before signing up for this type of policy (or any policy), you should ask:

- Are the advertised discount amounts guaranteed? If not, how widely do they vary?
- Can your insurer increase your rates based on your driving habits?
- How often will the rates change?
- Will the insurer use your driving data for purposes other than setting your insurance rates? Will your data be sold to third parties?
- Will your privacy be protected? How?
- Does the device include a GPS? If so, how does your insurer protect and use that data?

offer various discounts. Drivers under 25 can qualify for reduced rates by completing a driver training program or maintaining good grades in school. When young drivers are away at school without a car, families are likely to get reduced premiums since the student will not be using the vehicle on a regular basis.

Installing security devices such as a fuel shutoff switch, a second ignition switch, or an alarm system will decrease your chances of theft and lower your insurance costs. Being a nonsmoker can qualify you for lower automobile insurance premiums. Discounts are also offered for participating in a carpool and insuring two or more vehicles with the same company. Ask your insurance agent about other methods for lowering your automobile insurance rates.

Increasing the amount of deductibles will result in a lower premium. Also, some people believe an old car is not worth the amount paid for collision and comprehensive coverage and therefore dispense with them. However, before doing this, be sure to compare the value of your car for getting you to school or work with the cost of these coverages.

If you change your driving habits, get married, or alter your driving status in other ways, be sure to notify the insurance company. Premium savings can result. Also, some employers make group automobile insurance available to workers. Before you buy a motor vehicle, find out which makes and models have the lowest insurance costs. This information can result in a purchasing decision with many financial benefits.

Are you interested in "pay as you go car insurance"? Read the *Financial Literacy for My Life: Pay as You Go Car Insurance* feature to determine if it fits your lifestyle.

PFP Sheet 50
Automobile Insurance Comparison

✓ PRACTICE QUIZ 10-6

1. What factors influence how much a person pays for automobile insurance?
2. What actions can a person take to reduce the cost of automobile insurance?

Your Personal Finance Roadmap and Dashboard:

Home and Auto Insurance

PERCENT OF PERSONAL PROPERTY
COVERAGE

A personal finance dashboard can help you determine if you have proper coverage for household belongings. Homeowner's insurance protects you against financial loss in case your home is damaged or destroyed.

Your household belongings, such as furniture, appliances, and clothing, are covered by the personal property portion of a homeowner's insurance policy up to a portion of the insured value of the home. That portion may range from 55 to 75 percent.

YOUR SITUATION

Have you established a specific and measurable portion of coverage for your household belongings? Do you have adequate additional living expense coverage if a fire or other event damages your home? Some policies limit additional living expense coverage to 10 to 20 percent of the home's total coverage amount. Have you considered a personal property floater for additional property insurance that covers the damage or loss of a specific item of high

value? Other insurance actions you might consider during various stages of your life include:

First Steps

- Obtain appropriate auto insurance coverage based on vehicle value, driving habits, and financial situation.
- Consider renter's insurance to cover personal property and liability risks.
- Determine additional home property and motor vehicle insurance coverage based on current life situation.
- Prepare inventory (list, receipts, photos, video) of personal belongings.

Next Steps

- Review home insurance policy to determine possible coverage changes and discounts.
- Assess auto insurance coverage based on changes in household and vehicle situation.

Later Steps

- Determine potential changes in driving habits that might affect auto insurance costs.
- Update home and property insurance coverage based on housing situation.

> **YOUR** next step . . . select one or more of the items above and create an action plan to implement those financial planning activities.

✓ SUMMARY OF LEARNING OBJECTIVES

LO10-1

Develop a risk management plan using insurance.
An understanding of various risk management actions can reduce the chance of financial loss. The four general risk management techniques are risk avoidance, risk reduction, risk assumption, and risk shifting. In planning a personal insurance program, set your goals, make a plan to reach your goals, put your plan into action, and review your results.

LO10-2

Discuss the importance of property and liability insurance. Your knowledge of property and liability insurance coverages should include awareness that owners of homes and automobiles face the risks of (1) property damage or loss and (2) legal actions by others for the costs of injuries or property damage. Property and liability insurance offer protection from financial losses that may arise from a wide variety of situations faced by owners of homes and users of automobiles.

LO10-3

Explain the insurance coverage and policy types available to homeowners and renters. Appropriate homeowner's or renter's insurance coverage is a fundamental aspect of personal financial planning. Homeowner's insurance includes protection for the building and other structures, additional living expenses, personal property, and personal liability. Renter's insurance includes the same coverages excluding protection for the building and other structures, which is the concern of the building owner.

LO10-4

Analyze factors that influence the amount of coverage and the cost of home insurance. Awareness of methods to reduce homeowner's or renter's insurance costs can result in big savings. The amount of home insurance coverage is determined by the replacement cost of your dwelling and personal belongings. The cost of home insurance is influenced by the location of the home, the type of structure,

the coverage amount, the policy type, the discounts, and insurance company differences.

LO10-5

Identify the important types of automobile insurance coverage. Your understanding of the main types of auto insurance coverages is vital for successful financial planning. Automobile insurance is used to meet states' financial responsibility laws and to protect drivers against financial losses associated with bodily injury and property damage. The major types of automobile insurance coverages are bodily injury liability, medical payments, uninsured motorist, property damage liability, collision, and comprehensive physical damage.

LO10-6

Evaluate factors that affect the cost of automobile insurance. Various actions can be taken to reduce auto insurance costs. The cost of automobile insurance is affected by the amount of coverage, automobile type, rating territory, driver classification, differences among insurance companies, and premium discounts.

KEY TERMS

actual cash value (ACV)   357

assigned risk pool   365

bodily injury liability   359

coinsurance clause   356

collision   361

comprehensive physical
    damage   362

deductible   345

driver classification   365

endorsement   352

financial responsibility law   359

hazard   343

homeowner's insurance   349

household inventory   350

insurance   343

insurance company   343

insured   343

insurer   343

liability   349

medical payments coverage
    (homeowner)   352

medical payments coverage   360

negligence   349

no-fault system   361

peril   343

personal property floater   350

policy   343

policyholder   343

premium   343

property damage liability   361

pure risk   344

rating territory   365

replacement value   357

risk   343

self-insurance   344

speculative risk   344

strict liability   349

umbrella policy   352

uninsured motorists
    protection   360

vicarious liability   349

SELF-TEST PROBLEMS

1. A person with homeowner's insurance incurs roof damage of $17,000. The policy has a $500 deductible. What amount would the insurance pay for the claim?

2. A driver lost control of the vehicle, hit a parked car, and damaged a storefront. The damage to the parked car was $4,300, and the damage to the store was $15,400. If the driver has 50/100/15 vehicle insurance coverage, what amount will the insurance company pay? Is the driver responsible for any of the damages?

3. In Problem 2, what if the driver had 50/100/20 vehicle insurance coverage? What amount will the insurance company pay? Is the driver responsible for any of the damages?

4. Homeowner has a replacement cost policy from an insurance company. What it would cost the company to replace homeowner's personal belongings that originally cost $50,000? The replacement cost for items has increased 10 percent.

Self-Test Solutions

1. The claim would be settled for $16,500 ($17,000 minus the $500 deductible).

2. Of the total damages of $19,700, the insurance company would pay $15,000. The driver would be responsible for $4,700 (19,700 − $15,000).

3. Since the total damage was less than $20,000, the insurance will pay the entire amount of $19,700. The driver would not pay any amount.

4. The insurance company will pay $55,000 ($50,000 × 1.10).

 FINANCIAL PLANNING PROBLEMS

1. *Calculating Property Loss Claim Coverage.* Most home insurance policies cover jewelry for $1,000 and silverware for $2,500 unless items are covered with additional insurance. If $3,800 worth of jewelry and $2,800 worth of silverware were stolen from a family, what amount of the claim would not be covered by insurance?   **LO10-2**

2. *Computing Actual Cash Value Coverage.* What amount would a person with actual cash value (ACV) coverage receive for two-year-old furniture destroyed by a fire? The furniture would cost $1,000 to replace today and had an estimated life of five years.   **LO10-3**

3. *Determining Replacement Cost.* What would it cost an insurance company to replace a family's personal property that originally cost $42,000? The replacement costs for the items have increased 15 percent.   **LO10-3**

4. *Calculating a Coinsurance Claim.* If Carissa has a $130,000 home insured for $100,000, based on the 80 percent coinsurance provision, how much would the insurance company pay on a $5,000 claim?   **LO10-4**

5. *Determining the Claim Amount (with Deductibles).* For each of the following situations, what amount would the insurance company pay?   **LO10-4**

    a. Wind damage of $835; the insured has a $500 deductible.

    b. Theft of a home entertainment system worth $1,150; the insured has a $250 deductible.

    c. Vandalism that does $425 of damage to a home; the insured has a $500 deductible.

6. *Computing Claims.* When Carolina's house burned down, she lost household items worth a total of $50,000. Her house was insured for $160,000, and her homeowner's policy provided coverage for personal belongings up to 55 percent of the insured value of the house. Calculate how much insurance coverage Carolina's policy provides for her personal possessions and whether she will receive payment for all of the items destroyed in the fire.   **LO10-3**

7. *Calculating Insurance Discounts.* Matt and Kristin are newly married and living in their first house. The yearly premium on their homeowner's insurance policy is $450 for the coverage they need. Their insurance company offers a 5 percent discount if they install dead-bolt locks on all exterior doors. The couple can also receive a 2 percent discount if they install smoke detectors on each floor. They have contacted a locksmith, who will provide and install dead-bolt locks on the two exterior doors for $60 each. At the local hardware store, smoke detectors cost $8 each, and the new house has two floors. Kristin and Matt can install them themselves. What discount will Matt and Kristin receive if they install the dead-bolt locks? If they install smoke detectors?   **LO10-3**

8. *Computing Discount Payback.* In the preceding problem, assuming their insurance rates remain the same, how many years will it take Matt and Kristin to earn back in discounts the cost of the dead bolts? The cost of the smoke detectors?   **LO10-3**

9. *Calculating Auto Liability Claim Coverage.* Becky has 25/50/10 automobile insurance coverage. If two other people are awarded $35,000 each for injuries in an auto accident in which Becky was judged at fault, how much of this judgment would the insurance cover?   **LO10-5**

10. *Determining a Property Damage Liability Claim.* Kurt has 50/100/15 auto insurance coverage. One evening he lost control of his vehicle, hitting a parked car and damaging a storefront along the street. Damage to the parked car was $5,400, and damage to the store was $12,650. What amount will the insurance company pay for the damages? What amount will Kurt have to pay?   **LO10-5**

11. *Calculating Future Value of Insurance Savings.* Beverly and Kyle currently insure their cars with separate companies, paying $650 and $575 a year. If they insured both cars with the same company, they would save 10 percent on the annual premiums. What would be the future value of the annual savings over 10 years based on an annual interest rate of 6 percent?   **LO10-6**

12. *Determining What Amount the Insurance Company Will Pay for the Damages.* Eric and Susan just purchased their first home, which cost $130,000. They purchased a homeowner's policy to insure the home for $120,000 and personal property for $75,000. They declined any coverage for additional living expenses. The deductible for the policy is $500.   **LO10-3**

Soon after Eric and Susan moved into their new home, a strong windstorm caused damage to their roof. They reported the roof damage to be $17,000. While the roof was under repair, the couple had to live in a nearby hotel for three days. The hotel bill amounted to $320. Assuming the insurance company settles claims using the replacement value method, what amount will the insurance company pay for the damages to the roof?

LO10-6 **13.** *Determining What Amount the Insurance Company Will Pay for the Accident.* Eric's Ford Mustang and Susan's Toyota Prius are insured with the same insurance agent. They have 50/100/15 vehicle insurance coverage. The very week of the windstorm, Susan had an accident. She lost control of her car, hit a parked car, and damaged a storefront. The damage to the parked car was $4,300 and the damage to the store was $15,400. What amount will the insurance company pay for Susan's car accident?

DIGITAL FINANCIAL LITERACY: CAREER IN THE INSURANCE INDUSTRY

According to the Insurance Information Institute, employment of insurance brokers and sales agents is expected to grow 9 percent by the year 2024. Careers such as actuary and underwriter are considered one of the best jobs for young professionals.

If you enjoy interacting with people and can provide excellent customer service, then you can consider a rewarding career in the industry. Most insurance companies provide ongoing training, encourage professional development, and offer opportunities to advance in your career. Most insurance professionals have a bachelor's degree in business, insurance, economics, or finance.

Action items:

1. Gather information about a career in the insurance industry. Research several of the following websites:
   - investprogram.org
   - iicf.org
   - iii.orgindependentagent.com
2. Prepare a 1- to 2-page report providing answers related to:
   - average salaries
   - training programs
   - advancement opportunities
   - flexible scheduling

FINANCIAL PLANNING CASE

We Rent, So Why Do We Need Insurance?

"Have you been down in the basement?" Nathan asked his wife, Erin, as he entered their apartment.

"No, what's up?" responded Erin.

"It's flooded because of all that rain we got last weekend!" he exclaimed.

"Oh no! We have the extra furniture my mom gave us stored down there. Is everything ruined?" Erin asked.

"The couch and coffee table are in a foot of water; the loveseat was the only thing that looked OK. Boy, I didn't realize the basement of this building wasn't waterproof. I'm going to call our landlady to complain."

As Erin thought about the situation, she remembered that when they moved in last fall, Kathy, their landlady, had informed them that her insurance policy covered the building but not the property belonging to each tenant. Because of this, they had purchased renter's insurance. "Nathan, I think our renter's insurance will cover the damage. Let me give our agent a call."

When Erin and Nathan purchased their insurance, they had to decide whether they wanted to be insured for cash value or for replacement costs. Replacement was more expensive, but it meant they would collect enough to go out and buy new household items at today's prices. If they had opted for cash value, the couch Erin's mother had paid $1,000 for five years ago would be worth less than $500 today.

Erin made the call and found out their insurance did cover the furniture in the basement, and at replacement value after they paid the deductible. The $300 they had invested in renter's insurance last year was well worth it!

Not every renter has as much foresight as Erin and Nathan. Fewer than 4 in 10 renters have renter's insurance. Some aren't even aware they need it. They may assume they are covered by the landlord's insurance, but they aren't. This mistake can be costly.

Think about how much you have invested in your possessions and how much it would cost to replace them. Start with your home entertainment system that you bought last year. Experts suggest that people who rent start thinking about these things as soon as they move into their first apartment. Your policy should cover your personal belongings and provide funds for living expenses if you are dispossessed by a fire or other disaster.

Questions

1. Why is it important for people who rent to have insurance?

2. Does the building owner's property insurance ever cover the tenant's personal property?

3. What is the difference between cash value and replacement value?

4. When shopping for renter's insurance, what coverage features should you look for?

YOUR PERSONAL FINANCIAL PLAN

OBTAINING HOME AND AUTO INSURANCE

Creating an insurance plan, including appropriate coverage for your home, personal property, and motor vehicles, helps to avoid financial difficulties.

Your Short-Term Financial Planning Activity

Task Create a record of current and needed insurance coverage.

Research

1) Use Personal Financial Planning Sheets 46 and 48 to list your current insurance policies for your home, automobile(s), disability income, health and life insurance. Are your coverages adequate, or do you need additional insurance to protect yourself?

2) Contact two or three insurance agents to obtain information about homeowner's or renter's insurance. Use Personal Financial Planning Sheet 49 to compare the coverage and costs.

3) Contact two or three insurance agents to obtain information about auto insurance. Use Financial Planning Sheet 50 to compare costs and coverage for various insurance costs.

Outcome Create a visual presentation (PowerPoint presentation, video, chart, or another format of your choice) and show the types of coverages you have and what process you followed when selecting and comparing various insurance coverages.

Your Long-Term Financial Planning Activity

Task Develop a list of sources of information that could help you to reduce your future home and auto insurance costs.

Research

1) Research the material in the sections "Home Insurance Cost Factors" and "Automobile Insurance Costs." Explore these topics on the internet and take notes.

2) Talk to several homeowners about the actions they take to reduce the cost of their homeowner's insurance.

3) Develop a plan to monitor changes in your life situation that would affect the need to change home or auto insurance coverages.

Outcome Prepare a video or other visual presentation to communicate your findings.

Note: All *Personal Financial Planner* sheets are available at the end of the book and in an Excel spreadsheet format in *Connect Finance.*

CONTINUING CASE

Property and Motor Vehicle Insurance

Newlyweds Jamie Lee and Ross have had several milestones in the past year. They are newlyweds, recently purchased their first home, and now have twins on the way!

Jamie Lee and Ross have to seriously consider their insurance needs. With a family, a home, and now babies on the way, they need to develop a risk management plan to help them should an unexpected event arise.

Current financial situation

Assets (Jamie Lee and Ross combined)*:*
Checking account: $4,300
Savings account: $22,200
Emergency fund savings account: $20,500
IRA balance: $26,000
Car: $10,000 (Jamie Lee) and $18,000 (Ross)

Liabilities (Jamie Lee and Ross combined)*:*
Student loan balance: $0
　Credit card balance: $2,000
　Car loans: $6,000

Income:
Jamie Lee: $50,000 gross income ($37,500 net income after taxes)
Ross: $75,000 gross income ($64,000 net income after taxes)

Monthly Expenses (Jamie Lee and Ross combined)*:*
Mortgage: $1,252
Property taxes and insurance: $500
Utilities: $195
Food: $400
Gas/maintenance: $275
Credit card payment: $250
Car loan payment: $289
Entertainment: $300

Questions

1. Based on their current life status, what are some of the goals Jamie Lee and Ross should set to achieve when developing their insurance plan?

2. What four questions should Jamie Lee and Ross ask themselves as they develop the risk management plan?

3. Once Jamie Lee and Ross put their insurance plan into action, what should they do to maintain their plan?

4. Jamie and Ross decided to conduct a checkup on their homeowner's insurance policy. They noticed that they had omitted covering Jamie Lee's diamond wedding band set from their policy. What if it got lost or stolen? It was a major purchase and, besides the emotional value, the cost to replace the diamond jewelry would be very high. What type of policy should Jamie Lee and Ross consider to cover the diamond wedding rings?

5. Mr. Ferrell, Jamie Lee and Ross's insurance agent, suggested a flood insurance policy in addition to their regular homeowner's policy. Jamie Lee and Ross looked quizzically at the agent because they do not live within 2 miles of a body of water. What is the basis for Mr. Ferrell's claim for the necessity of the flood policy?

6. Using *Personal Financial Planner Sheet 47,* Home Inventory, create a record of belongings for Jamie Lee and Ross. Consider items of value that may be located in each of the rooms of the house, and determine a dollar amount for each item. What is the total cost of the items?

7. Considering the value of Jamie Lee's and Ross's automobiles, what type of automobile insurance coverage would you suggest for them?

8. What financial strategy would you suggest to Jamie Lee and Ross to enable them to save money on their insurance premiums?

 ## DAILY SPENDING DIARY

"My spending takes most of my money. So after adding car insurance payments, my budget is really tight."

Directions

As you continue (or start using) the *Daily Spending Diary* sheets, you should be able to make better choices for your spending priorities. The financial data you develop will help you better understand your spending patterns and help you plan for achieving financial goals.

Analysis Questions

1. What information from your *Daily Spending Diary* might encourage you to use your money differently?

2. How can your spending habits be developed to assure that you will be able to afford appropriate home and auto insurance coverage?

The *Daily Spending Diary* is located in at the end of Chapter 1 and on the library resource site in *Connect.*

Health, Disability, and Long-Term Care Insurance

11

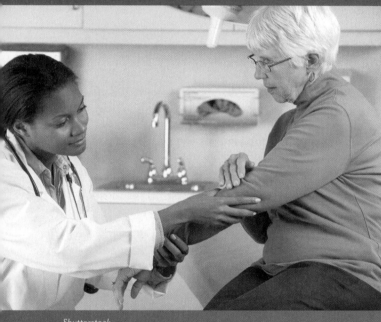

Shutterstock

Financial Literacy
IN YOUR LIFE

▶ **What if you . . .** needed regular cash income lost as a result of an accident or a lengthy illness? What if you could not work for months or years because you were too sick or injured? What actions would you take?

You might . . . consider purchasing disability income insurance. After all, your earning power is your most valuable resource. During the disability, you might face huge expenses for the medical treatment and special care the disability may require.

Now, what would you do Purchase a good disability insurance plan that pays you when you are unable to work at your regular job. A good disability plan will also make partial disability payments when you return to work on a part-time basis. Your Personal Finance Roadmap and Dashboard at the end of the chapter will help you determine the right amount of income needed during a disability.

---

my life | KEEP FIT AND HEALTHY FOREVER?

You are young. You are healthy. And it's easy to take good health for granted. However, as you get older, staying healthy can become a challenge. Because health insurance premiums have outpaced inflation for more than a decade, you are paying more for your health insurance premiums and copayments every time you visit a doctor. Health, disability, and long-term care insurance are an important part of your financial planning. How can you best plan for your health, disability, and long-term care insurance as you grow older?

For each of the following statements, select Agree, Neutral, or Disagree to indicate your personal response regarding these health and disability income insurance topics.

1. The best way to avoid the high cost of illness for me and my family is to stay well.   Agree   Neutral   Disagree

2. To safeguard my family's economic security, medical expense insurance and disability income insurance should be a part of my overall insurance program.   Agree   Neutral   Disagree

3. With today's high cost of health care, it makes sense for me to be as fully insured as I can afford.   Agree   Neutral   Disagree

4. My membership in an HMO should cover office visits, routine checkups, hospital and surgical care, eye exams, laboratory and X-ray service, and mental health services.   Agree   Neutral   Disagree

5. I am aware of various state and federal health care programs.   Agree   Neutral   Disagree

6. I realize that for all age groups, disability is more likely than death.   Agree   Neutral   Disagree

As you study this chapter, you will encounter "My Life" boxes with additional information and resources related to these items.

Health Care Costs

LO11-1

Explain why the costs of health insurance and health care have been increasing.

Health insurance is one way people protect themselves against economic losses due to illness, accident, or disability. Health coverage is available through private insurance companies, service plans, health maintenance organizations, and government programs. Employers often offer health insurance, called *group health insurance,* as part of an employee benefits package, and health care providers sell it to individuals.

Affordable health care has become one of the most important social issues of our time. News broadcasts abound with special reports on "America's health care crisis" or politicians demanding "universal health insurance." "Unless we fix our health care system—in both the public and private sectors—rising health care costs will have severe, adverse consequences for the federal budget as well as the U.S. economy in the future." This is one of the key messages that politicians have been delivering across the country in town-hall-style meetings, in speeches, and on radio and television programs.

Consequently, on March 23, 2010, President Barack Obama signed the Patient Protection and Affordable Care Act, and the Health Care and Education Reconciliation Act on March 30, 2010. The Obama administration believed that this comprehensive health care reform should:

- Reduce long-term growth of health care costs for businesses and government.
- Protect families from bankruptcy or debt because of health care costs.
- Guarantee choice of doctors and health plans.
- Invest in prevention and wellness.
- Improve patient safety and quality of care.
- Assure affordable, quality health coverage for all Americans.
- Maintain coverage when you change or lose your job.
- End barriers to coverage for people with preexisting medical conditions.

The health care debate continues. Polls have suggested both that the public is opposed to reform as passed and that the public is firmly behind the reforms in place, and opponents have vowed that the debate will continue into the future. The Republicans labeled the act "a fiscal Frankenstein," "a decisive step in the weakening of the United States," and "one of the worst offenses of social engineering legislation in the history of the United States," while the Democrats hailed the law as "a new day in America," and that it would "improve the quality of life for millions of American families."

Regardless, the expenditures for health care continue to increase as shown in Exhibit 11-1.

smart money minute

Although you can get health care at many different places, including a hospital's emergency department, it is best for you to get routine care and recommended preventive services from a primary care provider. There are big differences between visits to your primary care provider and visits to the emergency department, such as cost, time spent waiting for care, and follow-up.

HIGH MEDICAL COSTS

What do an aging and overweight population, the cost of prescription drugs, the growing number of uninsured, and advancements in medical technology have in common? These and other factors all add up to rising health costs. The United States has the highest per capita medical expenditures of any country in the world. We spend twice as much on health care as the average for the 24 industrialized countries in Europe and North America. The average per capita cost for health care was estimated to be $12,641 in 2021. It seems that, year after year, there is a third sure thing for U.S. citizens besides death and taxes: higher health costs.

Health care costs were estimated at $4.2 trillion in 2021 (see Exhibit 11-1), or 18.2 percent of GDP. The latest projections from the Centers for Medicare and Medicaid Services show that under the present tax legislation, by 2028 annual health care spending is expected to grow to $6.2 trillion, or almost 19.7 percent of GDP. Yet about 26.1 million people, or 8 percent of adults and children, have no health insurance.[1]

RAPID INCREASE IN MEDICAL EXPENDITURES   From the time federally sponsored health care began in 1965, U.S. health care expenditures rose from $41.6 billion, or about 6 percent of GDP, to over $4.0 trillion in 2020, about 17.7 percent of GDP. Under the current law, national health spending is projected to grow at an average of 5.4 percent per year from 2016 to 2028. These projections do not consider the impact of COVID-19 because of the highly uncertain nature of the pandemic.[2]

EXHIBIT 11-1 U.S. national health expenditures, 1960–2028

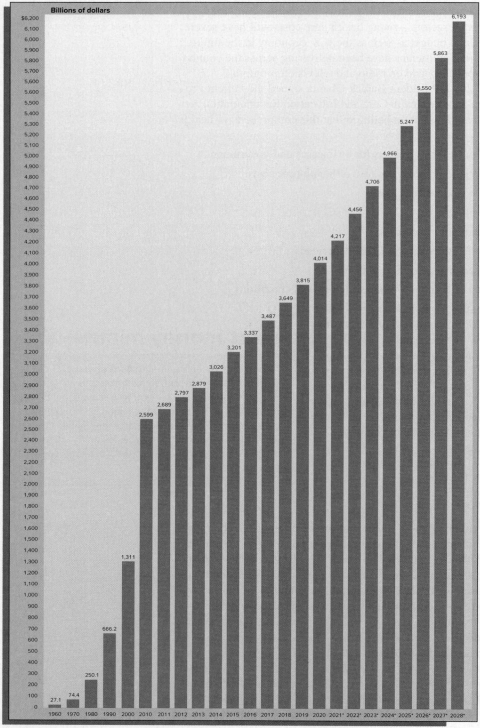

* Projected

Sources: U.S. Department of Health and Human Services and the Centers for Medicare and Medicaid Services, www.cms.gov, accessed January 20, 2021.

HIGH ADMINISTRATIVE COSTS In the United States, administrative costs consume nearly 11 percent of health care dollars, compared to 1 percent under Canada's socialized system. These costs include activities such as enrolling beneficiaries in a health plan, paying health insurance premiums, checking eligibility, obtaining authorizations for specialist referrals, and filing reimbursement claims.

WHY DOES HEALTH CARE COST SO MUCH?

The high and rising costs of health care are attributable to many factors including:

- The use of sophisticated, expensive technologies.
- Duplication of tests and sometimes duplication of technologies that yield similar results.
- Increases in the variety and frequency of treatments, including allegedly unnecessary tests.
- The increasing number and longevity of elderly people.
- Regulations that result in cost shifting rather than cost reduction.
- The increasing number of accidents and crimes that require emergency medical services.
- Limited competition and restrictive work rules in the health care delivery system.
- Labor intensiveness and rapid average earnings growth for health care professionals and executives.
- Using more expensive medical care than necessary, such as going to an emergency room with a bad cold.
- Built-in inflation in the health care delivery system.
- Aging baby boomers' use of more health care services, whether they're going to the doctor more often or snapping up pricier drugs, from Celebrex to Viagra.
- Other major factors that cost billions of dollars each year, including fraud, administrative waste, malpractice insurance, excessive surgical procedures, a wide range of prices for similar services, and double health coverage.

According to the Government Accountability Office, fraud and abuse account for nearly 10 percent of all dollars spent on health care. Because third parties—private health insurers and government—pay such a large part of the nation's health care bill, hospitals, doctors, and patients often lack the incentive to make the most economical use of health care services.

WHAT IS BEING DONE ABOUT THE HIGH COSTS OF HEALTH CARE?

In the private sector, concerned groups such as employers, labor unions, health insurers, health care professionals, and consumers have undertaken a wide range of innovative activities to contain the costs of health care. These activities include:

- Programs to carefully review health care fees and charges and the use of health care services.
- The establishment of incentives to encourage preventive care and provide more services out of hospitals, where this is medically acceptable.
- Involvement in community health planning to help achieve a better balance between health needs and health care resources.

personal fintech

ELECTRONIC HEALTH RECORDS (EHRs)

EHRs are a history of your health care or treatment that your doctor, other health care providers, medical office staff, or hospital keeps on a computer.

- EHRs can help lower the chances of medical errors, eliminate duplicate tests, and may improve your overall quality of care.
- Your doctor's EHRs may be able to link to a hospital, lab, pharmacy, other doctors, or immunization information systems, so the people who care for you can have a more complete history of your health.

HOW TO . . . Appeal Health Insurance Claim Decisions

If your health insurer has denied coverage for medical care you received, you have a right to appeal the claim and ask that the company reverse that decision. You can be your own health care advocate. Here's what you can do.

Step 1: Review your policy and explanation of benefits.

Step 2: Contact your insurer and keep detailed records of your contacts (copies of letters, time and date of conversations).

Step 3: Request documentation from your doctor or employer to support your case.

Step 4: Write a formal complaint letter explaining what care was denied and why you are appealing through use of the company's internal review process.

Step 5: If the internal appeal is not granted through step 4, file a claim with your state's insurance department. For more information, visit nclnet.org or statehealthfacts.org.

- The encouragement of prepaid group practices and other alternatives to fee-for-service arrangements.
- Community health education programs that motivate people to take better care of themselves.
- Physicians encouraging patients to pay cash for routine medical care and lab tests.

WHAT CAN YOU DO TO REDUCE PERSONAL HEALTH CARE COSTS?

As health care costs continue to rise, there are a few steps that you can take to reduce your own medical costs.

- Consider participating in a flexible spending account if your employer offers it.
- Consider a high-deductible health plan that provides medical insurance coverage and a tax-free opportunity to save for future medical needs.
- Ask your physician and pharmacist if a less expensive generic drug is available.
- Consider using a mail-order or legitimate online pharmacy, especially if you will take a drug for a long period.
- Most states offer free or low-cost coverage for children under 19 who do not have health insurance. Visit www.insurekidsnow.gov or call 1-877-KIDS-NOW for more information.
- Many states offer State Pharmacy Assistance Programs that help pay for prescription drugs based on financial need, age, or medical condition.
- If your doctor wants you to return for a follow-up visit, ask if it is really necessary or can you follow up by phone.
- If your doctor suggests a nonurgent procedure, ask for information and some time to think about it. Research the suggested treatment on Web MD (www.webmd.com) and compare costs on Health Care Blue Book (www.healthcarebluebook.com) or New Choice Health (www.newchoicehealth.com).
- Review billing statements from medical providers for billing errors.
- Appeal unfair decisions by your health plan. (Read the accompanying How To. . . feature box.)
- Practice preventive care and stay well.

Financial Literacy for My Life

SEVEN WAYS TO KEEP MEDICAL COSTS AND DEBT IN CHECK

Here are steps you can take to keep medical debt in check:

1. **Review medical bills carefully**
   If you don't recognize the provider, check the date of service to see if you had a medical treatment on that day. For more complicated procedures, ask for an itemized bill from the provider to check how much you were charged for each service. Some providers who bill you directly may have been associated with a hospital where you were treated, so you may not have known you were receiving services from them at the time you were being treated.

2. **Get documentation**
   Prepare an organized record of all bills. If you need to dispute a bill, send a written notice to the provider and include a copy of all relevant documents, such as records from doctors' offices or credit card statements. Do not send original documents.

3. **Check your health insurance policy and make sure your provider has your correct insurance information**
   You should know what your insurance covers, and what it doesn't—but first your insurance information needs to be up-to-date and accurate! A small mix-up can lead to big bills for expenses that your insurance should have covered.

4. **Act quickly to resolve or dispute the medical bills that you receive**
   If you have verified you owe the bill, try to resolve it right away. Verify whether an insurer is paying for all or part of a bill. If you delay the bill and let it end up in collections, it can have a significant impact on your credit score. If you don't owe the bill, act quickly to dispute it.

5. **Negotiate your bill**
   Hospitals may negotiate the amount of the bill with you. The bill may be reduced if you pay the whole amount immediately. Some hospitals and doctors often charge a reduced rate for people without insurance. The hospital might also offer a plan that enables you to pay off the debt in installments at no interest. It doesn't hurt to ask.

6. **Get financial assistance or support**
   Many hospitals have financial assistance programs, which may be called "charity care," if you are unable to pay your bill. Check the deadlines, which can vary.

7. **Don't put medical bills on your credit card, if you can't pay them**
   If you can't immediately pay off a high debt on your credit card bill, you will be charged high interest, and it will look like regular debt to other creditors. Instead, ask your medical provider for a payment plan with little or no interest.

Source: www.consumerfinance.gov/about-us/blog/consumer-advisory-7-ways-to-keep-medical-debt-in-check/accessed April 5, 2021.

The best way to avoid the high cost of illness is to stay well. The prescription is the same as it has always been:

1. Eat a balanced diet and keep your weight under control.
2. Avoid smoking and don't drink to excess.
3. Get sufficient rest, relaxation, and exercise.
4. Drive carefully and watch out for accident and fire hazards in the home.
5. Maintain a healthy lifestyle at home and at work.
6. Get your recommended health screenings and manage chronic conditions.

Read the *Financial Literacy for My Life: Seven Ways to Keep Medical Costs and Debt in Check* feature to learn how you can keep medical costs and medical debt under control.

 PRACTICE QUIZ 11-1

1. What are the reasons for rising health care expenditures?
2. What are various groups doing to curb the high costs of health care?
3. What can individuals do to reduce health care costs?

Health Insurance and Financial Planning

WHAT IS HEALTH INSURANCE?

Health insurance is a form of protection to alleviate the financial burdens individuals suffer from illness or injury. According to the Centers for Medicare and Medicaid Services, health insurance includes both medical expense insurance and disability income insurance.

HEALTH INSURANCE   Health insurance, like other forms of insurance, reduces the financial burden of risk by dividing losses among many individuals. It works in the same way as life insurance, homeowner's insurance, and automobile insurance. You pay the insurance company a specified premium, and the company guarantees you some degree of financial protection. Like the premiums and benefits of other types of insurance, the premiums and benefits of health insurance are figured on the basis of average experience. To establish rates and benefits, insurance company actuaries rely on general statistics that tell them how many people in a certain population group will become ill and how much their illnesses will cost.

Medical expense insurance and disability income insurance, discussed in this chapter's last section, are an important part of your financial planning. To safeguard your family's economic security, both protections should be a part of your overall insurance program.

There are many ways individuals or groups of individuals can obtain health insurance protection. Planning a health insurance program takes careful study because the protection should be shaped to the needs of the individual or family. For many families, the task is simplified because the group health insurance they obtain at work already provides a foundation for their coverage.

GROUP HEALTH INSURANCE   Group plans comprise about 90 percent of all the health insurance issued by health and life insurance companies. Most of these plans are employer sponsored, and the employer often pays part or most of their cost. However, not all employers provide health insurance to their employees. The Tax Cuts and Jobs Act of 2017 requires large employers (more than 50 employees) to provide health insurance coverage to all employees. Because insurance premiums have outpaced inflation for more than a decade, employers are increasing the share paid by employees and offering cheaper plans.

In June 2018, the U.S. Department of Labor expanded access to affordable health coverage options for small businesses and their employees through Association Health Plans (AHPs). These plans allow small businesses and self-employed workers to join together to obtain health care coverage as if they were a single large employer, which can be less expensive and better meet the needs of their employees. AHPs cannot charge higher premiums or deny coverage because of preexisting conditions or cancel coverage because an employee becomes ill.

Other organizations, such as labor unions and professional associations, also offer group plans. Group insurance will cover you and your immediate family. Group insurance seldom requires evidence that you are insurable, if you enroll when you first become eligible for coverage.

The *Health Insurance Portability and Accountability Act of 1996 (HIPAA)* legislates new federal standards for health insurance portability, nondiscrimination in health insurance, and guaranteed renewability. The law provides tax breaks for long-term care insurance and authorizes various government agencies to investigate Medicare/Medicaid fraud and abuses.

This landmark legislation gives millions of workers the comfort of knowing that if they change jobs, they need not lose their health insurance. For example, a parent with a sick child can move from one group plan to another without lapses in health insurance and without paying more than other employees for coverage. In addition to providing health care portability, this law created a stable source of funding for fraud control activities.

The protection group insurance provides varies from plan to plan. The plan may not cover all of your health insurance needs; therefore, you will have to consider supplementing it with individual health insurance.

INDIVIDUAL HEALTH INSURANCE Individual health insurance covers either one person or a family. If the kind of health insurance you need is not available through a group, you should obtain an individual policy—a policy tailored to your particular needs—from the company of your choice. This requires careful shopping, because coverage and cost vary from company to company. For example, the premiums for similar coverage can vary up to 50 percent for the same person, according to Mark Gurda, president of Castle Group Health in Northbrook, Illinois. Moreover, the rules and regulations vary from state to state.

Find out what your group insurance will pay for and what it won't. Make sure you have enough insurance, but don't waste money by overinsuring. Remember, the opportunity cost of not being adequately insured can be extremely high.

SUPPLEMENTING YOUR GROUP INSURANCE A sign that your group coverage needs supplementing would be its failure to provide benefits for the major portion of your medical care bills, mainly hospital, doctor, and surgical charges. If, for example, your group policy will pay only $1,000 per day toward a hospital room and the cost in your area is $1,500, you should look for an individual policy that covers most of the remaining amount. Similarly, if your group policy will pay only about half the going rate for surgical procedures in your area, you need individual coverage for the other half.

In supplementing your group health insurance, consider the health insurance benefits your employer-sponsored plan provides for family members. Most group policy contracts have a **coordination of benefits (COB)** provision. The COB is a method of integrating the benefits payable under more than one health insurance plan so that the benefits received from all sources are limited to 100 percent of allowable medical expenses.

If you have any questions about your group plan, you should be able to get answers from your employer, union, or association. If you have questions about an individual policy, talk with your insurance company representative. Since the cost of not being insured is very high, make sure to maintain your health insurance if you lose your job.

MEDICAL COVERAGE AND DIVORCE

Medical coverage of nonworking spouses is a concern when couples divorce. Under federal law, coverage under a former spouse's medical plan can be continued for 36 months if the former spouse works for a company with 20 or more employees.

Premiums will be totally paid by the individual and can run more than $12,000 annually. If there are children and the custodial parent doesn't work, the working parent usually can still cover the children under an employer's group plan.

The federal *Consolidated Omnibus Budget Reconciliation Act of 1986 (COBRA)* requires many employers to offer employees and dependents who would otherwise lose

smart money minute

You can get health care coverage through:

- A group coverage plan at your job or your spouse or partner's job
- Your parents' insurance plan, if you are under 26 years old
- A plan you purchase on your own directly from a health insurance company or through the Health Insurance Marketplace
- Government programs such as Medicare, Medicaid, or Children's Health Insurance Program (CHIP)
- The Veterans Administration or TRICARE for military personnel
- Your state, if it provides a health insurance plan
- Continuing employer coverage from your former employer, on a temporary basis under the Consolidated Omnibus Budget Reconciliation Act (COBRA).

coordination of benefits (COB) A method of integrating the benefits payable under more than one health insurance plan.

Financial Literacy for My Life

ALL YOU NEED TO KNOW ABOUT COBRA

Here's what you need to know about COBRA's continuation coverage. Remember, since your employer does not pay for COBRA coverage, you will pay the monthly premiums.

- In general, COBRA coverage requirements only apply to employers with 20 or more employees.

- If your family was covered under your employer coverage, they may also qualify for COBRA coverage.

- In most situations, you should get a notice from your employer's benefits administrator or the health plan telling you that your coverage is ending and offering you the right to take COBRA coverage.

- You have limited time to sign up for COBRA coverage. In most cases, you have 60 days after your last day of coverage to sign up for COBRA.

- COBRA coverage usually lasts for 18 months but could last up to 36 months. If you recently lost your employer health coverage, you may be eligible for a 65 percent reduction of your COBRA premium for up to 15 months.

WHERE CAN I GET MORE INFORMATION?

- Call your employer's benefit administrator for questions about your specific COBRA coverage options.

- If your health plan coverage was from a private employer, you can visit the Department of Labor's website or call 1-866-444-3272.

- If your coverage was with the federal government, you can visit the Office of Personnel Management's website at www.opm.gov/healthcare-insurance/healthcare/temporary-continuation-of-coverage.

STATE COVERAGE SIMILAR TO COBRA COVERAGE

- Many states have laws similar to COBRA that apply to insurance bought by employers with fewer than 20 employees. Contact your state department of insurance to ensure that "state continuation coverage" applies to you.

Source: U.S. Department of Labor website at https://www.dol.gov/general/topic/health-plans/cobra, accessed April 5, 2021.

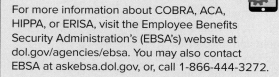

personal fintech

For more information about COBRA, ACA, HIPPA, or ERISA, visit the Employee Benefits Security Administration's (EBSA's) website at dol.gov/agencies/ebsa. You may also contact EBSA at askebsa.dol.gov, or, call 1-866-444-3272.

group health insurance the option to continue their group coverage for a set period of time. Employees of private companies and state and local governments are covered by this law; employees of the federal government and religious institutions are not. Read the *Financial Literacy for My Life: All You Need to Know about COBRA*" feature to learn about COBRA's continuation coverage. Also, see Exhibit 11-2 for qualifying events, qualified beneficiaries, and maximum period of continuation coverage.

Exhibit 11-2 shows the specific qualifying events, the qualified beneficiaries who are entitled to elect continuation coverage, and the maximum period of continuation coverage that must be offered, based on the type of qualifying event. Note that an event is a qualifying event only if it would cause the qualified beneficiary to lose coverage under the plan.

EXHIBIT 11-2 Who is entitled to continuation coverage?

Qualifying Event	Qualified Beneficiaries	Maximum Period of Continuation Coverage
Termination (for reasons other than gross misconduct) or reduction in hours of employment	Employee, Spouse, Dependent child	18 months
Employee enrollment in Medicare	Spouse, Dependent child	36 months
Divorce or legal separation	Spouse, Dependent child	36 months
Death of employee	Spouse, Dependent child	36 months
Loss of "dependent child" status under the plan	Spouse, Dependent child	36 months

Source: https://www.dol.gov/sites/default/files/ebsa/about-ebsa/our-activities/resource-center/publications/an-employees-guide-to-health-benefits-under-cobra.pdf, accessed April 5, 2021.

✔ **PRACTICE QUIZ 11-2**

1. What is health insurance, and what is its purpose?
2. What are group health and individual health insurance?
3. What is a coordination of benefits provision?

Types of Health Insurance Coverage

With today's high cost of health care, it makes sense to be as fully insured as you can afford. Combining the group plan available where you work with the individual policies insurance companies offer will enable you to put together enough coverage to give you peace of mind. A good health insurance plan should:

- Offer basic coverage for hospital and doctor bills.
- Provide at least 120 days' hospital room and board in full.
- Provide at least a $1 million lifetime maximum for each family member.
- Pay at least 80 percent for out-of-hospital expenses.
- Impose no unreasonable exclusions.
- Limit your out-of-pocket expenses to no more than $4,000 to $6,000 a year, excluding dental, optical, and prescription costs.

Several types of health insurance coverage are available under group and individual policies.

LO11-3

Analyze the benefits and limitations of the various types of health care coverage.

my life **3**

With today's high cost of health care, it makes sense for me to be as fully insured as I can afford.

Premiums are lower on employer-provided health insurance plans because risk is spread over a large group of employees. Take advantage of the lower costs that employer-sponsored plans offer, but expect to pay part of the premium out of your paycheck.

TYPES OF MEDICAL COVERAGE

HOSPITAL EXPENSE INSURANCE   **Hospital expense insurance** pays part or the full amount of hospital bills for room, board, and other charges. Frequently, a maximum amount is allowed for each day in the hospital, up to a maximum number of days. More people have hospital insurance than any other kind of health insurance.

SURGICAL EXPENSE INSURANCE   **Surgical expense insurance** pays part or the full amount of the surgeon's fees for an operation. A policy of this kind usually lists a number of specific operations and the maximum fee allowed for each. The higher the maximum fee allowed in the policy, the higher the premium charged. People often buy surgical expense insurance in combination with hospital expense insurance.

PHYSICIAN EXPENSE INSURANCE   **Physician expense insurance** helps pay for physician's care that does not involve surgery. Like surgical expense insurance, it lists maximum benefits for specific services. Its coverage may include visits to the doctor's office, X rays, and lab tests. This type of insurance is usually bought in combination with hospital and surgical insurance. The three types of insurance combined are called **basic health insurance coverage.**

MAJOR MEDICAL EXPENSE INSURANCE   **Major medical expense insurance** protects against the large expenses of a serious injury or a long illness. It adds to the protection offered by basic health insurance coverage. The costs of a serious illness

hospital expense insurance Pays part or all of hospital bills for room, board, and other charges.

surgical expense insurance Pays part or all of the surgeon's fees for an operation.

physician expense insurance Provides benefits for doctors' fees for nonsurgical care, x-rays, and lab tests.

basic health insurance coverage Combination of hospital expense insurance, surgical expense insurance, and physician expense insurance.

major medical expense insurance Pays most of the costs exceeding those covered by the hospital, surgical, and physician expense policies.

deductible An amount the insured must pay before benefits become payable by the insurance company.

coinsurance A provision under which both the insured and the insurer share the covered losses.

can easily exceed the benefits under hospital, surgical, and physician expense policies. Major medical pays the bulk of the additional costs. The maximum benefits payable under major medical insurance are high—up to $1 million. Because major medical insurance offers such a wide range of benefits and provides high maximums, it contains two features to help keep the premium within the policyholder's means.

One of these features is a **deductible** provision that requires the policyholder to pay a basic amount before the policy benefits begin—for example, the first $1,000 per year under an individual plan and a lesser amount under a group plan. (Sometimes part or all of the deductible amount is covered by the benefits of a basic hospital and surgical plan.) The other feature is a **coinsurance** provision that requires the policyholder to share expenses beyond the deductible amount. Many policies pay 75 or 80 percent of expenses above the deductible amount; the policyholder pays the rest.

> ## EXAMPLE: Deductibles and Coinsurance
>
> Ariana's policy includes an $2,000 deductible and a coinsurance provision requiring her to pay 20 percent of all bills. If her total is $3,800, for instance, the company will first exclude $2,000 from coverage, which is Ariana's deductible. It will then pay 80 percent of the remaining $1,800 or $1,440. Therefore, Ariana's total costs are $2,360 ($2,000 for the deductible and $360 for the coinsurance).

stop-loss order A provision under which an insured pays a certain amount, after which the insurance company pays 100 percent of the remaining covered expenses.

comprehensive major medical insurance A type of major medical insurance that has a very low deductible and is offered without a separate basic plan.

hospital indemnity policy Pays stipulated daily, weekly, or monthly cash benefits during hospital confinement.

Some major medical policies contain a **stop-loss,** or out-of-pocket limit, provision. This requires the policyholder to pay up to a certain amount, after which the insurance company pays 100 percent of all remaining covered expenses. Typically, the out-of-pocket payment is between $4,000 and $6,000. (See Exhibit 11-3.)

COMPREHENSIVE MAJOR MEDICAL INSURANCE **Comprehensive major medical insurance** is a type of major medical insurance that has a very low deductible amount and is offered without a separate basic plan. This all-inclusive health insurance helps pay hospital, surgical, medical, and other bills. Many major medical policies have specific maximum benefits for certain expenses, such as hospital room and board and the cost of surgery.

HOSPITAL INDEMNITY POLICIES A **hospital indemnity policy** pays benefits only when you are hospitalized, but these benefits, stipulated in the policy, are paid to you in cash and you can use the money for medical, nonmedical, or supplementary expenses. While such policies have limited coverage, their benefits can have wide use. The hospital indemnity policy is not a substitute for basic or major medical protection but a supplement to it. Many people buy hospital indemnity policies in the hope that they will make money if they get sick, but the average benefit return does not justify the premium cost.

DENTAL EXPENSE INSURANCE *Dental expense insurance* provides reimbursement for the expenses of dental services and supplies and encourages preventive dental care. The coverage normally provides for oral examinations (including X rays and cleanings), fillings, extractions, inlays, bridgework, and dentures, as well as oral surgery, root canal therapy, and orthodontics. As with other insurance plans, dental insurance may have a deductible and a coinsurance provision, stating that the policyholder pays from 20 to 50 percent after the deductible.

VISION CARE INSURANCE A recent development in health insurance coverage is *vision care insurance*. An increasing number of insurance companies and prepayment plans are offering this insurance, usually to groups.

Vision and eye health problems are second among the most prevalent chronic health care concerns, affecting more than 160 million Americans. Good vision care insurance

EXHIBIT 11-3 How you and your insurer share costs

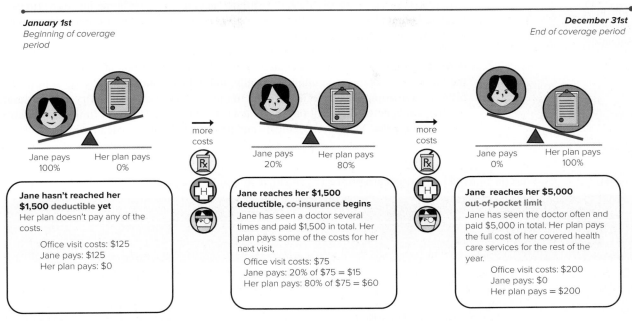

Jane's Plan: Deductible: $1,500   Co-insurance: 20%   Out-of-pocket Limit: $5,000

January 1st
Beginning of coverage period

December 31st
End of coverage period

Jane pays 100%   Her plan pays 0%

more costs

Jane pays 20%   Her plan pays 80%

more costs

Jane pays 0%   Her plan pays 100%

Jane hasn't reached her $1,500 deductible yet
Her plan doesn't pay any of the costs.

Office visit costs: $125
Jane pays: $125
Her plan pays: $0

Jane reaches her $1,500 deductible, co-insurance begins
Jane has seen a doctor several times and paid $1,500 in total. Her plan pays some of the costs for her next visit,

Office visit costs: $75
Jane pays: 20% of $75 = $15
Her plan pays: 80% of $75 = $60

Jane reaches her $5,000 out-of-pocket limit
Jane has seen the doctor often and paid $5,000 in total. Her plan pays the full cost of her covered health care services for the rest of the year.

Office visit costs: $200
Jane pays: $0
Her plan pays = $200

Source: "Glossary of Health Coverage and Medical Terms," www.healthcare.gov/sbc-glossary/, accessed April 5, 2021.

should cover diagnosing and treating eye diseases such as glaucoma, periodic eye examinations, eyeglasses, contact lenses, and eye surgery.

In considering vision and dental coverage, you should analyze their costs and benefits. Sometimes these coverages cost more than they are worth.

OTHER INSURANCE POLICIES   Dread disease, trip accident, death insurance, and cancer policies, which are usually sold through the mail, in newspapers and magazines, or by door-to-door salespeople working on commission, are notoriously poor values. Their appeal is based on unrealistic fears, and a number of states have prohibited their sale. Such policies provide coverage only for specific conditions and are no substitute for comprehensive insurance.

LONG-TERM CARE INSURANCE

Long-term care insurance (LTC), virtually unknown 50 years ago, is growing faster than any other form of insurance in the country. *Long-term care* is day-in, day-out assistance that you might need if you ever have an illness or a disability that lasts a long time and leaves you unable to care for yourself. You may or may not need lengthy care in a nursing home, but you may need help at home with daily activities such as dressing, bathing, and doing household chores.

Most older Americans will be cared for at home; family members and friends are the sole caregivers for 70 percent of the elderly population. A recent study by Americans for Long-Term Care Security (ALTCS) found that one out of five Americans over age 50 is at risk of needing some form of long-term care within the next 12 months. The same study revealed that more than half of the U.S. population will need long-term care during their lives.[3] While older people are more likely to need long-term care, your need for long-term care can come at any age. In fact, the U.S. Government Accountability Office estimates that 40 percent of the 13 million people receiving long-term care services are between the ages of 18 and 64.

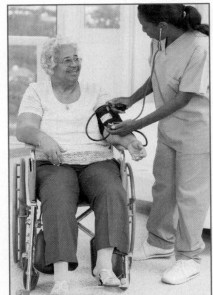

Long-term care insurance provides coverage for the expense of daily help that you may need if you become seriously ill or disabled and are unable to care for yourself.
Rolf Bruderer/Blend Images

long-term care insurance (LTC) Pays for the cost of day-in, day-out care for long-term illness or disability.

Long-term care can be very expensive. As a national average, a year in a nursing home can cost over $105,000; a semiprivate room in some regions can cost as much as $400,000 (in some parts of Alaska). Bringing an aide into your home just three times a week to help with dressing, bathing, preparing meals, and similar household chores can easily cost more than $3,000 a month.

The annual premium for LTC policies can range from under $2,000 up to $16,000, depending on your age and the choices you make. The older you are when you enroll, the higher your annual premium. Typically, individual insurance plans are sold to the 50-to-80 age group, pay benefits for a maximum of 2 to 6 years, and carry a dollar limit on the total benefits they will pay. Exhibit 11-4 summarizes the very limited long-term care coverage that Medicare, Medigap, and private health insurance provide.

EXHIBIT 11-4 Coverage limits of long-term care offered by health insurance

Long-Term Care Service	Public	Private	
	Medicare	Medigap Insurance	Private Health Insurance
Overview	Limited coverage for nursing home care following a hospital stay and home health if you require a nurse or other skilled provider	Insurance purchased to cover Medicare cost sharing	Varies, but generally only covers services for a short time following a hospital stay, surgery, or while recovering from an injury
Nursing home care	Pays in full for days 1–20 if you are in a skilled nursing facility following a recent 3-day hospital stay. If your need for skilled care continues, Medicare may pay for the difference between the total daily cost and your copayment of $137.50* per day for days 21–100. Does not pay after day 100.	May cover the $137.50 per day copayment if your nursing home stay meets all other Medicare requirements	Varies, but limited
Assisted living facility (and similar facility options)	Does not pay	Does not pay	Does not pay
Continuing care retirement community	Does not pay	Does not pay	Does not pay
Adult day services	Not covered	Not covered	Not covered
Home health and personal care	Limited to reasonable, necessary part-time or intermittent skilled nursing care and home health aide services, some therapies if a doctor orders them, and a Medicare-certified home health agency provides them. Does not pay for ongoing personal care or only help with activities of daily living (also called "custodial care")	Not covered under current policies. Some policies sold prior to 2009 offered an at-home recovery benefit that pays up to $1,600 per year for short-term at-home assistance with activities of daily living (bathing, dressing, personal hygiene, etc.) for those recovering from an illness, injury, or surgery	Varies, but limited

*As of October 10, 2020.
Source: U.S. Department of Health and Human Services website at https://longtermcare.acl.gov/costs-how-to-pay/what-is-covered-by-health-disability-insurance/coverage-limits-chart.html, accessed January 16, 2021.

Long-term care insurance is not for everyone; it is rarely recommended for people under 60. If you are over 60, you may consider it if you wish to protect your assets, but if you have substantial wealth ($2 million or more) or very little (less than $250,000), the premium can be a waste of money. However, if your employer pays the premium, the Health Insurance Portability and Accountability Act of 1996 treats a long-term care premium as a tax-deductible expense for the employer.

Explore services available in your community to help meet long-term care needs. Care given by family members can be supplemented by visiting nurses, home health aides, friendly visitor programs, home-delivered meals, chore services, adult day care centers, and respite services for caregivers who need a break from daily responsibilities.

These services are becoming more widely available. Some or all of them may be found in your community. Exhibit 11-5 lists sources of information for long-term care.

MAJOR PROVISIONS IN A HEALTH INSURANCE POLICY

All health insurance policies have certain provisions in common. Be sure you understand what your policy covers. Even the most comprehensive policy may be of little value if a provision in small print limits or denies benefits.

An insurance company usually allows you a minimum of 10 days to review your health insurance policy, so be sure to check the major provisions that affect your coverage. Deductible, coinsurance, and stop-loss provisions were discussed under major medical expense insurance. Other major provisions are described in the following sections.

ELIGIBILITY The eligibility provision defines who is entitled to benefits under the policy. Age, marital status, and dependency requirements are usually specified in this provision. For example, foster children usually are not automatically covered under the family contract, but stepchildren may be. Check with your insurance company to be sure.

ASSIGNED BENEFITS When you assign benefits, you sign a paper allowing your insurance company to make payments to your hospital or doctor. Otherwise, the payments will be made to you when you turn in your bills and claim forms to the company.

INTERNAL LIMITS A policy with internal limits will pay only a fixed amount for your hospital room no matter what the actual rate is, or it will cover your surgical expenses only to a fixed limit no matter what the actual charges are. For example, if your

EXHIBIT 11-5 Long-term care contacts

Use these resources to get more information about long-term care.

- Visit longtermcare.acl.gov to learn about planning for long-term care.
- Visit medicare.gov/nhcompare to compare nursing homes or medicare.gov/homehealth-compare to compare home health agencies in your area.
- Call 1-800-MEDICARE (1-800-633-4227). TTY users should call 1-877-486-2048.
- Call your state insurance department to get information about long-term care insurance. Visit medicare.gov/contacts or call 1-800-MEDICARE to get the phone number.
- Call your State Health Insurance Assistance Program (SHIP).
- Call the National Association of Insurance Commissioners at 1-866-470-6242 to get a copy of "A Shopper's Guide to Long-Term Care Insurance."
- Visit the Eldercare Locator, a public service of the U.S. Administration on Aging, at eldercare.gov to find your local Aging and Disability Resource Center (ADRC). You can also call 1-800-677-1116. ADRCs offer a full range of long-term care services and support in a single, coordinated program.

policy has an internal limit of $600 per hospital day and you are in a $1,000-a-day hospital room, you will have to pay the difference.

COPAYMENT   **Copayment** is a type of cost sharing. Most major medical plans define *copayment* as the amount the patient must pay for medical services after the deductible has been met. You pay a flat dollar amount each time you receive a covered medical service. Copayments of $15 to $30 for prescriptions and $20 to $30 for doctors' office visits are common. This is different from coinsurance, which is the percentage of your medical costs for which you are responsible after paying your deductible. The amount of copayment does not vary with the cost of service.

copayment A provision under which the insured pays a flat dollar amount each time a covered medical service is received after the deductible has been met.

SERVICE BENEFITS   In a service benefits provision, insurance benefits are expressed in terms of entitlement to receive specified hospital or medical care rather than entitlement to receive a fixed dollar amount for each procedure. For example, you are entitled to X rays, not $40 worth of X rays per visit. Service benefits are always preferable to a coverage stated in dollar amounts.

BENEFIT LIMITS   The benefit limits provision defines the maximum benefits possible, in terms of either a dollar amount or a number of days in the hospital. Many policies today have benefit limits ranging from $250,000 to unlimited payments.

EXCLUSIONS AND LIMITATIONS   The exclusions and limitations provision specifies the conditions or circumstances for which the policy does not provide benefits. For example, the policy may exclude coverage for cosmetic surgery or routine checkups.

COORDINATION OF BENEFITS   As discussed earlier, the coordination-of-benefits provision prevents you from collecting benefits from two or more group policies that would in total exceed the actual charges. Under this provision, the benefits from your own and your spouse's policies are coordinated to allow you up to 100 percent payment of your covered charges.

GUARANTEED RENEWABLE   With this policy provision, the insurance company cannot cancel a policy unless you fail to pay premiums when due. Also, it cannot raise premiums unless a rate increase occurs for all policyholders in that group.

CANCELLATION AND TERMINATION   This provision explains the circumstances under which the insurance company can terminate your health insurance policy. It also explains your right to convert a group contract into an individual contract.

HEALTH INSURANCE TRADE-OFFS

The benefits of health insurance policies differ, and the differences can have a significant impact on your premiums. Consider the following trade-offs.

REIMBURSEMENT VERSUS INDEMNITY   A reimbursement policy provides benefits based on the actual expenses you incur. An indemnity policy provides specified benefits, regardless of whether the actual expenses are greater or less than the benefits.

EXAMPLE: Reimbursement versus Indemnity

Katie and Seth are both charged $200 for an office visit to the same specialist. Katie's reimbursement policy has a deductible of $300. Once she has met the deductible, the policy will cover the full cost of such a visit. Seth's indemnity policy will pay him $125, which is what his plan provides for a visit to any specialist.

INTERNAL LIMITS VERSUS AGGREGATE LIMITS   A policy with internal limits stipulates maximum benefits for specific expenses, such as the maximum reimbursement for daily hospital room and board. Other policies may limit only the total amount of coverage, such as $1 million major expense benefits, or it may have no limits.

DEDUCTIBLES AND COINSURANCE   The cost of a health insurance policy can be greatly affected by the size of the deductible (the set amount that the policyholder must pay toward medical expenses before the insurance company pays benefits). It can also be affected by the term of the coinsurance provision (which states what percentage of the medical expenses the policyholder must pay in addition to the deductible amount).

OUT-OF-POCKET LIMIT   Some policies limit the amount of money you must pay for the deductible and coinsurance. After you have reached that limit, the insurance company covers 100 percentage of any additional costs. Out-of-pocket limits help you lower your financial risk, but they also increase your premiums.

BENEFITS BASED ON REASONABLE AND CUSTOMARY CHARGES   Some policies consider the average fee for a service in a particular geographical area. They then use the amount to set a limit on payments to policyholders, If the standard cost of a certain procedure is $1,500 in your part of the country, then your policy won't pay more than that amount.

The medical costs of giving birth can be high. However, most people have the basic health insurance coverage to minimize out-of-pocket costs.
Ariel Skelley/Marc Romanelli/Blend Images, LLC

WHICH COVERAGE SHOULD YOU CHOOSE?

Now that you are familiar with the types of health insurance available and some of their major provisions, how do you choose one? The type of coverage you choose will be affected by the amount you can afford to spend on the premiums and the level of benefits that you feel you want and need. It may also be affected by the kind of coverage your employer offers, if you are covered through your employer.

For medical insurance, you have three choices. You can buy (1) basic, (2) major medical, or (3) both basic and major medical. If your budget is very limited, it is a toss-up between choosing a basic plan or a major medical plan. In many cases, either plan will handle a major share of your hospital and doctor bills. In the event of an illness involving catastrophic costs, however, you will need the protection a major medical policy offers. Ideally, you should get a basic plan and a major medical supplementary plan or a comprehensive major medical policy that combines the values of both these plans in a single policy.

✔️ **PRACTICE QUIZ 11-3**

PFP Sheet 51
Health Care
Insurance

1. What are several types of health insurance coverage available under group and individual policies?
2. What are the major provisions of a health insurance policy?
3. How do you decide which coverage to choose?
4. How can you analyze the costs and benefits of your health insurance policy?

Private Sources of Health Insurance and Health Care

Health insurance is available from more than 800 private insurance companies. Moreover, service plans such as Blue Cross Blue Shield, health maintenance organizations, preferred provider organizations, government programs such as Medicare, fraternal organizations, and trade unions provide health insurance.

LO11-4

Evaluate private sources of health insurance and health care.

PRIVATE INSURANCE COMPANIES

More than 800 private insurance companies sell health insurance through either group or individual policies. Of these two types, group health insurance represents about 90 percent of all medical expense insurance and 80 percent of all disability income insurance.

The policies that insurance companies issue provide for payment either directly to the insured for reimbursement of expenses incurred or, if assigned by the insured, to the provider of services.

Most private insurance companies sell health insurance policies to employers, who in turn offer them as fringe benefits to employees and employees' dependents. The premiums may be partially paid by employers. The Health Insurance Portability and Accountability Act, as discussed earlier, requires employers to keep detailed records of all employees and dependents covered by the company's health plan.

As of September 23, 2012, all health insurance companies and group health plans are required to give you a summary of the health plan's benefits and coverage. See Exhibit 11-6 for a uniform Summary of Benefits and Coverage (SBC).

HOSPITAL AND MEDICAL SERVICE PLANS

Blue Cross An independent membership corporation that provides protection against the cost of hospital care.

Blue Shield An independent membership corporation that provides protection against the cost of surgical and medical care.

managed care Prepaid health plans that provide comprehensive health care to members.

health maintenance organization (HMO) A health insurance plan that provides a wide range of health care services for a fixed, prepaid monthly premium.

The Blue Cross Blue Shield Association is a national federation of 36 independent community-based and locally operated Blue Cross Blue Shield companies. The Association owns and manages the Blue Cross Blue Shield trademarks and names in more than 170 countries, and it grants licenses to independent companies to use the trademarks and names in various geographical areas. Each state has its own Blue Cross Blue Shield. The Blues plans, the nation's oldest and largest family of health benefits companies, play an important role in providing private health insurance to more than 106 million Americans.

Blue Cross plans provide *hospital care benefits* on essentially a "service-type" basis. Through a separate contract with each member hospital, Blue Cross reimburses the hospital for covered services provided to the insured.

Blue Shield plans provide benefits for *surgical and medical services* performed by physicians. The typical Blue Shield plan provides benefits similar to those provided under the benefit provisions of hospital-surgical policies issued by insurance companies.

HEALTH MAINTENANCE ORGANIZATIONS

During the 1970s and 1980s, increasing health care costs spurred the growth of managed care. **Managed care** refers to prepaid health plans that provide comprehensive health care to members. Managed care is offered by health maintenance organizations, preferred provider organizations, exclusive provider organizations, point-of-service plans, and traditional indemnity insurance companies.

HMOs are based on the premise that preventive medical services will minimize future medical problems.
Rocketclips/123RF

A recent industry survey estimated that 85 percent of employed Americans are enrolled in some form of managed care. Managed care companies now provide information that helps you better manage your health care needs. Health plans have launched internet programs that allow you to access medical research, support groups, and professional advice, and to exchange e-mail with health care providers. The best-known managed care plans are health maintenance organizations and preferred provider organizations, which offer a wide range of preventive services.

Prepaid managed care is designed to make the provision of health care services cost-effective by controlling their use. Health maintenance organizations are an alternative to basic and major medical insurance plans. A **health maintenance organization (HMO)** is a health insurance plan that directly employs or contracts with selected physicians, surgeons, dentists, and optometrists to provide health care services in exchange for a

EXHIBIT 11-6 Sample summary of benefits and coverage (SBC)

Insurance Company 1: Plan Option 1	Coverage Period: 01/01/2022–12/31/2022
Summary of Benefits and Coverage: What This Plan Covers and What It Costs:	
Coverage for Individual + Spouse/Type: PPO	

This is only a summary. If you want more detail about your coverage and costs, contact your insurance company for complete terms in the policy or plan document.

Important Questions	Answers	Why This Matters
What is the overall deductible?	$500 person/$1,000 family. Doesn't apply to preventive care.	You must pay all the costs up to the deductible amount before this plan begins to pay for covered services you use. Check your policy or plan document to see when the deductible starts over (usually, but not always, January 1). See how much you pay for covered services after you meet the deductible.
Are there other deductibles for specific services?	Yes. $300 for prescription drug coverage. There are no other specific deductibles.	You must pay all the costs for the services up to the specific deductible amount before this plan begins to pay for these services.
Is there an out-of-pocket limit on my expenses?	Yes. For participating providers $2,500 person/$5,000 family. For non-participating providers $4,000 person/$8,000 family.	The out-of-pocket limit is the most you could pay during a coverage period (usually one year) for your share of the cost of covered services. This limit helps you plan for health care expenses.
What is not included in the out-of-pocket limit?	Premiums, balance-billed charges, and health care this plan doesn't cover.	Even though you pay these expenses, they don't count toward the out-of-pocket limit.
Is there an overall annual limit on what the plan pays?	No	The plan document describes any limits on what the plan will pay for specific covered services, such as office visits.
Does this plan use a network of providers?	Yes. Ask for a list of participating providers.	If you use an in-network doctor or other health care provider, this plan will pay some or all of the costs of covered services. Be aware, your in-network doctor or hospital may use an out-of-network provider for some services. Plans use the term in-network, preferred, or participating for providers in their network.
Do I need a referral to see a specialist?	No	You can see the specialist you choose without permission from this plan.
Are there services this plan doesn't cover?	Yes	Some of the services are not covered. See your policy or plan document for additional information about excluded services.

Source: Centers for Medicare and Medicaid Services, https://www.cms.gov/CCIIO/Resources/Regulations-and-Guidance/Downloads/SBC-Sample-Completed.pdf, accessed July 14, 2018 and https://www.dol.gov/sites/dolgov/files/EBSA/laws-and-regulations/laws/affordable-care-act/for-employers-and-advisers/sbc-completed-new.pdf, accessed February 3, 2021.

fixed, prepaid monthly premium. HMOs operate on the premise that maintaining health through preventive care will minimize future medical problems.

The preventive care HMOs provide includes periodic checkups, screening programs, diagnostic testing, and immunizations. HMOs also provide a comprehensive range of other health care services. These services are divided into two categories: basic and supplemental. *Basic health services* include inpatient, outpatient, maternity, mental health, substance abuse, and emergency care. *Supplemental services* include vision, hearing, and pharmaceutical care, which are usually available for an additional fee.

Your membership in a typical HMO should cover office visits, routine checkups, hospital and surgical care, eye exams, laboratory and X-ray services, hemodialysis for kidney failure, and mental health services.

PREFERRED PROVIDER ORGANIZATIONS

preferred provider organization (PPO) A group of doctors and hospitals that agree to provide health care at rates approved by the insurer.

A **preferred provider organization (PPO)** is a group of doctors and hospitals that agree to provide health care at rates approved by the insurer. In return, PPOs expect prompt payment and the opportunity to serve an increased volume of patients. The premiums for PPOs are slightly higher than those for HMOs. An insurance company or your employer contracts with a PPO to provide specified services at predetermined fees to PPO members.

Preferred provider organizations combine the best elements of the fee-for-service and HMO systems. PPOs offer the services of doctors and hospitals at discount rates or give breaks in copayments and deductibles. PPOs provide their members with essentially the same benefits HMOs offer. However, while HMOs require members to seek care from HMO providers only (except for emergency treatment), PPOs allow members to use a preferred provider—or another provider for a higher copayment—each time a medical need arises. This combination of allowing free choice of physicians and low-cost care makes PPOs popular.

exclusive provider organization (EPO) A network that renders medical care from affiliated health care providers.

The **exclusive provider organization (EPO)** is the extreme form of the PPO. Services rendered by nonaffiliated providers are not reimbursed. Therefore, if you belong to an EPO, you must receive your care from affiliated providers or pay the entire cost yourself. Providers typically are reimbursed on a fee-for-service basis according to a negotiated discount or fee schedule.

point-of-service plan (POS) A network of selected contracted, participating providers; also called an *HMO-PPO hybrid* or *open-ended HMO.*

A **point-of-service plan (POS),** sometimes called an *HMO-PPO hybrid* or *open-ended HMO,* combines characteristics of both HMOs and PPOs. POSs use a network of selected, contracted, participating providers. Employees select a primary care physician, who controls referrals for medical specialists. If you receive care from a plan provider, you pay little or nothing, as in an HMO, and do not file claims. Medical care provided by out-of-plan providers will be reimbursed, but you must pay significantly higher copayments and deductibles. Hybrid plans are useful if you want to try managed care but don't want to be locked into a network of doctors. A drawback is that they cost more than HMOs.

The distinction among HMOs, PPOs, EPOs, and POSs is becoming blurred. PPOs and POS plans combine features from both fee-for-service and HMOs. PPOs and POS plans offer more flexibility than HMOs in choosing physicians and other providers. POS plans have primary care physicians who coordinate patient care, but, in most cases, PPOs do not. Premiums tend to be somewhat higher in PPOs and POS plans than in traditional HMOs. As cost reduction pressures mount and these alternative delivery systems try to increase their market share, each tries to make its system more attractive. The evolution of health care plans will likely continue so that it will become increasingly difficult to characterize a particular managed care delivery system as adhering to any particular model.

Exhibit 11-7 summarizes the main features of HMOs, EPOs, PPOs, and POS plans.

HOME HEALTH CARE AGENCIES

Home health care providers furnish and are responsible for the supervision and management of preventive medical care in a home setting in accordance with a medical order. Rising hospital care costs, new medical technology, and the increasing number of

EXHIBIT 11-7 How health plans compare

	HMO	EPO	PPO	Point-of-service
What's the cost?	Generally lowest of all plans	Usually lower than PPO	Generally highest of all plans	Usually lower than PPO
Do I have to use providers in the network?	Yes (except for emergencies and for care that isn't available in network)	Yes (except for emergencies and for care that isn't available in network)	No (but you'll have to pay more if you go out of network)	No (but you'll have to pay more if you go out of network)
Do I have to choose a primary care physician?	Yes	No	No	Usually
Do I need a referral to a specialist?	Yes	No	No	Usually

Source: https://www.tdi.texas.gov/pubs/consumer/cb005.html, accessed April 5, 2021.

elderly and infirm people have helped make home care one of the fastest-growing areas of the health care industry.

Spending on home health care has been growing at an annual rate of about 20 percent over the past few years. This rapid growth reflects (1) the increasing proportion of older people in the U.S. population, (2) the lower costs of home health care compared to the costs of institutional health care, (3) insurers' active support of home health care, and (4) Medicare's promotion of home health care as an alternative to institutionalization. Home health care consists of home health agencies, home care aide organizations, and hospices, facilities that care for the terminally ill.

EMPLOYER SELF-FUNDED HEALTH PLANS

Some companies choose to self-insure. The company runs its own insurance plan, collecting premiums from employees and paying medical benefits as needed. However, these companies must cover any costs that exceed the income from premiums. Unfortunately, not all corporations have the financial assets necessary to cover these situations, which can mean a financial disaster for the company and its employees.

NEW HEALTH CARE ACCOUNTS

Health savings accounts (HSAs), which Congress authorized in 2003, are the newest addition to the alphabet soup of health insurance available to American workers. Now you and your employer must sort through HSAs, health reimbursement accounts (HRAs), and flexible spending accounts (FSAs). Each has its own rules about how money is spent, how it can be saved, and how it is taxed.

How do FSAs, HRAs, and HSAs differ? FSAs allow you to contribute pretax dollars to an account managed by your employer. You use the money for health care spending but forfeit anything left over at the end of the year.

HRAs are tied to high-deductible policies. They are funded *solely* by your employer and give you a pot of money to spend

smart money minute

HEALTH SAVINGS ACCOUNTS

You can't contribute to your HSA once your Medicare coverage begins. To avoid a tax penalty, you should stop contributing to your HSA at least six months before you apply for Medicare.

Source: *Medicare & You* (Washington, D.C.: The Centers for Medicare and Medicaid Services, 2021), p. 20.

EXHIBIT 11-8 Comparison of HSAs, FSAs, and HRAs

Health Savings Accounts (HSAs)	Flexible Spending Accounts (Arrangements) (FSAs)	Health Reimbursement Accounts (HRAs)
• Employer sponsored.	• Employer sponsored.	• Employer sponsored.
• Set aside tax-free dollars you can use to pay for medical expenses that are not covered by insurance.	• Set aside tax-free dollars you can use to pay for medical expenses that are not covered by insurance.	• Funded solely by your employer to spend on your health care.
• Tied to a high-deductible policy.	• Not tied to a high-deductible policy.	• Tied to high-deductible policies.
• Unspent money can be carried over and accumulate year to year.	• Money left over can't be carried over; if you don't use it, you lose it to your employer.	• Reimbursement of claims is tax-deductible for employers.
• Can invest the funds in stocks, bonds, and mutual funds.		• The maximum annual contribution is determined by your employer's plan document.
• The money grows tax-free but can be spent only on health care.		• Can carry over unspent money from year to year, but you lose the balance if you change jobs.
• You own the funds; you take any unspent funds with you if you leave the employer.		• Premiums tend to be lower than for traditional insurance but higher than for HSAs.

on health care. You can carry over unspent money from year to year, but you lose the balance if you switch jobs. Premiums tend to be lower than for traditional insurance but higher than for HSAs.

HSAs allow you to contribute money to a tax-free account that can be used for out-of-pocket health care expenses if you buy high-deductible health insurance policies. With HSAs, you can invest the funds in stocks, bonds, and mutual funds. The money grows tax-free but can be spent only on health care. And it's your money. Any unspent funds stay in your account year to year, and you take it all with you if you leave the company.

You can't contribute to your HSA once your Medicare coverage begins. However, you may use money that's already in your HSA after you enroll in Medicare to help pay for deductibles, premiums, copayments, or coinsurance.

Exhibit 11-8 summarizes the important features of HSAs, FSAs, and HRAs. Also, read the accompanying *Financial Literacy for My Life: HSAs: How They Will Work in 2021* feature to learn how HSAs will work in 2021.

In addition to the private sources of health insurance and health care discussed in this section, government health care programs cover over 55 million people. The next section discusses these programs.

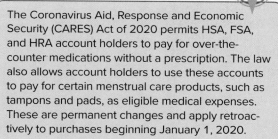

smart money minute

The Coronavirus Aid, Response and Economic Security (CARES) Act of 2020 permits HSA, FSA, and HRA account holders to pay for over-the-counter medications without a prescription. The law also allows account holders to use these accounts to pay for certain menstrual care products, such as tampons and pads, as eligible medical expenses. These are permanent changes and apply retroactively to purchases beginning January 1, 2020.

  PRACTICE QUIZ 11-4

1. What are the major sources of health insurance and health care?
2. What are Blue Cross Blue Shield plans? What benefits does each plan provide?
3. What are the differences among HMOs, PPOs, EPOs, and POSs?
4. What are home health care agencies?
5. What are employer self-funded health plans?

HSAS: HOW THEY WORK IN 2021

1. Your company offers a health insurance policy with an *annual deductible* of at least $1,400 for individual coverage or $2,800 for family coverage.

2. You can put *pretax dollars* into an HSA each year, up to the amount of the deductible—but no more than $7,200 for family coverage or $3,600 for individual coverage.

3. You withdraw the money from your HSA tax-free, but it can only go for your *family's medical expenses*. After the deductible and copays are met, insurance still typically *covers 80 percent* of health costs.

4. HSA plans are required to have maximum *out-of-pocket spending limits,* $7,000 for individuals, $14,000 for families. That's when your company's insurance kicks in again at 100 percent coverage.

5. Your *company can match* part or all of your HSA contributions if it wishes, just as it does with 401(k)s.

6. You can invest your HSA in stocks, bonds, or mutual funds. *Unused money remains* in your account at the end of the year and *grows tax free*.

7. You can also take your HSA with you if you *change jobs or retire*.

8. To help you *shop for health care* now that you're spending your own money, employers say they will give you detailed information about prices and quality of doctors and hospitals in your area.

Source: Internal Revenue Service, https://www.irs.gov, accessed April 5, 2021.

Government Health Care Programs

The health insurance coverage discussed thus far is normally purchased through private companies. Some consumers, however, are eligible for health insurance coverage under programs offered by federal and state governments.

Federal and state governments offer health coverage in accordance with laws that define the premiums and benefits they can offer. Specific requirements as to age, occupation, length of service, and family income may be used to determine eligibility for coverage. The two best-known sources of government health insurance are Medicare and Medicaid.

MEDICARE

Medicare, established in 1965, is a federal health insurance program for people 65 or older, people of any age with permanent kidney failure, and people with certain disabilities. The program is administered by the Centers for Medicare and Medicaid Services (formerly known as the Health Care Financing Administration). Local Social Security Administration offices take applications for Medicare, assist beneficiaries in filing claims, and provide information about the program.

Originally, Medicare had two parts: hospital insurance (Part A) and medical insurance (Part B). In December 2003, the Medicare Prescription Drug, Improvement, and Modernization Act created the Medicare Advantage program (Part C) and Medicare prescription drug benefit program (Part D).

Medicare *hospital insurance* (Part A) helps pay for inpatient hospital care, inpatient care in a skilled nursing facility, home health care, and hospice care. Hospital insurance is financed from a portion of the Social Security tax. Part A pays for all covered services for inpatient hospital care after you pay a single annual deductible. Most people over 65 are eligible for free Medicare hospital insurance.

Medicare *medical insurance* (Part B) helps pay for doctors' services and a variety of other medical services and supplies not covered by hospital insurance. Each year, as soon as you meet the annual medical insurance deductible, medical insurance will pay 80 percent of the approved charges for the covered services that

LO11-5

Appraise the sources of government health care programs.

Medicare A federal health insurance program for people 65 or older, people of any age with permanent kidney failure, and people with certain disabilities. The program is administered by the Centers for Medicare and Medicaid Services.

 my life **5**

I am aware of various state and federal health care programs.

Two sources of state and federal health care programs are Medicaid and Medicare. For a brief summary of Medicare Parts A, B, C, and D, examine Exhibit 11-9. For additional information, visit medicare.gov or call 1-800-Medicare (1-800-633-4227).

smart money minute

MEDICARE—BEFORE AND AFTER

1965: Medicare enacted into law. By 1969, Medicare represents about 0.7 percent of gross domestic product.

2004: Medicare provides benefits to 41.7 million elderly and disabled. Total cost of $308.9 billion. Represents 2.6 percent of gross domestic product.

2006: Prescription drug coverage (Medicare Part D) takes full effect (results from Medicare Modernization Act of 2003).

2026: Part A Hospital Insurance trust fund reserves projected to be depleted. (Program will be able to pay 79 percent of benefits.)

2035: Total Medicare costs (including prescription drug coverage) projected to represent 7.5 percent of gross domestic product.

you receive during the rest of the year. You must sign up for Part B coverage. This voluntary medical insurance is financed from the monthly premiums paid by people who have enrolled in it and from general federal revenues.

The Balanced Budget Act of 1997 created the Medicare + Choice program. The act expanded managed care options by encouraging wider availability of HMOs and allowed other types of health plans to participate in Medicare. It gave you the option to remain in the original Medicare (Parts A and B) or to enroll in a Medicare Advantage Plan. The Medicare Prescription Drug, Improvement, and Modernization Act of 2003 renamed the Medicare + Choice program as Medicare Advantage (Part C). This plan may be less expensive than the original Medicare and offers extra benefits. The plan is run by private health care providers who receive a set amount from Medicare for your health care regardless of how many or how few services you use.

The law also provides Medicare beneficiaries with prescription drug discounts (Part D). This voluntary, comprehensive Medicare drug coverage became effective on January 1, 2006. Most seniors pay about $50 per month for this new drug benefit and pay a copayment or coinsurance for each prescription. As with Medicare Part B enrollment, there is a penalty for not enrolling in the Medicare drug benefit in the first six months that you are eligible. People with the lowest incomes will pay no premiums or deductibles and small or no copayments. For a brief summary of Medicare Parts A, B, C, and D, see Exhibit 11-9.

While Medicare enjoys broad support among seniors and the American people, it faces many policy challenges. These challenges include addressing the affordability of

EXHIBIT 11-9 A Brief Look at Medicare

Medicare is health insurance for people age 65 or older, under age 65 with certain disabilities, and any age with end-stage renal disease (permanent kidney failure requiring dialysis or a kidney transplant).
   Most people get their Medicare health care coverage in one of two ways. Your costs vary depending on your plan's coverage, and the services you use.

Original Medicare Plan		or	Medicare Advantage Plans (Like HMOs and PPOs)
Part A (Hospital)	**Part B (Medical)**		**Called "Part C," this option combines your Part A (Hospital) and Part B (Medical)**
Medicare provides this coverage. Part B is optional. You have your choice of doctors. Your costs may be higher than in Medicare Advantage Plans.			Private insurance companies approved by Medicare provide this coverage. Generally, you must see doctors in the plan. Your costs may be lower than in the Original Medicare Plan, and you may get extra benefits.

+

Part D (Prescription Drug Coverage)

You can choose this coverage. Private companies approved by Medicare run these plans. Plans cover different drugs. Medically necessary drugs must be covered.

+

Medigap (Medicare Supplement Insurance) Policy

You can choose to buy this private coverage (or an employer or union may offer similar coverage) to fill in gaps in Part A and Part B coverage. Costs vary by policy and company.

+

Part D (Prescription Drug Coverage)

Most Part C plans cover prescription drugs. If they don't, you may be able to choose this coverage. Plans cover different drugs. Medically necessary drugs must be covered.

For information about Medicare, visit www.medicare.gov or call 1-800-MEDICARE (1-800-633-4227).

Source: *Medicare & You* (Washington, DC: The Centers for Medicare and Medicaid Services, 2021), p. 4, accessed April 4, 2021.

health and long-term care for the beneficiaries, financing the program over the long term, and examining the role of government versus the private sector in the Medicare program.

WHAT IS NOT COVERED BY MEDICARE? Although Medicare is very helpful for meeting medical costs, it does not cover everything. In addition to the deductibles and coinsurance mentioned earlier, Medicare does not cover some medical expenses at all, including:

- Acupuncture.
- Care in a skilled nursing facility (SNF) beyond 100 days per benefit period.
- Skilled nursing care in facilities not approved by Medicare.
- Intermediate and custodial nursing care (the kind many nursing home residents need).
- Most screening tests, vaccinations, and some diabetic supplies.
- Private-duty nursing.
- Routine checkups, dental care, most immunizations, cosmetic surgery, routine foot care, eyeglasses, and hearing aids.
- Care received outside the United States except in Canada and Mexico, and then only in limited circumstances.
- Services Medicare does not consider medically necessary.
- Physician charges above Medicare's approved amount. The government has a fee schedule for physician charges and places limits on charges in excess of the Medicare-approved amount when the physician does not accept Medicare's approved amount as payment in full.

Exhibit 11-10 compares features of different Medicare options. For a more complete description of Medicare coverage and costs, visit the Medicare website or ask your local Social Security Administration office for a copy of the Medicare handbook, *Medicare & You*. For more information, call the Medicare Hotline at 1-800-633-4227; or visit Medicare on Facebook (facebook.com/Medicare), Twitter (twitter.com/Medicaregov), and blog.medicare.gov.

MEDIGAP Medicare was never intended to pay all medical costs. To fill the gap between Medicare payments and medical costs not covered by Medicare, many companies sell Medigap insurance policies. **Medigap** or **MedSup insurance** is not sold or serviced by the federal government or state governments. Contrary to the claims made by some advertising and insurance agents, Medicare supplement insurance is not a government-sponsored program.

Most states now have 10 standardized Medicare supplement policies, designated by the letters *A* through *N*. These standardized policies make it easier to compare the costs of policies issued by different insurers. All Medicare policies must cover certain gaps in Medicare coverage, such as the daily coinsurance amount for hospitalization. In addition to the basic benefits that must now be included in all newly issued Medicare supplement policies in most states, you should consider other policy features. Some Medigap policies offer coverage for services that Medicare does not cover, like medical care when you travel outside the United States. Generally, Medigap policies do not cover long-term care, vision or dental care, hearing aids, eyeglasses, or private-duty nursing. In some states, you may be able to buy another type of Medigap policy called Medicare SELECT. If you buy this policy, you have rights to change your mind within 12 months and switch to a standard Medigap policy. For more information, visit www.medicare.gov/publications to view the booklet "Choosing a Medigap Policy: A Guide to Health Insurance for People with Medicare," or call 1-800-633-4227.

personal fintech

COVID-19 AND MEDICARE

Medicare covers:

- the lab tests and COVID-19 vaccines. You pay no out-of-pocket costs.
- the COVID-19 antibody tests if you are diagnosed with the infection.
- all medically necessary hospitalizations, but you still pay any hospital deductibles, copays, or coinsurance.

In addition, Medicare Advantage Plans and Prescription Drug Plans may waive or relax prior authorization requirements.

Medigap (MedSup) insurance Supplements Medicare by filling the gap between Medicare payments and medical costs not covered by Medicare.

EXHIBIT 11-10 A comparison of various Medicare plans

	Current Options	New Options (Medicare and Advantage)	Plan Description
Original Medicare	✓	✓	• You choose your health care providers. • Medicare pays your providers for covered services. • Most beneficiaries choose Medicare supplemental insurance to cover deductible and copayments.
Medicare health maintenance organization (HMO)	✓	✓	• You must live in the plan's service area. • You agree to use the plan's network of doctors, hospitals, and other health providers, except in an emergency. • Medicare pays the HMO to provide all medical services.
Preferred provider organization (PPO)		✓	• Works like an HMO, except you have the choice to see a health provider out of the network. • If you do see an out-of-network provider, you will pay a higher cost.
Provider-sponsored organization (PSO)		✓	• Works like a Medicare HMO, except the networks are managed by health care providers (doctors and hospitals) rather than an insurance company.
Private fee for service		✓	• Medicare pays a lump sum to a private insurance health plan. • Providers can bill more than what the plan pays; you are responsible for paying the balance. • The plan may offer more benefits than original Medicare.
Medical savings account (MSA)		✓	• Medicare MSAs are a special type of savings account that can be used to pay medical bills. • Centers for Medicare and Medicaid Services (CMS) will make an annual lump-sum deposit into enrollee's account (only Medicare can deposit funds into this account). • MSAs work with a special private insurance company and carry a very high deductible. • Funds withdrawn for nonmedical purposes are taxable and subject to a penalty.

Source: *Medicare & You* (Washington, DC: The Centers for Medicare and Medicaid Services, 2021), accessed April 5, 2021.

MEDICAID

Medicaid A program of medical assistance to low-income individuals and families.

Title XIX of the Social Security Act provides for a program of medical assistance to certain low-income individuals and families. In 1965 the program, known as **Medicaid,** became federal law.

Medicaid is administered by each state within certain broad federal requirements and guidelines. Financed by both state and federal funds, it is designed to provide medical assistance to groups or categories of persons who are eligible to receive payments under one of the cash assistance programs such as Temporary Assistance for Needy Families and Supplemental Security Income. The states may also provide Medicaid to medically needy individuals, that is, to persons who fit into one of the categories eligible for public assistance.

Many members of the Medicaid population are also covered by Medicare. Where such dual coverage exists, most state Medicaid programs pay for the Medicare premiums, deductibles, and copayments and for services not covered by Medicare. Medicaid differs from Medicare because eligibility for Medicaid depends on having very low income and assets. Once a person is eligible, Medicaid provides more benefits than does Medicare. Because Medicaid coverage is so comprehensive, people using it do not need to purchase supplemental insurance.

To qualify for federal matching funds, state programs must include inpatient hospital services; outpatient hospital services; laboratory and X-ray services; skilled nursing and home health services for individuals age 21 and older; family planning services; early and periodic screening, diagnosis, and treatment for individuals under 21; and physicians' services in the home, office, hospital, nursing home, or elsewhere.

HEALTH INSURANCE AND THE PATIENT PROTECTION AND AFFORDABLE CARE ACT OF 2010

Americans have been debating for years that the nation needs health care reform to ensure that we get high-quality, affordable health care. The Patient Protection and Affordable Care Act of 2010 (ACA) set aside $635 billion over 10 years to help finance this reform. Here are the key provisions of the act. The act:

- Offered tax credits for small businesses to make employee coverage more affordable.
- Prohibited denying coverage to children with preexisting medical conditions.
- Provided access to affordable insurance for those who are uninsured because of a preexisting condition through a temporary subsidized high-risk pool.
- Banned insurance companies from dropping people from coverage when they get sick.
- Eliminated copayments for preventive services and exempts preventive services from deductibles under the Medicare program.
- Required new health plans to allow young people up to their 26th birthday to remain on their parents' insurance policy.
- Prohibited health insurance companies from placing lifetime caps on coverage.
- Restricted the use of annual limits to ensure access to needed care in all plans.
- Required new private plans to cover preventive services with no copayment and with preventive services being exempt from deductibles.
- Ensured consumers in new plans have access to an effective internal and external appeals process to appeal decisions by their health insurance plans.
- Provided aid to states in establishing offices of health insurance consumer assistance to help individuals with the filing of complaints and appeals.
- Increased funds for community health centers to allow for nearly a doubling of the number of patients seen by the centers.
- Provided new investments to increase the number of primary care practitioners, including doctors, nurses, nurse practitioners, and physician assistants.
- Required health insurance companies to submit justification for all requested premium increases.
- Created state-based health insurance marketplaces (also called *insurance exchanges*) through which individuals can purchase coverage, with subsidies available to lower-income individuals.
- Expanded the Medicaid program for the nation's poorest individuals.
- Required employers with more than 20 employees to provide health insurance to their employees or pay penalties.[4]

The law was expansive and was to be implemented over several years, but all major provisions took effect in January 2014. On June 28, 2012, the Supreme Court, in a 5 to 4 vote, upheld the legality of the landmark Affordable Care Act.

An ethical dilemma: Is a government-run health care system that provides universal health care to all the most ethical? The current health care issues and the health care reform will have long-term effects on federal and state governments, insurance companies, health care providers, pharmaceutical companies, and, most important, patients. Most Americans believe that an ethical health care system should provide high, if not

smart money minute

the highest, quality of health care and freedom of choice, and it must be affordable and available to all citizens. Will "Obamacare" have long-term positive or negative effects on the general population? Only time will tell!

THE AFFORDABLE CARE ACT AND THE INDIVIDUAL SHARED RESPONSIBILITY PROVISION

Under the Affordable Care Act, the federal government, state governments, insurers, employers, and individuals share the responsibility for health insurance coverage. Many people already have qualifying health insurance coverage (called minimum essential coverage) and do not need to do anything more than maintain that coverage.

THE HEALTH INSURANCE MARKETPLACE   The Affordable Care Act also created the Health Insurance Marketplace, sometimes known as the health insurance "exchange" or "Obamacare exchange." The Health Insurance Marketplace makes buying health care coverage easier and more affordable. Since 2014, the Marketplace has allowed you to compare health plans, get answers to questions, find out if you are eligible for tax credits for private insurance, and enroll in a health plan that meets your needs. If you already have Medicare, you are covered and don't need to do anything about the Marketplace. No matter how you get Medicare, whether through original Medicare or a Medicare Advantage plan (like an HMO or PPO), you don't have to make any changes.

WHAT DO COLLEGE STUDENTS NEED TO KNOW ABOUT THE MARKETPLACE?   As a college student, you have several choices for health coverage. If you're covered by your school's student health plan, in most cases, you're considered covered.

A Marketplace health plan You can choose to buy a health plan through the Health Insurance Marketplace. Most people qualify for financial help to lower their premium costs. Visit HealthCare.gov to apply and find out if you can get lower costs for health coverage.

Coverage on a parent's plan You may be able to stay on or get added to your parent's health plan until you turn 26.

High-deductible health plans If you're under 30, you can buy a high-deductible health plan to protect yourself from the high costs of an accident or serious illness. These plans usually have lower monthly premiums, but high deductibles. You pay for most care yourself, up to a certain amount. After that, the insurance company pays its share for covered services.

Medicaid and the Children's Health Insurance Program (CHIP) coverage Medicaid is a combined state and federal program that provides coverage to people with limited income. CHIP provides low-cost health coverage up to age 19 in families that earn too much money to qualify for Medicaid. When you apply for coverage at HealthCare.gov, you'll find out if you qualify for coverage through Medicaid or CHIP.

For more information, visit HealthCare.gov, or call the Marketplace Call Center at 1-800-318-2596. TTY users can call 1-855-889-4325. You have the right to file a complaint if you feel you've been discriminated against. Visit www.cms.gov/About-CMS/Agency-Information/Aboutwebsite/CMSNondiscriminationNotice.html, or call the Marketplace Call Center at 1-800-318-2596 for more information. TTY users can call 1-855-889-4325.

FIGHT AGAINST MEDICARE/MEDICAID FRAUD AND ABUSE

Nearly 70 percent of consumers believe the Medicare program would not go broke if fraud and abuse were eliminated. Moreover, nearly 80 percent are not aware of any efforts to reduce health care fraud and abuse. In 1997 President Bill Clinton introduced the Medicare/Medicaid Anti-Waste, Fraud and Abuse Act, which established tough new requirements for health care providers that wish to participate in the Medicare/Medicaid program.

GOVERNMENT AND PRIVATE CONSUMER HEALTH INFORMATION WEBSITES

Health information, whether online or in print, should come from a trusted, credible source. Government sources, hospitals, universities, and medical journals and books provide evidence-based information sources you can trust. There are thousands of medical websites; some provide reliable health information, some don't. Choosing websites to trust is an important part of using the internet.

Recent studies indicate that consumers are seeking information on health and health care online to supplement traditional medical counsel. Many legitimate providers of reliable health and medical information, including the federal Food and Drug Administration, are taking advantage of the Web's popularity by offering brochures and in-depth information on specific topics at their websites.

With more than 60 central websites on eight separate domains, the Department of Health and Human Services (HHS) maintains one of the richest and most reliable sources of information on the internet (www.hhs.gov). HHS documents on the web include information on health issues, research-related data, and access to HHS services, including interactive sites. Major HHS health information websites include the following:

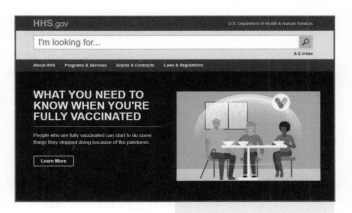

The Department of Health and Human Services maintains one of the richest and most reliable sources of information on the internet.
Source: U.S. Department of Health & Human Services

HEALTHFINDER Healthfinder includes links to more than 1,600 websites, including over 250 federal sites and 1,000 state, local, not-for-profit, university, and other consumer health resources. Topics are organized in a subject index. With more than 7 million hits in its first two months of operation, Healthfinder is among consumers' favorite websites. (www.hhs.gov).

MEDLINEPLUS MedlinePlus, the world's most extensive collection of published medical information, is coordinated by the National Library of Medicine. Originally designed for health professionals and researchers, MedlinePlus is also valuable for students and for those seeking more specific information about health care (www.medlineplus.gov/).

NIH HEALTH INFORMATION PAGE This website provides a single access point to the consumer health information resources of the National Institutes of Health, including the NIH Health Information Index, NIH publications and clearinghouses, and the Combined Health Information Database (www.nih.gov).

FDA: THE FOOD AND DRUG ADMINISTRATION The Food and Drug Administration (FDA) website provides information about the safety of various foods, drugs, cosmetics, and medical devices (www.fda.gov).

OTHER SOURCES Other good sources of health information include:

- Sites that end in ".gov," sponsored by the federal government. Many of these have already been covered, but we would also direct you to the Centers for Disease Control and Prevention (www.cdc.gov).
- Sites that end in ".edu," which are run by universities or medical schools, such as Johns Hopkins University School of Medicine (www.hopkinsmedicine.org/som/) and the University of California Health System (health.universityofcalifornia.edu/about/),

smart money minute

FIGHTING FRAUD CAN PAY

You may get a reward of up to $1,000 if you meet all these conditions:

- You report suspected Medicare fraud.
- The Inspector General's Office reviews your suspicion.
- The suspected fraud you report isn't already being investigated.
- Your report leads directly to the recovery of at least $100 of Medicare money.

For more information, call 1-800-MEDICARE (1-800-633-4227), or Office of the Inspector General at 1-800-447-8477.

and other health care facility sites, like the Mayo Clinic (www.mayoclinic.org/) and Cleveland Clinic (my.clevelandclinic.org/).

- Sites that end in ".org" that are maintained by not-for-profit groups whose focus is research and teaching the public about specific diseases or conditions, such as the American Diabetes Association (www.diabetes.org/), the American Cancer Society (www.cancer.org/), and the American Heart Association (www.heart.org/).

- Medical and scientific journals, such as *The New England Journal of Medicine* (www.nejm.org/) and the *Journal of the American Medical Association* (JAMA; jamanetwork.com/journal.aspx), although these aren't written for consumers and could be hard to understand.

Sites whose addresses end in ".com" are usually commercial sites and are often selling products.

✔ PRACTICE QUIZ 11-5

1. What are the two sources of government health insurance?
2. What benefits do Part A and Part B of Medicare provide?
3. What is Medigap, or MedSup, insurance?

Disability Income Insurance

LO11-6

Recognize the need for disability income insurance.

disability income insurance Provides payments to replace income when an insured person is unable to work.

Because you feel young and healthy now, you may overlook the very real need for disability income insurance. Disability income insurance protects your most valuable asset: your ability to earn income. People are more likely to lose their incomes due to disability than they are to die. The fact is, for all age groups, disability is more likely than death.

Disability income insurance provides regular cash income lost by employees as the result of an accident or illness. Disability income insurance is probably the most neglected form of available insurance protection. Many people who insure their houses, cars, and other property fail to insure their most valuable resource: their earning power. Disability can cause even greater financial problems than death. In fact, disability is often called "the living death." Disabled persons lose their earning power while continuing to incur normal family expenses. In addition, they often face huge expenses for the medical treatment and special care their disabilities require.

Every year, 12 percent of the adult U.S. population suffers a long-term disability. One out of every seven workers will suffer a five-year or longer period of disability before age 65, and if you are 35 now, your chances of experiencing a three-month or longer disability before you reach age 65 are 50 percent, according to the National Association of Insurance Commissioners. If you have no disability income protection, you are betting that you will not become disabled, and that could be a very costly bet.

DEFINITION OF DISABILITY

Disability has several definitions. Some policies define it simply as the inability to do your regular work. Others have stricter definitions. For example, a dentist who is unable to do his or her regular work because of a hand injury but can earn income through related duties, such as teaching dentistry, would not be considered permanently disabled under certain policies.

Good disability plans pay when you are unable to work at your regular job; poor disability plans pay only when you are unable to work at any job. A good disability plan will also make partial disability payments when you return to work on a part-time basis.

DISABILITY INSURANCE TRADE-OFFS

Following are some important trade-offs you should consider in purchasing disability income insurance.

WAITING OR ELIMINATION PERIOD   Benefits don't begin on the first day you become disabled. Usually there is a waiting or elimination period of between 30 and 90 days. Some waiting periods may be as long as 180 days. Generally, disability income policies with longer waiting periods have lower premiums. If you have substantial savings to cover three to six months of expenses, the reduced premiums of a policy with a long waiting period may be attractive. But if you need every paycheck to cover your bills, you are probably better off paying the higher premium for a short waiting period. Short waiting periods, however, are very expensive.

DURATION OF BENEFITS   The maximum time a disability income policy will pay benefits may be a few years, to age 65, or for life. You should seek a policy that pays benefits for life. If you became permanently disabled, it would be financially disastrous if your benefits ended at age 55 or 65.

AMOUNT OF BENEFITS   You should aim for a benefit amount that, when added to your other income, will equal 60 to 70 percent of your gross pay. Of course, the greater the benefits, the greater the cost.

ACCIDENT AND SICKNESS COVERAGE   Consider both accident and sickness coverage. Some disability income policies will pay only for accidents, but you want to be insured for illness, too.

GUARANTEED RENEWABILITY   Ask for noncancelable and guaranteed renewable coverage. Either coverage will protect you against your insurance company dropping you if your health becomes poor. The premium for these coverages is higher, but the coverages are well worth the extra cost. Furthermore, look for a disability income policy that waives premium payments while you are disabled.

See whether you qualify for a lower premium if you agree to forgo part of your monthly benefit when Social Security, company retirement benefits, or worker's compensation benefits begin. Most disability income policies coordinate their benefits with these programs.

SOURCES OF DISABILITY INCOME

Before you buy disability income insurance, remember that you may already have some form of such insurance. This coverage may come to you through your employer, Social Security, or worker's compensation.

EMPLOYER   Many, but not all, employers provide disability income protection for their employees through group insurance plans. Your employer may have some form of wage continuation policy that lasts a few months or an employee group disability plan that provides long-term protection. In most cases, your employer will pay part or all of the cost of this plan.

I realize that for all age groups, disability is more likely than death.

No matter your age, you are more likely to lose your income due to disability than you are to die. What would happen if your paychecks suddenly stopped because you were too sick or injured to work? What if you could not work for months or years? For additional information, visit www.ssa.gov/disabilityssi/.

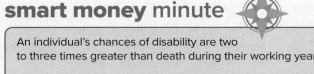

smart money minute

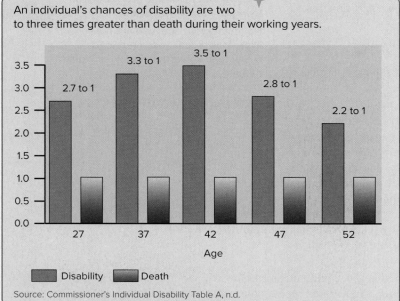

An individual's chances of disability are two to three times greater than death during their working years.

Disability   Death

Source: Commissioner's Individual Disability Table A, n.d.

SOCIAL SECURITY Most salaried workers in the United States participate in the Social Security program. In this program, your benefits are determined by your salary and by the number of years you have been covered under Social Security. Your dependents also qualify for certain benefits. However, Social Security has strict rules. You must be totally disabled for 12 months or more, and you must be unable to do *any* work.

WORKER'S COMPENSATION If your accident or illness occurred at your place of work or resulted from your type of employment, you could be entitled to worker's compensation benefits in your state. Like Social Security benefits, these benefits are determined by your earnings and work history.

Other possible sources of disability income include Veterans Administration pension disability benefits, civil service disability benefits for government workers, state vocational rehabilitation benefits, state welfare benefits for low-income people, Temporary Assistance for Needy Families, group union disability benefits, automobile insurance that provides benefits for disability from an auto accident, and private insurance. Exhibit 11-11 will help you identify the sources and amount of income available to you if you become disabled.

The availability and extent of these and other disability income sources vary widely in different parts of the country. Be sure to look into such sources carefully before calculating your need for additional disability income insurance.

The *Financial Literacy for My Life: Consumer Tips on Health and Disability Insurance* feature provides some consumer tips on health and disability insurance.

DETERMINING YOUR DISABILITY INCOME INSURANCE REQUIREMENTS

Once you have found out what your benefits from the numerous public and private disability income sources would be, you should determine whether those benefits are sufficient to meet your disability income needs. If the sum of your disability benefits approaches your after-tax income, you can safely assume that should disability strike, you'll be in good shape to pay your day-to-day bills while recuperating.

You should know how long you would have to wait before the benefits begin (the waiting or elimination period) and how long they would be paid (the benefit period).

What if, as is often the case, Social Security and other disability benefits are not sufficient to support your family? In that case, you may want to consider buying disability income insurance to make up the difference.

Don't expect to insure yourself for your full salary. Most insurers limit benefits from all sources to no more than 70 to 80 percent of your take-home pay. For example, if you earn $700 a week, you could be eligible for disability insurance of about $490 to $560 a week. You will not need $700, because while you are disabled, your work-related expenses will be eliminated and your taxes will be far lower or may even be zero.

The *Financial Literacy for My Life: Disability Income Policy Checklist* box shows you how to compare different features among disability income policies.

Financial Literacy for My Life

CONSUMER TIPS ON HEALTH AND DISABILITY INSURANCE

1. If you pay your own premiums directly, try to arrange to pay them on an annual or quarterly basis rather than on a monthly basis. It is often cheaper.

2. Policies should be delivered to you within 30 days. If not, contact your insurer and find out, in writing, why. If a policy is not delivered in 60 days, contact the state department of insurance.

3. When you receive a policy, take advantage of the free-look provision. You have 10 days to look it over and obtain a refund if you decide it is not for you.

4. Unless you have a policy with no internal limits, read over your contract every year to see whether its benefits are still in line with medical costs.

5. Don't replace a policy because you think it is out of date. Switching may subject you to new waiting periods and new exclusions. Rather, add to what you have if necessary.

6. On the other hand, don't keep a policy because you've had it a long time. You don't get any special credit from the company for being an old customer.

7. Don't try to make a profit on your insurance by carrying overlapping coverage. Duplicate coverage is expensive. Besides, most group policies now contain a coordination-of-benefits clause limiting benefits to 100 percent.

8. Use your health emergency fund to cover small expenses.

9. If you're considering the purchase of a dread disease policy such as cancer insurance, understand that it is supplementary and will pay for only one disease. You should have full coverage before you consider it. Otherwise, it's a gamble.

10. Don't lie on your insurance application. If you fail to mention a preexisting condition, you may not get paid. You can usually get paid even for that condition after one or two years have elapsed if you have had no treatment for the condition during that period.

11. Keep your insurance up to date. Some policies adjust to inflation better than others. Some insurers check that benefits have not been outdistanced by inflation. Review your policies annually.

12. Never sign a health insurance application (such applications are lengthy and detailed for individually written policies) until you have recorded full and complete answers to every question.

Source: Health Insurance Association of America.

EXHIBIT 11-11
Disability income worksheet

How much income will you have available if you become disabled?	Monthly Amount	After Waiting	For a Period of
Sick leave or short-term disability	_____	_____	_____
Group long-term disability	_____	_____	_____
Social Security	_____	_____	_____
Other government programs	_____	_____	_____
Individual disability insurance	_____	_____	_____
Credit disability insurance	_____	_____	_____
Other income:	_____	_____	_____
Savings	_____	_____	_____
Spouse's income	_____	_____	_____
Total monthly income while disabled:	$ _____		_____

Financial Literacy for My Life

DISABILITY INCOME POLICY CHECKLIST

Different disability income policies may have different features. The following checklist will help you compare policies you may be considering.

	Policy A	Policy B			Policy A	Policy B
1. How is disability defined? Inability to perform your own job?	____	____	**5.** What percentage of your income will the maximum benefit replace?		____	____
Inability to perform any job?	____	____	**6.** Is the policy noncancelable, guaranteed renewable, or conditionally renewable?		____	____
2. Does the policy cover Accident?	____	____	**7.** How long must you be disabled before premiums are waived?		____	____
Illness?	____	____	**8.** Is there an option to buy additional coverage, without evidence of insurability, at a later date?		____	____
3. Are benefits available For total disability?	____	____				
For partial disability?	____	____				
Only after total disability?	____	____	**9.** Does the policy offer an inflation adjustment feature?		____	____
Without a prior period of total disability?	____	____	If so, what is the rate of increase?		____	____
4. Are full benefits paid, whether or not you are able to work, for loss of Sight?	____	____	How often is it applied?		____	____
Speech?	____	____	For how long?		____	____
Hearing?	____	____				
Use of limbs?	____	____				

	Policy A		Policy B	
10. What does the policy cost?	**With Inflation Feature**	**Without Inflation Feature**	**With Inflation Feature**	**Without Inflation Feature**
For a waiting period of ___ (30–180) days, and	_____	_____	_____	_____
For a benefit period of ___ (1 yr–lifetime)?	_____	_____	_____	_____
Total	_____	_____	_____	_____

Source: Health Insurance Association of America, Washington, DC.

PFP Sheet 52
Disability Income Insurance

PRACTICE QUIZ 11-6

1. What is disability income insurance?
2. What are the three main sources of disability income?
3. How can you determine the amount of disability income insurance you need?

Your Personal Finance Roadmap and Dashboard:

Health, Disability, and Long-Term Care Insurance

INCOME PERCENT COVERED BY DISABILITY

A personal finance dashboard with key performance indicators can help you monitor your financial situation and guide you toward financial independence. Disability can be more disastrous financially than death. If you are disabled, you lose your earning power, but you still have living expenses and often huge expenses for medical care.

YOUR SITUATION

Do you know how disability is defined? When do your benefits begin? How long do your benefits last? What is the amount of your benefits? Can benefits be reduced by Social Security disability and workers' compensation payments? Are the benefits adjusted for inflation? You should aim for benefit amounts that, when added to your other income, equal 70 or 80 percent of your gross pay. Other personal financial planning actions you might consider during various stages of your life include:

◯ First Steps

- Stay on your parents' health care insurance plan if you meet current qualifications.
- Most states offer free or low-cost coverage for children who do not have health insurance. Call 1-877-543-7669 for more information.

- Take meaningful action to ensure your own good health: avoid smoking, drinking, bad nutrition, and lack of exercise.
- Get health care coverage from your employer.
- Consider HMOs for lower copayments and deductibles.
- Don't give your insurance identification numbers to companies you don't know.
- Consider purchasing disability income insurance.
- Consider participating in a flexible spending account if your employer offers it.

◯ Next Steps

- If you lose your group coverage from an employer due to unemployment or divorce, continue your coverage through the COBRA Act.
- Consider PPOs, which offer lower copayments like HMOs, but give you more flexibility.
- Consider purchasing long-term care insurance.

◯ Last Steps

- Consider enrolling in a Part D drug plan when you are first eligible.
- Only give your Medicare number to your physician or other approved Medicare providers.
- Review your Medicare statements to ensure that your account is not billed for services you did not receive.

YOUR Next Step . . . select one or more of the items above and create an action plan to implement those financial planning activities.

SUMMARY OF LEARNING OBJECTIVES

LO11-1

Explain why the costs of health insurance and health care have been increasing. Your health care costs, except during 1994–1996, have gone up faster than the rate of inflation. Among the reasons for high and rising health care costs are the use of expensive technologies, duplication of tests and sometimes technologies, increases in the variety and frequency of treatments, unnecessary tests, the increasing number and longevity of elderly people, regulations that shift rather than reduce costs, the increasing number of accidents and crimes requiring emergency services, limited competition, and restrictive work rules in the health care delivery system, rapid earnings growth among health care professionals, built-in inflation in the health care delivery system, and other factors.

LO11-2

Define *health insurance* and *disability income insurance* and explain their importance in financial planning. Health insurance is protection that provides payment of benefits for a covered sickness or injury. Disability income insurance protects your most valuable asset: the ability to earn income.

Health insurance and disability income insurance are two protections against economic losses due to illness, accident, or disability. Both protections should be a part of your overall insurance program to safeguard your family's economic security.

Disability can cause even greater financial problems than death. In fact, disability is often called "the living death." Disabled persons lose their earning power while continuing to incur normal family expenses. In addition, they often face huge expenses for the medical treatment and special care their disabilities require.

LO11-3

Analyze the benefits and limitations of the various types of health care coverage. Five basic types of health insurance are available to you under group and individual

policies: hospital expense insurance, surgical expense insurance, physician's expense insurance, major medical expense insurance, and comprehensive major medical insurance. The benefits and limitations of each policy differ. Ideally, you should get a basic plan and a major medical supplementary plan, or a comprehensive major medical policy that combines the values of both of these plans in a single policy.

Major provisions of a health insurance policy include eligibility requirements, assigned benefits, inside limits, copayment, service benefits, benefit limits, exclusions and limitations, coordination of benefits, guaranteed renewability, and cancellation and termination.

LO11-4

Evaluate private sources of health insurance and health care. Health insurance and health care are available from private insurance companies, hospital and medical service plans such as Blue Cross Blue Shield, health maintenance organizations (HMOs), preferred provider organizations (PPOs), exclusive provider organizations (EPOs), point-of-service plans (POSs), home health care agencies, and employer self-funded health plans.

LO11-5

Appraise the sources of government health care programs. The federal and state governments offer health coverage in accordance with laws that define the premiums and benefits. Two well-known government health programs are Medicare and Medicaid.

LO11-6

Recognize the need for disability income insurance. Disability income insurance provides regular cash income you lose as the result of an accident or illness. Sources of disability income insurance include the employer, Social Security, worker's compensation, the Veterans Administration, the federal and state governments, unions, and private insurance.

 KEY TERMS

SELF-TEST PROBLEMS

1. The MacDonald family has health insurance coverage that pays 75 percent of out-of-hospital expenses after a $1,000 deductible per person. Mrs. MacDonald incurred doctor and prescription medication expenses of $1,380. What amount would the insurance company pay?

2. Under Rose's PPO, emergency room care at a network hospital is 80 percent covered after the member has met a $1,000 annual deductible. Assume that Rose went to a hospital within her PPO network and that she has not met her annual deductible yet. Her total emergency room bill was $1,850. What amount did Rose have to pay? What amount did the PPO cover?

3. Gene, an assembly line worker at an automobile manufacturing plant, has take-home pay of $900 a week. He is injured in an accident that kept him off work for 18 weeks. His disability insurance coverage replaces 65 percent of his earnings after a six-week waiting period. What amount would he receive in disability benefits?

Self-Test Solutions

1. Total expenses = $1,380

   Deductible   = −1,000

                 $ 380

   Insurance company will pay 75 percent of $380 or $380 × .75 = $285.

2. Total bill $1,850

   Deductible   − 1,000

                 $ 850

   Rose pays $850 × .20 = $170 + $1,000 = $1,170.

   PPO pays $850 × .80 = $680.

3. Insurance will replace 65 percent of $900 or $900 × .65 = $585 per week.

   Insurance will pay for 18 − 6, or 12 weeks or $585 × 12 = $7,020.

FINANCIAL PLANNING PROBLEMS

1. *Calculating the Effect of Inflation on Health Care Costs.* If per capita spending on health care was about $8,000 and if this amount increased by 5 percent a year, what would be the amount of per capita spending for health care in 10 years?   **LO11-1**

2. *Calculating the Amount of Reimbursement from an Insurance Company.* The Kelleher family has health insurance coverage that pays 80 percent of out-of-hospital expenses after a $500 deductible per person. If one family member has doctor and prescription medication expenses of $1,100, what amount would the insurance company pay?   **LO11-3**

3. *Comparing the Costs of a Regular Health Insurance Policy and an HMO.* A health insurance policy pays 65 percent of physical therapy costs after a $200 deductible. In contrast, an HMO charges $15 per visit for physical therapy. How much would a person save with the HMO if he or she had 10 physical therapy sessions costing $50 each?   **LO11-3**

4. *Calculating the Cost of Health Care Coverage with and without a Stop-Loss Policy.* Sarah's comprehensive major medical health insurance plan at work has a deductible of $750. The policy pays 85 percent of any amount above the deductible. While on a hiking trip, she contracted a rare bacterial disease. Her medical costs for treatment, including medicines, tests, and a six-day hospital stay, totaled $8,893. A friend told her that she would have paid less if she had a policy with a stop-loss feature that capped her out-of-pocket expenses at $3,000. Was her friend correct? Show your computations. Then determine which policy would have cost Sarah less and by how much.   **LO11-3**

5. *Calculating the Amount of Disability Benefits.* Georgia, a widow, has take-home pay of $600 a week from her part-time job. Her disability insurance coverage replaces 70 percent of her earnings after a four-week waiting period. What amount would she receive in disability benefits if an illness kept Georgia off work for 16 weeks?   **LO11-6**

LO11-3 6. *Calculating the Cost of In-Network Care with a PPO.* Stephanie was injured in a car accident and was rushed to the emergency room. She received stitches for a facial wound and treatment for a broken finger. Under Stephanie's PPO plan, emergency room care at a network hospital is 80 percent covered after the member has met a $300 annual deductible. Assume that Stephanie went to a hospital within her PPO network. Her total emergency room bill was $850. What amount did Stephanie have to pay? What amount did the PPO cover?

Use the following information to answer Problems 7, 8, and 9:

Evaluating Health Insurance Options. Ronald started his new job as controller with Aerosystems today. Carole, the employee benefits clerk, gave Ronald a packet that contains information on the company's health insurance options. Aerosystems offers its employees the choice between a private insurance company plan (Blue Cross/Blue Shield), an HMO, and a PPO. Ronald needs to review the packet and make a decision on which health care program fits his needs. The following is an overview of that information.

a. The monthly premium cost to Ronald for the *Blue Cross Blue Shield plan* will be $42.32. For all doctor office visits, prescriptions, and major medical charges, Ronald will be responsible for 20 percent and the insurance company will cover 80 percent of covered charges. The annual deductible is $500.

b. The *HMO* is provided to employees free of charge. The copayment for doctors' office visits and major medical charges is $10. Prescription copayments are $5. The HMO pays 100 percent after Ronald's copayment. There is no annual deductible.

c. The *POS* requires that the employee pay $24.44 per month to supplement the cost of the program with the company's payment. If Ron uses health care providers within the plan, he pays the copayments as described above for the HMO. He can also choose to use a health care provider out of the service and pay 20 percent of all charges after he pays a $500 deductible. The POS will pay for 80 percent of those covered visits. There is no annual deductible for in-network expenses.

Ronald decided to review his medical bills from the previous year to see what costs he had incurred and to help him evaluate his choices. He visited his general physician four times during the year at a cost of $125 for each visit. He also spent $65 and $89 on prescriptions during the year. Using these costs as an example, what would Ron pay for each of the plans described above? (For the purposes of the POS computation, assume that Ron visited a physician outside of the network plan. Assume he had his prescriptions filled at a network-approved pharmacy.)

LO11-4 7. *Evaluating Health Insurance Options.* What annual medical costs will Ronald pay using the sample medical expenses provided if he were to enroll in the Blue Cross Blue Shield plan?

LO11-4 8. *Evaluating Health Insurance Options.* What total costs will Ronald pay if he enrolls in the HMO plan?

LO11-4 9. *Evaluating Health Insurance Options.* If Ronald selects the POS plan, what would annual medical costs be?

LO11-3 10. *Calculating Out-of-Pocket Costs.* Ariana's health insurance policy includes an $800 deductible and a coinsurance provision requiring her to pay 20 percent of all bills. Her total bill is $3,800. What is Ariana's total cost?

LO11-4 11. *Calculating Health Care Costs over Time.* In 2020, Mark spent $9,500 on his health care. If this amount increased by 6 percent per year, what would be the amount Mark will spend in 2030? (*Hint:* Use the compounded sum future value table in Chapter 1, Exhibit 1-8.)

LO11-4 12. *Calculating Health Care Costs over Time.* In 2012, per capita spending on health care in the United States was about $9,000. If this amount increased by 7 percent a year, what would be the amount of per capita spending for health care in eight years? (*Hint:* Use the Time Value of Money table in the Chapter 1 Appendix, Exhibit 1-A.)

DIGITAL FINANCIAL LITERACY: SHOULD YOU CARE ABOUT HEALTH CARE COSTS?

You are a young and healthy college student. Why should you be concerned about health care costs now? You should. Your health costs now and the future can be affected by your personal health habits. Many health problems result from poor habits, such as lack of exercise or inadequate diet, and may take years to develop. By establishing good habits now, you can reduce the likelihood of future health problems and related expenses.

Action items:

1. List health care services that you and other members of your family have used during the past year. Assign an

approximate dollar cost to each of these services, and identify the financial resources (savings, health insurance, government sources, etc.) you used to pay for them.

2. Choose a current issue of *Consumer Reports, Bloomberg Businessweek,* or *Kiplinger's Personal Finance* and summarize an article that updates the costs of health care. How might you use this information to reduce your health care costs?

FINANCIAL PLANNING CASE

Making Sense of Medicare

Eugenio Costa, 65, received a 127-page booklet from Uncle Sam called *Medicare and You 2021*. It doesn't have much of a plot, but it might be the most important reading he does this year.

For seniors or their adult children, the booklet outlines the choices Medicare recipients face in the fast-changing world of health care. But Medicare is mind-numbingly complicated, and it is easy to get lost in a maze of options.

Eugenio is fully aware, however, that Medicare, Medicare HMO (Medicare + Choice), or Medigap do not cover long-term nursing home or at-home care. For that, he will have to buy private insurance, which can cost thousands of dollars a year if he signs up now.

All of these choices allow seniors to tailor a plan to their needs. But it also makes picking insurance much more complicated. Eugenio knows that a mistake can be costly in terms of both health and money.

Questions

1. What factors should Eugenio Costa consider in making the choice among various types of Medicare, Medigap, or HMO health care insurance policies?

2. Visit the following websites for Medicare resources to obtain general information, guides on buying Medigap or HMO coverage, and price quotations with insurance company ratings on Medigap insurance carriers.

General Information

Medicare
1-800-633-4227
www.medicare.gov
ElderCare Locator
1-800-677-1116

Guides on Buying Medigap or HMO Coverage

Medicare Rights Center
www.medicarerights.org

Quotes and Ratings on Medigap Carriers

Insure.com
1-800-324-6370
www.lifequotes.com

YOUR PERSONAL FINANCIAL PLAN

COMPARING HEALTH INSURANCE PLANS

Changing programs and regulations influence your ability to be properly covered for health care and disability insurance coverage. Awareness of policy types, coverages, and limitations will help you plan this phase of your financial plan.

Your Short-Term Financial Planning Activity

Task Assess your health habits and what you can do to reduce medical costs.

Research

1) List health care services that you and other members of your family have used during the past year. Assign an approximate dollar cost to each of these services, and identify the financial resources (savings, health insurance, government sources, etc.) you used to pay for them.

2) Use Personal Financial Planning Sheet 51 to investigate the coverages you have for hospital costs, surgery costs, physician fees, lab tests, etc. What are the deductibles, coinsurance, and maximum limits? What items are not covered?

3) Visit insure.com, healthfinder.gov, or ncqa.org to compare the cost of health insurance programs available from various sources.

4) Use Personal Financial Planning Sheet 52 to evaluate your need for expanded disability insurance. Visit the Social Security Administration's web page to determine your approximate monthly Social Security disability benefits should you become disabled in the coming year.

Outcome Add these documents and files to your portfolio or files to your Personal Financial Plan online folder.

Your Long-Term Financial Planning Activity

Task Identify possible future needs for supplemental Medicare and long-term care insurance coverages.

Research

1) Visit ssa.gov, medicare.gov, or naic.org to determine if you will need disability income insurance. Also, read the material in "Disability Insurance Trade-Offs" and "Financial Literacy for My Life: Consumer Tips on Health and Disability Insurance."

2) Visit ahip.org, or mib.com to develop a plan for reducing health care and medical insurance costs. Why do the expenditures for health care continue to increase, and what can you do to reduce personal health care costs?

Outcome In a two-page report, describe if you will purchase disability income insurance. If so, why? If not, then why not? Explain what you will personally do to keep healthy and reduce costs of health care.

Note: All *Personal Financial Planner* sheets are available at the end of the book and in an Excel spreadsheet format in *Connect Finance*.

CONTINUING CASE

Health, Disability, and Long-Term Care Insurance

Jamie Lee and Ross, happy newlyweds with a new home and twins on the way, are anxiously awaiting their new bundles of joy. Ross was a little nervous, and understandably so, as he wondered if everything would go smoothly with Jamie's pregnancy. Fortunately for them, they coordinated benefits from the medical insurance group plan offered by Ross's employment at the graphics agency and Jamie Lee's own plan, although Ross's plan would be their primary. His employer offers a health care savings plan, but Ross previously had not realized the need to participate in this benefit.

Jamie Lee has had good maternity care so far, but they both felt a need to review their health insurance policies with the potential of extensive medical expenses just on the horizon. Would their salaries be enough to pay for the expenses that were not covered, or even the deductibles for out-of-network doctors?

Current Medical Insurance Provisions

Jamie Lee and Ross have a PPO, or *preferred provider organization* plan.

In-Network Medical Care: Jamie Lee and Ross currently have a $20 copayment on regular preventive care doctor visits and a $40 copayment on specialists that are preferred providers or participating members from the PPO plan's list.

Out-of-Network Medical Care: Jamie Lee and Ross have the choice of seeking medical care from the professional of their choice outside the PPO member list, but will incur a deductible of $500 per person/$1,000 per family, per year. After the deductible is met, there is a coinsurance of 80 percent/20 percent, whereas the insurance company would cover 80 percent of the allowable medical fees and the policyholders would be responsible for 20 percent of the allowable medical fees. Medical fees that are not allowed under the medical plan provisions would be 100 percent the policyholder's responsibility.

Out-of-Pocket Limits: Their health insurance plan provides an out-of-pocket limit of $20,000 per year.

Questions

1. Using the text as a guide, list some of the strategies that Ross and Jamie Lee can use to better prepare financially for the arrival of the twins.

2. How could Jamie Lee and Ross prepare for the birth of the twins with their existing PPO plan?

3. Jamie Lee and Ross learned that the hospital that they plan to use for the delivery is not a participating hospital. What will their financial responsibility be for the nonparticipating hospital expenses?

4. The doctor's office has estimated the hospital expense for Jamie Lee and the babies' delivery, without complications, to be approximately $18,000. Based on their health insurance policy, how much would Jamie Lee and Ross owe for this out-of-network hospital stay?

5. Surprise! The babies arrived five weeks early and Jamie Lee and Ross are the proud parents of *triplets*! There are two boys and a girl, and as they were preterm, they will need to spend a few extra days in the hospital for observation. How will Ross and Jamie Lee make provisions for adding the babies to their health insurance policy now that they have arrived?

DAILY SPENDING DIARY

"Some of my eating habits not only waste money but are also not best for my health or for my health insurance."

Directions

Continue your *Daily Spending Diary* to record and monitor your spending in various categories. Your comments should reflect what you have learned about your spending patterns and help you consider possible changes you might want to make in your spending habits.

Analysis Questions

1. What spending actions might directly or indirectly affect your health and physical well-being?

2. What amounts (if any) are currently required from your spending for the cost of health and disability insurance?

A *Daily Spending Diary* sheet is located at the end of Chapter 1 and on the library resource site in *Connect*.

Life Insurance

12

Rido/Shutterstock

Financial Literacy
IN YOUR LIFE

▶ **What if you . . .** were to die unexpectedly and leave your family with the financial burden of planning a funeral and preparing for the loss of your income?

You might . . . make adjustments now to make sure your family is financially secure by reviewing your life insurance needs.

Now, what would you do? Review your current assets, expected future expenses, and existing life insurance coverage to check for any shortfalls. One method to help you get started is by using the Your Personal Finance Roadmap and Dashboard feature at the end of the chapter.

Life Insurance: An Introduction

LO12-1

Define *life insurance* and describe its purpose and principle.

Before the recent pandemic, many families viewed life insurance as just another discretionary expense, assuming money was available for the premiums. As the U.S. saw the death toll rise to over 600,000 lives, the need for being financially prepared started to take on a new meaning and gained greater focus.

Although it is impossible to put a price on your life, now or someday soon, you will probably own some life insurance—through a group plan where you work, as a veteran, or through a policy you will buy. Perhaps you will consider the purchase of additional life insurance to keep pace with inflation or to provide for a growing family. If so, you should prepare for that purchase by learning as much as possible about life insurance and how it can help you meet your needs.

Most American families face a substantial loss when one spouse dies unexpectedly. Unfortunately, 45 percent of widows and 37 percent of widowers say their spouse was inadequately insured. Life for the surviving spouse becomes a financial struggle.

Life insurance is one of the most important and expensive purchases you may ever make. Deciding whether you need it and choosing the right policy from dozens of options takes time, research, and careful thought. This chapter will help you make decisions about life insurance. It describes what life insurance is and how it works, the major types of life insurance coverage, and how you can use life insurance to protect your family.

Consumer awareness of life insurance has changed little over the years. Life insurance is still more often sold than bought. In other words, while most people actively seek to buy insurance for their property and health, they avoid a life insurance purchase until an agent approaches them. Still, recently, over 39.4 million policies, with face value of about $3.1 trillion, were sold in one year. Two out of three households now have life insurance. At the beginning of 2020, 258 million policies were in force, with a total value of $19.8 trillion.[1]

my life | **1**

I need life insurance because someone depends on me for financial support.

Most Americans need life insurance, and many who already have it may need to update their coverage. If you are providing financial support for a spouse, children, aging parents, or siblings, or if you have significant debt, you should consider buying life insurance.

smart money minute

You can receive a free *Life Insurance Buyer's Guide* from the National Association of Insurance Commissioners. Visit their website at www.naic.org. The guide helps you get the most for your money and answers questions about buying life insurance, deciding how much is needed, and finding the right kind of insurance.

WHAT IS LIFE INSURANCE?

Life insurance is rather simple to understand. It works in the following three steps:

1) A person joins a risk-sharing group (an insurance company) by purchasing a contract (a policy).

2) Under the policy, the insurance company promises to pay a sum of money at the time of the policyholder's death to the person or persons (the beneficiaries) selected by the policyholder. In the case of an endowment policy, the money is paid to the policyholder (the insured) if he or she is alive on the future date (the maturity date) named in the policy.

3) The insurance company makes this promise in return for the insured's agreement to pay a sum of money (the premium) periodically.

THE PURPOSE OF LIFE INSURANCE

Most people buy life insurance to protect someone who depends on them from financial losses caused by their death. That someone could be the nonworking spouse and children of a single-income family. It could be the spouse of a two-income family. It could also be an aging parent. It could be a business partner or a corporation.

Life insurance proceeds are typically used to:

- Pay off a home mortgage or other debts at the time of death.
- Provide lump-sum payments to children when they reach a specified age.
- Provide an education or income for children.
- Cover medical expenses and funeral costs.
- Make charitable bequests after death.

EXHIBIT 12-1   Top Reasons For Not Owning Life Insurance

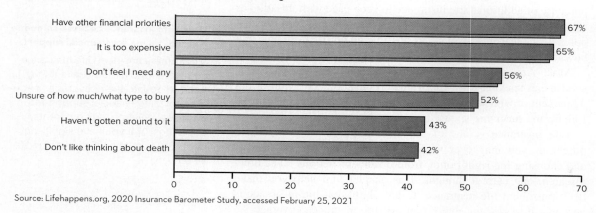

Source: Lifehappens.org, 2020 Insurance Barometer Study, accessed February 25, 2021

Most people buy life insurance to protect someone who depends on them from financial losses caused by their death.
wavebreakmedia/Shutterstock

- Provide a retirement income.
- Accumulate savings.
- Establish a regular income for survivors.
- Set up an estate plan.
- Make estate and death tax payments.

Life insurance is one of the few ways to provide liquidity at the time of death. Despite the need to provide for loved ones, only 54 percent of adult consumers had life insurance, according to the *2020 Insurance Barometer Study* for Life Happens and LIMRA. However, due to the recent pandemic, the survey also found that 36 percent of people surveyed intended to buy life insurance in the next 12 months, up from a low of 10 percent in 2014. Another important question asked by the survey was why participants were less likely to buy insurance. The results are shown in Exhibit 12-1. It is important to note that many of these reasons may pale in comparison to leaving a family with very few resources.

THE PRINCIPLE OF LIFE INSURANCE

The principle of home insurance, discussed in Chapter 10, can be applied to the lives of persons. From records covering many years and including millions of lives, mortality tables have been prepared to show the number of deaths among various age groups during any year. In the 1950s, the life insurance industry developed and the National Association of Insurance Commissioners (NAIC) approved a mortality table known as the Commissioners 1958 Standard Ordinary (CSO) Mortality Table. In 2001, the NAIC approved a new Standard Ordinary Mortality Table that separated the experience by gender. Since then, the tables have been modified to include preferred and standard lives. Preferred would be someone with better health habits (nonsmoker, not overweight, etc.)

HOW LONG WILL YOU LIVE?

No one really knows how long a particular person will live. But life expectancy in the United States has been steadily increasing since 1900. One major reason for the increase

EXHIBIT 12-2 Life expectancy tables, all races, 2018

This table helps insurance companies determine insurance premiums. *Use the table to find the average number of additional years a 25-year-old male and female are expected to live.*

Expectation of Life in Years				Expectation of Life in Years		
Age	Male	Female		Age	Male	Female
0	76.2	81.2		50	29.9	33.5
1	75.7	80.7		55	25.7	29.0
5	71.8	76.7		60	21.8	24.8
10	66.8	71.8		65	18.1	20.7
15	61.9	66.8		70	14.6	16.8
20	57.1	61.9		75	11.3	13.1
25	52.4	57.0		80	8.4	9.8
30	47.8	52.2		85	6.0	7.0
35	43.3	47.5		90	4.1	4.8
40	38.7	42.7		95	2.8	3.2
45	34.2	38.1		100	2.0	2.2

Source: CDC/NCHS, "National Vital Statistics Report," *Volume 69, Number 12, United States Life Tables, 2018,* November 17, 2020, p. 3, accessed at www.cdc.gov/nchs/fastats/life-expectancy.htm, accessed February 25, 2021.

is constantly improving medical care as well as overall knowledge of ways to have a healthier lifestyle. The fact remains, however, that the number of years that you have already lived is the biggest factor in determining how many years you have remaining. Historically, women have outlived men. For example, in 1900 the life expectancy of a man was 46.3 years and of a woman 48.3 years. By 2018, life expectancy had increased to 76.2 years for males and 81.2 for females. Further, projections now indicate that by 2050, life expectancy will increase to 80 for males and 83 for females. Exhibit 12-2 shows the most recent life expectancy table, issued in 2020 by the Centers for Disease Control and Prevention. The life expectancy shown does not indicate the age at which a person has the highest probability of dying. For example, the exhibit shows that the additional years of life expectancy of a female at age 25 is 57 years. This does not mean 25-year-old females will probably die at age 82 years. It means 57 is the average number of additional years females alive at age 25 may expect to live.

 PRACTICE QUIZ 12-1

1. How can the internet help you create a life insurance plan?
2. What is the purpose of life insurance?
3. What is the principle of life insurance?
4. What do life expectancy tables indicate?

Determining Your Life Insurance Needs

LO12-2

Determine your life insurance needs.

You should consider a number of factors before you buy life insurance. These factors include your present and future sources of income, other savings and income protection, group life insurance, group annuities (or other pension benefits), net worth, and Social Security. First, however, you should determine whether you *need* life insurance.

EVALUATING YOUR NEED FOR LIFE INSURANCE

If your death would cause financial stress for your spouse, children, parents, or anyone else you want to protect, you should consider purchasing life insurance. Your stage in the life cycle and the type of household you live in will influence this decision. Single persons living alone or with their parents usually have little or no need for life insurance. Consider Brian Reynolds, 28, a bachelor who does not smoke, is in excellent health, and has no dependents. Brian owns a $100,000 condominium with a $90,000 mortgage. Since his employer provides a $100,000 group term life policy, he needs no additional life insurance. Larry Lucas, 32, and his wife, Liz, 30, are professionals, each earning $45,000 a year. The Lucases have no dependents. This two-earner couple may have a moderate need for life insurance, especially if they have a mortgage or other large debts. Households with small children usually have the greatest need for life insurance.

DETERMINING YOUR LIFE INSURANCE OBJECTIVES

Before you consider types of life insurance policies, you must decide what you want your life insurance to do for you and your dependents.

- How much money do you want to leave to your dependents if you were to die today?
- Will you require more or less insurance protection to meet their needs as time goes on?
- When would you like to be able to retire?
- What amount of income do you believe you and your spouse would need in retirement?
- How much are you able to pay for your insurance program?
- Are the demands on your family budget for other living expenses likely to be greater or lower as time goes on?

When you have considered these questions and developed some approximate answers, you are ready to select the types and amounts of life insurance policies that will help you accomplish your objectives.

Once you have decided what you want your life insurance to accomplish, the next important decision is how much to buy. Exhibit 12-3 shows the average face amount of individual life insurance policies purchased in recent years.

ESTIMATING YOUR LIFE INSURANCE REQUIREMENTS

How much life insurance should you buy? This question is important for every person who owns or intends to purchase life insurance. Because of the various factors involved, the question

my life | **2**

I am aware of several general methods for determining the amount of life insurance I may need now or in the future.

The most difficult part of buying life insurance is determining how much you need. But with some effort you can come up with a good estimate that takes into account your specific financial situation. Visit various insurance needs calculators online, including the nonprofit Life and Health Insurance Foundation at www.lifehappens.org. The average insured adult American has about $163,000 in life insurance coverage, or about three times his or her gross annual income.[2]

EXHIBIT 12-3 Average face amount of individual life insurance policies purchased

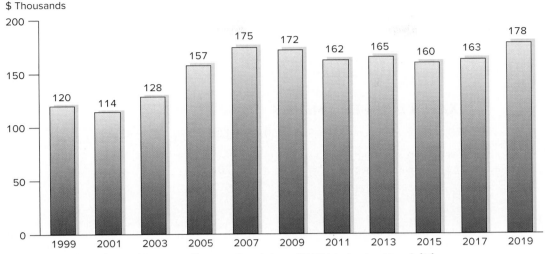

$ Thousands

Source: ACLI tabulation of National Association of Insurance Commissioners (NAIC) data. American Council of Life Insurers, 2020 Fact Book, Fig. 7.2, p. 93, accessed February 27, 2021.

cannot be answered by mathematics alone. Nevertheless, an insurance policy puts a price on the life of the insured person. Therefore, methods are needed to estimate what that price should be.

There are many general methods for determining the amount of insurance you may need. We will provide six; including the multiple of income method, the easy method, the DINK method, the "nonworking" spouse method, the "family need" method, and online calculators.

THE MULTIPLE OF INCOME METHOD   The multiple of income method uses your annual income as the sole factor. The method identifies your insurance needs as a range between five and ten times your income. This is one of the most basic methods to calculate, but it does leave out quite a few important factors. For example, family size, current assets, living expenses, and expected additional sources of income are excluded from the calculation.

EXAMPLE: The Multiple of Income Method

Low: $50,000 current income × 5 = $250,000

Your figures:
$_____ current income × 5 = $_____

High: $50,000 current income × 10 = $500,000

Your figures:
$_____ current income × 10 = $_____

This method assumes that you are looking for a basic benchmark to determine your insurance needs.

THE EASY METHOD   The easy method is based on the multiple of income method, but with a slight modification. Simple as this method is, it is remarkably useful. It uses the insurance agent's rule of thumb that a "typical family" will need approximately 70 percent of your salary for seven years before they adjust to the financial consequences of your death. In other words, for a simple estimate of your life insurance needs, just multiply your current gross income by 7 (7 years) and 0.70 (70 percent). For example:

EXAMPLE: The Easy Method

$50,000 current income × 7 = $350,000; $350,000 × 0.70 = $245,000

Your figures:

$_____ current income × 7 = $_____ × 0.70 = $_____

This method assumes your family is "typical." You may need more insurance if you have four or more children, if you have above-average family debt, if any member of your family suffers from poor health, or if your spouse has poor employment potential. On the other hand, you may need less insurance if your family is smaller.

THE DINK (DUAL INCOME, NO KIDS) METHOD   If you have no dependents and you and your spouse have similar income levels, you have simple insurance needs. All you need to do is ensure that your spouse will not be unduly burdened by debts should you die. The insurance needs cover one-half of the family debt, plus estimated funeral expenses. Here is an example of the DINK method.

EXAMPLE: The DINK Method

	Example	Your Figures
Funeral expenses (estimated)	$ 5,000	$_____
One-half of mortgage	55,000	_____
One-half of auto loan	10,000	_____
One-half of credit card balance	2,000	_____
One-half of personal debt	1,000	_____
Other debts	1,000	_____
	_____	_____
Total insurance needs	$74,000	$_____

This method assumes your spouse will continue to work after your death. If your spouse suffers poor health or is employed in an occupation with an uncertain future, you should consider adding an insurance cushion to see him or her through hard times.

THE "NONWORKING" SPOUSE METHOD   Insurance experts have estimated that extra costs of up to $10,000 a year may be required to replace the services of a homemaker in a family with small children. These extra costs may include the cost of a housekeeper, child care, more meals out, transportation, laundry services, and so on.

They do not include the lost potential earnings of the surviving spouse, who often must take time away from the job to care for the family.

To estimate how much life insurance a homemaker should carry, multiply the number of years before the youngest child reaches age 18 by $10,000. For example:

EXAMPLE: The "Nonworking" Spouse Method

7 years (years before the youngest child is 18) × $10,000 = $70,000

Your figures:
_____ years × $10,000 = $_____

If there are teenage children, the $10,000 figure can be reduced. If there are more than two children under age 13, or anyone in the family suffers poor health or has special needs, the $10,000 figure should be adjusted upward. Also, be aware that the $10,000 figure can vary greatly based upon recent estimates of the nonworking spouse's duties and proposed wages as reported in the nearby *Smart Money Minute* box.

smart money minute

According to a survey by Salary.com, stay-at-home moms should have an equivalent annual wage of $178,201 in 2019, an increase of 9.6 percent from the prior year.

Source: "How much is a mother really worth?" Salary.com (www .salary.com/articles/mother-salary/), accessed February 25, 2021.

THE "FAMILY NEED" METHOD The first four methods assume you and your family are "typical" and ignore important factors such as Social Security and your liquid assets. Exhibit 12-4 provides a detailed worksheet for making a thorough estimation of your life insurance needs.

Although this method is quite thorough, you may believe it does not address all of your special needs. If so, you should obtain further advice from an insurance expert or a financial planner.

As you determine your life insurance needs, don't forget to consider the life insurance you may already have. You may have ample coverage through your employer and through any mortgage and credit life insurance you have purchased.

In our dynamic economy, inflation and interest rates change often. Therefore, experts recommend that you reevaluate your insurance coverage every two years. Also, be sure to update your insurance whenever your situation changes substantially. For example, the birth of another child, an increase in your home mortgage, or the needs of an aging parent can boost your insurance needs.

ONLINE CALCULATORS AND APPS

There are numerous online calculators that can provide estimates of insurance needs. Many of the premier financial websites offer life insurance estimators. These may provide a slightly more impartial view of your insurance needs versus using an online calculator via an insurance company website.

Here are some helpful websites with online calculators:

- http://www.bankrate.com/calculators/insurance/life-insurance-calculator.aspx
- https://www.calcxml.com/calculators/life-insurance-calculator
- www.nerdwallet.com/life-insurance

Life insurance estimators on insurance company websites can also be used as a comparison. However, remember that these will typically provide a higher estimate of insurance needs. Thus, the higher the estimate, the higher the premium and commission for the agent.

EXHIBIT 12-4 The "family need" method worksheet to calculate your life insurance needs

What you have now (A)	
Bank accounts	+$_____
Taxable investments and savings, other than your home and other real estate	+$_____
Real estate you own other than your primary residence	+$_____
Individual life insurance policies	+$_____
Group life insurance policies	+$_____
Total of what you have now	= A $_____

What your dependents may need (B)	
Debt and expenses due at your death	
Funeral and burial expenses	+$_____
Final income taxes	+$_____
Estate probate and administration costs	+$_____
Mortgages and loans not covered by insurance	+$_____
Credit card debt	+$_____
Subtotal	$_____
Living expenses	
75% of your total family income (before tax) × the number of years your dependents will need it	+$_____
Emergency fund (3 to 6 months of income)	+$_____
Children's education	
Average annual potential cost × average number of years in college × number of children	+$_____
Total of what your dependents may need	= B $_____

Total of what your dependents may need (B)	B $_____
Total of what you have now (A)	−A $_____
How much estimated life insurance you need (B − A)	= C $_____

If C is **positive,** you may need *more* life insurance.

If C is **negative** *and* your estimates are realistic, your dependents may be able to manage without additional life insurance.

Source: *TIAA-CREF Life Insurance Company*, "Four Step Guide to Life Insurance," September 2017, p. 6.

Apps can also be handy for calculating insurance needs. There are many apps on the market and more are being added each day.

Here are some of the more popular apps today:

- *Life Happens*
- *Fabric*
- *Tomorrow*
- *Lemonade Insurance*

PFP Sheet 53
Life Insurance

PRACTICE QUIZ 12-2

1. How do you evaluate the need for life insurance?
2. What determines your life insurance objectives?
3. What are the six methods of estimating your life insurance requirements?

Types of Life Insurance Companies and Policies

TYPES OF LIFE INSURANCE COMPANIES

You can purchase the new or extra life insurance you need from two types of life insurance companies: stock life insurance companies, owned by shareholders, and mutual life insurance companies, owned by their policyholders. About 85 percent of U.S. life insurance companies are stock companies, and about 15 percent are mutuals.[3]

Stock companies generally sell **nonparticipating** (or *nonpar*) policies, while mutual companies specialize in the sale of **participating** (or *par*) policies. A participating policy has a somewhat higher premium than a nonparticipating policy, but a part of the premium is refunded to the policyholder annually. This refund is called the *policy dividend.*

There has been long and inconclusive debate about whether stock companies or mutual companies offer less expensive life insurance. You should check with both stock and mutual companies to determine which type offers the best policy for your particular needs at the lowest price.

If you wish to pay exactly the same premium each year, you should choose a nonparticipating policy with its guaranteed premiums. Indeed, about 70 percent of individual life insurance policies purchased recently were nonparticipating. However, you may prefer life insurance whose annual price reflects the company's experience with its investments, the health of its policyholders, and its general operating costs, that is, a participating policy.

Nevertheless, as with other forms of insurance, price should not be your only consideration in choosing a life insurance policy. You should consider the financial stability, reliability, and service the insurance company provides. Currently about 800 insurance companies in the United States sell life insurance.[4]

TYPES OF LIFE INSURANCE POLICIES

Both mutual insurance companies and stock insurance companies sell two basic types of life insurance: temporary and permanent insurance. Temporary insurance can be term, renewable term, convertible term, or decreasing term insurance. Permanent insurance is known by different names, including *whole life, straight life, ordinary life,* and *cash value life insurance.* As you will learn in the next section, permanent insurance can be limited payment, variable, adjustable, or universal life insurance. Other types of insurance policies—group life and credit life insurance—are generally temporary forms of insurance. Exhibit 12-5 shows the major types and subtypes of life insurance.

TERM LIFE INSURANCE

Term insurance is protection for a specified period of time, usually 1, 5, 10, or 20 years or up to age 95, which would have a significant cost. A term insurance policy pays a benefit only if you die during the period it covers. If you stop paying the premiums, the insurance stops. Term insurance is therefore sometimes called *temporary life insurance.*

LO12-3

Distinguish between the types of life insurance companies and analyze various types of life insurance policies.

nonparticipating policy Life insurance that does not provide policy dividends; also called a *nonpar policy.*

participating policy Life insurance that provides policy dividends; also called a *par policy.*

term insurance Life insurance protection for a specified period of time; sometimes called *temporary life insurance.*

EXHIBIT 12-5

Major types and subtypes of life insurance

Term (temporary)	Whole (permanent)	Other Types
• Renewable term	• Limited payment	• Group life
• Multiyear level term	• Single premium	• Credit life
• Convertible term	• Modified life	• Endowment life
• Decreasing term	• Variable life	
• Return of premium	• Adjustable life	
• Re-entry term	• Universal life	

smart money minute

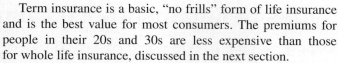

According to LIMRA, consumers overestimate the cost of insurance, which reduces the chances they will buy a policy due to perceived cost.

my life 3

Although term life insurance premiums increase as I get older, I can reduce my coverage as my children grow up and my assets increase.

Term insurance makes the most sense when your need for it is going to diminish in the future, such as when your children graduate from college or when a debt is paid off. Typically, term insurance offers the greatest amount of coverage for the lowest initial premium and is a good choice for young families on a tight budget.

Term insurance is a basic, "no frills" form of life insurance and is the best value for most consumers. The premiums for people in their 20s and 30s are less expensive than those for whole life insurance, discussed in the next section.

You need insurance coverage most while you are raising young children. Although term life insurance premiums increase as you get older, you can reduce your coverage as your children grow up and your assets (the value of your savings, investments, home, autos, etc.) increase.

Here are various options in choosing your term insurance.

RENEWABILITY OPTION The coverage of term insurance ends at the conclusion of the term, but you can continue it for another term if you have a renewability option. For example, many term insurance policies are renewable at your option for successive five-year periods to age 70 without medical reexamination. The premiums will increase every five years when you renew the policy, then remain level during each five-year period.

MULTIYEAR LEVEL TERM (OR STRAIGHT TERM) *Multiyear level term life* is a very popular type of policy. It has become popular because the policyholder pays the same premium amount for the life of the policy. This makes it much easier to budget for insurance needs. Most recently, 68 percent of the individual life insurance policies issued were level term.[5] One form of multiyear level term is *Term to 65* life insurance. Coverage expires at age 65, or sooner if the death benefit is paid.

CONVERSION OPTION If you have convertible term insurance, you can exchange it for a whole life policy without a medical examination and at a higher premium. The premium for the whole life policy stays the same for the rest of your life. Consider this option if you want cash-value life insurance and can't afford it now but expect to be able to do so in the future.

DECREASING TERM INSURANCE Term insurance is also available in a form that pays less to the beneficiary as time passes. The premiums will typically remain constant, while the payout amount of the insurance will decrease. This type of insurance was originally designed to be paired with a debt repayment, such as a mortgage on a home. For example, a decreasing term contract for 30 years might be appropriate as coverage of a mortgage loan balance on a house, because the coverage will decrease as the balance on the mortgage decreases. The insurance period you select might depend on your age, the term of the debt, or other assets that you currently own. Decreasing term insurance will help keep the premiums at a constant amount and, therefore, not be subjected to dramatic increases due to the age of the policyholder. You could get the same result by purchasing annual renewable term policies of diminishing amounts during the period of the mortgage loan. Additionally, an annual renewable policy would offer more flexibility to change coverage if you were to sell or remortgage the house.

RETURN OF PREMIUM Return-of-premium (ROP), or money-back, term policies refund every penny you paid in premiums if you outlive the 15-, 20-, or 30-year term of the policy. However, ROP policies cost 30 percent to 50 percent more than traditional term life. Does an ROP policy make sense for you? Read the *Financial Literacy for My Life: Return-of-Premium Policies* feature.

RE-ENTRY TERM INSURANCE Re-entry term insurance is highly desirable for healthy people who would like reduced rates on term insurance. In exchange for

RETURN-OF-PREMIUM POLICIES

Many people may believe that life insurance policies are a waste of money. If you don't end up needing it, you've thrown the money away; if you do need it, well, . . . you're dead, so you don't personally see the payments. To combat this attitude and indifference to having insurance, many insurance companies now offer return-of-premium (ROP), or money-back, term policies. These policies refund every penny paid in premiums if you outlive the term of the policy.

For those of you who think there has to be a catch, your instincts are correct. According to PolicyGenius, these policies cost more—some 30 percent more—than traditional term life. A healthy 30-year-old man might pay $387 annually for a basic $500,000, 30-year term policy versus $510 for one with the ROP feature. You can get policies for a shorter term, but they cost so much more per year—sometimes six or seven times as much—that many financial advisors would discourage buying them. Not all insurance companies offer these policies, but some big players in the industry certainly do, including AIG, Anico, Mutual of Omaha, and Prudential.

Does an ROP policy make sense for you? Carol Marie Cropper at *Bloomberg BusinessWeek* advises that it "depends on your answer to two questions: Would you earn more buying a cheaper term policy and investing the savings? Are you likely to cancel before the 30 (or however many) years are up?"

One key thing to remember: You get a return on your policy, but *only* if you pay the premiums for the entire term. If you drop the policy before, as most buyers of term life do, you'll get less, or perhaps nothing, in return. This is the way that companies make money on these policies. If you think about signing up, you'll want to take this into consideration.

If you've decided to use insurance as a part of your investment portfolio, you should look at all types of policies. Some may cost even more than these ROP policies, but because they pay interest or dividends or allow you to invest in mutual funds, they have the potential for higher returns. You should invest in whatever best fits your personal investment portfolio and strategy.

periodic good medical examinations, you can renew these policies at a lower rate than unhealthy people in the same age category. Eventually, however, age-related issues will probably impede renewal at the preferred rates.

If you want to compare rates and avoid a high-pressure pitch for permanent insurance, contact a low-load, no-commission insurer. One life insurance advisor recommends either USAA Life & Health Insurance Company (1-800-531-8000) or Ameritas Life Insurance Corporation (1-800-552-3553); both give quotes over the phone.

WHOLE LIFE INSURANCE

The most common type of permanent life insurance is the **whole life policy** (also called a *straight life policy,* a *cash-value life policy,* or an *ordinary life policy*), for which you pay a specified premium each year for as long as you live. In return, the insurance company promises to pay a stipulated sum to the beneficiary when you die. The amount of your premium depends primarily on the age at which you purchase the insurance.

One important feature of the whole life policy is its cash value. **Cash value** (or *cash surrender value*) is an amount, which increases each year, that you receive if you give up the insurance. Hence, cash-value policies provide a death benefit *and* a savings account. Insurance salespeople often emphasize the "forced savings" aspect of cash-value insurance. A table in the whole life policy enables you to tell exactly how much cash value the policy has at any given time (see Exhibit 12-6).

Cash-value policies may make sense for people who intend to keep the policies for the long term or for people who must be forced to save. But you should not have too low a death benefit just because you would like the savings component of a cash-value life policy. Experts suggest that you explore other savings and investment strategies before investing your money in a permanent life insurance policy.

The insurance company accumulates a substantial reserve during the early years of the whole life policy to pay the benefits in the later years, when your chances of dying are greater. At first, the annual premium for whole life insurance is higher than that for term insurance. However, the premium for a whole life policy remains constant throughout your lifetime, whereas the premium for a term policy increases with each renewal.

whole life policy An insurance plan in which the policyholder pays a specified premium each year for as long as he or she lives; also called a *straight life policy, cash-value life policy,* or *ordinary life policy.*

cash value The amount received after giving up a life insurance policy.

EXHIBIT 12-6

An example of guaranteed cash value

Plan and Additional Benefits	Amount	Premium	Years Payable
Whole life (premiums payable to age 90)	$10,000	$229.50	55
Waiver of premium (to age 65)		4.30	30
Accidental death (to age 70)	10,000	7.80	35

A premium is payable on the policy date and every 12 policy months thereafter. The first premium is $241.60.

Explanation for Table of Guaranteed Values: To cancel the policy in the 10th year, the insured would get $1,719 in savings (cash value). He or she could use the $1,719 to purchase a $3,690 paid-up life policy or purchase an extended term policy that would be in effect for 19 years and 78 days.

Table of Guaranteed Values

End of Policy Year	Cash or Loan Value	Paid-up Insurance	Extended Term Insurance	
			Years	Days
1	$ 14	$ 30	0	152
2	174	450	4	182
3	338	860	8	65
4	506	1,250	10	344
5	676	1,640	12	360
6	879	2,070	14	335
7	1,084	2,500	16	147
8	1,293	2,910	17	207
9	1,504	3,300	18	177
10	1,719	3,690	19	78
11	1,908	4,000	19	209
12	2,099	4,300	19	306
13	2,294	4,590	20	8
14	2,490	4,870	20	47
15	2,690	5,140	20	65
16	2,891	5,410	20	66
17	3,095	5,660	20	52
18	3,301	5,910	20	27
19	3,508	6,150	19	358
20	3,718	6,390	19	317
60	4,620	7,200	18	111
Age 65	5,504	7,860	16	147

Paid-up additions and dividend accumulations increase the cash values; indebtedness decreases them.

Direct Beneficiary: Helen M. Benson, wife of the insured
Owner: Thomas A. Benson, the insured
Insured: Thomas A. Benson
Policy Date: November 1, 2021
Date of Issue: November 1, 2021

Age and Sex: 37 Male
Policy Number: 000/00

Source: Sample Life Insurance Policy (Washington, DC: American Council of Life Insurance, n.d.), p. 2.

Financial Literacy for My Life

LIFE INSURANCE CLASSIFICATIONS

Your premium can vary widely based upon your overall health when applying for life insurance. Medical history, a physical exam, and a blood test may be required. Here is a listing of some of the guidelines for a preferred classification (the lowest rates):

Blood Pressure: May not exceed 140/90. Someone with 150/90 can qualify for standard rates.

High Cholesterol: 220 mg/dL or less with medication. 300–350 mg/dL may qualify for standard rates.

Anxiety: If the anxiety is managed by one medication prescribed by a primary care physician, the applicant will typically qualify for preferred status.

Obesity: BMI (body mass index) is the most common metric used. BMI of 26–28 can typically qualify for the best rates. BMI of 35–38 or higher will usually be classified for standard rates.

Acid Reflux: The risk with acid reflux is that it can lead to ulcers or even cancer. If mild to moderate reflux is treated with over-the-counter medications or prescriptions, preferred rates may still be available. More severe cases may qualify for standard rates.

Source: www.lifehappens.org.

Several types of whole life insurance have been developed to meet different objectives. A few of the more popular types are discussed next.

LIMITED PAYMENT POLICY   One type of whole life policy is called the *limited payment policy*. With this plan, you pay premiums for a stipulated period, usually 20 or 30 years, or until you reach a specified age, such as 60 or 65 (unless your death occurs earlier). Your policy then becomes "paid up," and you remain insured for life. The company will pay the face amount of the policy at your death. Because the premium payment period for a limited payment policy is shorter than that for a whole life policy, the annual premium is higher. For example, recently, a 25-year-old female in excellent health buying a $100,000, 10-year life policy would pay $144.25 per month. The same $100,000 policy would cost $99.88 per month for a 20-year payment option. These rates could be significantly higher depending upon her health classification. How do you qualify for preferred risk rates? See the *Financial Literacy for My Life: Life Insurance Classifications* feature.

A special form of the limited payment plan is the single-premium policy. In this type of contract, you make only one very large premium payment.

MODIFIED LIFE INSURANCE POLICY   Modified life insurance policies are attractive to people who want whole life policies, but find the premiums too high to handle on their current budget. They typically allow lower premiums for 5 to 10 years and then the premiums will increase significantly for the remainder of the life of the insured. Make sure that you think your budget will be able to handle the future increase.

VARIABLE LIFE INSURANCE POLICY   The cash values of a *variable life* insurance policy fluctuate according to the yields earned by a separate fund, which can be a stock fund, a money market fund, or a bond fund. A minimum death benefit is guaranteed, but the death benefit can rise above that minimum depending on the earnings of the dollars invested in the separate fund. Hence, policyholders, not insurance companies, assume the investment risk. The premium payments for a variable life policy are fixed.

When you purchase a variable life policy, you assume the risk of poor investment performance. Therefore, the cash value of a variable life policy is not guaranteed. Life insurance agents selling variable life policies must be registered representatives of a broker-dealer licensed by the National Association of Securities Dealers and registered with the Securities and Exchange Commission. If you are interested in a variable life policy, be sure your agent gives you a prospectus that includes an extensive disclosure about the policy.

ADJUSTABLE LIFE INSURANCE POLICY (OR FLEXIBLE PREMIUM ADJUSTABLE LIFE INSURANCE)   The *adjustable life* insurance policy is another relatively recent type of whole life insurance. You can change such a policy as your needs change. For example, if you want to increase or decrease your coverage, you can change either the premium payments or the period of coverage.

universal life A whole life policy that combines term insurance and investment elements.

UNIVERSAL LIFE   Subject to certain minimums, **universal life** insurance, first introduced in 1979, has a minimum amount that must be paid to cover the insurance portion. The amount of insurance can be changed more easily in a universal life policy than in a traditional policy. Additional contributions can be added to the cash value account. The cash value account is invested in short-term investments. Thus, the universal life policy clearly combines some elements of term insurance with an investment option.

Like the details of other types of policies, the details of universal life policies vary from company to company. The key distinguishing features of universal life policies are explicit, separate accounting reports to policyholders of (1) the charges for the insurance element, (2) the charges for company expenses (commissions, policy fees, etc.), and (3) the rate of return on the investment (cash value) of the policy. The rate of return is flexible; it is guaranteed to be not less than a certain amount (usually 2 percent), but it may be more, depending on the insurance company's decision.

What are the differences between universal life and whole life insurance? While both policy types have cash value, universal life gives you more direct control. With universal life, you control your outlay and can change your premium without changing your coverage. Whole life, in contrast, requires you to pay a specific premium every year, or the policy will lapse. Universal life allows you access to your cash value by a policy loan or withdrawal. Whole life allows only for policy loans.

Because your primary reason for buying a life insurance policy is the insurance component, the cost of that component should be your main consideration. Thus, universal life policies that offer a high rate of return on the cash value but charge a high price for the insurance element generally should be avoided.

Over the years, many variations on term and whole life insurance have been developed. The details of these policies may differ among companies. Therefore, check with individual companies to determine the best policy for your needs. Exhibit 12-7 compares some important features of term, whole life, and universal life policies.

OTHER TYPES OF LIFE INSURANCE POLICIES

GROUP LIFE INSURANCE   In recent decades, *group life insurance* has grown in popularity. A group insurance plan insures a large number of persons under the terms of a single policy without requiring medical examinations. In general, the principles that apply to other forms of insurance also apply to group insurance.

Fundamentally, group insurance is term insurance, which was described earlier. Usually the cost of group insurance is split between an employer and the employees so that the cost of insurance per $1,000 is the same for each employee, regardless of age. For older employees, the employer pays a larger portion of the costs of the group policy.

However, group life insurance is not always a good deal. Insurance advisors offer countless stories about employer-sponsored plans, or group plans offered through professional associations, offering coverage that costs 20, 50, or even 100 percent more than policies their clients could buy on the open market.

ENDOWMENT LIFE INSURANCE   *Endowment life insurance* provides coverage from the beginning of the contract to maturity and guarantees payment of a specified sum to the insured, even if he or she is still living at the end of the endowment period.

EXHIBIT 12-7 Comparing the major types of life insurance

	Term Life	Whole Life	Universal Life
Premium	Lower initially, increasing with each renewal.	Higher initially than term; normally doesn't increase.	Flexible premiums, after minimum cost of insurance.
Protects for	A specified period.	Entire life if you keep the policy.	A flexible time period.
Policy benefits	Death benefits only.	Death benefits and eventually a cash and loan value.	Death benefits and potentially a cash and loan value.
Advantages	Low outlay. Initially, you can purchase a larger amount of coverage for a lower premium.	Helps you with financial discipline. Generally fixed premium amount. Cash value accumulation. You can take loan against policy.	More flexibility. Takes advantages of current interest rates. Offers the possibility of improved mortality rates (increased life expectancy because of advancements in medicine, which may lower policy costs).
Disadvantages	Premium increases with age. No cash value.	Costly if you surrender early. Usually no cash value for at least three to five years. May not meet short-term needs.	Same as whole life. Greater risks due to program flexibility. Low interest rates can affect cash value and premiums.
Options	May be renewable or convertible to a whole life policy.	May pay dividends. May provide a reduced paid-up policy. Partial cash surrenders permitted.	May pay dividends. Minimum death benefit. Partial cash surrenders permitted.

The face value of the policy is paid to beneficiaries upon the death of the insured. The endowment period typically has a duration of 10 to 20 years or the attainment of a specified age. Recently, these types of insurance policies have been used as a way to save for college for beneficiaries. The guaranteed payout will be paid at a specified time as determined at the start of the policy. Should the insured die, the beneficiary will receive a death benefit for the face value of the policy. Either way, the beneficiary will have money for college.

personal fintech

Using a website or an app, calculate the amount and the cost of life insurance for you or a family member.

CREDIT LIFE INSURANCE *Credit life insurance* is used to repay a personal debt should the borrower die before doing so. It is based on the belief that "no person's debts should live after him or her." It was introduced in the United States in 1917, when installment financing and purchasing became popular.

Credit life insurance policies for auto loans and home mortgages are not the best buy for the protection they offer. Instead, buy less expensive decreasing term insurance, discussed earlier. In fact, some experts claim that credit life insurance policies are the nation's biggest ripoff.

Exhibit 12-8 shows the growth of individual and group life insurance in the United States.

EXHIBIT 12-8 Growth of individual, group, and credit life insurance in force in the United States

By the end of 2019, total life insurance coverage in the United States reached $19.8 trillion. Most group life insurance contracts are issued to employers, though many are issued to unions, professional associations, and other groups.

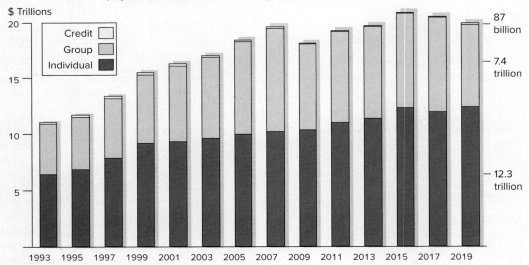

Note: NAIC does not endorse any analysis or conclusions based on use of its data. Data represent U.S. life insurers and, as of 2003, fraternal benefit societies.
Source: ACLI tabulations of National Association of Insurance Commissioners (NAIC) data. *American Council of Life Insurers, 2020 Life Insurers Fact Book, Fig. 7.1, p. 92,* https://www.acli.com/Tools/Industry%20Facts/Life%20Insurers%20Fact%20Book/Documents/FB15_Chapter7_LI.pdf, accessed February 27, 2021.

INDUSTRIAL LIFE INSURANCE   With industrial life insurance policies, also known as home service or debit insurance, agents collect weekly, bimonthly, or monthly premiums. Industrial life insurance is the least popular form, and its appeal continues to drop rapidly.

 **PRACTICE QUIZ 12-3**

1. What are the two types of life insurance companies?
2. What are the major types and subtypes of life insurance?
3. What are the main differences between whole life and term policies?

Important Provisions in a Life Insurance Contract

LO12-4

Select important provisions in life insurance contracts.

Life insurance policies today contain numerous provisions whose terminology can be confusing. Therefore, an understanding of these provisions is very important for the insurance buyer.

Your life insurance policy is valuable only if it meets your objectives. When your objectives change, however, it may not be necessary to change or give up the policy. Study the policy carefully and discuss its provisions with your agent. Following are some of the most common provisions.

PAYMENTS TO LIFE INSURANCE POLICIES

A policyholder must ensure that premiums are paid to keep the policy in effect. There are certain provisions that involve how these payments can be made.

POLICY REINSTATEMENT   A lapsed policy can be put back in force, or reinstated, if it has not been turned in for cash. To reinstate the policy, you must again qualify as an acceptable risk, and you must pay overdue premiums with interest. There is a time limit on reinstatement, usually one or two years.

THE GRACE PERIOD   When you buy a life insurance policy, the insurance company agrees to pay a certain sum of money under specified circumstances and you agree to pay a certain premium regularly. The *grace period* allows 28 to 31 days to elapse, during which time you may pay the premium without penalty. After that time, the policy lapses if you have not paid the premium.

AUTOMATIC PREMIUM LOAN   With an automatic premium loan option, if you do not pay the premium within the grace period, the insurance company automatically pays it out of the policy's cash value if that cash value is sufficient in your whole life policy. This prevents you from inadvertently allowing the policy to lapse.

GUARANTEED INSURABILITY OPTION   This option allows you to buy specified additional amounts of life insurance at stated intervals without proof of insurability. Thus, even if you do not remain in good health, you can increase the amount of your insurance as your income rises. This option is desirable if you anticipate the need for additional life insurance in the future.

CLAUSES IN LIFE INSURANCE POLICIES

A policyholder must review the policy carefully for certain clauses. Many clauses are designed to protect the insured and their beneficiaries.

NONFORFEITURE CLAUSE   One important feature of a whole life policy is the **nonforfeiture clause**. This provision prevents the forfeiture of accrued benefits if you choose to drop the policy. For example, if you decide not to continue paying premiums, you can exercise specified options with your cash value. (See Exhibit 12-6 for cash value example.)

INCONTESTABILITY CLAUSE   The **incontestability clause** stipulates that after the policy has been in force for a specified period (usually two years), the insurance company cannot dispute its validity during the lifetime of the insured for any reason, including fraud. One reason for this provision is that the beneficiaries, who cannot defend the company's contesting of the claim, should not be forced to suffer because of the acts of the insured.

SUICIDE CLAUSE   The **suicide clause** provides that if the insured dies by suicide during the first two years the policy is in force, the death benefit will equal the amount of the premium paid. Generally, after two years, the suicide becomes a risk covered by the policy, and the beneficiaries of a suicide receive the same benefit that is payable for death from any other cause.

PAYMENTS FROM LIFE INSURANCE POLICIES

These provisions specify circumstances that relate to how payments are made on your policy.

nonforfeiture clause A provision that allows the insured not to forfeit all accrued benefits.

incontestability clause A provision stating that the insurer cannot dispute the validity of a policy after a specified period.

suicide clause A provision stating that if the insured dies by suicide during the first two years the policy is in force, the death benefit will equal the amount of the premium paid.

beneficiary A person designated to receive something, such as life insurance proceeds, from the insured.

NAMING YOUR BENEFICIARY   An important provision in every life insurance policy is the right to name your beneficiary. A **beneficiary** is a person who is designated to receive something, such as life insurance proceeds, from the insured. In your policy, you can name one or more persons as contingent beneficiaries who will receive your policy proceeds if the primary beneficiary dies at the same time or before you do.

MISSTATEMENT OF AGE PROVISION   The misstatement of age provision says that if the company finds out that your age was incorrectly stated, it will pay the benefits your premiums would have bought if your age had been correctly stated. The provision sets forth a simple procedure to resolve what could otherwise be a complicated legal matter.

my life **4**

An important provision in every life insurance policy is the right to name my beneficiary.

You decide who receives the benefits of your life insurance policy: your spouse, your child, or even your business partner. You can also name one or more contingent beneficiaries.

POLICY LOAN PROVISION   A loan from the insurance company is available on a whole life policy after the policy has been in force for a certain number of years, as stated in the policy. This feature, known as the *policy loan provision,* permits you to borrow any amount up to the cash value of the policy. However, a policy loan reduces the death benefit by the amount of the loan plus interest if the loan is not repaid.

JOINT LIFE OPTIONS   These policies seek to insure two lives, usually spouses. A *first-to-die life insurance* policy pays a death benefit upon death of the first spouse. This is usually intended to provide for the surviving spouse. A *second-to-die life insurance* policy, also called *survivorship life,* pays a death benefit when the second spouse dies. Usually a second-to-die policy is intended to pay estate taxes.

RIDERS TO LIFE INSURANCE POLICIES

rider A document attached to a policy that modifies its coverage.

An insurance company can change the provisions of a policy by attaching a rider to it. A **rider** is any document attached to the policy that modifies its coverage by adding or excluding specified conditions or altering its benefits. For instance, a whole life insurance policy may include a waiver of premium disability benefit, an accidental death benefit, or both.

smart money minute

The most common rider is waiver of premium. Nearly 98 percent of individual policies provide this option.

WAIVER OF PREMIUM DISABILITY BENEFIT   Under this provision, the company waives any premiums that are due after the onset of total and permanent disability. In effect, the company pays the premiums. The disability must occur before you reach a certain age, usually 60.

The waiver of premium rider is sometimes desirable. Don't buy it, however, if the added cost will prevent you from carrying needed basic life insurance. Some insurance companies include this rider automatically in all policies issued through age 55.

double indemnity A benefit under which the company pays twice the face value of the policy if the insured's death results from an accident.

ACCIDENTAL DEATH BENEFIT   Under this provision, the insurance company pays twice the face amount of the policy if the insured's death results from an accident. The accidental death benefit is often called **double indemnity**. Accidental death must occur within a certain time period after the injury, usually 90 days, and before the insured reaches a certain age, usually 60 or 65.

The accidental death benefit is expensive. Moreover, your chances of dying in the exact manner stated in the policy are very small, so the chances that your beneficiary will collect the double payment are also small.

COST-OF-LIVING PROTECTION   This special rider is designed to help prevent inflation from eroding the purchasing power of the protection your policy provides.

CALCULATING THE EFFECT OF INFLATION ON A LIFE INSURANCE POLICY

Inflation can be described as an increase in the cost of a variety of goods and services. This has the effect of reducing the amount of goods and services that we can buy in the future. Therefore, inflation reduces the purchasing power of a fixed amount of money. The chart below shows the effect that inflation at different percentages could have on $100,000. For example, if you were to purchase a $100,000 life insurance policy today and inflation averaged 3 percent over 10 years, the value of the goods and services your beneficiary would be able to purchase is $74,409.

Note: The calculations for time value of money can be used to calculate the amounts presented above.

Follow these steps to determine the effect that 2 percent inflation would have after five years:

1. Review Exhibit 1-A, Future Value of $1 after a Given Number of Time Periods.
2. Locate the table factor for 2 percent and five years. The factor is 1.104.
3. Divide the $100,000 original amount by the 1.104 table factor:

$$\$100,000/1.104 = \$90,580$$

Now, It's Your Turn. Using Exhibit 1-A, Future Value of $1 after a Given Number of Time Periods, calculate the purchasing power of $100,000 after 10 years assuming 2 percent inflation.

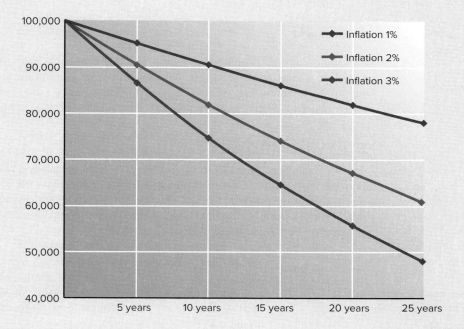

Answer: $82,034 ($100,000 / 1.219)

A *loss, reduction,* or *erosion of purchasing power* refers to the impact inflation has on a fixed amount of money. As inflation increases the costs of goods and services, that fixed amount will not buy as much in the future as it does today. The *Financial Literacy Calculations: Calculating the Effect of Inflation on a Life Insurance Policy* feature shows the effects of inflation on a $100,000 life insurance policy. However, your insurance needs are likely to be smaller in later years.

ACCELERATED BENEFITS *Accelerated benefits,* also known as *living benefits,* are life insurance policy proceeds paid to the terminally ill policyholder *before* he or she dies. The benefits may be provided for directly in the policies, but more often they are added by riders or attachments to new or existing policies. In most cases, the amount of the payout ranges between 25 and 95 percent of the death benefit. Any amounts paid out will reduce the death benefit that the beneficiary will receive upon the death of the insured.

National Life Insurance, John Hancock, and Columbus Life Insurance now sell a new life insurance policy with an accelerated benefits rider that promises to pay out all or part of the death benefit should you need it for long-term care.

Now that you know the various types of life insurance policies and the major provisions, including clauses, riders, and payment options, you are ready to make your buying decisions.

 PRACTICE QUIZ 12-4

1. What are the most common provisions in life insurance contracts?
2. What is a beneficiary?
3. What is a rider?
4. Describe the concept of double indemnity.

Buying Life Insurance

LO12-5

Create a plan to buy life insurance.

You should consider a number of factors before buying life insurance. As discussed earlier in this chapter, these factors include your present and future sources of income, other savings and income protection, group life insurance, group annuities (or other pension benefits), Social Security, and, of course, the financial strength of the company.

FROM WHOM TO BUY?

Look for insurance coverage from financially strong companies with professionally qualified representatives. It is not unusual for a relationship with an insurance company to extend over a period of 20, 30, or even 50 years. For that reason alone, you should choose carefully when deciding on an insurance company or an insurance agent. Fortunately, you have a choice of sources.

my life 5

The life insurance company I choose is essential to my beneficiaries' financial future.

Make sure that your insurance company and its agents are licensed in your state. Contact the National Association of Insurance Commissioners (NAIC) at 444 North Capitol St., NW, Washington, DC 20001, or visit www.naic.org. You can request several consumer protection and life insurance publications from the NAIC.

SOURCES   Protection is available from a wide range of private and public sources, including insurance companies, financial institutions and their representatives, and private groups such as employers, labor unions, and professional or fraternal organizations.

With life expectancies going up, life insurance rates should be coming down, right? That has been the case for over a decade, as term life premiums dropped by about half. But now the industry is tightening its guidelines, and that could spell a hike of 5 to 25 percent for many applicants. Some insurers are raising rates outright, says Bob Barney, president of Compulife Software, which provides rate comparisons. Others are simply making it harder to qualify for their best rate. Insurers are also getting pickier about cholesterol levels, family history of disease, even driving records, says Byron Udell, CEO of AccuQuote.

RATING INSURANCE COMPANIES   Some of the strongest, most reputable insurance companies in the nation provide excellent insurance coverage at reasonable costs. In fact, the financial strength of an insurance company may be a major factor in holding down premium costs for consumers.

Locate an insurance company by checking the reputations of local agencies. Ask members of your family, friends, or colleagues about the insurers they prefer.

EXHIBIT 12-9

Rating systems of major rating agencies
You should deal with companies rated superior or excellent.

	A. M. Best	Standard & Poor's, Duff & Phelps	Moody's	Weiss Research	Fitch Ratings
Superior	A + + A +	AAA	Aaa	A +	AAA
Excellent	A A−	AA + AA AA−	Aa1 Aa2 Aa3	A A− B +	AA + AA AA−
Good	B + + B +	A + A A−	A1 A2 A3	B B− C +	A + A A−
Adequate	B B−	BBB + BBB BBB−	Baa1 Baa2 Baa3	C C− D +	BBB + BBB BBB−
Below average	C + + C +	BB + BB BB−	Ba1 Ba2 Ba3	D D− E +	BB + BB BB−
Weak	C C− D	B + B B−	B1 B2 B3	E E−	B + B B−
Nonviable	E F	CCC CC C, D	Caa Ca C	F	CCC DD SR*

*Suspended rating.

For a more official review, consult *Best's Agents Guide* or *Best's Insurance Reports* at your public library or online at www.ambest.com. Exhibit 12-9 describes the rating systems used by A. M. Best and the other big four rating agencies. As a rule, you should deal with companies rated superior or excellent. In addition, *Consumer Reports, Kiplinger's Personal Finance,* and *Money* periodically provide satisfaction ratings on various types of insurance and insurance companies.

CHOOSING YOUR INSURANCE AGENT An insurance agent handles the technical side of insurance. However, that's only the beginning. The really important part of the agent's job is to apply his or her knowledge of insurance to help you select the proper kind of protection within your financial boundaries.

Not all agents are paid the same way. Some insurance companies, such as GEICO and USAA, use salaried agents. Firms such as Allstate and State Farm use primarily "captive agents," who may be salaried or paid on commission. Either way, they sell only those companies' policies. Independent agents represent multiple carriers and can offer more choices. They collect conventional commissions from insurance companies. Is one kind of agent better than another? In theory, independent agents have an edge because they're not limited to just one insurance company's products. But they may be tempted to direct consumers to companies that pay them the most. Truth is, you can get a good policy from any of the different types of insurance agents.

Choosing a good agent is among the most important steps in building your insurance program. How do you find an agent? One of the best ways to begin is by asking your parents, friends, neighbors, and others for their recommendations. However, note

		Yes	No
1.	Is your agent available when needed? Clients sometimes have problems that need immediate answers.	☐	☐
2.	Does your agent advise you to have a financial plan? Each part of the plan should be necessary to your overall financial protection.	☐	☐
3.	Does your agent pressure you? You should be free to make your own decisions about insurance coverage.	☐	☐
4.	Does your agent keep up with changes in the insurance field? Agents often attend special classes or study on their own so that they can serve their clients better.	☐	☐
5.	Is your agent happy to answer questions? Does he or she want you to know exactly what you are paying for with an insurance policy?	☐	☐

that you will seldom have the same agent all your life. The *How To* feature, "Choose an Insurance Agent," offers guidelines for choosing an insurance agent.

You may also want to investigate an agent's membership in professional groups. Agents who belong to a local Life Underwriters Association are often among the more experienced agents in their communities. A **chartered life underwriter (CLU)** is a life insurance agent who has passed a series of college-level examinations on insurance and related subjects. Such agents are entitled to use the designation CLU after their names. Other professional designations that life insurance agents may earn include life underwriter training council fellow (LUTCF), chartered financial consultant (ChFC), certified financial planner (CFP), financial services specialist (FSS), or member of the Registry of Financial Planning Practitioners. Agents who have passed a series of examinations on property and casualty insurance are designated as *chartered property and casualty underwriters* (CPCUs).

Once you have found an agent, you must decide which policy is right for you. The best way to do this is to talk to your agent, which does not obligate you to buy insurance.

COMPARING POLICY COSTS

Each life insurance company designs the policies it sells to make them attractive and useful to many policyholders. One policy may have features another policy doesn't; one company may be more selective than another company; one company may get a better return on its investments than another company. These and other factors affect the prices of life insurance policies.

In brief, five factors affect the price a company charges for a life insurance policy: the company's cost of doing business, the return on its investments, the mortality rate it expects among its policyholders, the features the policy contains, and competition among companies with comparable policies.

Underwriting uses many attributes of individuals such as age, gender, health, occupations, and even hobbies to determine the appropriate premiums to charge for

chartered life underwriter (CLU) A life insurance agent who has passed a series of college-level examinations on insurance and related subjects.

underwriting The process that insurance companies use to determine the premiums that will be charged and whom they will insure.

insurance. The work of underwriting is completed by actuaries. Actuaries help determine who will be a higher risk and whether they want to charge higher premiums or deny coverage. Actuaries use sophisticated statistical models to help them determine the chance of loss for the insurers.

The prices of life insurance policies therefore vary considerably among life insurance companies. Moreover, a particular company will not be equally competitive for all policies. Thus, one company might have a competitively priced policy for 24-year-olds but not for 35-year-olds.

Ask your agent to give you interest-adjusted indexes. An **interest-adjusted index** is a method of evaluating the cost of life insurance by taking into account the time value of money. Highly complex mathematical calculations and formulas combine premium payments, dividends, cash-value buildup, and present value analysis into an index number that makes possible a fairly accurate cost comparison among insurance companies. The lower the index number, the lower the cost of the policy. The Consumer Federation of America Insurance Group offers a computerized service for comparing policy costs. Visit them at www.consumerfed.org.

Price quote services offer convenient and free, no-obligation premium comparisons. Many life insurance companies provide free price quotes for term insurance. An agent will run your age, health status, and occupation through computer data banks covering about 650 different policies and send you the names of the five policies suitable for you and sold in your state. TermQuote in Dayton, Ohio, represents about 100 insurance companies, and Select Quote in San Francisco represents about 50 insurance companies. Here are the web addresses and telephone numbers of some price quote services.

- TermQuote (www.termquote.com)
- InstantQuote (www.instantquote.com)
- QuickQuote (www.quickquote.com)
- SelectQuote (www.selectquote.com)

These services are not always unbiased, since most sell life insurance themselves; they may recommend more coverage than you need. Ask them to quote you the rate each insurer charges most of its policyholders, not the best rate, for which few persons qualify.

The *Financial Literacy Calculations: Determining the Cost of Insurance* feature shows how to use an interest-adjusted index to compare the costs of insurance.

interest-adjusted index A method of evaluating the cost of life insurance by taking into account the time value of money.

OBTAINING A POLICY

A life insurance policy is issued after you submit an application for insurance and the insurance company accepts the application. The application usually has two parts. In the first part, you state your name, age, and gender, what type of policy you desire, how much insurance you want, your occupation, and so forth. In the second part, you give your medical history. While a medical examination is frequently required for ordinary policies, usually no examination is required for group insurance.

The company determines your insurability by means of the information in your application, the results of the medical examination, and the inspection report. Of all applicants, 98 percent are found to be insurable, though some may have to pay higher premiums because of an existing medical condition.

EXAMINING A POLICY

BEFORE THE PURCHASE When you buy a life insurance policy, read every word of the contract and, if necessary, ask your agent for a point-by-point explanation of the language. Many insurance companies have rewritten their contracts to make them more understandable. These are legal documents, and you should be familiar with what they promise, even though they use technical terms.

Financial Literacy Calculations

DETERMINING THE COST OF INSURANCE

In determining the cost of insurance, don't overlook the time value of money. You must include as part of your cost the interest (opportunity cost) you would earn on money if you did not use it to pay insurance premiums. For many years, insurers did not assign a time value to money while making their sales presentations. Only recently has the insurance industry widely adopted interest-adjusted cost estimates.

If you fail to consider the time value of money, you may get the false impression that the insurance company is giving you something for nothing.

For example, suppose you are 35 and have a $10,000 face amount, 20-year, limited-payment, participating policy:

Annual premium	$200, or $4,000 over the 20-year period ($200 × 20)
Dividends	$1,700 (used to build up cash value) over the 20-year period
Net premium	$2,300 ($4,000 − $1,700)
Cash value of policy	$4,500 at the end of 20 years
Excess value	$2,200 ($4,500 − $2,300)

If you disregard the interest your premiums could otherwise have earned, you might get the impression that the insurance company is giving you $2,200 more than you paid ($4,500 − $2,300). But if you consider the time value of money (or its opportunity cost), the insurance company is not giving you $2,200. What if you had invested the annual premiums in a conservative stock mutual fund?

At an 8 percent annual yield, your account would have accumulated to $9,152 in 20 years (see Exhibit 1-B). Therefore, instead of having received $2,200 from the insurance company, you have paid $4,552 for 20 years of insurance protection:

Annual premium (20 years)	$4,000
Time value of money	+$5,152 ($9,152 − $4,000)
Total cost of policy	$9,152
Cash value (end of 20 years)	−$4,500
Net cost of insurance	$4,652 ($9,152 − $4,500)

Be sure to request interest-adjusted indexes from your agent. If he or she doesn't give them to you, look for another agent. As you have seen in the example, you can compare the costs among insurance companies by combining premium payments, dividends, cash value buildup, and present value analysis into an index number.

AFTER THE PURCHASE   After you buy new life insurance, you have a 10-day "free-look" period during which you can change your mind. *Note:* Some states now offer a longer free-look period.

- When you receive your new policy, read it carefully.
- If you are not satisfied for any reason, you may return the new policy within 10 days after you receive it.
- Mail it to the company's home office, submit by secure email, or give it back to the agent who sold it to you.
- Be sure to get a dated receipt from the post office or the agent.
- The company must return your premium within 30 days from the date you returned the policy. If the insurance company keeps your money longer, legally it is responsible for a 10 percent penalty—payable to you.

It's a good idea to give your beneficiaries and your lawyer a photocopy of your policy. Your beneficiaries should know where the policy is kept, because to obtain the insurance proceeds, they will have to send it to the company upon your death, along with a copy of the death certificate.

smart money minute

Insurance has its own vocabulary. Make sure you understand all of the terms (dividends, premiums, riders, beneficiaries, mortality charge) before shopping for a policy and definitely before making a final purchasing decision.

1. Why is it important to know the ratings of the insurance company?
2. How do insurance companies price their products?
3. How do insurance companies determine your insurability?
4. What should you do in examining a policy before and after the purchase?

PFP Sheet 54
Life Insurance
Comparison

Life Insurance Proceeds

A well-planned life insurance program can serve two purposes: (1) to provide a financial death benefit to those who depend upon them or (2) to provide funds to the insured while the insured is still living. Typically, the insured will have to choose between these two options because taking money from the insurance policy will usually reduce the death benefit paid out.

LO12-6

Evaluate the payout options for life insurance.

DEATH (OR SURVIVOR) BENEFITS

The two main objectives of a death (or survivor) benefit are (1) to cover the immediate expenses resulting from the death of the insured and (2) to protect dependents against a loss of income resulting from the premature death of the primary wage earner. Thus, selecting the appropriate settlement option is an important part of designing a life insurance program. The most common settlement options are lump-sum payment, proceeds left with the company, limited installment payment, and life income option.

LUMP-SUM PAYMENT The insurance company pays the face amount of the policy in one installment to the beneficiary or to the estate of the insured. This form of settlement is the most widely used option.

PROCEEDS LEFT WITH THE COMPANY The life insurance proceeds are left with the insurance company at a specified rate of interest. The company acts as trustee and pays the interest to the beneficiary. The guaranteed minimum interest rate paid on the proceeds varies among companies.

LIMITED INSTALLMENT PAYMENT This option provides for payment of the life insurance proceeds in periodic installments for a specified number of years after your death. The first type is *fixed period,* where equal payments are made for a specified number of years after death. The second type is *fixed amount.* These are paid out at the same amount until all benefits and earned interest have been exhausted.

annuity A contract that provides a regular income, typically for as long as the person lives.

LIFE INCOME OPTION Under the life income option, payments are made to the beneficiary for as long as she or he lives. An **annuity** is the basis for this option. An annuity is a financial contract written by an insurance company that provides a regular income. Generally, the payments are received monthly. The payments may begin at once (immediate annuity) or at some future date (deferred annuity). The amount of each payment is based primarily on the gender and attained age of the beneficiary at the time of the insured's death. As with the life insurance principle discussed earlier, the predictable mortality experience of a large group of individuals is fundamental to the annuity principle.

 6

I am aware of the different payout options in a life insurance policy.

The choice of determining how insurance proceeds will be paid is typically a factor of how you believe the beneficiary will be able to financially handle the payout.

VARIABLE ANNUITY CHARGES

You will pay several charges when you invest in a variable annuity. Be sure you understand all the charges before you invest. *These charges will reduce the value of your account and the return on your investment.* Often, they will include the following:

Surrender Charges. If you withdraw money from a variable annuity within a certain period after a purchase payment (typically within 6 to 8 years, but sometimes as long as 10 years), the insurance company usually will assess a "surrender" charge, which is a type of sales charge. This charge is used to pay your insurance agent a commission for selling the variable annuity to you. Generally, the surrender charge is a percentage of the amount withdrawn and declines gradually over a period of several years, known as the *"surrender period."* For example, a 7 percent charge might apply in the first year after a purchase payment, 6 percent in the second year, 5 percent in the third year, and so on until the eighth year, when the surrender charge no longer applies. Often, contracts will allow you to withdraw part of your account value each year—10 percent or 15 percent of your account value, for example—without paying a surrender charge.

Mortality and Expense Risk Charge. This charge is equal to a certain percentage of your account value, typically in the range of 1.25 percent per year. This charge compensates the insurance company for insurance risks it assumes under the annuity contract. Profit from the mortality and expense risk charge is sometimes used to pay the insurer's costs of selling the variable annuity, such as

a commission paid to your insurance agent for selling the variable annuity to you.

Administrative Fees. The insurer may deduct charges to cover record-keeping and other administrative expenses. This may be charged as a flat account maintenance fee (perhaps $25 or $30 per year) or as a percentage of your account value (typically in the range of 0.15 percent per year).

Underlying Fund Expenses. You will also indirectly pay the fees and expenses imposed by the mutual funds that are the underlying investment options for your variable annuity.

Fees and Charges for Other Features. Special features offered by some variable annuities, such as a stepped-up death benefit, a guaranteed minimum income benefit, or long-term care insurance, often carry additional fees and charges.

Other charges, such as initial sales loads or fees for transferring part of your account from one investment option to another, may also apply. You should ask your insurance agent to explain to you all charges that may apply. You can also find a description of the charges in the prospectus for any variable annuity that you are considering.

As a consumer, the best way to arm yourself against the pressures of annuity marketers is to know the common sales pitches and how to respond to them. In the end, you still might want a variable annuity. But make that decision after careful consideration of the product and alternative solutions—not because someone pressured you into it.

INCOME FROM LIFE INSURANCE POLICIES

As you have seen so far, life insurance can provide a sum of money at death to a named beneficiary. There are times when the insured may need money for expenses such as college, retirement, or medical needs. Whole life policies have a cash value balance. The insured may either take a loan on this balance or surrender the policy and receive the amount of the cash value. If a loan is taken and not paid back, it will typically reduce the death benefit paid to the beneficiary.

Variable life insurance policies were designed to be an insurance policy combined with a separate investment product. Many people choose to supplement their retirement income by withdrawing some of the investment portion as an annuity to provide regular income. The appeal of variable annuities increased during the mid-1990s due to a rising stock market. A fixed annuity states that the annuitant (the person who is to receive the annuity) will receive a fixed amount of income over a certain period or for life. With a variable annuity, the monthly payments vary because they are based on the income received from stocks or other investments.

Variable annuities offer many optional features, including a stepped-up death benefit, a guaranteed minimum income benefit, or long-term care insurance. The features often come with additional fees and charges. Read the *Financial Literacy for My Life: Variable Annuity Charges* feature to understand these charges.

Financial Literacy for My Life

TEN GOLDEN RULES FOR BUYING LIFE INSURANCE

Remember that your need for life insurance coverage will change over time. Your income may go up or down, or your family size might change. Therefore, it is wise to review your coverage periodically to ensure that it keeps up with your changing needs.

Follow these rules when buying life insurance	Done
1. Understand and know what your life insurance needs are before you make any purchase, and make sure the company you choose can meet those needs.	☐
2. Buy your life insurance from a company that is licensed in your state.	☐
3. Select an agent who is competent, knowledgeable, and trustworthy.	☐
4. Shop around and compare costs.	☐
5. Buy only the amount of life insurance you need and can afford.	☐
6. Ask about lower premium rates for nonsmokers.	☐
7. Read your policy and make sure you understand it.	☐
8. Inform your beneficiaries about the kinds and amount of life insurance you own.	☐
9. Keep your policy in a safe place at home, and keep your insurance company's name and your policy number in a safe deposit box.	☐
10. Check your coverage periodically, or whenever your situation changes, to ensure that it meets your current needs.	☐

Source: American Council of Life Insurance, 1001 Pennsylvania Avenue, NW, Washington, DC 20004-2599.

SWITCHING POLICIES

Think twice if your agent suggests that you replace the whole life or universal life insurance you already own. According to a study by the Consumer Federation of America, consumers lose billions of dollars each year because they don't hold their cash-value life insurance policies long enough or because they purchase the wrong policies. The author of the study, James Hunt, Vermont's former insurance commissioner, notes that half of those who buy whole or universal life policies drop them within 10 years.

Before you give up this protection, make sure you are still insurable (check medical and any other qualification requirements). Remember that you are now older than you were when you purchased your policy, and a new policy will therefore cost more. Moreover, the older policy may have provisions that are not duplicated in some of the new policies. This does not mean you should reject the idea of replacing your present policy; rather, you should proceed with caution. We recommend that you ask your agent or company for an opinion about the new proposal to get both sides of the argument.

The insurance industry is regulated by state insurance commissioners. Recently many states passed new laws to protect consumers from overzealous sales agents. The National Association of Insurance Commissioners, state regulators, and insurance companies plan to develop new standards to protect consumers.

The *Financial Literacy for My Life: Ten Golden Rules for Buying Life Insurance* feature presents important guidelines for purchasing life insurance.

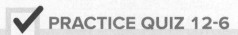

PRACTICE QUIZ 12-6

1. What are the four most common settlement options?
2. Should you switch life insurance policies?
3. What is an annuity?
4. What makes a variable annuity different?

Your Personal Finance Roadmap and Dashboard:

Life Insurance

NUMBER OF TIMES INCOME
FOR LIFE INSURANCE COVERAGE

Your need for life insurance will change with your stage in life. For example, if you are single or live with your parents, you may not need life insurance, unless you have a debt or want to provide for your parents, a friend, a relative, or charity. However, as children are born, your need for life insurance will increase. As children grow older and leave the nest, you will probably need less insurance.

YOUR SITUATION

Do you know if you need life insurance? Have you taken time to consider why you need life insurance and to find a sales agent who is knowledgeable and trustworthy? Have you evaluated the advantages and disadvantages of term life, whole life, and other life insurance options available to you? Personal financial planning actions you might consider depending upon your stage in life include:

First Steps

- Generally, young single people with no dependents don't need life insurance.

- Buy term insurance if you have debts or dependents who need financial support from you.
- If your spouse can live on his/her income alone and you don't have a mortgage, your only insurance need may be to cover final expenses at your death.
- Buy term insurance if you have any dependents who need your financial support.

Next Steps

- As children arrive, you'll need more life insurance.
- Reevaluate your life insurance coverage if you are promoted or change jobs.
- If you are providing financial support for aging parents or siblings, keep adequate life insurance coverage.

Later Steps

- As children grow older and leave, you'll probably need less insurance.
- Maintain adequate life insurance coverage to protect the widow or widower.
- If you have dependents and have enough assets to provide for them, then you don't need life insurance.

YOUR Next Step . . . select one or more of the items above and create an action plan to implement those financial planning activities.

LO12-1

Define *life insurance* and describe its purpose and principle. Life insurance is a contract between an insurance company and a policyholder under which the company agrees to pay a specified sum to a beneficiary upon the insured's death. Most people buy life insurance to protect someone who depends on them from financial losses caused by their death. Fundamental to the life insurance principle is the predictable mortality experience of a large group of individuals.

LO12-2

Determine your life insurance needs. In determining your life insurance needs, you must first determine your insurance objectives and then use the multiple of income method, the easy method, the DINK method, the "nonworking" spouse method, or the "family need" method. The "family need" method is recommended. You should consider a number of factors before you buy insurance, including your present and future sources of income, other savings and income protection, group life insurance, group annuities (or other pension benefits), and Social Security.

LO12-3

Distinguish between the types of life insurance companies, and analyze various types of life insurance policies. The two types of life insurance companies are stock companies, owned by stockholders, and mutual companies, owned by policyholders. In general, stock companies sell nonparticipating policies and mutual companies sell participating policies. The three basic types of life insurance are term, whole life, and endowment policies. Many variations and combinations of these types are available. You should check with both stock and mutual companies to determine which type offers the best policy for your particular needs at the lowest price.

Nevertheless, as with other forms of insurance, price should not be your only consideration in choosing a life

insurance policy. You should also consider the financial stability, reliability, and service the insurance company provides.

LO12-4

Select important provisions in life insurance contracts. The naming of the beneficiary, the grace period, policy reinstatement, the incontestability clause, the suicide clause, automatic premium loans, the misstatement of age provision, and the policy loan provision are important provisions in most life insurance policies. Common riders in life insurance policies are the waiver of premium disability benefit, the accidental death benefit, the guaranteed insurability option, cost of living protection, and accelerated benefits.

LO12-5

Create a plan to buy life insurance. Before buying life insurance, consider your present and future sources of income, group life insurance, group annuities (or other pension benefits), and Social Security. Then compare the costs of several life insurance policies. Examine your policy before and after the purchase.

LO12-6

Evaluate the payout options for life insurance. Choose appropriate settlement options based on the needs of your beneficiary. The most common settlement options are lump-sum payment, proceeds left with the company, limited installment payment, and life income option. Online computer services provide a wealth of information about all topics related to life insurance. An annuity can provide regular payments to your beneficiaries with the life income option. An annuity can also be used to provide you with a regular income for expenses in later years.

KEY TERMS

SELF-TEST PROBLEMS

1. Suppose that yours is a typical family. Your annual income is $55,000. Use the easy method to determine your need for life insurance.

2. Using the "nonworking" spouse method, what should be the life insurance needs for the nonworking spouse in a family whose youngest child is 3 years old?

3. Suppose your annual premium for a $20,000, 20-year limited-payment policy is $450 over the 20-year period. The cash value of your policy at the end of 20 years is $8,500. Assume that you could have invested the annual premium in a mutual fund yielding 7 percent annually. What is the net cost of your insurance for the 20-year period?

Self-Test Solutions

1. Current gross income   = $55,000
   Multiply gross income by 7 years   = $385,000
   Take 70 percent of $385,000   = $385,000 × .70
   Approximate insurance needed   = $269,500

2. Youngest child's age   =   3 years
   15 years before the child is 18 years old.   = $150,000
   Insurance needed = 15 × $10,000

3. Premiums paid over 20 years   = $450 × 20 = $9,000
   Time value of 20-year annual payments of
   $420 at 7 percent yield.
   (see Exhibit 1-B; use a factor of 40.995)   =   40.995 × $450 = $18,448
   Cash value   = $8,500
   Net cost of insurance   = $18,448 − $8,500 = $9,948

FINANCIAL PLANNING PROBLEMS

LO12-1   1. *Calculating Life Expectancy.* Using Exhibit 12-2, determine the life expectancy of a 40-year-old male.

LO12-1   2. *Calculating Life Expectancy.* Using Exhibit 12-2, determine the average number of additional years males alive at age 35 may expect to live.

LO12-1   3. *Calculating Life Expectancy.* Using Exhibit 12-2, determine the life expectancy of a 60-year-old female.

LO12-2   4. *Calculating the Amount of Life Insurance Needed Using the Multiple of Income Method.* You have a gross annual income of $62,000. Use the multiple of income method to determine the minimum amount of life insurance you should carry.

LO12-2   5. *Calculating the Amount of Life Insurance Needed Using the Multiple of Income Method.* You have a gross annual income of $65,000. Use the multiple of income method to determine the maximum amount of life insurance you should carry.

LO12-2   6. *Calculating the Amount of Life Insurance Needed Using the Easy Method.* You are the wage earner in a "typical family," with $70,000 gross annual income. Use the easy method to determine how much life insurance you should carry.

LO12-2   7. *Calculating the Amount of Life Insurance Needed Using the Easy Method.* Suppose that yours is a typical family. Your annual income is $65,000. Using the easy method, what should be your need for life insurance?

LO12-2   8. *Estimating Life Insurance Needs Using the DINK Method.* You and your spouse are in good health and have reasonably secure jobs. Each of you makes about $40,000 annually. You own a home with a $100,000 mortgage, and you owe $11,000 on car loans, $2,000 in personal debt, and $3,000 in credit card loans. You have no other debt. You have no plans to increase the size of your family in the near future. You estimate that funeral expenses will be $5,000. Estimate your total insurance needs using the DINK method.

LO12-2   9. *Estimating Life Insurance Needs Using the DINK Method.* You are a dual-income, no-kids family. You and your spouse have the following debts: Mortgage = $190,000; Auto loan = $10,000; Credit card balance = $2,000; and other debts = $4,000. Further, you estimate that your funeral will cost $6,000. Your spouse expects to continue to work after your death. Using the DINK method, what should be your need for life insurance?

10. *Using the "Nonworking" Spouse Method to Determine Life Insurance Needs.* Tim and Allison are married and have two children, ages 4 and 6. Allison is a "nonworking" spouse who devotes all of her time to household activities. Estimate how much life insurance Tim and Allison should carry to cover Allison. LO12-2

11. *Using the "Nonworking" Spouse Method to Determine Life Insurance Needs.* Using the "nonworking" spouse method, what should be the life insurance needs for a nonworking spouse whose youngest child is 5 years old? LO12-2

12. *Using the "Nonworking" Spouse Method to Determine Life Insurance Needs.* Using the "nonworking" spouse method, what should be the life insurance needs for a nonworking spouse whose youngest child is 8 years old? LO12-2

13. *Calculating the Effect of Inflation on a Life Insurance Policy.* Susan has purchased a whole life policy with a death benefit of $200,000. Assuming that she dies in 10 years and the average inflation has been 2 percent, what is the value of the purchasing power of the proceeds? LO12-4

14. *Calculating the Effect of Inflation on a Life Insurance Policy.* Allen has purchased a whole life policy with a death benefit of $150,000. Assuming that he dies in eight years and the average inflation has been 1 percent, what is the value of the purchasing power of the proceeds? LO12-4

15. *Determining the Cost of Insurance.* Suppose you are 45 and have a $50,000 face amount, 15-year, limited-payment, participating policy (dividends will be used to build up the cash value of the policy). Your annual premium is $1,000. The cash value of the policy is expected to be $12,000 in 15 years. Using time value of money and assuming you could invest your money elsewhere for a 7 percent annual yield, calculate the net cost of insurance. LO12-5

16. *Determining the Cost of Insurance.* Suppose you are 30 and have a $25,000 face amount, 20-year, limited-payment, participating policy (dividends will be used to build up the cash value of the policy). Your annual premium is $325. The cash value of the policy is expected to be $3,000 in 20 years. Using time value of money and assuming you could invest your money elsewhere for a 5 percent annual yield, calculate the net cost of insurance. LO12-5

17. *Calculating a Mortality and Expense Risk Charge.* Your variable annuity has a mortality and expense risk charge at an annual rate of 3.00 percent of account value. Your average account value during the year is $25,000. What are your mortality and expense risk charges for the year? LO12-6

18. *Calculating Administrative Fees.* Your variable annuity charges administrative fees at an annual rate of 0.215 percent of account value. Your average account value during the year is $60,000. What is the administrative fee for the year? LO12-6

DIGITAL FINANCIAL LITERACY. . .

LIFE INSURANCE AFTER A PANDEMIC

Most of us know someone who contracted COVID-19 and recovered. Some of us may know someone who did not fare as well and may still have long-term symptoms or even passed away due to the virus.

During the pandemic, there was a slight increase in the number of applications for new policies. The insurance companies were hesitant to cover people that had recently recovered from COVID-19 or may still be experiencing symptoms.

It's still too early to tell how the pandemic will effect premiums. However, now is definitely a good time to assess your overall insurance needs, especially if you have been putting it off.

Action items:

1) Locate a recent article that discusses life insurance after the pandemic. Using the information from the article, survey three people about their opinions and concerns about life insurance costs and coverage since the pandemic.

2) Based on your research, create a visual presentation, video summary, or short report on what you anticipate will happen to demand for life insurance and the associated premiums.

FINANCIAL PLANNING CASE

Life Insurance for Young Married People

Jeff and Ann are both 28 years old. They have been married for three years, and they have a son who is almost 2. They expect their second child in a few months.

Jeff is a junior software developer. He has just received a $60-a-week raise. His income is $1,100 a week, which, after taxes, leaves him with $3,600 a month. His company provides $50,000 of life insurance, a medical/hospital/surgical plan, and a major medical plan. All of these group plans protect him as long as he stays with the company.

When Jeff received his raise, he decided that part of it should be used to add to his family's protection. Jeff and Ann talked to their insurance agent, who reviewed the insurance Jeff obtained through his job. Under Social Security, they also had some basic protection against the loss of Jeff's income if he became totally disabled or if he died before the children were 18.

But most of this protection was only basic, a kind of floor for Jeff and Ann to build on. For example, monthly Social Security payments to Ann would be approximately $1,700 if Jeff died leaving two children under age 18. Yet the family's total expenses would soon be higher after the birth of the second baby. Although the family's expenses would be lowered if Jeff died, they would be at least $500 a month more than Social Security would provide.

Questions

1. In your opinion, do Jeff and Ann need additional insurance? Why or why not?

2. What type of policy would you suggest for Jeff and Ann? Why?

PERSONAL FINANCIAL PLANNER IN ACTION

DETERMINING LIFE INSURANCE NEEDS

Providing for the financial needs of dependents is the primary goal of a life insurance program. Comparing policy types, coverage amounts, and other provisions will help you meet this financial purpose.

Your Short-Term Financial Planning Activities	Resources and Apps
1. Determine life insurance needs for your current life situation.	PFP Sheet 53 www.lifehappens.org www.bankrate.com/calculators.aspx www.msn.com/en-us/money Human Life Value Calculator App
2. Compare rates and coverages for different life insurance policies and companies.	PFP Sheet 54 https://thebalance.com/personal-insurance-4073983 www.quickquote.com www.insure.com www.accuquote.com
3. Evaluate the various payout options from life insurance in your financial plan.	www.lifeinsurancehub.net www.reliaquote.com www.annuities.com www.invest-faq.com
Your Long-Term Financial Planning Activities	
1. Identify information sources to monitor changes in life insurance coverages and costs offered by life insurance companies.	www.lifehappens.org Tomorrow App
2. Develop a plan for reassessing life insurance needs as family and household situations change.	www.insurance.com Life Happens App

CONTINUING CASE

Life Insurance

Surprise! Jamie Lee and Ross were stunned to find that their family of two has grown to a family of five! They were surprised to find on the delivery date that they were the proud parents of *triplets*.

Ross immediately had worries about being able to provide for the growing family: diapers, formula, college expenses times three! What if something happened to him or Jamie Lee? How would the surviving parent be able to provide for such a large family?

Current Financial Situation

Assets (Jamie Lee and Ross combined)**:**
Checking account: $2,500
Savings account: $16,000
Emergency fund savings account: $19,100
IRA balance: $25,000
Car: $11,500 (Jamie Lee) and $19,000 (Ross)

Liabilities (Jamie Lee and Ross combined)**:**
Student loan balance: $0
Credit card balance: $3,500
Car loans: $7,000

Income:
Jamie Lee: $45,000 gross income ($31,500 net income after taxes)

Ross: $73,000 gross income ($60,800 net income after taxes)

Monthly Expenses:
Mortgage: $1,225
Property taxes: $400
Homeowner's insurance: $200
Utilities: $160
Food: $500
Gas/maintenance: $275
Credit card payment: $275
Car loan payment: $289
Entertainment: $125

Questions

1. Within days of the triplets' arrival, Jamie Lee and Ross began researching and comparing various agencies for the purchase of a life insurance policy. What characteristics should Ross look for when choosing a life insurance agency? What sources could he reference for help?

2. Jamie Lee and Ross need to ensure that the surviving spouse and the children will not have financial hardship in the event of a loss. Using the Easy Method and considering Ross's salary in the calculation, how much life insurance will they need?

3. With so many policy variations from which to choose, Ross and Jamie Lee are unsure which company is offering the most competitive rates. How will they be able to compare the rates between the various companies?

4. Jamie Lee and Ross have a limited budget for life insurance, given that they also have the additional present-day expenses of the triplets to consider. What type of life insurance would you recommend for the family at this life stage and what are its associated advantages and disadvantages?

 # DAILY SPENDING DIARY

"I'm not sure spending for life insurance is necessary for my life situation."

Directions

As you continue to record and monitor spending in various categories, be sure to consider how various decisions will affect your long-term financial security. Various comments you record might remind you to consider possible changes you might want to make in your spending habits.

Analysis Questions

1. Are there any spending amounts or items that you might consider reducing or eliminating?

2. What actions might you consider now or in the future regarding spending on life insurance?

A *Daily Spending Diary* sheet is located at the end of Chapter 1 and on the library resource site in *Connect*.

13 Investing Fundamentals

Lars A. Niki

Financial Literacy
IN **YOUR LIFE**

▶ **What if you . . .** have just gotten a new job. As part of your orientation, the human resources manager asks if you want to participate in the company's 401(k) retirement plan.

You might . . . want to ask (1) if your employer matches your contribution,

(2) how much the employer's contribution is, and (3) what types of investments you can choose for your retirement account.

Now, what would you do? Assuming the employer matches your contributions and you can choose the investments in your plan, you should consider participating in the plan. Once enrolled in the plan, you can usually choose different investments, which means that you need to learn about how to evaluate different types of investments. This is also a good time to complete a financial checkup and make sure you're ready to invest. The Your Personal Finance Roadmap and Dashboard feature at the end of this chapter can help you take this step.

---

my life | WHY INVEST?

There is no better time to begin an investment program than now. The reason is quite simple. If you start an investment program now and let the earnings from your investments compound, there's a good chance you won't have to worry about finances when you reach retirement age.

While reading this chapter won't magically make you a millionaire, it does provide some of the tools you need to begin investing. For each of the following statements, select Yes, No, or Maybe.

1.	My investment goals are written down.	Yes	No	Maybe
2.	I understand how the factors of safety and risk affect an investment decision.	Yes	No	Maybe
3.	I use asset allocation to minimize risks when investing.	Yes	No	Maybe
4.	I am actively involved in my investment program.	Yes	No	Maybe
5.	I know how to evaluate different investment alternatives.	Yes	No	Maybe

As you study this chapter, you will encounter "My Life" boxes with additional information and resources related to these items.

Preparing for an Investment Program

The old saying goes, "I've been rich and I've been poor, and believe me, rich is better." While being rich doesn't guarantee happiness, the creation of wealth does provide financial security. In addition, the creation of wealth can provide a safety net for unexpected emergencies. Also, the act of saving and investing money will allow you to retire on your terms when and where you choose. Regardless of the reason, the creation of wealth is a worthy goal. And yet, just dreaming of being rich doesn't make it happen.

By studying the basic investment principles presented in this chapter, along with the information on stocks, bonds, mutual funds, real estate, and other alternatives in the remaining investment chapters, you can create an investment plan that is custom-made for you.

LO13-1

Describe why you should establish an investment program.

ESTABLISHING INVESTMENT GOALS

For most people, the first step is to establish investment goals. To be useful, investment goals must be *written, specific,* and *measurable.* They must also be tailored to your particular financial needs. The following questions will help you establish valid investment goals.

1. How much money do you need to satisfy your investment goals?
2. How long will it take you to obtain the money?
3. How much risk are you willing to assume in an investment program?
4. What possible economic or personal conditions could alter your investment goals?
5. Are you willing to make the sacrifices necessary to reach your investment goals?
6. What will the consequences be if you don't reach your investment goals?
7. Considering your economic circumstances, are your investment goals reasonable?

Your investment goals are always oriented toward the future. For some people, it helps to create goals to satisfy the following five basic needs:

- Emergencies—money for unexpected events in your life.
- Short-term—goals that can be attained within the next year.
- Intermediate—goals that can be attained within one to five years.
- Long-term—goals that will take longer than five years.
- Retirement—goals that will provide the money you need after you quit working.

For example, you may establish a short-term goal of accumulating $2,500 in a savings account over the next 12 months. You may then use the $2,500 to purchase stocks or mutual funds to help you attain your intermediate or long-term investment goals.

Many people don't think they need to worry about retirement goals when they are in their 20s, 30s, or 40s. Often, they wait until they are in their 50s to start planning for retirement. Or, they just retire without a plan and hope they have enough money to pay for the necessities. Not planning for retirement is one of the *biggest* mistakes you can make. By starting as soon as possible, you can take advantage of the time value of money concept that was discussed in Chapter 1. The time value of money—as you will see later in this section—is built on two important concepts. First, you save or invest on a regular basis over a long period of time. Second, your savings and investments "grow" because they pay interest, dividends, or increase in value and are added to the amounts you save and invest. When combined, the amounts you save or invest and the earnings on your savings and investments over a long period of time create a well-funded retirement plan. That's why it is important to start as soon as possible. Simply put: Don't Wait—Start Now!

my life   1

My investment goals are written down.

If you answered yes to this question at the beginning of the chapter, that's good. If not, *Personal Financial Planner Sheet 55* can help you develop investment goals that will help you achieve financial security both now and in the future.

PERFORMING A FINANCIAL CHECKUP

Before you begin an investment program, your personal financial affairs should be in good shape. In this section, we examine several factors you should consider before making your first investment.

ETHICAL CONCERNS: PAYING YOUR BILLS ON TIME

From both legal and ethical standpoints, you have an obligation to pay for credit purchases. Moreover, business firms that extend credit expect you to pay for a product or service purchased using credit. There are serious consequences if you don't pay for products or services purchased on credit.

For example,

- Merchandise can be repossessed.
- A business can sue to recover the cost of the product or service.

- Your credit score can be lowered to reflect late or missed payments.
- The cost of additional credit, if available, may be higher because of lower credit scores or late or missed payments.

WORK TO BALANCE YOUR BUDGET   For most people, debt is one of the biggest obstacles that keeps them from obtaining the life they want. Many people regularly spend more than they make. They purchase items on credit or use the cash advance provision on their credit cards. Then they must make monthly installment payments and pay finance charges, often over 20 percent. Under these circumstances, it makes no sense to start an investment program until credit and installment purchases, along with the accompanying finance charges, are reduced or eliminated. A good rule of thumb is to limit consumer credit payments to no more than 20 percent of your net (after-tax) income. Eventually, the amount of cash remaining after the bills are paid will increase and can be used to start a savings program or finance investments.

For help with budgeting, you may want to review the material on budgeting in Chapter 3. You may also want to consider using software or a mobile app to help manage your spending. Four popular apps are

- Quicken (www.quicken.com)
- Mint (www.mint.com)
- YNAB (www.youneedabudget.com)
- EveryDollar (www.everydollar.com)

Each of these apps can help you track your income and spending. While some apps are free, there may be small monthly or annual fees for more advanced features that can help you manage your money.

MANAGE YOUR CREDIT CARD DEBT   While all cardholders have reasons for using their credit cards, the important point to remember is that it is *very* easy to get in trouble by using your credit cards. Consider the following statistics:

- The typical American has three credit cards.[1]
- For U.S. families, the average balance on credit cards was $5,897 in late 2020.[2]

According to Experian, one of the nation's largest credit bureaus, data for American consumers shows they were managing their credit card balances and avoiding late payments even during the midst of a pandemic.[3] Still, paying off credit card debt of over $5,800 can be a big hurdle that limits your ability to save and invest for the future. And the problem becomes worse if you just pay the minimum payment each month. For example, it will take almost six years to pay off a $1,000 credit card debt. This figure is based on an 18 percent annual percentage interest rate and a $40 minimum payment.[4]

When you apply for a credit card, consider the annual percentage rate. Obviously, the lower the annual percentage rate, the better. Also, note whether there is an annual fee or not. Again an obvious conclusion: A credit card with no annual fee is better than a card with an annual fee.

To avoid the financial problems associated with excessive credit card debt, experts suggest that you take control of your personal finances. Helpful hints include:

- Pay your credit card balance in full each month.
- Don't use your credit cards to pay for many small purchases during the month.
- Don't use the cash advance provision that accompanies most credit cards.

smart money minute

- For most people, one or two cards are enough.
- If you think you are in trouble regarding paying off your debt, get help.

Organizations like Credit.org (www.credit.org) or the National Foundation for Credit Counseling (nfcc.org) can often help you work out a plan to pay down or eliminate your credit card debt.

START AN EMERGENCY FUND   An **emergency fund** is an amount of money you can obtain quickly in case of immediate need. The need for an emergency fund became obvious during 2020 and the first part of 2021 when the world experienced the worst pandemic since the early 1900s. Many workers lost their jobs when nonessential businesses were required to shut down during a portion of 2020. Even after businesses began to reopen, the work week for many employees was reduced along with their take-home pay. Even with government stimulus packages and increased unemployment benefits, people without adequate emergency funds or savings were forced to scramble to find ways to pay for everyday necessities.

The amount of money to be put away in the emergency fund varies from person to person. However, most financial planners agree that an amount equal to three months' living expenses is reasonable. For example, Debbie Martin's monthly expenses total $1,600. Before Debbie can begin investing, she must save at least $4,800 ($1,600 × 3 months = $4,800). There are times when you may want to increase the amount. If you think you are about to lose your job, for example, an emergency fund equal to three months' living expenses may not be enough to tide you over until you find new employment. The money in your emergency fund should be kept in a savings account or a money market account that earns interest but is still available if you need it for emergencies.

HAVE ACCESS TO OTHER SOURCES OF CASH FOR EMERGENCY NEEDS   You may also want to establish a line of credit at a bank, savings and loan association, or credit union. A **line of credit** is a short-term loan that is approved before the money is actually needed. Because the paperwork has already been completed and the loan has been preapproved, you can later obtain the money as soon as you need it. The cash advance provision offered by major credit card companies can also be used in an emergency. However, both lines of credit and credit cards have a ceiling, or maximum dollar amount, that limits the amount of available credit. If you have already exhausted both of these sources of credit on everyday expenses, they will not be available in an emergency.

ECONOMIC FACTORS THAT CAN AFFECT YOUR PERSONAL FINANCES

While the typical personal finance course is not an economics course, it does help to have a basic understanding of how the nation's economy affects your personal financial situation. Let's begin with a basic definition for economics. **Economics** is the study of how wealth is created and distributed. Experts often use economics to explain the choices the government, businesses, *and* individuals make and what is important to each group. For example, assume you want to save money to pay off your credit card debt, and you also want to take a weekend trip to New York City. Because you can't afford to do both, you must decide which is the most important. The decision you make is an example of the concept of opportunity costs—what a person gives up by making a choice—defined in Chapter 1.

Major factors that can affect the economy, your personal financial plan, and the value of your investments include actions the federal government may take to maintain a healthy economy. For example, to offset the effects of a recession, the government may use *fiscal policy* to alter the tax structure and levels of government spending—specific

emergency fund An amount of money you can obtain quickly in case of immediate need.

line of credit A short-term loan that is approved before the money is actually needed.

economics The study of how wealth is created and distributed.

actions designed to influence the amount that citizens and businesses save, invest, and spend. In addition to fiscal policy, the Federal Reserve may use *monetary policy* to determine the level of interest rates that both consumers and businesses pay to borrow money. Both fiscal policy and monetary policy are used on a regular basis to stabilize the economy and encourage economic growth.

A nation's business cycle also affects your personal finances. Many economists define a **business cycle** as the increase and decrease in a nation's economic activity. While all industrialized nations seek sustained economic growth, full employment, and price stability, the fact is that a nation's economy fluctuates from year to year. If you were to graph the economic growth rate for a country like the United States, it would resemble a roller-coaster ride with peaks (strong economy) and low points (weak economy). For example, the U.S. economy experienced a recession in the first part of 2020. What happened? Answer: The Covid-19 pandemic accompanied with nonessential business closures and high unemployment. This recession was severe because it affected so many people. Compared to other recessions, the 2020 recession was a short recession because the economy experienced economic growth in the third and fourth quarters of 2020 as businesses reopened and people went back to work. Still, most experts believed there would be lingering effects for businesses and individuals before the economy returned to pre-pandemic economic growth—even though vaccines became available in late 2020.

business cycle The increase and decrease in a nation's economic activity.

The possibility of another economic crisis underscores the importance of managing your personal finances *and* your investment program. Here are five steps you can take to manage your money—especially if you think the economy is headed for a downturn:

1. *Establish a larger than usual emergency fund.* Under normal circumstances, an emergency fund of three months' living expenses is considered adequate, but you may want to increase your fund in anticipation of a crisis.

2. *Know what you owe.* Make a list of all your debts and the amount of the required monthly payments, and then identify the debts that *must* be paid. Typically, these include the mortgage or rent, medicine, utilities, food, and transportation.

3. *Reduce spending.* Cut back to the basics and reduce the amount of money spent on entertainment, dining at restaurants, and vacations.

4. *Notify credit card companies and lenders if you are unable to make payments.* Although not all lenders are willing to help, many will work with you and lower your interest rate, reduce your monthly payment, or extend the time for repayment.

5. *Monitor the value of your investment and retirement accounts.* Tracking the value of your stock, mutual fund, and other investments, for example, will help you decide which investments to sell if you need cash for emergencies.

Above all, don't panic. While financial problems are stressful, staying calm and considering all the options may help reduce the stress.

GETTING THE MONEY NEEDED TO START AN INVESTMENT PROGRAM

Once you have established your investment goals and completed your financial checkup, it's time to start investing—assuming you have enough money to finance your investments. Unfortunately, the money doesn't automatically appear.

PRIORITY OF INVESTMENT GOALS Quick question: How badly do you want to achieve your investment goals? The answer to this question is extremely important. While many people will promote the benefits of financial security and tell you to start investing as soon as possible, you are the one who must actually perform the financial checkup and save the money needed to start investing. Consider the following questions to determine if you are really motivated to build a long-term investment program:

- Are you willing to sacrifice some immediate purchases to provide financing for your investments?

- Can you control your spending in order to obtain the money needed for your investment program?

- Are you motivated to save money on a weekly, monthly, or annual basis?

Your answer to each question is important, but the word "you" is the key component in each of the above questions. You are the one who must make the "right" choices. Take Rita Johnson, a 42-year-old nurse in a large St. Louis hospital. As part of a divorce settlement in 2020, she received a cash payment of almost $72,000. At first, she was tempted to spend this money on a trip to Europe, a new BMW, and new furniture. But after some careful planning, she decided to save $35,000 in a certificate of deposit and invest the remainder in two mutual funds that contained a combination of stocks and bonds. On May 31, 2022, these investments had grown to $92,000.

What is important to you? What do you value? Each of these questions affects your investment goals. At one extreme are people who save or invest as much of each paycheck as they can. At the other extreme are people who live paycheck to paycheck, spend everything they make, and run out of money before their next paycheck. Most people find either extreme unacceptable and take a more middle-of-the-road approach. These people often spend money on the items that make their lives more enjoyable and still save enough to fund an investment program.

For many people, the easiest way to begin an investment program is to participate in an employer-sponsored retirement account—often referred to as a 401(k) or a 403(b) account. Many employers will match part or all of your contributions to a retirement account. For example, an employer may contribute $0.50 for every $1.00 the employee contributes. And while the amount of the "match" varies, some employers still match $1.00 for every $1.00 employees contribute up to a certain percentage of their annual salary. *Be warned:* Many employers have reduced or eliminated the matching provisions in their employee retirement plans in order to reduce the cost of their salary and benefit programs.

Some additional suggestions to help you obtain the money you need to establish an investment program are described in the nearby *How To . . . Obtain the Money Needed to Establish an Investment Program* feature.

HOW THE TIME VALUE OF MONEY AFFECTS YOUR INVESTMENTS

If you invest $1,800 each year for 40 years and your investment earns 8 percent a year, how much would your investment be worth at the end of the 40th year? Would you believe your investment would be worth $466,302? That's a lot of money—especially considering you only invested $72,000 ($1,800 investment each year × 40 years = $72,000). Where did the rest of the money come from? The money you invested each year earned 8 percent, or a total of $394,302 ($466,302 − $72,000 = $394,302).

You may be thinking $1,800 (that's $150 a month) couldn't possibly be worth almost a half a million dollars in 40 years, but $1,800 invested each year that earns 8 percent each year can really grow over a long period of time. Keep in mind that the time value of money is based on two factors. You must save or invest money each year. You must also allow your earnings to accumulate and resist the temptation to spend the earnings on immediate purchases. The numbers are real, and you can check it out by using a future value formula or a future value table discussed in the Chapter 1 Appendix, or you can use a financial calculator. While the formula or table will work, most people prefer using a calculator like the one at keisan.casio.com/exec/system/1234231998 because it is so easy. Just insert the values in the app and press Execute to obtain the answer. Another example and a tryout problem are provided in the *Financial Literacy*

Most people find it difficult to save or invest money. Following are some suggestions for obtaining the money you need to begin investing.

Suggestion	Suggested Action
1. Pay yourself first.	Each month, pay your monthly bills, save or invest a reasonable amount of money, and use the money left over for personal and entertainment expenses.
2. Take advantage of employer-sponsored retirement programs.	Sign up for a retirement program at work because many employers will match part or all of the contributions.
3. Participate in an elective savings program.	Elect to have money withheld from your paycheck each payday and automatically deposited in a savings or investment account.
4. Make a special savings effort one or two months each year.	Many financial planners recommend that you cut back to the basics for one or two months each year.

Calculations: Using the Time Value of Money to Calculate Investment Returns feature. Take a look at the example, and then use the tryout problem to reinforce this important concept. By using this same calculator, you can enter amounts for how much you plan to save or invest each year, an estimated return on your money, and the number of years before you need or want the money. The answer can help you refine both your financial goals and your long-term financial plan. For many people, these calculators are a real motivator and encourage them to continue to save or invest money each year and search for quality investments that provide larger returns.

Also, the rate of return makes a difference. As noted above, a $1,800 yearly investment that earns 8 percent is worth $466,302 at the end of 40 years. But if the same $1,800 annual investment earns only 2 percent each year, your investment is worth $108,724 at the end of the same 40-year period. There's a huge difference between an investment that earns 8 percent and one that earns 2 percent. To see the difference, look at Exhibit 13-1. The second column shows the total amount invested at the end of selected time periods. The third column shows the value of investments and earnings if your investments earn 2 percent. The fourth column shows the value of your investments and earnings if your investments earn 8 percent. The search for higher returns is one reason many investors choose stocks and mutual funds, which offer higher potential returns compared to

	Total Amount of Annual Investments	Total Amount of Investments and Earnings at 2 Percent	Total Amount of Investments and Earnings at 8 Percent
10 years	$18,000	$19,710	$26,076
20 years	36,000	43,735	82,372
30 years	54,000	73,023	203,910
40 years	72,000	108,724	466,302

EXHIBIT 13-1
The amount of money accumulated over different time periods if you invested $1,800 each year and chose an investment that earned 2 percent or an investment that earned 8 percent

Financial Literacy Calculations

USING THE TIME VALUE OF MONEY TO CALCULATE INVESTMENT RETURNS

$3,000 invested each year at 5 percent for 25 years equals $143,181.

Question: How do you calculate this amount?

Answer: While this problem can be solved using a future value formula or a future value table—both illustrated in the Chapter 1 Appendix—today many people use a future value calculator that can be found on many internet websites.
   To work this problem, follow these steps:

1. Use a search engine like Google, Yahoo!, or Bing and enter the term "future value calculator." (To illustrate how easy it is to work the problem described above,

we used the calculator at keisan.casio.com/exec/system/1234231998.)

2. To solve the problem, enter the interest rate, number of years, annual payment frequency, and payment amount, and select the option for payments made at the end of the period.

3. For most internet calculators, once all the information has been entered, you simply click on "execute" or "calculate."

Now, It's Your Turn. Using an internet future value calculator, determine the future value of a $1,500 annual investment that earns 10 percent a year for 20 years.

Tryout problem answer: $85,913

certificates of deposit or savings accounts. *Be warned:* Investments with higher returns are not guaranteed. In order to obtain higher returns, you must be willing to accept more risk and sacrifice some safety.

The investment earnings illustrated in this section are taxable under current Internal Revenue Service guidelines. To take advantage of tax-free growth options, you may want to invest your money in a traditional individual retirement account (IRA), a Roth IRA, one of the tax-free investments described later in the text, or a 401(k) or 403(b) retirement account offered through your employer. The details about different types of retirement accounts are presented in Chapter 18.

PFP Sheet 55
Investment Goals

✔ PRACTICE QUIZ 13-1

1. Why should an investor develop specific investment goals?
2. What factors should you consider when performing a financial checkup?
3. Explain the time value of money concept and how it affects your investment program.
4. Using the information in the *Financial Literacy Calculations* feature "Using the Time Value of Money to Calculate Investment Returns," calculate the future value of your investments if you invest $1,200 each year for 18 years. Assume your investments earn 7 percent each year.

Factors Affecting the Choice of Investments

LO13-2

Assess how safety, risk, income, growth, and liquidity affect your investment decisions.

Millions of Americans buy stocks, bonds, or mutual funds, purchase real estate, or make similar investments. And they all have reasons for investing their money. Some people want to supplement their retirement income when they reach age 65, while others want to become millionaires before age 40. Although each investor may have specific, individual goals for investing, all investors must consider a number of factors before choosing an investment alternative.

SAFETY AND RISK

For most people, the perfect investment is one with no risk and above average returns. Unfortunately, the perfect investment does not exist, because of the relationship between safety and risk. The safety and risk factors are two sides of the same coin. *Safety* in an investment means minimal risk of loss. On the other hand, *risk* in an investment means a measure of uncertainty about the outcome.

Investments range from very safe to very risky. At one end of the investment spectrum are very safe investments that attract conservative investors. Investments in this category include government bonds, certificates of deposit, and certain stocks, mutual funds, and corporate bonds. Real estate may also sometimes be a very safe investment. At the other end of the investment spectrum are speculative investments. A **speculative investment** is a high-risk investment made in the hope of earning a relatively large profit in a short time. Such investments offer the possibility of larger dollar returns, but if they are unsuccessful, you may lose most or all of your initial investment. Speculative stocks, certain bonds, some mutual funds, some real estate, commodities, options, and collectibles are high-risk investments.

speculative investment A high-risk investment made in the hope of earning a relatively large profit in a short time.

THE RISK–RETURN TRADE-OFF

Some risk is associated with all investments. In fact, you may experience two types of risks with investments.

- First, investors often choose some investments because they provide a predictable source of income. For example, you may choose to purchase a corporate bond because the bond pays a specific amount of interest every six months. If the corporation experiences financial difficulties, it may default on interest payments. In other words, there is a risk that you will not receive future income payments.

- A second type of risk associated with many investments is that an investment will decrease in value. For example, the value of Occidental Petroleum decreased over 70 percent during 2020 when investors became concerned about the effect of lower demand for its oil, gas, and petroleum products, falling oil prices in the world oil markets, and a drop in the value of the firm's oil and gas assets.[5]

Exhibit 13-2 lists a number of factors related to safety and risk that can affect an investor's choice of investments.

Conservative Investments with Less Risk	Speculative Investments with Higher Risks
People with no financial training or investment background	Investors with financial training and investment background
Older investors	Younger investors
Lower-income investors	Higher-income investors
Families with children	Married couples with no children or single individuals
Employees worried about job loss	Employees with secure employment positions

EXHIBIT 13-2
Factors that can affect your tolerance for risk and your investment choices

Financial Literacy for My Life

A QUICK TEST TO MEASURE INVESTMENT RISK TOLERANCE

To find tools to measure your risk tolerance and to help you decide the type of investments to include in your investment portfolio, use an internet search engine like Google or Yahoo! and enter the words "risk tolerance quiz."

One useful source is the Investment Risk Tolerance Quiz provided by Rutgers University at https://njaes.rutgers.edu/money/assessment-tools/investment-risk-tolerance-quiz.pdf.

Just by collecting your answers to a few questions, most sites will provide information about how much money you should invest in safe investments versus more risk-oriented, speculative investments. Invest a few minutes to answer the 13 questions in the Investment Risk Tolerance Quiz. Then use the grid at the bottom of the quiz to determine your risk tolerance.

EVALUATING YOUR TOLERANCE FOR RISK When investing, not everyone has the same tolerance for risk. Some people will seek investments that offer the least risk. For example, Ana Luna was injured in a work-related accident three years ago. After a lengthy lawsuit, she received a legal settlement totaling $420,000. When she thought about the future, she knew she needed to get a job, but realized she would be forced to acquire new employment skills. She also realized she had received a great deal of money that could be invested to provide a steady source of income, not only for the next two years while she obtained job training but also for the remainder of her life. Having never invested before, she quickly realized her tolerance for risk was minimal.

When people choose investments that have a higher degree of risk, they expect larger returns. Simply put, one basic rule sums up the relationship between the factors of safety and risk: *The potential return on any investment should be directly related to the risk the investor assumes.* To help you determine how much risk you are willing to assume, take the test for risk tolerance presented in the *Financial Literacy for My Life: A Quick Test to Measure Investment Risk Tolerance* feature.

Often, beginning investors are afraid of the risk associated with many investments. But it helps to remember that without risk, it is impossible to obtain larger returns that really make an investment program grow. The key is to determine how much risk you are willing to assume, and then choose quality investments that offer higher returns without an unacceptably high risk.

CALCULATING RETURN ON AN INVESTMENT When you invest, you expect a return on your investment. For example, if you purchase a one-year certificate of deposit (CD) *guaranteed* by the FDIC (Federal Deposit Insurance Corporation), your CD may earn 1.5 percent a year. At the end of one year, you receive your initial investment plus 1.5 percent interest. Another investment alternative, such as a mutual fund, may earn 7 percent a year. In this case, you receive an additional 5.5 percent return when compared to the CD because you chose to invest in a mutual fund that increased in value. While most investors don't like to think about it, an investor must assume more risk because the mutual fund could decrease in value for a number of reasons, and your original investment or any possible returns are *not guaranteed.*

rate of return The total income you receive on an investment over a specific period of time divided by the original amount invested.

To determine how much you actually earn on an investment over a specific period of time, you can calculate your rate of return. To calculate **rate of return**, the total income you receive on an investment over a specific period of time is divided by the original amount invested.

EXAMPLE: Rate of Return (Procter & Gamble)

Assume that you invest $6,400 in stock issued by consumer-goods giant Procter & Gamble. Also assume its stock pays you $40 in dividends this year and that the stock is worth $6,950 at the end of one year. Your rate of return is 9.2 percent, as illustrated below.

$$\text{Rate of return} = \frac{\text{Increase (+) or decrease (−) in value + Annual income}}{\text{Original investment}}$$

$$\text{Rate of return} = \frac{\$550 + \$40}{\$6,400}$$

$$= \frac{\$590}{\$6,400}$$

$$= 0.092$$

$$= 9.2\%$$

Note: If an investment decreases in value, the formula used to calculate the rate of return is the same, but the answer is a negative number. Also, if based on projections for the value of the stock and future dividends, the rate of return you calculate is only as good as the projections used in the calculations.

COMPONENTS OF THE RISK FACTOR

When choosing an investment, you must carefully evaluate changes in the risk factor. In fact, the overall risk factor can be broken down into five components.

INFLATION RISK There is a risk that the financial return on an investment will not keep pace with the inflation rate. To see how inflation reduces your buying power, let's assume you deposited $10,000 in a bank account that earns 2 percent interest. At the end of one year, your money will have earned $200 ($10,000 × 2% = $200). Assuming an inflation rate of 3 percent, it will cost you an additional $300 ($10,000 × 3% = $300), or a total of $10,300, to purchase the same amount of goods you could have purchased for $10,000 a year earlier. Thus, even though you earned $200, you lost $100 in purchasing power. And after paying taxes on the $200 interest, your loss of purchasing power is even greater.

INTEREST RATE RISK The interest rate risk associated with government or corporate bonds is the result of changes in interest rates in the economy, increases or decreases in interest rates for bonds of comparable quality, and the financial condition of the corporation or government entity that issued the bonds. For example, assume you purchase a $1,000 Amazon corporate bond that pays 3.15 percent interest. Also, assume you hold it for three years before deciding to sell your bond. If bond interest rates for new bonds of comparable quality increase to 4.5 percent during the three years you own the Amazon bond, the market value of your bond that pays 3.15 percent will decrease. No investor will buy your 3.15 percent bond for $1,000 since they can purchase a $1,000 bond of comparable quality that pays 4.5 percent. As a result, you will have to sell your bond for less than $1,000 or hold it until maturity.

my life 2

I understand how the factors of safety and risk affect an investment decision.

While some people are afraid of investment risk, the fact is that you must choose investments with acceptable risk in order to generate higher returns.

To help determine the amount of risk you are comfortable with, why not take a look at the material on measuring investment risk presented in the *Financial Literacy for My Life* feature, "A Quick Test to Measure Investment Risk Tolerance."

On the other hand, if bond interest rates for new, comparable bonds decrease to 2.5 percent during the three-year period you own the Amazon bond, the market value of your bond that pays 3.15 percent will increase. In this situation, you must decide if you will sell your bond at the higher price or hold it until maturity and collect the $1,000 face value.

BUSINESS FAILURE RISK   The risk of business failure is associated with investments in stock, corporate bonds, and mutual funds that invest in stocks or bonds. With each of these investments, you face the possibility that bad management, unsuccessful products, competition, the economy, or a host of other factors will cause a business to be less profitable than originally anticipated. Lower profits usually mean lower dividends or no dividends at all. If the business continues to operate at a loss, even interest payments and repayment of bonds may be questionable. The business may even fail and be forced to file for bankruptcy, in which case your investment may become totally worthless. Before ignoring the possibility of business failure, consider the plight of employees and investors who owned JCPenney bonds or stock. Because of a decline in sales and massive debt, the company filed for bankruptcy in 2020. At the time of publication, the company had emerged from bankruptcy and was closing stores, reducing expenses, and attempting to increase sales. Still, Penney's bonds and stock were trading at record low levels. In fact, many bondholders and stockholders are still wondering if the retailer will survive.

Of course, the best way to protect yourself against such losses is to carefully evaluate (and continue to evaluate) the companies that issue the stocks and bonds you purchase. It also helps to purchase different types of investments. Business failure risk can also affect the value of mutual funds that invest in stocks and corporate bonds or municipal bonds issued by local and state governments.

MARKET RISK   Two different types of risk—systematic and unsystematic—can affect the market value of stocks, bonds, mutual funds, real estate, and other investments. *Systematic* risk occurs because of overall risks in the market and the economy. Factors such as an economic crisis, increasing interest rates, changes in consumer purchasing power, political activity, a pandemic, natural disasters, and wars all represent sources of systematic risk. Because this type of risk affects the entire market, it is not possible to eliminate the risk through diversification. On the other hand, *unsystematic* risk affects a specific company or a specific industry. Because this type of risk affects one company or one industry, unsystematic risk can be reduced by diversifying an investment portfolio. For example, an investor who owns 30 different stocks in different industries can reduce unsystematic risk because the portfolio is well diversified. Anything that happens to one company in the investor's portfolio is not likely to wipe out the value of the entire portfolio.

The prices of stocks, bonds, mutual funds, and other investments may also fluctuate because of the behavior of investors in the marketplace. Fluctuations of this type may have nothing to do with the fundamental changes in the financial health of corporations or the corporations that issue the bonds or stocks contained in a mutual fund.

GLOBAL INVESTMENT RISK   Today more investors are investing in stocks and bonds issued by foreign firms and in international mutual funds because investing in international securities can diversify your portfolio. For example, when the U.S. markets are in decline, other markets around the world may be increasing. An investor can purchase stocks or bonds issued by individual foreign firms or purchase shares in an international mutual fund. For investors with less than $200,000 to invest and who don't have the expertise required to evaluate foreign firms or who are unaccustomed to the risks in foreign investments, international mutual funds offer more safety.

INVESTMENT INCOME

Investors sometimes purchase certain investments because they want a predictable source of income. The safest investments—savings accounts, certificates of deposit, and securities issued by the U.S. government—are also the most predictable sources of income. With these investments, you know exactly how much income will be paid on a specific date.

If investment income is a primary objective, you can also choose municipal bonds, corporate bonds, preferred stocks, or selected common stock issues. When purchasing these investments, most investors are concerned about the issuer's ability to continue making periodic interest or dividend payments. For example, some corporations, such as Colgate Palmolive and Coca-Cola, are very proud of their long record of consecutive dividend payments. Colgate Palmolive has paid dividends since 1895; Coca-Cola has paid dividends since 1920.

Other investments that may provide income potential are mutual funds and real estate rental property. Although the income from mutual funds is not guaranteed, you can choose funds whose primary objective is income. Income from rental property is not guaranteed, because the possibility of either vacancies or unexpected repair bills always exists.

INVESTMENT GROWTH

Question: What do Facebook, Amazon, and Netflix have in common?
Answer: According to many financial experts, these three companies are "growth" stocks because each firm's stock has the potential to increase in value.

Often the greatest opportunity for growth is an investment in common stock. Companies with better than average earnings potential, sales revenues that are increasing, and managers who can solve the problems associated with rapid expansion are often considered to be growth companies. These same companies generally pay little or nothing in dividends. Thus, investors often sacrifice immediate cash dividends in return for increased stock values in the future.

For most growth companies, profits that would normally be paid to stockholders are reinvested in the companies. The money the companies keep can provide at least part of the financing they need for future growth and expansion and control the cost of borrowing money. As a result, they grow at an even faster pace.

Other investments that may offer growth potential include selected mutual funds and real estate. For example, many mutual funds are referred to as growth funds or aggressive growth funds because of the growth potential of the individual securities included in the fund.

INVESTMENT LIQUIDITY

Liquidity is the ability to buy or sell an investment quickly without substantially affecting the investment's value. Investments range from near-cash investments to frozen investments from which it is sometimes hard to get your money. Checking and savings accounts are very liquid because you can get cash by writing a check or withdrawing money from your savings account. Certificates of deposit impose penalties for withdrawing money before the maturity date.

With other investments, you may be able to sell quickly, but market conditions, economic conditions, or a number of other factors may prevent you from regaining the amount you originally invested. For example, the owner of real estate may have to lower the asking price to find a buyer. And it may be difficult to find a buyer for investments in collectibles such as antiques and paintings.

liquidity The ability to buy or sell an investment quickly without substantially affecting the investment's value.

PRACTICE QUIZ 13-2

1. Explain the following statement: "safety and risk are two sides of the same coin."
2. In your own words, describe the risk–return trade-off.
3. What are the five components of the risk factor?
4. How do income, growth, and liquidity affect your choice of an investment?

Asset Allocation and Investment Alternatives

LO13-3

Explain how asset allocation and different investment alternatives affect your investment plan.

By now, you are probably thinking, How can I choose the right investment for me? Good question. To help answer that question, consider the following:

- For the last 30 years, stocks as measured by the Standard & Poor's 500 Index have returned 11.47 percent a year—well ahead of the nation's inflation rate.[6]
- Over the 10-year period from 2009 to 2019, stocks measured by the Standard & Poor's 500 index averaged 14.09 percent annual growth.[7]
- Over the five-year period from 2015 to 2020, stocks as measured by the Standard & Poor's 500 Index have averaged 12.37 percent annual growth.[8]
- Since 1926, stocks had positive gains in 70 years.[9]
- Since 1926, stocks lost money in 25 years.[10]

The preceding statistics are impressive, and it would be easy to think that everyone should invest in stocks because they offer the largest returns when compared to bonds, certificates of deposits, savings accounts, and other more conservative investments. And yet, as indicated by the last bulleted item, stocks can lose money or decline in value. For more proof that stocks can decrease in value, ask an investor what happened to the value of their stock investments on March 16, 2020. That's the day when the Dow Jones Industrial Average declined almost 3,000 points—the worst one-day point decline in history.[11] The drop in value that day was caused by a number of factors, including the fear of the COVID-19 pandemic, the effect of declining oil prices on the economy, and many other factors. Simply put, investors were scared, *and* they sold stocks. In reality, stocks may have a place in every investment portfolio, but always remember stock returns are not guaranteed, there is more risk involved with stocks than with more conservative investments, and there is more to establishing a long-term investment program than just picking a bunch of stocks. Before making the decision to purchase stocks, consider the factors of asset allocation, the time period that your investments will work for you, and your age.

ASSET ALLOCATION AND DIVERSIFICATION

asset allocation The process of spreading your assets among several different types of investments (sometimes referred to as asset classes) to lessen risk.

Asset allocation is the process of spreading your assets among several different types of investments (sometimes referred to as asset classes) to lessen risk. While the term *asset allocation* is a fancy way of saying it, simply put, it really means that you need to diversify and avoid the pitfall of putting all your eggs in one basket—a common mistake made by investors. The diversification provided by investing in *different* asset classes provides a measure of safety and reduces risk, because a loss in one type of investment is usually offset by gains from other types of investments. Typical asset classes include:

- Stocks issued by large corporations (large cap)
- Stocks issued by medium-size corporations (midcap)

- Stocks issued by small companies (small cap)
- Foreign stocks
- Bonds
- Cash

Note: Mutual funds can also be included as an asset class, but the typical mutual fund will invest in the securities in the preceding list or in a combination of those securities.

How difficult is it to find the right mix of asset classes? It is surprisingly easy! According to noted financial expert and author William Bernstein, if you had invested in the stocks and bonds that make up the widely quoted indexes for large-cap U.S. stocks, small-cap U.S. stocks, foreign stocks, and high-quality U.S. bonds (25 percent in each of these asset classes), you would have beaten over 90 percent of all professional money managers and with considerably less risk over a 10- or 20-year period.[12] And Bernstein is not alone. Today, most financial experts recommend asset allocation as a valued tool that can reduce the risk associated with long-term investment programs.

The percentage of your investments that should be invested in each asset class is determined by

- Your age,
- Investment goals,
- Ability to tolerate risk,
- How much you can save and invest each year,
- The dollar value of your current investments,
- The economic outlook for the economy,
- And several other factors.

Important Question: Based on the preceding factors, what percentage of your assets do you want to invest in stocks and bonds? What percentage of your assets do you want to put in certificates of deposit and cash? For many investors, the answers to these questions are often tied to their tolerance for risk. Remember the basic rule presented earlier in this chapter: *The potential return on any investment should be directly related to the risk the investor assumes.*

Generally, younger investors invest more heavily in stocks and mutual funds that invest in stocks. A typical asset allocation for a 28-year-old investor is illustrated in Exhibit 13-3.

smart money minute

The more you make, the more challenging your investment goals can be. Here are household income levels for U.S. families.

Annual Income	Percentage of American Population
Over $100,000	34 percent
$75,000 to $99,999	12 percent
$50,000 to $74,999	17 percent
$25,000 to $49,999	20 percent
Under $25,000	17 percent

Source: "Table A-2, Households by Total Money Income," U.S. Bureau of the Census website, https://www.census.gov/library/publications/2020/demo/p60-270.html, accessed September 15, 2020.

Asset Allocation by Investment Category

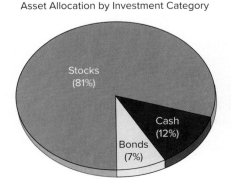

Stocks (81%)

Cash (12%)

Bonds (7%)

EXHIBIT 13-3

Suggested asset allocation for a young investor

Source: Bankrate.com (http://bankrate.com/calculators/retirement/asset-allocation.aspx), accessed December 14, 2020.

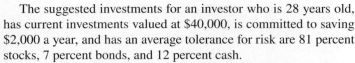

I use asset allocation to minimize risks when investing.

You may want to use one of the asset allocation calculators available on the internet to determine what percentage of your assets should be in different types of investments. To find an asset allocation calculator, use a search engine like Yahoo!, Google, or Bing and enter "asset allocation calculator" in the search box.

The suggested investments for an investor who is 28 years old, has current investments valued at $40,000, is committed to saving $2,000 a year, and has an average tolerance for risk are 81 percent stocks, 7 percent bonds, and 12 percent cash.

Keep in mind some people find that their other goals may affect their ability to begin or continue an investment program. For example, if you are 28 and just got married, your goals may include starting a family, buying your first home, and buying furniture. That's why it is important to look at the big picture and establish what's important to you. With that in mind, don't forget how important it is to start saving and investing sooner rather than later.

As investors get older, their asset allocations change and typically become more conservative. Assume this same investor is now 60 years old, has current investments valued at $200,000, is still saving $2,000 a year, and still has an average tolerance for risk. The asset calculator at Bankrate.com suggests that the 60-year-old investor should have 52 percent stocks, 21 percent bonds, and 27 percent cash. In addition to financial goals, other goals also change. A person in midlife or retirement may be more concerned about planning for retirement or making sure they have enough money to live on when they do retire than someone in their late 20s.

You can use the asset allocation calculator at https://www.bankrate.com/calculators/retirement/asset-allocation.aspx to determine your own asset mix. It's easy because all you have to do is enter your information, and press Calculate. Then you can use the suggestions to either build your own investment portfolio or fine-tune your existing portfolio.

To help you decide how much risk is appropriate for your investment portfolio, many financial planners suggest that you think of your investment portfolio as a pyramid consisting of four levels, as illustrated in Exhibit 13-4. In Exhibit 13-4, cash, CDs, and other conservative investments provide the foundation for your financial security. After the foundation is established in level 1, most investors choose from the investments in levels 2 and 3. Be warned: Many investors may decide the investments in level 4 are too speculative for their investment program. While the investments at this level may provide high dollar returns, they also have an unacceptable level of risk for many investors.

It may be necessary to adjust your asset allocation from time to time. Often, the main reasons for making changes are because of the amount of time that your investments have to work for you and your age.

THE TIME FACTOR   The amount of time that your investments have to work for you is another important factor when managing your investment portfolio. Review the

EXHIBIT 13-4   Typical investments for financial security, safety and income, growth, and speculation

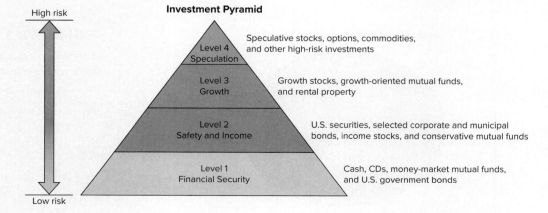

investment returns presented earlier in this section. Over a long period of time, stocks have returned more than other investment alternatives. And yet, during the same period, there were years when stocks decreased in value.[13] The point is that if you invested at the wrong time and then couldn't wait for the investment to recover, you would lose money.

The amount of time you have before you need to withdraw money from your investments is crucial. If you can leave your investments alone and let them work for 5 to 10 years or more, then you can invest in stocks and mutual funds. On the other hand, if you need your investment money in two years, you should probably invest in short-term government bonds, highly rated corporate bonds, certificates of deposit, or savings accounts. By taking a more conservative approach for short-term investments, you reduce the possibility of having to sell your investments at a loss because of a recession, a staggering economy, a pandemic, or world events that affect the financial markets.

YOUR AGE A final factor to consider when choosing investments is your age. Younger investors tend to invest a large percentage of their nest egg in growth-oriented investments. If their investments take a nosedive, they have time to recover. As you get older, your goals will change and you may want to use asset allocation to diversify your portfolio. On the other hand, older investors tend to be more conservative and invest in government bonds, high-quality corporate bonds, and very safe corporate stocks or mutual funds. Older investors don't have as much time to recover if their investments take a nosedive. As a result, a smaller percentage of their nest egg is placed in growth-oriented investments.

How much of your portfolio should be in growth-oriented investments? Many financial planners suggest that you subtract your age from 100, and the difference is the percentage of your assets that should be invested in growth investments. For example, if you are 40 years old, subtract 40 from 100, which gives you 60. Therefore, 60 percent of your assets should be invested in growth-oriented investments, while the remaining 40 percent should be kept in safer, more conservative investments. While this calculation is quick and easy and does provide a rough estimate to determine what percentage of your investment should be growth investments, asset allocation calculators like the one used in Exhibit 13-3 may provide more information about the different types of investments needed to create a diversified portfolio.

AN OVERVIEW OF INVESTMENT ALTERNATIVES

Once you have considered the risks involved when investing, asset allocation, the length of time your investments can work for you, and your age, it's time to consider which investment alternative is right for you. The remainder of this section provides a brief overview of different investment alternatives. The remaining investment chapters provide more detailed information on stocks, bonds, mutual funds, real estate, and other investment alternatives.

STOCK OR EQUITY FINANCING **Equity capital** is money that a business obtains from its owners. If a business is a sole proprietorship or a partnership, it acquires equity capital when the owners invest their own money in the business. For a corporation, equity capital is provided by stockholders, who buy shares of its stock. Since all stockholders are owners, they share in the success of the corporation. This can make buying stock an attractive investment opportunity.

equity capital Money that a business obtains from its owners.

However, you should consider at least two factors before investing in stock. *First,* a corporation is not required to repay the money obtained from the sale of stock or to repurchase the stock at a later date. Assume you purchased 100 shares of Southwest Airlines stock. Later you decide to sell your Southwest stock. Your stock is sold to another investor, not back to the company. In many cases, stockholders sell stock because they think its price is going to decrease in value. At the same time, other stockholders buy that stock because they think its price is going to increase. This creates a situation in which either the sellers or the buyers earn a profit while the other party to the transaction experiences a loss.

Second, a corporation is under no legal obligation to pay dividends to stockholders. A **dividend** is a distribution of money, stock, or other property that a corporation pays to stockholders. Dividends are paid out of earnings, but if a corporation that usually pays dividends has a bad year, its board of directors can vote to reduce or even omit dividend payments to help pay necessary business expenses. Corporations may also retain earnings to make additional financing available for expansion, acquisitions, research and product development, or other business activities.

There are two basic types of stock: *common stock* and *preferred stock.* A share of common stock represents the most basic form of corporate ownership. People often purchase common stock because this type of investment can provide (1) a source of income if the company pays dividends and (2) growth potential if the dollar value of the stock increases.

The most important priority an investor in preferred stock enjoys is receiving cash dividends before common stockholders are paid any cash dividends. This factor is especially important when a corporation is experiencing financial problems and cannot pay cash dividends to both preferred and common stockholders. Other factors you should consider before purchasing either common or preferred stock are discussed in Chapter 14.

CORPORATE AND GOVERNMENT BONDS   There are two types of bonds an investor should consider. A **corporate bond** is a corporation's written pledge to repay a specified amount of money, along with interest. A **government bond** is the written pledge of a government or a municipality to repay a specified sum of money, along with interest. Thus, when you buy a bond, you are loaning a corporation or government entity money for a period of time. Regardless of who issues the bond, you need to consider two questions before investing in bonds.

First, will the bond be repaid at maturity? The **maturity date** is the date on which a corporation, government, or municipality will repay the borrowed money. For example, assume you purchase a $1,000 Clorox Company corporate bond that pays 3.90 percent interest. The maturity date is May 15, 2028—the date the corporation will repay your investment. The maturity dates for most bonds range between 1 and 30 years. An investor who purchases a bond has two options: Keep the bond until maturity and then redeem it, or sell the bond to another investor before maturity. In either case, the value of the bond is closely tied to the ability of the corporation or government entity to repay the bond at maturity. A bond's value can decrease if a corporation experiences financial problems and investors are concerned about the prospects of repayment at maturity. Also, the value of a bond may increase or decrease before it reaches maturity because of changes in interest rates in the economy. To review how interest rates affect the value of a bond, review the material on interest rate risk discussed in the previous section, Factors Affecting the Choice of Investments. *Second,* will the corporation or government entity be able to maintain interest payments to bondholders until maturity? Bondholders normally receive interest payments every six months. For example, investors who purchase the Clorox bond in the previous example earn 3.90 percent each year until maturity. To calculate the amount of interest, you can use the formula below.

Dollar amount of annual interest = Face value × Interest rate.

If you own the Clorox bond that pays 3.90 percent, you will receive $39 each year until maturity ($1,000 × .0390 = $39). Because interest payments on bonds are paid every six months, investors would receive a check for $19.50 every six months for each bond they own.

Receiving periodic interest payments until maturity is one method of making money on a bond investment. Investors also use two other methods that can provide more liberal returns on bond investments. Chapter 15 discusses each of these methods and provides more details on evaluating bond investments.

dividend A distribution of money, stock, or other property that a corporation pays to stockholders.

corporate bond A corporation's written pledge to repay a specified amount of money with interest.

government bond A written pledge of a government or a municipality to repay a specified sum of money, along with interest.

maturity date The date on which a corporation, government, or municipality will repay the borrowed money.

HOW TO . . .   **Open an Account with a Brokerage Firm**

Often people never begin investing because they don't know how to open a brokerage account. In reality, it's easier than you think, if you follow the steps below.

Take This Step	Suggested Action
1. Establish an emergency fund and develop investment goals.	In a nutshell, you should establish an emergency fund equal to at least three months of living expenses. Your goals must be specific, measurable, and tailored to your particular financial needs. Don't skip this step—it's important.
2. Choose the type of brokerage account that meets your needs.	Before making this decision, research the following three types of accounts: • A taxable account with no immediate or deferred tax benefits. • A traditional IRA account with immediate tax benefits but that requires you to pay taxes when money is withdrawn. There is a penalty if money is withdrawn before you reach age 59½. Once you reach age 72 (70½ if you turned 70½ before Jan 1, 2020), you are required to take annual Required Minimum Distributions (RMDs) from your retirement accounts. • A Roth IRA with no immediate tax benefits, and the ability to withdraw your contributions at any time and tax-free withdrawals of earnings when you reach age 59½ or older and your account has been open for at least five years.
3. Save some money.	While some brokerage firms do not require a minimum deposit, other firms may require an initial deposit of up to $2,000. The minimum amount also may depend on whether you are opening a taxable, traditional IRA, or Roth IRA account.
4. Research different brokerage firms.	All brokerage firms have a website where you can get information about commissions, fees, available research, financial advice, and other important topics. Don't just choose the last company you saw advertised on TV. Do the research.
5. Do the paperwork.	Once you have made the choice, you can go online and follow the steps required to open an account. You can also talk to the firm's representative by going to a branch office or by telephone.

MUTUAL FUNDS A **mutual fund** pools the money from many investors—its shareholders—to invest in a variety of securities. When choosing a mutual fund, *professional management* is an especially important factor for investors with little or no previous investment experience. Another reason investors choose mutual funds is *diversification.* Since mutual funds invest in a number of different securities, an occasional loss in one security is often offset by gains in other securities. As a result, the diversification provided by a mutual fund reduces risk.

> **mutual fund** Pools the money of many investors—its shareholders—to invest in a variety of securities.

The goals of one investor often differ from those of another. The managers of mutual funds realize this and tailor their funds to meet their clients' needs and objectives. As a result of all the different investment alternatives, mutual funds range from very conservative to extremely speculative investments.

Many investors choose mutual funds for their retirement accounts, including traditional IRAs, Roth IRAs, and retirement plans sponsored by your employer. As mentioned earlier in this chapter, many employees contribute a portion of their salary to a retirement account. And in many cases, the employer matches the employee's contribution.

Although investing money in a mutual fund provides professional management, even the best managers can make errors in judgment. *The responsibility for choosing the right mutual fund is still based on your evaluation of a mutual fund investment.*

One of the major concerns for investors who choose mutual funds is fees. Mutual fund fees may include sales charges, redemption fees, management fees, and other fees. Knowing these fees is important because they reduce your investment return. Together, all the different management fees and fund operating costs are often referred to as an **expense ratio**. Many financial planners recommend that you choose a mutual fund with an expense ratio of 1 percent or less. This is an important factor to consider when evaluating a mutual fund. Chapter 16 presents more information on the different types of mutual funds, the costs involved, and techniques for evaluating mutual fund investments.

In order to buy stocks, bonds, mutual funds, and other financial securities, you will need to open a brokerage account. This sounds complicated, but it isn't. Please see the nearby *How To . . . Open an Account with a Brokerage Firm* feature on opening a brokerage account for details.

expense ratio All the different management fees and fund operating costs for a specific mutual fund.

REAL ESTATE   As a rule, real estate increases in value and eventually sells at a profit, but there are no guarantees. Although many beginning investors believe real estate values increase by 10 or 15 percent a year, in reality the nationwide average annual increase is about 3 to 5 percent over a long period of time. This growth rate makes real estate a long-term investment and not a get-rich-quick scheme. Success often depends on the economy, interest rates, and many other factors, if you invest in residential or commercial property. It also helps to remember that real estate values can decrease because of an economic crisis or recession.

Success in real estate investments depends on how well you evaluate alternatives. Experts often tell would-be investors that the three most important factors when evaluating a potential real estate investment are *location, location,* and *location.* Other factors may also determine whether or not a piece of real estate is a good investment. For example, you should answer the following questions before making a decision to purchase any property:

1. Is the property priced competitively with similar properties?
2. What type of financing is available, if any?
3. How much are the taxes?
4. Does the property need repairs?
5. What is the condition of the buildings and houses in the immediate area?
6. Why are the present owners selling the property?
7. Is there a chance that the property will decrease in value?

Chapter 17 presents additional information on how to evaluate a real estate investment.

OTHER INVESTMENT ALTERNATIVES   As defined earlier in this chapter, a speculative investment is a high-risk investment made in the hope of earning a relatively large profit in a short time. By its very nature, any investment may be speculative; that is, it may be quite risky. However, a true speculative investment is speculative because of the methods investors use to earn a quick profit. Typical speculative investments include:

- Options
- Commodities
- Derivatives

- Bitcoin and other cryptocurrencies
- Precious metals and gemstones
- Antiques and collectibles

Without exception, investments of this kind are normally referred to as speculative for one reason or another. For example, the gold market has many unscrupulous dealers who sell worthless gold-plated lead coins to unsuspecting, uninformed investors. With any speculative investment, it is extremely important to deal with reputable dealers and recognized investment firms. It pays to be careful. Chapter 14 presents information on options. Chapter 17 discusses precious metals, gemstones, and collectibles.

smart money minute

When it comes to planning your financial future, take nothing for granted—ask questions, demand answers, and make sure you understand the consequences of your investment choices before you commit your hard-earned money.

A PERSONAL PLAN FOR INVESTING

Earlier in this chapter, we examined how safety, risk, income, growth, and liquidity affect your investment choices. In the preceding section, we looked at investment alternatives. Now let's compare the factors that affect the choice of investments with each alternative. Exhibit 13-5 compares the alternatives in terms of safety, risk, income, growth, and liquidity.

With this type of information, it is now possible to begin building a personal plan for investing. Most people use a series of steps like those listed in Exhibit 13-6. And while each step is important, establishing investment goals (step 1), evaluating risk and potential return for each investment alternative (step 5), and continued evaluation (step 8) may be the most important.

EXHIBIT 13-5 Factors used to evaluate typical investment alternatives

	Type of Investment	Safety	Risk	Income	Growth	Liquidity
Traditional Investments	Common stock	Average	Average	Average	High	Average
	Preferred stock	Average	Average	High	Average	Average
	Corporate bonds	Average	Average	High	Low	Average
	Government bonds	High	Low	Low	Low	High
	Mutual funds	Average	Average	Average	Average	Average
	Real estate	Average	Average	Average	Average	Low
Speculative Investments	Options	Low	High	N/A	Low	Average
	Commodities	Low	High	N/A	Low	Average
	Derivatives	Low	High	N/A	Low	Average
	Precious metals, gemstones, antiques, and collectibles	Low	High	N/A	Low	Low

N/A = Not applicable.

EXHIBIT 13-6
Steps for effective investment planning

1. Establish your investment goals.
2. Determine the amount of money you need to obtain your goals.
3. Specify the amount of money you currently have available to fund your investments.
4. List different investments that you want to evaluate.
5. Evaluate (a) the risk factor and (b) the potential return for all investments.
6. Reduce possible investments to a reasonable number.
7. Choose at least two different investments.
8. Continue to evaluate your investment program.

PFP Sheet 56
Investment Risk

 PRACTICE QUIZ 13-3

1. How can asset allocation help you build an investment program to reach your financial goals?
2. How do the time your investments have to work for you and your age affect your investment program?
3. Of all the investment alternatives presented in this section, which one do you think would help you obtain your investment goals? Explain your answer.
4. What factors does an asset allocation calculator consider when recommending the percentage of stocks, bonds, and cash you should have in your investment portfolio?

Factors That Reduce Investment Risk

LO13-4

Recognize the importance of your role in a personal investment program.

In this section, we examine the factors that can spell the difference between success and failure for an investor. We begin by considering your role in the investment process.

YOUR ROLE IN THE INVESTMENT PROCESS

An informed investor has a much better chance of choosing the types of investments that will increase in value. But you have to be willing to work and learn if you want to be an informed investor.

EVALUATE POTENTIAL INVESTMENTS   Let's assume you have $25,000 to invest. Also assume your investment will earn a 10 percent return the first year. At the end of one year, you will have earned $2,500 and your investment will be worth $27,500. Now ask yourself: How long would it take to earn $2,500 if I had to work for this amount of money at a job? For some people it might take a month; for others, it might take longer. The point is that if you want this type of return, you should be willing to work for it. When choosing an investment, the work is the time needed to research different investments so that you can make an informed decision. In fact, much of the information in the remaining investment chapters will help you learn how to evaluate different investment opportunities.

MONITOR THE VALUE OF YOUR INVESTMENTS   Would you believe that some people invest their money, but don't track the value of their investments? They don't know if their investments have increased or decreased in value. They don't know if they should sell their investments or continue to hold them. A much better approach is to monitor the value of your investments.

Regardless of which type of investment you choose, monitoring your investment will help you determine if it increases or decreases in value. The *Financial Literacy Calculations: Monitoring the Value of Your Investment* feature presents further information on monitoring the value of your investments.

Financial Literacy Calculations

MONITORING THE VALUE OF YOUR INVESTMENT

To monitor the value of their investments, many investors use a simple chart like the one illustrated here. To construct a chart like this one, place the original purchase price of your investment on the side of the chart. Then use dollar increments of a logical amount to show increases and decreases in dollar value.

Place individual dates along the bottom of the chart. For stocks, bonds, mutual funds, and similar investments, you may want to graph every two weeks and chart current values on, say, a Friday. For longer-term investments like real estate, you can chart current values every six months. It is also possible to use computer software or websites to chart the value of your investments and your investment portfolio.

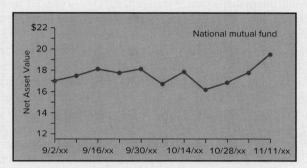

A WORD OF CAUTION

If an investment is beginning to have a large increase or decrease in value, you should watch that investment more

closely. You can still continue to chart at regular intervals, but you may want to check dollar values more frequently—in some cases, daily.

NOW IT'S YOUR TURN

Using the dates and the dollar amounts below, construct a graph to illustrate the price movements for a share of stock issued by Jordan Technology.

Date	Price
June 1	$19
June 15	$17
June 29	$18
July 13	$20
July 27	$22
August 10	$24
August 24	$22

KEEP ACCURATE AND CURRENT RECORDS Accurate recordkeeping can help you spot opportunities to maximize profits or reduce dollar losses when you sell your investments. Accurate recordkeeping can also help you decide whether you want to invest additional funds in a particular investment. At the very least, you should keep purchase records for each of your investments that include the actual dollar cost of the investment, plus any commissions or fees you paid, along with records of income (dividends, interest payments, rental income, etc.) you receive from your investment holdings. It is also useful to keep a list of the sources of information (internet addresses, business periodicals, research publications, etc.), along with copies of the material you used to evaluate each investment. Then, when it is time to reevaluate an existing investment, you will know where to begin your search for current information. Accurate recordkeeping is also necessary for tax purposes.

 my life | **4**

I am actively involved in my investment program.

You should be involved in and informed about your investment program. Read up on companies or government entities that issued the stocks, bonds, or securities that you own. Then take the time to continually evaluate the investments you own. Stay current by reading economic and financial news. Finally, develop a list of additional activities you can use to stay active in your investment plan.

OTHER FACTORS THAT IMPROVE INVESTMENT DECISIONS

To achieve their financial goals, many people seek professional help. In many cases, they turn to stockbrokers, lawyers, accountants, bankers, or insurance agents. However, these professionals are specialists in one specific field and may not be qualified to provide the type of advice required to develop a thorough financial plan. *Be warned: Some of the above professionals also earn commissions on the investments they recommend.*

The fact they are receiving commissions may influence which investments they recommend for their clients.

Another source of investment help is a financial planner who has had training in securities, insurance, taxes, real estate, and estate planning. Because financial planners have knowledge, expertise, and experience that you don't possess, they can help you make decisions and establish an investment program. While financial planners can receive commissions for the investment products they recommend, many charge consulting fees instead. For more information on the type of services financial planners provide, you may want to review the material in the Chapter 3 Appendix.

If you choose to use a financial planner or other professional, keep in mind that you are the one who must make the final decisions with the help of the professional. After all, it is your money *and* your financial future.

Regardless of whether you are making your own decisions or have professional help, you must consider the tax consequences of selling your investments. Taxes were covered in Chapter 4, and it is not our intention to cover them again. However, to reduce the amount of taxes you pay the Internal Revenue Service, it helps to consider how long you have owned an investment before deciding to sell an investment in a taxable account. Under current tax laws, short-term investment gains (investments held for one year or less) are taxed at ordinary tax rates just like your salary or other sources of ordinary income. On the other hand, long-term capital gains (investments held for more than one year) are taxed at reduced tax rates. Long-term capital gains are taxed at 0, 15, or 20 percent. The actual rate you pay is determined by your total income earned for a specific year.

It is also possible to avoid paying taxes or defer paying taxes on investment gains if your investments are held in a Roth IRA, traditional IRA, or specific types of retirement plans. To learn more, you may want to read the material on retirement plans presented in Chapter 18 or visit brokerage firm websites that offer different types of retirement accounts. For more information on how investment gains or losses are taxed, you can also visit the Internal Revenue Service website at www.irs.gov.

personal fintech

Some investors make their own decisions; others use professional account executives. Still others use a financial planner. Now, there's another choice: A robo advisor. Robo advisors are automated online software platforms that provide investment advice. To use a robo advisor, clients supply information about their short- and long-term goals, their risk tolerance, and their current financial situation. Then, the robo advisor uses the information to make suggestions and manage the client's portfolio. Today, many financial service companies, including Vanguard, Wealthfront, Robinhood, and Merrill, offer robo advisors that can help you plan and attain your financial goals.

How About You?   Would you use a robo advisor to help plan your financial future?

✔ PRACTICE QUIZ 13-4

1. What is your role in the investment process?
2. Why should you monitor the value of your investment?
3. Assume that you have $10,000 that can be invested. Would you make your own decisions or seek professional help? Explain your answer.

Sources of Investment Information

LO13-5

Use various sources of financial information to reduce risks and increase investment returns.

With most investments, more information is available than you can read and comprehend. Therefore, you must be selective in the type of information you use for evaluation purposes. Regardless of the number or availability of sources, always determine how reliable and accurate the information is. Following are sources of information you can use to evaluate your present and future investments.

THE INTERNET

Today more people have access to personal finance and investment information provided by internet sites than ever before. For example, you can obtain interest rates for certificates of deposit; current price information for stocks, bonds, and mutual funds; and brokers' recommendations to buy, hold, or sell corporate or government securities. You can even trade securities online with a click of your computer's mouse. You can also use financial planning software and financial calculators available on many personal finance websites to develop a personal financial plan. Finally, search engines like Yahoo!, Google, and Bing allow you to do a word search for any personal finance topic or investment alternative you want to explore.

Federal, state, and local governments; brokerage firms and investment companies; banks and other financial institutions; and corporations also each have a home page where you can obtain valuable investment information. For example, go to the General Mills website (www.generalmills.com) or the Coca-Cola website (https://www.coca-colacompany.com/) and click on the tab for "Investors" to obtain current financial information.

While it is impossible to list all the internet sites related to personal finance, those listed in Exhibit 13-7 will get you started. We will examine other specific internet sites in the remaining investment chapters.

smart money minute

With any investment, whether promoted in person, by mail, by telephone, or on the internet, a wise investor should always slow down, ask questions, and get written information. Take notes so you have a record of what you were told, and do your own research.

Source: Securities and Exchange Commission (SEC), www.sec.gov, accessed January 19, 2021.

EXHIBIT 13-7 Useful internet sites for personal financial planning

These websites provide information that you can use to establish a financial plan and begin an investment program.

Sponsor and Description	Web Address
The **Bloomberg** website provides current financial and economic news along with well-researched articles about the financial markets, business trends, and politics.	bloomberg.com
The **CNN/Business** website provides current financial news and material that can help you sharpen your personal finance and investment skills.	money.cnn.com
The **Financial Industry Regulatory Authority** is a great site for investors who want to learn more about investing and use different calculators to fine-tune their financial plan. The resources on this site can also help you budget, protect your identity, and learn about investment fraud.	finra.org
The **Investor.gov** website provides both general and detailed information about investing. You can also check to see if a broker or salesperson is licensed or has received investor complaints. Especially useful is the information on how to invest under the tab "Introduction to Investing."	investor.gov
The **Kiplinger** website contains a number of tools to help beginners become better investors. You may also want to study the information in the "Investing" and "Wealth Creation" sections on the site.	kiplinger.com
The **Motley Fool** website provides lighthearted but excellent educational materials. You may also want to study the information in the "Investing Basics" section on the site.	fool.com
The **Quicken** website provides information about software products and mobile apps that help you track your finances.	quicken.com
The **Securities and Exchange Commission** provides investment and financial information reported by companies that issue financial securities. You may also want to take a look at the "Education" section to see information specifically included for individual investors.	sec.gov
The **Yahoo! Finance** website is a go-to source for up-to-date financial information about the financial data needed to evaluate stocks or mutual funds. This site also provides news stories about the economy and specific businesses.	finance.yahoo.com

EXHIBIT 13-8
A reading list for successful investing

Although individual investors have their favorite sources for investment information, it is quite likely that most successful investors use some of the following newspapers, periodicals, and news programs on a regular basis.

Newspapers	*Business and General Periodicals*
• Metropolitan newspapers	• *Barron's*
• *The Wall Street Journal*	• *Bloomberg Businessweek*
• *The New York Times*	• *Fortune*
• *Financial Times*	• *Forbes*
• *USA Today*	• *The Economist*
Television	*Personal Financial and Consumer Publications*
• CNBC	• *Kiplinger's Personal Finance Magazine*
• MSNBC	• *Money*
• *Bloomberg*	• *Worth*

NEWSPAPERS AND NEWS PROGRAMS

One of the most readily available sources of information for the average investor is the financial pages of a metropolitan newspaper or *The Wall Street Journal.* In addition to limited stock coverage, newspapers may provide information on mutual funds, corporate and government bonds, other investment alternatives, and general economic news. Information on how to read price quotations for stocks, bonds, and mutual funds is presented in the remaining investment chapters.

It is also possible to obtain economic and investment information on radio or television. Many stations broadcast investment and economic information as part of their regular news programs. For example, CNBC provides ongoing market coverage, investment information, and economic news. See Exhibit 13-8 for publications and news programs used by successful investors.

BUSINESS PERIODICALS AND GOVERNMENT PUBLICATIONS

Barron's, Bloomberg Businessweek, Fortune, Forbes, and similar business periodicals provide not only general news about the overall economy but detailed financial information about individual corporations. In addition to business periodicals, more general magazines such as *Time* and *Newsweek* provide investment information as a regular feature. Finally, *Money, Kiplinger's Personal Finance, Worth,* and similar periodicals provide information and advice designed to improve your investment skills. In addition to print versions, most of the above magazines also have an online version. Many magazines may also be available in college or public libraries.

The U.S. government is the world's largest provider of information. Much of this information is of value to investors and is either free or available at minimal cost. For example, the Securities and Exchange Commission (www.sec.gov) provides access to financial information that is reported by corporations that issue stocks and bonds. The Federal Reserve (www.federalreserve.gov), and the Bureau of Economic Analysis (www.bea.gov) also provide information that can help investors to understand the financial markets and the economy.

CORPORATE REPORTS

The federal government requires corporations selling new issues of securities to disclose information about corporate earnings, assets and liabilities, products or services, and the qualifications of top management in a *prospectus* that they must give to investors.

In addition to the prospectus, publicly owned corporations send their stockholders an annual report. Annual reports contain a statement of financial position, which describes changes in assets, liabilities, and owners' equity. These reports also include an income statement, which provides dollar amounts for sales, expenses, and profits or losses. Finally, annual reports contain a statement of cash flows to report corporate operating, investing, and financing activities. An annual report and additional information about a corporation can be obtained by accessing a corporation's website or contacting the investor relations department of a corporation.

INVESTOR SERVICES AND NEWSLETTERS

Investors can subscribe to services that provide investment information both online and in a print version. To gain access to online information, you may need to create an account or register on the company's website. While some information from investor services may be free, there may be fees for the more detailed information you may need to evaluate different investment alternatives. For example, the following three services are available for investors who invest in stocks, bonds, and mutual funds.

1. *Value Line* (www.valueline.com). These reports supply detailed information about major corporations—earnings, sales, cash, liabilities, total returns, and other financial data. Research about specific mutual funds is also provided by Value Line.

2. *Standard & Poor's* (https://www.standardandpoors.com). Standard & Poor's reports help investors and financial professionals evaluate potential investments in corporate and government bonds, stocks, mutual funds, and other financial securities.

3. *Morningstar Investment Reports* (www.morningstar.com). Morningstar tracks thousands of stocks and mutual funds and issues reports on safety, financial performance, and other important information that investors can use to evaluate a corporate stock or a mutual fund.

my life 5

I know how to evaluate different investment alternatives.

Once you identify the sources of information that are most useful for evaluating a specific investment, make photocopies of the information. That way, you can refer back to the information when needed. Also, you can go back to those same sources when it's time to reevaluate your investment choices. To help sort through the wealth of information available, use *Personal Financial Planner Sheet 57.*

Keep in mind that many investors find many of the services and newsletters described here too expensive for personal subscriptions, but this information may be available from stockbrokers or financial planners. This type of information is also available at many public and college libraries.

This discussion of investment information is not exhaustive, but it gives you some idea of the amount and scope of the information available to serious investors. More detailed information about sources of investment information is provided in the remaining investment chapters.

 PRACTICE QUIZ 13-5

 PFP Sheet 57
Investment Information Sources

1. What do you think is the most readily available source of information for the average investor? Explain your answer.
2. Briefly describe the sources of information you can use to evaluate a potential investment to increase profits and reduce risk.

Your Personal Finance Roadmap and Dashboard:

Investing

MY FINANCIAL CHECKUP IS COMPLETE AND
I'M READY TO INVEST

Once you have established your investment goals and completed your financial checkup, it's time to start investing—assuming you have enough money to finance your investments. Unfortunately, the money doesn't automatically appear.

Your Situation

Have you established specific and measurable investment goals? Have you performed a financial checkup to see if you are ready to begin investing? Do you have money to invest? Are you participating in your employer's 401(k) retirement plan? All four questions are important and should be answered before you begin to invest.

First Steps

- Establish both short-term and long-term investment and financial goals.
- Work to balance your budget.
- Start an emergency fund.

- Save a reasonable amount of money from each paycheck.
- Explore different retirement plans.
- Begin investing after evaluation of different types of investments.

Next Steps

- Revise investment and financial goals.
- Continue to evaluate new and current investments.
- Increase your amount of savings and investments.
- Get serious about planning for retirement.

Later Steps

- Revise investment and financial goals.
- Continue planning for retirement within a specific number of years.
- Increase your amount of savings and investments.
- Consider conservative investment options.
- Continue to evaluate current investments.

YOUR Next Step . . . select one or more of the items above and create an action plan to implement those financial planning activities.

SUMMARY OF LEARNING OBJECTIVES

LO13-1

Describe why you should establish an investment program. Investment goals must be written, specific, and measurable. Often individuals create specific goals for emergencies; short-term, intermediate-term, and long-term goals; and retirement. Before beginning an investment program, you should perform a financial checkup to make sure your personal financial affairs are in order. This process begins with learning to live within your means, including managing your credit card debt. The next step is to accumulate an emergency fund equal to at least three months' living expenses. Then it is time to save the money needed to establish an investment program. Because of the time value of money, your investments can grow to substantial amounts over a long period of time.

LO13-2

Assess how safety, risk, income, growth, and liquidity affect your investment decisions. All investors must consider the factors of safety, risk, income, growth, and liquidity. Especially important is the relationship between safety and risk. Often, investors may experience two types of risk: a risk you will not receive periodic income payments and a risk that an investment will decrease in value. As a result, all investors must evaluate their tolerance for risk. Basically, this concept can be summarized as follows: *The potential return for any investment should be directly related to the risk the investor assumes.* To determine how much you actually earn on an investment over a specific period of time, investors often calculate a rate of return.

The risk factor can be broken down into five components: inflation risk, interest rate risk, business failure risk, market risk, and global investment risk. Income, growth, and liquidity may also affect your choice of investments.

LO13-3

Explain how asset allocation and different investment alternatives affect your investment plan. Asset allocation is the process of spreading your assets among several different types of investments to lessen risk. Typical asset classes include large-cap stocks,

midcap stocks, small-cap stocks, foreign stocks, bonds, and cash. The percentage of your investments that should be invested in each asset class is determined by your age, investment goals, ability to tolerate risk, how much you can save and invest each year, the dollar value of your current investments, the economic outlook for the economy, and several other factors.

Typical long-term investment alternatives include stocks, bonds, mutual funds, and real estate. More speculative investment alternatives include options, commodities, derivatives, bitcoins and cryptocurrencies, and collectibles. Before choosing a specific investment, you should evaluate all potential investments on the basis of safety, risk, income, growth, and liquidity. With all of these factors in mind, the next step is to develop a personal plan for investing to help you accomplish your goals.

LO13-4

Recognize the importance of your role in a personal investment program. It is your responsibility to evaluate and to monitor the value of your investments. Accurate record keeping can also help you spot opportunities to maximize profits or reduce losses when you sell your investments. These same detailed records can help you decide whether you want to invest additional funds in a particular investment. To achieve their financial goals, many people seek professional help. If you choose to use a financial planner or other professional, keep in mind that you are the one who must make the final decisions with the help of the professionals. Finally, it is your responsibility to determine how taxes affect your investment decisions.

LO13-5

Use various sources of financial information to reduce risks and increase investment returns. Because more information on investments is available than most investors can read and comprehend, you must be selective in the type of information you use for evaluation purposes. Sources of information include the internet, newspapers and news programs, business periodicals, government publications, corporate reports, investor services, and newsletters.

KEY TERMS

asset allocation   462

business cycle   453

corporate bond   466

dividend   466

economics   452

emergency fund   452

equity capital   465

expense ratio   468

government bond   466

line of credit   452

liquidity   461

maturity date   466

mutual fund   467

rate of return   458

speculative investment   457

KEY FORMULAS

Topic	Formula
Rate of return	$\text{Rate of return} = \dfrac{\text{Increase }(+)\text{ or decrease }(-)\text{ in value} + \text{Annual income}}{\text{Original investment}}$

Example:

$$\text{Rate of return} = \frac{\$200 + \$50}{\$5,000}$$

$$= \frac{\$250}{\$5,000}$$

$$= 0.05$$

$$= 5\%$$

Interest calculation for a bond	Dollar amount of annual interest = Face value × Interest rate

Example:

$$\text{Dollar amount of annual interest} = \$1,000 \times 4\%$$

$$= \$1,000 \times 0.04$$

$$= \$40$$

SELF-TEST PROBLEMS

1. For Alicia Thompson, the last few years have been a financial nightmare. It all started when she lost her job. Because she had no income and no emergency fund, she began using her credit cards to obtain the cash needed to pay everyday living expenses. Finally, after an exhaustive job search, she has a new job that pays $51,000 a year. While her monthly take-home pay is $2,975, she must now establish an emergency fund, pay off her $7,300 credit card debt, and start saving the money needed to begin an investment program.

   a. If monthly expenses are $2,150, what is the minimum amount of money Alicia should save for an emergency fund?

   b. What steps should Alicia take to pay the $7,300 credit card debt?

   c. Alicia has decided that she will save and invest $2,000 a year for the next five years. If her savings and investments earn 3 percent each year, how much money will she have at the end of five years? (Use the future value calculator discussed in the *Financial Literacy Calculations: Using the Time Value of Money to Calculate Investment Returns* feature to complete this problem).

2. Matt Jackson paid $1,000 for a corporate bond issued by Chevron Corporation. The annual interest rate for the bond is 2.36 percent.

   a. What is the annual interest amount for the Chevron bond?

   b. Since the annual interest for this bond is paid every six months, or semiannually, how much will Matt receive for his Chevron bond each six months?

   c. If comparable new bonds pay 3 percent interest, will Matt's bond increase or decrease in value?

Self-Test Solutions

1. a. The minimum emergency fund is $6,450. *Note:* This is the *minimum* emergency fund, and the amount could be increased because of personal or economic circumstances.

   $$\text{Minimum emergency fund} = \text{Monthly expenses} \times 3 \text{ months}$$
   $$= \$2,150 \times 3$$
   $$= \$6,450$$

   b. To pay her $7,300 credit card debt, Alicia should take the following actions: (1) Talk to the credit card companies and ask if they will lower the interest rate she is paying; (2) pay at least the minimum balance on all credit cards to ensure that she does not get behind on any payments; and (3) pay off the credit card with the highest interest rate first, then work on the remaining credit cards.

   c. If Alicia's savings and investments earn 3 percent each year, she will have accumulated $10,618, determined by using the future value calculator discussed in the *Financial Literacy Calculations* feature.

2. a. The annual interest amount for the Chevron bond is $23.60.

$$\text{Amount of annual interest} = \text{Face value} \times \text{Interest rate}$$
$$= \$1{,}000 \times 2.36\%$$
$$= \$1{,}000 \times 0.0236$$
$$= \$23.60$$

b. Every six months Matt will receive $11.80 for each Chevron bond he owns.

$$\text{Semiannual Payment} = \text{Annual interest amount per bond} \div 2$$
$$= \$23.60 \div 2$$
$$= \$11.80$$

c. If comparable new bonds pay 3 percent interest, Matt's Chevron bond that pays 2.36 percent will decrease in value because investors will opt for a comparable bond that pays the higher interest rate. In this situation, he must decide if he will sell his bond at the lower price or hold it until maturity and collect the $1,000 face value.

 FINANCIAL PLANNING PROBLEMS

1. *Calculating the Amount for an Emergency Fund.* Beth and Bob Martin have total take-home pay of $5,600 a month. Their monthly expenses total $4,230. Calculate the minimum amount this couple needs to establish an emergency fund. LO13-1

2. *Determining Profit or Loss from an Investment.* Two years ago, you purchased 220 shares of IBM stock for $124 a share. Today, you sold your IBM stock for $142 a share. For this problem, ignore commissions that would be charged to buy and sell your IBM shares and dividends you might have received as a shareholder. LO13-1

    a. What is the amount of profit you earned on each share of IBM stock?

    b. What is the total amount of profit for your IBM investment?

3. *Determining the Time Value of Money.* Using a future value calculator available on the internet or the future value formula or the table included in the Chapter 1 Appendix, complete the following table. Then answer the questions that follow the table. *Hint:* To calculate the total amount of interest or earnings, subtract the amount of your total investment from the value at the end of the time period. LO13-1

Annual Deposit	Rate of Return	Number of Years	Investment Value at End of Time Period	Total Amount of Investment	Total Amount of Interest or Earnings
$2,000	4%	15			
$2,000	8%	15			
$2,000	4%	25			
$2,000	8%	25			

    a. In the above situations, describe the effect that the rate of return has on the investment value at the end of the selected time period.

    b. In the above situations, describe the effect that the number of years has on the investment value at the end of the selected time period.

4. *Calculating Rate of Return.* Assume that at the beginning of the year, you purchase an investment for $5,600 that pays $125 annual income. Also assume the investment's value has increased to $5,900 by the end of the year. LO13-2

    a. What is the rate of return for this investment?

    b. Is the rate of return a positive or a negative number?

5. *Calculating Rate of Return.* Assume that at the beginning of the year, you purchase an investment for $8,200 that pays $80 annual income. Also assume that the investment's value has increased to $9,000 at the end of the year. LO13-2

    a. What is the rate of return for this investment?

    b. Is the rate of return a positive or a negative number?

LO13-2 **6.** *Calculating Rate of Return.* Assume that at the beginning of the year, you purchase an investment for $5,100 that pays $100 annual income. Also assume the investment's value has decreased to $4,700 by the end of the year.

    a. What is the rate of return for this investment?

    b. Is the rate of return a positive or a negative number?

LO13-2 **7.** *Determining Interest.* Assume that you purchased a $1,000 corporate bond. The interest rate is 3.70 percent. What is the dollar amount of annual interest you will receive each year?

LO13-2 **8.** *Determining Interest.* Three years ago you purchased a $1,000 Kroger corporate bond that pays 3.95 percent annual interest. What is the total dollar amount of interest that you received from your bond investment over the three-year period?

LO13-2 **9.** *Determining Interest.* Jackie Martin purchased five $1,000 corporate bonds issued by Starbucks. The bonds pay 2.45 percent annual interest and mature in 2026. What is the total dollar amount of interest Jackie will receive for her five bonds each year?

LO13-2 **10.** *Determining Interest and the Effect of Changing Interest Rates on a Bond Investment.* Assume that three years ago, you purchased a $1.000 corporate bond that pays 3.85 percent. Also assume that three years after your bond investment, comparable bonds are paying 4.50 percent.

    a. What is the annual dollar amount of interest that you receive from your bond investment?

    b. Assuming that comparable bonds are now paying 4.50 percent, will your bond increase or decrease in value?

    c. In your own words, explain why your bond increased or decreased in value.

LO13-2 **11.** *Determining Interest and the Effect of Changing Interest Rates on a Bond Investment.* Eight years ago, Burt Brownlee purchased a government bond that pays 3.0 percent interest. The face value of the bond was $1,000.

    a. What is the dollar amount of annual interest that Burt received from his bond investment each year?

    b. Assuming that comparable bonds are now paying 2.40 percent, will Burt's bond increase or decrease in value?

    c. In your own words, explain why Burt's bond increased or decreased in value.

DIGITAL FINANCIAL LITERACY: A CAREER IN FINANCIAL PLANNING

A personal financial advisor provides advice to help individuals manage their finances and plan their financial future. According to the U.S. Bureau of Labor Statistics, the need for financial planners is expected to increase about 4 percent a year between now and 2029, and financial planners earn salaries that are above average. Most financial planners have a bachelor's degree in finance, economics, insurance, or business; the most qualified financial planners have advanced training and have passed an exam to become a Certified Financial Planner (CFP). Individuals who pass the CFP exam are certified by the Certified Financial Board of Standards.

Action items:

1. Locate more information about a career in financial planning. You may want to begin your search for career information by visiting the Certified Financial Planning (CFP) Board website at https://www.cfp.net/.

2. Describe in a one- to two-page report what type of qualifications and work experience you must have to become a CFP. Also indicate in your report if you would be interested in a career in financial planning based on the information you have obtained on the CFP website.

FINANCIAL PLANNING CASE

First Budget, Then Invest for Success!

John and Nina Hartwick, married 17 years, have a 13-year-old daughter. Eight years ago, they purchased a home on which they owe about $240,000. They also owe $6,000 on a two-year-old automobile. All of their furniture and their second car are paid for, but they owe a total of $5,320 on two credit cards. John is employed as an engineer and makes $85,000 a year. Mary works from home as a part-time graphic designer and earns about $22,000 a year. Their combined monthly income after deductions and their portion of employer-sponsored health care is $6,200.

About six months ago, the Hartwicks had what they now describe as a "financial meltdown." It all started one Monday afternoon when the transmission on their second car had to be

replaced. Although they thought it would be an easy fix, the mechanic told them that the transmission would need a complete overhaul. Unfortunately, the warranty on the automobile's drive train components was for 5 years or 50,000 miles. Since this car was just over 6 years old, they would have to pay for the repair, and the mechanic said it would cost about $2,800 to rebuild the transmission. They thought about buying a new car, but they didn't think they could afford or want two car payments. At the time, they had about $3,500 in their savings account, which they had been saving for their summer vacation, and now they had to use their vacation money to fix the transmission.

For the Hartwicks, the fact that they didn't have enough money to take a vacation was a wake-up call. They realized they were now in their late 30s and had serious cash problems. According to John, "We don't waste money, but there just never seems to be enough money to do the things we want to do." But according to Nina, "The big problem is that we never have enough money to start an investment program that could pay for our daughter's college education or fund our retirement."

They decided to take a big first step in an attempt to solve their financial problems. They began by examining their monthly expenses for the past month. The table shows what they found.

Income (cash inflow)		
John's take-home salary	$4,950	
Nina's take-home salary	$1,250	
Total income		$6,200
Cash outflows		
Monthly fixed expenses:		
Home mortgage payment, including taxes and insurance	$1,570	
Roth IRA contribution	200	
Automobile loan	315	
Automobile insurance	130	
Life insurance premium	140	
Total fixed expenses		$2,355
Monthly variable expenses:		
Food and household necessities	$ 880	
Electricity	240	
Natural gas	175	
Water and trash collection	55	
Telephone, internet, and cable TV	420	
Family clothing allowance	230	
Gasoline and automobile repairs	215	
Personal and health care	150	
Recreation and entertainment	800	
Gifts and donations	350	
Minimum payment on credit cards	80	
Total variable expenses		$3,595
Total monthly expenses		$5,950
Surplus for savings or investments		$ 250

Once the Hartwicks realized they had a $250 surplus each month, they began to replace the $2,800 they had taken from their savings account to pay for repairing the transmission repair. Now it was time to take the next step.

Questions

1. How would you rate the financial health of the Hartwicks before their second automobile broke down?

2. The Hartwicks' take-home pay is $6,200 a month. Yet, after all expenses are paid, there is only a $250 surplus each month. Based on the information presented in this case, what expenses, if any, seem out of line and could be reduced to increase the surplus at the end of each month?

3. Given that both John and Nina Hartwick are in their late 30s and want to retire when they reach age 65, what type of investment goals would be most appropriate for them?

4. How does the time value of money and the asset allocation concept affect the types of long-term goals and the investments that a couple like the Hartwicks might use to build their financial nest egg?

5. Based on the different investments described in this chapter, what specific types of investments (stocks, bonds, mutual funds, real estate, etc.) would you recommend for the Hartwicks? Why?

 # YOUR PERSONAL FINANCIAL PLAN

DEVELOPING AN INVESTMENT PLAN

An investment program should consider safety, risk, current income, growth potential, liquidity, and taxes. Your ability to set financial goals and select investment vehicles is crucial to long-term financial prosperity.

Your Short-Term Financial Planning Activity

Task Develop specific and measurable short- and long-term goals to help you obtain financial security.

Research

1) Perform a financial checkup to determine actions that you should take before you begin investing.

2) Based on the results of your financial checkup, use PFP Sheet 55 (Investment Goals) to establish specific and measurable investment goals.

Outcome Create a three-column chart that summarizes your short-term and long-term goals. Use the first column to list your short-term goals. Use the second column to list your long-term goals. The third column can be used to indicate whether a specific goal is completed or is in progress. Then attach your summary chart to PFP Sheet 55. Update both your chart and PFP Sheet 55 on a frequent basis to monitor your progress or make changes if necessary to improve your financial planning.

Your Long-Term Financial Planning Activity

Task Develop a list of sources of information that could help you evaluate risk for different long-term investments.

Research

1) Use the information in the section "Components of the Risk Factor" to complete PFP Sheet 56 (Investment Risk).

2) Use the information in the section "Sources of Investment Information" and information from the internet to complete PFP Sheet 57 (Investment Information Sources).

3) Based on information in PFP Sheet 55 and 56, pick two types of investments (CDs. stocks, bonds, mutual funds, etc.) you would choose to achieve your goals.

Outcome In a two- to three-page report, describe each type of investment you chose. In your report, be sure to include the reasons behind your choices, the risk involved with each type, and the sources of investment information you could use to evaluate each type of investment.

CONTINUING CASE

Investing Fundamentals

The triplets are now three and a half years old, and Jamie Lee and Ross, both 38, are finally beginning to settle into a regular routine now that the triplets are a little more self-sufficient. The first three years were a blur of diapers, feedings, baths, mounds of laundry, and crying babies!

Jamie Lee and Ross finally had a welcomed dinner out on their own as Ross's parents were minding the triplets. They were having a conversation about their future and the future of the triplets. College expenses ($150,000) and their eventual retirement seem to be a major worry for both of them. They both have also dreamed of owning a beach house when they retire. That could be another $350,000, thirty years from now. They wondered how they could possibly afford all of this.

They agreed that it was time to talk to an investment counselor but wanted to organize all of their financial information and discuss their family's financial goals before setting up the appointment.

Current Financial Situation

Assets (Jamie Lee and Ross combined):
Checking account: $4,500
Savings account: $20,000
Emergency fund savings account: $21,000
IRA balance: $46,000
Car: $8,500 (Jamie Lee) and $14,000 (Ross)

Liabilities (Jamie Lee and Ross combined):
Student loan balance: $0
Credit card balance: $4,000
Car loans: $2,000

Income:
Jamie Lee: $45,000 gross income ($31,500 net income after taxes)
Ross: $80,000 gross income ($64,500 net income after taxes)

Monthly Expenses:
Mortgage: $1,225
Property taxes: $400
Homeowner's insurance: $200
IRA contribution $300
Utilities: $250
Food: $600
Baby essentials (clothing, toys, etc.): $200
Gas/maintenance: $275
Credit card payment: $400
Car loan payment: $289
Entertainment: $125

Questions

1. Looking back to Chapter 1 and Exhibit 1-6, "Goals and Actions for Personal Financial Literacy," what type of attitudes and abilities would help Jamie Lee and Ross build for the future?

2. After reviewing Jamie Lee and Ross's current financial situation, suggest specific and measurable short-term and long-term financial goals that they can implement at this stage.

3. Use the questions below to assess the validity of the short- and long-term financial goals that you created for Jamie Lee and Ross.

Financial Question	Short-Term Goals	Long-Term Goals
How much money do they need to satisfy their investment goals?		
How will they obtain the money?		
How long will it take them to obtain the money?		
How much risk should they assume in their investment program?		
What possible economic or personal conditions could alter their investment goals?		
Considering current economic conditions, are their investment goals reasonable?		
Are they willing to make the sacrifices necessary to ensure that they meet their investment goals?		

4. Using the formula in this chapter for determining the amount of growth investments investors should have and considering that they are both 38 years old, how much of Jamie Lee and Ross's assets should be allocated to growth investments? How should the remaining investments be distributed, and what is the risk associated with each type of investment?

5. Jamie Lee and Ross need to evaluate their emergency fund of $21,000. Will their present emergency fund be sufficient to cover them should one of them lose their job?

6. Jamie Lee and Ross agree that by accomplishing their short-term goals, they can budget $7,000 a year toward their long-term investment goals. They are estimating that with the investments recommended by their financial advisor, they will see an average annual return of 7 percent on their investments. The triplets will begin college in 15 years and will need $150,000 for tuition. Using Exhibit 1-B, "Future Value," in the Time Value of Money Appendix located after Chapter 1 or a future value calculator available on the internet, decide whether Jamie Lee and Ross will be on track to reaching their long-term financial goals of having enough money from their investments to pay the triplets' $150,000 tuition.

 DAILY SPENDING DIARY

"While I have a fairly large amount in a savings account, I should think about investing some of this money in other ways."

Directions

The use of your *Daily Spending Diary* can provide an important foundation for monitoring and controlling your spending. This will enable you to use money more wisely now and in the future.

Analysis Questions

1. Explain how the use of a *Daily Spending Diary* could result in starting an investment program.
2. Based on your *Daily Spending Diary,* describe actions you might take to identify and achieve various investment goals.

A *Daily Spending Diary* sheet is located at the end of Chapter 1 and on the library resource site in *Connect.*

14 Investing in Stocks

grafficx/Getty Images

LEARNING OBJECTIVES

LO14-1 Identify the most important features of common and preferred stocks.

LO14-2 Explain how you can evaluate stock investments.

LO14-3 Analyze the numerical measures that cause a stock to increase or decrease in value.

LO14-4 Describe how stocks are bought and sold.

LO14-5 Explain the trading techniques used by long-term investors and short-term speculators.

Financial Literacy IN **YOUR LIFE**

▶ **What if you . . .** have no experience in investing but have just inherited 50 shares of Apple stock? At the time of your inheritance, your Apple stock is worth more than $11,000!

You might . . . sell the stock, or you could keep the stock.

Now, what would you do? If you sell the Apple stock, you may have to pay taxes on profits if the stock has increased in value since you inherited it, but the remaining cash after the stock is sold can be used to pay bills, to fund your college education, or for any other purpose you choose. You could also choose to keep the stock, and it may increase in value and become the foundation for a long-term investment plan. These are choices that could change your life. Your decision to keep or sell may have something to do with your current financial condition. Keep those factors in mind as you read this chapter, and then review the Your Personal Finance Roadmap and Dashboard feature that concludes the chapter.

my life | **WHY STOCKS?**

There is more to investing in stocks than just luck. In fact, the best investors are the ones who "invest" the time to research a stock investment before they invest their money. And they continue to evaluate their investment after they have made their decision to purchase a specific stock. Before beginning this chapter, respond to the following statements.

1. I know how to make money with stock investments.	Yes	No	Maybe
2. I can evaluate stock investments.	Yes	No	Maybe
3. I know how investors use financial ratios to evaluate a specific stock.	Yes	No	Maybe
4. I know what factors to consider when choosing an account executive and a brokerage firm.	Yes	No	Maybe
5. I can explain the difference between long-term and short-term investment techniques.	Yes	No	Maybe

As you study this chapter, you will encounter "My Life" boxes with additional information and resources related to these statements.

Common and Preferred Stocks

Today, investors—especially beginning investors—face two concerns when they begin an investment program. First, they don't know where to get the information they need to evaluate potential investments. In reality, more information is available for most corporate stock issues than most investors can read.

Second, beginning investors sometimes worry that they won't know what the information means when they find it, yet common sense goes a long way when evaluating potential investments. For example, consider the following questions:

1. Is an increase in sales revenues a healthy sign for a corporation? (*Answer: yes*)

2. Should a firm's after-tax income increase or decrease over time? (*Answer: increase*)

3. Should a corporation's earnings per share increase or decrease over time? (*Answer: increase*)

Although the answers to these questions are obvious, you will find more detailed answers to these and other questions in this chapter. In fact, that's what this chapter is all about. We want you to learn how to evaluate a stock and to make money from your investment decisions.

LO14-1

Identify the most important features of common and preferred stocks.

WHY CORPORATIONS ISSUE COMMON STOCK

common stock The most basic form of ownership for a corporation.

Common stock is the most basic form of ownership for a corporation. Corporations issue common stock to finance their business start-up costs and help pay for expansion and their ongoing business activities. Corporate managers prefer selling common stock as a method of financing for several reasons.

equity financing Money received from the sale of shares of ownership in a business.

A FORM OF EQUITY   Corporations prefer selling stock because the money doesn't have to be repaid, and the company doesn't have to buy back shares from stockholders. Stock is equity financing. **Equity financing** is money received from the sale of shares of ownership in a business. *Important point:* A stockholder who buys common stock may sell his or her stock to another person. The selling price is determined by how much a buyer is willing to pay for the stock. The price for a share of stock changes when information about the firm or its future prospects is released to the general public. For example, information about future sales revenues, earnings, expansion or mergers, or other important developments within the firm can increase or decrease the price for a share of the company's stock.

dividend A distribution of money, stock, or other property that a corporation pays to stockholders.

DIVIDENDS NOT MANDATORY   *Important point:* Dividends are paid out of profits, and dividend payments must be approved by the corporation's board of directors. A **dividend** is a distribution of money, stock, or other property that a corporation pays to stockholders. Dividend policies vary among corporations, but most firms distribute between 30 and 70 percent of their earnings to stockholders. However, some corporations follow a policy of smaller or no dividend distributions to stockholders. In general, these are rapidly growing firms, like Netflix (entertainment services for television), Amazon (online retail), and Alphabet (the parent company of internet search engine Google) that retain a large share of their earnings and profits for research and development, expansion, or acquisitions. On the other hand, utility companies, such as Consolidated Edison and American Electric Power (AEP) and other financially secure corporations, may distribute up to 70 to 90 percent of their earnings. Always remember that the board of directors may vote to reduce or omit dividend payments because the corporation had a bad year or for any other reason.

VOTING RIGHTS AND CONTROL OF THE COMPANY   In return for the financing provided by selling common stock, management must make concessions to stockholders that may restrict corporate policies. For example, the common stockholders elect the board of directors and must approve major changes in corporate policies. Stockholders may vote in person at the corporation's annual meeting or by proxy. A **proxy** is a legal form that lists the issues to be decided at a stockholders' meeting and requests that stockholders transfer their voting rights to some individual or individuals.

proxy A legal form that lists the issues to be decided at a stockholders' meeting and requests that stockholders transfer their voting rights to some individual or individuals.

WHY INVESTORS PURCHASE COMMON STOCK

In the search for investments that offered larger returns, Patricia Nelson invested $10,000 in McDonald's Corporation on February 8, 2011. Ten years later, Nelson's investment had increased to $28,075.[1] During the 10-year period, she earned an average of just over 10 percent a year. What happened? Well, three factors account for her investment's increase in value. First, Nelson made the decision to look at McDonald's stock as an investment alternative when she noticed that the local McDonald's where she often had breakfast was always busy. Second, she spent more than 20 hours evaluating the firm and its financial performance. She also looked at what stock advisory services said about the company and learned all she could about McDonald's before investing her $10,000. Finally, McDonald's Corporation did its part. The fast-food chain continued to sell food items in record numbers while managing to improve its operating and marketing activities. Will Nelson's investment continue to increase in value? Will McDonald's stock continue to increase in value? Both good questions, but that's why successful investors like Nelson *continue* to evaluate their stock investments—even if they are enjoying above-average returns.

THE PSYCHOLOGY OF STOCK INVESTING Why do people invest in stocks? Good question. The simple answer is that investors want the larger returns that stocks offer, even though they are aware of increased risk and the potential for losses. Just for a moment review the statistics that were presented in Chapter 13:

- For the past 30 years, stocks as measured by the Standard & Poor's 500 Stock Index have returned 11.47 percent.[2]
- Over the 10-year period from 2009 to 2019, stocks measured by the Standard & Poor's 500 Index have averaged 14.09 percent.[3]
- Since 1926, stocks lost money in 25 years.[4]

While the first two items are pretty impressive, investors sometimes forget that stocks can decrease in value. Before you invest in stock, consider the last item one more time: *Since 1926, stocks lost money in 25 years.* For more proof that stocks can decrease in value, ask an investor what happened to the value of their stock investments on March 16, 2020. That's the day when the Dow Jones Industrial Average declined almost 3,000 points—the worst one-day point decline in history.[5] The fact is that stocks and the stock market are volatile, and investors often experience wide price swings from one day to the next. The market's volatility underscores the importance of a long-term investment program that will allow you to weather the ups and downs in the market. In fact, the key to success with any investment program is to allow your investments to grow over a long period of time. The sooner you start investing, the more time your investments have to work for you.

Another reason why financial experts recommend a long-term investment program is lower taxation for investments held longer than a year. Short-term investments—stocks held for one year or less—are taxed as ordinary income. Generally, tax rates for short-term investments range from 10 to 37 percent, depending on your total taxable income. On the other hand, long-term investments—stocks held for more than one year—are taxed at a lower rate. Under current tax laws, long-term investments are taxed at 0, 15, or 20 percent, depending on your total taxable income from all sources. While paying lower taxes on long-term investments doesn't seem like a big deal, those tax savings can be used to buy other stock investments that can provide additional dividend income and appreciate in value.

From a psychological standpoint, many investors have trouble making the decision to buy or sell a stock. The following suggestions can be used to reduce anxiety when you make stock investment decisions:

- *Evaluate each investment.* Too often, investors purchase or sell a stock without doing their homework. A much better approach is to become an expert and learn all that you can about the company (and its stock).
- *Analyze the firm's finances.* Look at the company's financial information. Examine trends for sales, profits, dividends, and other important financial information. More specific information on how to evaluate a firm's finances is provided later in the chapter.
- *Track the firm's product line.* If the firm's products become obsolete and the company fails to introduce new products, its sales—and ultimately, profits—may take a nosedive.
- *Monitor economic developments.* An economic recovery or an economic recession may cause the value of a stock investment to increase or decrease. Also, watch the unemployment rate, inflation rate, interest rates, and similar economic indicators.
- *Be patient.* The secret of success for making money with stocks is often time. If you choose quality stocks based on quality research and in some cases hold onto the stocks before selling, eventually your stock investments will provide average or even above-average returns.

smart money minute

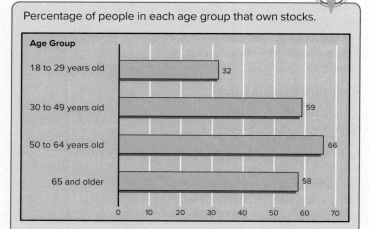

Percentage of people in each age group that own stocks.

Age Group

- 18 to 29 years old — 32
- 30 to 49 years old — 59
- 50 to 64 years old — 66
- 65 and older — 58

Source: "What Percentage of Americans Own Stock," the Gallup website at https://news.gallup.com/poll/266807/percentage-americans-owns-stock.aspx, accessed June 4, 2020.

How do you make money by buying common stock? Basically, there are two ways: income from dividends and dollar appreciation of stock value. In addition to dividend income and dollar appreciation, a stock split may affect the value of a corporation's stock.

INCOME FROM DIVIDENDS Investors must be concerned about the corporation's ability to earn profits and pay dividends in the future. Keep in mind that if a corporation isn't profitable, it is unlikely that stockholders will continue to receive income from dividends. Also remember the corporation's board members are under no legal obligation to pay dividends. Still, most board members like to keep stockholders happy (and prosperous). Therefore, board members usually declare dividends if the corporation's after-tax profits are sufficient for them to do so.

Corporate dividends for common stock may take the form of cash, additional stock, or company property. However, the last type of dividend is extremely unusual. If the board of directors declares a cash dividend, each common stockholder receives an equal amount per share. Although dividend policies vary, most corporations pay dividends on a quarterly basis.

Notice in Exhibit 14-1 that Starbucks declared a quarterly dividend of $0.45 per share to stockholders who owned the stock on the record date of February 18, 2021. The **record date** is the date on which a stockholder must be registered on the corporation's books in order to receive dividend payments. When a stock is traded around the record date, the company must determine whether the buyer or the seller is entitled to the dividend. According to the Securities and Exchange Commission, *dividends remain with the stock until one business day before the record date.* On the day before the record date, the stock begins selling *ex-dividend.* The term **ex-dividend** describes a situation when a stock trades "without dividend," and the seller—not the buyer—is entitled to a declared dividend payment.

For example, Starbucks declared a quarterly dividend of $0.45 per share to stockholders who owned its stock on Thursday, February 18. The stock went ex-dividend on Wednesday, February 17, *one business day* before the February 18 date. A stockholder who purchased the stock on Wednesday, February 17, or after was not entitled to this

record date The date on which a stockholder must be registered on the corporation's books in order to receive dividend payments.

ex-dividend A situation when a stock trades "without dividend," and the seller—not the buyer—is entitled to a declared dividend payment.

EXHIBIT 14-1

Information about corporate dividends
Corporate dividend information is available on the corporation's website or other investment sites. The numbers above each of the columns correspond to the numbered entries in the list of explanations.

1	2	3	4
Company	Amount of Dividend	Record Date	Payable Date
Starbucks	$0.45	Thursday, February 18	Friday, March 5

1. Name of the company that will pay the dividend: Starbucks
2. The dollar amount of the dividend: $0.45 per share
3. The record date: Thursday, February 18, 2021. Stockholders must be registered on the corporate books by the record date in order to receive this quarterly dividend. The stock begins selling "ex-dividend" Wednesday, February 17, 2021—one business day before the record date.
4. The payable date: Friday, March 5. The quarterly dividend is actually paid to stockholders of record on this date.

Source: The Nasdaq website at https://www.nasdaq.com/market-activity/stocks/sbux/dividend-history, accessed February 8, 2021.

quarterly dividend payment. Starbucks made the actual dividend payment on Friday, March 5, to stockholders who owned the stock on the record date. Investors are generally very conscious of the date on which a stock trades without the dividend, and the dollar value of the stock may go down by the amount of the quarterly dividend.

DOLLAR APPRECIATION OF STOCK VALUE   In most cases, you purchase stock and then hold onto that stock for a period of time. If the stock's price increases, you must decide whether to sell the stock at the higher price or continue to hold it. If you decide to sell the stock, the dollar amount of difference between the purchase price and the selling price represents your profit.

Let's assume that on February 9, 2020, you purchased 100 shares of Clorox stock at a cost of $167 a share. Your cost for the stock was $16,700 plus $25 in commission charges, for a total investment of $16,725. (*Note:* Commissions, a topic covered later in this chapter, are charged when you buy stock and when you sell stock.) Let's also assume you held your 100 shares until February 9, 2021, and then sold them for $190 a share. In addition to the stock increasing in value, the company paid dividends totaling $4.39 per share. Exhibit 14-2 shows your return on the investment.[6] In this case, you made money because of dividend payments and because the value of a share of Clorox stock increased from $167 to $190 a share. Of course, if the stock's value had decreased, or if the firm's board of directors had reduced or voted to omit dividends, your return might have been less than the original investment.

WHAT HAPPENS WHEN A CORPORATION SPLITS ITS STOCK?   A **stock split** is a procedure in which the shares of stock owned by existing stockholders are divided into a larger number of shares. For example, the board of directors of Apple approved a 4-for-1 stock split in late 2020. After the stock split, a stockholder who had previously owned 100 shares now owned 400 shares. Most common stock splits are 2-for-1, 3-for-1, and 3-for-2.

Why do corporations split their stock? In many cases, a firm's management has a theoretical ideal price range for the firm's stock. If the price of the stock rises above the ideal range, a stock split brings the price back in line. Also, a decision to split a company's stock and the resulting lower price may make the stock more attractive to the investing public. This attraction is based on the belief that most corporations split their stock only when their financial future is improving and revenues and profits are on the upswing.

stock split A procedure in which the shares of stock owned by existing stockholders are divided into a larger number of shares.

EXHIBIT 14-2

Sample stock transaction for Clorox

Assumptions

100 shares of common stock purchased February 9, 2020, sold February 9, 2021; total dividends of $4.39 per share for the investment period.

Costs when purchased		Return when sold	
100 shares @ $167	= $16,700	100 shares @ $190	= $19,000
Plus commission	+ 25	Minus commission	− 25
Total investment	$16,725	Total return	$18,975

Transaction summary	
Total return	$18,975
Minus total investment	−16,725
Profit from stock sale	$2,250
Plus dividends	+ 439
Total return for the transaction	$2,689

Note: The percentage of return for this investment was 16.1 percent ($2,689 total return ÷ $16,725 original investment = 0.161 = 16.1 percent.)

EXHIBIT 14-3

Effect of a 2-for-1 stock split on capitalization and earnings per share for common stock issued by Martin & Martin, Inc.

Assume that the firm has 2 million shares before the split and 4 million shares after the split.

	Total Capitalization	Annual Earnings	Number of Shares	Earnings per Share
Before the split	$100 million	$4 million	2 million	$2
After the split	$100 million	$4 million	4 million	$1

my life 1

I know how to make money with stock investments.

Basically, there are two methods investors can use to earn a financial return on stock investments: (1) income from dividends and (2) dollar appreciation of stock value.

Keep in mind that while you can make money on a short-term basis with stock investments, a better approach is to invest in quality stocks for a long period of time. If you start early, when you are in your 20s or 30s, your stock investments have more time to grow and appreciate in value.

Be warned: There are no guarantees that a stock's price will go up after a split. Investors often think that a stock split leads to immediate or long-term profits. Nothing could be further from the truth. Here's why: The total market *capitalization*—the current value of the company's stock and other securities—does not change just because a corporation splits its stock. Notice the effect of a 2-for-1 stock split on common stock issued by Martin & Martin Inc., illustrated in Exhibit 14-3. Total capitalization ($100 million) and annual earnings ($4 million) are unaffected by the stock split. The earnings per share declines to $1 per share because annual earnings are divided by twice as many shares. In simple terms, the earnings "pie" is the same size but has been sliced up into more pieces. The 2-for-1 stock split does affect the price for a share of Martin & Martin stock. If the share was $40 before the split, the adjusted price is $20 per share after the split. Again, the reason for the decrease in stock price is that there are now twice as many shares. If a stock's price does increase after a stock split, it increases because of the firm's financial performance and not just because there are more shares of stock.

PREFERRED STOCK

In addition to, or instead of, purchasing common stock, you may purchase preferred stock. **Preferred stock** is a type of stock that gives the owner the advantage of receiving cash dividends before common stockholders are paid any dividends. *Important point:* Dividends on preferred stock, as on common stock, may be omitted by action of the board of directors. Still, this is the most important priority an investor in preferred stock enjoys. Unlike the amount of the dividend on common stock, the dollar amount of the dividend on preferred stock is known before the stock is purchased.

Preferred stocks are often referred to as "middle" investments because they represent an investment midway between common stock (an ownership position for the stockholder) and corporate bonds (a lender position for the bondholder). When compared to corporate bonds, the dividend yield on preferred stocks is often higher than the yield on bonds. However, preferred stock dividends are less secure than interest payments on corporate bonds. When compared to common stocks, preferred stocks are safer investments that offer more secure dividends. They are often purchased by individuals who need a predictable source of income greater than that offered by common stock investments. They are also purchased by other corporations, because corporations receive a tax break on the dividend income paid by other corporations. For all other investors, preferred stocks lack the growth potential that common stocks offer and the safety of many corporate bond issues.

Like common stock, preferred stock is equity financing. This type of stock does not represent a legal debt that must be repaid. Still, if the firm is dissolved or declares bankruptcy, preferred stockholders do have first claim on the corporation's assets after creditors and bondholders are paid. In reality, preferred stockholders don't receive anything in most bankruptcies because creditors have a priority claim and must be paid before preferred stockholders receive anything.

preferred stock A type of stock that gives the owner the advantage of receiving cash dividends before common stockholders are paid any dividends.

N

PRACTICE QUIZ 14-1

1. Why do corporations issue common stock?
2. Describe the two reasons why investors purchase common stock.
3. Why do corporations split their stock?
4. What is the most important priority a preferred stockholder has compared to common stockholders?

Evaluating a Stock Issue

Many investors are unwilling to spend the time required to become a good investor. They wouldn't buy a home or a car without a test drive, but for some unknown reason they invest without doing their homework. The truth is that there is no substitute for a few hours of detective work when choosing an investment. A logical place to start the evaluation process for stock is with the classification of different types of stock investments.

LO14-2

Explain how you can evaluate stock investments.

CLASSIFICATION OF STOCK INVESTMENTS

When evaluating a stock investment, stockbrokers, financial planners, and investors often classify stocks into different categories (see Exhibit 14-4). *Be warned:* Regardless of a stock's classification, a stock is a speculative investment because there are no guarantees. Before investing in stocks, it may be useful to review the risk–return trade-off

Type of Stock	Characteristics of This Type of Investment
Blue chip	A safe investment that generally attracts conservative investors.
Cyclical	A stock that follows the business cycle of advances and declines in the economy.
Defensive	A stock that provides consistent dividends and stable earnings during declines in the economy.
Growth	A stock issued by a corporation that has the potential of earning profits above the average profits of all firms in the economy.
Income	An investment that pays higher-than-average dividends.
Large cap	A stock issued by a corporation that has a large market capitalization, in excess of $10 billion.
Midcap	A stock issued by a corporation that has market capitalization of between $2 and $10 billion.
Micro cap	A stock issued by a company that has a market capitalization of between $50 and $300 million.
Small cap	A stock issued by a company that has a market capitalization of between $300 million and $2 billion.
Penny stock	The Securities and Exchange Commission now defines a penny stock as a stock that sells for $5 or less per share.
Value stock	A stock that is attractive to investors because it may be undervalued based on its fundamentals, including dividends, earnings, sales revenues and other factors.

EXHIBIT 14-4

Classification of stock investments
Investors often classify stock into 11 categories.

that was discussed in Chapter 13. You may also want to review the concept of asset allocation that was discussed in Chapter 13 because some of the stock classifications just described may help you diversify your stock portfolio and reduce potential risk.

THE INTERNET

In this section, we examine some websites that are logical starting points when evaluating a stock investment, but there are many more than those described. Let's begin with information about corporations that is available on the internet.

Today most corporations have a website, and the information these sites provide is often useful because it is easily accessible. All you have to do is type in the corporation's URL address or use a search engine like Google, Yahoo!, or Bing to locate the corporation's home page. In fact, the information on the corporate website may be more up to date and thorough than printed material obtained from the corporation or outside sources. By clicking on a button, such as the Investor Relations link, you can access information on the firm's sales, earnings, assets, liabilities, and other financial factors that could affect the value of the company's stock.

You can also use websites or search engines to obtain information about stock investments. For example, the Yahoo! Finance website (finance.yahoo.com) provides a wealth of information. You can even use the Yahoo! stock screener to help you pick stock investments. You can also get current stock prices by entering a corporation's stock symbol and clicking on the Quote Lookup button. If you don't know the symbol, just begin entering the corporation's name and the symbol will be displayed. Notice in Exhibit 14-5 that you can obtain price information for the last trade for a share of The Coca-Cola Company common stock, the high and low price for the day, and a 52-week price range. You can also obtain information about the firm's P-E ratio, earnings per share, dividends, and dividend yield—all topics discussed later in this chapter.

By clicking on the Company Outlook, Chart, Statistics, Profile, Historical Data, Financials, Analysis, or other tabs at the top of the Yahoo! Finance screen for each corporation, it is possible to obtain even more information that you can use to evaluate a stock investment in a specific corporation.

How about picking a company like Amazon (symbol AMZN) or Home Depot (symbol HD) and going exploring on the internet? To begin, enter the internet address for Yahoo! Finance. Then enter the name or the symbol for one of the above corporations. See Exhibit 14-6 for four additional websites that provide detailed information about corporate stocks.

EXHIBIT 14-5

Stock price information available on the Internet
Current information about the price for a share of Coca-Cola common stock is presented here.

The Coca-Cola Company (KO) — NYSE 49.89 +0.19 (+0.38%) As of 11:55AM EST Market Open			
Previous Close:	49.70	Day's Range:	49.57–50.58
Open:	50.41	52 Week Range:	36.27–60.13
Bid	49.95 × 1100	Volume	14,065,310
Ask	49.97 × 1100	Avg. Volume	17,822,612
1y Target Est	57.02	Market Cap	214.485B
Beta	0.62	P-E (ttm)	25.86
EPS (ttm)	1.93	Forward Div & Yield	1.64 (3.30%)
Earnings Date	Feb. 10, 2021	Ex-Dividend Date	Nov. 30, 2020

Source: Yahoo! Finance, http://finance.yahoo.com, accessed February 10, 2021.

Website and Description	Web Address
Market Watch: Current price information, news, corporate profiles, analyst estimates, and detailed analysis about individual corporate stock issues and other financial securities.	www.marketwatch.com
Reuters: News site that provides information about business, the economy, and detailed information about individual corporations, including current news about specific companies.	www.reuters.com/finance/
Value Line: Many experienced investors rely on Value Line's research to provide information on a corporation's activities, performance, and investment outlook. Value Line reports may be available from public and college libraries, brokerage firms, or online.	www.valueline.com
Morningstar: Detailed research that can be used to sort, screen, graph, and report on individual common stocks and mutual funds. Some information is free, but a subscription is required for more detailed information.	www.morningstar.com

EXHIBIT 14-6

Four websites that can help you evaluate a corporation's stock

STOCK ADVISORY SERVICES

Stock advisory services provide both printed and online materials to evaluate potential stock investments. In choosing among the stock advisory services that charge fees for their information, you must consider the quality of the information they provide. The information ranges from simple alphabetical listings to newsletters to detailed financial reports.

For stocks, Value Line, Morningstar, and Zacks are three of the most popular and respected advisory services. Here we will examine a portion of the detailed report for Walmart that is available from the Value Line Investment Survey (see Exhibit 14-7).

While there is a lot of information about Walmart in Exhibit 14-7, it helps to break down the entire Value Line report into different sections. For example:

- Overall ranks for safety, timeliness, and technical strength, along with current price information, historical prices, total return, and target price projections for a company are included toward the top of the report.

- Detailed information about sales per share, earnings per share, dividends, total sales, net profit, capital structure, and other important financial information is included in the middle and along the left side of the report.

- Information about the type of business and prospects for the future is provided toward the bottom and in the lower right-hand corner.

Other stock advisory services, like Morningstar and Zacks, provide the same types of information as that in Exhibit 14-7. It is the investor's job to interpret such information and decide whether the company's stock is a good investment. You may want to use the information in Exhibit 14-7 to complete the Financial Planning Case at the end of the chapter.

smart money minute

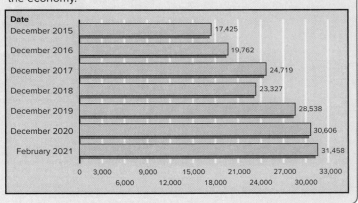

One of the oldest and most recognized measures of stock market activity is the Dow Jones Industrial Average (DJIA). This measure is an average of 30 stocks that are considered leaders in the economy.

Date	
December 2015	17,425
December 2016	19,762
December 2017	24,719
December 2018	23,327
December 2019	28,538
December 2020	30,606
February 2021	31,458

EXHIBIT 14-7   Value Line report for Walmart

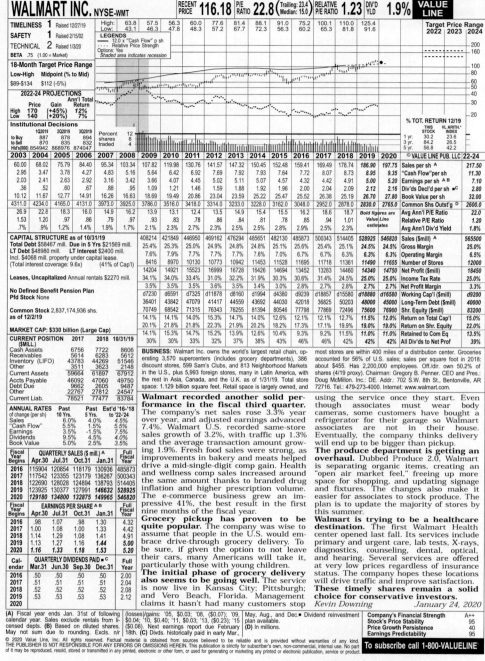

Source: "Walmart," the *Value Line website* at https://research.valueline.com/api/report?documentID=2185-VL_20200124_VLIS_WMT_2814_01-2DAT3I3MQN8K30F0EV7770M880&symbol=WMT, accessed February 10, 2021.

NEWSPAPER COVERAGE AND CORPORATE NEWS

Although some newspapers have eliminated or reduced their financial coverage, *The Wall Street Journal* and some metropolitan newspapers still contain some information about corporate stocks. Although not all newspapers print exactly the same information, they usually provide the basic information. Stocks are listed alphabetically, so your first task is to move down the table to find the name of the stock you're interested in. Then, read across the table to its stock symbol and price information.

As mentioned in Chapter 13, the federal government requires corporations selling new issues of securities to disclose information about corporate earnings, assets and liabilities, products or services, and the qualifications of top management in a prospectus. After stock is sold to the public, the federal government also requires that corporations periodically report financial information to the Securities and Exchange Commission (SEC). By accessing the SEC website (www.sec.gov), you can view this information. You can also obtain additional information about investing in stocks and other investments by visiting the Investor.gov website (https://www.investor.gov/).

In addition to the prospectus and the information reported to the SEC, publicly owned corporations provide detailed financial data and information about the company in an annual report. An annual report can be an excellent tool to learn about a company and its financial statements, its management, its past performance, and its goals. You can read an annual report by visiting the corporation's website or obtain a copy by contacting the investor relations department of a corporation.

Finally, many periodicals, including *Bloomberg Businessweek, Fortune, Forbes, Money, Kiplinger's Personal Finance,* and similar publications, contain information about stock investing in both print and online versions.

 2

I can evaluate stock investments.

In most cases, the search for a quality stock investment begins with a specific company. It may be a company that produces a product or a service that you purchased and really like. Then most good investors begin to "dig" for facts about the company and its financial outlook. To practice your skills at evaluating a potential stock investment, choose a stock you believe could help you achieve your financial goals and complete *Personal Financial Planner Sheet 58,* "Corporate Stock Evaluation."

 PRACTICE QUIZ 14-2

 PFP Sheet 58 Corporate Stock Evaluation

1. How would you define (a) a blue-chip stock, (b) a cyclical stock, (c) a defensive stock, (d) a growth stock, (e) an income stock, (f) a large-cap stock, (g) a midcap stock, (h) a small-cap stock, (i) a micro-cap stock, (j) a penny stock, and (k) a value stock?
2. Which type of stock could help you achieve your investment and financial goals? Justify your choice.
3. What sources of information would you use to evaluate a corporate stock issue?

Numerical Measures That Influence Investment Decisions

Many investors rely on numerical measures and different calculations to decide if it is the right time to buy or sell a stock. We begin this section by examining the relationship between a stock's price and a corporation's earnings.

WHY CORPORATE EARNINGS ARE IMPORTANT

Many analysts believe that a corporation's ability to generate earnings in the future is one of the most significant factors that account for an increase or decrease in the price of a stock. Simply put, higher earnings generally equate to higher stock prices. The reverse is also true. If a corporation's earnings decline, generally the stock's price will also decline. It also helps to remember that the price for a share of stock is determined by what another investor is willing to pay for it. In fact, there are times when investors may pay a high, inflated price for a share of stock. For example, the term **stock market bubble** is used to describe a situation when stocks are trading at prices above their actual worth. Consider what happened in 2021 when the price for a share of

LO14-3

Analyze the numerical measures that cause a stock to increase or decrease in value.

stock market bubble A situation in which stocks are trading at prices above their actual worth.

GameStop stock increased from $18 to over $400 a share within a three-week period. This dramatic price increase was caused by social media posts by a few investors that encouraged other investors to buy the stock. What many investors didn't realize was that the company was losing money-—over $4 per share at the time the stock's price was skyrocketing. Although the stock topped out at over $400 a share, shares quickly decreased in value. While some people made huge profits, a lot more investors lost money when the bubble burst. The bubble for a specific stock can burst when a company reduces or omits dividend payments to stockholders or lowers earnings expectations, or when stockholders begin to sell the stock for any other reason, including an economic slowdown, high unemployment rates, higher interest rates, and other factors that affect the economy.

Many investors consider earnings per share when evaluating the financial health of a corporation. **Earnings per share** is a corporation's after-tax income divided by the number of outstanding shares of a firm's common stock.

earnings per share A corporation's after-tax income divided by the number of outstanding shares of a firm's common stock.

EXAMPLE: Earnings per Share (Johnson & Johnson)

In a recent year, Johnson & Johnson has after-tax earnings of $15,119 million. Also assume that Johnson & Johnson has issued 2,645 million shares of common stock. This means Johnson & Johnson's earnings per share are $5.72, as illustrated below.

$$\text{Earnings per share} = \frac{\text{After-tax income}}{\text{Number of shares outstanding}}$$
$$= \frac{\$15,119 \text{ million}}{2,645 \text{ million}}$$
$$= \$5.72$$

No meaningful average for this measure exists, because the number of shares of a firm's stock is subject to change because of stock splits, stock dividends, or a company's decision to repurchase shares of its stock. *As a general rule, however, an increase in earnings per share is a healthy sign for any corporation and its stockholders.*

Another calculation, the price-earnings (P-E) ratio, can be used to evaluate a potential stock investment. The **price-earnings ratio** is the price of a share of stock divided by the corporation's earnings per share of stock.

price-earnings ratio The price of a share of stock divided by the corporation's earnings per share of stock.

EXAMPLE: Price-Earnings (P-E) Ratio (Johnson & Johnson)

Assume Johnson & Johnson's common stock is selling for $172 a share. As determined earlier, the corporation's earnings per share are $5.72. Johnson & Johnson's price-earnings ratio is 30, as illustrated below.

$$\text{Price-Earnings (P-E) ratio} = \frac{\text{Price per share}}{\text{Earnings per share}}$$
$$= \frac{\$172}{\$5.72}$$
$$= 30$$

A price-earnings ratio gives investors an idea of how much they are paying for a company's earning power. The higher the price-earnings ratio, the more investors are paying for earnings. For example, if Johnson & Johnson has a P-E ratio of 30, investors are paying $30 for each dollar the firm earns.

P-E ratios need to be interpreted carefully. Although it can go higher or lower, the average P-E ratio for the stock market generally is between 15 and 25 for any specific year. Stocks with high price-earnings ratios are often issued by young, fast-growing corporations or mature companies that continue to innovate and introduce new products. For these stocks, a high price-earnings ratio above the average P-E ratio for the market often indicates investor optimism because of the expectation of higher earnings in the future. If earnings do increase, the stock usually becomes more valuable. A high P-E ratio can also indicate a stock is overvalued. On the other hand, a stock with a low price-earnings ratio below the average P-E ratio for the market indicates investors have lower earnings expectations for a company's stock. If future earnings don't maintain the same level of growth or increase, the stock will become less valuable. A low P-E ratio can also indicate that a stock is undervalued. Stocks with low P-E ratios tend to be issued by large, established corporations or corporations in mature industries. When researching a stock, it is helpful to compare the P-E ratios of one company to other companies in the same industry. It is also possible to compare a company's P-E ratio against the company's own historical P-E ratios or to the market in general.

PROJECTED EARNINGS

Both earnings per share and the price-earnings ratio are based on historical numbers. In other words, this is what the company has done in the past. With this fact in mind, many investors will access investment websites that provide earnings estimates for major corporations. At the time of publication, for example, the Yahoo! Finance website provided the following earnings estimates for Visa, a world leader in electronic payment technology.[7]

	2021	2022
Yearly earnings estimates	$5.50 per share	$6.88 per share

From an investor's standpoint, a projected increase in earnings from $5.50 per share to $6.88 per share is a good sign. In the case of Visa, these estimates were determined by surveying more than 35 different analysts who track Visa. By using the same projected earnings amount, it is possible to calculate a price/earnings-to-growth (PEG) ratio. For more information about the price/earnings-to-growth ratio, read the *Financial Literacy Calculations: The Price/Earnings-to-Growth Ratio: A Look to the Future* feature.

DIVIDEND AND TOTAL RETURN CALCULATIONS

Today, many investors purchase stocks for dividend income. Because dividends are a distribution of a corporation's earnings, these same investors must be concerned about the firm's future earnings and the dividend payout. The **dividend payout** is the percentage of a firm's earnings paid to stockholders in cash. This ratio is calculated by dividing the annual dividend amount by the earnings per share.

dividend payout The percentage of a firm's earnings paid to stockholders in cash.

EXAMPLE: Dividend Payout (3M Company)

Assume you own stock issued by 3M Company and the corporation pays an annual dividend of $5.92. Also, assume that 3M earns $9.25 a share. The dividend payout is 64 percent, calculated as follows:

$$\text{Dividend payout} = \frac{\text{Annual dividend amount}}{\text{Earnings per share}}$$

$$= \frac{\$5.92}{\$9.25}$$

$$= 0.64 = 64\%$$

Financial Literacy Calculations

THE PRICE/EARNINGS-TO-GROWTH RATIO: A LOOK TO THE FUTURE

When evaluating a corporate stock, you may want to calculate a price/earnings-to-growth (PEG) ratio if you want to determine whether a stock is undervalued or not. Unlike the price-earnings ratio based on historical data, the PEG ratio includes a future projection for earnings per share in the calculation. If analysts estimate that Visa will earn $5.50 in 2021 and $6.88 in 2022, the first step is to determine the earnings per share growth stated as a percentage. This percentage is calculated below:

$$\$6.88 \ (2022) - \$5.50 \ (2021)$$
$$= \$1.38 \ \text{(projected change)}$$

$$\$1.38 \ \text{(projected change)} \div \$5.50 \ (2021)$$
$$= 0.25 = 25\%$$

For the next step, the 43 represents the current P-E ratio for Visa. Also, the percent sign (%) for annual EPS growth calculated in the first step is ignored. The following formula can then be used to calculate the PEG ratio:

$$\textbf{PEG ratio} = \frac{\text{Price-earnings ratio}}{\text{Annual EPS growth}}$$
$$= \frac{43}{25}$$
$$= 1.72$$

Generally, a PEG value less than 1 implies that a stock may be undervalued based on its projected growth rate. And a PEG value greater than 1 indicates that a stock may be overvalued based on its projected growth rate. With a PEG ratio of 1.72 (43 ÷ 25 = 1.72), Visa may be overvalued. *Caution: Your answer for the PEG ratio is only as good as the projection for earnings. If the projections are too high or too low, then the PEG ratio calculation can be an inaccurate predictor of a stock's value.*

Source: Values for Visa's stock were obtained from Yahoo! Finance, www.finance.yahoo.com, February 11, 2021.

dividend yield The annual dividend amount divided by the investment's current price per share.

For 3M, the dividend payout ratio indicates the company is paying 64 percent of its earnings to its stockholders. The 3M Company should be able to continue to pay dividends even if the company experiences a small decline in earnings.

One of the most common calculations investors use to monitor the value of their investments is the dividend yield. The **dividend yield** is the annual dividend amount divided by the investment's current price per share.

EXAMPLE: Dividend Yield (3M Company)

Assume 3M is currently selling for $180 a share and the annual dividend is $5.92 a share. The dividend yield is 3.3 percent, calculated as follows:

$$\text{Dividend yield} = \frac{\text{Annual dividend amount}}{\text{Price per share}}$$
$$= \frac{\$5.92}{\$180}$$
$$= 0.033 = 3.3\%$$

As a general rule, an increase in dividend yield is a healthy sign for any investment. A dividend yield of 3.3 percent is better than a 2 percent dividend yield.

Although the dividend yield calculation is useful, you should also consider whether the investment is increasing or decreasing in dollar value. **Total return** is a calculation that includes not only the yearly dollar amount of dividends but also any increase or decrease in the original purchase price of the investment. The following formula is used to calculate total return:

total return A calculation that includes the annual dollar amount of dividends as well as any increase or decrease in the original purchase price of the investment.

$$\text{Total return} = \text{Dividends} + \text{Capital gain}$$

While this concept may be used for any investment, let's illustrate it by using the assumptions for 3M stock presented in the preceding example.

EXAMPLE: Total Return (3M Company)

Assume that you own 100 shares of 3M stock that you purchased for $135 a share and that you hold your stock for five years before deciding to sell it at the current market price of $180 a share. Also, assume that during the five-year period, 3M paid total dividends of $26.22. Your total return for this investment would be $7,122, calculated as follows:

$$\text{Total return} = \text{Dividends} + \text{Capital gain}$$
$$= \$2,622 + \$4,500$$
$$= \$7,122$$

Dividends total $2,622 ($26.22 per-share dividend × 100 shares = $2,622). The capital gain of $4,500 results from the increase in the stock price from $135 a share to $180 a share ($45 per share increase × 100 shares = $4,500).

In this example, the investment increased in value and you received dividends. And while it may be obvious, we should point out that the larger the dollar amount of total return, the better.

The **annualized holding period yield** calculation takes into account the total return, the original investment, and the time the investment is held. The following formula is used to calculate the annualized holding period yield:

$$\text{Annualized holding period yield} = \frac{\text{Total return}}{\text{Original investment}} \times \frac{1}{N}$$

where

$$N = \text{Number of years investment is held}$$

> **annualized holding period yield** A yield calculation that takes into account the total return, the original investment, and the time the investment is held.

To illustrate this concept, let's return to your 3M investment, for which the total return was $7,122.

EXAMPLE: Annualized Holding Period Yield (3M Company)

Assume that five years ago you invested $13,500 to purchase 100 shares of 3M stock and that your total return when you sold your stock was $7,122. The annualized holding period yield is 10.6 percent for each of the five years you held the investment, as illustrated below:

$$\text{Annualized holding period yield} = \frac{\text{Total return}}{\text{Original investment}} \times \frac{1}{N}$$
$$= \frac{\$7,122}{\$13,500} \times \frac{1}{5}$$
$$= 0.106 = 10.6\%$$

Note: N in the above formula is the number of years the investment is held.

There is no meaningful average for annualized holding period yield, because individual investments vary. But an increase in annualized holding period yield is a healthy sign. For instance, an annualized holding period yield of 10.6 percent is better than one of 8 percent.

Financial Literacy Calculations

TIME VALUE OF MONEY CAN HELP YOU EVALUATE YOUR INVESTMENTS!

Many investors spend substantial time initially selecting an investment, but they don't continue to evaluate the investment to ensure that it continues to perform and meet their investment objectives.

Assume that you purchase a *growth* stock that does not pay dividends. In this situation, you plan to make money based upon an increase in the value of the stock over a long period of time. Your investment objective is to make at least 6 percent on your investment each year.

When you initially purchased the stock, you invested $2,400. Three years have passed and the value of your investment is now $2,700. You want to evaluate whether you are meeting your objective of earning 6 percent each year. In this situation, you can use the annualized holding period yield formula to evaluate the performance of your investment.

Step 1: *Subtract the value of the investment at the end of three years from your original investment.*

$2,700 Value at the end of 3 years − $2,400 Original investment = $300 Total return

Step 2: *Use the Annualized Holding Period Yield calculation to determine the annual return.*

Annualized holding period yield

$$= \frac{\text{Total return}}{\text{Original investment}} \times \frac{1}{N}$$

(where N = Number of years the investment is held)

$$= \frac{\$300}{\$2,400} \times \frac{1}{3}$$

$$= 0.042 = 4.2\%$$

CONCLUSION

Based upon the above calculations, the stock is not meeting your objective of earning at least 6 percent a year. You may want to reevaluate this investment and possibly sell it. Then, you could search for another investment that could help you obtain your objective of a 6 percent annual return.

OTHER FACTORS THAT INFLUENCE THE PRICE OF A STOCK

beta A measure reported in many financial publications that compares the volatility associated with a specific stock issue with the volatility of the overall stock market or an index like the Standard & Poor's 500 Stock Index

The **beta** is a measure reported in many financial publications that compares the volatility associated with a specific stock issue with the volatility of the overall stock market or an index like the Standard & Poor's 500 Stock Index. The beta for the S&P 500 is defined as 1.0. The majority of stocks have betas between 0.5 and 2.0. Generally, conservative stocks have low betas, while more speculative stocks have betas greater than 1.

EXAMPLE: Beta Calculation (Facebook)

Assume that Facebook has a beta of 1.30 and that the overall stock market increases by 10 percent. Based on the calculation below, Facebook will increase 13 percent when the market increases 10 percent.

Volatility for a stock = Beta for a specific stock × increase in overall market

= 1.30 × 10%

= 1.30 × 0.10

= 0.13 = 13%

Because individual stocks generally move in the same direction as the stock market, most betas are positive, but it is possible for a stock to have a negative beta. A negative beta occurs when a corporation's stock moves in the opposite direction compared to the stock market in general.

book value Determined by deducting all liabilities from the corporation's assets and dividing the remainder by the number of outstanding shares of common stock.

Although little correlation may exist between the market value of a stock and its book value, book value is widely reported in financial publications. Therefore, it deserves mention. The **book value** for a share of stock is determined by deducting all liabilities from the corporation's assets and dividing the remainder by the number of outstanding shares of common stock.

EXAMPLE: Book Value (First National)

If First National Corporation has assets of $670 million and liabilities of $375 million and has issued 12 million shares of common stock, the book value for one share of First National stock is $24.58, as follows:

$$\text{Book value} = \frac{\text{Assets} - \text{Liabilities}}{\text{Shares outstanding}}$$

$$= \frac{\$670 \text{ million} - \$375 \text{ million}}{12 \text{ million shares of stock}}$$

$$= \$24.58 \text{ per share}$$

Investors can also calculate a market price-to-book ratio (sometimes called a price-to-book ratio). The **market price-to-book ratio** is the market price of one share of stock divided by the book value for one share of stock.

EXAMPLE: Market Price-to-Book Ratio (First National)

Using First National's $24.58 per share book value and assuming the stock has a current price of $43 a share, the market price-to-book ratio would be 1.75, as follows:

$$\text{Market price-to-book ratio} = \frac{\text{Market price per share}}{\text{Book value per share}}$$

$$= \frac{\$43}{\$24.58}$$

$$= 1.75$$

While the average market price-to-book ratio varies from one industry to another, a statistic often quoted for this ratio is 3 to 1. A low market price-to-book ratio (less than the average) could mean that the stock is undervalued, and a high market price-to-book ratio (greater than the average) could mean that a stock is overvalued.

Some investors believe they have found a bargain when a stock's market value is about the same as or lower than its book value. *Be warned:* Book value and market price-to-book ratio calculations may be misleading, because the dollar amount of assets used in the above formula for book value may be understated or overstated on the firm's financial statements. Keep in mind that this is one calculation. A better way to evaluate individual stocks is to perform multiple calculations that were illustrated in this section to determine if a stock is a good investment choice or not.

market price-to-book ratio The current price of one share of stock divided by the book value for one share of stock.

INVESTMENT THEORIES

Investors sometimes use three different investment theories to determine a stock's value. **Fundamental analysis** is based on the assumption that a stock's intrinsic or real value is determined by the company's future earnings. If a corporation's expected earnings are higher than its present earnings, the corporation's stock should increase in value. If its expected earnings are lower than its present earnings, the stock should decrease in value. In addition to expected earnings, fundamentalists consider (1) the financial strength of the company, (2) the type of industry the company is in, (3) new product development, and (4) the economic growth of the overall economy. The goal of fundamental analysis is to find a stock's intrinsic value, which is a fancy way of trying to determine what you think a stock is really worth instead of what the stock is actually trading for in the marketplace. If you find a stock with an intrinsic value that is more than the current market price, it makes sense to buy the stock. One of the most famous and successful users of fundamental analysis is Warren Buffett, the chairman and CEO of Berkshire Hathaway. Mr. Buffett is well known for successfully employing

fundamental analysis An investment practice based on the assumption that a stock's intrinsic or real value is determined by the company's future earnings.

technical analysis An investment practice based on the assumption that a stock's market value is determined by the forces of supply and demand in the stock market as a whole.

efficient market hypothesis (EMH) An investment theory based on the assumption that stock price movements are purely random.

fundamental analysis to identify both stocks and corporations that are undervalued. His ability to use fundamental analysis has enabled him to become a billionaire.[8]

Technical analysis is based on the assumption that a stock's market value is determined by the forces of supply and demand in the stock market, *not* on the expected earnings or the intrinsic value of an individual corporation's stock. Technical analysis is also based on the assumption that past market trends can predict the future direction for the market as a whole. Typical technical factors are price movements, the total number of shares traded, the number of buy orders, and the number of sell orders over a period of time. Technical analysts, sometimes called *chartists,* construct charts or use computer programs to plot past price movements and other market averages. These charts allow them to observe trends and patterns for the market that enable them to predict the effect that changes in supply and demand will have on different securities.

The **efficient market hypothesis (EMH)** is an investment theory based on the assumption that stock price movements are purely random. Advocates of the efficient market hypothesis assume the stock market is completely efficient and buyers and sellers have considered all of the available information about an individual stock. According to this theory, it is impossible for an investor to outperform the average for the stock market as a whole over a long period of time. Advocates of the efficient market hypothesis also believe it is useless to identify undervalued or overvalued stocks, and the only way to achieve superior results is to pick riskier investments. Most investors reject the efficient market hypothesis on the assumption that, by means of the fundamental theory, technical analysis, or a combination of the two theories, they can improve their performance (and ultimately their financial returns) in the stock market.

my life 3

I know how investors use financial ratios to evaluate a specific stock.

Numbers, formulas, ratios! What do they all mean? For an investor, they could mean the difference between a profit and a loss on a stock investment. To provide more practice on these important calculations, complete the financial problems at the end of this chapter.

 PRACTICE QUIZ 14-3

1. Explain the relationship between earnings and a stock's market price.
2. Why are earnings per share and price-earnings calculations important?
3. What are the formulas for dividend payout, dividend yield, total return, annualized holding period yield, beta, book value, and market price-to-book value ratio?
4. Explain how fundamental analysis, technical analysis, or the efficient market hypothesis can be used to describe price movements for the stock market.

Buying and Selling Stocks

LO14-4

Describe how stocks are bought and sold.

primary market A market in which an investor purchases financial securities, via an investment bank or other representative, from the issuer of those securities.

To purchase common or preferred stock, you generally have to work through a brokerage firm. In turn, your brokerage firm must buy the stock in either the primary or the secondary market. In the **primary market**, you purchase financial securities, via an investment bank or other representative, from the issuer of those securities. An **investment bank** is a financial firm that assists corporations in raising funds, usually by helping to sell new security issues.

New security issues sold through an investment bank can be issued by corporations that have sold stocks and bonds before and need to sell additional securities to raise more financing. The new securities can also be initial public offerings. An **initial public offering (IPO)** occurs when a corporation sells stock to the general public for the first time. For example, DoorDash, Inc., a food delivery business that connects merchants, consumers, and dashers in the United States and internationally, used an IPO to raise over $3.3 billion in late 2020.[9] The promise of quick profits often lures investors to purchase IPO shares. On the day of the IPO, investors bought shares in DoorDash's IPO for just over $100 a share; three months later those shares were selling for just over $170 a share. Still, experts indicate that the company started by a group of college students in 2013 and now operating in all 50 states will need to increase revenues, control expenses, and become profitable in the near future for the value of its shares to continue to increase. Without continued growth and the ability to earn profits, share values could fall. *Be warned:* An IPO is generally classified as a high-risk investment—one made in the hope of earning a relatively large profit in a short time. Depending on the corporation selling the new security, IPOs may be too speculative for many people.

After a stock has been sold through the primary market, it is traded through the secondary market. The **secondary market** is a market for existing financial securities that are currently traded among investors. Once stocks are sold in the primary market, they can be sold time and again in the secondary market. Although a corporation does not receive money each time its stock is bought or sold in the secondary market, liquidity—the ability to obtain cash by selling stock investments—is one reason why investors purchase corporate stock. Without the liquidity provided by the secondary market, investors would not purchase stock in the primary market because there would be no way to sell shares to other investors.

SECONDARY MARKETS FOR STOCKS

When you purchase stock in the secondary market, the transaction is completed on a securities exchange or through the over-the-counter market.

SECURITIES EXCHANGES A **securities exchange** is a marketplace where member brokers who represent investors meet to buy and sell securities. The securities sold at a particular exchange must first be listed, or accepted for trading, at that exchange. Generally, the securities issued by nationwide corporations are traded at either the New York Stock Exchange (NYSE) or regional exchanges. The securities of very large corporations may be traded at more than one exchange. American firms may also be listed on foreign securities exchanges—in Tokyo, London, or Shanghai, for example.

The New York Stock Exchange is one of the largest securities exchanges in the world. Most NYSE members represent brokerage firms that charge commissions on security trades made by their representatives for their customers. Other members are called *designated market makers*. A **designated market maker (DMM)** buys *or* sells a particular stock in an effort to maintain an orderly market.

The stock of corporations that cannot meet the NYSE requirements, find it too expensive to be listed on the NYSE, or choose not to be listed on the NYSE is often traded on one of the regional exchanges or through the over-the-counter market.

THE OVER-THE-COUNTER MARKET Not all securities are traded on organized exchanges. Stocks issued by several thousand companies are traded in the over-the-counter market. The **over-the-counter (OTC) market** is a network of dealers who buy and sell the stocks of corporations that are not listed on a securities exchange. Today these stocks are not really traded over the counter. The term was coined more than 100 years ago when securities were sold "over the counter" in stores and banks.

Many stocks are traded through Nasdaq (pronounced "nazzdack"). **Nasdaq** is an electronic marketplace for buying and selling global stocks and securities. In addition to providing price information, this computerized system allows investors to buy and sell shares of companies listed on Nasdaq. When you want to buy or sell shares of a company that trades on Nasdaq—say, Microsoft—your account executive sends your order into the Nasdaq computer system, where it shows up on the screen with all the other orders from people who want to buy or sell Microsoft. Then a Nasdaq dealer or market maker matches buy and sell orders for Microsoft. Once a match is found, your order is completed.

investment bank A financial firm that assists corporations in raising funds, usually by helping to sell new security issues.

initial public offering (IPO) Occurs when a corporation sells stock to the general public for the first time.

secondary market A market for existing financial securities that are currently traded among investors.

securities exchange A marketplace where member brokers who represent investors meet to buy and sell securities.

designated market maker Buys or sells a particular stock in an effort to maintain an orderly market.

over-the-counter (OTC) market A network of dealers who buy and sell the stocks of corporations that are not listed on a securities exchange.

Nasdaq An electronic marketplace for buying and selling global stocks and securities.

smart money minute

account executive A licensed individual who buys or sells securities for clients; also called a *stockbroker.*

Nasdaq is known for its innovative, forward-looking growth companies—especially technology companies. Although many securities are issued by smaller companies, some large firms, including Intel, Microsoft, Amazon, Facebook, and Cisco Systems, also trade on Nasdaq.

BROKERAGE FIRMS AND ACCOUNT EXECUTIVES

An **account executive**, or *stockbroker,* is a licensed individual who buys or sells securities for his or her clients. Even though an account executive can buy and sell securities for you and should help you develop your investment program, you should be *actively* involved in your investment program. Avoid allowing your account executive to use his or her discretion without your approval when making investment decisions for you. *Finally, keep in mind that account executives generally are not liable for client losses that result from their recommendations.* In fact, most brokerage firms require new clients to sign a statement in which they promise to submit any complaints to an arbitration board. This arbitration clause generally prevents a client from suing an account executive or a brokerage firm.

SHOULD YOU USE A FULL-SERVICE, DISCOUNT, OR ONLINE BROKERAGE FIRM?

Although the distinctions between full-service, discount, and online brokerage firms have blurred in recent years, there is healthy competition between different types of brokerage firms. Many investors begin the search for a brokerage firm by looking at the commissions they charge to buy or sell stock for you. Another factor to consider is how much research information is available and if there is a cost for research information. Also, consider how much help you need when making an investment decision. Although there are many exceptions, the following information may help you decide whether to use a full-service, discount, or online brokerage firm.

• Full service	Beginning investors with little or no experience. Individuals who are uncomfortable making investment decisions.
• Discount	People who understand the "how to" of researching stocks and prefer to make their own decisions. Individuals who are uncomfortable trading stocks online.
• Online	People who understand the "how to" of researching stocks and prefer to make their own decisions. Individuals who are comfortable trading stocks online.

Finally, consider how easy it is to buy and sell stock and other securities when using a full-service, discount, or online brokerage firm. Questions to ask include:

1. Can I buy or sell stocks online or over the phone?
2. How easy is it to use the firm's website, and what services are available online?
3. Do you have a telephone number for customer assistance?
4. Is there a charge for statements, research reports, and other financial reports?
5. Are there any fees in addition to the commissions I pay when I buy or sell stocks?

EXHIBIT 14-8

Typical commission charges for online stock transactions

	Account Minimum	Internet Trades	Advantages
Charles Schwab	$0	$0	Extensive research and above average mobile app
E*Trade	0	0	Great customer service and extensive research
Fidelity	0	0	Strong customer service and extensive research provided by different advisory services
Merrill Edge	0	0	Robust third-party research and affiliated with Bank of America
Robinhood	0	0	Becoming more popular, but no retirement accounts and limited customer service
TD Ameritrade	0	0	Good customer service and high-quality trading platform

Source: Kevin Voight, "11 Best Online Brokers for Stock Trading of February 2021," https://www.nerdwallet.com/best/investing/online-brokers-for-stock-trading, February 9, 2021.

COMMISSION CHARGES

Today, there is a healthy competition among brokerage firms to attract investors. As illustrated in Exhibit 14-8, many brokerage firms don't charge commissions for internet trades. *Be warned:* Commission-free trade may be an introductory offer and only apply for a specific time period. Other restrictions, including a large minimum balance, may apply before you are entitled to free trades. For brokerage firms that charge commissions, a minimum commission ranging from $5 to $25 for buying *and* selling stock is common. Additional commission charges, if any, are based on the number of shares and the value of stock bought and sold.

Generally, full-service brokerage firms charge higher commissions than those charged by discount and online brokerage firms. In return for charging higher commissions, you have access to the same account executive each time you interact with the brokerage firm to buy or sell stocks. Your account executive can also help you develop a financial plan and help you make financial decisions. Keep in mind, many account executives often don't spend a lot of time with investors who only have a small amount of money to invest.

  my life | **4**

I know what factors to consider when choosing an account executive and a brokerage firm.

While all brokerage firms can buy and sell stocks and other securities for you, there are important differences. For help making the right choice, go to the brokerage firm's website. Take a look at the information contained on the websites for at least two different brokerage firms. You can use *Personal Financial Planner Sheet 59* to compare account executives and brokerage firms.

COMPLETING STOCK TRANSACTIONS

Once you have decided on a particular stock investment, it is time to execute an order to buy or sell. Today most investors buy or sell stocks online. It is also possible to trade stocks by using a brokerage firm's automated telephone system. Finally, you can contact a broker and execute a broker-assisted trade. Let's begin by examining three types of orders used to trade stocks.

personal fintech

Today you can practice your investing skills by playing a virtual stock game. To begin, research three different stocks that you think would be a good investment over the next year. Once your research is completed, use an internet search engine like Google, Yahoo!, or Bing and enter the words "virtual stock game" in the search box. Select one of the virtual stock games. Then enter the information required to play the game. Monitor the value of your investment portfolio for a specific time period. At the end of the time period, determine how much money you made or lost on your investments. For future reference, it's a good idea to make notes about what you learned, the mistakes you made, and what you would do differently if you were investing real money.

market order A request to buy or sell a stock at the current market price.

limit order A request to buy or sell a stock at a specified price or better.

stop-loss order An order to sell a particular stock at the next available opportunity after its market price reaches a specified amount.

A **market order** is a request to buy or sell a stock at the current market price. Since the stock exchange is an auction market, the account executive's representative will try to get the best price available, and the transaction will be completed as soon as possible. According to new rules issued by the Securities and Exchange Commission, payment for stocks is generally required within two business days after the transaction. For example, if you buy or sell stock on Monday, the transaction will settle on Wednesday—two business days after the transaction. Today it is common practice for investors to leave stock certificates with a brokerage firm. Because the stock certificates are in the broker's care, transfers when the stock is sold are much easier. The phrase "left in the street name" is used to describe investor-owned securities held by a brokerage firm.

A **limit order** is a request to buy or sell a stock at a specified price or better. When you purchase stock, a limit order ensures that you will buy at the best possible price but not above a specified dollar amount. When you sell stock, a limit order ensures that you will sell at the best possible price, but not below a specified dollar amount. For example, if you place a limit order to buy stock issued by The Walt Disney Company for $190 a share, the stock will not be purchased until the price drops to $190 a share or lower. Likewise, if your limit order is to sell Disney for $190 a share, the stock will not be sold until the price rises to $190 a share or higher. *Be warned:* Limit orders are executed if and when the specified price or better is reached and *all* other previously received orders have been fulfilled.

Many stockholders are certain they want to sell their stock if it reaches a specified price. A limit order does not guarantee this will be done. With a limit order, as mentioned above, previously received orders by other investors may be placed ahead of your order. If you want to guarantee that your order will be executed, you place a special type of order known as a stop-loss order. A **stop-loss order** (sometimes referred to as a stop order) is an order to sell a particular stock at the next available opportunity after its market price reaches a specified amount. This type of order is used to protect an investor against a sharp drop in price and thus stop the dollar loss on a stock investment. For example, assume you purchased stock issued by American Airlines for $28 a share. Two months after making your investment, the COVID-19 pandemic forces the company to reduce flights and curtail service to some destinations. Fearing that the market value of your stock will decrease, you enter a stop-loss order to sell your American Airlines stock at $23 a share. This means that if the price of the stock decreases to $23 or lower, the account executive will sell it. While a stop order does not guarantee that your stock will be sold at the price you specified, it does guarantee that it will be sold at the next available opportunity. Both limit and stop-loss orders may be good for one day, one week, one month, good until canceled (GTC), or a specified date.

PFP Sheet 59
Brokerage and Account Executive Comparison

 PRACTICE QUIZ 14-4

1. What is the difference between the primary market and the secondary market?
2. Assume you want to purchase stock. Would you use a full-service broker or a discount broker? Would you ever trade stocks online?
3. Describe the types of orders that are used to buy or sell stocks in the secondary market.

Financial Literacy for My Life

HOW DO I PICK A WINNING STOCK?

Good question! Now for some answers. Stock investors who are willing to do their homework can make sense out of all the information and numbers that are available. Below are some suggestions for pulling it all together.

1. LOOK AT THE INFORMATION AND NUMBERS.

There are many sources—this chapter, self-help investing books, and internet investment sites—that will help you learn the "how to" of researching a stock investment. Also, don't forget to use professional advisory services like Value Line, Morningstar, and Zacks that provide detailed stock research.

2. DEVELOP A PLAN OR A SYSTEM TO HELP ORGANIZE THE DATA.

With so much information available, you need to organize the information so that it makes sense. One suggestion is to use the *Personal Financial Planner Sheet 58*, "Corporate Stock Evaluation," as a starting point. You can customize this sheet by adding or deleting questions that help you to establish a database of information for each potential stock investment.

3. USE SOFTWARE AND FINANCIAL CALCULATORS TO FINE-TUNE YOUR INVESTMENT SELECTIONS.

Many investment websites have both software and financial calculators that will help you evaluate a corporate stock. For example, a website that helps you use different financial measures to identify potential stock investments is MSN Money's Stock Screener (www.msn.com/en-us/money/stockscreener).

Making informed investment decisions requires work and time. While each of the above suggestions will help you accumulate the information you need to make a more informed decision, a better approach is to use all three suggestions *and* any other available information to get a more complete picture of a corporation and the investment potential for its stock.

Long-Term and Short-Term Investment Strategies

As mentioned in the first part of this chapter, stocks have returned 11.47 percent a year—substantially more than other investment alternatives—over the last 30 years. And while there have been years when stocks declined in value, investing for the long term allows you to "get through the rough years" and "enjoy the good years" when your investments are earning higher returns.

Once you purchase stock, the investment may be classified as either long term or short term. Individuals who hold an investment for a long period of time are referred to as *investors*. Typically, long-term investors hold their investments for a year or longer. Individuals who routinely buy and then sell stocks within a short period of time are called *speculators* or *traders*.

LO14-5

Explain the trading techniques used by long-term investors and short-term speculators.

LONG-TERM TECHNIQUES

In this section, we discuss the long-term techniques of buy and hold, dollar cost averaging, direct investment programs, and dividend reinvestment programs.

BUY-AND-HOLD TECHNIQUE   Many long-term investors purchase stock and hold onto it for a number of years. When they do this, their investment can increase in value two ways. First, they are entitled to dividends *if the board of directors approves dividend payments to stockholders*. While stockholders can use dividends for immediate needs, another option is to reinvest the dividends in either the same stock or a different investment alternative. By reinvesting your dividends, even small amounts can

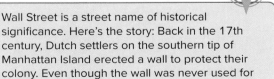

smart money minute

Wall Street is a street name of historical significance. Here's the story: Back in the 17th century, Dutch settlers on the southern tip of Manhattan Island erected a wall to protect their colony. Even though the wall was never used for defensive purposes, the name remains and is now recognized as one of the most famous streets in the financial world.

grow over a long period of time. Second, the price of the stock may go up. To see the effect of an increase in stock value over a period of time, you may want to review the sample stock transaction for Clorox illustrated in Exhibit 14-2. Over a 12-month period, both dividends *and* increase in value contributed to total profit for this investment. How do you know if you've picked the right stock to hold? See the *Financial Literacy for My Life: How Do I Pick a Winning Stock?* feature for some tips on selecting stocks to purchase.

dollar cost averaging A long-term technique used by investors who purchase an equal dollar amount of the same stock at equal intervals.

DOLLAR COST AVERAGING   **Dollar cost averaging** is a long-term technique used by investors who purchase an equal dollar amount of the same stock at equal intervals. Assume you invest $2,000 in Johnson & Johnson's common stock each year for a period of seven years. The results of your investment program are illustrated in Exhibit 14-9. The average cost for a share of stock, determined by dividing the total investment by the total number of shares, is $122.48 ($14,000 ÷ 114.3 = $122.48).

While many people don't realize it, they are using dollar cost averaging when they purchase shares of their company's stock or other investments through a payroll deduction plan or as part of an employer-sponsored retirement plan over an extended period of time.

Investors use dollar cost averaging to avoid the common pitfall of buying high and selling low. In the situation shown in Exhibit 14-9, you would lose money only if you sold your stock at less than the average cost of $122.48. Thus, with dollar cost averaging, you can make money if the stock is sold at a price higher than the average cost for a share of stock.

direct investment plan A plan that allows stockholders to purchase stock directly from a corporation without having to use an account executive or a brokerage firm.

dividend reinvestment plan A plan that allows current stockholders the option to reinvest or use their cash dividends to purchase stock of the corporation.

DIRECT INVESTMENT AND DIVIDEND REINVESTMENT PLANS   Today a large number of corporations offer direct investment plans. A **direct investment plan** allows you to purchase stock directly from a corporation without having to use an account executive or a brokerage firm. For example, McDonald's, Procter & Gamble, Amazon, and ExxonMobil allow investors to purchase stock directly from the corporation. Similarly, a **dividend reinvestment plan** allows you the option to reinvest your cash dividends to purchase stock of the corporation. For stockholders, the chief advantage of both types of plans is that these plans enable them to purchase stock without paying a commission charge to a brokerage firm. The fees (if any), minimum investment amounts, rules, and features for both direct investment and dividend reinvestment do vary from one corporation to the next.

EXHIBIT 14-9

Dollar cost averaging for Johnson & Johnson

Year	Investment	Stock Price	Shares Purchased
2015	$ 2,000	$ 100	20.0
2016	2,000	108	18.5
2017	2,000	128	15.6
2018	2,000	122	16.4
2019	2,000	124	16.1
2020	2,000	135	14.8
2021	2,000	155	12.9
Total	$14,000		114.3

Average cost = Total investment ÷ Total shares
= $14,000 ÷ 114.3
= $122.48

In addition to saving the commissions that would be paid to account executives, both types of plans enable investors to purchase a small number of shares (or even fractional shares) of a stock. Both plans are practical applications of dollar cost averaging. A number of websites provide information about direct investment or dividend reinvestment plans.

SHORT-TERM TECHNIQUES

Investors sometimes use more speculative, short-term techniques. In this section, we discuss day trading, buying stock on margin, selling short, and trading in options. *Be warned:* The methods presented in this section are quite risky; do not use them unless you fully understand the underlying risks.

DAY TRADING   A **day trader** is an individual who buys and then later sells stocks and other securities in a very short period of time. What could be easier? Buy a stock in the morning that has a great deal of momentum because of a projected revenue jump or an increase in earnings and then sell it a few hours later the same day or in just a few days? Sounds simple! Here's the problem—*most day traders lose money over a long period of time!*

Consider what happened when thousands of investors bought stocks issued by AMC and Blackberry in 2021. Like GameStop, interest in these two stocks was fueled by social media messages on the Reddit WallStreetBets website, and the price of each stock jumped to recent record levels almost overnight, despite the fact that each company was losing money. A few investors who bought before or right after the stock began to increase in value and sold at just the right time made huge profits. On the other hand, the majority of investors who paid too much for the stocks lost money when the bubble burst and prices began to fall.

Be warned: This is one of the most speculative techniques used today—much like going to Las Vegas and gambling. And yet, the lure of quick profits and the success stories of a few cause people to try their luck at day trading. Individuals should never use day trading if they don't fully understand the risks involved and cannot afford to lose money if the strategy doesn't work.

BUYING STOCK ON MARGIN   When buying stock on **margin**, you borrow part of the money needed to buy a particular stock. The margin requirement is set by the Federal Reserve Board and is subject to periodic change. The current margin requirement is 50 percent. This requirement means you may borrow up to half of the total stock purchase price. Although margin is regulated by the Federal Reserve, specific requirements and the interest rate charged on the loans used to fund margin transactions may vary among brokerage firms. Usually, your brokerage firm either lends the money or arranges the loan with another financial institution.

Investors buy on margin because the financial leverage created by borrowing money can increase the return on an investment. Because they can buy up to twice as much stock by buying on margin, they can earn larger returns. Suppose you expect the market price for a share of PepsiCo—the parent company of Pepsi and other drink products—to *increase* in the next three to four months. Let's say you have enough money to purchase 100 shares of the stock. However, if you buy on margin, you can purchase an additional 100 shares for a total of 200 shares.

day trader An individual who buys and then later sells stocks and other securities in a very short period of time.

margin A speculative technique whereby an investor borrows part of the money needed to buy a particular stock.

> ## EXAMPLE: Margin Transaction (PepsiCo)
>
> If the price of PepsiCo's stock increases by $4 a share, your profit will be
>
> | | |
> |---|---|
> | Without margin: | $400 = $4 increase per share × 100 shares |
> | With margin: | $800 = $4 increase per share × 200 shares |

In this example, the PepsiCo stock did exactly what it was supposed to do: It increased in market value. Because you used margin to purchase 200 shares, and your stock increased $4 per share, you made $800. Your actual profit would be reduced by commissions and the amount of interest your broker would charge for the margin loan needed to complete this transaction. Had the value of PepsiCo stock gone down, however, buying on margin would have increased your loss.

If the value of a margined stock *decreases* past a certain point, you may receive a *margin call* from the brokerage firm. After the margin call, you must pledge additional cash or securities to serve as collateral for the loan. If you don't have acceptable collateral or cash, the margined stock is sold and the proceeds are used to repay the loan. The exact price at which the brokerage firm issues the margin call is determined by the amount of money you borrowed when you purchased the stock and the rules established by the brokerage firm. Generally, the more money you borrow, the sooner you will receive a margin call if the price of the margined stock decreases.

In addition to facing the possibility of larger dollar losses if you use margin, you must pay interest on the money borrowed to purchase stock on margin. Interest charges can absorb the potential profits if the price of margined stock does not increase rapidly enough and the margined stocks must be held for long periods of time.

SELLING SHORT   Normally, you buy stocks and assume they will increase in value, a procedure referred to as *buying long*. But not all stocks increase in value all the time. In fact, the value of a stock may decrease for many reasons, including lower sales, lower profits, reduced dividends, product failures, increased competition, and product liability lawsuits. With this fact in mind, you may use a procedure called *selling short* to make money when the value of a stock is expected to decrease in value. **Selling short** is selling stock that has been borrowed from a brokerage firm and must be replaced at a later date. When you sell short, you sell today, knowing you must buy, or *cover* your short transaction, at a later date. To make money in a short transaction, you must take these steps:

> **selling short** Selling stock that has been borrowed from a brokerage firm and must be replaced at a later date.

1. Arrange to *borrow a certain number of shares of a particular stock* from a brokerage firm.

2. *Sell the borrowed stock,* assuming it will drop in value in a reasonably short period of time.

3. *Buy the stock at a lower price* than the price it sold for in step 2.

4. Use the stock purchased in step 3 to *replace the stock borrowed from the brokerage firm* in step 1.

When selling short, your profit is the difference between the amount received when the stock is sold in step 2 and the amount paid for the stock in step 3. For example, assume that you think ExxonMobil is overvalued at $60 a share. You also believe the stock will *decrease* in value over the next four to six months because of declining oil prices. You call your broker and arrange to borrow 100 shares of ExxonMobil stock (step 1). The broker then sells the borrowed stock for you at the current market price of $60 a share (step 2). Also assume that four months later ExxonMobil stock drops to $50 a share. You instruct your broker to purchase 100 shares of ExxonMobil stock at the current lower price (step 3). The newly purchased stock is given to the brokerage firm to repay the borrowed stock (step 4).

EXAMPLE: Selling Short (ExxonMobil)

Your profit from the ExxonMobil short transaction was $1,000 because the price declined from $60 to $50.

$6,000 selling price = $60 price per share × 100 shares (step 2)

$5,000 purchase price = $50 price per share × 100 shares (step 3)

$1,000 Profit from selling short

Note: For illustration purposes, no commission was included in the above example. In reality, the profits for this transaction would be reduced by any commissions charged by the brokerage firm to buy and sell the stock.

Before selling short, consider two factors. First, since the stock you borrow from your broker is actually owned by another investor, you must pay any dividends the stock earns before you replace the stock. After all, you borrowed the stock and then sold the borrowed stock. The dividends you are required to pay can absorb the profits from your short transaction if the price of the stock does not decrease rapidly enough. Second, to make money selling short, you must be correct in predicting that a stock will decrease in value. If the value of the stock increases, you lose because you must replace the borrowed stock with stock purchased at a higher price.

TRADING IN OPTIONS An **option** gives you the right—but not the obligation—to buy or sell a stock at a predetermined price during a specified period of time. If you think the market price of a stock will increase during a short period of time, you may decide to purchase a call option. A *call option* is sold by a stockholder and gives the purchaser the right to *buy* 100 shares of a stock at a guaranteed price before a specified expiration date. If the stock's price increases before the expiration date, the owner of a call option can purchase the stock at the lower price guaranteed by the call option and then sell it for a profit. In this example the investor's profit is reduced by commissions and the cost of the call option.

It is also possible to purchase a put option. A *put option* is the right to *sell* 100 shares of a stock at a guaranteed price before a specified expiration date. If the stock's price decreases before the expiration date, the owner of a put option can purchase the stock at the lower price and then sell it for a higher price that is guaranteed by the put option. With both call and put options, the price movement must occur before the expiration date, or you lose the money you paid for either type of option.

Because of the increased risk involved in option trading, a more detailed discussion of how you profit or lose money with options is beyond the scope of this book. *Be warned:* Amateurs and beginning investors should stay away from options unless they fully understand all of the risks involved. For the rookie, the lure of large profits over a short period of time may be tempting, but the risks are real.

option The right—but not the obligation—to buy or sell a stock at a predetermined price during a specified period of time.

 PRACTICE QUIZ 14-5

1. How can an investor make money using the buy-and-hold technique?
2. What is the advantage of using dollar cost averaging?
3. Explain the difference between direct investment plans and dividend reinvestment plans.
4. Why would an investor buy stock on margin?
5. Why would an investor use the selling-short technique?

Your Personal Finance Roadmap and Dashboard:

Managing Stock Investments

HAVE YOU SAVED ENOUGH MONEY TO OPEN
A BROKERAGE ACCOUNT AND PURCHASE
YOUR FIRST STOCK?

A personal finance dashboard allows you to assess your financial situation.

Beginning investors are often reluctant to begin investing because they don't have the money needed to open an account at a brokerage firm or buy their first stock. Second, they don't know how to research different investment alternatives.

YOUR SITUATION

Have you saved enough money to open a brokerage account? While some brokerage firms do not require a minimum deposit, other firms may require an initial deposit of up to $2,000. The minimum amount also may depend on whether you are opening a taxable, traditional IRA, or Roth IRA account. Next, you should research any potential investment. The material in this chapter, along with information available on websites can help you evaluate a specific stock that can help you obtain your financial goals.

First Steps

- Establish investment and financial goals.
- Work to balance your budget.
- Start an emergency fund.
- Save the money needed to begin investing.
- Consider investing in a Roth IRA or traditional IRA.
- Participate in an employer-sponsored 401(k) retirement account.
- Open a brokerage account and begin investing.

Next Steps

- Revise investment and financial goals.
- Continue to save money and invest in growth-oriented investments.
- Evaluate new investments before purchase.
- Evaluate all existing investments on a regular basis.

Later Steps

- Revise investment and financial goals.
- Begin planning for retirement within a specific number of years.
- Evaluate existing and new investments.
- Use asset allocation to make sure there is a balance between growth and conservative investments.

YOUR Next Step . . . select one or more of the items above and create an action plan to implement those financial planning activities.

SUMMARY OF LEARNING OBJECTIVES

LO14-1
Identify the most important features of common and preferred stocks. Both common and preferred stock are equity financing. Corporations sell common stock to finance their business start-up costs and help pay for business expansion and ongoing business activities. People invest in common stock because of dividend income and appreciation of value. In return for providing the money needed to finance the corporation, common stockholders have the right to elect the board of directors. They must also approve changes to corporate policies. The most important priority an investor in preferred stock enjoys is receiving cash dividends before any cash dividends are paid to common stockholders. Still, dividend distributions to both preferred and common stockholders must be approved by the board of directors.

LO14-2
Explain how you can evaluate stock investments. A number of factors can make a share of stock increase or decrease in value. Depending on specific characteristics associated with a stock investment, account executives, financial planners, and investors often classify a particular stock as blue chip, cyclical, defensive, growth, income, large cap, midcap, small cap, micro cap, penny, or value stock. When evaluating a particular stock issue, most investors begin with the information contained on the internet. Stock advisory services, annual reports, the SEC and other government websites, newspapers, and business and personal finance periodicals can all be used to help evaluate a stock investment.

LO14-3
Analyze the numerical measures that cause a stock to increase or decrease in value. Many analysts believe that a corporation's ability or inability to generate earnings in the future may be one of the most significant factors that account for an increase or decrease in the value of a stock. Generally, higher earnings equate to higher stock value, and lower earnings equate to lower stock value. It is also possible to calculate earnings per share and a price-earnings ratio to evaluate a stock investment. While both earnings per share and a price-earnings ratio are historical numbers based on

what a corporation has already done, it is possible to obtain earnings estimates for most corporations. Other calculations that help evaluate stock investments include dividend payout, dividend yield, total return, annualized holding period yield, beta, book value, and a market price-to-book ratio. Fundamental analysis, technical analysis, and the efficient market hypothesis can also be used to explain the price movements that occur in the stock market.

LO14-4
Describe how stocks are bought and sold. A corporation may sell a new stock issue in the primary market with the help of an investment bank. Once the stock has been sold in the primary market, it can be sold time and again in the secondary market. In the secondary market, investors buy or sell stock listed on a securities exchange or traded in the over-the-counter market. Most securities transactions are made through a brokerage firm. In some cases, an account executive, who works for the brokerage firm, will help complete your transaction. A growing number of investors are using discount brokerage firms or online firms to complete security transactions. While there are exceptions, brokerage firms may charge a commission for buying or selling stock. Additional commission charges, if any, are generally based on the number and value of the stock shares bought or sold and whether you use a full-service or discount broker or trade stocks online. To buy or sell stocks, you can use a market, limit, or stop-loss order.

LO14-5
Explain the trading techniques used by long-term investors and short-term speculators. Purchased stock may be classified as either a long-term investment or a speculative investment. Long-term investors typically hold their investments for a year or longer; speculators (sometimes referred to as *traders*) usually sell their investments within a shorter time period. Traditional trading techniques long-term investors use include the buy-and-hold technique, dollar cost averaging, direct investment plans, and dividend reinvestment plans. More speculative techniques include day trading, buying on margin, selling short, and trading in options.

KEY TERMS

KEY FORMULAS

Topic	Formula

Earnings per share

$$\text{Earnings per share} = \frac{\text{After-tax income}}{\text{Number of shares outstanding}}$$

Example:

$$\text{Earnings per share} = \frac{\$11,250,000}{3,750,000}$$

$$= \$3.00 \text{ per share}$$

Price-earnings (P-E) ratio

$$\text{P-E ratio} = \frac{\text{Price per share}}{\text{Earnings per share}}$$

Example:

$$\text{Price-earnings ratio} = \frac{\$54}{\$3.00}$$

$$= 18$$

Dividend payout

$$\text{Dividend payout} = \frac{\text{Annual dividend amount}}{\text{Earnings per share}}$$

Example:

$$\text{Dividend payout} = \frac{\$0.90}{\$1.28}$$

$$= 0.70 = 70\%$$

Dividend yield

$$\text{Dividend yield} = \frac{\text{Annual dividend amount}}{\text{Price per share}}$$

Example:

$$\text{Dividend yield} = \frac{\$2.00}{\$50.00}$$

$$= 0.04 = 4\%$$

Total return

$$\text{Total return} = \text{Dividends} + \text{Capital gain}$$

Example:

$$\text{Total return} = \$120 + \$710$$

$$= \$830$$

Annualized holding period yield

$$\text{Annualized holding period yield} = \frac{\text{Total return}}{\text{Original investment}} \times \frac{1}{N}$$

$N = $ Number of years investment is held

Example:

$$\text{Annualized holding period yield} = \frac{\$830}{\$2,600} \times \frac{1}{4}$$

$$= 0.08 = 8\%$$

Price/earnings to growth ratio (PEG)

$$\text{Price/earnings to growth ratio} = \frac{\text{Price-earnings ratio}}{\text{Annual EPS growth (\%)}}$$

Example:

$$\text{Price/earnings to growth ratio} = \frac{20}{24\%}$$

$$= 0.83$$

Note: The percent sign (%) is ignored in the above calculation.

Beta calculation

Volatility for a stock = Beta for a specific stock × Increase in overall market

Example:

Volatility for a stock = $1.25 \times 8\% = 0.10 = 10\%$

Book value

$$\text{Book value} = \frac{\text{Assets} - \text{Liabilities}}{\text{Shares outstanding}}$$

Example:

$$\text{Book value} = \frac{\$135,000,000 - \$60,000,000}{3,750,000}$$

$$= \$20 \text{ per share}$$

Market-to-book ratio

$$\text{Market-to-book ratio} = \frac{\text{Market value per share}}{\text{Book value per share}}$$

Example:

$$\text{Market-to-book ratio} = \frac{\$40}{\$32}$$

$$= 1.25$$

SELF-TEST PROBLEMS

1. Kristy Nguyen is trying to decide between two different stock investments, and she asks for your help. Information about each investment is below.

Company	Price per Share	Annual Dividend	After-Tax Income This Year	Projected Earnings Next Year	Number of Shares Outstanding
One Source Manufacturing	$24	$0.40	$35 million	$39 million	20 million shares
Down South Homes	$40	$0.56	$122 million	$90 million	140 million shares

   a. Calculate the dividend yield for each company.

   b. Calculate the earnings per share for each company.

   c. Calculate the price-earnings (P-E) ratio for each company.

   d. Based on this information, which company would you recommend?

2. Last year, Shanna Young purchased 100 shares of Iowa Farm Implement. During the last 12 months, she received dividends totaling $1.20 a share. During the 12-month period, the company earned $4.00 a share.

   a. For the 12-month period, what is the amount of total dividends that Ms. Young received?

   b. If a share of Iowa Farm Implement is selling for $52, what is the dividend yield?

   c. What was the dividend payout during this 12-month period?

3. Four years ago, David Robertson purchased 200 shares of Harrison Microchips. At the time, each share of Harrison Microchips was selling for $40. He also paid a $22 commission when the shares were purchased. Now, four years later, he has decided it's time to sell his investment. Harrison Microchips's share price when sold was $52.50. In addition, he paid a $34 commission to sell his shares. He also received total dividends of $2.20 per share over the four-year investment period.

    a. What was the total return for Mr. Robertson's investment?

    b. What is the annualized holding yield for his investment?

Self-Test Solutions

1. a. Calculate the dividend yield for each company.

One Source Manufacturing

$$\text{Dividend yield} = \text{Annual dividend amount} \div \text{Price per share}$$
$$= \$0.40 \div \$24$$
$$= 0.017 = 1.7 \text{ percent}$$

Down South Homes

$$\text{Dividend yield} = \text{Annual dividend amount} \div \text{Price per share}$$
$$= \$0.56 \div \$40$$
$$= 0.014 = 1.4 \text{ percent}$$

    b. Calculate the earnings per share for each company.

One Source Manufacturing

$$\text{Earnings per share} = \text{After-tax income} \div \text{Number of shares outstanding}$$
$$= \$35,000,000 \div 20,000,000$$
$$= \$1.75 \text{ per share}$$

Down South Homes

$$\text{Earnings per share} = \text{After-tax income} \div \text{Number of shares outstanding}$$
$$= \$122,000,000 \div \$140,000,000$$
$$= \$0.87 \text{ per share}$$

    c. Calculate the price-earnings (P-E) ratio for each company.

One Source Manufacturing

$$\text{P-E ratio} = \text{Price per share} \div \text{Earnings per share}$$
$$= \$24 \div \$1.75$$
$$= 13.7 = 14$$

Down South Homes

$$\text{P-E ratio} = \text{Price per share} \div \text{Earnings per share}$$
$$= \$40 \div \$0.87$$
$$= 45.9 = 46$$

    d. Based on this information, which company would you recommend?

Based on the calculations, One Source Manufacturing is a better investment because it has a higher dividend yield and higher earnings per share—both good signs. Also, One Source Manufacturing is expecting earnings to increase next year. During the same period, Down South Homes' earnings are projected to decline.

2. a. For the 12-month period, what is the amount of total dividends that Ms. Young received?

$$\text{Total dividends} = \text{Dividend per share} \times \text{Number of shares}$$
$$= \$1.20 \times 100$$
$$= \$120$$

    b. If a share of Iowa Farm Implement is selling for $52 a share, what is the dividend yield?

$$\text{Dividend yield} = \text{Annual dividend amount} \div \text{Price per share}$$
$$= \$1.20 \div \$52$$
$$= 0.023 = 2.3 \text{ percent}$$

    c. What is the dividend payout during this 12-month period?

$$\text{Dividend payout} = \text{Annual dividend amount} \div \text{Earnings per share}$$
$$= \$1.20 \div \$4.00$$
$$= 0.30 = 30 \text{ percent}$$

3. a. What was the total return for Mr. Robertson's investment?

$$\text{Total dividends} = \text{Annual dividends} \times \text{Number of shares}$$
$$= \$2.20 \times 200 \text{ shares}$$
$$= \$440$$

Purchase price = $40 × 200 shares = $8,000 + $22 commission = $8,022

Selling price = $52.50 × 200 shares = $10,500 − $34 commission = $10,466

Capital gain = $10,466 selling price − $8,022 purchase price = $2,444

Total return = $440 total dividends + $2,444 capital gain = $2,884

b. What is the annualized holding period yield for his investment? *Note:* In the formula below, *N* is the number of years the investment is held.

$$\text{Annualized holding period yield} = \frac{\text{Total return}}{\text{Original investment}} \times \frac{1}{N}$$
$$= \frac{\$2,884}{\$8,022} \times \frac{1}{4}$$
$$= 0.09 = 9 \text{ percent}$$

FINANCIAL PLANNING PROBLEMS

1. *Calculating Dividend Amounts.* Betty and John Martinez own 180 shares of McDonald's common stock. McDonald's annual dividend is $5.16 per share. What is the total of dividends the Martinez couple will receive for this year? **LO14-1**

2. *Determining the Number of Shares after a Stock Split.* The board of directors of Herbalife Nutrition approved a 2-for-1 stock split. After the split, how many shares of Herbalife stock will an investor have if he owned 210 shares before the split? **LO14-1**

3. *Calculating Total Return.* Tammy Jackson purchased 100 shares of All-American Manufacturing Company stock at $28.25 a share. One year later, she sold the stock for $36 a share. She paid her broker a $22 commission when she purchased the stock and a $15 commission when she sold it. During the 12 months she owned the stock, she received $110 in dividends. Calculate Tammy's total return on this investment. **LO14-1**

4. *Determining a Preferred Dividend Amount.* James Hayes owns 215 shares of Ohio Utility preferred stock. If this preferred stock issue pays $1.60 per share each year, what is the total dollar amount Mr. Hayes will receive in one year? **LO14-1**

5. *Calculating Dividend Payout.* Assume you own shares in Walmart and that the company currently earns $6.93 per share and pays annual dividend payments that total $2.16 a share each year. Calculate the dividend payout for Walmart. **LO14-3**

6. *Compounding Investment Returns.* Nancy Cardoza invested $4,200 in ExxonMobil stock because her research indicated the stock should average a 6 percent return for investors over the next four years. If ExxonMobil investors do earn 6 percent each year, what will her $4,200 investment be worth at the end of four years? (To solve this problem, you may want to use the formulas or tables in Exhibit 1-A in the appendix that follows Chapter 1 or use a future value calculator available on various websites.) **LO14-3**

7. *Compounding Dividend Amounts.* Carl Patterson likes investing in stocks that pay dividends. Carl owns 118 shares of a local utility company. The stock pays a regular annual dividend in the amount of $3.10 per share, and the company has indicated that the dividend will stay the same for a long time. If Carl reinvests his dividends each year and the dividends earn a return of 6 percent each year, how much will Carl accumulate in 15 years? (To solve this problem, you may want to use the formulas or tables in Exhibit 1-B in the appendix that follows Chapter 1 or use a future value calculator available on different websites.) **LO14-3**

8. *Calculating Return on Investment.* Two years ago, you purchased 100 shares of General Mills Corporation. Your purchase price was $52 a share, plus a total commission of $8 to purchase the stock. During the last two years, you have received the following dividend amounts: $1.96 per share for the first year and $2.02 per share the second year. Also, assume that at the end of two years, you sold your General Mills stock for $60 a share minus a total commission of $12 to sell the stock. **LO14-3**

   a. Calculate the dividend yield for your General Mills stock at the time you purchased it.

   b. Calculate the dividend yield for your General Mills stock at the time you sold it.

   c. Calculate the total return for your General Mills investment when you sold the stock at the end of two years.

   d. Calculate the annualized holding period yield for your General Mills investment at the end of the two-year period.

LO14-3 9. *Calculating Earnings per Share, Price-Earnings Ratio, and Book Value.* As a stockholder of Bozo Oil Company, you receive its annual report. In the financial statements, the firm has reported assets of $21 million, liabilities of $12 million, after-tax earnings of $2 million, and 1.25 million outstanding shares of common stock.

    a. Calculate the earnings per share of Bozo Oil's common stock.

    b. Assuming a share of Bozo Oil's common stock has a market value of $40, what is the firm's price-earnings ratio?

    c. Calculate the book value of a share of Bozo Oil's common stock.

LO14-3 10. *Calculating Beta.* Northwestern Electronics has a 1.40 beta. If the overall stock market increases by 8 percent, how much will the stock for Northwestern Electronics change?

LO14-3 11. *Calculating Ratios.* According to the financial statements for Samson Electronics, Inc., the firm has total assets valued at $310 million. It also has total liabilities of $190 million. Company records indicate that the firm has issued 2 million shares of stock.

    a. Based on the above information, calculate the book value for a share of Samson Electronics.

    b. If a share of Samson Electronics, Inc., currently has a market value of $50 a share, what is the market-to-book ratio?

    c. Based on the market-to-book ratio, is a share of Samson Electronics overpriced or underpriced? Explain your answer.

LO14-5 12. *Using Dollar Cost Averaging.* For four years, Mary Thomas invested $4,000 each year in America Bank stock. The stock was selling for $52 in 2018, for $48 in 2019, for $49 in 2020, and for $41 in 2021.

    a. What is Mary's total investment in America Bank?

    b. After four years, how many shares does Mary own?

    c. What is the average cost per share of Mary's investment?

LO14-5 13. *Using Margin.* Bill Campbell invested $4,000 and borrowed $4,000 to purchase shares in Kellogg. At the time of his investment, Kellogg stock was selling for $58 a share. Note: There were no commissions to buy or sell this stock.

    a. How many shares could he buy if he used his $4,000 and borrowed $4,000 on margin to buy Kellogg stock?

    b. Assuming Bill did use margin, sold his Kellogg stock for $65 a share, how much profit did he make on his Kellogg investment?

LO14-5 14. *Selling Short.* After researching Best Buy common stock, Sally Jackson is convinced the stock is overpriced. She contacts her account executive and arranges to sell short 200 shares of Best Buy. At the time of the sale, a share of common stock had a value of $120. Three months later, Best Buy is selling for $112 a share, and Sally instructs her broker to cover her short transaction. Total commissions to buy and sell the stock were $44. What is her profit for this short transaction?

 ## DIGITIAL FINANCIAL LITERACY

Tracking Dividends, Stock Prices, and Stock Splits

Although many investing websites provide historical data for dividends, stock prices, and stock splits that you can access with a simple click of your mouse, one site that is especially easy to use is Yahoo! Finance. To find information about historical prices, dividends, and stock splits, follow these steps. First go to Yahoo! Finance at finance.yahoo.com. Next enter the symbol for the stock you are evaluating and click enter. Then click on the tab for Historical Data. Information for stock prices, dividends, and stock splits is listed beginning with the most current date. To find dates when dividends were paid or stock splits occurred, scroll down through the prices until you find the information you want. If you want to go further back than the dates in the default setting, you can adjust the date setting to increase or reduce the time span for the information.

Action items:

Question 1: Most stocks declined in March of 2020 because of the COVID-19 pandemic. Many of the same stocks recovered by the end of the year. Using the Yahoo! Finance website at finance.yahoo.com, determine the closing price for a share of Facebook stock on March 16, 2020. Then compare the price for March 16 to the closing price for a share of Facebook stock on December 31, 2020. What is the dollar amount of difference between the two dates? *Hint:* The symbol for Facebook is FB.

Question 2: What is the total amount of dividends American Express paid stockholders during the last two years? *Hint:* The symbol for American Express is AXP.

Question 3: When was the last stock split for National Beverage? *Hint:* The symbol for National Beverage is FIZZ.

FINANCIAL PLANNING CASE

Research Information Available from Value Line

This chapter stressed the importance of evaluating potential investments. Now it's your turn to try your skill at evaluating a potential investment in the Walmart Corporation. Assume you could invest $10,000 in the common stock of this company. To help you evaluate this potential investment, carefully examine Exhibit 14-7, which reproduces the research report on Walmart from Value Line. The report was published on January 24, 2020.

Questions

1. Based on the research provided by Value Line, would you buy Walmart's stock? Justify your answer.

2. What other investment information would you need to evaluate Walmart's common stock? Where would you obtain this information?

3. On January 24, 2020, Walmart's common stock was selling for $116 a share. Using the internet, determine the current price for a share of Walmart's common stock. Based on this information, would your investment have been profitable if you had purchased the common stock for $116 a share? (*Hint:* Walmart's stock symbol is WMT.)

4. Assuming you purchased Walmart's stock on January 24, 2020, and based on your answer to question 3, would you want to hold or sell your Walmart stock? Explain your answer.

YOUR PERSONAL FINANCIAL PLAN

Investing in Stocks

Historically, stocks have outperformed many investment alternatives over a long period of time. Still, not all stocks are quality investments that will increase in value. The simple fact is that your ability to make money with stock investments is correlated to your ability to evaluate which stocks to choose and which stocks to avoid.

Your Short-Term Financial Planning Activity

Task Choose a brokerage firm that can provide research information, offer professional help, and execute your buy and sell orders.

Research

1) Review the material in the section "Buying and Selling Stocks" in this chapter.

2) Review the article "11 Best Online Brokers for Stock Trading," on the NerdWallet website at https://www.nerdwallet.com/best/investing/online-brokers-for-stock-trading or other articles available on the internet or available at your college library.

Outcome Use Personal Financial Planner Sheet (PFP) sheet 59 to compare different account executives and brokerage firms that you believe could help you obtain your financial goals. Summarize your findings in a two-page report for both brokerage firms. Attach PFP Sheet 59 with your report.

Your Long-Term Financial Planning Activity

Task Assume you want to invest $6,000 in a corporate stock. To help you decide on a specific stock, use the information in this chapter to determine the risk, potential growth, dividends, and recent market performance for one stock.

Research

1) Use the MSN Money stock screener at https://www.msn.com/en-us/money/stockscreener to research a stock you believe could help you obtain your long-term financial goals.

2) Use information from professional advisory services and other sources to evaluate the stock you chose in step 1. Then answer the questions on Personal Financial Planner Sheet (PFP) sheet 58.

Outcome Create a PowerPoint presentation, video, or storyboard to explain why you think this stock would be a good investment and any concerns you would have about investing $6,000 in this stock.

CONTINUING CASE

Investing in Stocks

The triplets are now entering high school, and Jamie Lee and Ross are comfortable with their financial and investment strategies. They budgeted throughout the years and are right on track to reach their long-term investment goals of paying the triplets' college tuition and accumulating enough to purchase a beach house to enjoy when Jamie Lee and Ross retire.

Recently, Ross inherited $50,000 from his uncle's estate. Ross would like to invest in several varieties of stocks or other investments to supplement their retirement income goals.

Jamie Lee and Ross have been watching a technology company that has an upcoming initial public offering and several other stocks for well-established companies, but they are unsure which stocks to invest in and are also wondering if their choices will fit into their moderate-risk investment strategies. They want to make the best decisions they can to maximize their investment returns.

Questions

1. What benefits could Jamie Lee and Ross expect if they invest in a company's IPO? Will they be guaranteed a large return from this investment? At this life stage, would you recommend that Jamie Lee and Ross invest in an IPO? Why or why not?

2. Jamie Lee's father suggested that they purchase stock in a company that he has owned shares in for decades. They want to take advantage of the stock tip, but Jamie Lee and Ross are trying to decide between purchasing the company's common stock and preferred stock. How would you describe the differences between common and preferred stock?

3. Currently, the economy is in the recovery stage. Referring to the *Classification of Stock Investments* chart found in Exhibit 14-4, what types of stock would you suggest for Jamie Lee and Ross to invest in, considering their current life stage and moderate-risk investment strategies? What characteristics are associated with the types of investments you suggested?

4. Suppose Jamie Lee and Ross are evaluating corporate stocks to add to their investment portfolio. Using the *Personal Financial Planner Sheet 58*, "Corporate Stock Evaluation," select a company from your own personal experiences, such as an automobile or technology company, and research the information needed to complete the worksheet.

   a. Based on your research, should Jamie Lee and Ross invest in this company? Provide support for your evaluation based on the *Personal Financial Planner Sheet 58* research findings for that company.

   b. If they decide to invest in the company you researched, how much should they allocate of their $50,000 inheritance?

   c. Regardless of your position on whether they should invest in your chosen company, if Jamie Lee and Ross went ahead and purchased shares of stock in that company, how many shares could they purchase with the $50,000?

   d. What would be the total transaction cost if they purchased the shares online? (List the source for your answer.)

DAILY SPENDING DIARY

"Investing in stock is not possible. I'm barely able to pay my various living expenses."

Directions

Your *Daily Spending Diary* will help you manage your expenses to create a better overall spending plan. Once you control your spending, you will be able to save the money needed to fund various types of investments.

Analysis Questions

1. What information from your daily spending diary can help you better achieve financial and investment goals?

2. Based on your observations of our society and the economy, what types of stocks might you consider for investing in now or in the near future?

A *Daily Spending Diary* sheet is located at the end of Chapter 1 and on the library resource site in *Connect*.

Investing in Bonds

15

Bloomberg/Getty Images

Financial Literacy
IN **YOUR LIFE**

▶ **What if you . . .** were worried about how the long-term effects of a recession would affect the nation's economy and the value of the stocks in your investment portfolio?

You might . . . consider selling some of your stocks and investing in corporate bonds or government bonds.

Now, what would you do? Evaluate all possible options before selling existing stocks and investing in more conservative corporate or government bonds. The information in this chapter and the material in the Your Personal Finance Roadmap and Dashboard feature at the end of this chapter will walk you through some of the questions you might consider as you decide if you should invest in bonds.

WHY BONDS?

While most beginning investors think bonds are for people who are retired and afraid of losing their money, there are valid reasons why you might want to invest in corporate or government bonds—regardless of your age. The fact is that bonds can provide a measure of safety and allow you to use asset allocation to diversify your investment portfolio. To begin, answer the questions below.

1. I understand the basics of corporate bonds.	Agree	Neutral	Disagree
2. I understand why corporations issue bonds.	Agree	Neutral	Disagree
3. I appreciate the advantages of investing in corporate bonds.	Agree	Neutral	Disagree
4. I sometimes think about investing in government and tax-free municipal bonds.	Agree	Neutral	Disagree
5. I know how to evaluate bond investments.	Agree	Neutral	Disagree

As you study this chapter, you will encounter "My Life" boxes with additional information and resources related to these items.

When it comes to investing, how do bonds fit in the "big picture"? Good question. Many people believe that the best investments are always stock investments. And while stocks have traditionally returned more than other investment alternatives, bonds are often considered a safer investment when compared to stocks or mutual funds that invest in stocks.

Assuming you thought the stock market was headed for a long period of decline, you could sell some or all of your stocks and use asset allocation to diversify your investment portfolio by purchasing corporate and government bonds. That's exactly what Joe Goode, a 38-year-old marketing manager for a sports equipment company, did in the last part of February 2020. He sold some of his stock investments and used $52,000 to purchase corporate and government bonds and increase the amount of cash in his savings account. At the time, Joe thought the stock market was too high because the nation's economy seemed to be plagued with a lot of problems, including the fear of a worldwide pandemic, a possible lockdown for nonessential businesses, and political turmoil. Although his friends thought he was crazy for taking such a conservative approach, he actually avoided a sharp downturn in the stock market during the three-month period of March, April, and May in 2020. According to Joe, he earned almost $400 because he received interest from the corporate and government bonds and his savings accounts. At the same time, he preserved his investment funds for a return to

the stock market when the economy turned around. Sure enough, when the stock market began to rebound three months later, Joe sold some of the bonds and used the cash to purchase, at much lower prices, a few of the same stocks he had sold in February. He also decided to keep some of his bond investments as a way to diversify his investment portfolio. Now, his current investment portfolio consists of about 65 percent stocks and growth mutual funds while the remainder is divided between corporate bonds and cash.

In addition to asset allocation, investors often choose bonds because they need current income provided by bond interest payments, and they expect to be repaid when the bonds mature. Some investors even choose specific bonds because the bond's maturity date coincides with their expected future expenses. For example, parents may want to pick bonds that mature when their first child begins college. Then, when the bonds are repaid at maturity, the money can be used to pay college tuition. We begin this chapter by describing the basic characteristics of corporate bonds that define the relationship between investors and corporations that sell bonds to obtain financing.

> **corporate bond** A corporation's written pledge to repay a specified amount of money with interest.

> **maturity date** For a corporate bond, the date on which the corporation is to repay the borrowed money.

Characteristics of Corporate Bonds

A **corporate bond** is a corporation's written pledge to repay a specified amount of money with interest. The **maturity date** of a corporate bond is the date on which the corporation is to repay the borrowed money. At the maturity date, a bondholder returns the bond to the corporation and receives cash equal to the bond's face value. Maturity dates for bonds generally range from 1 to 30 years after the date of issue. While different sources use different time periods to classify bonds, maturities for corporate bonds are often classified as short term (under 3 years), intermediate term (3 to 10 years), and long term (over 10 years).

The **face value** (sometimes referred to as par value) is the dollar amount the bondholder will receive at the bond's maturity. The usual face value of a corporate bond is $1,000, but the face value of some corporate bonds may be as high as $5,000 or even higher in some cases. The total face value of all the bonds in a bond issue usually runs into millions of dollars. Between the time of purchase and the maturity date, the corporation pays interest to the bondholder, usually every six months, at the stated interest rate. *Note:* The interest rate is sometimes referred to as the coupon rate in some financial publications.

The actual legal conditions for a corporate bond are described in a bond indenture. A **bond indenture** is a legally binding contract that details all of the conditions relating to a bond issue. Because corporate bond indentures are difficult for the average person to read and understand, a corporation issuing bonds appoints a trustee. The **trustee** is a financially independent firm that acts as the bondholders' representative. Usually, the trustee is a commercial bank or some other financial institution. The corporation must report to the trustee periodically regarding its ability to make interest payments and eventually redeem the bonds. In turn, the trustee transmits this information to the bondholders along with its own evaluation of the corporation's ability to pay interest until maturity and eventually repay the bondholders at maturity. If the corporation fails to live up to all the provisions in the indenture agreement, the trustee may bring legal action to protect the bondholders' interests.

LO15-1

Describe the characteristics of corporate bonds.

> **face value** The dollar amount the bondholder will receive at the bond's maturity.

> **bond indenture** A legally binding contract that details all of the conditions relating to a bond issue.

> **trustee** A financially independent firm that acts as the bondholders' representative.

 my life 1

I understand the basics of corporate bonds.

Before you read the next section, review how maturity date, face value, bond indenture, and the trustee affect an investment in corporate bonds.

 **PRACTICE QUIZ 15-1**

1. What is the usual face value for a corporate bond?
2. In your own words, define *maturity date* and *bond indenture*.
3. How does a trustee evaluate the provisions contained in a bond indenture?

Why Corporations Sell Corporate Bonds

LO15-2

Discuss why corporations issue bonds.

Let's begin this section with some basics of why corporations sell bonds. Corporations sell bonds to obtain borrowed money when they:

- Don't have enough money to pay for major purchases.
- Need to finance ongoing business activities.
- Find it is difficult or impossible to sell stock.
- Want to improve a corporation's financial leverage—the use of borrowed funds to increase the firm's return on investment.
- Use the interest paid to bond owners as a tax-deductible expense that reduces the taxes the corporation pays to federal and state governments.

Corporate bonds are often referred to as the "workhorse" of corporate finance. They are used by many corporations to raise capital because it often costs less to issue bonds than to sell a new stock issue. Although a corporation may use both bonds and stocks to finance its activities, there are important differences between the two types of financing. The most important differences are explained in Exhibit 15-1. Before issuing bonds, a corporation must decide what type of bond to issue and how the bond issue will be repaid.

TYPES OF BONDS

debenture A bond or unsecured debt instrument that is backed only by the reputation of the issuing corporation.

Most corporate bonds are debentures. A **debenture** is an unsecured bond or debt instrument that is backed only by the reputation of the issuing corporation. If the corporation fails to make either interest payments or repayment at maturity, investors who own debentures become general creditors, much like the firm's suppliers. In the event of corporate bankruptcy, general creditors, including debenture bondholders, can claim any asset not specifically used as collateral for a loan or other financial obligation.

mortgage bond A corporate bond secured by various assets of the issuing firm.

To make a bond issue more appealing to conservative investors, a corporation may issue a mortgage bond. A **mortgage bond** (sometimes referred to as a *secured bond*) is a corporate bond secured by various assets of the issuing firm. A mortgage bond is safer than a debenture because corporate assets or collateral may be sold to repay the bondholders if the corporation defaults on interest payments or repayment at maturity. Because of this added security, interest rates on mortgage bonds are usually lower than interest rates on unsecured debentures.

EXHIBIT 15-1

Important differences between bonds and stocks

Bonds	Stocks
Bonds are debt financing and must be repaid at maturity.	Stocks are equity financing, and the corporation doesn't have to repurchase stock or repay stockholders.
Interest payments for bonds are required.	Dividends for stocks are not required and are paid at the discretion of the board of directors.
Bondholders have a priority claim compared to stockholders in case of bankruptcy.	Stockholders are paid after bondholders and other creditors in case of bankruptcy.
Since bondholders usually do not have a right to vote, many corporate executives prefer to issue bonds to raise capital because they can retain control of the corporation.	Stockholders do have a right to vote on many corporate issues, including the right to elect the board of directors.

A third type of corporate bond is called a *subordinated debenture*. A **subordinated debenture** is an unsecured bond that gives bondholders a claim secondary to that of mortgage or debenture bondholders with respect to interest payments, repayment at maturity, and assets in the case of bankruptcy. Investors who purchase subordinated debentures usually enjoy higher interest rates than other bondholders because of the increased risk associated with this type of bond.

CONVERTIBLE BONDS AND NOTES   A **convertible bond** can be exchanged, at the owner's option, for a specified number of shares of the corporation's common stock. A **convertible corporate note** is a legal debt convertible to shares of common stock at the investor's option. This conversion feature allows investors to enjoy the lower risk of a corporate bond or note but also take advantage of the speculative nature of common stock. For example, assume you purchase a $1,000 convertible note issued by Southwest Airlines, the airline that serves many U.S. cities and nearby international destinations. The convertible notes pay 1.25 percent and mature in 2025. Each convertible note can be converted to 25.9909 shares of Southwest's common stock. This means you could convert the bond to common stock whenever the price of the company's common stock is $38.48 ($1,000 ÷ 25.9909 = $38.48) or higher.[1]

In reality, there is no guarantee that Southwest investors will convert to common stock even if the market value of the common stock does increase to $38.48 or higher. The reason for choosing not to exercise the conversion feature in this example is quite simple. As the market value of the common stock increases, the market value of a convertible bond or note *also* increases. By not converting to common stock, investors enjoy the added safety of the bond or note and interest income in addition to the increased market value caused by the price movement of the common stock.

The corporation gains three advantages by issuing convertible bonds or notes. First, the interest rate on a convertible bond or note is often 1 to 2 percent lower than nonconvertible bonds or notes because of the conversion feature which provides a benefit to the purchaser. Second, the conversion feature attracts investors who are interested in the speculative gain that conversion to common stock may provide. Third, if the investor converts to common stock, the corporation no longer has to redeem the bond or note at maturity.

Convertible bonds, like all potential investments, must be carefully evaluated. Remember, not all convertible bonds are quality investments.

HIGH-YIELD BOND   **High-yield bonds** are corporate bonds that pay higher interest but also have a higher risk of default. Before investing in high-yield bonds, keep in mind these investments are often referred to as "junk bonds" in the financial world. High-yield (junk) bonds are sold by companies with a poor earnings history, a questionable credit record, and lower ratings by major rating services, or by newer companies with an unproven ability to increase sales and earn profits. They are also frequently used in connection with leveraged buyouts—a situation where investors acquire a company and sell high-yield bonds to pay for the company.

While high-yield bonds do pay more interest than safer corporate bond issues, the corporation issuing high-yield bonds may not be able to pay interest each year, and the risks of default and nonpayment at maturity are real. So, why do investors purchase high-yield bonds? The answer: Corporations issuing high-yield bonds must offer investors interest rates that are three to four percentage points higher than safer bond issues. *Caution:* You should not invest in high-yield (junk) bonds unless you fully understand all of the risks associated with this type of investment.

subordinated debenture An unsecured bond that gives bondholders a claim secondary to that of other designated bondholders with respect to interest payments, repayment at maturity, and assets in the case of bankruptcy.

convertible bond A bond that can be exchanged, at the owner's option, for a specified number of shares of the corporation's common stock.

convertible corporate note A legal debt convertible to shares of common stock at the investor's option.

high-yield bonds Corporate bonds that pay higher interest but also have a higher risk of default.

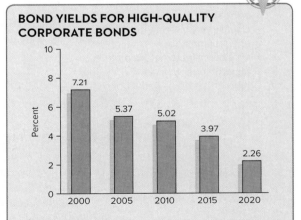

smart money minute

BOND YIELDS FOR HIGH-QUALITY CORPORATE BONDS

Year	Percent
2000	7.21
2005	5.37
2010	5.02
2015	3.97
2020	2.26

Source: "Moody's Yield on Seasoned Corporate Bonds," Federal Reserve Bank of St. Louis, https://fred.stlouisfed.org/graph/?id=AAA, accessed January 10, 2021.

PROVISIONS FOR REPAYMENT

call feature A feature that allows the corporation to call in, or buy, outstanding bonds from current bondholders before the maturity date.

sinking fund A fund to which annual or semiannual deposits are made for the purpose of redeeming a bond issue at maturity or a percentage of a bond issue before maturity.

serial bonds Bonds of a single issue that mature on different dates.

Today many corporate bonds are callable. A **call feature** allows the corporation to call in, or buy, outstanding bonds from current bondholders before the maturity date. For bondholders who purchased bonds for income, a problem is often created when a bond paying high interest is called. For example, if your bond that pays 6 percent annual interest is called by the corporation that issued the bond, it may be difficult for you to replace the bond with a new bond of the same quality that also pays the same 6 percent interest rate. This is especially true when overall interest rates in the economy are declining. If you choose to replace your bond, you may have to purchase a bond with a lower interest rate (and ultimately lower interest income from your new bond investment) or a bond with lower quality and more risk to obtain a 6 percent interest return. For the corporation, the money needed to call a bond may come from the firm's profits, the sale of additional stock, or the sale of a new bond issue that has a lower interest rate.

In most cases, corporations issuing callable bonds agree not to call them for the first 5 to 10 years. When a call feature is used, the corporation may have to pay the bondholders a *premium,* an additional amount above the face value of the bond. The amount of the premium, if any, is specified in the bond indenture; a $10 to $25 premium over the bond's face value is common.

A corporation may use one of two methods to ensure that it has sufficient funds available to redeem a bond issue. First, the corporation may establish a sinking fund. A **sinking fund** is a fund to which annual or semiannual deposits are made for the purpose of redeeming a bond issue at maturity or a percentage of the bonds in an issue before maturity. To retire a $275 million bond issue, Union Pacific Corporation agreed to establish a sinking fund and make annual payments in order to retire 95 percent of the bonds in the issue prior to the maturity date. If the corporation is required to retire a percentage of the bonds in an issue before maturity, it can use a call provision and the money in the sinking fund to redeem the bonds. If the terms of the sinking fund provision are not met, the trustee or bondholders may take legal action against the company.

I understand why corporations issue bonds.

To be an educated bond investor, you must understand that corporate bonds:

- Are sold for many reasons, including paying for major purchases and ongoing business activities, when it is impossible to sell stock, or to improve the firm's financial leverage.
- Can be debentures, mortgage bonds, subordinated debentures, convertible bonds, or high-yield bonds.
- Usually pay interest to bondholders until maturity.
- May be callable before maturity.
- May be repaid by using a sinking fund or issued as serial bonds.

Second, a corporation may issue serial bonds. **Serial bonds** are bonds of a single issue that mature on different dates. For example, Seaside Productions used a 20-year, $100 million bond issue to finance its expansion. None of the bonds mature during the first 10 years. Thereafter, 10 percent of the bonds mature each year until all the bonds are retired at the end of the 20-year period.

Detailed information about provisions for repayment, along with other vital information (including maturity date, interest rate, bond rating, call provisions, trustee, and details about security, if any), is available from Moody's Investors Service, Standard & Poor's Corporation, Fitch Ratings Service, and other financial service companies. More information about evaluating bonds is provided in the last section of this chapter.

✔ PRACTICE QUIZ 15-2

1. Why do corporations sell bonds?
2. What are the differences among a debenture, a mortgage bond, and a subordinated debenture?
3. Why would an investor purchase a convertible bond or a high-yield bond?
4. Describe three reasons a corporation would sell convertible bonds.
5. Explain the methods corporations can use to repay a bond issue.

ARE BOND FUNDS RIGHT FOR YOU?

Bond funds are an indirect way of owning bonds issued by corporations, the U.S. Treasury, or state, city, and local governments. Many financial experts recommend bond funds for investors because these investments offer two advantages: diversification and professional management. Diversification spells safety because an occasional loss incurred with one bond investment is usually offset by gains from other bond investments in the fund's portfolio. Also, professional managers should be able to do a better job of choosing bonds than individual investors.

Before investing, consider three factors. First, even the best fund managers make mistakes. Second, it may cost more to purchase bond funds than individual bonds. Finally, rising interest rates in the economy can cause the value of an individual bond with a fixed interest rate to decline. And since bond funds are made up of individual bonds, the share value for a bond fund is likely to decline if interest rates rise. Of course, the reverse is also true: If interest rates fall, the value of an individual bond with a fixed interest rate can increase. Thus, lower interest rates can cause shares in a bond fund to increase in value.

EVALUATING BOND FUNDS

Martha and Joseph Cordoza received $80,000 following the death of Joseph's grandmother. After some careful planning, they decided to invest $60,000 in two high-quality corporate bond funds. They used the remaining $20,000 to pay off some credit card debts and establish an emergency fund. During the next two years, they earned over 4 percent on their bond fund investments each year—not bad during a period when CDs were paying between 0.50 and 1 percent.

Martha and Joseph's 4 percent return wasn't just luck. They began by establishing an investment goal: Find a safe investment with minimal risk. After establishing their goal, Martha talked with an account executive at Merrill Lynch and asked for five suggestions that would enable the couple to attain their goal. Of the five original suggestions, three were highly rated bond funds.

Next, Martha and Joseph took a crucial step that many investors forget: They did their own research and didn't just rely on the account executive's suggestions. They used the internet to obtain both a prospectus and an annual report for each fund. Then they analyzed the performance of each bond fund using information from different bond websites. Based on the account executive's suggestions and their own research, they chose the "top" two bond funds.

The Cardozas spent almost 30 hours researching their investments, but they believe the time was well spent. When you consider the amount of money they made on their bond fund investments during the first two years—almost $5,000—they made over $160 an hour.

Why Investors Purchase Corporate Bonds

While bonds are not as popular as stocks, mutual funds that invest in stocks, or other investment alternatives, there are reasons why investors choose bonds.

LO15-3

Explain why investors purchase corporate bonds.

THE PSYCHOLOGY OF INVESTING IN BONDS

First, bonds are another way to use asset allocation to diversify your investment portfolio. As described in Chapter 13, *asset allocation* is the process of spreading your money among several different types of investments to lessen risk. And if diversification is your goal, you may also purchase bond funds. Many financial experts recommend bond funds for investors because they offer diversification and professional management. The advantages and disadvantages of bond funds are discussed in more detail in the *Financial Literacy for My Life: Are Bond Funds Right for You?* feature and in Chapter 16, "Investing in Mutual Funds."

Second, often investors consider government and corporate bonds a safer investment when compared to stocks, mutual funds that invest in stocks, or other investments because bonds represent a debt that must be repaid at maturity. Many investors believe that bonds are a "safe harbor" in troubled economic

smart money minute

The Securities and Exchange Commission website has information about bonds. For example, the brochure on *Saving and Investing: A Roadmap to Your Financial Security Through Saving and Investing* is an excellent publication that encourages people to begin saving and investing sooner rather than later. This same article also provides information about different investment alternatives—including corporate bonds.

Source: "Saving and Investing: A Roadmap to Your Financial Security," Securities and Exchange Commission, https://www.sec.gov/investor/pubs/sec-guide-to-savings-and-investing.pdf, accessed January 10, 2021.

times. For example, many stock investors lose money when the economy or the financial markets have a downturn. That's what happened to Sharon and Charles Martin, a couple in their early 50s. They lost almost $65,000 when they chose not to liquidate their stock investments over a 12-month period when the stock market experienced an unexpected downturn. If they had been diversified, used the principle of asset allocation, and invested some of their money in bonds or bond funds, they might have reduced their losses or even made some money, depending on the investments they chose.

Finally, corporate bonds may provide more growth and income potential than other conservative options. Savings accounts, certificates of deposit (discussed in Chapter 5), and bonds issued by the U.S. government and state and local governments (discussed later in this chapter) provide a safe place to invest your money. Unfortunately, they don't offer a lot of growth or income potential.

For specific suggestions to help determine whether bonds will help you achieve your financial goals, see Exhibit 15-2. Basically, investors purchase corporate bonds for three reasons: (1) interest income, (2) possible increase in value, and (3) repayment at maturity.

INTEREST INCOME

As mentioned earlier in this chapter, bondholders normally receive interest payments—usually every six months. The dollar amount of interest is determined by multiplying the face value of the bond by the interest rate.

EXAMPLE: Interest Calculation (Microsoft)

Assume you purchase a $1,000 corporate bond issued by Microsoft that matures in 2027. The interest rate for this bond is 3.3 percent. The annual interest is $33, as shown below.

$$\text{Dollar amount of annual interest} = \text{Face value} \times \text{Interest rate}$$
$$= \$1{,}000 \times 3.3\%$$
$$= \$1{,}000 \times 0.033$$
$$= \$33$$

You will receive $33 a year, paid in installments of $16.50 at the end of each six-month period for each bond you own.

EXHIBIT 15-2   Financial suggestions for bond investors

Financial Need	Suggestion
1. Asset allocation	Bonds are an excellent way to diversify your portfolio in order to lessen risk.
2. Income for current financial needs	Generally, bonds pay interest income semi-annually (every six months).
3. Long-term financial needs	Bonds can be purchased with staggered maturity dates that match your future financial needs.
4. Conservative investment in an economic downturn	Buy quality bonds to lock in income and avoid potential losses in other types of investments.

The method used to pay bondholders their interest depends on whether they own registered bonds or bearer bonds. A **registered bond** is registered in the owner's name by the issuing company. Generally, interest checks for registered bonds are mailed directly to the bondholder of record. Investors can also choose to have interest payments deposited directly into their brokerage account. Today, almost all ownership records for bonds are maintained by a process called *book entry*. With book entry, ownership of bonds is recorded electronically by a central depository, a custodian, or the brokerage firm. When book entry is used, brokerage firms are usually listed as the owners of bonds instead of individual investors. As a result, it is the brokerage firm's responsibility to maintain accurate ownership records for its individual clients. The advantage of book entry recording is that it is much easier to transfer ownership when the bondholder decides to sell a bond.

A second type of bond is a **bearer bond**, which is not registered in the investor's name. While U.S. corporations no longer issue bearer bonds, they may still be issued by corporations in foreign countries. *Be warned:* If you own a bearer bond, anyone—the rightful owner or a thief—can collect interest payments and the face value at maturity.

registered bond A bond that is registered in the owner's name by the issuing company.

bearer bond A bond that is not registered in the investor's name.

DOLLAR APPRECIATION OF BOND VALUE

Most beginning investors think a $1,000 bond is always worth $1,000. In reality, the price of a corporate bond may fluctuate until the maturity date. Changes in overall interest rates in the economy are the primary cause of most bond price fluctuations. The following three specific situations can affect bond prices:

- Actions by the Federal Reserve to either stimulate the economy or control inflation can lead to an increase or decrease in the interest rates that corporations and government entities pay when they issue new bonds.
- An interest rate increase or decrease for new bond issues can also cause the current market value of older bonds with fixed interest rates you already own to increase or decrease until they reach maturity.
- The value of a bond may also be affected by the financial condition of the company or government entity issuing the bond, the factors of supply and demand, an upturn or downturn in the economy, and the proximity of the bond's maturity date.

Changing bond prices that result from the changes in overall interest rates in the economy are an example of interest rate risk and market risk, discussed in Chapter 13. *In fact, there is an inverse relationship between a bond's price and overall interest rates in the economy.* In 2017, Apple, the maker of iPhones, computers, and other electronic gear, sold corporate bonds with a $1,000 face value that paid 3.35 percent interest each year. When issued, the 3.35 percent interest rate was competitive with the interest rates offered by other corporations issuing bonds of the same quality at that time. If overall interest rates fall, the price of the Apple bonds will increase due to their higher 3.35 percent interest rate. In fact, the price of this Apple bond increased to $1,130 in early 2021. The reason for the price increase was that interest rates for comparable bonds had decreased since this Apple bond was issued in 2017. If you own this bond, you must decide if you want to sell your bond at the current higher price. Or, if you prefer, you can hold your bond until maturity and receive interest payments each year and eventually be repaid the bond's face value at maturity. *Note:* While the interest rate for corporate bonds is fixed, the price and the yield for a bond may fluctuate up or down until maturity. In this case, **yield** is the rate of return earned by an investor who holds a bond for a stated period of time—usually a 12-month period. Changes in the yield for a bond are caused by an increase *or* a decrease in the price of the bond. The actual steps required to calculate yield are described later in this chapter.

yield The rate of return earned by an investor who holds a bond for a stated period of time—usually a 12-month period.

On the other hand, this inverse relationship also affects a bond's price if overall interest rates in the economy rise. For example, if overall interest rates for comparable bonds rise, the price of your $1,000 Apple bond will decrease due to its fixed 3.35 percent interest rate. Keep in mind, you can always sell your bond, but if the price has decreased below the price you paid, you will incur a loss. In this situation, many investors choose to hold the bond until maturity and collect the face value.

When interest rates in the economy increase or decrease, it is possible to calculate the approximate value of a bond with a fixed interest rate using a present value formula like the one in the appendix that follows Chapter 1 or a financial calculator. To solve the following example problem, we used the present value of a bond calculator at https://www.thecalculator.co/finance/Bond-Price-Calculator-606.html.

EXAMPLE: Present Value of a Bond (Apple)

Assume you purchase an Apple bond that pays 3.35 percent interest semiannually based on a face value of $1,000. Also, assume new corporate bond issues of comparable quality are currently paying 4 percent and the bond will mature in 5 years. What is the present value of the Apple bond?

Step 1: Go to https://www.thecalculator.co/finance/Bond-Price-Calculator-606.html.
Step 2: Enter the face value ($1,000), the interest rate (3.35 percent), the current market rate (4 percent), the compounding frequency (semiannual), and the years to maturity (5).
Step 3: Press *calculate*. The present value of the bond is $970.81.

If you purchase the Apple bond and keep it for 5 years until maturity, you will receive interest payments that total $167.50 ($33.50 annual interest × 5 years = $167.50). At maturity, you will receive $1,000. Since you paid $970.81 for the bond, you had a capital gain of $29.19 ($1000 face value − $970.81 original purchase price = $29.19). Your total return is $196.69 ($167.50 interest + $29.19 capital gain = $196.69).

BOND REPAYMENT AT MATURITY

Corporate bonds are repaid at maturity. After you purchase a bond, you have two options: You may keep the bond until maturity and then redeem it, or you may sell the bond at any time to another investor. Before investing in bonds, you should remember that the price of a corporate bond can decrease and that interest payments and eventual repayment may be a problem for a corporation that encounters financial difficulties or enters bankruptcy. For example, bonds issued by Hertz dropped in value due to questions concerning continued interest payments and the prospects for bond repayment at maturity when the demand for its cars and trucks virtually vanished during the COVID-19 pandemic. The situation for bondholders became worse when Hertz actually filed bankruptcy. Before investing in bonds, you may want to review the risk of business failure, and how it affects bond repayment, in Chapter 13.

To help diversify their bond investments, some investors use a concept called bond laddering. A **bond ladder** is a strategy where investors divide their investment dollars among bonds that mature at regular intervals in order to balance risk and return. To start your bond ladder, you purchase different bonds with maturities spread out over a number of years. For example, you might purchase bonds that mature in 1, 2, 3, 4, 5, 6, 7, 8, 9, and 10 years. When the first bond matures, you purchase a new bond that matures in 10 years. This new purchase continues the bond ladder. The short-term bonds that are

bond ladder A strategy where investors divide their investment dollars among bonds that mature at regular intervals in order to balance risk and return.

closer to maturity provide a high degree of stability because the bonds are not very sensitive to changing interest rates. The long-term bonds provide a higher return, but you must accept the risk that the prices of bonds with long-term maturities might change. By choosing bonds with different maturities, you realize greater returns than from holding only short-term bonds, but with lower risk than holding only long-term bonds. With a bond ladder, you can also take advantage of the concept of dollar-cost averaging that was discussed in Chapter 14.

A TYPICAL BOND TRANSACTION

Assume that on December 4, 2018, you purchased a 3.90 percent corporate bond that matures in 2028 with a face value of $1,000 issued by Clorox, a company known for consumer products in the United States and around the globe. Your cost for the bond was $990 plus a $10 commission charge, for a total investment of $1,000. Also, assume you held the bond until December 4, 2020, when you sold it at its current market value of $1,170 minus a $10 commission charge. Exhibit 15-3 shows the return on your investment.

After deducting commissions ($20) for buying and selling your Clorox bond, you experienced a profit of $160 because the value of the bond increased. The increase in the value of the bond resulted because interest rates for new bonds issued by similar companies decreased and the financial health of Clorox continued to improve during the two-year period in which you owned the bond. Also, bonds will generally increase in value the closer they get to the maturity date.

You also made money on your Clorox bond investment because of interest payments. For each of the two years you owned the bond, Clorox paid you $39 ($1,000 × 3.9% = $39) interest. Thus, you received interest payments totaling $78. In this example, you made a total return of $238 as follows:

$$\text{Total return} = \text{Interest} + \text{Capital gain}$$
$$= \$78 + \$160$$
$$= \$238$$

I appreciate the advantages of investing in corporate bonds.

Investors purchase corporate bonds for many different reasons, but basically there are three ways to make money with a bond investment: (1) interest income, (2) possible dollar appreciation of bond value, and (3) bond repayment at maturity. To learn more about why investors purchase bonds, use a web search engine such as Google, Bing, or Yahoo! to search for the phrase "reasons to purchase bonds."

EXHIBIT 15-3

Sample corporate bond transaction for Clorox

Assumption				
Interest, 3.90 percent; purchased December 4, 2018; sold December 4, 2020				
Costs when purchased			**Return when sold**	
1 bond @ $990	$ 990		1 bond @ $1,170	$1,170
Plus commission	+10		Minus commission	−10
Total investment	$1,000		Dollar return	$1,160
Transaction summary				
Dollar return			$ 1,160.00	
Minus total investment			$ 1,000.00	
Profit from bond sale			$ 160.00	
Plus interest ($39 for 2 years)			+ $ 78.00	
Total return on the investment			$ 238.00	

Financial Literacy Calculations

TIME VALUE OF MONEY: REINVESTING INTEREST CAN MAKE A DIFFERENCE!

How can the time value of money help you achieve your financial goals? Here's how Ty and Joe Nguyen used this concept to increase the dollar value of their investments.

The Facts: The Nguyens purchased 10 Procter & Gamble (P&G) bonds. They chose this investment because:

- The corporate bonds were issued by P&G, and each bond paid 5.5 percent or $55 each year until maturity in 2034.
- The bonds were rated "high grade" by Moody's.
- They could take advantage of the time value of money concept if they chose to reinvest their interest payments from the P&G bonds.

Conclusion: The Nguyens received $550 interest each year from their 10 P&G bonds. They also committed to reinvesting the $550 annual income they received each year. They used a time value of money table like Exhibit 1-B in the Chapter 1 Appendix of your text to estimate that if they earned 5 percent each year on their reinvested interest, they would accumulate $6,917.90 at the end of 10 years, as shown next.

Step 1: Locate the table factor for 5 percent and 10 years in Exhibit 1-B.

The table factor is 12.578.

Step 2: Multiply the annual interest from their 10 P&G bonds by the table factor.

$550 × 12.578 = $6,917.90

Ten years later, the Nguyens still have the P & G bonds that are still paying 5.5 percent interest. They also have an additional $6,917.90 because they reinvested their interest income.

Tryout Problem: Assume you invest in a bond issued by Visa that matures in 2035 and pays $41.50 interest each year. Also assume you choose to reinvest your interest income in an investment that earns 6 percent. What is the value of your *reinvested interest* at the end of 12 years? (Use Exhibit 1-B in the Chapter 1 Appendix for this calculation. *Note:* You can also use a financial calculator or the future value of money formula discussed in Chapter 1 to calculate your answer.)

Answer: $41.50 annual interest × 16.870 table factor = $700.11 total of reinvested interest.

THE MECHANICS OF A BOND TRANSACTION

Most bonds are sold through full-service brokerage firms, discount brokerage firms, or the internet. If you use a full-service brokerage firm, your account executive should provide both information and advice about bond investments. As with stock investments, the chief advantage of using a discount brokerage firm or trading online is lower commissions, but you must do your own research. As you will see later in this chapter, many sources of information can be used to evaluate bond investments.

While brokerage firms charge commissions (often called transaction costs) to buy and sell bonds, the actual amount you pay is often hard to determine. Unlike stocks where commissions are stated in plain language, commissions on bonds may be a combination of a stated dollar amount for each bond *plus* an additional commission (often called a markup when buying and a markdown when selling) calculated on the value of the bond you are buying or selling. If you want to know the exact dollar amount a brokerage firm is charging you to buy or sell a bond, the best advice is to ask the brokerage firm or your account executive.

 PRACTICE QUIZ 15-3

1. Describe the three reasons investors purchase bonds.
2. What are the differences between a registered bond and a bearer bond?
3. In what ways can interest rates in the economy affect the price of a corporate bond?
4. Why is the value of a bond closely tied to the issuing corporation's ability to repay its bond indebtedness?
5. How are corporate bonds bought and sold?

Government Bonds and Debt Securities

In addition to corporations, the U.S. government and state and local governments issue bonds to obtain financing. A **government bond** is a written pledge of a government or a municipality to repay a specified sum of money, along with interest. In this section, we discuss bonds issued by these three levels of government and look at why investors purchase these bonds.

U.S. TREASURY BILLS, NOTES, AND BONDS

Investors choose U.S. government securities because they are backed by the full faith and credit of the U.S. government and carry a decreased risk of default. Even with concerns about the size of the national debt, threats of downgrades by U.S. rating agencies, and the nation's economic problems, many investors in the United States and from around the globe still regard securities issued by the United States as a very conservative and safe investment.

Today, the U.S. Treasury Department issues five principal types of securities: Treasury bills, Treasury notes, Treasury bonds, Treasury Inflation-Protected Securities (TIPS), and U.S. government savings bonds. *Note:* Refer to Chapter 5 for a review of different types of U.S. savings bonds. Treasury bills, Treasury notes, Treasury bonds, TIPS, and savings bonds can be purchased through TreasuryDirect at www.treasurydirect.gov.

TreasuryDirect conducts auctions to sell Treasury securities. Buyers interested in purchasing these securities at such auctions may bid competitively or noncompetitively. If they bid competitively, they must specify the interest yield they are willing to accept. Most individual investors use noncompetitive bids once they have visited the website and opened an account. If you bid noncompetitively, you are willing to accept the interest yield determined at auction. For more information about the TreasuryDirect website, see Exhibit 15-4. Treasury securities may also be purchased directly from banks or brokers, which charge a commission.

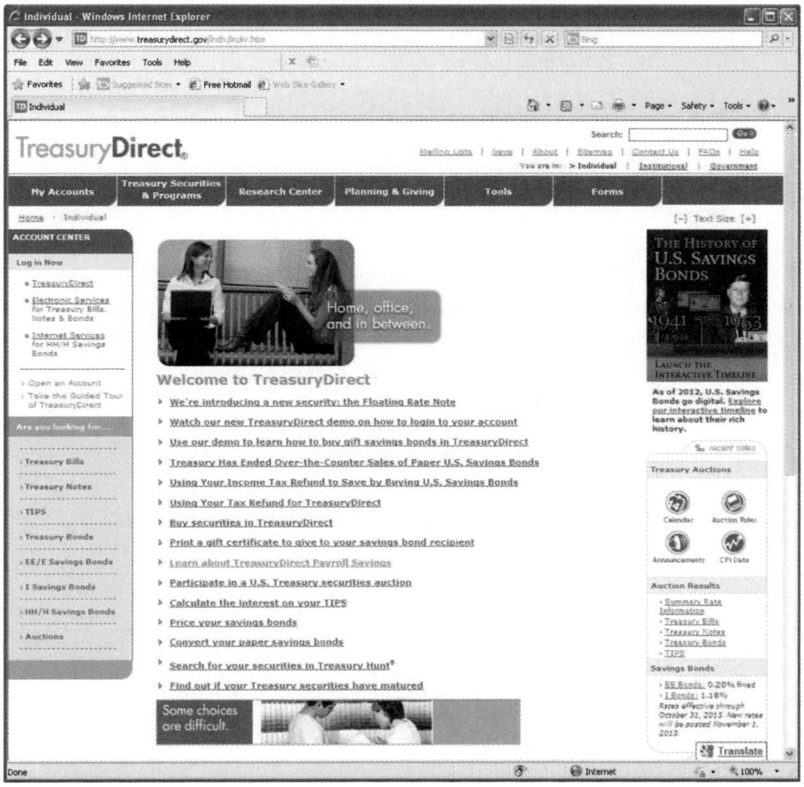

LO15-4

Discuss why federal, state, and local governments issue bonds and why investors purchase government bonds.

government bond A written pledge of a government or a municipality to repay a specified sum of money, along with interest.

EXHIBIT 15-4

The TreasuryDirect website provides information regarding U.S. Treasury securities
Source: The TreasuryDirect website at https://www.treasurydirect.gov/indiv/indiv.htm, accessed January 10, 2021.
U.S. Department of the Treasury.

Interest paid on U.S. government securities (and growth in principal for TIPS) is taxable for federal income tax purposes but is exempt from state and local taxation. *Be warned:* At the time of publication of your text, interest rates for securities issued by the U.S. Treasury are at record low levels. And yet investors often choose these securities because of the decreased risk of default. U.S. Treasury securities are also used by some investors as part of their efforts to use asset allocation to lessen overall risk. Current information on prices and interest rates appears on the TreasuryDirect website, the internet, and in *The Wall Street Journal* and other financial publications.

TREASURY BILLS   A *Treasury bill,* sometimes called a *T-bill,* is sold in a minimum unit of $100 with additional increments of $100 above the minimum. The maturity for T-bills may be as short as a few days or as long as one year. The Treasury Department currently only sells T-bills with 4-week, 8-week, 13-week, 26-week, and 52-week maturities. Another type of bill, the cash management bill, is issued in terms usually shorter than those of other T-bills.

T-bills are discounted securities, and the actual purchase price you pay is less than the maturity value of the T-bill. At maturity, you receive the maturity value, often referred to as the face value.

EXAMPLE: Discount and Purchase Amounts for a T-Bill

Assume you purchase 10 T-bills that will have a maturity value of $1,000. The bills have a stated interest rate of 1 percent. The discount amount ($10) is calculated in step 1. The purchase price after the discount ($990) is calculated in step 2.

$$\text{Step 1: Discount amount} = \text{Maturity value} \times \text{Interest rate}$$
$$= \$1,000 \times 1\%$$
$$= \$1,000 \times 0.01$$
$$= \$10$$
$$\text{Step 2: Purchase price} = \text{Maturity value} - \text{Discount amount}$$
$$= \$1,000 - \$10$$
$$= \$990$$

When your T-bills reach maturity, you are paid the maturity value. In reality, the return on T-bills is slightly higher than the stated interest rate. In the above example, you received $10 interest on a $990 investment, which represents a 1.01 percent current yield as illustrated below.

EXAMPLE: Yield Calculation for a T-Bill

To calculate the current yield, divide the discount amount by the purchase price. For the above example,

$$\text{Current yield for a T-bill} = \frac{\text{Discount amount}}{\text{Purchase price}}$$
$$= \frac{\$10}{\$990}$$
$$= 0.0101 = 1.01\%$$

The stated interest rate for the T-bill in the preceding examples is only for illustration purposes. In reality, the actual interest rate paid by the U.S. Treasury for T-bills can increase or decrease. For example, the interest rate for 13-week T-bills was 0.08 percent at the time of publication of this text. T-bills and other Treasury securities with longer maturities often have higher interest rates and may offer larger returns. *Remember:* While the rates (and the returns) are low compared to other investment alternatives, most investors purchase U.S. Treasury securities because they want to diversify their investment portfolio or reduce risk in their investment portfolio.

TREASURY NOTES   A *Treasury note* (sometimes called a *T-note*) is issued in $100 units with a maturity of more than 1 year but not more than 10 years. Typical maturities are 2, 3, 5, 7, and 10 years. Interest rates for Treasury notes are usually slightly higher than those for Treasury bills because investors must wait longer to get their money back, and therefore they demand a higher interest rate. Interest for Treasury notes is paid every six months until maturity. At maturity the face value of the note is paid to the owner. Notes can also be sold before maturity.

TREASURY BONDS   A *Treasury bond* is issued in minimum units of $100 and has a 20-year or 30-year maturity. Interest rates for Treasury bonds are generally higher than those for either Treasury bills or Treasury notes. Again, the primary reason for the higher interest rates is the length of time investors must hold Treasury bonds before maturity. Like interest on Treasury notes, interest on Treasury bonds is paid every six months until maturity. When a bond matures, the owner is paid the face value of the bond. Bonds can also be sold before maturity.

TREASURY INFLATION-PROTECTED SECURITIES (TIPS)   *Treasury Inflation-Protected Securities (TIPS)* are sold in minimum units of $100 with additional increments of $100 above the minimum. Currently, TIPS are sold with 5-, 10-, or 30-year maturities. The principal of TIPS increases with inflation and decreases with deflation, as measured by the consumer price index. When TIPS mature, you are paid the adjusted principal or original principal, whichever is greater. TIPS also pay interest twice a year, at a fixed rate. The rate is applied to the adjusted principal, so, like the principal, interest payments rise with inflation and fall with deflation. Interest income and growth in principal are exempt from state and local income taxes but are subject to federal income tax. Like other Treasury securities, TIPS can be held until maturity or sold before maturity.

FEDERAL AGENCY DEBT ISSUES

In addition to the bonds and securities issued by the Treasury Department, debt securities are issued by federal agencies and government-sponsored enterprises (GSEs), which include the Federal National Mortgage Association (sometimes referred to as Fannie Mae), the Government National Mortgage Association (sometimes referred to as Ginnie Mae), and the Federal Home Loan Mortgage Corporation (which somehow became known as Freddie Mac).

While some federal agencies or GSEs may have been created by the government or sponsored by the government, strictly speaking they are not actually part of the U.S. government. As a result, many of the securities they issue do not have the same guarantee that the bills, notes, bonds, and other securities issued by the U.S. Treasury have, and they often have a slightly higher interest rate when compared to the securities issued by the Treasury Department. Still, these

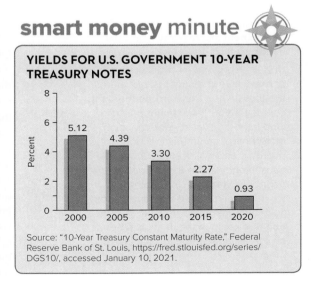

smart money minute

YIELDS FOR U.S. GOVERNMENT 10-YEAR TREASURY NOTES

Source: "10-Year Treasury Constant Maturity Rate," Federal Reserve Bank of St. Louis, https://fred.stlouisfed.org/series/DGS10/, accessed January 10, 2021.

debt issues are considered safe investments by most financial planners because of the relationship between the government and the agency or the GSE. In many cases, the agency or GSE is considered too large or too important to the nation's economy to be allowed to fail. Both Fannie Mae and Freddie Mac, for instance, received federal monies to avoid failure during the 2008 economic crisis. In addition to the slightly increased risk, there are other factors that should be considered before investing in agency or GSE securities. For example, the minimum denomination for a Ginnie Mae security is $25,000. Minimum investments in other federal agencies and GSEs vary, but tend to start lower.

Often brokers and account executives recommend agency or GSE debt instruments because the interest rate is usually higher than Treasury securities. However, you should know that there may be differences in how interest is paid when compared to Treasury securities and that many agency debt issues are also callable before the maturity date. Simply put, investing in agency debt is more complicated than buying and selling Treasury securities.

STATE AND LOCAL GOVERNMENT SECURITIES

municipal bond A debt security issued by a state or local government.

general obligation bond A bond backed by the full faith, credit, and unlimited taxing power of the government that issued it.

revenue bond A bond that is repaid from the income generated by the project it is designed to finance.

A **municipal bond**, sometimes called a *muni,* is a debt security issued by a state or local government. In the United States, there are 50 state governments. In addition, cities, counties, school districts, and special taxing districts may sell municipal bonds. Such securities are used to finance the ongoing activities of state and local governments and major projects such as airports, schools, toll roads, and toll bridges. They may be purchased through account executives, banks, or brokerage firms or in some cases directly from the government entity that issued them. State and local securities are classified as either general obligation bonds or revenue bonds. A **general obligation bond** is backed by the full faith, credit, and unlimited taxing power of the government that issued it. A **revenue bond** is repaid from the income generated by the project it is designed to finance.

If the risk of default worries you, you can purchase insured municipal bonds. There are two large private insurers: MBIA Inc. (Municipal Bond Insurance Association) and the Assured Guaranty Municipal Corporation. Even if a municipal bond issue is insured, however, financial experts worry about the insurer's ability to pay off in the event of default on a large bond issue or multiple defaults. Most experts advise investors to determine the underlying quality of a bond whether or not it is insured. Also, guaranteed municipal securities usually carry a slightly lower interest rate than uninsured bonds because of the reduced risk of default. While many investors think that municipal bonds are as safe as securities offered by the U.S. Treasury, they are not: There have been defaults. *Caution:* The majority of municipal bonds are safe investments, but it is your responsibility to evaluate different bond issues before investing your money.

Like a corporate bond, a municipal bond may be callable by the government unit that issued it. *Be warned:* Your municipal bond may be called if interest rates fall and the government entity that issued the bond can sell new bonds with lower rates. For example, thousands of bondholders who purchased high-yield municipal bonds in the first part of the 21st century were shocked to have their bonds called. Many were counting on another 5 to 20 years of high yields to finance their retirement. Although they were repaid the principal for the bond that was called, they faced the challenge of reinvesting their money when interest rates were at record lows. If the bond is not called, the investor has two options. First, the bond may be held until maturity, in which case the investor will be repaid its face value. Second, the bond may be sold to another investor before maturity.

my life 4

I sometimes think about investing in government and tax-free municipal bonds.

U.S. Treasury and municipal bonds are conservative investments, but there are times when they may be the right choice for your investment portfolio. One important reason for choosing government and municipal bonds might be asset allocation. Other reasons might include the outlook for the economy, your age, your tolerance for risk, and possible tax advantages. Take a moment and describe a situation that could make municipal bonds an attractive addition to your investment portfolio.

One of the most important features of municipal bonds is that the interest on them may be exempt from federal taxes—a factor especially important for wealthy investors. Whether or not the interest on municipal bonds is tax exempt often depends on how the funds obtained from their sale are used. *Caution:* It is your responsibility, as an investor, to determine whether or not interest from municipal bonds is taxable.

Municipal bonds exempt from federal taxation are generally exempt from state and local taxes only if you live in the state where they are issued. Although the interest income on municipal bonds may be exempt from taxation, you may have to pay both federal and state taxes on *capital gains* when *you* sell a municipal bond before maturity *and* at a profit, just like capital gains on other investments sold at a profit.

Because of their tax-exempt status, the interest rates on municipal bonds are lower than those on taxable bonds. By using the following formula, you can calculate the *taxable equivalent yield* for a municipal security:

$$\text{Taxable equivalent yield} = \frac{\text{Tax-exempt return}}{1.0 - \text{Your tax rate}}$$

EXAMPLE: Taxable Equivalent Yield

The taxable equivalent yield on a 3 percent tax-exempt municipal bond for a person in the 24 percent tax bracket is 3.95 percent, as follows:

$$\text{Taxable equivalent yield} = \frac{\text{Tax-exempt return}}{1.0 - \text{Your tax rate}}$$
$$= \frac{3\%}{1.0 - 0.24}$$
$$= \frac{0.03}{0.76}$$
$$= 0.0395 = 3.95\%$$

Once you have calculated the taxable equivalent yield, you can compare the return on tax-exempt securities with the return on taxable investments that include certificates of deposit, corporate bonds, stocks, mutual funds, and other investment alternatives. Exhibit 15-5 illustrates the yields for tax-exempt investments and their taxable equivalent yields.

The following information can be used to compare the return on tax-exempt investments with the returns offered by taxable investments.

EXHIBIT 15-5

Yields for tax-exempt investments

Equivalent Yields for Taxable Investments							
Tax-Exempt Yield	10% Tax Rate	12% Tax Rate	22% Tax Rate	24% Tax Rate	32% Tax Rate	35% Tax Rate	37% Tax Rate
2%	2.22%	2.27%	2.56%	2.63%	2.94%	3.08%	3.17%
3	3.33	3.41	3.85	3.95	4.41	4.62	4.76
4	4.44	4.55	5.13	5.26	5.88	6.15	6.35
5	5.56	5.68	6.41	6.58	7.35	7.69	7.94

PRACTICE QUIZ 15-4

1. What are the maturities for a Treasury bill, a Treasury note, a Treasury bond, and Treasury Inflation-Protected Securities?
2. What is the difference between a general obligation bond and a revenue bond?
3. What risks are involved when investing in municipal bonds?
4. What is the chief advantage of investing in municipal bonds?

The Decision to Buy or Sell Bonds

LO15-5

Describe how to evaluate bonds when making an investment.

One basic principle we have stressed throughout this text is the need to evaluate any potential investment. Certainly, corporate *and* government bonds are no exception. Only after you have determined how bonds can help you achieve your financial goals and completed your research should you purchase bonds. In this section, we examine methods you can use to evaluate bond investments.

THE INTERNET

When investing in bonds, you can use the internet in three ways. First, you can obtain current price information on specific bond issues to track the value of your investments. Second, it is possible to trade bonds online and pay lower commissions than you would pay a full-service or discount brokerage firm. Third, you can get information about a corporation or government entity that has issued bonds, and you can get recommendations to buy or sell bonds by accessing specific bond websites. *Be warned:* Bond websites are not as numerous as websites that provide information on stocks, mutual funds, or personal financial planning. And many of the better bond websites charge a fee, or you must register, to access their research and recommendations.

The following websites may provide the information you need to evaluate a bond investment:

- http://finra-markets.morningstar.com/BondCenter/
- http://finance.yahoo.com/bonds
- www.investinginbonds.com
- www.fmsbonds.com
- www.municipalbonds.com
- www.treasurydirect.gov

You may also want to visit the Moody's website (www.moodys.com), the Standard & Poor's website (www.standardandpoors.com), and the Fitch Ratings website (www.fitchratings.com) to obtain detailed information about both corporate and government bonds.

FINANCIAL COVERAGE FOR BOND TRANSACTIONS

Detailed information obtained from the Financial Industry Regulatory Authority website for a $1,000 Exxon Mobil corporate bond, which pays 2.275 percent interest and matures in 2026 is provided in Exhibit 15-6. Although there's a good chance you have purchased gasoline at an Exxon or Mobil station, what you may not realize is that Exxon is a giant corporation that produces crude oil, gasoline and other petroleum products, and natural gas in the United States, Canada, and many other

EXHIBIT 15-6

Bond information available by accessing the FINRA bond site

EXXON MOBIL CORPORATION

OVERVIEW

1. Price:	107
2. Coupon (%):	2.275
3. Maturity Date:	8/16/26
4. Lookup Symbol:	XOM4872077
5. Yield (%):	2.13
6. Standard & Poor's Rating:	AA
7. Payment Frequency:	Semiannual
8. First Coupon Date:	2/16/20
9. Type:	Corporate
10. Callable:	Yes

1. *Price* is quoted as a percentage of the face value: $1,000 × 107% = $1,070.

2. *Coupon (%)* is the rate of interest: 2.275 percent.

3. *Maturity Date* is the date when bondholders will receive repayment of the face value: August 16, 2026.

4. *Look Up Symbol* is the information you can use to determine the current price and other information about this bond issue on internet sites: XOM4872077.

5. *Yield (%)* is determined by dividing the dollar amount of annual interest by the current price of the bond: $22.75 ÷ $1,070 = 0.0213 = 2.13 percent.

6. *Standard & Poor's Rating* shows the rating issued by Standard & Poor's Ratings. This rating is used to assess the risk associated with this bond: AA.

7. *Payment Frequency* tells bondholders how often they will receive interest payments: semiannually.

8. *First Coupon Date* tells bondholders when the first interest payment was paid: February 16, 2020.

9. *Type*: Corporate.

10. *Callable* tells the bondholder if the bond is callable or not: Yes.

Source: The Financial Industry Regulatory Authority (FINRA) website http://finra-markets.morningstar.com/BondCenter/BondDetail.jsp?ticker=C844903&symbol=XOM4872077, accessed January 11, 2021.

countries around the globe. All of its activities require financing, and a large part of that financing comes from bond issues like the one described in Exhibit 15-6. Without this type of information, investors would not be able to evaluate the quality of bond investments like this one and determine if it is the right choice to help them achieve their financial goals.

In bond quotations, prices are given as a percentage of the face value, which is usually $1,000. Thus, to find the actual price for a bond, you must multiply the face value (usually $1,000) by the bond quotation.

EXAMPLE: Bond Price Calculation (Dell)

If a Dell corporate bond has a price quote of 109, the actual price for the bond is $1,090, as calculated below.

$$\text{Bond price} = \text{Face value} \times \text{Bond quotation}$$
$$= \$1,000 \times 109\%$$
$$= \$1,000 \times 1.09$$
$$= \$1,090$$

In addition to internet coverage of bond transactions, *The Wall Street Journal*, *Barron's*, and some metropolitan newspapers publish information on bonds. *Note:* Most bonds are traded in the over-the-counter market by bond dealers and brokers who trade bonds electronically or over the phone. Thus, the bonds whose prices are reported in the newspaper make up only a small portion of the bonds actually bought and sold each day.

In the United States, bond price quotations are based on the *clean price*. The clean price represents the price of a bond with no accrued or earned interest. On the other hand, the *dirty price* for a bond represents the price of the bond *plus* accrued interest earned since the last interest payment date. The dirty price is different from the clean price because bond owners earn interest for every day that they own a bond issue. Simply put, the clean price is the bond price without interest, while the dirty price is the bond plus interest. For example, assume that Maria Hernandez owns a $1,000 corporate bond that pays 5.0 percent interest. She receives her regular semiannual interest payment on June 1. Two months later, she decides to sell her bond. In this case, the buyer will pay Maria the dirty price, which includes the quoted clean price of the bond *plus* interest for the two-month period since Maria's last interest payment. When the next semiannual interest payment date arrives, the new owner of the bond will receive the full interest payment.

For government bonds, most financial publications include two price quotations. The first price quotation, or the *bid price,* is the price that a buyer is willing to pay for a government security. The second price quotation, or the *ask price,* represents the price at which a seller is willing to sell a government security. The difference between the bid and ask prices is called the *spread* and represents the dealer's profit on the transaction. A trade or transaction occurs when the buyer and seller agree on a price for the security.

personal fintech

If you invest in bonds to diversify your investments or to reduce risk, E*TRADE, Charles Schwab, TD Ameritrade, and other brokerage firms provide apps to help you choose just the right bonds for your investment portfolio. To use TD Ameritrade's Bond Wizard app at https://www.tdameritrade.com/research/bonds-and-cds/bond-wizard.html, all you need to do is answer a few questions and you'll receive a list of bonds that fit your objectives, including maturity dates for different bonds, quality ratings, and taxable or nontaxable alternatives. The app will also help you build a customized bond ladder to improve your average returns and reduce the risks associated with long-term bond investments.

ANNUAL REPORTS

As pointed out earlier in this chapter, bondholders must be concerned about the financial health of the corporation or government entity that issues bonds. To understand how important financial information is when evaluating a bond issue, consider the following two questions:

1. Will the bond be repaid at maturity?
2. Will you receive interest payments until maturity?

HOW TO . . .   Evaluate Corporate, Government, and Municipal Bonds

When investing in bonds, there are a lot of factors to consider. To help you decide whether a bond is a good investment that will help you reach your financial goals, use the suggestions below.

Take This Step	Suggested Action
✓ 1. **Determine what type of bond you want.**	Bonds are issued by the federal government, state and local governments, and corporations. Regardless of who issues the bond, you should always evaluate a potential bond investment.
✓ 2. **To help narrow the field of potential bond investments, use a bond screener.**	Most brokerage firms provide information on bond investments to help you choose the right bond that meets your needs. For example, both E*TRADE and Charles Schwab have bond screeners to help you choose a quality bond investment. By entering the type of bond you want, interest rate, maturity date, and other criteria, most bond screeners will display bonds that match your criteria.
✓ 3. **Dig in deeper to find more information.**	Many of the sources of bond information discussed in this chapter can be used to gather important information about the financial health of the issuer of a specific bond issue. Hint: You can use Personal Financial Planner Sheet 60, Corporate Bond Evaluation, to record the information you find.
✓ 4. **Use a financial calculator to determine if a bond is a good investment or not.**	You can use a bond calculator to help evaluate your bond. For example, the calculator at https://www.calculatestuff.com/financial/bond-yield-calculator can be used to calculate current yield and yield to maturity for different bond issues. You can find other bond calculators by using an internet search engine such as Google, Bing, or Yahoo! and entering the term "bond calculator" in the search window.

While it may be difficult to answer these questions with 100 percent accuracy, the information contained in a firm's annual report is a logical starting point. You can find a great deal of information about the firm's bond issues and its current financial condition in its annual report, and you can find other financial information by accessing a corporation's website and locating the tab for "investor relations." You can also obtain a corporation's annual report by requesting a report by phone or mail. Regardless of how you obtain an annual report, you should look for signs of financial strength or weakness. Is the firm profitable? Are sales revenues increasing? Are the firm's long-term liabilities increasing? In fact, there are many questions you should ask before making a decision to buy a corporate bond. Often, information on municipal bonds is more difficult to find. Sources include the government entity that issued the bond and the professional advisory services listed earlier in this section.

To help you determine the right questions to ask when evaluating a bond issue, examine the *How To . . . Evaluate Corporate, Government, and Municipal Bonds* feature. Also, you may want to read the material on bond ratings and perform the calculations described in the remainder of this section before investing your money.

BOND RATINGS

To determine the quality and risk associated with bond issues, investors rely on the bond ratings provided by Moody's Investors Service Inc., Standard & Poor's Corporation, and Fitch Ratings. These companies rank thousands of corporate and municipal bonds.

EXHIBIT 15-7 Description of bond ratings provided by Moody's Investors Service and Standard & Poor's Corporation

Quality	Moody's	Standard & Poor's	Description
High grade	Aaa	AAA	Bonds that are judged to be of the highest quality by Moody's and Standard & Poor's.
	Aa	AA	Bonds that are judged to be of high quality by all standards. Together with the first group, they comprise what are generally known as *high-grade* bonds.
Medium grade	A	A	Bonds that possess many favorable investment attributes and are to be considered upper-medium-grade obligations.
	Baa	BBB	Bonds that are considered medium-grade obligations but adverse economic conditions could lead to a weakened capacity to meet financial obligations.
Speculative	Ba	BB	Bonds that are judged to have speculative elements; their future may be determined by economic or adverse conditions.
	B	B	Bonds that generally lack characteristics of a safe investment and are subject to high risk of nonpayment of interest and principal.
Problematic or Default	Caa	CCC	Bonds that are of poor standing, vulnerable and dependent on a favorable business environment, and subject to very high credit risk.
	Ca	CC	Bonds that represent obligations that are highly speculative and near default.
	C		Moody's rating given to bonds that are typically in default and regarded as having extremely poor prospects for recovery of principal or interest.
		C	Standard & Poor's rating given to bonds that are highly vulnerable to nonpayment.
		D	Bond issues in default.

Sources: "S&P Global Ratings Definitions," Standard & Poor's, https://www.standardandpoors.com/en_US/web/guest/article/-/view/sourceId/504352, accessed November 20, 2020; and "Ratings Symbols and Definitions," Moody's, https://www.moodys.com/ratings-process/Ratings-Definitions/002002, accessed November 20, 2020.

As Exhibit 15-7 illustrates, bond ratings generally range from AAA (the highest) to D (the lowest) for Standard & Poor's and Aaa (the highest) to C (the lowest) for Moody's. For both Moody's and Standard & Poor's, the first two categories (high grade and medium grade) represent investment-grade securities. Investment-grade securities are suitable for conservative investors who want a safe investment that provides a predictable source of income. Bonds in the speculative category are considered speculative in nature and are often referred to as high-yield bonds. Finally, the C and D categories are used to rank bonds where there are poor prospects of repayment or even continued payment of interest. Bonds in these categories may be in default.

So how important are the bond ratings provided by Moody's, Standard & Poor's, and other companies that provide bond ratings? Answer: Very Important. Bond ratings are often one of the most important factors bond investors use to determine if they will invest in a bond or not. Consider the following two bonds:

- A Johnson & Johnson corporate bond that has a 3.2 percent yield, a current price of $1,403, and is rated AAA by Standard & Poor's
- An American Airlines bond that has a 6.3 percent yield, a current price of $690, and is rated B by Standard & Poor's

Which bond would you choose? At first glance, the American Airlines bond with a 6.3 percent current yield and a $690 price seems like the best choice. And yet, consider the B rating issued by Standard & Poor's. The B rating is given to corporate bond issues that generally lack characteristics of a safe investment and are subject to high risk of nonpayment of interest and principal. On the other hand, the Johnson & Johnson bond is rated AAA by Standard & Poor's—the highest rating given to corporate bonds. While the current yield for the Johnson & Johnson bond is less than the current yield for the American Airlines bond, the ratings indicate there is a great deal less risk with the Johnson & Johnson bond. After everything is considered, the choice between these two bonds may depend on your tolerance for risk. And there are other factors you should consider before making a decision to purchase either bond, including the economy, the financial condition of each company, and the effect of the COVID-19 pandemic on both companies.

Generally, U.S. government securities issued by the Treasury Department and various federal agencies are not graded because they are considered risk-free for practical purposes. The rating of municipal bonds is similar to that of corporate bonds.

BOND YIELD CALCULATIONS

Earlier in the chapter, the *yield* for a bond investment was defined as the rate of return earned by an investor who holds a bond for a stated period of time, usually a 12-month period. Two methods are used to measure the yield on a bond investment: the current yield and the yield to maturity.

The **current yield** is determined by dividing the annual income amount generated by an investment by the investment's current market value. For bonds, the following formula may help you complete this calculation:

$$\text{Current yield on a corporate bond} = \frac{\text{Annual income amount}}{\text{Current market value}}$$

current yield Determined by dividing the annual dollar amount of income generated by an investment by the investment's current market value.

EXAMPLE: Current Yield Calculation (Boeing)

Assume you own a Boeing corporate bond with a face value of $1,000. The bond pays 3.01 percent interest ($30.10) each year until the bond's maturity in 2026. Also assume the current market price of the Boeing bond is $1,030.

Because the current market value is more than the bond's face value, the current yield decreases to 2.92 percent, as shown below.

$$\text{Current yield} = \frac{\text{Annual income amount}}{\text{Current market value}}$$

$$= \frac{\$30.10}{\$1,030}$$

$$= 0.0292 = 2.92\%$$

This calculation allows you to compare the current yield on a bond investment with the yields of other investment alternatives, which include savings accounts, certificates of deposit, common stock, preferred stock, and mutual funds. Naturally, the higher the current yield, the better! A current yield of 4 percent is better than a current yield of 2.92 percent. Before choosing a bond because of a high current yield, keep in mind that there are other factors to consider. One very important factor to consider is the risk associated with a potential bond investment. For example, the Boeing bond in the previous example is rated BBB by Standard & Poor's. The BBB rating indicates that this investment is a medium-grade bond, but adverse economic conditions could lead to a weakened capacity to meet financial obligations. On the other hand, a more conservative investor may choose a bond with a lower current yield that has a higher rating and less risk.

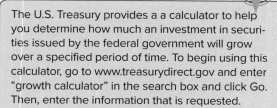

EXAMPLE: Yield to Maturity (Boeing)

Assume you purchased the $1,000 Boeing corporate bond that pays 3.01 percent interest in the previous example on May 1, 2020, for $1,030 and held the bond for six years until its maturity on May 1, 2026. The yield to maturity is 2.47 percent, as illustrated below.

$$\text{Yield to maturity} = \frac{\text{Dollar amount of annual interest} + \dfrac{\text{Face value} - \text{Market value}}{\text{Number of periods}}}{\dfrac{\text{Market value} + \text{Face value}}{2}}$$

$$= \frac{\$30.10 + \dfrac{\$1,000 - \$1,030}{6}}{\dfrac{\$1,030 + \$1,000}{2}}$$

$$= \frac{\$25.10}{\$1,015}$$

$$= 0.0247 = 2.47\%$$

Note: It is also possible to calculate yield to maturity using a financial calculator.

yield to maturity A yield calculation that takes into account the relationship among a bond's maturity value, the time to maturity, the current price, and the dollar amount of interest.

The **yield to maturity** takes into account the relationship among a bond's maturity value, the time to maturity, the current price, and the dollar amount of interest. This calculation is often reported in financial publications and on the internet, but you can approximate a bond's yield to maturity using the formula below.

$$\text{Yield to maturity} = \frac{\text{Dollar amount of annual interest} + \dfrac{\text{Face value} - \text{Market value}}{\text{Number of periods}}}{\dfrac{\text{Market value} + \text{Face value}}{2}}$$

smart money minute

The U.S. Treasury provides a a calculator to help you determine how much an investment in securities issued by the federal government will grow over a specified period of time. To begin using this calculator, go to www.treasurydirect.gov and enter "growth calculator" in the search box and click Go. Then, enter the information that is requested.

my life **5**

I know how to evaluate bond investments.

How do you choose the right bond to help you meet your investment objectives? Although there are many sources of information about bond investments, most serious investors use the internet to obtain current price information, bond ratings, and other important information about bond issues.

In this situation, the yield to maturity takes into account two types of return on the bond. First, you will receive interest income from your purchase date until the maturity date. Second, at maturity you will receive a payment for the face value of the bond. If you purchased the bond at a price above the face value, the yield to maturity will be lower than the stated interest rate. For example, the Boeing bond in the above example has a $1,000 face value and a stated interest rate of 3.01 percent. Because you purchased the bond for $1,030, the yield to maturity decreased to 2.47 percent. If you purchased the bond at a price below the face value, the yield to maturity will be more than the stated interest rate. Remember, the actual price you pay for a bond may be higher or lower than the face value because of many factors, including increases or decreases in comparable interest rates on similar investments, changes in the economy, and the financial condition of the company.

The yield to maturity calculation is an annualized rate of return if the bond is held until maturity. If the bond is sold before maturity, the yield for the investor may be higher or lower, depending on the price the bond is sold for and the length of time the bond is held. Like the current yield, the yield to maturity allows you to compare returns on a bond investment with similar investments. Also, like the current yield, the higher the yield to maturity, the better. A yield to maturity of 2.47 percent is better than a yield to maturity of 2 percent.

Financial Literacy Calculations

THE TIMES INTEREST EARNED RATIO: ONE TOOL TO HELP YOU EVALUATE BOND ISSUES

After evaluating the Home Depot Corporation, Shira and Mathew Matson wanted to purchase the firm's long-term corporate bonds. But she was concerned about the corporation's ability to make future interest payments. To determine Home Depot's ability to pay interest, she used a formula called the *times interest earned ratio*, illustrated below.

$$\text{Times interest earned} = \frac{\text{Operating income before interest and taxes}}{\text{Interest expense}}$$

For example, the Home Depot Corporation had interest expense of $1,201 million and operating income before interest and taxes of $15,843 million for the latest year for which actual figures were available at the time of this publication. The times interest earned ratio for Home Depot Corporation is 13.19 to 1, as follows:

$$\text{Times interest earned} = \frac{\$15,843 \text{ million}}{\$1,201 \text{ million}}$$

$$= 13.19 \text{ to } 1$$

Although the average for the times interest earned ratio varies from industry to industry, a higher number is better than a lower number. Home Depot is earning 13.19 times the amount required to pay the annual interest on its bonds, notes, and other financial obligations. With a times interest earned ratio of 13.19 to 1, Home Depot could experience a substantial drop in earnings and still meet its financial obligations.

Source: Based on information contained in Home Depot Corporation's 2019 annual report.

OTHER SOURCES OF INFORMATION

Investors can use two additional sources of information to evaluate potential bond investments. First, many business periodicals provide information about the economy, changes in interest rates for home mortgages, business loans, and bonds, and articles about corporations and government at the federal, state, and local levels. For example, *Barron's, Bloomberg Businessweek, Fortune, Forbes,* and similar business periodicals often provide detailed financial information about corporations that may have issued bonds. You can locate many of these periodicals on the internet or at your college or public library.

Second, a number of federal agencies provide information on the internet or in printed form that may be useful to bond investors. Reports and research published by the Federal Reserve System (www.federalreserve.gov), the U.S. Treasury (www.treasury.gov), and the Bureau of Economic Analysis (www.bea.gov) may be used to assess the nation's economy. You can also obtain information that corporations have reported to the Securities and Exchange Commission by accessing the SEC website (www.sec.gov). Finally, state and local governments will provide information about specific municipal bond issues.

 PRACTICE QUIZ 15-5

PFP Sheet 60
Corporate Bond Evaluation

1. What type of financial information is contained in the investor relations section of a corporation's website? How could this information be used to evaluate a bond issue?
2. What is the market value for a bond with a face value of $1,000 and a bond quotation of 77?
3. How important are bond ratings when evaluating a bond issue?
4. Why should you calculate the current yield and yield to maturity on a bond investment?
5. How can business periodicals and government publications help you evaluate a bond issue?

Your Personal Finance Roadmap and Dashboard:

Investing in Bonds

ASSET ALLOCATION

BONDS AND ASSET ALLOCATION

While some investors think of bonds as an investment for retired individuals, there are other valid reasons to choose bonds for your investment portfolio. In fact, many investors use bonds to diversify their investment portfolio.

YOUR SITUATION

Bonds are an excellent way to use asset allocation to diversify your investments—especially if you think your other investments may decline in value because of a downturn in the nation's economy or a slump in the financial markets. Do you need to diversify your investments? Other personal financial planning actions you might consider during various stages of your life include:

 First Steps

- Create a financial plan that includes your investment and financial goals.
- Work to balance your budget.
- Start an emergency fund.
- Save a reasonable amount of money from each paycheck.

- Participate in an employer-sponsored 401(k) retirement account and/or open a Roth IRA or Traditional IRA.
- Open a brokerage account and begin investing.
- Begin using asset allocation to diversify your investments.

 Next Steps

- Revise your financial plan and investment and financial goals.
- Evaluate all existing investments on a regular basis.
- Continue to save money and invest.
- Choose investments that match your tolerance for risk.
- Consider adding bonds or bond funds to diversify your investments.
- Begin to plan for retirement in 25 to 35 years.

Later Steps

- Determine current financial status and the number of years until retirement.
- Revise your financial plan and investment and financial goals.
- Use asset allocation to diversify all your investments.
- Begin to increase the amount of money invested in bonds and other conservative investments and decrease the amount invested in more speculative investments, including some stocks and mutual funds that invest in stocks.
- Evaluate existing investments on a regular basis.

YOUR Next Step . . . select one or more of the items above and create an action plan to implement those financial planning activities.

SUMMARY OF LEARNING OBJECTIVES

LO15-1

Describe the characteristics of corporate bonds. A corporate bond is a corporation's written pledge to repay a specified amount of money with interest. All of the details about a bond (face value, interest rate, maturity date, repayment, etc.) are contained in the bond indenture. The trustee is the bondholder's representative.

LO15-2

Discuss why corporations issue bonds. Corporations issue bonds and other securities to pay for major purchases and to help finance their ongoing activities. Firms also issue bonds when it is difficult or impossible to sell stock, to improve a corporation's financial leverage, and to reduce taxes paid to federal and state governments. Bonds may be debentures, mortgage bonds, subordinated debentures, convertible bonds, or high-yield (junk) bonds. Many bonds are callable. A call provision can be used to buy back bonds before the maturity date. To ensure that the money will be available when needed to repay bonds, many corporations establish a sinking fund. Corporations can also issue serial bonds that mature on different dates.

LO15-3

Explain why investors purchase corporate bonds. Investors purchase corporate bonds for three reasons: (1) interest income, (2) possible increase in value, and (3) repayment at maturity. They are also an excellent way to use asset allocation to diversify your investment portfolio. The method used to pay bondholders their interest depends on whether they own registered bonds or bearer bonds. Because bonds can increase or decrease in value, it is possible to purchase a bond at a discount and hold the bond until it appreciates in value. Changes in overall interest rates in the economy and changes in the financial condition of the corporation are the primary causes of most bond price fluctuations. You can lose money on your investment if your bond decreases in value. You can also choose to hold the bond until maturity, when the corporation will repay the bond's face value. Corporate bonds are sold by full-service and discount brokerage firms and online.

LO15-4

Discuss why federal, state, and local governments issue bonds and why investors purchase government bonds. Bonds issued by the U.S. Treasury are used to finance the national debt and the ongoing activities of the federal government. Currently, the U.S. Treasury issues five principal types of securities: Treasury bills, Treasury notes, Treasury bonds, Treasury Inflation-Protected Securities (TIPS), and savings bonds. Federal agencies, government-sponsored enterprises, and state and local governments also issue bonds to finance their ongoing activities and special projects. Typical activities and projects include home mortgage financing, airports, schools, toll roads, and toll bridges. U.S. Treasury securities can be purchased through TreasuryDirect, brokerage firms, and banks. Municipal bonds are generally sold through the government entity that issued them or through banks or brokerage firms. One of the most important features of municipal bonds is that interest on them may be exempt from federal taxes.

LO15-5

Describe how to evaluate bonds when making an investment. Today it is possible to trade bonds online and obtain research information via the internet. Some local newspapers, *The Wall Street Journal,* and *Barron's* provide bond investors with information they need to evaluate a bond issue. Detailed financial information can also be obtained by accessing a corporation's website or requesting a print copy of the corporation's annual report. Information about municipal bonds can be obtained from the entity that issued the bonds or from internet sites. To determine the quality of a bond issue, most investors study the financial information and ratings provided by Standard & Poor's, Moody's, and Fitch Bond Ratings.

Investors can also calculate a current yield and a yield to maturity to evaluate a decision to buy or sell bond issues. The current yield is determined by dividing the annual income amount by a bond's current market value. The yield to maturity takes into account the relationship among a bond's maturity value, the time to maturity, the current price, and the dollar amount of interest.

KEY TERMS

bearer bond   529

bond indenture   523

bond ladder   530

call feature   526

convertible bond   525

convertible corporate note   525

corporate bond   523

current yield   543

debenture   524

face value   523

general obligation bond   536

government bond   533

high-yield bonds   525

maturity date   523

mortgage bond   524

KEY FORMULAS

Topic	Formula
Annual interest *Example*:	Dollar amount of annual interest = Face value × Interest rate $= \$1{,}000 \times 4.2\%$ $= \$1{,}000 \times 0.042$ $= \$42$
Purchase price for a Treasury bill *Example*:	Step 1: Discount amount = Maturity value × Interest rate $= \$1{,}000 \times 0.50\%$ $= \$1{,}000 \times 0.005$ $= \$5$ Step 2: Purchase price = Maturity value − Discount amount $= \$1{,}000 - \$5$ $= \$995$
Current yield for a 52-week T-bill *Example*:	$\text{Current yield} = \dfrac{\text{Discount amount}}{\text{Purchase price}}$ $\text{Current yield} = \dfrac{\$5}{\$995}$ $= 0.00503 = 0.503\%$
Taxable equivalent yield (24% tax rate) *Example*:	$\text{Taxable equivalent yield} = \dfrac{\text{Tax-exempt yield}}{1.0 - \text{Your tax rate}}$ $\text{Taxable equivalent yield} = \dfrac{0.04}{1.0 - 0.24}$ $= 0.053 = 5.3\%$
Bond price *Example*:	Bond price = Face value × Bond quotation $= \$1{,}000 \times 93\%$ $= \$1{,}000 \times 0.93$ $= \$930$
Current yield on a corporate bond *Example*:	$\text{Current yield} = \dfrac{\text{Annual income amount}}{\text{Current market value}}$ $\text{Current yield} = \dfrac{\$50}{\$930}$ $= 0.054 = 5.4\%$
Yield to maturity	$\text{Yield to maturity} = \dfrac{\text{Dollar amount of annual interest} + \dfrac{\text{Face value} - \text{Market value}}{\text{Number of periods}}}{\dfrac{\text{Market value} + \text{Face value}}{2}}$

Topic	Formula

Example:

$$\text{Yield to maturity} = \frac{\$60 + \dfrac{\$1{,}000 - \$900}{10}}{\dfrac{\$900 + \$1{,}000}{2}}$$

$$= 0.074 = 7.4\%$$

Times interest earned

Example:

$$\text{Times interest earned} = \frac{\text{Operating income before interest and taxes}}{\text{Interest expense}}$$

$$= \frac{\$4{,}800 \text{ million}}{\$1{,}066 \text{ million}}$$

$$= 4.50 \text{ to } 1$$

SELF-TEST PROBLEMS

1. Charlie Nelson is 50 years old and wants to diversify her investment portfolio and must decide if she should invest in tax-free municipal bonds or corporate bonds. The tax-free bonds are highly rated and pay 3.25 percent. The corporate bonds are more speculative and pay 5 percent.

   a. If Ms. Nelson is in the 32 percent tax bracket, what is the taxable equivalent yield for the municipal bond?

   b. If you were Ms. Nelson, would you choose the municipal bonds or corporate bonds? Justify your answer.

2. James Gomez purchased ten $1,000 corporate bonds issued by Kohl's. The annual interest rate for the bonds is 4.00 percent.

   a. What is the annual interest amount for each Kohl's bond?

   b. If the bonds have a current price quotation of 106, what is the current price of this bond?

   c. Given the above information, what is the current yield for a Kohl's bond?

3. Matt Redburn has decided to invest $1,000 and purchase 52-week T-bills with some excess cash he doesn't need for the next year. He knows that T-bills are discounted securities, but he is confused about the purchase price and current yield and asks for your help.

   a. If the T-bill has a stated interest rate of 0.40 percent, what is the purchase price?

   b. What is the current yield for the T-bill?

Self-Test Solutions

1. a. The taxable equivalent yield is 4.78 percent for the municipal bond.

$$\text{Taxable equivalent yield} = \frac{\text{Tax-exempt yield}}{1.0 - \text{Your tax rate}}$$

$$= \frac{0.0325}{0.68}$$

$$= 0.0478 = 4.78\%$$

   b. The taxable equivalent yield for the municipal bond (4.78 percent) is only slightly lower than the current yield on the corporate bond (5 percent). Because Ms. Nelson is 50 years old and will probably retire in 10 to 15 years, the highly rated municipal bond is a better choice than the more speculative corporate bond.

2. a. The annual interest amount is $40 for each Kohl's bond.

$$\text{Dollar amount of annual interest} = \text{Face value} \times \text{Interest rate}$$

$$= \$1{,}000 \times 4.00\%$$

$$= \$40$$

b. The current bond price for the Kohl's bond is $1,060.

$$\text{Bond price} = \text{Face value} \times \text{Bond quote}$$
$$= \$1,000 \times 106\%$$
$$= \$1,060$$

c. The current yield for the Kohl's bond is 3.77 percent.

$$\text{Current yield} = \frac{\text{Annual income amount}}{\text{Current market value}}$$
$$= \frac{\$40}{\$1,060}$$
$$= 0.0377 = 3.77\%$$

3. a. The purchase price for the 52-week T-bill is $996.

$$\text{Step 1: Discount amount} = \text{Maturity value} \times \text{Interest rate}$$
$$= \$1,000 \times 0.40\%$$
$$= \$1,000 \times 0.0040$$
$$= \$4$$
$$\text{Step 2: Purchase price} = \text{Maturity value} - \text{Discount amount}$$
$$= \$1,000 - \$4$$
$$= \$996$$

b. The current yield for the T-bill is 0.402%.

$$\text{Current yield} = \frac{\text{Discount amount}}{\text{Purchase price}}$$
$$= \frac{\$4}{\$996}$$
$$= 0.00402 = 0.402\%$$

FINANCIAL PLANNING PROBLEMS

LO15-2 **1.** *Analyzing Convertible Bonds.* Jackson Metals, Inc., issued a $1,000 convertible corporate bond. Each bond is convertible to 32 shares of the firm's common stock.

    a. What price must the common stock reach before investors would consider converting their bond to common stock?

    b. If you owned a bond in Jackson Metals, would you convert your bond to common stock if the stock's price did reach the conversion price? Explain your answer.

LO15-3 **2.** *Calculating Interest.* Calculate the annual interest and the semiannual interest payment for the following corporate bond issues with a face value of $1,000.

Annual Interest Rate	Annual Interest Amount	Semiannual Interest Payment
3.60%		
4.30%		
2.25%		
2.80%		

3. *Determining the Approximate Value for a Bond.* To solve the problem below, use the present value of a bond calculator at https://www.thecalculator.co/finance/Bond-Price-Calculator-606.html. Note: Each bond below has a face value of $1,000. LO15-3

Interest Rate When Issued	Years to Maturity	Frequency of Payments	Interest Rate for Comparable Bond	Approximate Present Value
5%	10	Semiannual	4%	
4.1%	8	Annual	5%	
3.2%	6	Semiannual	4%	

4. *Calculating Total Return.* Jean Miller purchased a $1,000 corporate bond for $880. The bond paid 3 percent annual interest. Three years later, she sold the bond for $960. Calculate the total return for Ms. Miller's bond investment. LO15-3

5. *Calculating Total Return.* Mark Crane purchased a $1,000 corporate bond five years ago for $1,060. The bond paid 2.5 percent annual interest. Five years later, he sold the bond for $950. Calculate the total return for Mr. Crane's bond investment. LO15-3

6. *Calculating Bond Yield for a T-Bill.* Sandra Waterman purchased a 52-week, $1,000 T-bill issued by the U.S. Treasury. The purchase price was $984. LO15-4

    a. What is the amount of the discount?

    b. What is the amount Ms. Waterman will receive when the T-bill matures?

    c. What is the current yield for the 52-week T-bill at the time of purchase?

7. *Calculating Total Return.* James McCulloch purchased a 30-year U.S. Treasury bond four years ago for $1,000. The bond paid 2.1 percent annual interest. Four years later he sold the bond for $1,040. LO15-4

    a. What is the annual interest amount for the bond?

    b. What is the total interest Mr. McCulloch earned during the four-year period?

    c. What is the total return for Mr. McCulloch's bond investment?

8. *Calculate the Purchase Price for a T-Bill.* Calculate the purchase price for a 52-week, $1,000 Treasury bill with a stated interest rate of 1.10 percent. LO15-4

9. *Calculating Tax-Equivalent Yield.* Assume you are in the 35 percent tax bracket and purchase a 2.8 percent, tax-exempt municipal bond. Use the formula presented in this chapter to calculate the taxable equivalent yield for this investment. LO15-4

10. *Calculating Tax-Equivalent Yield.* Assume you are in the 32 percent tax bracket and purchase a 3.15 percent, tax-exempt municipal bond. Use the formula presented in this chapter to calculate the taxable equivalent yield for this investment. LO15-4

11. *Determining Bond Prices.* What is the current price for a $1,000 bond that has a price quote of 108? LO15-5

12. *Calculating Current Yields.* Calculate the interest amount and current yield for the following $1,000 bonds: LO15-5

Interest Rate	Interest Amount	Current Market Value	Current Yield
4%		$1,040	
3.6%		$920	
2.9%		$1,050	

13. *Calculating the Times Interest Earned Ratio.* Assume Northern Electronic Manufacturing has operating income before interest and taxes of $925 million. It also has interest expense of $124 million. Calculate the times interest earned ratio for this company. LO15-5

14. *Calculating Yields.* Assume that 10 years ago you purchased a $1,000 bond for $920. The bond pays 3.1 percent interest and will mature this year. LO15-5

    a. Calculate the current yield on your bond investment at the time of the purchase.

    b. Determine the yield to maturity on your bond investment at the time of purchase.

15. *Calculating Yields.* Assume you purchased a high-yield corporate bond with a face value of $1,000 at its current market price of $850. It pays 5 percent interest and will mature in eight years. LO15-5

    a. Determine the current yield on your bond investment at the time of purchase.

    b. Determine the yield to maturity on your bond investment at the time of purchase.

DIGITAL FINANCIAL LITERACY: TREASURYDIRECT WEBSITE

For investors who want to buy U.S. Treasury securities, the TreasuryDirect website is a treasure trove of information. Detailed information about Treasury bills, notes, bonds, Treasury Inflation-Protected Securities (TIPS), and savings bonds is provided. You can also open an account and buy securities online without having to use an account executive or broker at a bank or brokerage firm. More information is provided in the website's Research Center and the Planning & Giving section. There is even a section for tools and calculators to help you plan your financial future.

Action items:

1. Visit the TreasuryDirect website at https://treasurydirect. gov/indiv/indiv.htm. Explore the differences between

the different investment options. Also, take a look at the material in the Research Center, Planning & Giving section, and Tools sections.

2. Create a visual presentation (PowerPoint presentation, video, storyboard, or other format) to explain (a) the different investment options available from the U.S. Treasury, (b) why people invest in Treasury securities, and (c) if you think Treasury securities are a good investment alternative to help you achieve your financial goals at this time in your life.

FINANCIAL PLANNING CASE

A Lesson from the Past

Back in 2018, Betty Wallace, a 47-year-old single mother, got a telephone call from a Wall Street account executive who said that other clients had given him her name. Then he told her his brokerage firm was selling a new corporate bond issue in Great Resources Exploration, a company heavily engaged in oil exploration in the southern United States and off the Texas and Louisiana coast. The bonds in this issue paid investors 6.7 percent a year. The bonds in this issue were also convertible to 18.5 shares of the company's stock. He then said that the minimum investment was $5,000 and that if she wanted to take advantage of this "once in a lifetime" opportunity, she had to move fast. To Betty, it was an opportunity too good to pass up, and she bit hook, line, and sinker. She sent the account executive a check—and never heard from him again. When she went to the library to research her bond investment, she found there was no such company as Great Resources Exploration. She lost her $5,000 and quickly vowed she would never invest in bonds again. From now on, she would put her money in the bank, where it was guaranteed.

Over the next four years, she continued to deposit money in the bank and accumulated more than $46,000. Things seemed to be pretty much on track until her certificate of deposit (CD) matured. When she went to renew the CD, the bank officer told her interest rates had fallen and current CD interest rates ranged between 0.5 and 2 percent.

Betty decided to shop around for higher rates. She called several local banks and got pretty much the same answer. Then a friend suggested that she talk to Peter Manning, an account executive for Fidelity Investments. Manning told her there were conservative corporate bonds and quality stock issues that offered higher returns. But, he warned her, these investments were *not* guaranteed. If she wanted higher returns, she would have to take some risks.

While Betty wanted higher returns, she also remembered how she had lost $5,000 investing in fictitious corporate bonds. When she told Peter Manning about her bond investment in the fictitious Great Resources Exploration, he pointed out that she

made some pretty serious mistakes. For starters, she bought the bonds over the phone from someone she didn't know, and she bought them without doing any research. He assured her the bonds and stocks he would recommend were issued by real companies, and she would be able to find a lot of information on each of his recommendations at the library or on the internet. For starters, he suggested the following three investments:

1. A PepsiCo corporate note that pays 2.625 percent annual interest and matures on July 29, 2029. This note has a current market value of $1,110 and is rated A by Moody's.

2. An AT&T corporate note that pays 4.125 percent annual interest and matures on February 17, 2026. This note has a current market value of $1,150 and is rated Baa by Moody's.

3. American Electric Power common stock (listed on the New York Stock Exchange) and selling for $81 a share with annual dividends of $2.96 per share and a current yield of 3.7 percent.

Questions

1. According to Betty Wallace, the chance to invest in Great Resources Exploration was "too good to pass up." Unfortunately, it was too good to be true, and she lost $5,000. Why do you think so many people are taken in by get-rich-quick schemes?

2. Over the past four to five years, investors have been forced to look for ways to squeeze additional income from their investment portfolios. Do you think investing in corporate bonds or notes or quality stocks is the best way to increase income? Why or why not?

3. Using information obtained in the library or on the internet, answer the following questions about Peter Manning's investment suggestions.

    a. What does the rating for the PepsiCo note mean?

    b. What does the rating for the AT&T corporate note mean?

    c. How would you describe the common stock issued by American Electric Power?

4. Based on your research, which investment would you recommend to Betty Wallace? Why?

5. Using the internet, a current newspaper, *The Wall Street Journal,* or *Barron's,* determine the current market value for each of the three investments suggested in this case. Based on this information, would these investments have been profitable if Betty had purchased the PepsiCo corporate note for $1,110, the AT&T corporate note for $1,150, or American Electric Power stock for $81 a share? Hint: You may want to use the Finra website at http://finra-markets.morningstar.com/BondCenter/Default.jsp to determine current bond values and the Yahoo Finance website at https://finance.yahoo.com/ to determine the current value for American Electric Power.

YOUR PERSONAL FINANCIAL PLAN

INVESTING IN BONDS

Including bonds in an investment portfolio can be useful for achieving short-term and long-term financial goals when certain life situations, business conditions, and economic trends arise.

Your Short-Term Financial Planning Activity

Task Evaluate the difference between corporate bonds and stocks and determine if bonds could help you achieve your financial goals.

Research

1) Review the material in Exhibit 15-1 to understand the differences between bond and stock investments.

2) Read the article "What Are Corporate Bonds" at the Securities and Exchange website (https://www.investor.gov/introduction-investing/general-resources/news-alerts/alerts-bulletins/investor-bulletins/what-are).

3) Use the internet to locate other sources of information about why investors choose bond investments.

Outcome Create a visual presentation (PowerPoint presentation, video, storyboard, or other format) to explain how bonds differ from stocks. Also, describe under what circumstances bonds could help you meet your short-term financial goals.

Your Long-Term Financial Planning Activity

Task Evaluate at least two different corporate bonds that could help you obtain your long-term financial goals.

Research

1) Review the material in the section "The Decision to Buy or Sell Bonds" in this chapter.

2) Use the search tab at the Finra.org website at http://finra-markets.morningstar.com/BondCenter/ and enter the names of two corporate bonds that you think would be good investments.

3) Use the internet and other sources of information to answer the questions on PFP Sheet 60 (Corporate Bond Evaluation) for each bond you chose.

Outcome In a two- to three-page report, describe each bond you evaluated. In your report, be sure to explain if you would invest $10,000 in either of the bonds you researched. Also, explain what information from your research supports your decision to invest or not invest in these bonds. Attach the corporate bond evaluation sheets for each bond as part of your final report.

CONTINUING CASE

Investing in Bonds

With the triplets now in high school, Jamie Lee and Ross have made good decisions so far concerning their financial and investment strategies. They budgeted throughout the years and are right on track to reach their long-term investment goals of paying the triplets' college tuition and accumulating enough to purchase a beach house to enjoy when Jamie Lee and Ross retire.

The pair are still researching where best to invest the $50,000 that Ross recently inherited from his uncle's estate. Ross and Jamie Lee would like to invest in several varieties of stocks, bonds, or other investment securities to supplement their retirement income goals.

Jamie Lee and Ross have been researching stock investment opportunities that may offer lucrative returns, but they know there is risk involved. They are aware that they must develop a plan to assess the risk of the various investment types so they may have the proper balance between high, moderate, and low-risk investment alternatives.

They decide that at this stage of their lives, it might be wise to speak to an investment counselor, and they contact Mr. Jay Hall, who has been highly recommended by a trusted colleague and friend of Ross throughout the years.

Mr. Hall assesses their desired risk for investments and recommends bonds for the low-risk portion of their investment portfolio.

Questions

1. Based on Exhibit 15-1, what are the important differences between stocks and bonds?

Bonds	Stocks

2. Why are bonds a good option for the conservative investor?

3. Jamie Lee and Ross were unaware that there was so much to learn about the different types of bonds. Using the information found in the text, compare the four types of corporate bonds: *Debenture Bond, Mortgage Bond, Subordinate Debenture Bond, and Convertible Bond*. Which bond investment type would you recommend for Jamie Lee and Ross? Why?

Debenture Bond	Mortgage Bond	Subordinate Debenture Bond	Convertible Bond

4. Using the *Personal Financial Planner Sheet 60*, Corporate Bond Evaluation, and the suggested websites listed in this chapter, choose two different corporate bonds that you feel would be a good investment for Jamie Lee and Ross. Then complete *Personal Financial Planner Sheet 60* for each bond that you chose.

DAILY SPENDING DIARY

"How do I know if investing in bonds would be the right option for me?"

Directions

Your *Daily Spending Diary* will help you maintain a record of your expenses to better understand your spending habits. As you record daily spending, your comments should reflect what you have learned about your spending patterns and help you consider possible changes you might want to make.

Analysis Questions

1. How might changes in your spending activities allow you to increase funds available for investing?

2. In what types of situations might investing in bonds be appropriate?

A *Daily Spending Diary* sheet is located at the end of Chapter 1 and on the library resource site in *Connect*.

Investing in Mutual Funds

16

LEARNING OBJECTIVES

LO16-1 Describe the characteristics of mutual fund investments.

LO16-2 Classify mutual funds by investment objective.

LO16-3 Explain how to evaluate mutual funds for investment purposes.

LO16-4 Describe how and why mutual funds are bought and sold.

Financial Literacy
IN YOUR LIFE

▶ **What if you . . .** had just received a refund check from the Internal Revenue Service?

You might . . . spend the money, or you could invest the money in mutual funds.

Now, what would you do? While the actual decision depends on many factors, including your current financial situation and your investment goals, many financial planners would suggest a decision to invest at least part of the money from your refund check is a great option. While there are many investment alternatives, mutual funds are a very popular choice. The Your Personal Finance Roadmap and Dashboard feature at the end of this chapter can help you determine if you are ready to begin investing in mutual funds.

---

my life	**WHY MUTUAL FUNDS?**

Why do almost half of U.S. households invest in mutual funds? Here are three reasons: (1) it's an easy way to invest, (2) mutual funds offer professional management, and (3) funds can help you diversify your investment dollars. Before beginning this chapter, respond to the questions below.

	Yes	No
1. I understand the reasons investors choose fund investments.	_____	_____
2. I can identify the types of funds that will help me achieve my investment goals.	_____	_____
3. I know how to evaluate a fund investment.	_____	_____
4. I know how I can make money with fund investments.	_____	_____

As you study this chapter, you will encounter "My Life" boxes with additional information and resources related to these items.

Consider this! James Martin, a single dad, had always worked hard for his money. And when it came time to invest, he did his homework. After accumulating a $5,000 emergency fund and an additional $7,500 for investment purposes, he purchased shares in the T. Rowe Price Dividend Growth fund based on research information available on the Morningstar and MarketWatch websites. According to research information, the fund managers choose investments that provide dividend income and long-term capital growth. Although he researched other funds that were more aggressive, he felt comfortable with the type of investments in this T. Rowe Price fund. Did his research efforts pay off? You bet! Over the last five years, he earned an average return of just over 16 percent each year.

Why Investors Purchase Mutual Funds

LO16-1

Describe the characteristics of mutual fund investments.

mutual fund Pools the money of many investors—its shareholders—to invest in a variety of securities.

If you ever thought about buying stocks or bonds but decided not to, your reasons were probably like most other people's: You didn't know enough to make a good decision; and, you lacked enough money to diversify your investments among several choices. These same two reasons explain why people invest in mutual funds. By pooling your money with money from other investors, a mutual fund can do for you what you can't do on your own. A **mutual fund** pools the money of many investors—its shareholders—to invest in a variety of securities. Because of professional management and diversification, mutual funds are an excellent choice for many individuals.

Mutual funds can also be used for retirement accounts, including traditional individual retirement accounts, Roth IRAs, and employer-sponsored 401(k) and 403(b) retirement accounts. For example, many employees contribute a portion of their salary to a 401(k) retirement account. And in many cases, the employer matches the employee's contribution. A common match would work like this: For every $1 the employee invests, the employer contributes an additional $0.50. All monies—both the employee's and employer's contributions—are often invested in mutual funds that are selected by the employee. *Caution:* Although some employers have reduced or eliminated matching provisions, some employers still match employee contributions.

Today, many investors use firms like Morgan Stanley to create a financial plan to generate the income needed to satisfy their long-term goals.
Bastian Kienitz/Shutterstock

The notion of investing your money in a mutual fund may be new to you, but mutual funds have been around for a long time. Fund investing began in Europe in the late 1700s and became popular in the United States before the Great Depression in 1929. After the depression, government regulations increased, the number of funds grew, and the amount invested in funds continued to increase. New types of funds, including index funds, aggressive growth funds, and social responsibility and green funds were created to meet the needs of a larger and more demanding group of investors. During this same time period, the cost of investing in funds decreased, while the popularity of fund investing increased.

The following statistics illustrate how popular mutual fund investments are to individuals.

1. In the United States, over 100 million individuals own mutual funds.

2. Over 59 million U.S. households—almost half of all households—own mutual funds.

3. The typical mutual fund investor owns shares in four different funds.[1]

THE PSYCHOLOGY OF INVESTING IN FUNDS

The major reasons investors purchase mutual funds are *professional management* and *diversification.* Most investment companies do everything possible to convince you that they can do a better job of picking securities than you can. Sometimes these claims are true, and sometimes they are just so much hot air. Still, investment companies do have professional fund managers with years of experience who devote large amounts of time to picking just the "right" securities for their funds' portfolios. *Be warned:* Even the best portfolio managers make mistakes. So you, the investor, must be careful!

The diversification mutual funds offer spells safety because an occasional loss incurred with one investment contained in a mutual fund is usually offset by gains from other investments in the fund. For example, consider the diversification provided in the portfolio of the Fidelity Blue Chip Growth Fund, shown in Exhibit 16-1. An investment in the $45 billion fund represents ownership in at least 10 different industries. In addition, the companies in the fund's portfolio are often market leaders, as seen by the fund's top holdings. With more than 490 different companies included in the fund's investment portfolio, investors enjoy diversification coupled with Fidelity's stock selection expertise.

For beginning investors or investors without a great deal of money to invest, the diversification offered by funds is especially important because there is no other practical way to purchase the individual stocks issued by a large number of corporations.

EXHIBIT 16-1

Fidelity Blue Chip Growth
Fund top holdings

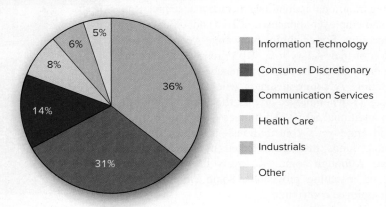

Top 5 industries included in this Fidelity fund

- Information Technology — 36%
- Consumer Discretionary — 31%
- Communication Services — 14%
- Health Care — 8%
- Industrials — 6%
- Other — 5%

Top 5 companies in this Fidelity fund

Apple	9%
Amazon	8%
Microsoft	6%
Alphabet (Google)	5%
Facebook	4%

Source: The Fidelity website (fidelity.com), accessed January 23, 2020 and the MarketWatch Website (marketwatch.com), accessed January 23, 2021.

closed-end fund A fund whose shares are issued by an investment company only when the fund is organized.

exchange-traded fund (ETF) A fund that generally invests in the stocks or other securities contained in a specific stock or securities index.

CHARACTERISTICS OF MUTUAL FUNDS

Today, mutual funds may be classified as either closed-end funds, exchange-traded funds, or open-end funds.

CLOSED-END FUNDS A **closed-end fund** is a fund whose shares are issued by an investment company only when the fund is organized. As a result, only a certain number of shares are available to investors. After all the shares originally issued have been sold, an investor can purchase shares only from another investor who is willing to sell. Closed-end funds are actively managed by professional fund managers, in accordance with the fund's investment objective and policies, and they may be invested in stocks, bonds, and other securities. Shares are traded on the floors of securities exchanges or in the over-the-counter market during the day like individual corporate stocks. Like the prices of stocks, the prices of shares for closed-end funds are determined by the factors of supply and demand, by the value of stocks and other investments contained in the fund's portfolio, and by investor expectations. There are approximately 500 closed-end funds.[2]

EXCHANGE-TRADED FUNDS An **exchange-traded fund (ETF)** is a fund that generally invests in the stocks or other securities contained *in a specific stock or securities index*. While most investors think of an ETF as investing in the stocks

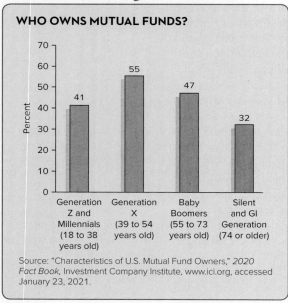

smart money minute

WHO OWNS MUTUAL FUNDS?

Generation Z and Millennials (18 to 38 years old): 41
Generation X (39 to 54 years old): 55
Baby Boomers (55 to 73 years old): 47
Silent and GI Generation (74 or older): 32

Source: "Characteristics of U.S. Mutual Fund Owners," *2020 Fact Book*, Investment Company Institute, www.ici.org, accessed January 23, 2021.

contained in the Standard & Poor's 500 stock index, the Dow Jones Industrial Average, or the Nasdaq 100 index, today there are many different types of ETFs available that attempt to track all kinds of indexes that include:

- midcap stocks,
- small-cap stocks,
- fixed-income securities,
- stocks issued by companies in specific industries,
- stocks issued by corporations in different countries, and
- commodities.

Like a closed-end fund, shares of an exchange-traded fund are traded on a securities exchange or in the over-the-counter market at any time during the business day. Like the price for shares in closed-end funds, the price for shares in ETFs is determined on a stock exchange or in the over-the-counter market. Consequently, two investors buying or selling shares in the same ETF fund at different times on the same day may pay or receive different prices for their shares. Share prices for ETFs are determined by supply and demand, by the value of stocks and other investments contained in the fund's portfolio, and by investor expectations. With both closed-end funds and ETFs, an investor can purchase as little as one share, because both types are traded like individual corporate stock issues.

Although exchange-traded funds are similar to closed-end funds, there is an important difference. Most closed-end funds are actively managed, with portfolio managers making the selection of stocks and other securities contained in a closed-end fund. Almost all exchange-traded funds, on the other hand, normally invest in the stocks, bonds, or securities included in a specific index. *Note:* There are a *few* ETFs that are actively managed with portfolio managers buying stocks, bonds, and other securities. The vast majority of exchange-traded funds tends to mirror the performance of the index, moving up or down as the individual stocks or securities contained in the index move up or down. Therefore, there is less need for a portfolio manager to make investment decisions. Because of passive management, fees associated with owning ETF shares are generally less when compared to both closed-end and open-end funds. In addition to lower fees, there are other advantages to investing in ETFs, which include:

- There is no minimum investment amount, because shares are traded on an exchange and not purchased from an investment company, which often requires a minimum investment of $250 to $3,000, or more to open an account.
- You can use limit orders and the more speculative techniques of selling short and margin—all discussed in Chapter 14—to buy and sell ETF shares.

Because they are traded like stocks, investors must pay commissions when they buy *and* sell shares. Although increasing in popularity, there are only about 2,200 exchange-traded funds.[3]

OPEN-END FUNDS There are just over 9,400 open-end funds.[4] An **open-end fund** is a mutual fund whose shares are issued and redeemed by the investment company at the request of investors. Investors are free to buy and sell shares at the net asset value. The **net asset value (NAV)** per share is equal to the current market value of securities contained in the mutual fund's portfolio minus the mutual fund's liabilities, divided by the number of shares outstanding:

$$\text{Net asset value} = \frac{\text{Value of the fund's portfolio} - \text{Liabilities}}{\text{Number of shares outstanding}}$$

open-end fund A mutual fund whose shares are issued and redeemed by the investment company at the request of investors

net asset value (NAV) The current market value of the securities contained in the mutual fund's portfolio minus the mutual fund's liabilities, divided by the number of shares outstanding.

EXAMPLE: Net Asset Value: New American Frontiers Fund

Assume the portfolio of stocks, bonds, and other securities contained in the New American Frontiers mutual fund has a current market value of $655 million. The fund also has liabilities totaling $5 million. If this mutual fund has 30 million shares outstanding, the net asset value per share is $21.67, as illustrated below.

$$\text{Net asset value} = \frac{\text{Value of the fund's portfolio} - \text{Liabilities}}{\text{Number of shares outstanding}}$$

$$= \frac{\$655 \text{ million} - \$5 \text{ million}}{30 \text{ million shares}}$$

$$= \$21.67 \text{ per share}$$

For most mutual funds, the net asset value is calculated at the close of trading each day. From a practical standpoint, this means that you can place an order to buy or sell shares in an open-end fund during the day, *but* your shares will not be bought or sold until the end of the trading day. The inability to trade a fund until the end of the day can be a problem. For example, assume you own shares in an open-end fund that is heavily invested in technology and online retailing. Reports surface that the government is concerned that large firms in technology and online retailing are "too big" and are systematically eliminating competition. Fearing government reports will lower the value of shares in your fund, you decide to sell. Since you own shares in an open-end fund, your order to sell will not be executed until the end of the day. Thus, you are locked in and cannot reduce your dollar loss. By contrast, if you owned shares in either a closed-end fund or an exchange-traded fund, you could sell your shares during the day because both closed-end funds and ETFs are traded on an exchange or in the over-the-counter market at any time during the day.

Most open-end funds provide their investors with a wide variety of services, including payroll deduction programs, automatic reinvestment programs, automatic withdrawal programs, and the option to change shares in one fund to another fund within the same fund family—all topics discussed later in this chapter.

LOAD FUNDS AND NO-LOAD FUNDS   Before investing in mutual funds, you should compare the cost of this type of investment with the cost of other investment alternatives, such as stocks or bonds. With regard to cost, mutual funds are classified as load funds or no-load funds. A **load fund** (sometimes referred to as an *"A" fund*) is a mutual fund in which investors pay a commission every time they purchase shares. The commission, sometimes referred to as the *sales load charge,* may be as high as 8½ percent of the purchase price. While many exceptions exist, the average load charge for mutual funds is between 2 and 5 percent.

load fund A mutual fund in which investors pay a commission (as high as 8½ percent) every time they purchase shares.

EXAMPLE: Sales Load Calculation

Let's assume you decide to invest $10,000 in the Davis New York Venture fund. This fund charges a sales load of 4.75 percent that you must pay when you purchase shares. The dollar amount of the sales load charge on your $10,000 investment is $475, as calculated below.

$$\text{Dollar amount of sales load} = \text{Original investment} \times \text{Sales load percentage}$$

$$= \$10,000 \times 4.75\%$$

$$= \$10,000 \times 0.0475$$

$$= \$475$$

After paying the $475 sales load, the amount available for investment is reduced to $9,525 ($10,000 − $475 = $9,525). The "stated" advantage of a load fund is that the fund's sales force (account executives, financial planners and advisors, or people in the brokerage divisions of banks and other financial institutions) will explain the investment objective of the fund and provide additional information to investors and offer advice as to when shares of the fund should be bought or sold.

A **no-load fund** is a mutual fund for which the individual investor pays no sales charge. No-load funds don't charge commissions when you buy shares, because they have no salespeople. If you want to buy shares of a no-load fund, you must deal directly with the investment company. The usual means of contact is by the internet, telephone, or mail. You can also purchase shares in a no-load fund from many brokerage firms, including Charles Schwab, Fidelity, TD Ameritrade, and E*Trade.

As an investor, you must decide whether to invest in a load fund or a no-load fund. Some investment salespeople have claimed that load funds outperform no-load funds. But many financial analysts suggest there is no significant performance difference between mutual funds that charge commissions and those that do not. In fact, according to numerous research studies, with the data cross-checked to the verify the findings, no-load funds actually outperform load funds.[5]

Since no-load funds offer the same investment opportunities load funds offer, you should investigate them further before deciding which type of mutual fund is best for you. The chief reason no-load funds may be a better choice is because of the amount of the sales charge that is deducted from your investment when you purchase shares in a load fund. Although the sales load charge should not be the decisive factor, the possibility of saving up to 8½ percent of your investment is a factor to consider. Depending on the load fund's performance, it may take an investor a year or more just to "catch up" and cover the cost of the sales load charge. Does the above information imply that all no-load funds are superior to all load funds? No. Which is better depends on which fund you choose. A mutual fund that charges a 4 percent sales load but has above-average annual returns over a long period of time may provide better returns than a no-load fund that has average performance.

Instead of charging investors a fee when they purchase shares in a mutual fund, some mutual funds charge a **contingent deferred sales load** on withdrawals. This type of fund is sometimes referred to as a *"B" fund* or a *back-end load fund.* These fees range from 1 to 5 percent and often depend on how long you own the mutual fund before making a withdrawal.

no-load fund A mutual fund for which the individual investor pays no sales charge.

contingent deferred sales load A 1 to 5 percent charge that shareholders pay when they withdraw their investment from a mutual fund.

EXAMPLE: Contingent Deferred Sales Load: MFS Global Equity Fund

Assume you withdraw $5,000 from B shares that you own in the MFS Global Equity Fund within a year of your original purchase date. You must pay a 4 percent contingent deferred sales fee. Your fee is $200, as illustrated below.

$$\text{Contingent deferred sales load} = \text{Withdrawal amount} \times \text{Contingent deferred sales load percentage}$$
$$= \$5,000 \times 4\%$$
$$= \$5,000 \times 0.04$$
$$= \$200$$

After the fee is deducted from your $5,000 withdrawal, you will receive $4,800 ($5,000 − $200 = $4,800). *Generally,* the deferred charge declines until there is no withdrawal charge if you own the shares in the fund for more than five to seven years. It is also common for some fund investment companies to convert B shares to A shares after a specified number of years. This type of conversion usually results in lower ongoing expenses and fees for the shareholder. In recent years, class B shares have declined in popularity as investors have chosen other options to purchase mutual fund shares.

MANAGEMENT FEES AND OTHER CHARGES   In addition to the possibility of paying a sales charge to purchase a fund, you should consider different ongoing fees you will pay each year. For example, investment companies that sponsor mutual funds charge *management fees*. This fee, which is disclosed in the fund's prospectus, is a fixed percentage of the fund's asset value. While fees vary considerably, the average is 0.5 to 2 percent of the fund's assets. *Note:* While it's obvious that fund managers must be paid, the management fee is paid by shareholders regardless of the fund's performance.

12b-1 fee A fee that an investment company charges to defray the costs of marketing and selling fund shares and commissions paid to brokers who sell shares in the mutual fund.

The investment company may also charge an annual **12b-1 fee** (sometimes referred to as a *distribution fee*) to defray the costs of marketing and selling fund shares. Typically, 12b-1 fees are used to pay brokers and others who sell the fund shares. This fee may also pay for advertising, printing information for new investors, and shareholder service fees. Approved by the Securities and Exchange Commission, annual 12b-1 fees (including service fees) are calculated on the value of a fund's assets and cannot exceed 1 percent of the fund's assets per year. *Note:* For a fund to be called a "no-load" fund, its 12b-1 fee must not exceed 0.25 percent of its assets.

Unlike the one-time sales load fees that some mutual funds charge when you purchase or sell shares, the 12b-1 fee is an ongoing fee that is charged on an annual basis. Assuming there is no difference in performance offered by two different mutual funds, one of which charges a 12b-1 fee while the other doesn't, choose the latter fund. The 12b-1 fee is so lucrative for investment companies that a number of them have begun selling Class C shares that often charge a higher 12b-1 fee and may even charge a small contingent deferred sales fee.

Exhibit 16-2 reproduces a portion of the prospectus for the Davis New York Venture Fund. A summary of expenses (sometimes called a fee table) is included in a prospectus and must contain details relating to sales fees, management fees, 12b-1 fees, and other expenses. Notice that this exhibit has two separate parts. The first part describes shareholder transaction expenses to buy shares. For this fund, the maximum sales charge is 4.75 percent. The second part describes the fund's annual operating expenses.

expense ratio All the different management fees, 12b-1 fees, if any, and fund operating costs for a specific mutual fund.

- Management fees are 0.53 percent for A, B, and C shares.
- The 12b-1 fee for Class A shares is 0.23 percent compared to 1 percent for Class B and C shares.

Together, all the different management fees, 12b-1 fees, if any, and additional operating costs for a specific fund are referred to as an **expense ratio**. Since it is important to keep fees and expenses as low as possible, you should examine a fund's expense ratio as one more factor to consider when evaluating a mutual fund. *As a guideline, many financial planners recommend that you choose a mutual fund with an expense ratio of 1 percent or less.* The expense ratio, as reported in Exhibit 16-2, for the Davis New York Venture Fund is 0.90 percent for Class A shares compared to 1.99 percent for Class B and 1.70 percent for Class C shares. When compared to Class A shares (with commissions charged when shares are purchased), Class B and C shares, with their ongoing, higher 12b-1 fees, may be more expensive and cost you a lot of money over a period of years.

By now, you are probably asking yourself, "Should I purchase a no-load fund or Class A shares, Class B shares, or Class C shares in a load fund?" There are no easy answers, but your professional financial advisor or broker or representative from the investment company that sponsors the fund can help you determine if a mutual fund can help you achieve your financial goals. You can also do your own research to determine which type of fund is right for you. Factors to consider include

- whether you want to invest in a load fund or a no-load fund,
- financial returns over selected time periods,

my life | 1

I understand the reasons investors choose fund investments.

While investors choose mutual funds because of professional management and diversification, these same investors often complain about fees and charges. As you can tell from reading this section, there are a lot of different fees that can take away from your profits on fund investments. To make sure you know the amount of fees you will be expected to pay, review the fee table contained in a fund's prospectus. Also, take a second look at the fee information summarized in Exhibit 16-3.

EXHIBIT 16-2 Summary of expenses paid to invest in the Davis New York Venture mutual fund

Shareholder Fees *(fees paid directly from your investment)*	Class A Shares	Class B Shares	Class C Shares
Maximum sales charge (load) imposed on purchases (*as a percentage of offering price*)	4.75%	None	None
Maximum deferred sales charge (load) (*as a percentage of the lesser of the net asset value of the shares redeemed or the total cost of such shares*)	0.50%*	4.00%	1.00%
Redemption fee (*as a percentage of total redemption proceeds*)	None	None	None

Annual fund operating expenses *(expenses that you pay each year as a percentage of the value of your investment)*	Class A Shares	Class B Shares	Class C Shares
Management fees	0.53%	0.53%	0.53%
Distribution and/or service (12b-1) fees	0.23%	1.00%	1.00%
Other expenses	0.14%	0.46%	0.17%
Total annual operating expenses	0.90%	1.99%	1.70%

*Only applies if you buy shares valued at $1 million or more without a sales charge and sell the shares within one year of purchase

Source: Excerpted from Davis Funds, Davis New York Venture Fund Summary Prospectus, November 30, 2020, p. 1.

- quality of stocks, bonds, and securities in the fund,
- management fees, 12b-1 fees, and expense ratios, and
- how long you plan to own the fund.

As you will see later in this chapter, a number of sources of information can help you make your investment decisions. Exhibit 16-3 summarizes information for load

EXHIBIT 16-3 Typical fees associated with mutual fund investments

Type of Fee or Charge	Customary Amount
Load fund	Up to 8½ percent of the purchase. Average load is 2–5 percent of the purchase
No-load fund	No sales charge
Contingent deferred sales load	1–5 percent of withdrawals, depending on how long you own the fund before making a withdrawal
Management fee	0.5–2 percent per year of the fund's assets
12b-1 fee	Cannot exceed 1 percent of the fund's assets per year
Expense ratio	Amount investors pay for all fees and operating costs
Class A shares	Commission charge when shares are purchased
Class B shares	Commission charge when money is withdrawn during the first five to seven years
Class C shares	May have higher ongoing 12b-1 fees and a small contingent deferred sales fee

Financial Literacy for My Life

TIME VALUE OF MONEY: SHOULD YOU CHOOSE A MUTUAL FUND OR A SAVINGS ACCOUNT?

Choosing an appropriate investment alternative can be a difficult decision. Of course, there are many factors to consider, but two deserve special attention. First, you need to evaluate your tolerance for risk. One basic rule that was discussed in Chapter 13 is worth remembering. Simply put: *The potential return on any investment should be directly related to the risk the investor assumes.*

Second, your time horizon for investing should also be considered. If you need your money in a short period of time, you should consider conservative investments with less risk. If you can leave your investments alone and let them work for 5 to 10 years, you can invest in stocks or mutual funds.

THE TIME VALUE OF MONEY CONCEPT

Assume you have just received an inheritance of $50,000. You are considering two different options. First, you can purchase a certificate of deposit (CD) that is guaranteed. The CD is projected to earn 1 percent for the next 20 years. Second, you could invest in an index fund that will average an 8 percent return over the next 20 years. How much additional earnings would you receive by choosing the index fund instead of the savings account?

THE SOLUTION

To solve the problem, you need to use Exhibit 1-A (Future Value Table) in the Chapter 1 Appendix. You can also solve this problem by using a future value calculator available on many websites. (*Note:* Depending on the method used to solve this problem, answers may be slightly different because table factors have been rounded off.)

Step 1: $50,000 invested at 1 percent for 20 years has increased to $61,000, as shown below.

> $50,000 investment × 1.220 (Table Factor for 1 percent) = $61,000

Step 2: $50,000 invested at 8 percent for 20 years has increased to $233,050, as shown below.

> $50,000 initial investment × 4.661 (Table Factor for 8 percent) = $233,050

CONCLUSION

You earned an additional $172,050 ($233,050 − $61,000 = $172,050) by investing in the index fund. While the total amount for the index fund is substantially more than the earnings for the certificate of deposit, keep in mind that the index fund is *not* guaranteed, and you should consider your tolerance for risk before investing in a mutual fund.

---

charges, no-load charges, and Class A, Class B, and Class C shares. In addition, it reports typical contingent deferred sales loads, management fees, 12b-1 fees, and expense ratios.

 PRACTICE QUIZ 16-1

1. What are two major reasons investors purchase mutual funds?
2. How do a closed-end fund, an exchange-traded fund, and an open-end fund differ?
3. What are the typical sales fees charged for load and no-load mutual funds?
4. What is the difference among Class A, B, and C shares?
5. What are the typical management fees, 12b-1 fees, and expense ratios?

Classifications of Mutual Funds

LO16-2

Classify mutual funds by investment objective.

The managers of mutual funds tailor their investment portfolios to achieve specific investment objectives that match the objectives of different types of investors. For example, a young investor may pick funds that contain growth stocks like Facebook, Amazon, or Alphabet (the parent company of Google) in the technology sector. These same investors are not so concerned with risk or a possible downturn in the economy because they are working and don't plan on retiring until they are 65 or even older.

On the other hand, older investors, who are retired, may be more concerned about safety because they depend on their investments to provide the income they need for living expenses. In their situation, they may choose government and corporate bond funds or very conservative stock funds that have a long history of paying dividends.

Usually, a fund's objectives are plainly disclosed in its prospectus. For example, the objectives of the Vanguard U.S. Growth fund are described as follows:

> The investment seeks to provide long-term capital appreciation. The fund invests mainly in large-capitalization stocks of U.S. companies considered to have above-average earnings growth potential and reasonable stock prices in comparison with expected earnings. Under normal circumstances, at least 80% of its assets will be invested in securities issued by U.S. companies. The fund uses multiple investment advisors.[6]

While it may be helpful to categorize mutual funds into different categories, different sources of investment information may use different categories for the same mutual fund. In most cases, the name of the category gives a pretty good clue as to the types of investments included within the category. The *major* fund categories are described below in alphabetical order.

STOCK FUNDS

- *Aggressive growth funds* seek rapid growth by purchasing stocks whose prices are expected to increase dramatically in a short period of time. Turnover within an aggressive growth fund is high because managers are buying individual stocks of smaller growth companies. Investors in these funds experience wide price swings because of the underlying speculative nature of the stocks in the fund's portfolio and more risk than other types of funds.

- *Equity income funds* invest in stocks issued by companies with a long history of paying dividends. The major objective of these funds is to provide income to shareholders. These funds are attractive investment choices for conservative or retired investors.

- *Global stock funds* invest in stocks of companies throughout the world, including the United States.

- *Growth funds* invest in companies expecting higher-than-average revenue and earnings growth. While similar to aggressive growth funds, growth funds tend to invest in larger, well-established companies. As a result, the prices for shares in a growth fund are less volatile compared to aggressive growth funds.

- *Index funds* invest in the same companies included in an index like the Standard & Poor's 500 Stock Index or NASDAQ 100 Index. Since fund managers pick the stocks issued by the companies included in the index, an index fund should provide approximately the same performance as the index. Also, since index funds are cheaper to manage, they often have lower management fees and expense ratios.

- *International funds* (sometimes referred to as foreign funds) invest in foreign stocks sold in securities markets throughout the world; thus, if the economy in one region or nation is in a slump, profits can still be earned in others. Unlike global funds, which invest in stocks issued by companies in both foreign nations and the United States, a true international fund invests outside the United States.

- *Large-cap funds* invest in the stocks of companies with total capitalization of $10 billion or more. Large-capitalization stocks are generally invested in stable, well-established companies and are likely to have minimal fluctuation in their value.

- *Midcap funds* invest in companies with total capitalization of $2 to $10 billion whose stocks offer more security than small-cap funds and more growth potential than funds that invest in large corporations.

I can identify the types of funds that will help me achieve my investment goals.

Often investors begin the search for a mutual fund by attempting to match their financial objectives with a specific fund's objective. The fund's objective is always contained in the prospectus available by accessing the investment company's website, making a phone call, or requesting a prospectus by mail. In addition, many financial websites and publications provide information about a fund's objective (along with a lot of other useful information).

smart money minute

- *Regional funds* seek to invest in stocks traded within one specific region of the world, such as the European region, the Latin American region, or the Pacific region.

- *Sector funds* invest in companies within the same industry. Examples of sectors include health and biotechnology, science, technology, and natural resources.

- *Small-cap funds* invest in smaller, lesser-known companies with a total capitalization of less than $2 billion. Because these companies are small and innovative, these funds offer higher growth potential. They are more speculative than funds that invest in larger, more established companies.

- *Socially responsible funds* avoid investing in companies that may cause harm to people, animals, and the environment. Typically, these funds do not invest in companies that produce tobacco, nuclear energy, or weapons or in companies that have a history of discrimination. These funds invest in companies that have a history of making ethical decisions, establishing policies to reduce pollution, and other socially responsible activities.

BOND FUNDS

- *High-yield bond funds* (often referred to as junk-bond funds) invest in high-yield, high-risk corporate bonds.

- *Intermediate corporate bond funds* invest in investment-grade corporate debt with maturities between 3 and 10 years.

- *Intermediate U.S. government bond funds* invest in U.S. Treasury securities with maturities between 2 and 10 years.

- *Long-term corporate bond funds* invest in investment-grade corporate bond issues with maturities in excess of 10 years.

- *Long-term U.S. government bond funds* invest in U.S. Treasury securities with maturities in excess of 10 years.

- *Municipal bond funds* invest in municipal bonds that may provide investors with tax-free interest income.

- *Short-term corporate bond funds* invest in investment-grade corporate bond issues with maturities less than three years.

- *Short-term U.S. government bond funds* invest in U.S. Treasury securities with maturities less than two years.

- *World bond funds* invest in bonds and other debt securities offered by foreign companies and governments.

OTHER FUNDS

- *Asset allocation funds* invest in various asset classes, including, but not limited to, stocks, bonds, fixed-income securities, and money market instruments. These funds seek high total return by maintaining precise amounts within each type of asset classification.

- *Balanced funds* invest in stocks, bonds, and money-market securities with the primary objectives of conserving principal, providing income, and achieving long-term growth. Often the percentage of stocks and bonds is stated in the fund's prospectus.

- *Funds of funds* invest in shares of other mutual funds. The main advantage of a fund of funds is increased diversification and asset allocation because this type of fund purchases shares in many different funds. Higher expenses and fees are quite common with this type of fund.

- *Money market funds* invest in certificates of deposit, government securities, and other safe and highly liquid investments.

- *Target-date funds* (sometimes referred to as lifestyle or life-cycle funds) are popular with investors planning for retirement by a specific date. Typically, these funds initially invest in more risk-oriented securities (stocks) and become increasingly conservative and income oriented (bonds and CDs) as the specified date approaches and investors are closer to retirement.

A **family of funds** exists when one investment company manages a group of mutual funds. Each fund within the family has a different financial objective. For instance, one fund may be a long-term government bond fund and another a growth stock fund. Most investment companies offer exchange privileges that enable shareholders to switch among the mutual funds in a fund family. Especially in volatile markets, the ability to switch from one fund to another fund can be a real advantage. Assume you think the financial markets and the economy are headed for a downturn, you may switch your investment in the Fidelity Blue Chip Growth fund (a higher-risk investment) to the Fidelity Money Market fund (a very conservative investment). Moves like this enable you to avoid a drop in the value of your investments and can preserve your investment funds when the market is declining. When the market stabilizes, you can switch back from the money market fund to more growth-oriented investments. The ability to switch from one fund to another fund can also help you use asset allocation to diversify your investments. For example, if you think you have too much in international funds, you may want to sell some shares and reinvest in funds that invest in U.S. companies.

Investors may give instructions to switch from one fund to another within the same family by using the internet, by making a telephone call, or by sending a letter. Charges for exchanges, if any, generally are small for each transaction. For funds that do charge, the fee may be as low as $5 per transaction.

THE BENEFITS OF PORTFOLIO CONSTRUCTION

While you are reading this section, keep in mind one important fact: There are a lot of funds that are available, and eventually you must choose the funds you believe will help you obtain your financial goals. To decide which funds are right for you, first, you must decide what type of fund(s) you want. Choices include stock funds, bond funds, or the other funds that were described earlier in this section. You can choose more than one type of fund and even other investment alternatives, including individual stocks, individual bonds, real estate, or more speculative investments, to construct an investment portfolio. **Portfolio construction** is the process of choosing different types of stocks, bonds, funds, and other investment alternatives to obtain larger returns while reducing risk. Using the portfolio construction concept is a very personalized process, and the choice of investments is often determined by your goals, your tolerance for risk, your age, how much money you have to invest, how long before you retire, and other factors. People who use portfolio construction are much more involved in their investment program and are willing to invest the time and effort to build a portfolio that is more suited to their particular needs—especially when they are planning for retirement. In addition to personal factors, the nation's economy, world economy, unemployment rate, inflation rates, interest rates, and a host of other factors that could affect your investment portfolio must be considered.

family of funds A group of mutual funds managed by one investment company.

portfolio construction The process of choosing different types of stocks, bonds, funds, and other investment alternatives to obtain larger returns while reducing risk.

For many investors, a very important component of your investment portfolio is a 401(k) or 403(b) retirement plan. Because it is so important and can affect your financial future, consider the following three factors.

1. *Do you want to participate in the retirement account?* The answer to this question is a definite yes for two reasons. The reasons are simple: Employer-sponsored retirement accounts—as explained in Chapter 18—provide a way to reduce the amount of current income tax that is withheld from your paycheck. Therefore, there are immediate tax savings. A second reason for participating in a retirement plan is because many employers will match your contributions. A common match would work like this: For every $1.00 the employee contributes, the employer contributes an additional $0.50. All monies—both the employer's and your contributions—are then invested in mutual funds that are selected by you. *Note:* Many employers that match place a limit on how much of the employee's salary can be matched each year.

2. *Which mutual funds do you want to invest in?* Most retirement plans allow you to choose the mutual funds for your plan from a number of different fund options. When making your choices, keep in mind your long-term goals and the time value of money concept that was discussed in Chapter 1. The time value of money concept is especially important because the investments in your plan will grow because you (and your employer) continue to contribute money to your retirement account *and* because quality investments should increase in value over a long period of time.

3. *What is your stage in life?* The actual choice of investments for your retirement account should be determined by your age, how long before you retire, and your tolerance for risk. Typically, younger workers choose more risk-oriented funds that have greater potential for growth over a long period of time. Older workers closer to retirement tend to choose more conservative funds with less risk.

 PRACTICE QUIZ 16-2

1. How important is the investment objective as stated in a fund's prospectus?
2. Why do you think fund managers offer so many different kinds of funds?
3. What is a family of funds? How is it related to shareholder exchanges?
4. What are the benefits of portfolio construction?

How to Decide to Buy or Sell Mutual Funds

LO16-3

Explain how to evaluate mutual funds for investment purposes.

Often the decision to buy or sell shares in mutual funds is "too easy" because investors assume they do not need to evaluate these investments. Why question what the professional portfolio managers decide to do? Yet professionals do make mistakes. The responsibility for choosing the right mutual fund rests with *you*. After all, you are the only one who knows how much risk you are willing to assume and how a particular mutual fund can help you achieve your goals.

Fortunately, a lot of information is available to help you evaluate a specific mutual fund. Let's begin with one basic question: Do you want a managed fund or an index fund?

MANAGED FUNDS VERSUS INDEXED FUNDS

Most mutual funds are managed funds. In other words, there is a professional fund manager (or team of managers) that chooses the securities that are contained in the fund. The fund manager also decides when to buy and sell securities in the fund. One important question is how long the present fund manager has been managing the fund. The benchmark for a good fund manager is the ability to increase share value when the economy is good and retain that value when the economy is bad. For example, most funds reported double-digit returns during 2019. Yet, many of those same funds experienced declines in share value during the first six months of 2020 because of the COVID-19 pandemic that led to nonessential business closures, high unemployment rates, and falling oil prices. While there are no guarantees, if a fund has performed well under its present manager over a 5-year, 10-year, or longer period, there is a strong likelihood that it will continue to perform well under that manager in the future. On the other hand, if the fund has a new manager, his or her decisions may affect the performance of the fund.

Instead of investing in a managed fund, some investors choose to invest in an index fund. Why? The answer to that question is simple: Over many years, the majority of funds fail to outperform the Standard & Poor's 500 stock index or other comparable indices. The exact statistics vary depending on the year and the specific fund, but on average the Standard & Poor's 500 stock index outperforms 50 to 80 percent of large-cap funds over a long period of time.[7] The main reason why funds fail to outperform the Standard & Poor's 500 stock index or other indices is the fees that managed funds charge. And while lower fees may not sound significant, don't be fooled. One of the chief reasons why investors choose index funds is because they have lower fees than managed funds. Even a small difference in fees can make a huge difference over a long period of time. For example, assume two different investors each invest $10,000. One investor chooses an index fund that has annual expenses of 0.20 percent; the other chooses a managed fund that has annual expenses of 1.20 percent. Both funds earn 10 percent a year. At the end of 35 years, the index fund is worth $263,683, while the managed fund is worth $191,431. That's a difference of $72,252.[8] Thus, even though the two funds earned the same 10 percent a year, the difference in annual expenses made a "big" difference in the amount of money each investor had at the end of 35 years.

Over a long period of time, it's hard to beat an index like the Standard & Poor's 500 Stock Index. If the individual securities included in an index increase in value, the index goes up. Because an index mutual fund is a mirror image of a specific index, the dollar value of a share in an index fund also increases when the index increases. Unfortunately, the reverse is true. If the index goes down, the value of a share in an index fund goes down.

The concept behind index funds is based on the efficient market hypothesis discussed in Chapter 14, which states that it is impossible to consistently beat the market without raising your risk level. John Bogle, founder of the Vanguard mutual funds, created one of the first index funds in 1976 as a low-cost alternative to managed mutual funds. Today, the Vanguard 500 Index fund is one of the largest mutual funds in the world.[9] Index funds, sometimes called "passive" funds, do have managers, but they simply buy the stocks, bonds, or securities contained in the index.

As mentioned earlier, investors choose index funds because they have a lower expense ratio than managed funds. As defined earlier in this chapter, the total fees charged by a mutual fund is called the *expense ratio*. (Remember, financial planners recommend that you choose a mutual fund with an expense rate of 1 percent or less.) If a fund's expense ratio is 1.20 percent, then the fund has to earn at least that amount on its investment holdings each year just to break even. With few exceptions, the expense ratios for index funds are lower than the expense ratios for managed funds. Typical expense ratios for an index fund are 0.25 percent or less.

Which type of fund is best? The answer depends on which managed mutual fund you choose. Consider the following:

- Managed funds can outperform index funds, especially if you own the fund for a short period of time, but it's hard for a managed fund to continue outperforming the index. Moreover, over a long period of time, higher fees can reduce your returns in a managed fund.

- If you pick a managed fund that has significantly better performance than an index, then you made the right choice. If, on the other hand, the index (and the index fund) outperforms the managed fund—which happens most of the time—an index fund is a better choice.

Open an Investment Account and Begin Investing in Funds

You may want to use the seven suggestions contained here to open an investment account and begin investing in funds.

Take This Step	Suggested Action
1. Determine your investment goals and perform a financial checkup.	Without investment goals, you don't know what you want to accomplish. For more information on establishing goals, review the material in Chapter 13. Also, make sure your budget is balanced and you have an emergency fund.
2. Save the money you need to purchase funds.	Although the amount may be lower, $250 to $3,000 is usually required to open an account with a brokerage firm or an investment company.
3. Research different brokerage firms and investment companies.	When choosing a brokerage firm or investment company, use the internet to find information about available funds, fees, available research information, and requirements to open an account.
4. Choose the type of account that is appropriate for you.	Choices include a taxable account, a traditional IRA retirement account, a Roth IRA, or an employer-sponsored retirement account. More information is provided in Chapter 18, "Starting Early: Retirement Planning."
5. Find a fund with an objective that matches your objective.	Use the internet, professional advisory services, and investment publications to identify funds with objectives that match your objectives.
6. Once you identify two to five possible funds, evaluate each alternative before buying shares.	Sources of detailed information include the internet, professional advisory services, the fund's annual report and prospectus, and financial publications—all sources described later in this chapter. You may want to use *Personal Financial Planner Sheet 62* to help you evaluate each individual fund investment.
7. After all your research and evaluation, purchase shares in a fund that will help you obtain your investment goals.	Evaluate your investments on a regular basis. If necessary, sell funds that no longer are helping you achieve your financial goals.

With both investments, the key is how well you can research a specific investment alternative using the sources of information that are described in the remainder of this section.

See the *How To . . . Open an Investment Account and Begin Investing in Funds* feature for tips on opening an investment account and investing in funds.

THE INTERNET

Many investors have found a wealth of information about mutual fund investments on the internet. Basically, there are three ways to access information. First, you can obtain current market values for mutual funds by accessing an investment website such as Yahoo! Finance (finance.yahoo.com). The Yahoo! Finance site has a box where you can enter the symbol of the mutual fund you want to research. If you don't know the symbol, just begin entering the mutual fund's name in the "Quote Lookup" box, and the symbol will be displayed. In addition to current market values, you can obtain a price history for a mutual fund and a profile that includes specific holdings that the fund owns, performance data, comparative data, Morningstar rating, and information about risk.

Second, most investment companies that sponsor mutual funds have a website. To obtain information, all you have to do is access an internet search engine and type in the name of the fund. Generally, the fund's prospectus, annual report, statistical information about individual funds, procedures for opening an account, promotional literature, how much money is required to open an account, and different investor services are provided. How about picking one of the fund families listed in Exhibit 16-4 and going exploring on the internet? While the three investment companies listed in Exhibit 16-4 are quite large, there are many smaller investment companies that also sell funds. A word of caution: Investment companies want you to become a shareholder. As a result, the websites for *some* investment companies read like a sales pitch. Read beyond the glowing descriptions and look at the facts before investing your money.

Many investors often use the research provided by investment companies as a first step to identify potential mutual fund investments. For example, Fidelity has a fund screener to help investors choose mutual funds. To begin the search process, investors enter criteria, including what type of fund, the Morningstar rating, expected return, risk, etc. Then the Fidelity computer matches the criteria with different potential fund investments. If you would like to use this fund screener, go to https://fundresearch.fidelity.com/fund-screener/.[10]

Finally, professional advisory services, covered in the next section, offer online research reports for mutual funds. Professional advisory services provide some of the most detailed information that can be used to evaluate mutual funds.

smart money minute

MORNINGSTAR "STAR" RATINGS

Morningstar rates mutual funds from 1 (the lowest rating) to 5 (the highest rating) stars on how well they've performed in comparison with similar funds over different time periods.

Within each Morningstar fund category, only the top 10 percent of funds receive the five-star rating. And the bottom 10 percent receive the one-star rating. The other funds within each category are given ratings of two, three, or four stars, depending on past performance.

Source: Morningstar, Inc., http://www.morningstar.com/InvGlossary/morningstar_rating_for_funds.aspx, accessed January 27, 2021.

EXHIBIT 16-4

Information about three of the largest mutual fund asset management companies based in the United States

Mutual Fund Company	Website Information	Assets under Management	Basic Information
BlackRock	https://www.blackrock.com	$7.3 trillion	BlackRock's purpose is to help more and more people experience financial well-being. The largest investment company (ranked by assets under management) in the United States offers a wide selection of load, no-load, and exchange-traded funds to help shareholders achieve their financial goals.
The Vanguard Group	www.vanguard.com	$6.1 trillion	The Vanguard group has always been known as the leader in low-cost investing and has almost 200 different mutual funds. Many investors choose Vanguard because of its index funds and low expense ratios.
Fidelity Investments	www.fidelity.com	$3.3 trillion	Because Fidelity is a fund supermarket, investors have access to approximately 10,000 funds from both Fidelity and other mutual fund companies.

Source: World's Top Asset Management Firms 2020, The ADV Ratings Website (https://www.advratings.com/top-asset-management-firms), assessed January 25, 2021.

PROFESSIONAL ADVISORY SERVICES

As pointed out in the last section, a number of professional advisory services provide detailed information on mutual funds. Morningstar Inc., Refinitiv Lipper (often referred to as just Lipper), and Value Line are three widely used sources of such information. While in the past much of the research information for mutual funds was available only in libraries, today most professional advisory services are using the internet to provide research information online. Although excellent free information may be available, you may be required to register and pay a fee for the more detailed information you may need to research a fund investment. Still, many investors have found that the research reports provided by Morningstar, Lipper, and Value Line are well worth the cost. For example, Exhibit 16-5 illustrates research information about the Calvert Balanced A Fund provided by Morningstar (https://www.morningstar.com/funds/xnas/csifx/quote). Information including fund symbol, current net asset value (NAV), one-day return, total assets, expenses, manager tenure, category of fund, investment style, turnover, and other important information are displayed at the top of Exhibit 16-5. Further down, you can also find a graph that displays the growth of a $10,000 investment over a period of time, and information about total return.

EXHIBIT 16-5

Information about the Calvert Balanced A Fund available from the Morningstar website

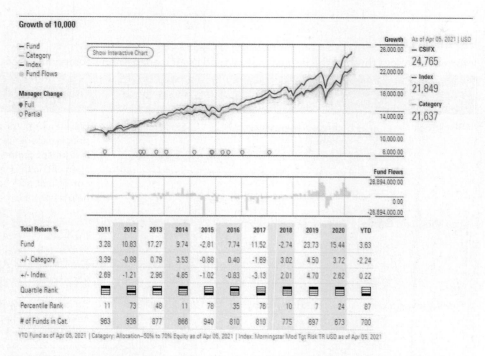

Even more detailed information is available by clicking on the different tabs located below the name of the fund. The descriptions below provide basic information for some of the more important tabs.

Fund analysis tab	Provides in-depth information reported by professional analysts. To access this premium content, you will need to subscribe or take advantage of a free-trial offer.
Performance tab	Provides detailed information about how this fund has performed over selected time periods and also compares the fund's performance with selected benchmarks, including other asset-allocation funds.
Risk tab	Describes the current Morningstar ratings for risk and risk return analysis.
Price tab	Explains the cost of investing in this fund, including load fees, management fees, 12b-1 fees, expense ratio, and an example of what the expenses for this fund would be for different time periods.
Portfolio tab	Provides information about the type of securities included in the fund.
People tab	Describes the current fund manager or team of managers and how long this manager or team of managers has managed the fund.
Parent tab	Includes information about the dollar amount of assets under management and the number of funds the investment company offers.

Keep in mind, professional advisory services update their reports on a regular basis to reflect the fund's performance or an upturn or downturn in the economy. And research firms like Lipper and Value Line, as well as Morningstar Inc., will also tell you if a fund is a poor performer that offers poor investment potential.

In addition, various mutual fund newsletters provide financial information to subscribers for a fee. All of the professional advisory services are rather expensive, but some reports may be available from brokerage firms or libraries.

MUTUAL FUND PROSPECTUS AND ANNUAL REPORT

An investment company sponsoring a mutual fund must give potential investors a prospectus. A fund's prospectus is also available on the investment company's website, by calling a toll-free phone number, or by mail.

According to financial experts, investors should read the prospectus completely before investing. Keep in mind, a commonsense approach to reading a fund's prospectus can provide valuable insights. As pointed out earlier, the prospectus summarizes the fund's objective. Also, the fee table provides a summary of the fees a fund charges. In addition to information about fund objective and fees, the prospectus should provide the following:

- A statement describing the risk factors associated with the fund;
- A description of the fund's past performance;

my life 3

I know how to evaluate a fund investment.

How do you evaluate a fund? For many investors, the answer is a professional advisory service like Morningstar, Lipper, or Value Line. Why not take a look at the information available for a fund you think would help you obtain your financial goals? To begin the search, go to www.morningstar.com and enter the symbol for a specific fund. If you don't know the symbol, just enter the name of the fund, and the symbol will be displayed. Then click on the Quote link and read the available information about your potential investment.

- A statement describing the type of investments contained in the fund's portfolio;
- Information about dividends and capital gain distributions;
- Information about the fund's management;
- Information on limitations or requirements, if any, the fund must honor when choosing investments;
- The process investors can use to open an account and buy or sell shares in the fund;
- A description of services provided to investors and fees for services, if any; and
- Information about how often the fund's investment portfolio changes (sometimes referred to as its turnover ratio) and tax consequences of a fund's trading activities.

Many investors will also access a fund's annual report by using the internet. A fund's annual report may contain a letter from the president of the investment company, from the fund manager, or both. The annual report also contains detailed financial information about the fund's assets and liabilities, performance, statement of operations, and statement of changes in net assets. Next, the annual report includes a schedule of investments. Finally, the fund's annual report should include a letter from the fund's independent auditors that provides an opinion as to the accuracy of the fund's financial statements.

NEWSPAPERS AND FINANCIAL PUBLICATIONS

Although many newspapers have reduced or eliminated mutual fund coverage, many large, metropolitan newspapers and *The Wall Street Journal* often provide news and information about mutual fund investments. In addition, these same publications may provide basic information for current prices and performance. Typical coverage includes the name of a fund family and names of specific funds within the family, current net asset value for a fund, and percentage of year-to-date (YTD) return. This same information (along with more detailed information) is available online.

Investment-oriented magazines such as *Bloomberg Businessweek, Forbes, Fortune, Kiplinger's Personal Finance,* and *Money* provide information about mutual funds and investing. Depending on the publication, coverage ranges from detailed articles that provide in-depth information to simple listings of which funds to buy or sell. And many investment-oriented magazines also have websites that provide information about mutual funds.

The material in Exhibit 16-6 is a portion of the information available in a *Kiplinger's* article entitled "Kiplinger's 25 Favorite No-Load Mutual Funds."

EXHIBIT 16-6

A portion of *Kiplinger's* 25 Favorite No-Load Mutual Funds

Large-Company Stock Funds

Fund Name	Symbol	1-Yr Return	3-Yr Return	5-Yr Return	10-Yr Return	20-Yr Return	Expense Ratio
DF Dent Midcap Growth	**DFDMX**	27.86%	21.89%	21.21%	16.98%	–%	0.98%
Dodge & Cox Stock	**DODGX**	53.97	13.82	16.07	14.26	9.37	0.52
Fidelity Blue Chip Growth	**FBGRX**	45.71	30.38	28.14	20.39	11.22	0.78
Mairs & Power Growth	**MPGFX**	41.98	18.40	15.26	15.04	10.27	0.64
T. Rowe Price Dividend Growth	**PRDGX**	32.72	17.51	15.77	14.62	9.08	0.63
Vanguard Equity-Income	**VEIPX**	34.29	11.31	11.89	12.88	8.51	0.28
S&P 500-Stock Index	–	36.45%	18.16%	17.35%	15.35%	8.79%	–

Source: Kiplinger's 25 Favorite No-Load Mutual Funds, Kiplinger website at https://www.kiplinger.com/kiplinger-tools/ investing/t041-s000-kiplingers-25-favorite-fund/index.php, accessed August 24, 2021.

The article provides basic information for each of the 25 recommended no-load funds, including:

- fund category,
- fund name and fund symbol,
- annual return for 1 year,
- total annualized returns for 3, 5, 10, and 20 years, and
- expense ratio for each fund

The point of the *Kiplinger* article is to provide suggestions for high-quality, no-load funds run by managers who take a long-term view and have proved that they can weather an economic storm. The funds illustrated in Exhibit 16-6 have no sales charges and below-average fees. Even though these funds are recommended by the editors at *Kiplinger's,* investors still need to dig deeper and examine more detailed research information to determine whether the funds described in this article could help them achieve their investment goals.

In addition to mutual fund information in financial publications, a number of mutual fund guidebooks are available online, at your local bookstore, or at your public library.

 PRACTICE QUIZ 16-3

1. Many financial experts say that purchasing a mutual fund is "too easy." Do you think this statement is true or false? Explain your answer.
2. In your own words, describe the difference between a managed fund and an index fund. Which fund would you choose for your investment program?
3. How can the following sources of information help you evaluate a mutual fund?
   a. The internet
   b. Professional advisory services
   c. The prospectus
   d. The annual report
   e. Newspapers and financial publications

 PFP Sheet 61
Mutual Fund
Investment
Information

PFP Sheet 62
Mutual Fund
Evaluation

The Mechanics of a Mutual Fund Transaction

For many investors, funds have become the investment of choice. They may be part of a 401(k) or 403(b) retirement account, a Roth IRA, or a traditional IRA retirement account, all topics discussed in Chapter 18. Funds can also be owned in a taxable account by purchasing shares through account executives or salespeople who work for a brokerage firm or directly from an investment company or brokerage firm that sponsors a mutual fund. As you will see later in this section, it's easy to purchase shares in a fund. Although the amount may be lower, for $250 to $3,000 you can open an account and begin investing. And there are other advantages that encourage investors to purchase shares in funds. Unfortunately, there are also disadvantages. Exhibit 16-7 summarizes the advantages and disadvantages of mutual fund investments.

One advantage of any investment is the opportunity to make money on your investment. In the next section, we examine how you can make money by investing in closed-end funds, exchange-traded funds, or open-end funds.

LO16-4

Describe how and why mutual funds are bought and sold.

EXHIBIT 16-7

Advantages and dis-
advantages of investing in
mutual funds

Advantages

- Ease of buying and selling shares
- Professional management
- Diversification
- Multiple withdrawal options
- Distribution or reinvestment of income and capital gain distributions
- Switching privileges within the same fund family
- Services that include online trades, toll-free telephone numbers, complete records of all transactions, and savings and checking accounts

Disadvantages

- Purchase/withdrawal costs
- Ongoing management fees and 12b-1 fees
- Poor performance that may not match the Standard & Poor's 500 stock index or some other index
- Inability to control when capital gain distributions occur and complicated tax-reporting issues
- Potential market risk associated with all investments
- Some sales personnel are aggressive or unethical

income dividends The earnings a fund pays to shareholders from its dividend and interest income.

capital gain distributions The payments made to a fund's shareholders that result from the sale of securities in the fund's portfolio.

RETURN ON INVESTMENT

As with other investments, the purpose of investing in a closed-end fund, exchange-traded fund, or open-end fund is to earn a financial return. Shareholders in such funds can receive a return in one of three ways. First, all three types of funds may pay income dividends. **Income dividends** are the earnings a fund pays to shareholders from its dividend and interest income. Second, investors may receive capital gain distributions. **Capital gain distributions** are the payments made to a fund's shareholders that result from the sale of securities in the fund's portfolio. These amounts generally are paid once a year. *Note:* The majority of index exchange-traded funds don't usually pay end-of-the-year capital gain distributions. Third, as with stock and bond investments, you can buy shares in funds at a low price and then sell them after the price has increased. For example, assume you purchased shares in the T. Rowe Price Communications and Technology Fund at $160 per share and sold your shares two years later at $195 per share. In this case, you made $35 ($195 selling price minus $160 purchase price = $35 gain) per share. With this financial information along with the dollar amounts for income dividends and capital gain distributions, you can also calculate a total return for your mutual fund investment—see the *Financial Literacy Calculations: Calculating Total Return for Mutual Funds* feature.

When shares in a mutual fund are sold, the profit that results from an increase in value is referred to as a capital gain. Note the difference between a capital gain distribution and a capital gain. A *capital gain distribution* occurs when *the fund* distributes profits that result from *the fund* selling securities in the portfolio at a profit. On the other hand, a *capital gain* is the profit that results when *you* sell your shares in the fund for more than *you* paid for them. Of course, if the price of a fund's shares goes down between the time of your purchase and the time of sale, you incur a loss.

Financial Literacy Calculations

CALCULATING TOTAL RETURN FOR MUTUAL FUNDS

In Chapter 14, we defined *total return* as a value that includes not only the yearly dollar amount of income but also any increase or decrease in market value from the original purchase price of an investment. For funds, you can use the following calculation to determine the dollar amount of total return.

Income dividends
+ Capital gain distributions
+ Change in share market value when sold
  Dollar amount of total return

For example, assume you purchased 100 shares of Majestic Growth Fund for $25 per share for a total investment of $2,500. During the next 12 months, you received income dividends of $0.40 a share and capital gain distributions of $0.95. Also, assume you sold your investment at the end of 12 months for $27 a share. As illustrated below, the dollar amount for total return is $335.

Income dividends = 100 × $0.40 =	$ 40
Capital gain distributions = 100 × $0.95 =	+ 95
Change in share value = $27 − $25 = $2 × 100 =	+ 200
Dollar amount of total return	$ 335

To calculate the percentage of total return, divide the dollar amount of total return by the original cost of your investment. The percentage of total return for the above example is 13.4 percent, as follows:

$$\text{Percentage of total return} = \frac{\text{Dollar amount of total return}}{\text{Original cost of your investment}}$$

$$= \frac{\$335}{\$2,500}$$

$$= 0.134, \text{ or } 13.4\%$$

Now it's your turn. Use the following information for the New Frontiers Natural Resources fund to calculate the dollar amount of total return and percentage of total return over a 12-month period.

Number of shares: 100
Purchase price: $36.00 a share
Income dividends: $0.70 a share
Capital gain distribution: $0.80 a share
Sale price: $40.00 a share

What is your total return on your fund investment, and what is the percentage of total return?

Answer: The total return is $550 and the percentage of total return is 15.3 percent.

TAXES AND MUTUAL FUNDS

Income dividends, capital gain distributions, and financial gains and losses from the sale of closed-end, exchange-traded, or open-end funds are subject to taxation. When you pay taxes is determined by the type of account you own. For example, if your mutual fund shares are part of a 401(k) retirement account or traditional IRA account, taxation is postponed until you begin making withdrawals. Assuming all qualifications are met, you can even eliminate taxes on reinvested income, capital gain distributions, and profits from the sale of shares for funds held in a Roth individual retirement account. On the other hand, if your shares are part of a taxable account, then taxes must be paid each year. For taxable accounts, investment companies are required to send each shareholder a statement specifying how much he or she received in dividends and capital gain distributions at the end of each calendar year. Although investment companies may provide this information as part of their year-end statement, most funds also use IRS Form 1099 DIV.

smart money minute

TAXATION OF YEAR-END DISTRIBUTIONS

A fund often pays income dividends and capital gain distributions at the end of the calendar year. For investors who purchase shares in a taxable account at the end of the year, this creates a "taxing" problem because the dividend income and capital gain distributions are taxed in the same year they are received and must be reported on their tax return. To make matters worse, the net asset value per share usually decreases by the amount of the dividend and capital gain distribution.

The following information provides general guidelines on how mutual fund transactions are taxed.

- Income dividends are reported on your federal tax return and are taxed as income.

- Capital gain distributions result from the *fund* selling securities it has held for more than a year in its portfolio at a profit. For the taxpayer, capital gain distributions are reported on your tax return and are taxed as long-term capital gains regardless of how long you own shares in the mutual fund.[11]

- Capital gains or losses that result from *you* selling shares in a mutual fund are reported on your federal tax return. How long you hold the shares determines whether your gains or losses are taxed as a short-term or long-term capital gain. Gains for short-term investments—fund shares you held for one year or less—are taxed as ordinary income. Gains for long-term investments—fund shares you held for more than a year—are taxed as a long-term capital gain. Under current tax laws, long-term capital gains are taxed at 0, 15, or 20 percent, depending on your total taxable income from all sources.

While paying lower taxes on long-term capital gains doesn't seem like a big deal, those tax savings can be used to buy more shares in funds you own, in different funds, or in other types of investments.

Two specific problems develop with taxation of mutual funds. First, almost all investment companies allow you to reinvest dividend income and capital gain distributions from the fund to buy additional shares instead of receiving cash. Even though you didn't receive cash because you chose to reinvest your dividends and capital gain distributions, they are still reported as current income on your federal tax return if they are paid from a fund held in a taxable account.

Second, when you purchase shares of stock, corporate bonds, or other investments in a taxable account, you decide when you sell. Thus, you can pick the tax year when you pay tax on capital gains or deduct capital losses. Mutual funds, on the other hand, buy and sell securities within the fund's portfolio on a regular basis during any 12-month period. At the end of the year, profits that result from the mutual fund's buying and selling activities are paid to shareholders in the form of capital gain distributions. Unlike the investments you manage, you have no control over when the mutual fund sells securities and when you will be taxed on capital gain distributions.

turnover ratio The percentage of a fund's holdings that have changed or "been replaced" during a 12-month period.

Because capital gain distributions are taxable, one factor to consider when choosing a mutual fund is its turnover. For a mutual fund, the **turnover ratio** measures the percentage of a fund's holdings that have changed or "been replaced" during a 12-month period. Simply put, turnover is a measure of a fund's trading activity. *Caution:* For shares held in a taxable account, a mutual fund with a high turnover ratio can result in increased capital gain distributions and higher income tax bills for investors. A higher turnover ratio can also result in higher fund expenses, which may reduce your investment returns.

To ensure having all of the documentation you need for tax reporting purposes, it is essential that *you* keep accurate records. These same records will help you monitor the value of your mutual fund investments and make more intelligent decisions with regard to buying and selling these investments. For more information on taxes and how they affect your investments, see Chapter 4 or visit the IRS website at www.irs.gov.

PURCHASE OPTIONS

Because closed-end funds and exchange-traded funds are traded on securities exchanges or in the over-the-counter market, it is possible to buy shares in these funds from another investor. In this situation, transactions are completed with the help of a brokerage firm. You can purchase shares of an open-end, *no-load* fund by contacting the investment company that sponsors the fund. You can purchase shares of an open-end, *load* fund through an account executive or salesperson who is authorized to sell them or directly from the investment company that sponsors the fund.

You can also purchase both no-load and load funds from mutual fund supermarkets available through most brokerage firms. A mutual fund supermarket offers at least two advantages. First, instead of dealing with numerous investment companies that sponsor mutual funds, you can make one toll-free phone call or use the internet to obtain information, purchase shares, and sell shares in a large number of different mutual funds. Second, you receive one statement from the brokerage firm instead of receiving a statement from each investment company you deal with. One statement can be a real plus, because it provides the information you need to monitor the value of your investments in one place and in the same format.

Because of the unique nature of open-end fund transactions, we will examine how investors buy and sell shares in this type of mutual fund. To purchase shares in an open-end mutual fund from an investment company, you may use four options:

- Regular account transactions
- Voluntary savings plans
- Contractual savings plans
- Reinvestment plans

The most popular and least complicated method of purchasing shares in an open-end fund is through a regular account transaction. When you use a regular account transaction, you decide how much money you want to invest and when you want to invest, and you simply buy as many shares as possible.

The chief advantage of the voluntary savings plan is that it allows you to make smaller purchases than the minimum purchases required by the regular account method described above. At the time of the initial purchase, you declare an intent to make regular minimum purchases of the fund's shares. Although there is no penalty for not making purchases, most investors feel an "obligation" to make purchases on a periodic basis, and, as pointed out throughout this text, small monthly investments are a great way to save for long-term financial goals. For most voluntary savings plans, the minimum purchase ranges from $25 to $100 for each purchase after the initial investment required to open the account. Funds try to make investing as easy as possible. Most offer payroll deduction plans, and many will deduct, upon proper shareholder authorization, a specified amount from a shareholder's bank account. Also, many investors can choose mutual funds as a vehicle to invest money that is contributed to a 401(k), 403(b), or individual retirement account. When part of a retirement plan at work, the amount used to purchase shares is often a percentage of the employee's pay that is deducted each pay period. As mentioned earlier, Chapter 18 provides more information on the tax advantages of different types of retirement accounts.

Not as popular as they once were, contractual savings plans (sometimes referred to as *periodic payment plans*) require you to make regular purchases over a specified period of time, usually 10 to 20 years. These plans are sometimes referred to as *front-end load plans* because almost all of the commissions are paid in the first few years of the contract period. You will incur penalties if you do not fulfill the purchase requirements. For example, if you drop out of a contractual savings plan before completing the purchase requirements, you may sacrifice the prepaid commissions. In some cases, contractual savings plans combine mutual fund shares and life insurance to make these plans more attractive. Many financial experts and government regulatory agencies are critical of contractual savings plans. As a result, the Securities and Exchange Commission and many states have imposed new disclosure rules on investment companies that offer contractual savings plans.

personal fintech

Today there are a lot of apps that can help you invest! To help you screen different apps, use the internet to gather information, and then choose just the right app to help you manage your money. To get started, read a *Forbes* article entitled "The 15 Best Investment Apps for Everyday Investors" at https://www.forbes.com/sites/jaimecatmull/2019/10/07/the-15-best-investment-apps-for-everyday-investors/?sh=758bcb95145b. You will probably recognize the names of some of the apps described in the article, including Acorns, Personal Capital, Betterment, and brokerage firms E*Trade and TD Ameritrade. Others may be new apps that you don't recognize, but they are still worth a look to see how they can help you obtain your financial goals.

reinvestment plan A service provided by an investment company in which income dividends and capital gain distributions are automatically reinvested to purchase additional shares of the fund.

You may also purchase shares in an open-end fund by using the fund's reinvestment plan. A **reinvestment plan** is a service provided by an investment company in which income dividends and capital gain distributions are automatically reinvested to purchase additional shares of the fund. Most reinvestment plans allow shareholders to use reinvested money to purchase shares without having to pay additional sales charges or commissions. *Reminder:* When your dividends or capital gain distributions are reinvested in a taxable account, you must still report these transactions as taxable income.

All four purchase options allow you to buy shares over a long period of time. As a result, you can use the principle of *dollar cost averaging,* which was explained in Chapter 14. Dollar cost averaging allows you to average many individual purchase prices over a long period of time. This method helps you avoid the problem of buying high and selling low. With dollar cost averaging, you can make money if you sell your mutual fund shares at a price higher than their *average* purchase price.

WITHDRAWAL OPTIONS

Because closed-end funds and exchange-traded funds are traded on securities exchanges or in the over-the-counter market, it is possible to sell shares in such a fund to another investor. Shares in an open-end fund can be sold on any business day to the investment company that sponsors the fund. In this case, the shares are redeemed at their net asset value. All you have to do is give proper notification and the investment company will send you a check or electronically transfer the money to your bank account. With some funds, you can even write checks to withdraw money from the fund.

In addition, most open-end funds have provisions that allow investors with shares that have a minimum net asset value (usually at least $5,000) to use four options to systematically withdraw money. First, you may withdraw a specified, fixed dollar amount each investment period. Normally, an investment period is three months. A second option allows you to liquidate or "sell off" a certain number of shares each investment period. Since the net asset value of shares in a fund varies from one period to the next, the amount of money you receive will also vary. A third option allows you to withdraw a fixed percentage of asset growth. Under this option, your principal remains untouched and, assuming you withdraw less than 100 percent of asset growth, your fund continues to grow.

EXAMPLE: Withdrawal Calculation

You arrange to receive 60 percent of the asset growth from your fund investment, and the asset growth amounts to $1,500 in a particular investment period. For that period, you will receive a check for $900, as shown below.

$$\text{Amount you receive} = \text{Investment growth} \times \text{Percentage of growth withdrawn}$$
$$= \$1,500 \times 60\%$$
$$= \$1,500 \times 0.60$$
$$= \$900$$

A final option allows you to withdraw all asset growth earned by the fund during an investment period. Because the amount you receive is determined by how much your investment grew during the investment period, payments will vary from one investment period to the next. Under this option, your principal remains untouched.

✔ PRACTICE QUIZ 16-4

1. How can you make money when investing in mutual funds?
2. What are the differences among income dividends, capital gain distributions, and capital gains?
3. How would you purchase or sell a closed-end fund? An exchange-traded fund?
4. What options can you use to purchase shares in an open-end mutual fund from an investment company?
5. What options can you use to withdraw money from an open-end mutual fund?

Your Personal Finance Roadmap and Dashboard:

Investing in Mutual Funds

Have You Saved Enough Money
to Invest in Mutual Funds?

Because of professional management and diversification, beginning investors often choose mutual funds. Still, you must choose the right fund that will help you achieve your financial objectives. Then you must evaluate each fund alternative before investing your money.

Your Situation

Are you ready to invest in mutual funds? A very important step is to save the money you need to begin investing. Two suggestions may help you accumulate the money you need. First, have a specified amount of money from your paycheck deposited in a savings or investment account. Second, if you receive a tax refund check, use the money to invest in funds. Although the amount may be lower, most brokerage firms and investment companies require investors to have $250 to $3,000 to open an account. Other personal financial planning actions you might consider during various stages of your life include:

📍 First Steps

- Establish investment and financial goals.
- Work to balance your budget.
- Establish an emergency fund.

- Save the money needed to begin investing.
- Participate in an employer-sponsored 401(k) retirement account.
- Learn about the advantages of a Roth IRA or traditional IRA.
- Open an account with a brokerage firm or an investment company.
- Evaluate different fund investments that offer a potential for growth.
- Begin investing.

📍 Next Steps

- Revise investment and financial goals.
- Continue to save money and participate in retirement and IRA accounts.
- Continue to evaluate all existing investments.
- Use asset allocation to diversify investments in stocks, bonds, and funds with different objectives.

📍 Later Steps

- Revise investment and financial goals.
- Evaluate all existing investments on a regular basis.
- Determine current financial status and the number of years until retirement.
- Continue to save and use asset allocation to make sure that there is a balance between growth-oriented and conservative funds.

YOUR next step . . . select one or more of the items above and create an action plan to implement those financial planning activities

SUMMARY OF LEARNING OBJECTIVES

LO16-1

Describe the characteristics of mutual fund investments. The major reasons investors choose mutual funds are professional management and diversification. Mutual funds are also a convenient way to invest money. There are three types of mutual funds. A closed-end fund is a mutual fund whose shares are issued only when the fund is organized. An exchange-traded fund (ETF) is a fund that invests in the stocks and securities contained in a specific stock or securities index. Both closed-end funds and exchange-traded funds are traded on a securities exchange or in the over-the-counter market. An open-end fund is a mutual fund whose shares are sold and redeemed by the investment company at the net asset value (NAV) at the request of investors. Mutual funds are also classified as load or no-load funds. A load fund charges a commission every time you purchase shares. No commission is charged to purchase shares in a no-load fund. Mutual funds can also be classified as A shares (commissions charged when shares are purchased), B shares (commissions charged when money is withdrawn during the first five years to seven years), and C shares (usually no commission to buy or sell shares, but often higher, ongoing 12b-1 fees). Other possible fees include management fees, contingent deferred fees, and 12b-1 fees. Together all the different fees are reported as an expense ratio.

LO16-2

Classify mutual funds by investment objective. The managers of mutual funds tailor their investment portfolios to achieve specific investment objectives that match the objectives of different types of investors. The major categories of stock mutual funds, in terms of the types of securities in which they invest, are aggressive growth, equity income, global, growth, index, international, large-cap, midcap, regional, sector, small-cap, and socially responsible. There are also bond funds that include high-yield, intermediate corporate, intermediate U.S. government, long-term corporate, long-term U.S. government, municipal, short-term corporate, short-term U.S. government, and world. Finally, other funds invest in a mix of different stocks, bonds, and other investment securities that include asset allocation funds, balanced funds, funds of funds, target-date funds, and money market funds. Today many investment companies use a family-of-funds concept, which allows shareholders to switch their investments among funds as different funds offer more potential, financial reward, or security. Portfolio construction is the process of choosing different types of stocks, bonds, funds, and other

investment alternatives to obtain larger returns while reducing risks. For many investors, a very important component of their investment portfolio is a 401(k) or 403(b) retirement plan.

LO16-3

Explain how to evaluate mutual funds for investment purposes. The responsibility for choosing the "right" mutual fund rests with you, the investor. One of the first questions you must answer is whether you want a managed fund or an index fund. Most mutual funds are managed funds, with a professional fund manager (or team of managers) who chooses the securities contained in the fund. An index fund invests in the securities that are contained in an index, such as the Standard & Poor's 500 stock index. Statistically, the majority of managed mutual funds have failed to outperform the Standard & Poor's 500 stock index or other indices over a long period of time. The information on the internet, from professional advisory services, in the fund prospectus and annual report, and in newspapers and financial publications can all help you evaluate a mutual fund.

LO16-4

Describe how and why mutual funds are bought and sold. The advantages and disadvantages of mutual funds have made mutual funds the investment of choice for many investors. Although the amount may be lower, for $250 to $3,000 you can open an account and begin investing. The shares of a closed-end fund or exchange-traded fund are bought and sold on organized securities exchanges or the over-the-counter market with the help of a brokerage firm. The shares of an open-end fund may be purchased through an account executive or salesperson who is authorized to sell them or from the investment company that sponsors the fund. The shares in an open-end fund can be sold to the investment company that sponsors the fund. Shares of closed-end funds, ETFs, and open-end funds can also be bought and sold by investing through a mutual fund supermarket.

Shareholders in mutual funds can receive a return in one of three ways: income dividends, capital gain distributions when the *fund* buys and sells securities in the fund's portfolio at a profit, and capital gains when the *shareholder* sells shares in the mutual fund at a higher price than the price paid. Unless your mutual fund account is part of an individual retirement account, or 401k or 403(b) retirement account, income dividends, capital gain distributions, and capital gains are subject to taxation. A number of purchase and withdrawal options are available.

KEY TERMS

capital gain distributions   576

closed-end fund   558

contingent deferred sales
   load   561

exchange-traded fund (ETF)   558

expense ratio   562

family of funds   567

Income dividends   576

load fund   560

mutual fund   556

net asset value (NAV)   559

no-load fund   561

open-end fund   559

portfolio construction   567

reinvestment plan   580

turnover ratio   578

12b-1 fee   562

KEY FORMULAS

Topic	Formula
Net asset value	$\text{Net asset value} = \dfrac{\text{Value of the fund's portfolio} - \text{Liabilities}}{\text{Number of shares outstanding}}$
Example:	$\text{Net asset value} = \dfrac{\$245 \text{ million} - \$5 \text{ million}}{8 \text{ million shares}}$
	$= \$30 \text{ per share}$
Dollar amount of sales load	$\text{Dollar amount of sales load} = \text{Original investment} \times \text{Sales load stated as a percentage}$
Example:	$\text{Dollar amount of sales load} = \$20,000 \times 5\%$
	$= \$20,000 \times 0.05$
	$= \$1,000$
Contingent deferred sales load	$\text{Contingent deferred sales load} = \text{Withdrawal amount} \times \text{Contingent deferred sales load as a percentage}$
Example:	$\text{Contingent deferred sales load} = \$12,000 \times 4\%$
	$= \$12,000 \times 0.04$
	$= \$480$

Total return

    Income dividends

$+$ Capital gain distributions

$+$ Change in market value

    Dollar amount of total return

Example:

Dollar amount of total return =	$ 140	Income dividends
	+ 90	Capital gain distributions
	+ 220	Change in market value
	$ 450	Dollar amount of total return

Topic	Formula
Percentage of total return	$\text{Percentage of total return} = \dfrac{\text{Dollar amount of total return}}{\text{Original cost of your investment}}$
Example:	$\text{Percentage of total return} = \dfrac{\$450}{\$4,500}$
	$= 0.10, \text{ or } 10\%$
Withdrawal calculation	$\text{Amount you receive} = \text{Investment growth} \times \text{Percentage of growth withdrawn}$
Example:	$\text{Amount you receive} = \$2,000 \times 30\%$
	$= \$2,000 \times 0.30$
	$= \$600$

SELF-TEST PROBLEMS

1. Three years ago, Dorothy Schwartz's mutual fund portfolio was worth $243,000. Now, because of an upturn in the economy, the value of her investment portfolio has increased to $320,000. Even though her investments have increased in value, she wonders if it is time to change her investment holdings, which consist of either aggressive growth funds or growth funds.

   a. How much money has Ms. Schwartz gained in the last three years?

   b. Given the above information, calculate the percentage of gain.

   c. If you were in Dorothy Schwartz's position, what actions would you take to evaluate your investment portfolio?

2. Two years ago, Bill Crandall purchased 500 shares in the no-load Vanguard Dividend Growth fund—a Morningstar four-star fund that invests in corporations that are currently paying dividends and is a fund that will provide a steady stream of dividend income. His rationale for choosing this fund was that he wanted a fund that was conservative and highly rated. Each share in the fund cost $33. At the end of the two years, he received income dividends and capital gain distributions that total $1.66 a share for the two-year period. At the end of two years, the shares in the fund were selling for $38.

   a. How much did Mr. Crandall invest in this fund?

   b. At the end of two years, what is the total return for this fund?

   c. What is the percentage of total return?

Self-Test Solutions

1. a. Dollar gain = $320,000 Current value − $243,000 Value three years ago

      = $77,000

   b. Percentage of gain = $77,000 Dollar gain ÷ $243,000 Value three years ago

      = 0.32 = 32%

   c. While Ms. Schwartz has several options, any decision should be based on careful research and evaluation. First, she could do nothing. While she has gained a substantial amount of money ($77,000, or 32 percent), she may want to hold onto her existing investments if she believes the economy is still improving and the value of her funds will increase. Second, she could sell (or exchange) some or all of her shares in specific funds and add different funds to increase her asset allocations. Finally, she could sell shares in some of her funds and place the cash she receives in a savings or money market account or purchase a certificate of deposit (CD) if she believes the economy is beginning to decline. Deciding which option Ms. Schwartz should take may depend on the economic conditions at the time you answer this question.

2. a. Total investment = Price per share × Number of shares

         = $33 × 500

         = $16,500

   b. Dividends & Distributions = $1.66 × 500 = $830

      Change in share value = $38 − $33 = $5 Gain per share

      Total increase in value = $5 Gain per share × 500 = $2,500 Gain in value

      Total return = $830 Income dividends + $2,500 Gain in value

         = $3,330 Total return

   c. Percentage of total return = $\dfrac{\$3,330}{\$16,500 \text{ Investment}}$

         = 0.202 = 20.2%

FINANCIAL PLANNING PROBLEMS

LO16-1   1. *Calculating Net Asset Value.* Given the following information, calculate the net asset value for the Boston Equity mutual fund.

Total assets	$870 million
Total liabilities	$4 million
Total number of shares	42 million

2. *Calculating Net Asset Value.* Given the following information, calculate the net asset value for the New Empire small-cap mutual fund.   LO16-1

Total assets	$910 million
Total liabilities	$20 million
Total number of shares	60 million

3. *Calculating Sales Fees.* Julie Martin is investing $35,000 in the Invesco Charter mutual fund. The fund charges a 5.50 percent commission when shares are purchased. Calculate the amount of commission Julie must pay.   LO16-1

4. *Calculating Sales Fees.* Bill Matthews is investing $11,300 in the Washington Mutual fund. The fund charges a 5.75 percent commission when shares are purchased. Calculate the amount of commission Bill must pay.   LO16-1

5. *Calculating Contingent Deferred Sales Loads.* Ted Paulson needed money to pay for unexpected medical bills. To obtain $12,000, he decided to sell some of his shares in the Ridgemoor Capital Appreciation Fund. When he called the investment company, he was told that the following fees would be charged to sell his B shares: LO16-1

First year	5 percent withdrawal fee
Second year	4 percent withdrawal fee
Third year	3 percent withdrawal fee
Fourth year	2 percent withdrawal fee
Fifth year	1 percent withdrawal fee

If he has owned the fund for 21 months and withdraws $12,000 to pay medical bills, what is the amount of the contingent deferred sales load?

6. *Calculating Contingent Deferred Sales Loads.* Nina Collins purchased the New Dimensions bond fund. While this fund doesn't charge a front-end load, it does charge a contingent deferred sales load of 4 percent for any withdrawals in the first five years. If Nina withdraws $5,600 during the second year, how much is the contingent deferred sales load?   LO16-1

7. *Determining Management Fees.* Mathew Johnston invested a total of $94,000 in the New Colony Pacific Region mutual fund. The management fee for this particular fund is 0.80 percent of the total asset value. Calculate the management fee Mathew must pay this year.   LO16-1

8. *Calculating 12b-1 Fees.* Jane Ramirez owns shares in the Touchstone Small Cap fund that have a current value of $31,300. The fund charges an annual 12b-1 fee of 0.25 percent. What is the amount of the 12b-1 fee Ms. Ramirez must pay?   LO16-1

9. *Calculating Mutual Fund Fees.* In the prospectus for the Brazos Aggressive Growth fund, the fee table indicates that the fund has a 12b-1 fee of 0.35 percent and an expense ratio of 1.55 percent that is collected once a year on December 1. Joan and Don Norwood have shares valued at $113,250 on December 1.   LO16-1

  a. What is the amount of the 12b-1 fee this year?

  b. What is the amount they will pay for expenses this year?

10. *Finding Total Return.* Assume that one year ago you bought 100 shares of a mutual fund for $33.10 per share, you received a $0.42 per-share capital gain distribution during the past 12 months, and the market value of the fund is now $40.25. Calculate the total return for this investment if you were to sell it now.   LO16-4

11. *Finding Percentage of Total Return.* Given the information in question 10, calculate the percentage of total return for your $3,310 investment.   LO16-4

12. *Finding Total Return.* Assume that one year ago, you bought 210 shares of a mutual fund for $24 per share and that you received an income dividend of $0.31 cents per share and a capital gain distribution of $1.04 per share during the past 12 months. Also assume the market value of the fund is now $26.50 a share. Calculate the total return for this investment if you were to sell it now.   LO16-4

13. *Finding Percentage of Total Return.* Given the information in question 12, calculate the percentage of total return for your $5,040 investment.   LO16-4

14. *Using Dollar Cost Averaging.* Over a four-year period, Matt Ewing purchased shares in the ClearBridge Large-Cap Value Fund. Using the following information, answer the questions below. You may want to review the concept of dollar cost averaging in Chapter 14 before completing this problem.   LO16-4

Year	Investment Amount	Price per Share
2018	$3,000	$27 per share
2019	$3,000	$35 per share
2020	$3,000	$32 per share
2021	$3,000	$34 per share

a. At the end of four years, what is the total amount invested?

b. At the end of four years, what is the total number of mutual fund shares purchased?

c. At the end of four years, what is the average cost for each mutual fund share?

LO16-4 **15.** *Calculating Withdrawal Amounts.* Since Toni Brookfield is retired, she has used income from her investment in the Alger Mid Cap growth fund to supplement her other retirement income. During one three-month period, the fund grew by $1,300. If she withdraws 70 percent of the growth, how much will she receive?

DIGITAL FINANCIAL LITERACY: TRACKING THE VALUE OF YOUR INVESTMENT PORTFOLIO

Which would you choose: stock funds, bond funds, or other types of funds? Once you make your investment choices, you still have a problem because you know you should track the value and performance of your investments to determine if you want to keep, sell, or buy more shares in the funds you selected. Today, an increasing number of investors solve this problem by using an investment app to track their investment portfolio. Most investment apps are easy to use and can help you track investment values, monitor performance, and reduce fees and risk.

Action items:

1. Read the article "5 Best Investment Apps to Manage Your Portfolio" at https://www.forbes.com/advisor/investing/best-investment-managing-apps/ or similar articles about investment apps or portfolio construction.

2. Select at least two different investment apps described in the *Forbes* article or similar articles. Then create a two- to three-minute presentation that includes a PowerPoint presentation or a short video that describes the apps you chose and how they could help you manage your investments.

FINANCIAL PLANNING CASE

Mutual Fund Research Can Make a *Big* Difference

This chapter stressed the importance of evaluating potential mutual fund investments. Now it's your turn to try your skill at evaluating a potential fund investment. To complete this case assignment, you need to begin by picking a specific fund. You can choose any type of fund you think will help you achieve your personal financial goals. For help choosing a fund, you may want to use the fund screeners at the Yahoo! Finance website (screener.finance.yahoo.com/funds.html) or MarketWatch (https://www.marketwatch.com/tools/mutual-fund/screener) or Fidelity (https://fundresearch.fidelity.com/fund-screener/). Once you have selected your fund, use information from the internet, professional advisory services, newspapers, or financial publications to research your fund. *Hint:* Before completing this assignment, you may want to review the material in the section "How to Decide to Buy or Sell Mutual Funds" in this chapter. Then complete the following assignment.

Assignment

1. Explain the process you used to choose your fund.

2. Describe the specific sources of information you used to evaluate your fund. Were the sources of information helpful or not?

3. Based on your research, answer all of the questions on *Personal Financial Planner Sheet 62,* Mutual Fund Evaluation, that is located at the end of your text.

4. In a one- to two-page report, explain your decision to buy or not buy the fund you chose to research. Be sure to indicate whether this fund could help you obtain your personal financial goals and what you have learned about evaluating a mutual fund. Include the completed *Personal Financial Planner Sheet 62*, Mutual Fund Evaluation, with your report.

YOUR PERSONAL FINANCIAL PLAN

INVESTING IN MUTUAL FUNDS

Using mutual funds for diversification and asset allocation provides investors with convenience and professional management. The variety of mutual funds contributes to your ability to achieve various long-term and short-term financial goals.

Your Short-Term Financial Planning Activity

Task Create a plan to choose information sources that can be used to evaluate fund investments.

Your Long-Term Financial Planning Activity

Task Assume you want to invest $5,000 in a fund. To help you decide if this is the right investment choice, research the performance, costs, and fees for a specific fund.

Research

1) Review the material in the section "How to Decide to Buy or Sell Mutual Funds" in this chapter.

2) Read the article "Best Mutual Fund Research Sites" at https://www.thebalance.com/best-mutual-fund-research-sites-2466453 or other articles available on the internet.

Outcome Use *Personal Financial Planner (PFP) Sheet 61*, Mutual Fund Investment Information to help determine which sites can help you evaluate a mutual fund. Then prepare a PowerPoint or storyboard presentation of the pros and cons of each source of information you included in *PFP Sheet 61*.

Research

1) Use the Fidelity Fund Screener at https://fundresearch.fidelity.com/fund-screener/ to find a fund that you believe could help you obtain your long-term financial goals.

2) Use the information on the Fidelity site and other sources to answer the questions on *Personal Financial Planner (PFP) Sheet 62*, Mutual Fund Evaluation.

Outcome Summarize your findings in a two-page report. In your report, be sure to explain if you would invest $5,000 in the fund you researched. Attach *PFP Sheet 62* to your final report.

 CONTINUING CASE

Investing in Mutual Funds

Jamie Lee and Ross did several weeks' worth of research trying to choose just the right stock in which to invest. After all, a $50,000 inheritance was a lot of money, and they wanted to make the most informed investment choices they could. They discovered, by doing their homework, the corporate stocks they were researching did not seem like they were going to have the promising financial returns that Jamie Lee and Ross were hoping for unless they chose speculative investments with more risk. They were aware that they would be taking a chance with corporate stock investments, but they were both nervous about "putting all of their eggs in one basket" and wanted to be more confident in making their investment choices. But how could they be more assured?

They decided to speak to their professional investment advisor, who suggested that investing in mutual funds might be a way to lessen the risk by joining a pool of other investors in a variety of securities chosen by a professional mutual fund manager. This way, Jamie Lee and Ross can eliminate the pressure of choosing the right corporate stocks, and they minimize the chances of losing their investment money by diversifying their portfolio.

A mutual fund sounded like the sensible investment choice for them, but which mutual fund would be tailored to their investment strategy? Jamie Lee and Ross are in their late-40s and well on their way to reaching their long-term investment goals, as they committed to reaching their goals early on in their marriage. They set their sights on having the triplets graduate from college debt-free and saving enough to purchase a beach house when they retire. They are looking for a mutual fund that will provide both growth and investment income while maintaining the moderate-risk investment path that they are on, as they have some time to go before retirement.

Current Financial Situation

Assets (Jamie Lee and Ross combined):
Checking account: $7,500
Savings account: $83,000 (including the $50,000 inheritance)
Emergency fund savings account: $45,000
House: $410,000
IRA balance: $78,000
Life insurance cash value: $110,000
Investments (stocks, bonds): $230,000
Car: $18,500 (Jamie Lee) and $24,000 (Ross)

Liabilities (Jamie Lee and Ross combined):
Mortgage balance: $73,000
Student loan balance: $0
Credit card balance: $0
Car loans: $0

Income:
Jamie Lee: $45,000 gross income ($31,500 net income after taxes)
Ross: $135,000 gross income ($97,200 net income after taxes)

Monthly Expenses:
Mortgage: $1,225
Property taxes: $500
Homeowner's insurance: $300
IRA contribution: $300
Utilities: $550
Food: $600
Gas/maintenance: $275
Entertainment: $300
Life insurance: $375

Questions

1. It has been suggested by Jamie Lee and Ross's professional investment advisor they should perform a financial checkup before investing in mutual funds, even though they are investing $50,000 that was inherited from Ross's late uncle's estate. Is it a good time to invest the inheritance, or should Jamie Lee and Ross perform their financial checkup to make sure their budget is balanced?

2. While researching the classifications of mutual funds, Jamie Lee and Ross have been reading quite a lot about stock funds. Knowing Jamie Lee and Ross's stage in life, what different types of stock funds would you recommend they invest their $50,000 inheritance in? Why?

3. The investment advisor recommended looking into managed funds, which could help take the burden of the decision-making on when to buy and sell off Jamie Lee and Ross. But Jamie Lee and Ross were considering index funds, which have lower expense ratios. Using your text as a guide, compare managed funds and index funds. Which fund would you recommend for Jamie Lee and Ross? Why?

Managed Funds	Index Funds

4. Jamie Lee and Ross are ready to evaluate a mutual fund more closely. Choose a mutual fund that is available through one of the investment companies described in Exhibit 16-4 or one that has been recommended by a friend or family member, and complete *Personal Financial Planner Sheet 62,* Mutual Fund Evaluation. Would you recommend this mutual fund for Jamie Lee and Ross? Why or why not?

DAILY SPENDING DIARY

"I must choose between spending money on something now or investing for the future."

Directions

Monitoring your daily spending will help you improve your financial planning. You will also have better information that enables you to take control of your spending and make better financial choices.

Analysis Questions

1. Are there any spending items that you might consider revising to allow you to increase the amount you invest?

2. Based on your investment goals and the amount of money you have available to invest, what types of mutual funds would you consider?

A *Daily Spending Diary* sheet is located at the end of Chapter 1 and on the library resource site in *Connect.*

Investing in Real Estate and Other Investment Alternatives

17

Santiago Cornejo/Shutterstock

LEARNING OBJECTIVES

LO17-1   Identify types of real estate investments.

LO17-2   Evaluate the advantages of real estate investments.

LO17-3   Assess the disadvantages of real estate investments.

LO17-4   Analyze the risks and rewards of investing in precious metals, gems, and collectibles.

Financial Literacy
IN YOUR LIFE

▶ **What if you . . .** have a well-balanced portfolio of stocks, bonds, and mutual funds but lack any investment in real estate, gold, or collectibles? While some financial experts recommend buying precious metals as part of a balanced portfolio, others suggest having only a small portion of your investments in alternative investments.

You might . . . consider further diversifying your portfolio by adding real estate, gold, silver, or collectibles to your investments. However, be cautious because values of these investments vary widely and can change quickly.

Now, what would you do? If you decide to invest in alternative investments, find a reputable financial advisor to help you choose an appropriate investment. If you purchase coins, for example, check the U.S. Mint website at www.usmint.gov and make sure you research the seller with the state consumer protection agency and the Better Business Bureau. You will be able to monitor your progress using the Your Personal Finance Roadmap and Dashboard feature at the end of the chapter.

my life   ALL THAT GLOWS AND GLITTERS!

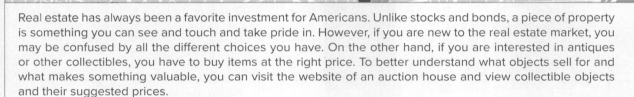

Real estate has always been a favorite investment for Americans. Unlike stocks and bonds, a piece of property is something you can see and touch and take pride in. However, if you are new to the real estate market, you may be confused by all the different choices you have. On the other hand, if you are interested in antiques or other collectibles, you have to buy items at the right price. To better understand what objects sell for and what makes something valuable, you can visit the website of an auction house and view collectible objects and their suggested prices.

You can now start to assess your investment knowledge and skills. For each of the following statements, indicate your choice.

1. An example of a direct real estate investment is
   a. a home mortgage.
   b. a real estate syndicate.
   c. a real estate investment trust.
2. Generally, an indirect investment in real estate is
   a. only for the wealthy.
   b. a hedge against inflation.
   c. a good tax shelter.
3. One of the disadvantages of investing in real estate is that
   a. it is illiquid.
   b. it provides no financial leverage.
   c. it almost always declines in value.
4. Drawbacks of finding collectibles on the internet include the
   a. inability to comparison shop.
   b. lack of a wide range of sellers.
   c. inability to examine items for flaws.

As you study this chapter, you will encounter "My Life" boxes with additional information and resources related to these items.

Investing in Real Estate

Traditionally, Americans have invested in real estate. It is an asset that we can see, touch, and smell, and it is generally a good hedge against inflation. However, as you will see, the choices in real estate investment can be bewildering for the new investor.

Real estate investments are classified as direct or indirect. In a **direct investment**, the investor holds legal title to the property. Direct real estate investments include single-family dwellings, duplexes, apartments, land, and commercial property.

With an **indirect investment**, investors appoint a trustee to hold legal title on behalf of all the investors in the group. Limited partnerships and syndicates, real estate investment trusts, mortgages, and mortgage pools are examples of indirect real estate investments.

Exhibit 17-1 summarizes the advantages and disadvantages of the two types of investments.

DIRECT REAL ESTATE INVESTMENTS

YOUR HOME AS AN INVESTMENT   If you can answer yes to the following questions, you are probably ready to buy your own home.

- Do you have at least two years of regular, steady income?
- Is your income reliable?
- Do you have good credit?
- Do you have just a few long-term debts, such as car payments?
- Have you saved enough money for a down payment?
- Can you pay a mortgage every month?
- Can you pay other costs, such as insurance and taxes?
- Can you set aside money for other costs of home ownership, such as closing costs, moving costs, new furniture, repairs, and home improvement?

What home you can afford depends on your income, credit rating, current monthly expenses, down payment, and the interest rate.

Your home is, first, a place to live; second, it is an income tax shelter if you have a mortgage on it; finally, it is a possible hedge against inflation. In addition, according to National Association of Realtors (NAR) former president Cathy Whatley, "Home ownership brings about a sense of belonging, an emotional connection not just to the home itself but also to the neighborhood and community in which homeowners live and work."

The tax deductions you can take for mortgage interest and property taxes greatly increase the financial benefits of home ownership. However, the Tax Cuts and Jobs Act

LO17-1

Identify types of real estate investments.

direct investment
Investment in which the investor holds legal title to property.

indirect investment
Investment in which a trustee holds legal title to property on behalf of the investors.

Direct

Indirect

Types of real estate investments

- Your home
- Vacation home
- Commercial property
- Raw land
- Foreclosures

Possible Advantages
- Hedge against inflation
- Limited financial liability
- No management headaches
- Financial leverage

Possible Disadvantages
- Illiquidity
- Lack of diversification
- No tax shelters
- New tax law provisions

- Real estate syndicates or limited partnerships
- REITs
- 1st and 2nd mortgages
- Participation certificates

EXHIBIT 17-1

Types, advantages, and disadvantages of real estate investments of 2017 reduces the tax benefits of owning your home. It reduces the property tax and mortgage interest deductions. For example, the limit on a deductible mortgage has now been reduced from $1 million to $750,000 for couples filing a joint return.

EXAMPLE: Tax Benefits of Home Ownership

Assessed value of your home	= $180,000
Amount of loan	= $150,000
Term of loan	= 30 years
Interest rate	= 7%
Property tax rate	= 1.5% of assessed value
Mortgage interest paid in Year 5	= $9,877
Property tax paid in Year 5 (1.5% on $180,000)	= $2,700
Total deduction on your federal income tax ($9,877 + $2,700)	= $12,577
Assumed tax bracket	= 28%
Federal income tax lowered by ($12,577 × .28)	= $3,521.56

Is your home a hedge against inflation? Yes, according to the National Association of Realtors. Over the past 30 years, the median price of existing homes has increased an average of more than 6 percent every year, and some home values nearly double every 10 years, according to historical data from the National Association of Realtors' existing-home sales series. A Federal Reserve study has shown that the average home-owner's net worth is 46 times the net worth of the average renter.

But let the home buyer beware: During the Great Recession, housing prices tumbled across the country. Indeed, about $7 *trillion* in household wealth was lost as average house prices decreased by nearly 33 percent from their peak in 2007.

Even though the global pandemic shattered the U.S. economy in 2020, the housing market remained strong. The year 2020 was record-breaking for the U.S. housing market. According to Zillow, 5.64 million homes were sold in 2020, up 5.6 percent from 2019. In 2021, sales were expected to grow 7 percent as the mortgage rates remained relatively low. According to Sam Khater, chief economist at Freddie Mac, 72 million millennials "will remain in the driver's seat for the next few years." Generation Z (born after 1995, 23 million strong and growing rapidly), which followed the millennials, has strong feelings and attachments to home ownership, and 86 percent of that generation wants to own a home.

Exhibit 17-2 shows annual home ownership rates for the United States by age groups.

While near-term increases aren't expected to match the gains of the past, economists say demographics should hold prices roughly in line with disposable-income gains during the coming decade. That's expected to be 5.5 percent to 6 percent, says David Berson, chief economist at Fannie Mae. Over time, prices have risen at a rate 1 percent above inflation, notes Doug Duncan, chief economist at the Mortgage Bankers Association.

Housing will continue to be a not-so-liquid investment that promises steady returns over time. Just how much depends on your timing—and location, location, location.

YOUR VACATION HOME   If you have a vacation home, the after-tax cost of owning it has risen steadily. How much depends largely on whether the Internal Revenue Service

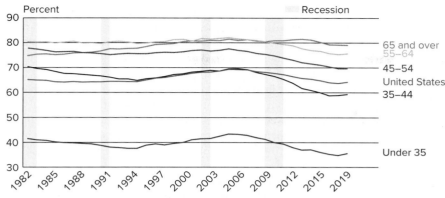

Sources: https://www.census.gov/housing/hvs/data/charts/fig07.pdf, accessed January 14, 2021.

EXHIBIT 17-2
Annual home ownership rates by age groups: 1982–2019

views the property as your second home or as a rental property. It is deemed a second home as long as you don't rent it for more than 14 days a year. In that case, you can write off your mortgage interest and property tax. If you rent the vacation home regularly, the size of your deductions is determined by whether you actively manage it and by the size of your income. According to one certified public accountant, "The primary reason you buy a vacation home is because you want to use it. Tax reasons . . . are way down on the list."

More second-home buyers today are blurring the line between vacation and rental properties, justifying the purchase by planning to rent it out and figuring it's sure to appreciate. But if you're really looking for an investment property, do the math.

The National Association of Realtors reports that the typical vacation-home owner is 47 years old, while the median age of investment property owners is 45. While 80 percent of vacation-home owners purchased their home to use for vacations, other owners reported that it was a good investment opportunity as well.

During the COVID-19 pandemic, Americans were able to work from anywhere and sought less congested places. Consequently, there were more vacation home buyers from suburbs, rural areas, small towns, and resort areas.

 1

An example of a direct real estate investment is . . .

In a direct real estate investment, you hold the legal title to the property. Direct investments include single-family houses, duplexes, apartments, land, and commercial property.

COMMERCIAL PROPERTY   The term **commercial property** refers to land and buildings that produce lease or rental income. Such property includes duplexes, apartments, hotels, office buildings, stores, and many other types of commercial establishments. After a home, the real property investment most widely favored by small investors is the duplex, fourplex, or small apartment building. Many investors have acquired sizable commercial properties by first investing in a duplex and then "trading up" to larger units as equity in the original property increases.

A January 2021 Commercial Real Estate Trends and Outlook study by the National Association of Realtors revealed that COVID-19 pandemic had stalled the commercial real estate market, but the market continued to recover gradually. Still, sales, leasing, and construction activity remained below 2019 levels. The recovery was uneven, with stronger investor interest in land, multifamily, and industrial properties than for hotels, retail, and office properties.

Under current tax laws, deductions such as mortgage interest, depreciation, property taxes, and other expenses of rental property are limited to the amount of rental income you receive. Any excess deductions are considered a passive loss and, with some exceptions, can be used only to offset income from a similar investment such as another rental property. A **passive activity** is a business or trade in which you do not materially participate, such as rental activity. **Passive loss** is the total amount of losses from a passive activity minus the total income from the passive activity.

commercial property Land and buildings that produce lease or rental income.

passive activity A business or trade in which the investor does not materially participate.

passive loss The total amount of losses from a passive activity minus the total income from the passive activity.

Do you want to invest in a tangible asset?
Arina Habich/Alamy Stock Photo

UNDEVELOPED LAND   If land investments have promised tremendous gains, they have also posed enormous risks. With their money riding on a single parcel, investors could end up owning overpriced cropland in the event of a building slowdown or an economic downturn. Furthermore, land usually does not produce any cash flow.

Many investors buy land with the intention of subdividing it. Purchases of this kind are speculative because they involve many risks. You must be certain that water, sewers, and other utilities will be available. The most common and least expensive way to obtain water and sewer service is to hook onto existing facilities of an adjoining city or town.

INVESTING IN FORECLOSURES   U.S. home foreclosures have set new records in the midst of the economic downturn. Is now a good time to invest in foreclosures? This is a difficult question to answer since local market conditions vary from one region to another. However, if you do invest in a foreclosure, make sure that your loan is preapproved. The financing for a foreclosure is more difficult and more expensive than financing your primary residence. Also, be aware of any unpaid liens, including mortgage debt, taxes, construction loans, home equity lines of credit, and second or third mortgages. Any outstanding foreclosure liens and fees will become your financial responsibility.

If you want a clean and clear title to the property, buy it after the property has been repossessed by the creditor. According to John T. Reed, editor of Real Estate Investor's *Monthly Newsletter,* "You can buy foreclosures for as cheap as 30 percent or 40 percent below market, but most foreclosures sell for 5 percent below market." So forget about buying foreclosed properties for pennies on the dollar. Remember, too, that real estate laws for each state are different. Therefore, you should understand the laws and procedures before you invest your money in foreclosed properties.

Investing in a foreclosure may be profitable, but make sure to protect your own property from being foreclosed. Read the *Financial Literacy for My Life: Beware of Foreclosure Rescue Scams* feature.

INDIRECT REAL ESTATE INVESTMENTS

Indirect real estate investments include investing in real estate syndicates, real estate investment trusts, and participation certificates.

Bernice R. Hecker, a Seattle anesthesiologist, made her first real estate investment in 1985. She joined a partnership that bought an office building in Midland, Texas. "Why real estate? Probably superstition," she said. "I wanted a tangible asset. I felt I could evaluate a piece of property much more readily" than stocks, bonds, or a cattle ranch.

Dr. Hecker used a real estate syndicate, one of the three basic indirect methods of investing in real estate: (1) real estate syndicates, partnerships that buy properties; (2) real estate investment trusts (REITs), stockholder-owned real estate companies; and (3) participation certificates sold by federal and state agencies. Indirect real estate investments are sold by most brokerage firms, such as Merrill Lynch.

REAL ESTATE SYNDICATES OR LIMITED PARTNERSHIPS   A **syndicate** is a temporary association of individuals or firms organized to perform a specific task that requires a large amount of capital. The syndicate may be organized as a corporation, as a trust, or, most commonly, as a limited partnership.

The limited partnership works as follows: It is formed by a general partner, who has unlimited liability for its liabilities. The general partner then sells participation units to the limited partners, whose liability is generally limited to the extent of their initial investment, say, $5,000 or $10,000. Limited liability is particularly important in real estate syndicates, because their mortgage debt obligations may exceed the net worth of the participants.

syndicate A temporary association of individuals or firms organized to perform a specific task that requires a large amount of capital.

Financial Literacy for My Life

BEWARE OF FORECLOSURE RESCUE SCAMS!

Foreclosure rescue and mortgage modification scams are a growing problem that could cost you thousands of dollars—or even your home. Scammers will make promises that they can't keep, such as guaranteeing to "save" your home or lower your mortgage payments, usually for a fee, sometimes even claiming that they have direct contact with your mortgage company.

TIPS TO AVOID SCAMS

If you're struggling to pay your mortgage, keep the following tips in mind:

- Beware of anyone seeking to charge you in advance for mortgage modification services. In most cases, charging fees in advance of a mortgage modification is illegal.
- Only your mortgage company has the discretion to grant a loan modification. Therefore, no third party can guarantee or preapprove your mortgage modification application.
- Beware of individuals and companies using mail and/or phone solicitations that claim to be from your mortgage company, but insist that payments be sent to an alternate contact or address that is different from the information in your mortgage statement.
- Paying a third party to assist with your application may not improve your likelihood of receiving a mortgage modification. Beware of individuals or companies that ask you for payment, or tout their success rate. In particular, avoid any businesses that:
  - pressure you to sign papers you haven't had a chance to read thoroughly or that you don't understand;
  - offer to buy your house for cash for much lower than the selling price of similar houses in your neighborhood.

- Beware of individuals or companies that offer money-back guarantees or insist on up-front fees and can accept payment only by cashier's check or wire transfer.
- Beware of individuals or companies that advise you to stop making your mortgage payments or discontinue contact with your mortgage company.
- Do not sign over the deed to your property to any individual or organization unless you are working directly with your mortgage company to forgive your debt.
- You can apply for mortgage assistance on your own or with free help from a HUD-approved housing counseling agency. For more information and help with your application, call a housing counselor at 888-995-HOPETM (4673). To find a HUD-approved housing counseling agency near you, access HUD's database for Foreclosure Avoidance Counseling.

ADDITIONAL RESOURCES:

- Call 888-995-HOPE (4673) to report a suspected scam and to get mortgage help.
- The Federal Trade Commission (FTC) is the nation's consumer protection agency. If a business doesn't make good on its promises or cheats, the FTC wants to know.
- Submit a CFPB complaint online with the Consumer Financial Protection Bureau (CFPB), or call 1-855-411-CFPB (2372).

Sources: Board of Governors of the Federal Reserve System, https://www.federalreserve.gov/pubs/foreclosurescamtips/foreclosurescamtips.pdf, accessed May 8, 2021.

In addition to limited liability, a real estate syndicate provides professional management for its members. A syndicate that owns several properties may also provide diversification.

REAL ESTATE INVESTMENT TRUSTS   Another way to invest in real estate is the **real estate investment trust (REIT)**, which is similar to a mutual fund or an investment company and trades on stock exchanges or over the counter. Like mutual funds, REITs pool investor funds. These funds, along with borrowed funds, are invested in real estate or used to make construction or mortgage loans.

There are three types of REITs: equity REITs, mortgage REITs, and hybrid REITs. *Equity REITs* own and operate income-producing real estate. They increasingly have become real estate operating companies engaged in leasing, maintaining, and developing real property and tenant services. About 90 percent of REITs are equity REITs,

real estate investment trust (REIT) A firm that pools investor funds and invests them in real estate or uses them to make construction or mortgage loans.

smart money minute

Most frequently asked questions about REITs, such as, "Who invests in REITs?" "Why should you invest in REITs?" and "What should you look for before investing in a REIT?" are answered on the National Association of Real Estate Investment Trusts website at www.reit.com, or call 1-800-3NAREIT.

The REIT story is an economic success story. Investing in commercial real estate is a reality for all investors.
Prawel Gaul/Getty Images

and their revenues mostly come from rents. *Mortgage REITs,* about 7 percent of all REITs, loan money to real estate owners or invest in existing mortgages. *Hybrid REITs* are combinations of mortgage and equity REITs.

You can buy or sell shares in REITs as easily as you buy or sell shares in any other publicly traded company. REIT shares are traded on all of the major stock exchanges, including the New York Stock Exchange and NASDAQ. As in the case of equity investments in other publicly traded companies, you have no personal liability for the debts of the REITs in which you invest.

Federal law requires REITs to:

- Distribute at least 90 percent of their taxable annual earnings to shareholders.
- Refrain from engaging in speculative, short-term holding of real estate to sell for quick profits.
- Hire independent real estate professionals to carry out certain management activities.
- Have at least 100 shareholders; no more than half the shares may be owned by five or fewer people.
- Invest at least 75 percent of the total assets in real estate.

Today, REITs invest in apartment buildings, hospitals, hotels, industrial facilities, nursing homes, office buildings, shopping malls, storage centers, student housing, and timberlands. Most REITs specialize in one property type only, such as shopping malls, timberlands, or self-storage facilities.

You may choose from among more than 1,100 REITs. Further information on REITs is available from the National Association of Real Estate Investment Trusts, 1875 I Street, N.W., Suite 600, Washington, DC 20006-5413, online at www.reit.com, or by phone at 1-800-3NAREIT.

INVESTING IN FIRST AND SECOND MORTGAGES   Mortgages and other debt contracts are commonly purchased by more well-to-do investors. The purchaser of a mortgage may take on some sort of risk that is unacceptable to the financial institutions from which mortgage financing is ordinarily obtained. Perhaps the mortgage is on a property for which there is no ready market. The title to the property may not be legally clear, or the title may not be insurable. Nevertheless, many people purchase such mortgages. These investments may provide relatively high rates of return due to their special risk characteristics.

participation certificate (PC)
An equity investment in a pool of mortgages that have been purchased by a government agency, such as Ginnie Mae.

PARTICIPATION CERTIFICATES   If you want a risk-proof real estate investment, participation certificates (PCs) are for you. A **participation certificate (PC)** is an equity investment in a pool of mortgages or student loans that have been purchased by one of several government agencies. Participation certificates are sold by federal agencies such as the Government National Mortgage Association (Ginnie Mae), the Federal Home Loan Mortgage Corporation (Freddie Mac), the Federal National Mortgage Association (Fannie Mae), and the Student Loan Marketing Association (Sallie Mae). A few states issue "little siblings," such as the State of New York Mortgage Agency (Sonny Mae) and the New England Education Loan Marketing Corporation (Nellie Mae).

Maes and Macs are guaranteed by agencies closely tied to the federal government, making them as secure as U.S. Treasury bonds and notes. At one time, you needed a minimum of $25,000 to invest in PCs. Thanks to Maes and Macs mutual funds, you now need as little as $1,000 to buy shares in a unit trust or a mutual fund whose portfolio

Financial Literacy for My Life

UNCLE SAM AND HIS FAMILY

The government securities named Maes and Macs can offer safety and relatively high yields.

1. **Ginnie Mae—Government National Mortgage Association (GNMA).** Established in 1968, the GNMA introduced the first mortgage-backed securities in 1970 and still dominates this market. The residential mortgage-backed securities are packaged in pools and then resold to investors as certificates ($25,000) or as shares by mutual funds. Regular payments to investors are guaranteed by the GNMA, an agency of the Department of Housing and Urban Development. Ginnie Maes are backed by the full faith and credit of the federal government. The average life of mortgages is 12 years.

2. **Freddie Mac—Federal Home Loan Mortgage Corporation (FHLMC).** Created by Congress in 1970, the agency issues mortgage-backed securities similar to Ginnie Maes. The pools of fixed-rate home mortgages are made up of conventional home loans rather than mortgages insured by the FHA or the VA. The timely payment of interest and the *ultimate* payment of principal are guaranteed. Over five decades, Freddie Mac has provided more than $11 *trillion* to help more than 69 million homeowners and 11 million renters.

3. **Fannie Mae—Federal National Mortgage Association (FNMA).** Created in 1938, the agency issues mortgage-backed securities similar to Ginnie Maes and Freddie Macs. Newly issued Fannie Mae certificates require a minimum investment of $25,000; the older certificates (whose principal has been partially paid off) require an investment of as little as $10,000. FNMA has been a publicly traded company since 1968.

4. **Sallie Mae—Student Loan Marketing Association (SLM Corporation).** This agency was created by Congress in 1972 to provide a national secondary market for government-guaranteed student loans. It issues bonds, each backed by Sallie Mae as a whole rather than as specific pools of loans. Sallie Mae bonds are considered as safe as government Treasuries. Brokers sell bonds having minimum denominations of $10,000. You can also buy shares of Sallie Mae *stock;* the corporation is government chartered but publicly owned, and its shares are traded on the New York Stock Exchange.

5. **Sonny Mae (SONYMA)—State of New York Mortgage Agency.** Since 1970, Sonny Mae has issued bonds backed by fixed-rate, single-family home mortgages and uses proceeds to subsidize below-market-rate mortgages for first-time home buyers. As with ordinary bonds, interest on Sonny Maes is paid only until the bonds mature. Sonny Maes are exempt from federal income tax, and New York State residents do not pay state income tax on them.

6. **Nellie Mae—New England Education Loan Marketing Corporation.** A nonprofit corporation created in 1982 by the Commonwealth of Massachusetts. Provides a secondary market for federally guaranteed student loans issued in Massachusetts and New Hampshire. It has been a wholly owned subsidiary of Sallie Mae since 1999. The AAA-rated Nellie Mae bonds mature in three years and are sold in minimum denominations of $5,000.

consists entirely of these securities. Either way, you assume the role of a mortgage or student loan lender. Each month, as payments are made on the mortgages or loans, you receive interest and principal by check, or, if you wish, the mutual fund will reinvest the amount for you.

See the *Financial Literacy for My Life: Uncle Sam and His Family* feature, which describes various types of participation certificates sold by federal and state agencies.

 PRACTICE QUIZ 17-1

1. What are four examples of direct investments in real estate?
2. What are four examples of indirect investments in real estate?
3. What is a syndicate? An REIT? A participation certificate (PC)?

Advantages of Real Estate Investments

LO17-2

Evaluate the advantages of real estate investments.

For many types of real estate investments, blanket statements about their investment advantages and disadvantages are not possible. However, certain types of real estate investments may possess some of the advantages discussed in this section.

A POSSIBLE HEDGE AGAINST INFLATION

Real property equity investments usually (but not always) provide protection against purchasing power risk, also known as inflation. In some areas, the prices of homes have increased consistently.

my life 2

Generally, an investment in real estate is . . .

Before you invest in real estate, you should weigh the advantages and disadvantages. Real estate investments provide some protection against inflation. Historically, real estate continues to increase in value or at least holds its value, thus protecting you from declining purchasing power.

EASY ENTRY

You can gain entry to a shopping center or a large apartment building investment by investing $5,000 as a limited partner. (A limited partner's liability is restricted by the amount of his or her investment. A limited partner cannot take part in the management of the partnership.) The minimum capital requirements for the total venture may be as high as $1 million or more, which is beyond the limits of a typical real estate investor.

LIMITED FINANCIAL LIABILITY

If you are a limited partner, you are not liable for losses beyond your initial investment. This can be important if the venture is speculative and rewards are not assured. General partners, however, must bear all financial risks.

NO MANAGEMENT CONCERNS

If you have invested in limited partnerships, REITs, mortgages, or participation certificates, you need not worry about paperwork and accounting, maintenance chores, and other administrative duties.

FINANCIAL LEVERAGE

Financial leverage is the use of borrowed funds for investment purposes. It enables you to acquire a more expensive property than you could on your own. This is an advantage when property values and incomes are rising. Assume you buy a $100,000 property with no loan and then sell it for $120,000. The $20,000 gain represents a 20 percent return on your $100,000 investment. Now assume you invest only $10,000 of your own money and borrow the other $90,000 (90 percent financing). Now you have made $20,000 on your $10,000 investment, or a 200 percent return. Of course, you will have to deduct the interest paid on the borrowed money.

✔ PRACTICE QUIZ 17-2

1. What are the advantages of real estate investments?
2. How is financial leverage calculated?

Disadvantages of Real Estate Investments

Real estate investments have several disadvantages. However, these disadvantages do not affect all kinds of real estate investments to the same extent.

LO17-3

Assess the disadvantages of real estate investments.

ILLIQUIDITY

Perhaps the largest drawback of direct real estate investments is the absence of large, liquid, and relatively efficient markets for them. Whereas stocks or bonds generally can be sold in a few minutes at the market price, this is not the case for real estate. It may take months to sell commercial property or limited partnership shares.

DECLINING PROPERTY VALUES

As discussed earlier, real property investments usually provide a hedge against inflation. But during deflationary and recessionary periods, the value of such investments may decline. For example, thousands of developers, lenders, and investors were victims of a deflation in commercial real estate in the 1980s and in 2007–2009.

LACK OF DIVERSIFICATION

Diversification in direct real estate investments is difficult because of the large size of most real estate projects. REITs, Ginnie Maes, Freddie Macs, and other syndicates, however, do provide various levels of diversification.

LACK OF A TAX SHELTER

The Tax Reform Act of 1986 limits taxpayers' ability to use losses generated by real estate investments to offset income gained from other sources. Thus, investors cannot deduct their real estate losses from income generated by wages, salaries, dividends, and interest. In short, the tax shelter aspect of real estate syndicates no longer exists.

Beginning in 2018, the Tax Cuts and Jobs Act of 2017 limits the mortgage interest deduction to $750,000 (down from $1 million) for your primary residence if you file a joint return; it doubled the standard deduction, which would reduce the number of households that would deduct mortgage interest; and finally, the law places limits on who can claim, and how often they can claim, the capital gains exclusions when selling a house.

my life 3

One of the disadvantages of investing in real estate is . . .

Unfortunately, there are several possible disadvantages to real estate investments. One of these is that real estate is an illiquid investment, which means that it cannot be easily converted into cash without a loss in value. It may take months or even years to sell real property or shares in a limited partnership.

LONG DEPRECIATION PERIOD

Before the Tax Reform Act of 1986 went into effect, commercial real estate could be depreciated within 18 years. Under the accelerated cost recovery system (ACRS), adopted in 1980, an investor was allowed to use accelerated depreciation methods to recover the costs. Now investors must use the straight-line depreciation method over 27½ years for residential real estate and over 31½ years for all other types of real estate.

Other provisions of the 1986 act affect real estate investments, and all reduce the value of the tax credits for such investments. Investors are not allowed to take losses in excess of the actual amounts they invest. Furthermore, the investment tax credit has been eliminated entirely for all types of real estate except low-income housing projects.

MANAGEMENT PROBLEMS

Although investments in limited partnerships, REITs, mortgages, and participation certificates do not create management problems, buying individual properties does. Along with the buildings come the responsibilities of management: finding reliable tenants, buying new carpeting, fixing the furnace when it breaks down in the middle of the night, and so on. Many people aren't willing to take on these responsibilities. "This is one reason I dislike small real estate investments," says one financial planner. "There should be a large enough amount of money that it is very important to you and you pay a lot of attention to it. Otherwise it won't work."

If you believe investing in real estate is too risky or too complicated, you might want to consider other tangible investments such as gold and other precious metals, gems, and collectibles. But remember, these investments entail both risk and reward.

 **PRACTICE QUIZ 17-3**

1. What are the disadvantages of real estate investments?
2. What depreciation method is used for residential real estate?

Investing in Precious Metals, Gems, and Collectibles

LO17-4

Analyze the risks and rewards of investing in precious metals, gems, and collectibles.

When the economy picks up, some investors predict higher inflation. Therefore, many think precious metals such as gold, platinum, and silver will regain some of their glitter. In this section, we discuss several methods for buying precious metals.

GOLD

Gold prices tend to be driven up by factors such as fear of war, political instability, and inflation. On the other hand, easing of international tensions or disinflation causes a decline in gold prices. High interest rates also depress gold prices because they make it very expensive to carry gold as an investment.

Many people have acquired gold directly. Many others have invested in gold through a number of other kinds of investments that serve a variety of purposes. Some of these investments promise quick profits at high risk, others preserve capital, and still others provide income from dividends or interest. But all of them are subject to daily gold price fluctuations. Exhibit 17-3 shows gold price fluctuations between 1976 and February 2021. Gold soared to $1,908 an ounce in midday trading on August 22, 2011, and dropped to $1,751 on April 12, 2021. It's still below its inflation-adjusted peak of about $2,200, which it hit in 1980. More gold is in jewelry than in government reserves.

GOLD BULLION   Gold bullion includes gold bars and wafers. The basic unit of gold bullion is 1 kilogram (32.15 troy ounces) of 0.995 fine gold. Coin dealers, precious metals dealers, and some banks sell gold bullion in amounts ranging from 5 grams (16/100 of a troy ounce) to 500 ounces or more. According to industry specialists Gold Bars Worldwide, there are 94 accredited bar manufacturers and brands in 26 countries, producing a total of more than 400 types of standard gold bars. They normally contain 99.5 percent fine gold. The Gold Bars Worldwide website, www.goldbarsworldwide.com, provides a wealth of information about the international gold bar market. On small bars, dealers and banks add a 5 to 8 percent premium over the pure gold bullion value; on larger bars, the premium is usually 1 to 2 percent. Gold bullion poses storage and insurance problems, and unless the gold bar or wafer remains in the custody of the bank or dealer that sells it initially, it must be reassayed (retested for fineness) before being sold.

EXHIBIT 17-3

Fluctuations in the price of gold since 1976

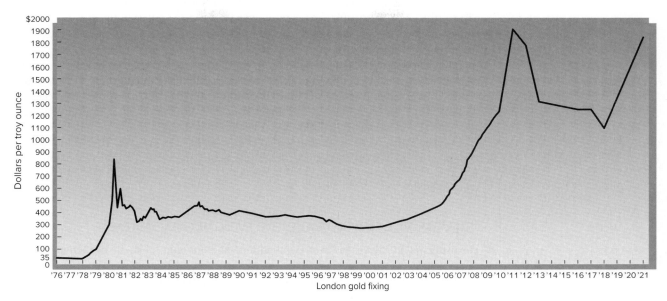

London gold fixing

GOLD BULLION COINS   You can avoid storage and assaying problems by investing in gold bullion coins. In the early 1980s, before South Africa's political problems intensified, South African krugerrands were the most popular gold bullion coins in the United States. Popular gold bullion coins today include Australia's kangaroo nugget, the Canadian gold maple leaf, the Mexican 50 peso, the Austrian 100 koronas, the British sovereign, Chinese Panda, and Austria's Vienna Philharmonic. The American eagle gold coin, the first gold bullion coin ever produced by the U.S. government, was first issued in late 1986. Today, the U.S. Mint produces gold, silver, and platinum bullion coins and guarantees their precious metal content. The Mint produces two types of bullion coins:

- *Proof bullion coins,* which are specially minted for collectors and usually sold in a protective display case directly by the Mint.
- *Uncirculated bullion coins,* which are minted for investment purposes and sold to a select number of authorized buyers based on the current market price (the spot price) for the precious metal plus a small premium charged by the Mint.

Foreign governments also mint coins, but they may not be produced to the same standards as U.S. coins, and they aren't guaranteed by the U.S. government. The value of foreign bullion coins depends primarily upon the coin's melt value—the basic intrinsic bullion value of a coin if it were melted and sold. A bullion coin's condition—its "grade"—isn't the most relevant factor in determining its price.

Most brokers require a minimum order of 10 coins and charge a commission of at least 2 percent. Don't confuse bullion coins with commemorative or numismatic coins, whose value depends on their rarity, design, and finish rather than on their fine gold content. Many dealers sell both.

GOLD STOCKS   In addition to investing in gold bullion and gold bullion coins, you may invest in gold by purchasing the common stocks of gold mining companies. Over 300 gold mining companies are listed on the U.S. stock exchanges. Among the gold mining stocks listed on U.S. stock exchanges are those of Barrick Gold Corp., Goldcorp Inc., Newmont Mining Corp., and Golden Star Resources Ltd. Because such stocks often move in a direction opposite to that of the stock market as a whole, they may provide excellent portfolio diversification. You may also wish to examine exchange traded funds (ETFs) for precious metals.

GOLD CERTIFICATES   Historically, gold certificates were issued by the U.S. Treasury from the Civil War until 1933. Denominated in dollars, these certificates were used as part of the gold standard and could be exchanged for an equal value of gold. These U.S. Treasury gold certificates have been out of circulation for many years, and they have become collectibles. They were initially replaced by silver certificates and later by Federal Reserve notes.

Nowadays, gold certificates offer you a method of holding gold without taking physical delivery. Issued by individual banks, particularly in countries like Germany and Switzerland, they confirm your ownership while the bank holds the metal on your behalf. You save on storage and personal security problems and gain liquidity because you can sell portions of the holdings (if need be) by simply telephoning the custodian bank. The Perth Mint in Australia also runs a certificate program that is guaranteed by the government of Western Australia and is distributed in a number of countries.

Read the nearby *Financial Literacy for My Life* feature, "Is Gold a Solid Investment?"

SILVER, PLATINUM, PALLADIUM, AND RHODIUM

Investments in silver, platinum, palladium, and rhodium, like investments in gold, are used as a hedge against inflation and as a safe haven during political or economic upheavals. During the last 90 years, silver prices ranged from a historic low of 24.25 cents an ounce in 1932, to over $50 an ounce in early 1980, and then back to $27.49 an ounce on May 15, 2021.

Three lesser-known precious metals, platinum, palladium, and rhodium, are also popular investments. All have industrial uses as catalysts, particularly in automobile production. Some investors think increased car sales worldwide could mean higher prices for these metals. In early 2021, platinum sold for about $1,115 an ounce and palladium for about $2,306 an ounce. The rhodium price in June 2008 was about $9,750 per ounce, but it dropped to only $500 in late 2006 and then rose to $28,000 in May 2021. Remember, however, if you are *selling* your collection to precious metals dealers, you will get considerably less than these prices.

As discussed earlier, finding storage for your precious metals can be tricky. While $20,000 in gold, for example, occupies only as much space as a paperback book, $20,000 in silver weighs more than 70 pounds and could require a few safe-deposit boxes. Such boxes, moreover, are not insured against fire and theft.

You should remember too that, unlike stocks, bonds, and other interest-bearing investments, precious metals sit in vaults earning nothing. And whether you profit on an eventual sale depends entirely on how well you call the market.

No wonder the Commodity Futures Trading Commission advises not to take cash from your retirement accounts and invest it in gold, silver, or other precious metals without consulting licensed or registered financial, tax, or legal advisors. Since the Coronavirus Aid, Relief, and Economic Security Act (CARES Act) was passed in response to the COVID-19 pandemic in 2020, a growing number of precious metals promoters and dealers are encouraging investors to convert their savings into gold or silver IRAs. (Individual retirement accounts are discussed in Chapter 18.)

PRECIOUS STONES

Precious stones include diamonds, sapphires, rubies, and emeralds. Precious stones appeal to investors because of their small size, ease of concealment, great durability, and potential as a hedge against inflation. Inflation and investor interest in

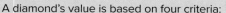

smart money minute

A diamond's value is based on four criteria:

- **Color** often is graded on a scale established by the Gemological Institute of America (GIA). On the GIA scales, color is rated from D to Z, with D at the top.
- **Cut** refers to the quality of how the diamond has been shaped, taking into account the diamond's proportions, polish, and symmetry.
- **Clarity** measures the natural imperfections in the stone. On the GIA scales, clarity is rated from flawless to I3. A diamond can be described as "flawless" only if it has no visible surface or internal imperfections when viewed under 10-power magnification by a skilled diamond grader.
- **Carat** refers to the stone's weight.

Financial Literacy for My Life

IS GOLD A SOLID INVESTMENT?

It's true that people sometimes use gold to diversify their investment portfolio: It helps hedge against inflation and economic uncertainty. How much gold to buy, in what form, at what price, and from whom, are important questions to answer before you make that investment. Some gold promoters don't deliver what they promise and may push you into an investment that isn't right for you.

ALL GOLD IS NOT CREATED EQUAL

There are several ways to invest in gold.

1. Gold Stocks and Funds—You can buy stock in a gold mining firm or purchase a mutual fund that invests in gold bullion. Gold stocks and mutual funds may offer more liquidity than actual gold, and there is no need for you to store or insure gold. However, any gold stock or mutual fund may carry inherent risk and may drop in value regardless of the price of gold.

2. Bullion and Bullion Coins—Bullion is a bulk quantity of precious metal, usually gold, platinum, or silver, assessed by weight and typically cast as ingots or bars. Dealers and some banks and brokerage firms sell bullion. Bullion coins are struck from precious metal—usually gold, platinum, or silver—and kept as an investment. The value of bullion coins is determined mostly by their precious metals content rather than by rarity and condition. Prices may change throughout the day, depending on the prices for precious metals in the world markets. Coin dealers and some banks, brokerage firms, and precious metal dealers buy and sell bullion coins. The U.S. Mint has produced gold and silver bullion coins for investment purposes since 1986 and began producing platinum bullion coins in 1997. The U.S. Mint guarantees the precious metal weight, content, and purity of the coins.

3. Collectible Coins—These coins have some historic or aesthetic value to coin collectors. Most collectible coins have a market value that exceeds their face value or their metal content. This collectible value is often called numismatic value. The coin dealers who sell collectible coins often have valuable coins graded by professional services, but grading can be subjective.

INVESTIGATE BEFORE YOU INVEST

Whether you are buying gold stocks and funds, bullion and bullion coins, or collectible coins, the Federal Trade Commission offers these cautions.

- If you are buying bullion coins or collectible coins, ask for the coin's melt value—the basic intrinsic bullion value of a coin if it were melted and sold. The melt value for virtually all bullion coins and collectible coins is widely available.

- Consult with a reputable dealer or financial advisor you trust who has specialized knowledge.

- Get an independent appraisal of the specific gold product you're considering. The seller's appraisal might be inflated.

- Consider additional costs. You may need to buy insurance, a safe-deposit box, or rent offsite storage to safeguard bullion. These costs will reduce the investment potential of bullion.

- Some sellers deliver bullion or bars to a secured facility rather than to a consumer. When you buy metals without taking delivery, take extra precautions to ensure that the metal exists, is of the quality described, and is properly insured.

- Walk away from sales pitches that minimize risk or sales representatives who claim that risk disclosures are mere formalities. Reputable sales reps are honest about the risk of particular investments. Always get a receipt for your transaction.

- Refuse to "act now." Any sales pitch that urges you to buy immediately is a signal to walk away and hold on to your money.

- Check out the seller by entering the company's name in a search engine online. Read about other investors' experiences with the company. In addition, contact your state attorney general and local consumer protection agency. This research is prudent, although it isn't fool-proof.

To summarize, before you invest, investigate: Take your time, do some research, get details, be skeptical, find out who you are dealing with, and ask if the investment has a track record.

Sources: Federal Trade Commission, www.consumer.ftc.gov/articles/0136 -investing-collectible-coins, accessed June 12, 2018, and www.consumer.ftc .gov/articles/0134-investing-gold, accessed June 12, 2018.

tangible assets helped increase diamond prices 40-fold between 1970 and 1980. A few lucky investors made fortunes, and brokerage and diamond firms took up the investment diamond business.

Whether you are buying precious stones to store in a safe-deposit box or to wear around your neck, there are a few risks to keep in mind. Diamonds and other precious stones are not easily turned into cash. It is difficult to determine whether you are getting a good stone. Diamond prices can be affected by the whims of De Beers Consolidated Mines of

South Africa Ltd., which controls 85 percent of the world's supply of rough diamonds, and by political instability in diamond-producing countries. Moreover, you should expect to buy at retail and sell at wholesale, a difference of at least 10 to 15 percent and perhaps as much as 50 percent.

The best way to know exactly what you are getting, especially if you are planning to spend more than $10,000, is to insist that your stone be certified by an independent geological laboratory, one not connected with a diamond-selling organization. (The acknowledged industry leader in this area is the Gemological Institute of America.) The certificate should list the stone's characteristics, including its weight, color, clarity, and quality of cut. The grading of diamonds, however, is not an exact science, and recent experiments have shown that when the same diamond is submitted twice to the same institute, it can get two different ratings.

Michael Roman, former chairman of the Jewelers of America, a trade group representing 12,000 retailers, stated that his group did not recommend diamonds as an investment and scoffed at the notion that local retail jewelers were realizing huge profits on diamond sales to misguided customers. He also did not believe in certification unless the stone in question was a high-grade diamond weighing at least one carat.

collectibles Rare coins, works of art, antiques, stamps, rare books, and other items that appeal to collectors and investors.

COLLECTIBLES

Collectibles include rare coins, works of art, antiques, stamps, rare books, sports memorabilia, rugs, Chinese ceramics, paintings, and other items that appeal to collectors and investors. Each of these items offers the knowledgeable collector/investor both pleasure and the opportunity for profit. Many collectors have discovered only incidentally that items they bought for their own pleasure had gained greatly in value while they owned them.

COLLECTIBLES ON THE WEB   Before the era of the internet, author and antiques collector David Maloney had to search far and wide to find a 1950s cut crystal Val St. Lambert pitcher. No one in his hometown of Frederick, Maryland, carried fancy glassware, he says, "and I would spend days driving around to yard sales and little shops." Recently, though, Maloney logged onto the internet and, in only 15 seconds, found a store in Pennsylvania that carries 40 styles of his prized crystal.

my life **4**

Drawbacks of finding collectibles on the Internet include . . .

Before the era of the World Wide Web, finding items to add to your collections could be very time-consuming. The internet has made buying and selling collectibles efficient and convenient, and the number of websites for collectors has exploded. Unfortunately, as an online buyer, you cannot assess a dealer face-to-face or examine the objects for flaws or trademarks.

Whether you collect glassware, home-run baseballs, or Ming vases, you no longer need to travel to far-flung antiques fairs or pore over trade magazines to add to your collection. The world of collectibles has expanded onto the web, bringing unprecedented efficiency and convenience to a collector's market. The explosion of online collecting and the success of the biggest auction site, eBay, prompted Guernsey's Auction House to open the bidding for Mark McGwire's 70th home-run baseball to online buyers as well as those in the salesroom. (It went for $3 million to an anonymous phone bidder.)

It's easy to see why the web has such appeal. Buyers can target obscure items with a few keystrokes, and sellers can reach a much larger, more varied market. Of course, online buyers can't kick the tires or size up dealers face to face. But fraud is rampant, and preventive measures are increasing.

Although you can find antique armoires and vintage cars, dealers say the web is best suited to smaller items, such as books, coins, stamps, buttons, and textiles, that can be easily scanned for viewing and shipped by mail.

Prices aren't necessarily cheaper on the web, but it's much easier to compare them, and most sites don't charge a buyer's commission. To purchase an early edition of Mark Twain's *The Adventures of Tom Sawyer,* for example, use a search engine to view descriptions of dealers' inventories. The site will provide details on the condition, publisher, and price of the book. Most editions of *Tom Sawyer* published in

Many collectors have been surprised to learn that their old belongings have attained considerable value over the years.
parema/Getty Images

PREVENTING FRAUD

Looking for an online investment opportunity that is "unaffected by the volatile stock market," guarantees "virtually unlimited profits," "minimizes or eliminates risk factors," and is "IRA approved"?

"Forget it," advises Jodie Bernstein, director of the Federal Trade Commission's Bureau of Consumer Protection. "Claims that an investment is IRA approved are a tip-off to a rip-off. You must be just as careful when investing in opportunities touted on the Net as you are when you make other investments. You should check out these with state securities regulators and other investment professionals." For more information about investing on the internet, Bernstein suggests that you contact the following organizations:

- Federal Trade Commission (www.ftc.gov)
- North American Securities Administrators Association Inc. (www.nasaa.org)
- Commodity Futures Trading Commission (www.cftc.gov)
- National Association of Securities Dealers (www.nasd.com)
- Securities and Exchange Commission (www.sec.gov)
- National Association of Investors Corporation (www.better-investing.org)
- The Motley Fool (www.fool.com)
- Alliance for Investor Education (www.investoreducation.org)
- The Online Investor (www.theonlineinvestor.com)
- National Fraud Information Center (www.fraud.org)

the 20th century sell for about $10, but a first British edition from 1898 lists for $350. Because the internet has opened up a wider market, items that probably wouldn't sell at a local antiques show can find an appropriate home.

Still, virtual collecting has drawbacks. Buyers can't examine objects for flaws or trademarks. Many knowledgeable old-time dealers aren't computer literate, while some collectors prefer the thrill of hunting in out-of-the-way junk shops. "The average person still wants to see and feel the antiques," says Terry Kovel, author of *Kovel's Antiques & Collectibles Price List.* "An awful lot of antiques purchases are emotional, because someone walks into a store and sees an object they had as a kid."

A more serious concern, perhaps, is the security risk of buying online when you don't know who's getting your cash or credit card number. Collectors do take gambles, but for many happy hunters, the increased selection and convenience of shopping on the web far outweigh its dangers.

Also, read the *Financial Literacy for My Life: Preventing Fraud* feature.

CAVEAT EMPTOR Collecting can be a good investment and a satisfying hobby, but for many Americans it has recently become a financial disaster. For example, as the market for paintings by Pablo Picasso and Andy Warhol has exploded, forgeries have become a significant problem. Art experts and law enforcement officials say that a new generation of collectors is being victimized by forgeries more sophisticated, more expensive, and more difficult to detect than ever before.

Forgeries or not, art prices are booming. For example, a single painting, a van Gogh called *Portrait of Dr. Gachet,* which sold for an all-time record of $82.5 million in 1990, had been up for sale privately for months. The minimum asking price: $80 million. An 1889 self-portrait believed to be the last painted by van Gogh sold for $71.5 million.

Nostalgia and limited availability will also fuel certain markets. With failed airlines and railroads becoming distant memories, count on Pan Am wing pins and Pullman porter badges to go up in value. Fanaticism, combined with a dwindling supply, will also push up prices of rock-and-roll record albums.

smart money minute

Many buyers of collectible coins make the *mistake* of putting faith in "buy back" offers for these coins. Dishonest sellers fail to honor the option, or fail to disclose commissions and other fees attached to the option. In these cases, you may find that your real options for *action* are to hold the collectible coins or sell them at a loss on the open market. You may achieve *success* if you sell your collection at a later time, though that is not guaranteed.

personal fintech

When buying jewelry, precious stones, or collectibles, compare quality, price, and service from several different sellers. Consider asking family members, friends, or coworkers for recommendations. Check a seller's reputation by doing online search. Enter the seller's name and the words "complaint" or "review" in a search engine. Ask for the store's refund and return policy.

Collecting for investment purposes is very different from collecting as a hobby. Like investing in real estate or the stock market, investing in collectibles should be approached with care. Don't consider collectibles as your savings plan for retirement, and be especially careful if you buy from online auctions.

Investment counselors caution that collectibles do not provide interest or dividends, that it may be difficult to sell them at the right price on short notice, and that if they become valuable enough, they must be appraised periodically and insured against loss or theft.

See the *How To . . . Buy Authentic Indian Arts and Crafts for Fun or Investment* feature for some tips on evaluating a particular type of Native American arts and crafts.

HOW TO . . .   Buy Authentic Indian Arts and Crafts for Fun or Investment

Whether you're drawn to the beauty of turquoise and silver jewelry or the earth-toned colors of American Indian pottery, having some knowledge about Native American arts and crafts can help you get the most for your money. Be aware also that because American Indian arts and crafts are prized and often command higher prices, a few unscrupulous sellers misrepresent imitation arts and crafts as genuine.

BUYING TIPS

Native American arts and crafts are sold through many outlets, including tourist stores, gift shops, and art galleries. Here are some tips to help you shop wisely:

Buying Tips

Familiarize yourself with the Indian Arts and Crafts Act of 1990.

Buy from an established dealer.

Get a receipt that includes all the vital information about the value of your purchase, including any verbal representations.

Before buying Indian arts and crafts at powwows, annual fairs, juried competitions, and other events, check the event requirements for information about the authenticity of the products being offered for sale.

Know your recourse if you have a complaint.

Why Is This important

The Indian Arts and Crafts Act of 1990 helps ensure that buyers of American Indian arts and crafts products get what they pay for by making it illegal to misrepresent that a product is made by an Indian. You can obtain more information about the Indian Arts and Crafts Act and related regulations by visiting the website of the Indian Arts and Crafts Board, www .iacb.doi.gov, or by calling the Board's toll-free number, 1-888-ART-FAKE.

Well-established and reputable dealers should always be able to give you a written guarantee or written verification of authenticity.

Your receipt will help protect you and your investment. If the salesperson told you that the piece of jewelry you're buying is sterling silver and natural turquoise and was handmade by an American Indian artisan, insist that this information appear on your receipt as proof of what you have been told.

Many legitimate events list the requirements in newspaper ads, promotional flyers, and printed programs. If the event organizers make no statements about the authenticity of Indian arts and crafts being offered for sale, get written verification of authenticity for any item you purchase that claims to be authentic.

Even in specialized markets, there are associations that protect consumers. The Indian Arts and Crafts Board receives and refers valid complaints about violations of the Indian Arts and Crafts Act to the FBI for investigation and to the Department of Justice for legal action. To file a complaint under the Act or to get free information about the Act, call the Indian Arts and Crafts Board, U.S. Department of the Interior, toll free at 1-888-278-3253 or use the online complaint form at www.iacb.doi.gov.

Financial Literacy for My Life

INVESTING IN BITCOIN AND OTHER VIRTUAL CURRENCY-RELATED INVESTMENTS

The U.S. Commodity Futures Trading Commission (CFTC) warns of possible risks associated with investing or speculating in virtual currencies or recently launched Bitcoin futures and options.

Bitcoin, the world's largest cryptocurrency, is a decentralized, peer-to-peer virtual currency that is used like money—it can be exchanged for traditional currencies such as the U.S. dollar, or used to purchase goods or services, usually online. Unlike traditional currencies, Bitcoin operates without central authority or banks, and it is not backed by any government.

Virtual currency is a digital representation of value that functions as a medium of exchange, a unit of account, or a store of value, but it does not have legal tender status. Virtual currencies are sometimes exchanged for U.S. dollars or other currencies around the world. Their value is completely derived by market forces of supply and demand, and they are more volatile than traditional fiat currencies.

WHAT MAKES VIRTUAL CURRENCY RISKY?

Purchasing virtual currencies on the market—spending dollars to purchase Bitcoin for your personal wallet, for example—comes with a number of risks, including:

- Cryptocurrency markets are not regulated or supervised by a government agency.
- Platforms in the cryptocurrency market lack critical system safeguards, including customer protections.
- There can be volatile market price swings or flash crashes.
- Cryptocurrency markets can be manipulated.
- There are cyber risks, such as hacking customer wallets.
- Platforms selling from their own accounts can put customers at an unfair disadvantage.

It's also important to note that market changes that affect the cash market price of a virtual currency may ultimately affect the price of virtual currency futures and options.

BEWARE OF RELATED FRAUD

Virtual currencies are commonly targeted by hackers and criminals who commit fraud. There is no assurance of recourse if your virtual currency is stolen. Be careful how and where you store your virtual currency. The CFTC has received complaints about virtual currency exchange scams, as well as Ponzi and "pyramid" schemes. If you decide to buy virtual currencies, remember these tips:

- If someone tries to sell you an investment in options or futures on virtual currencies, including Bitcoin, verify they are registered with the CFTC. Visit SmartCheck.gov to check registrations or learn more about common investment frauds.
- Remember that much of the virtual currency cash market operates through internet-based trading platforms that may be unregulated and unsupervised.
- Do not invest in products or strategies you do not understand.
- Be sure you understand the risks and how the product can lose money, as well as the likelihood of loss. Only speculate with money you can afford to lose.
- There is no such thing as a guaranteed investment or trading strategy. If someone tells you there is no risk of losing money, do not invest.
- Investors should conduct extensive research into the legitimacy of virtual currency platforms and digital wallets before providing credit card information, wiring money, or offering sensitive personal information.

If you believe you may have been the victim of fraud, contact CFTC at 866.366.2382 or visit CFTC.gov/TipOrComplaint.

Source: https://www.cftc.gov/sites/default/files/idc/groups/public/@customerprotection/documents/file/customeradvisory_urvct121517.pdf, accessed February 7, 2021.

Author's Note: On February 9, 2021, Bitcoin prices soared to a record high of more than $48,000 after Elon Musk disclosed that he had purchased $1.5 billion of the cryptocurrency and might start permitting the use of Bitcoin to purchase Tesla products.

Curious about investing in Bitcoin and cryptocurrencies? Read the *Financial Literacy for My Life: Investing in Bitcoin and Other Virtual Currency–Related Investments* feature for a few tips.

 PRACTICE QUIZ 17-4

1. What are several methods for buying precious metals?
2. Why do precious stones appeal to investors?
3. What are collectibles?
4. How can you protect yourself from fraudulent practices in the collectibles market?

PFP Sheet 77
Investments—Summary

Your Personal Finance Roadmap and Dashboard:

Investing in Alternative Materials

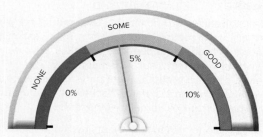

PORTFOLIO DIVERSIFICATION: PRECIOUS METALS, GEMS, AND COLLECTIBLES

You can achieve investment diversification by including a variety of assets in your portfolio—for example, stocks, bonds, mutual funds, real estate, collectibles, and precious metals. Financial experts recommend placing about 10 percent of your investment portfolio in precious metals and other collectibles.

YOUR SITUATION

Are all of your investment eggs in one basket? Do you know that spreading your assets among several different types of investments lessens risk? Are you reducing investment risk by investing in a variety of assets? Is your portfolio properly diversified? What percentage of your assets do you want to invest in stocks, bonds, real estate, and precious metals? Other personal financial planning actions you might consider during various stages of your life include:

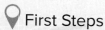 First Steps

- Establish investment and financial goals.
- Work to balance your budget.

- Start an emergency fund.
- Save a reasonable amount of money from each paycheck.
- Revise investment and financial goals.
- Pay off any college loans and other debts.
- Explore different retirement plans.
- Begin investing after careful evaluation of different types of investments.

 Next Steps

- Revise investment and financial goals.
- Continue to evaluate new and current investments.
- Increase your amount of savings and investments.

Later Steps

- Revise investment and financial goals.
- Begin planning for retirement within a specific number of years.
- Increase your amount of savings and investments.
- Consider conservative investment options.
- Continue to evaluate current investments.

YOUR Next Step . . . select one or more of the items above and create an action plan to implement those financial planning activities.

SUMMARY OF LEARNING OBJECTIVES

LO17-1

Identify types of real estate investments. Real estate investments are classified as direct or indirect. Direct real estate investments, in which you hold legal title to the property, include a home, a vacation home, commercial property, and undeveloped land. Indirect real estate investments include real estate syndicates, REITs, mortgages, and participation certificates.

LO17-2

Evaluate the advantages of real estate investments. Real estate investments offer a hedge against inflation, easy entry, limited financial liability, no management headaches, and financial leverage.

LO17-3

Assess the disadvantages of real estate investments. Real estate investments may have the disadvantages of illiquidity, declining values, lack of diversification, lack of a tax shelter, a long depreciation period, and management problems.

LO17-4

Analyze the risks and rewards of investing in precious metals, gems, and collectibles. Some investors prefer to invest in precious metals such as gold, platinum, and silver; precious stones such as diamonds; or collectibles such as stamps, rare coins, works of art, antiques, rare books, and Chinese ceramics. Collectibles do not provide current income, and they may be difficult to sell quickly.

KEY TERMS

collectibles   604

commercial property   593

direct investment   591

indirect investment   591

participation certificate (PC)   596

passive activity   593

passive loss   593

real estate investment trust
   (REIT)   595

syndicate   594

SELF-TEST PROBLEMS

1. You bought a rental property for $150,000 cash. Later you sell the property for $180,000. What was your return on investment?

2. Suppose you invested just $20,000 of your own money and had a $130,000 mortgage with an interest rate of 7.5 percent. After one year you sold the property for $180,000. (a) What is your gross profit? (b) What is your net profit? (c) What is your percent rate of return on investment?

3. Assume your home is assessed at $200,000. You have a $150,000 loan for 15 years at 5 percent. Your property tax rate is 2 percent of the assessed value. Assume you are in a 28 percent federal income tax bracket. By what amount is your federal income tax lowered?

Self-Test Solutions

1. Selling price   = $180,000
   Purchase price = $150,000
   Profit   = $30,000

   Return on investment $\dfrac{\text{Profit}}{\text{Purchase price}}$ $\dfrac{\$30,000}{\$150,000} = .20$, or 20%

2. a. Gross profit = Selling price − Purchase price
          = $180,000 − $150,000 = $30,000

   b. Net profit = Gross profit − Interest paid in one year
          = $30,000 − ($130,000 × .075 × 1)
          = $30,000 − $9,750 = $20,250

   c. Percent return on investment = $\dfrac{\text{Net profit}}{\text{Amount invested}} = \dfrac{\$20,250}{\$20,000} = 1.01$ *or* 101%

3. Assessed value of your home   = $200,000

    Amount of loan   = $150,000

    Term of loan   = 15 years

    Interest rate   = 5%

    Property tax rate   = 2% of assessed value

    Mortgage interest for one year $= \$150,000 \times .05 \times 1$

                = $7,500

    Property tax paid for one year $= \$200,000 \times .02$

                = $4,000

    Total deduction on your federal income tax   = $7,500 + $4,000

                = $11,500

    Assumed tax bracket   = 28%

    Federal income tax lowered by ($11,500 × .28)   = $3,220

FINANCIAL PLANNING PROBLEMS

LO17-1   **1.** *Calculating the Return on Investment.* Dave bought a rental property for $200,000 cash. One year later, he sold it for $240,000. What was the return on his $200,000 investment?

LO17-1   **2.** *Calculating the Return on Investment Using Financial Leverage.* (Refer to Problem 1.) Suppose Dave invested only $20,000 of his own money and borrowed $180,000 interest-free from his rich father. What was his return on investment?

LO17-1   **3.** *Calculating the Rate of Return on Investment.* Rani bought a rental property for $100,000 with no borrowed funds. Later, she sold the building for $120,000. What was her return on investment?

LO17-1   **4.** *Calculating the Rate of Return on Investment Using Financial Leverage.* Suppose Shaan invested just $10,000 of his own money and had a $90,000 mortgage with an interest rate of 8.5 percent. After three years, he sold the property for $120,000.

    a. What is his gross profit?

    b. What is his net profit or loss?

    c. What is the rate of return on investment?

Problems 5 and 6 are based on the following scenario: Felice bought a duplex apartment at a cost of $150,000. Her mortgage payments on the property are $940 per month, $121 of which can be deducted from her income taxes. Her real estate taxes total $1,440 per year, and insurance costs $900 per year. She estimates that she will spend $1,000 each year per apartment for maintenance, replacing appliances, and other costs. The tenants will pay for all utilities.

LO17-1   **5.** *Calculating Profit or Loss on a Rental Property.* What monthly rent must she charge for each apartment to break even?

LO17-1   **6.** *Calculating Profit or Loss on a Rental Property.* What must she charge to make $2,000 in profit each year?

Problems 7 and 8 are based on the following scenario: Assume your home is assessed at $200,000. You have a $150,000 loan for 30 years at 6 percent. Your property tax rate is 1.5 percent of the assessed value. In year one, you would pay $9,000 in mortgage interest and $3,000 in property tax (1.5 percent on $200,000 assessed value).

LO17-1   **7.** *Calculating Net Profit after Taxes.* What is the total deduction you can take on your federal income tax return?

LO17-1   **8.** *Calculating Net Profit after Taxes.* Assuming you are in a 28 percent tax bracket, by what amount would you have lowered your federal income tax?

Problems 9 and 10 are based on the following scenario: Audra owns a rental house. She makes mortgage payments of $600 per month, which include insurance, and pays $1,800 per year in property taxes and maintenance. Utilities are paid by the renter.

LO17-1   **9.** *Determining the Monthly Rent.* How much should Audra charge for monthly rent to cover her costs?

LO17-1   **10.** *Determining the Monthly Rent.* What should Audra charge for monthly rent to make $1,000 profit each year?

Problems 11 and 12 are based on the following scenario: In 1978 Juan bought 50 ounces of gold for $1,750 as protection against rising inflation. He sold half the gold in 1980 at a price of $800 an ounce. Juan sold the other half in 1982 when the price was $400 an ounce.

11. *Calculating a Return on Investment.* What was Juan's profit in 1980 and in 1982? LO17-4

12. *Calculating a Return on Investment.* What would Juan's profit have been if he had sold all of his gold in 1980? LO17-4

Problems 13, 14, and 15 are based on the following scenario: Prema purchased 15 ounces of gold in 2005 for $422 per ounce in order to try to diversify her investment portfolio. She sold a third of her holdings in gold in 2009 at a price of $944 per ounce. She sold the rest of her gold holdings in 2010 for $1,254 per ounce.

13. *Calculating a Return on Investment.* What is Prema's profit in 2009 and 2010? LO17-4

14. *Calculating a Return on Investment.* What would her profit have been if she sold all the gold holdings in 2009? LO17-4

15. *Calculating a Return on Investment.* What if she sold everything in 2010? LO17-4

DIGITAL FINANCIAL LITERACY. . .

INVESTING IN PRECIOUS METALS

Bullion is a bulk quantity of precious metal, usually gold, platinum, or silver, assessed by weight and typically cast as ingots or bars. Dealers and some banks and brokerages sell bullion. Bullion coins are struck from precious metal—usually gold, platinum, or silver—and kept as an investment. They are not used in daily commerce. The value of bullion coins is determined mostly by their precious metals content rather than by rarity and condition. Prices may change throughout the day, depending on the prices for precious metals in the world markets. Coin dealers and some banks, brokerage firms, and precious metal dealers buy and sell bullion coins. The U.S. Mint has produced gold and silver bullion coins for investment purposes since 1986 and began producing platinum bullion coins in 1997. The U.S. Mint guarantees the precious metal weight, content, and purity of the coins they produce.

Action items:

1) Listen to business news on the internet, radio, or television. What are the current quotes for an ounce of gold and an ounce of silver? Are the prices of precious metals going up or down? How do the latest prices compare with the prices quoted in the chapter? What might be some reasons for fluctuations in the prices of precious metals?

2) Check out the seller by entering the company's name in a search engine online. Read about other people's experiences with the company. Try to communicate offline if possible to clarify any details. In addition, contact your **state attorney general** and **local consumer protection agency**. This kind of research is prudent, although it isn't foolproof; it may be too soon for someone to realize they've been defrauded or to have lodged a complaint with the authorities.

FINANCIAL PLANNING CASE

Bogus Brushstroke: Art Fraud

Richard received a letter inviting him to participate in a drawing for a free original lithograph by a famous artist. He was asked to return a postcard with his name, address, and phone number. After he returned the postcard, he was telephoned for more information, including his credit card number.

At some point, the caller asked Richard to buy a print, using such glowing terms as "fabulous opportunity," "one-time offer," "limited edition," and "excellent work of a famous artist." The artist, the caller said, was near death and the print's value would increase after the artist's death. He was assured that when the artist died, the company that the caller represented would gladly buy back the print at two to three times what he paid for it and that he could always resell the print elsewhere at a substantial profit. He was told that he would receive a certificate of the "authenticity" of the print. And he was promised a trial examination period with a 30-day money-back guarantee.

Questions

1. Does the offer seem genuine to you? Explain your answer.

2. How can Richard protect himself against a phony offer? List at least five suggestions that you would give him.

3. If Richard bought the work of art and discovered fraud, how should he try to resolve his dispute with the company that sold it to him? Where should he complain if the dispute is not resolved?

YOUR PERSONAL FINANCIAL PLAN

COMPARING OTHER TYPES OF INVESTMENTS

Real estate and collectibles allow investors to achieve greater potential returns. However, these sometimes speculative ventures must be considered carefully in relation to your personal financial situation.

Your Short-Term Financial Planning Activity

Task Identify types of real estate and other investments that might serve your various financial goals and life situations.

Research

1) Review Exhibit 17-1 to understand the differences between direct and indirect real estate investments. What are possible advantages and disadvantages of owning and investing in real estate?

2) Visit the National Real Estate Investor website at nreionline.com, or locate other sources of information about why investors choose real estate investments.

Outcome Prepare a two-page report that summarizes the various types of direct and indirect real estate investments available for investors.

Your Long-Term Financial Planning Activity

Task Identify real estate and other investments that might serve you in the future.

Research

1) Call a few real estate and stock brokerage firms in your area to find out whether any real estate investment trusts or real estate partnerships are available for investors. Also, read the Financial Literacy for My Life: Is Gold a Solid Investment? feature.

2) Research current commercial real estate sections of local newspapers. How many listings do you find for duplexes? For fourplexes and small apartment buildings? Then, develop a plan for selecting and monitoring real estate.

Outcome Prepare a report or visual presentation that summarizes the various types of real estate investments available to investors.

Note: All *Personal Financial Planner* sheets are available at the end of the book and in an Excel spreadsheet format in *Connect Finance*.

CONTINUING CASE

Investing in Real Estate and Other Investment Alternatives

"Whew! Time really does fly!" Jamie Lee thought as she unpacked from her third weekend in a row visiting colleges with the triplets. It seemed like just yesterday that Jamie Lee and Ross brought the little newborns home from the hospital, and now they are preparing to send the three off to college.

So much to consider. In-state universities or community college for the first few years? Either way, years of saving and safe investment strategies helped Jamie Lee and Ross get the triplets ready for college, although they still do want to make the wisest financial choices. After all, putting three through school is still a major undertaking, even for the most well-prepared.

The triplets are leaning toward the state university, which will help with tuition, compared to the out-of-state schools, although it is still a two-hour car drive from home. This translates into room and board times three for the next four years.

"Should we invest in a small house or condominium for the triplets to live in during their college years?" Jamie Lee wondered. She had a hobby of watching all of the home shows on television, such as *Home Reno Nation* and *Flip This Flop,* which made the purchase of a fixer-upper an attractive thought and a possible investment opportunity in the long run.

Jamie Lee and Ross decide to make an appointment with their investment counselor, Jay Hall, and real estate broker, Annie O'Halloran, to discuss their options, as they were unfamiliar with real estate investment opportunities.

Current Financial Situation

Assets (Jamie Lee and Ross combined):
Checking account: $5,000
Savings account: $47,000
Emergency fund savings account: $40,000
House: $475,000
IRA balance: $85,000
Life insurance cash value: $125,000
Investments (stocks, bonds): $700,000
Car: $14,500 (Jamie Lee) and $18,000 (Ross)

Liabilities (Jamie Lee and Ross combined):
Mortgage balance: $47,000
Credit card balance: $0
Car loans: $0

Income:
Jamie Lee: $45,000 gross income ($31,500 net income after taxes)
Ross: $135,000 gross income ($97,200 net income after taxes)

Monthly Expenses:
Mortgage: $1,225
Property taxes: $500
Homeowner's insurance: $300
IRA contribution: $300
Utilities: $250
Food: $600
Gas/maintenance: $275
Entertainment: $300
Life insurance: $375

Questions

1. Compare *direct investment* and *indirect investment* real estate classifications. If Jamie Lee and Ross purchase a small house or condominium for the triplets to stay in during their college years, which type of investment classification would they fall under?

2. Mr. Hall discusses the financial liabilities that Jamie Lee and Ross would undertake with the triplets living in a college dorm room that are on top of the usual tuition and book expenses. Assume that the triplets' rent for the dorm room is $7,500 per student per year based on double occupancy and a shared bathroom. What is the total amount that Jamie Lee and Ross would owe for the entire four years for the three to stay in the dorms?

3. If Jamie Lee and Ross decide to purchase a small house for the triplets to live in for the four years they are in college, what are some of the financial benefits for Jamie Lee and Ross?

4. Jamie Lee and Ross understand that purchasing the second home for the triplets to use during the college years is not all about saving money by avoiding paying the dorm rent. What are some of the liabilities that Jamie Lee and Ross can expect that are directly connected to owning the second home that might make them second-guess the purchase?

 # DAILY SPENDING DIARY

"Saving funds to buy additional real estate is a goal that I'm considering."

Directions

Maintaining a *Daily Spending Diary* can provide important information for monitoring and controlling spending. Taking time to reconsider your spending habits can result in achieving better long-term satisfaction from your finances.

Analysis Questions

1. What changes in your daily spending patterns could help you increase the amount you have available for investing?

2. When might you consider investing in real estate, precious metals, or collectibles?

A *Daily Spending Diary* sheet is located at the end of Chapter 1 and on the library resource site in *Connect*.

18 Starting Early: Retirement Planning

Financial Literacy
IN YOUR LIFE

▶ **What if . . .** you determine that your retirement income during your retirement years will not be sufficient to maintain your lifestyle? If so, you are not alone. Even though 75 percent of workers expect to live as well as, if not better than, they do now when they retire, only 20 percent of those surveyed have begun to save seriously for retirement.

You might . . . want to seek advice from a qualified financial advisor who has your best interests ahead of their own. You might want to review your assets, life insurance, retirement living expenses, housing options, employer and personal pension plans, and annuities.

Now, what would you do? Consider saving at least 20 percent of your income, reducing your expenses, working extra hours, retiring later, or delaying your Social Security benefits. You might also consider moving to a less expensive home. You will be able to monitor your progress using the Your Personal Finance Roadmap and Dashboard feature at the end of the chapter.

my life | STARTING NOW FOR A SECURE RETIREMENT?

Most of us know it is smart to save money for those big-ticket items we really want to buy—a new smart home theatre or car or home. Yet you may not realize that probably the most expensive thing you will ever buy in your lifetime is your retirement. Perhaps you've never thought of "buying" your retirement. Yet that is exactly what you do when you put money into a retirement nest egg. You are paying today for the cost of your retirement tomorrow. The cost of those future years is getting more expensive for most Americans, for two reasons. First, we live longer after we retire. Many of us will spend 15, 20, even 30 years in retirement—and we are more active. Second, you may have to provide a greater share of the cost of your retirement because fewer employers are providing traditional pension plans, and they are contributing less to those plans. Many retirement plans today, such as the popular 401(k), are paid for primarily by you, not the employer. You may not have a retirement plan at work, or you may be self-employed. This makes you responsible for choosing retirement investments.

For every 10 years you delay before starting to save for retirement, you will need to save three times as much each month to catch up. That's why, no matter how young you are, the sooner you begin saving for retirement the better. Whether you are 18 or 58, you can take steps toward a better, more secure future.

As you start (or expand) your retirement planning activities, consider the following statements. For each, select Yes, No, or Uncertain to indicate your personal response regarding these retirement planning activities.

1.	I can depend on Social Security and my company pension to pay for my basic living expenses.	Yes	No	Uncertain
2.	Reviewing my assets to ensure they are sufficient for retirement is a sound idea.	Yes	No	Uncertain
3.	My spending patterns during retirement will probably not change that much.	Yes	No	Uncertain
4.	The place where I live during retirement can have a significant impact on my financial needs.	Yes	No	Uncertain
5.	My Social Security benefits will be reduced if I retire before age 65.	Yes	No	Uncertain
6.	To supplement my retirement income, I may want to work part-time or start a new part-time career after I retire.	Yes	No	Uncertain

As you study this chapter, you will encounter "My Life" boxes with additional information and resources related to these items.

Why Retirement Planning?

LO18-1

Recognize the importance of retirement planning.

A 2020 report from the Insured Retirement Institute (IRI)[1] found that saving for retirement is not the most pressing financial priority for most millennials. The oldest are in their late 30s, focused on their next career move, or maybe with children in elementary or middle school, and the youngest are just starting their career in a very challenging employment environment, many saddled with student debt.

Other significant findings from the IRI report reveal that:

- Only 55 percent of millennials are confident that Social Security will provide them with meaningful retirement income.
- More than 70 percent millennials believe they will be able to finally retire when they want to, while 16 percent believe they wouldn't be able to retire due to a lack of financial security.
- Sixty-five percent of millennials believe they will generate enough income from savings in a retirement plan, but 50 percent are not currently contributing to a plan.
- Eighty percent millennials have money saved for retirement, but nearly half have saved less than $10,000.[2]

Retirement can be a rewarding phase of your life. However, a successful, happy retirement doesn't just happen; it takes planning and continual evaluation. Thinking about retirement in advance can help you anticipate future changes and gain a sense of control over the future. According to the Securities and Exchange Commission, the easiest ways to boost your retirement savings are to take advantage of your employer's matching some or all of your contributions to the retirement plan, focus on low fees and expenses, and save by regular, automatic deductions from your paycheck.

The ground rules for retirement planning are changing rapidly. Reexamine your retirement plans if you hold any of these misconceptions:

my life | 1

I can depend on Social Security and my company pension to pay for my basic living expenses.

While Social Security replaces about 40 percent of the average worker's preretirement earnings, most financial advisors suggest that you will need 70 to 90 percent of preretirement earnings to live comfortably. Even if you are lucky enough to have a company pension, you will still need to save.

- My expenses will drop when I retire.
- My retirement will last only 15 years.
- I can depend on Social Security and my company pension to pay for my basic living expenses.
- My pension benefits will increase to keep pace with inflation.
- My employer's health insurance plan and Medicare will cover my medical expenses.
- There's plenty of time for me to start saving for retirement.
- Saving just a little bit won't help.

It is vital to engage in basic retirement planning activities throughout your working years and to update your retirement plans periodically. While it is never too late to begin sound financial planning, you can avoid many unnecessary and serious difficulties by starting this planning early. Saving now for the future requires tackling the trade-offs between spending and saving.

TACKLING THE TRADE-OFFS

Although exceptions exist, the old adage "You can't have your cake and eat it too" is particularly true in planning for retirement. For example, if you buy state-of-the-art home entertainment systems, drive expensive cars, and take extravagant vacations now, don't expect to retire with plenty of money.

Only by saving now and curtailing current spending can you ensure a comfortable retirement later. Yet saving money doesn't come naturally to many young people.

Ironically, although the time to begin saving is when you are young, the people who are in the best position to save are middle aged.

Seventy-five percent of workers expect to live as well as, if not better than, they do now when they retire, but only 20 percent of those surveyed have begun to save seriously for retirement.

THE IMPORTANCE OF STARTING EARLY

Consider this: If from age 25 to 65 you invest $300 per month and earn an average of 9 percent return a year, you'll have $1.4 million in your retirement fund at age 65. Waiting just 10 years until age 35 to begin your $300-a-month investing will yield about $550,000, while if you wait 20 years to begin this investment, you will have only $201,000 at age 65. Exhibit 18-1 shows how even a $2,000 annual investment earning just 4 percent will grow.

For 40 years, your life, and probably your family's life, revolves around your job. One day you retire, and practically every aspect of your life changes. There's less money, more time, and no daily structure.

You can expect to spend about 16 to 30 years in retirement—too many years to be bored, lonely, and broke. You want your retirement years to be rewarding, active, and rich in new experiences. It's never too early to begin planning for retirement; some experts even suggest starting while you are in school. Be certain you don't let your 45th birthday roll by without a comprehensive retirement plan. Remember, the longer you wait, the less you will be able to shape your life in retirement.

Consider this: Centenarians are the fastest-growing segment of our population. The second fastest is the age group 85+. While in 1950 there were only 2,300 centenarians, currently there are more than 82,000 centenarians in the United States, or a little more than two centenarians per 10,000 in population; about 83 percent are women, 17 percent men.

Retirement planning has both emotional and financial components. Emotional planning for retirement involves identifying your personal goals and setting out to meet them. Financial planning for retirement involves assessing your postretirement needs and income and plugging any gaps you find. Financial planning for retirement is critical for several reasons:

1. You can expect to live in retirement for 16 to 30 years. At age 65, the average life expectancy is 18 years for a man and almost 20 years for a woman.

2. Social Security and a private pension, if you have one, are most often insufficient to cover the cost of living.

3. Inflation may diminish the purchasing power of your retirement savings. Even a 3 percent rate of inflation will cause prices to double every 24 years.

You should anticipate your retirement years by analyzing your long-range goals. What does retirement mean to you? Does it mean an opportunity to stop work and relax, or does it mean time to travel, develop a hobby, or start a second career? Where and how

With more free time, many retirees spend more money on leisure activities.
Lucigerma/Shutterstock

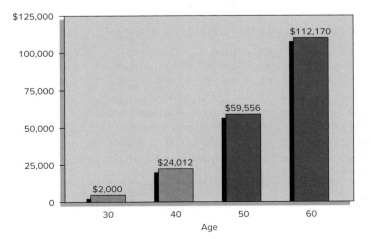

EXHIBIT 18-1

It's never too early to start planning for retirement
Start young. A look at the performance of $2,000 per year of retirement plan investments over time, even at 4 percent, shows the value of starting early.

do you want to live during your retirement? Once you have considered your retirement goals, you are ready to evaluate their cost and assess whether you can afford them.

THE POWER OF COMPOUNDING

No matter where you choose to invest your money—cash, mutual funds, stocks, bonds, or real estate—the key to saving for retirement is to make your money work for you. It does this through the power of compounding. Compounding investment earnings is what can make even small investments become larger given enough time.

You already know the principle of compounding. Money you put into a savings account earns interest. Then you earn interest on the money you originally put in, plus on the interest you've accumulated. As the size of your savings account grows, you can earn interest on a bigger and bigger pool of money.

The following example shows how investment grows at different annual rates of return over different time periods. Notice how the amount of gain gets bigger each 10-year period. That's because interest is being earned on a bigger and bigger pool of money.

EXAMPLE: Power of Compounding: The Time Value of Money

The value of $1,000 compounded at various rates of return over time.

Years	4%	6%	8%	10%
10	$ 1,480	$1,791	$ 2,159	$ 2,594
20	2,191	3,207	4,661	6,727
30	3,243	5,743	10,063	17,449

Also notice that when you double your rate of return from 4 percent to 8 percent, the result after 30 years is over three times what you would have accumulated with a 4 percent return. That's the power of compounding!

The real power of compounding comes with time. The earlier you start saving, the more your money can work for you. Look at it another way. For every 10 years you delay before starting to save for retirement, you will need to save three times as much each month to catch up. That's why no matter how young you are, the sooner you begin saving for retirement, the better.

THE BASICS OF RETIREMENT PLANNING

Before you decide where you want to be financially, you have to find out where you are. Your first step, therefore, is to analyze your current assets and liabilities. Then estimate your spending needs and adjust them for inflation. Next, evaluate your planned retirement income. Finally, increase your income by working part-time, if necessary. An attorney, for example, might teach some law courses after retirement. Recent articles and other retirement information can be found online. For further information, see the Chapter 3 Appendix. Exhibit 18-2 shows online sources for retirement planning. Also, read the *Financial Literacy for My Life* feature, "Planning for Retirement While You Are Still Young."

What if you did not start early to prepare for your retirement? Is there any way you can prepare for retirement when there is little time left? Yes, here are some tips. Some are painful, but these will help you toward your goal.

- It's never too late to start. It's only too late if you don't start at all.
- Save everything you can into your tax-sheltered retirement plans and personal savings. Try to put away at least 20 percent of your income.

PLANNING FOR RETIREMENT WHILE YOU ARE STILL YOUNG: THE TIME VALUE OF MONEY

Retirement probably seems vague and far off at this stage of your life. Besides, you have other things to buy right now. Yet there are some crucial reasons to start preparing now for retirement.

- You'll probably have to pay for more of your own retirement than earlier generations. The sooner you get started, the better.

- You have one huge ally—time. Let's say that you put $1,000 at the beginning of each year into an IRA from age 20 through age 30 (11 years) and then never put in another dime. The account earns 7 percent annually. When you retire at age 65, you'll have $168,515 in the account. A friend doesn't start until age 30 but saves the same amount annually for 35 years straight. Despite putting in three times as much money, your friend's account grows to only $138,237.

- You can start small and grow. Even setting aside a small portion of your paycheck each month will pay off in big dollars later.

- You can afford to invest more aggressively. You have years to overcome the inevitable ups and downs of the market.

Developing the habit of saving for retirement is easier when you are young.

Source: U.S. Department of Labor, www.dol.gov/ebsa/, accessed May 14, 2021.

- Reduce expenses. Put the savings into your nest egg.
- Take a second job or work extra hours.
- Make sure your investments are part of the solution, not part of the problem. To boost your returns, diversify your holdings and keep an eye on fees. But don't take risks you can't afford, and don't trade too much.
- Retire later. You may not need to work full-time beyond your planned retirement age. Part-time may be enough.
- Refine your goal. You may have to live a less expensive lifestyle in retirement.
- Delay taking Social Security. Benefits will be higher when you start taking them.
- Make use of your home. Rent out a room or move to a less expensive home and save the profits.
- Sell assets that are not producing much income or growth, such as undeveloped land or a vacation home, and invest in income-producing assets.

EXHIBIT 18-2
Using a personal computer for retirement planning

General Websites

American Savings Education Council, www.choosetosave.org

Longevity Game, www.northwesternmutual.com/learning-center/tools/the-longevity-game

RothIRA.com, www.rothira.com

Online Planning Software

Financial Engines, www.financialengines.com

Financial Calculator Websites

Kiplinger, www.kiplinger.com (search for *retirement calculator*)

Money, time.com/money/page/money-calculators/

AARP, www.aarp.org/work/retirement-planning/retirement_calculator.html

Choose to Save, www.choosetosave.org/ballpark/

Financial Industry Regulatory Authority, www.finra.org/investors/tools

Source: U.S. Department of Labor, www.dol.gov/ebsa, accessed May 14, 2021.

 **PRACTICE QUIZ 18-1**

1. How can the internet assist you in retirement planning?
2. Why is retirement planning important?
3. What are the four basic steps in retirement planning?

Conducting a Financial Analysis

LO18-2

Analyze your current assets and liabilities for retirement.

As you learned in Chapter 3, your assets include everything you own that has value: cash on hand and in checking and savings accounts; the current value of your stocks, bonds, and other investments; the current value of your house, car, jewelry, and furnishings; and the current value of your life insurance and pensions. Your liabilities are everything you owe: your mortgage, car payments, credit card balances, taxes due, and so forth. The difference between the two totals is your *net worth,* a figure you should increase each year as you move toward retirement. Use Exhibit 18-3 to calculate your net worth now and at retirement.

REVIEW YOUR ASSETS

Reviewing your assets to ensure they are sufficient for retirement is a sound idea. Make any necessary adjustments in your investments and holdings to fit your circumstances. In reviewing your assets, consider the following factors.

my life 2

Reviewing my assets to ensure they are sufficient for retirement is a sound idea.

It is a good idea to review your assets on a regular basis. You may need to make adjustments in your saving, spending, and investing in order to stay on track. As you review your assets, consider your housing, life insurance, and other investments. Each will have an important effect on your retirement income.

reverse annuity mortgage (RAM) A mortgage in which the lender uses the borrower's house as collateral to buy an annuity for the borrower from a life insurance company; also called an *equity conversion*.

HOUSING   If you own your house, it is probably your biggest single asset. The amount tied up in your house, however, may be out of line with your retirement income. You might consider selling your house and buying a less expensive one. The selection of a smaller, more easily maintained house can also decrease your maintenance costs. The difference saved can be put into a savings account or certificates of deposit or into other income-producing investments. If your mortgage is largely or completely paid off, you may be able to get an annuity to provide you with extra income during retirement. In this arrangement, a lender uses your house as collateral to buy an annuity for you from a life insurance company. Each month, the lender pays you (the homeowner) from the annuity after deducting the mortgage interest payment. The mortgage principal, which was used to obtain the annuity, is repaid to the lender by probate after your death. This special annuity is known as a **reverse annuity mortgage (RAM)** or *equity conversion*.

The amount of money available depends on your age, the value of your home, and interest rates. For example, a 75-year-old couple with a $150,000 condominium in Chicago or the suburbs could receive a monthly check of about $900 for the next 10 years or $599 each year for as long as either partner lives in the home.

Before you get a reverse mortgage of any kind, consider the following:

- There are origination fees, closing costs, servicing fees, and mortgage insurance premiums.
- Interest rates may change over the life of the mortgage.
- Interest on reverse mortgages is not deductible on your income tax return until the loan is paid off.
- You are still responsible for property taxes, insurance, utilities, maintenance, and other expenses.

	Sample Figures	Your Figures
Assets: What We Own		
Cash:		
Checking account	$ 800	_____
Savings account	4,500	_____
Investments:		
U.S. savings bonds (current cash-in value)	5,000	_____
Stocks, mutual funds	4,500	_____
Life insurance:		
Cash value, accumulated dividends	10,000	_____
Company pension rights:		
Accrued pension benefit	20,000	_____
Property:		
House (equity)	50,000	_____
Furniture and appliances	8,000	_____
Collections and jewelry	2,000	_____
Automobile	3,000	_____
Other:		
Loan to brother	1,000	_____
Gross assets	$ 108,800	_____
Liabilities: What We Owe		
Current unpaid bills	$ 600	_____
Home mortgage (remaining balance)	9,700	_____
Auto loan	1,200	_____
Property taxes	1,100	_____
Home improvement loan	3,700	_____
Total liabilities	$ 16,300	_____
Net worth = Gross assets – Total liabilities =	$ 92,500	

EXHIBIT 18-3
Review your assets, liabilities, and net worth
Reviewing your assets to ensure they are sufficient for retirement is a sound idea.
Net worth: Assets of $108,800 minus liabilities of $16,300 equals $92,500.

- If your spouse has not signed the loan agreement, your spouse may not get any money from the reverse mortgage.
- You may leave fewer or no assets for your heirs.

For more information about reverse mortgages, go to www.aarp.org/money/credit-loans-debt/reverse_mortgages/. AARP's booklet *Home Made Money: A Consumer's Guide to Reverse Mortgages* is available online or by calling (888) 687-2277 and asking for publication D 15601. Or you may call the Housing and Urban Development office at 1-800-569-4287 for a list of counselors.

LIFE INSURANCE   You may have set up your life insurance to provide support and education for your children. Now you may want to convert some of this asset into cash or income (an annuity). Another possibility is to reduce premium payments by decreasing the face value of your insurance. This will give you extra money to spend on living expenses or to invest for additional income.

OTHER INVESTMENTS   Evaluate any other investments you have. When you chose them, you may have been more interested in making your money grow than in getting an early return. Has the time come to take the income from your investments? You may now want to take dividends rather than reinvest them.

After thoroughly reviewing your assets, estimate your spending needs during your retirement years.

YOUR ASSETS AFTER DIVORCE

Any divorce is difficult, particularly when it comes to a division of marital assets. Your pension benefits are considered marital property, which must be divided in a divorce. Even if a person is not ready to retire, pension benefits are considered a marital asset subject to the division of property. Any retirement fund money, including a 401(k) plan or a profit-sharing plan set aside during a marriage, and the dollar growth of a pension plan during a marriage are considered marital property.

Division of pension benefits generally depends on the length of the marriage. "In a five-year marriage, the percentage of one person's assets given to the spouse is usually small," says Howard Sharfstein, divorce attorney. "In an eight-year marriage about 25 percent of the monetary assets earned by one partner may be given to the other partner. In a marriage that lasts more than 15 years, there's generally a 50-50 split of the marital assets."[3]

Be warned: Many retirement planning strategies accommodate the traditional husband-wife-kids family unit. But millions of nontraditional households have unique retirement needs. Nearly half of all American marriages end in divorce, creating difficulties for millions of adults thinking about their retirement years.

 PRACTICE QUIZ 18-2

1. How can you calculate your net worth today and at retirement?
2. What assets are considered marital assets?

Retirement Living Expenses

LO18-3

Estimate your retirement spending needs.

The exact amount of money you will need in retirement is impossible to predict. However, you can estimate the amount you will need by considering the changes you anticipate in your spending patterns and in where and how you live.

Your spending patterns will probably change. A study conducted by the Bureau of Labor Statistics on how families spend money shows that retired families use a greater share for food, housing, and medical care than nonretired families. Although no two families adjust their spending patterns to changes in the life cycle in the same manner, the tabulation in Exhibit 18-4 can guide you in anticipating your own future spending patterns.

The following expenses may be lowered or eliminated:

- *Work expenses.* You will no longer make payments into your retirement fund. You will not be buying gas and oil for the drive back and forth to work or for train or bus fares. You may be buying fewer lunches away from home.
- *Clothing expenses.* You will probably need fewer clothes after you retire, and your dress may be more casual.

	Age 65–74		Age 75 & Older	
	Average $ Amount	**Percent**	**Average $ Amount**	**Percent**
Pretax annual income	$ 52,366	100	$ 35,467	100
Annual expenditures	$ 48,855	100	$ 36,673	100
Housing	$ 15,838	32.4	$ 13,375	36.5
Food	$ 6,284	12.0	$ 4,349	11.9
Clothing	$ 1,417	2.9	$ 683	1.9
Transportation	$ 8,338	17.1	$ 5,091	13.9
Health care	$ 5,456	12.2	$ 5,708	15.6
Entertainment	$ 2,988	6.1	$ 1,626	4.4
Pensions and Social Security	$ 2,788	5.7	$ 800	2.2
Other*	$ 6,074	11.6	$ 5,041	13.7

*Includes cash contributions, alcohol, tobacco, personal care products and services, reading, education, life and personal insurance, and miscellaneous expenses.
Source: Ann C. Foster, "A Closer Look at Spending Patterns of Older Americans," *Beyond the Numbers: Prices and Spending*, vol. 5, no. 4 (U.S. Bureau of Labor Statistics, March 2016), https://www.bls.gov/opub/btn/volume 5/spending-patterns-of-older-americans.htm, accessed June 8, 2018.

EXHIBIT 18-4
How "average" older (65–74 and 75+) households spend their money
Retired families spend a greater share of their income for food, housing, and medical care than nonretired families.

- *Housing expenses.* If you have paid off your house mortgage by the time you retire, your cost of housing may decrease (although increases in property taxes and insurance may offset this gain).

- *Federal income taxes.* Your federal income taxes will probably be lower. No federal tax has to be paid on some forms of income, such as railroad retirement benefits and certain veterans' benefits. Under the U.S. Civil Service Retirement System, your retirement income is not taxed until you have received the amount you have invested in the retirement fund. After that, your retirement income is taxable. A retirement credit is allowed for some sources of income, such as annuities. You will probably pay taxes at a lower rate because your taxable income will be lower.

my life 3

My spending patterns during retirement will probably not change that much.

When you are retired, you may spend more money on recreation, health insurance, and medical care than you will as a young adult. At the same time, you may spend less money on transportation and clothing. Your federal income taxes may be lower as well.

You can also estimate which of the following expenses may increase:

- *Insurance.* The loss of your employer's contribution to health and life insurance will increase your own payments. Medicare, however, may offset part of this increased expense.

- *Medical expenses.* Although medical expenses vary from person to person, they tend to increase with age.

- *Expenses for leisure activities.* With more free time, many retirees spend more money on leisure activities. You may want to put aside extra money for a retirement trip or other large recreational expenses.

- *Gifts and contributions.* Many retirees who continue to spend the same amount of money on gifts and contributions find their spending in this area takes a larger share of their smaller income. Therefore, you may want to reevaluate such spending.

EXHIBIT 18-5
Your monthly present expenses and your estimated monthly retirement expenses
Don't forget inflation in calculating the prices of goods and services in retirement.

Monthly Expenses		
Item	**Present**	**Retirement**
Fixed expenses:		
Rent or mortgage payment	$ _____	$ _____
Taxes	_____	_____
Insurance	_____	_____
Savings	_____	_____
Debt payment	_____	_____
Other	_____	_____
Total fixed expenses	_____	_____
Variable expenses:		
Food and beverages	_____	_____
Household operation and maintenance	_____	_____
Furnishings and equipment	_____	_____
Clothing	_____	_____
Personal	_____	_____
Transportation	_____	_____
Medical care	_____	_____
Recreation and education	_____	_____
Gifts and contributions	_____	_____
Other	_____	_____
Total variable expenses	_____	_____
Total expenses	_____	_____

Using the worksheet in Exhibit 18-5, list your present expenses and estimate what these expenses would be if you were retired. To make a realistic comparison, list your major spending categories, starting with fixed expenses such as rent or mortgage payments, utilities, insurance premiums, and taxes. Then list variable expenses—food, clothing, transportation, and so on, as well as miscellaneous expenditures such as medical expenses, entertainment, vacations, gifts, contributions, and unforeseen expenses.

Be sure you have an emergency fund for unforeseen expenses. Even when you are living a tranquil life, unexpected events can occur. Build a cushion to cope with inflation. Estimate high in calculating how much the prices of goods and services will rise.

ADJUST YOUR EXPENSES FOR INFLATION

You now have a list of your likely monthly (and annual) expenses if you were to retire today. With inflation, however, those expenses will not be fixed. The potential loss of buying power due to inflation is what makes planning ahead so important. (See Exhibit 18-6.) During the 1970s and the early 1980s, the cost of living increased an average of 6.1 percent a year, though the annual increase slowed to less than 3 percent between 1983 and 2013. According to the U.S. Bureau of Labor Statistics, the annual inflation rate in the United States was 4.2 percent in April 2021.

Financial Literacy Calculations

HOW MUCH INFLATION IS IN YOUR FUTURE?

Years to Retirement	ESTIMATED ANNUAL RATE OF INFLATION BETWEEN NOW AND RETIREMENT									
	3%	4%	5%	6%	7%	8%	9%	10%	11%	12%
5	1.2	1.2	1.3	1.3	1.4	1.5	1.5	1.6	1.7	1.8
8	1.3	1.4	1.5	1.6	1.7	1.8	2.0	2.1	2.3	2.5
10	1.4	1.5	1.6	1.8	2.0	2.2	2.4	2.6	2.8	3.1
12	1.5	1.6	1.8	2.0	2.3	2.5	2.8	3.1	3.5	3.9
15	1.6	1.8	2.1	2.4	2.8	3.2	3.6	4.2	4.8	5.5
18	1.8	2.0	2.4	2.8	3.4	4.0	4.7	5.6	6.5	7.7
20	2.0	2.2	2.7	3.2	3.9	4.7	5.6	6.7	8.1	9.6
25	2.1	2.7	3.4	4.3	5.4	6.8	8.6	10.8	13.6	17.0

1. Choose from the first column the approximate number of years until your retirement.

2. Choose an estimated annual rate of inflation. The rate of inflation cannot be predicted accurately and will vary from year to year.

3. Find the inflation factor corresponding to the number of years until your retirement and the estimated annual inflation rate. (Example: 10 years to retirement combined with a 4 percent estimated annual inflation rate yields a 1.5 inflation factor.)

4. Multiply the inflation factor by your estimated retirement income and your estimated retirement expenses. (Example: $6,000 × 1.5 = $9,000)

   Total annual inflated retirement income: $ _____.

   Total annual inflated retirement expenses: $ _____.

Sources: The above figures are from a compound interest table showing the effective yield of lump-sum investments after inflation that appeared in Charles D. Hodgman, ed., *Mathematical Tables from the Handbook of Chemistry and Physics* (Cleveland: Chemical Rubber Publishing, 1959); *Citicorp Consumer Views*, July 1985, pp. 2–3, Citicorp, 1985; *Financial Planning Tables*, A. G. Edwards, August 1991.

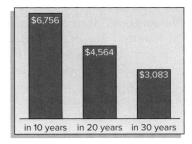

$6,756 — in 10 years
$4,564 — in 20 years
$3,083 — in 30 years

EXHIBIT 18-6

The Effects of Inflation
This chart shows you what $10,000 will be worth in 10, 20, and 30 years, assuming a 4 percent rate of inflation.
Source: TIAA-CREF.

To help you plan for this likely increase in your expenses, use the inflation factor table in the accompanying *Financial Literacy Calculations* feature, "How Much Inflation Is in Your Future?"

 PRACTICE QUIZ 18-3

1. How can you estimate the amount of money you will need during retirement?
2. What expenses are likely to increase or decrease during retirement?
3. How might you adjust your expenses for inflation?

Planning Your Retirement Housing

LO18-4

Identify your retirement housing needs.

Think about where you will want to live. If you think you will want to live in another city, it's a good idea to plan vacations now in areas you might enjoy later. When you find one that appeals to you, visit that area during various times of the year to experience the year-round climate. Meet the people. Check into available activities, transportation, and taxes. Be realistic about what you will have to give up and what you will gain.

Where you live in retirement can influence your financial needs. You must make some important decisions about whether or not to stay in your present community and in your current home. Everyone has unique needs and preferences; only you can determine the location and housing that are best for you.

Consider what moving involves. Moving is expensive, and if you are not satisfied with your new location, returning to your former home may be impossible. Consider the social aspects of moving. Will you want to be near your children, other relatives, and good friends? Are you prepared for new circumstances?

my life 4

The place where I live during retirement can have a significant impact on my financial needs.

Even if you do not move to a new location, housing needs may change during retirement. Many retirees want a home that is easy and inexpensive to maintain, such as a smaller house, a condominium, or an apartment.

TYPE OF HOUSING

Housing needs often change as people grow older. The ease and cost of maintenance and nearness to public transportation, shopping, worship center, and entertainment often become more important to people when they retire.

Many housing alternatives exist, several of which were discussed in Chapter 9. Staying in their present home, whether a single-family dwelling, a condominium, or an apartment, is the alternative preferred by most people approaching retirement. A recent survey of over 5,000 men and women revealed that 92 percent wanted to own their homes in retirement.

DeLoma Foster of Greenville, South Carolina, has seen the future, and she wants to be prepared. DeLoma, 69, has osteoporosis, just as her mother did. Although she's not having difficulty now, she knows the debilitating bone condition eventually could make it difficult, if not impossible, to navigate steep stairs, cramped bathrooms, and narrow doorways. So two years ago, she and her husband, Clyde, a 72-year-old retired textile executive, moved into a novel type of home, one that can comfortably accommodate them no matter what disabilities old age may bring. Called a "universal design home," their residence is on the cutting edge of an architectural concept that an aging population may well embrace. The only house of its kind in the neighborhood, it has wide doors, pull-out cabinet shelves, easy-to-reach electrical switches, and dozens of other features useful for elderly persons or those with disabilities. Yet these features are incorporated into the design unobtrusively.

Apart from aesthetics, universal design is appealing because it allows people to stay in their homes as they grow older and more frail. "The overwhelming majority of people would prefer to grow old in their own homes in their own communities," says Jon Pynoos, a gerontologist at the University of Southern California in Los Angeles. Recognizing this trend, building suppliers now offer everything from lever door handles to faucets that turn on automatically when you put your hand beneath the spigot. Remodeling so far is creating the biggest demand for these products. But increasingly, contractors are building universal design homes from scratch, which generally costs less than completely retrofitting an existing house.

During retirement, will you want to be near your children, grandchildren, other relatives, and good friends?
Shutterstock

With the many choices available, determining where to live in retirement is itself turning into a time-consuming job. But whether you want to race cars, go on a safari, or stay home to paint, the goal is to end up like Edna Cohen. "Don't feel bad if I die tomorrow," she says. "I've had a wonderful life." Who could ask for more?

Whatever retirement housing alternative you choose, make sure you know what you are signing and understand what you are buying.

AVOIDING RETIREMENT HOUSING TRAPS

Too many people make the move without doing enough research, and often it's a huge mistake. How can retirees avoid being surprised by hidden tax and financial traps when they move? Here are some tips from retirement specialists on how to uncover hidden taxes and other costs of a retirement area before moving:

- Write or call the local chamber of commerce to get an economic profile and details on area property taxes.
- Contact the state's tax department to find out state income, sales, and inheritance taxes and special exemptions for retirees. If your pension will be taxed by the state you're leaving, check whether the new state will give you credit for those taxes.
- Subscribe to the Sunday edition of a local newspaper.
- Call a local CPA to find out which taxes are rising.
- Check with local utilities to estimate your energy costs. Visit the area in as many seasons as possible. Talk to retirees and other local residents about costs of health care, auto insurance, food, and clothing.
- Rent for a while instead of buying immediately.

 **PRACTICE QUIZ 18-4**

1. What are some housing options for retirees?
2. How can retirees avoid retirement housing traps?

 **PFP Sheet 63**
Retirement Planning

Planning Your Retirement Income

Once you have determined your approximate future expenses, you must evaluate the sources and amounts of your retirement income. Possible sources of income for many retirees are Social Security, other public pension plans, employer pension plans, personal retirement plans, and annuities.

LO18-5

Determine your planned retirement income.

SOCIAL SECURITY

Social Security is the most widely used source of retirement income; it covers almost 97 percent of U.S. workers. Many Americans think of Social Security as benefiting only retired people. But it is actually a package of protection, providing retirement, survivors', and disability benefits. The package protects you and your family while you work and after you retire. As of February 2021, more than 69.7 million people, one out of every five Americans, collect over $1.1 trillion in some kind of Social Security benefit.

The Social Security Administration estimates that 47 percent of individuals age 65 and older would live in poverty without Social Security benefits, four times as many as live in poverty today.

smart money minute

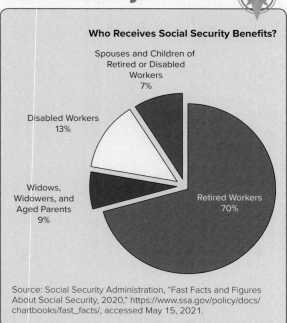

Who Receives Social Security Benefits?

Spouses and Children of Retired or Disabled Workers
7%

Disabled Workers
13%

Widows, Widowers, and Aged Parents
9%

Retired Workers
70%

Source: Social Security Administration, "Fast Facts and Figures About Social Security, 2020," https://www.ssa.gov/policy/docs/chartbooks/fast_facts/, accessed May 15, 2021.

smart money minute

If your full retirement age is 66 years and 4 months, and you make the mistake of receiving benefits starting at age 62, you would only get 73.3% of your full benefit. The reduction will be greater in future years as the full retirement age increases. *Action:* You might consider taking the action of putting off your benefits until your full retirement age or later. You will enjoy the success of a higher benefit amount for the rest of your life.

Source: Social Security Administration, *"Understanding the Benefits,"* January 2021.

Social Security should not be the only source of your retirement income, however. It should be only a small part of your plan, or you won't live a very exciting retired life. Even the Social Security Administration cautions that Social Security was never intended to provide 100 percent of retirement income.

WHEN AND WHERE TO APPLY Most people qualify for reduced Social Security retirement benefits at age 62; widows or widowers can begin collecting Social Security benefits earlier.

About four months before the date you want your benefits to start, apply for Social Security benefits online or by telephoning the Social Security office at 1-800-772-1213. The payments will not start unless you apply for them.

WHAT INFORMATION WILL YOU NEED? The Social Security office will tell you what proof you need to establish your particular case. Generally, you will be asked to provide the following.

- Proof of your age.
- Your Social Security card or Social Security number.
- Your most recent W-2 withholding form, or your tax return, if you are self-employed.
- Your marriage license if you are applying for your spouse's benefits.
- The birth certificates of your children if you are applying for their benefits.
- Proof of U.S. citizenship, or lawful immigration status if you (or a child) were not born in the United States.

WHAT IF YOU RETIRE AT 62 INSTEAD OF FULL RETIREMENT AGE? Your Social Security benefits will be reduced if you retire before the full retirement age. Currently there is a permanent reduction of five-ninths of 1 percent for each month you receive payments before the full retirement age. Thus, if you retire at 62, your monthly payments will be permanently reduced by 20 percent of what they would be if you waited until the full retirement age to retire. However, if you wait until the full retirement age to collect Social Security, your benefits will not decrease. If you work after the full retirement age, your benefits will increase by one-fourth of 1 percent for each month past the full retirement age that you delay retirement, but only up to age 70.

Because of longer life expectancies, the full retirement age will be increased in gradual steps until it reaches 67. This change started in 2003 and affects people born in 1938 and later. Look at Exhibit 18-7 to determine your full retirement age.

WHEN TO START RECEIVING RETIREMENT BENEFITS Would it be better for you to start getting benefits early with a smaller monthly amount for more years, or wait for a larger monthly payment over a shorter time period? The answer is personal and depends on several factors, such as your current cash needs, your current health, and family longevity. Also, consider if you plan to work in retirement and if you have other sources of retirement income. You must also study your future

HOW TO . . .
CHOOSE A SOCIAL SECURITY BENEFIT CALCULATOR

Use any of the three calculators below to estimate your potential benefit amounts using different retirement dates and different levels of potential future earnings. The calculators will show your retirement benefits as well as disability and survivor benefit amounts on your record if you should become disabled or die today. The calculators, along with others, can be found on the Social Security Administration website at www.ssa.gov/planners/benefitcalculators.html

- The Quick and Online calculators can be used from the screen.
- The Detailed Calculator must be downloaded. There are both PC and Mac versions.
- Calculator estimates will differ from those on your Social Security statement if you use different assumptions.
- If you are eligible for a pension based on work that was not covered by Social Security, your benefit amount may be reduced.

1. **Quick Calculator.** Simple, rough estimate calculator. You input your date of birth and this year's earnings. (You must be over age 21 to use this calculator.)
2. **Online Calculator.** You input your date of birth and your complete earnings history. You may project your future earnings. (This calculation is similar to that shown on your Social Security Statement.)
3. **Detailed Calculator.** This program provides the most precise estimates. It must be downloaded and installed on your computer. (This includes reduction for Government Pension Offset.)

Source: Social Security Administration, www.socialsecurity.gov/estimator, and ssa.gov/pubs/EN-05-10024.pdf, accessed May 15, 2021.

Year of Birth	Full Retirement Age
1937 or earlier	65
1938	65 and 2 months
1939	65 and 4 months
1940	65 and 6 months
1941	65 and 8 months
1942	65 and 10 months
1943–54	66
1955	66 and 2 months
1956	66 and 4 months
1957	66 and 6 months
1958	66 and 8 months
1959	66 and 10 months
1960 and later	67

Although the full retirement age is rising, you should still apply for Medicare benefits within three months of your 65th birthday. If you wait longer, your Medicare medical insurance (Part B) and prescription drug coverage (Part D) may cost you more money.

Source: Social Security Administration, *Social Security: Understanding the Benefits* (Washington, D.C., January 2021), accessed May 15, 2021.

EXHIBIT 18-7

Age to receive full Social Security benefits
Because of longer life expectancies, the full retirement age will be increased in gradual steps until it reaches 67. In 2021, if you were born before 1954, you are already eligible for your full Social Security benefits.

financial needs and obligations, and calculate your future Social Security benefits. Weigh all the facts carefully before making this crucial decision. This decision affects the monthly benefit you will receive for the rest of your life, and it may affect benefit protection for your survivors.

my life 5

My Social Security benefits will be reduced if I retire before age 65.

Most people can begin collecting Social Security retirement benefits at age 62. However, the monthly amount at age 62 is less than it would be if you waited until full retirement age. The full retirement age is being increased in gradual steps. For people born in 1960 and later, the full retirement age is 67.

ESTIMATING YOUR RETIREMENT BENEFITS The Social Security Administration now provides a history of your earnings and an estimate of your future monthly benefits online. The statement includes an estimate, in today's dollars, of how much you will get each month from Social Security when you retire—at age 62, 65, or 70—based on your earnings to date and your projected future earnings. Use the *How To . . . Choose a Social Security Benefit Calculator* to estimate your potential monthly benefits.

HOW TO BECOME ELIGIBLE To qualify for Social Security retirement benefits, you must have the required number of quarters of coverage. The number of quarters you need depends on your year of birth. People born after 1928 need 40 quarters to qualify for benefits.

TAXABILITY OF SOCIAL SECURITY BENEFITS Up to 85 percent of your Social Security benefits may be subject to federal income tax for any year in which your adjusted gross income plus your nontaxable interest income and one-half of your Social Security benefits exceed a base amount. For current information, go online (irs.gov) or telephone the Internal Revenue Service at 1-800-829-3676 for Publication 554, *Tax Benefits for Older Americans,* and Publication 915, *Tax Information on Social Security.*

IF YOU WORK AFTER YOU RETIRE Your Social Security benefits may be reduced if you earn above a certain amount a year, depending on your age and the amount you earn. You will receive all of your benefits for the year if your employment earnings do not exceed the annual exempted amount.

BENEFITS INCREASE AUTOMATICALLY Social Security benefits increase automatically each January if the cost of living increased during the preceding year. Each year, the cost of living is compared with that of the year before. If it has increased, Social Security benefits increase by the same percentage.

SPOUSE'S BENEFITS The full benefit for a spouse is one-half of the retired worker's full benefit. If your spouse takes benefits before age 65, the amount of the spouse's benefit is reduced to a low of 37.5 percent at age 62. However, a spouse who is taking care of a child who is under 16 or has a disability gets full (50 percent) benefits, regardless of age.

If you are eligible for both your own retirement benefits and for benefits as a spouse, Social Security pays your own benefit first. If your benefit as a spouse is higher than your retirement benefit, you'll get a combination of benefits equal to the higher spouse benefit.

INTERNET ACCESS You can create a *my Social Security* account if you're age 18 or older and have a Social Security number, valid email, and U.S. mail address. To create your personal and confidential account, visit www.ssa.gov/myaccount. You'll need to provide some personal information to confirm your identity, and then choose a username and password.

To view and print the Social Security Administration's publications, forms, reports, and program history, with links to information for employers, employees, children, parents, and teachers, visit the agency at www.ssa.gov.

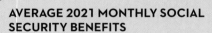

smart money minute

AVERAGE 2021 MONTHLY SOCIAL SECURITY BENEFITS

- Retired worker: $1,543
- Retired couple: $2,596
- Disabled worker: $1,277
- Disabled worker with a spouse and children: $2,224
- Widow or widower: $1,453
- Young widow or widower with two children: $3,001

Source: *Social Security: Understanding the Benefits* (Washington, D.C., Social Security Administration, January 2021), accessed May 15, 2021.

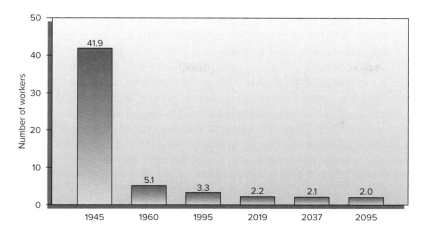

EXHIBIT 18-8
The number of workers per beneficiary has plummeted
Source: Social Security Administration, "Fast Facts and Figures about Social Security, 2020," accessed May 15, 2021.

THE FUTURE OF SOCIAL SECURITY   According to the 2020 OASDI Trustees Report, "Social Security is not sustainable over the long term at current benefit and tax rates." Recently, Social Security paid more in benefits and expenses than it collected in taxes and other income. The 2020 report projects this pattern to continue for the next 75 years. The trustees estimate that the trust funds will be exhausted by 2035. At that point, payroll taxes and other income will flow into the fund but will be sufficient to pay only 79 percent of program costs.

Many people are concerned about the future of Social Security. They contend that enormous changes since Social Security started over 86 years ago have led to promises that are impossible to keep. Longer life expectancies mean retirees collect benefits over a greater number of years. More workers are retiring early, thus entering the system sooner and staying longer. The flood of baby boomers who began retiring early in the 21st century will mean fewer workers to contribute to the system. In 1945, 42 workers supported every recipient. By 2019, that number had dropped to 2.2. The Social Security Administration estimates the number will drop to 2.1 workers by 2037 and 2.0 workers by 2095 (see Exhibit 18-8).

OTHER PUBLIC PENSION PLANS

Besides Social Security, the federal government administers several other retirement plans (for federal government and railroad employees). Employees covered under these plans are not covered by Social Security. The Veterans Administration provides pensions for many survivors of men and women who died while in the armed forces and disability pensions for eligible veterans. The Railroad Retirement System is the only retirement system administered by the federal government that covers a single private industry. Many state, county, and city governments operate retirement plans for their employees.

Do you have a question about your retirement plan and are not sure where to turn for help? Then go to the PensionHelp America website at www.pensionhelp.org. PensionHelp America can connect you with counseling projects, government agencies, and legal service providers that offer free information and assistance. By leading you through a series of questions, PensionHelp America will guide you to the help you need.

EMPLOYER PENSION PLANS

Another possible source of retirement income is the pension plan your company offers. With employer plans, your employer contributes to your retirement benefits, and sometimes you contribute too. Contributions and earnings on those contributions accumulate tax free until you receive them.

smart money minute

PROTECT YOURSELF FROM SOCIAL SECURITY PHONE SCAMS

Remember, Social Security will NEVER:

- suspend your Social Security number because someone else has used it in a crime;
- threaten you with arrest or other legal action unless you immediately pay a fine or fee;
- require payment by retail gift card, wire transfer, internet currency, or mailing cash;
- promise a benefit increase or other assistance in exchange for payment; or
- send official letters or reports containing your personal information via email.

Source: https://oig.ssa.gov/sites/default/files/Fraud%20Advisory%20-%20ss%20Scam%20Call%20Update%201-8-2021_0.pdf?utm_medium=email&utm_source=govdelivery, January 10, 2021.

Since private pension plans vary, you should find out (1) when you become eligible for pension benefits and (2) what benefits you will be entitled to. Most employer plans are defined-contribution or defined-benefit plans.

DEFINED-CONTRIBUTION PLAN   Over the last two decades, the defined-contribution plan has grown rapidly, while the number of defined-benefit plans has generally dropped. A **defined-contribution plan** has an individual account for each employee; therefore, these plans are sometimes called *individual account plans*. The plan document describes the amount the employer will contribute, but it does not promise any particular benefit. When a plan participant retires or otherwise becomes eligible for benefits, the benefit is the total amount in the participant's account, including past investment earnings on amounts put into the account.

Defined-contribution plans include the following:

1. *Money-purchase pension plans.* Your employer promises to set aside a certain amount for you each year, generally a percentage of your earnings.
2. *Stock bonus plans.* Your employer's contribution is used to buy stock in your company for you. The stock is usually held in trust until you retire, at which time you can receive your shares or sell them at their fair market value.
3. *Profit-sharing plans.* Your employer's contribution depends on the company's profits.
4. *Salary reduction or 401(k) plans.* Under a **401(k) plan**, your employer makes nontaxable contributions to the plan for your benefit and as a tax-deferred method of saving for retirement. Sometimes your employer matches a portion of the funds contributed by you. If your employer is a tax-exempt institution such as a hospital, university, or museum, the salary reduction plan is called a *Section 403(b) plan.* Or, if you are a government employee, you may have a *Section 457 plan.* These plans are often referred to as *tax-sheltered annuity (TSA) plans.*

defined-contribution plan A retirement savings plan—profit sharing, money purchase, Keogh, or 401(k)—that provides an individual account for each participant; also called an *individual account plan.*

401(k) (TSA) plan A plan under which employees can defer current taxation on a portion of their salary.

smart money minute

Despite increasing wealth, most Americans have only modest savings relative to their retirement income needs, and a substantial portion of their savings is held in 401(k) accounts.

Source: Insured Retirement Institute, www.irionline.org, accessed March 7, 2021.

The Economic Growth and Tax Relief Reconciliation Act (the EGTRRA) was passed by Congress in 2001. The Act increased the employee contribution limit for 401(k) and other employer-sponsored retirement plans. For example, you can contribute $19,500 to your 401(k), 403(b), or Section 457(b) plan in 2021 ($26,000 if you are 50 or older. This provision is intended to allow older workers to make up for lost time and catch up on their contributions).

An Example: How Funds Accumulate   All earnings in a tax-sheltered annuity (TSA) grow without current federal taxation. Dollars saved on a pretax basis while your earnings grow tax deferred will enhance the growth of your funds (see Exhibit 18-9).

One caution! Don't overlook your 401(k) plan fees. Fees and expenses paid by your plan may substantially reduce the growth in your account and, ultimately, your account balance. Your account balance will determine the amount of retirement income you will receive from the plan. For example, assume you are a 30-year-old with $25,000 in a 401(k) plan. If your account earns 7 percent and incurs fees of 0.5 percent a year, without another contribution, your payout at age 65 will be $227,000. But if the same account incurs fees of 1.5 percent, your payout at age 65 will be only $163,000. *That extra 1 percent per year reduces your payout by 28 percent.*

Tax Benefits of a TSA   With a TSA, your investment earnings are tax deferred. Your savings compound at a faster rate and provide you with a greater sum than in an account without this advantage. Ordinary income taxes will be due when you receive the income. The following table illustrates the difference between saving in a conventional savings

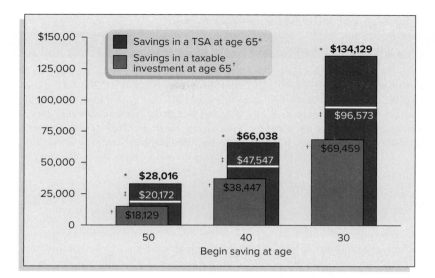

EXHIBIT 18-9

An early start + tax-deferred growth = greater savings

All earnings in a tax-sheltered annuity grow without current federal taxation.

*Tax-deferred growth: Assumes a 28 percent tax bracket, a $100 contribution per month, and a 6 percent tax-deferred annual return.

†Taxable growth: Assumes a 28 percent tax bracket, a $72 contribution ($100 – $28 paid in taxes) per month, and a 6 percent taxable annual return (a 4.32 percent after-tax earnings rate). A 10 percent federal tax penalty may be due on amounts withdrawn before age 59½.

‡Net after 28 percent tax at retirement.

Source: Massachusetts Mutual Life Insurance Company.

plan and a tax-deferred TSA for a single person earning $28,000 a year from their part-time job. Notice how you can increase your take-home pay with a TSA.

EXAMPLE: Tax Benefits of a TSA

	Without a TSA	With a TSA
Your income	$28,000	$28,000
TSA contribution	–0	–2,400
Taxable income	$28,000	$25,600
Estimated federal income taxes	–5,319	–4,647
Gross take-home pay	$22,681	$20,953
After-tax savings contributions	–2,400	–0
Net take-home pay	$20,281	$20,953
Increase in take-home pay with a TSA		$672

> **vesting** An employee's right to at least a portion of the benefits accrued under an employer pension plan, even if the employee leaves the company before retiring.

What happens to your benefits under an employer pension plan if you change jobs? One of the most important aspects of such plans is vesting. **Vesting** is your right to at least a portion of the benefits you have accrued under an employer pension plan (within certain limits), even if you leave the company before you retire.

DEFINED-BENEFIT PLAN In a **defined-benefit plan**, the plan document specifies the benefits promised to the employee at the normal retirement age. The plan itself does not specify how much the employer must contribute annually. The plan's actuary determines the annual employer contribution required so that the plan fund will be sufficient to pay the promised benefits as each participant retires. If the fund is inadequate, the employer must make additional contributions. Because of their actuarial aspects,

> **defined-benefit plan** A pension plan that specifies the benefits the employee will receive at the normal retirement age.

EXHIBIT 18-10   Comparison of defined-benefit and defined-contribution plans

	Defined Benefit Plan	Defined Contribution Plan
Employer contributions and/or matching contributions	Employer funded. Federal rules set amounts that employers must contribute to plans in an effort to ensure that plans have enough money to pay benefits when due. There are penalties for failing to meet these requirements.	There is no requirement that the employer contribute, except in the SIMPLE 401(k) and Safe Harbor 401(k)s, money purchase plans, SIMPLE IRA, and SEP plans. The employer may choose to match a portion of the employee's contributions or to contribute without employee contributions. In some plans, employer contributions may be in the form of employer stock.
Employee contributions	Generally, employees do not contribute to these plans.	Many plans require the employee to contribute in order for an account to be established.
Managing the investment	Plan officials manage the investment, and the employer is responsible for ensuring that the amount it has put in the plan plus investment earnings will be enough to pay the promised benefit.	The employee often is responsible for managing the investment of the account, choosing from investment options offered by the plan. In some plans, plan officials are responsible for investing all the plan's assets.
Amount of benefits paid upon retirement	A promised benefit is based on a formula in the plan, often using a combination of the employee's age, years worked for the employer, and salary.	The benefit depends on contributions made by the employee and the employer, performance of the account's investments, and fees charged to the account.
Type of retirement benefit payments	Traditionally, these plans pay the retiree monthly annuity payments that continue for life. Plans may offer other payment options.	The retiree may transfer the account balance into an individual retirement account (IRA) from which the retiree withdraws money or may receive it as a lump sum payment. Some plans also offer monthly payments through an annuity.
Guarantee of benefits	The federal government, through the Pension Benefit Guaranty Corporation (PBGC), guarantees some amount of benefits.	No federal guarantee of benefits.
Leaving the company before retirement age	If an employee leaves after vesting in a benefit but before the plan's retirement age, the benefit generally stays with the plan until the employee files a claim for it at retirement. Some defined benefit plans offer early retirement options.	The employee may transfer the account balance to an individual retirement account (IRA) or, in some cases, another employer plan, where it can continue to grow based on investment earnings. The employee also may take the balance out of the plan but will owe taxes and possibly penalties, thus reducing retirement income. Plans may cash out small accounts.

defined-benefit plans tend to be more complicated and more expensive to administer than defined-contribution plans. Most companies nationwide are switching their retirement plans to defined contributions from defined benefits. Exhibit 18-10 compares important features of defined-benefit and defined-contribution plans.

PLAN PORTABILITY AND PROTECTION   Some pension plans allow portability. This feature enables you to carry earned benefits from one employer's pension plan to another's when you change jobs.

The Employee Retirement Income Security Act of 1974 (ERISA) sets minimum standards for pension plans in private industry and protects more than 50 million workers. Under this act, the federal government has insured part of the payments promised to retirees from private defined-benefit pensions. ERISA established the Pension Benefit Guaranty Corporation (PBGC), a quasi-governmental agency, to provide pension insurance. The PBGC protects employees' pensions to some degree if a firm defaults. Since 1974, the PBGC has protected the pension benefits of over 34 million workers, retirees, and their families. The PBGC's board of directors includes the secretaries of the U.S. Departments of Labor, the Treasury, and Commerce.

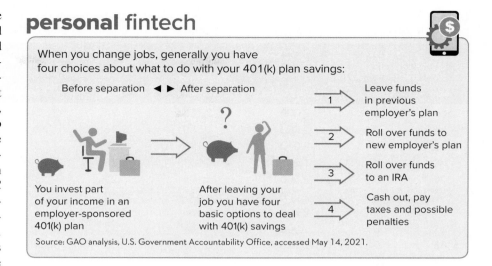

personal fintech

When you change jobs, generally you have four choices about what to do with your 401(k) plan savings:

Before separation ◀ ▶ After separation

You invest part of your income in an employer-sponsored 401(k) plan

After leaving your job you have four basic options to deal with 401(k) savings

1 Leave funds in previous employer's plan

2 Roll over funds to new employer's plan

3 Roll over funds to an IRA

4 Cash out, pay taxes and possible penalties

Source: GAO analysis, U.S. Government Accountability Office, accessed May 14, 2021.

PERSONAL RETIREMENT PLANS

In addition to the retirement plans offered by Social Security, other public pension plans, and employer pension plans, many individuals have set up personal retirement plans. The two most popular personal retirement plans are individual retirement accounts (IRAs) and Keogh accounts.

INDIVIDUAL RETIREMENT ACCOUNTS The **individual retirement account (IRA),** which entails the establishment of a trust or a custodial account, is a retirement savings plan created for an individual. The Taxpayer Relief Act of 1997 included several provisions designed to help you save for retirement. The act expanded rules on traditional (classic) IRAs and created several new types of IRAs.

Furthermore, the EGTRRA of 2001 increased the amount of money you can contribute to an IRA from $2,000 in 2001 to $6,000 in 2021. If you are 50 or older, you can contribute $1,000 more than the regular limits in 2021.

Whether or not you are covered by a pension plan, you may still make nondeductible IRA contributions, and all of the income your IRA earns will compound tax deferred until you withdraw money from the IRA. Remember, the biggest benefit of an IRA lies in its tax-deferred earnings growth; the longer the money accumulates tax deferred, the bigger the benefit.

Exhibit 18-11 shows the power of tax-deferred compounding of earnings, an important advantage offered by an IRA. Consider how compounded earnings transformed the lives of two savers, Abe and Ben. As the exhibit shows, Abe regularly invested $2,000 a year in an IRA for 10 years, from ages 25 to 35. Then Abe sat back and let compounding work its magic. Ben started making regular $2,000 annual contributions at age 35 and contributed for 30 years until age 65. As you can see, Abe retired with a much larger nest egg—over $192,000 more than Ben's. Moral? Get an early start on your plan for retirement.

Your investment opportunities for IRA funds are not limited to savings accounts and certificates of deposit. You can put your IRA funds in many kinds of investments—mutual funds, annuities, stocks, bonds, U.S.-minted gold and silver coins, real estate, and so forth. Only investments in life insurance, precious metals, collectibles, and securities bought on margin are prohibited.

individual retirement account (IRA) A special account in which the employee sets aside a portion of his or her income; taxes are not paid on the principal or interest until money is withdrawn from the account.

EXHIBIT 18-11   Tackling the trade-offs (saving now versus saving later): The time value of money

Get an early start on your plan for retirement.

	Saver Abe				Saver Ben		
Age	Years	Contributions	Year-End Value	Age	Years	Contributions	Year-End Value
25	1	$ 2,000	$ 2,188	25	1	$ 0	$ 0
26	2	2,000	4,580	26	2	0	0
27	3	2,000	7,198	27	3	0	0
28	4	2,000	10,061	28	4	0	0
29	5	2,000	13,192	29	5	0	0
30	6	2,000	16,617	30	6	0	0
31	7	2,000	20,363	31	7	0	0
32	8	2,000	24,461	32	8	0	0
33	9	2,000	28,944	33	9	0	0
34	10	2,000	33,846	34	10	0	0
35	11	0	37,021	35	11	2,000	2,188
36	12	0	40,494	36	12	2,000	4,580
37	13	0	44,293	37	13	2,000	7,198
38	14	0	48,448	38	14	2,000	10,061
39	15	0	52,992	39	15	2,000	13,192
40	16	0	57,963	40	16	2,000	16,617
41	17	0	63,401	41	17	2,000	20,363
42	18	0	69,348	42	18	2,000	24,461
43	19	0	75,854	43	19	2,000	28,944
44	20	0	82,969	44	20	2,000	33,846
45	21	0	90,752	45	21	2,000	39,209
46	22	0	99,265	46	22	2,000	45,075
47	23	0	108,577	47	23	2,000	51,490
48	24	0	118,763	48	24	2,000	58,508
49	25	0	129,903	49	25	2,000	66,184
50	26	0	142,089	50	26	2,000	74,580
51	27	0	155,418	51	27	2,000	83,764
52	28	0	169,997	52	28	2,000	93,809
53	29	0	185,944	53	29	2,000	104,797
54	30	0	203,387	54	30	2,000	116,815
55	31	0	222,466	55	31	2,000	129,961
56	32	0	243,335	56	32	2,000	144,340
57	33	0	266,162	57	33	2,000	160,068
58	34	0	291,129	58	34	2,000	177,271
59	35	0	318,439	59	35	2,000	196,088
60	36	0	348,311	60	36	2,000	216,670
61	37	0	380,985	61	37	2,000	239,182
62	38	0	416,724	62	38	2,000	263,807
63	39	0	455,816	63	39	2,000	290,741
64	40	0	498,574	64	40	2,000	320,202
65	41	0	545,344	65	41	2,000	352,427
		$20,000				$62,000	
Value at retirement*			$545,344	Value at retirement*			$352,427
Less total contributions			−20,000	Less total contributions			−62,000
Net earnings			$525,344	Net earnings			$290,427

*The table assumes a 9 percent fixed rate of return, compounded monthly, and no fluctuation of the principal. Distributions from an IRA are subject to ordinary income taxes when withdrawn and may be subject to other limitations under IRA rules.

Source: *The Franklin Investor* (San Mateo, CA: Franklin Distributors Inc., January 1989).

Regular (Traditional or Classic) IRA   This arrangement lets you contribute up to $6,000 in 2021 ($7,000 if over 50). Whether the contribution is tax deductible depends on your tax filing status, your income, and your participation in an employer-provided retirement plan.

Roth IRA   With a **Roth IRA**, contributions are not tax deductible, but earnings accumulate tax free. You may contribute up to the amounts shown in the above paragraph (reduced by the amount contributed to a traditional IRA). You can make contributions even after age 70½. Five years after you establish your Roth IRA, you can take tax-free, penalty-free distributions if you are at least 59½ or will use the fund for first-time home buyer expenses.

> **Roth IRA** A retirement account for which contributions are not tax deductible, but earnings accumulate tax free.

Your Roth IRA is exclusively for you. Your interest in the account is nonforfeitable. You can't borrow from your Roth IRA. If you use your Roth IRA as collateral for a loan, the part you pledge as collateral will be taxed as a withdrawal.

In 2021, if you are a single taxpayer, your Roth IRA contribution limit is reduced when your adjusted gross income (AGI) is more than $125,000. You cannot contribute when your AGI reaches $140,000. If you are filing jointly, the amounts are $198,000 and $208,000, respectively.

You may convert your traditional IRA to a Roth IRA. Depending on your current age and your anticipated tax bracket in retirement, it may be a good idea to convert. Is a tax-deductible IRA or a Roth IRA better for you? If you are saving for a first-time home purchase or retirement at age 59½, and these events are at least five years away, the Roth IRA allows for penalty-free withdrawals as well as tax-free distributions.

myRA   myRA, developed by the U.S. Department of the Treasury, is a Roth IRA that invests in a new U.S. Treasury retirement savings bond. myRA offers a simple, safe, and affordable method to start saving for retirement. It can be a good option if you have not started saving for retirement because you:

- don't have a retirement saving plan at work,
- don't have other options available to start savings for retirement,
- feel the cost of opening and maintaining a retirement savings account is too high, or
- are concerned about complicated investment options and losing money.

Spousal IRA   A *spousal IRA* lets you contribute up to the amounts shown above on behalf of your nonworking spouse if you file a joint tax return. As in the traditional IRA, whether or not this contribution is tax deductible depends on your income and on whether you or your spouse participates in an employer-provided retirement plan.

Rollover IRA   A *rollover IRA* is a traditional IRA that accepts rollovers of all or a portion of your taxable distribution from a retirement plan or from another IRA. A rollover IRA may also let you roll over to a Roth IRA. To avoid a mandatory 20 percent federal income tax withholding, the rollover must be made directly to a similar employer-provided retirement plan or to an IRA. If you receive the money yourself, you must roll it over within 60 days. However, you will receive only 80 percent of the amount you request as a distribution (distribution minus the mandatory 20 percent withholding tax). Unless you add additional money to the rollover accumulation to equal the 20 percent withheld, the IRS will consider the 20 percent withheld to be taxable income. If you are under 59½, the 20 percent withholding will be considered an early distribution subject to a 10 percent penalty tax. The 80 percent you roll over will not be taxed until you take it out of the IRA.

The 2001 law made retirement savings more portable, permitting workers to roll money between 401(k)s, 403(b)s, and governmental 457s. That's especially good now for those with a 457. Before, you could not even transfer savings into an IRA when you left a job. You can now also roll regular deductible IRA savings into a 401(k).

Financial Literacy for My Life

CONFLICTS OF INTEREST IN RETIREMENT ADVICE COST SAVERS BILLIONS OF DOLLARS

Since Congress enacted the Employee Retirement Income Security Act (ERISA) in 1974, there has been a dramatic shift from employer-sponsored defined benefit plans to self-directed IRAs and 401(k)s. These changes have increased the need for good retirement advice, yet until 2016 the ERISA rules governing retirement investment advice had not been meaningfully updated since 1975. While many investment advisors acted in their customers' best interest, not everyone was legally obligated to do so. Instead, the broken regulatory system had allowed misaligned incentives to steer customers into investments that have higher fees or lower returns—costing some middle-class families tens of thousands of dollars of their retirement savings.

Analysis by the President's Council of Economic Advisers (CEA) in 2015 showed that:

- Working and middle-class families receiving conflicted advice earn returns roughly 1 percentage point lower each year (for example, conflicted advice reduces what would be a 6 percent annual return to a 5 percent return).

- An estimated $1.7 trillion of IRA assets were invested in products that generally provide payments that generate conflicts of interest. Thus, CEA estimated that the annual cost of conflicted advice is about $17 billion each year.

- A typical worker who receives conflicted advice when rolling over a 401(k) balance to an IRA at age 45 will lose an estimated 17 percent from their account by age 65. In other words, if a worker has $100,000 in retirement savings at age 45, without conflicted advice it would grow to an estimated $216,000 by age 65 adjusted for inflation, but if they receive conflicted advice it would grow to $179,000—a loss of $37,000, or 17 percent.

Source: The White House at www.whitehouse.gov/the-press-office/2016/04/06/fact-sheet-middle-class-economics-strengthening-retirement-security-0, accessed May 14, 2021.

A 2016 landmark federal rule requires financial advisors to act solely in your best interest, not their own. Read the *Financial Literacy for My Life* feature on how this new rule will affect your lifetime savings during retirement years.

Education IRA   Created in 1997, the Education IRA, renamed the *Coverdell Education Savings Account* after the late Senator Paul Coverdell, has also been enhanced. You can now give $2,000 a year to each child—up from $500—for the Education IRA. The contributions must be made in cash, and they are not deductible. These accounts grow tax-free and can be invested any way you choose. Coverdells can now be used for elementary and secondary school costs, including books, tuition, and tutoring.

Simplified Employee Pension–IRA (SEP–IRA)   A *SEP–IRA plan* is simply an individual retirement account funded by the employer. Each employee sets up an IRA account at a bank or a brokerage house. Then the employer makes an annual contribution of up to $58,000 in 2021 (indexed to cost-of-living adjustments in the future).

The SEP–IRA is the simplest type of retirement plan if you are fully or partially self-employed. Your contributions, which can vary from year to year, are tax deductible, and earnings accumulate on a tax-deferred basis. A SEP–IRA has no IRS filing requirements, so paperwork is minimal. Exhibit 18-12 summarizes various IRA options.

IRA Withdrawals   When you retire, you will be able to withdraw your IRA in a lump sum, withdraw it in installments over your life expectancy, or place it in an annuity that guarantees payments over your lifetime. If you take the lump sum, the entire amount will be taxable as ordinary income, and the only tax break you will have is standard five-year income averaging. IRA withdrawals made before age 59½ are subject to a 10 percent tax in addition to ordinary income tax, unless the participant dies or becomes disabled. You can avoid this tax if you roll over your IRA.

You cannot keep money in most retirement plans indefinitely. Except for Roth IRAs, most tax-qualified retirement plans, including 403(b), 401(k), and other IRAs, are

Type of Plan	Plan Features
Regular or traditional IRA	• Tax-deferred interest and earnings. • Annual limit on individual contributions. • Limited eligibility for tax-deductible contributions.
Roth IRA	• Tax-deferred interest and earnings. • Annual limit on individual contributions. • Withdrawals are tax free in specific cases. • Contributions do not reduce current taxes.
Spousal IRA	• Tax-deferred interest and earnings. • Both working spouse and nonworking spouse can contribute up to the annual limit. • Limited eligibility for tax-deductible contributions.
Rollover IRA	• Traditional IRA that accepts rollovers of all or a portion of your taxable distribution from a retirement plan. • You can roll over to a Roth IRA.
Education IRA (Coverdell Education Savings Account)	• Tax-deferred interest and earnings. • 10 percent early withdrawal penalty is waived when money is used for higher-education expenses. • Annual limit on individual contributions. • Contributions do not reduce current taxes.
Employer-sponsored retirement plan (SEP–IRA)	• "Pay yourself first" payroll reduction contributions. • Pretax contributions. • Tax-deferred interest and earnings.

EXHIBIT 18-12
Summary of IRA options

Sources: Adapted from "12 Easy Retirement Planning Tips for Women," VALIC, An American General Company, April 1998, p. 20; and *BusinessWeek,* January 28, 2002, p. 111.

required by the IRS to begin what is known as "minimum lifetime distributions" at age 72. If you have retired, you must either receive the entire balance of your tax-qualified plan or start receiving periodic distributions by April 1 of the year following the year in which you reach 72 or retire, if later.

The amount of the minimum required distribution is based on your life expectancy at the time of the distribution. The IRS provides single- and joint-life expectancy tables for calculating required distribution amounts. The penalties for noncompliance in this case are severe. Insufficient distributions may be subject to an excise tax of 50 percent on the amount not withdrawn as required.

KEOGH PLANS The new tax package of 2001 did not forget the self-employed. A **Keogh plan,** named for U.S. Representative Eugene James Keogh of New York, also known as an HR10 or a *self-employed retirement plan,* is a qualified pension plan developed for self-employed people and their employees. Generally, Keogh plans cannot discriminate in favor of a self-employed person or any employee. Both defined-contribution and defined-benefit Keogh plans have tax-deductible contribution limits, and other restrictions also apply to Keogh plans. These plans are more complicated to set up and maintain, but offer more advantages than SEP–IRAs. Therefore, you should obtain professional tax advice before using this type of retirement plan. Whether you have an employer pension plan or a personal retirement plan, you must start withdrawing

Keogh plan A qualified pension plan in which tax-deductible contributions fund the retirement of self-employed people and their employees; also called a *self-employed retirement plan.*

at age 70½ or the IRS will charge you a penalty. In general, with a Keogh plan, you may contribute 25 percent of your annual income, up to a maximum of $58,000 (as of 2021), to this tax-deferred retirement plan.

ANNUITIES

annuity A contract that provides a regular income, typically for as long as the person lives.

In Chapter 12 you learned what an annuity is and how annuities provide lifelong security. You can outlive the proceeds of your IRA, your Keogh plan, or your investments, but an **annuity** provides guaranteed income for life. Who should consider an annuity? One financial planner uses them for clients who have fully funded all other retirement plan options, including 401(k), 403(b), Keogh, and profit-sharing plans, but still want more money for retirement.

You can buy an annuity with the proceeds of an IRA or a company pension or as supplemental retirement income. You can buy an annuity with a single payment or with periodic payments. You can buy an annuity that will begin payouts immediately, or, as is more common, you can buy one that will begin payouts at a later date.

To the extent that annuity payments exceed your premiums, these payments are taxed as ordinary income as you receive them, but earned interest on annuities accumulates tax free until the payments begin. Annuities may be fixed, providing a specific income for life, or variable, with payouts above a guaranteed minimum level dependent on investment return. Either way, the rate of return on annuities is often pegged to market rates.

TYPES OF ANNUITIES   *Immediate annuities* are generally purchased by people of retirement age. Such annuities provide income payments at once. They are usually purchased with a lump-sum payment.

With *deferred annuities,* income payments start at some future date. Interest builds up on the money you deposit. Younger people often use such annuities to save money toward retirement. If you are buying a deferred annuity, you may wish to obtain a contract that permits flexible premiums. With such an annuity, your contributions may vary from year to year.

A deferred annuity purchased with a lump sum is known as a *single-premium deferred annuity.* In recent years, such annuities have been popular because of the tax-free buildup during the accumulation period.

The cash value of your life insurance policy may be converted to an annuity. If you are over 65 and your children have completed their education and are financially self-sufficient, you may no longer need all of your life insurance coverage. An option in your life insurance policy lets you convert its cash value to a lifetime income.

OPTIONS IN ANNUITIES   You can decide on the terms under which your annuity pays you and your family. Exhibit 18-13 summarizes the major options and their uses.

WHICH ANNUITY OPTION IS THE BEST?   The straight life annuity gives more income per dollar of outlay than any other type. But payments stop when you die, whether a month or many years after the payout begins.

Should you get an annuity with a guaranteed return? Opinions differ. Some experts argue that it is a mistake to diminish your monthly income just to make sure your money is returned to your survivors. Some suggest that if you want to ensure that your spouse or someone else continues to receive annuity income after your death, you might choose the joint-and-survivor annuity. Such an annuity pays its installments until the death of the last designated survivor.

You have still another choice to make: how your annuity premiums are to be invested. With a fixed-dollar annuity, the money you pay is invested in bonds and mortgages that have a guaranteed return. Such an annuity guarantees you a fixed amount each payout period. With a variable annuity, the money you pay is generally invested in common

EXHIBIT 18-13 Annuity income options

This exhibit gives you an approximate idea of how different income options compare. The amount of income you actually receive is based on factors such as how you invest, your age, your sex, and the income option you choose. Market conditions at any given time, especially interest rates, influence income amounts.

Income Option	Description	Common Uses	Typical Monthly Income*
Lifetime income. Also called *life income* or *life only*.	You receive income payments for the rest of your life. The income ceases upon your death.	Provides the most income per dollar invested of any lifetime option. Frequently used by single people with limited sources of additional income.	$923.71 per month for life.
Lifetime income with a minimum number of payments guaranteed. Also called *life with period certain*.	You receive income for the rest of your life. If you die before you receive a specific number of payments, your beneficiary will receive the balance of the number of income payments you choose.	Appropriate if you want a life income but dislike the risk of lost income in the event of premature death. People with heirs often consider this option.	$791.49 per month for life, 240-month minimum.
Lifetime income for two people. Also called *joint and survivor*.	Income payments are received for as long as either of the two people are alive. Upon the death of either person, income continues as a percentage of the original amount. Common percentages chosen for the survivor are 50, 66²/₃, and 100%.	Often chosen by couples, who may choose the 100% option when there is little other income, or 50% or 66²/₃% when there is other income. Lifetime income with period certain and installment refund† options are also available for joint-income plans.	$774.06 per month for as long as at least one of the people is alive, assuming the 100% option.

Note: The numbers above are hypothetical, and your actual income may differ. Only a portion of each payment would be taxable.
*Assumes a 65-year-old male with a 65-year-old spouse who invests $100,000 and begins receiving income immediately.
†In an installment refund annuity, you receive an income for the rest of your life. However, if you die before receiving as much money as you paid in, your beneficiary receives regular income until the total payments equal that amount.
Source: Building Your Future with Annuities: A Consumer Guide (Fidelity Investments and U.S. Department of Agriculture, August 1991), p. 12.

stocks or other equities. The income you receive will depend on the investment results. Exhibit 18-14 compares variable and fixed annuities.

An annuity guarantees lifetime income, but you have a choice regarding the form it will take. Discuss all of the possible options with your insurance agent. The features, as well as the costs and fees, of annuities differ from policy to policy. Ask about sales and administrative charges, purchase and withdrawal fees, and interest rate guarantees. Also, as explained in Chapter 12, be sure to check the financial health of the insurance company.

WILL YOU HAVE ENOUGH MONEY DURING RETIREMENT?

Now that you have reviewed all the possible sources of your retirement income, estimate what your annual retirement income will be. Don't forget to inflate incomes or investments that increase with the cost of living (such as Social Security) to what they will be when you retire. (Use the inflation factor table in the *Financial Literacy Calculations* box in this chapter.) Remember, inflation is a major uncontrollable variable for retirees.

Now compare your total estimated retirement income with your total inflated retirement expenses. If your estimated income exceeds your estimated expenses and a large portion of your planned income will automatically increase with the cost of living

EXHIBIT 18-14
A comparison of variable and fixed annuities
The costs, fees, and other features of annuities differ from policy to policy.

	Variable	Fixed
Tax-deferred earnings	Yes	Yes
Variety of income options	Yes	Yes
Annual investment ceiling	No	No
Investment flexibility	Yes	No
Potential for higher returns	Yes	No
Increased investment risk	Yes	No
Hedge against inflation	Yes	No
Security of principal and earnings	No	Yes
Guaranteed interest rate	No	Yes
Control over type of investment in the annuity	Yes	No

during your retirement, you are in good shape. (You should evaluate your plans every few years between now and retirement to be sure your planned income is still adequate to meet your planned expenses.)

If, however, your planned retirement income is less than your estimated retirement expenses, now is the time to take action to increase your retirement income. Also, if a large portion of your retirement income is fixed and will not increase with inflation, you should make plans for a much larger retirement income to meet your rising expenses during retirement. Exhibit 18-15 summarizes the government and private sources of retirement income.

EXHIBIT 18-15   Sources of retirement income

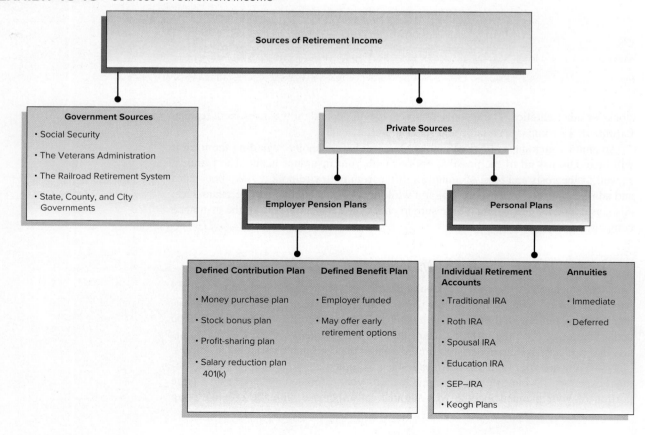

✔️ **PRACTICE QUIZ 18-5**

1. What are possible sources of income for retirees?
2. What are examples of defined-contribution plans? How do they differ from defined-benefit plans?
3. What are the two most popular personal retirement plans?
4. What are annuities? What options are available in annuities? Which option is best?

PFP Sheet 64
Retirement Plan Comparison

PFP Sheet 65
Retirement Income Forecast

Living on Your Retirement Income

The first step in stretching your retirement income is to make sure you are receiving all of the income to which you are entitled. Examine the possible sources of retirement income mentioned earlier to see whether you could qualify for more programs or additional benefits. What assets or valuables could you use as a cash or income source?

As you planned retirement, you estimated a budget or spending plan, but you may find your actual expenses at retirement are higher than anticipated. To stay within your income, you may also need to make some changes in your spending plans. For example, you can use your skills and time instead of your money. There are probably many things you can do yourself instead of paying someone else to do them. Take advantage of free and low-cost recreation such as walks, picnics, public parks, lectures, museums, libraries, art galleries, art fairs, gardening, and church and club programs.

LO18-6

Develop a balanced budget based on your retirement income.

TAX ADVANTAGES

Be sure to take advantage of all the tax savings retirees receive. For more information, go online (irs.gov) or ask your local IRS office for a free copy of *Tax Benefits for Older Americans.* If you have any questions about your taxes, get free help from someone at the IRS. You may need to file a quarterly estimated income tax return beginning with the first quarter of your first year of retirement or arrange for withholding on Social Security and pension payments.

Pursuing a personal interest or hobby during retirement can keep your mind and body active and healthy.
Andersen Ross/Blend Images LLC

WORKING DURING RETIREMENT

You may want to work part-time or start a new part-time career after you retire. Work can provide you with a greater sense of usefulness, involvement, and self-worth and may be the ideal way to add to your retirement income. You may want to pursue a personal interest or hobby, or you can contact your state or local agency on aging for information about employment opportunities for retirees.

If you decide to work part-time after you retire, you should be aware of how your earnings will affect your Social Security income. As long as you do not earn more than the annually exempt amount, your Social Security payments will not be affected. But if you earn more than the annual exempt amount, your Social Security payments will be reduced. Check with your local Social Security office for the latest information.

my life 6

To supplement my retirement income, I may want to work part-time or start a new part-time career after I retire.

Retirees can use their skills and time instead of spending money. Some people decide to work part-time after they retire; some even take new part-time or new full-time jobs. Many people prefer to keep active and pursue new careers.

INVESTING FOR RETIREMENT

The guaranteed-income part of your retirement fund consists of money paid into lower-yield, very safe investments. This part of your fund may already be taken care of through Social Security and retirement plans, as discussed earlier. To offset inflation, your retirement assets must earn enough to keep up with, and even exceed, the rate of inflation.

DIPPING INTO YOUR NEST EGG

Suppose you have $10,000 in a retirement plan account or an IRA. Your money is invested in stocks and bonds that earn an average annual return of 6.4 percent. In 20 years, your account will grow, with compounding, to $34,581. If you withdraw this amount after you reach age 59½ (the age at which you can receive money without a 10 percent penalty) and pay 25 percent income tax on that amount, you will keep nearly $25,900. However, if you close your retirement plan account before age 59½, your account balance will decrease from $10,000 to $6,750 after paying the 10 percent penalty and 25 percent income tax. In addition, your account grows for the next 20 years but at a lower rate of growth, because you are paying taxes on your investment earnings. As a result, the value of your account after 20 years will be approximately $23,300, assuming the same rate of return and tax bracket. The tax consequences of early withdrawal will cost you 33 percent of your account balance at retirement.

When should you draw on your savings? The answer depends on your financial circumstances, your age, and how much you want to leave to your heirs. Your savings may be large enough to allow you to live comfortably on the interest alone. Or you may need to make regular withdrawals to help finance your retirement. Dipping into savings isn't wrong, but you must do so with caution.

How long would your savings last if you withdrew monthly income? If you have $10,000 in savings that earns 5.5 percent interest, compounded quarterly, you could take out $68 every month for 20 years before reducing this nest egg to zero. If you have $40,000, you could collect $224 every month for 30 years before exhausting your nest egg. For different possibilities, see Exhibit 18-16.

EXHIBIT 18-16 Dipping into your nest egg

Dipping into savings isn't wrong; however, you must do so with caution.

Starting Amount of Nest Egg	You Can Reduce Your Nest Egg to Zero by Withdrawing This Much Each Month for the Stated Number of Years					Or You Can Withdraw This Much Each Month and Leave Your Nest Egg Intact
	10 Years	15 Years	20 Years	25 Years	30 Years	
$10,000	$ 107	$ 81	$ 68	$ 61	$ 56	$ 46
15,000	161	121	102	91	84	69
20,000	215	162	136	121	112	92
25,000	269	202	170	152	140	115
30,000	322	243	204	182	168	138
40,000	430	323	272	243	224	184
50,000	537	404	340	304	281	230
60,000	645	485	408	364	337	276
80,000	859	647	544	486	449	368
100,000	1,074	808	680	607	561	460

Note: Based on an interest rate of 5.5 percent per year, compounded quarterly.
Source: Select Committee on Aging, U.S. House of Representatives.

EXHIBIT 18-17   Major sources of retirement income: Advantages and disadvantages

The income needed to live during retirement can come from various sources.

Source	Advantages	Disadvantages
Social Security		
In planning	Forced savings. Portable from job to job. Cost shared with employer.	Increasing economic pressure on the system as U.S. population ages.
At retirement	Inflation-adjusted survivorship rights.	Minimum retirement age specified.
		Earned income may partially offset benefits.
Employee Pension Plans		
In planning	Forced savings.	May not be portable.
	Cost shared or fully covered by employer.	No control over how funds are managed.
At retirement	Survivorship rights.	Cost-of-living increases may not be provided on a regular basis.
Individual Saving and Investing (including housing, IRA, and Keogh plans)		
In planning	Current tax savings (e.g., IRAs).	Current needs compete with future needs.
	Easily incorporated into family (home equity).	Penalty for early withdrawal (IRAs and Keoghs).
	Portable.	
	Control over management of funds.	
At retirement	Inflation resistant.	Some sources taxable.
	Can usually use as much of the funds as you wish, when you wish (within certain requirements).	Mandatory minimum withdrawal restrictions (IRAs and Keoghs).
Post-retirement Employment		
In planning	Special earning skills can be used as they are developed.	Technology and skills needed to keep up may change rapidly.
At retirement	Inflation resistant.	Ill health can mean loss of this income source.

Exhibit 18-17 summarizes major sources of retirement income and their advantages and disadvantages. Finally, use the *Financial Literacy for My Life: Retirement Checklist* to assess your financial condition as you approach retirement.

 PRACTICE QUIZ 18-6

1. What is the first step in stretching your retirement income?
2. How should you invest to obtain retirement income?

Financial Literacy for My Life

RETIREMENT CHECKLIST

As you approach retirement, assess your financial condition using the following checklist. Don't wait too long or you will miss one or more opportunities to maximize your future financial independence.

		Yes	No
1.	Do you talk regularly and frankly to family members about finances and agree on your goals and the lifestyle you will prefer as you get older?	☐	☐
2.	Do you know what your sources of income will be after retirement, how much to expect from each source, and when?	☐	☐
3.	Do you save according to your plan, shifting from growth-producing to safe, income-producing investments?	☐	☐
4.	Do you know where your health insurance will come from after retirement and what it will cover?	☐	☐
5.	Do you review your health insurance and consider options such as converting to cash or investments?	☐	☐
6.	Do you have your own credit history?	☐	☐
7.	Do you have a current will or a living trust?	☐	☐
8.	Do you know where you plan to live in retirement?	☐	☐
9.	Do you anticipate the tax consequences of your retirement plans and of passing assets on to your heirs?	☐	☐
10.	Do your children or other responsible family members know where your important documents are and whom to contact if questions arise?	☐	☐
11.	Do you have legal documents, such as a living will or a power of attorney, specifying your instructions in the event of your death or incapacitating illness?	☐	☐

TIMELINE FOR RETIREMENT

At age 50 Begin making catch-up contributions, an extra amount that those over 50 can add, to 401(k) and other retirement accounts.

At 59½ No more tax penalties on early withdrawals from retirement accounts, but leaving money in means more time for it to grow.

At 62 The minimum age to receive Social Security benefits, but delaying means a bigger monthly benefit.

At 65 Eligible for Medicare.

At 67 Eligible for full Social Security benefits if born in 1960 or later.

At 72 Start taking minimum withdrawals from most retirement accounts by this age; otherwise, you may be charged heavy tax penalties in the future.

Your Personal Finance Roadmap and Dashboard:

Retirement Planning

PERCENT OF PRERETIREMENT EARNINGS

You have several retirement savings opportunities available to you—from IRAs and SEPs to 401(k)s and 403(b)s. These options are especially important now that traditional pensions and other employer-funded retirement plans have become increasingly rare.

YOUR SITUATION

Have you figured out how much money you should save for retirement? Most financial advisors suggest that you will need 70 to 90 percent of pre-retirement earnings to live comfortably. Are you taking advantage of retirement savings programs at work, especially those where your employer matches contributions? Have you made sure that your investments are diversified? Other personal financial planning actions you might consider during various stages of your life include:

◉ First Steps

- Stop procrastinating and start planning for retirement now.
- Starting savings small is better than not starting at all.
- Work part-time and start your Roth IRA account.
- If you begin saving later, you'll have to save and invest more each month.
- You can typically afford to take a little more risk with your investments.
- If you are putting off retirement planning because you don't know how, speak to a professional who does.
- Take full responsibility of your financial future.

- Put together a retirement plan and save more.
- Try to put aside 10 percent of your income for retirement. (If your employer matches 3 percent, then you should be saving 7 percent, for a total of 10 percent.)
- About 80 percent of your 401(k) assets should be in equities and 20 percent in fixed income.

◉ Next Steps

- You've been diligent about contributing to a savings account, but is it enough?
- Are you sure your money is invested properly? Are there better options for you?
- Make your retirement a priority and determine how much you'll need during retirement.
- Try to put aside 15 to 20 percent of your income for retirement.
- About 60 to 70 percent of your 401(k) assets should be in stocks and 30 to 40 percent in bonds.
- Reassess your financial needs in retirement.

◉ Later Steps

- If you are already near or past your retirement date, it is still not too late.
- Consider how you are receiving your income and how long it will last.
- Revise your income distribution strategy.
- Consider the impact of inflation, taxes, and long-term care expense.
- Try to extend your working years and work at least part-time during retirement.
- Consider converting the equity in your home into income.
- Be sure to rebalance your investment portfolio as needed.

> **YOUR** next step . . . select one or more of the items above and create an action plan to implement those financial planning activities.

SUMMARY OF LEARNING OBJECTIVES

LO15-1

Describe the characteristics of corporate bonds. A corporate bond is a corporation's written pledge to repay a specified amount of money with interest. All of the details about a bond (face value, interest rate, maturity date, repayment, etc.) are contained in the bond indenture. The trustee is the bondholder's representative.

LO15-2

Discuss why corporations issue bonds. Corporations issue bonds and other securities to pay for major purchases and to help finance their ongoing activities. Firms also issue bonds when it is difficult or impossible to sell stock, to improve a corporation's financial leverage, and to reduce taxes paid to federal and state governments. Bonds may be debentures, mortgage bonds, subordinated debentures, convertible bonds, or high-yield (junk) bonds. Many bonds are callable. A call provision can be used to buy back bonds before the maturity date. To ensure that the money will be available when needed to repay bonds, many corporations establish a sinking fund. Corporations can also issue serial bonds that mature on different dates.

LO15-3

Explain why investors purchase corporate bonds. Investors purchase corporate bonds for three reasons: (1) interest income, (2) possible increase in value, and (3) repayment at maturity. They are also an excellent way to use asset allocation to diversify your investment portfolio. The method used to pay bondholders their interest depends on whether they own registered bonds or bearer bonds. Because bonds can increase or decrease in value, it is possible to purchase a bond at a discount and hold the bond until it appreciates in value. Changes in overall interest rates in the economy and changes in the financial condition of the corporation are the primary causes of most bond price fluctuations. You can lose money on your investment if your bond decreases in value. You can also choose to hold the bond until maturity, when the corporation will repay the bond's face value. Corporate bonds are sold by full-service and discount brokerage firms and online.

LO15-4

Discuss why federal, state, and local governments issue bonds and why investors purchase government bonds. Bonds issued by the U.S. Treasury are used to finance the national debt and the ongoing activities of the federal government. Currently, the U.S. Treasury issues five principal types of securities: Treasury bills, Treasury notes, Treasury bonds, Treasury Inflation-Protected Securities (TIPS), and savings bonds. Federal agencies, government-sponsored enterprises, and state and local governments also issue bonds to finance their ongoing activities and special projects. Typical activities and projects include home mortgage financing, airports, schools, toll roads, and toll bridges. U.S. Treasury securities can be purchased through TreasuryDirect, brokerage firms, and banks. Municipal bonds are generally sold through the government entity that issued them or through banks or brokerage firms. One of the most important features of municipal bonds is that interest on them may be exempt from federal taxes.

LO15-5

Describe how to evaluate bonds when making an investment. Today it is possible to trade bonds online and obtain research information via the internet. Some local newspapers, *The Wall Street Journal,* and *Barron's* provide bond investors with information they need to evaluate a bond issue. Detailed financial information can also be obtained by accessing a corporation's website or requesting a print copy of the corporation's annual report. Information about municipal bonds can be obtained from the entity that issued the bonds or from internet sites. To determine the quality of a bond issue, most investors study the financial information and ratings provided by Standard & Poor's, Moody's, and Fitch Bond Ratings.

Investors can also calculate a current yield and a yield to maturity to evaluate a decision to buy or sell bond issues. The current yield is determined by dividing the annual income amount by a bond's current market value. The yield to maturity takes into account the relationship among a bond's maturity value, the time to maturity, the current price, and the dollar amount of interest.

KEY TERMS

bearer bond   529

bond indenture   523

bond ladder   530

call feature   526

convertible bond   525

convertible corporate note   525

corporate bond   523

current yield   543

debenture   524

face value   523

general obligation bond   536

government bond   533

high-yield bonds   525

maturity date   523

mortgage bond   524

KEY FORMULAS

Topic	Formula
Annual interest	Dollar amount of annual interest = Face value × Interest rate
Example:	$= \$1,000 \times 4.2\%$
	$= \$1,000 \times 0.042$
	$= \$42$
Purchase price for a Treasury bill	Step 1: Discount amount = Maturity value × Interest rate
Example:	$= \$1,000 \times 0.50\%$
	$= \$1,000 \times 0.005$
	$= \$5$
	Step 2: Purchase price = Maturity value − Discount amount
	$= \$1,000 - \$5$
	$= \$995$
Current yield for a 52-week T-bill	$\text{Current yield} = \dfrac{\text{Discount amount}}{\text{Purchase price}}$
Example:	$\text{Current yield} = \dfrac{\$5}{\$995}$
	$= 0.00503 = 0.503\%$
Taxable equivalent yield (24% tax rate)	$\text{Taxable equivalent yield} = \dfrac{\text{Tax-exempt yield}}{1.0 - \text{Your tax rate}}$
Example:	$\text{Taxable equivalent yield} = \dfrac{0.04}{1.0 - 0.24}$
	$= 0.053 = 5.3\%$
Bond price	Bond price = Face value × Bond quotation
Example:	$= \$1,000 \times 93\%$
	$= \$1,000 \times 0.93$
	$= \$930$
Current yield on a corporate bond	$\text{Current yield} = \dfrac{\text{Annual income amount}}{\text{Current market value}}$
Example:	$\text{Current yield} = \dfrac{\$50}{\$930}$
	$= 0.054 = 5.4\%$
Yield to maturity	$\text{Yield to maturity} = \dfrac{\text{Dollar amount of annual interest} + \dfrac{\text{Face value} - \text{Market value}}{\text{Number of periods}}}{\dfrac{\text{Market value} + \text{Face value}}{2}}$

Topic	Formula

Example:

$$\text{Yield to maturity} = \frac{\$60 + \dfrac{\$1,000 - \$900}{10}}{\dfrac{\$900 + \$1,000}{2}}$$

$$= 0.074 = 7.4\%$$

Times interest earned

$$\text{Times interest earned} = \frac{\text{Operating income before interest and taxes}}{\text{Interest expense}}$$

Example:

$$= \frac{\$4,800 \text{ million}}{\$1,066 \text{ million}}$$

$$= 4.50 \text{ to } 1$$

SELF-TEST PROBLEMS

1. Charlie Nelson is 50 years old and wants to diversify her investment portfolio and must decide if she should invest in tax-free municipal bonds or corporate bonds. The tax-free bonds are highly rated and pay 3.25 percent. The corporate bonds are more speculative and pay 5 percent.

   a. If Ms. Nelson is in the 32 percent tax bracket, what is the taxable equivalent yield for the municipal bond?

   b. If you were Ms. Nelson, would you choose the municipal bonds or corporate bonds? Justify your answer.

2. James Gomez purchased ten $1,000 corporate bonds issued by Kohl's. The annual interest rate for the bonds is 4.00 percent.

   a. What is the annual interest amount for each Kohl's bond?

   b. If the bonds have a current price quotation of 106, what is the current price of this bond?

   c. Given the above information, what is the current yield for a Kohl's bond?

3. Matt Redburn has decided to invest $1,000 and purchase 52-week T-bills with some excess cash he doesn't need for the next year. He knows that T-bills are discounted securities, but he is confused about the purchase price and current yield and asks for your help.

   a. If the T-bill has a stated interest rate of 0.40 percent, what is the purchase price?

   b. What is the current yield for the T-bill?

Self-Test Solutions

1. a. The taxable equivalent yield is 4.78 percent for the municipal bond.

$$\text{Taxable equivalent yield} = \frac{\text{Tax-exempt yield}}{1.0 - \text{Your tax rate}}$$

$$= \frac{0.0325}{0.68}$$

$$= 0.0478 = 4.78\%$$

   b. The taxable equivalent yield for the municipal bond (4.78 percent) is only slightly lower than the current yield on the corporate bond (5 percent). Because Ms. Nelson is 50 years old and will probably retire in 10 to 15 years, the highly rated municipal bond is a better choice than the more speculative corporate bond.

2. a. The annual interest amount is $40 for each Kohl's bond.

$$\text{Dollar amount of annual interest} = \text{Face value} \times \text{Interest rate}$$

$$= \$1,000 \times 4.00\%$$

$$= \$40$$

b. The current bond price for the Kohl's bond is $1,060.

$$\text{Bond price} = \text{Face value} \times \text{Bond quote}$$
$$= \$1,000 \times 106\%$$
$$= \$1,060$$

c. The current yield for the Kohl's bond is 3.77 percent.

$$\text{Current yield} = \frac{\text{Annual income amount}}{\text{Current market value}}$$
$$= \frac{\$40}{\$1,060}$$
$$= 0.0377 = 3.77\%$$

3. a. The purchase price for the 52-week T-bill is $996.

$$\text{Step 1: Discount amount} = \text{Maturity value} \times \text{Interest rate}$$
$$= \$1,000 \times 0.40\%$$
$$= \$1,000 \times 0.0040$$
$$= \$4$$
$$\text{Step 2: Purchase price} = \text{Maturity value} - \text{Discount amount}$$
$$= \$1,000 - \$4$$
$$= \$996$$

b. The current yield for the T-bill is 0.402%.

$$\text{Current yield} = \frac{\text{Discount amount}}{\text{Purchase price}}$$
$$= \frac{\$4}{\$996}$$
$$= 0.00402 = 0.402\%$$

FINANCIAL PLANNING PROBLEMS

LO15-2 **1.** *Analyzing Convertible Bonds.* Jackson Metals, Inc., issued a $1,000 convertible corporate bond. Each bond is convertible to 32 shares of the firm's common stock.

    a. What price must the common stock reach before investors would consider converting their bond to common stock?

    b. If you owned a bond in Jackson Metals, would you convert your bond to common stock if the stock's price did reach the conversion price? Explain your answer.

LO15-3 **2.** *Calculating Interest.* Calculate the annual interest and the semiannual interest payment for the following corporate bond issues with a face value of $1,000.

Annual Interest Rate	Annual Interest Amount	Semiannual Interest Payment
3.60%		
4.30%		
2.25%		
2.80%		

3. *Determining the Approximate Value for a Bond.* To solve the problem below, use the present value of a bond calculator at https://www.thecalculator.co/finance/Bond-Price-Calculator-606.html. Note: Each bond below has a face value of $1,000. LO15-3

Interest Rate When Issued	Years to Maturity	Frequency of Payments	Interest Rate for Comparable Bond	Approximate Present Value
5%	10	Semiannual	4%	
4.1%	8	Annual	5%	
3.2%	6	Semiannual	4%	

4. *Calculating Total Return.* Jean Miller purchased a $1,000 corporate bond for $880. The bond paid 3 percent annual interest. Three years later, she sold the bond for $960. Calculate the total return for Ms. Miller's bond investment. LO15-3

5. *Calculating Total Return.* Mark Crane purchased a $1,000 corporate bond five years ago for $1,060. The bond paid 2.5 percent annual interest. Five years later, he sold the bond for $950. Calculate the total return for Mr. Crane's bond investment. LO15-3

6. *Calculating Bond Yield for a T-Bill.* Sandra Waterman purchased a 52-week, $1,000 T-bill issued by the U.S. Treasury. The purchase price was $984. LO15-4

   a. What is the amount of the discount?

   b. What is the amount Ms. Waterman will receive when the T-bill matures?

   c. What is the current yield for the 52-week T-bill at the time of purchase?

7. *Calculating Total Return.* James McCulloch purchased a 30-year U.S. Treasury bond four years ago for $1,000. The bond paid 2.1 percent annual interest. Four years later he sold the bond for $1,040. LO15-4

   a. What is the annual interest amount for the bond?

   b. What is the total interest Mr. McCulloch earned during the four-year period?

   c. What is the total return for Mr. McCulloch's bond investment?

8. *Calculate the Purchase Price for a T-Bill.* Calculate the purchase price for a 52-week, $1,000 Treasury bill with a stated interest rate of 1.10 percent. LO15-4

9. *Calculating Tax-Equivalent Yield.* Assume you are in the 35 percent tax bracket and purchase a 2.8 percent, tax-exempt municipal bond. Use the formula presented in this chapter to calculate the taxable equivalent yield for this investment. LO15-4

10. *Calculating Tax-Equivalent Yield.* Assume you are in the 32 percent tax bracket and purchase a 3.15 percent, tax-exempt municipal bond. Use the formula presented in this chapter to calculate the taxable equivalent yield for this investment. LO15-4

11. *Determining Bond Prices.* What is the current price for a $1,000 bond that has a price quote of 108? LO15-5

12. *Calculating Current Yields.* Calculate the interest amount and current yield for the following $1,000 bonds: LO15-5

Interest Rate	Interest Amount	Current Market Value	Current Yield
4%		$1,040	
3.6%		$920	
2.9%		$1,050	

13. *Calculating the Times Interest Earned Ratio.* Assume Northern Electronic Manufacturing has operating income before interest and taxes of $925 million. It also has interest expense of $124 million. Calculate the times interest earned ratio for this company. LO15-5

14. *Calculating Yields.* Assume that 10 years ago you purchased a $1,000 bond for $920. The bond pays 3.1 percent interest and will mature this year. LO15-5

   a. Calculate the current yield on your bond investment at the time of the purchase.

   b. Determine the yield to maturity on your bond investment at the time of purchase.

15. *Calculating Yields.* Assume you purchased a high-yield corporate bond with a face value of $1,000 at its current market price of $850. It pays 5 percent interest and will mature in eight years. LO15-5

   a. Determine the current yield on your bond investment at the time of purchase.

   b. Determine the yield to maturity on your bond investment at the time of purchase.

For investors who want to buy U.S. Treasury securities, the TreasuryDirect website is a treasure trove of information. Detailed information about Treasury bills, notes, bonds, Treasury Inflation-Protected Securities (TIPS), and savings bonds is provided. You can also open an account and buy securities online without having to use an account executive or broker at a bank or brokerage firm. More information is provided in the website's Research Center and the Planning & Giving section. There is even a section for tools and calculators to help you plan your financial future.

Action items:

1. Visit the TreasuryDirect website at https://treasurydirect. gov/indiv/indiv.htm. Explore the differences between

the different investment options. Also, take a look at the material in the Research Center, Planning & Giving section, and Tools sections.

2. Create a visual presentation (PowerPoint presentation, video, storyboard, or other format) to explain (a) the different investment options available from the U.S. Treasury, (b) why people invest in Treasury securities, and (c) if you think Treasury securities are a good investment alternative to help you achieve your financial goals at this time in your life.

FINANCIAL PLANNING CASE

A Lesson from the Past

Back in 2018, Betty Wallace, a 47-year-old single mother, got a telephone call from a Wall Street account executive who said that other clients had given him her name. Then he told her his brokerage firm was selling a new corporate bond issue in Great Resources Exploration, a company heavily engaged in oil exploration in the southern United States and off the Texas and Louisiana coast. The bonds in this issue paid investors 6.7 percent a year. The bonds in this issue were also convertible to 18.5 shares of the company's stock. He then said that the minimum investment was $5,000 and that if she wanted to take advantage of this "once in a lifetime" opportunity, she had to move fast. To Betty, it was an opportunity too good to pass up, and she bit hook, line, and sinker. She sent the account executive a check—and never heard from him again. When she went to the library to research her bond investment, she found there was no such company as Great Resources Exploration. She lost her $5,000 and quickly vowed she would never invest in bonds again. From now on, she would put her money in the bank, where it was guaranteed.

Over the next four years, she continued to deposit money in the bank and accumulated more than $46,000. Things seemed to be pretty much on track until her certificate of deposit (CD) matured. When she went to renew the CD, the bank officer told her interest rates had fallen and current CD interest rates ranged between 0.5 and 2 percent.

Betty decided to shop around for higher rates. She called several local banks and got pretty much the same answer. Then a friend suggested that she talk to Peter Manning, an account executive for Fidelity Investments. Manning told her there were conservative corporate bonds and quality stock issues that offered higher returns. But, he warned her, these investments were *not* guaranteed. If she wanted higher returns, she would have to take some risks.

While Betty wanted higher returns, she also remembered how she had lost $5,000 investing in fictitious corporate bonds. When she told Peter Manning about her bond investment in the fictitious Great Resources Exploration, he pointed out that she

made some pretty serious mistakes. For starters, she bought the bonds over the phone from someone she didn't know, and she bought them without doing any research. He assured her the bonds and stocks he would recommend were issued by real companies, and she would be able to find a lot of information on each of his recommendations at the library or on the internet. For starters, he suggested the following three investments:

1. A PepsiCo corporate note that pays 2.625 percent annual interest and matures on July 29, 2029. This note has a current market value of $1,110 and is rated A by Moody's.

2. An AT&T corporate note that pays 4.125 percent annual interest and matures on February 17, 2026. This note has a current market value of $1,150 and is rated Baa by Moody's.

3. American Electric Power common stock (listed on the New York Stock Exchange) and selling for $81 a share with annual dividends of $2.96 per share and a current yield of 3.7 percent.

Questions

1. According to Betty Wallace, the chance to invest in Great Resources Exploration was "too good to pass up." Unfortunately, it was too good to be true, and she lost $5,000. Why do you think so many people are taken in by get-rich-quick schemes?

2. Over the past four to five years, investors have been forced to look for ways to squeeze additional income from their investment portfolios. Do you think investing in corporate bonds or notes or quality stocks is the best way to increase income? Why or why not?

3. Using information obtained in the library or on the internet, answer the following questions about Peter Manning's investment suggestions.

   a. What does the rating for the PepsiCo note mean?

   b. What does the rating for the AT&T corporate note mean?

   c. How would you describe the common stock issued by American Electric Power?

4. Based on your research, which investment would you recommend to Betty Wallace? Why?

5. Using the internet, a current newspaper, *The Wall Street Journal,* or *Barron's,* determine the current market value for each of the three investments suggested in this case. Based on this information, would these investments have been profitable if Betty had purchased the PepsiCo corporate note for $1,110, the AT&T corporate note for $1,150, or American Electric Power stock for $81 a share? Hint: You may want to use the Finra website at http://finra-markets.morningstar.com/BondCenter/Default.jsp to determine current bond values and the Yahoo Finance website at https://finance.yahoo.com/ to determine the current value for American Electric Power.

YOUR PERSONAL FINANCIAL PLAN

INVESTING IN BONDS

Including bonds in an investment portfolio can be useful for achieving short-term and long-term financial goals when certain life situations, business conditions, and economic trends arise.

Your Short-Term Financial Planning Activity

Task Evaluate the difference between corporate bonds and stocks and determine if bonds could help you achieve your financial goals.

Research

1) Review the material in Exhibit 15-1 to understand the differences between bond and stock investments.

2) Read the article "What Are Corporate Bonds" at the Securities and Exchange website (https://www.investor.gov/introduction-investing/general-resources/news-alerts/alerts-bulletins/investor-bulletins/what-are).

3) Use the internet to locate other sources of information about why investors choose bond investments.

Outcome Create a visual presentation (PowerPoint presentation, video, storyboard, or other format) to explain how bonds differ from stocks. Also, describe under what circumstances bonds could help you meet your short-term financial goals.

Your Long-Term Financial Planning Activity

Task Evaluate at least two different corporate bonds that could help you obtain your long-term financial goals.

Research

1) Review the material in the section "The Decision to Buy or Sell Bonds" in this chapter.

2) Use the search tab at the Finra.org website at http://finra-markets.morningstar.com/BondCenter/ and enter the names of two corporate bonds that you think would be good investments.

3) Use the internet and other sources of information to answer the questions on PFP Sheet 60 (Corporate Bond Evaluation) for each bond you chose.

Outcome In a two- to three-page report, describe each bond you evaluated. In your report, be sure to explain if you would invest $10,000 in either of the bonds you researched. Also, explain what information from your research supports your decision to invest or not invest in these bonds. Attach the corporate bond evaluation sheets for each bond as part of your final report.

CONTINUING CASE

Investing in Bonds

With the triplets now in high school, Jamie Lee and Ross have made good decisions so far concerning their financial and investment strategies. They budgeted throughout the years and are right on track to reach their long-term investment goals of paying the triplets' college tuition and accumulating enough to purchase a beach house to enjoy when Jamie Lee and Ross retire.

The pair are still researching where best to invest the $50,000 that Ross recently inherited from his uncle's estate. Ross and Jamie Lee would like to invest in several varieties of stocks, bonds, or other investment securities to supplement their retirement income goals.

Jamie Lee and Ross have been researching stock investment opportunities that may offer lucrative returns, but they know there is risk involved. They are aware that they must develop a plan to assess the risk of the various investment types so they may have the proper balance between high, moderate, and low-risk investment alternatives.

They decide that at this stage of their lives, it might be wise to speak to an investment counselor, and they contact Mr. Jay Hall, who has been highly recommended by a trusted colleague and friend of Ross throughout the years.

Mr. Hall assesses their desired risk for investments and recommends bonds for the low-risk portion of their investment portfolio.

Questions

1. Based on Exhibit 15-1, what are the important differences between stocks and bonds?

Bonds	Stocks

2. Why are bonds a good option for the conservative investor?

3. Jamie Lee and Ross were unaware that there was so much to learn about the different types of bonds. Using the information found in the text, compare the four types of corporate bonds: *Debenture Bond, Mortgage Bond, Subordinate Debenture Bond, and Convertible Bond*. Which bond investment type would you recommend for Jamie Lee and Ross? Why?

Debenture Bond	Mortgage Bond	Subordinate Debenture Bond	Convertible Bond

4. Using the *Personal Financial Planner Sheet 60,* Corporate Bond Evaluation, and the suggested websites listed in this chapter, choose two different corporate bonds that you feel would be a good investment for Jamie Lee and Ross. Then complete *Personal Financial Planner Sheet 60* for each bond that you chose.

DAILY SPENDING DIARY

"How do I know if investing in bonds would be the right option for me?"

Directions

Your *Daily Spending Diary* will help you maintain a record of your expenses to better understand your spending habits. As you record daily spending, your comments should reflect what you have learned about your spending patterns and help you consider possible changes you might want to make.

Analysis Questions

1. How might changes in your spending activities allow you to increase funds available for investing?

2. In what types of situations might investing in bonds be appropriate?

A *Daily Spending Diary* sheet is located at the end of Chapter 1 and on the library resource site in *Connect.*

SUMMARY OF LEARNING OBJECTIVES

LO16-1

Describe the characteristics of mutual fund investments. The major reasons investors choose mutual funds are professional management and diversification. Mutual funds are also a convenient way to invest money. There are three types of mutual funds. A closed-end fund is a mutual fund whose shares are issued only when the fund is organized. An exchange-traded fund (ETF) is a fund that invests in the stocks and securities contained in a specific stock or securities index. Both closed-end funds and exchange-traded funds are traded on a securities exchange or in the over-the-counter market. An open-end fund is a mutual fund whose shares are sold and redeemed by the investment company at the net asset value (NAV) at the request of investors. Mutual funds are also classified as load or no-load funds. A load fund charges a commission every time you purchase shares. No commission is charged to purchase shares in a no-load fund. Mutual funds can also be classified as A shares (commissions charged when shares are purchased), B shares (commissions charged when money is withdrawn during the first five years to seven years), and C shares (usually no commission to buy or sell shares, but often higher, ongoing 12b-1 fees). Other possible fees include management fees, contingent deferred fees, and 12b-1 fees. Together all the different fees are reported as an expense ratio.

LO16-2

Classify mutual funds by investment objective. The managers of mutual funds tailor their investment portfolios to achieve specific investment objectives that match the objectives of different types of investors. The major categories of stock mutual funds, in terms of the types of securities in which they invest, are aggressive growth, equity income, global, growth, index, international, large-cap, midcap, regional, sector, small-cap, and socially responsible. There are also bond funds that include high-yield, intermediate corporate, intermediate U.S. government, long-term corporate, long-term U.S. government, municipal, short-term corporate, short-term U.S. government, and world. Finally, other funds invest in a mix of different stocks, bonds, and other investment securities that include asset allocation funds, balanced funds, funds of funds, target-date funds, and money market funds. Today many investment companies use a family-of-funds concept, which allows shareholders to switch their investments among funds as different funds offer more potential, financial reward, or security. Portfolio construction is the process of choosing different types of stocks, bonds, funds, and other

investment alternatives to obtain larger returns while reducing risks. For many investors, a very important component of their investment portfolio is a 401(k) or 403(b) retirement plan.

LO16-3

Explain how to evaluate mutual funds for investment purposes. The responsibility for choosing the "right" mutual fund rests with you, the investor. One of the first questions you must answer is whether you want a managed fund or an index fund. Most mutual funds are managed funds, with a professional fund manager (or team of managers) who chooses the securities contained in the fund. An index fund invests in the securities that are contained in an index, such as the Standard & Poor's 500 stock index. Statistically, the majority of managed mutual funds have failed to outperform the Standard & Poor's 500 stock index or other indices over a long period of time. The information on the internet, from professional advisory services, in the fund prospectus and annual report, and in newspapers and financial publications can all help you evaluate a mutual fund.

LO16-4

Describe how and why mutual funds are bought and sold. The advantages and disadvantages of mutual funds have made mutual funds the investment of choice for many investors. Although the amount may be lower, for $250 to $3,000 you can open an account and begin investing. The shares of a closed-end fund or exchange-traded fund are bought and sold on organized securities exchanges or the over-the-counter market with the help of a brokerage firm. The shares of an open-end fund may be purchased through an account executive or salesperson who is authorized to sell them or from the investment company that sponsors the fund. The shares in an open-end fund can be sold to the investment company that sponsors the fund. Shares of closed-end funds, ETFs, and open-end funds can also be bought and sold by investing through a mutual fund supermarket.

Shareholders in mutual funds can receive a return in one of three ways: income dividends, capital gain distributions when the *fund* buys and sells securities in the fund's portfolio at a profit, and capital gains when the *shareholder* sells shares in the mutual fund at a higher price than the price paid. Unless your mutual fund account is part of an individual retirement account, or 401k or 403(b) retirement account, income dividends, capital gain distributions, and capital gains are subject to taxation. A number of purchase and withdrawal options are available.

KEY TERMS

capital gain distributions   576

closed-end fund   558

contingent deferred sales
  load   561

exchange-traded fund (ETF)   558

expense ratio   562

family of funds   567

Income dividends   576

load fund   560

mutual fund   556

net asset value (NAV)   559

no-load fund   561

open-end fund   559

portfolio construction   567

reinvestment plan   580

turnover ratio   578

12b-1 fee   562

KEY FORMULAS

Topic	Formula
Net asset value	$\text{Net asset value} = \dfrac{\text{Value of the fund's portfolio} - \text{Liabilities}}{\text{Number of shares outstanding}}$
Example:	$\text{Net asset value} = \dfrac{\$245 \text{ million} - \$5 \text{ million}}{8 \text{ million shares}}$
	$= \$30 \text{ per share}$
Dollar amount of sales load	$\text{Dollar amount of sales load} = \text{Original investment} \times \text{Sales load stated as a percentage}$
Example:	$\text{Dollar amount of sales load} = \$20,000 \times 5\%$
	$= \$20,000 \times 0.05$
	$= \$1,000$
Contingent deferred sales load	$\text{Contingent deferred sales load} = \text{Withdrawal amount} \times \text{Contingent deferred sales load as a percentage}$
Example:	$\text{Contingent deferred sales load} = \$12,000 \times 4\%$
	$= \$12,000 \times 0.04$
	$= \$480$

Total return

$$
\begin{array}{l}
\text{Income dividends} \\
+ \text{ Capital gain distributions} \\
\underline{+ \text{ Change in market value}} \\
\text{Dollar amount of total return}
\end{array}
$$

Example:

Dollar amount of total return =	$ 140	Income dividends
	+ 90	Capital gain distributions
	+ 220	Change in market value
	$ 450	Dollar amount of total return

Topic	Formula
Percentage of total return	$\text{Percentage of total return} = \dfrac{\text{Dollar amount of total return}}{\text{Original cost of your investment}}$
Example:	$\text{Percentage of total return} = \dfrac{\$450}{\$4,500}$
	$= 0.10, \text{ or } 10\%$
Withdrawal calculation	$\text{Amount you receive} = \text{Investment growth} \times \text{Percentage of growth withdrawn}$
Example:	$\text{Amount you receive} = \$2,000 \times 30\%$
	$= \$2,000 \times 0.30$
	$= \$600$

SELF-TEST PROBLEMS

1. Three years ago, Dorothy Schwartz's mutual fund portfolio was worth $243,000. Now, because of an upturn in the economy, the value of her investment portfolio has increased to $320,000. Even though her investments have increased in value, she wonders if it is time to change her investment holdings, which consist of either aggressive growth funds or growth funds.

   a. How much money has Ms. Schwartz gained in the last three years?

   b. Given the above information, calculate the percentage of gain.

   c. If you were in Dorothy Schwartz's position, what actions would you take to evaluate your investment portfolio?

2. Two years ago, Bill Crandall purchased 500 shares in the no-load Vanguard Dividend Growth fund—a Morningstar four-star fund that invests in corporations that are currently paying dividends and is a fund that will provide a steady stream of dividend income. His rationale for choosing this fund was that he wanted a fund that was conservative and highly rated. Each share in the fund cost $33. At the end of the two years, he received income dividends and capital gain distributions that total $1.66 a share for the two-year period. At the end of two years, the shares in the fund were selling for $38.

   a. How much did Mr. Crandall invest in this fund?

   b. At the end of two years, what is the total return for this fund?

   c. What is the percentage of total return?

Self-Test Solutions

1. a. Dollar gain = $320,000 Current value − $243,000 Value three years ago

      = $77,000

   b. Percentage of gain = $77,000 Dollar gain ÷ $243,000 Value three years ago

      = 0.32 = 32%

   c. While Ms. Schwartz has several options, any decision should be based on careful research and evaluation. First, she could do nothing. While she has gained a substantial amount of money ($77,000, or 32 percent), she may want to hold onto her existing investments if she believes the economy is still improving and the value of her funds will increase. Second, she could sell (or exchange) some or all of her shares in specific funds and add different funds to increase her asset allocations. Finally, she could sell shares in some of her funds and place the cash she receives in a savings or money market account or purchase a certificate of deposit (CD) if she believes the economy is beginning to decline. Deciding which option Ms. Schwartz should take may depend on the economic conditions at the time you answer this question.

2. a. Total investment = Price per share × Number of shares

      = $33 × 500

      = $16,500

   b. Dividends & Distributions = $1.66 × 500 = $830

      Change in share value = $38 − $33 = $5 Gain per share

      Total increase in value = $5 Gain per share × 500 = $2,500 Gain in value

      Total return = $830 Income dividends + $2,500 Gain in value

      = $3,330 Total return

   c. Percentage of total return = $\dfrac{\$3,330}{\$16,500 \text{ Investment}}$

      = 0.202 = 20.2%

FINANCIAL PLANNING PROBLEMS

LO16-1 1. *Calculating Net Asset Value.* Given the following information, calculate the net asset value for the Boston Equity mutual fund.

Total assets	$870 million
Total liabilities	$4 million
Total number of shares	42 million

584

2. *Calculating Net Asset Value.* Given the following information, calculate the net asset value for the New Empire small-cap mutual fund.   LO16-1

Total assets	$910 million
Total liabilities	$20 million
Total number of shares	60 million

3. *Calculating Sales Fees.* Julie Martin is investing $35,000 in the Invesco Charter mutual fund. The fund charges a 5.50 percent   LO16-1
commission when shares are purchased. Calculate the amount of commission Julie must pay.

4. *Calculating Sales Fees.* Bill Matthews is investing $11,300 in the Washington Mutual fund. The fund charges a 5.75 percent   LO16-1
commission when shares are purchased. Calculate the amount of commission Bill must pay.

5. *Calculating Contingent Deferred Sales Loads.* Ted Paulson needed money to pay for unexpected medical bills. To obtain   LO16-1
$12,000, he decided to sell some of his shares in the Ridgemoor Capital Appreciation Fund. When he called the investment
company, he was told that the following fees would be charged to sell his B shares:

First year	5 percent withdrawal fee
Second year	4 percent withdrawal fee
Third year	3 percent withdrawal fee
Fourth year	2 percent withdrawal fee
Fifth year	1 percent withdrawal fee

If he has owned the fund for 21 months and withdraws $12,000 to pay medical bills, what is the amount of the contingent
deferred sales load?

6. *Calculating Contingent Deferred Sales Loads.* Nina Collins purchased the New Dimensions bond fund. While this fund   LO16-1
doesn't charge a front-end load, it does charge a contingent deferred sales load of 4 percent for any withdrawals in the first
five years. If Nina withdraws $5,600 during the second year, how much is the contingent deferred sales load?

7. *Determining Management Fees.* Mathew Johnston invested a total of $94,000 in the New Colony Pacific Region mutual   LO16-1
fund. The management fee for this particular fund is 0.80 percent of the total asset value. Calculate the management fee
Mathew must pay this year.

8. *Calculating 12b-1 Fees.* Jane Ramirez owns shares in the Touchstone Small Cap fund that have a current value of $31,300.   LO16-1
The fund charges an annual 12b-1 fee of 0.25 percent. What is the amount of the 12b-1 fee Ms. Ramirez must pay?

9. *Calculating Mutual Fund Fees.* In the prospectus for the Brazos Aggressive Growth fund, the fee table indicates that the   LO16-1
fund has a 12b-1 fee of 0.35 percent and an expense ratio of 1.55 percent that is collected once a year on December 1. Joan
and Don Norwood have shares valued at $113,250 on December 1.

   a. What is the amount of the 12b-1 fee this year?

   b. What is the amount they will pay for expenses this year?

10. *Finding Total Return.* Assume that one year ago you bought 100 shares of a mutual fund for $33.10 per share, you received   LO16-4
a $0.42 per-share capital gain distribution during the past 12 months, and the market value of the fund is now $40.25.
Calculate the total return for this investment if you were to sell it now.

11. *Finding Percentage of Total Return.* Given the information in question 10, calculate the percentage of total return for your   LO16-4
$3,310 investment.

12. *Finding Total Return.* Assume that one year ago, you bought 210 shares of a mutual fund for $24 per share and that you   LO16-4
received an income dividend of $0.31 cents per share and a capital gain distribution of $1.04 per share during the past
12 months. Also assume the market value of the fund is now $26.50 a share. Calculate the total return for this investment if
you were to sell it now.

13. *Finding Percentage of Total Return.* Given the information in question 12, calculate the percentage of total return for your   LO16-4
$5,040 investment.

14. *Using Dollar Cost Averaging.* Over a four-year period, Matt Ewing purchased shares in the ClearBridge Large-Cap Value   LO16-4
Fund. Using the following information, answer the questions below. You may want to review the concept of dollar cost averaging in Chapter 14 before completing this problem.

Year	Investment Amount	Price per Share
2018	$3,000	$27 per share
2019	$3,000	$35 per share
2020	$3,000	$32 per share
2021	$3,000	$34 per share

a. At the end of four years, what is the total amount invested?

b. At the end of four years, what is the total number of mutual fund shares purchased?

c. At the end of four years, what is the average cost for each mutual fund share?

LO16-4 **15.** *Calculating Withdrawal Amounts.* Since Toni Brookfield is retired, she has used income from her investment in the Alger Mid Cap growth fund to supplement her other retirement income. During one three-month period, the fund grew by $1,300. If she withdraws 70 percent of the growth, how much will she receive?

DIGITAL FINANCIAL LITERACY: TRACKING THE VALUE OF YOUR INVESTMENT PORTFOLIO

Which would you choose: stock funds, bond funds, or other types of funds? Once you make your investment choices, you still have a problem because you know you should track the value and performance of your investments to determine if you want to keep, sell, or buy more shares in the funds you selected. Today, an increasing number of investors solve this problem by using an investment app to track their investment portfolio. Most investment apps are easy to use and can help you track investment values, monitor performance, and reduce fees and risk.

Action items:

1. Read the article "5 Best Investment Apps to Manage Your Portfolio" at https://www.forbes.com/advisor/investing/best-investment-managing-apps/ or similar articles about investment apps or portfolio construction.

2. Select at least two different investment apps described in the *Forbes* article or similar articles. Then create a two- to three-minute presentation that includes a PowerPoint presentation or a short video that describes the apps you chose and how they could help you manage your investments.

FINANCIAL PLANNING CASE

Mutual Fund Research Can Make a *Big* Difference

This chapter stressed the importance of evaluating potential mutual fund investments. Now it's your turn to try your skill at evaluating a potential fund investment. To complete this case assignment, you need to begin by picking a specific fund. You can choose any type of fund you think will help you achieve your personal financial goals. For help choosing a fund, you may want to use the fund screeners at the Yahoo! Finance website (screener.finance.yahoo.com/funds.html) or MarketWatch (https://www.marketwatch.com/tools/mutual-fund/screener) or Fidelity (https://fundresearch.fidelity.com/fund-screener/). Once you have selected your fund, use information from the internet, professional advisory services, newspapers, or financial publications to research your fund. *Hint:* Before completing this assignment, you may want to review the material in the section "How to Decide to Buy or Sell Mutual Funds" in this chapter. Then complete the following assignment.

Assignment

1. Explain the process you used to choose your fund.

2. Describe the specific sources of information you used to evaluate your fund. Were the sources of information helpful or not?

3. Based on your research, answer all of the questions on *Personal Financial Planner Sheet 62,* Mutual Fund Evaluation, that is located at the end of your text.

4. In a one- to two-page report, explain your decision to buy or not buy the fund you chose to research. Be sure to indicate whether this fund could help you obtain your personal financial goals and what you have learned about evaluating a mutual fund. Include the completed *Personal Financial Planner Sheet 62*, Mutual Fund Evaluation, with your report.

YOUR PERSONAL FINANCIAL PLAN

INVESTING IN MUTUAL FUNDS

Using mutual funds for diversification and asset allocation provides investors with convenience and professional management. The variety of mutual funds contributes to your ability to achieve various long-term and short-term financial goals.

Your Short-Term Financial Planning Activity

Task Create a plan to choose information sources that can be used to evaluate fund investments.

Your Long-Term Financial Planning Activity

Task Assume you want to invest $5,000 in a fund. To help you decide if this is the right investment choice, research the performance, costs, and fees for a specific fund.

Research

1) Review the material in the section "How to Decide to Buy or Sell Mutual Funds" in this chapter.

2) Read the article "Best Mutual Fund Research Sites" at https://www.thebalance.com/best-mutual-fund-research-sites-2466453 or other articles available on the internet.

Outcome Use *Personal Financial Planner (PFP) Sheet 61*, Mutual Fund Investment Information to help determine which sites can help you evaluate a mutual fund. Then prepare a PowerPoint or storyboard presentation of the pros and cons of each source of information you included in *PFP Sheet 61*.

Research

1) Use the Fidelity Fund Screener at https://fundresearch.fidelity.com/fund-screener/ to find a fund that you believe could help you obtain your long-term financial goals.

2) Use the information on the Fidelity site and other sources to answer the questions on *Personal Financial Planner (PFP) Sheet 62*, Mutual Fund Evaluation.

Outcome Summarize your findings in a two-page report. In your report, be sure to explain if you would invest $5,000 in the fund you researched. Attach *PFP Sheet 62* to your final report.

 CONTINUING CASE

Investing in Mutual Funds

Jamie Lee and Ross did several weeks' worth of research trying to choose just the right stock in which to invest. After all, a $50,000 inheritance was a lot of money, and they wanted to make the most informed investment choices they could. They discovered, by doing their homework, the corporate stocks they were researching did not seem like they were going to have the promising financial returns that Jamie Lee and Ross were hoping for unless they chose speculative investments with more risk. They were aware that they would be taking a chance with corporate stock investments, but they were both nervous about "putting all of their eggs in one basket" and wanted to be more confident in making their investment choices. But how could they be more assured?

They decided to speak to their professional investment advisor, who suggested that investing in mutual funds might be a way to lessen the risk by joining a pool of other investors in a variety of securities chosen by a professional mutual fund manager. This way, Jamie Lee and Ross can eliminate the pressure of choosing the right corporate stocks, and they minimize the chances of losing their investment money by diversifying their portfolio.

A mutual fund sounded like the sensible investment choice for them, but which mutual fund would be tailored to their investment strategy? Jamie Lee and Ross are in their late-40s and well on their way to reaching their long-term investment goals, as they committed to reaching their goals early on in their marriage. They set their sights on having the triplets graduate from college debt-free and saving enough to purchase a beach house when they retire. They are looking for a mutual fund that will provide both growth and investment income while maintaining the moderate-risk investment path that they are on, as they have some time to go before retirement.

Current Financial Situation

Assets (Jamie Lee and Ross combined):
Checking account: $7,500
Savings account: $83,000 (including the $50,000 inheritance)
Emergency fund savings account: $45,000
House: $410,000
IRA balance: $78,000
Life insurance cash value: $110,000
Investments (stocks, bonds): $230,000
Car: $18,500 (Jamie Lee) and $24,000 (Ross)

Liabilities (Jamie Lee and Ross combined):
Mortgage balance: $73,000
Student loan balance: $0
Credit card balance: $0
Car loans: $0

Income:
Jamie Lee: $45,000 gross income ($31,500 net income after taxes)
Ross: $135,000 gross income ($97,200 net income after taxes)

Monthly Expenses:
Mortgage: $1,225
Property taxes: $500
Homeowner's insurance: $300
IRA contribution: $300
Utilities: $550
Food: $600
Gas/maintenance: $275
Entertainment: $300
Life insurance: $375

Questions

1. It has been suggested by Jamie Lee and Ross's professional investment advisor they should perform a financial checkup before investing in mutual funds, even though they are investing $50,000 that was inherited from Ross's late uncle's estate. Is it a good time to invest the inheritance, or should Jamie Lee and Ross perform their financial checkup to make sure their budget is balanced?

2. While researching the classifications of mutual funds, Jamie Lee and Ross have been reading quite a lot about stock funds. Knowing Jamie Lee and Ross's stage in life, what different types of stock funds would you recommend they invest their $50,000 inheritance in? Why?

3. The investment advisor recommended looking into managed funds, which could help take the burden of the decision-making on when to buy and sell off Jamie Lee and Ross. But Jamie Lee and Ross were considering index funds, which have lower expense ratios. Using your text as a guide, compare managed funds and index funds. Which fund would you recommend for Jamie Lee and Ross? Why?

Managed Funds	Index Funds

4. Jamie Lee and Ross are ready to evaluate a mutual fund more closely. Choose a mutual fund that is available through one of the investment companies described in Exhibit 16-4 or one that has been recommended by a friend or family member, and complete *Personal Financial Planner Sheet 62,* Mutual Fund Evaluation. Would you recommend this mutual fund for Jamie Lee and Ross? Why or why not?

DAILY SPENDING DIARY

"I must choose between spending money on something now or investing for the future."

Directions

Monitoring your daily spending will help you improve your financial planning. You will also have better information that enables you to take control of your spending and make better financial choices.

Analysis Questions

1. Are there any spending items that you might consider revising to allow you to increase the amount you invest?

2. Based on your investment goals and the amount of money you have available to invest, what types of mutual funds would you consider?

A *Daily Spending Diary* sheet is located at the end of Chapter 1 and on the library resource site in *Connect*.

SUMMARY OF LEARNING OBJECTIVES

LO17-1

Identify types of real estate investments. Real estate investments are classified as direct or indirect. Direct real estate investments, in which you hold legal title to the property, include a home, a vacation home, commercial property, and undeveloped land. Indirect real estate investments include real estate syndicates, REITs, mortgages, and participation certificates.

LO17-2

Evaluate the advantages of real estate investments. Real estate investments offer a hedge against inflation, easy entry, limited financial liability, no management headaches, and financial leverage.

LO17-3

Assess the disadvantages of real estate investments. Real estate investments may have the disadvantages of illiquidity, declining values, lack of diversification, lack of a tax shelter, a long depreciation period, and management problems.

LO17-4

Analyze the risks and rewards of investing in precious metals, gems, and collectibles. Some investors prefer to invest in precious metals such as gold, platinum, and silver; precious stones such as diamonds; or collectibles such as stamps, rare coins, works of art, antiques, rare books, and Chinese ceramics. Collectibles do not provide current income, and they may be difficult to sell quickly.

KEY TERMS

collectibles   604

commercial property   593

direct investment   591

indirect investment   591

participation certificate (PC)   596

passive activity   593

passive loss   593

real estate investment trust
   (REIT)   595

syndicate   594

SELF-TEST PROBLEMS

1. You bought a rental property for $150,000 cash. Later you sell the property for $180,000. What was your return on investment?

2. Suppose you invested just $20,000 of your own money and had a $130,000 mortgage with an interest rate of 7.5 percent. After one year you sold the property for $180,000. (a) What is your gross profit? (b) What is your net profit? (c) What is your percent rate of return on investment?

3. Assume your home is assessed at $200,000. You have a $150,000 loan for 15 years at 5 percent. Your property tax rate is 2 percent of the assessed value. Assume you are in a 28 percent federal income tax bracket. By what amount is your federal income tax lowered?

Self-Test Solutions

1. Selling price   = $180,000
   Purchase price = $150,000
   Profit   = $30,000

   Return on investment $\dfrac{\text{Profit}}{\text{Purchase price}}$ $\dfrac{\$30,000}{\$150,000} = .20$, or 20%

2. a. Gross profit = Selling price − Purchase price
      = $180,000 − $150,000 = $30,000

   b. Net profit = Gross profit − Interest paid in one year
      = $30,000 − ($130,000 × .075 × 1)
      = $30,000 − $9,750 = $20,250

   c. Percent return on investment = $\dfrac{\text{Net profit}}{\text{Amount invested}} = \dfrac{\$20,250}{\$20,000} = 1.01$ *or* 101%

3. Assessed value of your home = $200,000

Amount of loan = $150,000

Term of loan = 15 years

Interest rate = 5%

Property tax rate = 2% of assessed value

Mortgage interest for one year = $150,000 × .05 × 1

= $7,500

Property tax paid for one year = $200,000 × .02

= $4,000

Total deduction on your federal income tax = $7,500 + $4,000

= $11,500

Assumed tax bracket = 28%

Federal income tax lowered by ($11,500 × .28) = $3,220

FINANCIAL PLANNING PROBLEMS

LO17-1 **1.** *Calculating the Return on Investment.* Dave bought a rental property for $200,000 cash. One year later, he sold it for $240,000. What was the return on his $200,000 investment?

LO17-1 **2.** *Calculating the Return on Investment Using Financial Leverage.* (Refer to Problem 1.) Suppose Dave invested only $20,000 of his own money and borrowed $180,000 interest-free from his rich father. What was his return on investment?

LO17-1 **3.** *Calculating the Rate of Return on Investment.* Rani bought a rental property for $100,000 with no borrowed funds. Later, she sold the building for $120,000. What was her return on investment?

LO17-1 **4.** *Calculating the Rate of Return on Investment Using Financial Leverage.* Suppose Shaan invested just $10,000 of his own money and had a $90,000 mortgage with an interest rate of 8.5 percent. After three years, he sold the property for $120,000.

   a. What is his gross profit?

   b. What is his net profit or loss?

   c. What is the rate of return on investment?

Problems 5 and 6 are based on the following scenario: Felice bought a duplex apartment at a cost of $150,000. Her mortgage payments on the property are $940 per month, $121 of which can be deducted from her income taxes. Her real estate taxes total $1,440 per year, and insurance costs $900 per year. She estimates that she will spend $1,000 each year per apartment for maintenance, replacing appliances, and other costs. The tenants will pay for all utilities.

LO17-1 **5.** *Calculating Profit or Loss on a Rental Property.* What monthly rent must she charge for each apartment to break even?

LO17-1 **6.** *Calculating Profit or Loss on a Rental Property.* What must she charge to make $2,000 in profit each year?

Problems 7 and 8 are based on the following scenario: Assume your home is assessed at $200,000. You have a $150,000 loan for 30 years at 6 percent. Your property tax rate is 1.5 percent of the assessed value. In year one, you would pay $9,000 in mortgage interest and $3,000 in property tax (1.5 percent on $200,000 assessed value).

LO17-1 **7.** *Calculating Net Profit after Taxes.* What is the total deduction you can take on your federal income tax return?

LO17-1 **8.** *Calculating Net Profit after Taxes.* Assuming you are in a 28 percent tax bracket, by what amount would you have lowered your federal income tax?

Problems 9 and 10 are based on the following scenario: Audra owns a rental house. She makes mortgage payments of $600 per month, which include insurance, and pays $1,800 per year in property taxes and maintenance. Utilities are paid by the renter.

LO17-1 **9.** *Determining the Monthly Rent.* How much should Audra charge for monthly rent to cover her costs?

LO17-1 **10.** *Determining the Monthly Rent.* What should Audra charge for monthly rent to make $1,000 profit each year?

Problems 11 and 12 are based on the following scenario: In 1978 Juan bought 50 ounces of gold for $1,750 as protection against rising inflation. He sold half the gold in 1980 at a price of $800 an ounce. Juan sold the other half in 1982 when the price was $400 an ounce.

11. *Calculating a Return on Investment.* What was Juan's profit in 1980 and in 1982?   **LO17-4**

12. *Calculating a Return on Investment.* What would Juan's profit have been if he had sold all of his gold in 1980?   **LO17-4**

Problems 13, 14, and 15 are based on the following scenario: Prema purchased 15 ounces of gold in 2005 for $422 per ounce in order to try to diversify her investment portfolio. She sold a third of her holdings in gold in 2009 at a price of $944 per ounce. She sold the rest of her gold holdings in 2010 for $1,254 per ounce.

13. *Calculating a Return on Investment.* What is Prema's profit in 2009 and 2010?   **LO17-4**

14. *Calculating a Return on Investment.* What would her profit have been if she sold all the gold holdings in 2009?   **LO17-4**

15. *Calculating a Return on Investment.* What if she sold everything in 2010?   **LO17-4**

DIGITAL FINANCIAL LITERACY. . .

INVESTING IN PRECIOUS METALS

Bullion is a bulk quantity of precious metal, usually gold, platinum, or silver, assessed by weight and typically cast as ingots or bars. Dealers and some banks and brokerages sell bullion. Bullion coins are struck from precious metal—usually gold, platinum, or silver—and kept as an investment. They are not used in daily commerce. The value of bullion coins is determined mostly by their precious metals content rather than by rarity and condition. Prices may change throughout the day, depending on the prices for precious metals in the world markets. Coin dealers and some banks, brokerage firms, and precious metal dealers buy and sell bullion coins. The U.S. Mint has produced gold and silver bullion coins for investment purposes since 1986 and began producing platinum bullion coins in 1997. The U.S. Mint guarantees the precious metal weight, content, and purity of the coins they produce.

Action items:

1) Listen to business news on the internet, radio, or television. What are the current quotes for an ounce of gold and an ounce of silver? Are the prices of precious metals going up or down? How do the latest prices compare with the prices quoted in the chapter? What might be some reasons for fluctuations in the prices of precious metals?

2) Check out the seller by entering the company's name in a search engine online. Read about other people's experiences with the company. Try to communicate offline if possible to clarify any details. In addition, contact your **state attorney general** and **local consumer protection agency**. This kind of research is prudent, although it isn't foolproof; it may be too soon for someone to realize they've been defrauded or to have lodged a complaint with the authorities.

FINANCIAL PLANNING CASE

Bogus Brushstroke: Art Fraud

Richard received a letter inviting him to participate in a drawing for a free original lithograph by a famous artist. He was asked to return a postcard with his name, address, and phone number. After he returned the postcard, he was telephoned for more information, including his credit card number.

At some point, the caller asked Richard to buy a print, using such glowing terms as "fabulous opportunity," "one-time offer," "limited edition," and "excellent work of a famous artist." The artist, the caller said, was near death and the print's value would increase after the artist's death. He was assured that when the artist died, the company that the caller represented would gladly buy back the print at two to three times what he paid for it and that he could always resell the

print elsewhere at a substantial profit. He was told that he would receive a certificate of the "authenticity" of the print. And he was promised a trial examination period with a 30-day money-back guarantee.

Questions

1. Does the offer seem genuine to you? Explain your answer.

2. How can Richard protect himself against a phony offer? List at least five suggestions that you would give him.

3. If Richard bought the work of art and discovered fraud, how should he try to resolve his dispute with the company that sold it to him? Where should he complain if the dispute is not resolved?

YOUR PERSONAL FINANCIAL PLAN

COMPARING OTHER TYPES OF INVESTMENTS

Real estate and collectibles allow investors to achieve greater potential returns. However, these sometimes speculative ventures must be considered carefully in relation to your personal financial situation.

Your Short-Term Financial Planning Activity

Task Identify types of real estate and other investments that might serve your various financial goals and life situations.

Research

1) Review Exhibit 17-1 to understand the differences between direct and indirect real estate investments. What are possible advantages and disadvantages of owning and investing in real estate?

2) Visit the National Real Estate Investor website at nreionline.com, or locate other sources of information about why investors choose real estate investments.

Outcome Prepare a two-page report that summarizes the various types of direct and indirect real estate investments available for investors.

Your Long-Term Financial Planning Activity

Task Identify real estate and other investments that might serve you in the future.

Research

1) Call a few real estate and stock brokerage firms in your area to find out whether any real estate investment trusts or real estate partnerships are available for investors. Also, read the Financial Literacy for My Life: Is Gold a Solid Investment? feature.

2) Research current commercial real estate sections of local newspapers. How many listings do you find for duplexes? For fourplexes and small apartment buildings? Then, develop a plan for selecting and monitoring real estate.

Outcome Prepare a report or visual presentation that summarizes the various types of real estate investments available to investors.

Note: All *Personal Financial Planner* sheets are available at the end of the book and in an Excel spreadsheet format in *Connect Finance.*

 CONTINUING CASE

Investing in Real Estate and Other Investment Alternatives

"Whew! Time really does fly!" Jamie Lee thought as she unpacked from her third weekend in a row visiting colleges with the triplets. It seemed like just yesterday that Jamie Lee and Ross brought the little newborns home from the hospital, and now they are preparing to send the three off to college.

So much to consider. In-state universities or community college for the first few years? Either way, years of saving and safe investment strategies helped Jamie Lee and Ross get the triplets ready for college, although they still do want to make the wisest financial choices. After all, putting three through school is still a major undertaking, even for the most well-prepared.

The triplets are leaning toward the state university, which will help with tuition, compared to the out-of-state schools, although it is still a two-hour car drive from home. This translates into room and board times three for the next four years.

"Should we invest in a small house or condominium for the triplets to live in during their college years?" Jamie Lee wondered. She had a hobby of watching all of the home shows on television, such as *Home Reno Nation* and *Flip This Flop,* which made the purchase of a fixer-upper an attractive thought and a possible investment opportunity in the long run.

Jamie Lee and Ross decide to make an appointment with their investment counselor, Jay Hall, and real estate broker, Annie O'Halloran, to discuss their options, as they were unfamiliar with real estate investment opportunities.

Current Financial Situation

Assets (Jamie Lee and Ross combined):
Checking account: $5,000
Savings account: $47,000
Emergency fund savings account: $40,000
House: $475,000
IRA balance: $85,000
Life insurance cash value: $125,000
Investments (stocks, bonds): $700,000
Car: $14,500 (Jamie Lee) and $18,000 (Ross)

Liabilities (Jamie Lee and Ross combined):
Mortgage balance: $47,000
Credit card balance: $0
Car loans: $0

Income:
Jamie Lee: $45,000 gross income ($31,500 net income after taxes)
Ross: $135,000 gross income ($97,200 net income after taxes)

Monthly Expenses:
Mortgage: $1,225
Property taxes: $500
Homeowner's insurance: $300
IRA contribution: $300
Utilities: $250
Food: $600
Gas/maintenance: $275
Entertainment: $300
Life insurance: $375

Questions

1. Compare *direct investment* and *indirect investment* real estate classifications. If Jamie Lee and Ross purchase a small house or condominium for the triplets to stay in during their college years, which type of investment classification would they fall under?

2. Mr. Hall discusses the financial liabilities that Jamie Lee and Ross would undertake with the triplets living in a college dorm room that are on top of the usual tuition and book expenses. Assume that the triplets' rent for the dorm room is $7,500 per student per year based on double occupancy and a shared bathroom. What is the total amount that Jamie Lee and Ross would owe for the entire four years for the three to stay in the dorms?

3. If Jamie Lee and Ross decide to purchase a small house for the triplets to live in for the four years they are in college, what are some of the financial benefits for Jamie Lee and Ross?

4. Jamie Lee and Ross understand that purchasing the second home for the triplets to use during the college years is not all about saving money by avoiding paying the dorm rent. What are some of the liabilities that Jamie Lee and Ross can expect that are directly connected to owning the second home that might make them second-guess the purchase?

 DAILY SPENDING DIARY

"Saving funds to buy additional real estate is a goal that I'm considering."

Directions

Maintaining a *Daily Spending Diary* can provide important information for monitoring and controlling spending. Taking time to reconsider your spending habits can result in achieving better long-term satisfaction from your finances.

Analysis Questions

1. What changes in your daily spending patterns could help you increase the amount you have available for investing?

2. When might you consider investing in real estate, precious metals, or collectibles?

A *Daily Spending Diary* sheet is located at the end of Chapter 1 and on the library resource site in *Connect*.

SUMMARY OF LEARNING OBJECTIVES

LO18-1
Recognize the importance of retirement planning. Retirement planning is important because you will probably spend many years in retirement. Social Security and a private pension may be insufficient to cover the cost of living, and inflation may erode the purchasing power of your retirement savings. Many young people are reluctant to think about retirement, but they should start retirement planning now, before they reach age 45.

LO18-2
Analyze your current assets and liabilities for retirement. Analyze your current assets (everything you own) and your current liabilities (everything you owe). The difference between your assets and your liabilities is your net worth. Review your assets to ensure they are sufficient for retirement.

LO18-3
Estimate your retirement spending needs. Since the spending patterns of retirees change, it is impossible to predict the exact amount of money you will need in retirement. However, you can estimate your expenses. Some of those expenses will increase; others will decrease. The expenses that are likely to be lower or eliminated are

work-related expenses, clothing, housing expenses, federal income taxes, and commuting expenses.

LO18-4
Identify your retirement housing needs. Where you live in retirement can influence your financial needs. You are the only one who can determine the location and housing that are best for you. Would you like to live in your present home or move to a new location? Consider the social aspects of moving.

LO18-5
Determine your planned retirement income. Estimate your retirement expenses and adjust those expenses for inflation using the appropriate inflation factor. Your possible sources of income during retirement include Social Security, other public pension plans, employer pension plans, personal retirement plans, and annuities.

LO18-6
Develop a balanced budget based on your retirement income. Compare your total estimated retirement income with your total inflated retirement expenses. If your income approximates your expenses, you are in good shape; if not, determine additional income needs and sources.

KEY TERMS

annuity 640	individual retirement account (IRA) 635	Roth IRA 637
defined-benefit plan 633	Keogh plan 639	vesting 633
defined-contribution plan 632	reverse annuity mortgage (RAM) 620	401(k) (TSA) plan 632

SELF-TEST PROBLEMS

1. Beverly is planning for her retirement. She has determined that her car is worth $10,000, her home is worth $150,000, her personal belongings are worth $100,000, and her stocks and bonds are worth $300,000. She owes $50,000 on her home and $5,000 on her car. Calculate her net worth.

2. Calculate how much money an average older household, 65–74 years, with an annual income of $50,000 spends on food each year. (*Hint:* Use Exhibit 18-4.)

3. You have $100,000 in your retirement fund that is earning 5.5 percent per year, compounding quarterly. How many dollars in withdrawals per month would keep your nest egg intact forever? (*Hint:* Use Exhibit 18-16.)

DIGITAL FINANCIAL LITERACY: CREATE YOUR PERSONAL MY SOCIAL SECURITY ACCOUNT

A free and secure My Social Security account provides personalized tools for everyone, whether you receive benefits or not. You can use your account to request a replacement Social Security card, check the status of an application, estimate future benefits, or manage the benefits you already receive. All from anywhere!

To create a my Social Security account, you'll be asked to:

1. Verify your identity by providing personal information about yourself and answering questions that only you are likely to know.

2. Create a username and password you'll use to access your online account.

3. Confirm your email address or phone number by entering a one-time security code within 10 minutes of receiving it in order to help keep your personal information safe.

Action items:

1. If you are not receiving benefits:

- Get your Social Security statement
- Get personalized retirement benefit estimates
- Get estimates for spouse's benefits
- Get proof that you do not receive benefits
- Check your application status

2. If you are receiving benefits:

- Set up or change direct deposit
- Get a Social Security 1099 (SSA-1099) form
- Opt out of mailed notices for those available online
- Print a benefit verification letter
- Change your address

FINANCIAL PLANNING CASE

Planning for Retirement

Is a bad day fishing better than a good day at the office? Yes, according to a retired dad, Chuck. With his company pension, at least he didn't have to worry about money. In the good old days, if you had a decent job, you'd hang onto it, and then your company's pension combined with Social Security payments would be enough to live on comfortably. Chuck's son, Rob, does not have a company pension, and he is not sure whether Social Security will even exist when he retires. So when it comes to retirement, the sooner someone in Rob's position starts saving, the better.

Take Maureen, a salesperson for a computer company, and Therese, an accountant for a lighting manufacturer. Both start their jobs at age 25. Maureen starts saving for retirement right away by investing $300 a month at 9 percent until age 65. But Therese does nothing until age 35. At 35 she begins investing the same $300 a month at 9 percent until age 65. What a shocking difference! Maureen has accumulated $1.4 million, while Therese has only $549,223 in her retirement fund. The moral? The sooner you start, the more you'll have for your retirement. Women especially need to start sooner, because they typically have lower salaries, and, ultimately, lower pensions.

Laura Tarbox, owner and president of Tarbox Equity, explains how to determine your retirement needs and how your budget might change when you retire. Tarbox advises that the old rule of thumb that you need 60 to 70 percent of pre-retirement income is too low an estimate. She cautions that most people will want to spend very close to what they were spending before retiring. Some expenses might be lower, such as clothing for work, dry cleaning, commuting expenses, and so forth. Other expenses, though, such as insurance, travel, and recreation, may increase during retirement.

Questions

1. In the past, many workers chose to stay with their employers until retirement. What was the major reason for employees' loyalty?

2. How did Maureen amass $1.4 million for retirement, while Therese could only accumulate $549,223?

3. Why do women need to start early to save for retirement?

4. How is net worth determined?

5. What expenses may increase or decrease during retirement?

YOUR PERSONAL FINANCIAL PLAN

PLANNING FOR RETIREMENT

Long-term financial security is a common goal of most people. Retirement planning should consider both personal decisions (location, housing, activities) and financial factors (investments, pensions, living expenses).

Your Short-Term Financial Planning Activity

Task Identify personal and financial retirement needs.

Research

1) Search the internet, and read newspaper or magazine articles to determine what expenses are likely to increase or decrease during retirement. How might this information affect your retirement planning decisions?

2) Use PFP Sheet 64 to compare the benefits and costs of a traditional IRA, Roth IRA, and other pension plans.

Outcome Create a portfolio file for completed PFP sheets and other documents, or set up a computer folder of Excel PFP sheets.

Your Long-Term Financial Planning Activity

Task Plan actions to achieve your retirement goals.

Research

1) Visit seniorhousing.org or aarp.org and gather information about your housing options during retirement. Then use PFP Sheet 63 to evaluate current and expected needs when you retire.

2) Use PFP Sheet 65 to estimate future income needs and identify appropriate investments to meet those needs.

3) Visit choosetosave.org or ftc.gov and explore the variety of issues related to expanding personal interests and increasing contributions to retirement accounts.

Outcome Create a checklist of the advantages and disadvantages of your housing choice.

Note: All *Personal Financial Planner* sheets are available at the end of the book and in an Excel spreadsheet format in *Connect Finance*.

 CONTINUING CASE

Starting Early: Retirement Planning

Jamie Lee and Ross, now in their 50s and still very active, have plenty of time on their hands now that the triplets are away at college. They both realized that time has just flown by; over 24 years have passed since they married!

Looking back over the past years, they realize they have worked hard, Jamie Lee as the proprietor of a cupcake café and Ross self-employed as a web page designer. They have enjoyed raising their family and have striven to make financially sound decisions. Now they are looking forward to a retirement that is just around the corner. They saved regularly and invested wisely over the years. They have rebounded nicely from the recent economic crisis, as they watched their investments closely and adjusted their strategies when they felt it was necessary. They purchase vehicles with cash and do not carry credit card balances, choosing instead to use them for convenience only. The triplets are pursuing their master's degrees and have tuition covered through work-study programs at the university.

Jamie Lee and Ross are just a few short years from realizing their goals of retiring at 65 and purchasing the home at the beach!

Current Financial Situation

Assets (Jamie Lee and Ross combined):
Checking account: $5,500
Savings account: $53,000
Emergency fund savings account: $45,000
House: $475,000
IRA balance: $92,000
Life insurance cash value: $125,000
Investments (stocks, bonds): $750,000
Car: $12,500 (Jamie Lee) and $16,000 (Ross)

Liabilities (Jamie Lee and Ross combined):
Mortgage balance: $43,000
Credit card balance: $0
Car loans: $0

Income:
Jamie Lee: $45,000 gross income ($31,500 net income after taxes)
Ross: $135,000 gross income ($97,200 net income after taxes)

Monthly Expenses:
Mortgage: $1,225
Property taxes: $500
Homeowner's insurance: $300
IRA contribution: $300
Utilities: $250
Food: $600
Gas/maintenance: $275
Entertainment: $300
Life insurance: $375

SUMMARY OF LEARNING OBJECTIVES

LO18-1

Recognize the importance of retirement planning. Retirement planning is important because you will probably spend many years in retirement. Social Security and a private pension may be insufficient to cover the cost of living, and inflation may erode the purchasing power of your retirement savings. Many young people are reluctant to think about retirement, but they should start retirement planning now, before they reach age 45.

LO18-2

Analyze your current assets and liabilities for retirement. Analyze your current assets (everything you own) and your current liabilities (everything you owe). The difference between your assets and your liabilities is your net worth. Review your assets to ensure they are sufficient for retirement.

LO18-3

Estimate your retirement spending needs. Since the spending patterns of retirees change, it is impossible to predict the exact amount of money you will need in retirement. However, you can estimate your expenses. Some of those expenses will increase; others will decrease. The expenses that are likely to be lower or eliminated are

work-related expenses, clothing, housing expenses, federal income taxes, and commuting expenses.

LO18-4

Identify your retirement housing needs. Where you live in retirement can influence your financial needs. You are the only one who can determine the location and housing that are best for you. Would you like to live in your present home or move to a new location? Consider the social aspects of moving.

LO18-5

Determine your planned retirement income. Estimate your retirement expenses and adjust those expenses for inflation using the appropriate inflation factor. Your possible sources of income during retirement include Social Security, other public pension plans, employer pension plans, personal retirement plans, and annuities.

LO18-6

Develop a balanced budget based on your retirement income. Compare your total estimated retirement income with your total inflated retirement expenses. If your income approximates your expenses, you are in good shape; if not, determine additional income needs and sources.

KEY TERMS

annuity 640	individual retirement account (IRA) 635	Roth IRA 637
defined-benefit plan 633	Keogh plan 639	vesting 633
defined-contribution plan 632	reverse annuity mortgage (RAM) 620	401(k) (TSA) plan 632

SELF-TEST PROBLEMS

1. Beverly is planning for her retirement. She has determined that her car is worth $10,000, her home is worth $150,000, her personal belongings are worth $100,000, and her stocks and bonds are worth $300,000. She owes $50,000 on her home and $5,000 on her car. Calculate her net worth.

2. Calculate how much money an average older household, 65–74 years, with an annual income of $50,000 spends on food each year. (*Hint:* Use Exhibit 18-4.)

3. You have $100,000 in your retirement fund that is earning 5.5 percent per year, compounding quarterly. How many dollars in withdrawals per month would keep your nest egg intact forever? (*Hint:* Use Exhibit 18-16.)

Self-Test Solutions

1.

Assets		Liabilities	
Car	$ 10,000	Mortgage	$ 50,000
Home	$150,000	Car	$ 5,000
Personal belongings	$100,000	Total liabilities	$ 55,000
Stocks and bonds	$300,000		
Total assets	$560,000		

Net worth	=	Assets	−	Liabilities	
	=	$560,000	−	$55,000 =	$505,000

2. Average older household (65–74 years), with an annual income of $50,000 spends about 12 percent of their income on food. Thus, $50,000 × 12 percent = $6,000.

3. Referring to Exhibit 18-16, students will find that at a withdrawal rate of $460 a month, the nest egg of $100,000 would stay intact forever.

FINANCIAL PLANNING PROBLEMS

1. *Calculating Net Worth.* Shelly's assets include money in checking and savings accounts, investments in stocks and mutual funds, and personal property, including furniture, appliances, an automobile, a coin collection, and jewelry. Shelly calculates that her total assets are $108,800. Her current unpaid bills, including an auto loan, credit card balances, and taxes total $16,300. Calculate Shelly's net worth. `LO18-2`

2. *Calculating Net Worth.* Ted owns a Lexus worth $40,000. He owns a home worth $275,000. He has a checking account with $800 in it and a savings account with $1,900 in it. He has a mutual fund worth $110,000. His personal assets are worth $90,000. He still owes $25,000 on his car and $150,000 on his home, and he has a balance on his credit card of $1,600. What is Ted's net worth? `LO18-3`

3. *Calculating the Amount Spent on Housing.* Calculate approximately how much money an older (age 65–74) household with an annual income of $45,000 spends on housing each year. (*Hint:* Use Exhibit 18-4.) `LO18-3`

4. *Calculating the Amount Spent on Health Care.* Using Exhibit 18-4, calculate approximately how much money the household from Problem 3 spends on health care. `LO18-5`

5. *Calculating an IRA Accumulation.* When Jamal graduated from college recently, his parents gave him $1,000 and told him to use it wisely. Jamal decided to use the money to start a retirement account. After doing some research about different options, he put the entire amount into a tax-deferred IRA that pays 11 percent interest, compounded annually. Calculate how much money Jamal will have in his IRA at the end of 10 years, assuming that the interest rate remains the same and that he does not deposit any additional money. Show your calculations in the form of a chart. `LO18-5`

6. *Calculating an IRA Accumulation.* Janine is 25 and has a good job at a biotechnology company. Janine estimates that she will need $875,000 in her *total* retirement nest egg by the time she is 65 in order to have retirement income of $20,000 a year. (She expects that Social Security will pay her an additional $15,000 a year.) She currently has $5,000 in an IRA, an important part of her retirement nest egg. She believes her IRA will grow at an annual rate of 8 percent, and she plans to leave it untouched until she retires at age 65. How much will Janine's IRA be worth when she needs to start withdrawing money from it when she retires? (*Hint:* Use Exhibit 1–A in the Chapter 1 Appendix.) `LO18-5`

7. *Calculating an IRA Accumulation.* In the above problem, how much money will Janine have to accumulate in her company's 401(k) plan over the next 40 years in order to reach her retirement income goal? `LO18-5`

8. *Calculating Retirement Amount.* Calculate how much you would have in 10 years if you saved $2,000 a year at an annual rate of 10 percent with the company contributing $500 a year. `LO18-6`

9. *Calculating Net Pay and Spendable Income.* Assume your gross pay per pay period is $2,000 and you are in the 33 percent tax bracket. Calculate your net pay and spendable income if you save $200 per pay period after paying income tax on $2,000. `LO18-6`

10. *Calculating Net Pay and Spendable Income.* In the above example, calculate your net pay and spendable income if you save $200 per pay period in a tax-sheltered annuity. `LO18-6`

11. *Dipping into Your Nest Egg.* You have $50,000 in your retirement fund that is earning 5.5 percent per year, compounded quarterly. How many dollars in withdrawals per month would reduce this nest egg to zero in 20 years? `LO18-6`

12. *Dipping into Your Nest Egg.* In the above example, how many dollars per month can you withdraw for as long as you live and still leave this nest egg intact? `LO18-6`

DIGITAL FINANCIAL LITERACY: CREATE YOUR PERSONAL MY SOCIAL SECURITY ACCOUNT

A free and secure My Social Security account provides personalized tools for everyone, whether you receive benefits or not. You can use your account to request a replacement Social Security card, check the status of an application, estimate future benefits, or manage the benefits you already receive. All from anywhere!

To create a my Social Security account, you'll be asked to:

1. Verify your identity by providing personal information about yourself and answering questions that only you are likely to know.

2. Create a username and password you'll use to access your online account.

3. Confirm your email address or phone number by entering a one-time security code within 10 minutes of receiving it in order to help keep your personal information safe.

Action items:

1. If you are not receiving benefits:

- Get your Social Security statement
- Get personalized retirement benefit estimates
- Get estimates for spouse's benefits
- Get proof that you do not receive benefits
- Check your application status

2. If you are receiving benefits:

- Set up or change direct deposit
- Get a Social Security 1099 (SSA-1099) form
- Opt out of mailed notices for those available online
- Print a benefit verification letter
- Change your address

FINANCIAL PLANNING CASE

Planning for Retirement

Is a bad day fishing better than a good day at the office? Yes, according to a retired dad, Chuck. With his company pension, at least he didn't have to worry about money. In the good old days, if you had a decent job, you'd hang onto it, and then your company's pension combined with Social Security payments would be enough to live on comfortably. Chuck's son, Rob, does not have a company pension, and he is not sure whether Social Security will even exist when he retires. So when it comes to retirement, the sooner someone in Rob's position starts saving, the better.

Take Maureen, a salesperson for a computer company, and Therese, an accountant for a lighting manufacturer. Both start their jobs at age 25. Maureen starts saving for retirement right away by investing $300 a month at 9 percent until age 65. But Therese does nothing until age 35. At 35 she begins investing the same $300 a month at 9 percent until age 65. What a shocking difference! Maureen has accumulated $1.4 million, while Therese has only $549,223 in her retirement fund. The moral? The sooner you start, the more you'll have for your retirement. Women especially need to start sooner, because they typically have lower salaries, and, ultimately, lower pensions.

Laura Tarbox, owner and president of Tarbox Equity, explains how to determine your retirement needs and how your budget might change when you retire. Tarbox advises that the old rule of thumb that you need 60 to 70 percent of pre-retirement income is too low an estimate. She cautions that most people will want to spend very close to what they were spending before retiring. Some expenses might be lower, such as clothing for work, dry cleaning, commuting expenses, and so forth. Other expenses, though, such as insurance, travel, and recreation, may increase during retirement.

Questions

1. In the past, many workers chose to stay with their employers until retirement. What was the major reason for employees' loyalty?

2. How did Maureen amass $1.4 million for retirement, while Therese could only accumulate $549,223?

3. Why do women need to start early to save for retirement?

4. How is net worth determined?

5. What expenses may increase or decrease during retirement?

YOUR PERSONAL FINANCIAL PLAN

PLANNING FOR RETIREMENT

Long-term financial security is a common goal of most people. Retirement planning should consider both personal decisions (location, housing, activities) and financial factors (investments, pensions, living expenses).

Your Short-Term Financial Planning Activity

Task Identify personal and financial retirement needs.

Research

1) Search the internet, and read newspaper or magazine articles to determine what expenses are likely to increase or decrease during retirement. How might this information affect your retirement planning decisions?

2) Use PFP Sheet 64 to compare the benefits and costs of a traditional IRA, Roth IRA, and other pension plans.

Outcome Create a portfolio file for completed PFP sheets and other documents, or set up a computer folder of Excel PFP sheets.

Your Long-Term Financial Planning Activity

Task Plan actions to achieve your retirement goals.

Research

1) Visit seniorhousing.org or aarp.org and gather information about your housing options during retirement. Then use PFP Sheet 63 to evaluate current and expected needs when you retire.

2) Use PFP Sheet 65 to estimate future income needs and identify appropriate investments to meet those needs.

3) Visit choosetosave.org or ftc.gov and explore the variety of issues related to expanding personal interests and increasing contributions to retirement accounts.

Outcome Create a checklist of the advantages and disadvantages of your housing choice.

Note: All *Personal Financial Planner* sheets are available at the end of the book and in an Excel spreadsheet format in *Connect Finance*.

CONTINUING CASE

Starting Early: Retirement Planning

Jamie Lee and Ross, now in their 50s and still very active, have plenty of time on their hands now that the triplets are away at college. They both realized that time has just flown by; over 24 years have passed since they married!

Looking back over the past years, they realize they have worked hard, Jamie Lee as the proprietor of a cupcake café and Ross self-employed as a web page designer. They have enjoyed raising their family and have striven to make financially sound decisions. Now they are looking forward to a retirement that is just around the corner. They saved regularly and invested wisely over the years. They have rebounded nicely from the recent economic crisis, as they watched their investments closely and adjusted their strategies when they felt it was necessary. They purchase vehicles with cash and do not carry credit card balances, choosing instead to use them for convenience only. The triplets are pursuing their master's degrees and have tuition covered through work-study programs at the university.

Jamie Lee and Ross are just a few short years from realizing their goals of retiring at 65 and purchasing the home at the beach!

Current Financial Situation

Assets (Jamie Lee and Ross combined):
Checking account: $5,500
Savings account: $53,000
Emergency fund savings account: $45,000
House: $475,000
IRA balance: $92,000
Life insurance cash value: $125,000
Investments (stocks, bonds): $750,000
Car: $12,500 (Jamie Lee) and $16,000 (Ross)

Liabilities (Jamie Lee and Ross combined):
Mortgage balance: $43,000
Credit card balance: $0
Car loans: $0

Income:
Jamie Lee: $45,000 gross income ($31,500 net income after taxes)
Ross: $135,000 gross income ($97,200 net income after taxes)

Monthly Expenses:
Mortgage: $1,225
Property taxes: $500
Homeowner's insurance: $300
IRA contribution: $300
Utilities: $250
Food: $600
Gas/maintenance: $275
Entertainment: $300
Life insurance: $375

Questions

1. Looking over Jamie Lee and Ross's assets, which ones could be valuable to them for income as retirement approaches?

2. Using the *Personal Financial Planner* Sheet 63, "Retirement Planning," evaluate Jamie Lee and Ross's housing needs as they begin to look at retirement properties at the beach. Using the internet, research retirement options for Jamie Lee and Ross at the beach of your choice. What are the prices for a small residence that would suit their needs during their retirement years?

3. Jamie Lee and Ross estimate that they will have $1 million in liquid assets to withdraw from at the start of their retirement. They plan to be in retirement for 30 years. Using the chart in Exhibit 18-16, "Dipping into Your Nest Egg," how much can Jamie Lee and Ross withdraw each month and still leave their nest egg intact? How much can they withdraw each month that will reduce their nest egg to zero?

 DAILY SPENDING DIARY

"Keeping track of my daily spending gets me to start thinking about saving and investing for retirement."

Directions

The consistent use of a *Daily Spending Diary* can provide you with ongoing information that will help you manage your spending, saving, and investing activities. Taking time to reconsider your spending habits can result in achieving better satisfaction from your available finances.

Analysis Questions

1. What portion of your net income is set aside for saving or investing for long-term financial security?

2. What types of retirement planning activities might you start to consider at this point of your life?

A *Daily Spending Diary* sheet is located at the end of Chapter 1 and on the library resource site in *Connect*.

Estate Planning

19

scyther5/Getty Images

LEARNING OBJECTIVES

LO19-1 Analyze the personal aspects of estate planning.

LO19-2 Assess the legal aspects of estate planning.

LO19-3 Distinguish among various types and formats of wills.

LO19-4 Appraise various types of trusts and estates.

LO19-5 Evaluate the effects of federal and state taxes on estate planning.

Financial Literacy IN **YOUR LIFE**

▶ **What if you . . .** have not given enough thought to your estate planning because you believe that estate planning is for the rich and famous? Even if you have not accumulated a lot of wealth, you should consider preparing an estate plan so that your hard-earned money goes to those you wish to provide with financial security.

You might . . . want to get legal advice when preparing a will, even though writing a will can be as simple as typing how you want your assets to be transferred to loved ones or charitable organizations. Remember, in most states, you have to be at least 18 years old to write a will.

Now, what would you do? Contact an estate planning attorney to prepare legal documents for your estate. These documents might include a will, a living will, a health care proxy, a letter of last instruction, a social media will, or a trust. You will be able to monitor your progress using the Your Personal Finance Roadmap and Dashboard feature at the end of the chapter.

my life | WHERE THERE IS A WILL

Do you think of estates belonging only to the rich or elderly? The fact is, however, everyone has an estate. During your working years, your financial goal is to build your estate by acquiring and accumulating money for your current and future needs. However, as you grow older, your point of view will change. Instead of working to acquire assets, you will start to think about what will happen to your hard-earned wealth after you die.

What are your current attitudes toward estate planning? For each of the following statements, select Agree, Neutral, or Disagree to indicate your personal response regarding these estate planning situations.

1. I believe estate planning is only for the rich and famous.	Agree	Neutral	Disagree
2. If I die intestate (without a valid will), my legal state of residence will control the distribution of my estate.	Agree	Neutral	Disagree
3. In addition to my will, I should prepare a letter of last instruction.	Agree	Neutral	Disagree
4. If I establish a trust, it will avoid probate and transfer my assets immediately to my beneficiaries.	Agree	Neutral	Disagree
5. I can reduce my taxable estate by giving away assets to *anyone* during my lifetime.	Agree	Neutral	Disagree

As you study this chapter, you will encounter "My Life" boxes with additional information and resources related to these items.

Why Estate Planning?

LO19-1

Analyze the personal aspects of estate planning.

estate Everything one owns.

Your **estate** consists of everything you own, including bank accounts, stocks, bonds, real estate, and personal property. While you work, your objective is to accumulate funds for your future and for your dependents. As you grow older, your point of view will change. The emphasis in your financial planning will shift from accumulating assets to distributing them wisely. Your hard-earned wealth should go to those whom you wish to support and not to the various taxing agencies.

Contrary to widely held notions, estate planning, which includes wills and trusts, is useful not only to rich and elderly people. Trusts can be used for purposes other than tax advantages, such as choosing a guardian for children and avoiding family fights over personal belongings. Furthermore, most people can afford the expense of using them.

This chapter discusses a subject most people would rather avoid: death—your own or that of your spouse. Many people give little or no thought to setting their personal and financial affairs in order.

As you learned in Chapter 18, most people today live longer than those of previous generations and have ample time to think about and plan for the future. Yet a large percentage of people do little or nothing to provide for those who will survive them.

Planning for your family's financial security in the event of your death or the death of your spouse is not easy. Therefore, the objective of this chapter is to help you initiate discussions about questions you should ask before that happens. Does your spouse, for instance, know what all of the family's resources and debts are? Does your family have enough insurance protection?

The question of whether your family can cope financially without your or your spouse's income and support is a difficult one. This chapter can't provide all of the answers, but it supplies a basis for sound estate planning for you and your family.

| my life | 1

I believe estate planning is only for the rich and famous.

Contrary to popular belief, estate planning is useful not only to the rich, famous, and elderly. Because everyone has an estate (owns something), estate planning is important.

WHAT IS ESTATE PLANNING?

Estate planning is a definite plan for the administration and disposition of one's property during one's lifetime and at one's death. Thus, it involves both handling your property while you are alive and dealing with what happens to that property after your death.

Estate planning is an essential part of retirement planning and an integral part of financial planning. It has two components. The first consists of building your estate through savings, investments, and insurance. The second involves transferring your estate, at your death, in the manner you have specified. As this chapter explains, an estate plan is usually implemented by a will and one or more trust agreements.

Nearly every adult engages in financial decision-making and must keep important records. Whatever your status—single or married, male or female, taxi driver or corporate executive—you must make financial decisions that are important to you. Those decisions may be even more important to others in your family. Knowledge in certain areas and good recordkeeping can simplify those decisions.

At first, planning for financial security and estate planning may seem complicated. Although many money matters require legal and technical advice, if you and your spouse learn the necessary skills, you will find yourselves managing your money affairs more efficiently and wisely. Begin by answering the questionnaire in the *Financial Literacy for My Life: Estate Planning Checklist* feature to see how much you and your family know about your own money affairs. You and your family should be able to answer some of these questions. The questions can be bewildering if the subjects are unfamiliar to you, but after reading this chapter, you'll be able to answer most of them.

estate planning A definite plan for the administration and disposition of one's property during one's lifetime and at one's death.

IF YOU ARE MARRIED

If you are married, your estate planning involves the interests of at least two people, and more if you have children. Legal requirements and responsibilities can create problems for married people that are entirely different from those of single people. Situations become more complex. Possessions accumulate. The need for orderliness and clarity increases.

Your death will mean a new lifestyle for your spouse. If you have no children or if the children are grown and lead separate lives, your spouse will once again be single. The surviving spouse must confront problems of grief and adjustment. Daily life must continue. At the same time, the estate must be settled. If not, catastrophic financial consequences may result.

Financial Literacy for My Life

ESTATE PLANNING CHECKLIST

Do you and your family members know the answers to the following questions?

1. Where are your previous years' income tax returns?

2. Where is your safe deposit box located? Where is the key to it kept?

3. What kinds and amounts of life insurance protection do you have?

4. Can you locate your insurance policies—life, health, property, casualty, and auto?

5. Who are the beneficiaries and contingent beneficiaries of your life insurance policies?

6. What type of health insurance protection do you have, and what are the provisions of your health insurance policy?

7. Do you and your spouse have current wills? Who was the attorney who drafted them? Where are they kept?

8. Do you have a separate record of the important papers you keep in your safe deposit box? Where is this record located?

9. Do you have a record of your spouse's and children's Social Security numbers?

10. Where are your marriage certificate and the birth certificates of all members of your family?

11. Do you know the name, address, and phone number of your life insurance agent (or the phone number and web address of the company if you obtained the policy online)?

12. Do you know the principal financial resources and liabilities of your estate?

13. Are you knowledgeable about simple, daily, and compound interest rates? About retirement funds and property ownership?

14. Have you given any thought to funerals and burial arrangements?

15. What papers and records will be important to other people when you die?

16. Do you understand the functions of a bank trust department and the meaning of joint ownership?

Source: *Planning with Your Beneficiaries* (Washington, DC: American Council of Life Insurance, Education, and Community Services, n.d.), p. 2.

Most people have various assets and many possessions that make up their estate.
Imagenet/Shutterstock

If children survive you, making sure that your estate can be readily analyzed and distributed may be even more critical. If relatives or friends are beneficiaries, bequests have to be made known quickly and clearly.

Your desires and information about your estate have to be accessible, understandable, and legally documented. Otherwise, your beneficiaries may encounter problems, and your intentions may not be carried out.

IF YOU NEVER MARRIED

Never having been married does not eliminate the need to organize your financial affairs. For people who live alone, as for married people, it is essential that important documents and personal information be consolidated and accessible.

Remember that in the event of your death, difficult questions and situations will confront some person at a time of severe emotional strain. That person may not be prepared to face them objectively. Probably the single most important thing you can do is take steps to see that your beneficiaries have the information and the knowledge they need to survive emotionally and financially when you die.

Everyone should take such steps. However, the need to take them is especially great if you are only 5 or 10 years away from retirement. By then, your possessions will probably be of considerable value. Your savings and checking account balances will probably be substantial. Your investment plans will have materialized. If you stop and take a look at where you are, you may be pleasantly surprised at the value of your estate.

NEW LIFESTYLES

Millions of nontraditional households have unique estate planning problems. Nearly half of all American marriages end in divorce, creating difficulties for millions of adults contemplating estate planning. Single parents and other single persons all have formidable estate planning challenges. Financial planners and estate attorneys universally offer such households the following smart advice: Plan early, and get expert help. The law provides plenty of protection for married couples, but it is rife with pitfalls for almost everyone else.

Single parents, divorced or not, must plan for their own death as part of retirement and estate planning. David Scott Sloan, chairman of trusts and estates at Sherburne, Powers & Needham, a law firm in Boston, says that simply leaving money to your children can result in a huge estate tax bill, sharply decreasing the funds available if your estate is worth more than $11.7 million in 2021. Sloan recommends setting up a trust for the children's benefit.

Unmarried couples face formidable retirement and estate planning challenges. A partner lacks any legal right to the companion's assets upon the companion's disability or death or upon the breakup of the partnership. Unmarried couples also cannot use the so-called marital deduction, which allows spouses to pass on everything they own to their surviving spouse tax free. Estate planning is even more important for unmarried couples. For example, if no beneficiary is named on your pension plan, the plan sponsor is required to give the proceeds to your closest blood relative. If you want your partner to receive the plan proceeds after you die, make sure he or she is named the beneficiary. Also, check to see whether the plan allows unmarried partners to receive joint-and-survivor benefits.

THE OPPORTUNITY COST OF RATIONALIZING

Daily living often gets in the way of thinking about death. You mean to organize things that others need to know in case you die, but you haven't done this yet. One of your rationalizations may be that you are not sure what information you need to provide.

Think about the outcome of your delay. Your beneficiary will meet people who offer specific types of assistance—morticians, clergy, lawyers, insurance agents, clerks of federal government agencies, and so on. These people will probably be strangers—sympathetic, courteous, and helpful, but disinterested. Also, your bereaved beneficiary may find it difficult to reveal confidences to them. Today, however, the information survivors need is as close as the telephone. Call LIMRA International, a financial services research organization, at 1-800-235-4672 to order their booklet, *What Do You Do Now?*

The moral is to plan your estate while you are in good health and think through the provisions carefully. Last-minute "death-bed" estate planning may fail to carry out your wishes.

 PRACTICE QUIZ 19-1

PFP Sheet 66
Estate Planning

1. If you needed information about estate planning, would you go to the library or online? Why?
2. Why is estate planning an important component of financial planning?
3. Why is estate planning important for single as well as married individuals? For "new" lifestyle individuals?

Legal Aspects of Estate Planning

When death occurs, proof of claims must be produced or the claims will not be processed. If no thought was given to gathering the necessary documents beforehand (with a sufficient number of copies), a period of financial hardship may follow until

LO19-2

Assess the legal aspects of estate planning.

Preparing a will can make things easier for your family after your death and ensure that your estate is distributed according to your wishes.
wavebreakmedia/Shutterstock

proof is obtained. If needed documentation cannot be located, irretrievable loss of funds may occur. Your heirs may experience emotionally painful delays until their rights have been established.

Important papers include the following:

1. Birth certificates—yours, your spouse's, and your children's.
2. Marriage certificates—always important, but especially important if you or your spouse were married previously—and divorce papers.
3. Legal name changes—judgment of court documents pertaining to any legal changes in the names that appear on birth certificates (especially important to protect the adopted children of a previous marriage or children who have been adopted through adoption agencies).
4. Military service records—the standard DD–214 (Armed Forces of the United States Report of Transfer or Discharge) or any other official statement of your military service details, if appropriate.

Here is a list of additional important documents.

- Social Security documents
- Veteran documents
- Insurance policies
- Transfer records of joint bank accounts
- Safe deposit box records
- Registration of automobiles
- Title to stock and bond certificates

will The legal declaration of a person's mind as to the disposition of his or her property after death.

intestate Without a valid will.

You should have several copies of certain documents because when you submit a claim, the accompanying proof often becomes a permanent part of the claim file and is not returned. Remember too that in some circumstances, children may be required to furnish proof of their parents' birth, marriage, or divorce.

WILLS

One of the most vital documents every adult should have is a written will. A **will** is the legal declaration of a person's mind as to the disposition of his or her property after death. Thus, a will is a way to transfer your property according to your wishes after you die. Although wills are simple to create, about half of all Americans die without one. When singer-songwriter Prince died in 2016, he left no will. Prince, however, is not alone. Other famous people who died intestate include Abraham Lincoln, Howard Hughes, Jimi Hendrix, Elvis Presley, Martin Luther King, Jr., Walt Disney, John D. Rockefeller, and Clark Gable.

my life 2

If I die intestate (without a valid will), my legal state of residence will control the distribution of my estate.

A will is the most practical first step in estate planning; it makes clear how you want your property to be distributed after you die. If you die intestate, your estate could be distributed differently than what you would like.

Whether you prepare a will before you die or neglect to take that sensible step, you still have a will. If you fail to prepare your own will, the state in which you legally reside steps in and controls the distribution of your estate without regard for wishes you may have had but failed to define in legal form. Thus, if you die **intestate**—without a valid will—the state's law of descent and distribution becomes your copy of the will, as shown in Exhibit 19-1.

Consider the opportunity cost of a husband and father who died without a will. By default, he has authorized his estate to be disposed of according to the provisions of the fictitious document

EXHIBIT 19-1
Your will: If you don't write one
If you die without a will, the state's law of descent and distribution becomes your will.

My Last Will and Testament

Being of sound mind and memory, I, ___, do hereby publish this as my last Will and Testament.

FIRST

I give my wife only one-third of my possessions, and I give my children the remaining two-thirds.

A. I appoint my wife as guardian of my children, but as a safeguard I require that she report to the Probate Court each year and render an accounting of how, why, and where she spent the money necessary for the proper care of my children.

B. As a further safeguard, I direct my wife to produce to the Probate Court a Performance Bond to guarantee that she exercise proper judgment in the handling, investing, and spending of the children's money.

C. As a final safeguard, my children shall have the right to demand and receive a complete accounting from their mother of all of her financial actions with their money as soon as they reach legal age.

D. When my children reach age 18, they shall have full rights to withdraw and spend their shares of my estate. No one shall have any right to question my children's actions on how they decide to spend their respective shares.

SECOND

Should my wife remarry, her second husband shall be entitled to one-third of everything my wife possesses. Should my children need some of this share for their support, the second husband shall not be bound to spend any part of his share on my children's behalf.

A. The second husband shall have the sole right to decide who is to get his share, even to the exclusion of my children.

THIRD

Should my wife predecease me or die while any of my children are minors, I do not wish to exercise my right to nominate the guardian of my children.

A. Rather than nominating a guardian of my preference, I direct my relatives and friends to get together and select a guardian by mutual agreement.

B. In the event that they fail to agree on a guardian, I direct the Probate Court to make the selection. If the court wishes, it may appoint a stranger acceptable to it.

FOURTH

Under existing tax law, certain legitimate avenues are open to me to lower estate and inheritance taxes rates. Since I prefer to have my money used for government purposes rather than for the benefit of my wife and children, I direct that no effort be made to lower taxes.

IN WITNESS WHEREOF, I have set my hand to this, my LAST WILL AND TESTAMENT, this ___ day of ___ 20 ___.

in Exhibit 19-1. The wording in this exhibit represents a pattern of distribution that could occur unless you prepare a valid will specifying otherwise.

This does not happen only to a husband. It could happen to anyone. To avoid such consequences, make a will! Consulting an attorney for this purpose can spare your heirs many difficulties, especially since the passage of the Economic Recovery Tax Act of 1981. This act created estate planning opportunities and problems for many people. It also created some difficult choices as to types of wills.

personal fintech

RULES TO REMEMBER WHEN WRITING A WILL

In most states, you must be 18 years of age or older to write your will.

- A will must be written in sound judgment and mental capacity to be valid.
- The document must clearly state that it is your will.
- The will must name an executor, who ensures your estate is distributed according to your wishes.
- It is not necessary to notarize or record your will, but these can safeguard against any claims that your will is invalid. For it to be valid, you must sign a will in the presence of at least two witnesses.

THE EFFECT OF MARRIAGE OR DIVORCE ON YOUR WILL   If you already have a will and are about to be married or divorced, review your will with an attorney for necessary changes. Upon divorce, only provisions favoring a former spouse are automatically revoked; provisions favoring family members of your ex-spouse, such as stepchildren, nieces, nephews, or in-laws, are not affected.

If you marry after you have made a will, the will is revoked automatically unless certain conditions are met. For example, marriage does not revoke a will if:

- The will indicates an intent that it not be revoked by a subsequent marriage, or
- The will was drafted under circumstances indicating that it was in contemplation of marriage.

Because your existing will's legal status may be uncertain, you are better off drawing a new will to fit your new circumstances.

COST OF A WILL   Legal fees for drafting a will vary with the complexities of your estate and family situation. A standard will costs between $500 and $800. The price varies from place to place, but generally the cost of writing a will is less than that for writing a living trust (to be discussed later in the chapter). Look for an attorney experienced in drafting wills and in estate planning. If your will is not complex, you may visit online sites such as Legal Zoom which allows you to easily, conveniently, and cheaply write your own will.

probate The legal procedure of proving a valid or invalid will.

Probate is the legal procedure of proving a valid or invalid will. It is the process by which an executor manages and distributes your property after you die according to your will's provisions. A probate court generally validates wills and makes sure debts are paid. You should avoid probate because it is expensive, lengthy, and public. As you'll read later, a living trust avoids probate and is less expensive, quicker, and private.

 PRACTICE QUIZ 19-2

1. What are the legal aspects of estate planning?
2. What is a will? Why is it an important estate planning tool?
3. How does marriage or divorce affect a will?

Types and Formats of Wills

LO19-3

Distinguish among various types and formats of wills.

simple will A will that leaves everything to the spouse; also called an *I love you will.*

TYPES OF WILLS

A brief review of the types of wills will be helpful, since the tax effects of these wills differ. The four types of wills are the simple will, the traditional marital share will, the exemption trust will, and the stated dollar amount will.

SIMPLE WILL   A **simple will**, sometimes called an *I love you will,* leaves everything to the spouse. Such a will is sufficient for most smaller estates. However, if you have a large or complex estate, especially one involving business interests that you want to pass on to your children, a simple will may not meet your objectives. It may also create higher overall taxation because everything would be taxed in your spouse's subsequent estate.

TRADITIONAL MARITAL SHARE WILL

The **traditional marital share will** leaves one-half of the **adjusted gross estate** (the gross estate minus debts and costs) to the spouse outright as a marital share. The other half of the adjusted gross estate might go to children or other heirs or be held in trust for the family. A trust can provide the spouse with a lifelong income and would not be taxed at the spouse's death.

Under this type of will, half of your estate is taxed at your death and half at your spouse's death. This results in the lowest overall amount of federal estate taxes on estates above a certain size (twice the exemption amount). However, there are other considerations. State inheritance taxes may be greater, especially at the first death, due to conflicting federal and state exemption and beneficiary classifications. Also, under this type of will, unlike a simple will or an exemption trust, federal estate taxes may have to be paid up front at the first death that will involve the loss of use of money. If your spouse has considerable assets in his or her own right, it might not be prudent to increase your spouse's estate by any amount. In such a situation, a will that equalizes estates might be better. Finally, the nine community-property states severely limit your options as to how to allocate your money.

EXEMPTION TRUST WILL

The **exemption trust will** has been gaining in popularity due to its increased exemption. Under this type of will, everything passes to your spouse with the exception of an amount equal to the exemption, which would pass into trust. The amount passed to your spouse can be by will, trust, or other means. The exemption trust can provide your spouse with a lifelong income.

There would be little or no tax at your death due to the combination of the exemption and the marital deduction. The main advantage of the exemption trust will is that it eliminates future taxation of the exemption amount and any growth in it, which may be important if property values appreciate considerably.

STATED DOLLAR AMOUNT WILL

The **stated dollar amount will** allows you to pass on to your spouse any amount that satisfies your family objectives. These objectives may or may not include tax considerations. For example, you could pass on the stated amount of $11,700,000 (in 2021). However, the stated amount might instead be related to anticipated income needs or to the value of personal items.

State law may dictate how much you must leave your spouse. Most states require that your spouse receive a certain amount, usually one-half or one-third. Some states require that such interests pass outright, and others permit life interests. The stated dollar amount will may satisfy such requirements and pass the balance to others. You may, for example, decide to pass most of your estate to your children, thereby avoiding subsequent taxation of your spouse's estate. It may also make sense to pass interests in a business to children who are involved in the business.

Such plans may increase taxes at your death, since not all of your property passes to your spouse. However, the taxes at your spouse's subsequent death would be lower. You can also leave your spouse an outright amount equal to the exemption with a life estate in the balance, or a life estate in trust.

The stated dollar amount has one major shortcoming: The will may leave specific dollar amounts to listed heirs and the balance to the surviving spouse. Although these amounts may be reasonable when the will is drafted, they can soon become obsolete. What if estate values suddenly decrease due to a business setback or a drop in the stock market? Consider an individual with an extensive equities portfolio who drafted a will in 2019. During the COVID-19 global pandemic, the value of the portfolio may have shrunk by one-third in just a few weeks. None of that decrease will be borne by those who were left specific dollar amounts. The entire decrease will be borne by the surviving spouse. Therefore, you should use percentages instead of designated amounts.

traditional marital share will A will in which the grantor leaves one-half of the adjusted gross estate to the spouse.

adjusted gross estate The gross estate minus debts and costs.

exemption trust will A will in which everything passes to the spouse except the exemption amount.

stated dollar amount will A will that allows you to pass on to your spouse any amount that satisfies your family objectives.

smart money minute

holographic will A handwritten will.

formal will A will that is usually prepared with an attorney's assistance.

beneficiary A person who has been named to receive property under a will.

statutory will A formal will on a preprinted form.

executor Appointed representative who ensures that your desires expressed in your will are carried out.

WHICH TYPE OF WILL IS BEST FOR YOU? The four types of wills just discussed are your basic choices. Which one is best for you?

Prior to the Economic Recovery Tax Act of 1981, many experts advocated the traditional marital share will. Today many attorneys believe the exemption trust will is best. However, there is no one ideal will. Which will is best for you depends on factors such as the size of your estate, the future appreciation of your estate, inflation, the respective ages of you and your spouse, cash on hand, and—most important—your objectives.

FORMATS OF WILLS

Wills may be holographic or formal. A **holographic will** is a handwritten will that you prepare yourself. It should be written, dated, and signed entirely in your handwriting; no printed or typed information should be on its pages. Some states, however, may not recognize a holographic will.

A **formal will** is usually prepared with an attorney's assistance. It may be either typed or on a preprinted form. You must sign the will and acknowledge it as your will in the presence of two witnesses, neither of whom is a **beneficiary** (a person you have named to receive property under the will). The witnesses must then sign the will in your presence.

A **statutory will** is one type of formal will. It is a preprinted form that may be obtained from lawyers and online stores. There are serious risks in using this or any other preprinted form. One risk is that such a form usually requires you to conform to rigid *p*rovisions, some of which may not be in the best interests of your beneficiaries. Also, if you change the preprinted wording, you may violate the law regarding wills, which may cause the changed sections or even the entire will to be declared invalid. There is also a risk that the form is out of date with respect to current law. It is always prudent to seek legal assistance in developing these documents.

WRITING YOUR WILL

The way to transfer your property according to your wishes is to write a will specifying those wishes. Joint ownership is no substitute for a will. Although jointly owned property passes directly to the joint owner and may be appropriate for some assets, such as your home, only a will allows you to distribute your property as a whole exactly as you wish. Select a person who will follow your instructions (your **executor** or *executrix*). By naming your own executor, you will eliminate the need for a court-appointed administrator, prevent unnecessary delay in the distribution of your property, and minimize estate taxes and settlement costs. See the *Financial Literacy for My Life: The Ten Commandments of Making Your Will* feature for guidance on important aspects of making a will.

If you have a will drawn, you are testate in the eyes of the law, and an executor (named in your will) will carry out your wishes in due time.
Ariel Skelley/Getty Images

SELECTING AN EXECUTOR Select an executor or executrix who is both willing and able to carry out the complicated tasks associated with executing a will. These tasks are preparing an inventory of assets, collecting any money due, paying off any debts, preparing and filing all income and estate tax returns, liquidating and reinvesting other assets to pay off debts and provide income for your family while the estate is being administered, distributing the estate, and making a final accounting to your beneficiaries and to the probate court.

Financial Literacy for My Life

THE 10 COMMANDMENTS OF MAKING YOUR WILL

1. Work closely with your spouse as you prepare your will. Seek professional help so that your family objectives can be met regardless of who dies first.

2. Write your will to conform with your current wishes. When your circumstances change (e.g., when you retire or move to another state), review your will and, if appropriate, write a new one.

3. Do not choose a beneficiary as a witness. If such a person is called on to validate your will, he or she may not be able to collect an inheritance.

4. If you are remarrying, consider signing a prenuptial agreement to protect your children. If you sign such an agreement before the wedding, you and your intended spouse can legally agree that neither of you will make any claim on the other's estate. The agreement can be revoked later, if you both agree.

5. Consider using percentages rather than dollar amounts when you divide your estate. For example, if you leave $50,000 to a friend and the rest to your spouse, your spouse will suffer if your estate shrinks to $60,000.

6. Both you and your spouse should have a will, and those wills should be separate documents.

7. Be flexible. Don't insist that your heirs keep stock or run a cattle ranch. If you do so, they may suffer if economic conditions change.

8. Sign the original copy of your will and keep it in a safe place; keep an unsigned copy at home for reference.

9. Alter your will by preparing a new will or adding a codicil. Don't change beneficiaries by writing on the will itself; this may invalidate the will.

10. Select an executor or executrix who is both willing and able to carry out the complicated tasks associated with the job.

Who can be an executor? Any U.S. citizen over 18 who has not been convicted of a felony can be named the executor of a will. Your executor can be a family member, a friend, an attorney, an accountant, or the trust department of a bank. Fees for executors, whether professionals or friends, are set by state law. Exhibit 19-2 summarizes typical duties of an executor.

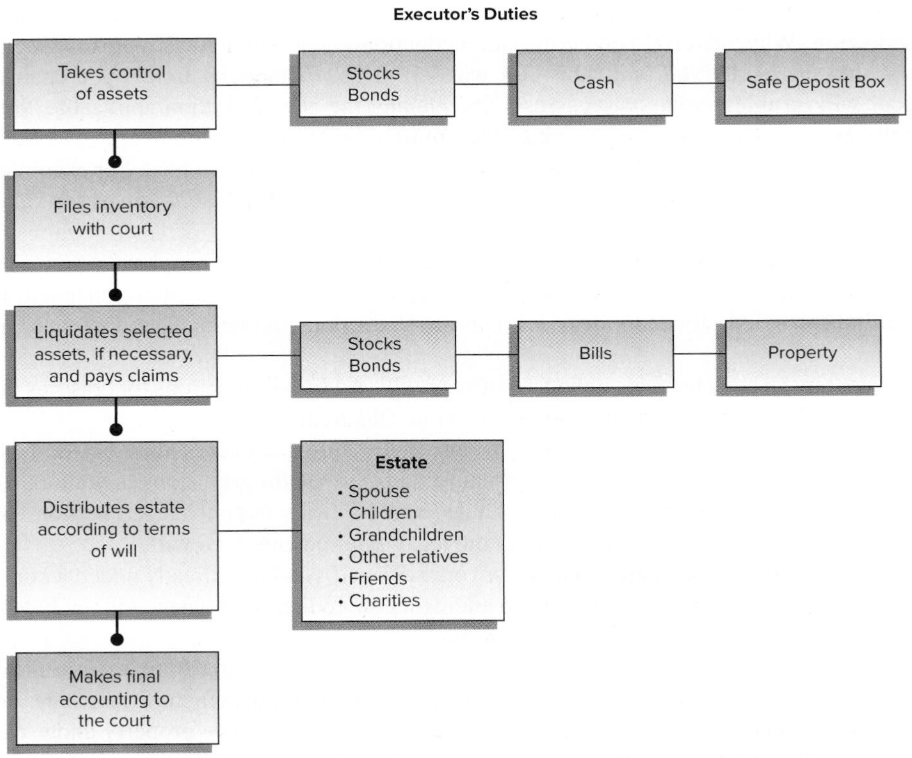

Executor's Duties

EXHIBIT 19-2

Major responsibilities of an executor

An executor is someone who is willing and able to perform the complicated tasks involved in carrying out your will.

Source: American Bankers Association, *Trust Services from Your Bank,* rev. ed. (Washington, DC: American Bankers Association, 1978), p. 9.

SELECTING A GUARDIAN   In addition to disposing of your estate, your will should name a guardian and/or trustee to care for minor children if both parents die at the same time, such as in an automobile accident or a plane crash. A **guardian** is a person who assumes the responsibilities of providing the children with personal care and of managing the estate for them. A **trustee,** on the other hand, is a person or an institution that holds or generally manages property for the benefit of someone else under a trust agreement.

You should take great care in selecting a guardian for your children. You want a guardian whose philosophy on raising children is similar to yours and who is willing to accept the responsibility.

Most states require a guardian to post a bond with the probate court. The bonding company promises to reimburse the minor's estate up to the amount of the bond if the guardian uses the property of the minor for his or her own gain. The bonding fee (usually several hundred dollars) is paid from the estate. However, you can waive the bonding requirement in your will.

Through your will, you may want to provide funds to raise your children. You could, for instance, leave a lump sum for an addition to the guardian's house and establish monthly payments to cover your children's living expenses.

The guardian of the minor's estate manages the property you leave behind for your children. This guardian can be a person or the trust department of a financial institution, such as a bank. Property that you place in trust for your children can be managed by the trustee rather than by the guardian of the minor's estate.

Each executor or a trustee has a fiduciary relationship to the beneficiaries of the will. This relationship dictates that beneficiaries' interests are paramount. The executor or trustee must not take advantage of his or her position.

ALTERING OR REWRITING YOUR WILL

If you do have a will, you should review it periodically. This is necessary even if you have already done some planning and your will refers to the old 50 percent marital deduction. Why? The 100 percent marital deduction is not automatic. Congress would not alter or rewrite your will; this task was left to you. Therefore, unless you change your will or unless your state passes a law making the new definition applicable, you will have to rewrite your will to make the unlimited marital deduction apply. Because many choices are of a personal nature, few, if any, states will get involved. For example, some people may not want to leave the entire estate to their spouse, perhaps for valid tax reasons.

You should review your will if you move to a different state; if you have sold property mentioned in the will; if the size and composition of your estate have changed; if you have married, divorced, or remarried; or if new potential heirs have died or been born.

Don't make any changes on the face of your will. Additions, deletions, or erasures on a will that has been signed and witnessed can invalidate the will.

If only a few changes are needed in your will, adding a codicil may be the best choice. A **codicil** is a document that explains, adds, or deletes provisions in your existing will. It identifies the will being amended and confirms the unchanged sections of the will. To be valid, it must conform to the legal requirements for a will.

If you wish to make major changes in your will or if you have already added a codicil, preparing a new will is preferable to adding a new codicil. In the new will, include a clause revoking all earlier wills and codicils.

If you are rewriting a will because of a remarriage, consider drafting a **prenuptial agreement.** This is a documentary agreement between spouses before marriage. In such agreements, one or both parties often waive a right to receive property under the other's will or under state law. Be sure to consult an attorney in drafting a prenuptial agreement.

LIVING WILL AND ADVANCE DIRECTIVES

Advance directives are legal documents that allow you to state what kind of health care you want if you are too ill to speak for yourself. Advance directives most often include the following:

- a living will,
- a health care proxy (durable power of attorney), and
- a letter of last instruction (after-death wishes).

Wills have existed for thousands of years; the oldest known will was written by the Egyptian pharaoh Uah in 2448 BC. Recently a new type of will, called a living will, has emerged.

A **living will** provides for your wishes to be followed if you become so physically or mentally disabled that you are unable to act on your own behalf. A living will is not a substitute for a traditional will. It enables an individual, while well, to express the intention that life be allowed to end if he or she becomes terminally ill. Many states recognize living wills, and you may consider writing one when you draw a conventional will. Exhibit 19-3 is an example of a typical living will.

living will A document that enables an individual, while well, to express the intention that life be allowed to end if he or she becomes terminally ill.

EXHIBIT 19-3
A living will
Many states recognize living wills.

To My Family, My Physician, My Lawyer, My Clergyman;

To Any Medical Facility in Whose Care I Happen to Be;

To Any Individual Who May Become Responsible for My Health or Welfare;

Living Will Declaration

Declaration made this _____ day of _____ (month, year)

I, _____, being of sound mind, willfully and voluntarily make known my desire that my dying shall not be artificially prolonged under the circumstances set forth below, do hereby declare

If at any time I should have an incurable injury, disease, or illness regarded as a terminal condition by my physician and if my physician has determined that the application of life-sustaining procedures would serve only to artificially prolong the dying process and that my death will occur whether or not life-sustaining procedures are utilized, I direct that such procedures be withheld or withdrawn and that I be permitted to die with only the administration of medication or the performance of any medical procedure deemed necessary to provide me with comfort care.

In the absence of my ability to give directions regarding the use of such life-sustaining procedures, it is my intention that this declaration shall be honored by my family and physician as the final expression of my legal right to refuse medical or surgical treatment and accept the consequences from such refusal.

I understand the full import of this declaration, and I am emotionally and mentally competent to make this declaration.

Signed _____

City, County, and State of Residence _____

The declarant has been personally known to me, and I believe him or her to be of sound mind.

Witness _____

Witness _____

Source: *Don't Wait until Tomorrow* (Hartford, CT: Aetna Life and Casualty Company, n.d.), p. 11.

To ensure the effectiveness of a living will, discuss your intention of preparing such a will with the people closest to you. You should also discuss this with your family doctor. Sign and date your document before two witnesses. Witnessing shows that you signed of your own free will.

Give copies of your living will to those closest to you, and have your family doctor place a copy in your medical file. Keep the original document readily accessible, and look it over periodically—preferably once a year—to be sure your wishes have remained unchanged. To verify your intent, re-date and initial each subsequent endorsement.

Most lawyers will do the paperwork for a living will at no cost if they are already preparing your estate plan. You can also get the necessary forms from nonprofit advocacy groups. For example, Aging With Dignity (www.agingwithdignity.org) lets you download a plain-English version called Five Wishes that's valid in 42 states and in the District of Columbia. National Hospice and Palliative Care (www.caringinfo.org) is a national nonprofit organization that operates the national crisis and information hotline dealing with end-of-life issues. It also provides documents, such as living wills and medical powers of attorney, geared to specific states. Working through end-of-life issues is difficult, but it can help avoid forcing your family to make a decision in a hospital waiting room—or worse, having your last wishes ignored.

A living will can become a problem. A once-healthy person may have a change of heart and prefer to remain alive even as death seems imminent. Living wills call for careful thought, but they do provide you with a choice as to the manner of your death.

ETHICAL WILL

ethical will A document that dispenses emotional and spiritual wealth to heirs.

Renewed interest in another type of will has emerged since the September 11, 2001, terrorist attacks. An **ethical will** is a way to pass on your values and beliefs to your heirs. Even though it is not a legally binding document, ethical wills help with estate planning.

Before taking a trip to California shortly after September 11, 2001, Kim Payfrock, 42, wrote letters to her two sons and two stepsons, ages 11 to 17. The letters expressed her love for them as well as her joys and regrets in life. "I was nervous about flying and wanted them to open the letters if anything happened to me," says Payfrock, who is an activity coordinator at an assisted-living community in Minneapolis. "This was a way to leave them my thoughts, to give them a part of myself."[1]

Payfrock didn't know it at the time, but she had written each of her children an *ethical will*. "It's a way to pass on your values, share lessons learned, express love, and address any regrets," says Barry Baines, the medical director of a hospice in Minneapolis and author of *Ethical Will: Putting Your Values on Paper*. Preparing such a document is not easy, since it requires earnest self-examination. But writers and recipients of ethical wills say the result is an invaluable legacy.[2]

SOCIAL MEDIA WILL

Social media is part of daily life, so what happens to the online content that you created once you die? If you are active online, you should consider creating a statement of how you would like your online identity to be handled, like a social media will or digital asset plan. You should appoint someone you trust as an online executor. This person will be responsible for the closure of your email addresses, social media profiles, and blogs after you die. Take these steps to help you write a social media will:

- Review the privacy policies and the terms and conditions of each website where you have a presence.

- State how you would like your profile to be handled. You may want to completely cancel your profile or keep it up for friends and family to visit. Some sites allow users to create a memorial profile where other users can still see your profile but can't post anything new.

- Give the social media executor a document that lists all the websites where you have a profile, along with your usernames and passwords.
- State in your will that the online executor should have a copy of your death certificate. The online executor may need this as proof in order for websites to take any actions on your behalf.

POWER OF ATTORNEY

Related to the concept of a living will is a durable power of attorney also known as a health care proxy. A **durable power of attorney** is a legal document authorizing someone to act on your behalf. At some point in your life, you may become ill or incapacitated. You may then wish to have someone attend to your needs and your personal affairs. You can assign a durable power of attorney to anyone you choose.

The person you name can be given limited power or a great deal of power. The power given can be special—to carry out certain acts or transactions—or it can be general—to act completely for you. A conventional power of attorney is automatically revoked in a case of legal incapacity.

LETTER OF LAST INSTRUCTION

In addition to your will, you should prepare a *letter of last instruction*. This document, also known as after-death wishes, though not legally enforceable in some states, can provide your heirs with important information. It should contain the details of your funeral arrangements. It should also contain the names of the people who are to be notified of your death and the locations of your bank accounts, safe deposit box, and other important items listed earlier in this chapter.

durable power of attorney A legal document authorizing someone to act on one's behalf.

my life **3**

In addition to a will, I should prepare a letter of last instruction.

Even though a letter of last instruction is not legally binding, it can provide heirs with important information. It should contain preferences for funeral arrangements as well as the names of the people who are to be informed of the death. For information on topics such as letters of last instruction, wills, trusts, living wills, and powers of attorney, visit www.nolo.com.

 PRACTICE QUIZ 19-3

1. Distinguish among the four types of wills.
2. What are the two formats of wills?
3. What are the steps in writing your will?
4. What is an ethical will?
5. What is a power of attorney?
6. What is a letter of last instruction?

 **PFP Sheet 67** Will Planning

Types of Trusts and Estates

A trust is a property arrangement in which a trustee, such as a person or a bank trust department, holds title to, takes care of, and in most cases manages property for the benefit of someone else. The creator of the trust is called the **trustor** or *grantor*. A bank, as trustee, charges a modest fee for its services, generally based on the value of the trust assets. All trust assets added together are known as an *estate*.

It is a good idea to discuss with your attorney the possibility of establishing a trust as a means of managing your estate. Basically, a **trust** is a legal arrangement through which a trustee holds your assets for your benefit or that of your beneficiaries. Trusts

LO19-4

Appraise various types of trusts and estates.

trustor The creator of a trust; also called the *grantor*.

trust A legal arrangement through which one's assets are held by a trustee.

are used for everything from protecting assets from creditors to managing property for young children, disabled elders, or even the family pets.

Trusts are either revocable or irrevocable. If you establish a **revocable trust**, you retain the right to end the trust or change its terms during your lifetime. Revocable trusts avoid the often lengthy probate process, but they do not provide shelter from federal or state estate taxes. You might choose a revocable trust if you think you may need its assets for your own use at a later time or if you want to monitor the performance of the trust and the trustee before the arrangement is made irrevocable by your death. If you establish an **irrevocable trust**, you cannot change its terms or end it. The trust becomes, for tax purposes, a separate entity, and the assets can't be removed, nor can changes be made by the grantor. Therefore, an irrevocable trust offers tax advantages not offered by a revocable trust. Irrevocable trusts often are used by individuals with large estates to reduce estate taxes and avoid probate.

revocable trust A trust whose terms the trustor retains the rights to change.

irrevocable trust A trust that cannot be altered or ended by its creator.

BENEFITS OF ESTABLISHING TRUSTS

Your individual circumstances dictate whether it makes sense to establish a trust. Here are some common reasons for setting up a trust. You can use a trust to:

- Reduce or otherwise provide for payment of estate taxes,
- Avoid probate and transfer your assets immediately to your beneficiaries,
- Free yourself from management of your assets while you receive a regular income from the trust,
- Provide income for a surviving spouse or other beneficiaries, and
- Ensure that your property serves a desired purpose after your death.

Trustee services are commonly provided by banks and, in some instances, by life insurance companies. An estate attorney can advise you about the right type of trust for you.

my life 4

If I establish a trust, it will avoid probate and transfer my assets immediately to my beneficiaries.

Basically, a trust is a legal arrangement that helps manage the assets of your estate for your benefit or that of your beneficiaries. One of the benefits of establishing a trust is that it avoids probate and transfers your assets immediately to your beneficiaries.

TYPES OF TRUSTS

There are many types of trusts, some of which are described in detail below. Each of these types has particular advantages. Choose the type of trust that is most appropriate for your family situation.

CREDIT-SHELTER TRUST   A **credit-shelter trust** is perhaps the most common estate planning trust. It is also known as a *bypass trust,* a *"residuary" trust,* an *A/B trust,* an *exemption equivalent trust,* or a *family trust.* It is designed to allow married couples, who can leave everything to each other tax free, to take full advantage of the exemption that allows $11.7 million (in 2021) in every estate to pass free of federal estate taxes. Thus, under the Tax Cuts and Jobs Act of 2017, for a married couple, only an estate of more than $23.4 million is taxed at the 40 percent rate. These exemptions, however, expire on December 31, 2025.

credit-shelter trust A trust that allows married couples to leave everything to each other tax free.

disclaimer trust A trust designed for a couple who do not yet have enough assets to need a credit-shelter trust but may need one in the future.

DISCLAIMER TRUST   A **disclaimer trust** is appropriate for a couple who do not yet have enough assets to need a credit-shelter trust but may need one in the future. For example, a newly practicing physician who will soon finish paying off college loans might want to take this approach. With a disclaimer trust, the surviving spouse is left everything but has the right to disclaim some portion of the estate. Anything disclaimed goes into a credit-shelter trust. This approach gives the surviving spouse the flexibility to shelter any wealth from estate taxes. However, if the estate fails to grow as expected, the survivor isn't locked into a trust structure.

LIVING, OR INTER VIVOS, TRUST A **living trust**, or *inter vivos trust,* is a property management arrangement that you establish while you are alive. Well-structured estate plans often start with a living trust that becomes irrevocable at death, dividing itself into several other types of trusts, such as a credit-shelter trust. You simply transfer some property to a trustee, giving him or her instructions regarding its management and disposition while you are alive and after your death.

In the past several years, many people have opted for a living trust instead of a will, or in addition to one. But bare-bones living trusts, which start at $2,000, are overhyped and often misunderstood. (See the *How To . . . Make Sure a Living Trust Offer Is Trustworthy* feature.) They do not, for example, bypass estate taxes or protect you from creditors. What they do is avoid probate—which, in states such as Florida and California, can drag on for a couple of years and eat up as much as 5 to 10 percent of the estate's assets in administrative fees. With a living trust, you can change the terms while you're living, and your successor trustee, usually a family member, distributes the property without court interference when you die.

> **living trust** A trust that is created and provides benefits during the trustor's lifetime.

 HOW TO . . .   **Make Sure a Living Trust Offer Is Trustworthy**

Misinformation and misunderstanding about estate taxes and the length or complexity of probate provide the perfect cover for scam artists who have created an industry out of older people's fears that their estates could be eaten up by costs or that the distribution of their assets could be delayed for years. Some unscrupulous businesses are advertising seminars on living trusts or sending postcards inviting consumers to call for in-home appointments to learn whether a living trust is right for them. In these cases, it's not uncommon for the salesperson to exaggerate the benefits or the appropriateness of the living trust and claim—falsely—that locally licensed lawyers will prepare the documents.

Other businesses are advertising living trust "kits": consumers send money for these do-it-yourself products but receive nothing in return. Still other businesses are using estate planning services to gain access to consumers' financial information and to sell them other financial products, such as insurance annuities.

What's a consumer to do? It's true that for some people, a living trust can be a useful and practical tool. But for others, it can be a waste of money and time. Because state laws and requirements vary, "cookie-cutter" approaches to estate planning aren't always the most efficient way to handle your affairs. Before you sign any papers to create a will, a living trust, or any other kind of trust, do the following:

- Explore all your options with an experienced and licensed estate planning attorney or financial advisor. Generally, state law requires that an attorney draft the trust.
- Avoid high-pressure sales tactics and high-speed sales pitches by anyone who is selling estate planning tools or arrangements.
- Avoid salespeople who give the impression that AARP is selling or endorsing their products. AARP does not endorse any living trust product.
- Do your homework. Get information about your local probate laws from the clerk (or registrar) of wills.
- If you opt for a living trust, make sure it's properly funded—that is, that the property has been transferred from your name to the trust. If the transfers aren't done properly, the trust will be invalid, and the state will determine who inherits your property and serves as guardian for your minor children.
- If someone tries to sell you a living trust, ask whether the seller is an attorney. Some states limit the sale of living trust services to attorneys.
- Remember the *cooling off rule*. If you buy a living trust in your home or somewhere other than the seller's permanent place of business (say, at a hotel seminar), the seller must give you a written statement of your right to cancel the deal within three business days. The cooling off rule provides that during the sales transaction, the salesperson must give you two copies of a cancellation form (one for you to keep and one to return to the company) and a copy of your contract or receipt. The contract or receipt must be dated, show the name and address of the seller, and explain your right to cancel. You can write a letter and exercise your right to cancel

within three days, even if you don't receive a cancellation form. You do not have to give a reason for canceling. Stopping payment on your check if you do cancel in these circumstances is a good idea. If you pay by credit card and the seller does not credit your account after you cancel, you can dispute the charge with the credit card issuer.

- Check out the organization with the Better Business Bureau in your state or the state where the organization is located before you send any money for any product or service. Although this is prudent, it is not foolproof: there may be no record of complaints if an organization is too new or has changed its name.

FOR MORE INFORMATION

To learn more about estate planning strategies, talk with an experienced estate planning attorney or financial advisor and check out the following resources.

AARP: 1-800-424-3410; www.aarp.org. Ask for a copy of *Product Report: Wills & Living Trusts.* AARP does not sell or endorse living trust products.

American Bar Association, 312-988-5522; www.americanbar.org/groups/public_education/resources/resources_for_the_public.html.

Council of Better Business Bureaus Inc., 703-276-0100; www.bbb.org/.

National Academy of Elder Law Attorneys Inc., 703-942-5711, www.naela.org/.

National Consumer Law Center, 617-542-8010; www.consumerlaw.org/.

Source: Federal Trade Commission.

Living trusts are a must if you own property in more than one state, since your heirs will not be subjected to multiple probate proceedings. Unlike wills, which become public as soon as they are filed with the probate court, living trusts are private documents. They can be handy for other situations as well, such as disinheriting estranged family members. The biggest mistake made in estate planning? You sign the documents setting up the trust but don't follow through with the tedious task of retitling all of your property, such as real estate, stocks and bonds, and bank accounts, in the specific name of the trust. A living trust has the following advantages:

- It ensures privacy. A will is a public record; a trust is not.
- The property held in the trust avoids probate at your death. It eliminates probate costs and delays.
- It enables you to review your trustee's performance and make changes if necessary.
- It can remove management responsibilities from your shoulders.
- It is less subject to dispute by disappointed heirs than a will is.
- It can guide your family and doctors if you become terminally ill or incompetent.

However, a living trust can be complicated and involves higher costs than creating a will, and funding a trust can be time consuming.

TESTAMENTARY TRUST An irrevocable trust, a **testamentary trust** is established by your will and becomes effective upon your death. Such a trust can be valuable if your beneficiaries are inexperienced in financial matters or if the potential estate tax is substantial. Like a living trust, a testamentary trust provides the benefits of asset management, financial bookkeeping, protection of the beneficiaries, and minimizing of estate taxes. However, it does not protect your assets from the probate process.

testamentary trust A trust established by the creator's will that becomes effective upon his or her death.

Newly acquired property can always be added to your trust. But what if you forget to change the title on some of your assets? A simple pourover will, written when the trust agreement is drafted, is the answer. A *pourover* will is a simple document stating that anything you may have neglected to place in your trust during your lifetime should be placed in it at your death. While assets passing under a pourover will are generally probated, a small amount may be excluded from a probate.

LIFE INSURANCE TRUST In many families, the proceeds of life insurance policies are the largest single asset of the estate. A **life insurance trust** is established while you are living. The trust receives your life insurance benefits upon your death and administers them in an agreed-on manner. Such a trust can be canceled if your family or financial circumstances change or if you wish to make new plans for the future.

Although common estate planning tools, life insurance trusts "aren't for the faint of heart," says one tax attorney. They require careful monitoring so that they don't run afoul of gift tax rules.

As you can see, trusts are complicated; therefore, you should seek a competent estate attorney in preparing this legal document. The purpose of all types of trusts is to preserve your estate for your heirs. (Read the *Financial Literacy for My Life: Other Types of Trusts* feature.)

life insurance trust A trust whose assets are derived at least in part from the proceeds of life insurance.

ESTATES

As mentioned earlier, your estate is everything you own (see Exhibit 19-4). It includes all of your property—tangible and intangible, however acquired or owned, whether inside or outside the country. It may include jointly owned property, life insurance, and employee benefits. Thus, an important step in estate planning is taking inventory of everything you own, such as:

1. Cash, checking accounts, savings accounts, CDs, and money market funds.
2. Stocks, bonds (including municipals and U.S. savings bonds), mutual funds, commodity futures, and tax shelters.
3. Life insurance, employee benefits, and annuities.
4. Your home and any other real estate, land and buildings, furniture, and fixtures.
5. Farms, grain, livestock, machinery, and equipment.
6. Proprietorship, partnership, and close corporation interests.
7. Notes, accounts, and claims receivable.
8. Interests in trusts and powers of appointment.
9. Antiques, works of art, collectibles, cars, boats, planes, personal effects, and everything else.

smart money minute

In common-law states (most states), spouses are not considered co-owners of property unless it has been jointly titled. Surviving spouses are entitled to inherit a portion of the deceased spouse's property.

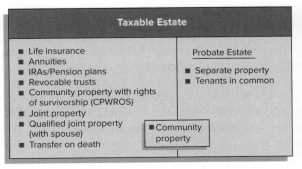
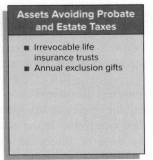

EXHIBIT 19-4

What is your estate?
This exhibit shows which assets are included in your probate estate, the much larger number of assets included in your taxable estate, and the very few assets that can avoid both probate and estate taxes.

Source: *Planning Your Estate* (A. G. Edwards, 1996), p. 6.

OTHER TYPES OF TRUSTS

GRANTOR RETAINED ANNUITY TRUST (GRAT)

If you are worried about estate taxes, consider one of today's most popular alternatives. A grantor retained annuity trust (GRAT) not only shelters valuable assets that you can pass on to your heirs with minimal taxes but also lets you receive an annuity for as long as the trust lasts.

MARITAL-DEDUCTION TRUST

With a marital-deduction trust, you can leave to your spouse any money that doesn't go into a credit-shelter trust. Whatever the amount, it is free of estate tax when you die, since it qualifies for the marital deduction. Perhaps the most popular form of marital trust is the *qualified terminable interest property trust,* or *Q-TIP.* Here, the surviving spouse gets all trust income, which must be distributed at least once a year, and sometimes receives access to the principal as well. When the spouse dies, the assets go to whomever you specified in the trust documents. The trust assets are then taxed as part of the surviving spouse's estate.

SELF-DECLARATION TRUST

A self-declaration trust is a variation of the living trust. Its unique feature is that the creator of the trust is also the trustee. The trust document usually includes a procedure for removing the creator of the trust as the trustee without going to court. Typically, one or more physicians or family members, or a combination of physicians and family members, have removal power. If the creator of the trust is removed, a named successor trustee takes over.

CHARITABLE REMAINDER TRUST

With a charitable remainder trust, you retain the right to the income but transfer that right to the charity upon death. If you have highly appreciated assets, it is a great way to improve your cash flow during your retirement and pursue a charitable interest at the same time. The biggest drawback is that you have to give away the asset irrevocably.

QUALIFIED PERSONAL RESIDENCE TRUST

A qualified personal residence trust (QPRT) lets you get your home or vacation home out of your estate. You give your home to a trust but live in it for a term of, say, 10 years.

At the end of that time, the home belongs to the continuing trust or to the trust beneficiaries, depending on how the trust is written.

CHARITABLE LEAD TRUST

A charitable lead trust pays a specified charity income from a donated asset for a set number of years. When the term is up, the principal goes to the donor's beneficiaries with reduced estate or gift taxes. Such a trust has high setup and operating costs, however, which may make it impractical unless the assets involved are substantial. For this reason, it is a vehicle for very wealthy people, giving them a way to keep an asset in the family but greatly reducing the cost of passing it on.

GENERATION-SKIPPING TRUST

A generation-skipping trust allows you to directly leave a substantial amount of money to your grandchildren or great-grandchildren. If you have a large estate, you should explore a generation-skipping (or dynasty) trust. Over time, it can save millions of dollars in taxes and can be used to help all of those family members who come after you.

SPENDTHRIFT TRUST

If your beneficiary is too young or is unable to handle money wisely, consider a spendthrift trust. Here the beneficiary receives small amounts of money at specified intervals. It prevents the beneficiary from squandering money or losing it in a bad investment.

OTHER TYPES

There are still other types of specialized trusts. For example, a *pourover trust* is usually dormant during your lifetime, but it can be activated if you become disabled. It can be used to manage your insurance, qualified pension or profit-sharing plan proceeds, and your probate estate. A *QDOT (qualified domestic trust)* is for spouses who are not U.S. citizens. It provides the same marital deduction benefit that is available to citizen spouses. A *GRUT (grantor retained unitrust)* and a *personal residence GRIT (grantor retained income trust)* permit grantors to use favorable rules for determining the amount of gift made to the trust.

---

community property Any property that has been acquired by either spouse during the marriage.

In the community-property states (Arizona, California, Idaho, Louisiana, Nevada, New Mexico, Texas, Wisconsin, and Washington), where each spouse owns 50 percent of the property, half of the community assets are included in each spouse's estate. **Community property** is "any property that has been acquired by either of the spouses during the marriage, but not by gift, devise, bequest or inheritance, or, often, by the income therefrom." In the other, non–community-property states, property is included in the estate of the spouse who owns it. The way you own property can make a tax difference.

JOINT OWNERSHIP Joint ownership of property between spouses is very common. Joint ownership may also exist between parents and children, other relatives, or any two or more persons. While joint ownership may avoid *probate* (official proof of a will), creditor attachment, and inheritance taxes in some states, it does not avoid federal estate taxes. In fact, it may increase them.

There are three types of joint ownership, and each has different tax and estate planning consequences. First, if you and your spouse own property as *joint tenants with the right of survivorship (JT/WROS),* the property is considered owned 50-50 for estate tax purposes and will automatically pass to your spouse at your death, and vice versa. No gift tax is paid on creating such ownership, nor, due to the unlimited marital deduction, is any estate tax paid at the first death. However, this type of joint ownership may result in more taxes overall at the surviving spouse's later death than would be the case with a traditional marital share will, discussed earlier.

Second, if you and your spouse or anyone else own property as *tenants in common,* each individual is considered to own a proportionate share for tax purposes, and only your share is included in your estate. That share does not go to the other tenants in common at your death but is included in your probate estate and subject to your decision as to who gets it. While there are no gift or estate tax consequences between spouse joint owners, gifts of joint interests to children or others can create taxation.

Tenancy by the entirety, the third type of joint ownership, is limited to married couples. Under this type of joint ownership, both spouses own the property; when one spouse dies, the other gets it automatically. Neither spouse may sell the property without the consent of the other.

Joint ownership is a poor substitute for a will. It gives you less control over the disposition and taxation of your property. Your state laws govern the types and effects of joint ownership. Some states require that survivorship rights be spelled out in the deed, or at least abbreviated (e.g., JT/WROS). Only your attorney can advise you on these matters.

LIFE INSURANCE AND EMPLOYEE BENEFITS Life insurance proceeds are free of income tax, excluded from probate, and wholly or partially exempt from most state inheritance taxes. However, these proceeds are included in your estate for federal estate tax purposes if the policy contains any incidents of ownership such as the right to change beneficiaries, surrender the policy for cash, or make loans on the policy.

Assignment of ownership to your beneficiary or a trust can remove a life insurance policy from your estate. But if your spouse is the intended beneficiary, you do not need to assign ownership, since the proceeds will be free of estate tax due to the marital deduction.

Death benefits from qualified pension, profit-sharing, or Keogh plans are excluded from your estate unless they are payable to it or unless your beneficiary elects the special provision for averaging income tax in lump-sum distributions.

If there is "too much" money in your qualified retirement plan when you and your spouse die, your heirs could lose up to 80 percent in federal and state income taxes, estate tax, and the "excess accumulation" tax. Proper estate planning can minimize such confiscatory taxes.

LIFETIME GIFTS AND TRUSTS Gifts or trusts with strings attached, such as retaining the income, use, or control of the property, are fully included in your estate at their date-of-death value, whether your rights are expressed or implied. For example, if you transfer title of your home to a child but continue to live in it, the home is taxed in your estate. Or if you put property in trust and retain a certain amount of control over the income or principal, the property is included in your estate even though you cannot obtain it yourself. Also, if you are the beneficiary of a trust established by someone else and you have general rights to the principal during life or the power to appoint it to anyone at death, that amount is included in your estate.

SETTLING YOUR ESTATE

If you have had a will drawn, you are *testate* in the eyes of the law, and an executor (named in your will) will carry out your wishes in due time. If you have not named an executor, the probate court (the court that supervises the distribution of estates) will appoint an administrator to carry out the instructions in your will.

If you don't have a will, you become *intestate* at your death. In that case, your estate is put under the control of a court-appointed administrator for distribution according to the laws of the state in which you reside.

Some assets pass outside of the will directly to your beneficiaries. These assets that avoid probate include proceeds from life insurance; annuities; investments in your individual retirement account (IRA); qualified retirement plans such as 401(k)s, 403(b)s, or SEPs; and trust property. Jointly owned property, such as home, cars, bank accounts, and so forth, automatically passes to the surviving co-owner without probate.

PFP Sheet 68
Trust Comparison

 PRACTICE QUIZ 19-4

1. Differentiate among the various types of trusts.
2. What is included in an estate?
3. What are the three types of joint ownership?

Federal and State Estate Taxes

LO19-5

Evaluate the effects of federal and state taxes on estate planning.

The tax aspects of estate planning have changed considerably due to recent major changes in the federal tax structure. The maximum tax rate on estates and gifts, for example, is gradually declining. However, as Exhibit 19-5 shows, estate settlement costs can quickly deplete an estate.

You can reduce your taxable estate by giving away assets to anyone during your lifetime. (But don't give away assets just to reduce your estate tax liability if you may need those assets in your retirement.) No gift tax is due on gifts of up to $15,000 (in 2021) to any one person in any one year. (A married couple, acting together, may give up to $30,000 to any one person in one year.)

> **EXAMPLE: Reducing an Estate by Gifting**
>
> Suppose that on December 31, 2021, Michael gave $15,000 worth of shares of a stock mutual fund to his son. On January 2, 2024, these shares are worth $31,000. As a result of this gift in 2021, Michael has removed from his estate the $15,000 gift plus $16,000 of appreciation, for a total of $31,000, assuming Michael is alive in 2024. All of this has been accomplished at no gift tax cost.

EXHIBIT 19-5

The erosion of probate and estate taxes

	Gross Estate	Settlement Costs	Net Estate	Shrinkage
Elvis Presley	$ 10,165,434	$ 7,374,635	$ 2,790,799	73%
John D. Rockefeller	26,905,182	17,124,988	9,780,194	64
Clark Gable	2,806,526	1,101,038	1,705,488	39
Walt Disney	23,004,851	6,811,943	16,192,908	30

Source: Public court records, state probate courts.

TYPES OF TAXES

Federal and state governments levy various types of taxes that you must consider in planning your estate. The four major taxes of this kind are estate taxes, estate and trust income taxes, inheritance taxes, and gift taxes.

ESTATE TAXES   An **estate tax** is a federal tax levied on the value of the inheritance of a deceased person to transmit his or her property and life insurance at death. Estate taxes, levied since 1916, have undergone extensive revision since the mid-1970s. The Economic Recovery Tax Act of 1981 made important tax concessions, particularly the unlimited marital deduction and the increased exemption equivalent. Fewer than 1 percent of estates pay an estate tax. Therefore, only about 1,800 estates were expected to owe estate tax in 2021.

Under the Tax Cuts and Jobs Act of 2017, with intelligent estate planning and properly drawn wills, you may leave all of your property to your surviving spouse free of federal estate taxes. The surviving spouse's estate in excess of $23.4 million (in 2021) faces estate tax of 40 percent. In addition to the 40 percent federal estate tax, 12 states and the District of Columbia impose an estate tax while six states impose an inheritance tax. Maryland has both.

All limits have been removed from transfers between spouses during their lifetimes as well as at death. Whatever you give your spouse is exempt from gift and estate taxes. Gift tax returns need not be filed for interspousal gifts. There is still the possibility, however, that such gifts will be included in your estate if they were given within three years of your death.

ESTATE AND TRUST FEDERAL INCOME TAXES

In addition to the federal estate tax, estates and certain trusts must file federal income tax returns with the Internal Revenue Service. Generally, taxable income for estates and trusts is computed in much the same manner as taxable income for individuals. Under the Tax Reform Act of 1986, trusts and estates must pay quarterly estimated taxes, and new trusts must use the calendar year as the tax year.

INHERITANCE TAXES   An **inheritance tax** is levied on an heir to receive all or part of the estate and life insurance proceeds of a deceased person. The tax payable depends on the net value of the property and insurance received. It also depends on the relationship of the heir to the deceased.

Inheritance taxes are imposed only by the state governments. Some states levy an inheritance tax, but the state laws differ widely as to exemptions, rates of taxation, and the treatment of property and life insurance. A reasonable average for state inheritance taxes would be 4 to 10 percent of your estate, with the higher percentages on larger amounts. Only six states, New Jersey, Maryland, Nebraska, Iowa, Kentucky, and Pennsylvania, impose an inheritance tax.

Over the past few years, many states have been phasing out their inheritance tax provisions, usually over a period of three or four years. This apparently reflects a desire to retain older and wealthy citizens as residents and to discourage them from leaving the states where they have lived most of their lives to seek tax havens in states such as Florida and Nevada. Increasingly, state legislatures have been questioning the equity of

my life   5

I can reduce my taxable estate by giving away assets to anyone during my lifetime.

Yes. You can reduce your taxable estate by giving away assets to anyone, but don't give away assets if you may need those assets during your retirement years.

estate tax A federal tax on the right of a deceased person to transfer property and life insurance at death.

inheritance tax A tax levied on the right of an heir to receive an estate.

Dealing with the financial aspects of a person's death can be a difficult burden. Reproduction of form permitted under General Public License Agreement (GPL). Source: www.irs.gov, accessed May 15, 2021.

further taxes at death and are opting instead for sales and income taxes to provide state revenues.

GIFT TAXES   The federal and state governments levy a **gift tax** on the value of the gift to others. A property owner can avoid estate and inheritance taxes by giving property during his or her lifetime. For this reason, the federal tax laws provide for taxes on gifts of property. The tax rates on gifts used to be only 75 percent of the tax rates on estates, but since 1976 the gift tax rates have been the same as the estate tax rates. Indeed, the tax rates are now called *unified transfer tax rates*.

Many states have gift tax laws. The state gift tax laws are similar to the federal gift tax laws, but the exemptions and dates for filing returns vary widely among the states.

As discussed earlier, the Tax Cuts and Jobs Act allows you to give up to $15,000 each year to any person without incurring gift tax liability or having to report the gift to the IRS. Note that the Taxpayer Relief Act of 1997 increased this amount in $1,000 increments, depending on rates of inflation in future years. Gifts from a husband or a wife to a third party are considered as having been made in equal amounts by each spouse. Consequently, a husband and wife may give as much as $30,000 per year to anyone without incurring tax liability.

Exhibit 19-6 summarizes the important provisions of the Tax Cuts and Jobs Act of 2017, the Economic Growth and Tax Relief Reconciliation Act of 2001, and the American Taxpayer Relief Act of 2012 pertaining to estate planning.

smart money minute

One common estate planning *mistake* is not to make gifts during your lifetime to reduce your estate taxes. You can take *action*: start gifting up to $15,000 every year to any person or an organization of your choice. *Success!* Your estate tax will be lower at your death.

TAX AVOIDANCE AND TAX EVASION

A poorly arranged estate may be subject to unnecessarily large taxation. Therefore, you should study the tax laws and seek advice to avoid estate taxes larger than those the lawmakers intended you to pay. You should have a clear idea of the distinction between tax avoidance and tax evasion. *Tax avoidance* is the use of legal methods to reduce or escape taxes; *tax evasion* is the use of illegal methods to reduce or escape taxes.

CHARITABLE GIFTS AND BEQUESTS   Gifts made to certain recognized charitable or educational organizations are exempt from gift, estate, and inheritance taxes. Accordingly, such gifts or bequests (gifts through a will) represent one method of reducing or avoiding estate and inheritance taxes.

CALCULATING THE TAX

The estate tax is applied not to your total gross estate but to your net taxable estate at death. *Net taxable estate* is your testamentary net worth after subtracting your debts, liabilities, probate costs, and administration costs. These items, all of which are taken off your estate before calculating your tax, are cash requirements to be paid by your estate.

DEBTS AND LIABILITIES   In arriving at your taxable estate, the amount of your debts and other creditor obligations are subtracted. You are liable for the payment of these debts while living; your estate will be liable at your death. Your debts may include mortgages, collateralized loans, margin accounts, bank loans, notes payable, installment and charge accounts, and accrued income and property taxes. They may also include your last-illness and funeral expenses.

PROBATE AND ADMINISTRATION COSTS   Your estate administration costs will include fees for attorneys, accountants, appraisers, executors or administrators

EXHIBIT 19-6 Estate tax law changes

The Tax Cuts and Jobs Act of 2017 and the Economic Growth and Tax Relief Reconciliation Act of 2001 brought important and significant changes to the federal estate, gift, and generation-skipping transfer (GST) taxes.

Tax Year	Highest Estate Tax Rate (%)	Gift Exemption ($ million)	Estate Exemption Unified or Credit Amount ($ million)	GST Tax Exemption ($ million)	Notes
2001	55	0.675	0.675	0.675	
2002	50	1.00	1.00	1.00*	Estate tax exemption rises to $1 million; top estate tax cut to 50%.
2003	49	1.00	1.00	1.00*	Top estate tax cut to 49%.
2004	48	1.00	1.50	1.50	Estate tax exemption rises to $1.5 million; top estate tax rate cut to 48%.
2005	47	1.00	1.50	1.50	Top estate tax cut to 47%.
2006	46	1.00	2.00	2.00	Exemption rises to $2 million; top rate declines to 46%.
2007	45	1.00	2.00	2.00	Top rate declines to 45%.
2008	45	1.00	2.00	2.00	No change.
2009	45	1.00	3.50	3.50	Exemption rises to $3.5 million.
2010	0	1.00	Repeal	Repeal	Estate tax completely repealed.
2011	35	1.00	5.00	5.00	
2012	35	5.12	5.12	5.12	
2013	40	5.25	5.25	5.25	Exemption rises to $5.25 million. Top estate tax rises to 40%.
2014	40	5.34	5.34	5.34	
2015	40	5.43	5.43	5.43	
2016	40	5.45	5.45	5.45	
2017	40	5.49	5.49	5.49	
2018	40	11.18	11.18	11.18	Indexed for inflation each year after 2018 through 2025. These amounts are doubled for a married couple.
2019	40	11.40	11.40	11.40	
2020	40	11.58	11.58	11.58	
2021	40	11.70	11.70	11.70	

*Adjusted annually for inflation.

Source: Internal Revenue Service, www.irs.gov/businesses/small-businesses-self-employed/estate-tax, accessed February 11, 2021.

and trustees, court costs, bonding and surety costs, and miscellaneous expenses. These administration costs may run 5 to 8 percent of your estate, depending on its size and complexity. While the percentage usually decreases as the size of the estate increases, it may be increased by additional complicating factors, such as handling a business interest.

Next, deductions are made for bequests to qualified charities and for property passing to your spouse (the marital deduction). That leaves your net taxable estate, to which the rates shown in Exhibit 19-6 are applied to determine your gross estate tax.

Inheritance and estate taxes in your own state are additional costs, and these costs are not deductible in arriving at your taxable estate. In fact, you may have to pay inheritance taxes in two or more states, depending on the location of your property.

PAYING THE TAX

If, after having used various estate tax reduction techniques, you must still pay an estate tax, you should consider the best way to pay it. The federal estate tax is due and payable in cash nine months after your death. State taxes, probate costs, debts, and expenses also usually fall due within that time. These often result in a real cash bind, because people rarely keep a lot of cash on hand. They derived their wealth from putting their money to work in businesses, real estate, or other investments. Estate liquidity—having enough cash to pay taxes and costs without selling assets or borrowing heavily—is often a problem.

One way to handle the estate tax is to set aside or accumulate enough cash to pay it when it falls due. However, you may die before you have accumulated enough cash, and the cash you accumulate may be subject to income tax during your lifetime and to estate tax at your death.

Another way to handle the estate tax is for your family to sell assets to pay taxes. The first assets to be sold might be stocks, bonds, gold or silver coins, and similar liquid assets. However, these assets may be the source of your family's income after your death, and the market for them may be down. Assets such as real estate may also be sold, but prices on forced sales are usually only a fraction of the fair value.

Your family could consider borrowing; however, it is unusual to find a commercial lender that will lend money to pay back-taxes. If you do find one, it may require personal liability. In any event, borrowing does not solve the problem; it only prolongs it, adding interest costs in the process.

Borrowing from the IRS itself in the form of deferred payments or installments may be possible for reasonable cause. Tax extension and installment payment provisions are helpful, but they still leave a tax debt to be paid by your heirs at your death. Paying that debt, even over an extended period of time, could be a real burden and severely restrict their income and flexibility.

Life insurance may be a reasonable, feasible, and economical means of paying your estate tax. Instead of forcing your family to pay off the estate tax and other debts and costs by borrowing or selling, you can, through insurance, provide your family with tax-free cash at a fraction of the cost of borrowing.

PFP Sheet 69
Estate Tax
Estimate

 **PRACTICE QUIZ 19-5**

1. What are the four types of taxes to consider in planning your estate?
2. How is estate tax calculated?
3. What are the various ways to handle the payment of estate tax?

Your Personal Finance Roadmap and Dashboard:

Estate Planning

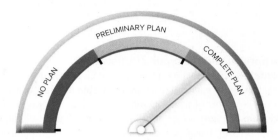

ESTATE PLANNING PROGRESS

Estate planning is essential not only to ensure that your assets are distributed in the way you choose, but also to make sure that your loved ones are not left with difficult or costly problems. Planning for your estate and taxes as well as writing a will are just a few of the steps you can take to have a secure financial future for yourself and your loved ones.

YOUR SITUATION

Have you prepared a valid will? Do you have several copies of the documents needed for processing insurance claims and settling your estate? Have you selected an executor who is willing to perform the tasks involved in carrying out a will? If you have children, have you selected a guardian to take care of them in the event that you and your spouse die at the same time? Have you prepared a power of attorney and a letter of last instruction? Other personal financial planning actions you might consider during various stages of your life include:

First Steps

- You may not be wealthy, but make sure to prepare a will.
- Prepare a durable power of attorney and a living will.
- Carry a card in your wallet that states you have advance directives.

- Give a copy of your advance directives to family members and/or friends, and give your doctor a copy for your medical record.

Next Steps

- Make a list and share detailed financial information about your assets with your spouse.
- Decide who will take care of your children if you and your spouse die in an accident.
- Review your power of attorney every few years.
- Keep the original copies of your living will, durable power of attorney, and letter of last instruction where they are easily found.

Later Steps

- Review your estate plan. With a proper estate plan, you can avoid underfunded and backlogged courts.
- Tell your children what you intend to leave for them in your will and why.
- Review your advance directives to be sure that you are still satisfied with your decisions and that your health care proxy is still willing and able to carry out your plans.
- Provide a copy of your advance directives to a hospital and/or your nursing home.
- Plan your funeral. Do you want an elaborate funeral? Will you leave your assets to heirs? Spare your loved ones from the decision-making during their period of grief.

YOUR next step . . . select one or more of the items above and create an action plan to implement those financial planning activities.

SUMMARY OF LEARNING OBJECTIVES

LO19-1

Analyze the personal aspects of estate planning. Estate planning is an essential part of retirement planning and an integral part of financial planning. The first part of estate planning consists of building your estate; the second part consists of transferring your estate at your death in the manner you have specified. The personal aspects of estate planning depend on whether you are single or married. If you are married, your estate planning involves the interests of at least two people, and more if there are children. Never having been married does not eliminate the need to organize your financial affairs.

LO19-2

Assess the legal aspects of estate planning. In the event of death, proof of claims must be produced or the claims will not be processed. Among the papers needed are birth certificates, marriage certificates, legal name changes, and military service records. Every adult should have a written will, which is the legal declaration of a person's mind as to the disposition of his or her property after death. Thus, a will is a way to transfer your property according to your wishes after you die.

LO19-3

Distinguish among various types and formats of wills. The four types of wills are the simple will, the traditional marital share will, the exemption trust will, and the stated dollar amount will. A will can be simple or complex depending on your personal and financial circumstances.

A *simple will* leaves everything to the spouse. Such a will is sufficient for most smaller estates. However, if you have a large or complex estate, a simple will may not meet your objectives. It may also create higher overall taxation because everything would be taxed in your spouse's subsequent estate.

LO19-4

Appraise various types of trusts and estates. Establishing a trust can be an excellent way to manage your estate. Trusts are revocable or irrevocable. Popular forms of trusts include credit-shelter trusts, grantor retained annuity trusts, disclaimer trusts, marital-deduction trusts, living trusts, self-declaration trusts, testamentary trusts, life insurance trusts, charitable remainder trusts, qualified personal residence trusts, charitable lead trusts, generation-skipping trusts, and spendthrift trusts. An attorney's help is needed to establish a trust.

If you establish a *revocable trust,* you retain the right to end the trust or change its terms during your lifetime. If you establish an *irrevocable trust,* you cannot change its terms or end it. However, an irrevocable trust offers tax advantages not offered by a revocable trust.

LO19-5

Evaluate the effects of federal and state taxes on estate planning. The tax aspects of estate planning have changed considerably due to recent major changes in the federal tax structure. The four major federal and state taxes you must consider in planning your estate are estate taxes, estate and trust income taxes, inheritance taxes, and gift taxes.

The federal estate tax is due and payable in cash nine months after your death. State taxes, probate costs, debts, and expenses also usually fall due within that time.

KEY TERMS

adjusted gross estate   661

beneficiary   662

codicil   664

community property   672

credit-shelter trust   668

disclaimer trust   668

durable power of attorney   667

estate   654

estate planning   655

estate tax   675

ethical will   666

executor   662

exemption trust will   661

formal will   662

gift tax   676

guardian   664

holographic will   662

inheritance tax   675

intestate   658

irrevocable trust   668

life insurance trust   671

living trust   669

living will   665

prenuptial agreement   664

probate   660

revocable trust   668

simple will   660

stated dollar amount will   661

statutory will   662

testamentary trust   670

traditional marital share will   661

trust   667

trustee   664

trustor   667

will   658

SELF-TEST PROBLEMS

1. In 2021, you gave $15,000 worth of stock to your best friend. In 2022, the stock is valued at $25,000.

   a. What was the gift tax in 2021?

   b. What is the total amount removed from your estate in 2022?

2. On December 31, 2021, George gives $15,000 to his son and $15,000 to his son's wife. One day later, on January 1, 2022, George gives another $15,000 to his son and another $15,000 to his son's wife. George made no other gifts to his son and his son's wife in 2021 and 2022. What is the gift tax?

Self-Test Solutions

1. a. Since you can give up to $15,000 to anyone in 2021, there is no gift tax.

   b. Total amount removed from your estate in 2022 is $15,000 + $10,000 = $25,000.

2. There is no gift tax in 2021 or in 2022 since George gave $15,000 to his son and his son's wife in each of the two years.

FINANCIAL PLANNING PROBLEMS

Problems 1, 2, and 3 are based on the following scenario: In 2021, Joshua gave $15,000 worth of XYZ stock to his son. In 2022, the XYZ shares are worth $25,000.

1. *Calculating the Gift Tax.* What was the gift tax in 2021? **LO19-5**
2. *Calculating the Gift Tax.* What is the total amount removed from Joshua's estate in 2022? **LO19-5**
3. *Calculating the Gift Tax.* What will be the gift tax in 2021? **LO19-5**
4. *Calculating the Gift Tax.* In 2021, you gave a $15,000 cash gift to your best friend. What is the gift tax? **LO19-5**

Problems 5, 6, and 7 are based on the following scenario: Barry and his wife Mary have accumulated over $4 million during their 45 years of marriage. They have three children and five grandchildren.

5. *Calculating the Gift Tax.* How much money can Barry and Mary gift to their children in 2021 without any gift tax liability? **LO19-5**
6. *Calculating the Gift Tax.* How much money can Barry and Mary gift to their grandchildren? **LO19-5**
7. *Calculating the Gift Tax.* What is the total amount removed from Barry and Mary's estate? **LO19-5**
8. *Calculating the Estate Tax.* The date of death for a widow was 2021. If the estate was valued at $2,129,000 and the estate was taxed at 40 percent, what was the heir's tax liability? **LO19-5**
9. *Calculating the Estate Tax.* Joel and Rachel are both retired. Married for 50 years, they've amassed an estate worth $10 million. The couple has no trusts or other types of tax-sheltered assets. If Joel or Rachel dies in 2021, how much federal estate tax would the surviving spouse have to pay, assuming that the estate is taxed at the 40 percent rate? **LO19-5**

DIGITAL FINANCIAL LITERACY. . .

MAKING A WILL

One of the most important documents that every adult should have is a written will. This legal document specifies how you want your property to be distributed after your death. If you die intestate—without a will—your legal state of residence steps in and controls the distribution of your estate without regard for any wishes you may have had. In most states, you must:

- be 18 years of age or older,
- be of sound judgment and mental capacity,
- sign your will in the presence of at least two witnesses.

Action items:

1. Gather more information about making a will. You may want to visit legalzoom.com, nolo.com, aarp.org, or legalinfo.org.

2. Using this information, prepare a report on the following: (*a*) Who needs a will? (*b*) What are the elements of a will (naming a guardian, naming an executor, preparing a will, updating a will, estate taxes, where to keep your will, living will, etc.)? (*c*) How is this web page helpful in preparing your own will?

FINANCIAL PLANNING CASE

Estate Planning

A married couple, Linda and Charles, have just learned about the death of their friend, Lloyd, and wondered whether Lloyd had provided for his family. Charles admits he doesn't even have a will. What would happen to their children if Charles died today?

Rick Fenelli, an estate planning attorney, explains that the first step in estate planning is to identify all of your assets. He reminds Linda and Charles that most people forget that estate planning is not just for the rich and famous.

Linda and Charles believe their net worth is not much, even though they own a home, a savings account, 401(k)s, and a few IRAs. Their attorney friend calculates that Linda and Charles have a net worth of about $1 million. The couple is startled. The attorney explains that they already have a will even though they never wrote one. The will is written by the state and it's called "probate." Dying without a will is called "dying intestate."

Questions

1. What triggered Charles and Linda to start thinking about planning their estate?
2. According to attorney Rick Fenelli, what is the first step in estate planning?
3. Who writes your will if you don't?

YOUR PERSONAL FINANCIAL PLAN

DEVELOPING AN ESTATE PLAN

Most people do not think they have enough assets to do estate planning. However, the planned transfer of resources with the use of a will, trusts, and other legal vehicles is a necessary phase of your total financial plan.

Your Short-Term Financial Planning Activity

Task Investigate the cost of a will and costs of different types of trusts.

Research

1) Review the section in this chapter about "Types and Formats of Wills." Distinguish among the types and formats of wills. Which type of will might be the most appropriate for you?
2) Use Personal Financial Planning Sheet 67 to compare costs and features of different types of wills.
3) Use the IRS and other websites to identify recent tax law changes that may affect your financial planning decisions.
4) Use Personal Financial Planning Sheet 68 to compare the features of different types of trusts. Also, review the material in Financial Literacy for My Life: Other Types of Trusts.

Outcome Create a visual presentation (PowerPoint presentation, video, a chart, or information graphic report) to explain different types of wills and trusts and their costs.

Your Long-Term Financial Planning Activity

Task Develop a plan for actions to take related to estate planning.

Resource

1) Use the Personal Financial Planning Sheet 66, and respond to the important questions to form a basis for making and implementing an estate plan.
2) Explore internet sources to identify saving and investing decisions that would minimize future estate taxes. Also, use Personal Financial Planning Sheet 69 to estimate the estate tax based on your financial situation.

Outcome Write a two- to three-page report on various estate planning topics such as estate planning worksheets, whether you need an estate plan, when to update your plan, estate taxes, wills, executors, trusts, etc.

Note: All *Personal Financial Planner* sheets are available at the end of the book and in an Excel spreadsheet format in *Connect Finance.*

CONTINUING CASE

Estate Planning

Jamie Lee and Ross are in their mid-50s and enjoying planning for their next phase in life: retirement! The triplets are finishing their college educations and will be starting careers of their own in no time at all. As they prepare their children for the next chapter in their lives, Jamie Lee and Ross emphasize the importance of preparing for the future and draw on their own experiences when

FINANCIAL PLANNING CASE

Estate Planning

A married couple, Linda and Charles, have just learned about the death of their friend, Lloyd, and wondered whether Lloyd had provided for his family. Charles admits he doesn't even have a will. What would happen to their children if Charles died today?

Rick Fenelli, an estate planning attorney, explains that the first step in estate planning is to identify all of your assets. He reminds Linda and Charles that most people forget that estate planning is not just for the rich and famous.

Linda and Charles believe their net worth is not much, even though they own a home, a savings account, 401(k)s, and a few IRAs. Their attorney friend calculates that Linda and Charles have a net worth of about $1 million. The couple is startled. The attorney explains that they already have a will even though they never wrote one. The will is written by the state and it's called "probate." Dying without a will is called "dying intestate."

Questions

1. What triggered Charles and Linda to start thinking about planning their estate?
2. According to attorney Rick Fenelli, what is the first step in estate planning?
3. Who writes your will if you don't?

YOUR PERSONAL FINANCIAL PLAN

DEVELOPING AN ESTATE PLAN

Most people do not think they have enough assets to do estate planning. However, the planned transfer of resources with the use of a will, trusts, and other legal vehicles is a necessary phase of your total financial plan.

Your Short-Term Financial Planning Activity

Task Investigate the cost of a will and costs of different types of trusts.

Research

1) Review the section in this chapter about "Types and Formats of Wills." Distinguish among the types and formats of wills. Which type of will might be the most appropriate for you?
2) Use Personal Financial Planning Sheet 67 to compare costs and features of different types of wills.
3) Use the IRS and other websites to identify recent tax law changes that may affect your financial planning decisions.
4) Use Personal Financial Planning Sheet 68 to compare the features of different types of trusts. Also, review the material in Financial Literacy for My Life: Other Types of Trusts.

Outcome Create a visual presentation (PowerPoint presentation, video, a chart, or information graphic report) to explain different types of wills and trusts and their costs.

Your Long-Term Financial Planning Activity

Task Develop a plan for actions to take related to estate planning.

Resource

1) Use the Personal Financial Planning Sheet 66, and respond to the important questions to form a basis for making and implementing an estate plan.
2) Explore internet sources to identify saving and investing decisions that would minimize future estate taxes. Also, use Personal Financial Planning Sheet 69 to estimate the estate tax based on your financial situation.

Outcome Write a two- to three-page report on various estate planning topics such as estate planning worksheets, whether you need an estate plan, when to update your plan, estate taxes, wills, executors, trusts, etc.

Note: All *Personal Financial Planner* sheets are available at the end of the book and in an Excel spreadsheet format in *Connect Finance*.

CONTINUING CASE

Estate Planning

Jamie Lee and Ross are in their mid-50s and enjoying planning for their next phase in life: retirement! The triplets are finishing their college educations and will be starting careers of their own in no time at all. As they prepare their children for the next chapter in their lives, Jamie Lee and Ross emphasize the importance of preparing for the future and draw on their own experiences when

Endnotes

CHAPTER 6

1. Polonius quote from William Shakespeare's *Hamlet*.
2. Peter Pae, "Credit Junkies," *The Wall Street Journal,* December 26, 1991, p. 1.
3. Joseph Weber, "AmEx Gets Serious Competition from Merrill in the Race to Sign Up Affluent Cardholders," bloomberg.com., May 3, 1999.
4. Adapted from Guide to Online Payments, Federal Trade Commission, www.ftc.gov, accessed March 8, 2013.
5. The Federal Trade Commission, The Co-signer's Notice.
6. * Exhibit 6-8A shows a sample letter to dispute a billing error.

CHAPTER 7

1. National Credit Union Administration, *Credit Union Trends Report,* February 2016.
2. Thomas Leary quoted in "FTC Testifies about Credit Counseling Abuses Testimony Says that Some Firms Are Deceiving Consumers." www.ftc.gov

CHAPTER 7: APPENDIX

1. www.newyorkfed.org/householdcredit/, 2020 Q3, *Quarterly Report on Household Debt and Credit,* accessed February 15, 2021.
2. http://studentaid.ed.gov/types/loans/interest-rates.

CHAPTER 11

1. Centers for Medicare and Medicaid at www.cms.gov, accessed January 15, 2021.
2. Ibid.
3. Seema Verma, administrator for the Centers for Medicare and Medicaid.
4. Adapted from Guide to Online Payments, Federal Trade Commission, www.ftc.gov, accessed March 8, 2013.

CHAPTER 12

1. American Council of Life Insurers, 2020 Life Insurance Fact Book, p. 94, Table 7.1, www.acli.com, accessed February 25, 2021.
2. Ibid.
3. Ibid.
4. Ibid.
5. Ibid.

CHAPTER 13

1. Stefani Wendel, "State of Credit: 2020: Consumer Credit During COVID-19," Experian, https://www.experian.com/blogs/insights/2020/10/state-credit-2020/, accessed January 18, 2021.
2. Ibid.
3. Ibid.
4. Bankrate, www.bankrate.com/calculators/credit-cards/credit-card-minimum-payment.aspx, accessed January 12, 2021.
5. John Devine, "7 Stocks that Have Dropped the Most in 2020," U.S. News and World Report, https://money.usnews.com/investing/stock-market-news/slideshows/stocks-that-have-dropped-the-most-in-2020?slide=2, accessed October 5, 2020.
6. The S&P 500 Historical Annaul Returns [1970-2020], the FINASKO website, https://finasko.com/sp-500-returns/, accessed December 9, 2020.
7. Ibid.

8. Ibid.
9. "Vanguard Portfolio Allocation Models," Vanguard Group, https://personal.vanguard.com/us/insights/saving-investing/model-portfolio-allocation, accessed January 18, 2021.
10. Ibid.
11. Kimberly Amadeo, "How Does the 2020 Stock Market Crash Compare with Others?" The Balance website, https://www.thebalance.com/fundamentals-of-the-2020-market-crash-4799950, accessed April 27, 2020.
12. William J. Bernstein, "The Online Asset Allocator," *Efficient Frontier,* www.efficientfrontier.com/aa/, accessed December 9, 2020.
13. "Vanguard Portfolio Allocation Models," Vanguard Group, https://personal.vanguard.com/us/insights/saving-investing/model-portfolio-allocation, accessed December 9, 2020.

CHAPTER 14

1. "The McDonald's Investment Calculator" at the McDonald's web site at https://corporate.mcdonalds.com/corpmcd/investors/stock-information.html, accessed February 9, 2021.
2. The S&P 500 Historical Annual Returns [1970-2020], the FINASKO website, https://finasko.com/sp-500-returns/, accessed December 9, 2020.
3. Ibid.
4. "Vanguard Portfolio Allocation Models," Vanguard Group, https://personal.vanguard.com/us/insights/saving-investing/model-portfolio-allocation, accessed January 18, 2021.
5. Kimberly Amadeo, "How Does the 2020 Stock Market Crash Compare with Others?" The Balance website, https://www.thebalance.com/fundamentals-of-the-2020-market-crash-4799950, accessed April 27, 2020.
6. "Historical Data," Yahoo! Finance, http://finance.yahoo.com, accessed February 9, 2021.
7. Yahoo! Finance, https://finance.yahoo.com/quote/V/analysis?p=V, accessed February 11, 2021.
8. "Fundamental Analysis," Investopedia.com, www.investopedia.com/terms/f/fundamentalanalysis.asp, accessed February 11, 2021.
9. Crystal Tse and Katie Roof, "DoorDash Hits $38 Billion Valuation in Above-Range IPO," the Bloomberg web site at https://www.bloombergquint.com/business/doordash-is-said-to-raise-3-37-billion-in-above-range-ipo, accessed December 9, 2020.

CHAPTER 15

1. Ambrogio Visconti, "Southwest Airlines Co.'s 1.250% Convertible Notes," Global Legal Chronicle website at http://www.globallegalchronicle.com/southwest-airlines-co-s-1-250-convertible-notes, May 1, 2020.

CHAPTER 16

1. "2020 Fact Book," Investment Company Institute, www.ici.org, accessed January 23, 2021.
2. Ibid.
3. Ibid.
4. Ibid.
5. Daniel Cross, "Breaking Down Load Versus No-Load Mutual Funds," the MutualFund.com website, https://mutualfunds.com/no-load-funds/breaking-down-load-versus-no-load-mutual-funds/, accessed January 22, 2021.
6. "Vanguard U.S. Growth Fund," The Yahoo! Finance website, https://finance.yahoo.com/quote/VWUSX/profile?p=VWUSX, accessed January 24, 2021.

offering advice to the three. They have always been candid with their children and have included them in most of their financial decisions over the years, hoping that their focus on saving for the future will also become a way of life for their children.

Jamie Lee and Ross have also included the triplets in their estate planning, realizing that they are an important part of the entire asset management process. They all understand that preparation is key, as you never can predict what lies in the future.

Lately, Jamie Lee and Ross have been hearing many stories about acquaintances who are passing away without leaving a will or a plan for their estate, which made Jamie Lee and Ross anxious to review their own estate plan with an attorney. They do not want to think about eventually passing on, but they know that death is inevitable and that planning for it is essential to careful financial planning.

Current Financial Situation

Assets *(Jamie Lee and Ross combined):*
Checking account: $5,500
Savings account: $53,000
Emergency fund savings account: $45,000
House: $475,000
IRA balance: $92,000
Life insurance cash value: $125,000
Investments (stocks, bonds): $750,000
Car: $12,500 (Jamie Lee) and $16,000 (Ross)

Liabilities *(Jamie Lee and Ross combined):*
Mortgage balance: $43,000
Credit card balance: $0
Car loans: $0

Income:
Jamie Lee: $45,000 gross income ($31,500 net income after taxes)
Ross: $135,000 gross income ($97,200 net income after taxes)

Monthly Expenses:
Mortgage: $1,225
Property taxes: $500
Homeowner's insurance: $300
IRA contribution: $300
Utilities: $250
Food: $600
Gas/maintenance: $275
Entertainment: $300
Life insurance: $375

Questions

1. What is an estate? Based on the information provided, what components make up Jamie Lee and Ross's estate?

2. Jamie Lee and Ross are now having the attorney draw up a will for each of them.

   a. What is the purpose of having a will?

   b. Do they need to have an attorney to draft a will?

   c. What type of will would you recommend they have, based on their marital and family status?

3. The attorney suggested that Jamie Lee and Ross assemble all of their legal documents in a place where their heirs would be able to access them when it is necessary. What legal documents would you suggest that Jamie Lee and Ross compile so they will be accessible should the need arise?

4. For your own safekeeping, file the following important documents where they can be accessed should the need arise.

   a. Complete the *Personal Financial Planner* Sheet 66, "Estate Planning," with your own personal information as a follow-up to question 3.

   b. Using the websites listed in the Planner as a guide, complete *Personal Financial Planner* Sheet 67, "Will Planning," for your personal use.

 DAILY SPENDING DIARY

"This current spending information allows me to better plan for the future needs of my family."

Directions

Your *Daily Spending Diary* can provide you with ongoing information that will help you manage your current finances while planning for future family needs.

Analysis Questions

1. What information from your spending patterns can help you plan for the long-term needs of you and family members?

2. What estate planning activities are you planning to take action on in the next few years?

A *Daily Spending Diary* sheet is located at the end of Chapter 1 and on the library resource site in *Connect*.

Endnotes

CHAPTER 6

1. Polonius quote from William Shakespeare's *Hamlet*.
2. Peter Pae, "Credit Junkies," *The Wall Street Journal,* December 26, 1991, p. 1.
3. Joseph Weber, "AmEx Gets Serious Competition from Merrill in the Race to Sign Up Affluent Cardholders," bloomberg.com., May 3, 1999.
4. Adapted from Guide to Online Payments, Federal Trade Commission, www.ftc.gov, accessed March 8, 2013.
5. The Federal Trade Commission, The Co-signer's Notice.
6. * Exhibit 6-8A shows a sample letter to dispute a billing error.

CHAPTER 7

1. National Credit Union Administration, *Credit Union Trends Report,* February 2016.
2. Thomas Leary quoted in "FTC Testifies about Credit Counseling Abuses Testimony Says that Some Firms Are Deceiving Consumers." www.ftc.gov

CHAPTER 7: APPENDIX

1. www.newyorkfed.org/householdcredit/, 2020 Q3, *Quarterly Report on Household Debt and Credit,* accessed February 15, 2021.
2. http://studentaid.ed.gov/types/loans/interest-rates.

CHAPTER 11

1. Centers for Medicare and Medicaid at www.cms.gov, accessed January 15, 2021.
2. Ibid.
3. Seema Verma, administrator for the Centers for Medicare and Medicaid.
4. Adapted from Guide to Online Payments, Federal Trade Commission, www.ftc.gov, accessed March 8, 2013.

CHAPTER 12

1. American Council of Life Insurers, 2020 Life Insurance Fact Book, p. 94, Table 7.1, www.acli.com, accessed February 25, 2021.
2. Ibid.
3. Ibid.
4. Ibid.
5. Ibid.

CHAPTER 13

1. Stefani Wendel, "State of Credit: 2020: Consumer Credit During COVID-19," Experian, https://www.experian.com/blogs/insights/2020/10/state-credit-2020/, accessed January 18, 2021.
2. Ibid.
3. Ibid.
4. Bankrate, www.bankrate.com/calculators/credit-cards/credit-card-minimum-payment.aspx, accessed January 12, 2021.
5. John Devine, "7 Stocks that Have Dropped the Most in 2020," U.S. News and World Report, https://money.usnews.com/investing/stock-market-news/slideshows/stocks-that-have-dropped-the-most-in-2020?slide=2, accessed October 5, 2020.
6. The S&P 500 Historical Annaul Returns [1970-2020], the FINASKO website, https://finasko.com/sp-500-returns/, accessed December 9, 2020.
7. Ibid.

8. Ibid.
9. "Vanguard Portfolio Allocation Models," Vanguard Group, https://personal.vanguard.com/us/insights/saving-investing/model-portfolio-allocation, accessed January 18, 2021.
10. Ibid.
11. Kimberly Amadeo, "How Does the 2020 Stock Market Crash Compare with Others?" The Balance website, https://www.thebalance.com/fundamentals-of-the-2020-market-crash-4799950, accessed April 27, 2020.
12. William J. Bernstein, "The Online Asset Allocator," *Efficient Frontier,* www.efficientfrontier.com/aa/, accessed December 9, 2020.
13. "Vanguard Portfolio Allocation Models," Vanguard Group, https://personal.vanguard.com/us/insights/saving-investing/model-portfolio-allocation, accessed December 9, 2020.

CHAPTER 14

1. "The McDonald's Investment Calculator" at the McDonald's web site at https://corporate.mcdonalds.com/corpmcd/investors/stock-information.html, accessed February 9, 2021.
2. The S&P 500 Historical Annual Returns [1970-2020], the FINASKO website, https://finasko.com/sp-500-returns/, accessed December 9, 2020.
3. Ibid.
4. "Vanguard Portfolio Allocation Models," Vanguard Group, https://personal.vanguard.com/us/insights/saving-investing/model-portfolio-allocation, accessed January 18, 2021.
5. Kimberly Amadeo, "How Does the 2020 Stock Market Crash Compare with Others?" The Balance website, https://www.thebalance.com/fundamentals-of-the-2020-market-crash-4799950, accessed April 27, 2020.
6. "Historical Data," Yahoo! Finance, http://finance.yahoo.com, accessed February 9, 2021.
7. Yahoo! Finance, https://finance.yahoo.com/quote/V/analysis?p=V, accessed February 11, 2021.
8. "Fundamental Analysis," Investopedia.com, www.investopedia.com/terms/f/fundamentalanalysis.asp, accessed February 11, 2021.
9. Crystal Tse and Katie Roof, "DoorDash Hits $38 Billion Valuation in Above-Range IPO," the Bloomberg web site at https://www.bloombergquint.com/business/doordash-is-said-to-raise-3-37-billion-in-above-range-ipo, accessed December 9, 2020.

CHAPTER 15

1. Ambrogio Visconti, "Southwest Airlines Co.'s 1.250% Convertible Notes," Global Legal Chronicle website at http://www.globallegalchronicle.com/southwest-airlines-co-s-1-250-convertible-notes, May 1, 2020.

CHAPTER 16

1. "2020 Fact Book," Investment Company Institute, www.ici.org, accessed January 23, 2021.
2. Ibid.
3. Ibid.
4. Ibid.
5. Daniel Cross, "Breaking Down Load Versus No-Load Mutual Funds," the MutualFund.com website, https://mutualfunds.com/no-load-funds/breaking-down-load-versus-no-load-mutual-funds/, accessed January 22, 2021.
6. "Vanguard U.S. Growth Fund," The Yahoo! Finance website, https://finance.yahoo.com/quote/VWUSX/profile?p=VWUSX, accessed January 24, 2021.

7. "Percentage of Large-Cap Funds that Underperformed the S&P 500 Index," "Investing: Index Funds," Spiva Statistics & Reports website, https://us.spindices.com/spiva/#/reports, accessed January 25, 2021.

8. Kevin Voigt, "Mutual Fund Calculator: Find What Fees Will Cost You," The Nerdwallet website, https://www.nerdwallet.com/blog/investing/mutual-fund-calculator/, accessed October 26, 2020.

9. John Bogle, "A Look Back at the Life of Vanguard's Founder," The Vanguard Group, https://about.vanguard.com/who-we-are/a-remarkable-history/founder-Jack-Bogle-tribute/, accessed January 26, 2021.

10. "Fidelity Fund Screener," The Fidelity Website, https://fundresearch.fidelity.com/fund-screener/, accessed January 27, 2021.

11. Investment Income and Expenses (Publication 550), The Internal Revenue Service website, https://www.irs.gov/forms-pubs/about-publication-550, accessed January 26, 2021.

CHAPTER 18

1. www.irionline.org/resources/resources-detail-view/boomer-2016

2. Cathy Weatherford quoted in "Jackson Supports National Retirement Planning Week April 8-12 to Promote Financial Education, Literacy Across the Country," *Business Wire,* April 5, 2013.

3. Howard Sharfstein, a partner in Schulte Roth & Zabel of New York.

CHAPTER 19

1. *Businessweek,* "The Virtues and Values of an Ethical Will," April 7, 2002.

2. Excerpted from Kate Murphy, "The Virtues and Values of an Ethical Will," *Bloomberg Businessweek,* April 7, 2002, p. 83.

Index

Preface

The following *Personal Financial Planner* sheets are designed to help you create and implement a personal financial plan.

Items to consider when using this *Personal Financial Planner*

1. Since these sheets are designed to adapt to every personal financial situation, some are appropriate for you at this time, while others may not be used until later in life.

2. The sheets are referenced to the textbook materials. To help you use these sheets with the appropriate text material, the following textbook icon (appearing, as appropriate, with the Practice Quizzes) will refer you to the appropriate sheet.

Sheet 15
Personal
Balance Sheet

3. Some sheets will be used more than once (such as preparing a personal cash flow statement or a budget). You are encouraged to create additional copies from the Excel templates on the library resource site in *Connect*.

4. To provide online information for financial planning activities, suggested websites and apps are presented on the sheets.

5. Finally, remember that personal financial planning is an ongoing activity. With the use of these sheets, textbook material, and your efforts, an organized and satisfying personal economic existence can be yours.

Table of Contents

Personal Data

Purpose: To provide quick reference for vital household data.

Instructions: Provide the personal and financial data requested below. This sheet is also available in an Excel spreadsheet format on the library resource site in *Connect*.

Suggested websites: www.kiplinger.com   www.moneycafe.com   www.money.com

Name	_____	_____
Birth date	_____	_____
Marital status	_____	_____
Address	_____	_____
Phone	_____	_____
Email	_____	_____
Social Security no.	_____	_____
Driver's license no.	_____	_____
Place of employment	_____	_____
Address	_____	_____
Phone	_____	_____
Position	_____	_____
Length of service	_____	_____
Checking acct. no.	_____	_____
Financial institution	_____	_____
Address	_____	_____
Phone	_____	_____

Dependent Data

Name	Birth date	Relationship	Social Security no.
_____	_____	_____	_____
_____	_____	_____	_____
_____	_____	_____	_____
_____	_____	_____	_____

What's Next for Your Personal Financial Plan?

- Identify financial planning experts (insurance agent, banker, investment advisor, tax preparer, others) you might contact for financial planning information or assistance.
- With other household members, create financial goals and discuss activities for achieving those goals.

2

Financial Institutions and Advisors

Purpose: To create a directory of personal financial institutions and financial planning professionals.

Instructions: Supply the information required in the spaces provided. This sheet is also available in an Excel spreadsheet format on the library resource site in *Connect*.

Suggested websites: www.20somethingfinance.com   www.thebalance.com

Attorney

Name _____
Address _____
_____
Phone _____
Website _____
Email _____

Primary Financial Institution

Name _____
Address _____
_____
Phone _____
Website _____
Checking acct. no. _____
Savings acct. no. _____
Loan no. _____

Insurance (Home/Auto)

Agent _____
Company _____
Address _____
_____
Phone _____
Website _____
Policy no. _____
Email _____

Credit Card 1

Issuer _____
Address _____
_____
Phone _____
Website _____
Acct. no. _____
Exp. date _____
Credit limit _____

Credit Card 2

Issuer _____
Address _____
_____
Phone _____
Website _____
Acct. no. _____
Exp. date _____
Credit limit _____

Tax Preparer

Name _____
Firm _____
Address _____
_____
Phone _____
Website _____
Email _____

Insurance (Life/Health)

Agent _____
Company _____
Address _____
_____
Phone _____
Website _____
Email _____
Policy no. _____

Investment Broker

Name _____
Address _____
_____
Phone _____
Website _____
Email _____
Acct. no. _____

Real Estate Agent

Name _____
Company _____
Address _____
_____
Phone _____
Website _____
Email _____

Investment Company

Name _____
Address _____
_____
Phone _____
Acct. no. _____
Email _____
Website _____

What's Next for Your Personal Financial Plan?

- Talk to personal and professional contacts to determine factors to consider when selecting financial planning advisors.
- Identify additional financial planning contacts that you might consider using in the future.

Name: _____   Date: _____

Current Economic Conditions

Purpose: To monitor selected economic indicators that might influence your saving, investing, spending, and borrowing decisions.

Instructions: Using *The Wall Street Journal,* an online search, and other sources of economic information, obtain current data for various economic factors. This sheet is also available in an Excel spreadsheet format on the library resource site in *Connect.*

Suggested websites: www.bls.gov   www.federalreserve.gov   www.wsj.com   www.ft.com

Suggested app: The Wall Street Journal

Economic Factor	Recent Trends	Possible Financial Planning Actions
Example: Mortgage rates	*Decline in mortgage rates*	• *Consider buying a home.* • *Consider refinancing an existing mortgage.*
Interest rates		
Consumer prices		
Other: _____		
Other: _____		
Other: _____		

What's Next for Your Personal Financial Plan?

• Determine economic factors that could affect your personal financial decisions.

• Identify actions to take as a result of current economic trends.

Suggested App:

• The Wall Street Journal

Name: _____ **Date:** _____

Setting Personal Financial Goals

Purpose: To identify personal financial goals and create an action plan.
Instructions: Based on personal and household needs and values, identify specific goals that require action. This sheet is also available in an Excel spreadsheet format on the library resource site in _Connect_.
Suggested websites: www.20somethingfinance.com   www.wisebread.com   thefinancialdiet.com
Suggested apps: Qapital, Buxfer

Short-Term Monetary Goals (less than one year)

Description	Amount needed	Months to achieve	Action to be taken	Priority
Example: Pay off credit card debt	_$850_	_10_	_Use money from pay raise._	_High_

Intermediate- and Long-Term Monetary Goals (two years and longer)

Description	Amount needed	Months to achieve	Action to be taken	Priority

Nonmonetary Goals

Description	Time frame	Actions to be taken
Example: Set up system for personal financial records and documents	_Next 2–3 months_	• _Locate personal and financial records and documents._ • _Set up spreadsheet for spending, saving, and borrowing categories._

What's Next for Your Personal Financial Plan?

• Based on a specific financial goal, calculate the savings deposits necessary to achieve those goals.
• Analyze current economic trends that might influence saving, spending, investing, and borrowing decisions.

Suggested Apps:
• **Qapital, Buxfer**

Time Value of Money Calculations

Purpose: To calculate future and present value amounts related to financial planning decisions.

Instructions: Use a financial calculator, app, website, or future/present value tables to compute the time value of money. This sheet is also available in an Excel spreadsheet format on the library resource site in *Connect*.

Suggested websites: www.dinkytown.net   www.kiplinger.com/tools   www.grunderware.com

Suggested app: Financial and TVM Calculator

Future Value of a Single Amount

(Use Exhibit 1-A in Chapter 1 Appendix)

- To determine future value of a single amount
- To determine interest lost when cash purchase is made

$$FV = PV\,(1 + i)^n$$

current amount	times	future value factor	equals	future value amount
$ _____	×	$ _____	=	$ _____

Future Value of a Series of Deposits

(Use Exhibit 1-B in Chapter 1 Appendix)

- To determine future values of regular savings deposits
- To determine future value of regular retirement deposits

$$FV = \text{Annuity}\,\frac{(1 + i)^n - 1}{i}$$

regular deposit amount	times	future value of annuity factor	equals	future value amount
$ _____	×	$ _____	=	$ _____

Present Value of a Single Amount

(Use Exhibit 1-C in Chapter 1 Appendix)

- To determine an amount to be deposited now that will grow to desired amount

$$PV = \frac{FV}{(1 + i)^n}$$

future amount desired	times	present value factor	equals	present value amount
$ _____	×	$ _____	=	$ _____

Present Value of a Series of Deposits

(Use Exhibit 1-D in Chapter 1 Appendix)

- to determine an amount that can be withdrawn on a regular basis

$$PV = \text{Annuity}\,\frac{1 - \dfrac{1}{(1 + i)^n}}{i}$$

regular amount to be withdrawn	times	present value of annuity factor	equals	present value amount
$ _____	×	$ _____	=	$ _____

Note: A financial calculator, spreadsheet software, a time value of money app, or an online time value of money calculator may be used for future value and present value calculations.

What's Next for Your Personal Financial Plan?

- Identify financial goals that require time value of money calculations.
- Research current interest rates to determine a rate that you might use when calculating time value of money for your personal financial goals.

Suggested App:

- Financial and TVM Calculator

Name: _____ **Date:** _____

Career Research Sheet

Purpose: To become familiar with work activities and career requirements for a field of employment of interest to you.

Instructions: Using websites, personal interviews, and other sources, obtain information for one or more career areas of interest to you. This sheet is also available in an Excel spreadsheet format on the library resource site in *Connect*.

Suggested websites: www.mappingyourfuture.org   www.careeronestop.org

Suggested app: Job Search Organizer

Career Area/Job Title		
Nature of the work General activities and duties		
Working conditions Physical surroundings, hours, mental and physical demands		
Training and other qualifications		
Job outlook Future prospect for employment in this field		
Earnings Starting and advanced		
Additional information		
Questions that require further research		
Sources of additional information Websites, publications, trade associations, professional organizations, government agencies, other career sources		

What's Next for Your Personal Financial Plan?

- Identify employment activities and industries of interest to you.
- Discuss existing and future career opportunities with friends, relatives, and professional contacts.

Suggested App:
- Job Search Organizer

Career Contacts

Purpose: To create a record of your professional contacts.

Instructions: Record the requested information for use when researching career areas and employment opportunities. This sheet is also available in an Excel spreadsheet format on the library resource site in *Connect*.

Suggested websites: www.linkedin.com   www.careerjournal.com

Suggested app: LinkedIn

Name _____

Organization _____

Address _____

_____

Phone _____

Website _____   Email _____

Date of contact _____

Contact situation _____

Contact's career situation _____

Areas of specialization _____

Major accomplishments _____

Name _____

Organization _____

Address _____

_____

Phone _____

Website _____   Email _____

Date of contact _____

Contact situation _____

Contact's career situation _____

Areas of specialization _____

Major accomplishments _____

What's Next for Your Personal Financial Plan?

- Identify people whom you might contact to obtain career information.
- Prepare specific questions to ask about career fields and career planning activities.

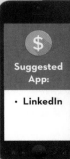

Suggested App:

- LinkedIn

Résumé Planning

Purpose: To summarize your education, training, work background, and other experiences for use when preparing a résumé.

Instructions: List dates, organizations, and other data for the categories below. This sheet is also available in an Excel spreadsheet format on the library resource site in *Connect*.

Suggested websites: www.monster.com   www.myperfectresume.com   https://resumegenius.com/

Suggested app: Builder Résumé

Education

Degree/programs completed	School/location	Dates

Professional Experience

Title	Organization	Dates	Responsibilities

Other Experience

Title	Organization	Dates	Responsibilities

Campus/Community Activities

Organization/location	Dates	Involvement

Honors/Awards

Title	Organization/location	Dates

References

Name	Title	Organization	Address	Phone

Note: See Exhibit 2-B for résumé format suggestions.

Suggested App:

· Builder Résumé

What's Next for Your Personal Financial Plan?

· Create a preliminary résumé and ask others for suggested improvements.

· Conduct online research to obtain samples of effective résumé formats and to avoid common résumé mistakes.

Cover Letter Planning

Purpose: To outline an employment cover letter.

Instructions: Prepare the preliminary version of a cover letter for a specific employment position. This sheet is also available in an Excel spreadsheet format on the library resource site in *Connect*.

Suggested websites: www.monster.com   resumegenius.com   www.thebalancecareers.com

Name	_____
Title	_____
Organization	_____
Address	_____
Phone	_____
Email	_____
Information about employment position available	_____
Organizational information	_____

Introduction: Get attention of reader with an overview of how your background connects to the available position, mention of a person who recommended you for the position, a story that communicates some unique aspect of your background, or evidence of your desire to work in that industry.

Development: Emphasize how your experience, knowledge, and skills will benefit the needs of the organization in the future.

Conclusion: Request an interview; restate any distinctive qualities; tell how you may be contacted.

Note: See sample cover letter (Exhibit 2-C).

What's Next for Your Personal Financial Plan?

- Conduct online research for examples of effective cover letters.
- Prepare a preliminary cover letter and obtain comments for improvements from others.

10

Prospective Employer Research

Purpose: To obtain information about an organization for which an employment position is available.

Instructions: Conduct research to obtain the information requested below. This sheet is also available in an Excel spreadsheet format on the library resource site in *Connect*.

Suggested websites: www.careerbuilder.com   www.hoovers.com   www.annualreports.com

Suggested app: Job Search

Organization _____

Address _____

_____

Contact _____

Title _____

Phone _____

Email _____

Website _____

Title of position _____

Major products, services, and customers

_____

Locations of main offices, factories, and other facilities

_____

Major historical developments of the company

_____

Recent company and industry developments

_____

Required skills and experience

_____

Major responsibilities and duties

_____

Employee benefits

_____

Other comments

_____

What's Next for Your Personal Financial Plan?

- Create a list of information sources to research prospective employers.
- Conduct online research about specific organizations in which you are interested.

Name: _____   **Date:** _____

Interview Preparation

Purpose: To organize information and ideas for a job interview.

Instructions: Prepare information for the items listed. This sheet is also available in an Excel spreadsheet format on the library resource site in *Connect*.

Suggested websites: www.glassdoor.com   www.careerbuilder.com   www.careercontessa.com

Suggested app: 101 HR Interview Questions

Organization _____

Address _____

_____

Contact _____

Title _____

Phone _____

Email _____

Website _____

Title of position _____

Date/time/location of interview _____

_____

Required skills and experience

_____

Major responsibilities and duties

_____

Questions you expect to be asked

_____

Major ideas you plan to emphasize (main theme, stories of experiences)

_____

Questions you plan to ask

_____

Other comments

_____

What's Next for Your Personal Financial Plan?

- Search online for commonly asked interview questions. Prepare preliminary answers for potential questions.
- Have others ask you questions in a practice interview setting.

Suggested App:

- **101 HR Interview Questions**

12

Employee Benefits Comparison

Purpose: To assess the financial and personal value of employment benefits.

Instructions: When comparing different employment situations or when selecting benefits, consider the factors listed below. This sheet is also available in an Excel spreadsheet format on the library resource site in *Connect*.

Suggested websites: www.benefitnews.com   www.dol.gov/ebsa

Suggested app: 401(k)

Organization		
Location		
Phone		
Contact/title/email		
Health insurance		
Company/coverage		
Cost to be paid by employee		
Disability income insurance		
Company/coverage		
Cost to be paid by employee		
Life insurance		
Company/coverage		
Cost to be paid by employee		
Pension/retirement		
Employer contributions		
Vesting period		
Tax benefits		
Employee contributions		
Other benefits/estimated market value		
• Vacation time		
• Tuition reimbursement		
• Child/dependent care		
• Other _____		
Website to access benefit information		

Suggested App:

• **401(k)**

What's Next for Your Personal Financial Plan?

• Talk to several people about their employee benefits.

• Conduct research to obtain information on employee benefits required by law and those commonly provided in various industries.

Name: _____   Date: _____

Career Development and Advancement

Purpose: To develop a plan for career advancement.

Instructions: Prepare responses for the items below. This sheet is also available in an Excel spreadsheet format on the library resource site in *Connect*.

Suggested websites: www.careerjournal.com   www.thebalancecareers.com   www.careercontessa.com

Suggested app: Monster Job Search

Current position _____

Address _____

_____

Phone _____

Website _____

Current responsibilities and duties

Accomplishments

Career goal within the next year

• Required skills and experience

• Plans to achieve that goal

Career goal within the next two years

• Required skills and experience

• Plans to achieve that goal

Career goal within the next five years

• Required skills and experience

• Plans to achieve that goal

What's Next for Your Personal Financial Plan?

• Talk with others about their career development activities.

• Prepare a list of formal and informal career development activities in which you might participate.

Suggested App:

• Monster Job Search

Financial Documents and Records

Purpose: To develop a system for storing personal financial documents and records.

Instructions: Indicate the location of the following records, and create files for the eight major categories of financial documents. This sheet is also available in an Excel spreadsheet format on the library resource site in *Connect*.

Suggested websites: www.bankrate.com   www.kiplinger.com   www.usa.gov

Suggested app: Finovera

Item	Home File	Safe Deposit Box	Computer File, Online, Other (specify)
1. Money management records			
• budget, financial statements			
2. Personal/employment records			
• current résumé, Social Security card			
• educational transcripts			
• birth, marriage, divorce certificates			
• citizenship, military papers, passport			
• adoption, custody papers			
3. Tax records			
4. Financial services/consumer credit records			
• unused, canceled checks			
• savings, passbook statements			
• savings certificates			
• credit card information, statements			
• credit contracts			
5. Consumer purchase, housing, and automobile records			
• warranties, receipts			
• owner's manuals			
• lease or mortgage papers, title deed, property tax info			
• automobile title			
• auto registration			
• auto service records			
6. Insurance records			
• insurance policies			
• home inventory			
• medical information (health history)			
7. Investment records			
• broker statements			
• dividend reports			
• stock/bond certificates			
• rare coins, stamps, and collectibles			
8. Estate planning and retirement			
• will			
• pension, Social Security info			

Suggested App:

• Finovera

What's Next for Your Personal Financial Plan?

• Select a location for storing your financial documents and records.

• Decide if some older documents may no longer be needed.

PERSONAL FINANCIAL PLANNER

14

Name: _____ Date: _____

Personal Balance Sheet

Purpose: To determine your current financial position.
Instructions: List the current value of assets in the categories below; list the amounts owed for liabilities; subtract total liabilities from total assets to determine net worth. This sheet is also available in an Excel spreadsheet format on the library resource site in *Connect*.
Suggested websites: time.com/money   www.thesimpledollar.com
Suggested apps: Simple Balance Sheet, Personal Capital

Balance Sheet as of _____

Assets

Liquid assets

Checking account balance _____

Savings/money market accounts, funds _____

Cash value of life insurance _____

Other _____ _____

Total liquid assets .... _____

Household assets and possessions

Current market value of home _____

Market value of automobiles _____

Furniture _____

Computer, electronics _____

Jewelry _____

Other _____ _____

Other _____ _____

Total household assets .... _____

Investment assets

Savings certificates _____

Stocks and bonds _____

Retirement accounts _____

Mutual funds _____

Other _____ _____

Total investment assets ....

Total assets .... [_____]

Liabilities

Current liabilities

Charge account and credit card balances _____

Loan balances _____

Other _____ _____

Other _____ _____

Total current liabilities ....

Long-term liabilities

Mortgage _____

Other _____ _____

Total long-term liabilities ....

Total liabilities .... [_____]

Net Worth

(assets minus liabilities) [_____]

What's Next for Your Personal Financial Plan?

- Compare net worth to previous balance sheets to assess your financial progress.
- Decide how often you will prepare a balance sheet.

PERSONAL FINANCIAL PLANNER

15

Suggested Apps:

- Simple Balance Sheet, Personal Capital

PERSONAL FINANCIAL PLANNER

16

Personal Cash Flow Statement

Purpose: To maintain a record of cash inflows and outflows for a month.

Instructions: Record inflows and outflows of cash for a one-month period. This sheet is also available in an Excel spreadsheet format on the library resource site in *Connect*.

Suggested websites: cashmoneylife.com   www.thesimpledollar.com   www.choosetosave.org/asec/

Suggested apps: Expensify, Spending Tracker, Every Dollar

For month ending _____

Cash Inflows

Salary (take-home)	_____
Other income:	_____
Other income:	_____
Total Income	[_____]

Cash Outflows

Fixed expenses

Mortgage or rent	_____
Loan payments	_____
Insurance	_____
Other _____	_____
Other _____	_____
Total variable outflows	_____

Variable expenses

Food	_____
Clothing	_____
Electricity	_____
Telephone	_____
Water	_____
Transportation	_____
Personal care	_____
Medical expenses	_____
Recreation/entertainment	_____
Gifts	_____
Donations	_____
Other _____	_____
Other _____	_____
Total fixed outflows	_____
Total outflows	[_____]

Surplus/Deficit . . . . [_____]

Allocation of surplus

Emergency fund savings	_____
Financial goals savings	_____
Other savings _____	_____

What's Next for Your Personal Financial Plan?

- Decide which areas of spending need to be delayed, reduced, or eliminated.
- Evaluate your spending patterns for preparing a budget.

Suggested Apps:

- **Expensify, Spending Tracker, Every Dollar**

Cash Budget

Purpose: To compare projected and actual spending for one month.

Instructions: Estimate projected spending based on your cash flow statement, and maintain records for actual spending for these same budget categories. This sheet is also available in an Excel spreadsheet format on the library resource site in *Connect*.

Suggested websites: www.betterbudgeting.com   www.mymoney.gov

Suggested apps: Home Budget and YNAB (You Need A Budget)

Income	Budgeted Amounts Dollar	Budgeted Amounts Percent	Actual Amounts	Variance
Salary				
Other _____				
Total income		100%		
Expenses	<<<<<<<<<<<<<	<<<<<<<<<<<<<<<<	<<<<<<<<<<<<<<<<	<<<<<<<<<<<<<<<<
Fixed expenses	<<<<<<<<<<<<<	<<<<<<<<<<<<<<<<	<<<<<<<<<<<<<<<<	<<<<<<<<<<<<<<<<
Mortgage or rent				
Property taxes				
Loan payments				
Insurance				
Other _____				
Total fixed expenses				
Emergency fund/savings	<<<<<<<<<<<<<	<<<<<<<<<<<<<<<<	<<<<<<<<<<<<<<<<	<<<<<<<<<<<<<<<<
Emergency fund				
Savings for _____				
Savings for _____				
Total savings				
Variable expenses	<<<<<<<<<<<<<	<<<<<<<<<<<<<<<<	<<<<<<<<<<<<<<<<	<<<<<<<<<<<<<<<<
Food				
Utilities				
Clothing				
Transportation costs				
Personal care				
Medical and health care				
Entertainment				
Education				
Gifts/donations				
Miscellaneous				
Other _____				
Other _____				
Total variable expenses				
Total expenses		100%		

What's Next for Your Personal Financial Plan?

• Evaluate if your current budget is appropriate for your situation.

• Assess if your budgeting and money management activities are helping you achieve your financial goals.

Suggested Apps:

• Home Budget, YNAB (You Need a Budget)

Name: _____   Date: _____

18

PERSONAL FINANCIAL PLANNER

Annual Budget Summary

Purpose: To prepare an overview of your annual spending patterns.

Instructions: Record the monthly budget amount in the first column and actual monthly spending in the appropriate column. This sheet is also available in an Excel spreadsheet format on the library resource site in *Connect*.

Suggested websites: www.mymoney.gov   www.bls.gov/cex

Suggested app: Mint

Expense	Monthly Budget	Actual Spending					
		Jan	Feb	Mar	Apr	May	Jun
Savings							
Mortgage/rent							
Housing costs							
Telephone							
Food (at home)							
Food (away)							
Clothing							
Transportation							
Credit payments							
Insurance							
Health care							
Recreation							
Reading/education							
Gifts/donations							
Miscellaneous							
Other _____							
Other _____							
Total							

Expense	Actual Spending						Year Totals	
	Jul	Aug	Sep	Oct	Nov	Dec	Actual	Budget
Savings								
Mortgage/rent								
Housing costs								
Telephone								
Food (at home)								
Food (away)								
Clothing								
Transportation								
Credit payments								
Insurance								
Health care								
Recreation								
Reading/education								
Gifts/donations								
Miscellaneous								
Other _____								
Other _____								
Total								

Suggested App:
• Mint

What's Next for Your Personal Financial Plan?

• Decide which areas of spending need to be delayed, reduced, or eliminated.

• Evaluate your spending patterns to determine any revisions to your budget.

College Education Savings Plan

Purpose: To estimate future costs of college and calculate needed savings.

Instructions: Complete the information and calculations requested below. This sheet is also available in an Excel spreadsheet format on the library resource site in *Connect*.

Suggested website: www.kiplinger.com   www.smartypig.com

Suggested app: My Piggy Bank Savings Tracker

Estimated Cost of College Education

Current cost of college education $ _____

(including tuition, fees, room, board, books, travel, and other expenses)

Future value for _____ years until starting college at an expected
annual inflation of _____ percent (use future value of $1, Exhibit 1-A in
Chapter 1 Appendix or a financial calculator)   × $ _____

Projected future cost of college adjusted for inflation .... = $ _____

Estimated Annual Savings Needed

Projected future cost of college adjusted for inflation .... **(A)** $ _____

Future value of a series of deposits for _____ years until starting college
and expected annual rate of return on savings and investments of
_____ percent (use Exhibit 1-B in Chapter 1 Appendix or a financial calculator)   **(B)** $ _____

Estimated annual deposit to achieve needed education fund .... **A** divided by **B** $ _____

What's Next for Your Personal Financial Plan?

- Identify savings and investment plans to achieve long-term goals.

- Ask others for suggested actions to save for long-term goals.

Current Income Tax Estimate

Purpose: To estimate your current federal income tax liability.
Instructions: Based on last year's tax return, estimates for the current year, and current tax regulations and rates, estimate your current tax liability. This sheet is also available in an Excel spreadsheet on the library resource site in *Connect*.
Suggested websites: www.irs.gov   turbotax.intuit.com/tax-tools/calculators/taxcaster/
Suggested app: TaxCaster

Gross income (wages, salary, investment income, and other ordinary income)		$	
Less Adjustments to income (see current tax regulations)		− $	
Equals Adjusted gross income		= $	
Less Standard deduction **or**	Itemized deduction		
	medical expenses (exceeding 7.5% of AGI)		$
	state/local income & property taxes		$
	mortgage, home equity loan interest		$
	contributions		$
	casualty and theft losses		$
	other itemized deductions (see current tax regulations)		$
Amount − $	**Total**		− $
Equals Taxable income		= $	
Estimated tax (based on current tax tables or tax schedules)		$	
Less Tax credits		− $	
Plus Other taxes		+ $	
Equals Total tax liability		= $	
Less Estimated withholding and payments		− $	
Equals Tax due (or refund)		= $	

What's Next for Your Personal Financial Plan?

- Develop a system for filing and storing various tax records related to income, deductible expenses, and current tax forms.
- Using www.irs.gov and other online sources, identify recent changes in tax laws that may affect your financial planning decisions.

Suggested App:
- **TaxCaster**

Name: _____   Date: _____

Tax Preparer Comparison

Purpose: To compare the services and costs of different income tax return preparation sources.
Instructions: Using online sources and contacting tax preparation services, obtain the information requested below. This sheet is also available in an Excel spreadsheet on the library resource site in *Connect*.
Suggested websites: turbotax.intuit.com/tax-tools/   www.hrblock.com

	Local Tax Service	National Tax Service	Local Accountant
Company name			
Address			
Telephone			
Email			
Website			
Cost of preparing Form 1040 with Schedule A (itemized deductions)			
Cost of preparing state or local tax return			
Cost of electronic filing			
Assistance provided if IRS questions your return			
Other services provided			

What's Next for Your Personal Financial Plan?

- Talk with people about their experiences when using a tax preparation service.
- Compare the costs and benefits of using a tax preparation service with using tax software.

Tax Planning Activities

Purpose: To consider actions that prevent tax penalties and may result in tax savings.

Instructions: Consider which of the following actions are appropriate to your tax situation. This sheet is also available in an Excel spreadsheet on the library resource site in *Connect*.

Suggested websites: www.irs.gov   turbotax.intuit.com/tax-tools/

Suggested apps: IRS2go, Credit Karma Tax

	Action to Be Taken (if applicable)	Completed
Filing Status/Withholding		
• Change filing status because of changes in life situation.		
• Change amount of withholding because of changes in tax situation.		
• Plan to make estimated tax payments (due the 15th of April, June, September, and January).		
Tax Records/Documents		
• Organize home files for ease of maintaining and retrieving data.		
• Send current mailing address and correct Social Security number to IRS, place of employment, and other sources of income.		
Annual Tax Activities		
• Be certain all needed data and current tax forms are available well before deadline.		
• Research tax code changes and uncertain tax areas.		
Tax Savings Actions		
• Consider tax-exempt and tax-deferred investments.		
• If you expect to have the same or lower tax rate next year, accelerate deductions into the current year.		
• If you expect to have the same or lower tax rate next year, delay the receipt of income until next year.		
• If you expect to have a higher tax rate next year, delay deductions because they will have a greater benefit.		
• If you expect to have a higher tax rate next year, accelerate the receipt of income to have it taxed at the current lower rate.		
• Start or increase use of tax-deferred retirement plans.		
• Other		

Suggested Apps:
• IRS2go, Credit Karma Tax

What's Next for Your Personal Financial Plan?

• Conduct online research to identify saving and investing decisions that would minimize future income taxes.

• Develop a plan for actions related to your current and future tax situation.

Name: _____   Date: _____

Planning the Use of Financial Services

Purpose: To assess current financial services and to determine services that may be needed in the future.

Instructions: List currently used services with financial institution information (name, address, phone, website) and services that may be needed in the future. This sheet is also available in an Excel spreadsheet format on the library resource site in *Connect*.

Suggested websites: www.bankrate.com   www.cuna.org   www.findabetterbank.com www.nerdwallet.com

Financial Services and Apps	Current Financial Services Used	Additional Financial Services Needed
Payment services (checking, debit card, online payments, apps)	Financial institution:	
	Address:	
	Phone:	
	Website:	
Savings plans (savings account, certificates of deposit, savings bonds)	Financial institution:	
	Address:	
	Phone:	
	Website:	
Credit accounts (credit cards, personal loans, mortgage)	Financial institution:	
	Address:	
	Phone:	
	Website:	
Other financial services (investments, trust account, tax planning, apps)	Financial institution:	
	Address:	
	Phone:	
	Website:	

What's Next for Your Personal Financial Plan?

• Assess whether the current financial services used and sources of these services are appropriate for your situation.

• Determine additional financial services you may use in the future.

Saving to Achieve Financial Goals

Purpose: To monitor savings for achieving financial goals.

Instructions: Record savings plan information along with the balance on a periodic basis. This sheet is also available in an Excel spreadsheet format on the library resource site in *Connect*.

Suggested websites: www.fdic.gov   www.savingsbonds.gov   https://americasaves.org

Suggested app: My Piggy Bank Savings Tracker

Regular Savings Account

Acct. no. _____
Financial institution
_____
Address _____
_____
Phone _____
Website _____

Savings goal/Amount needed/Date needed:

_____

Initial deposit: Date _____ $ _____
Balance: Date _____ $ _____
                     Date _____ $ _____
                     Date _____ $ _____
                     Date _____ $ _____

Certificate of Deposit

Acct. no. _____
Financial institution
_____
Address _____
_____
Phone _____
Website _____

Savings goal/Amount needed/Date needed:

_____

Initial deposit: Date _____ $ _____
Balance: Date _____ $ _____
                     Date _____ $ _____
                     Date _____ $ _____
                     Date _____ $ _____

Money Market fund/account

Acct. no. _____
Financial institution
_____
Address _____
_____
Phone _____
Website _____

Savings goal/Amount needed/Date needed:

_____

Initial deposit: Date _____ $ _____
Balance: Date _____ $ _____
                     Date _____ $ _____
                     Date _____ $ _____
                     Date _____ $ _____

U.S. Savings Bonds, other savings plan

Purchase location _____

Address _____
_____
Phone _____
Website _____

Savings goal/Amount needed/Date needed:

_____

Purchase date: _____   Maturity date: _____
Amount: _____   Maturity date: _____

Purchase date: _____   Maturity date: _____
Amount: _____   Maturity date: _____

Suggested App:
• My Piggy Bank Savings Tracker

What's Next for Your Personal Financial Plan?

• Assess your progress toward achieving various savings goals. Evaluate existing and new savings goals.

• Plan actions to expand savings amounts for your savings goals.

Name: _____   Date: _____

Savings Plan Comparison

 25

Purpose: To compare the benefits and costs of different savings plans.
Instructions: Obtain online information from financial service providers for the items requested below. This sheet is also available in an Excel spreadsheet format on the library resource site in *Connect*.
Suggested websites: www.bankrate.com   www.depositaccounts.com   www.nerdwallet.com

Type of savings plan: (regular savings account, certificate of deposit, money market account, other _____)			
Financial service provider			
Address/phone			
Website			
Annual interest rate			
Annual percentage yield (APY)			
Frequency of compounding			
Insured by FDIC, NCUA, other			
Maximum amount insured			
Minimum initial deposit			
Minimum time period savings must be on deposit			
Penalties for early withdrawal			
Service charges, transaction fees, other costs or fees			

What's Next for Your Personal Financial Plan?

- Based on this savings plan analysis, determine the best types for your current and future financial situation.
- When analyzing savings plans, what factors should you carefully investigate?

Name: _____   Date: _____

Payment Account Comparison

Purpose: To compare the benefits and costs associated with different checking/payment accounts.

Instructions: Obtain online information from financial service providers for the items requested below. This sheet is also available in an Excel spreadsheet format on the library resource site in *Connect.*

Suggested websites: www.bankrate.com   www.nerdwallet.com

Suggested app: MoneyPass (ATM locator)

Financial Service Provider			
Address			
Phone			
Website			
Type of account			
Minimum balance for "free" checking; monthly fee for going below minimum balance			
Debit card availability, fees			
"Free" checking accounts for full-time students?			
Online banking services; app features			
Other fees/costs			
• printing of checks			
• stop payment order			
• overdrawn account			
• certified check			
• ATM, other charges			
Banking hours; location of branch offices, ATM network			
Other information, services, fees			

What's Next for Your Personal Financial Plan?

• Are your payment activities best served by your current payment methods (checking account, debit card, online payments, app)?

• Talk with others about their online payment and app experiences.

Payment Account Cost Analysis

Purpose: To compare the inflows and outflows of a checking account.

Instructions: Record the interest earned (inflows) and the costs and fees (outflows) as requested below. *Note: Not all items will apply to every checking account.* This sheet is also available in an Excel spreadsheet format on the library resource site in *Connect.*

Suggested websites: www.bankrate.com   www.nerdwallet.com/best/banking/checking-accounts

Inflows (earnings)

Step 1

Multiply average monthly balance $ _____
by average rate of return _____ % to determine annual earnings

Outflows (costs)

Step 2

Monthly service charge
$ _____ × 12 = $ _____

Average number of checks written per month _____ × charge per check (if applicable) × 12 = $ _____

Average number of deposits per month _____ × charge per deposit (if applicable) × 12 = $ _____

Fee incurred when going below minimum balance _____ × times below minimum = $ _____

Lost interest: opportunity cost
_____ % × required minimum balance $ _____ = $ _____

= [_____]

Total estimated inflow

$ [_____]

Total estimated outflow

$ [_____]

Estimated inflows less outflows =

Net earnings for account _____

− Net cost for account _____

+/−$ _____

Note: This calculation does not take into account charges and fees for such services as overdrafts, stop payments, ATM use, and check printing. Be sure to also consider those costs when selecting a checking account.

What's Next for Your Personal Financial Plan?

- What actions can you take to minimize checking/payment account costs?
- Talk to others about the actions they take to minimize checking account costs.

Name: _____   **Date:** _____

Checking Account Reconciliation

Purpose: To determine the adjusted cash balance for your checking account.
Instructions: Enter data from your bank statement and checkbook for the amounts requested. This sheet is also available in an Excel spreadsheet format on the library resource site in *Connect.*
Suggested websites: www.bankrate.com   www.thebalance.com

Date of bank statement _____

Balance on bank statement $ _____

Step 1

Subtract total of outstanding checks, payments, and withdrawals

Check No.	Amount	Check No.	Amount
_____	_____	_____	_____
_____	_____	_____	_____
_____	_____	_____	_____
_____	_____	_____	−$ _____

Step 2

Add deposits in transit (deposits you have made but have not been reported on this statement)

Date	Amount	Date	Amount
_____	_____	_____	_____

+ $ _____

Adjusted bank statement balance . . . . $ _____ ←

Current balance in your checkbook   _____

Step 3

Subtract fees or other charges listed on your bank statement

Item	Amount	Item	Amount
_____	_____	_____	_____
_____	_____	_____	− $ _____

Subtract ATM withdrawals, debit card payments, and other automatic payments.   − $ _____

Step 4

Add interest earned   + $ _____
Add direct deposits   + $ _____

Adjusted checkbook balance . . . . $ _____ ←

(The two adjusted balances should be the same; if not, carefully check your math and check to see that deposits and checks recorded in your checkbook and on your statement are for the correct amounts.)

What's Next for Your Personal Financial Plan?

- Develop a plan to monitor your payment records.
- Research actions to reduce banking service costs.

Consumer Credit Usage

Purpose: To create a record of current consumer debt balances.
Instructions: Record account names, numbers, and payments for current consumer debts. This sheet is also available in an Excel spreadsheet format on the library resource site in *Connect*.
Suggested websites: www.bankrate.com   www.ftc.gov   https://credit.org

Automobile, Education, Personal, and Installment Loans

Financial institution	Account number	Current balance	Monthly payment
_____	_____	_____	_____
_____	_____	_____	_____
_____	_____	_____	_____
_____	_____	_____	_____
_____	_____	_____	_____

Charge Accounts and Credit Cards

_____	_____	_____	_____
_____	_____	_____	_____
_____	_____	_____	_____
_____	_____	_____	_____
_____	_____	_____	_____

Other Loans (overdraft protection, home equity, life insurance loan)

_____	_____	_____	_____
_____	_____	_____	_____
_____	_____	_____	_____
	Totals	_____	_____

$$\text{Debt payment} - \text{to} - \text{income ratio} = \frac{\text{Total monthly payments}}{\text{net(after-tax)income}}$$

What's Next for Your Personal Financial Plan?

- Talk to others to determine how they first established credit.
- Survey three or four individuals to determine actions to minimize credit use.

Name: _____   Date: _____

Credit Card Comparison

Purpose: To compare the costs and benefits of different credit cards and credit accounts.

Instructions: Analyze online information, credit applications, and information from financial institutions to obtain the items requested below. This sheet is also available in an Excel spreadsheet format on the library resource site in *Connect*.

Suggested websites: www.nerdwallet.com   www.wallethub.com

Type of credit/charge account			
Name of company/account			
Address/phone			
Website			
Type of purchases that can be made			
Annual fee (if any)			
Annual percentage rate (APR) (interest calculation information)			
Credit limit for new customers			
Minimum monthly payment			
Other costs: • Credit report • Late fee • Other _____			
Restrictions (age, minimum annual income)			
Other information for consumers to consider			
Rewards program			

What's Next for Your Personal Financial Plan?

• Assess the advantages and disadvantages of using credit and debit cards.

• Determine the types of credit cards you might use in the future.

Name: _____   Date: _____

Consumer Loan Comparison

Purpose: To compare the costs associated with different loan sources.

Instructions: Obtain online information and information from a bank, credit union, and online lender to compare loans based on the items below. This sheet is also available in an Excel spreadsheet format on the library resource site in *Connect*.

Suggested websites: www.eloan.com   www.bankrate.com

Amount of loan $ _____

Type of financial institution			
Name			
Address			
Phone			
Website			
Amount of down payment			
Length of loan (months)			
What collateral is required?			
Amount of monthly payment			
Total amount to be repaid (monthly amount × number of months + down payment)			
Total finance charge/cost of credit			
Annual percentage rate (APR)			
Other costs • Credit life insurance • Credit report • Other _____			
Is a cosigner required?			
Other information			

What's Next for Your Personal Financial Plan?

• Ask several individuals how they would compare loans at different financial institutions.

• Survey several friends and relatives to determine whether they ever cosigned a loan. If yes, ask about their experience.

Unit Pricing Worksheet

Purpose: To calculate the unit price for a consumer purchase.

Instructions: Use online information, advertisements, and store visits to calculate and compare unit prices. This sheet is also available in an Excel spreadsheet format on the library resource site in *Connect*.

Suggested websites: www.consumer.gov   www.consumerworld.org

Suggested apps: Grocery Gadget, AnyList

Item _____

Date	Store/Location	Brand	Total price	÷	Size	=	Unit Price	Unit of Measurement
_____	_____	_____	_____		_____		_____	_____
_____	_____	_____	_____		_____		_____	_____
_____	_____	_____	_____		_____		_____	_____
_____	_____	_____	_____		_____		_____	_____
_____	_____	_____	_____		_____		_____	_____
_____	_____	_____	_____		_____		_____	_____

Highest unit price

Store _____

Date _____

Lowest unit price

Store _____

Date _____

Difference: _____

_____

Wisest consumer buy/best overall store

_____

Reasons

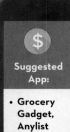

What's Next for Your Personal Financial Plan?

• Talk to others for suggestions for wise buying actions.

• Conduct research to determine local and online shopping locations that provide the best value.

Name: _____   Date: _____

Consumer Purchase Comparison

Purpose: To research and evaluate brands and purchase locations for a major consumer item.

Instructions: When considering a major consumer purchase, use online research, ads, catalogs, store visits, and other sources to obtain the information below. This sheet is also available in an Excel spreadsheet format on the library resource site in *Connect*.

Suggested websites: www.consumerreports.org   clark.com

Suggested app: Red Laser

Product:

_____

Exact description (size, model, features, etc.):

_____

Conduct online research to obtain information and buying suggestions regarding the product.

Source _____   Source _____

Date _____   Date _____

_____

What buying suggestions are presented in these information sources?

_____

Which brands are recommended in these information sources? Why?

_____

Contact or visit two or three stores or online sources that sell the product to obtain the following information:

	Buying location	**Buying location**	**Buying location**
Business name			
Address (if applicable)			
Phone/website			
Brand name/cost			
Product difference from item above			
Guarantee/warranty offered (describe)			

Which brand and at which store would you buy this product? Why?

What's Next for Your Personal Financial Plan?

- Which consumer information sources might be most valuable for future buying decisions?
- List guidelines you might use in the future when making major purchases.

Suggested App:
- **Red Laser**

Name: _____ Date: _____

Transportation Needs

Purpose: To assess current and future transportation needs.

Instructions: Based on current and expected needs, complete the information requested below. This sheet is also available in an Excel spreadsheet format on the library resource site in *Connect.*

Suggested websites: www.thoughtco.com/cars-4132715   www.kbb.com

Suggested app: KBB

Current situation: Date _____

	Vehicle 1		Vehicle 2
Year/Model	_____	Year/Model	_____
Mileage	_____	Mileage	_____
Condition	_____	Condition	_____
Needed repairs	_____	Needed repairs	_____
Estimated annual costs		**Estimated annual costs**	
Gas, oil, repairs	_____	Gas, oil, repairs	_____
Insurance	_____	Insurance	_____
Loan balance	_____	Loan balance	_____
Estimated market value	_____	Estimated market value	_____

Expected and projected changes in transportation needs
_____

Personal desires and concerns regarding current transportation

Analysis of Future Desired Transportation Situation

_____

Description of possible future vehicle purchase

_____

Time when future vehicle purchase is desired

_____

Financing resources needed

_____

Available and projected financial resources

_____

Concerns that must be overcome

_____

Realistic time when transportation choice may be achieved

_____

Suggested App:

• **KBB**

What's Next for Your Personal Financial Plan?

• Talk to others about their experiences with public transportation.

• Identify financial and personal factors that affect your transportation spending decisions.

Name: _____   Date: _____

Used-Car Comparison

Purpose: To research and evaluate different used cars.

Instructions: When considering a used-car purchase, use online research, advertisements, and visits to new and used-car dealers to obtain the information below. This sheet is also available in an Excel spreadsheet format on the library resource site in *Connect*.

Suggested websites: www.carbuyingtips.com   www.kbb.com

Suggested app: Edmunds

Automobile (year, make, model)			
Dealer/source name			
Address			
Phone			
Website			
Cost			
Mileage			
Condition of auto			
Condition of tires			
Audio system			
Air conditioning			
Other options			
Warranty (if applicable)			
Items in need of repair			
Inspection items: • any rust, major dents?			
• oil or fluid leaks?			
• condition of brakes?			
• proper operation of heater, wipers, other accessories?			
Other information			

Suggested App:

• Edmunds

What's Next for Your Personal Financial Plan?

• Maintain a record of automobile operating costs.

• Prepare a plan for regular maintenance of your vehicle.

Name: _____ Date: _____

Buying or Leasing a Motor Vehicle

Purpose: To compare costs of buying and leasing an automobile or other motor vehicle.

Instructions: Obtain costs related to leasing and buying a vehicle. This sheet is also available in an Excel spreadsheet format on the library resource site in *Connect*.

Suggested websites: www.leasesource.com   www.leaseguide.com

Suggested app: Car Lease and Loan Calculator

Purchase Costs

Total vehicle cost, including sales tax ($ _____)

Down payment (or full amount if paying cash) $ _____

Monthly loan payment $ _____ times _____ months
(this item is zero if vehicle is not financed) $ _____

Opportunity cost of down payment (or total cost of the vehicle if bought for cash)

$ _____ times number of years of financing/ownership times

_____ percent (interest rate which funds could earn) $ _____

Less: estimated value of vehicle at end of loan term/ownership $ _____

Total cost to buy .... $

Leasing Costs

Security deposit $ _____ $ _____

Monthly lease payments $ _____ times _____ months $ _____

Opportunity cost of security deposit:

$ _____ times _____ years times _____ percent $ _____

End-of-lease charges (if applicable)* $ _____

Total cost to lease .... $

*Such as charges for extra mileage.

Suggested App:

• Car Lease and Loan Calculator

What's Next for Your Personal Financial Plan?

• Prepare a list of future actions to use when buying, financing, or leasing a car.

• Maintain a record of operating costs and maintenance actions for your vehicle.

Comparing Cash and Credit Purchases

Purpose: To compare the costs and benefits of cash and credit.

Instructions: When considering a major consumer purchase, complete the information requested below. This sheet is also available in an Excel spreadsheet format on the library resource site in *Connect.*

Suggested websites: www.consumerreports.org   www.daveramsey.com

Suggested app: ShopSavvy

Item/Description _____

Cash Price

Selling price	$ _____
Sales tax	$ _____
Additional charges (delivery, setup, service contract)	$ _____
Discounts (employee, senior citizen or student discounts, discounts for paying cash)	$ _____
Net cost of item times percent interest that could be earned times years of use to determine opportunity cost	$ _____
Total financial and economic cost when paying cash	$

Credit Price

Down payment	$ _____
Financing: monthly payment times months	$ _____
Additional financing charges (application fee, credit report, credit life insurance)	$ _____
Product-related charges (delivery, setup)	$ _____
Discounts that may apply	−$ _____
Total financial and economic cost when using credit	$

Other Considerations

Will cash used for the purchase be needed for other purposes?

Will this credit purchase result in financial difficulties?

Do alternatives exist for this purchasing and payment decision?

Note: Use Sheet 33 to compare brands, stores, features, and prices when making a major consumer purchase.

What's Next for Your Personal Financial Plan?

- Develop a plan to save for major purchases in the future.
- Create a list of factors to consider when comparing cash and credit purchases.

Suggested
App:

- ShopSavvy

Name: _____   Date: _____

Auto Operation Costs

Purpose: To calculate or estimate the cost of owning and operating an automobile or other vehicle.
Instructions: Maintain records related to the cost of categories listed below. This sheet is also available in an Excel spreadsheet format on the library resource site in *Connect*.
Suggested websites: www.consumerreports.org   www.autobytel.com
Suggested app: Car Expenses Manager

Model year _____   Make, size, model _____

Fixed Ownership Costs

Depreciation*

Purchase price $ _____ divided by estimated life of
_____ years $ _____

Interest on auto loan

Annual cost of financing vehicle if buying on credit $ _____

Insurance for the vehicle

Annual cost of liability and property $ _____

License, registration fee, and taxes $ _____

Cost of registering vehicle for state and city license fees $ _____

Total fixed costs (A) .... $ _____

Variable Costs

Gasoline

_____ estimated miles per year divided by _____
miles per gallon of _____ times the average price of
$ _____ per gallon $ _____

Oil changes

Cost of regular oil changes during the year $ _____

Tires

Cost of tires purchased during the year $ _____

Maintenance/repairs

Cost of planned or other unexpected maintenance $ _____

Parking and tolls

Regular fees for parking and highway toll charges $ _____

Total variable costs (B) .... $ _____

Total costs (A+B) $ _____

Divided by miles per year _____

Equals cost per mile $ _____

*This estimate of vehicle depreciation is based on a straight-line approach—equal depreciation each year. A more realistic approach would be larger amounts in the early years of ownership, such as 25–30 percent in the first year, 30–35 percent in the second; most cars lose 90 percent of their value by the time they are seven years old.

What's Next for Your Personal Financial Plan?

- Talk to others to obtain suggestions for reducing auto operation costs.
- Prepare a list of auto service businesses that provide the best value.

Legal Services Comparison

Purpose: To compare costs of services from different sources of legal assistance.

Instructions: Using online information and contacting various sources of legal services (lawyer, prepaid legal service, legal aid society), compare costs and services. This sheet is also available in an Excel spreadsheet format on the library resource site in *Connect.*

Suggested websites: www.ftc.gov   www.fraud.org   www.nolo.com

Type of legal service			
Organization name			
Address			
Phone			
Website/email			
Contact person			
Recommended by			
Areas of specialization			
Cost of initial consultation			
Cost of simple will			
Cost of real estate closing			
Cost method for other services—flat fee, hourly rate, or contingency basis			
Other information			

What's Next for Your Personal Financial Plan?

- Determine the best alternative for your legal needs.
- Maintain a file of legal documents and other financial records.

Name: _____ Date: _____

Housing Needs

Purpose: To assess current and future plans for housing.
Instructions: Based on current and expected future needs, complete the information requested below. This sheet is also available in an Excel spreadsheet format on the library resource site in *Connect*.
Suggested websites: www.thebalance.com/home-buying-4074010   lifehacker.com   www.realtor.com
Suggested app: Redfin

Current situation _____   Date _____

Renting

Location _____

Description _____

_____

Advantages _____

_____

Disadvantages _____

_____

Rent $ _____

Lease expiration _____

Buying

Location _____

Description _____

_____

Advantages _____

_____

Disadvantages _____

_____

Mortgage payment $ _____

Balance $ _____

Current market value _____

Expected and projected changes in housing needs
_____

Personal desires and concerns regarding current housing situation
_____

Analysis of Future Desired Housing Situation

Description of future housing situation	
Time when future situation is desired	
Financing resources needed/available	
Concerns that must be overcome	
Realistic time when housing of choice may be achieved	

Suggested App:

• **Redfin**

What's Next for Your Personal Financial Plan?

• List personal factors that would affect your decision to rent or buy.
• Talk with various people about factors that affect their housing decisions.

Renting or Buying Housing

Purpose: To compare cost of renting and buying your place of residence.

Instructions: Obtain estimates for comparable housing units for the data requested below. This sheet is also available in an Excel spreadsheet format on the library resource site in *Connect*.

Suggested websites: www.homefair.com   www.nerdwallet.com/mortgages/rent-vs-buy-calculator

Suggested app: Realtor.com

Rental Costs

Annual rent payments (monthly rent $ _____ × 12)	$ _____
Renter's insurance	$ _____
Interest lost on security deposit (deposit times after-tax savings account interest rate)	$ _____
Total annual cost of renting	$

Buying Costs

Annual mortgage payments	$ _____
Property taxes (annual costs)	$ _____
Homeowner's insurance (annual premium)	$ _____
Estimated maintenance and repairs	$ _____
After-tax interest lost because of down payment/closing costs	$ _____
Less: financial benefits of home ownership	
Growth in equity	$ – _____
Tax savings for mortgage interest (annual mortgage interest times tax rate)	$ – _____
Tax savings for property taxes (annual property taxes times tax rate)	$ – _____
Estimated annual depreciation	$ – _____
Total annual cost of buying	$

What's Next for Your Personal Financial Plan?

• Determine whether renting or buying is most appropriate for you at the current time.

• Prepare a list of circumstances or actions that might change your housing needs.

Suggested App:

• Realtor.com

Apartment Rental Comparison

Purpose: To evaluate and compare rental housing alternatives.

Instructions: When in the market for an apartment, obtain information to compare costs and facilities of three apartments. This sheet is also available in an Excel spreadsheet format on the library resource site in *Connect*.

Suggested websites: https://www.rentjungle.com/comparerent/   www.apartmentguide.com/blog/

Suggested app: PadMapper

Name of renting person or apartment building			
Address			
Phone			
Email, website			
Monthly rent			
Amount of security deposit			
Length of lease			
Utilities included in rent			
Parking facilities			
Storage area in building			
Laundry facilities			
Distance to schools			
Distance to public transportation			
Distance to shopping			
Pool, recreation area, other facilities			
Estimated utility costs: • electric • telephone • gas • water			
Other costs			
Other information			

What's Next for Your Personal Financial Plan?

- Which of these rental units would best serve your current housing needs?
- What additional information should be considered when renting an apartment?

Suggested App:
• PadMapper

PERSONAL FINANCIAL PLANNER

42

Housing Mortgage Affordability

Purpose: To estimate the amount of affordable mortgage payment, mortgage amount, and home purchase price.

Instructions: Enter the amounts requested, and perform the required calculations. This sheet is also available in an Excel spreadsheet format on the library resource site in *Connect.*

Suggested websites: www.kiplinger.com   www.mortgagecalculator.org

Suggested app: Mortgage Calculator

Step 1

Determine your monthly gross income (annual income divided by 12). $ _____

Step 2

With a down payment of at least 5 percent, lenders use 33 percent of monthly gross income as a guideline for PITI (principal, interest, taxes, and insurance), and 38 percent of monthly gross income as a guideline for PITI plus other debt payments (enter 0.33 or 0.38).   × _____

Step 3

Subtract other debt payments (such as payments on an auto loan), if applicable.   − _____

Subtract estimated monthly costs of property taxes and homeowners' insurance.   − _____

Affordable monthly mortgage payment .... $ _____

Step 4

Divide this amount by the monthly mortgage payment per $1,000 based on current mortgage rates (see Exhibit 9–9). For example, for a 10 percent, 30-year loan, the number would be $8.78).   ÷ _____

Multiply by $1,000.   × $1,000 _____

Affordable mortgage amount .... $ _____

Step 5

Divide your affordable mortgage amount by 1 minus the fractional portion of your down payment (for example, 0.9 for a 10 percent down payment).   ÷ _____

Affordable home purchase price .... $ _____

Note: The two ratios used by lending institutions (Step 2) and other loan requirements are likely to vary based on a variety of factors, including the type of mortgage, the amount of the down payment, your income level, and current interest rates. For example, with a down payment of 10 percent or more and a credit score of at least 720, the ratios might increase to 40/45 or 45/50 percent in the above analysis.

What's Next for Your Personal Financial Plan?

- Identify actions you might need to take to qualify for a mortgage.
- Discuss your mortgage qualifications with a mortgage broker or other lender.

Suggested App:

- **Mortgage Calculator**

Mortgage Comparison

Purpose: To compare the services and costs for different home mortgage sources.

Instructions: When obtaining a mortgage, obtain the information requested below from different mortgage companies. This sheet is also available in an Excel spreadsheet format on the library resource site in *Connect*.

Suggested websites: www.bankrate.com   www.hsh.com

Suggested app: Mortgage Rates

Amount of mortgage $ _____	Down payment $ _____	Years _____
Company		
Address		
Phone		
Website		
Contact person, email		
Application fee, credit report, property appraisal fees		
Loan origination fee		
Other fees, charges (commitment, title, tax transfer)		
Fixed-rate mortgage (%)		
Monthly payment		
Discount points		
Adjustable-rate mortgage (%)		
• Time until first rate change		
• Frequency of rate change		
Monthly payment		
Discount points		
Payment cap		
Interest rate cap		
Rate index used		
Commitment period		
Other information		

Suggested App:

• **Mortgage Rates**

What's Next for Your Personal Financial Plan?

• What additional information should be considered when selecting a mortgage?

• Which mortgage company would best serve your needs?

Mortgage Refinance Analysis

Purpose: To determine savings associated with refinancing a mortgage.

Instructions: Record financing costs and amount saved with new mortgage in the areas provided below. This sheet is also available in an Excel spreadsheet format on the library resource site in *Connect*.

Suggested websites: www.interest.com   www.mortgage101.com

Suggested app: Refinance Calculator

Costs of Refinancing:

Points	$ _____
Application fee	$ _____
Credit report	$ _____
Attorney fees	$ _____
Title search	$ _____
Title insurance	$ _____
Appraisal fee	$ _____
Inspection fee	$ _____
Other fees	$ _____

Total refinancing costs .... **(A)** $ _____

Monthly savings:

Current monthly mortgage payment $ _____

Less:

New monthly payment $ _____

Monthly savings .... **(B)** $ _____

Number of months to cover finance costs

Refinance costs (A) divided by monthly savings (B)

(A) _____ ÷ (B) _____ = _____ months

What's Next for Your Personal Financial Plan?

- Monitor changing mortgage rates to determine if any actions are necessary.

- Talk with a mortgage broker about expected trends in mortgage rates.

Suggested App:

- Refinance Calculator

Name: _____ Date: _____

Insurance Policies and Needs

Purpose: To establish a record of current and needed insurance coverage.

Instructions: List current insurance policies and areas where new or additional coverage is needed. This sheet is also available in an Excel spreadsheet format on the library resource site in *Connect*.

Suggested websites: www.thebalance.com/personal-insurance-4073983   www.iii.org

Current Coverage	Needed Additional Coverage
Property insurance	
Company _____	
Policy no. _____	
Coverage amounts _____	
Deductible _____	
Annual premium _____	
Agent _____	
Address _____	
Phone _____	
Website/email _____	
Automobile insurance	
Company _____	
Policy no. _____	
Coverage amounts _____	
Deductible _____	
Annual premium _____	
Agent _____	
Address _____	
Phone _____	
Website/email _____	
Disability income insurance	
Company _____	
Policy no. _____	
Coverage _____	
Contact _____	
Phone _____	
Website/email _____	
Health insurance	
Company _____	
Policy no. _____	
Policy provisions _____	
Contact _____	
Phone _____	
Website/email _____	
Life insurance	
Company _____	
Policy no. _____	
Type of policy _____	
Amount of coverage _____	
Cash value _____	
Agent _____	
Phone _____	
Website/email _____	

What's Next for Your Personal Financial Plan?

- Talk with others to determine the types of insurance they have.
- Conduct an online search for types of insurance on which you need additional information.

Name: _____   Date: _____

Home Inventory

Purpose: To create a record of personal belongings for use when settling home insurance claims.

Instructions: For areas of the home, list your possessions including a description (model, serial number), cost, and date of acquisition. Also consider photographs and videos of your possessions. This sheet is also available in an Excel spreadsheet format on the library resource site in *Connect*.

Suggested websites: www.iii.org

Suggested app: All My Stuff

Item, description	Cost	Date acquired
Attic		
_____		
_____		
Bathroom		
_____		
_____		
Bedrooms		
_____		
_____		
Family room		
_____		
_____		
Living room		
_____		
_____		
Hallways		
_____		
_____		
Kitchen		
_____		
_____		
Dining room		
_____		
_____		
Basement		
_____		
_____		
Garage		
_____		
_____		
Other items		
_____		
_____		

Suggested App:
• All My Stuff

What's Next for Your Personal Financial Plan?

• Determine common items that may be overlooked when preparing a home inventory. Take photos, create a video of your personal property.

• Talk to an insurance agent to determine how best to document your property in the event of an insurance claim.

Property Insurance

Purpose: To determine property insurance needed for a home or apartment.

Instructions: Estimate the value and your needs for the categories below. This sheet is also available in an Excel spreadsheet format on the library resource site in *Connect.*

Suggested websites: www.thebalance.com/personal-insurance-4073983
www.insure.com   www.iii.org

Real Property

(this section not applicable to renters, condo owners.)

Current replacement value of home $ _____

Personal Property

Estimated value of appliances, furniture, clothing,
and other household items (conduct an inventory) $ _____

Type of coverage for personal property

    actual cash value ☐

    replacement value ☐

Additional coverage for items with limits on standard personal property coverage such as jewelry, firearms, silverware, photographic, electronic and computer equipment

Item	**Amount**
_____	_____
_____	_____
_____	_____

Personal Liability

Amount of additional personal liability coverage
desired for possible personal injury claims $ _____

Specialized Coverages

If appropriate, investigate flood or earthquake coverage
excluded from home insurance policies $ _____

Note: Use Sheet 49 to compare companies, coverages,
and costs for apartment or home insurance.

What's Next for Your Personal Financial Plan?

- Talk to others about the amount of coverage for their home and property.
- Research the main factors that affect home insurance costs in your region.

Name: _____ Date: _____

Apartment/Home Insurance Comparison

Purpose: To research and compare companies, coverages, and costs for apartment or home insurance.

Instructions: Contact three insurance agents or online companies to obtain the information requested below. This sheet is also available in an Excel spreadsheet format on the library resource site in *Connect*.

Suggested websites: www.netquote.com   www.iii.org   www.insurancequotes.org/home-insurance/

Type of building: ☐ apartment   ☐ house   ☐ condominium

Location: _____

Type of construction _____ Age of building _____

Company name			
Agent's name, address, and phone			
Email, website			
Coverage:	Premium	Premium	Premium
Dwelling $ Other structures $ (does not apply to apartment/condo coverage)			
Personal property $			
Additional living expenses $			
Personal liability Bodily injury $ Property damage $			
Medical payments Per person $ Per accident $			
Deductible amount			
Other coverage $			
Service charges or fees			
Total Premium			

What's Next for Your Personal Financial Plan?

- Conduct a survey to determine common reasons that renters do not have renter's insurance.
- Determine cost differences for home insurance among different local agents and online companies.

Automobile Insurance Comparison

Purpose: To research and compare companies, coverages, and costs for auto insurance.

Instructions: Contact three insurance agents or online companies to obtain the information requested below. This sheet is also available in an Excel spreadsheet format on the library resource site in *Connect*.

Suggested websites: www.thebalance.com/personal-insurance-4073983   https://insure.it

Suggested app: Car Insurance

Automobile (year, make, model, engine size) _____

Driver's age _____ Sex _____ Total miles driven in a year _____

Full- or part-time drive? _____ Driver's education completed? _____

Accidents or traffic violations within the past three years? _____

Company name			
Agent's name, address, and phone			
Email, website			
Policy length (6 months, 1 year)			
Coverage:	**Premium**	**Premium**	**Premium**
Bodily injury liability Per person $			
Per accident $			
Property damage liability per accident $			
Collision deductible $			
Comprehensive deductible $			
Medical payments per person $			
Uninsured motorist Per person $			
Per accident $			
Other coverage			
Service charges			
Total Premium			

Suggested App:

• Car Insurance

What's Next for Your Personal Financial Plan?

• Research actions that you might take to reduce automobile insurance costs.

• Determine cost differences for auto insurance among different local agents and online companies.

Name: _____   **Date:** _____

Health Care Insurance

Purpose: To assess current and needed medical and health care insurance.

Instructions: Assess current and needed medical and health care insurance. Investigate your existing medical and health insurance, and determine the need for additional coverages. This sheet is also available in an Excel spreadsheet format on the library resource site in *Connect*.

Suggested websites: www.insure.com   www.lifehappens.org   www.ehealthinsurance.com

Suggested app: Healthcare Bluebook

Insurance company
_____

Address
_____

Type of coverage   ☐ Individual health policy   ☐ Group health policy

                        ☐ HMO   ☐ PPO   ☐ Other _____

Premium amount (monthly/quarterly/semiannually/annually)
_____

Main coverages
_____

Amount of coverage for
_____

• Hospital costs
_____

• Surgery costs
_____

• Physician's fees
_____

• Lab tests
_____

• Outpatient expenses
_____

• Maternity
_____

• Major medical
_____

Other items covered/amounts
_____

Policy restrictions (deductible, coinsurance, maximum limits)
_____

Items not covered by this insurance
_____

Of items not covered, would supplemental coverage be appropriate for your personal situation?
_____

What actions related to your current (or proposed additional) coverage are necessary?
_____

What's Next for Your Personal Financial Plan?

• Talk to others about the impact of their health insurance on other financial decisions.

• Search online to determine the availability and cost of health insurance for a person in your life situation.

PERSONAL FINANCIAL PLANNER

Suggested App:

• Healthcare Bluebook

Name: _____ Date: _____

Disability Income Insurance

Purpose: To determine financial needs and insurance coverage related to disability situations.

Instructions: Use the categories below to determine your potential income needs and disability insurance coverage. This sheet is also available in an Excel spreadsheet format on the library resource site in *Connect*.

Suggested websites: www.ssa.gov   www.lifehappens.org

Suggested app: myCigna

Monthly Expenses

	Current	When Disabled
Mortgage (or rent)	$ _____	$ _____
Utilities	$ _____	$ _____
Food	$ _____	$ _____
Clothing	$ _____	$ _____
Insurance payments	$ _____	$ _____
Debt payments	$ _____	$ _____
Auto/transportation	$ _____	$ _____
Medical/dental care	$ _____	$ _____
Education	$ _____	$ _____
Personal allowances	$ _____	$ _____
Recreation/entertainment	$ _____	$ _____
Contributors, donations	$ _____	$ _____
Total monthly expenses when disabled		$ _____

Substitute Income   Monthly Benefit*

	Monthly Benefit*
Group disability insurance	$ _____
Social Security	$ _____
State disability insurance	$ _____
Worker's compensation	$ _____
Credit disability insurance (in some auto loan or home mortgages)	$ _____
Other income (investments, etc.)	$ _____
Total projected income when disabled	$ _____

If projected income when disabled is less than expenses, additional disability income insurance should be considered.

*Most disability insurance programs have a waiting period before benefits start, and they may have a limit as to how long benefits are received.

Suggested App:
• myCigna

What's Next for Your Personal Financial Plan?

• Survey several people to determine if they have disability insurance.

• Talk to an insurance agent to compare the costs of disability income insurance from several insurance companies.

Name: _____   Date: _____

Life Insurance

Purpose: To estimate life insurance coverage needed to cover expected expenses and future family living costs.

Instructions: Estimate the amounts for the categories listed. This sheet is also available in an Excel spreadsheet format on the library resource site in *Connect*.

Suggested websites: www.insure.com   www.lifehappens.org   www.lemonade.com
www.thebalance.com/understanding-and-choosing-life-insurance-1289279

Suggested app: Life Happens Needs Calculator

Household expenses to be covered

Final expenses (funeral, estate taxes, etc.)   (1) $ _____

Payment of consumer debt amounts   (2) $ _____

Emergency fund   (3) $ _____

College fund   (4) $ _____

Expected living expenses:

   Average living expense $ _____

   Spouse's income after taxes $ – _____

   Annual Social Security benefits $ – _____

   Net annual living expenses   (a) $ _____

   Years until spouse is 90   _____

   Investment rate factor (see below)   (b) _____

Total living expenses (a × b)   (5) $ _____

Total monetary needs (1 + 2 + 3 + 4 + 5) $ _____

Less: Total current investments $ – _____

Life insurance needs $ _____

Investment Rate Factors   Years until Spouse Is 90

	25	30	35	40	45	50	55	60
Conservative investment	20	22	25	27	30	31	*f*	35
Aggressive investment	16	17	19	20	21	21	22	23

Note: Use Sheet 54 to compare life insurance policies.

What's Next for Your Personal Financial Plan?

- Survey several people to determine their reasons for buying life insurance.
- Talk to an insurance agent to compare the rates charged by different companies and for different age categories.

PERSONAL FINANCIAL PLANNER
53

Suggested App:
- Life Happens Needs Calculator

54

Life Insurance Comparison

Purpose: To research and compare companies, coverages, and costs for different insurance policies.

Instructions: Analyze ads, find online information, and contact life insurance agents to obtain the information requested below. This sheet is also available in an Excel spreadsheet format on the library resource site in *Connect*.

Suggested websites: www.insure.com   www.accuquote.com   www.selectquote.com

Suggested app: Lemonade

Age			
Company			
Agent's name, address, and phone			
Email, website			
Type of insurance (term, straight/whole, limited payment, endowment, universal)			
Type of policy (individual, group)			
Amount of coverage			
Frequency of payment (monthly, quarterly, semiannually, annually)			
Premium amount			
Other costs: • Service charges • Physical exam			
Rate of return (annual percentage increase in cash value; not applicable for term policies)			
Benefits of insurance as stated in ad or by agent			
Potential problems or disadvantages of this coverage			

Suggested App:
• **Lemonade**

What's Next for Your Personal Financial Plan?

• Talk to a life insurance agent to obtain information on the methods used to determine the amount of life insurance a person should have.

• Determine possible life insurance needs for your future.

Investment Goals

Purpose: To determine specific goals for an investment program.

Instructions: Based on short- and long-term objectives for your investments, enter the items requested below. This sheet is also available in an Excel spreadsheet format on the library resource site in *Connect*.

Suggested websites: www.fool.com   www.betterinvesting.org

Suggested app: Acorns - Invest Spare Change

Description of Goal	Amount	Date Needed	Investment Goal (safety, growth, income)	Level of Risk (high, medium, low)	Possible Investments to Achieve This Goal

What's Next for Your Personal Financial Plan?

- Use the suggestions in Chapter 13 to perform a financial checkup.
- Discuss the importance of investment goals and financial planning with other household members.

Suggested App:
- Acorns – Invest Spare Change

Name: _____   Date: _____

Investment Risk

Purpose: To assess the risk of different investments in relation to your personal risk tolerance and financial goals.

Instructions: List various investments you are considering based on the risk associated with each. This sheet is also available in an Excel spreadsheet format on the library resource site in *Connect*.

Suggested websites: www.marketwatch.com   https://finance.yahoo.com

Suggested app: Personal Capital

	Type of Risk			
Level of Risk	Loss of market value (market risk)	Inflation risk	Interest rate risk	Liquidity risk
High risk				
Moderate risk				
Low risk				

Suggested App:

• **Personal Capital**

What's Next for Your Personal Financial Plan?

• Identify current economic trends that might increase or decrease the risk associated with your choice of investments.

• Based on the risk associated with the investments you chose, which investment would you choose to achieve your investment goals?

Investment Information Sources

Purpose: To identify and assess the value of different investment information sources.

Instructions: Obtain samples of investment information from three sources that you might consider to guide you in your investment decisions. This sheet is also available in an Excel spreadsheet format on the library resource site in *Connect*.

Suggested websites: morningstar.com   https://finance.yahoo.com

Suggested app: The Motley Fool

	Source 1	Source 2	Source 3
Information source, organization			
Address			
Phone, email			
Website			
Overview of information provided (main features)			
Cost			
Ease of access			
Evaluation: • reliability • clarity • value of information compared to cost			

What's Next for Your Personal Financial Plan?

- Based on the information that you provided, select one source that you believe is not only easy to use, but also provides quality information that would help you obtain your financial goals.

- Choose a specific investment and use the best information source to conduct a more thorough evaluation of this chosen investment alternative.

Suggested App:

- **The Motley Fool**

Name: _____   Date: _____

Corporate Stock Evaluation

Purpose: To identify a corporate stock that could help you obtain your investment goals.

Instructions: Use online research and other sources to answer these questions. This sheet is also available in an Excel spreadsheet format on the library resource site in *Connect*.

Suggested websites: https://finance.yahoo.com   www.marketwatch.com

Suggested app: Yahoo! Finance

Note: No checklist can serve as a complete guide for choosing a common or preferred stock investment. However, the following questions will help you evaluate a potential stock investment. Use online research and other sources to answer these questions about a corporate stock that you believe could help you obtain your investment goals.

Category 1: The Basics

1. What is the corporation's name? _____
2. What are the corporation's address and telephone number? _____
3. Have you evaluated the latest annual report and quarterly report?   ☐ Yes   ☐ No
4. What information about the corporation is available on the Internet? _____
5. Where is the stock traded? _____
6. What types of products or services does this firm provide? _____
7. Briefly describe the prospects for this company. (Include significant factors like product development, plans for expansion, plans for mergers, etc.)
_____

Category 2: Dividend Income

8. Is the corporation currently paying dividends? If so, how much? _____
9. What is the current yield for this stock? _____
_____
10. Has the dividend amount increased or decreased over the past five years? _____
11. How does the yield for this investment compare with those for other potential investments?
_____

Category 3: Financial Performance

12. What are the firm's earnings per share for the last year? _____
13. Have the firm's earnings increased over the past five years? _____
14. What is the firm's current price-earnings ratio? _____

15. How does the firm's current price-earnings ratio compare with firms in the same industry?
_____
16. What are the firm's projected earnings for the next year? _____
_____
17. Have sales increased over the last five years?
_____
_____
18. What is the stock's current price? _____
_____
19. What are the 52-week high and low prices for this stock? _____
20. Will an uptick or downturn in the nation's (or world's) economy affect the value of this stock or the company's performance?   ☐ Yes   ☐ No
21. Do the analysts that cover this stock indicate this is a good time to invest in this stock? _____
_____
22. Briefly describe any other information that you obtained from Morningstar, Value Line, Standard & Poor's, or other sources of information. _____
_____
_____

A Word of Caution

When you use a checklist, there is always a danger of overlooking other relevant information. This checklist is not all-inclusive, but it does provide some questions that you should answer before making a decision to invest. Quite simply, it is a place to start. If you need more information, *you* are responsible for obtaining it and for determining how it affects your potential investment.

What's Next for Your Personal Financial Plan?

• Identify additional factors that might affect your decision to invest in this corporation's stock.

• Develop a plan for monitoring an investment's value once a stock is purchased.

Brokerage and Investment App Comparison

Purpose: To compare the benefits and costs of different brokerage firms and investment apps.

Instructions: Compare the services provided by a brokerage firm and an Investment App based on the factors listed below. This sheet is also available in an Excel spreadsheet format on the library resource site in *Connect*.

Suggested websites: stockbrokers.com   www.placetrade.com   www.nerdwallet.com

Suggested app: Stash

Brokerage firm's name		
Contact person's name		
Address		
Email		
Website		
How much money is required to open an account?		
What types of retirement accounts are offered?		
Can I talk with a real person when I need assistance?		
Online services offered (trades, apps, robo-advisors)		
Minimum commission charge		
Commission on 100 shares of stock at $50/share		
Fees for other investments: • Corporate bonds • Mutual funds • Stock options		
Other fees: • Annual account fee • Inactivity fee • Other		

Suggested App:

• Stash

What's Next for Your Personal Financial Plan?

• Using the information you obtained, choose a brokerage firm that you believe will help you obtain your investment goals.

• Access the website for the brokerage firm you have chosen and answer the questions in the "Should You Use a Full-Service, Discount, or Online Brokerage Firm?" section of Chapter 14 in your text.

Name: ______________________ Date: ______________

Corporate Bond Evaluation

Purpose: To determine if a specific corporate bond might be appropriate for your financial goals.

Instructions: Use an online search or library sources to answer the questions below. This sheet is also available in an Excel spreadsheet format on the library resource site in *Connect.*

Suggested website: finra-markets.morningstar.com/BondCenter/Default.jsp

Suggested app: BondEvalue

Category 1: Information about the Corporation

1. What is the corporation's name? ______________________
2. What are the corporation's website address and telephone number? ______________________
3. What types of products or services does this firm provide? ______________________
4. Briefly describe the prospects for this company. (Include significant factors like product development, plans for expansion, plans for mergers, etc.) ______________________

Category 2: Bond Basics and Financial Performance

5. What type of bond is this? ______________________
6. What is the face value for this bond? ______________________
7. What is the interest rate for this bond? ______________________
8. What is the dollar amount of annual interest for this bond? ______________________
9. When are interest payments made to bondholders? ______________________
10. What is the current price of the bond? ______________________
11. What is the current yield for the bond? ______________________
12. Is the corporation currently paying interest as scheduled? ☐ Yes ☐ No
13. What is the maturity date for this bond? ______________________
14. What is the Moody's rating for this bond? ______________________
15. What is the Standard & Poor's rating for this bond? ______________________
16. What do these ratings mean? ______________________
17. What was the original issue date? ______________________
18. Who is the trustee for this bond issue? ______________________
19. Is the bond callable? If so, when? ______________________
20. Is the bond secured with collateral? If so, what? ☐ Yes ☐ No ______________________
21. What are the firm's earnings per share for the last year? ______________________
22. Have the firm's earnings increased over the past five years? ______________________
23. What are the firm's projected earnings for the next year? ______________________
24. Do the analysts indicate that this is a good time to invest in this company? ______________________
25. Briefly describe any other information that you obtained from Moody's, Standard & Poor's, or other sources of information. ______________________

A Word of Caution

When you use a checklist, there is always a danger of overlooking other relevant information. This checklist is not all-inclusive, but it does provide some questions that you should answer before making a decision to invest in bonds. Quite simply, it is a place to start. If you need other information, *you* are responsible for obtaining it and for determining how it affects your potential investment.

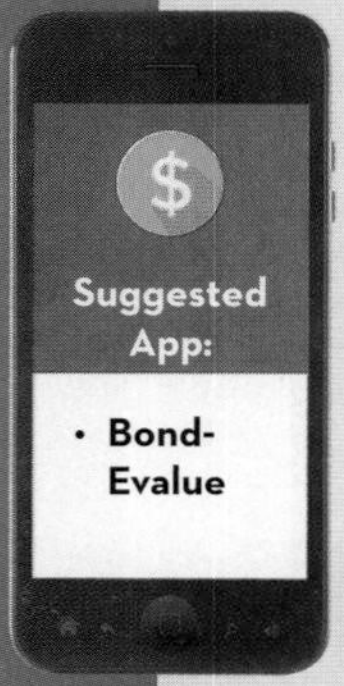

What's Next for Your Personal Financial Plan?

- Talk with people who have invested in government, municipal, or corporate bonds to obtain information on these investments.
- Discuss with other household members why bonds might be a valid choice for your investment program.

Mutual Fund Investment Information

Purpose: To identify and assess the value of mutual fund investment information sources.

Instructions: Obtain samples of several investment information sources that you might consider to guide you in your investment decisions. This sheet is also available in an Excel spreadsheet format on the library resource site in *Connect*.

Suggested websites: www.morningstar.com   https://imealliance.com/

Suggested app: myCAMS

	Source 1	Source 2	Source 3
Information source, organization			
Website or location where information can be found			
Overview of information provided (main features)			
Cost, if any			
Ease of access			
Evaluation • Reliability • Clarity • Value of information compared to cost			

What's Next for Your Personal Financial Plan?

- Talk with friends and relatives to determine what information sources they use to evaluate mutual funds.
- Choose one information source and describe how the information could help you obtain your investment goals.

Suggested
App:

· myCAMS

Name: _____   Date: _____

Mutual Fund Evaluation

Purpose: To determine whether a specific mutual fund could help you achieve your investment goals.

Instructions: Use online research and other sources to answer the questions below. This sheet is also available in an Excel spreadsheet format on the library resource site in *Connect*.

Suggested websites: www.morningstar.com   https://finance.yahoo.com/mutualfunds/

Suggested app: Morningstar

Category 1: Fund Characteristics

1. What is the fund's name? What is the fund's ticker symbol?
   _____

2. What is this fund's Morningstar rating?
   _____

3. What is the minimum investment?
   _____

4. Does the fund allow telephone or internet exchanges?
   ☐ Yes   ☐ No

5. Is there a fee for exchanges?   ☐ Yes   ☐ No

Category 2: Costs

6. Is there a front-end load charge? If so, how much is it?
   _____

7. Is there a redemption fee? If so, how much is it?
   _____

8. How much is the annual management fee?
   _____

9. Is there a 12b-1 fee? If so, how much is it?
   _____

10. What is the fund's expense ratio?
    _____

Category 3: Diversification

11. What is the fund's objective?
    _____

12. What types of securities does the fund's portfolio include?
    _____

13. How many different securities does the fund's portfolio include?
    _____

14. How many types of industries does the fund's portfolio include? _____

15. What are the fund's five largest holdings?

Category 4: Fund Performance

16. How long has the fund manager been with the fund?
    _____

17. How would you describe the fund's performance over the past 12 months?
    _____

18. How would you describe the fund's performance over the past five years?
    _____

19. How would you describe the fund's performance over the past 10 years?
    _____

20. What is the current net asset value for this fund?
    _____

21. What is the high net asset value for this fund over the last 12 months? _____

22. What is the low net asset value for this fund over the last 12 months? _____

23. What do the experts say about this fund?
    _____

Category 5: Conclusion

24. Based on the above information, do you think an investment in this fund will help you achieve your investment goals?   ☐ Yes   ☐ No

25. Explain your answer to question 24.
    _____

A Word of Caution

When you use a checklist, there is always a danger of overlooking relevant information. This checklist is not a cure-all, but it does provide some questions that you should answer before making a mutual fund investment decision. Quite simply, it is a place to start. If you need other information, *you* are responsible for obtaining it and for determining how it affects your potential investment.

Suggested App:
• Morning-star

What's Next for Your Personal Financial Plan?

• Identify additional factors that may affect your decision to invest in this fund.

• Develop a plan for monitoring an investment's value once mutual funds are purchased.

Name: _____   Date: _____

Retirement Planning

Purpose: To consider housing alternatives for retirement living and to plan retirement activities.

Instructions: Evaluate current and expected needs and personal interests based on the items below. This sheet is also available in an Excel spreadsheet format on the library resource site in *Connect*.

Suggested websites: www.aarp.org   www.thebalance.com/retirement-planning-4073976

Suggested app: Retirement Planner

Retirement Housing Plans

Description of current housing situation (size, facilities, location)

_____

_____

Time until retirement _____ years

Description of retirement housing needs

_____

Checklist of Retirement Housing Alternatives

_____ present home	_____ professional companionship arrangement
_____ house sharing	_____ commercial rental
_____ accessory apartment	_____ board and care home
_____ elder cottage housing	_____ congregate housing
_____ rooming house	_____ continuing care retirement community
_____ single-room occupancy	_____ assisted-living facility
_____ caretaker arrangement	_____ nursing home

Personal and financial factors that will influence the retirement housing decision

Financial planning actions to be taken related to retirement housing

_____

Retirement Activities

What plans do you have to work part-time or do volunteer work?

_____

What recreational activities do you plan to continue or start? (location, training, equipment needs)

_____

What plans do you have for travel or educational study?

What's Next for Your Personal Financial Plan?

- Survey local senior housing facilities to determine the types of services available.
- Make a list with the best housing options for seniors.

Suggested App:

• Retirement Planner

64

Retirement Plan Comparison

Purpose: To compare benefits and costs for different retirement plans (401k, IRA, Roth IRA, Keogh, SEP).

Instructions: Analyze online information, and contact your employer and financial institutions to obtain the information below. This sheet is also available in an Excel spreadsheet format on the library resource site in *Connect*.

Suggested websites: www.thebalance.com/retirement-planning-4073976   www.aarp.org

Suggested app: 401(k)

Type of plan			
Name of financial institution or employer			
Address			
Phone/email			
Website			
Type of investments			
Minimum initial deposit			
Minimum additional deposits			
Employer contributions			
Current rate of return			
Service charges/fees			
Safety insured? By whom?			
Amount			
Payroll deduction available			
Tax benefits			
Penalty for early withdrawal: • IRS penalty (10%) • other penalties			
Other features or restrictions			

Suggested App:

· 401(k)

What's Next for Your Personal Financial Plan?

• Survey local employers to obtain information about the types of retirement plans available to employees.

• Talk to representatives of financial institutions to obtain suggestions for retirement plan investments.

Retirement Income Forecast

Purpose: To determine the amount needed to save each year to have the necessary funds for retirement living costs.

Instructions: Estimate the information requested below. This sheet is also available in an Excel spreadsheet format on the library resource site in *Connect*.

Suggested websites: www.ssa.gov   www.pensionplanners.com   brentmark.com

Suggested app: RetirePlan

Estimated Annual Retirement Living Expenses

Estimated annual living expenses
if you retired today $ _____

Future value for _____ years
until retirement at expected annual
income of _____% (use future
value of $1)   × _____

**Projected annual retirement living
expenses adjusted for inflation** .... (A) $ _____

Estimated Annual Income at Retirement

Social Security income $_____

Company pension, personal
retirement account income $ _____

Investment and other income $ _____

Total retirement income .... (B) $ _____

Additional Retirement Plan Contributions (if B is less than A)

Annual shortfall of income after
retirement (A − B) $ _____

Expected annual rate of return on
invested funds after retirement,
percentage expressed as a decimal $ _____

Needed investment fund after retirement A − B .... (C) $ _____

Future value factor of a series of deposits for _____ years
until retirement and an expected annual rate of return before
retirement of _____ %   (D) $ _____

**Annual deposit to achieve needed investment
fund (C divided by D)** .... $ _____

What's Next for Your Personal Financial Plan?

• Survey retired people and others near retirement to obtain information about sources of retirement income.

• Evaluate investment options for an individual retirement account and other retirement plans.

Suggested
App:

• RetirePlan

PERSONAL FINANCIAL PLANNER

Name: _____ Date: _____

Estate Planning

Purpose: To develop a plan for estate planning and related financial activities.

Instructions: Respond to the questions below for planning and implementing an estate plan. This sheet is also available in an Excel spreadsheet format on the library resource site in *Connect*.

Suggested websites: www.nolo.com   www.estateplanning.com

Suggested app: ACTEC Wealth Advisor

Are your financial records, including recent tax forms, insurance policies, and investment and housing documents, organized and easily accessible?	
Do you have a safe deposit box? Where is it located? Where is the key?	
Location of life insurance policies. Name and address of insurance company and agent.	
Is your will current? Location of copies of your will. Name, address, phone, and email of your lawyer.	
Name, address, phone, and email of your executor.	
Do you have a listing of the current value of assets owned and liabilities outstanding?	
Have any funeral and burial arrangements been made?	
Have you created any trusts? Name and location of financial institution.	
Do you have any current information on gift and estate taxes?	
Have you prepared a letter of last instruction? Where is it located?	

Suggested App:

• ACTEC Wealth Advisor

What's Next for Your Personal Financial Plan?

- Talk to several people about actions they recommend for estate planning.
- Create a list of situations in which a will would need to be revised.

Name: _____ Date: _____

Will Planning

Purpose: To compare costs and features of different types of wills.

Instructions: Obtain information for the areas listed based on your current and future situation; contact attorneys regarding the cost of these wills. This sheet is also available in an Excel spreadsheet format on the library resource site in *Connect*.

Suggested websites: nnepa.com   estateplanninglinks.com   www.thebalance.com/wills-4073967

Type of Will	Features That Would Be Appropriate for My Current or Future Situation	Cost; Attorney, Address, Phone, Email, Website

What's Next for Your Personal Financial Plan?

- Create a list of items that you believe would be desirable to include in a will.
- Obtain the cost of preparing a will from different legal sources.

Trust Comparison

Purpose: To compare the features of different types of trusts.

Instructions: Research features of various trusts to determine their value for your current or future situation. This sheet is also available in an Excel spreadsheet format on the library resource site in *Connect*.

Suggested websites: www.estateplanning.com   www.savewealth.com

Suggested app: Trusts & Estates Plus

Type of Trust	Benefits	Possible Value for My Situation

Suggested App:

· **Trusts & Estates Plus**

What's Next for Your Personal Financial Plan?

· Talk to legal and financial planning experts to determine the costs and benefits of wills and trusts.

· Talk to one or more lawyers to obtain information about the type of trust recommended for your situation.

Estate Tax Estimate

Purpose: To estimate the estate tax based on your financial situation.

Instructions: Enter the data requested below to calculate the tax based on current tax rates. This sheet is also available in an Excel spreadsheet format on the library resource site in *Connect*.

Suggested websites: www.irs.gov   www.savewealth.com

Gross Estate Values

Personal property	$ _____
Real estate	$ _____
Joint ownership	$ _____
Business interests	$ _____
Life insurance	$ _____
Employee benefits	$ _____
Controlled gifts/trusts	$ _____
Prior taxable gifts	$ _____
Total estate values	$ _____

Deductible Debts, Costs, Expenses

Mortgages and secured loans	$ _____
Unsecured notes and loans	$ _____
Bills and accounts payable	$ _____
Funeral and medical expenses	$ _____
Probate administration costs	$ _____
Total deductions	−$ _____
Marital deduction	−$ _____
Taxable estate	=$ _____
Gross estate tax*	$ _____

Allowable Credits

Unified credit	$ _____
Gift tax credit	$ _____
State tax credit	$ _____
Foreign tax credit	$ _____
Prior tax credit	$ _____
Total tax credits	−$ _____
Net estate tax	$ _____

*Consult the Internal Revenue Service (www.irs.gov) for current rates and regulations related to estate taxes.

What's Next for Your Personal Financial Plan?

- Research the history of the estate tax law to determine how it has changed over the years.
- Research the inheritance and gift tax laws in your state.

Financial Data Summary

Date > > > > > > > > > > > >					
Balance sheet summary					
Assets					
Liabilities					
Net worth					
Cash flow summary					
Inflows					
Outflows					
Surplus/deficit					
Budget summary					
Budget					
Actual					
Variance					
Date > > > > > > > > > > > >					
Balance sheet summary					
Assets					
Liabilities					
Net worth					
Cash flow summary					
Inflows					
Outflows					
Surplus/deficit					
Budget summary					
Budget					
Actual					
Variance					

Name: _____   **Date:** _____

Savings/Investment Portfolio Summary

Description	Organization Contact/Phone/ Website	Purchase Price/Date	Value/ Date	Value/ Date	Value/ Date	Value/ Date

Progress Check—Major Financial Goals and Activities

Some financial planning activities require a short-term perspective. Others may require ongoing efforts over a period of time, such as purchasing a vacation home. This sheet is designed to help you monitor these long-term, ongoing financial activities.

Major Financial Objective	Desired Completion Date	Initial Actions and Date	Progress Checks (date, progress made, and other actions to be taken)

Money Management, Budgeting, and Tax Planning—Summary

As you complete the ***Personal Financial Planner*** sheets, transfer financial data, goals, and planned actions to the following summary sheet. For example:

Sheet	Actions to Be Taken	Planned Completion Date	Completed (✓)
14 (Financial documents and records)	Locate and organize all personal financial documents	Within 2–3 months	
20 (Current income tax estimate)	Sort current tax data, compute estimate to determine tax amount	February 15	✓

(Text Chapters 1, 2, 3, 4; Sheets 1–22)

Sheet	Actions to Be Taken	Planned Completion Date	Completed (✓)

Banking Services and Consumer Credit—Summary

74

(Text Chapters 5, 6, 7; Sheets 23–31)

Sheet	Actions to Be Taken	Planned Completion Date	Completed (✓)

Consumer Buying and Housing—Summary

(Text Chapters 8–9; Sheets 32–45)

Sheet	Actions to Be Taken	Planned Completion Date	Completed (✓)

76 Insurance—Summary

(Text Chapters 10, 11, 12; Sheets 46–54)

Sheet	Actions to Be Taken	Planned Completion Date	Completed (✓)

Investments—Summary

(Text Chapters 13, 14, 15, 16, 17; Sheets 55–62)

Sheet	Actions to Be Taken	Planned Completion Date	Completed (✓)

Retirement and Estate Planning—Summary

(Text Chapters 18–19; Sheets 63–69)

Sheet	Actions to Be Taken	Planned Completion Date	Completed (✓)